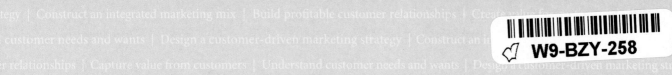

ango notes

nership with **Audible** Education

Hear it. Get It.

Study on the go with VangoNotes.

Just download chapter reviews from your text and listen to them on any mp3 player. Now wherever you are--whatever you're doing--you can study by listening to the following for each chapter of your textbook:

Big Ideas: Your "need to know" for each chapter

Practice Test: A gut check for the Big Ideas--tells you if you need to keep studying

Key Terms: Audio "flashcards" to help you review key concepts and terms

Rapid Review: A quick drill session--use it right before your test

VangoNotes.com

Reviewers Agree: Kotler and Armstrong's Text

Creates More Value for You

A unique, integrative, and intuitive customer value framework:

"The authors do a superb job of covering customer value. It is a conspicuous cornerstone of the book. The concept is well integrated into each chapter."

"The [text's] establishment of a framework for marketing, with customer value and satisfaction at its core, is very good—students can really relate to it."

"[The customer value framework] is effective because it emphasizes the core of the marketing concept in focusing on the customer. Other texts lack in addressing issues of customer relationships, customer lifetime value, and measuring return on marketing."

"I think that Kotler and Armstrong really have a tiger by the tail in emphasizing customer value and relationships as their dominant theme."

The content depth and quality you'd expect from Kotler and Armstrong:

"Excellent and thorough coverage of a vast topic. Easy to read with lots of good examples. Topical and up-to-date."

"Serious and well-written; much deeper and more comprehensive than other books."

"It is comprehensive, integrates global and ethics issues, and offers excellent examples that are both current and relevant."

"Kotler and Armstrong have stayed contemporary with everything going on in the field."

An interesting, relevant, and readable text:

"Kotler and Armstrong is current and straightforward, with lots of practical applications."

"Kotler and Armstrong is quite refreshing—it draws the reader into the fascinating areas of marketing via use of real-life examples right off the bat."

"I love the diversity of the products and companies chosen for the company examples and cases, examples that all ages can relate to that are of interest to young professionals."

"Well-covered basics; integrated, intriguing examples; vivid color splashed all over the place . . ."

Value-adding supplements:

"I was very impressed with the quality and relevance of the videos."

"I'm starting to use the videos a lot and I like them, and the students like them too. I use the supplemental Web site also…."

"I have aggressively sought to utilize various assessment tools in my curriculum and have been very pleased with the Kotler/Armstrong support and value-added materials. I find the students often list them as "most helpful" in course evaluations."

It's the best marketing text available:

"The strengths of Kotler and Armstrong are that the focus is on the customer—which is very important—and that they define marketing in an understandable manner. I am impressed."

"Kotler and Armstrong are superior in their coverage of this material. I feel my students would be better off with Kotler and Armstrong's text."

"Kotler and Armstrong have the best text on the market."

Principles of Marketing

Principles
of Marketing

twelfth edition

PHILIP KOTLER
Northwestern University

GARY ARMSTRONG
University of North Carolina

PEARSON
Prentice
Hall

Upper Saddle River, New Jersey 07458

Library of Congress Cataloging-in-Publication Data

Kotler, Philip.
  Principles of marketing / Philip Kotler, Gary Armstrong. — 12th ed.
     p. cm.
  ISBN 978-0-13-239002-6 (alk. paper)
  1. Marketing. I. Armstrong, Gary (Gary M.) II. Title.
  HF5415 . K636 2008
  658.8—dc22

                                                        2007000562

VP/Editorial Director: Jeff Shelstad
Editor in Chief: David Parker
Product Development Manager: Ashley Santora
Project Manager: Melissa Pellerano
Editorial Assistant: Christine Ietto
Development Editor: Keri Miksza
Assistant Editor, Media: Ashley Lulling
Marketing Manager: Anne Howard
Marketing Assistant: Laura Cirigliano
Associate Director, Production Editorial: Judy Leale
Managing Editor: Renata Butera
Production Editor: Angela Pica
Permissions Coordinator: Charles Morris
Associate Director, Manufacturing: Vinnie Scelta
Manufacturing Buyer: Diane Peirano
Manager, Creative Services: Christy Mahon
Interior Design: Christy Mahon
Cover Design: Christy Mahon
Director, Image Resource Center: Melinda Patelli
Manager, Rights and Permissions: Zina Arabia
Manager, Visual Research: Beth Brenzel
Manager, Cover Visual Research & Permissions: Karen Sanatar
Image Permission Coordinator: Robert Farrell
Photo Researcher: Sheila Norman
Illustrations: Carlisle Publishing Services
Composition: Carlisle Publishing Services
Full-Service Project Management: Carlisle Publishing Services/Lynn Steines
Printer/Binder: R. R. Donnelley–Willard
Typeface: 9/11 Melior

Credits and acknowledgments borrowed from other sources and reproduced, with permission, in this textbook appear on page C-1.

Pearson Education LTD.
Pearson Education Singapore, Pte. Ltd
Pearson Education, Canada, Ltd
Pearson Education–Japan

Pearson Education Australia PTY, Limited
Pearson Education North Asia Ltd
Pearson Educación de Mexico, S.A. de C.V.
Pearson Education Malaysia, Pte. Ltd.

10 9 8 7 6 5 4 3 2 1
ISBN-13: 978-0-13-239002-6
ISBN-10:   0-13-239002-7

Dedication

To Kathy, Betty, Mandy, Matt, KC, Keri, Delaney, Molly, and Macy; and Nancy, Amy, Melissa, and Jessica

About the Authors

As a team, Philip Kotler and Gary Armstrong provide a blend of skills uniquely suited to writing an introductory marketing text. Professor Kotler is one of the world's leading authorities on marketing. Professor Armstrong is an award-winning teacher of undergraduate business students. Together they make the complex world of marketing practical, approachable, and enjoyable.

PHILIP KOTLER is the S. C. Johnson & Son Distinguished Professor of International Marketing at the Kellogg Graduate School of Management, Northwestern University. He received his master's degree at the University of Chicago and his Ph.D. at M.I.T., both in economics. Dr. Kotler is the author of *Marketing Management* (Prentice Hall), now in its twelfth edition and the world's most widely used marketing textbook in graduate schools of business worldwide. He has authored dozens of other successful books and has written more than 100 articles in leading journals. He is the only three-time winner of the coveted Alpha Kappa Psi award for the best annual article in the *Journal of Marketing*.

Professor Kotler was named the first recipient of two major awards: the *Distinguished Marketing Educator of the Year Award* given by the American Marketing Association and the *Philip Kotler Award for Excellence in Health Care Marketing* presented by the Academy for Health Care Services Marketing. His numerous other major honors include the Sales and Marketing Executives International *Marketing Educator of the Year Award*; The European Association of Marketing Consultants and Trainers *Marketing Excellence Award*; the *Charles Coolidge Parlin Marketing Research Award*; and the *Paul D. Converse Award*, given by the American Marketing Association to honor "outstanding contributions to science in marketing." In a recent *Financial Times* poll of 1,000 senior executives across the world, Professor Kotler was ranked as the fourth "most influential business writer/guru" of the twenty-first century.

Dr. Kotler has served as chairman of the College of Marketing of the Institute of Management Sciences, a director of the American Marketing Association, and a trustee of the Marketing Science Institute. He has consulted with many major U.S. and international companies in the areas of marketing strategy and planning, marketing organization, and international marketing. He has traveled extensively throughout Europe, Asia, and South America, advising companies and governments about global marketing practices and opportunities.

GARY ARMSTRONG is the Crist W. Blackwell Distinguished Professor of Undergraduate Education in the Kenan-Flagler Business School at the University of North Carolina at Chapel Hill. He holds undergraduate and master's degrees in business from Wayne State University in Detroit, and he received his Ph.D. in marketing from Northwestern University. Dr. Armstrong has contributed numerous articles to leading business journals. As a consultant and researcher, he has worked with many companies on marketing research, sales management, and marketing strategy.

But Professor Armstrong's first love is teaching. His Blackwell Distinguished Professorship is the only permanent endowed professorship for distinguished undergraduate teaching at the University of North Carolina at Chapel Hill. He has been very active in the teaching and administration of Kenan-Flagler's undergraduate program. His administrative posts have included Chair of Marketing, Associate Director of the Undergraduate Business Program, Director of the Business Honors Program, and many others. He works closely with business student groups and has received several campuswide and Business School teaching awards. He is the only repeat recipient of school's highly regarded Award for Excellence in Undergraduate Teaching, which he has received three times. Professor Armstrong recently received the UNC Board of Governors Award for Excellence in Teaching, the highest teaching honor bestowed by the sixteen-campus University of North Carolina system.

Brief Contents

Contents

Message from the Authors

Welcome to the twelfth edition of *Principles of Marketing!* With each new edition, we work to bring you the freshest and most authoritative insights into the fascinating world of marketing. As we present this new edition, we want to again thank you and the millions of other marketing students and professors who have used our text over the years. You've been our inspiration. With your help, this book remains a market leader and international best seller. Thank you.

The goal of every marketer is to create more value for customers. So it makes sense that our goal for the twelfth edition is to create more value for you—*our* customer. How does this text bring you more value? First, it builds on a unique, integrative, and intuitive marketing framework: Simply put, marketing is the art and science of creating value *for* customers in order to capture value *from* customers in return. Marketers lead the way in developing and managing profitable, value-based customer relationships. We introduce this customer-value framework in the first two chapters and then build upon it throughout the book.

Beyond the strengthened customer-relationships framework, we emphasize four additional customer-value themes. First, we expand our emphasis on *building strong brands and brand value*. After all, customer value and profitable customer relationships are built upon strong brands. Second, we focus on the importance of *measuring and managing return on marketing*—of capturing value in return for the customer value that the company creates. Third, we present all of the latest developments in the *marketing technologies* that are rapidly changing how marketers create and communicate customer value. Finally, we emphasize the importance of *socially responsible marketing around the globe*. As the world becomes an increasingly smaller place, marketers must be good at marketing their brands globally and in socially responsible ways that create long-term value to society as a whole.

In addition to providing all the latest marketing thinking, to add even more value, we've worked to make learning about and teaching marketing easier and more exciting for both students and instructors. The twelfth edition presents marketing in a complete yet practical, exciting, and easy-to-digest way. For example, to help bring marketing to life, we've filled the text with interesting examples and stories about real companies and their marketing practices. Moreover, the integrated, cutting-edge teaching and learning package lets you customize your learning and teaching experience. We highlight the twelfth edition's many new features and enhancements in the pages that follow.

So, the twelfth edition *creates more value for you*—more value in the content, more value in the supplements, more value in learning, and more value in YOUR classroom. We think that it's the best edition yet. We hope that you'll find *Principles of Marketing* the very best text from which to learn about and teach marketing.

Sincerely,

Gary Armstrong
University of North Carolina–Chapel Hill

Philip Kotler
Northwestern University

The Twelfth Edition—Creating More Value for You!

The goal of *Principles of Marketing*, twelfth edition, is to introduce new marketing students to the fascinating world of modern marketing in an innovative yet practical and enjoyable way. Like any good marketer, we're out to create more value for you, *our* customer. We've poured over every page, table, figure, fact, and example in an effort to make this the best text from which to learn about and teach marketing.

Today's marketing is all about creating customer value and building profitable customer relationships. It starts with understanding consumer needs and wants, deciding which target markets the organization can serve best, and developing a compelling value proposition by which the organization can win, keep, and grow targeted consumers. If an organization does these things well, it will reap the rewards in terms of market share, profits, and customer equity.

Marketing is much more than just an isolated business function—it is a philosophy that guides the entire organization. The marketing department cannot create customer value and build profitable customer relationships by itself. This is a companywide undertaking that involves broad decisions about who the company wants as its customers, which needs to satisfy, what products and services to offer, what prices to set, what communications to send, and what partnerships to develop. Marketing must work closely with other company departments and with other organizations throughout its entire value-delivery system to delight customers by creating superior customer value.

Marketing: Creating Customer Value and Relationships

From beginning to end, *Principles of Marketing* develops an innovative customer-value and customer-relationships framework that captures the essence of today's marketing.

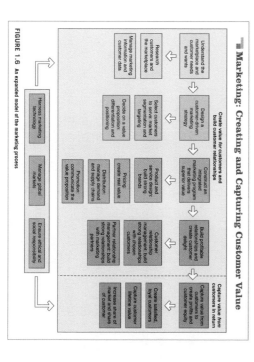

Marketing: Creating and Capturing Customer Value

Create value for customers and build customer relationships

| Understand the marketplace and customer needs and wants | Design a customer-driven marketing strategy | Construct an integrated marketing program that delivers superior value | Build profitable relationships and create customer delight |
| | | | |

Research customers and the marketplace

Manage marketing information and customer data

Select customers to serve: market segmentation and targeting

Decide on a value proposition: differentiation and positioning

Product and service design: build strong brands

Pricing: create real value

Distribution: manage demand and supply chains

Promotion: communicate the value proposition

Customer relationship management: build strong relationships with chosen customers

Partner relationship management: build strong relationships with marketing partners

Capture value from customers in return

Create satisfied, loyal customers

Capture customer lifetime value

Increase share of market and share of customer

Harness marketing technology

Manage global markets

Ensure ethical and social responsibly

FIGURE 1.6 An expanded model of the marketing process

Five Major Value Themes

The twelfth edition builds on five major value themes:

- **Creating value for customers in order to capture value from customers in return.** Today's marketers must be good at *creating customer value* and *managing customer relationships*. They must attract targeted customers with strong value propositions. Then, they must keep and grow customers by delivering superior customer value and effectively managing the company-customer interface. Today's outstanding marketing companies understand the marketplace and customer needs, design value-creating marketing strategies, develop integrated marketing programs that deliver customer value and delight, and build strong customer relationships. In return, they capture value from customers in the form of sales, profits, and customer loyalty.

This innovative customer-value *framework* is introduced at the start of Chapter 1 in a five-step marketing process model, which details how marketing *creates* customer value and *captures* value in return. The framework is carefully explained in the first two chapters, providing students with a solid foundation. The framework is then integrated throughout the remainder of the text.

■ **Building and managing strong, value-creating brands.** Well-positioned brands with strong brand equity provide the basis upon which to build customer value and profitable customer relationships. Today's marketers must position their brands powerfully and manage them well.

■ **Managing return on marketing to recapture value.** In order to capture value from customers in return, marketing managers must be good at measuring and managing the return on their marketing investments. They must ensure that their marketing dollars are being well spent. In the past, many marketers spent freely on big, expensive marketing programs, often without thinking carefully about the financial and customer response returns on their spending. But all that is changing rapidly. Measuring and managing return on marketing investments has become an important part of strategic marketing decision making.

■ **Harnessing new marketing technologies.** New digital and other high-tech marketing developments are dramatically changing how marketers create and communicate customer value. Today's marketers must know how to leverage new computer, information, communication, and distribution technologies to connect more effectively with customers and marketing partners in this digital age.

■ **Marketing in a socially responsible way around the globe.** As technological developments make the world an increasingly smaller place, marketers must be good at marketing their brands globally and in socially responsible ways that create not just short-term value for individual customers but also long-term value for society as a whole.

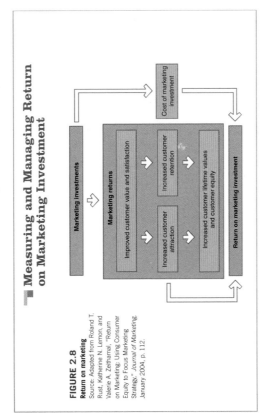

■ **Measuring and Managing Return on Marketing Investment**

FIGURE 2.8
Return on marketing
Source: Adapted from Roland T. Rust, Katherine N. Lemon, and Valerie A. Zeithaml, "Return on Marketing: Using Consumer Equity to Focus Marketing Strategy," *Journal of Marketing*, January 2004, p. 112.

Important Changes and Additions

We've thoroughly revised the twelfth edition of *Principles of Marketing* to reflect the major trends and forces impacting marketing in this era of customer value and relationships. Here are just some of the major changes you'll find in this edition.

■ This new edition builds on and extends the innovative **customer-value framework** from previous editions. No other marketing text presents such a clear and comprehensive customer-value approach.

■ The integrated marketing communications chapters have been completely restructured to reflect sweeping shifts in how today's marketers communicate value to customers.

■ A newly revised Chapter 14—Communicating Customer Value—addresses today's **shifting integrated marketing communications model**. It tells how marketers are now adding a host new-age media—everything from interactive TV and the Internet to iPods and cell phones to reach targeted customers with more personalized messages.

■ Advertising and public relations are now combined in Chapter 15, which includes important new discussions on "Madison & Vine" (the merging of advertising and entertainment to break through the clutter), return on advertising, and other important topics. A restructured Chapter 16 now combines personal selling and sales promotion.

■ The new Chapter 17—**Direct and Online Marketing**—provides focused new coverage of direct marketing and its fastest-growing arm, marketing on the Internet. The new chapter includes a section on new digital direct-marketing technologies, such as mobile phone marketing, podcasts and vodcasts, and interactive TV.

- Harrah's, the world's largest casino operator, maintains a vast customer database and uses CRM to manage day-to-day customer relationships and build customer loyalty

- Dunkin' Donuts targets the "Dunkin' Tribe"—not the Starbucks snob but the average Joe

- Tiny nicher Bike Friday creates customer evangelists—delighted customers who can't wait to tell others about the company

- Apple Computer founder Steve Jobs used dazzling customer-driven innovation to first start the company and then to remake it again 20 years later

- Staples held back its now-familiar "Staples: That was easy" repositioning campaign for more than a year. First, it had to *live* the slogan.

- Ryanair—Europe's original, largest, and most profitable low-fares airline—appears to have found a radical new pricing solution: Fly free!

- The NBA has become one of today's hottest global brands, jamming down one international slam dunk after another

- Dove—with its Campaign for Real Beauty campaign featuring candid and confident images of real women of all types—is on a bold mission to create a broader and healthier view of beauty

These and countless other examples and illustrations throughout each chapter reinforce key concepts and bring marketing to life.

Valuable Learning Aids

A wealth of chapter-opening, within-chapter, and end-of-chapter learning devices help students to learn, link, and apply major concepts:

- *Previewing the Concepts.* A section at the beginning of each chapter briefly previews chapter concepts, links them with previous chapter concepts, outlines chapter learning objectives, and introduces the chapter-opening vignette.

- *Chapter-opening marketing stories.* Each chapter begins with an engaging, deeply developed marketing story that introduces the chapter material and sparks student interest.

- *Real Marketing highlights.* Each chapter contains two highlight features that provide an in-depth look at real marketing practices of large and small companies.

- *Reviewing the Concepts.* A summary at the end of each chapter reviews major chapter concepts and chapter objectives.

- *Reviewing the Key Terms.* Key terms are highlighted within the text, clearly defined in the margins of the pages in which they first appear, and listed at the end of each chapter.

- *Discussing the Concepts and Applying the Concepts.* Each chapter contains a set of discussion questions and application exercises covering major chapter concepts.

- *Focus on Technology.* Application exercises at the end of each chapter provide discussion on important and emerging marketing technologies in this digital age.

- *Focus on Ethics.* Situation descriptions and questions highlight important issues in marketing ethics at the end of each chapter.

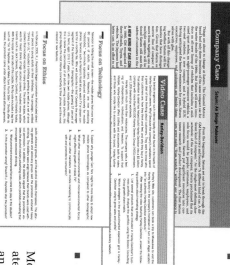

- *Company Cases.* All new or revised company cases for class or written discussion are provided at the end of each chapter. These cases challenge students to apply marketing principles to real situations.

- *Video Shorts.* Short vignettes and discussion questions appear at the end of every chapter, to be used with the set of 4- to 7-minute videos that accompany this edition.

- *Marketing Plan appendix.* Appendix 1 contains a sample marketing plan that helps students to apply important marketing planning concepts.

- *Marketing by the Numbers appendix.* A new Appendix 2 introduces students to the marketing financial analysis that helps to guide, assess, and support marketing decisions.

More than ever before, the twelfth edition of *Principles of Marketing* creates value for you—it gives you all you need to know about marketing in an effective and enjoyable totallearning package!

A Valuable Supplements Package

A successful marketing course requires more than a well-written book. Today's classroom requires a dedicated teacher and a fully integrated teaching system. A total package of teaching and learning supplements extends this edition's emphasis on creating value for both the student and instructor. The following aids support *Principles of Marketing*.

Supplements for Instructors

The following supplements are available to adopting instructors.

Instructor's Manual with Video Case Notes (ISBN: 0-13-239003-5)

The instructor's handbook for this text provides suggestions for using features and elements of the text. This *Instructor's Manual* includes a chapter overview, objectives, a detailed lecture outline (incorporating key terms, text art, chapter objectives, and references to various pedagogical elements), and support for end-of-chapter material. Also included within each chapter is a section that offers barriers to effective learning, student projects/assignments, as well as an outside example, all of which provide a springboard for innovative learning experiences in the classroom. Video Case Notes, offering a brief summary of each segment, along with answers to the case questions in the text, as well as teaching ideas on how to present the material in class are also offered in the Instructor's Manual.

Visit the Instructor's Resource Center Online (www.prenhall.com/irc) for these additional elements:

- "Professors on the Go!" serves to bring key material upfront in the manual, where an instructor who is short on time can take a quick look and find key points and assignments to incorporate into the lecture, without having to page through all the material provided for each chapter.

- Annotated Instructor's Notes, which serve as a quick reference for the entire supplements package. Suggestions for using materials from the Instructor's Manual, PowerPoint slides, Test Item File, Video Library, and online material are offered for each section within every chapter.

- More Quantitative Exercises, based on the concepts covered in Appendix 2: Marketing by the Numbers. An additional set of exercises are offered here, not found in the textbook. Suggested answers are provided as well.

Test Item File (ISBN: 0-13-239004-3)

Featuring more than 3,000 questions, 175 questions per chapter, this Test Item File has been written specifically for the twelfth edition. Each chapter consists of multiple-choice, true/false, short-answer, and essay questions, with page references and difficulty level provided for each question. New to this edition is the introduction of small-business cases, offering ten essay questions per chapter. Additionally, the questions are offered in two categories—General Concept and Application. The application questions provide real-life situations that take students beyond basic chapter concepts and vocabulary and ask them to apply their newly learned marketing skills.

Instructor's Resource Center

Register. Redeem. Login.

The Web site www.prenhall.com/irc is where instructors can access a variety of print, media, and presentation resources available with this text in downloadable, digital format. For most texts, resources are also available for course management platforms such as Blackboard, WebCT, and Course Compass.

It gets better. Once you register, you will not have additional forms to fill out or multiple usernames and passwords to remember to access new titles and/or editions. As a registered faculty member, you can log in directly to download resource files and receive immediate access and instructions for installing Course Management content to your campus server.

Need help? Our dedicated technical support team is ready to assist instructors with questions about the media supplements that accompany this text. Visit 247.prenhall.com/ for answers to frequently asked questions and toll-free user support phone numbers.

All instructor resources in one place. It's your choice. Available via a password-protected site at www.prenhall.com/kotler or on CD-ROM (0-13-239007-8). Resources include:

- *Instructor's Manual:* View chapter-by-chapter or download the entire manual as a .zip file.
- *Test Item File:* View chapter-by-chapter or download the entire test item file as a .zip file.
- *TestGen EQ for PC/Mac:* Download this easy-to-use software; it's preloaded with the twelfth edition test questions and a user's manual.
- *Image bank (on CD only):* Access many of the images, ads, and illustrations featured in the text. Ideal for PowerPoint customization.
- *PowerPoints:* When it comes to PowerPoints, Prentice Hall knows one size does not fit all. That's why we offer instructors more than one option.

  PowerPoint BASIC: This simple presentation includes only basic outlines and key points from each chapter. No animation or forms of rich media are integrated, which makes the total file size manageable and easier to share online or via e-mail. BASIC was also designed for instructors who prefer to customize PowerPoints and want to be spared from having to strip out animation, embedded files, or other media rich features.

  PowerPoint MEDIA RICH (on CD only): This media-rich alternative includes basic outlines and key points from each chapter, plus advertisements and art from the text, images not included in the text, discussion questions, Web links, and embedded video snippets from the accompanying video library. This is the best option for a complete presentation solution. Instructors can further customize this presentation using the image library featured on the Instructor's Resource Center on CD-ROM.

  PowerPoints for Classroom Response Systems (CRS): These Q&A style slides are designed for classrooms using "clickers" or classroom response systems. Instructors who are interested in making CRS a part of their course should contact their Prentice Hall representative for details and a demonstration. CRS is a fun and easy way to make your classroom more interactive.

- *Online Courses:* See OneKey below. Compatible with BlackBoard and WebCT.

TestGen Test Generating Software

Prentice Hall's test-generating software is available from the *IRC Online* (www.prenhall. com/kotler) or from the *IRC on CD-ROM*.

- PC/Mac compatible; preloaded with all of the Test Item File questions.
- Manually or randomly view test bank questions and drag -and drop to create a test.

- Add or modify test bank questions using the built-in Question Editor.
- Print up to 25 variations of a single test and deliver the test on a local area network using the built-in QuizMaster feature.
- Free customer support is available at media.support@pearsoned.com or call 1-800-6-PROFESSOR between 8:00 a.m. and 5:00 p.m. CST.

Custom Videos

The video library features 20 exciting segments for this edition. All segments are available online (www.prenhall.com/kotlervideo), on VHS (ISBN: 0-13-239012-4), and on DVD (ISBN: 0-13-239011-6). Here are just a few of the videos offered:

- GE and pricing strategies
- Harley-Davidson and how brand image is managed through global marketing strategies
- NineMSN and its strategies in direct marketing
- American Express and the modern marketing environment
- The NFL and the importance of social responsibility
- Eaton's approach to B2B issues, including buyer behavior
- Hasbro's views on distribution channels and logistics management
- Wild Planet's strategies in the consumer markets

Transparencies (ISBN: 0-13-239006-X)

Features 15 to 20 color acetates per chapter selected from the media-rich set of PowerPoints, which includes images from the text.

AdCritic.com

Prentice Hall and AdAge are bringing the most current ads and commentary from advertising experts into your classroom. Only Prentice Hall can offer students 16 weeks of access to a special AdCritic.com site that includes AdAge's encyclopedia of articles at a deeply discounted rate. An access code is available only when shrink-wrapped with a Prentice Hall text, so be sure and specify the appropriate package with your local bookstore in advance. Please visit www.prenhall.com/marketing for a tour of the AdCritic site.

Supplements for Students

OneKey

Available through Course Compass, Blackboard, and WebCT, classroom resources for students are available in one spot. Resources include:

- Quizzing for review
- Case Pilot to aid in analyzing cases
- Marketing Toolkit: Interactive Modules to aid in review of understanding key concepts
- Marketing Updates: Bringing current articles to the classroom
- Critical Thinking Problems
- Learning Modules
- Much more

OneKey requires an access code, which professors can ask to be shrink-wrapped with new copies of this text. Please contact your local sales representative for the correct ISBN. Codes may also be purchased separately at www.prenhall.com/marketing.

Study Guide (ISBN: 0-13-238987-8)

The twelfth edition study guide provides students on the go with a valuable resource. It consists of detailed chapter outlines, student exercises, plus exercises correlated to award-winning print advertisements. There is also a section providing suggested answers for all exercises, offering the students feedback on their responses. The study guide can be packaged at a low cost with new copies of this text. The study guide can also be purchased separately at www.prenhall. com/marketing.

Companion Website

The Web site www.prenhall.com/kotler offers two student quizzes per chapter. The Concept Check Quiz is to be administered prior to reviewing the chapter, in order to assess the student's initial understanding. The Concept Challenge Quiz is to be administered after reviewing the chapter.

More Valuable Resources

Announcing SafariX Textbooks Online—Where the Web meets textbooks for student savings!

Principles of Marketing, twelfth edition, is also available as a WebBook! SafariX WebBooks offer study advantages no print textbook can match. With an Internet-enhanced SafariX WebBook, students can search the entire text for key concepts; navigate easily to a page number, reading assignment, or chapter; or bookmark important pages or sections for quick review at a later date. Some key features:

- Digital textbook delivery that saves students off the print edition's suggested list price
- Internet-based service, making textbook content available anytime, anywhere there is a Web connection
- Easy navigation, which makes finding pages and completing assignments easy and efficient
- Search, bookmark, and note-taking tools that save study time and reduce frustration by making critical information immediately accessible. Organizing study notes has never been easier!
- Ability to print pages on the fly, making critical content available for offline study and review.

Prentice Hall is pleased to be the first publisher to offer students a new choice in how they purchase and access required or recommended course textbooks. For details and a demonstration, visit www.prenhall.com/safarix.

Classroom Response Systems (CRS)

This exciting new wireless polling technology makes classrooms, no matter how large or small, even more interactive because it enables instructors to pose questions to their students, record results, and display those results instantly. Students answer questions using compact remote-control-style transmitters. Prentice Hall has partnerships with leading classroom response systems providers and can show you everything you need to know about setting up and using a CRS system. We'll provide the classroom hardware, software, and support and show you how your students can save.

- Enhance interactivity
- Capture attention
- Get instant feedback
- Access comprehension

Learn more at www.prenhall.com/crs.

VangoNotes

Study on the go with VangoNotes—chapter reviews from your text in downloadable mp3 format. Now wherever you are—whatever you're doing—you can study by listening to the following for each chapter of your textbook:

- *Big Ideas:* Your "need to know" for each chapter
- *Practice Test:* A gut check for the Big Ideas—tells you if you need to keep studying
- *Key Terms:* Audio "flashcards" to help you review key concepts and terms
- *Rapid Review:* A quick drill session—use it right before your test

VangoNotes are **flexible;** download all the material directly to your player, or only the chapters you need. And they're **efficient.** Use them in your car, at the gym, walking to class, or wherever. So get yours today at VangoNotes.com. And get studying.

Acknowledgments

No book is the work only of its authors. We greatly appreciate the valuable contributions of several people who helped make this new edition possible. We owe very special thanks to Keri Miksza for her deep and valuable involvement and advice throughout every phase of the project. We thank Andrew Norman of Drake University for his skillful development of company cases and for his assistance in preparing selected marketing stories. Thanks also go to Laurie Babin of the University of Southern Mississippi for her dedicated efforts in preparing the new Marketing by the Numbers appendix; Deborah Utter of Boston University for her able development of the end-of-chapter material; Marian Burk Wood for her help in creating the Marketing Plan appendix; and Mandy Roylance for her good work on the video cases.

Many reviewers at other colleges and universities provided valuable comments and suggestions for this and previous editions. We are indebted to the following colleagues for their thoughtful inputs:

Twelfth Edition Reviewers

Roger Berry, California State University, Dominguez Hills

Glenn Chappell, Coker College

Glenn L. Christensen, Brigham Young University

Kathleen Conklin, St. John Fisher College

Mary Conran, Temple University

Philip Gelman, College of DuPage

Hugh Guffey, Auburn University

Pat Jacoby, Purdue University

Carol Johanek, Washington University

Dolly D. Loyd, University of Southern Mississippi

Kerri Lum, Kapiolani Community College

Thomas R. Keen, Caldwell College

Dmitri Kuksov, Washington University in St. Louis

Larry Maes, Davenport University

Wendy Martin, Judson College, Illinois

Patrick H. McCaskey, Millersville University

June McDowell-Davis, Catawba College/High Point University

H. Lee Meadow, Indiana University East

John Mellon, College Misericordia University

William Renforth, Angelo State University

Melinda Schmitz, Pamlico Community College

Lynne Smith, Carroll Community College

Donna Tillman, California Polytechnic University, Pomona

Janice Trafflet, Bucknell University

Rafael Valiente, University of Miami

Douglas E Witt, Brigham Young University

Larry Zigler, Highland Community College

Former Reviewers

Ron Adams, University of North Florida

Sana Akili, Iowa State University

Mark Alpert, University of Texas at Austin

Mark Anderson, Eastern Kentucky University

Allan L. Appell, San Francisco State University

Laurie Babin, University of Southern Mississippi

Michael Ballif, University of Utah

Pat Bernson, County College of Morris

Amit Bhatnagar, University of Wisconsin

Thomas Brashear, University of Massachusetts, Amherst

Fred Brunel, Boston University

Jeff Bryden, Bowling Green University

David J. Burns, Youngstown State University

Sang T. Choe, University of Southern Indiana

Mary Conran, Temple University

Alicia Cooper, Morgan State University

Preyas Desai, Purdue University

Kenny Herbst, Saint Joseph's University

Terry Holmes, Murray State University

Eileen Kearney, Montgomery County Community College

Tina Kiesler, California State University at North Ridge

Bruce Lammers, California State University at North Ridge

J. Ford Laumer, Auburn University

Kenneth Lawrence, New Jersey Institute of Technology

Richard Leventhal, Metropolitan State College, Denver

Tamara Mangleburg, Florida Atlantic University

Patricia M. Manninen, North Shore Community College

H. Lee Meadow, Northern Illinois University

Mohan K. Menon, University of Southern Alabama

Martin Meyers, University of Wisconsin, Stevens Point

William Mindak, Tulane University

David M. Nemi, Niagra County Community College

Carl Obermiller, Seattle University

Howard Olsen, University of Nevada at Reno

Betty Parker, Western Michigan University

Vanessa Perry, George Washington University

Abe Qastin, Lakeland College

Paul Redig, Milwaukee Area Technical College

Roberta Schultz, Western Michigan University

Alan T. Shao, University of North Carolina, Charlotte

Martin St. John, Westmoreland County Community College

Karen Stone, Southern New Hampshire University

John Stovall, University of Illinois, Chicago

Jeff Streiter, SUNY Brockport

Ruth Taylor, Texas State University

Donna Tillman, California State Polytechnic University

Simon Walls, University of Tennessee

Mark Wasserman, University of Texas

Alvin Williams, University of Southern Mississippi

Andrew Yap, Florida International University

Irvin A. Zaenglein, Northern Michigan University

We also owe a great deal to the people at Prentice Hall who helped develop this book. Project Manager Melissa Pellerano provided valuable support and assistance and ably managed many facets of this complex revision project. We would also like to thank Angela Pica, Production Editor; Jeff Shelstad, Editorial Director; Judy Leale, Associate Director of Production; and Christy Mahon, Manager of Creative Services. We are proud to be associated with the fine professionals at Prentice Hall.

Finally, we owe many thanks to our families for all of their support and encouragement— Kathy, Betty, Mandy, Matt, KC, Keri, Delaney, Molly, and Macy from the Armstrong family and Nancy, Amy, Melissa, and Jessica from the Kotler family. To them, we dedicate this book.

Philip Kotler

Gary Armstrong

Principles of Marketing

1

Marketing
Managing Profitable Customer Relationships

Previewing the Concepts

Welcome to the exciting world of marketing. In this chapter, to start you off, we will first introduce you to the basic concepts. We'll start with a simple question: What *is* marketing? Simply put, marketing is managing profitable customer relationships. The aim of marketing is to create value for customers and to capture value in return. Chapter 1 is organized around five steps in the marketing process—from understanding customer needs, to designing customer-driven marketing strategies and programs, to building customer relationships and capturing value for the firm. Understanding these basic concepts, and forming your own ideas about what they really mean to you, will give you a solid foundation for all that follows.

To set the stage, let's first look at NASCAR. In only a few years, NASCAR has swiftly evolved from a pastime for beer-guzzling Bubbas into a national marketing phenomenon. How? By creating high-octane value for its millions of fans. In return, NASCAR captures value from these fans, both for itself and for its many sponsors. Read on and see how NASCAR does it.

When you think of NASCAR, do you think of tobacco-spitting rednecks and run-down race tracks? Think again! These days, NASCAR (the National Association for Stock Car Auto Racing) is much, much more. In fact, it's one great marketing organization. And for fans, NASCAR is a lot more than stock car races. It's a high-octane, totally involving experience.

As for the stereotypes, throw them away. NASCAR is now the second-highest rated regular season sport on TV—only the NFL draws more viewers—and races are seen in 150 countries in 23 languages. NASCAR fans are young, affluent, and decidedly family oriented—40 percent are women. What's more, they are 75 million strong—according to one survey, one in three Americans follows NASCAR. Most important, fans are passionate about NASCAR. A hardcore NASCAR fan spends nearly $700 a year on NASCAR-related clothing, collectibles, and other items. NASCAR has even become a cultural force, as politicians scramble to gain the favor of a powerful demographic dubbed "NASCAR dads."

What's NASCAR's secret? Its incredible success results from a single-minded focus: creating lasting customer relationships. For fans, the NASCAR relationship develops through a careful blend of live racing events, abundant media coverage, and compelling Web sites.

Each year, fans experience the adrenalin-charged, heart-stopping excitement of NASCAR racing firsthand by attending national tours to some two dozen tracks around the country. NASCAR races attract the largest crowds of any U.S. sporting event. About 240,000 people attended the recent Daytona 500, far more than attended the Super Bowl, and the Allstate Brickyard 400 sells out its more than 300,000 seats each year. Last year alone, NASCAR events captured 306 million television viewers.

At these events, fans hold tailgate parties, camp and cook out, watch the cars roar around the track, meet the drivers, and swap stories with other NASCAR enthusiasts. Track facilities even include RV parks next to and right inside the racing oval. Marvels one sponsor, "[In] what other sport can you drive your beat-up RV or camper into the stadium and sit on it to watch the race?" NASCAR really cares about its customers and goes out of its way to show them a good time. For example, rather than fleecing fans with over-priced food and beer, NASCAR tracks encourage fans to bring their own. Such actions mean that NASCAR might lose a sale today, but it will keep the customer tomorrow.

To further the customer relationship, NASCAR makes the sport a wholesome family affair. The environment is safe for kids—uniformed security guards patrol the track to keep things in line. The family atmosphere extends to the drivers, too. Unlike the aloof and often distant athletes in other sports, NASCAR drivers seem like regular guys. They are friendly and readily available to mingle with fans and sign autographs. Fans view drivers as good role models, and the long NASCAR tradition of family involvement creates the next generation of loyal fans.

Can't make it to the track? No problem. An average NASCAR event reaches 18 million TV viewers. Well-orchestrated coverage and in-car cameras put fans in the middle of the action, giving them vicarious thrills that keep them glued to the screen. "When the network gets it right, my surround-sound bothers my neighbors but makes my ears happy," says Angela Kotula, a 35-year-old human resources professional.

NASCAR also delivers the NASCAR experience through its engaging Web sites. NASCAR.com serves up a glut of information and entertainment—in-depth news, driver bios, background information, online games, community discussions, and merchandise. True die-hard fans can subscribe to TrackPass to get up-to-the-minute audio and video highlights. TrackPass with PitCommand even delivers a real-time data feed, complete with the GPS locations of cars and data from drivers' dashboards.

But a big part of the NASCAR experience is the feeling that the sport, itself, is personally accessible. Anyone who knows how to drive feels that he or she, too, could be a champion NASCAR driver. As 48-year-old police officer Ed Sweat puts it: "Genetics did not bless me with the height of a basketball player, nor was I born to have the bulk of a

Objectives

After studying this chapter, you should be able to

1. define marketing and outline the steps in the marketing process

2. explain the importance of understanding customers and the marketplace, and identify the five core marketplace concepts

3. identify the key elements of a customer-driven marketing strategy and discuss the marketing management orientations that guide marketing strategy

4. discuss customer relationship management, and identify strategies for creating value *from* customers and capturing value *for* customers in return

5. describe the major trends and forces that are changing the marketing landscape in this age of relationships

lineman in the NFL. But . . . on any given Sunday, with a rich sponsor, the right car, and some practice, I could be draftin' and passin', zooming to the finish line, trading paint with Tony Stewart. . . . Yup, despite my advancing age and waistline, taking Zocor, and driving by a gym . . . I could be Dale Jarrett!"

Ultimately, such fan enthusiasm translates into financial success for NASCAR, and for its sponsors. Television networks pay on average $555 million per year for the rights to broadcast NASCAR events. With everything from NASCAR-branded bacon and its own series of Harlequin romance novels to NASCAR-branded bikinis, the sport is third in licensed merchandise sales, behind only the NFL and the NCAA. NASCAR itself sells $2 billion in merchandise a year. And marketing studies show that NASCAR's fans are more loyal to the sport's sponsors than fans of any other sport. They are three times more to likely seek out and buy sponsor's products and services than nonfans, and 72 percent of NASCAR fans consciously purchase sponsors' products because of the NASCAR connection.

Just ask Ted Wuebben, a big fan of NASCAR driver Rusty Wallace, whose car is sponsored by Miller beer. "I only drink Miller Lite," he says, "not because it tastes great or it's less filling, but because of Rusty." Or talk to dental hygienist Jenny German, an ardent fan of driver Jeff Gordon. According to one account: "She actively seeks out any product he endorses. She drinks Pepsi instead of Coke, eats Edy's ice cream for dessert, and owns a pair of Ray-Ban sunglasses. 'If they sold underwear with the number 24 on it, I'd have it on,' German says."

Because of such loyal fan relationships, NASCAR has attracted more than 250 big-name sponsors, from Wal-Mart, Home Depot, and Target to Procter & Gamble, UPS, Coca-Cola, and the U.S. Army. In all, corporations spend more than $1 billion a year for NASCAR sponsorships and promotions. Sprint Nextel is shelling out $750 million over a span of ten years to be a NASCAR sponsor and to put its name on the Nextel Cup series. "I could pay you $1 million to try and not run into our name at a NASCAR race and you would lose," says a Nextel spokesperson. Other sponsors eagerly pay up to $20 million per year to sponsor a top car and to get their corporate colors and logos emblazoned on team uniforms and on the hoods or side panels of team cars. Or they pay $3 million to $5 million a year to become the "official" (fill-in-the-blank) of NASCAR racing. Is it worth the price? Office Depot certainly thinks so. It began sponsoring a car when its surveys showed that 44 percent of rival Staples' customers would switch office supply retailers if Office Depot hooked up with NASCAR.

So if you're still thinking of NASCAR as rednecks and moonshine, you'd better think again. NASCAR is a premier marketing organization that knows how to create customer value that translates into deep and lasting customer relationships. "Better than any other sport," says a leading sports marketing executive, "NASCAR listens to its fans and gives them what they want." In turn, fans reward NASCAR and its sponsors with deep loyalty and the promise of lasting profits.[1]

Today's successful companies have one thing in common: Like NASCAR, they are strongly customer focused and heavily committed to marketing. These companies share a passion for satisfying customer needs in well-defined target markets. They motivate everyone in the organization to help build lasting customer relationships through superior customer value and satisfaction. As Wal-Mart founder Sam Walton once asserted: "There is only one boss. The customer. And he can fire everybody in the company from the chairman on down, simply by spending his money somewhere else."

What Is Marketing?

Marketing, more than any other business function, deals with customers. Although we will soon explore more-detailed definitions of marketing, perhaps the simplest definition is this one: Marketing is managing profitable customer relationships. The twofold goal of marketing is to attract new customers by promising superior value and to keep and grow current customers by delivering satisfaction.

Wal-Mart has become the world's largest retailer, and one of the world's largest companies, by delivering on its promise, "Always low prices. Always!" At Disney theme parks, "imagineers" work wonders in their quest to "make a dream come true today." Dell leads the personal computer industry by consistently making good on its promise to "be direct." Dell makes it easy for customers to custom-design their own computers and have them delivered quickly to their doorsteps or desktops. These and other highly successful companies know that if they take care of their customers, market share and profits will follow.

Sound marketing is critical to the success of every organization. Large for-profit firms such as Procter & Gamble, Toyota, Target, Apple, and Marriott use marketing. But so do not-for-profit organizations such as colleges, hospitals, museums, symphony orchestras, and even churches.

You already know a lot about marketing—it's all around you. You see the results of marketing in the abundance of products in your nearby shopping mall. You see marketing in the advertisements that fill your TV screen, spice up your magazines, stuff your mailbox, or enliven your Web pages. At home, at school, where you work, and where you play, you see marketing in almost everything you do. Yet, there is much more to marketing than meets the consumer's casual eye. Behind it all is a massive network of people and activities competing for your attention and purchases.

This book will give you a complete introduction to the basic concepts and practices of today's marketing. In this chapter, we begin by defining marketing and the marketing process.

Marketing Defined

What *is* marketing? Many people think of marketing only as selling and advertising. And no wonder—every day we are bombarded with television commercials, direct-mail offers, sales calls, and Internet pitches. However, selling and advertising are only the tip of the marketing iceberg.

Today, marketing must be understood not in the old sense of making a sale—"telling and selling"—but in the new sense of *satisfying customer needs.* If the marketer understands consumer needs; develops products and services that provide superior customer value; and prices, distributes, and promotes them effectively, these products will sell easily. In fact, according to management guru Peter Drucker, "The aim of marketing is to make selling unnecessary."[2] Selling and advertising are only part of a larger "marketing mix"—a set of marketing tools that work together to satisfy customer needs and build customer relationships.

Broadly defined, marketing is a social and managerial process by which individuals and organizations obtain what they need and want through creating and exchanging value with others. In a narrower business context, marketing involves building profitable, value-laden exchange relationships with customers. Hence, we define **marketing** as the process by which companies create value for customers and build strong customer relationships in order to capture value from customers in return.[3]

The Marketing Process

Figure 1.1 presents a simple five-step model of the marketing process. In the first four steps, companies work to understand consumers, create customer value, and build strong customer relationships. In the final step, companies reap the rewards of creating superior customer value. By creating value *for* consumers, they in turn capture value *from* consumers in the form of sales, profits, and long-term customer equity.

In this and the next chapter, we will examine the steps of this simple model of marketing. In this chapter, we will review each step but focus more on the customer relationship steps—understanding customers, building customer relationships, and capturing value from customers. In Chapter 2, we'll look more deeply into the second and third steps—designing marketing strategies and constructing marketing programs.

FIGURE 1.1 A simple model of the marketing process

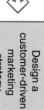

Understand the marketplace and customer needs and wants

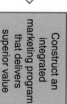

Design a customer-driven marketing strategy

Construct an integrated marketing program that delivers superior value

Build profitable relationships and create customer delight

Capture value from customers to create profits and customer equity

Create value *for* customers and build customer relationships

Capture value *from* customers in return

Understanding the Marketplace and Customer Needs

As a first step, marketers need to understand customer needs and wants and the marketplace within which they operate. We now examine five core customer and marketplace concepts: (1) *needs, wants, and demands*; (2) *marketing offerings (products, services, and experiences)*; (3) *value and satisfaction*; (4) *exchanges and relationships*; and (5) *markets*.

Customer Needs, Wants, and Demands

The most basic concept underlying marketing is that of human needs. Human **needs** are states of felt deprivation. They include basic *physical* needs for food, clothing, warmth, and safety; *social* needs for belonging and affection; and *individual* needs for knowledge and self-expression. These needs were not created by marketers; they are a basic part of the human makeup.

Wants are the form human needs take as they are shaped by culture and individual personality. An American *needs* food but *wants* a Big Mac, french fries, and a soft drink. A person in Mauritius *needs* food but *wants* a mango, rice, lentils, and beans. Wants are shaped by one's society and are described in terms of objects that will satisfy needs. When backed by buying power, wants become **demands**. Given their wants and resources, people demand products with benefits that add up to the most value and satisfaction.

Outstanding marketing companies go to great lengths to learn about and understand their customers' needs, wants, and demands. They conduct consumer research and analyze mountains of customer data. Their people at all levels—including top management—stay close to customers. For example, at Southwest Airlines, all senior executives handle bags, check in passengers, and serve as flight attendants once every quarter. Harley-Davidson's chairman regularly mounts his Harley and rides with customers to get feedback and ideas. And at Build-A-Bear, one of the country's fastest-growing retailers, founder and chief executive Maxine Clark visits two or three of her more than 200 stores each week, meeting customers, chatting with employees, and just getting to know the preteens who buy her products. "I'm on a lot of online buddy lists," she says.[4]

Market Offerings—Products, Services, and Experiences

Consumers' needs and wants are fulfilled through a **market offering**—some combination of products, services, information, or experiences offered to a market to satisfy a need or want. Market offerings are not limited to physical *products*. They also include *services*, activities or benefits offered for sale that are essentially intangible and do not result in the ownership of anything. Examples include banking, airline, hotel, tax preparation, and home repair services. More broadly, market offerings also include other entities, such as *persons, places, organizations, information*, and *ideas*. For example, beyond promoting its banking services, LaSalle Bank runs ads asking people to donate used or old winter clothing to the Salvation Army. In this case, the "market offering" is helping to keep those who are less fortunate warm.

Many sellers make the mistake of paying more attention to the specific products they offer than to the benefits and experiences produced by these products. These sellers suffer from **marketing myopia**. They are so taken with their products that they focus only on existing wants and lose sight of underlying customer needs.[5] They forget that a product is only a tool to solve a consumer problem. A manufacturer of quarter-inch drill bits may think that the customer needs a drill bit. But what the customer *really* needs is a quarter-inch hole. These sellers will have trouble if a new product comes along that serves the customer's need better or less expensively. The customer will have the same *need* but will *want* the new product.

Smart marketers look beyond the attributes of the products and services they sell. By orchestrating several services and products, they create *brand experiences* for consumers. For example, Walt Disney World is an experience; so is a ride on a Harley-Davidson motorcycle. And you don't just watch a NASCAR race; you immerse yourself in the NASCAR experience. Says A. G. Lafley, CEO of Procter & Gamble, "Consumers want more than attributes and benefits, and even solutions. They want delightful shopping, usage, and service experiences they look forward to, time after time." P&G's Mr. Clean brand "Doesn't ask, 'How can we help to get customers' floors and toilets cleaner?' No, the more inspiring questions is, 'How can we give customers their Saturday mornings back?'"[6]

Needs
States of felt deprivation.

Wants
The form human needs take as shaped by culture and individual personality.

Demands
Human wants that are backed by buying power.

Market offering
Some combination of products, services, information, or experiences offered to a market to satisfy a need or want.

Marketing myopia
The mistake of paying more attention to the specific products a company offers than to the benefits and experiences produced by these products.

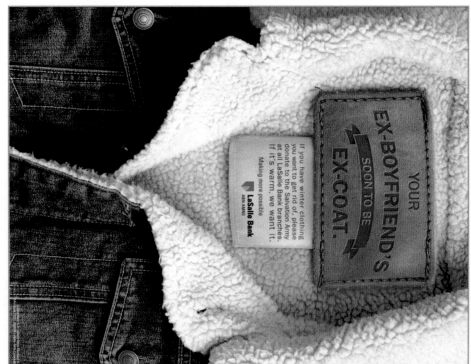

Similarly, Hewlett-Packard recognizes that a personal computer is much more than just a collection of wires and electrical components. It's an intensely personal user experience: "There is hardly anything that you own that is *more* personal. Your personal computer is your backup brain. It's your life. . . . It's your astonishing strategy, staggering proposal, dazzling calculation. It's your autobiography, written in a thousand daily words."[7]

Customer Value and Satisfaction

Consumers usually face a broad array of products and services that might satisfy a given need. How do they choose among these many market offerings? Customers form expectations about the value and satisfaction that various market offerings will deliver and buy accordingly. Satisfied customers buy again and tell others about their good experiences. Dissatisfied customers often switch to competitors and disparage the product to others.

Marketers must be careful to set the right level of expectations. If they set expectations too low, they may satisfy those who buy but fail to attract enough buyers. If they raise expectations too high, buyers will be disappointed. Customer value and customer satisfaction are key building blocks for developing and managing customer relationships. We will revisit these core concepts later in the chapter.

Exchanges and Relationships

Marketing occurs when people decide to satisfy needs and wants through exchange relationships.

Exchange is the act of obtaining a desired object from someone by offering something in return. In the broadest sense, the marketer tries to bring about a response to some market offering. The response may be more than simply buying or trading products and services. A political candidate, for instance, wants votes, a church wants membership, an orchestra wants an audience, and a social action group wants idea acceptance.

Marketing consists of actions taken to build and maintain desirable exchange *relationships* with target audiences involving a product, service, idea, or other object. Beyond simply attracting new customers and creating transactions, the goal is to retain customers and grow their business with the company. Marketers want to build strong relationships by consistently delivering superior customer value. We will expand on the important concept of managing customer relationships later in the chapter.

Markets

The concepts of exchange and relationships lead to the concept of a market. A **market** is the set of actual and potential buyers of a product. These buyers share a particular need or want that can be satisfied through exchange relationships.

Marketing means managing markets to bring about profitable customer relationships. However, creating these relationships takes work. Sellers must search for buyers, identify their needs, design good market offerings, set prices for them, promote them, and store and deliver them. Activities such as product development, research, communication, distribution, pricing, and service are core marketing activities.

■ Market offerings are not limited to physical products. For example, LaSalle Bank runs ads asking people to donate used or old winter clothing to the Salvation Army. In this case, the "marketing offer" is helping to keep those who are less fortunate warm.

Exchange
The act of obtaining a desired object from someone by offering something in return.

Market
The set of all actual and potential buyers of a product or service.

FIGURE 1.2
Elements of a modern marketing system

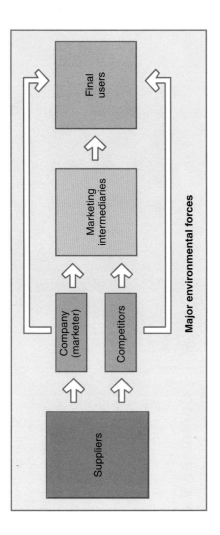

Although we normally think of marketing as being carried on by sellers, buyers also carry on marketing. Consumers do marketing when they search for the goods they need at prices they can afford. Company purchasing agents do marketing when they track down sellers and bargain for good terms.

Figure 1.2 shows the main elements in a modern marketing system. In the usual situation, marketing involves serving a market of final consumers in the face of competitors. The company and the competitors send their respective offers and messages to consumers, either directly or through marketing intermediaries. All of the actors in the system are affected by major environmental forces (demographic, economic, physical, technological, political/legal, and social/cultural).

Each party in the system adds value for the next level. All of the arrows represent relationships that must be developed and managed. Thus, a company's success at building profitable relationships depends not only on its own actions but also on how well the entire system serves the needs of final consumers. Wal-Mart cannot fulfill its promise of low prices unless its suppliers provide merchandise at low costs. And Ford cannot deliver high quality to car buyers unless its dealers provide outstanding sales and service.

Designing a Customer-Driven Marketing Strategy

Once it fully understands consumers and the marketplace, marketing management can design a customer-driven marketing strategy. We define **marketing management** as the art and science of choosing target markets and building profitable relationships with them. The marketing manager's aim is to find, attract, keep, and grow target customers by creating, delivering, and communicating superior customer value.

To design a winning marketing strategy, the marketing manager must answer two important questions: *What customers will we serve (what's our target market)?* and *How can we serve these customers best (what's our value proposition)?* We will discuss these marketing strategy concepts briefly here, and then look at them in more detail in the next chapter.

Marketing management
The art and science of choosing target markets and building profitable relationships with them.

Selecting Customers to Serve

The company must first decide *who* it will serve. It does this by dividing the market into segments of customers (*market segmentation*) and selecting which segments it will go after (*target marketing*). Some people think of marketing management as finding as many customers as possible and increasing demand. But marketing managers know that they cannot serve all customers in every way. By trying to serve all customers, they may not serve any customers well. Instead, the company wants to select only customers that it can serve well and profitably. For example, Nordstrom stores profitably target affluent professionals; Family Dollar stores profitably target families with more modest means.

Some marketers may even seek *fewer* customers and reduced demand. For example, many power companies have trouble meeting demand during peak usage periods. In these

and other cases of excess demand, companies may practice *demarketing* to reduce the number of customers or to shift their demand temporarily or permanently. For instance, to reduce demand for space on congested expressways in Washington, D.C., the Metropolitan Washington Council of Governments has set up a Web site encouraging commuters to carpool and use mass transit (www.commuterconnections.org).[8]

Thus, marketing managers must decide which customers they want to target and the level, timing, and nature of their demand. Simply put, marketing management is *customer management* and *demand management*.

Choosing a Value Proposition

The company must also decide how it will serve targeted customers—how it will *differentiate and position* itself in the marketplace. A company's *value proposition* is the set of benefits or values it promises to deliver to consumers to satisfy their needs. Saab promises driving performance and excitement: "Born from jets . . . you can learn what it's like to fly without ever leaving the ground." By contrast, Subaru provides safety: "Air bags save lives. All-wheel drive saves air bags. It's what makes a Subaru a Subaru." Propel Fitness Water by Gatorade is "made for bodies in motion." Red Bull energy drink, on the other hand, helps you fight mental and physical fatigue. It captures 70 percent of the energy drink market by promising "It gives you wiiings!"

Such value propositions differentiate one brand from another. They answer the customer's question "Why should I buy your brand rather than a competitor's?" Companies must design strong value propositions that give them the greatest advantage in their target markets.

■ Value propositions: Red Bull Energy Drink "vitalizes both body and mind. It Gives You Wiiings."

Marketing Management Orientations

Marketing management wants to design strategies that will build profitable relationships with target consumers. But what *philosophy* should guide these marketing strategies? What weight should be given to the interests of customers, the organization, and society? Often, these interests conflict.

There are five alternative concepts under which organizations design and carry out their marketing strategies: the *production, product, selling, marketing,* and *societal marketing concepts.*

The Production Concept

The **production concept** holds that consumers will favor products that are available and highly affordable. Therefore, management should focus on improving production and distribution efficiency. This concept is one of the oldest orientations that guides sellers.

The production concept is still a useful philosophy in some situations. For example, computer maker Lenovo dominates the highly competitive, price-sensitive Chinese PC market through low labor costs, high production efficiency, and mass distribution. However, although useful in some situations, the production concept can lead to marketing myopia. Companies adopting this orientation run a major risk of focusing too narrowly on their own operations and losing sight of the real objective—satisfying customer needs and building customer relationships.

Production concept
The idea that consumers will favor products that are available and highly affordable and that the organization should therefore focus on improving production and distribution efficiency.

The Product Concept

The **product concept** holds that consumers will favor products that offer the most in quality, performance, and innovative features. Under this concept, marketing strategy focuses on making continuous product improvements.

Product concept

The idea that consumers will favor products that offer the most quality, performance, and features and that the organization should therefore devote its energy to making continuous product improvements.

Product concept

Product quality and improvement are important parts of most marketing strategies. However, focusing *only* on the company's products can also lead to marketing myopia. For example, some manufacturers believe that if they can "build a better mousetrap, the world will beat a path to their door." But they are often rudely shocked. Buyers may well be looking for a better solution to a mouse problem but not necessarily for a better mousetrap. The better solution might be a chemical spray, an exterminating service, or something that works better than a mousetrap. Furthermore, a better mousetrap will not sell unless the manufacturer designs, packages, and prices it attractively; places it in convenient distribution channels; brings it to the attention of people who need it; and convinces buyers that it is a better product.

The Selling Concept

Selling concept

The idea that consumers will not buy enough of the firm's products unless it undertakes a large-scale selling and promotion effort.

Many companies follow the **selling concept**, which holds that consumers will not buy enough of the firm's products unless it undertakes a large-scale selling and promotion effort. The concept is typically practiced with unsought goods—those that buyers do not normally think of buying, such as insurance or blood donations. These industries must track down prospects and sell them on product benefits.

Such aggressive selling, however, carries high risks. It focuses on creating sales transactions rather than on building long-term, profitable customer relationships. The aim often is to sell what the company makes rather than making what the market wants. It assumes that customers who are coaxed into buying the product will like it. Or, if they don't like it, they will possibly forget their disappointment and buy it again later. These are usually poor assumptions.

The Marketing Concept

Marketing concept

The marketing management philosophy that achieving organizational goals depends on knowing the needs and wants of target markets and delivering the desired satisfactions better than competitors do.

The **marketing concept** holds that achieving organizational goals depends on knowing the needs and wants of target markets and delivering the desired satisfactions better than competitors do. Under the marketing concept, customer focus and value are the *paths* to sales and profits. Instead of a product-centered "make and sell" philosophy, the marketing concept is a customer-centered "sense and respond" philosophy. It views marketing not as "hunting," but as "gardening." The job is not to find the right customers for your product, but to find the right products for your customers.

Figure 1.3 contrasts the selling concept and the marketing concept. The selling concept takes an *inside-out* perspective. It starts with the factory, focuses on the company's existing products, and calls for heavy selling and promotion to obtain profitable sales. It focuses primarily on customer conquest—getting short-term sales with little concern about who buys or why.

In contrast, the marketing concept takes an *outside-in* perspective. As Herb Kelleher, Southwest Airlines' colorful CEO, puts it, "We don't have a marketing department; we have a customer department." And in the words of one Ford executive, "If we're not customer driven, our cars won't be either."[9] The marketing concept starts with a well-defined market, focuses on customer needs, and integrates all the marketing activities that affect customers. In turn, it yields profits by creating lasting relationships with the right customers based on customer value and satisfaction.

Implementing the marketing concept often means more than simply responding to customers' stated desires and obvious needs. *Customer-driven* companies research current cus-

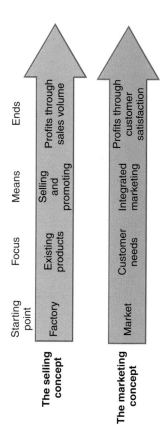

FIGURE 1.3
The selling and marketing concepts contrasted

	Starting point	Focus	Means	Ends
The selling concept	Factory	Existing products	Selling and promoting	Profits through sales volume
The marketing concept	Market	Customer needs	Integrated marketing	Profits through customer satisfaction

tomers deeply to learn about their desires, gather new product and service ideas, and test proposed product improvements. Such customer-driven marketing usually works well when a clear need exists and when customers know what they want.

In many cases, however, customers *don't* know what they want or even what is possible. For example, even 20 years ago, how many consumers would have thought to ask for now-commonplace products such as cell phones, notebook computers, iPods, digital cameras, 24-hour online buying, and satellite navigation systems in their cars? Such situations call for *customer-driving* marketing—understanding customer needs even better than customers themselves do and creating products and services that meet existing and latent needs, now and in the future. As an executive at 3M puts it: "Our goal is to lead customers where they want to go before *they* know where they want to go."

The Societal Marketing Concept

The **societal marketing concept** questions whether the pure marketing concept overlooks possible conflicts between consumer *short-run wants* and consumer *long-run welfare*. Is a firm that satisfies the immediate needs and wants of target markets always doing what's best for consumers in the long run? The societal marketing concept holds that marketing strategy should deliver value to customers in a way that maintains or improves both the consumer's *and the society's* well-being.

Consider the fast-food industry. You may view today's giant fast-food chains as offering tasty and convenient food at reasonable prices. Yet many consumer nutritionists and environmental groups have voiced strong concerns. They point to fast feeders such as Hardee's, who are promoting monster meals such as the Monster Thickburger—two 1/3-pound slabs of Angus beef, four strips of bacon, three slices of

American cheese, and mayonnaise on a buttered bun, delivering 1,420 calories and 102 grams of fat. And McDonald's and Burger King still cook their fried foods in oils that are high in artery-clogging trans fats. Such unhealthy fare, the critics claim, is leading consumers to eat too much of the wrong foods, contributing to a national obesity epidemic. What's more, the products are wrapped in convenient packaging, but this leads to waste and pollution. Thus, in satisfying short-term consumer wants, the highly successful fast-food chains may be harming consumer health and causing environmental problems in the long run.[10]

As Figure 1.4 shows, companies should balance three considerations in setting their marketing strategies: company profits, consumer wants, *and* society's interests. Johnson & Johnson does this well. Its concern for societal interests is summarized in a company document called

Societal marketing concept

A principle of enlightened marketing that holds that a company should make good marketing decisions by considering consumers' wants, the company's requirements, consumers' long-run interests, and society's long-run interests.

■ Customer-driving marketing: Even 20 years ago, how many consumers would have thought to ask for now-commonplace products such as cell phones, personal digital assistants, notebook computers, iPods, and digital cameras? Marketers must often understand customer needs even better than the customers themselves do.

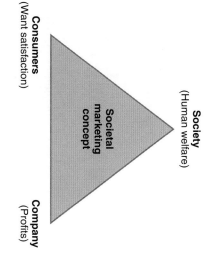

FIGURE 1.4
Three considerations underlying the societal marketing concept

Society
(Human welfare)

Societal
marketing
concept

Consumers
(Want satisfaction)

Company
(Profits)

"Our Credo," which stresses honesty, integrity, and putting people before profits. Under this credo, Johnson & Johnson would rather take a big loss than ship a bad batch of one of its products.

Consider the tragic tampering case in which eight people died in 1982 from swallowing cyanide-laced capsules of Tylenol, a Johnson & Johnson brand. Although Johnson & Johnson believed that the pills had been altered in only a few stores, not in the factory, it quickly recalled all of its product and launched an information campaign to instruct and reassure consumers. The recall cost the company $100 million in earnings. In the long run, however, the company's swift recall of Tylenol strengthened consumer confidence and loyalty, and today Tylenol remains one of the nation's leading brands of pain reliever.

Johnson & Johnson management has learned that doing what's right benefits both consumers and the company. Says former CEO Ralph Larsen, "The Credo should not be viewed as some kind of social welfare program . . . it's just plain good business. If we keep trying to do what's right, at the end of the day we believe the marketplace will reward us." Thus, over the years, Johnson & Johnson's dedication to consumers and community service has made it one of America's most-admired companies *and* one of the most profitable.[11]

Our Credo

We believe our first responsibility is to the doctors, nurses and patients, to mothers and fathers and all others who use our products and services. In meeting their needs everything we do must be of high quality. We must constantly strive to reduce our costs in order to maintain reasonable prices. Customers' orders must be serviced promptly and accurately. Our suppliers and distributors must have an opportunity to make a fair profit.

We are responsible to our employees, the men and women who work with us throughout the world. Everyone must be considered as an individual. We must respect their dignity and recognize their merit. They must have a sense of security in their jobs. Compensation must be fair and adequate, and working conditions clean, orderly and safe. We must be mindful of ways to help our employees fulfill their family responsibilities. Employees must feel free to make suggestions and complaints. There must be equal opportunity for employment, development and advancement for those qualified. We must provide competent management, and their actions must be just and ethical.

We are responsible to the communities in which we live and work and to the world community as well. We must be good citizens — support good works and charities and bear our fair share of taxes. We must encourage civic improvements and better health and education. We must maintain in good order the property we are privileged to use, protecting the environment and natural resources.

Our final responsibility is to our stockholders. Business must make a sound profit. We must experiment with new ideas. Research must be carried on, innovative programs developed and mistakes paid for. New equipment must be purchased, new facilities provided and new products launched. Reserves must be created to provide for adverse times. When we operate according to these principles, the stockholders should realize a fair return.

Johnson & Johnson

■ The societal marketing concept: Johnson & Johnson's Credo stresses putting people before profits. Johnson & Johnson's quick product recall following a tragic Tylenol tampering incident some years ago cost the company $100 million in earnings but strengthened consumer confidence and loyalty.

Preparing an Integrated Marketing Plan and Program

The company's marketing strategy outlines which customers the company will serve and how it will create value for these customers. Next, the marketer develops an integrated marketing program that will actually deliver the intended value to target customers. The marketing program builds customer relationships by transforming the marketing strategy into action. It consists of the firm's *marketing mix*, the set of marketing tools the firm uses to implement its marketing strategy.

The major marketing mix tools are classified into four broad groups, called the *four Ps* of marketing; product, price, place, and promotion. To deliver on its value proposition, the firm must first create a need-satisfying market offering (product). It must decide how much it will charge for the offer (price) and how it will make the offer available to target consumers (place). Finally, it must communicate with target customers about the offer and persuade them of its merits (promotion). The firm must blend all of these marketing mix tools into a comprehensive, *integrated marketing program* that communicates and delivers the intended value to chosen customers. We will explore marketing programs and the marketing mix in much more detail in later chapters.

Building Customer Relationships

The first three steps in the marketing process—understanding the marketplace and customer needs, designing a customer-driven marketing strategy, and constructing marketing programs—all lead up to the fourth and most important step: building profitable customer relationships.

Customer Relationship Management

Customer relationship management (*CRM*) is perhaps the most important concept of modern marketing. Until recently, CRM has been defined narrowly as a customer data management activity. By this definition, it involves managing detailed information about individual customers and carefully managing customer "touch points" in order to maximize customer loyalty. We will discuss this narrower CRM activity in a later chapter dealing with marketing information.

More recently, however, customer relationship management has taken on a broader meaning. In this broader sense, **customer relationship management** is the overall process of building and maintaining profitable customer relationships by delivering superior customer value and satisfaction. It deals with all aspects of acquiring, keeping, and growing customers.

Relationship Building Blocks: Customer Value and Satisfaction

The key to building lasting customer relationships is to create superior customer value and satisfaction. Satisfied customers are more likely to be loyal customers and to give the company a larger share of their business.

CUSTOMER VALUE Attracting and retaining customers can be a difficult task. Customers often face a bewildering array of products and services from which to choose. A customer buys from the firm that offers the highest **customer perceived value**—the customer's evaluation of the difference between all the benefits and all the costs of a market offering relative to those of competing offers.

For example, Toyota Prius hybrid automobile owners gain a number of benefits. The most obvious benefit is fuel efficiency. However, by purchasing a Prius, the owners also may receive some status and image values. Driving a Prius makes owners feel and appear more environmentally responsible. When deciding whether to purchase a Prius, customers will weigh these and other perceived values of owning the car against the money, effort, and psychic costs of acquiring it. Moreover, they will compare the value of owning a Prius against that of owning another hybrid or nonhybrid brand. They will select the brand that gives them the greatest perceived value.

Customers often do not judge product values and costs accurately or objectively. They act on *perceived value*. For example, is the Prius really the most economical choice? In reality, it might take years to save enough in reduced fuel costs to offset the car's higher sticker price. However, Prius buyers perceive that they are getting real value. A recent survey of the ownership experiences of 69,000 new car buyers showed that the Prius was rated as most "delightful" in terms of fuel economy, and that Prius owners perceived more overall value for their money than buyers of any other hybrid car.[12]

CUSTOMER SATISFACTION Customer satisfaction depends on the product's perceived performance relative to a buyer's expectations. If the product's performance falls short of expectations, the customer is dissatisfied. If performance matches expectations, the customer is satisfied. If performance exceeds expectations, the customer is highly satisfied or delighted.

Outstanding marketing companies go out of their way to keep important customers satisfied. Most studies show that higher levels of customer satisfaction lead to greater customer loyalty, which in turn results in better company performance. Smart companies aim to *delight* customers by promising only what they can deliver, then delivering *more* than they promise. Delighted customers

---

GET THE FEELING

The next generation gas/electric Prius with hybrid Synergy Drive. Best emission rating for a gas-powered production vehicle. Best estimated.

Best economy in a mid-size car. All with the best interests of the earth in mind. Take a deep breath everyone. The Prius is here. **toyota.com**

©2005 Toyota Motor Sales, U.S.A., Inc. *Based on production vehicles only. California Air Resources Board SULEV rating.

Lifetime supply of fresh air with every purchase.

The power to move forward.

PRIUS CARB NOW

TOYOTA

Customer relationship management
The overall process of building and maintaining profitable customer relationships by delivering superior customer value and satisfaction.

Customer perceived value
The customer's evaluation of the difference between all the benefits and all the costs of a market offering relative to those of competing offers.

Customer satisfaction
The extent to which a product's perceived performance matches a buyer's expectations.

■ Perceived customer value: When deciding whether to purchase a Prius, customers will weigh its benefits against the benefits of owning another hybrid or non-hybrid brand.

Real Marketing   Bike Friday: Creating Customer Evangelists

Delighting customers: Bike Friday has built a core of delighted "customer evangelists" who can't wait to tell others about their Bike Friday experiences.

1.1 Margaret Day loves to talk about her bicycle—almost as much as she loves to ride it. And that's a good thing for custom-cycle maker Bike Friday: Day, a 70-something Australian, has made about 100 customer referrals worth more than $300,000 in sales since she purchased her first bike in 1995. "I simply cannot stop telling people about the Bike Friday," she says. Her most recent referral, in March, garnered almost $5,000 worth of bicycle sales for the company.

You can't buy that kind of loyalty, but you can cultivate it—and that's precisely what Green Gear Cycling (known as Bike Friday after its signature product) has done. Through bike clubs, newsletters, Web forums, and a referral rewards program, it has built a community of delighted customer evangelists whose word-of-mouth testimony has proven more effective for the company than mounting an expensive advertising campaign. "We get key customers who are excited to be involved," says Bike Friday's Lynette Chiang. "They attract others and this creates community."

Chiang is Bike Friday's chief Customer Evangelist, the company's official World Traveler and marketing chief. Her job is to create customer delight and build customer relationships. "The role of the evangelist is to make a connection with a human being. In selling loyalty and a brand, you need to understand that brands need to be built for the long haul." Bike Friday is a small company with an even smaller mar-

keting budget. So its customer evangelism strategy has been crucial to the company's success.

It doesn't hurt that the unusual styling of the custom-fit, high-end travel bikes catches plenty of eyes—and prospects. Bike Friday bikes fold in seconds, pack into a standard airline suitcase, and ride like a

not only make repeat purchases, they become "customer evangelists" who tell others about their good experiences with the product (see Real Marketing 1.1).

For companies interested in delighting customers, exceptional value and service are more than a set of policies or actions—they are a companywide attitude, an important part of the overall company culture. Consider the following example:[13]

A man bought his first new Lexus—a $45,000 piece of machinery. He could afford a Mercedes, a BMW, or a Cadillac, but he bought the Lexus. He took delivery of his new honey and started to drive it home, luxuriating in the smell of the leather interior and the glorious handling. On the interstate, he put the pedal to the metal and felt the Gs in the pit of his stomach. The lights, the windshield washer, the gizmo cup holder that popped out of the center console, the seat heater that warmed his bottom on a cold winter morning—he tried all of these with mounting pleasure. On a whim, he turned on the radio. His favorite classical music station came on in splendid quadraphonic sound that ricocheted around the interior. He pushed the second button; it was his favorite news station. The third button brought his favorite talk station that kept him awake on long trips. The fourth button was set to his daughter's favorite rock station. In fact, every button was set to his specific tastes. The customer knew the car was smart, but was it psychic? No. The mechanic at Lexus had noted the radio settings on his trade-in and duplicated them on the new Lexus. The customer was delighted. This was his car now—through and through! No one told the mechanic to do it. It's just part of the Lexus philosophy: Delight a customer and continue to delight that customer, and you will have a

full-size performance bike. The curiosity factor has proven a powerful way to reach new customers, particularly in the company's early years when marketing money was tight. "The nature of anything custom is you will have or generate an interest group, community group, or cult," says Chiang. "We call it a community." Creating relationships and community makes sense, given the nature of the company's target market. "Bike Friday's customers are not fickle teens," says one observer, "but 40-something, well-heeled professionals who travel extensively and cherish personalized service." The Bike Friday Web site, newsletter, and catalog are filled with pictures of happy owners biking all over the world.

Bike Friday has cultivated this community in a number of ways, most notably through its 30 Bike Friday Clubs of America (and Beyond). Chiang describes these groups as self-perpetuating loyalty centers in the field, whose activities provide a social outlet for riders and help to generate referrals. The clubs are free to anyone, regardless of what brand of bike they ride. However, it usually doesn't take long for the Bike Friday enthusiasts in the clubs to convert the non-believers.

The "Community" page on the Bike Friday Web site welcomes new owners into the fold: "Come get to know the rest of the community," it suggests. "Buying your Bike Friday travel bike was just the beginning. Now you are automatically a member of a family of Bike Friday enthusiasts crisscrossing the globe on their little wheels." The site also invites the faithful to send photos and share travel stories. "We want to see you using your new bike," it says. To create interaction, Bike Friday also operates Yak!, an e-mail discussion list that lets owners swap tips, tricks, and travel ideas relating to Bike Friday. Besides creating chat, the discussion list provides great feedback. Chiang reads the forum daily, looking for ways to create even more customer delight.

Bike Friday enthusiasts usually can't wait to tell others about their Bike Friday experiences. So the company formalizes the process through a referral awards program. Customers receive a set of 12 prepaid postage cards with their name and that of the Bike Friday expert who sold them their bike. Whenever customers meet someone whose interest is piqued by their bike, they fill out a card and drop it in the mail. Bike Friday then mails information to the contact. It also captures this interaction in its database so that riders who make a referral receive a bonus if their prospect purchases a bike. Customers can choose either a $50 check or $75 credit toward future products. Evangelist Margaret Day accumulated enough referral credits to purchase a $2,000 bike last year.

All of this customer delight has paid off handsomely for Bike Friday, creating what is essentially a voluntary customer sales force. Delighted customers can be far more persuasive than ads and other formal marketing communications. "These people have battle-tested your product or service," says a marketing communications expert. "They're so passionate about it, and they tell things in their own words to others." So far, Bike Friday's referral program has accounted for more than one-third of its 10,000 customers. Last year alone, 29 percent of the company's sales came from referrals. "We did a lot more press releases and advertisements early on," explains Hanna Scholz, Bike Friday's marketing manager. "But we realized our customers were our best advertisers—if we made them happy."

Sources: Portions adapted from "The Power of One," *CMO*, October 2005, accessed at www.cmomagazine.com/read/100105/power_one.html. Other quotes and information from Ben McConnell and Jackie Huba, "The Evangelist with the Folding Bicycle," October 2002, accessed at www.creatingcustomerevangelists.com/resources/evangelists/lynette_chiang.asp; and www.bikefriday.com, November 2006.

customer for life. What the mechanic did cost Lexus nothing. Not one red cent. Yet it solidified the relationship that could be worth high six figures to Lexus in customer lifetime value. Such relationship-building passions in dealerships around the country have made Lexus the nation's top-selling luxury vehicle.

However, although the customer-centered firm seeks to deliver high customer satisfaction relative to competitors, it does not attempt to *maximize* customer satisfaction. A company can always increase customer satisfaction by lowering its price or increasing its services. But this may result in lower profits. Thus, the purpose of marketing is to generate customer value profitably. This requires a very delicate balance: The marketer must continue to generate more customer value and satisfaction but not "give away the house."

Customer Relationship Levels and Tools

Companies can build customer relationships at many levels, depending on the nature of the target market. At one extreme, a company with many low-margin customers may seek to develop *basic relationships* with them. For example, Procter & Gamble does not phone or call on all of its Tide consumers to get to know them personally. Instead, P&G creates relationships through brand-building advertising, sales promotions, a 1-800 customer response number, and its Tide FabricCare Network Web site (www.Tide.com). At the other extreme, in markets with few customers and high margins, sellers want to create *full partnerships* with key customers. For example, P&G customer teams work closely with Wal-Mart, Safeway, and other large retailers. In between these two extreme situations, other levels of customer relationships are appropriate.

Today, most leading companies are developing customer loyalty and retention programs. Beyond offering consistently high value and satisfaction, marketers can use specific marketing tools to develop stronger bonds with consumers. For example, many companies now offer *frequency marketing programs* that reward customers who buy frequently or in large amounts. Airlines offer frequent-flyer programs, hotels give room upgrades to their frequent guests, and supermarkets give patronage discounts to "very important customers." Some of these programs can be spectacular. To cater to its very best customers, Neiman Marcus created its InCircle Rewards program:

InCircle members, who must spend at least $5,000 a year using their Neiman Marcus credit cards to be eligible, earn points with each purchase—one point for each dollar charged. They then cash in points for anything from a New York lunch experience for two at one of the "Big Apple's hottest beaneries" (5,000 points) or a Sony home theater system (25,000 points) to a three-day personalized bullfighting course, including travel to a ranch in Northern Baja for some practical training (50,000 points). For 500,000 points, InCircle members can get a six-night Caribbean cruise, and for 1.5 million points, a Yamaha grand piano. Among the top prizes (for 5 million points!) are a J. Mendal custommade sable coat valued at $200,000 and a private concert in the InCircle's home by jazz instrumentalist Chris Botti.[14]

■ Relationship building tools: Neiman Marcus created its InCircle Rewards program to cater to its very best customers.

Other companies sponsor *club marketing programs* that offer members special benefits and create member communities. For example, Harley-Davidson sponsors the Harley Owners Group (H.O.G.), which gives Harley riders "an organized way to share their passion and show their pride." H.O.G membership benefits include two magazines (*Hog Tales* and *Enthusiast*), a *H.O.G. Touring Handbook*, a roadside assistance program, a specially designed insurance program, theft reward service, a travel center, and a "Fly & Ride" program enabling members to rent Harleys while on vacation. The worldwide club now numbers more than 1,500 local chapters and over one million members.[15]

To build customer relationships, companies can add structural ties as well as financial and social benefits. A business marketer might supply customers with special equipment or online linkages that help them manage their orders, payroll, or inventory. For example, McKesson Corporation, a leading pharmaceutical wholesaler, has set up a Supply Management Online system that helps retail pharmacy customers manage their inventories, order entry, and shelf space. The system also helps McKesson's medical-surgical supply and equipment customers optimize their supply purchasing and materials management operations.[16]

The Changing Nature of Customer Relationships

Dramatic changes are occurring in the ways in which companies are relating to their customers. Yesterday's companies focused on mass marketing to all customers at arm's length. Today's companies are building more direct and lasting relationships with more carefully selected customers. Here are some important trends in the way companies are relating to their customers.

Relating with More Carefully Selected Customers

Few firms today still practice true mass marketing—selling in a standardized way to any customer who comes along. Today, most marketers realize that they don't want relationships with every customer. Instead, companies now are targeting fewer, more profitable customers. Called *selective relationship management*, many companies now use customer profitability analysis to weed out losing customers and to target winning ones for pampering. Once they identify profitable customers, firms can create attractive offers and special handling to capture these customers and earn their loyalty.

But what should the company do with unprofitable customers? If it can't turn them into profitable ones, it may even want to "fire" customers that are too unreasonable or that cost more to serve than they are worth. For example, banks now routinely assess customer profitability based on such factors as an account's average balances, account activity, services usage, branch visits, and other variables. For most banks, profitable customers with large balances are pampered with premium services, whereas unprofitable, low-balance ones get the cold shoulder. ING DIRECT, however, selects accounts differently. It seeks relationships with customers who don't need or want expensive pampering while firing those who do.[17]

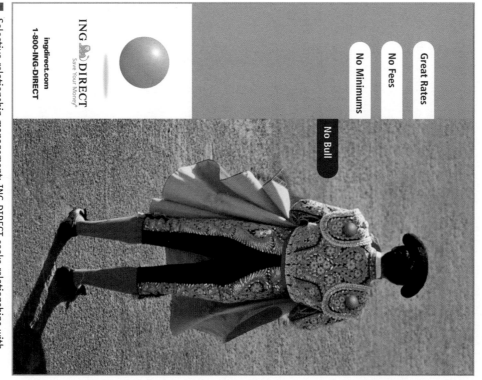

ING DIRECT is the fast-food chain of financial services. With a handful of offerings including savings accounts, CDs, and home equity loans, the bank is about as no-frills as it gets. Yet its profits are downright gaudy, soaring more than 200 percent just last year. ING's secret? Selective relationship management. The bank lures low-maintenance customers with high interest rates. Then, to offset that generosity, the bank does 75 percent of its transactions online, avoids amenities, and offers bare-bones service. In fact, ING routinely "fires" overly demanding customers. By ditching clients who are too time consuming, the company has driven its cost per account to a third of the industry average.

CEO Arkadi Kuhlmann explains: "We need to keep expenses down, which doesn't work when customers want a lot of [hand-holding]. If the average customer phone call costs us $5.25 and the average account revenue is $12 per month, all it takes is 100,000 misbehaving customers for costs to go through the roof. So when a customer calls too many times or wants too many exceptions to the rule, our sales associate can basically say: Look, this doesn't fit you. You need to go back to your community bank and get the kind of contact you're comfortable with. . . . It's all about finding customers who are comfortable with a self-serve business; we try to get you in and out fast. While this makes for some unhappy customers, [those are the] ones you want out the door anyway."

■ Selective relationship management: ING DIRECT seeks relationships with customers who don't need or want expensive pampering, routinely "firing" overly demanding customers. The bank lures low-maintenance customers with high interest rates and no fees or minimums. "No Bull!"

Relating for the Long Term

Just as companies are being more selective about which customers they choose to serve, they are serving chosen customers in a deeper, more lasting way. Today's companies are going beyond designing strategies to *attract* new customers and create *transactions* with them. They are using customer relationship management to *retain* current customers and build profitable, long-term *relationships* with them. The new view is that marketing is the science and art of finding, retaining, *and* growing profitable customers.

Why the new emphasis on retaining and growing customers? In the past, growing markets and an upbeat economy meant a plentiful supply of new customers. However, companies today face some new marketing realities. Changing demographics, more sophisticated competitors, and overcapacity in many industries mean that there are fewer customers to go around. Many companies are now fighting for shares of flat or fading markets.

As a result, the costs of attracting new consumers are rising. In fact, on average, it can cost five to ten times as much to attract a new customer as it does to keep a current customer satisfied. For example, one recent study found that it costs a financial services institution $280 to acquire a new customer but only $57 to keep one. Given these new realities, companies now go all out to keep profitable customers.[18]

Relating Directly

Beyond connecting more deeply with their customers, many companies are also connecting more *directly*. In fact, direct marketing is booming. Consumers can now buy virtually any product without going to a store—by telephone, mail-order catalogs, kiosks, and online. Business purchasing agents routinely shop on the Web for items ranging from standard office supplies to high-priced, high-tech computer equipment.

Some companies sell *only* via direct channels—firms such as Dell, Amazon.com, and GEICO—to name only a few. Other companies use direct connections to supplement their other communications and distribution channels. For example, Sony sells PlayStation consoles and game cartridges through retailers, supported by millions of dollars of mass-media advertising. However, Sony uses its www.PlayStation.com Web site to build relationships with game players of all ages. The site offers information about the latest games, news about events and promotions, game guides and support, and even online forums in which game players can swap tips and stories.

Some marketers have hailed direct marketing as the "marketing model of the next century." They envision a day when all buying and selling will involve direct connections between companies and their customers. Others, although agreeing that direct marketing will play a growing and important role, see it as just one more way to approach the marketplace. We will take a closer look at the world of direct marketing in Chapter 17.

Partner Relationship Management

When it comes to creating customer value and building strong customer relationships, today's marketers know that they can't go it alone. They must work closely with a variety of marketing partners. In addition to being good at *customer relationship management*, marketers must also be good at **partner relationship management**. Major changes are occurring in how marketers partner with others inside and outside the company to jointly bring more value to customers.

Partners Inside the Company

Traditionally, marketers have been charged with understanding customers and representing customer needs to different company departments. The old thinking was that marketing is done only by marketing, sales, and customer support people. However, in today's more connected world, marketing no longer has sole ownership of customer interactions. Every functional area can interact with customers, especially electronically. The new thinking is that every employee must be customer focused. David Packard, late cofounder of Hewlett-Packard, wisely said, "Marketing is far too important to be left only to the marketing department."[19]

Today, rather than letting each department go its own way, firms are linking all departments in the cause of creating customer value. Rather than assigning only sales and marketing people to customers, they are forming cross-functional customer teams. For example, Procter & Gamble assigns "customer development teams" to each of its major retailer accounts. These teams—consisting of sales and marketing people, operations specialists, market and financial analysts, and others—coordinate the efforts of many P&G departments toward helping the retailer be more successful.

Marketing Partners Outside the Firm

Changes are also occurring in how marketers connect with their suppliers, channel partners, and even competitors. Most companies today are networked companies, relying heavily on partnerships with other firms.

Partner relationship management
Working closely with partners in other company departments and outside the company to jointly bring greater value to customers.

Marketing channels consist of distributors, retailers, and others who connect the company to its buyers. The *supply chain* describes a longer channel, stretching from raw materials to components to final products that are carried to final buyers. For example, the supply chain for personal computers consists of suppliers of computer chips and other components, the computer manufacturer, and the distributors, retailers, and others who sell the computers.

Through *supply chain management*, many companies today are strengthening their connections with partners all along the supply chain. They know that their fortunes rest not just on how well they perform. Success at building customer relationships also rests on how well their entire supply chain performs against competitors' supply chains. These companies don't just treat suppliers as vendors and distributors as customers. They treat both as partners in delivering customer value. On the one hand, for example, Lexus works closely with carefully selected suppliers to improve quality and operations efficiency. On the other hand, it works with its franchise dealers to provide top-grade sales and service support that will bring customers in the door and keep them coming back.

Beyond managing the supply chain, today's companies are also discovering that they need *strategic* partners if they hope to be effective. In the new, more competitive global environment, going it alone is going out of style. *Strategic alliances* are booming across almost all industries and services. For example, Dell joins forces with software creators such as Oracle and Microsoft to help boost business sales of its servers and their software. And Volkswagen is working jointly with agricultural processing firm Archer Daniels Midland to further develop and utilize biodiesel fuel. Sometimes, even competitors work together for mutual benefit:

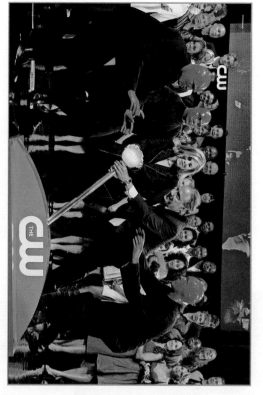

■ Partner relationship management: Time Warner and CBS merged the competing WB and UPN networks into a single, larger one called The CW, which "keeps the best of both networks."

Until recently, Time Warner and CBS ran competing cable networks (WB and UPN, respectively). But both companies struggled to attract enough viewers to make their modest networks profitable. So the two competitors shuttered their individual networks and merged them into a single, larger one, a 50–50 joint venture called CW, which targets the profitable 18–34 age group. The new network will cherry-pick the strongest shows from the old WB and UPN networks—like WB's *Smallville and Gilmore Girls* plus UPN's *Veronica Mars and America's Next Top Model*. Dubbed by the partners as "the new fifth network," CW should be profitable from the start. "You keep the best of both networks," says a CBS executive. "That's a pretty good way to start a network."[20]

As Jim Kelly, former CEO at UPS, puts it, "The old adage 'If you can't beat 'em, join 'em,' is being replaced by 'join 'em and you can't be beat.'"[21]

Capturing Value from Customers

The first four steps in the marketing process involve building customer relationships by creating and delivering superior customer value. The final step involves capturing value in return, in the form of current and future sales, market share, and profits. By creating superior customer value, the firm creates highly satisfied customers who stay loyal and buy more. This, in turn, means greater long-run returns for the firm. Here, we discuss the outcomes of creating customer value: customer loyalty and retention, share of market and share of customer, and customer equity.

Creating Customer Loyalty and Retention

Good customer relationship management creates customer delight. In turn, delighted customers remain loyal and talk favorably to others about the company and its products. Studies show big differences in the loyalty of customers who are less satisfied, somewhat satisfied, and completely satisfied. Even a slight drop from complete satisfaction can create an enormous drop in loyalty. Thus, the aim of customer relationship management is to create not just customer satisfaction, but customer delight.[22]

Companies are realizing that losing a customer means losing more than a single sale. It means losing the entire stream of purchases that the customer would make over a lifetime of patronage. For example, here is a dramatic illustration of **customer lifetime value:**

Customer lifetime value
The value of the entire stream of purchases that a customer would make over a lifetime of patronage.

Stew Leonard, who operates a highly profitable four-store supermarket in Connecticut and New York, says that he sees $50,000 flying out of his store every time he sees a sulking customer. Why? Because his average customer spends about $100 a week, shops 50 weeks a year, and remains in the area for about 10 years. If this customer has an unhappy experience and switches to another supermarket, Stew Leonard's has lost $50,000 in revenue. The loss can be much greater if the disappointed customer shares the bad experience with other customers and causes them to defect. To keep customers coming back, Stew Leonard's has created what the *New York Times* has dubbed the "Disneyland of Dairy Stores," complete with costumed characters, scheduled entertainment, a petting zoo, and animatronics throughout the store. From its humble beginnings as a small dairy store in 1969, Stew Leonard's has grown at an amazing pace. It's built 29 additions onto the original store, which now serves more than 250,000 customers each week. This legion of loyal shoppers is largely a result of the store's passionate approach to customer service. Rule #1 at Stew Leonard's—The customer is always right. Rule #2—If the customer is ever wrong, reread Rule #1![23]

■ Customer lifetime value: To keep customers coming back, Stew Leonard's has created the "Disneyland of dairy stores." Rule #1—The customer is always right. Rule #2—If the customer is ever wrong, reread Rule #1.

Stew Leonard is not alone in assessing customer lifetime value. Lexus estimates that a single satisfied and loyal customer is worth $600,000 in lifetime sales. The customer lifetime value of a Taco Bell customer exceeds $12,000.[24] Thus, working to retain and grow customers makes good economic sense. In fact, a company can lose money on a specific transaction but still benefit greatly from a long-term relationship.

This means that companies must aim high in building customer relationships. Customer delight creates an emotional relationship with a product or service, not just a rational preference. L.L. Bean, long known for its outstanding customer service and high customer loyalty, preaches the following "golden rule": "Sell good merchandise, treat your customers like human beings, and they'll always come back for more." A customer relationships expert agrees: "If you want your customers to be more loyal, you must prove that you have their best interests at heart. Your concern for the customer's welfare must be so strong that it even occasionally trumps (gasp!) your own concern for immediate profits."[25]

Growing Share of Customer

Share of customer
The portion of the customer's purchasing that a company gets in its product categories.

Beyond simply retaining good customers to capture customer lifetime value, good customer relationship management can help marketers to increase their **share of customer**—the share they get of the customer's purchasing in their product categories. Thus, banks want to increase "share of wallet." Supermarkets and restaurants want to get more "share of stomach." Car companies want to increase "share of garage" and airlines want greater "share of travel."

To increase share of customer, firms can offer greater variety to current customers. Or they can train employees to cross-sell and up-sell in order to market more products and services to existing customers. For example, Amazon.com is highly skilled at leveraging relationships with its 50 million customers to increase its share of each customer's purchases. Originally an online bookseller, Amazon.com now offers customers music, videos, gifts, toys, consumer electronics, office products, home improvement items, lawn and garden products, apparel and accessories, jewelry, and an online auction. In addition, based on each customer's purchase history, the company recommends related products that might be of interest. In this way, Amazon.com captures a greater share of each customer's spending budget.

Building Customer Equity

We can now see the importance of not just acquiring customers, but of keeping and growing them as well. One marketing consultant puts it this way: "The only value your company will ever create is the value that comes from customers—the ones you have now and the ones you will have in the future. Without customers, you don't have a business."[26] Customer relationship management takes a long-term view. Companies want not only to create profitable customers, but to "own" them for life, capture their customer lifetime value, and earn a greater share of their purchases.

What Is Customer Equity?

The ultimate aim of customer relationship management is to produce high *customer equity*.[27] **Customer equity** is the combined discounted customer lifetime values of all of the company's current and potential customers. Clearly, the more loyal the firm's profitable customers, the higher the firm's customer equity. Customer equity may be a better measure of a firm's performance than current sales or market share. Whereas sales and market share reflect the past, customer equity suggests the future. Consider Cadillac:

In the 1970s and 1980s, Cadillac had some of the most loyal customers in the industry. To an entire generation of car buyers, the name "Cadillac" defined American luxury. Cadillac's share of the luxury car market reached a whopping 51 percent in 1976. Based on market share and sales, the brand's future looked rosy. However, measures of customer equity would have painted a bleaker picture. Cadillac customers were getting older (average age 60) and average customer lifetime value was falling. Many Cadillac buyers were on their last car. Thus, although Cadillac's market share was good, its customer equity was not. Compare this with BMW. Its more youthful and vigorous image didn't win BMW the early market share war. However, it did win BMW younger customers with higher customer lifetime values. The result: In the years that followed, BMW's market share and profits soared while Cadillac's fortunes eroded badly. Thus, market share is not the answer. We should care not just about current sales but also about future sales. Customer lifetime value and customer equity are the name of the game. Recognizing this, Cadillac is now making the Caddy cool again by targeting a younger generation of consumers with

Customer equity
The total combined customer lifetime values of all of the company's customers.

Cadillac is cool again. To increase lifetime value and customer equity, Cadillac's highly successful Break Through ad campaign targets a younger generation of consumer.

new high-performance models and its highly successful Break Through advertising campaign. Sales are up 37 percent over the past four years. More important, the future looks promising.[28]

Building the Right Relationships with the Right Customers

Companies should manage customer equity carefully. They should view customers as assets that need to be managed and maximized. But not all customers, not even all loyal customers, are good investments. Surprisingly, some loyal customers can be unprofitable, and some disloyal customers can be profitable. Which customers should the company acquire and retain? "Up to a point, the choice is obvious: Keep the consistent big spenders and lose the erratic small spenders," says one expert. "But what about the erratic big spenders and the consistent small spenders? It's often unclear whether they should be acquired or retained, and at what cost."[29]

The company can classify customers according to their potential profitability and manage its relationships with them accordingly. Figure 1.5 classifies customers into one of four relationship groups, according to their profitability and projected loyalty.[30] Each group requires a different relationship management strategy. "Strangers" show low profitability and little projected loyalty. There is little fit between the company's offerings and their needs. The relationship management strategy for these customers is simple: Don't invest anything in them.

"Butterflies" are profitable but not loyal. There is a good fit between the company's offerings and their needs. However, like real butterflies, we can enjoy them for only a short while and then they're gone. An example is stock market investors who trade shares often and in large amounts, but who enjoy hunting for the best deals without building a regular relationship with any single brokerage company. Efforts to convert butterflies into loyal customers are rarely successful. Instead, the company should enjoy the butterflies for the moment. It should use promotional blitzes to attract them, create satisfying and profitable transactions with them, and then cease investing in them until the next time around.

"True friends" are both profitable and loyal. There is a strong fit between their needs and the company's offerings. The firm wants to make continuous relationship investments to delight these customers and nurture, retain, and grow them. It wants to turn true friends into "true believers," who come back regularly and tell others about their good experiences with the company.

"Barnacles" are highly loyal but not very profitable. There is a limited fit between their needs and the company's offerings. An example is smaller bank customers who bank regularly but do not generate enough returns to cover the costs of maintaining their accounts. Like barnacles on the hull of a ship, they create drag. Barnacles are perhaps the most problematic customers. The company might be able to improve their profitability by selling them more, raising their fees, or reducing service to them. However, if they cannot be made profitable, they should be "fired" (see Real Marketing 1.2).

The point here is an important one: Different types of customers require different relationship management strategies. The goal is to build the *right relationships* with the *right customers*.

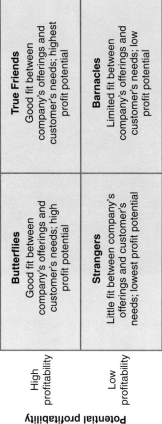

FIGURE 1.5
Customer relationship groups

■ The New Marketing Landscape

As the world spins on, dramatic changes are occurring in the marketplace. Richard Love of Hewlett-Packard observes, "The pace of change is so rapid that the ability to change has now become a competitive advantage." Yogi Berra, the legendary New York Yankees catcher, summed it up more simply when he said, "The future ain't what it used to be." As the marketplace changes, so must those who serve it.

In this section, we examine the major trends and forces that are changing the marketing landscape and challenging marketing strategy. We look at four major developments: the new digital age, rapid globalization, the call for more ethics and social responsibility, and the growth in not-for-profit marketing.

The New Digital Age

The recent technology boom has created a new digital age. The explosive growth in computer, telecommunications, information, transportation, and other technologies has had a major impact on the ways companies bring value to their customers.

Now, more than ever before, we are all connected to each other and to things near and far in the world around us. Where it once took weeks or months to travel across the United States, we can now travel around the globe in only hours or days. Where it once took days or weeks to receive news about important world events, we now see them as they are occurring through live satellite broadcasts. Where it once took weeks to correspond with others in distant places, they are now only moments away by phone or the Internet.

The technology boom has created exciting new ways to learn about and track customers and to create products and services tailored to individual customer needs. Technology is also helping companies to distribute products more efficiently and effectively. And it's helping them to communicate with customers in large groups or one-to-one.

Through videoconferencing, marketing researchers at a company's headquarters in New York can look in on focus groups in Chicago or Paris without ever stepping onto a plane. With only a few clicks of a mouse button, a direct marketer can tap into online data services to learn anything from what car you drive to what you read to what flavor of ice cream you prefer. Or, using today's powerful computers, marketers can create their own detailed customer databases and use them to target individual customers with offers designed to meet their specific needs.

Technology has also brought a new wave of communication and advertising tools—ranging from cell phones, iPods, DVRs, Web sites, and interactive TV to video kiosks at airports and shopping malls. Marketers can use these tools to zero in on selected customers with carefully targeted messages. Through the Internet, customers can learn about, design, order, and pay for products and services, without ever leaving home. Then, through the marvels of express delivery, they can receive their purchases in less than 24 hours. From virtual reality displays that test new products to online virtual stores that sell them, the technology boom is affecting every aspect of marketing.

Perhaps the most dramatic new technology is the **Internet**.

■ Technology has brought a new wave of marketing tools.

Internet

A vast public web of computer networks that connects users of all types all around the world to each other and to an amazingly large information repository.

The Internet links individuals and businesses of all types to each other and to information all around the world. It allows anytime, anywhere connections to information, entertainment, and communication. Companies are using the Internet to build closer relationships with customers and marketing partners. Beyond competing in traditional market*places*, they now have access to exciting new market*spaces*.

The Internet has now become a truly a global phenomenon. The number of Internet users worldwide is expected to reach 1.8 billion by 2010.[31] This growing and diverse Internet population means that all kinds of people are now going to the Web for information and to buy products and services.

Real Marketing

Best Buy: Building the Right Relationships with the Right Customers

1.2 "The customer is always right." Right? After all, that slogan has become the guiding principle of most successful marketing firms. But these days, more and more marketers are discovering a new truth: Some customers can be way, way wrong—as in unprofitable. Increasingly, these companies are taking special care of their profitable customers while shunning those they lose money on.

Consider Best Buy, the nation's leading consumer electronics retailer. Since its humble beginnings in 1966 as a small Minnesota home and car stereo chain, Best Buy has transformed itself into a profitable 941-store, $30-billion megaretailer. Today's Best Buy stores are huge, warehouse-like emporiums featuring a treasure trove of goods—from consumer electronics, home office equipment, and appliances to software, CDs, and DVDs—all at low discount prices.

Despite the company's success, however, Best Buy now faces storm clouds on the horizon. Wal-Mart, the world's largest retailer, and Dell, the largest computer maker, are rapidly encroaching on Best Buy's profitable consumer electronics turf. A decade ago, neither of these competitors even appeared on the list of top consumer electronics retailers. By last year, however, Wal-Mart had shot up to the number two position, with $20 billion in consumer electronics sales versus Best Buy's $30 billion. Dell was in fourth place but rising quickly. Best Buy CEO Brad Anderson fears that Best Buy could end up in what retailers call the "unprofitable middle," unable to compete against Wal-Mart's massive buying power for price-sensitive store shoppers or against Dell's direct model for more affluent online customers.

To better differentiate itself in this more crowded marketplace, Best Buy has rolled out a new strategy designed to better identify and serve its best customers. The strategy draws on the research of consultant Larry Selden, a Columbia University business professor. Selden argues that a company should see itself as a portfolio of *customers*, not product lines. His research has identified two basic types of customers: angels and demons. Angel customers are profitable,

Best Buy's customer-centricity strategy: Serve the angel customers while exorcizing the demons. Stores targeting upper-income "Barrys" steer them into the Magnolia Home Theater Center, a comfy store within a store that mimics media rooms popular with home theater fans.

whereas demon customers may actually cost a company more to serve than it makes from them. In fact, Selden claims, serving the demons often wipes out the profits earned by serving the angels.

Following this logic, Best Buy assigned a task force to analyze its customers' purchasing habits. Sure enough, the analysts found a host of angels—some 20 percent of Best Buy's customers who produced the bulk of its profits. According to the *Wall Street Journal:* "Best Buy's angels are customers who boost profits at the consumer-electronics giant by snapping up high-definition televisions, portable electronics, and newly released DVDs without waiting for markdowns or rebates."

The task force also found demons: "The [demons are Best Buy's] worst customers . . . the underground of bargain-hungry shoppers intent on wringing every nickel of savings out of the big retailer. They buy products, apply for rebates, return the purchases, then buy them back at returned-merchandise discounts. They load up on 'loss leaders,' severely discounted merchandise designed to boost store traffic, then

These days, it's hard to find a company that doesn't use the Web in a significant way. Most traditional "brick-and-mortar" companies have now become "click-and-mortar" companies. They have ventured online to attract new customers and build stronger relationships with existing ones. The Internet also spawned an entirely new breed of "click-only" companies—the so-called "dot-coms." Today, online consumer buying is growing at a healthy rate. Some 65 percent of American online users now use the Internet to shop.[32] Business-to-business e-commerce is also booming. It seems that almost every business has set up shop on the Web. Giants such as GE, Siemens, Microsoft, Dell, and many others have moved quickly to exploit the B-to-B power of the Internet.

Thus, the technology boom is providing exciting new opportunities for marketers. We will explore the impact of the new digital age in future chapters, especially Chapter 17.

flip the goods at a profit on eBay. They slap down rock-bottom price quotes from Web sites and demand that Best Buy make good on its lowest-price pledge." CEO Anderson learned that these demon customers could account for up to 100 million of Best Buy's 500 million customer visits each year. "They can wreak enormous economic havoc," he says.

So, after deciding that the customer was *not* always right, Anderson set out to ditch the demon customers. Best Buy started testing a "Customer Centricity" strategy in 100 of its stores. It began by combing through these stores' sales records and customer databases to distinguish between good and bad customers. To attract the angels, the stores began stocking more merchandise and offering better service to them. For example, the stores set up digital photo centers and a "Geek Squad," which offers one-on-one in-store or at-home computer assistance to high-value buyers. It established a Reward Zone loyalty program, in which regular customers can earn points toward discounts on future purchases. To discourage the demons, it removed them from its marketing lists, reduced the promotions and other sales tactics that tended to attract them, and installed a 15 percent restocking fee.

However, Best Buy didn't stop there. Customer analysis revealed that its best customers fell into five groups: "Barrys," high-income men; "Jills," suburban moms; "Buzzes," male technology enthusiasts; "Rays," young family men on a budget; and small business owners. The company instructed each Customer Centricity store to analyze the customers in its market area and to align its product and service mix to reflect the make-up of these customers. Further, it trained store clerks in the art of serving the angels and exorcising the demons.

Store clerks receive hours of training in identifying desirable customers according to their shopping preferences and behavior. [At one store targeting upper-income Barrys,] . . . blue-shirted sales clerks prowl the DVD aisles looking for promising candidates. The goal is to steer them into [the store's Magnolia Home Theater Center, a store within a store that features premium home-theater systems and knowledgeable, no-pressure home-theater consultants.] Unlike the television sections at most Best Buy stores, the [center] has easy chairs, a leather couch, and a basket of popcorn to mimic the media rooms popular with home-theater fans. At stores popular with young Buzzes, Best Buy is setting up videogame areas with leather chairs and game players hooked to mammoth, plasma-screen televisions. The games are conveniently stacked outside the playing area, the glitzy new TVs a short stroll away.

Will Best Buy's new strategy work? Anderson realizes that his unconventional strategy is risky and that Best Buy must be careful. For one thing, tailoring store formats to fit local customers is expensive—the costs in the test stores have been about 1 percent to 2 percent higher. Moreover, shunning customers—good or bad—can be very risky. "The most dangerous image I can think of is a retailer that wants to fire customers," he notes—before letting them go, Best Buy first tries to turn its bad customers into profitable ones. "The trickiest challenge may be to deter bad customers without turning off good ones," observes an industry analyst.

However, early results show the Customer Centricity test stores have "clobbered" the traditional Best Buy stores—with many posting sales gains more than triple those of stores with conventional formats. Since rolling out the new strategy two years ago, sales have climbed 26 percent and profits have surged 43 percent. "Growing our company through customer centricity continues to be our top priority," says Anderson.

So, is the customer always right? Not necessarily. Although this might hold true for a company's best customers, it simply doesn't apply to others. As one marketer put it, "The customer is always right, but they aren't all the right customers." Best Buy knows that the goal is to develop the best customer portfolio, one built on the right relationships with the right customers. As one store manager puts it: "The biggest thing now is to build better relationships with [our best] customers."

Sources: Quotes and extracts from Gary McWilliams, "Analyzing Customers, Best Buy Decides Not All Are Welcome," *Wall Street Journal,* November 8, 2004, p. A1; "Gunning for the Best Buy," *Knight Ridder Tribune Business News,* May 28, 2006, p. 1; and Shirley A. Lazo, "Let's Go Shopping," *Barron's,* June 26, 2006, p. 28. Additional information from Laura Heller, "At Crossroads, Best Buy Charges Ahead with Customer Centricity," *DSN Retailing Today,* January 10, 2005, p.13; Joshua Freed, "The Customer Is Always Right? Not Anymore," July 5, 2004, accessed at www.sfgate.com; Laura Heller, "Doing to Demographics What's Never Been Done Before," *DSN Retailing Today,* September 6, 2004, p. 44; Matthew Boyle, "Best Buy's Giant Gamble," *Fortune,* April 3, 2006, pp. 69–75; "Best Buy Co., Inc.," *Hoover's Company Records,* April 15, 2006, p. 10209; and www.bestbuy.com, November 2006.

Rapid Globalization

As they are redefining their relationships with customers and partners, marketers are also taking a fresh look at the ways in which they connect with the broader world around them. In an increasingly smaller world, many marketers are now connected *globally* with their customers and marketing partners.

Today, almost every company, large or small, is touched in some way by global competition. A neighborhood florist buys its flowers from Mexican nurseries, while a large U.S. electronics manufacturer competes in its home markets with giant Japanese rivals. A fledgling Internet retailer finds itself receiving orders from all over the world at the same time that an American consumer-goods producer introduces new products into emerging markets abroad.

■ Many U.S. companies have developed truly global operations. Coca-Cola offers more than 400 different brands in more than 200 countries including BPM energy drink in Ireland, bitter Mare Rosso in Spain, Sprite Ice Cube in Belgium, Fanta in Chile, and NaturAqua in Hungary.

American firms have been challenged at home by the skillful marketing of European and Asian multinationals. Companies such as Toyota, Siemens, Nestlé, Sony, and Samsung have often outperformed their U.S. competitors in American markets. Similarly, U.S. companies in a wide range of industries have developed truly global operations, making and selling their products worldwide. Coca-Cola offers a mind-boggling 400 different brands in more than 200 countries. Even MTV has joined the elite of global brands, delivering localized versions of its pulse-thumping fare to teens in 419 million homes in 164 countries around the globe.[33]

Today, companies are not only trying to sell more of their locally produced goods in international markets, they also are buying more supplies and components abroad. For example, Isaac Mizrahi, one of America's top fashion designers, may choose cloth woven from Australian wool with designs printed in Italy. He will design a dress and e-mail the drawing to a Hong Kong agent, who will place the order with a Chinese factory. Finished dresses will be airfreighted to New York, where they will be redistributed to department and specialty stores around the country.

Thus, managers in countries around the world are increasingly taking a global, not just local, view of the company's industry, competitors, and opportunities. They are asking: What is global marketing? How does it differ from domestic marketing? How do global competitors and forces affect our business? To what extent should we "go global"? We will discuss the global marketplace in more detail in Chapter 19.

The Call for More Ethics and Social Responsibility

Marketers are reexamining their relationships with social values and responsibilities and with the very Earth that sustains us. As the worldwide consumerism and environmentalism movements mature, today's marketers are being called upon to take greater responsibility for the social and environmental impact of their actions. Corporate ethics and social responsibility have become hot topics for almost every business. And few companies can ignore the renewed and very demanding environmental movement.

The social-responsibility and environmental movements will place even stricter demands on companies in the future. Some companies resist these movements, budging only when forced by legislation or organized consumer outcries. More forward-looking companies, however, readily accept their responsibilities to the world around them. They view socially responsible actions as an opportunity to do well by doing good. They seek ways to profit by serving the best long-run interests of their customers and communities.

Some companies—such as Patagonia, Ben & Jerry's, Honest Tea, and others—are practicing "caring capitalism," setting themselves apart by being civic-minded and responsible. They are building social responsibility and action into their company value and mission statements. For example, when it comes to environmental responsibility, outdoor gear marketer Patagonia is "committed to the core." "Those of us who work here share a strong commitment to protecting undomesticated lands and waters," says the company's Web site. "We believe in using business to inspire solutions to the environmental crisis." Patagonia backs these words with actions. Each year it pledges at least 1 percent of its sales or 10 percent of its profits, whichever is greater, to the protection of the natural environment.[34] We will revisit the topic of marketing and social responsibility in greater detail in Chapter 20.

The Growth of Not-for-Profit Marketing

In the past, marketing has been most widely applied in the for-profit business sector. In recent years, however, marketing also has become a major part of the strategies of many not-for-profit organizations, such as colleges, hospitals, museums, zoos, symphony orchestras, and even churches. The nation's more than 1.2 million nonprofits face stiff competition for support and membership.[35] Sound marketing can help them to attract membership and support. Consider the marketing efforts of the San Francisco Zoo:

The San Francisco Zoological Society aggressively markets the zoo's attractions to what might be its most important customer segment—children of all ages. It starts with a well-designed "product." The expanded Children's Zoo is specially designed to encourage parent-child interaction and discussions about living together with animals. The zoo provides close-up encounters with critters ranging from companion animals and livestock to the wildlife in our backyards and beyond. Children can groom livestock or collect eggs at the Family Farm, peer through microscopes in the Insect Zoo, crawl through a child-sized burrow at the Meerkats and Prairie Dogs exhibit, and lots more. To get the story out, attract visitors, and raise funds, the zoo sponsors innovative advertising, an informative Web site, and exciting family events. The most popular event is the annual ZooFest for Kids. "Bring your children, parents, grandparents, and friends to participate in the San Francisco Zoo's most popular annual family fundraiser—ZooFest for Kids!" the zoo invites. "Get your face painted, enjoy up-close encounters with animals, eat yummy treats, and much, much more." ZooFest planners market the event to local businesses, which supply food and entertainment. The event usually nets about $50,000, money that goes to support the Zoo's conservation and education programs. "With music in the air and tables heaped high with food," notes one observer, "ZooFest for Kids [has] a magic about it befitting the beginning of Summer"—magic created by good marketing.[36]

■ Not-for-profit marketing: The San Francisco Zoological Society aggressively markets the zoo's attractions to what might be its most important customer segment—children of all ages.

Similarly, private colleges, facing declining enrollments and rising costs, are using marketing to compete for students and funds. Many performing arts groups—even the Lyric Opera Company of Chicago, which has seasonal sellouts—face huge operating deficits that they must cover by more aggressive donor marketing. Finally, many long-standing not-for-profit organizations—the YMCA, the Salvation Army, the Girl Scouts—have lost members and are now modernizing their missions and "products" to attract more members and donors.[37]

Government agencies have also shown an increased interest in marketing. For example, the U.S. military has a marketing plan to attract recruits to its different services, and various government agencies are now designing *social marketing campaigns* to encourage energy conservation and concern for the environment or to discourage smoking, excessive drinking, and drug use. Even the once-stodgy U.S. Postal Service has developed innovative marketing to sell commemorative stamps, promote its priority mail services against those of its competitors, and lift its image. In all, the U.S. Government is the nation's 27th largest advertiser, with an annual advertising budget of more than $1.2 billion.[38]

So, What Is Marketing? Pulling It All Together

At the start of this chapter, Figure 1.1 presented a simple model of the marketing process. Now that we've discussed all of the steps in the process, Figure 1.6 presents an expanded model that will help you pull it all together. What is marketing? Simply put, marketing is the process of building profitable customer relationships by creating value for customers and capturing value in return.

The first four steps of the marketing process focus on creating value for customers. The company first gains a full understanding of the marketplace by researching customer needs and managing marketing information. It then designs a customer-driven marketing strategy based on the answers to two simple questions. The first question is "What consumers will we serve?" (market segmentation and targeting). Good marketing companies know that they cannot serve all customers in every way. Instead, they need to focus their resources on the customers they can serve best and most profitably. The second marketing strategy question is "How can we best serve targeted customers?" (differentiation and positioning). Here, the marketer outlines a value proposition that spells out what values the company will deliver in order to win target customers.

With its marketing strategy decided, the company now constructs an integrated marketing program—consisting of a blend of the four marketing mix elements, or the four Ps—that transforms the marketing strategy into real value for customers. The company develops product offers and creates strong brand identities for them. It prices these offers to create real customer value and distributes the offers to make them available to target consumers. Finally, the company designs promotion programs that communicate the value proposition to target consumers and persuade them to act on the market offering.

Perhaps the most important step in the marketing process involves building value-laden, profitable relationships with target customers. Throughout the process, marketers practice customer relationship management to create customer satisfaction and delight. In creating customer value and relationships, however, the company cannot go it alone. It must work closely with marketing partners both inside the company and throughout the marketing system. Thus, beyond practicing good customer relationship management, firms must also practice good partner relationship management.

The first four steps in the marketing process create value *for* customers. In the final step, the company reaps the rewards of its strong customer relationships by capturing value *from* customers. Delivering superior customer value creates highly satisfied customers who will buy more and will buy again. This helps the company to capture customer lifetime value and greater share of customer. The result is increased long-term customer equity for the firm.

Finally, in the face of today's changing marketing landscape, companies must take into account three additional factors. In building customer and partner relationships, they must harness marketing technology, take advantage of global opportunities, and ensure that they act in an ethical and socially responsible way.

Figure 1.6 provides a good roadmap to future chapters of the text. Chapters 1 and 2 introduce the marketing process, with a focus on building customer relationships and capturing value from customers. Chapters 3, 4, 5, and 6 address the first step of the marketing process—understanding the marketing environment, managing marketing information, and understanding consumer and business buyer behavior. In Chapter 7, we look more deeply into the two major marketing strategy decisions: selecting which customers to serve (segmentation and targeting) and deciding on a value proposition (differentiation and positioning). Chapters 8 through 17 discuss the marketing mix variables, one by one. Chapter 18

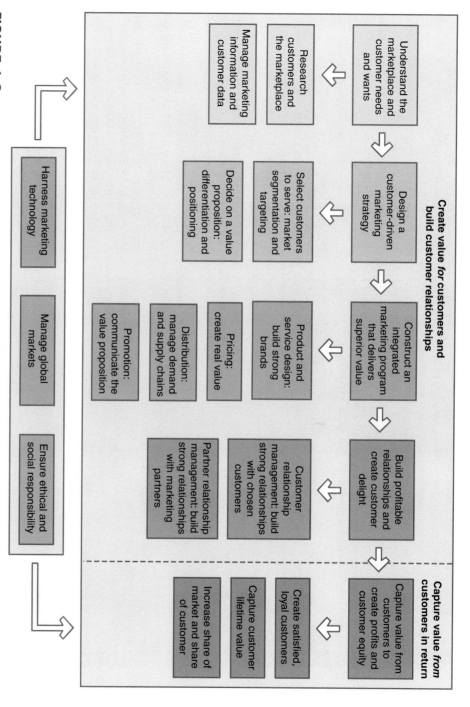

FIGURE 1.6 An expanded model of the marketing process

Create value *for* customers and build customer relationships

Understand the marketplace and customer needs and wants
- Research customers and the marketplace
- Manage marketing information and customer data

Design a customer-driven marketing strategy
- Select customers to serve: market segmentation and targeting
- Decide on a value proposition: differentiation and positioning

Construct an integrated marketing program that delivers superior value
- Product and service design: build strong brands
- Pricing: create real value
- Distribution: manage demand and supply chains
- Promotion: communicate the value proposition

Build profitable relationships and create customer delight
- Customer relationship management: build strong relationships with chosen customers
- Partner relationship management: build strong relationships with marketing partners

Capture value *from* customers in return

Capture value from customers to create profits and customer equity
- Create satisfied, loyal customers
- Capture customer lifetime value
- Increase share of market and share of customer

- Harness marketing technology
- Manage global markets
- Ensure ethical and social responsibility

Reviewing the Concepts

Today's successful companies—whether large or small, for-profit or not-for-profit, domestic or global—share a strong customer focus and a heavy commitment to marketing. The goal of marketing is to build and manage profitable customer relationships. Marketing seeks to attract new customers by promising superior value and to keep and grow current customers by delivering satisfaction. Marketing operates within a dynamic global environment that can quickly make yesterday's winning strategies obsolete. To be successful, companies must be strongly market focused.

1. Define marketing and outline the steps in the marketing process.

Marketing is the process by which companies create value for customers and build strong customer relationships in order to capture value from customers in return.

The marketing process involves five steps. The first four steps create value for customers. First, marketers need to understand the marketplace and customer needs and wants. Next, marketers design a customer-driven marketing strategy with the goal of getting, keeping, and growing target customers. In the third step, marketers construct a marketing program that actually delivers superior value. All of these steps form the basis for the fourth step, building profitable customer relationships and creating customer delight. In the final step, the company reaps the rewards of strong customer relationships by capturing value from customers.

2. Explain the importance of understanding customers and the marketplace, and identify the five core marketplace concepts.

Outstanding marketing companies go to great lengths to learn about and understand their customers' needs, wants, and demands. This understanding helps them to design want-satisfying market offerings and build value-laden customer relationships by which they can capture customer lifetime value and greater share of customer. The result is increased long-term customer equity for the firm.

The core marketplace concepts are needs, wants, and demands; market offerings (products, services, and experiences); value and satisfaction; exchange and relationships; and markets. Wants are the form taken by human needs when shaped by culture and individual

sums up customer-driven marketing strategy and creating competitive advantage in the marketplace. Then, the final two chapters examine special marketing considerations: global marketing and marketing ethics and social responsibility.

personality. When backed by buying power, wants become demands. Companies address needs by putting forth a value proposition, a set of benefits that they promise to consumers to satisfy their needs. The value proposition is fulfilled through a market offering that delivers customer value and satisfaction, resulting in long-term exchange relationships with customers.

3. Identify the key elements of a customer-driven marketing strategy and discuss marketing management orientations that guide marketing strategy.

To design a winning marketing strategy, the company must first decide *who* it will serve. It does this by dividing the market into segments of customers (*market segmentation*) and selecting which segments it will cultivate (*target marketing*). Next, the company must decide *how* it will serve targeted customers (how it will *differentiate and position* itself in the marketplace).

Marketing management can adopt one of five competing market orientations. The *production concept* holds that management's task is to improve production efficiency and bring down prices. The *product concept* holds that consumers favor products that offer the most in quality, performance, and innovative features; thus, little promotional effort is required. The *selling concept* holds that consumers will not buy enough of the organization's products unless it undertakes a large-scale selling and promotion effort. The *marketing concept* holds that achieving organizational goals depends on determining the needs and wants of target markets and delivering the desired satisfactions more effectively and efficiently than competitors do. The *societal marketing concept* holds that generating customer satisfaction *and* long-run societal well-being are the keys to both achieving the company's goals and fulfilling its responsibilities.

4. Discuss customer relationship management, and identify strategies for creating value *for* customers and capturing value *from* customers in return.

Broadly defined, *customer relationship management* is the process of building and maintaining profitable customer relationships by delivering superior customer value and satisfaction. The aim of customer relationship management is to produce high *customer equity*, the total

combined customer lifetime values of all of the company's customers. The key to building lasting relationships is the creation of superior *customer value and satisfaction.*

Companies want not only to acquire profitable customers, but to build relationships that will keep them and grow "share of customer." Different types of customers require different customer relationship management strategies. The marketer's aim is to build the *right relationships* with the *right customers*. In return for creating value *for* targeted customers, the company captures value *from* customers in the form of profits and customer equity.

In building customer relationships, good marketers realize that they cannot go it alone. They must work closely with marketing partners inside and outside the company. In addition to being good at customer relationship management, they must also be good at *partner relationship management.*

5. Describe the major trends and forces that are changing the marketing landscape in this new age of relationships.

As the world spins on, dramatic changes are occurring in the marketing arena. The boom in computer, telecommunications, information, transportation, and other technologies has created exciting new ways to learn about and track customers and to create products and services tailored to individual customer needs.

In an increasingly smaller world, many marketers are now connected *globally* with their customers and marketing partners. Today, almost every company, large or small, is touched in some way by global competition. Today's marketers are also reexamining their ethical and societal responsibilities. Marketers are being called upon to take greater responsibility for the social and environmental impact of their actions. Finally, in the past, marketing has been most widely applied in the for-profit business sector. In recent years, however, marketing also has become a major part of the strategies of many not-for-profit organizations, such as colleges, hospitals, museums, zoos, symphony orchestras, and even churches.

Pulling it all together, as discussed throughout the chapter, the major new developments in marketing can be summed up in a single word: *relationships.* Today, marketers of all kinds are taking advantage of new opportunities for building relationships with their customers, their marketing partners, and the world around them.

Reviewing the Key Terms

Discussing the Concepts

1. You can define marketing and its functions in many ways. In your own words, explain marketing to someone who has not yet read this chapter.

2. What is the difference between a need, a want, and a demand? Describe the need versus the want for the following products: Gatorade, Nike, iPod.

3. What are the five different marketing management orientations? Which orientation do you believe your college follows when marketing its undergraduate program?

4. Customer value is consumers' evaluation of the difference between total benefits and total costs. When a consumer orders a T-shirt from an online retailer such as landsend.com, what are the total benefits and total costs?

5. What is customer equity? How can a company increase its customer equity?

6. How has the Internet changed consumers? Marketers?

Applying the Concepts

1. When companies have close competitors, they try to choose value propositions that will differentiate them from others in the market. Choose three fast-food restaurants and describe their value propositions. Are they strongly differentiating themselves?

2. What are the four customer relationship groups? Is there a way marketers can move a Stranger to a True Friend? Explain how Apple and BMW would move their Strangers to True Friends.

3. A cell phone company spends $148.50 in total costs to acquire a new user. On average, this new user spends $60 a month for calling and related services, and the cell phone company generates an 18 percent profit margin in each of the 25 months that the user is expected to stay with the service. What is the Customer Lifetime Value of this user to the cell phone company?

Focus on Technology

Visit www.oddcast.com and you will find animated characters that interact with customers on various linked sponsor Web sites. The characters, referred to as VHosts, help customers navigate the site and find important information. A VHost can be set up to speak any one of 64 languages and to have a variety of facial characteristics, skin tones, and hair styles. More than 5,000 companies currently use Oddcast's technology, including major brands such as ESPN, L'Oreal, and NBC.

1. What is the appeal of the VHost for a marketer?

2. What might be a concern for the marketer?

3. After visiting the site, as a consumer, what are your thoughts regarding the VHosts?

4. What specific target markets might benefit most from a VHost?

Focus on Ethics

In this digital age, marketers have more thorough data and can use the data for very precise market targeting. In fact, the United States military has developed a database of millions of high school and college students for recruiting. With the database, the military can more effectively target potential recruits. In addition to names and addresses, the data for each young person includes such things as favorite subjects, grade point averages, and consumer purchases. Currently, more than 100 groups, including the American Civil Liberties Union and Rock the Vote are demanding that the database be abandoned and that the military not continue to collect this information for marketing purposes.

1. Do you think the military has a right to improve its recruiting through a more elaborate database of their potential "customers"?

2. Do you think the database is an invasion of privacy?

3. How else might the military improve its recruiting?

See: "Military Database of Potential Recruits Rankles Privacy Groups," *Advertising Age*, October 31, 2005, p. 9.

Video Case

Dunkin' Donuts

For more than 50 years, Dunkin' Donuts has offered customers throughout the United States, and around the world, a consistent experience—the same donuts, the same coffee, the same store décor—each time a customer drops in. Although the chain now offers iced coffee, breakfast sandwiches, smoothies, gourmet cookies, and Dunkin' Dawgs in addition to the old standbys, devoted customers argue that it's the coffee that sets Dunkin' Donuts apart. To keep customers coming back, the chain still relies on the recipe that founder Bill Rosenberg crafted more than 50 years ago.

The company is so concerned about offering a consistent, high-quality cup of coffee that managers in Dunkin' Donuts' "Tree-to-Cup" program monitor the progress of its coffee beans from the farm to the restaurant. The result? Dunkin' Donuts sells more cups of coffee than any other retailer in the United States—30 cups a second, nearly one billion cups each year. Building on that success, the company plans to more than triple its current number of stores, amassing 15,000 franchises by the year 2015.

After viewing the video featuring Dunkin' Donuts, answer the following questions about managing profitable customer relationships.

1. How does Dunkin' Donuts build long-term customer relationships?

2. What is Dunkin' Donuts' value proposition?

3. How is Dunkin' Donuts growing its share of customers?

In the late 1990s, it was all about the dot-coms. While venture capital poured into the high-tech sector and the stock prices of dot-com startups rose rapidly, the performance of traditional companies paled in comparison. This era seemed like a very bad time to start a chain of brick-and-mortar mall stores selling stuffed animals. Indeed, when Maxine Clark founded Build-A-Bear Workshop in 1996, many critics thought that she was making a very poor business decision.

But as the company nears the end of its first decade, it has more cheerleaders than naysayers. In 2005, one retail consultancy named Build-A-Bear one of the five hottest retailers. The company hit number 25 on *BusinessWeek's* Hot Growth list of fast-expanding small companies. And CEO Maxine Clark won Fast Company's Customer-Centered Leader Award. How does a small startup company achieve such accolades?

THE PRODUCT

On paper, it all looks simple. Maxine Clark opened the first company store in 1996. Since then, the company has opened more than 200 stores and has custom-made more than 30 million teddy bears and other stuffed animals. Annual revenues reached $359 million for 2005 and are growing at a steady and predictable 20 percent annually. Annual sales per square foot are $600, roughly double the average for U.S. mall stores. The company plans to open approximately 30 new stores each year in the United States and Canada and to franchise an additional 20 stores per year internationally. The company's stock price has soared 56 percent since it went public in November of 2004. On top of all this, the company's Internet sales are exploding.

What all these numbers don't illustrate is *how* the company is achieving such success. That success comes not from the tangible object that children clutch as they leave a store. It comes from what Build-A-Bear is really selling: the experience of participating in the creation of personalized entertainment.

When children enter a Build-A-Bear store, they step into a cartoon land, a genuine fantasy world organized around a child-friendly assembly line comprised of clearly labeled work stations. The process begins at the "Choose Me" station where customers select an unstuffed animal from a bin. At the "Stuff Me" station, the animal literally comes to life. A friendly employee inserts a metal tube into the animal, extending from a large tumbler full of "fluff." The child operates a foot pedal that blows in the stuffing. She or he decides how full the animal should be. Other stations include "Hear Me" (where customers decide whether or not to include a "voice box"), "Stitch Me" (where the child stitches the animal shut), "Fluff Me" (where the child can give the animal a blow-dry spa treatment), "Dress Me" (filled with accessories galore), and "Name Me" (where a birth certificate is created with the child-selected name).

Unlike most retail stores, waiting in line behind other customers is not an unpleasant activity. In fact, because the process is much of the fun, waiting actually enhances the experience. By the time children leave the store, they have a product unlike any they've ever bought or received. They have a product that they have created. More than just a stuffed animal that they can have and hold, it's entrenched with the memory created on their visit to the store.

Obviously, kids love Build-A-Bear. But parents love it too. The cost of the experience starts as low as $10. And although options and accessories can push that price up, the average bear leaves the store costing around $25. Many parents consider this a bargain when they see how each of those dollars translates into their child's delight.

WHY THE CONCEPT WORKS

The outside observer might assume that Build-A-Bear is competing with other toy companies, or with other makers of stuffed animals, such as the Vermont Teddy Bear Company. Touting its product as the only bear made in America and guaranteed for life, Vermont Teddy Bear handmakes all of its bears at a central factory in Vermont. Quality is the key selling point. Vermont Teddy Bear sells direct to the consumer through catalogues and its Internet site. Although it does offer customization options, most of its sales come from off-the-shelf bears in a variety of preestablished costumes and outfits. Whether choosing a customized or a premade bear, the customer receives the bear in the mail, in a box, without the experience of seeing the bear being made or taking part in the creation process. Vermont Teddy Bears start at $50 and can top $90, a price range that reinforces the brand's high-quality position.

Although Vermont Teddy Bear has achieved great success since it sold its first bear in 1981, Maxine Clark does not consider it to be a serious Build-A-Bear competitor. "Our concept is based on customization," says Clark. "Most things today are high-tech and hard-touch. We are soft-touch. We don't think of ourselves as a toy store—we think of ourselves as an experience." As evidence, Clark points out that, unlike the rest of the toy industry, Build-A-Bear sales do not peak during the holiday season, but are evenly distributed throughout the year.

Product personalization has long been popular in many industries. Harley-Davidson has developed a very strong brand and intense customer loyalty by allowing each customer to personalize his or her own motorcycle. Dell has achieved industry leadership by doing the same. Even in the fashion sector, mass-producers such as Nike and Levi's have joined the trend by allowing customers to customize products through their Web site. Jaison Blair, research analyst for Rochdale Securities, has stated that the customization feature is so satisfying, it "builds fiercely loyal customers."

Although not very common in the toy industry, Maxine Clark asserts that personalization is emerging because it lets customers be creative and express themselves. It provides far more value for the customer than they receive from mass-produced products. "It's empowerment—it lets the customer do something in their control," she adds. Build-A-Bear has capitalized on this concept by not just allowing for customization, but by making it a key driver of customer value. The extensive customer involvement in the personalization process is more of the "product" than the resulting item.

Although Build-A-Bear has performed impressively, some analysts question whether or not it is just another toy industry fad, comparing the brand to Beanie Babies and Cabbage Patch Kids. Maxine Clark has considered this, and she is confident that the Build-A-Bear product and experience will evolve as quickly as the fickle tastes of children. Although some outfits and accessories might be trendy (the company added Spiderman costumes to the bear-size clothing line at the peak of the movie's popularity), accessories assortments are changed 11 times each year.

KNOWING THE CUSTOMER

Maxine Clark has been viewed as the strategic visionary—and even the genius—who has made the Build-A-Bear concept work. But her success as CEO derives from more than just business skills relating to strategy development and implementation. Clark attributes her success to "never forgetting what it's like to be a customer." Given that Clark has no children of her own, this is an amazing feat indeed. Understanding customers is certainly not a new concept, and Clark has employed both low-tech and high-tech methods for making Build-A-Bear a truly customer-centric organization.

To put herself in the customer's shoes, Clark walks where they walk. Every week, she visits two or three of the more than 200 Build-A-Bear stores. She doesn't do this just to see how the stores are running operationally. She takes the opportunity to interact with her customer base by chatting with preteens and parents. She actually puts herself on the front line, assisting employees in serving customers. She even hands out business cards.

As a result, Clark receives thousands of e-mails each week, and she's added to the buddy lists of preteens all over the world. Clark doesn't take this honor lightly, and she tries to respond to as many of those messages as possible via her BlackBerry. Also, to capitalize on these customer communications, she has created what she calls the "Virtual Cub Advisory Council," a panel of children on her e-mail list. And what does Clark get in return from all this high-tech communication? "Ideas," she says, "I used to feel like I had to come up with all the ideas myself, but it's so much easier relying on my customers for help."

From the location of stores to accessories that could be added to the Build-A-Bear line, Build-A-Bear actually puts customer ideas into practice. As the ideas come in, Clark polls the Cub Council to get real-time feedback from cus-

tomers throughout the areas where the company does business, Miniscooters, mascot bears at professional sports venues, and sequined purses are all ideas generated by customers that have become very successful additions.

The future holds great potential as more ideas are being considered and implemented. Soon, Build-A-Bear Workshops will house in-store galleries of bear-sized furniture designed by kids for kids. The company will add NASCAR to the sports licensing agreements that it currently has with the NBA, MLB, NHL, and NFL. And Clark will give much more attention to a new line of stores called "Friends 2B Made," a concept built around the personalization of dolls rather than stuffed animals.

Although Maxine Clark may communicate with only a fraction of her customers, she sees this as the basis for a personal connection with all customers. "With each child that enters our store, we have an opportunity to build a lasting memory," she says. "Any business can think that way, whether you're selling a screw, a bar of soap, or a bear."

Questions for Discussion

1. Give examples of needs, wants, and demands that Build-A-Bear customers demonstrate, differentiating each of these three concepts. What are the implications of each on Build-A-Bear's actions?

2. In detail, describe all facets of Build-A-Bear's product. What is being exchanged in a Build-A-Bear transaction?

3. Which of the five marketing management concepts best describes Build-A-Bear Workshop?

4. Discuss in detail the value that Build-A-Bear creates for its customers.

5. Is Build-A-Bear likely to be successful in continuing to build customer relationships? Why or why not?

Sources: Parija Bhatnagar, "The Next Hot Retailers?" CNNMoney.com, January 9, 2006; Lucas Conley, "Customer-Centered Leader: Maxine Clark," Fast Company, October 2005, p. 54; Ray Allegrezza, "Kids Today," Kids Today, April 1, 2006, p. 10; "The Mini-Me School of Marketing," Brand Strategy, November 2, 2005, p. 12; Michael O'Rourke, "Build-a-Bear Assembles Dreams," San Antonio Express-News, February 4, 2006, p. 1E; Dody Tsiantar, "Not Your Average Bear," Time, July 3, 2005; Roger Crockett, "Build-A-Bear Workshop: Retailing Gets Interactive with Toys Designed by Tots," BusinessWeek, June 6, 2005, p. 77; and "Build-A-Bear Workshop, Inc. Reports Strong Sales and Net Income Growth in Fiscal 2005 Fourth Quarter and Full Year," press release through Business Wire, February 16, 2006.

Company and Marketing Strategy

Partnering to Build Customer Relationships

Previewing the Concepts

In the first chapter, we explored the marketing process by which companies create value for consumers in order to capture value in return. On this leg of our journey, we dig deeper into steps two and three of the marketing process—designing customer-driven marketing strategies and constructing marketing programs. To begin, we look at the organization's overall strategic planning. Next, we discuss how marketers, guided by the strategic plan, work closely with others inside and outside the firm to serve customers. We then examine marketing strategy and planning—how marketers choose target markets, position their market offerings, develop a marketing mix, and manage their marketing programs. Finally, we look at the important step of measuring and managing return on marketing investment.

Let's look first at Nike. During the past several decades, Nike has forever changed the rules of sports marketing strategy. In the process, it has built the Nike swoosh into one of the world's best-known brand symbols. But the Nike we know today is far, far different from the brash young start-up company of 40 years ago. As Nike has grown and matured—moving from maverick to mainstream—its marketing strategy has matured as well. To stay on top in the intensely competitive sports apparel business, Nike will have to keep finding fresh ways to bring value to its customers.

The Nike "swoosh"—it's everywhere! Just for fun, try counting the swooshes whenever you pick up the sports pages or watch a pickup basketball game or tune into a televised golf match. Through innovative marketing, Nike has built the ever-present swoosh into one of the best-known brand symbols on the planet. But 40-some years ago, when young CPA Phil Knight and college track coach Bill Bowerman cofounded the company, Nike was just a brash, young upstart in the athletic footwear industry.

In those early days, Knight and Bowerman ran Nike by the seat of their pants. In 1964, the pair chipped in $500 apiece to start Blue Ribbon Sports. In 1970, Bowerman dreamed up a new sneaker tread by stuffing a piece of rubber into his wife's waffle iron. The Waffle Trainer quickly became the nation's best-selling training shoe. In 1972, the company became Nike, named after the Greek goddess of victory. The swoosh was designed by a graduate student for a fee of $35. By 1979, Nike owned 50 percent of the U.S. running shoe market. It all seemed easy then. Running was in, sneakers were hot, and Nike had the right stuff.

During the 1980s, under Phil Knight's leadership, Nike revolutionized sports marketing. To build its brand image and market share, Nike spent lavishly on big-name endorsements, splashy promotional events, and in-your-face "Just Do It" ads. At Nike, however, good marketing meant more than just promotional hype and promises—it meant consistently building strong relationships with customers based on real value. Nike's initial success resulted from the technical superiority of its running and basketball shoes. To this day, Nike leads the industry in research-and-development spending.

But Nike gave customers much more than good athletic gear. Customers didn't just wear their Nikes, they *experienced* them. As the company stated on its Web page (www.nike.com), "Nike has always known the truth—it's not so much the shoes but where they take you." Beyond shoes, apparel, and equipment, Nike marketed a way of life, a sports culture, a just-do-it attitude. As Phil Knight said at the time: "Basically, our culture and our style is to be a rebel." The company was built on a genuine passion for sports, a maverick disregard for convention, and a belief in hard work and serious sports performance.

Throughout the 1980s and 1990s, still playing the role of the upstart underdog, Nike sprinted ahead of its competition. Between 1988 and 1997, Nike's revenues grew at an annual rate of 21 percent; annual return to investors averaged an eye-popping 47 percent. Nike leveraged its brand strength, moving aggressively into new product categories, sports, and regions of the world. The company slapped its familiar swoosh logo on everything from sunglasses and soccer balls to batting gloves and hockey sticks. Nike invaded a dozen new sports, including baseball, golf, ice and street hockey, skateboarding, wall climbing, and hiking. It seemed that things couldn't be going any better.

In the late 1990s, however, Nike stumbled and its sales slipped. The whole industry suffered a setback, as a "brown shoe" craze for hiking and outdoor shoe styles ate into the athletic sneaker business. Moreover, Nike's creative juices seemed to run dry. Ho-hum new sneaker designs collected dust on retailer shelves as buyers seeking a new look switched to competing brands. To make matters worse, Nike was fighting off allegations that it was overcommercializing sports and exploiting child labor in Asian sweatshops.

But Nike's biggest obstacle may have been its own incredible success. The brand appeared to suffer from big-brand backlash, and the swoosh may have become too common to be cool. As sales moved past the $10 billion mark, Nike moved from maverick to mainstream. Rooting for Nike was like rooting for Microsoft. Instead of antiestablishment, Nike was the establishment. Once the brat of sports marketing, Nike now had to grow up and act its age.

And grow up it has. In recent years, Nike's marketing strategy has matured. The company still spends hundreds of millions of dollars each year on very creative advertising, innovative brand-building promotions, and big-name endorsers. For example, Nike signed basketball phenom LeBron James to a $90 million endorsement contract a few years back, and in the Athens Olympics, Nike athletes brought home 50 gold medals plus dozens more silver and bronze.

But Nike has toned down its antiestablishment attitude—its marketing is a bit less edgy. And the company is now devoting much more attention to mundane marketing details. "Gone are the days when Nike execs, working on little more than hunches, would do just about anything and spend just about any amount in the quest for publicity and market share," says one Nike observer. "More and more, Nike is searching for the right balance between its creative and its business sides, relying on a newfound financial and managerial discipline to drive growth."

The new Nike has returned to the basics—focusing on innovation, methodically assessing new market opportunities, developing new product lines, and reworking its information and distribution systems. According to the industry expert:

In the old days, Nike operated pretty much on [marketing] instinct. It took a guess as to how many pairs of shoes to churn out and hoped it could cram

Objectives

After studying this chapter, you should be able to

1. explain companywide strategic planning and its four steps
2. discuss how to design business portfolios and develop growth strategies
3. explain marketing's role in strategic planning and how marketing works with its partners to create and deliver customer value
4. describe the elements of a customer-driven marketing strategy and mix, and the forces that influence it
5. list the marketing management functions, including the elements of a marketing plan, and discuss the importance of measuring and managing return on marketing investment

them all onto retailers' shelves. Not anymore. Nike has overhauled its computer systems to get the right number of sneakers to more places in the world more quickly. [It] also overhauled its supply-chain system, which often left retailers either desperately awaiting delivery of hot shoes or struggling to get rid of the duds. The old jerry-built compilation strung together 27 different computer systems worldwide, most of which couldn't talk with the others. . . . Nike has spent $500 million to build a new system. [Now, according to Nike,] the percentage of shoes it makes without a firm order from a retailer has fallen from 30 percent to 3 percent, while the lead time for getting new sneaker styles to market has been cut from nine months to six months.

The old seat-of-the-pants Nike had difficulty going global; at the new Nike, more than 50 percent of sales now come from international markets, and these markets are growing rapidly. The old Nike also stumbled with its acquisitions, trying to force its own superheated marketing culture onto them. The new Nike has learned to give its acquired brands some independence. As a result, acquisitions such as Cole Haan dress shoes, Converse retro-style sneakers, Hurley International skateboard gear, Bauer in-line and hockey skates, and Starter Official affordable sneakers now account for more than 13 percent of Nike's revenues and a quarter of its sales growth.

The new, more-mature Nike is once again achieving stunning results. In the past five years, Nike's sales have grown more than 50 percent to almost $15 billion; profits have more than doubled. The company captures some 36 percent of the U.S. athletic shoe market; the next-biggest competitor is Adidas (which recently acquired Reebok) at 21 percent. A relative newcomer to soccer, Nike is now virtually neck-and-neck in the European soccer market with longtime leader Adidas. Nike's evolving marketing prowess over the years has also been good for investors. An investment of $1,000 in Nike in 1980 would be worth more than $64,000 today. And founder Phil Knight's 23 percent stake in Nike is worth almost $6 billion, making him one of the world's richest people.

To stay on top, however, Nike must keep its marketing strategy fresh, finding new ways to deliver the kind of innovation and value that built the brand so powerfully in the past. No longer the rebellious, antiestablishment upstart, Nike must continually reassess and rekindle its meaning to customers. Says Knight, "Now that we've [grown so large], there's a fine line between being a rebel and being a bully. [To our customers,] we have to be beautiful as well as big."[1]

Marketing strategies and programs are guided by broader, companywide strategic plans. Thus, to understand the role of marketing, we must first understand the organization's overall strategic planning process. Like Nike, all companies must look ahead and develop long-term strategies to meet the changing conditions in their industries and to ensure long-term survival.

Companywide Strategic Planning: Defining Marketing's Role

Each company must find the game plan for long-run survival and growth that makes the most sense given its specific situation, opportunities, objectives, and resources. This is the focus of **strategic planning**—the process of developing and maintaining a strategic fit between the organization's goals and capabilities and its changing marketing opportunities.

Strategic planning sets the stage for the rest of the planning in the firm. Companies usually prepare annual plans, long-range plans, and strategic plans. The annual and long-range plans deal with the company's current businesses and how to keep them going. In contrast, the strategic plan involves adapting the firm to take advantage of opportunities in its constantly changing environment.

At the corporate level, the company starts the strategic planning process by defining its overall purpose and mission (see Figure 2.1). This mission then is turned into detailed supporting objectives that guide the whole company. Next, headquarters decides what portfolio of businesses and products is best for the company and how much support to give each one. In turn, each business and product develops detailed marketing and other departmental plans

Strategic planning
The process of developing and maintaining a strategic fit between the organization's goals and capabilities and its changing marketing opportunities.

Corporate level

| Defining the company mission | ⇨ | Setting company objectives and goals | ⇨ | Designing the business portfolio | ⇢ | Planning marketing and other functional strategies |

Business unit, product, and market level

FIGURE 2.1 Steps in strategic planning

that support the companywide plan. Thus, marketing planning occurs at the business-unit, product, and market levels. It supports company strategic planning with more detailed plans for specific marketing opportunities.[2]

Defining a Market-Oriented Mission

An organization exists to accomplish something. At first, it has a clear purpose or mission, but over time its mission may become unclear as the organization grows, adds new products and markets, or faces new conditions in the environment. When management senses that the organization is drifting, it must renew its search for purpose. It is time to ask: What is our business? Who is the customer? What do consumers value? What *should* our business be? These simple-sounding questions are among the most difficult the company will ever have to answer. Successful companies continuously raise these questions and answer them carefully and completely.

Many organizations develop formal mission statements that answer these questions. A **mission statement** is a statement of the organization's purpose—what it wants to accomplish in the larger environment. A clear mission statement acts as an "invisible hand" that guides people in the organization. Studies have shown that firms with well-crafted mission statements have better organizational and financial performance.[3]

Some companies define their missions myopically in product or technology terms ("We make and sell furniture" or "We are a chemical-processing firm"). But mission statements should be *market oriented* and defined in terms of customer needs. Products and technologies eventually become outdated, but basic market needs may last forever.

A market-oriented mission statement defines the business in terms of satisfying basic customer needs. For example, Nike isn't just a shoe and apparel manufacturer—it wants "to bring inspiration and innovation to every athlete* in the world. (*If you have a body, you are an athlete.)" Likewise, eBay's mission isn't simply to hold online auctions and trading. Its mission is "to provide a global trading platform where practically anyone can trade practically anything—you can get it on eBay." It wants to be a unique Web community in which people can shop around, have fun, and get to know each other, for example, by chatting at the eBay Café. Table 2.1 provides several other examples of product-oriented versus market-oriented business definitions.[4]

Management should avoid making its mission too narrow or too broad. A pencil manufacturer that says it is in the communication equipment business is stating its mission too broadly. Missions should be *realistic*. Singapore Airlines

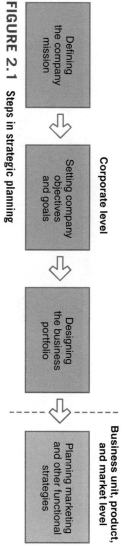

searchebay.com/hula skirts
/portable video games
/mystery novels
/baseball tickets
/all-terrain tires
/dome tents
/stain removers
/ranch land
/hedge trimmers
/golf shoes
/video cellphones
/flip-flops
/digital sports watches
/horseshoe sets
/laptops
/swimming trunks
/digital cameras
/sprinklers
/sun hats
/lawnmowers
/artificial turf

you can get it on **ebay**.

Mission statement
A statement of the organization's purpose—what it wants to accomplish in the larger environment.

■ Mission statements: eBay's mission is "to provide a global trading platform where practically anyone can trade practically anything—you can get *it* on eBay."

TABLE 2.1 Market-Oriented Business Definitions

Company	Product-Oriented Definition	Market-Oriented Definition
Amazon.com	We sell books, videos, CDs, toys, consumer electronics, hardware, housewares, and other products.	We make the Internet buying experience fast, easy, and enjoyable—we're the place where you can find and discover anything you want to buy online.
America Online	We provide online services.	We create customer connectivity, anytime, anywhere.
Disney	We run theme parks.	We create fantasies—a place where America still works the way it's supposed to.
eBay	We hold online auctions.	We provide a global marketplace where practically anyone can trade practically anything—a unique Web community in which people can shop around, have fun, and get to know each other.
Home Depot	We sell tools and home repair and improvement items.	We empower consumers to achieve the homes of their dreams.
Charles Schwab	We are a brokerage firm.	We are the guardian of our customers' financial dreams.
Revlon	We make cosmetics.	We sell lifestyle and self-expression; success and status; memories, hopes, and dreams.
Ritz-Carlton Hotels	We rent rooms.	We create the Ritz-Carlton experience—one that enlivens the senses, instills well-being, and fulfills even the unexpressed wishes and needs of our guests.
Wal-Mart	We run discount stores.	We deliver low prices every day and give ordinary folks the chance to buy the same things as rich people.

would be deluding itself if it adopted the mission to become the world's largest airline. Missions should also be *specific*. Many mission statements are written for public relations purposes and lack specific, workable guidelines. Too often, they "are platitudes incorporating quality and customer satisfaction, often with an 'employees are our most important assets' kicker," say one analyst. "They're too long to remember, too vague to be meaningful, and too dull to inspire."[5] Such generic statements sound good but provide little real guidance or inspiration.

Missions should fit the *market environment*. The Girl Scouts of America would not recruit successfully in today's environment with its former mission: "to prepare young girls for motherhood and wifely duties." Today, its mission is to be the place "where girls grow strong." The organization should also base its mission on its *distinctive competencies*. Finally, mission statements should be *motivating*. A company's mission should not be stated as making more sales or profits—profits are only a reward for undertaking a useful activity. A company's employees need to feel that their work is significant and that it contributes to people's lives. For example, Microsoft's aim is to help people to "realize their potential"—"your potential, our passion" says the company. Wal-Mart's mission is to "Give ordinary folks the chance to buy the same things as rich people."

Setting Company Objectives and Goals

The company needs to turn its mission into detailed supporting objectives for each level of management. Each manager should have objectives and be responsible for reaching them. For example, Monsanto operates in the agricultural biotechnology business. It defines its business . . . improving the future of farming . . . improving the future of food . . . abundantly and safely." It seeks to help feed the world's exploding population while at the same time sustaining the environment. Monsanto ads ask us to "Imagine innovative agriculture that creates incredible things today."

This mission leads to a hierarchy of objectives, including business objectives and marketing objectives. Monsanto's overall objective is to build profitable customer relationships by developing better agricultural products and getting them to market faster at lower costs. It does this by researching products that safely help crops produce more nutrition and higher yields without chemical spraying. But research is expensive and requires improved profits to plow back into research programs. So improving profits becomes another major Monsanto objective. Profits can be improved by increasing sales or reducing costs. Sales can be increased by improving the company's share of the U.S. market, by entering new foreign markets, or both. These goals then become the company's current marketing objectives.[6]

Imagine innovative agriculture that creates incredible things today.

imagine

learn more at monsanto.com

MONSANTO imagine

■ Monsanto defines its mission as "improving the future of farming . . . improving the future of food . . . abundantly and safely." Its ads ask us to "Imagine innovative agriculture that creates incredible things today." This mission leads to specific business and marketing objectives.

Business portfolio
The collection of businesses and products that make up the company.

Portfolio analysis
The process by which management evaluates the products and businesses making up the company.

Growth-share matrix
A portfolio-planning method that evaluates a company's strategic business units in terms of their market growth rate and relative market share. SBUs are classified as stars, cash cows, question marks, or dogs.

ment evaluates the products and businesses making up the company. The company will want to put strong resources into its more profitable businesses and phase down or drop its weaker ones.

Management's first step is to identify the key businesses making up the company. These can be called the strategic business units. A *strategic business unit* (SBU) is a unit of the company that has a separate mission and objectives and that can be planned independently from other company businesses. An SBU can be a company division, a product line within a division, or sometimes a single product or brand.

The next step in business portfolio analysis calls for management to assess the attractiveness of its various SBUs and decide how much support each deserves. Most companies are well advised to "stick to their knitting" when designing their business portfolios. It's usually a good idea to focus on adding products and businesses that fit closely with the firm's core philosophy and competencies.

The purpose of strategic planning is to find ways in which the company can best use its strengths to take advantage of attractive opportunities in the environment. So most standard portfolio-analysis methods evaluate SBUs on two important dimensions—the attractiveness of the SBU's market or industry and the strength of the SBU's position in that market or industry. The best-known portfolio-planning method was developed by the Boston Consulting Group, a leading management consulting firm.[7]

THE BOSTON CONSULTING GROUP APPROACH Using the Boston Consulting Group (BCG) approach, a company classifies all its SBUs according to the **growth-share matrix** shown in Figure 2.2. On the vertical axis, *market growth rate* provides a measure of market attractiveness.

Marketing strategies and programs must be developed to support these marketing objectives. To increase its U.S. market share, Monsanto might increase its products' availability and promotion. To enter new foreign markets, the company may cut prices and target large farms abroad. These are its broad marketing strategies. Each broad marketing strategy must then be defined in greater detail. For example, increasing the product's promotion may require more salespeople and more advertising; if so, both requirements need to be spelled out. In this way, the firm's mission is translated into a set of objectives for the current period.

Designing the Business Portfolio

Guided by the company's mission statement and objectives, management now must plan its **business portfolio**—the collection of businesses and products that make up the company. The best business portfolio is the one that best fits the company's strengths and weaknesses to opportunities in the environment. Business portfolio planning involves two steps. First, the company must analyze its *current* business portfolio and decide which businesses should receive more, less, or no investment. Second, it must shape the *future* portfolio by developing strategies for growth and downsizing.

Analyzing the Current Business Portfolio

The major activity in strategic planning is business **portfolio analysis**, whereby management evaluates the products and businesses making up the company. The company will

FIGURE 2.2
The BCG growth-share matrix

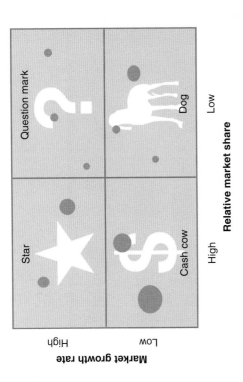

On the horizontal axis, *relative market share* serves as a measure of company strength in the market. The growth-share matrix defines four types of SBUs:

Stars. Stars are high-growth, high-share businesses or products. They often need heavy investment to finance their rapid growth. Eventually their growth will slow down, and they will turn into cash cows.

Cash cows. Cash cows are low-growth, high-share businesses or products. These established and successful SBUs need less investment to hold their market share. Thus, they produce a lot of cash that the company uses to pay its bills and to support other SBUs that need investment.

Question marks. Question marks are low-share business units in high-growth markets. They require a lot of cash to hold their share, let alone increase it. Management needs to think hard about which question marks it should try to build into stars and which should be phased out.

Dogs. Dogs are low-growth, low-share businesses and products. They may generate enough cash to maintain themselves but do not promise to be large sources of cash.

The ten circles in the growth-share matrix represent a company's ten current SBUs. The company has two stars, two cash cows, three question marks, and three dogs. The areas of the circles are proportional to the SBU's dollar sales. This company is in fair shape, although not in good shape. It wants to invest in the more promising question marks to make them stars and to maintain the stars so that they will become cash cows as their markets mature. Fortunately, it has two good-sized cash cows. Income from these cash cows will help finance the company's question marks, stars, and dogs. The company should take some decisive action concerning its dogs and its question marks. The picture would be worse if the company had no stars, if it had too many dogs, or if it had only one weak cash cow.

Once it has classified its SBUs, the company must determine what role each will play in the future. One of four strategies can be pursued for each SBU. The company can invest more in the business unit in order to *build* its share. Or it can invest just enough to *hold* the SBU's share at the current level. It can *harvest* the SBU, milking its short-term cash flow regardless of the long-term effect. Finally, the company can *divest* the SBU by selling it or phasing it out and using the resources elsewhere.

As time passes, SBUs change their positions in the growth-share matrix. Each SBU has a life cycle. Many SBUs start out as question marks and move into the star category if they succeed. They later become cash cows as market growth falls, then finally die off or turn into dogs toward the end of their life cycle. The company needs to add new products and units continuously so that some of them will become stars and, eventually, cash cows that will help finance other SBUs.

PROBLEMS WITH MATRIX APPROACHES The BCG and other formal methods revolutionized strategic planning. However, such centralized approaches have limitations. They can be difficult, time consuming, and costly to implement. Management may find it difficult to define SBUs and measure market share and growth. In addition, these approaches focus on classifying *current* businesses but provide little advice for *future* planning.

Formal planning approaches can also place too much emphasis on market-share growth or growth through entry into attractive new markets. Using these approaches, many companies plunged into unrelated and new high-growth businesses that they did not know how to manage—with very bad results. At the same time, these companies were often too quick to abandon, sell, or milk to death their healthy mature businesses. As a result, many companies that diversified too broadly in the past now have narrowed their focus and gotten back to the basics of serving one or a few industries that they know best.

Because of such problems, many companies have dropped formal matrix methods in favor of more customized approaches that are better suited to their specific situations. Moreover, unlike former strategic-planning efforts, which rested mostly in the hands of senior managers at company headquarters, today's strategic planning has been decentralized. Increasingly, companies are placing responsibility for strategic planning in the hands of cross-functional teams of divisional managers who are close to their markets.

For example, consider The Walt Disney Company. Most people think of Disney as theme parks and wholesome family entertainment. But in the mid-1980s, Disney set up a powerful, centralized strategic planning group to guide the company's direction and growth. Over the next two decades, the strategic planning group turned The Walt Disney Company into a huge but diverse collection of media and entertainment businesses. The newly transformed company proved hard to manage and performed unevenly. Recently, Disney's new chief executive disbanded the centralized strategic planning unit, decentralizing its functions to divisional managers (see Real Marketing 2.1).

2.1 The Walt Disney Company: Strategic Planning for a Happy-Ever-After Ending

When you think of The Walt Disney Company, you probably think first of theme parks and animated films. And no wonder. Since the release of its first Mickey Mouse cartoon more than 75 years ago, Disney has grown to become the undisputed master of family entertainment. It perfected the art of movie animation. From pioneering films such as *Snow White and the Seven Dwarfs*, *Fantasia*, and *Pinocchio* to more recent features such as *Monsters, Inc.*, *Finding Nemo*, *The Incredibles*, *Valiant*, and *Cars*, Disney has brought pure magic to the theaters, living rooms, and hearts and minds of audiences around the world.

But perhaps nowhere is the Disney magic more apparent than at the company's premier theme parks. Each year, some 43 million people flock to The Walt Disney World Resort alone—14 times more than visit Yellowstone National Park—making it the world's number one tourist attraction. What brings so many people to The Walt Disney World Resort? Part of the answer lies in its many attractions. The resort's four major theme parks—Magic Kingdom, Epcot, Disney-MGM Studios, and Disney's Animal Kingdom—brim with such attractions as the Twilight Zone Tower of Terror, Soarin' Over California, the Kilimanjaro Safaris, and Big Thunder Mountain Railroad.

But the real "Disney Magic" lies in the company's obsessive dedication to its mission to "make people happy" and to "make a dream come true." Disney goes to extremes to fulfill guests' expectations and dreams. Its theme parks are so highly regarded for outstanding customer service that many of America's leading corporations send managers to Disney University to learn how Disney does it.

You might be surprised to learn, however, that theme parks and movies are only part of a much bigger Disney story. Parks and resorts account for only about 25 percent of today's Disney empire; movies and entertainment make up another 28 percent. The rest comes from a diverse portfolio of businesses that have been acquired by Disney over the past two decades.

In fact, The Walt Disney Company has become a real study in strategic planning. In 1985, Disney's then-new chief officer, Michael Eisner, set up a high-powered, centralized strategic planning unit, charged with seeking out and nurturing new growth opportunities

For more than 75 years, The Walt Disney Company has been the undisputed master of family entertainment. But it will take masterful strategic planning—along with some big doses of the famed "Disney Magic"—to give the modern Disney a happy-ever-after ending.

(continues)

(continued)

and setting the company's strategic path. Throughout the late 1980s and the 1990s, seeking growth, the strategic planning group engineered a series of major acquisitions, including the mid-1990s purchase of Capital Cities/ABC, which almost doubled Disney's size.

By the early 2000s, the group had transformed The Walt Disney Company into a $30 billion international media and entertainment colossus. The company now owns all or part of hundreds of companies and divisions, organized into four major business groups:

Studio Entertainment: Four television production companies, eight movie and theatrical production companies, and a distribution company (including Walt Disney Pictures, Touchstone Pictures, Hollywood Pictures, Miramax Films, Dimension Films, and Buena Vista Theatrical Productions); and four music labels (Walt Disney Records, Hollywood Records, Buena Vista Records, and Lyric Street Records).

Media Networks: A major broadcast television network (ABC, plus ten company-owned television stations); a dozen cable television networks (including the Disney Channel, Toon Disney, SOAPnet, ESPN, A&E, the History Channel, Lifetime Television, E! Entertainment, and ABC Family); three radio networks (ESPN Radio, ABC Radio, and Disney Radio, plus more than seventy radio stations); and the Walt Disney Internet Group (nineteen Internet sites including Disney Online, Disney's Daily Blast, ABC.com, ESPN.com, Family.com, NASCAR.com, and NBA.com).

Parks and Resorts: Eleven parks and thirty-five resort hotels on three continents (including Disneyland Resort Paris, Tokyo Disney Resort, and Hong Kong Disneyland); Disney Cruise Line; Disney Vacation Club; and ESPN Zone.

Consumer Products: Three Disney Merchandise Licensing divisions; four Disney Publishing divisions (including Hyperion Books, Disney Press, and *Disney Adventures*, the number one children's magazine in the United States); the Baby Einstein Company (developmental media for infants); four Disney Retail groups (including Disney Stores Worldwide and Disney Direct Marketing); and Buena Vista Games (Disney content for the interactive gaming community).

Whew! That's an impressive list. However, for Disney, managing this diverse portfolio of businesses has become a real *Monsters, Inc.* During the last half of the 1980s, the smaller, more focused Disney experienced soaring sales and profits. Revenues grew at an average rate of 23 percent annually; net income grew at 50 percent annually.

In contrast, at least until recently, the larger, more complex Disney has struggled for consistent profitability and growth.

Disney's centralized strategic planning group frequently bore the blame for the transformed company's uneven performance. Operating from on high, the group reached for the stars—overreached, according to some. Many critics assert that the company has grown too large, too diverse, and too distant from the core strengths that made it so successful in earlier years. At the same time, the strategic planning group reviewed and often rejected the strategies proposed by the company's business unit managers. The group was criticized for "having too much power and quashing ideas that weren't its own," notes one analyst. It even came to be called by some "the business prevention department."

In 2004, disagreements over Disney's long-term strategic direction erupted into high-level boardroom brawls, resulting in Eisner's ouster as chairman and resignation as CEO. Tellingly, less than two weeks after assuming the reins at The Walt Disney Company, new Chief Executive Robert Iger set a priority of decentralizing the company's strategic planning. In a move popular with most Disney executives, Iger broke up the centralized strategic planning group, returning most of the group's functions to Disney's division managers. He is betting that the individual business units, which are closer to their markets, can do a better job of planning growth strategies than the centralized unit did. As part of an expected corporate overhaul, Iger will no doubt take a fresh look at Disney's disparate portfolio of businesses.

Thus, for Disney, bigger isn't necessarily better. And more decentralized strategic planning seems to make better sense than on-high planning. One thing seems certain: Creating just the right blend of businesses to make up the new Magic Kingdom won't be easy. It will take masterful strategic planning—along with some big doses of the famed "Disney magic"—to give the modern Disney story a happy-ever-after ending.

Sources: Merissa Marr, "Disney Cuts Strategic-Planning Unit," *Wall Street Journal*, March 28, 2005, p. A3; Jacqueline Doherty, "Better Days for Disney," *Barron's*, March 21, 2005, p. 14; Laura M. Holson, "Disney Intends to Overhaul Planning Unit," *New York Times*, March 26, 2005, p. C2; Robert Niles, "Disney Slams Universal in 2005 Theme Park Attendance," December 27, 2005, accessed at www.themeparkinsider. com/flume/200512/2/; Juliana Koranteng, "Parks Persist in the Face of Calamity," *Amusement Business*, January 2006, pp. 6–7; "The Walt Disney Company," *Hoover Company Records*, June 15, 2006, p. 11603; and information from www.disney.go.com, November 2006.

Developing Strategies for Growth and Downsizing

Beyond evaluating current businesses, designing the business portfolio involves finding businesses and products the company should consider in the future. Companies need growth if they are to compete more effectively, satisfy their stakeholders, and attract top talent. "Growth is pure oxygen," states one executive. "It creates a vital, enthusiastic corporation where people see genuine opportunity." At the same time, a firm must be careful not to make growth itself an objective. The company's objective must be "profitable growth."

Marketing has the main responsibility for achieving profitable growth for the company. Marketing must identify, evaluate, and select market opportunities and lay down strategies for capturing them. One useful device for identifying growth opportunities is the **product/market expansion grid**, shown in Figure 2.3.[8] We apply it here to Starbucks:

Product/market expansion grid

A portfolio-planning tool for identifying company growth opportunities through market penetration, market development, product development, or diversification.

More than 20 years ago, Howard Schultz hit on the idea of bringing a European-style coffeehouse to America. People needed to slow down, he believed—to "smell the coffee" and enjoy life a little more. The result was Starbucks. This coffeehouse doesn't just sell coffee, it sells *The Starbucks Experience.* "There's the Starbucks ambience," notes an analyst, "The music. The comfy velvety chairs. The smells. The hissing steam." Says Starbucks Chairman Schultz, "We aren't in the coffee business, serving people. We are in the people business, serving coffee." People around the globe now flock to

FIGURE 2.3
The product/market expansion grid

	Existing products	New products
Existing markets	Market penetration	Product development
New markets	Market development	Diversification

Starbucks, making it a powerhouse premium brand. Some 35 million customers now visit the company's more than 11,000 stores worldwide each week. Starbucks gives customers what it calls a "third place"—away from home and away from work.

Growth is the engine that keeps Starbucks perking—the company targets (and regularly achieves) jaw-dropping revenue growth exceeding 20 percent each year. Starbucks' success, however, has drawn a full litter of copycats, ranging from direct competitors such as Caribou Coffee to fast-food merchants (such as McDonald's McCafé) and even discounters (Wal-Mart's Kicks Coffee). To maintain its phenomenal growth in an increasingly overcaffeinated marketplace, Starbucks must brew up an ambitious, multipronged growth strategy.

■ Strategies for growth: To maintain its phenomenal growth in an increasingly overcaffeinated marketplace, Starbucks has brewed up an ambitious multipronged growth strategy.

Market penetration
A strategy for company growth by increasing sales of current products to current market segments without changing the product.

Market development
A strategy for company growth by identifying and developing new market segments for current company products.

First, Starbucks management might consider whether the company can achieve deeper **market penetration**—making more sales to current customers without changing its products. It might add new stores in current market areas to make it easier for more customers to visit. In fact, Starbucks is adding an average of 34 stores a week, 52 weeks a year—its ultimate goal is 30,000 stores worldwide. Improvements in advertising, prices, service, menu selection, or store design might encourage customers to stop by more often, stay longer, or to buy more during each visit. For example, Starbucks has added drive-through windows to many of its stores. A Starbucks Card that lets customers prepay for coffee and snacks or give the gift of Starbucks to family and friends. And to get customers to hang around longer, Starbucks offers wireless Internet access in most of its stores.

Second, Starbucks management might consider possibilities for **market development**—identifying and developing new markets for its current products. For instance, managers could review new *demographic markets*. Perhaps new groups—such as seniors or ethnic groups—could be encouraged to visit Starbucks coffee shops for the first time or to buy more from them. Managers also could review new *geographical markets*. Starbucks is now expanding swiftly into new U.S. markets, especially smaller cities. And it's expanding rapidly in new global markets. In 1996, Starbucks had only 11 coffeehouses outside North America. It now has more than 3,000, with plenty of room to grow. "We're just scratching the surface in China," says Starbucks's CEO. "We have 150 stores and the potential for more than 2,000 there."

Product development
A strategy for company growth by offering modified or new products to current market segments.

Third, management could consider **product development**—offering modified or new products to current markets. For example, Starbucks has introduced new reduced-calorie options, such as Frappuccino Light Blended Beverages. It recently added Chantico, an indulgent chocolate beverage, to its menu to draw in more non-coffee drinkers. To capture consumers who brew their coffee at home, Starbucks has also pushed into America's supermarket aisles. It has a cobranding deal with Kraft, under which Starbucks roasts and packages its coffee and Kraft markets and distributes it. And the company is forging ahead into new consumer categories. For example, it has brought out a line of Starbucks coffee liqueurs.

Diversification
A strategy for company growth through starting up or acquiring businesses outside the company's current products and markets.

Fourth, Starbucks might consider **diversification**—starting up or buying businesses outside of its current products and markets. For example, in 1999, Starbucks purchased Hear Music, which was so successful that it spurred the creation of the new Starbucks entertainment division. Beginning with just selling and playing compilation CDs, Hear Music now has its own XM Satellite Radio station. It is also installing kiosks (called Media Bars) in select Starbucks stores that let customers download music and burn their own CDs while sipping their lattes. As a next step, Starbucks is investing in Hear Music retail outlets, which will be music stores first and coffee shops second.

In a more extreme diversification, Starbucks has partnered with Lion's Gate to coproduce movies and then market them in Starbucks coffee houses. Starbucks supported the partnership's first film, *Akeelah and the Bee*, by sprinkling flashcards around the stores, stamping the movie's logo on its coffee cups, and placing spelling-bee caliber words on the store chalkboards. This new venture has left some analysts asking whether Starbucks is diversifying too broadly, at the risk of losing its market focus. They are asking, "What do movies have to do with Starbucks coffee and the Starbucks experience?"[9]

Downsizing
Reducing the business portfolio by eliminating products of business units that are not profitable or that no longer fit the company's overall strategy.

Companies must not only develop strategies for *growing* their business portfolios but also strategies for **downsizing** them. There are many reasons that a firm might want to abandon products or markets. The market environment might change, making some of the company's products or markets less profitable. The firm may have grown too fast or entered areas where it lacks experience. This can occur when a firm enters too many foreign markets without the proper research or when a company introduces new products that do not offer superior customer value. Finally, some products or business units simply age and die. One marketing expert summarizes the problem this way:

Companies spend vast amounts of money and time launching new brands, leveraging existing ones, and acquiring rivals. They create line extensions and brand extensions, not to mention channel extensions and subbrands, to cater to the growing number of niche segments in every market. . . . Surprisingly, most businesses do not examine their brand portfolios from time to time to check if they might be selling too many brands, identify weak ones, and kill unprofitable ones. They tend to ignore loss-making brands rather than merge them with healthy brands, sell them off, or drop them. Consequently, most portfolios have become [jammed] with loss-making and marginally profitable brands. Moreover, the surprising truth is that most brands don't make money for companies. Many corporations generate less than 80 to 90 percent of their profits from fewer than 20 percent of the brands they sell, while they lose money or barely break even on many of the other brands in their portfolios.[10]

When a firm finds brands or businesses that are unprofitable or that no longer fit its overall strategy, it must carefully prune, harvest, or divest them. Weak businesses usually require a disproportionate amount of management attention. Managers should focus on promising growth opportunities, not fritter away energy trying to salvage fading ones.

Planning Marketing: Partnering to Build Customer Relationships

The company's strategic plan establishes what kinds of businesses the company will operate in and its objectives for each. Then, within each business unit, more detailed planning takes place. The major functional departments in each unit—marketing, finance, accounting, purchasing, operations, information systems, human resources, and others—must work together to accomplish strategic objectives.

Marketing plays a key role in the company's strategic planning in several ways. First, marketing provides a guiding *philosophy*—the marketing concept—that suggests that company strategy should revolve around building profitable relationships with important consumer groups. Second, marketing provides *inputs* to strategic planners by helping to identify attractive market opportunities and by assessing the firm's potential to take advantage of them. Finally, within individual business units, marketing designs *strategies* for reaching the unit's objectives. Once the unit's objectives are set, marketing's task is to help carry them out profitably.

Customer value and satisfaction are important ingredients in the marketer's formula for success. However, as we noted in Chapter 1, marketers alone cannot produce superior value for customers. Although it plays a leading role, marketing can be only a partner in attracting, keeping, and growing customers. In addition to *customer relationship management*, marketers must also practice *partner relationship management*. They must work closely with partners in other company departments to form an effective *value chain* that serves the customer. Moreover, they must partner effectively with other companies in the marketing system to form a competitively superior *value-delivery network*. We now take a closer look at the concepts of a company value chain and value-delivery network.

Value chain

The series of departments that carry out value-creating activities to design, produce, market, deliver, and support a firm's products.

Partnering with Other Company Departments

Each company department can be thought of as a link in the company's **value chain**.[11] That is, each department carries out value-creating activities to design, produce, market, deliver, and support the firm's products. The firm's success depends not only on how well each department performs its work but also on how well the activities of various departments are coordinated.

For example, Wal-Mart's goal is to create customer value and satisfaction by providing shoppers with the products they want at the lowest possible prices. Marketers at Wal-Mart play an important role. They learn what customers need and stock the stores' shelves with the

desired products at unbeatable low prices. They prepare advertising and merchandising programs and assist shoppers with customer service. Through these and other activities, Wal-Mart's marketers help deliver value to customers.

However, the marketing department needs help from the company's other departments. Wal-Mart's ability to offer the right products at low prices depends on the purchasing department's skill in developing the needed suppliers and buying from them at low cost. Wal-Mart's information technology department must provide fast and accurate information about which products are selling in each store. And its operations people must provide effective, low-cost merchandise handling.

A company's value chain is only as strong as its weakest link. Success depends on how well each department performs its work of adding customer value and on how well the activities of various departments are coordinated. At Wal-Mart, if purchasing can't wring the lowest prices from suppliers, or if opera-

■ The value chain: Wal-Mart's ability to offer the right products at low prices depends on the contributions of people in all of the company's departments—marketing, purchasing, information systems, and operations.

tions can't distribute merchandise at the lowest costs, then marketing can't deliver on its promise of lowest prices.

Ideally, then, a company's different functions should work in harmony to produce value for consumers. But, in practice, departmental relations are full of conflicts and misunderstandings. The marketing department takes the consumer's point of view. But when marketing tries to develop customer satisfaction, it can cause other departments to do a poorer job *in their terms*. Marketing department actions can increase purchasing costs, disrupt production schedules, increase inventories, and create budget headaches. Thus, the other departments may resist the marketing department's efforts.

Yet marketers must find ways to get all departments to "think consumer" and to develop a smoothly functioning value chain. Marketing managers need to work closely with managers of other functions to develop a system of functional plans under which the different departments can work together to accomplish the company's overall strategic objectives. The idea is to "maximize the customer experience across the organization and its various customer touch points," says a marketing consultant. Jack Welch, GE's highly regarded former CEO, told his employees: "Companies can't give job security. Only customers can!" He emphasized that all GE people, regardless of their department, have an impact on customer satisfaction and retention. His message: "If you are not thinking customer, you are not thinking."[12]

Partnering with Others in the Marketing System

In its quest to create customer value, the firm needs to look beyond its own value chain and into the value chains of its suppliers, distributors, and, ultimately, customers. Consider McDonald's. McDonald's nearly 32,000 restaurants worldwide serve more than 50 million customers daily, capturing more than a 40 percent share of the burger market.[13] People do not swarm to McDonald's only because they love the chain's hamburgers. In fact, consumers typically rank McDonald's behind Burger King and Wendy's in taste. Consumers flock to the McDonald's *system*, not just to its food products. Throughout the world, McDonald's finely-tuned system delivers a high standard of what the company calls QSCV—quality, service, cleanliness, and value. McDonald's is effective only to the extent that it successfully partners with its franchisees, suppliers, and others to jointly deliver exceptionally high customer value.

More companies today are partnering with the other members of the supply chain to improve the performance of the customer **value-delivery network**. For example, Toyota knows the importance of building close relationships with its suppliers. In fact, it even includes the phrase "achieve supplier satisfaction" in its mission statement.

Achieving satisfying supplier relationships has been a cornerstone of Toyota's stunning success. U.S. competitors often alienate their suppliers through self-serving, heavy-handed dealings. "The [U.S. automakers] set annual cost-reduction targets [for the parts they buy]," says one supplier. "To realize those targets, they'll do anything. [They've unleashed] a reign of terror, and it gets worse every year." Says another, "[Ford] seems to send its people to 'hate school' so that they learn how to hate suppliers." By contrast, in survey after survey, auto suppliers rate Toyota as their most preferred customer. Rather than bullying suppliers, Toyota partners with them and helps them to meet its very high expectations. It learns about their businesses, conducts joint improvement activities, helps train their employees, gives daily performance feedback, and actively seeks out supplier concerns. Says one delighted Toyota supplier, "Toyota helped us dramatically improve our production system. We started by making one component, and as we improved, [Toyota] rewarded us with orders for more components. Toyota is our best customer."

Value-delivery network
The network made up of the company, suppliers, distributors, and ultimately customers who "partner" with each other to improve the performance of the entire system.

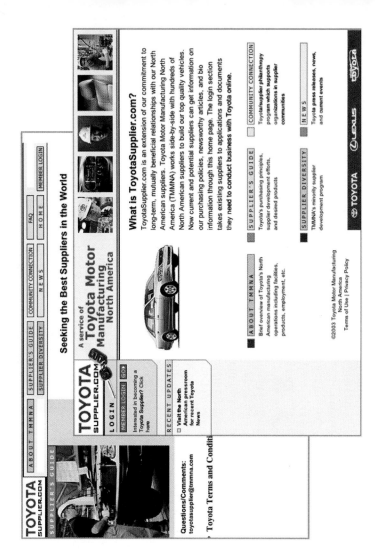

■ Toyota partners with its suppliers and helps them meet its very high expectations. Creating satisfied suppliers helps Toyota produce lower-cost, higher-quality cars, which in turn results in more satisfied customers.

Such high supplier satisfaction means that Toyota can rely on suppliers to help it improve its own quality, reduce costs, and develop new products quickly. For example, when Toyota recently launched a program to reduce prices by 30 percent on 170 parts that it would buy for its next generation of cars, suppliers didn't complain. Instead, they pitched in, trusting that Toyota would help them achieve the targeted reductions, in turn making them more competitive and profitable in the future. In all, creating satisfied suppliers helps Toyota to produce lower-cost, higher-quality cars, which in turn results in more satisfied customers.[14]

Increasingly in today's marketplace, competition no longer takes place between individual competitors. Rather, it takes place between the entire value-delivery networks created by these competitors. Thus, Toyota's performance against Ford depends on the quality of Toyota's overall value-delivery network versus Ford's. Even if Toyota makes the best cars, it might lose in the marketplace if Ford's dealer network provides more customer-satisfying sales and service.

Marketing Strategy and the Marketing Mix

The strategic plan defines the company's overall mission and objectives. Marketing's role and activities are shown in Figure 2.4, which summarizes the major activities involved in managing a customer-driven marketing strategy and the marketing mix.

Consumers stand in the center. The goal is to create value for customers and build strong and profitable customer relationships. Next comes **marketing strategy**—the marketing logic by which the company hopes to create this customer value and achieve these profitable relationships. The company decides which customers it will serve (segmentation and targeting) and how it will serve them (differentiation and positioning). It identifies the total market, then divides it into smaller segments, selects the most promising segments, and focuses on serving and satisfying customers in these segments.

Guided by marketing strategy, the company designs an integrated *marketing mix* made up of factors under its control—product, price, place, and promotion (the four Ps). To find the best marketing strategy and mix, the company engages in marketing analysis, planning, implementation, and control. Through these activities, the company watches and adapts to the actors and forces in the marketing environment. We will now look briefly at each activity. Then, in later chapters, we will discuss each one in more depth.

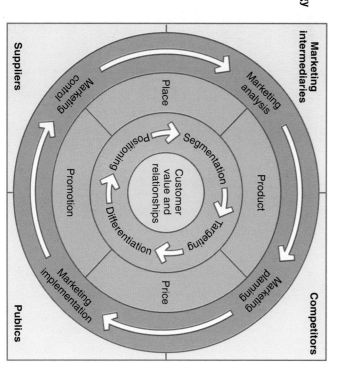

FIGURE 2.4
Managing marketing strategy and the marketing mix

Customer-Driven Marketing Strategy

As we emphasized throughout Chapter 1, to succeed in today's competitive marketplace, companies need to be customer centered. They must win customers from competitors, then keep and grow them by delivering greater value. But before it can satisfy consumers, a company must first understand their needs and wants. Thus, sound marketing requires a careful customer analysis.

Companies know that they cannot profitably serve all consumers in a given market—at least not all consumers in the same way. There are too many different kinds of consumers with too many different kinds of needs. And most companies are in a position to serve some segments better than others. Thus, each company must divide up the total market, choose the best segments, and design strategies for profitably serving chosen segments. This process involves *market segmentation, target marketing, differentiation, and market positioning*.

Market Segmentation

Market segmentation

Dividing a market into distinct groups of buyers who have distinct needs, characteristics, or behavior and who might require separate products or marketing programs.

Market segment

A group of consumers who respond in a similar way to a given set of marketing efforts.

The market consists of many types of customers, products, and needs. The marketer has to determine which segments offer the best opportunities. Consumers can be grouped and served in various ways based on geographic, demographic, psychographic, and behavioral factors. The process of dividing a market into distinct groups of buyers who have different needs, characteristics, or behaviors, who might require separate products or marketing programs is called **market segmentation.**

Every market has segments, but not all ways of segmenting a market are equally useful. For example, Tylenol would gain little by distinguishing between low-income and high-income pain reliever users if both respond the same way to marketing efforts. A **market segment** consists of consumers who respond in a similar way to a given set of marketing efforts. In the car market, for example, consumers who want the biggest, most comfortable car regardless of price make up one market segment. Consumers who care mainly about price and operating economy make up another segment. It would be difficult to make one car model that was the first choice of consumers in both segments. Companies are wise to focus their efforts on meeting the distinct needs of individual market segments.

Market Targeting

Market targeting

The process of evaluating each market segment's attractiveness and selecting one or more segments to enter.

After a company has defined market segments, it can enter one or many of these segments. **Market targeting** involves evaluating each market segment's attractiveness and selecting one or more segments in which it can profitably generate the greatest customer value and sustain it over time.

A company with limited resources might decide to serve only one or a few special segments or "market niches." Such "nichers" specialize in serving customer segments that major competitors overlook or ignore. For example, Ferrari sells only 1,500 of its very high-performance cars in the United States each year, but at very high prices—from an eye-opening $287,020 for its Ferrari Superamerica model to an absolutely astonishing $2 million for its FXX super sports car, which can be driven only on race tracks (it sold 10 in the United States last year). Most nichers aren't quite so exotic. White Wave, maker of Silk Soymilk, has found its niche as the nation's largest soymilk producer. And by operating in the shadows of soft drink giants like Coca-Cola and Pepsi, nicher Jones Soda has learned that small can be beautiful—and very profitable (see Real Marketing 2.2).

Alternatively, a company might choose to serve several related segments—perhaps those with different kinds of customers but with the same basic wants. Pottery Barn, for example, targets kids, teens, and adults with the same lifestyle-themed merchandise in different outlets: the original Pottery Barn, Pottery Barn Kids, and PB Teen. Or a large company might decide to offer a complete range of products to serve all market segments. Most companies enter a new market by serving a single segment, and if this proves successful, they add segments. Large companies eventually seek full market coverage. They want to be the General Motors of their industry. GM says that it makes a car for every "person, purse, and personality." The leading company normally has different products designed to meet the special needs of each segment.

Market Differentiation and Positioning

After a company has decided which market segments to enter, it must decide how it will differentiate its market offering for each targeted segment and what positions it wants to occupy in

Real Marketing

2.2 Jones Soda: Staying True to Your Niche

Every great product has a secret formula. Coca-Cola's legendary recipe is locked deep within the vaults beneath its Atlanta headquarters. KFC mixes different parts of its 11 herbs and spices at three separate facilities to safeguard the Colonel's secret blend. And McDonald's hunted down its original special-sauce mix for Big Macs last year as part of its turnaround effort.

Jones Soda, the small Seattle soft drink maker, has its own secret ingredient—one that has created buzz, produced 30 percent yearly revenue growth in a flat beverage market, drawn major distribution partners such as Starbucks and Target, and brought in $34 million in annual revenue. That ingredient: a small but growing following of devout customers. These are not just any customers—Jones Soda knows its niche. It targets young buyers—12- to 24-year-olds—who appreciate the brand's wacky, irreverent attitude. By focusing on these customers, listening to them, and giving them what they want, Jones Soda is thriving in the shadows of the soft drink giants.

Virtually everything about a Jones Soda, from labels to flavors, comes from its carefully targeted customers. That's important because "the reality is that consumers don't need our s___," founder and CEO Peter van Stolk says unapologetically. The world isn't necessarily clamoring for another soda, even if it tastes like blue bubble gum. So how do you sell an unnecessary product? If you're van Stolk, a 41-year-old former ski instructor who started Jones 10 years ago, you hand the product over to customers. Strategy gurus might call that a good example of how to "cocreate unique value." Van Stolk has a more down-to-earth but no less profound way to describe it: "People get fired up about Jones because it's theirs."

It all started with the Web site Jones Soda launched in 1997. Hundreds of comments poured in from customers, and van Stolk quickly took up their suggestions and online votes for neon colors, wacky names (like Fufu Berry, Whoop Ass, MF Grape, Happy, Bugjuice, and Bada Bing!), and offbeat flavors (including blue bubblegum, crushed melon, and twisted lime—or even strange seasonal flavors like fruitcake or turkey and gravy). Even the "Deep Thoughts"—like quotes found on the Web site and underneath bottle caps ("It's not broken, it just needs duct tape")—come straight from Jones enthusiasts.

Van Stolk also encouraged customers to submit photos, and the eccentric and strangely captivating images on Jones's stark black-and-white bottle labels have come largely from fans. And as the site became flooded with hundreds of thousands of cute, but useless, baby snapshots, he launched myJones to offer customers 12-packs of soda customized with their own photos and sayings for $34.95. MyJones has since blossomed into one of the cornerstones of the Jones Soda brand.

Jones also stays close to its 12- to 24-year-old customers with a pair of roving RVs. The two flame-festooned vehicles spend nine months out of the year visiting Jones-friendly sites, from small skate parks in the middle of nowhere to major extreme-games competitions such as the X Games. The RVs also turn up in places where they're less welcome, such as high schools to which they weren't invited. "The more deviant you can be, the better," says RV driver Chris King, 32, on a crackling cell phone. "Kids love to see you get kicked out of places. I, personally am banned from Nassau County in New York." The idea is simple. Kids come in and grab a bunch of

Jones Soda sticks closely to its niche—virtually everything about a Jones Soda, from labels to flavors, come directly from its carefully targeted customers.

Jones Soda stuff—buttons, stickers, key chains—while King studies them for a mental inventory of what's hot and what's not.

Whereas its mainstream competitors work at making something for everyone, Jones Soda understands the importance of sticking to its niche. As only van Stolk can put it, "The customer's not always right. [Bleep] that. If you're always trying to cater to everyone, you have no soul." To van Stolk, the Web site, the labels, the RVs, and the various stunts just add up to being in sync with target customers. "It's the difference between being real and saying you're real," van Stolk says, taking a not-so-subtle swipe at a certain "Real Thing" megarival. "If you're able to listen to customers from their perspective," he says, "not everything they say will make sense. Not everything they do will be right. But you'll know more about what you have to do because of it."

Staying so close to customers will become more of a challenge as Jones grows and its customers start buying its soda at the likes of Panera Bread, Target, Barnes & Noble, and Starbucks instead of the local skate shop. But so far, Jones Soda has learned that small can be beautiful—and very profitable. Over the past two years, sales have soared 67 percent; profits have more than quadrupled.

Sources: Adapted from Ryan Underwood, "Cracking Jones Soda's Secret Formula," *Fast Company,* March 2005, pp. 74–75. Additional information from Christopher Steiner, "Soda Jerk," *Forbes,* April 11, 2005, p. 74; Kate MacArthur, "Quirky Jones Soda and Steps into Mainstream," *Advertising Age,* March 27, 2006, p. 1; and www.jonessoda.com, accessed December 2006.

■ Market positioning: Whether it's an everyday moment or the moment of a lifetime, "life takes Visa."

Positioning

Arranging for a product to occupy a clear, distinctive, and desirable place relative to competing products in the minds of target consumers.

Differentiation

Actually differentiating the market offering to create superior customer value.

Marketing mix

The set of controllable tactical marketing tools—product, price, place, and promotion—that the firm blends to produce the response it wants in the target market.

those segments. A product's *position* is the place the product occupies relative to competitors in consumers' minds. Marketers want to develop unique market positions for their products. If a product is perceived to be exactly like others on the market, consumers would have no reason to buy it.

Positioning is arranging for a product to occupy a clear, distinctive, and desirable place relative to competing products in the minds of target consumers. As one positioning expert puts it, positioning is "how you differentiate your product or company—why a shopper will pay a little more for your brand."[15] Thus, marketers plan positions that distinguish their products from competing brands and give them the greatest advantage in their target markets.

BMW makes "the ultimate driving machine"; Ford is "built for the road ahead"; and Kia promises "the power to surprise."

MasterCard gives you "priceless experiences"; and whether its an everyday moment or the moment of a lifetime, "life takes Visa." Target says "expect more, pay less." And at Caesar's Palace in Las Vegas, you can "live famously." Such deceptively simple statements form the backbone of a product's marketing strategy.

In positioning its product, the company first identifies possible customer value differences that provide competitive advantages upon which to build the position. The company can offer greater customer value either by charging lower prices than competitors do or by offering more benefits to justify higher prices. But if the company *promises* greater value, it must then *deliver* that greater value. Thus, effective positioning begins with **differentiation**, actually differentiating the company's market offering so that it gives consumers more value. Once the company has chosen a desired position, it must take strong steps to deliver and communicate that position to target consumers. The company's entire marketing program should support the chosen positioning strategy.

Developing an Integrated Marketing Mix

After deciding on its overall marketing strategy, the company is ready to begin planning the details of the marketing mix, one of the major concepts in modern marketing. The **marketing mix** is the set of controllable, tactical marketing tools that the firm blends to produce the response it wants in the target market. The marketing mix consists of everything the firm can do to influence the demand for its product. The many possibilities can be collected into four groups of variables known as the "four *P*s": *product, price, place, and promotion.* Figure 2.5 shows the marketing tools under each *P.*

Product means the goods-and-services combination the company offers to the target market. Thus, a Ford Escape consists of nuts and bolts, spark plugs, pistons, headlights, and thousands of other parts. Ford offers several Escape models and dozens of optional features. The car comes fully serviced and with a comprehensive warranty that is as much a part of the product as the tailpipe.

Price is the amount of money customers have to pay to obtain the product. Ford calculates suggested retail prices that its dealers might charge for each Escape. But Ford dealers rarely charge the full sticker price. Instead, they negotiate the price with each customer, offering discounts, trade-in allowances, and credit terms. These actions adjust prices for the current competitive situation and bring them into line with the buyer's perception of the car's value.

Place includes company activities that make the product available to target consumers. Ford partners with a large body of independently owned dealerships that sell the company's many different models. Ford selects its dealers carefully and supports them strongly. The dealers keep an inventory of Ford automobiles, demonstrate them to potential buyers, negotiate prices, close sales, and service the cars after the sale.

FIGURE 2.5
The four P's of the marketing mix

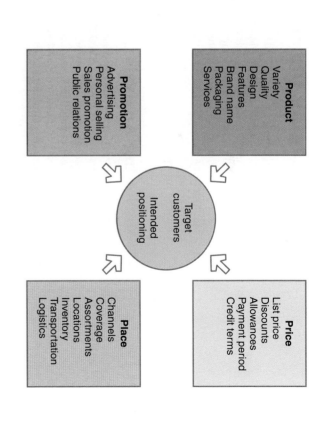

Product
Variety
Quality
Design
Features
Brand name
Packaging
Services

Price
List price
Discounts
Allowances
Payment period
Credit terms

Target customers
Intended positioning

Promotion
Advertising
Personal selling
Sales promotion
Public relations

Place
Channels
Coverage
Assortments
Locations
Inventory
Transportation
Logistics

Promotion means activities that communicate the merits of the product and persuade target customers to buy it. Ford Motor Company spends almost $2.4 billion each year on advertising, more than $600 per vehicle, to tell consumers about the company and its many products.[16] Dealership salespeople assist potential buyers and persuade them that Ford is the best car for them. Ford and its dealers offer special promotions—sales, cash rebates, low financing rates—as added purchase incentives.

An effective marketing program blends all of the marketing mix elements into an integrated marketing program designed to achieve the company's marketing objectives by delivering value to consumers. The marketing mix constitutes the company's tactical tool kit for establishing strong positioning in target markets.

Some critics think that the four Ps may omit or underemphasize certain important activities. For example, they ask, "Where are services?" Just because they don't start with a *P* doesn't justify omitting them. The answer is that services, such as banking, airline, and retailing services, are products too. We might call them *service products*. "Where is packaging?" the critics might ask. Marketers would answer that they include packaging as just one of many product decisions. All said, as Figure 2.5 suggests, many marketing activities that might appear to be left out of the marketing mix are subsumed under one of the four Ps. The issue is not whether there should be four, six, or ten Ps so much as what framework is most helpful in designing integrated marketing programs.

There is another concern, however, that is valid. It holds that the four Ps concept takes the seller's view of the market, not the buyer's view. From the buyer's viewpoint, in this age of customer relationships, the four Ps might be better described as the four Cs:[17]

4Ps	4Cs
Product	Customer solution
Price	Customer cost
Place	Convenience
Promotion	Communication

Thus, while marketers see themselves as selling products, customers see themselves as buying value or solutions to their problems. And customers are interested in more than just the price; they are interested in the total costs of obtaining, using, and disposing of a product. Customers want the product and service to be as conveniently available as possible. Finally, they want two-way communication. Marketers would do well to think through the four Cs first and then build the four Ps on that platform.

Managing the Marketing Effort

In addition to being good at the *marketing* in marketing management, companies also need to pay attention to the *management*. Managing the marketing process requires the four marketing management functions shown in Figure 2.6—*analysis, planning, implementation, and control*. The company first develops companywide strategic plans, and then translates them into marketing and other plans for each division, product, and brand. Through implementation, the company turns the plans into actions. Control consists of measuring and evaluating the results of marketing activities and taking corrective action where needed. Finally, marketing analysis provides information and evaluations needed for all of the other marketing activities.

Marketing Analysis

Managing the marketing function begins with a complete analysis of the company's situation. The marketer should conduct a **SWOT analysis,** by which it evaluates the company's overall strengths (S), weaknesses (W), opportunities (O), and threats (T) (see Figure 2.7). Strengths include internal capabilities, resources, and positive situational factors that may help the company to serve its customers and achieve its objectives. Weaknesses include internal limitations and negative situational factors that may interfere with the company's performance. Opportunities are favorable factors or trends in the external environment that the company may be able to exploit to its advantage. And threats are unfavorable external factors or trends that may present challenges to performance.

The company must analyze its markets and marketing environment to find attractive opportunities and identify environmental threats. It must analyze company strengths and weaknesses as well as current and possible marketing actions to determine which opportunities it can best pursue. The goal is to match the company's strengths to attractive opportunities in the environment, while eliminating or overcoming the weaknesses and minimizing the threats. Marketing analysis provides inputs to each of the other marketing management functions. We discuss marketing analysis more fully in Chapter 3.

Marketing Planning

Through strategic planning, the company decides what it wants to do with each business unit. Marketing planning involves deciding on marketing strategies that will help the company attain its overall strategic objectives. A detailed marketing plan is needed for each business, product, or brand. What does a marketing plan look like? Our discussion focuses on product or brand marketing plans.

Table 2.2 outlines the major sections of a typical product or brand marketing plan. (See Appendix 1 for a sample marketing plan.) The plan begins with an executive summary, which quickly overviews major assessments, goals, and recommendations. The main section of the plan presents a detailed SWOT analysis of the current marketing situation as well as potential threats and opportunities. The plan next states major objectives for the brand and outlines the specifics of a marketing strategy for achieving them.

SWOT analysis
An overall evaluation of the company's strengths (S), weaknesses (W), opportunities (O), and threats (T).

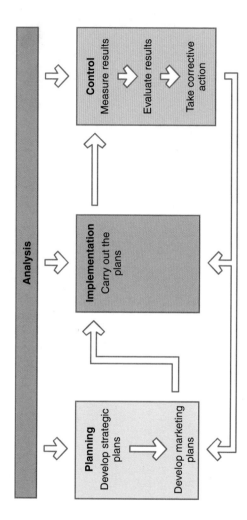

FIGURE 2.6
Marketing analysis, planning, implementation, and control

FIGURE 2.7
SWOT analysis

	Positive	Negative
Internal	**Strengths** Internal capabilities that may help a company reach its objectives	**Weaknesses** Internal limitations that may interfere with a company's ability to achieve its objectives
External	**Opportunities** External factors that the company may be able to exploit to its advantage	**Threats** Current and emerging external factors that may challenge the company's performance

A *marketing strategy* consists of specific strategies for target markets, positioning, the marketing mix, and marketing expenditure levels. It outlines how the company intends to create value for target customers in order to capture value in return. In this section, the planner explains how each strategy responds to the threats, opportunities, and critical issues spelled out earlier in the plan. Additional sections of the marketing plan lay out an action program for implementing the marketing strategy along with the details of a supporting *marketing budget*. The last section outlines the controls that will be used to monitor progress, measure return on marketing investment, and take corrective action.

Marketing Implementation

Planning good strategies is only a start toward successful marketing. A brilliant marketing strategy counts for little if the company fails to implement it properly. **Marketing implementation** is the process that turns marketing *plans* into marketing *actions* in order to accomplish strategic marketing objectives. Whereas marketing planning addresses the *what* and *why* of marketing activities, implementation addresses the *who*, *where*, *when*, and *how*.

Many managers think that "doing things right" (implementation) is as important as, or even more important than, "doing the right things" (strategy). The fact is that both are critical to success, and companies can gain competitive advantages through effective implementation. One firm can have essentially the same strategy as another, yet win in the marketplace through faster or better execution. Still, implementation is difficult—it is often easier to think up good marketing strategies than it is to carry them out. "Despite the enormous time and energy that goes into strategy development, . . . companies on average deliver only 63 percent of the financial performance their strategies promise," declares a marketing consultant. "To close the strategy-to-performance gap, [companies need] better planning *and* execution."[18]

In an increasingly connected world, people at all levels of the marketing system must work together to implement marketing strategies and plans. [companies need] better planning and execution.ing implementation for the company's power tools, outdoor equipment, and other products

requires day-to-day decisions and actions by thousands of people both inside and outside the organization. Marketing managers make decisions about target segments, branding, packaging, pricing, promoting, and distributing. They talk with engineering about product design, with manufacturing about production and inventory levels, and with finance about funding and cash flows. They also connect with outside people, such as advertising agencies to plan ad campaigns and the news media to obtain publicity support. The sales force urges Home Depot, Lowe's, Wal-Mart, and other retailers to advertise Black & Decker products, provide ample shelf space, and use company displays.

Successful marketing implementation depends on how well the company blends its people, organizational structure, decision and reward systems, and company culture into a cohesive action program that supports its strategies. At all levels, the company must be staffed

Marketing implementation
The process that turns marketing strategies and plans into marketing actions in order to accomplish strategic marketing objectives.

■ Marketers must continually plan their analysis, implementation, and control activities.

TABLE 2.2 Contents of a Marketing Plan

Section	Purpose
Executive summary	Presents a brief summary of the main goals and recommendations of the plan for management review, helping top management to find the plan's major points quickly. A table of contents should follow the executive summary.
Current marketing situation	Describes the target market and company's position in it, including information about the market, product performance, competition, and distribution. This section includes: • A *market description* that defines the market and major segments, then reviews customer needs and factors in the marketing environment that may affect customer purchasing. • A *product review* that shows sales, prices, and gross margins of the major products in the product line. • A review of *competition* that identifies major competitors and assesses their market positions and strategies for product quality, pricing, distribution, and promotion. • A review of *distribution* that evaluates recent sales trends and other developments in major distribution channels.
Threats and opportunities analysis	Assesses major threats and opportunities that the product might face, helping management to anticipate important positive or negative developments that might have an impact on the firm and its strategies.
Objectives and issues	States the marketing objectives that the company would like to attain during the plan's term and discusses key issues that will affect their attainment. For example, if the goal is to achieve a 15 percent market share, this section looks at how this goal might be achieved.
Marketing strategy	Outlines the broad marketing logic by which the business unit hopes to achieve its marketing objectives and the specifics of target markets, positioning, and marketing expenditure levels. How will the company create value for customers in order to capture value from customers in return? This section also outlines specific strategies for each marketing mix element and explains how each responds to the threats, opportunities, and critical issues spelled out earlier in the plan.
Action programs	Spells out how marketing strategies will be turned into specific action programs that answer the following questions: *What* will be done? *When* will it be done? *Who* will do it? *How much* will it cost?
Budgets	Details a supporting marketing budget that is essentially a projected profit-and-loss statement. It shows expected revenues (forecasted number of units sold and the average net price) and expected costs (of production, distribution, and marketing). The difference is the projected profit. Once approved by higher management, the budget becomes the basis for materials buying, production scheduling, personnel planning, and marketing operations.
Controls	Outlines the control that will be used to monitor progress and allow higher management to review implementation results and spot products that are not meeting their goals. It includes measures of return on marketing investment.

by people who have the needed skills, motivation, and personal characteristics. The company's formal organization structure plays an important role in implementing marketing strategy; so do its decision and reward systems. For example, if a company's compensation system rewards managers for short-run profit results, they will have little incentive to work toward long-run market-building objectives.

Finally, to be successfully implemented, the firm's marketing strategies must fit with its company culture, the system of values and beliefs shared by people in the organization. A study of America's most successful companies found that these companies have almost cultlike cultures built around strong, market-oriented missions. At companies such as Dell, Nordstrom, Citicorp, and P&G, "employees share such a strong vision that they know in their hearts what's right for their company."[19]

Marketing Department Organization

The company must design a marketing organization that can carry out marketing strategies and plans. If the company is very small, one person might do all of the research, selling, advertising, customer service, and other marketing work. As the company expands, a market-

Marketing control
The process of measuring and evaluating the results of marketing strategies and plans and taking corrective action to ensure that objectives are achieved.

Marketing audit
A comprehensive, systematic, independent, and periodic examination of a company's environment, objectives, strategies, and activities to determine problem areas and opportunities and to recommend a plan of action to improve the company's marketing performance.

ing department emerges to plan and carry out marketing activities. In large companies, this department contains many specialists. Thus, GE and Microsoft have product and market managers, sales managers and salespeople, market researchers, advertising experts, and many other specialists. To head up such large marketing organizations, many companies have now created a *chief marketing officer* (or CMO) position.

Modern marketing departments can be arranged in several ways. The most common form of marketing organization is the *functional organization*. Under this organization, different marketing activities are headed by a functional specialist—a sales manager, advertising manager, marketing research manager, customer service manager, or new-product manager. A company that sells across the country or internationally often uses a *geographic organization*. Its sales and marketing people are assigned to specific countries, regions, and districts. Geographic organization allows salespeople to settle into a territory, get to know their customers, and work with a minimum of travel time and cost.

Companies with many very different products or brands often create a *product management organization*. Using this approach, a product manager develops and implements a complete strategy and marketing program for a specific product or brand. Product management first appeared at Procter & Gamble in 1929. A new company soap, Camay, was not doing well, and a young P&G executive was assigned to give his exclusive attention to developing and promoting this product. He was successful, and the company soon added other product managers.[20] Since then, many firms, especially consumer products companies, have set up product management organizations.

For companies that sell one product line to many different types of markets and customers that have different needs and preferences, a *market or customer management organization* might be best. A market management organization is similar to the product management organization. Market managers are responsible for developing marketing strategies and plans for their specific markets or customers. This system's main advantage is that the company is organized around the needs of specific customer segments.

Large companies that produce many different products flowing into many different geographic and customer markets usually employ some *combination* of the functional, geographic, product, and market organization forms. This ensures that each function, product, and market receives its share of management attention. However, it can also add costly layers of management and reduce organizational flexibility. Still, the benefits of organizational specialization usually outweigh the drawbacks.

Marketing organization has become an increasingly important issue in recent years. As we discussed in Chapter 1, many companies are finding that today's marketing environment calls for less focus on products, brands, and territories and more focus on customers and customer relationships. More and more companies are shifting their brand management focus toward *customer management*—moving away from managing just product or brand profitability and toward managing customer profitability and customer equity. And many companies now organize their marketing operations around major customers. For example, companies such as Procter & Gamble and Black & Decker have large teams, or even whole divisions, set up to serve large customers such as Wal-Mart, Target, Safeway, or Home Depot.

Marketing Control

Because many surprises occur during the implementation of marketing plans, the marketing department must practice constant marketing control. **Marketing control** involves evaluating the results of marketing strategies and plans and taking corrective action to ensure that objectives are attained. Marketing control involves four steps. Management first sets specific marketing goals. It then measures its performance in the marketplace and evaluates the causes of any differences between expected and actual performance. Finally, management takes corrective action to close the gaps between its goals and its performance. This may require changing the action programs or even changing the goals.

Operating control involves checking ongoing performance against the annual plan and taking corrective action when necessary. Its purpose is to ensure that the company achieves the sales, profits, and other goals set out in its annual plan. It also involves determining the profitability of different products, territories, markets, and channels.

Strategic control involves looking at whether the company's basic strategies are well matched to its opportunities. Marketing strategies and programs can quickly become outdated, and each company should periodically reassess its overall approach to the market-place. A major tool for such strategic control is a **marketing audit**. The marketing audit is a comprehensive, systematic, independent, and periodic examination of a company's environment, objectives, strategies, and activities to determine problem areas and opportunities. The audit provides good input for a plan of action to improve the company's marketing performance.[21]

The marketing audit covers *all* major marketing areas of a business, not just a few trouble spots. It assesses the marketing environment, marketing strategy, marketing organization, marketing systems, marketing mix, and marketing productivity and profitability. The audit is normally conducted by an objective and experienced outside party. The findings may come as a surprise—and sometimes as a shock—to management. Management then decides which actions make sense and how and when to implement them.

Measuring and Managing Return on Marketing Investment

Marketing managers must ensure that their marketing dollars are being well spent. In the past, many marketers spent freely on big, expensive marketing programs, often without thinking carefully about the financial returns on their spending. They believed that marketing produces intangible outcomes, which do not lend themselves readily to measures of productivity or return. But all that is changing:

> For years, corporate marketers have walked into budget meetings like neighborhood junkies. They couldn't always justify how well they spent past handouts or what difference it all made. They just wanted more money—for flashy TV ads, for big-ticket events, for, you know, getting out the message and building up the brand. But those heady days of blind budget increases are fast being replaced with a new mantra: measurement and accountability. Armed with reams of data, increasingly sophisticated tools, and growing evidence that the old tricks simply don't work, there's hardly a marketing executive today who isn't demanding a more scientific approach to help defend marketing strategies in front of the chief financial officer. Marketers want to know the actual return on investment (ROI) of each dollar. They want to know it often, not just annually. . . . Com-panies in every segment of American business have become obsessed with honing the science of measuring marketing performance. "Marketers have been pretty unaccountable for many years," notes one expert. "Now they are under big pressure to estimate their impact."[22]

In response, marketers are developing better measures of *return on marketing investment*. **Return on marketing investment** (or *marketing ROI*) is the net return from a marketing investment divided by the costs of the marketing investment. It measures the profits generated by investments in marketing activities.

Return on marketing investment (or marketing ROI)

The net return from a marketing investment divided by the costs of the marketing investment.

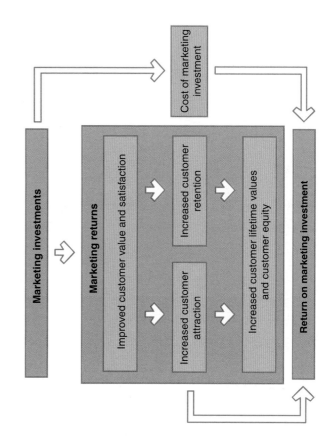

FIGURE 2.8
Return on marketing

Source: Adapted from Roland T. Rust, Katherine N. Lemon, and Valerie A. Zeithamal, "Return on Marketing: Using Consumer Equity to Focus Marketing Strategy," *Journal of Marketing*, January 2004, p. 112.

It's true that marketing returns can be difficult to measure. In measuring financial ROI, both the *R* and the *I* are uniformly measured in dollars. But there is as of yet no consistent definition of marketing ROI. "It's tough to measure, more so than for other business expenses," says one analyst. "You can imagine buying a piece of equipment, . . . and then measuring the productivity gains that result from the purchase," he says. "But in marketing, benefits like advertising impact aren't easily put into dollar returns. It takes a leap of faith to come up with a number." [23]

A company can assess return on marketing in terms of standard marketing performance measures, such as brand awareness, sales, or market share. Campbell Soup uses sales and share data to evaluate specific advertising campaigns. For example, analysis revealed that its recent Soup at Hand advertising campaign, which depicted real-life scenarios of consumers using the portable soup, nearly doubled both the product's trial rate

and repeat use rate after the first year. The Soup at Hand campaign received a Gold Effie, an advertising industry award based on marketing effectiveness. [24]

Many companies are assembling such measures into *marketing dashboards*—meaningful sets of marketing performance measures in a single display used to monitor strategic marketing performance. Just as automobile dashboards present drivers with details on how their cars are performing, the marketing dashboard gives marketers the detailed measures they need to assess and adjust their marketing strategies. [25]

Increasingly, however, beyond standard performance measures, marketers are using customer-centered measures of marketing impact, such as customer acquisition, customer retention, and customer lifetime value. Figure 2.8 views marketing expenditures as investments that produce returns in the form of more profitable customer relationships. [26] Marketing investments result in improved customer value and satisfaction, which in turn increases customer attraction and retention. This increases individual customer lifetime values and the firm's overall customer equity. Increased customer equity, in relation to the cost of the marketing investments, determines return on marketing investment.

Regardless of how it's defined or measured, the return on marketing investment concept is here to stay. "Marketing ROI is at the heart of every business," says an AT&T marketing executive. "[We've added another P to the marketing mix]—for *profit and loss* or *performance*. We absolutely have to . . . quantify the impact of marketing on the business. You can't improve what you can't measure." [27]

Reviewing the Concepts

In Chapter 1, we defined *marketing* and outlined the steps in the marketing process. In this chapter, we examined companywide strategic planning and marketing's role in the organization. Then, we looked more deeply into marketing strategy and the marketing mix and reviewed the major marketing management functions. So you've now had a pretty good overview of the fundamentals of modern marketing. In future chapters, we'll expand on these fundamentals.

■ **Return on marketing investment.** Companies can assess return on marketing in terms of standard marketing performance measures. Such analysis showed that Campbell's recent "Soup at Hand" advertising campaign nearly doubled both the product's trial rate and repeat use.

1. **Explain companywide strategic planning and its four steps.**

Strategic planning sets the stage for the rest of the company's planning. Marketing contributes to strategic planning, and the overall plan defines marketing's role in the company. Although formal planning offers a variety of benefits to companies, not all companies use it or use it well.

Strategic planning involves developing a strategy for long-run survival and growth. It consists of four steps: defining the company's mission, setting objectives and goals, designing a business portfolio, and developing functional plans. *Defining a clear company mission* begins with drafting a formal mission statement, which should be market oriented, realistic, specific, motivating, and consistent with the market environment. The mission is then transformed into detailed *supporting goals and objectives* to guide the entire company. Based on those goals and objectives, headquarters designs a *business portfolio*, deciding which businesses and products should receive more or fewer resources. In turn, each business and product unit must develop *detailed marketing plans* in line with the companywide plan.

2. Discuss how to design business portfolios and develop strategies for growth and downsizing.

Guided by the company's mission statement and objectives, management plans its *business portfolio*, or the collection of businesses and products that make up the company. The firm wants to produce a business portfolio that best fits its strengths and weaknesses to opportunities in the environment. To do this, it must analyze and adjust its *current* business portfolio and develop growth and downsizing strategies for adjusting the *future* portfolio. The company might use a formal portfolio-planning method. But many companies are now designing more customized portfolio-planning approaches that better suit their unique situations. The *product/market expansion grid* suggests four possible growth paths: market penetration, market development, product development, and diversification.

3. Assess marketing's role in strategic planning and explain how marketers partner with others inside and outside the firm to build profitable customer relationships.

Under the strategic plan, the major functional departments—marketing, finance, accounting, purchasing, operations, information systems, human resources, and others—must work together to accomplish strategic objectives. Marketing plays a key role in the company's strategic planning by providing a *marketing-concept philosophy* and *inputs* regarding attractive market opportunities. Within individual business units, marketing designs *strategies* for reaching the unit's objectives and helps to carry them out profitably.

Marketers alone cannot produce superior value for customers. A company's success depends on how well each department performs its customer value-adding activities and how well the departments work together to serve the customer. Thus, marketers must practice *partner relationship management*. They must work closely with partners in other company departments to form an effective *value chain* that serves the customer. And they must partner effectively with other

companies in the marketing system to form a competitively superior *value-delivery network*.

4. Describe the elements of a customer-driven marketing strategy and mix, and the forces that influence it.

Consumer value and relationships are at the center of marketing strategy and programs. Through market segmentation, market targeting, differentiation, and market positioning, the company divides the total market into smaller segments, selects segments it can best serve, and decides how it wants to bring value to target consumers. It then designs an *integrated marketing mix* to produce the response it wants in the target market. The marketing mix consists of product, price, place, and promotion decisions.

5. List the marketing management functions, including the elements of a marketing plan, and discuss the importance of measuring and managing return on marketing.

To find the best strategy and mix and to put them into action, the company engages in marketing analysis, planning, implementation, and control. The main components of a *marketing plan* are the executive summary, current marketing situation, threats and opportunities, objectives and issues, marketing strategies, action programs, budgets, and controls. To plan good strategies is often easier than to carry them out. To be successful, companies must also be effective at *implementation*—turning marketing strategies into marketing actions.

Much of the responsibility for implementation goes to the company's marketing department. Marketing departments can be organized in one or a combination of ways: *functional marketing organization, geographic organization, product management organization,* or *market management organization.* In this age of customer relationships, more and more companies are now changing their organizational focus from product or territory management to customer relationship management. Marketing organizations carry out *marketing control,* both operating control and strategic control. They use *marketing audits* to determine marketing opportunities and problems and to recommend short-run and long-run actions to improve overall marketing performance.

Marketing managers must ensure that their marketing dollars are being well spent. Today's marketers face growing pressures to show that they are adding value in line with their costs. In response, marketers are developing better measures of *return on marketing investment.* Increasingly, they are using customer-centered measures of marketing impact as a key input into their strategic decision making.

■ Reviewing the Key Terms

Discussing the Concepts

1. There are four major steps in strategic planning. Why is it important for a marketer to perform these steps in order?

2. The BCG growth-share matrix identifies four classifications of SBUs: stars, cash cows, question marks, and dogs. Briefly discuss why management may find it difficult to dispose of a "question mark."

3. Discuss the differences between the four growth strategies identified in the product/market expansion grid. Which option would a smaller company be pursuing if it decided to enter an existing market served by many large, well-known competitors? Assume that the product being introduced by this smaller company is a new offering for the organization, but that this new product offers a number of unique features.

4. Does the "4 Ps" marketing mix framework do an adequate job of describing marketer responsibilities in preparing and managing marketing programs? Why? Do you see any issues with this framework in relation to service products?

5. What is the importance of marketing implementation? How might a company have excellent planning and poor implementation?

6. What is return on marketing investment? Why is it difficult to measure?

Applying the Concepts

1. In a small group, discuss whether the following statement from Burton Snowboards North America, manufacturers and marketers of a leading snowboard brand, meets the five criteria of a good mission statement: "Burton Snowboards is a rider-driven company solely dedicated to creating the best snowboarding equipment on the planet."

2. A company's value chain and value-delivery network are critical to its success. Describe how Reebok relies on its value chain. Sketch Reebok's value-delivery network and highlight the importance of each member in the network.

3. Both Wal-Mart and Target sell merchandise at lower prices with lower margins and higher volumes. Based on your experience with these two retailers and visits to each of their Web sites, describe how the two discount store chains differ in their market segmentation, target marketing, and market positioning strategies.

Focus on Technology

Visit the Web sites of several car manufacturers and you will see the technological innovations and additions offered in today's vehicles. From navigation systems to audio enhancements and DVD systems, these technologies are enhancing today's cars. Microsoft, known mostly for its computer operating systems, has been working with Fiat to develop a new "infotainment" system known as Blue&Me. Currently offered only in limited Fiat models, the system integrates mobile phones, MP3 players, and an Internet connection through controls on the steering wheel. The new technology will also contain a navigation system, weather and traffic forecasts, and antitheft devices.

1. According to the product/market expansion grid, which strategy best describes Microsoft's expansion into automobile applications?

2. Why is Fiat an important member of Microsoft's value-delivery network?

3. Describe why this advanced technology is important to Fiat in terms of positioning its products.

Focus on Ethics

Tyson Foods Inc. has been a leading provider of poultry products for more than 60 years. Its corporate mission statement includes a set of core values that clearly state the importance of being a faith-friendly company and honoring God. Internally, Tyson connects with its employees and has placed 128 part-time chaplains in 78 plants across the United States. But Tyson also wants to send its faith-friendly message to consumers. To reinforce its "Powered by Tyson" campaign, it has recently begun to offer free downloadable prayer books on its Web site. According to Tyson, it provides these books to help consumers discover (or rediscover) the joy and power of saying a word of thanks at mealtime.

1. What do you think of Tyson's strategy to offer the downloadable booklets? Is there a reason to believe it is embracing religion only to make increased profit?

2. In your opinion, does religion belong in a corporate mission statement? Why or why not?

3. Many consumers see chicken as a commodity product with no real difference between brands. Does this strategy make you more or less likely to buy Tyson over another brand?

Video Case

Harley-Davidson

Few brands engender such intense loyalty as that found in the hearts of Harley-Davidson owners. Why? Because the company's marketers spend a great deal of time thinking about customers. They want to know who their customers are, how they think and feel, and why they buy a Harley. That attention to detail has helped build Harley-Davidson into a $5 billion company with more than 900,000 Harley Owners Group (HOG) members and 1,200 dealerships worldwide.

Harley sells much more than motorcycles. The company sells a feeling of independence, individualism, and freedom. To support that lifestyle, Harley-Davidson offers clothes and accessories both for riders and those who simply like to associate with the brand. Harley further extends the brand experience by offering travel adventures. Through

Harley's Web site, customers can book a trip to Milwaukee to visit the Harley-Davidson owners. Why? Because the company's hometown or turn a Las Vegas vacation into "an authentic Harley-Davidson adventure."

After viewing the video featuring Harley-Davidson, answer the following questions about marketing strategy.

1. List several products that are included in Harley-Davidson's business portfolio. Analyze the portfolio using the Boston Consulting Group growth-share matrix.

2. Which strategies in the product/market expansion grid is Harley-Davidson using to grow sales and profits?

3. List some of the members of Harley's value-delivery network.

Company Case

Trap-Ease America: The Big Cheese of Mousetraps

CONVENTIONAL WISDOM

One April morning, Martha House, president of Trap-Ease America, entered her office in Costa Mesa, California. She paused for a moment to contemplate the Ralph Waldo Emerson quote that she had framed and hung near her desk:

"If a man [can] . . . make a better mousetrap than his neighbor . . . the world will make a beaten path to his door."

Perhaps, she mused, Emerson knew something that she didn't. She *had* the better mousetrap—Trap-Ease—but the world didn't seem all that excited about it.

The National Hardware Show Martha had just returned from the National Hardware Show in Chicago. Standing in the trade show display booth for long hours and answering the same questions hundreds of times had been tiring. Yet, all the hard work had paid off. Each year, National Hardware Show officials held a contest to select the best new product introduced at that year's show. The Trap-Ease had won the contest this year, beating out over 300 new products.

Such notoriety was not new for the Trap-Ease mousetrap, however. *People* magazine had run a feature article on the trap, and the trap had been the subject of numerous talk shows and articles in various popular press and trade publications.

Despite all of this attention, however, the expected demand for the trap had not materialized. Martha hoped that this award might stimulate increased interest and sales.

BACKGROUND

A group of investors had formed Trap-Ease America in January after it had obtained worldwide rights to market the innovative mousetrap. In return for marketing rights, the group agreed to pay the inventor and patent holder, a retired

rancher, a royalty fee for each trap sold. The group then hired Martha to serve as president and to develop and manage the Trap-Ease America organization.

Trap-Ease America contracted with a plastics-manufacturing firm to produce the traps. The trap consisted of a square, plastic tube measuring about 6 inches long and 1-1/2 inches in diameter. The tube bent in the middle at a 30-degree angle, so that when the front part of the tube rested on a flat surface, the other end was elevated. The elevated end held a removable cap into which the user placed bait (cheese, dog food, or some other aromatic tidbit). The front end of the tube had a hinged door. When the trap was "open," this door rested on two narrow "stilts" attached to the two bottom corners of the door. (See Exhibit 1.)

The simple trap worked very efficiently. A mouse, smelling the bait, entered the tube through the open end. As it walked up the angled bottom toward the bait, its weight made the elevated end of the trap drop downward. This action elevated the open end, allowing the hinged door to swing closed, trapping the mouse. Small teeth on the ends of the stilts caught in a groove on the bottom of the trap, locking the door closed. The user could then dispose of the mouse while it was still alive, or the user could leave it alone for a few hours to suffocate in the trap.

Martha believed the trap had many advantages for the consumer when compared with traditional spring-loaded traps or poisons. Consumers could use it safely and easily with no risk of catching their fingers while loading it. It posed no injury or poisoning threat to children or pets. Furthermore, with Trap-Ease, consumers avoided the unpleasant "mess" they often encountered with the violent spring-loaded traps. The Trap-Ease created no "clean-up" problem. Finally, the user could reuse the trap or simply throw it away.

Martha's early research suggested that women were the best target market for the Trap-Ease. Men, it seemed, were

IT'S HUMANE!

TRAP EASE

Traps Mice Easily!

Never see or touch a dead mouse again.

| Clean | Safe | Easy to use |

TrapEase
AMERICA
The Big Cheese of Mousetraps®

Bait attracts mouse into trap. Weight of mouse trips trap.

---

more willing to buy and use the traditional, spring-loaded trap. The targeted women, however, did not like the traditional trap. These women often stayed at home and took care of their children. Thus, they wanted a means of dealing with the mouse problem that avoided the unpleasantness and risks that the standard trap created in the home.

To reach this target market, Martha decided to distribute Trap-Ease through national grocery, hardware, and drug chains such as Safeway, Kmart, Hechingers, and CB Drug. She sold the trap directly to these large retailers, avoiding any wholesalers or other middlemen.

The traps sold in packages of two, with a suggested retail price of $2.49. Although this price made the Trap-Ease about five to ten times more expensive than smaller, standard traps, consumers appeared to offer little initial price resistance. The manufacturing cost for the Trap-Ease, including freight and packaging costs, was about 31 cents per unit. The company paid an additional 8.2 cents per unit in royalty fees. Martha priced the traps to retailers at 99 cents per unit (two units to a package) and estimated that, after sales and volume discounts, Trap-Ease would produce net revenue from retailers of 75 cents per unit.

To promote the product, Martha had budgeted approximately $60,000 for the first year. She planned to use $50,000 of this amount for travel costs to visit trade shows and to make sales calls on retailers. She planned to use the remaining $10,000 for advertising. So far, however, because the mousetrap had generated so much publicity, she had not felt that she needed to do much advertising. Still, she had placed advertising in *Good Housekeeping* (after all, the trap had earned the *Good Housekeeping* Seal of Approval) and in other "home and shelter" magazines. Martha was the company's only salesperson, but she intended to hire more salespeople soon.

Martha had initially forecasted Trap-Ease's first-year sales at five million units. Through April, however, the company had only sold several hundred thousand units. Martha wondered if most new products got off to such a slow start, or if she was doing something wrong. She had detected some problems, although none seemed overly serious. For one, there had not been enough repeat buying. For another, she had noted that many of the retailers upon whom she called kept their sample mousetraps on their desks as conversation pieces—she wanted the traps to be used and demonstrated. Martha wondered if consumers were also buying the traps as novelties rather than as solutions to their mouse problems.

Martha knew that the investor group believed that Trap-Ease America had a "once-in-a-lifetime chance" with its innovative mousetrap, and she sensed the group's impatience with the company's progress so far. She had budgeted approximately $250,000 in administrative and fixed costs for the first year (not including marketing costs). To keep the investors happy, the company needed to sell enough traps to cover those costs and make a reasonable profit.

BACK TO THE DRAWING BOARD

In these first few months, Martha had learned that marketing a new product was not an easy task. Some customers were very demanding. For example, one national retailer had placed a large order with instructions that Trap-Ease America was to deliver the order to the loading dock at one of the retailer's warehouses between 1:00 and 3:00 P.M. on a specified day. When the truck delivering the order arrived after 3 P.M., the retailer had refused to accept the shipment. The retailer had told Martha it would be a year before she got another chance.

As Martha sat down at her desk, she realized she needed to rethink her marketing strategy. Perhaps she had missed something or made some mistake that was causing sales to be so slow. Glancing at the quotation again, she thought that perhaps she should send the picky retailer and other customers a copy of Emerson's famous quote.

Questions for Discussion

1. Martha and the Trap-Ease America investors believe they face a once-in-a-lifetime opportunity. What information do they need to evaluate this opportunity? How do you think the group would write its mission statement? How would *you* write it?

2. Has Martha identified the best target market for Trap-Ease? What other market segments might the firm target?

3. How has the company positioned the Trap-Ease for the chosen target market? Could it position the product in other ways?

4. Describe the current marketing mix for Trap-Ease. Do you see any problems with this mix?

5. Who is Trap-Ease America's competition?

6. How would you change Trap-Ease's marketing strategy? What kinds of control procedures would you establish for this strategy?

The Marketing Environment

Previewing the Concepts

In Part 1 (Chapters 1 and 2), you learned about the basic concepts of marketing and the steps in the marketing process for building profitable relationships with targeted consumers. In Part 2, we'll look deeper into the first step of the marketing process—understanding the marketplace and customer needs and wants. In this chapter, you'll discover that marketing does not operate in a vacuum but rather in a complex and changing environment. Other *actors* in this environment—suppliers, intermediaries, customers, competitors, publics, and others—may work with or against the company. Major environmental *forces*—demographic, economic, natural, technological, political, and cultural—shape marketing opportunities, pose threats, and affect the company's ability to serve customers and develop lasting relationships with them. To understand marketing, and to develop effective marketing strategies, you must first understand the environment in which marketing operates.

First, we'll look at an American icon, McDonald's. More than half a century ago, Ray Kroc spotted an important shift in U.S. consumer lifestyles and bought a small chain of restaurants. He built that chain into the vast McDonald's fast-food empire. But although the shifting marketing environment brought opportunities for McDonald's, it has also created challenges.

In 1955, Ray Kroc, a 52-year-old salesman of milk-shake mixing machines, discovered a string of seven restaurants owned by Richard and Maurice McDonald. Kroc saw the McDonald brothers' fast-food concept as a perfect fit for America's increasingly on-the-go, time-squeezed, family-oriented lifestyles. Kroc bought the small chain for $2.7 million, and the rest is history.

McDonald's grew quickly to become the world's largest fast-feeder. Its more than 31,800 restaurants worldwide now serve 50 million customers each day, racking up system-wide sales of almost $60 billion annually. The Golden Arches are one of the world's most familiar symbols, and other than Santa Claus, no character in the world is more recognizable than Ronald McDonald. "By making fast food respectable for middle-class families," says an industry analyst, "the Golden Arches did for greasy spoons what Holiday Inn did for roadside motels in the 1950s and what Sam Walton later did for the discount retail store."

But just as the changing marketplace has provided opportunities for McDonald's, it has also presented challenges. In fact, by early in this decade, the once-shiny Golden Arches had lost some of their luster, as the company struggled to address shifting consumer lifestyles. While McDonald's remained the nation's most-visited fast-food chain, its sales growth slumped, and its market share fell by more than 3 percent between 1997 and 2003. In 2002, the company posted its first-ever quarterly loss.

What happened? In this age of obesity lawsuits and $5 lattes, McDonald's seemed a bit out of step with the times. Consumers were looking for fresher, better-tasting food and more upscale atmospheres. As a result, McDonald's was losing share to what the industry calls "fast-casual" restaurants. New competitors such as Panera Bread, Baja Fresh, Pret a Manger, and Cosi were offering more imaginative meals in more fashionable surroundings. And for busy consumers who'd rather "eat-out-in," even the local supermarket offered a full selection of pre-prepared, ready-to-serve gourmet meals to go.

Americans were also seeking healthier eating options. Fast-food patrons complained about too few healthy menu choices. Worried about their health, many customers were eating less at fast-food restaurants. As the market leader, McDonald's bore the brunt of much of this criticism. In one lawsuit, the parents of two teenage girls even charged that McDonald's was responsible for their children's obesity and related health problems, including diabetes.

Reacting to these challenges, in early 2003, McDonald's announced a turn-around plan—the "Plan to Win"—to better align the company with the new market-place realities. The plan included the following initiatives:

s what i **eat** and what i **do**™

i'm lovin' it®™

Back to Basics—McDonald's began refocusing on what made it successful: consistent products and reliable service. It began pouring money back into existing stores, speeding up service, training employees, and monitoring restaurants to make sure they stay bright and clean. It's also "re-imaging" its restaurants, with clean, simple, more modern interiors and amenities such as wireless Internet access. McDonald's now promises to be a "forever young" brand.

If You Can't Lick 'Em, Join 'Em—To find new ways to compete better with the new breed of fast-casual competitors, and to expand its customer base, McDonald's has experimented with new restaurant concepts. For example, it has tested upscale *McCafe* coffee shops, which offer leather seating, a knowledgeable staff, and espresso in porcelain cups, along with made-to-order drinks, gourmet sandwiches, and Internet access. It is also testing a *Bistro Gourmet* concept in a handful of restaurants in the United States, which offers high-back leather chairs, a made-to-order omelet breakfast bar, and food served on real china. Kids can still get their Happy Meals, but parents can feast on more sophisticated fare, such as panini sandwiches, gourmet burgers, and crème brulee cheesecake.

"It's *what i eat and what i do . . . i'm lovin' it*"—McDonald's recently unveiled a major multifaceted education campaign to help consumers better understand the keys to living balanced, active lifestyles. The "it's what i eat and what i do . . . i'm lovin' it" theme underscores the important interplay between eating right and

Objectives

After studying this chapter, you should be able to

1. describe the environmental forces that affect the company's ability to serve its customers

2. explain how changes in the demographic and economic environments affect marketing decisions

3. identify the major trends in the firm's natural and technological environments

4. explain the key changes in the political and cultural environments

5. discuss how companies can react to the marketing environment

staying active. The company assembled a Global Advisory Council of outside experts in the areas of nutrition, wellness, and activity to provide input on its menu choice and variety, education outreach, and promoting physical fitness. McDonald's has introduced a trimmer, fitter Ronald McDonald. He has expanded his role as Chief Happiness Officer to be global ambassador of fun, fitness, and children's well-being, inspiring and encouraging kids and families around the world to eat well and stay active. McDonald's has also refreshed its GoActive.com Web site, which offers tips on how to lead a balanced active lifestyle as well as a Family Fitness Tool Kit. And the McDonald's Passport to Play in-school program, motivates children in 31,000 schools around the country to be more active in unique and fun ways during grade school physical education classes. Even the harshest McDonald's critics, although still skeptical, applaud these actions.

Improving the Fare—McDonald's has worked to provide more choice and variety on its menu. For example, it introduced a "Go Active! Happy Meal for adults featuring a Premium Salad, a bottle of Dasani water, and a Stepometer," which measures physical activity by tracking daily steps. It now offers Chicken McNuggets made with white meat, Chicken Selects wholebreast strips, low-fat "milk jugs," and a line of Premium Salads, such as its Fruit & Walnut Premium Salad, consisting of apple slices and seedless grapes with a side of low-fat vanilla yogurt and candied walnuts. Within only a year of introducing its Premium Salads, McDonald's became the world's largest salad seller—it has sold more than 516 million salads to date.

McDonald's efforts to realign itself with the changing marketing environment appear to be paying off. By almost any measure, the fast-food giant is now back in shape. The company is posting steady, even startling, sales and profit increases. Since announcing its Plan to Win, McDonald's has increased its sales by 33 percent and profits have tripled. It looks like customers and stockholders alike are humming the chain's catchy jingle, "I'm lovin' it." A former McDonald's CEO summed it up this way: "Ray Kroc used to say he didn't know what we would be selling in the year 2000, but whatever it was we would be selling the most of it. He recognized early on that consumer needs change and we want to change with them."[1]

Marketing environment
The actors and forces outside marketing that affect marketing management's ability to build and maintain successful relationships with target customers.

Microenvironment
The actors close to the company that affect its ability to serve its customers—the company, suppliers, marketing intermediaries, customer markets, competitors, and publics.

Macroenvironment
The larger societal forces that affect the microenvironment—demographic, economic, natural, technological, political, and cultural forces.

Marketers need to be good at building relationships with customers, others in the company, and external partners. To do this effectively, they must understand the major environmental forces that surround all of these relationships. A company's **marketing environment** consists of the actors and forces outside marketing that affect marketing management's ability to build and maintain successful relationships with target customers. Successful companies know the vital importance of constantly watching and adapting to the changing environment.

The environment continues to change rapidly, and both consumers and marketers wonder what the future will bring. More than any other group in the company, marketers must be the trend trackers and opportunity seekers. Although every manager in an organization needs to observe the outside environment, marketers have two special aptitudes. They have disciplined methods—marketing research and marketing intelligence—for collecting information about the marketing environment. They also spend more time in the customer and competitor environments. By carefully studying the environment, marketers can adapt their strategies to meet new marketplace challenges and opportunities.

The marketing environment is made up of a *microenvironment* and a *macroenvironment*. The **microenvironment** consists of the actors close to the company that affect its ability to serve its customers—the company, suppliers, marketing intermediaries, customer markets, competitors, and publics. The **macroenvironment** consists of the larger societal forces that affect the microenvironment—demographic, economic, natural, technological, political, and cultural forces. We look first at the company's microenvironment.

The Company's Microenvironment

Marketing management's job is to build relationships with customers by creating customer value and satisfaction. However, marketing managers cannot do this alone. Figure 3.1 shows the major actors in the marketer's microenvironment. Marketing success will require building

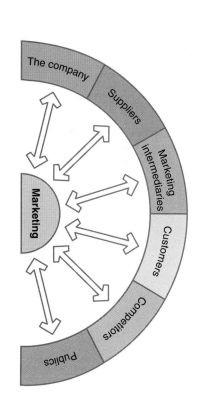

FIGURE 3.1
Actors in the microenvironment

relationships with other company departments, suppliers, marketing intermediaries, customers, competitors, and various publics, which combine to make up the company's value delivery network.

The Company

In designing marketing plans, marketing management takes other company groups into account—groups such as top management, finance, research and development (R&D), purchasing, operations, and accounting. All these interrelated groups form the internal environment. Top management sets the company's mission, objectives, broad strategies, and policies. Marketing managers make decisions within the strategies and plans made by top management. As we discussed in Chapter 2, marketing managers must work closely with other company departments. Other departments have an impact on the marketing department's plans and actions. And under the marketing concept, all of these functions must "think consumer." They should work in harmony to provide superior customer value and satisfaction.

Suppliers

Suppliers form an important link in the company's overall customer value delivery system. They provide the resources needed by the company to produce its goods and services. Supplier problems can seriously affect marketing. Marketing managers must watch supply availability—supply shortages or delays, labor strikes, and other events can cost sales in the short run and damage customer satisfaction in the long run. Marketing managers also monitor the price trends of their key inputs. Rising supply costs may force price increases that can harm the company's sales volume.

Most marketers today treat their suppliers as partners in creating and delivering customer value. Wal-Mart goes to great lengths to work with its suppliers. For example, it helps them to test new products in its stores. And its Supplier Development Department publishes a *Supplier Proposal Guide* and maintains a supplier Web site, both of which help suppliers to navigate the complex Wal-Mart buying process. "Wal-Mart talks tough and remains a demanding customer," says one supplier executive, but "it also helps you get there."2 It knows that good partnership relationship management results in success for Wal-Mart, suppliers, and, ultimately, its customers.

Marketing Intermediaries

Marketing intermediaries help the company to promote, sell, and distribute its products to final buyers. They include resellers, physical distribution firms, marketing services agencies, and financial intermediaries. *Resellers* are distribution channel firms that help the company find customers or make sales to them. These include wholesalers and retailers, who buy and resell merchandise. Selecting and partnering with resellers is not easy. No longer do manufacturers have many small, independent resellers from which to choose. They now face large and growing reseller organizations such as Wal-Mart, Target, Home Depot, Costco, and Best Buy. These organizations frequently have enough power to dictate terms or even shut the manufacturer out of large markets.

Marketing intermediaries Firms that help the company to promote, sell, and distribute its goods to final buyers; they include resellers, physical distribution firms, marketing service agencies, and financial intermediaries.

Physical distribution firms help the company to stock and move goods from their points of origin to their destinations. Working with warehouse and transportation firms, a company must determine the best ways to store and ship goods, balancing factors such as cost, delivery, speed, and safety. *Marketing services agencies* are the marketing research firms, advertising agencies, media firms, and marketing consulting firms that help the company target and promote its products to the right markets. *Financial intermediaries* include banks, credit companies, insurance companies, and other businesses that help finance transactions or insure against the risks associated with the buying and selling of goods.

Like suppliers, marketing intermediaries form an important component of the company's overall value delivery system. In its quest to create satisfying customer relationships, the company must do more than just optimize its own performance. It must partner effectively with marketing intermediaries to optimize the performance of the entire system.

Thus, today's marketers recognize the importance of working with their intermediaries as partners rather than simply as channels through which they sell their products. For example, when Coca-Cola signs on as the exclusive beverage provider for a fast-food chain, such as McDonald's, Wendy's, or Subway, it provides much more than just soft drinks. It also pledges powerful marketing support.

Coke assigns cross-functional teams dedicated to understanding the finer points of each retail partner's business. It conducts a staggering amount of research on beverage consumers and shares these insights with its partners. It analyzes the demographics of U.S. zip code areas and helps partners to determine which Coke brands are preferred in their areas. Coca-Cola has even studied the design of drive-through menu boards to better understand which layouts, fonts, letter sizes, colors, and visuals induce consumers to order more food and drink. Such intense partnering efforts have made Coca-Cola a run-away leader in the U.S. fountain soft drink market.[3]

■ Partnering with marketing intermediaries: Coca-Cola provides Subway with much more than just soft drinks. It also pledges powerful marketing support.

Customers

The company needs to study five types of customer markets closely. *Consumer markets* consist of individuals and households that buy goods and services for personal consumption. *Business markets* buy goods and services for further processing or for use in their production process, whereas *reseller markets* buy goods and services to resell at a profit. *Government markets* are made up of government agencies that buy goods and services to produce public services or transfer the goods and services to others who need them. Finally, *international markets* consist of these buyers in other countries, including consumers, producers, resellers, and governments. Each market type has special characteristics that call for careful study by the seller.

Competitors

The marketing concept states that to be successful, a company must provide greater customer value and satisfaction than its competitors do. Thus, marketers must do more than simply adapt to the needs of target consumers. They also must gain strategic advantage by positioning their offerings strongly against competitors' offerings in the minds of consumers.

No single competitive marketing strategy is best for all companies. Each firm should consider its own size and industry position compared to those of its competitors. Large firms

Wal-Mart congratulates our National Teacher of the Year.

Carol Olney
Whitesides Elementary School
Mt. Pleasant, S.C.
Wal-Mart National Teacher of the Year

Sarah Lyles
Student

"Nothing is impossible"

is the motto that drives Carol Olney. Her spirited approach is why her peers have chosen her to be Wal-Mart's 2004 National Teacher of the Year. This honor has earned her school a $25,000 donation from Wal-Mart to recognize the education and inspiration she provides her special-needs students.

Caring about education means supporting it. More than $4 million was awarded to 3,600 schools of Local and State Teachers of the Year by their neighborhood Wal-Mart stores and SAM'S CLUBs in 2004. This year Wal-Mart will give back more than $150 million overall to the communities we serve.

Visit us on the Web at www.walmartfoundation.org.

WAL*MART

■ Publics: Wal-Mart's Good. WORKS efforts, such as the Wal-Mart Teacher of the Year program, recognize the importance of community publics. "Supporting our communities is good for everyone," says the ad.

Public

Any group that has an actual or potential interest in or impact on an organization's ability to achieve its objectives.

with dominant positions in an industry can use certain strategies that smaller firms cannot afford. But being large is not enough. There are winning strategies for large firms, but there are also losing ones. And small firms can develop strategies that give them better rates of return than large firms enjoy.

Publics

The company's marketing environment also includes various publics. A **public** is any group that has an actual or potential interest in or impact on an organization's ability to achieve its objectives. We can identify seven types of publics.

- *Financial publics* influence the company's ability to obtain funds. Banks, investment houses, and stockholders are the major financial publics.

- *Media publics* carry news, features, and editorial opinions. They include newspapers, magazines, and radio and television stations.

- *Government publics.* Management must take government developments into account. Marketers must often consult the company's lawyers on issues of product safety, truth in advertising, and other matters.

- *Citizen-action publics.* A company's marketing decisions may be questioned by consumer organizations, environmental groups, minority groups, and others. Its public relations department can help it stay in touch with consumer and citizen groups.

- *Local publics* include neighborhood residents and community organizations. Large companies usually appoint a community relations officer to deal with the community, attend meetings, answer questions, and contribute to worthwhile causes.

- *General public.* A company needs to be concerned about the general public's attitude toward its products and activities. The public's image of the company affects its buying.

- *Internal publics* include workers, managers, volunteers, and the board of directors. Large companies use newsletters and other means to inform and motivate their internal publics. When employees feel good about their company, this positive attitude spills over to external publics.

A company can prepare marketing plans for these major publics as well as for its customer markets. Suppose the company wants a specific response from a particular public, such as goodwill, favorable word of mouth, or donations of time or money. The company would have to design an offer to this public that is attractive enough to produce the desired response.

◼ The Company's Macroenvironment

The company and all of the other actors operate in a larger macroenvironment of forces that shape opportunities and pose threats to the company. Figure 3.2 shows the six major forces in the company's macroenvironment. In the remaining sections of this chapter, we examine these forces and show how they affect marketing plans.

Part 2 Understanding the Marketplace and Consumers

FIGURE 3.2
Major forces in the company's macroenvironment

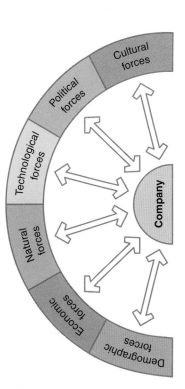

Demography
The study of human populations in terms of size, density, location, age, gender, race, occupation, and other statistics.

Demographic Environment

Demography is the study of human populations in terms of size, density, location, age, gender, race, occupation, and other statistics. The demographic environment is of major interest to marketers because it involves people, and people make up markets. The world population is growing at an explosive rate. It now exceeds 6.5 billion people and will exceed 8.1 billion by the year 2030.[4] The world's large and highly diverse population poses both opportunities and challenges.

Changes in the world demographic environment have major implications for business. For example, consider China. More than a quarter century ago, to curb its skyrocketing population, the Chinese government passed regulations limiting families to one child each. As a result, Chinese children—known as "little emperors and empresses"—are being showered with attention and luxuries under what's known as the "six-pocket syndrome." As many as six adults—two parents and four doting grandparents—may be indulging the whims of each "only child." Parents in the average Beijing household now spend about 40 percent of their income on their cherished only child. Among other things, this trend has created huge market opportunities for children's educational products.

Demographics and business: Chinese regulations limiting families to one child have resulted in what's known as the "six-pocket syndrome." Chinese children are being showered with attention and luxuries creating opportunities for marketers.

In China's increasingly competitive society, parents these days are desperate to give Junior an early edge. That's creating opportunities for companies peddling educational offerings aimed at kids. Disney, for example, is moving full speed into educational products. Magic English, a $225 Disney package that includes workbooks, flash cards, and 26 videodisks, has been phenomenally successful. Disney has also launched interactive educational CD-ROMs featuring the likes of Winnie the Pooh and *101 Dalmations'* Cruella DeVille. Disney isn't alone in catering to the lucrative Chinese coddled-kiddies market. For example, Time Warner is testing the waters in Shanghai with an interactive language course called English Time. The 200-lesson, 40-CD set takes as long as four years for a child to complete. Time Warner is expecting strong sales, despite the $3,300 price tag, which equals more than a year's salary for many Chinese parents.[5]

Interestingly, the one-child policy is creating another major Chinese demographic development—a rapidly aging population. In what some deem a potential "demographic earthquake," by 2024 an estimated 58 percent of the Chinese population will be over age 40. And because of the one-child policy, close to 75 percent of all Chinese households will be childless, either because they chose to have no children or because their only child has left

Baby boomers

The 78 million people born during the baby boom following World War II and lasting until the early 1960s.

---

the nest. The result is an aging society that will need to be more self-reliant, which in turn will cause a large growth in service markets such as senior education, leisure clubs, and nursing homes.[6]

Thus, marketers keep close track of demographic trends and developments in their markets, both at home and abroad. They track changing age and family structures, geographic population shifts, educational characteristics, and population diversity. Here, we discuss the most important demographic trends in the United States.

Changing Age Structure of the Population

The U.S. population stood at more than 300 million in 2006 and may reach almost 364 million by the year 2030.[7] The single most important demographic trend in the United States is the changing age structure of the population. The U.S. population contains several generational groups. Here, we discuss the three largest groups—the baby boomers, Generation X, and Generation Y—and their impact on today's marketing strategies.

THE BABY BOOMERS The post–World War II baby boom produced 78 million **baby boomers**, born between 1946 and 1964. Since then, the baby boomers have become one of the most powerful forces shaping the marketing environment. Today's baby boomers account for about 27.5 percent of the population, spend about $2.1 trillion annually, and hold three-quarters of the nation's financial assets. It has been estimated that when the last baby boomer turns 65 in 2029, the generation will control more than 40 percent of the nation's disposable income.[8]

As a group, the baby boomers are the most affluent Americans. However, although the more affluent boomers have grabbed most of the headlines, baby boomers cut across all walks of life, creating a diverse set of target segments for businesses. There are wealthy boomers but also boomers with more modest means. And almost 25 percent of the 78 million boomers belong to a racial or ethnic minority.

The youngest boomers are now in their early forties; the oldest are entering their sixties. The maturing boomers are rethinking the purpose and value of their work, responsibilities, and relationships. As they reach their peak earning and spending years, the boomers constitute a lucrative market for new housing and home remodeling, financial services, travel and entertainment, eating out, health and fitness products, and just about everything else.

It would be a mistake to think of the boomers as aging and slowing down. In fact, the boomers are spending $30 billion a year on *antiaging* products and services. And unlike previous generations, boomers are likely to postpone retirement. Rather than viewing themselves as phasing out, they see themselves as entering new life phases. "Boomers don't see themselves as old," says one expert. "They never grew up. They say that they feel seven to 10 years younger than they are. And they are not etching the typical life stages. Now it's, 'The kids are out of the house and I'm taking up in-line skating.'"[9]

Toyota recognizes these changing boomer life phases. Ads for its Toyota Highlander show empty-nest boomers and declare "For your newfound freedom." Similarly, Curves fitness centers targets older women, but not grandmas in rocking chairs. Curves' older regulars "want to be strong and fit," says the expert. "They just don't want to go into Gold's Gym and be surrounded by spandex-clad Barbie dolls."[10] And, as many boomers are rediscovering the excitement of life and have the means to play it out, the luxury RV market is exploding.

It seems that every younger boomer family needs an RV to take the classic American family vacation before the kids grow up and leave home. The older boomers, now empty nesters, use an RV to visit their grandchildren or to see America at their own pace. "RVs are selling like hotcakes," says an RV industry association executive. "And baby boomers are in their prime RV years."[11]

Perhaps no one is targeting the baby boomers more fervently than the financial services industry. In coming years, the aging boomers will transfer some $30 trillion in retirement nest eggs and other savings into new investments. They'll also be inheriting $8 trillion as their parents pass away. Thus, the boomers will be needing lots of money management help. In magazine ads targeting boomers, Ameriprise Financial suggests, "A generation as unique as this needs a new generation of personal financial planning." An Ameriprise marketer explains, "It's not just about the rational numbers. It's about how you are going to reinvent yourself for what could be 30 or 40 years of retirement."[12]

Fidelity Investments also takes a life phases approach in marketing to baby boomers, with ads featuring the likes of former Beatle Paul McCartney, the ultimate boomer icon:

> This notion of life as a series of fresh chapters animates commercials for Fidelity Investments. One ad chronicles the life of Paul McCartney through his phases as a Beatle, a member of Wings, a poet, and a father. [Says] Fidelity marketing executive Claire Huang: "He fit perfectly our model that you don't really retire—you just keep doing something new."

Do you have *dream* **a 401(k) plan?**

What do you dream of doing in retirement? Maybe you want to go back to school. Start a second career. Visit the Spanish Steps. Work on that short game. Or maybe you're not even sure.

That's precisely the reason why Ameriprise Financial created the *Dream Book.* It's a place to help you envision what exactly you want to do in the next phase of your life. And it's the perfect starting point for you and an Ameriprise financial advisor to develop a plan to help get you there.

Get started today by calling **1-800-Ameriprise** or visit **ameriprise.com/dream** for your complimentary copy of the *Dream Book.*

Get to What's next.™   Financial Planning ▸ Retirement ▸ Investments ▸ Insurance

The Personal Advisors of Ameriprise **Financial**

Financial advisory services and investments available through Ameriprise Financial Services, Inc., Member NASD and SIPC. © 2006 Ameriprise Financial Inc. All rights reserved.

■ Targeting the baby boomers: This ad promises retiring boomers that the company will "help you envision what exactly you want to do in the next phase of your life."

Generation X

The 45 million people born between 1965 and 1976 in the "birth dearth" following the baby boom.

GENERATION X The baby boom was followed by a "birth dearth," creating another generation of 49 million people born between 1965 and 1976. Author Douglas Copeland calls them **Generation X**, because they lie in the shadow of the boomers and lack obvious distinguishing characteristics. Others call them the "baby busters" or the "generation caught in the middle" (between the larger baby boomers and later Generation Ys).

The Generation Xers are defined as much by their shared experiences as by their age. Increasing parental divorce rates and higher employment for their mothers made them the first generation of latchkey kids. Having grown up during times of recession and corporate downsizing, they developed a more cautious economic outlook. They care about the environment and respond favorably to socially responsible companies. Although they seek success, they are less materialistic; they prize experience, not acquisition. They are cautious romantics who want a better quality of life and are more interested in job satisfaction than in sacrificing personal happiness and growth for promotion. For many of the 30 million Gen Xers that are parents, family comes first, career second.[13]

As a result, the Gen Xers are a more skeptical bunch. "Marketing to Gen Xers is difficult," says one marketer, "and it's all about word of mouth. You can't tell them you're good, and they have zero interest in a slick brochure that says so. . . . They have a lot of 'filters' in place." Another marketer agrees: "Sixty-three percent of this group will research products before they consider a purchase. [They are also] creating extensive communities to exchange information. Even though nary a handshake occurs, the information swap is trusted and thus is more powerful than any marketing pitch ever could be."[14]

Once labeled as "the MTV generation" and viewed as body-piercing slackers who whined about "McJobs," the Gen Xers have now grown up and are beginning to take over. The Gen Xers are displacing the lifestyles, culture, and materialistic values of the baby boomers. They represent close to $1.4 trillion in annual purchasing power. By the year 2010, they will have overtaken the baby boomers as a primary market for almost every product category.[15]

With so much potential, many companies are focusing on Gen Xers as an important target segment. For example, consider the banking industry:[16]

As the Gen Xers progress in their careers, start families, and settle into home ownership, banks are responding with programs to help them manage their finances. For example, home financing is a major issue. To help out, Washington Mutual (WaMu to its customers) ran a marketing campaign showing young home buyers how they can simplify the home buying process. The "Buying a Home" page on WaMu's Web site is an "all-you-ever-wanted-to-know" resource for new-home financing. Generation

Generation Y

The 72 million children of the baby boomers, born between 1977 and 1994.

Xers also worry about saving money for their children's college educations—one study showed that 26 percent of Gen Xers felt that education costs would be out of reach by the time their children were ready for college. To meet this need, the Life Stages section of WaMu's Web site offers "College Savings 101," and other educational planning tools. But marketing to Gen X consumers requires fresh approaches. So rather than bombarding them with brash marketing pitches, WaMu combines softer marketing approaches with community-oriented programs. For example, to gain favor with Gen Xers who have young families with small children, WaMu developed WaMoola for Schools. This program sets aside $1 for every new checking account opened during the year and then distributes the funds to local schools. Or customers can earn WaMoola points for their schools by making purchases with their Washington Mutual Visa Check Cards.

GENERATION Y

Generation Y (also called echo boomers). Born between 1977 and 1994, these children of the baby boomers now number 76 million, dwarfing the Gen Xers and almost equal in size to the baby boomer segment. The echo boom has created a large teen and young adult market. Teen spending alone has increased 30 percent in the past eight years, rising to $159 billion last year. Teens also influence an estimated $30 billion more each year in family spending. After years of bust, markets for teen and young-adult games, clothes, furniture, and food have enjoyed a boom.[17]

Generation Y oldsters have now graduated from college and are moving up in their careers. Like the trailing edge of the Generation Xers ahead of them, one distinguishing characteristic of Generation Y is their utter fluency and comfort with computer, digital, and Internet technology. Some 87 percent of teens use the Internet, up 24 percent over the past four years. More than half of the 87 percent go online every day, and 84 percent of teens own at least one networked device, such as a cell phone, blackberry, or computer. In all, they are an impatient, now-oriented bunch. "Blame it on the relentless and dizzying pace of the Internet, 24-hour cable news cycles, cell phones, and TiVo for creating the on-demand, gotta-get-it-now universe in which we live," says one observer. "Perhaps nowhere is the trend more pronounced than among the Gen Y set."[18]

Generation Y represents an attractive target for marketers. However, reaching this message-saturated segment effectively requires creative marketing approaches. For example, the popularity of action sports with Gen Yers has provided creative marketing opportunities for products ranging from clothes to video games, movies, and even beverages. Mountain Dew's edgy and irreverent positioning makes it a natural for the action-sport crowd. But more than just showing snowboarders, skateboarders, and surfers in its ads, Mountain Dew has become a true action-sports supporter. It sponsors the ESPN XGames, the Vans Triple Crown, and numerous action-sport athletes. It even started its own grassroots skate park tour, the Mountain Dew Free Flow Tour. As a result of these and other actions, Mountain Dew has become the beverage of choice for men ages 18 to 24.[19]

The automobile industry is aggressively targeting this future generation of car buyers. By 2010, Generation Y will buy one of every four new cars sold in the United States. Toyota even created a completely new brand—the Scion—targeted to Gen Yers (see Real Marketing 3.1). Scion and other automakers are using a variety of programs and pitches to lure Generation Y as they move into their key car-buying years.[20]

Recently, Toyota quietly began an unusual virtual promotion of its small, boxy Scion: It paid for the car's product placement in Whyville.net, an online interactive community populated almost entirely by 8- to 15-year-olds. Never mind that they cannot actually buy the car. Toyota is counting on Whyvillians to do two things—influence their parents' car purchases and maybe grow up with some Toyota brand loyalty. It may appear counterintuitive, but Toyota says the promotion is working. Ten days into the campaign, visitors to the site had used the word "Scion" in online chats more than 78,000 times; hundreds of virtual Scions were purchased, using "clams," the currency of Whyville; and the community meeting place, "Club Scion," was visited 33,741 times. These online Scion owners customized their cars, drove around the virtual Whyville, and picked up their Scion-less friends for a ride.

GENERATIONAL MARKETING

Do marketers need to create separate products and marketing programs for each generation? Some experts warn that marketers must be careful about turning off one generation each time they craft a product or message that appeals effectively to another.

Chapter 3 The Marketing Environment **71**

3.1 In the late 1990s, as Toyota's management team peered through the corporate windshield, it took great pride in the company's accomplishments in the U.S. market. Riding a wave of loyal baby boomers who had grown up with its Toyota and Lexus models, the company had become one of the nation's most powerful automobile brands.

Yet when the team looked down at the corporate dashboard, they saw the "check engine" light flashing. As the baby boomers had aged, the age of the average Toyota customer had risen as well. The median Toyota buyer was 49; the median Lexus buyer, 54. Too few younger customers were lining up to buy Toyotas. Gen Yers by the millions were now reaching driving age, and Toyota wasn't speaking their language. In fact, Toyota's strong reputation among the baby boomers for quality, efficiency, and value had translated to more youthful consumers as, well, "stodgy."

Other auto manufacturers were facing this same Gen Y problem. Honda's durable, easy-to-customize Civic had met with some success with younger buyers, but that brand's appeal was fading. Honda followed with the boxy Element, which one observer described as a "Swiss Army knife on wheels," and which Honda promoted as "a dorm room on wheels." The Element sold well but often attracted the wrong market—boomers and Gen Xers (average age 43) looking for something to transport their flowers and power tools. Toyota had also tried before with three vehicles in its Genesis Project: the frumpy Echo, an edgy Celica, and a pricey but impractical MR2 Spider. Each had failed to score with young people.

So, in the early 2000s, Toyota went back to the drawing board. The challenge was to keep Gen Y from seeing Toyota as "old people trying to make a young person's car." Success depended on understanding this new generation of buyers, a segment of strangers to most car marketers. "They demand authenticity, respect for their time, and products built just for them," observed a senior Toyota executive. "They are in their early 20s, new to us, and have changed every category they have touched so far. It's the most diverse generation ever seen."

The search for a new, more youthful model began in Toyota's own driveway. Following orders to "loosen up," Toyota engineers in Japan had designed and successfully introduced a boxy microvan, the bB, and a five-door hatchback, the "ist" (pronounced "east"). The company decided to rename these vehicles and introduce them in the United States. Thus was born Toyota's Gen Y brand, the Scion (Sighun). Following soon after, Toyota added the Scion tC coupe, which adds more power and driving pleasure to the Scion equation. In the Scion, Toyota created not just a new car brand, but new marketing approaches as well.

Accelerate to Memorial Day weekend in late May 2003. Twenty-something Toyota reps sporting goatees and sunglasses have set up shop near a major intersection in San Francisco's Haight-Ashbury district. Standing under banners heralding the new Scion brand, with hip-hop music blaring in the background, the reps encourage young passersby to test drive two new models, the Scion xA hatchback and the Scion xB van.

To target Gen Yers, with their "built-just-for-them" preferences, Toyota positioned the Scion on personalization. "Personalization begins here—what moves you?"

UNIDENTIFIED DRIVING OBJECT
Scion xA

what moves you
scion.com

Others caution that each generation spans decades of time and many socioeconomic levels. For example, marketers often split the baby boomers into three smaller groups—leading boomers, core boomers, and trailing boomers—each with its own beliefs and behaviors. Similarly, they split Generation Y into Gen Y adults and Gen Y teens. Thus, marketers need to form more precise age-specific segments within each group. More important, defining people by their birth date may be less effective than segmenting them by their lifestyle or life stage.

The Changing American Family

The "traditional household" consists of a husband, wife, and children (and sometimes grandparents). Yet, the once American ideal of the two-child, two-car suburban family has lately been losing some of its luster.

In the United States today, married couples with children make up only 23 percent of the nation's 111 million households; married couples without children make up 28 percent;

This was not your typical Toyota sales event—it was the opening round in a campaign to solve, finally, the Gen Y riddle. And it signaled the most unorthodox new-car campaign in the company's 70-year history—a campaign that was edgy, urban, and underground. To speak to Gen Y, Toyota shunned traditional marketing approaches and employed guerrilla tactics. Its young marketing team put up posters with slogans such as "No Clone Zone" and "Ban Normality," even projecting those slogans onto buildings at night. It held "ride-and-drive" events, like the one in San Francisco, to generate spontaneous test-drives by taking its cars to potential customers instead of waiting for them to find their way to showrooms. It put brochures in alternative publications such as *Urb* and *Tokion*, and it sponsored events at venues ranging from hip-hop nightclubs and urban pubs to library lawns.

Toyota assigned Dawn Ahmed and Brian Bolain, two young members of its product development staff, to head the U.S. promotional campaign. Understanding the "built-just-for-them" preferences of the Gen Y target market, Ahmed and Bolain decided to position the Scion on *personalization*. They appealed to the new youth-culture club of "tuners," young fans of tricked-out vehicles (such as BMW's wildly successful Mini Cooper) who wanted to customize their cars from bumper to bumper. "We saw that the tuner phenomenon was really spreading, and took that idea of customization to a totally different level," Ahmed notes. "It comes back to that thing of rational versus emotional," observes Bolain. "Scion buyers have all the rational demands of a Toyota buyer, but they also want more fun, personality, and character."

So, along with all of the traditional Toyota features—like lots of airbags, remote keyless entry, and a 160-watt Pioneer stereo with MP3 capability—the Scion offers lots of room for individual self-expression. The staff worked with after-market auto-parts suppliers to develop specially designed Scion add-ons. To create their own one-of-a-kind cars, customers can select from 40 different accessory products, such as LED interior lighting and illuminated cup holders, wake-the-dead stereo systems, and stiffer shocks. As Bolain points out, "We wanted the Scion to be a] blank canvas on which the consumer can make the car what they would like it to be."

Toyota dealers who have agreed to sell Scions provide special areas in their showrooms where customers can relax, check out the cars, and create their own customized Scions on computers linked to Scion's Web site. And Scion buyers do, indeed, customize their cars. The Scion xA and Scion xB start at "no haggle" prices around $13,000 and $14,000, respectively. But 48 percent of Scion buyers spend another $1,000 to $3,000 to customize their cars. Two-thirds of buyers labor at the Scion Web site, configuring just the car they want before ever walking into the dealership.

How is Toyota's Scion strategy working? The California launch was so successful that Toyota quickly rolled out the Scion nationally, finishing the process in June 2004. Scion blew past its first-year, 60,000-unit sales target by mid-2004, selling 100,000 units for the year. Toyota sold nearly 160,000 Scions the next year and sales remain brisk. Most importantly, the Scion is bringing a new generation of buyers into the Toyota family. Eighty percent of Scion buyers have never before owned a Toyota. And the average age of a Scion buyer is 31, the youngest in the automotive industry. That overstates the average age of a Scion driver, given that many parents are buying the car for their kids.

All this success, however, brings new challenges. For example, according to an industry analyst, Gen Y consumers "disdain commercialism and don't really want 'their brand' to be discovered." To maintain its appeal to these young buyers, as the brand becomes more mainstream, Scion will have to keep its models and messages fresh and honest. Says VP Jim Farley, "We want to [reach out to youthful buyers] without shouting 'Buy This Car.'"

Sources: Quotes from Lillie Guyer, "Scion Connects in Out-of-Way Places," *Advertising Age,* February 21, 2005, p. 38. Also see Brett Corbin, "Toyota's Scion Line Banks on Tech-Savvy Younger Drivers," *Business First,* June 18, 2004, p. 11; Nick Kurczewski, "Who's Your Daddy? Staid Toyota Gets a Hip Implant," *New York Times,* July 25, 2004, p. 12; Patrick Paternie, "Driven by Personality," *Los Angeles Times,* January 6, 2005, p. E34; Karl Greenberg, "Dawn Ahmed," *Brandweek,* April 11, 2005, p. 33; Chris Woodyard, "Outside-the-Box Scion Scores Big with Young Drivers," May 3, 2005, accessed at www.detnews.com/2005/autosinsider/0505/03/1auto-170121.htm; Mark Rechtin, "Scion's Delimma: Be Hip—But Avoid the Mainstream," *Automotive News,* May 22, 2006, pp. 42–45; and Julie Bosman, "Hey, Kid, You Want to Buy A Scion?" *New York Times,* June 14, 2006, p. C2.

and single parents comprise another 16 percent. A full 32 percent are nonfamily households—single live-alones or adult live-togethers of one or both sexes.[21]

More people are divorcing or separating, choosing not to marry, marrying later, or marrying without intending to have children. Marketers must increasingly consider the special needs of nontraditional households, because they are now growing more rapidly than traditional households. Each group has distinctive needs and buying habits.

The number of working women has also increased greatly, growing from under 40 percent of the U.S. workforce in the late 1950s to around 77 percent in 2000. However, research indicates that the trend may be slowing. After increasing steadily since 1976, the percentage of women with children under age one in the workforce has fallen during the past few years.[22] Meanwhile, more men are staying home with their children, managing the household while their wives go to work. According to the census, the number of stay-at-home dads has risen 18 percent since 1994.[23]

The significant number of women in the workforce has spawned the child day care business and increased consumption of career-oriented women's clothing, financial services, and convenience foods and services. An example is Dream Dinners, Inc., a national franchise chain created by a busy working mom who invited fellow busy moms to her catering kitchen to prepare make-ahead meals. People visiting a Dream Dinners store can prepare up to a dozen family meals in under two hours, with cleanup handled by the store's staff. Using workstations, they prepare healthy meals ranging from Kung Pao Chicken to New England Pot Roast, take them home in coolers, and store them in the freezer until needed. A dozen meals, each serving four to six people, cost under $200. With over 155 locations, Dream Dinners gives precious family time back to harried working parents.[24]

Introducing DREAM DINNERS.
All the *joy* of a family meal.
None of the hassle.

Dream Dinners lets you choose 12 wonderful entrées you assemble once a month and then serve to your family in the weeks ahead. Dream Dinners. *All the ingredients for a great meal.*

dreamdinners.com

■ Businesses like Dream Dinners have arisen to serve the growing number of working women. The chain was created by a busy working mom who invited fellow busy mothers to her catering kitchen to prepare make-ahead meals. With Dream Dinners, you get "All the joy of a family meal. None of the hassle."

Geographic Shifts in Population

This is a period of great migratory movements between and within countries. Americans, for example, are a mobile people, with about 14 percent of all U.S. residents moving each year. Over the past two decades, the U.S. population has shifted toward the Sunbelt states. The West and South have grown, while the Midwest and Northeast states have lost population.[25] Such population shifts interest marketers because people in different regions buy differently. For example, research shows that people in Seattle buy more toothbrushes per capita than people in any other U.S. city; people in Salt Lake City eat more candy bars; and people in Miami drink more prune juice.

Also, for more than a century, Americans have been moving from rural to metropolitan areas. In the 1950s, they made a massive exit from the cities to the suburbs. Today, the migration to the suburbs continues. And more and more Americans are moving to "micropolitan areas," small cities located beyond congested metropolitan areas. Drawing refugees from rural and suburban America, these smaller micros offer many of the advantages of metro areas—jobs, restaurants, diversions, community organizations—but without the population crush, traffic jams, high crime rates, and high property taxes often associated with heavily urbanized areas.[26]

The shift in where people live has also caused a shift in where they work. For example, the migration toward micropolitan and suburban areas has resulted in a rapid increase in the number of people who "telecommute"—work at home or in a remote office and conduct their business by phone, fax, modem, or the Internet. This trend, in turn, has created a booming SOHO (small office/home office) market. Almost a quarter of all Americans telecommuted at least one day a month last year, twice the number from 2000, with the help of electronic conveniences such as PCs, cell phones, fax machines, PDA devices, and fast Internet access.[27]

Many marketers are actively courting the home office segment of this lucrative SOHO market. For example, FedEx Kinko's is much more than just a self-service copy shop. Targeting small office/home office customers, it services as a well-appointed office outside the home. People can come to a FedEx Kinko's store to do all their office jobs: They can copy, send and receive faxes, use various programs on the computer, go on the Internet, order stationery and other printed supplies, ship packages, and even rent a conference room or conduct a teleconference. As more and more people join the work-at-home trend,

■ Geographic shifts: To serve the burgeoning small office/home office market, FedEx Kinko's has reinvented itself as the well-appointed office outside the home. "Our office is your office," says the company.

FedEx Kinko's offers an escape from the isolation of the home office. Its ads proclaim, "Our office is your office."

A Better-Educated, More White-Collar, More Professional Population

The U.S. population is becoming better educated. For example, in 2004, 85 percent of the U.S. population over age 25 had completed high school and 28 percent had completed college, compared with 69 percent and 17 percent in 1980. Moreover, nearly two-thirds of high school graduates now enroll in college within 12 months of graduating.[28] The rising number of educated people will increase the demand for quality products, books, magazines, travel, personal computers, and Internet services.

The workforce also is becoming more white-collar. Between 1950 and 1985, the proportion of white-collar workers rose from 41 percent to 54 percent, that of blue-collar workers declined from 47 percent to 33 percent, and that of service workers increased from 12 percent to 14 percent. Between 1983 and 1999, the proportion of managers and professionals in the workforce increased from 23 percent to more than 30 percent. Job growth is now strongest for professional workers and weakest for manufacturers. Between 2004 and 2014, the number of professional workers is expected to increase 21 percent and manufacturing is expected to decline 5 percent.[29]

Increasing Diversity

Countries vary in their ethnic and racial makeup. At one extreme is Japan, where almost everyone is Japanese. At the other extreme is the United States, with people from virtually all nations. The United States has often been called a melting pot—diverse groups from many nations and cultures have melted into a single, more homogenous whole. Instead, the United States seems to have become more of a "salad bowl" in which various groups have mixed together but have maintained their diversity by retaining and valuing important ethnic and cultural differences.

Marketers are facing increasingly diverse markets, both at home and abroad as their operations become more international in scope. The U.S. population is about 67 percent white, with Hispanics at 14.4 percent and African Americans at 13.4 percent. The U.S. Asian American population now totals about 4 percent of the population, with the remaining 1 percent made up of American Indian, Eskimo, and Aleut. Moreover, more than 34 million people living in the United States—more than 12 percent of the population—were born in another country. The nation's ethnic populations are expected to explode in coming decades. By 2050, Hispanics will comprise an estimated 24 percent of the U.S. population, with African Americans at 13 percent and Asians at 9 percent.[30]

Most large companies, from Procter & Gamble, Sears, Wal-Mart, Allstate, and Bank of America to Levi Strauss and General Mills, now target specially designed products, ads, and promotions to one or more of these groups. For example, Allstate worked with Kang & Lee Advertising, a leading multicultural marketing agency, to create an award-winning marketing campaign aimed at the single largest Asian group in the country—Chinese Americans. Creating culturally significant messages for this market was no easy matter. Perhaps the most daunting task was translating Allstate's iconic "You're In Good Hands With Allstate®" slogan into Chinese.[31]

There's nary a U.S.-born citizen who doesn't know that, when it comes to insurance, you are in good hands with Allstate. But to Chinese Americans, Allstate was not the first insurance company that came to mind. So Allstate asked Kang & Lee Advertising to help it translate the "good hands" concept into the Chinese market.

The trick was to somehow make the company's longtime brand identity relevant to this group. Problem was, the English slogan just doesn't make sense in any Chinese dialect. After months of qualitative consumer research and discussion with Chinese American Allstate agents, Kang & Lee came up with a Chinese-language version of the tag line, which, roughly translated, says "turn to our hands, relax your heart, and be free of worry." The campaign started in Seattle and New York and has since expanded to California. Studies in the first two cities show that awareness of Allstate in the Chinese American community had doubled within six month of the start of the campaign.

Diversity goes beyond ethnic heritage. For example, many major companies have recently begun to explicitly target gay and lesbian consumers. A Simmons Research study of readers of the National Gay Newspaper Guild's 12 publications found that, compared to the average American, respondents are 12 times more likely to be in professional jobs, almost twice as likely to own a vacation home, eight times more likely to own a notebook computer, and twice as likely to own individual stocks. More than two-thirds have graduated from college and 21 percent hold a master's degree. They are twice as likely as the general population to have a household income over $250,000. In all, the gay and lesbian market spent more than $640 billion on goods and services last year.[32]

With hit TV shows such as *Queer Eye for the Straight Guy* and *The Ellen DeGeneres Show*, and Oscar-winning movies such as *Brokeback Mountain* and *Capote*, the gay and lesbian community has increasingly emerged into the public eye. A number of media now provide companies with access to this market. For example, PlanetOut Inc., a leading global media company, exclusively serves the gay, lesbian, bisexual, and transgender (GLBT) community with several successful magazines (*Out, The Advocate, Out Traveler*) and Web sites (Gay.com, PlanetOut.com, Out&About.com). In 2005, media giant Viacom introduced Logo, a cable television network aimed at the gay men and lesbians and their friends and family. Logo is now available in 23 million U.S. households. More than 60 mainstream marketers have advertised on Logo, including Ameriprise Financial, Anheuser-Busch, Continental Airlines, Dell, eBay, General Motors, Johnson & Johnson, Orbitz, Sears, Sony, and Subaru. Here are examples of some gay and lesbian marketing efforts.[33]

With an estimated $65 billion in annual travel expenditures, the American gay and lesbian community is a much sought-after leisure travel segment. Some 53 percent of this segment spends $5,000 or more per person on vacations each year, and 98 percent say that a destination's "gay-friendly reputation" factors into their decision to travel there. Las Vegas, like other cities, aims to snag a larger slice of the gay and lesbian travel pie. The city recently unveiled its first gay promotional push. It placed ads from its universally appealing Vegas ad campaign, "What happens here, stays here," in leading gay publications: *The Advocate, Out,* and *Out Traveler.* It also placed ads on the Logo network, along with sponsorship of episodes of *Queer Eye for the Straight Guy.* Whereas other popular gay getaways, such as Key West, Florida and Palm Springs, California, promote themselves as places where guests will enjoy a largely gay community, Las Vegas urges gays to experience the same attractions that appeal to everyone else. "We're trying to attract this subculture here to immerse themselves into the Las Vegas experience," says the Las Vegas Convention and Visitors Authority's vice president of marketing. So far, the push seems to be work-

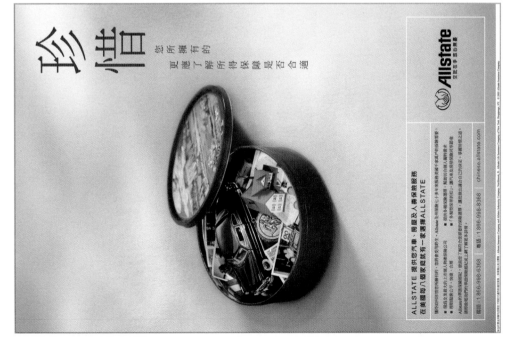

■ Multicultural marketing: Allstate created an award-winning marketing campaign aimed at the single largest Asian group in the country—Chinese Americans. The most daunting task: translating Allstate's iconic "You're In Good Hands With Allstate®" slogan into Chinese.

珍惜

您所擁有的

更應了解所得保障是否合適

ALLSTATE 提供您汽車、房產及人壽保險服務
在美國每八個家庭就有一家選擇ALLSTATE

■ 提供多種保障服務
■ 您的汽車保險可能為您省下更多
■ 專人協助您中英文雙語服務

■ 我們為您提供完善的服務
■ 擁有多項榮譽及獎項

chinese.allstate.com

電話·1-866-998-6368   售後·1-866-998-8366

ing. Gays and lesbians now rank Las Vegas as their second-favorite travel destination, behind only New York City.

IBM fields a paid, full-time sales team dedicated to bringing GLBT decision makers in contact with IBM. The company targeted the gay small-business community with an ad that ran in *The Advocate*, *Out*, and about 40 other gay-themed publications. The ad pictures a diverse group of men and women and links IBM's Armonk, New York headquarters with well-known gay communities: "Chelsea/Provincetown/The Castro/Armonk." The six people shown in the ad are among the 1,100 IBM employees who make up the company's GLBT Network. IBM launched the GLBT group three years ago when research showed that gay business owners are more likely to buy from gay salespeople. Over the past several years, IBM has received numerous awards acknowledging its commitment to the GLBT community.

Another attractive segment is the nearly 60 million people with disabilities in the United States—a market larger than African Americans or Hispanics—representing over $220 billion in annual spending power. This market is expected to grow as the baby boomers age. People with disabilities appreciate products that work for them. Explains Jim Tobias, president of Inclusive Technologies, a consultancy specializing in accessible products, "those with disabilities tend to be brand evangelists for products they love. Whereas consumers may typically tell 10 friends about a favorite product, people with disabilities might spread the word to 10 times that [many]."[34]

How are companies trying to reach these consumers? Many marketers now recognize that the worlds of people with disabilities and those without disabilities are one in the same. Says one marketer, "The 'us and them' paradigm is obsolete." Consider the following Avis example:[35]

A common theme in much of the recent crop of mainstream ads, in fact, is that the disability is virtually an afterthought. A recent New York Marathon-themed print ad for car rental company Avis features an image of a marathoner in a wheelchair, but the copy—"We honor participants of the New York Marathon for spirit, courage, and unrelenting drive"—addresses the racers at large. Since 2003, Avis has offered a suite of products and services that make vehicles more accessible to renters with disabilities, helping to make travel easier and less stressful for everyone. Most recently, Avis has become the official sponsor of the Achilles Track Club, an international organization that supports individuals with disabilities who want to participate in mainstream athletics. Says an Avis marketing executive, "The Achilles athletes themselves truly exemplify the character we strive for at Avis, with their 'we try harder' spirit. Some are amputees back from Iraq; others are visually impaired. But now all of them are setting their sights on what they can achieve."

■ Avis targets people with disabilities by offering a suite of products and services that make vehicles more accessible. It also sponsors the Achilles Track Club, which supports individuals with disabilities who want to participate in mainstream athletics.

Economic environment
Factors that affect consumer buying power and spending patterns.

Economic Environment

Markets require buying power as well as people. The **economic environment** consists of factors that affect consumer purchasing power and spending patterns. Nations vary greatly in their levels and distribution of income. Some countries have *subsistence economies*—they

As the population in the United States grows more diverse, successful marketers will continue to diversify their marketing programs to take advantage of opportunities in fast-growing segments.

consume most of their own agricultural and industrial output. These countries offer few markets for many different kinds of goods. At the other extreme are *industrial economies*, which constitute rich markets for many different kinds of goods. Marketers must pay close attention to major trends and consumer spending patterns both across and within their world markets. Following are some of the major economic trends in the United States.

Changes in Income

Throughout the 1990s, American consumers fell into a consumption frenzy, fueled by income growth, a boom in the stock market, rapid increases in housing values, and other economic good fortune. They bought and bought, seemingly without caution, amassing record levels of debt. However, the free spending and high expectations of those days were dashed by the recent recession of the early 2000s. In fact, we are now facing the age of the "squeezed consumer." Along with rising incomes in some segments have come increased financial burdens. Consumers now face repaying debts acquired during earlier spending splurges, increased household and family expenses, and saving ahead for college tuition payments and retirement.

These financially squeezed consumers have adjusted to their changing financial situations and are spending more carefully. *Value marketing* has become the watchword for many marketers. Rather than offering high quality at a high price, or lesser quality at very low prices, marketers are looking for ways to offer today's more financially cautious buyers greater value—just the right combination of product quality and good service at a fair price.

Marketers should pay attention to *income distribution* as well as average income. Income distribution in the United States is still very skewed. At the top are *upper-class* consumers, whose spending patterns are not affected by current economic events and who are a major market for luxury goods. There is a comfortable *middle class* that is somewhat careful about its spending but can still afford the good life some of the time. The *working class* must stick close to the basics of food, clothing, and shelter and must try hard to save. Finally, the *underclass* (persons on welfare and many retirees) must count their pennies when making even the most basic purchases.

Over the past three decades, the rich have grown richer, the middle class has shrunk, and the poor have remained poor. The top 1 percent of American families now control 33.4 percent of the nation's net worth, up 3.3 points from 1989. By contrast, the bottom 90 percent of families now control 30.4 percent of the net worth, down 3.5 points.[36]

This distribution of income has created a tiered market. Many companies—such as Nordstrom and Neiman-Marcus department stores—aggressively target the affluent. Others—such as Dollar General and Family Dollar stores—target those with more modest means. In fact, such dollar stores are now the fastest growing retailers in the nation. Still other companies tailor their marketing offers across a range of markets, from the affluent to the less affluent. For example, Levi-Strauss currently markets several different jeans lines. The Signature line of low-priced Levi's are found on the shelves of low-end retailers such as Wal-Mart and Target. Levi's moderately priced Red Tab line sells at retailers such as Kohl's and J.C. Penney. Boutique lines, such as Levi's [Capital E] and Warhol Factory X Levi's, sell in the Levi's Store and at high-end retailers such as Nordstrom and Urban Outfitters. You can buy Levi 501 jeans at any of three different price levels. The Red Tab 501s sell for around $35, the Levi's [Capital E] for about $100, and the Warhol Factory X Levi's for $250 or more.[37]

Changing Consumer Spending Patterns

Food, housing, and transportation use up the most household income. However, consumers at different income levels have different spending patterns. Some of these differences were noted over a century ago by Ernst Engel, who studied how people shifted their spending as their income rose. He found that as family income rises, the percentage spent on food declines, the percentage spent on housing remains about constant (except for such utilities as gas, electricity, and public services, which decrease), and both the percentage spent on most other categories and that devoted to savings increase. **Engel's laws** generally have been supported by later studies.

Changes in major economic variables such as income, cost of living, interest rates, and savings and borrowing patterns have a large impact on the marketplace. Companies watch these variables by using economic forecasting. Businesses do not have to be wiped out by an economic downturn or caught short in a boom. With adequate warning, they can take advantage of changes in the economic environment.

Engel's laws

Differences noted over a century ago by Ernst Engel in how people shift their spending across food, housing, transportation, health care, and other goods and services categories as family income rises.

Natural Environment

The **natural environment** involves the natural resources that are needed as inputs by marketers or that are affected by marketing activities. Environmental concerns have grown steadily during the past three decades. In many cities around the world, air and water pollution have reached dangerous levels. World concern continues to mount about the possibilities of global warming, and many environmentalists fear that we soon will be buried in our own trash.

Marketers should be aware of several trends in the natural environment. The first involves growing *shortages of raw materials*. Air and water may seem to be infinite resources, but some groups see long-run dangers. Air pollution chokes many of the world's large cities, and water shortages are already a big problem in some parts of the United States and the world. Renewable resources, such as forests and food, also have to be used wisely. Nonrenewable resources, such as oil, coal, and various minerals, pose a serious problem. Firms making products that require these scarce resources face large cost increases, even if the materials do remain available.

A second environmental trend is *increased pollution*. Industry will almost always damage the quality of the natural environment. Consider the disposal of chemical and nuclear wastes; the dangerous mercury levels in the ocean; the quantity of chemical pollutants in the soil and food supply; and the littering of the environment with nonbiodegradable bottles, plastics, and other packaging materials.

A third trend is *increased government intervention* in natural resource management. The governments of different countries vary in their concern and efforts to promote a clean environment. Some, like the German government, vigorously pursue environmental quality. Others, especially many poorer nations, do little about pollution, largely because they lack the needed funds or political will. Even the richer nations lack the vast funds and political accord needed to mount a worldwide environmental effort. The general hope is that companies around the world will accept more social responsibility, and that less expensive devices can be found to control and reduce pollution.

In the United States, the Environmental Protection Agency (EPA) was created in 1970 to set and enforce pollution standards and to conduct pollution research. In the future, companies doing business in the United States can expect continued strong controls from government and pressure groups. Instead of opposing regulation, marketers should help develop solutions to the material and energy problems facing the world.

Concern for the natural environment has spawned the so-called green movement. Today, enlightened companies go beyond what government regulations dictate. They are developing environmentally sustainable strategies and practices in an effort to create a world economy

■ Responding to consumer demands for more environmentally responsible products, GE is using "ecomagination" to create products for a better world.

Natural environment
Natural resources that are needed as inputs by marketers or that are affected by marketing activities.

that the planet can support indefinitely. They are responding to consumer demands with more environmentally responsible products. For example, GE is using its "ecomagination" to create products for a better world—cleaner aircraft engines, cleaner locomotives, cleaner fuel technologies.

Other companies are developing recyclable or biodegradable packaging, recycled materials and components, better pollution controls, and more energy-efficient operations. For example, HP is pushing legislation to force recycling of old TVs, computers, and other electronic gear:[38]

HP wants your old PCs back. A few years ago, when environmentalists in Washington State began agitating to banish high-tech junk from landfills and scrub the nation's air and water of lead, chromium, mercury, and other toxins prevalent in digital debris, they found an unexpected ally: Hewlett-Packard. Teaming up with greens and retailers, HP took on IBM, Apple Computer, and several major TV manufacturers, which were resisting recycling programs because of the costs. Aided by HP's energetic lobbying, the greens persuaded state lawmakers to adopt a landmark program that forces electronics companies to foot the bill for recycling their old equipment. With HP's help, the movement to recycle electronic refuse, or "e-waste," is now spreading across the nation. HP's efforts have made it the darling of environmentalists, but its agenda isn't entirely altruistic. Take-back laws play to the company's strategic strengths. For decades the computer maker has invested in recycling systems, giving it a head start against competitors. Last year, HP recycled more than 70,000 tons of product, the equivalent of about 10 percent of company sales. And it collected more than 2.5 million units of hardware to be refurbished for resale or donation. No other electronics maker has a recycling and resale program on this scale. "We see legislation coming," says HP's vice-president for corporate, social, and environmental responsibility. "A lot of companies haven't stepped up to the plate. . . . If we do this right, it becomes an advantage to us."

Thus, companies today are looking to do more than just good deeds. More and more, they are recognizing the link between a healthy ecology and a healthy economy. They are learning that environmentally responsible actions can also be good business (see Real Marketing 3.2).

Technological Environment

The **technological environment** is perhaps the most dramatic force now shaping our destiny. Technology has released such wonders as antibiotics, robotic surgery, miniaturized electronics, laptop computers, and the Internet. It also has released such horrors as nuclear missiles, chemical weapons, and assault rifles. It has released such mixed blessings as the automobile, television, and credit cards.

Our attitude toward technology depends on whether we are more impressed with its wonders or its blunders. For example, what would you think about having tiny little transmitters implanted in all of the products you buy that would allow tracking products from their point of production through use and disposal? On the one hand, it would provide many advantages to both buyers and sellers. On the other hand, it could be a bit scary. Either way, it's already happening:[39]

Envision a world in which every product contains a tiny transmitter, loaded with information. As you stroll through the supermarket aisles, shelf sensors detect your selections and beam ads to your shopping cart screen, offering special deals on related products. As your cart fills, scanners detect that you might be buying for a dinner party; the screen suggests a wine to go with the meal you've planned. When you leave the store, exit scanners total up your purchases and automatically charge them to your credit card. At home, readers track what goes into and out of your pantry, updating your shopping list when stocks run low. For Sunday dinner, you pop a Butterball turkey into your "smart oven," which follows instructions from an embedded chip and cooks the bird to perfection.

Seem far-fetched? Not really. In fact, it might soon become a reality, thanks to tiny radio-frequency identification (RFID) transmitters—or "smart chips"—that can be embedded in the products you buy. Beyond benefits to consumers, the RFID chips also give producers and retailers an amazing new way to track their products electronically—anywhere in the world, anytime, automatically—from factories, to

3.2

If a tree falls in the rain forest and no one is there to trumpet—if that wood is destined for an electric guitar. Gibson Guitar, the iconic guitar maker, has worked since the late 1980s to make its wood supply environmentally sustainable. Gibson's electric-guitar division recently switched to 100 percent fair-trade-certified wood. Other Gibson divisions, including Baldwin Piano, plan to follow suit.

Yet, unlike Starbucks, The Body Shop, and other businesses that eagerly brandish their green deeds, Gibson CEO Henry Juszkiewicz doesn't much care to flaunt his environmental credentials (the guy drives a Hummer, after all). What matters to him is ensuring that Gibson has enough exotic wood, mostly mahogany, to keep making guitars for generations.

"We're mercenaries. We're a company. We're for-profit," Juszkiewicz says in his Nashville office, packed with so many music-industry mementos it looks like his own private Hard Rock Cafe. "I'm not a conservationist." High-end guitar enthusiasts, after all, demand that their instruments be made of exotic woods. But prices for exotics can swing wildly, governed by an unsteady supply and the threat that some species may be placed on an extinction watch list.

Juszkiewicz wanted to eliminate the guesswork by building a network of growers rather than relying on brokers scouring world markets for the best prices. He approached the Rainforest Alliance, a nonprofit conservation group, to discuss buying wood from Mexican suppliers certified as sustainable. (Such growers are graded against environmental, labor, and community standards—and for responsible harvesting.)

But that hardly made a dent in Gibson's sourcing problems. So the company hired away two Rainforest Alliance employees to source wood in Costa Rica and Brazil. "Within the first year of hiring these guys, they were able to develop significant sources," Juszkiewicz says. "We went from less than 1 percent usage of certified product to something like 80 percent." Since then, Gibson has forged a direct relationship with growers in Guatemala. That provides both stability of supply and quality, because Gibson is able to instruct farmers on its exacting specifications.

Initially, Juszkiewicz says, Gibson paid a premium for purchasing wood this way. Now buying direct creates modest savings—and the relationships help curb traditional slash-and-burn harvesting,

Gibson Guitar works to make its exotic hardwood supply environmentally sustainable. The company has learned that environmentally friendly practices can also be good business.

which threatens supplies of precious woods. "In the short run, a slight price increase won't necessarily hurt them because a guitar is a higher-value product," says an industry expert. "In the long run, it helps ensure that they can tap this supply not just in five years but in fifty years."

Tensie Whelan, executive director of the Rainforest Alliance, says she's seeing a critical mass of CEOs discovering that environmentally friendly practices can be good business. But she still teases Juszkiewicz, one of the first: "He'll say he's a businessman, that he's just out to make money. But believe me, he's passionate about wanting to leave the world a better place."

Source: Adapted from Ryan Underwood, "In Tune with the Environment," *Fast Company,* February 2005, p. 26.

recently switched to 100 percent fair-trade-certified wood. Other Gibson divisions, including Baldwin Piano, plan to follow suit.

warehouses, to retail shelves, to recycling centers. RFID technology is already in use. Every time consumers flash an ExxonMobil Speed-Pass card to purchase gas at the pump or breeze through an automated toll booth, they're using an RFID chip. Many large firms are adding fuel to the RFID fire. Procter & Gamble plans to have the chips on products in broad distribution as soon as 2008. And at the request of mega-retailers such as Wal-Mart, Best Buy, and Albertson's, suppliers have now begun placing RFID tags on selected products.

The technological environment changes rapidly. Think of all of today's common products that were not available 100 years ago, or even 30 years ago. Abraham Lincoln did not know about automobiles, airplanes, radios, or the electric light. Woodrow Wilson did not know about television, aerosol cans, automatic dishwashers, air conditioners, antibiotics, or computers. Franklin Delano Roosevelt did not know about xerography, synthetic detergents, tape recorders, birth control pills, or earth satellites. John F. Kennedy did not know about personal computers, cell phones, iPods, or the Internet.

■ Technological environment: Technology is perhaps the most dramatic force shaping the marketing environment. Here, a herder makes a call on his cell phone.

New technologies create new markets and opportunities. However, every new technology replaces an older technology. Transistors hurt the vacuum-tube industry, xerography hurt the carbon-paper business, CDs hurt phonograph records, and digital photography hurt the film business. When old industries fought or ignored new technologies, their businesses declined. Thus, marketers should watch the technological environment closely. Companies that do not keep up will soon find their products outdated. And they will miss new product and market opportunities.

The United States leads the world in research and development spending. Total U.S. R&D spending reached an estimated $329 billion in 2006. The federal government was the largest R&D spender at about $132 billion.[40] Scientists today are researching a wide range of promising new products and services, ranging from practical solar energy, electric cars, and organ transplants to mind-controlled computers and genetically engineered food crops.

Today's research usually is carried out by research teams rather than by lone inventors like Thomas Edison, Samuel Morse, or Alexander Graham Bell. Many companies are adding marketing people to R&D teams to try to obtain a stronger marketing orientation. Scientists also speculate on fantasy products, such as flying cars, three-dimensional televisions, and space colonies. The challenge in each case is not only technical but also commercial—to make *practical, affordable* versions of these products.

As products and technology become more complex, the public needs to know that these are safe. Thus, government agencies investigate and ban potentially unsafe products. In the United States, the Food and Drug Administration (FDA) has set up complex regulations for testing new drugs. The Consumer Product Safety Commission sets safety standards for consumer products and penalizes companies that fail to meet them. Such regulations have resulted in much higher research costs and in longer times between new-product ideas and their introduction. Marketers should be aware of these regulations when applying new technologies and developing new products.

Political Environment

Marketing decisions are strongly affected by developments in the political environment. The **political environment** consists of laws, government agencies, and pressure groups that influence or limit various organizations and individuals in a given society.

Legislation Regulating Business

Even the most liberal advocates of free-market economies agree that the system works best with at least some regulation. Well-conceived regulation can encourage competition and ensure fair markets for goods and services. Thus, governments develop *public policy* to guide commerce—sets of laws and regulations that limit business for the good of society as a whole. Almost every marketing activity is subject to a wide range of laws and regulations.

INCREASING LEGISLATION Legislation affecting business around the world has increased steadily over the years. The United States has many laws covering issues such as competition, fair trade practices, environmental protection, product safety, truth in advertising, consumer privacy, packaging and labeling, pricing, and other important areas (see Table 3.1). The European Commission has been active in establishing a new framework of laws covering competitive behavior, product standards, product liability, and commercial transactions for the nations of the European Union.

Several countries have gone further than the United States in passing strong consumerism legislation. For example, Norway bans several forms of sales promotion—trading stamps, contests, premiums—as being inappropriate or unfair ways of promoting products.

Political environment
Laws, government agencies, and pressure groups that influence and limit various organizations and individuals in a given society.

TABLE 3.1 Major U.S. Legislation Affecting Marketing

Legislation	Purpose
Sherman Antitrust Act (1890)	Prohibits monopolies and activities (price fixing, predatory pricing) that restrain trade or competition in interstate commerce.
Federal Food and Drug Act (1906)	Forbids the manufacture or sale of adulterated or fraudulently labeled foods and drugs. Created the Food and Drug Administration.
Clayton Act (1914)	Supplements the Sherman Act by prohibiting certain types of price discrimination, exclusive dealing, and tying clauses (which require a dealer to take additional products in a seller's line).
Federal Trade Commission Act (1914)	Establishes a commission to monitor and remedy unfair trade methods.
Robinson-Patman Act (1936)	Amends Clayton Act to define price discrimination as unlawful. Empowers FTC to establish limits on quantity discounts, forbid some brokerage allowances, and prohibit promotional allowances except when made available on proportionately equal terms.
Wheeler-Lea Act (1938)	Makes deceptive, misleading, and unfair practices illegal regardless of injury to competition. Places advertising of food and drugs under FTC jurisdiction.
Lanham Trademark Act (1946)	Protects and regulates distinctive brand names and trademarks.
National Traffic and Safety Act (1958)	Provides for the creation of compulsory safety standards for automobiles.
Fair Packaging and Labeling Act (1966)	Provides for the regulation of packaging and labeling of consumer goods. Requires that manufacturers state what the package contains, who made it, and how much it contains.
Child Protection Act (1966)	Bans sale of hazardous toys and articles. Sets standards for child resistant packaging.
Federal Cigarette Labeling and Advertising Act (1967)	Requires that cigarette packages contain the following statement: "Warning: The Surgeon General Has Determined That Cigarette Smoking Is Dangerous to Your Health."
National Environmental Policy Act (1969)	Establishes a national policy on the environment. The 1970 Reorganization Plan established the Environmental Protection Agency.
Consumer Product Safety Act (1972)	Establishes the Consumer Product Safety Commission and authorizes it to set safety standards for consumer products as well as exact penalties for failure to uphold those standards.
Magnuson-Moss Warranty Act (1975)	Authorizes the FTC to determine rules and regulations for consumer warranties and provides consumer access to redress, such as the class action suit.
Nutrition Labeling and Education Act (1990)	Requires that food product labels provide detailed nutritional information.
Children's Television Act (1990)	Limits number of commercials aired during children's programs.
Americans with Disabilities Act (1991)	Makes discrimination against people with disabilities illegal in public accommodations, transportation, and telecommunications.
Telephone Consumer Protection Act (1991)	Establishes procedures to avoid unwanted telephone solicitations. Limits marketers' use of automatic telephone dialing systems and artificial or prerecorded voices.
Children's Online Privacy Protection Act (2000)	Prohibits Web sites or online services operators from collecting personal information from children without obtaining consent from a parent and allowing parents to review information collected from their children.
Do-Not-Call Implementation Act (2003)	Authorized the FTC to collect fees from sellers and telemarketers for the implementation and enforcement of a National Do-Not-Call Registry.

Thailand requires food processors selling national brands to also market low-price brands, so that low-income consumers can find economy brands on the shelves. In India, food companies must obtain special approval to launch brands that duplicate those already existing on the market, such as additional cola drinks or new brands of rice.

Understanding the public policy implications of a particular marketing activity is not a simple matter. For example, in the United States, there are many laws created at the national, state, and local levels, and these regulations often overlap. Aspirins sold in Dallas are governed both by federal labeling laws and by Texas state advertising laws. Moreover, regulations are constantly changing—what was allowed last year may now be prohibited, and what was prohibited may now be allowed. Marketers must work hard to keep up with changes in regulations and their interpretations.

Business legislation has been enacted for a number of reasons. The first is to *protect companies from each other.* Although business executives may praise competition, they sometimes try to neutralize it when it threatens them. So laws are passed to define and prevent unfair competition. In the United States, such laws are enforced by the Federal Trade Commission and the Antitrust Division of the Attorney General's office.

The second purpose of government regulation is to *protect consumers* from unfair business practices. Some firms, if left alone, would make shoddy products, invade consumer privacy, tell lies in their advertising, and deceive consumers through their packaging and pricing. Unfair business practices have been defined and are enforced by various agencies.

The third purpose of government regulation is to *protect the interests of society* against unrestrained business behavior. Profitable business activity does not always create a better quality of life. Regulation arises to ensure that firms take responsibility for the social costs of their production or products.

CHANGING GOVERNMENT AGENCY ENFORCEMENT International marketers will encounter dozens, or even hundreds, of agencies set up to enforce trade policies and regulations. In the United States, Congress has established federal regulatory agencies, such as the Federal Trade Commission, the Food and Drug Administration, the Federal Communications Commission, the Federal Energy Regulatory Commission, the Federal Aviation Administration, the Consumer Product Safety Commission, and the Environmental Protection Agency.

Because such government agencies have some discretion in enforcing the laws, they can have a major impact on a company's marketing performance. At times, the staffs of these agencies have appeared to be overly eager and unpredictable. Some of the agencies sometimes have been dominated by lawyers and economists who lacked a practical sense of how business and marketing work. In recent years, the Federal Trade Commission has added staff marketing experts, who can better understand complex business issues.

New laws and their enforcement will continue to increase. Business executives must watch these developments when planning their products and marketing programs. Marketers need to know about the major laws protecting competition, consumers, and society. They need to understand these laws at the local, state, national, and international levels.

Increased Emphasis on Ethics and Socially Responsible Actions

Written regulations cannot possibly cover all potential marketing abuses, and existing laws are often difficult to enforce. However, beyond written laws and regulations, business is also governed by social codes and rules of professional ethics.

SOCIALLY RESPONSIBLE BEHAVIOR Enlightened companies encourage their managers to look beyond what the regulatory system allows and simply "do the right thing." These socially responsible firms actively seek out ways to protect the long-run interests of their consumers and the environment.

The recent rash of business scandals and increased concerns about the environment have created fresh interest in the issues of ethics and social responsibility. Almost every aspect of marketing involves such issues. Unfortunately, because these issues usually involve conflicting interests, well-meaning people can honestly disagree about the right course of action in a given situation. Thus, many industrial and professional trade associations have suggested codes of ethics. And more companies are now developing policies, guidelines, and other responses to complex social responsibility issues.

The boom in Internet marketing has created a new set of social and ethical issues. Critics worry most about online privacy issues. There has been an explosion in the amount of personal digital data available. Users, themselves, supply some of it. They voluntarily place highly private information on social networking sites such as MySpace or on geneology sites, which are easily searched by anyone with a PC.

However, much of the information is systematically developed by businesses seeking to learn more about their customers, often without consumers realizing that they are under the microscope. Legitimate businesses plant cookies on consumers' PCs and collect, analyze, and share digital consumer information from every mouse click consumers make at their Web sites. Critics are concerned that companies may now know *too* much, and that some companies might use digital data to take unfair advantage of consumers. Although most companies fully disclose their Internet privacy policies, and most work to use data to benefit their customers, abuses do occur. As a result, consumer advocates and policymakers are taking action to protect consumer privacy.

Throughout the text, we present Real Marketing exhibits that summarize the main public policy and social responsibility issues surrounding major marketing decisions. These exhibits discuss the legal issues that marketers should understand and the common ethical and societal concerns that marketers face. In Chapter 20, we discuss a broad range of societal marketing issues in greater depth.

CAUSE-RELATED MARKETING   To exercise their social responsibility and build more positive images, many companies are now linking themselves to worthwhile causes. These days, every product seems to be tied to some cause. Buy a pink mixer from KitchenAid and support breast cancer research. Shop at EddieBauer.com and have a percentage of your purchase go to support your local grade school. Purchase Habitat Coffee and help Habitat for Humanity build a house for a needy family. Order the City Harvest Tasting Menu at Le Bernardin in New York City, and the restaurant donates $5 to City Harvest, which feeds the hungry by rescuing millions of pounds of edible food thrown away each year by the city's food businesses. Pay for these purchases with the right charge card and you can support a local cultural arts group or help fight heart disease.

Cause-related marketing has become a primary form of corporate giving. It lets companies "do well by doing good" by linking purchases of the company's products or services with fund-raising for worthwhile causes or charitable organizations. Companies now sponsor dozens of cause-related marketing campaigns each year. Many are backed by large budgets and a full complement of marketing activities.

Consider the cause-marketing activities of Home Depot. In 2006, the home improvement retailer received the Golden Halo Award, given each year by the Cause Marketing Forum to one business for its leadership and outstanding efforts in the field of cause marketing. Here's just one example of Home Depot's many cause-marketing initiatives:

Home Depot is a founding sponsor of KaBoom!, a nonprofit organization that envisions a great place to play within walking distance of every child in America through the construction of community playgrounds around the nation. Home Depot provides financial support, materials, and volunteers in an ongoing effort to help KaBoom! accomplish this mission. For example, last year, Home Depot announced that it would work with KaBoom! to create and refurbish 1,000 playspaces in 1,000 days, a commitment of $25 million and one million volunteer hours. Home Depot also works with its suppliers to develop cause-marketing initiatives that support KaBoom!. It recently partnered with Swing-N-Slide, a do-it-yourself backyard play system producer, to raise money by contributing $30 to KaBoom! for each Brookview No-Cut backyard playground kit sold at Home Depot. Swing-N-Slide also released a special edition of its Racing Roadster toddler swing in Home Depot orange. Home Depot donates 5 percent of the retail price of each Racing Roadster swing to KaBoom!.

■ Cause-related marketing: Home Depot links with KaBoom! to "create a great place to play within walking distance of every child in America." "Supporting KaBoom! helps Home Depot to build stronger relationships with customers by giving back to the communities its stores serve.

Such efforts "will help KaBoom! and Home Depot bring the gift of play to countless communities nationwide," says KaBoom!'s CEO. They will also help Home Depot to build closer relationships with consumers in the communities that its stores serve.[41]

Cause-related marketing has stirred some controversy. Critics worry that cause-related marketing is more a strategy for selling than a strategy for giving—that "cause-related" marketing is really "cause-exploitative" marketing. Thus, companies using cause-related marketing might find themselves walking a fine line between increased sales and an improved image, and facing charges of exploitation.

However, if handled well, cause-related marketing can greatly benefit both the company and the cause. The company gains an effective marketing tool while building a more positive public image. The charitable organization or cause gains greater visibility and important new sources of funding. Spending on cause-related marketing has skyrocketed from only $120 million in 1990 to more than 1.1 billion last year.[42]

Cultural Environment

The **cultural environment** is made up of institutions and other forces that affect a society's basic values, perceptions, preferences, and behaviors. People grow up in a particular society that shapes their basic beliefs and values. They absorb a worldview that defines their relationships with others. The following cultural characteristics can affect marketing decision making.

Persistence of Cultural Values

People in a given society hold many beliefs and values. Their core beliefs and values have a high degree of persistence. For example, most Americans believe in working, getting married, giving to charity, and being honest. These beliefs shape more specific attitudes and behaviors found in everyday life. *Core* beliefs and values are passed on from parents to children and are reinforced by schools, churches, businesses, and governments.

Secondary beliefs and values are more open to change. Believing in marriage is a core belief; believing that people should get married early in life is a secondary belief. Marketers have some chance of changing secondary values but little chance of changing core values. For example, family-planning marketers could argue more effectively that people should get married later in life than that they should not get married at all.

Shifts in Secondary Cultural Values

Although core values are fairly persistent, cultural swings do take place. Consider the impact of popular music groups, movie personalities, and other celebrities on young people's hairstyling and clothing norms. Marketers want to predict cultural shifts in order to spot new opportunities or threats. Several firms offer "futures" forecasts in this connection.

For example, the Yankelovich Monitor has tracked consumer value trends for years. At the dawn of the twenty-first century, it looked back to capture lessons from the past decade that might offer insight into the 2000s.[43] Yankelovich maintains that the "decade drivers" for the 2000s will primarily come from the baby boomers and Generation Xers. The baby boomers will be driven by four factors in the 2000s: "adventure" (fueled by a sense of youthfulness), "smarts" (fueled by a sense of empowerment and willingness to accept change), "intergenerational support" (caring for younger and older, often in nontraditional arrangements), and "retreading" (embracing early retirement with a second career or phase of their work life). Gen Xers will be driven by three factors: "redefining the good life" (being highly motivated to improve their economic well-being and remain in control), "new rituals" (returning to traditional values but with a tolerant mind-set and active lifestyle), and "cutting and pasting" (balancing work, play, sleep, family, and other aspects of their lives).

The major cultural values of a society are expressed in people's views of themselves and others, as well as in their views of organizations, society, nature, and the universe.

PEOPLE'S VIEWS OF THEMSELVES People vary in their emphasis on serving themselves versus serving others. Some people seek personal pleasure, wanting fun, change, and escape. Others seek self-realization through religion, recreation, or the avid pursuit of careers or other life goals. People use products, brands, and services as a means of self-expression, and they buy products and services that match their views of themselves.

The Yankelovich Monitor identifies several consumer segments whose purchases are motivated by self-views. Here are two examples:[44]

Cultural environment
Institutions and other forces that affect society's basic values, perceptions, preferences, and behaviors.

Do-It-Yourselfers—Recent Movers. Embodying the whole do-it-yourself attitude, these active consumers not only tackle home improvement projects on their own, but they also view the experience as a form of self-expression. They view their homes as their havens, especially when it's time to kick back and relax. Undertaking decorating, remodeling, and auto maintenance projects to save money and have fun, Do-It-Yourselfers view their projects as personal victories over the high-priced marketplace. Mostly Gen-X families with children at home, these consumers also enjoy playing board and card games and renting movies. As recent movers, they're actively spending to turn their new home into a castle.

Adventurers. These adventuresome individuals rarely follow a single path or do the same thing twice. These folks view the experience as far more exciting than the entertainment value. Although they may be appreciative of the arts (including movies, museums, photography, and music), they are more likely to engage in activities most think are too dangerous, and they like to view themselves doing things others wouldn't dare to do.

Marketers can target their products and services based on such self-views. For example, MasterCard targets Adventurers who might want to use their credits cards to quickly set up the experience of a lifetime. It tells these consumers, "There are some things in life that money can't buy. For everything else, there's MasterCard."

PEOPLE'S VIEWS OF OTHERS In past decades, observers have noted several shifts in people's attitudes toward others. Recently, for example, some trend trackers have seen a new wave of "cocooning," in which people are going out less with others and staying home more to enjoy the creature comforts of home and hearth.

Nearly half of major league baseball's 30 clubs are luring smaller crowds this year. Empty seats aren't just a baseball phenomenon. Rock concert attendance was off 12 percent. Entertainment promoters blame everything from unseasonable weather to high gas prices for the lousy attendance numbers. . . . But industry watchers also believe shifting consumer behavior is at work: Call it Cocooning in the Digital Age. With DVD players in most homes, broadband connections proliferating, scores of new video game titles being released each year, and nearly 400 cable channels, consumers can be endlessly entertained right in their own living room—or home theater. Add in the high costs and bother of going out, and more and more people are trading the bleachers for the couch.[45]

This trend suggests a greater demand for home improvement and entertainment products. "As the . . . 'nesting' or 'cocooning' trend continues, with people choosing to stay home and entertain more often, the trend of upgrading outdoor living spaces has [grown rapidly]," says a home industry analyst. People are adding bigger decks with fancy gas-ready barbeques, outdoor Jacuzzis, and other amenities that make the old house "home, sweet home" for family and friends.[46]

PEOPLE'S VIEWS OF ORGANIZATIONS People vary in their attitudes toward corporations, government agencies, trade unions, universities, and other organizations. By and large, people are willing to work for major organizations and expect them, in turn, to carry out society's work.

The late 1980s saw a sharp decrease in confidence in and loyalty toward America's business and political organizations and institutions. In the workplace, there has been an overall decline in organizational loyalty. During the 1990s, waves of company downsizings bred cynicism and distrust. And in this decade, corporate scandals at Enron, WorldCom, and Tyco; record-breaking profits for big oil companies during a time of all-time high prices at the pump; and other questionable activities have resulted in a further loss of confidence in big business. Many people today see work not as a source of satisfaction but as a required chore to earn money to enjoy their nonwork hours. This trend suggests that organizations need to find new ways to win consumer and employee confidence.

PEOPLE'S VIEWS OF SOCIETY People vary in their attitudes toward their society; patriots defend it, reformers want to change it, malcontents want to leave it. People's orientation to their society influences their consumption patterns and attitudes toward the marketplace. American patriotism has been increasing gradually for the past two decades. It surged, however, following the September 11th terrorist attacks and the Iraq war. For example, the summer following the start of the Iraq war saw a surge of pumped-up Americans visiting U.S. historic sites, ranging from the Washington, D.C. monuments, Mount Rushmore, the Gettysburg battlefield, and the *USS Constitution* ("Old Ironsides") to Pearl Harbor and the Alamo. Following these peak periods, patriotism in the United States still remains high. A recent global survey on "national pride" found that Americans ranked number one among the 34 democracies polled.[47]

Marketers respond with patriotic products and promotions, offering everything from floral bouquets to clothing with patriotic themes. Although most of these marketing efforts are tasteful and well received, waving the red, white, and blue can prove tricky. Except in cases where companies tie product sales to charitable contributions, such flag-waving promotions can be viewed as attempts to cash in on triumph or tragedy. Marketers must take care when responding to such strong national emotions.

PEOPLE'S VIEWS OF NATURE People vary in their attitudes toward the natural world. Some feel ruled by it, others feel in harmony with it, and still others seek to master it. A long-term trend has been people's growing mastery over nature through technology and the belief that nature is bountiful. More recently, however, people have recognized that nature is finite and fragile, that it can be destroyed or spoiled by human activities.

This renewed love of things natural has created a 63-million-person "lifestyles of health and sustainability" (LOHAS) market, consumers who seek out everything from natural, organic, and nutritional products to fuel-efficient cars and alternative medicine. In the words of one such consumer:[48]

I am not an early adopter, a fast follower, or a mass-market stampeder. But I am a gas-conscious driver. So that's why I was standing in a Toyota dealership . . . this week, the latest person to check out a hybrid car. Who needs $40 fill-ups? After tooling around in three different hybrid car brands—Toyota, Honda and a Ford—I thought: How cool could this be? Saving gas money and doing well by the environment. Turns out there's a whole trend-watchers' classification for people who think like that: LOHAS. Lifestyles of Health and Sustainability. Buy a hybrid. Shop at places like Whole Foods. Pick up the Seventh Generation paper towels at Albertsons. No skin off our noses. Conscientious shopping, with no sacrifice or hippie stigma.

Business has responded by offering more products and services catering to such interests. For example, food producers have found fast-growing markets for natural and organic foods. Consider Earthbound Farm, a company that grows and sells organic produce. It started in 1984 as a 2.5-acre raspberry farm in California's Carmel Valley. Founders Drew and Myra Goodman wanted to do the right thing by farming the land organically and producing food they'd feel good about serving to their family, friends, and neighbors. Today, Earthbound Farm has grown to become the world's largest producer of organic vegetables, with 30,000 acres under plow, annual sales of $278 million, and products available in 80 percent of America's supermarkets.

In total, the U.S. organic-food market will exceed $15.5 billion in sales this year, a 325 percent increase since 1997. Niche marketers, such as Whole Foods Market, have sprung up to serve this market, and traditional food chains such as Kroger and Safeway have added separate natural and organic food sections. Even pet owners are joining the movement as they

ORGANIC FOOD
IS MORE THAN OUR BUSINESS. IT'S OUR
PASSION.

More than 20 years ago, Earthbound Farm started as a backyard garden where we grew food we felt good about feeding our friends and family. And that meant farming organically. Today, Earthbound Farm's commitment to the health of those who enjoy our harvest is stronger than ever. We're proud that our work helps make the world a healthier place and makes it easier for you to choose delicious organic salads, fruits and vegetables every day.

Earthbound Farm • *Food to live by.* • www.ebfarm.com

Food to Live By: The Earthbound Farm Organic Cookbook is now available wherever books are sold. More than 250 delicious recipes from the farm that brings organic produce to millions of people every week.

© 2006 EARTHBOUND FARM

■ Riding the trend towards all things natural, Earthbound Farm has grown to become the world's largest producer of organic salads, fruits, and vegetables, with its product in 80 percent of America's supermarkets.

become more aware of what goes into Fido's food. Almost every major pet food brand now offers several types of natural foods.[49]

PEOPLE'S VIEWS OF THE UNIVERSE Finally, people vary in their beliefs about the origin of the universe and their place in it. Although most Americans practice religion, religious conviction and practice have been dropping off gradually through the years. Some futurists, however, have noted a renewed interest in spirituality, perhaps as a part of a broader search for a new inner purpose. People have been moving away from materialism and dog-eat-dog ambition to seek more permanent values—family, community, earth, faith—and a more certain grasp of right and wrong.

"Americans are on a spiritual journey, increasingly concerned with the meaning of life and issues of the soul and spirit," observes one expert. People say "they are increasingly looking to religion—Christianity, Judaism, Hinduism, Islam, and others—as a source of comfort in a chaotic world." This new spiritualism affects consumers in everything from the television shows they watch and the books they read to the products and services they buy. "Since consumers don't park their beliefs and values on the bench outside the marketplace," adds the expert, "they are bringing this awareness to the brands they buy. Tapping into this heightened sensitivity presents a unique marketing opportunity for brands."[50]

Responding to the Marketing Environment

Someone once observed, "There are three kinds of companies: those who make things happen, those who watch things happen, and those who wonder what's happened."[51] Many companies view the marketing environment as an uncontrollable element to which they must react and adapt. They passively accept the marketing environment and do not try to change it. They analyze the environmental forces and design strategies that will help the company avoid the threats and take advantage of the opportunities the environment provides.

Other companies take a *proactive* stance toward the marketing environment. Rather than simply watching and reacting, these firms take aggressive actions to affect the publics and forces in their marketing environment. Such companies hire lobbyists to influence legislation affecting their industries and stage media events to gain favorable press coverage. They run advertorials (ads expressing editorial points of view) to shape public opinion. They press lawsuits and file complaints with regulators to keep competitors in line, and they form contractual agreements to better control their distribution channels.

By taking action, companies can often overcome seemingly uncontrollable environmental events. For example, whereas some companies view the ceaseless online rumor mill as something over which they have no control, others work proactively to prevent or counter negative word of mouth.[52]

One e-mail recently circulating in Washington, D.C said that a former government lawyer knew a guy whose dog had to be put to sleep because he walked on a floor cleaned with Procter & Gamble's Swiffer Wetjet, licked his paws and developed liver disease. Although the claim was proved false by toxicologists, it has been neither quick nor easy for P&G to squelch the story. But P&G learned long ago that it was best to face a false rumor head-on. Years before, P&G endured a nasty rumor that the stars-and-moon trademark the company then displayed on its packaging was linked with Satanism. The rumor was disseminated through fliers and, much later, e-mails. At one point, fliers even claimed that P&G officials had appeared on TV talk shows confirming the rumor. Rather than letting the rumor lie, P&G reacted strongly by soliciting support from a range of religious leaders as well as from its employees, who worked to convince members of their own churches that the rumors were false. It publicized letters from the TV networks saying that no P&G executives had appeared on the TV shows. And once P&G identified people it said had spread the rumor—some of whom it says worked for competitors—it pressed charges to get them to confess and stop distributing the information. Some of them did confess, and litigation is still pending against others.

Marketing management cannot always control environmental forces. In many cases, it must settle for simply watching and reacting to the environment. For example, a company would have little success trying to influence geographic population shifts, the economic environment, or major cultural values. But whenever possible, smart marketing managers will take a *proactive* rather than *reactive* approach to the marketing environment.

Reviewing the Concepts

In this chapter and the next two chapters, you'll examine the environments of marketing and how companies analyze these environments to better understand the marketplace and consumers. Companies must constantly watch and manage the *marketing environment* in order to seek opportunities and ward off threats. The marketing environment consists of all the actors and forces influencing the company's ability to transact business effectively with its target market.

1. Describe the environmental forces that affect the company's ability to serve its customers.

The company's *microenvironment* consists of other actors close to the company that combine to form the company's value delivery network or that affect its ability to serve its customers. It includes the company's *internal environment*—its several departments and management levels—as it influences marketing decision making. *Marketing channel firms*—suppliers and marketing intermediaries, including resellers, physical distribution firms, marketing services agencies, and financial intermediaries—cooperate to create customer value. Five types of customer *markets* include consumer, business, reseller, government, and international markets. *Competitors* vie with the company in an effort to serve customers better. Finally, various *publics* have an actual or potential interest in or impact on the company's ability to meet its objectives.

The *macroenvironment* consists of larger societal forces that affect the entire microenvironment. The six forces making up the company's macroenvironment include demographic, economic, natural, technological, political, and cultural forces. These forces shape opportunities and pose threats to the company.

2. Explain how changes in the demographic and economic environments affect marketing decisions.

Demography is the study of the characteristics of human populations. Today's *demographic environment* shows a changing age structure, shifting family profiles, geographic population shifts, a better-educated and more white-collar population, and increasing diversity. The *economic environment* consists of factors that affect buying power and patterns. The economic environment is characterized by more con-

sumer concern for value and shifting consumer spending patterns. Today's squeezed consumers are seeking greater value—just the right combination of good quality and service at a fair price. The distribution of income also is shifting. The rich have grown richer, the middle class has shrunk, and the poor have remained poor, leading to a two-tiered market. Many companies now tailor their marketing offers to two different markets—the affluent and the less affluent.

3. Identify the major trends in the firm's natural and technological environments.

The *natural environment* shows three major trends: shortages of certain raw materials, higher pollution levels, and more government intervention in natural resource management. Environmental concerns create marketing opportunities for alert companies. The *technological environment* creates both opportunities and challenges. Companies that fail to keep up with technological change will miss out on new product and marketing opportunities.

4. Explain the key changes in the political and cultural environments.

The *political environment* consists of laws, agencies, and groups that influence or limit marketing actions. The political environment has undergone three changes that affect marketing worldwide: increasing legislation regulating business, strong government agency enforcement, and greater emphasis on ethics and socially responsible actions. The *cultural environment* is made up of institutions and forces that affect a society's values, perceptions, preferences, and behaviors. The environment shows trends toward digital "cocooning," a lessening trust of institutions, increasing patriotism, greater appreciation for nature, a new spiritualism, and the search for more meaningful and enduring values.

5. Discuss how companies can react to the marketing environment.

Companies can passively accept the marketing environment as an uncontrollable element to which they must adapt, avoiding threats and taking advantage of opportunities as they arise. Or they can take a *proactive* stance, working to change the environment rather than simply reacting to it. Whenever possible, companies should try to be proactive rather than reactive.

Reviewing the Key Terms

Discussing the Concepts

1. Assume you are a marketing manager for an automobile company. Your job is to reposition an SUV model that was once identified as a "fuel guzzler." The model now comes with a superefficient, nonpolluting hybrid engine. Which of the seven types of publics discussed in the chapter would have the greatest impact on your plans to the more fuel-efficient model?

2. What leading demographic factors must an Internet portal like AOL consider when marketing its products? Why is each factor so important to AOL?

3. Discuss the primary reasons why a company would hire a lobbyist in Washington D.C. Would it make sense for the same company to also hire lobbyists at the state level? Why?

4. Is it a certainty that a company will lose out on new opportunities if it does not keep up with new technology? Explain. Can you think of an industry segment where technology may not play an important role?

5. What can a mobile phones marketer do to take a more proactive approach to the changes in the marketing environment? Discuss specific forces, including macroenvironmental and microenvironmental forces.

6. Much of the U.S. culture is based on products from Hollywood, including movies and television shows. Choose a current top-rated television show and explain how it might affect the cultural environment.

Applying the Concepts

1. Go to Shonenjump.com and you will see a Web site devoted to Japanese Anime and Manga. In fact, these products are gaining in popularity in the U.S. market. What environmental forces are involved in the increased demand for this Japanese entertainment?

2. Most well-known cause-related marketing campaigns are launched by companies with substantial resources. In a small group, discuss how smaller companies with more limited resources can implement successful cause-related marketing efforts. How can such organizations help the charities with which they partner while successfully promoting their own products and services?

Focus on Technology

Television is hitting the small screen—the mobile phones that more than 80 percent of adults now carry. Networks are now producing "mobisodes," two-minute episodes produced exclusively for mobile phones. Services such as Verizon's Vcast let you watch TV or stream content for a monthly fee. Who will subscribe to this? Certainly the younger segment of the Generation Y demographic—the growing 57 percent of U.S. teens, ages 13 to 17 years, who now own mobile phones. Although this is below the percentage of all adults owning mobile phones, this group displays the most intense connectivity to their phones and the most interest in new features.

1. Explain why younger Gen Yers might be more likely to adapt new mobile phone technologies as compared to other demographic groups.

2. What other macroenvironmental and microenvironmental forces might affect the growth of mobile TV?

3. How can other marketers use mobile marketing to communicate with and promote to consumers?

Focus on Ethics

In February, 2005, R.J. Reynolds began a promotion that included direct-mail pieces to young adults on their birthdays. The campaign, entitled "Drinks on Us," included a birthday greeting as well as a set of drink coasters that included recipes for many drinks. The drink recipes, which were for mixed drinks of high alcohol content, included many distiller brands such as Jack Daniels, Southern Comfort, and Finlandia Vodka. With the recipe on one side of the coaster, the flip side included a tag line such as "Go 'til Daybreak, and Make Sure You're Sittin.'" Shortly after its release, the promotion came under attack from several attorney generals,

public advocacy groups, and the alcohol distillers themselves. The attorney generals and advocacy groups said the promotion endorsed heavy drinking. The distillers were angry because their brands were used without permission. In addition, the distillers argued that the promotion violates the alcohol industry advertising code, which prohibits marketing that encourages excessive drinking.

1. What prominent environmental forces come into play in this situation?

2. Is this promotion wrong? Should R.J. Reynolds stop the promotion?

Video Case

American Express

Understanding consumers and their needs can be a challenge. As the American population diversifies, and as consumers redefine their values and preferences, marketers work to provide relevant products and services that meet consumers' changing needs and wants. For American Express, keeping up with environmental shifts translates into creating new marketing offers. American Express issued its first charge card in 1958. Within five years, it had more than one million cards in use. Eight years later, the company introduced the American Express Gold Card.

The company now offers more than 20 consumer cards and 14 small-business cards, in addition to its customizable corporate cards. Some cards target very specific consumers. For example, the IN:CHICAGO, IN:NYC, and IN:LA cards offer cardholders special perks, including saving 10 percent at select retailers, spas, and nightclubs; skipping lines at some of these cities' hottest clubs; access to select VIP rooms; and saving on concert tickets. By targeting such specific consumers, American Express builds strong relationships with the right customers.

After viewing the video featuring American Express, answer the following questions about the marketing environment.

1. Visit the American Express Web site (www.americanexpress.com) to learn more about the different cards that American Express offers. Select three of the macroenvironmental forces discussed in the chapter. How do the different card options reflect the changes in those forces?

2. What sections of the Web site reflect American Express's efforts to deal with the various publics in its microenvironment?

3. Is American Express taking a proactive approach to managing its marketing environment? How?

Americans love their cars. In a country where SUVs sell briskly and the biggest sport is stockcar racing, you wouldn't expect a small, hybrid, sluggish vehicle to sell well. Despite such expectations, Honda successfully introduced the Insight in 1999 as a 2000 model. Toyota closely followed Honda's lead, bringing the 2001 Prius to market one year later. Introducing a fuel sipper in a market where vehicle size and horsepower reigned led one Toyota executive to profess, "Frankly, it was one of the biggest crapshoots I've ever been involved in." Considering these issues, it is nothing short of amazing that a mere five years later, the Prius is such a runaway success that Toyota Motor Sales U.S.A. President Jim Press has dubbed it "the hottest car we've ever had."

THE NUTS AND BOLTS OF THE PRIUS

Like other hybrids currently available or in development, the Prius (pronounced PREE-us, not PRY-us) combines a gas engine with an electric motor. Different hybrid vehicles employ this combination of power sources in different ways to boost both fuel efficiency and power. The Prius runs on only the electric motor when starting up and under initial acceleration. At roughly 15 mph, the gas engine kicks in. This means that the auto gets power from only the battery at low speeds, and from both the gas engine and electric motor during heavy acceleration. Once up to speed, the gas engine sends power directly to the wheels and, through the generator, to the electric motor or battery. When braking, energy from the slowing wheels—energy that is wasted in a conventional car—is sent back through the electric motor to charge the battery. At a stop, the gas engine shuts off, saving fuel. When starting up and operating at low speeds, the auto does not make noise, which seems eerie to some drivers and to pedestrians who don't hear it coming!

The original Prius was a small, cramped compact with a dull design. It had a total of 114 horsepower—70 from its four-cylinder gas engine and 44 from the electric motor. It went from 0 to 60 in a woeful 14.5 seconds. But it got 42 miles per gallon. Although the second-generation Prius, introduced as a 2004 model, benefited from a modest power increase, the car was still hardly a muscle car. But there were countless other improvements. The sleek, Asian-inspired design was much better looking than the first-generation Prius and came in seven colors. The interior was roomy and practical, with plenty of rear legroom and gobs of storage space.

The new Prius also provided expensive touches typically found only in luxury vehicles. A single push button brought the car to life. A seven-inch energy monitor touch screen displayed fuel consumption, outside temperature, and battery charge level. It also indicated when the car was running on gas, electricity, regenerated energy, or a combination of these. Multiple screens within the monitor also provided controls for air conditioning, audio, and a satellite navigation system. But perhaps the most important improvement was an increase in fuel efficiency to a claimed 60 miles per gallon in city driving.

A RUNAWAY SUCCESS

Apparently, consumers liked the improvements. In its inaugural year, the Prius saw moderate sales of just over 15,000

units—not bad considering Toyota put minimal promotional effort into the new vehicle. But for 2005, more than 107,000 Priuses were sold in the United States alone, making it Toyota's third-best-selling passenger car following the Camry and Corolla. Perhaps more significantly, Toyota announced that as of April, 2006, the Prius had achieved a major milestone, having sold over 500,000 units worldwide.

The rapid increase in demand for the Prius has created a rare automotive phenomenon. During a time period when most automotive companies have offered substantial incentives in order to move vehicles, many Toyota dealers have had no problem getting premiums of up to $5,000 over sticker price for the Prius. By June 2004, waiting lists for the Prius stretched to six months or more. At one point, spots on dealers' waiting lists were being auctioned on eBay for $500. By 2006, the Prius had become the "hottest" car in the United States, based on industry metrics of time spent on dealer lots, sales incentives, and average sale price relative to sticker price. In fact, demand for new Priuses is currently so strong, that Kelley Blue Book puts the price of a used 2005 Prius with 20,000 miles at $25,970, more than $4,500 higher than the original sticker price.

There are many reasons for the success of the Prius. For starters, Toyota's targeting strategy has been spot-on from the beginning. It focused first on early adopters, techies who were attracted by the car's advanced technology. Such buyers not only bought the car, but found ways to modify it by hacking into the Prius's computer system. Soon, owners were sharing their hacking secrets through chat rooms such as Priusenvy.com, boasting such modifications as using the dashboard display screen to play video games, show files from a laptop, watch TV, and look at images taken by a rearview camera. One savvy owner found a way to plug the Prius into a wall socket and boost fuel efficiency to as much as 100 miles per gallon.

By 2004, Toyota had skimmed off the market of techies and adopters. It knew that the second-generation Prius needed to appeal to a wider market. Toyota anticipated that environmentally conscious consumers as well as those desiring more fuel efficiency would be drawn to the vehicle. To launch the new Prius, Toyota spent more than $40 million spread over media in consumer-oriented magazines and TV. With the accuracy of a fortune teller, Toyota hit the nail right on the head. In the summer of 2004, gasoline prices began to rise—going to over $2 a gallon in some locations. By the summer of 2005, gas prices had skyrocketed to over $3 a gallon. As a result, buyers moved toward smaller SUVs, cars, and hybrids while sales of full-sized SUVs such as the Ford Expedition, Chevy Tahoe, and Hummer H2 fell significantly.

In addition to Toyota's effective targeting tactics, various external incentives have helped to spur Prius sales. For example, some states allow single-occupant hybrids in HOV (High Occupancy Vehicle) lanes. Some cities, including Albuquerque, Los Angeles, San Jose, and New Haven, provide free parking for hybrids. But the biggest incentives contribute real dollars toward the price of the Prius, making it more affordable. Currently, the federal government gives a tax break of up to $3,150. This tax break will expire under the current rules in 2007, but there are various other tax incentives for the Prius and other hybrid vehicles.

Some state governments are also getting in the game. West Virginia, New York, and various other states are offering tax breaks over and above any IRS kickbacks. The most generous is Colorado, giving a tax credit of up to $3,434. And if a chunk of money from these two sources isn't enough, employees of certain companies can cash in for even more. A select few companies are anteing up in order to do their bit for the environment. Eco-friendly Timberland contributes $3,000 as well as preferred parking spaces. Google and Hyperion Solutions, the California-based software company, each give employees a whopping $5,000 toward hybrids such as the Prius.

FUELING THE HYBRID CRAZE

Although Honda's Insight was the first to market in the United States, its sales have been miniscule compared to the Prius. Thus, after the 2006 model year, Honda will drop the Insight. And although Toyota's Japanese rival has had much better results with its Civic hybrid, its sales goal of 25,000 units for 2006 is less than one-fourth of the Prius's anticipated sales. The overall category of gas-electric vehicles in the United States appears to be hotter than ever, with unit sales up 140 percent from 2004 to 2005, to a total of 205,749 units. The Prius alone commands over 50 percent of the market and is largely responsible for category growth.

It appears that consumers like their green cars very green. Whereas sales of the ultra-high-mileage Prius and Civic have grown significantly each year since their introductions, less efficient (and more expensive) hybrid models such as the Honda Accord, Toyota Highlander, Ford Escape, and Mercury Mariner have had flat or even declining sales. Some analysts believe it is because consumers are doing the math and realizing that even with better fuel efficiency, they may not save money with a hybrid. In fact, a widely publicized report by Consumer Reports revealed that of six hybrid models studied, the Prius and the Civic were the only two to recover the price premium and save consumers money after five years and 75,000 miles.

However, although car makers are scaling back on some models, almost every automotive nameplate wants a piece of the growing pie. Ford blames the lack of success with the Escape and Mariner on a bogged promotional effort. With a lofty goal of producing 250,000 hybrids per year by 2010, it plans to put more money into campaigns for its existing models as well as introduce new models. General Motors also has big plans, beginning with the Saturn Vue Greenline, which will have the advantage of a low $2,000 price tag for the hybrid option. GM plans to extend the Saturn hybrid line to almost every vehicle in the lineup. It also plans to introduce hybrids in other divisions, including full-size trucks and SUVs. And while Subaru, Nissan, Hyundai, and Honda are all promoting upcoming hybrid models, Audi, BMW, and numerous others are busy developing hybrid vehicles of their own.

Even with all the activity from these automotive brands, Toyota is currently the clear leader in hybrid sales and will likely be for some time to come. 2006 Prius sales have actually dropped, but only because the company has dedicated production capacity to the 2006 Camry hybrid. The supply limitation has made demand for the Prius stronger than ever. In the past, Toyota Vice Chairman Fujio Cho had asserted that the company would not open a second plant for the production of hybrids, but he has quickly changed his tune. "[Given] the way American consumers have snapped up the [Prius]," he says, "I have been urging the company, almost as a matter of strategy, to produce [it] in the U.S." Given that Toyota plans to offer hybrid versions for all vehicle classes and quadruple worldwide hybrid sales to one million vehicles by 2012, it would seem that Mr. Cho's statement is conservative.

Questions for Discussion

1. What microenvironmental factors affected the introduction and relaunch of the Toyota Prius? How well has Toyota dealt with these factors?

2. Outline the major macroenvironmental factors—demographic, economic, natural, technological, political and cultural—that affected the introduction and relaunch of the Toyota Prius. How well has Toyota dealt with each of these factors?

3. Evaluate Toyota's marketing strategy so far. What has Toyota done well? How might it improve its strategy?

4. GM's marketing director for new ventures, Ken Stewart, says, "If you want to get a lot of hybrids on the road, you put them in vehicles that people are buying now." This tends to summarize the U.S. automakers' approach to hybrids. Would you agree with Mr. Stewart? Why or why not?

Sources: David Kushner, "How to Hack a Hybrid," Business 2.0 Magazine, July 13, 2006; "Toyota Prius Reaches Sales Milestone," Car and Driver, June 9, 2006, accessed online at www.caranddriver.com; Thane Peterson, "Harnessing Hybrid Tax Credits," Business Week, June 8, 2006, accessed at www.businessweek.com; Norihiko Shirouzu, "Toyota Seeks to Improve Prius and Plans to Produce Car in U.S.," Wall Street Journal, May 22, 2006, p. A2; Peter Valdes-Dapena, "Mad Market for Used Fuel Sippers," CNNMoney.com, May 18, 2006; John D. Stoll and Gina Chon, "Consumer Drive for Hybrid Autos Is Slowing Down," Wall Street Journal, April 7, 2006, p. A2; Matt Nauman, "Hybrid Sales Growth Slowing," San Jose Mercury News, April 14, 2006; "Toyota to Offer Hybrids for All Vehicle Classes by 2012," The Wall Street Journal, April 1, 2006, accessed at www.wsj.com; Peter Valdes-Dapena, "Toyota Tops Hottest Cars in America," CNNMoney.com, March 18, 2006; David Kiley and David Welch, "Invasion of the Hybrids," Business Week, January 10, 2006, accessed at www.businessweek.com; "Testing Toyota's Hybrid Car," GP, June 7, 2004; Gary S. Vasilash, "Is Toyota Prius the Most Important 2004 Model?" Motor Trend, November 11, 2003, accessed online at www. motortrend.com.

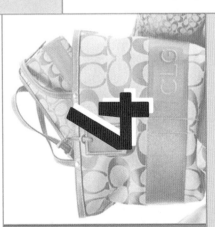

chapter

Managing Marketing Information

Previewing the Concepts

In the previous chapter, you learned about the complex and changing marketing environment. In this chapter, we'll continue our exploration of how marketers go about understanding the marketplace and consumers. We'll look at how companies develop and manage information about important marketplace elements—about customers, competitors, products, and marketing programs. We'll examine marketing information systems designed to give managers the right information, in the right form, at the right time to help them make better marketing decisions. We'll also take a close look at the marketing research process and at some special marketing research considerations. To succeed in today's marketplace, companies must know how to manage mountains of marketing information effectively.

We'll start the chapter with a story about Coach, a company long known for its classic, high-quality leather handbags and accessories. Until recently, Coach seemed to get along just fine in the mature and stable handbag industry without much consumer research. But when consumer needs and preferences shifted and sales slowed, all that changed. Read on to see how Coach used exhaustive marketing research to give itself an extreme strategic makeover.

Coach first opened its doors in 1941 as a family-owned, leather-goods workshop. Over the next 50 years, the company developed a strong following for its classically styled, high-quality leather handbags and accessories.

In those early years, it seemed, Coach didn't need a lot of marketing research to understand its customers. For most buyers, handbags were largely functional, used for carrying keys, a wallet, and cosmetics. Women typically bought only two purses a year—one for everyday use and one for special occasions. The everyday handbag lasted a long time and styles changed infrequently. Women didn't waste much time or energy on their purse-buying decisions.

Coach offered basic Coach handbag designs in understated colors, black and brown. The classic Coach bag's only ornamentation was a small gold latch and a small leather tag embossed with the Coach name. Over the years, with their understated styling and quality image, Coach handbags earned a reputation as classy but "traditional sturdy standbys." Conservative professionals, who liked the look, quality, and value of Coach's handbags, became the company's loyal core customers. Coach, by then a unit of Sara Lee Corporation, cruised along comfortably.

By the mid-1990s, however, Coach's world had changed dramatically and sales started to slow. As more and more women entered the workforce, they needed different types of bags to carry their work and their laptops. These increasingly influential women fueled the "mass luxury movement." They wanted the designer brands that only affluent women had been able to afford. And they wanted more stylish and colorful bags to spruce up the plain fashions of the day.

High-end designers such as Prada, Fendi, Gucci, and Chanel were responding to these trends. According to one analyst, the industry saw "a sharp uptick in demand for handbags with extra flair, such as bright colors, exotic leathers, and even materials such as wool, velvet, and fur." Many of these designer bags sold for more than $1,000, some for as much as $3,000. By comparison, Coach's traditional styles began to look downright plain.

It was time for an extreme makeover. But where to start? To gain a better understanding of the new handbag buyer, Coach began with marketing research—lots of marketing research. "Coach started thinking like a consumer-products company," says the analyst, "relentlessly testing the market to see what holes it could fill."

Based on extensive marketing research, Coach overhauled its strategy. In the process, it helped engineer a shift in the way women shop for handbags.

[Coach] decided to translate the elite notion of the handbag as a fashion statement into something the average American woman could afford, [dubbing] the strategy "accessible luxury." Coach [now] creates and markets new kinds of bags to fill what it calls "usage voids," activities that range from weekend getaways to dancing at nightclubs to trips to the grocery store. . . . Known for decades as a sturdy purveyor of conservative, long-lasting handbags, it has [now] successfully convinced women to buy weekend bags, evening bags, backpacks, satchels, clutches, totes, briefcases, diaper bags, coin purses, duffels, and a minihandbag that doubles as a bag-within-a-bag . . . [Coach now] updates its collections nearly every month with new colors, fabrics, and sizes. It prices bags lower than luxury designers but high enough for women to buy as a special treat.

As a starter, consumer research revealed that even Coach's conservative customers wanted more fashion pizzazz in their handbags. So, in early 2001, the company launched the "Signature" collection, stylish and colorful bags made of leather and fabric and covered in the letter C. Coach designers even began to use adjectives such as *sexy, fun, sophisticated, playful, grounded, luxurious,* and *quality driven* to describe Coach's customers and the company itself.

About that same time, research revealed another "usage void." Women were carrying small Coach cosmetic cases inside their larger handbags to hold essentials—such as keys, credit cards, and even cell phones—making them easier to find. However, when crammed into larger bags, these smaller cases caused bulges, making the larger bags appear misshapen and bulky. To fill the void, Coach designed a four-inch by six-inch zippered bag with a looped strap, which a woman could either dangle from her wrist or clip inside a larger bag. Coach called the new product the "wristlet" and introduced it at prices as low as $38. In only the first 10 months, women snapped up more than 100,000 wristlets. By 2004, Coach was selling more than a million wristlets a year in 75 styles.

Still more research revealed additional usage voids. For example, Coach's consumer researchers learned that women were increasingly interested in nonleather bags. They also faced the problem that customers did most of their handbag shopping only during the holiday season. To fill both voids, the company developed its

Objectives

After reading this chapter, you should be able to

1. explain the importance of information to the company and its understanding of the marketplace

2. define the marketing information system and discuss its parts

3. outline the steps in the marketing research process

4. explain how companies analyze and distribute marketing information

5. discuss the special issues some marketing researchers face, including public policy and ethics issues

"Hamptons Weekend" line, stylish fabric bags designed for summer weekend use. Unlike competitors' uninspired black nylon or basic canvas bags, the new Coach line featured an easily foldable shape, hot colors, and a durable, water-resistant material befitting a "relaxed-but-sophisticated" lifestyle. The new bags flew off the shelves at Coach's retail stores.

Now, Coach thinks that its research points to yet another market void. Researchers noticed that more women are now mixing formal clothing, stilettos, and diamonds with blue jeans and other casual clothes. This suggests an opportunity to get women to use formal accessories—including evening bags—during daylight hours. So Coach has introduced the "Madison" collection, sleek satin or bejeweled versions of its more traditional purses. Ads for the line show a casually dressed woman carrying a Madison bag in daylight, while also carrying a larger, casual tote bag. Coach also plans to offer a line of jewelry and is looking to add fragrances.

Thus, Coach watches its customers closely, looking for trends that might suggest new market voids to fill. Last year alone, Coach spent $3 million on marketing research, interviewing 14,000 women about everything from lifestyles to purse styles to strap lengths. According to a Coach executive, everything Coach does is thoroughly "girlfriend tested, down to the last stitch."

Such exhaustive marketing research has more than paid for itself. The company's sales, profits, and share prices are now soaring. Coach has achieved double-digit sales and earnings growth every period since spinning off from Sara Lee and going public in 2000. Over the past five years, sales are up over 177 percent and profits have increased sixfold. It looks like investors are going to need bigger purses.[1]

In order to produce superior customer value and satisfaction, companies need information at almost every turn. As the Coach story highlights, good products and marketing programs begin with solid information on consumer needs and wants. Companies also need an abundance of information on competitors, resellers, and other actors and forces in the marketplace.

With the recent explosion of information technologies, companies can now generate information in great quantities. For example, Wal-Mart maintains a huge database that can provide deep insights for marketing decisions. A few years ago, as Hurricane Ivan roared toward the Florida coast, reports one observer, the giant retailer "knew exactly what to rush onto the shelves of stores in the hurricane's path—strawberry Pop Tarts. By analyzing years of sales data from just prior to other hurricanes, [Wal-Mart] figured out that shoppers would stock up on Pop Tarts—which don't require refrigeration or cooking."[2]

In fact, today's managers often receive too much information. For example, Wal-Mart refreshes sales data from check-out scanners hourly, adding a billion rows of data a day, equivalent to about 96,000 DVD movies. That's a *lot* of data to analyze. Thus, running out of information is not a problem, but seeing through the "data smog" is. "In this oh-so-overwhelming Information Age," comments one observer, "it's all too easy to be buried, burdened, and burned out by data overload."[3]

Despite this data glut, marketers frequently complain that they lack enough information of the right kind. They don't need *more* information, they need *better* information. And they need to make better *use* of the information they already have. A former CEO at Unilever once said that if Unilever only knew what it knows, it would double its profits.[4] The meaning is clear: Many companies sit on rich information but fail

■ Information overload: "In this oh-so-overwhelming information age, it's all too easy to be buried, burdened, and burned out by data overload."

to manage and use it well. Companies must design effective marketing information systems that give managers the right information, in the right form, at the right time to help them make better marketing decisions.

Marketing information system (MIS)
People, equipment, and procedures to gather, sort, analyze, evaluate, and distribute needed, timely, and accurate information to marketing decision makers.

A **marketing information system (MIS)** consists of people, equipment, and procedures to gather, sort, analyze, evaluate, and distribute needed, timely, and accurate information to marketing decision makers. Figure 4.1 shows that the MIS begins and ends with information users—marketing managers, internal and external partners, and others who need marketing information. First, it interacts with these information users to *assess information needs*. Next, it *develops needed information* from internal company databases, marketing intelligence activities, and marketing research. Then it helps users to analyze information to put it in the right form for making marketing decisions and managing customer relationships. Finally, the MIS *distributes* the marketing information and helps managers *use* it in their decision making.

Assessing Marketing Information Needs

The marketing information system primarily serves the company's marketing and other managers. However, it may also provide information to external partners, such as suppliers, resellers, or marketing services agencies. For example, Wal-Mart gives key suppliers access to information on customer buying patterns and inventory levels. And Dell creates tailored Premium Pages for large customers, giving them access to product design, order status, and product support and service information. In designing an information system, the company must consider the needs of all of these users.

A good marketing information system balances the information users would *like* to have against what they really *need* and what is *feasible* to offer. The company begins by interviewing managers to find out what information they would like. Some managers will ask for whatever information they can get without thinking carefully about what they really need. Too much information can be as harmful as too little. Other managers may omit things they ought to know, or they may not know to ask for some types of information they should have. For example, managers might need to know about a new product that a competitor plans to introduce during the coming year. Because they do not know about the new product, they do not think to ask about it. The MIS must monitor the marketing environment in order to provide decision makers with information they should have to make key marketing decisions.

FIGURE 4.1
The marketing information system

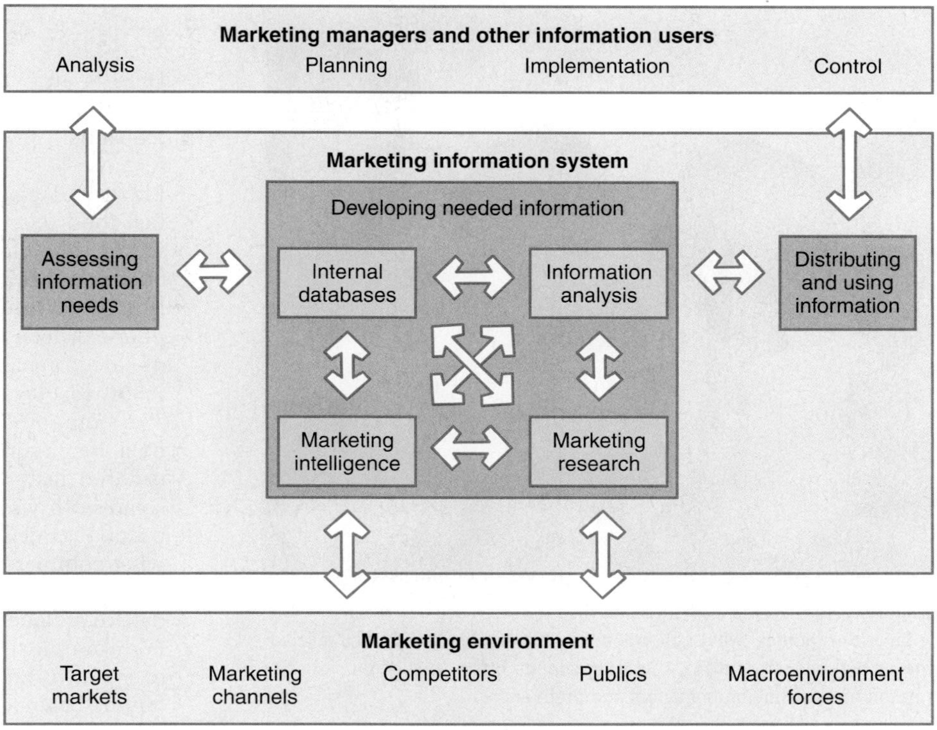
Marketing managers and other information users
Analysis
Planning
Implementation
Control
Marketing information system
Developing needed information
Assessing information needs
Internal databases
Information analysis
Distributing and using information
Marketing intelligence
Marketing research
Marketing environment
Target markets
Marketing channels
Competitors
Publics
Macroenvironment forces

Sometimes the company cannot provide the needed information, either because it is not available or because of MIS limitations. For example, a brand manager might want to know how competitors will change their advertising budgets next year and how these changes will affect industry market shares. The information on planned budgets probably is not available. Even if it is, the company's MIS may not be advanced enough to forecast resulting changes in market shares.

Finally, the costs of obtaining, processing, storing, and delivering information can mount quickly. The company must decide whether the benefits of having additional information are worth the costs of providing it, and both value and cost are often hard to assess. By itself, information has no worth; its value comes from its *use*. In many cases, additional information will do little to change or improve a manager's decision, or the costs of the information may exceed the returns from the improved decision. Marketers should not assume that additional information will always be worth obtaining. Rather, they should weigh carefully the costs of getting more information against the benefits resulting from it.

Developing Marketing Information

Marketers can obtain the needed information from *internal data*, *marketing intelligence*, and *marketing research*.

Internal Data

Internal databases

Electronic collections of consumer and market information obtained from data sources within the company network.

Many companies build extensive **internal databases,** electronic collections of consumer and market information obtained from data sources within the company network. Marketing managers can readily access and work with information in the database to identify marketing opportunities and problems, plan programs, and evaluate performance.

Information in the database can come from many sources. The accounting department prepares financial statements and keeps detailed records of sales, costs, and cash flows. Operations reports on production schedules, shipments, and inventories. The marketing department furnishes information on customer transactions, demographics, psychographics, and buying behavior. The customer service department keeps records of customer satisfaction or service problems. The sales force reports on reseller reactions and competitor activities, and marketing channel partners provide data on point-of-sale transactions. Harnessing such information can provide a powerful competitive advantage.

Here is an example of how one company uses its internal database to make better marketing decisions:

Pizza Hut claims to have the largest fast-food customer database in the world. The database contains detailed customer information data on 40 million U.S. households, gleaned from phone orders, online orders, and point-of-sale transactions at its more than 7,500 restaurants around the nation. The company can slice and dice the data by favorite toppings, what you ordered last, and whether you buy a salad with your cheese and pepperoni pizza. Pizza Hut also tracks in real time what commercials people are watching and responding to. It then uses all this data to enhance customer relationships. For example, it can target coupon offers to specific households based on past buying behaviors and preferences.[5]

■ Internal databases: Pizza Hut can slice and dice its extensive customer database by favorite toppings, what you ordered last, and whether you buy a salad with your cheese and pepperoni pizza, targeting coupon offers to specific households based on past buying behaviors and preferences.

Internal databases usually can be accessed more quickly and cheaply than other information sources, but they also present some problems. Because internal information was often collected for other purposes, it may be incomplete or in the wrong form for making marketing decisions. For example, sales and cost data used by the accounting department for preparing financial statements must be adapted for use in evaluating the value of specific customer segment, sales force, or channel performance. Data also ages quickly: Keeping the database current requires a major effort. In addition, a large company produces mountains of information, which must be well integrated and readily accessible so that managers can find it easily and use it effectively. Managing that much data requires highly sophisticated equipment and techniques.

Marketing Intelligence

Marketing intelligence is the systematic collection and analysis of publicly available information about competitors and developments in the marketplace. The goal of marketing intelligence is to improve strategic decision making, assess and track competitors' actions, and provide early warning of opportunities and threats.

Competitive intelligence gathering has grown dramatically as more and more companies are now busily snooping on their competitors. Techniques range from quizzing the company's own employees and benchmarking competitors' products to researching the Internet, lurking around industry trade shows, and even rooting through rivals' trash bins.

Much intelligence can be collected from people inside the company—executives, engineers and scientists, purchasing agents, and the sales force. The company can also obtain important intelligence information from suppliers, resellers, and key customers. Or it can get good information by observing competitors and monitoring their published information. It can buy and analyze competitors' products, monitor their sales, check for new patents, and examine various types of physical evidence. For example, one company regularly checks out competitors' parking lots—full lots might indicate plenty of work and prosperity; half-full lots might suggest hard times.

Some companies have even rifled their competitors' garbage, which is legally considered abandoned property once it leaves the premises. In one elaborate garbage-snatching incident, AirCanada was recently caught rifling through rival WestJet's dumpsters in efforts to find evidence that WestJet was illegally tapping into Air Canada's computers.[6] In another case, Procter & Gamble admitted to "dumpster diving" at rival Unilever's headquarters. "P&G got its mitts on just about every iota of info there was to be had about Unilever's [hair-care] brands," notes an analyst. However, when news of the questionable tactics reached top P&G managers, they were shocked. They immediately stopped the project and voluntarily set up negotiations with Unilever to right whatever competitive wrongs had been done. Although P&G claims it broke no laws, the company reported that the dumpster raids "violated our strict guidelines regarding our business policies."[7]

Competitors often reveal intelligence information through their annual reports, business publications, trade show exhibits, press releases, advertisements, and Web pages. The Internet is proving to be a vast new source of competitor-supplied information. Using Internet search engines, marketers can search specific competitor names, events, or trends and see what turns up. Moreover, most companies now place volumes of information on their Web sites, providing details to attract customers, partners,

■ Marketing Intelligence: Procter & Gamble admitted to "dumpster diving" at rival Unilever's Helene Curtis headquarters. When P&G's top management learned of the questionable practice, it stopped the project, voluntarily informed Unilever, and set up talks to right whatever competitive wrongs had been done.

Marketing intelligence
The systematic collection and analysis of publicly available information about competitors and developments in the marketing environment.

suppliers, investors, or franchisees. This can provide a wealth of useful information about competitors' strategies, markets, new products, facilities, and other happenings.

Something as simple as a competitor's job postings can be very revealing. For example, a few years back, while poking around on Google's company Web site, Microsoft's Bill Gates came across a help-wanted page describing all of the jobs available at Google. To his surprise, he noted that Google was looking for engineers with backgrounds that had nothing to do with its Web-search business but everything to do with Microsoft's core software businesses. Forewarned that Google might be preparing to become more than just a search engine company, Gates emailed a handful of Microsoft executives, saying, in effect, "We have to watch these guys. It looks like they are building something to compete with us." Notes a marketing intelligence consultant, companies "are often surprised that there's so much out there to know. They're busy with their day-to-day operations and they don't realize how much information can be obtained with a few strategic keystrokes."[8]

Intelligence seekers can also pore through any of thousands of online databases. Some are free. For example, the U.S. Security and Exchange Commission's database provides a huge stockpile of financial information on public competitors, and the U.S. Patent Office and Trademark database reveals patents competitors have filed. And for a fee, companies can subscribe to any of the more than 3,000 online databases and information search services such as Dialog, Hoover's, DataStar, LexisNexis, Dow Jones News Retrieval, ProQuest, and Dun & Bradstreet's Online Access.

The intelligence game goes both ways. Facing determined marketing intelligence efforts by competitors, most companies are now taking steps to protect their own information. For example, Unilever conducts widespread competitive intelligence training. Employees are taught not just how to collect intelligence information but also how to protect company information from competitors. According to a former Unilever staffer, "We were even warned that spies from competitors could be posing as drivers at the minicab company we used." Unilever even performs random checks on internal security. Says the former staffer, "At one [internal marketing] conference, we were set up when an actor was employed to infiltrate the group. The idea was to see who spoke to him, how much they told him, and how long it took to realize that no one knew him. He ended up being there for a long time."[9]

The growing use of marketing intelligence raises a number of ethical issues. Although most of the preceding techniques are legal, and some are considered to be shrewdly competitive, some may involve questionable ethics. Clearly, companies should take advantage of publicly available information. However, they should not stoop to snoop. With all the legitimate intelligence sources now available, a company does not need to break the law or accepted codes of ethics to get good intelligence.

Marketing Research

In addition to information about competitor and marketplace happenings, marketers often need formal studies of specific situations. For example, Budweiser wants to know what appeals will be most effective in its Super Bowl advertising. Or Samsung wants to know how many and what kinds of people will buy its next-generation plasma televisions. In such situations, marketing intelligence will not provide the detailed information needed. Managers will need marketing research.

Marketing research is the systematic design, collection, analysis, and reporting of data relevant to a specific marketing situation facing an organization. Companies use marketing research in a wide variety of situations. For example, marketing research can help marketers understand customer satisfaction and purchase behavior. It can help them to assess market potential and market share or to measure the effectiveness of pricing, product, distribution, and promotion activities.

Some large companies have their own research departments that work with marketing managers on marketing research projects. This is how Procter & Gamble, Kraft, Citigroup, and many other corporate giants handle marketing research. In addition, these companies—like their smaller counterparts—frequently hire outside research specialists to consult with management on specific marketing problems and conduct marketing research studies. Sometimes firms simply purchase data collected by outside firms to aid in their decision making.

The marketing research process has four steps (see Figure 4.2): defining the problem and research objectives, developing the research plan, implementing the research plan, and interpreting and reporting the findings.

Marketing research

The systematic design, collection, analysis, and reporting of data relevant to a specific marketing situation facing an organization.

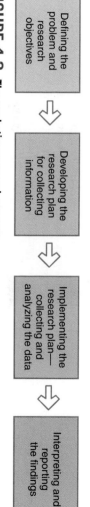

| Defining the problem and research objectives | ⇨ | Developing the research plan for collecting information | ⇨ | Implementing the research plan—collecting and analyzing the data | ⇨ | Interpreting and reporting the findings |

FIGURE 4.2 The marketing research process

Defining the Problem and Research Objectives

Marketing managers and researchers must work closely together to define the problem and agree on research objectives. The manager best understands the decision for which information is needed; the researcher best understands marketing research and how to obtain the information. Defining the problem and research objectives is often the hardest step in the research process. The manager may know that something is wrong, without knowing the specific causes.

After the problem has been defined carefully, the manager and researcher must set the **research objectives**. A marketing research project might have one of three types of objectives. The objective of **exploratory research** is to gather preliminary information that will help define the problem and suggest hypotheses. The objective of **descriptive research** is to describe things, such as the market potential for a product or the demographics and attitudes of consumers who buy the product. The objective of **causal research** is to test hypotheses about cause-and-effect relationships. For example, would a 10 percent decrease in tuition at a private college result in an enrollment increase sufficient to offset the reduced tuition? Managers often start with exploratory research and later follow with descriptive or causal research.

The statement of the problem and research objectives guides the entire research process. The manager and researcher should put the statement in writing to be certain that they agree on the purpose and expected results of the research.

Developing the Research Plan

Once the research problems and objectives have been defined, researchers must determine the exact information needed, develop a plan for gathering it efficiently, and present the plan to management. The research plan outlines sources of existing data and spells out the specific research approaches, contact methods, sampling plans, and instruments that researchers will use to gather new data.

Research objectives must be translated into specific information needs. For example, suppose Campbell Soup Company decides to conduct research on how consumers would react to the introduction of new heat-and-go microwavable cups for its Campbell's SpaghettiOs. Such packaging has been successful for Campbell's soups—including its Soup at Hand line of hand-held, shippable soups and its Chunky and Select soup line in microwavable bowls, dubbed "M'm! M'm! Good! To Go!" The containers would cost more but would allow consumers to heat their SpaghettiOs in a microwave oven and to eat them without using dishes. This research might call for the following specific information:

- The demographic, economic, and lifestyle characteristics of current SpaghettiOs users. (Busy working couples might find the convenience of the new packaging worth the price; families with children might want to pay less and wash the bowls.)

- Consumer-usage patterns for SpaghettiOs and related products: how much they eat, where, and when. (The new packaging might be ideal for adults eating lunch on the go, but less convenient for parents feeding lunch to several children.)

- Retailer reactions to the new packaging. (Failure to get retailer support could hurt sales of the new package.)

- Forecasts of sales of both new and current packages. (Will the new packaging create new sales or simply take sales from the current packaging? Will the package increase Campbell's profits?)

Campbell managers will need these and many other types of information to decide whether to introduce the new packaging.

The research plan should be presented in a *written proposal*. A written proposal is especially important when the research project is large and complex or when an outside firm carries it out. The proposal should cover the management problems addressed and the research objectives, the information to be obtained, and the way the results will help management decision making. The proposal also should include research costs.

Exploratory research

Marketing research to gather preliminary information that will help define problems and suggest hypotheses.

Descriptive research

Marketing research to better describe marketing problems, situations, or markets, such as the market potential for a product or the demographics and attitudes of consumers.

Causal research

Marketing research to test hypotheses about cause-and-effect relationships.

Secondary data
Information that already exists somewhere, having been collected for another purpose.

Primary data
Information collected for the specific purpose at hand.

To meet the manager's information needs, the research plan can call for gathering secondary data, primary data, or both. **Secondary data** consist of information that already exists somewhere, having been collected for another purpose. **Primary data** consist of information collected for the specific purpose at hand.

Gathering Secondary Data

Researchers usually start by gathering secondary data. The company's internal database provides a good starting point. However, the company can also tap a wide assortment of external information sources, including commercial data services and government sources (see Table 4.1).

Companies can buy secondary data reports from outside suppliers. For example, ACNielsen sells buyer data from a panel of 125,000 households in two dozen countries, with measures of trial and repeat purchasing, brand loyalty, and buyer demographics. Simmons sells information on more than 8,000 brands in 460 product categories, including detailed consumer profiles that assess everything from the products consumers buy and the brands they prefer, to

TABLE 4.1   Selected External Information Sources

For business data:

ACNielsen Corporation (www.acnielsen.com) provides supermarket scanner data on sales, market share, and retail prices; data on household purchasing; and data on television audiences (a unit of VNU NV).

Information Resources, Inc. (www.infores.com) provides supermarket scanner data for tracking grocery product movement and new product purchasing data.

Arbitron (www.arbitron.com) provides local-market and Internet radio audience and advertising expenditure information, among other media and ad spending data.

J.D. Power and Associates (www.jdpower.com) provides information from independent consumer surveys of product and service quality, customer satisfaction, and buyer behavior.

IMS Health (www.imshealth.com) tracks drug sales, monitors performance of pharmaceutical sales representatives, and offers pharmaceutical market forecasts.

Simmons Market Research Bureau (www.smrb.com) provides detailed analysis of consumer patterns in 400 product categories in selected markets.

Dun & Bradstreet (www.dnb.com) maintains a database containing information on more than 50 million individual companies around the globe.

comScore Networks (www.comscore.com) provides consumer behavior information and geodemographic analysis of Internet and digital media users around the world.

Thomson Dialog (www.dialog.com) offers access to more than 900 databases containing publications, reports, newsletters, and directories covering dozens of industries.

LexisNexis (www.lexisnexis.com) features articles from business, consumer, and marketing publications plus tracking of firms, industries, trends, and promotion techniques.

Factiva (www.factiva.com) specializes in in-depth financial, historical, and operational information on public and private companies.

Hoover's, Inc. (www.hoovers.com) provides business descriptions, financial overviews, and news about major companies around the world.

CNN (www.cnn.com) reports U.S. and global news and covers the markets and news-making companies in detail.

American Demographics (www.demographics.com) reports on demographic trends and their significance for businesses.

For government data:

Securities and Exchange Commission Edgar database (www.sec.gov) provides financial data on U.S. public corporations.

Small Business Administration (www.sba.gov) features information and links for small business owners.

Federal Trade Commission (www.ftc.gov) shows regulations and decisions related to consumer protection and antitrust laws.

Stat-USA (www.stat-usa.gov), a Department of Commerce site, highlights statistics on U.S. business and international trade.

U.S. Census (www.census.gov) provides detailed statistics and trends about the U.S. population.

U.S. Patent and Trademark Office (www.uspto.gov) allows searches to determine who has filed for trademarks and patents.

For Internet data:

ClickZ Stats/CyberAtlas (www.clickz.com/stats) brings together a wealth of information about the Internet and its users, from consumers to e-commerce.

Interactive Advertising Bureau (www.iab.net) covers statistics about advertising on the Internet.

Jupiter Research (www.jupiterresearch.com) monitors Web traffic and ranks the most popular sites.

their lifestyles, attitudes, and media preferences. The *Monitor* service by Yankelovich sells information on important social and lifestyle trends. These and other firms supply high-quality data to suit a wide variety of marketing information needs.[10]

Using commercial **online databases**, marketing researchers can conduct their own searches of secondary data sources. General database services such as Dialog, ProQuest, and LexisNexis put an incredible wealth of information at the keyboards of marketing decision makers. Beyond commercial Web sites offering information for a fee, almost every industry association, government agency, business publication, and news medium offers free information to those tenacious enough to find their Web sites. There are so many Web sites offering data that finding the right ones can become an almost overwhelming task.

Secondary data can usually be obtained more quickly and at a lower cost than primary data. Also, secondary sources can sometimes provide data an individual company cannot collect on its own—information that either is not directly available or would be too expensive to collect. For example, it would be too expensive for Campbell to conduct a continuing retail store audit to find out about the market shares, prices, and displays of competitors' brands. But it can buy the InfoScan service from Information Resources, Inc., which provides this information based on scanner and other data from 34,000 supermarkets in markets around the nation.

Secondary data can also present problems. The needed information may not exist—researchers can rarely obtain all the data they need from secondary sources. For example, Campbell will not find existing information about consumer reactions to new packaging that it has not yet placed on the market. Even when data can be found, they might not be very usable. The researcher must evaluate secondary information carefully to make certain it is *relevant* (fits research project needs), *accurate* (reliably collected and reported), *current* (up-to-date enough for current decisions), and *impartial* (objectively collected and reported).

Primary Data Collection

Secondary data provide a good starting point for research and often help to define research problems and objectives. In most cases, however, the company must also collect primary data. Just as researchers must carefully evaluate the quality of secondary information, they also must take great care when collecting primary data. They need to make sure that it will be relevant, accurate, current, and unbiased. Table 4.2 shows that designing a plan for primary data collection calls for a number of decisions on *research approaches, contact methods, sampling plan,* and *research instruments.*

Research Approaches

Research approaches for gathering primary data include observation, surveys, and experiments. Here, we discuss each one in turn.

Online databases
Computerized collections of information available from online commercial sources or via the Internet.

■ Commercial database services such as Simmons sell an incredible wealth of information on everything from the products consumers buy and the brands they prefer to their lifestyles, attitudes, and media preferences. Simmons is "the voice of the American consumer."

TABLE 4.2 Planning Primary Data Collection

Research Approaches	Contact Methods	Sampling Plan	Research Instruments
Observation	Mail	Sampling unit	Questionnaire
Survey	Telephone	Sample size	Mechanical instruments
Experiment	Personal	Sampling procedure	
	Online		

Observational research

The gathering of primary data by observing relevant people, actions, and situations.

Ethnographic research

A form of observational research that involves sending trained observers to watch and interact with consumers in their "natural habitat."

Observational research involves gathering primary data by observing relevant people, actions, and situations. For example, a bank might evaluate possible new branch locations by checking traffic patterns, neighborhood conditions, and the location of competing branches.

Researchers often observe consumer behavior to glean insights they can't obtain by simply asking customers questions. For instance, Fisher-Price has set up an observation lab in which it can observe the reactions of little tots to new toys. The Fisher-Price Play Lab is a sunny, toy-strewn space where lucky kids get to test Fisher-Price prototypes, under the watchful eyes of designers who hope to learn what will get kids worked up into a new-toy frenzy. And Kimberly-Clark invented a new way to observe behavior through the eyes of consumers:[11]

A few years back, Kimberly-Clark saw sales of its Huggies baby wipes slip just as the company was preparing to launch a line of Huggies baby lotions and bath products. When traditional research didn't yield any compelling insights, K-C's marketers decided they could get more useful feedback just from watching customers' daily lives. They came up with camera-equipped "glasses" to be worn by consumers at home, so that researchers could see what they saw. It didn't take long to spot the problems—and the opportunities. Although women in focus groups talked about changing babies at a diaper table, the truth was they changed them on beds, floors, and on top of washing machines in awkward positions. The researchers could see they were struggling with wipe containers and lotions requiring two hands. So the company redesigned the wipe package with a push-button one-handed dispenser and designed lotion and shampoo bottles that can be grabbed and dispensed easily with one hand.

Observational research can obtain information that people are unwilling or unable to provide. In some cases, observation may be the only way to obtain the needed information. In contrast, some things simply cannot be observed, such as feelings, attitudes and motives, or private behavior. Long-term or infrequent behavior is also difficult to observe. Because of these limitations, researchers often use observation along with other data collection methods.

A wide range of companies now use **ethnographic research.** Ethnographic research involves sending trained observers to watch and interact with consumers in their "natural habitat." Consider this example:[12]

Marriott hired design firm IDEO to help it take a fresh look at business travel and to rethink the hotel experience for an increasingly important customer: the young, tech-savvy road warrior. Rather than doing the usual customer surveys or focus group research, IDEO dispatched a team of consultants, including a designer, anthropologist, writer, and architect, on a six-week trip to mingle with customers and get an up-close and personal view of them. Covering 12 cities, the group hung out in hotel lobbies, cafes, and bars and asked guests to graph what they were doing hour by hour.

By "living with the natives," they learned that hotels are not generally good at serving small groups of business travelers. Hotel lobbies tend to be dark and better suited

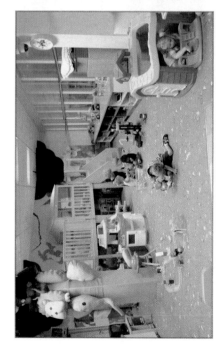

■ Observational research: Fisher-Price set up an observation lab in which it could observe the reactions of little tots to new toys.

to killing time than conducting casual business. Marriott lacked places where guests could comfortably combine work with pleasure outside their rooms. One IDEO consultant recalls watching a female business traveler drinking wine in the lobby while trying not to spill it on papers spread out on a desk. "There are very few hotel services that address [such] problems," he says. The result: Marriott is reinventing the lobbies of its Marriott and Renaissance Hotels, creating a "social zone," with small tables, brighter lights, and wireless Web access, that is better suited to meetings. Another area will allow solo travelers to work or unwind in larger, quiet, semiprivate spaces where they won't have to worry about spilling coffee on their laptops or papers. . . .

Ethnographic research often yields the kinds of details that just don't emerge from traditional research questionnaires or focus groups. "The beauty of ethnography," says a research expert, "is that it provides a richer understanding of consumers than does traditional research. Yes, companies are still using focus groups, surveys, and demographic data to glean insights into the consumer's mind. But closely observing people where they live and work . . . allows companies to zero in on their customers' unarticulated desires."[13]

SURVEY RESEARCH **Survey research**, the most widely used method for primary data collection, is the approach best suited for gathering *descriptive* information. A company that wants to know about people's knowledge, attitudes, preferences, or buying behavior can often find out by asking them directly.

The major advantage of survey research is its flexibility—it can be used to obtain many different kinds of information in many different situations. However, survey research also presents some problems. Sometimes people are unable to answer survey questions because they cannot remember or have never thought about what they do and why. People may be unwilling to respond to unknown interviewers or about things they consider private. Respondents may answer survey questions even when they do not know the answer in order to appear smarter or more informed. Or they may try to help the interviewer by giving pleasing answers. Finally, busy people may not take the time, or they might resent the intrusion into their privacy.

EXPERIMENTAL RESEARCH Whereas observation is best suited for exploratory research and surveys for descriptive research, **experimental research** is best suited for gathering *causal* information. Experiments involve selecting matched groups of subjects, giving them different treatments, controlling unrelated factors, and checking for differences in group responses. Thus, experimental research tries to explain cause-and-effect relationships.

For example, before adding a new sandwich to its menu, McDonald's might use experiments to test the effects on sales of two different prices it might charge. It could introduce the new sandwich at one price in one city and at another price in another city. If the cities are similar, and if all other marketing efforts for the sandwich are the same, then differences in sales in the two cities could be related to the price charged.

Contact Methods

Information can be collected by mail, telephone, personal interview, or online. Table 4.3 shows the strengths and weaknesses of each of these contact methods.

Survey research
Gathering primary data by asking people questions about their knowledge, attitudes, preferences, and buying behavior.

Experimental research
Gathering primary data by selecting matched groups of subjects, giving them different treatments, controlling related factors, and checking for differences in group responses.

TABLE 4.3
Strengths and Weaknesses of Contact Methods

	Mail	Telephone	Personal	Online
Flexibility	Poor	Good	Excellent	Good
Quantity of data that can be collected	Good	Fair	Good	Good
Control of interviewer effects	Excellent	Fair	Poor	Fair
Control of sample	Fair	Excellent	Good	Excellent
Speed of data collection	Poor	Excellent	Good	Excellent
Response rate	Fair	Good	Good	Good
Cost	Good	Fair	Poor	Excellent

Source: Adapted with permission of the authors, Donald S. Tull and Del I. Hawkins, *Marketing Research: Measurement and Method*, 7th ed. (New York: Macmillan Publishing Company, 1993).

MAIL, TELEPHONE, AND PERSONAL INTERVIEWING *Mail questionnaires* can be used to collect large amounts of information at a low cost per respondent. Respondents may give more honest answers to more personal questions on a mail questionnaire than to an unknown interviewer in person or over the phone. Also, no interviewer is involved to bias the respondent's answers.

However, mail questionnaires are not very flexible—all respondents answer the same questions in a fixed order. Mail surveys usually take longer to complete, and the response rate—the number of people returning completed questionnaires—is often very low. Finally, the researcher often has little control over the mail questionnaire sample. Even with a good mailing list, it is hard to control *who* at the mailing address fills out the questionnaire.

Telephone interviewing is the one of the best methods for gathering information quickly, and it provides greater flexibility than mail questionnaires. Interviewers can explain difficult questions and, depending on the answers they receive, skip some questions or probe on others. Response rates tend to be higher than with mail questionnaires, and interviewers can ask to speak to respondents with the desired characteristics or even by name.

However, with telephone interviewing, the cost per respondent is higher than with mail questionnaires. Also, people may not want to discuss personal questions with an interviewer. The method introduces interviewer bias—the way interviewers talk, how they ask questions, and other differences may affect respondents' answers. Finally, different interviewers may interpret and record responses differently, and under time pressures some interviewers might even cheat by recording answers without asking questions.

Personal interviewing takes two forms—individual and group interviewing. *Individual interviewing* involves talking with people in their homes or offices, on the street, or in shopping malls. Such interviewing is flexible. Trained interviewers can guide interviews, explain difficult questions, and explore issues as the situation requires. They can show subjects actual products, advertisements, or packages and observe reactions and behavior. However, individual personal interviews may cost three to four times as much as telephone interviews.

Group interviewing consists of inviting six to ten people to meet with a trained moderator to talk about a product, service, or organization. Participants normally are paid a small sum for attending. The moderator encourages free and easy discussion, hoping that group interactions will bring out actual feelings and thoughts. At the same time, the moderator "focuses" the discussion—hence the name **focus group interviewing.**

Researchers and marketers watch the focus group discussions from behind one-way glass, and comments are recorded in writing or on video for later study. Today, focus group researchers can even use videoconferencing and Internet technology to connect marketers in distant locations with live focus group action. Using cameras and two-way sound systems, marketing executives in a far-off boardroom can look in and listen, using remote controls to zoom in on faces and pan the focus group at will.

Focus group interviewing has become one of the major marketing research tools for gaining insights into consumer thoughts and feelings. However, focus group studies present some challenges. They usually employ small samples to keep time and costs down, and it may be hard to generalize from the results. Moreover, consumers in focus groups are not always open and honest in front of other people. "There's peer pressure in focus groups that gets in the way of finding the truth about real behavior and intentions," says one marketing executive.[14] Thus, although focus groups are still widely used, many researchers are tinkering with focus group design. For example, Cammie Dunaway, chief marketing officer at Yahoo!, prefers "immersion groups"—four or five people with whom Yahoo!'s product designers talk informally, without a focus group moderator present. That way, rather than just seeing videos of consumers reacting to a moderator, Yahoo! staffers can work directly with select customers to design new products and programs. "The outcome is richer if [consumers] feel included in our process, not just observed," says Dunaway.[15]

Still other researchers are changing the environments in which they conduct focus groups. To help consumers relax and to elicit more authentic responses, they use settings that are more comfortable and more relevant to the products being researched. For example, they might conduct focus groups for cooking products in a kitchen setting, or focus groups for home furnishings in a living room setting. One research firm offers facilities that look just like anything from a living room or play room to a bar or even a courtroom.

ONLINE MARKETING RESEARCH Advances in communication technologies have resulted in a number of high-tech contact methods. The latest technology to hit marketing research is the Internet. Increasingly, marketing researchers are collecting primary data through **online marketing research**—*Internet surveys, online panels, experiments, and online focus groups.* In

Focus group interviewing
Personal interviewing that involves inviting six to ten people to gather for a few hours with a trained interviewer to talk about a product, service, or organization. The interviewer "focuses" the group discussion on important issues.

Online marketing research
Collecting primary data through Internet surveys and online focus groups.

■ Focus group technology: Today, many researchers are employing videoconferencing and Internet technology to connect marketers with live focus group action. ActiveGroup allows researchers to view their focus groups and collaborate remotely from any location, no matter how distant. Says the company, "no traveling, no scheduling, no problems."

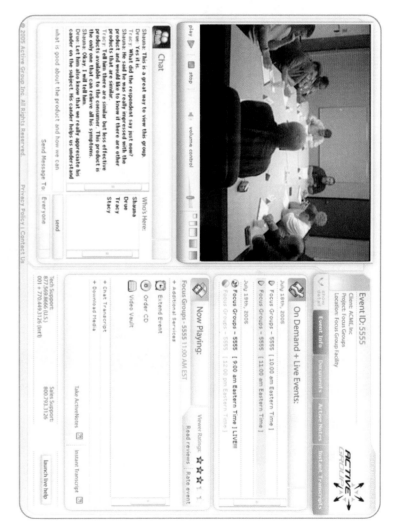

fact, by 2006, companies were spending an estimated 30 percent of their marketing research dollars online, making it the largest single data collection methodology.[16]

Online research can take many forms. A company can include a questionnaire on its Web site and offer incentives for completing it. Or it can use e-mail, Web links, or Web pop-ups to invite people to answer questions and possibly win a prize. The company can sponsor a chat room and introduce questions from time to time or conduct live discussions or online focus groups. A company can learn about the behavior of online customers by following their click streams as they visit the Web site and move to other sites. A company can experiment with different prices, use different headlines, or offer different product features on different Web sites or at different times to learn the relative effectiveness of its offerings. It can float "trial balloons" to quickly test new product concepts.

Web research offers some real advantages over traditional surveys and focus groups. The most obvious advantages are speed and low costs. Online focus groups require some advance scheduling, but results are practically instantaneous.[17]

Looking for better methods of predicting consumer acceptance to potential new products, Pepsi recently turned to Invoke Solutions, an online consumer research company, which maintained several instant-message-style online consumer panels of 80 to 100 people. Using the panels, Pepsi delved into attitudes among Gen Xers toward drinking mineral water. In just a few hours, the beverage marketer was able to gather and process detailed feedback from hundreds of consumers. At first, Pepsi marketers were jazzed that the group liked the idea of high levels of mineral content in water. But after further exchanges with the online panel, Pepsi beverage scientists on the scene squelched higher mineral levels; that would require adding sugar, which consumers didn't want, to make the taste acceptable. Using the online panels, "conclusions that could take three to four months to sort out through regular focus groups . . . got settled in a few hours," says an Invoke executive.

Internet research is also relatively low in cost. Participants can dial in for a focus group from anywhere in the world, eliminating travel, lodging, and facility costs. For surveys, the Internet eliminates most of the postage, phone, labor, and printing costs associated with other approaches. As a result, an Internet survey may be only 10 to 20 percent as expensive as mail, telephone, or personal surveys. Moreover, sample size has little influence on costs. Once the questionnaire is set up, there's little difference in cost between 10 and 10,000 respondents on the Web.

Online surveys and focus groups are also excellent for reaching the hard-to-reach—the often-elusive teen, single, affluent, and well-educated audiences. It's also good for reaching working mothers and other people who lead busy lives. They respond to it in their own space and at their own convenience. The Internet also works well for bringing together people from different parts of the country, especially those in higher-income groups who can't spare the time to travel to a central site.

Using the Internet to conduct marketing research does have some drawbacks. For one, restricted Internet access can make it difficult to get a broad cross section of Americans. However, with Internet household penetration now at 64 percent in the United States, this is less of a problem. Another major problem is controlling who's in the sample. Without seeing respondents, it's difficult to know who they really are.

Even when you reach the right respondents, online surveys and focus groups can lack the dynamics of more personal approaches. The online world is devoid of the eye contact, body language, and direct personal interactions found in traditional focus group research. And the Internet format—running, typed commentary and online "emoticons" (punctuation marks that express emotion, such as :-) to signify happiness)—greatly restricts respondent expressiveness. Although the impersonal nature of the Internet may shield people from excessive peer pressure, it also prevents people from interacting with each other and getting excited about a concept.

To overcome such sample and response problems, many online research firms use opt-in communities and respondent panels. For example, online research firm Greenfield Online provides access to 12 million opt-in panel members in more than 40 countries. Advances in technology—such as the integration of animation, streaming audio and video, and virtual environments—also help to overcome online research dynamics limitations.

Perhaps the most explosive issue facing online researchers concerns consumer privacy. Some fear that unethical researchers will use the e-mail addresses and confidential responses gathered through surveys to sell products after the research is completed. They are concerned about the use of electronic agents (such as Spambots or Trojans) that collect personal information without the respondents' consent. Failure to address such privacy issues could result in angry, less-cooperative consumers and increased government intervention. Despite these concerns, most industry insiders predict healthy growth for online marketing research.[18]

Sampling Plan

Marketing researchers usually draw conclusions about large groups of consumers by studying a small sample of the total consumer population. A **sample** is a segment of the population selected for marketing research to represent the population as a whole. Ideally, the sample should be representative so that the researcher can make accurate estimates of the thoughts and behaviors of the larger population.

Designing the sample requires three decisions. First, *who* is to be surveyed (what *sampling unit*)? The answer to this question is not always obvious. For example, to study the

Sample

A segment of the population selected for marketing research to represent the population as a whole.

■ Increasingly, companies are moving their research onto the Web. According to this Greenfield Online ad, in many ways, "it beats the old-fashioned kind."

TABLE 4.4
Types of Samples

PROBABILITY SAMPLE	
Simple random sample	Every member of the population has a known and equal chance of selection.
Stratified random sample	The population is divided into mutually exclusive groups (such as age groups), and random samples are drawn from each group.
Cluster (area) sample	The population is divided into mutually exclusive groups (such as blocks), and the researcher draws a sample of the groups to interview.
NONPROBABILITY SAMPLE	
Convenience sample	The researcher selects the easiest population members from which to obtain information.
Judgment sample	The researcher uses his or her judgment to select population members who are good prospects for accurate information.
Quota sample	The researcher finds and interviews a prescribed number of people in each of several categories.

decision-making process for a family automobile purchase, should the researcher interview the husband, wife, other family members, dealership salespeople, or all of these? The researcher must determine what information is needed and who is most likely to have it.

Second, *how many people* should be surveyed (what *sample size*)? Large samples give more reliable results than small samples. However, larger samples usually cost more, and it is not necessary to sample the entire target market or even a large portion to get reliable results. If well chosen, samples of less than 1 percent of a population can often give good reliability.

Third, *how* should the people in the sample be *chosen* (what *sampling procedure*)? Table 4.4 describes different kinds of samples. Using *probability samples*, each population member has a known chance of being included in the sample, and researchers can calculate confidence limits for sampling error. But when probability sampling costs too much or takes too much time, marketing researchers often take *nonprobability samples*, even though their sampling error cannot be measured. These varied ways of drawing samples have different costs and time limitations as well as different accuracy and statistical properties. Which method is best depends on the needs of the research project.

Research Instruments

In collecting primary data, marketing researchers have a choice of two main research instruments—the *questionnaire* and *mechanical devices*. The *questionnaire* is by far the most common instrument, whether administered in person, by phone, or online.

Questionnaires are very flexible—there are many ways to ask questions. *Closed-end questions* include all the possible answers, and subjects make choices among them. Examples include multiple-choice questions and scale questions. *Open-end questions* allow respondents to answer in their own words. In a survey of airline users, Southwest might simply ask, "What is your opinion of Southwest Airlines?" Or it might ask people to complete a sentence: "When I choose an airline, the most important consideration is. . . ." These and other kinds of open-end questions often reveal more than closed-end questions because respondents are not limited in their answers. Open-end questions are especially useful in exploratory research, when the researcher is trying to find out *what* people think but not measuring *how many* people think in a certain way. Closed-end questions, on the other hand, provide answers that are easier to interpret and tabulate.

Researchers should also use care in the *wording* and *ordering* of questions. They should use simple, direct, unbiased wording. Questions should be arranged in a logical order. The first question should create interest if possible, and difficult or personal questions should be asked last so that respondents do not become defensive. A carelessly prepared questionnaire usually contains many errors (see Table 4.5).

Although questionnaires are the most common research instrument, researchers also use *mechanical instruments* to monitor consumer behavior. Nielsen Media Research attaches *people meters* to television sets in selected homes to record who watches which programs. Retailers use *checkout scanners* to record shoppers' purchases.

TABLE 4.5
A "Questionable Questionnaire"

Suppose that a summer camp director has prepared the following questionnaire to use in interviewing the parents of prospective campers. How would you assess each question?

1. What is your income to the nearest hundred dollars? *People don't usually know their income to the nearest hundred dollars, nor do they want to reveal their income that closely. Moreover, a researcher should never open a questionnaire with such a personal question.*

2. Are you a strong or weak supporter of overnight summer camping for your children? *What do "strong" and "weak" mean?*

3. Do your children behave themselves well at a summer camp? Yes ( ) No ( ) *"Behave" is a relative term. Furthermore, are yes and no the best response options for this question? Besides, will people answer this honestly and objectively? Why ask the question in the first place?*

4. How many camps mailed or e-mailed information to you last year? This year? *Who can remember this?*

5. What are the most salient and determinant attributes in your evaluation of summer camps? *What are salient and determinant attributes? Don't use big words on me!*

6. Do you think it is right to deprive your child of the opportunity to grow into a mature person through the experience of summer camping? *A loaded question. Given the bias, how can any parent answer yes?*

Other mechanical devices measure subjects' physical responses. For example, advertisers use eye cameras to study viewers' eye movements while watching ads—at what points their eyes focus first and how long they linger on any given ad component. IBM's BlueEyes human recognition technology goes even further.

BlueEyes uses sensing technology to identify and interpret user reactions. The technology was originally created to help users to interact more easily with a computer. For example, IBM is perfecting an "emotion mouse" that will figure out computer users' emotional states by measuring pulse, temperature, movement, and galvanic skin response. Another BlueEyes technology records and interprets human facial reactions by tracking pupil, eyebrow, and mouth movement. BlueEyes offers a host of potential marketing uses. Retailers are already using the technology to study customers and their responses. And in the not-to-distant future, more than just measuring customers' physical reactions, marketers will be able to respond to them as well. An example: creating marketing machines that "know how you feel." Sensing through an emotion mouse that a Web shopper is frustrated, an Internet marketer offers a different screen display. An elderly man squints at a bank's ATM screen and the font size doubles almost instantly. A woman at a shopping center kiosk smiles at a travel ad, prompting the device to print out a travel discount coupon. Several users at another kiosk frown at a racy ad, leading a store to pull it. In the future, ordinary household devices—such as televisions, refrigerators, and ovens—may be able to do their jobs when we look at them and speak to them.[19]

Implementing the Research Plan

The researcher next puts the marketing research plan into action. This involves collecting, processing, and analyzing the information. Data collection can be carried out by the company's marketing research staff or by outside firms. The data collection phase of the marketing research process is generally the most expensive and the most subject to error. Researchers should watch closely to make sure that the plan is implemented correctly. They must guard against problems with contacting respondents, with respondents who refuse to cooperate or who give biased answers, and with interviewers who make mistakes or take shortcuts.

Researchers must also process and analyze the collected data to isolate important information and findings. They need to check data for accuracy and completeness and code it for analysis. The researchers then tabulate the results and compute statistical measures.

- Mechanical measures of consumer response: New technologies can record and interpret human facial reactions. In the not-too-distant future, marketers may be using machines that "know how you feel" to not just gauge customers' physical reactions, but to respond to them as well.

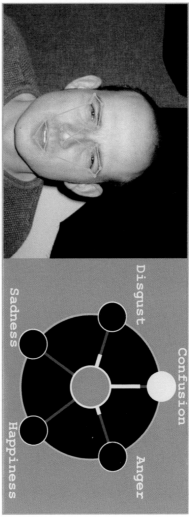

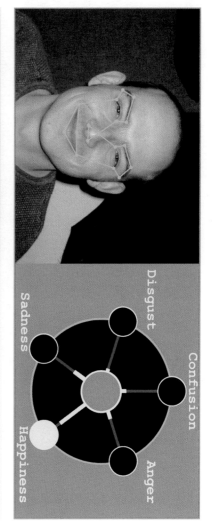

Interpreting and Reporting the Findings

The market researcher must now interpret the findings, draw conclusions, and report them to management. The researcher should not try to overwhelm managers with numbers and fancy statistical techniques. Rather, the researcher should present important findings that are useful in the major decisions faced by management.

However, interpretation should not be left only to the researchers. They are often experts in research design and statistics, but the marketing manager knows more about the problem and the decisions that must be made. The best research means little if the manager blindly accepts faulty interpretations from the researcher. Similarly, managers may be biased—they might tend to accept research results that show what they expected and to reject those that they did not expect or hope for. In many cases, findings can be interpreted in different ways, and discussions between researchers and managers will help point to the best interpretations. Thus, managers and researchers must work together closely when interpreting research results, and both must share responsibility for the research process and resulting decisions.

Analyzing Marketing Information

Information gathered in internal databases and through marketing intelligence and marketing research usually requires more analysis. And managers may need help applying the information to their marketing decisions. This help may include advanced statistical analysis to learn more about the relationships within a set of data. Such analysis allows managers to go beyond means and standard deviations in the data and to answer questions about markets, marketing activities, and outcomes.

Information analysis might also involve a collection of analytical models that will help marketers make better decisions. Each model represents some real system, process, or outcome. These models can help answer the questions of *what if* and *which is best*. Marketing scientists have developed numerous models to help marketing managers make better marketing mix decisions, design sales territories and sales call plans, select sites for retail outlets, develop optimal advertising mixes, and forecast new-product sales.

Customer Relationship Management (CRM)

The question of how best to analyze and use individual customer data presents special problems. Most companies are awash in information about their customers. In fact, smart companies capture information at every possible customer *touch point*. These touch points include customer purchases, sales force contacts, service and support calls, Web site visits, satisfaction surveys, credit and payment interactions, market research studies—every contact between the customer and the company.

The trouble is that this information is usually scattered widely across the organization. It is buried deep in the separate databases and records of different company departments. To overcome such problems, many companies are now turning to **customer relationship management (CRM)** to manage detailed information about individual customers and carefully manage customer "touch points" in order to maximize customer loyalty.

CRM first burst onto the scene in the early 2000s. Many companies rushed in, implementing overly ambitious CRM programs that produced disappointing results and many failures. More recently, however, companies are moving ahead more cautiously and implementing CRM systems that really work. A recent study by Gartner Group found that 60 percent of the businesses surveyed intend to adopt or expand their CRM usage over the next two years. By 2007, U.S. companies will spend an estimated $73.8 billion on CRM systems from companies such as Oracle, Microsoft, and SAS.[20]

CRM consists of sophisticated software and analytical tools that integrate customer information from all sources, analyze it in depth, and apply the results to build stronger customer relationships. CRM integrates everything that a company's sales, service, and marketing teams know about individual customers to provide a 360-degree view of the customer relationship.

Customer relationship management (CRM)
Managing detailed information about individual customers and carefully managing customer "touch points" in order to maximize customer loyalty.

CRM analysts develop *data warehouses* and use sophisticated *data mining* techniques to unearth the riches hidden in customer data. A data warehouse is a companywide electronic database of finely detailed customer information that needs to be sifted through for gems. The purpose of a data warehouse is not just to gather information, but to pull it together into a central, accessible location. Then, once the data warehouse brings the data together, the company uses high-powered data mining techniques to sift through the mounds of data and dig out interesting findings about customers.

By using CRM to understand customers better, companies can provide higher levels of customer service and develop deeper customer relationships. They can use CRM to pinpoint high-value customers, target them more effectively, cross-sell the company's products, and create offers tailored to specific customer requirements. For example, Harrah's Entertainment, the world's largest casino operator, maintains a vast customer database and uses its CRM system to manage day-to-day relationships with important customers at its 43 casinos around the world (see Real Marketing 4.1).

CRM benefits don't come without cost or risk, not only in collecting the original customer data but also in maintaining and mining it. The most common CRM mistake is to view CRM only as a technology and software solution. But technology alone cannot build profitable customer relationships. "CRM is not a technology solution—you can't achieve . . . improved customer relationships by simply slapping in some software," says a CRM expert. Instead, CRM is just one part of an effective overall *customer relationship management strategy.* "Focus on the *R,*" advises the expert. "Remember, a relationship is what CRM is all about."[21]

■ CRM: SAS customer intelligence software helps companies to keep a profitable, loyal customer base by leveraging customer information and developing targeted, personalized responses to customer needs.

When it works, the benefits of CRM can far outweigh the costs and risks. Based on a recent study by SAP, customers using its mySAP CRM software reported an average 10 percent increase in customer retention and a 30 percent increase in sales leads. Overall, 90 percent of the companies surveyed increased in value from use of the software and reported an attractive return on investment. The study's conclusion: "CRM pays off." "No question that companies are getting tremendous value out of this," says a CRM consultant. "Companies [are] looking for ways to bring disparate sources of customer information together, then get it to all the customer touch points." The powerful new CRM techniques can unearth "a wealth of information to target that customer, to hit their hot button."[22]

Distributing and Using Marketing Information

Marketing information has no value until it is used to make better marketing decisions. Thus, the marketing information system must make the information readily available to the managers and others who make marketing decisions or deal with customers. In some cases, this means providing managers with regular performance reports, intelligence updates, and reports on the results of research studies.

But marketing managers may also need nonroutine information for special situations and on-the-spot decisions. For example, a sales manager having trouble with a large customer may want a summary of the account's sales and profitability over the past year. Or a retail store manager who has run out of a best-selling product may want to know the current inventory levels in the chain's other stores. Increasingly, therefore, information distribution involves entering information into databases and making it available in a timely, user-friendly way.

Many firms use a company *intranet* to facilitate this process. The intranet provides ready access to research information, stored reports, shared work documents, contact information for employees and other stakeholders, and more. For example, iGo, a catalog and Web retailer, integrates incoming customer service calls with up-to-date database information about customers' Web purchases and e-mail inquiries. By accessing this information on the intranet while speaking with the customer, iGo's service representatives can get a well-rounded picture of each customer's purchasing history and previous contacts with the company.

In addition, companies are increasingly allowing key customers and value-network members to access account, product, and other data on demand through *extranets*. Suppliers, customers, resellers, and select other network members may access a company's extranet to update their accounts, arrange purchases, and check orders against inventories to improve customer service. For example, one insurance firm allows its 200 independent agents access to a Web-based database of claim information covering one million customers. This allows the agents to avoid high-risk customers and to compare claim data with their own customer databases. And Wal-Mart's RetailLink extranet system provides suppliers with a two-year history of every product's daily sales in every Wal-Mart store worldwide, letting them track when and where their products are selling and current inventory levels. Other retailers are rolling out similar data-sharing systems, including Lowe's (LowesLink) and Target (PartnersOnline).[23]

Thanks to modern technology, today's marketing managers can gain direct access to the information system at any time and from virtually any location. They can tap into the system while working at a home office, from a hotel room, or from the local Starbuck's through a wireless network—anyplace where they can turn on a laptop and link up. Such systems allow managers to get the information they need directly and quickly and to tailor it to their own needs. From just about anywhere, they can obtain information from company or outside databases, analyze it using statistical software, prepare reports and presentations, and communicate directly with others in the network.

Other Marketing Information Considerations

This section discusses marketing information in two special contexts: marketing research in small businesses and nonprofit organizations and international marketing research. Finally, we look at public policy and ethics issues in marketing research.

Real Marketing Harrah's Hits the CRM Jackpot

4.1 Companies everywhere covet the title "The world's greatest." Giant casino operator Harrah's Entertainment rightly claims that title in the gaming industry. Following its recent acquisition of Caesars Entertainment, Harrah's now captures a huge $7.1 billion in revenues from its 43 properties around the nation and world. The Harrah's portfolio includes such star-studded casino and gaming brands as Harrah's, Caesars, Horseshoe, Bally's, Flamingo, Showboat, and The World Series of Poker.

The recent Caesars acquisition only adds to the luster of what was an already very successful company. In the four years prior to the acquisition, Harrah's annual sales grew 37 percent and profits soared 76 percent. Harrah's stock is worth nearly two-and-a-half times its value five years ago, suggesting that Wall Street is betting on a bright future for the gaming giant.

Why has Harrah's been so successful? Everyone at Harrah's will quickly tell you that it's all about managing customer relationships. When you get right down to it, in physical terms, all casinos are pretty much alike. Most customers can't distinguish one company's slot machines, game tables, restaurants, and hotel rooms from another's. What sets Harrah's apart is the way it relates to its customers and creates customer loyalty. During the past decade, Harrah's has become *the* model for good CRM and customer-loyalty management.

At the heart of the Harrah's CRM strategy is its pioneering card-based Total Rewards program, the gaming industry's first and by far most successful loyalty program. Total Rewards members receive points based on the amount they spend at Harrah's facilities. They can then redeem the points for a variety of perks, such as cash, food, merchandise, rooms, and hotel show tickets. Total Rewards forms the basis for a two-part CRM process. First, the company uses Total Rewards to collect a mother lode of information about customers. Then, it mines this information to identify important customers and finely tune its market offerings to their specific needs.

Harrah's maintains a vast customer database. More than 80 percent of Harrah's customers worldwide—40 million customers in all—use a Total Rewards card. That's roughly one out of six adults in the United States alone. Information from every swipe of every card at each of Harrah's 43 casinos zips off to a central computer in

Customer relationship management: Harrah's CRM system helps the company to focus its branding, marketing, and service development strategies on the needs of its most important customers. "We're trying to figure out which products sell, and we're trying to increase our customer loyalty."

Memphis, Tennessee. That's a lot of information. Harrah's current data warehouse can store up to 30 terabytes (30 trillion bytes) of data, roughly three times the volume of data contained in the U.S. Library of Congress. Amazingly, Harrah's is rapidly reaching full information capacity and plans to double its data storage capabilities.

Marketing Research in Small Businesses and Nonprofit Organizations

Just like larger firms, small organizations need market information. Start-up businesses need information about their industries, competitors, potential customers, and reactions to new market offers. Existing small businesses must track changes in customer needs and wants, reactions to new products, and changes in the competitive environment.

Managers of small businesses and nonprofit organizations often think that marketing research can be done only by experts in large companies with big research budgets. True, large-scale research studies are beyond the budgets of most small businesses. However, many of the marketing research techniques discussed in this chapter also can be used by smaller organizations in a less formal manner and at little or no expense. Consider how one small-business owner conducted market research on a shoestring before even opening his doors:[24]

After a string of bad experiences with his local dry cleaner, Robert Byerley decided to open his own dry-cleaning business. But before jumping in, he conducted plenty of

Analyzing all this information gives Harrah's detailed insights into casino operations. For example, "visualization software" can generate a dynamic "heat map" of a casino floor, with machines glowing red when at peak activity, then turning blue and then white as the action moves elsewhere. More importantly, the information provides insights into the characteristics and behavior of individual customers—who they are, how often they visit, how long they stay, and how much they gamble and entertain.

From its Total Rewards data, Harrah's has learned that 26 percent of its customers produce 82 percent of revenues. And these best customers aren't the "high-rollers" that have long been the focus of the industry. Rather, they are ordinary folks from all walks of life—middle-aged and retired teachers, bankers, and doctors who have discretionary income and time. More often than not, these customers visit casinos for an evening, rather than staying overnight at the hotel, and they are more likely to play at the slots than at tables. What motivates them? It's mostly the intense anticipation and excitement of gambling itself.

Using such insights, Harrah's focuses its marketing and service development strategies on the needs of its best customers. For example, the company's advertising reflects the feeling of exuberance that target customers seek. The data insights also help Harrah's do a better job of managing day-to-day customer relationships. After a day's gaming, by the next morning, it knows which customers should be rewarded with free show tickets, dinner vouchers, or room upgrades.

In fact, Harrah's is now starting to process customer information in real time, from the moment customers swipe their rewards cards, creating the ideal link between data and the customer experience. Harrah's chief information officer calls this "operational CRM." Based on up-to-the-minute customer information, he explains, "the hotel clerk can see your history and determine whether you should get a room upgrade, based on booking levels in the hotel at that time and on your past level of play. A person might walk up to you while you're playing and offer you $5 to play more slots, or a free meal, or maybe just wish you a happy birthday."

Harrah's CRM and customer-loyalty efforts are paying off in spades. The company has found that happy customers are much more loyal—whereas customer spending decreases by 10 percent based on an unhappy casino experience, it increases by 24 percent with a happy experience. And Harrah's Total Rewards customers appear to be a happier bunch. Compared with nonmembers, member customers visit the company's casinos more frequently, stay longer, and spend more of their gambling and entertainment dollars in Harrah's rather than rival casinos. Since setting up Total Rewards, Harrah's has seen its share of customers' average annual gambling budgets rise 20 percent, and revenue from customers gambling at Harrah's rather than their "home casino" has risen 18 percent.

Harrah's CEO Gary Loveman calls Total Rewards "the vertebrae of our business" and says, "it touches, in some form or fashion, 85 percent of our revenue." He says that Harrah's "customer-loyalty strategy [and] relationship marketing . . . are constantly bringing us closer to our customers so we better understand their preferences, and from that understanding we are able to improve the entertainment experiences we offer." Another Harrah's executive puts it even more simply: "It's no different from what a good retailer or grocery store does. We're trying to figure out which products sell, and we're trying to increase our customer loyalty. Ka-ching! Through smart CRM investments, Harrah's has hit the customer-loyalty jackpot.

Sources: Quotes and other information from Phil Bligh and Doug Turk, "Cashing In on Customer Loyalty," *Customer Relationship Management*, June 1, 2004, p. 48; Thomas Hoffman, "Harrah's Bets on Loyalty Program in Caesars Deal," *Computerworld*, June 27, 2005, p. 10; Daniel Lyons, "Too Much Information," *Forbes*, December 13, 2004, p. 110; Suzette Parmley, "When Its Customers Return, a Casino Always Wins," *Philadelphia Inquirer*, April 15, 2005; Kai Ryssdal and Andrew Park, "Harrah's Database of Gamblers," transcript from *Marketplace*, August 4, 2005; Neal A. Martin, "A Tempting Wager," *Barron's*, April 10, 2006, pp. 28–30; John S. Webster, "Harrah's CTO Tim Stanley Plays 'Operational CRM'," June 7, 2006, accessed at www.computerworld.com; and Harrah's annual reports and other information accessed at http://investor.harrahs.com/phoenix.zhtml?c=84772&p=irol-reportsAnnual, August 2006.

market research. Making a careful tour of the town, he observed a dry-cleaning establishment in practically every strip mall. How would his stand out? To find an answer, Byerley spent an entire week in the library, researching the dry-cleaning industry. From government reports and trade publications, he learned it was a $16 billion-a-year industry dominated by mom-and-pop establishments. Better Business Bureau reports showed that dry cleaners accounted for a high number of complaints. The number one criticism: "Cleaners didn't stand behind what they did," he says. To get input from potential customers, using a marketing firm, Byerley held focus groups on the store's name, look, and brochure. He also took clothes to the 15 best cleaners in town and had focus-group members critique their work. In all, Byerley says he spent about $15,000 for the focus groups. Based on his research, he made a list of features for his new business. First on his list: His business would stand behind everything it did. Not on the list: cheap prices. Creating the perfect dry-cleaning establishment simply wasn't compatible with a discount operation.

His research complete, Byerley opened Bibbentuckers, a high-end dry cleaner positioned on high-quality service and convenience. Bibbentuckers featured a

■ Small businesses need market research, too. Before opening his own dry-cleaning business, Bibbentuckers owner Robert Byerley conducted plenty of low-budget market research, including talking with prospective customers. "You have to think like Procter & Gamble."

banklike drive-through area with curbside delivery. A computerized bar-code system read customer cleaning preferences and tracked clothes all the way through the cleaning process. Byerley added other differentiators, such as decorative awnings, refreshments, and TV screens. "I wanted a place people would be comfortable leaving their best clothes, a place that paired five-star service and quality with an establishment that didn't look like a dry cleaner," he says. The market research yielded results—Bibbentuckers' business took off, turning a profit after only four months. Today, it's a thriving three-store operation. "Too many small-business owners have a technician's mind-set rather than a marketing mind-set," says a small-business consultant. "You have to think like Procter & Gamble. What would they do before launching a new product? They would find out who their customer is and who their competition is."

Thus, managers of small businesses and nonprofit organizations can obtain good marketing information simply by *observing* things around them. For example, retailers can evaluate new locations by observing vehicle and pedestrian traffic. They can monitor competitor advertising by collecting ads from local media. They can evaluate their customer mix by recording how many and what kinds of customers shop in the store at different times. In addition, many small business managers routinely visit their rivals and socialize with competitors to gain insights.

Managers can conduct informal *surveys* using small convenience samples. The director of an art museum can learn what patrons think about new exhibits by conducting informal focus groups—inviting small groups to lunch and having discussions on topics of interest. Retail salespeople can talk with customers visiting the store; hospital officials can interview patients. Restaurant managers might make random phone calls during slack hours to interview consumers about where they eat out and what they think of various restaurants in the area.

Managers also can conduct their own simple *experiments*. For example, by changing the themes in regular fund-raising mailings and watching the results, a nonprofit manager can find out much about which marketing strategies work best. By varying newspaper advertisements, a store manager can learn the effects of things such as ad size and position, price coupons, and media used.

Small organizations can obtain most of the secondary data available to large businesses. In addition, many associations, local media, chambers of commerce, and government agencies provide special help to small organizations. The U.S. Small Business Administration offers dozens of free publications and a Web site (www.sbaonline.sba.gov) that give advice on topics ranging from starting, financing, and expanding a small business to ordering business cards. Other excellent Web resources for small businesses include the U.S. Census Bureau (www.census.gov) and the Bureau of Economic Analysis (www.bea.gov).

The business sections at local libraries can also be a good source of information. Local newspapers often provide information on local shoppers and their buying patterns. Finally, small businesses can collect a considerable amount of information at very little cost on the Internet. They can scour competitor and customer Web sites and use Internet search engines to research specific companies and issues.

In summary, secondary data collection, observation, surveys, and experiments can all be used effectively by small organizations with small budgets. Although these informal research methods are less complex and less costly, they still must be conducted carefully. Managers must think carefully about the objectives of the research, formulate questions in advance, recognize the biases introduced by smaller samples and less skilled researchers, and conduct the research systematically.[25]

International Marketing Research

International marketing researchers follow the same steps as domestic researchers, from defining the research problem and developing a research plan to interpreting and reporting the results. However, these researchers often face more and different problems. Whereas domestic researchers deal with fairly homogenous markets within a single country, international researchers deal with diverse markets in many different countries. These markets often vary greatly in their levels of economic development, cultures and customs, and buying patterns.

In many foreign markets, the international researcher may have a difficult time finding good secondary data. Whereas U.S. marketing researchers can obtain reliable secondary data from dozens of domestic research services, many countries have almost no research services at all. Some of the largest international research services do operate in many countries. For example, ACNielsen Corporation (owned by VNU NV, the world's largest marketing research company) has offices in more than 100 countries. And 67 percent of the revenues of the world's 25 largest marketing research firms comes from outside their home countries.[26] However, most research firms operate in only a relative handful of countries. Thus, even when secondary information is available, it usually must be obtained from many different sources on a country-by-country basis, making the information difficult to combine or compare.

Because of the scarcity of good secondary data, international researchers often must collect their own primary data. Here again, researchers face problems not found domestically. For example, they may find it difficult simply to develop good samples. U.S. researchers can use current telephone directories, census tract data, and any of several sources of socioeconomic data to construct samples. However, such information is largely lacking in many countries.

Once the sample is drawn, the U.S. researcher usually can reach most respondents easily by telephone, by mail, on the Internet, or in person. Reaching respondents is often not so easy in other parts of the world. Researchers in Mexico cannot rely on telephone, Internet, and mail data collection—most data collection is done door to door and concentrated in three or four of the largest cities. In some countries, few people have phones or personal computers. For example, whereas there are 1,118 telephone subscriptions and 544 PCs per thousand people in the United States, there are only 354 phone subscriptions and 54 PCs per thousand in Mexico. In Ghana, the numbers drop to 21 phone subscriptions and 3 PCs

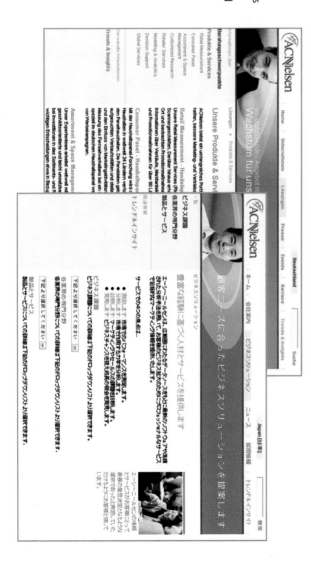

■ Some of the largest research services firms have large international organizations. ACNielsen has offices in more than 100 countries, here Germany and Japan.

per thousand people. In some countries, the postal system is notoriously unreliable. In Brazil, for instance, an estimated 30 percent of the mail is never delivered. In many developing countries, poor roads and transportation systems make certain areas hard to reach, making personal interviews difficult and expensive.[27]

Cultural differences from country to country cause additional problems for international researchers. Language is the most obvious obstacle. For example, questionnaires must be prepared in one language and then translated into the languages of each country researched. Responses then must be translated back into the original language for analysis and interpretation. This adds to research costs and increases the risks of error.

Translating a questionnaire from one language to another is anything but easy. Many idioms, phrases, and statements mean different things in different cultures. For example, a Danish executive noted, "Check this out by having a different translator put back into English what you've translated from English. You'll get the shock of your life. I remember [an example in which] 'out of sight, out of mind' had become 'invisible things are insane.' "[28]

Consumers in different countries also vary in their attitudes toward marketing research. People in one country may be very willing to respond; in other countries, nonresponse can be a major problem. Customs in some countries may prohibit people from talking with strangers. In certain cultures, research questions often are considered too personal. For example, in many Latin American countries, people may feel embarrassed to talk with researchers about their choices of shampoo, deodorant, or other personal care products. Similarly, in most Muslim countries, mixed-gender focus groups are taboo, as is videotaping female-only focus groups.

Even when respondents are *willing* to respond, they may not be *able* to because of high functional illiteracy rates. And middle-class people in developing countries often make false claims in order to appear well-off. For example, in a study of tea consumption in India, over 70 percent of middle-income respondents claimed that they used one of several national brands. However, the researchers had good reason to doubt these results—more than 60 percent of the tea sold in India is unbranded generic tea.

Despite these problems, the recent growth of international marketing has resulted in a rapid increase in the use of international marketing research. Global companies have little choice but to conduct such research. Although the costs and problems associated with international research may be high, the costs of not doing it—in terms of missed opportunities and mistakes—might be even higher. Once recognized, many of the problems associated with international marketing research can be overcome or avoided.

Public Policy and Ethics in Marketing Research

Most marketing research benefits both the sponsoring company and its consumers. Through marketing research, companies learn more about consumers' needs, resulting in more satisfying products and services and stronger customer relationships. However, the misuse of marketing research can also harm or annoy consumers. Two major public policy and ethics issues in marketing research are intrusions on consumer privacy and the misuse of research findings.

Intrusions on Consumer Privacy

Many consumers feel positive about marketing research and believe that it serves a useful purpose. Some actually enjoy being interviewed and giving their opinions. However, others strongly resent or even mistrust marketing research. A few consumers fear that researchers might use sophisticated techniques to probe our deepest feelings or peek over our shoulders and then use this knowledge to manipulate our buying (see Real Marketing 4.2). Or they worry that marketers are building huge databases full of personal information about customers. For example, consider a company called Acxiom:

Never heard of Acxiom? Chances are it's heard of you. Once upon a time in America, a savvy local store clerk knew that you had, say, three kids, an old Ford, a pool, and a passion for golf and yellow sweaters. Today Acxiom is that store clerk. It's the world's largest processor of consumer data, collecting and massaging more than a billion records a day. Acxiom's database on 96 percent of U.S. households gives marketers a so-called real-time, 360-degree view of their customers. How? Acxiom provides a 13-digit code for every person, "so we can identify you wherever you go," says the company's demographics guru. Each person is placed into one of 70 lifestyle clusters, ranging from "Rolling Stones" and "Single City Struggles" to "Timeless Elders." Acxiom's catalog offers businesses hundreds of lists, including a "pre-movers file," updated daily, of people preparing to change residences, as well as lists of people sorted by the frequency with which they use credit cards, the square footage of their homes, and their interest in the "strange and unusual." Its customers include eight of the country's top ten credit-card issuers, seven of the top ten retail banks, seven of the top 10 retailers, and all of the top 10 automakers. Acxiom may even know things about you that you don't know yourself.[29]

Other consumers may have been taken in by previous "research surveys" that actually turned out to be attempts to sell them something. Still other consumers confuse legitimate marketing research studies with telemarketing efforts and say "no" before the interviewer can even begin. Most, however, simply resent the intrusion. They dislike mail, telephone, or Web surveys that are too long or too personal or that interrupt them at inconvenient times.

Increasing consumer resentment has become a major problem for the research industry. One recent survey found that 70 percent of Americans say that companies have too much of consumers' personal information, and 76 percent feel that their privacy has been compromised if a company uses the collected personal information to sell them products. These concerns have led to lower survey response rates in recent years.[30]

Other studies found that 59 percent of consumers had refused to give information to a company because they thought it was not really needed or too personal, up from 42 percent five years earlier. And 71 percent of consumers believe that protecting information is more of a concern now than it was a few years ago. "Some shoppers are unnerved by the idea of giving up any information at all," says an analyst. When asked for something as seemingly harmless as a zip code, "one woman told me she always gives the zip code for Guam, and another said she never surrenders any information, not even a zip code, because "I don't get paid to help them with market research."[31]

The research industry is considering several options for responding to this problem. One example is the Council for Marketing and Opinion Research's "Your Opinion Counts" and "Respondent Bill of Rights" initiatives to educate consumers about the benefits of marketing research and to distinguish it from telephone selling and database building. The industry also has considered adopting broad standards, perhaps based on The International Chamber of Commerce's International Code of Marketing and Social Research Practice. This code outlines researchers' responsibilities to respondents and to the general public. For example, it says that researchers should make their names and addresses available to participants. It also bans companies from representing activities such as database compilation or sales and promotional pitches as research.[32]

Most major companies—including IBM, CitiGroup, American Express, Bank of America, and Microsoft—have now appointed a "chief privacy officer (CPO)," whose job is to safeguard the privacy of consumers who do business with the company. The chief privacy officer for Microsoft says that his job is to come up with data policies for the company to follow, make certain that every program the company creates enhances customer privacy, and inform and educate company employees about privacy issues and concerns. Similarly, IBM's CPO claims that her job requires "multidisciplinary thinking and attitude." She needs to get all company departments, from technology, legal, and accounting to marketing and communications working together to safeguard customer privacy.[33]

American Express, which deals with a considerable volume of consumer information, has long taken privacy issues seriously. The company developed a set of formal privacy principles in 1991, and in 1998 it became one of the first companies to post privacy policies on its Web site. Its online Internet privacy statement

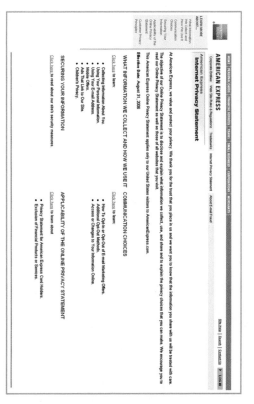

■ Consumer privacy. American Express was one of the first companies to post its privacy policies on the Web. "American Express respects your privacy and is committed to protecting it at all times."

Real Marketing | Video Mining

4.2 Stepping into a Gap store at the South Shore Shopping Plaza on a recent evening, Laura Munro became a research statistic. Twelve feet above her, a device resembling a smoke detector, mounted on the ceiling and equipped with a hidden camera, took a picture of her head and shoulders. The image was fed to a computer and shipped to a database in Chicago, where ShopperTrak, a consumer research firm, keeps count of shoppers nationwide using 40,000 cameras placed in stores and malls.

ShopperTrak is a leader in an emerging market research field called "video mining." Video miners use advanced computer software to sort through video images, plucking data of interest to marketers, without a human ever seeing the video. ShopperTrak says it doesn't take pictures of faces. The company worries that shoppers would perceive that as an invasion of privacy. But nearly all of its videotaping is done without the knowledge of the people being taped. "I didn't even know there was a camera up there," says Ms. Munro, who popped into the mall on her way home from work to find a gift for her 12-year-old daughter.

Using such video information, ShopperTrak calculates and sells many valuable tidbits of data. For example, by comparing the number of people taped entering the store with the number of transactions, it arrives at a so-called "conversion rate"—the percentage of shoppers that buys versus the percentage that only browses. At a broader level, by combining video data gleaned from 130 retail clients and 380 malls with consumer spending data obtained from

credit-card companies and banks, ShopperTrak can estimate sales and store traffic figures for the entire retail industry. Gap and other retail clients pay ShopperTrak for the store-level data. ShopperTrak sells the broader industry data to economists, bankers, and retailers.

More and more companies are now employing video miners to help them peek in on their customers. Video-tracking cameras, with lenses as small as a quarter, can provide data on everything from the density of shopping traffic in an aisle to the reactions of a shopper gazing at the latest plasma TV set. The cash register is a popular spot for cameras. But cameras can also be found in banks, fast-food outlets, and hotel lobbies (but not guest rooms).

Many companies now use video mining along with other traditional methods to help gain more rapid, accurate, and complete insights. For example, Kahn Research Group recently used video mining along with sales analysis and in-store behavioral tracking to determine what was and was not working to increase sales at Subway fast-food restaurants. Kahn's researchers hid golf-ball-sized cameras in several Subway restaurants to track customers' eye movements during the order process. Video analysis revealed that before and while sandwiches were being assembled, customers focused on the "sandwich artists" rather than on the menu board or promotional displays. In particular, drinks and sides received little customer notice. The researchers suggested that Subway move drinks and sides to a point where consumers would view them after making the major

Serving customers better or invading their privacy? Video miners use advanced computer software to sort through video images, plucking data of interest to marketers. Smile, you're being video mined!

tells customers in clear terms what information American Express collects and how it uses it, how it safeguards the information, and how it uses the information to market to its customers (with instructions on how to opt out).

In the end, if researchers provide value in exchange for information, customers will gladly provide it. For example, Amazon.com's customers do not mind if the firm builds a database of products they buy in order to provide future product recommendations. This saves time and provides value. Similarly, Bizrate users gladly complete surveys rating online seller sites because they can view the overall ratings of others when making purchase decisions. The best approach is for researchers to ask only for the information they need, to use it responsibly to provide customer value, and to avoid sharing information without the customer's permission.

Misuse of Research Findings

Research studies can be powerful persuasion tools; companies often use study results as claims in their advertising and promotion. Today, however, many research studies appear to be little more than vehicles for pitching the sponsor's products. In fact, in some cases, the

sandwich decision but before reaching the cash register. The research also revealed that promotions dangling from the ceiling were often ignored—Subway now uses table tents to remind customers to buy a snack for later.

Video mining software is fast—taking only hours to complete image interpretation tasks that might have taken weeks for humans to do. For example, Kahn's computers took only a couple of days to sift through 192 hours of tape on some 1,200 shoppers. Had Kahn tried to personally interview that many people, the process would have taken much longer, and the presence of the researchers might have annoyed shoppers and affected the results. "Nobody knew they were being recorded," says Greg Kahn of Kahn Research Group, "and our work didn't interfere with the store environment." Moreover, had people known they were being taped, he says, "I know many of the shoppers would have stuck their hands in front of the camera lens and refused to be recorded."

Video mining proponents say their research cameras are less invasive than security cameras, because their subjects aren't scrutinized as closely as security suspects. The images are studied only by the software and not by people, they say, and the videos are destroyed when the research is done. And marketers use the information to give their customers improved products and better service. "A driving force behind this technology is the fact that businesses want to be better prepared to serve their customers," says one marketing professor.

Still, the eavesdropping potential of video mining can be a bit unnerving. For example, VideoMining, another shopper-monitoring firm, set up cameras in two McDonald's restaurants to find out which customer types would find a new salad item most appealing. The research was done without consumers' knowledge. By measuring the shapes of people's faces, VideoMining's sensors were able to provide a breakdown of each salad buyers' race, gender, and age. The videos also revealed the length of time these customers spent waiting in line or looking at the menu before ordering. Looking ahead, the technology already exists for matching a photo with an individual's identity. Theoretically, retailers with customer databases built from the use of loyalty cards, store credit cards, and other in-house programs could link a transaction at a cash register with the face of a shopper appearing on the videotape. Smile, you're being video mined!

So, although video mining offers much promise for marketers and researchers, it also raises important privacy issues. People have pretty much learned to live with the approximately 29 million security cameras around the nation videotaping them in airports, government buildings, offices, schools, stores, busy intersections, and elsewhere. But few consumers are aware that they are being filmed for market research. Security is one thing, but the American public isn't likely to be as tolerant of secret market research using videotape.

Marketers appear to recognize this fact. ShopperTrak discloses its clients—the list includes, among others, Gap and its Banana Republic unit, The Limited and its Victoria's Secret chain, Payless ShoeSource, American Eagle Outfitters, and Children's Place Retail Stores. However, several other research companies that videotape shoppers say they sign agreements with clients in which they pledge not to disclose their names. Their clients want the taping to be secret, worrying that shoppers would feel alienated or complain of privacy invasion if they knew.

They're probably right to worry. Katherine Albrecht, founder and director of Caspian, a consumer-advocacy group, says consumers have "no idea such things as video tracking are going on," and they should be informed. When she tells them about such activities, she says the response she often hears is, "Isn't this illegal, like stalking? Shouldn't there be a law against it?" Robert Bulmash, a consumer-privacy advocate, says that being in a retailer's store doesn't give a retailer "the right to treat me like a guinea pig." He says he wonders about assurances that images are destroyed, because there isn't any way to verify such claims. The pictures "could be saved somewhere in that vast digital universe and some day come back to haunt us," he says.

Source: Portions adapted from Joseph Pereira, "Spying on the Sales Floor: Video Miners' Use Cameras Hidden in Stores to Analyze Who Shops, What They Like," Wall Street Journal, December 21, 2004, p. B1. Other information from Kelly Sitch, "Mining' Software Studies Shoppers," The Digital Collegian, January 11, 2005, accessed at www.collegian.psu.edu/archive/2005/01/01-11-05/dc/01-11-05dsciehealth-01.asp; Kahn Research Group (www.webehavior.com), July 2006; and www.videomining.com, July 2006.

research surveys appear to have been designed just to produce the intended effect. Few advertisers openly rig their research designs or blatantly misrepresent the findings; most abuses tend to be subtle "stretches." Consider the following examples:[35]

A study by Chrysler contends that Americans overwhelmingly prefer Chrysler to Toyota after test-driving both. However, the study included just 100 people in each of two tests. More importantly, none of the people surveyed owned a foreign car brand, so they appear to be favorably predisposed to U.S. brands.

A Black Flag survey asked: "A roach disk . . . poisons a roach slowly. The dying roach returns to the nest and after it dies is eaten by other roaches. In turn these roaches become poisoned and die. How effective do you think this type of product would be in killing roaches?" Not surprisingly, 79 percent said effective.

A poll sponsored by the disposable diaper industry asked: "It is estimated that disposable diapers account for less than 2 percent of the trash in today's landfills. In contrast, beverage containers, third-class mail, and yard waste are estimated to account for about 21 percent of the trash in landfills. Given this, in your opinion, would it be fair to ban disposable diapers?" Again, not surprisingly, 84 percent said no.

Thus, subtle manipulations of the study's sample or the choice or wording of questions can greatly affect the conclusions reached.

In other cases, so-called independent research studies are actually paid for by companies with an interest in the outcome. Small changes in study assumptions or in how results are interpreted can subtly affect the direction of the results. For example, at least four widely quoted studies compare the environmental effects of using disposable diapers to those of using cloth diapers. The two studies sponsored by the cloth diaper industry conclude that cloth diapers are more environmentally friendly. Not surprisingly, the other two studies, sponsored by the disposable diaper industry, conclude just the opposite. Yet both appear to be correct *given* the underlying assumptions used.

Recognizing that surveys can be abused, several associations—including the American Marketing Association, Marketing Research Association, and the Council of American Survey Research Organizations (CASRO)—have developed codes of research ethics and standards of conduct. For example, the CASRO Code of Standards and Ethics for Survey Research outlines researcher responsibilities to respondents, including confidentiality, privacy, and avoidance of harassment. It also outlines major responsibilities in reporting results to clients and the public.[36] In the end, however, unethical or inappropriate actions cannot simply be regulated away. Each company must accept responsibility for policing the conduct and reporting of its own marketing research to protect consumers' best interests and its own.

■ Reviewing the Concepts

In today's complex and rapidly changing marketplace, marketing managers need more and better information to make effective and timely decisions. This greater need for information has been matched by the explosion of information technologies for supplying information. Using today's new technologies, companies can now obtain great quantities of information, sometimes even too much. Yet marketers often complain that they lack enough of the *right* kind of information or have an excess of the *wrong* kind. In response, many companies are now studying their managers' information needs and designing information systems to help managers develop and manage market and customer information.

1. Explain the importance of information to the company and its understanding of the marketplace.

The marketing process starts with a complete understanding of the marketplace and consumer needs and wants. Thus, the company needs sound information in order to produce superior value and satisfaction for customers. The company also requires information on competitors, resellers, and other actors and forces in the marketplace. Increasingly, marketers are viewing information not only as an input for making better decisions but also as an important strategic asset and marketing tool.

2. Define the marketing information system and discuss its parts.

The *marketing information system (MIS)* consists of people, equipment, and procedures to gather, sort, analyze, evaluate, and distribute needed, timely, and accurate information to marketing decision makers. A well-designed information system begins and ends with users.

The MIS first assesses *information needs.* The marketing information system primarily serves the company's marketing and other managers, but it may also provide information to external partners. Then, the MIS *develops information* from internal databases, marketing intelligence activities, and marketing research. *Internal databases* provide information on the company's own operations and departments. Such data can be obtained quickly and cheaply but often needs to be adapted for marketing decisions. *Marketing intelligence* activities supply everyday information about developments in the external marketing environment. *Market research* consists of collecting information relevant to a specific marketing problem faced by the company. Lastly, the MIS *distributes information* gathered from these sources to the right managers in the right form and at the right time.

3. Outline the steps in the marketing research process.

The first step in the marketing research process involves *defining the problem and setting the research objectives,* which may be exploratory, descriptive, or causal research. The second step consists of *developing a research plan* for collecting data from primary and secondary sources. The third step calls for *implementing the marketing research plan* by gathering, processing, and analyzing the information. The fourth step consists of *interpreting and reporting the findings.* Additional information analysis helps marketing managers apply the information and provides them with sophisticated statistical procedures and models from which to develop more rigorous findings.

Both *internal* and *external* secondary data sources often provide information more quickly and at a lower cost than primary data sources, and they can sometimes yield information that a company cannot collect by itself. However, needed information might not exist in secondary sources. Researchers must also evaluate secondary information to ensure that it is *relevant, accurate, current,* and *impartial.* Primary research must also be evaluated for these features. Each primary data collection method—*observational, survey,* and *experimental*—has its own advantages and disadvantages. Each of the various primary research contact methods—mail, telephone, personal interview, and online—also has its own advantages and drawbacks. Similarly, each contact method has its pluses and minuses.

4. Explain how companies analyze and distribute marketing information.

Information gathered in internal databases and through marketing intelligence and marketing research usually requires more analysis. This may include advanced statistical analysis or the application of analytical models that will help marketers make better decisions. To analyze individual customer data, many companies have now acquired or developed special software and analysis techniques—called *customer relationship management (CRM)*—that integrate, analyze, and apply the mountains of individual customer data contained in their databases.

Marketing information has no value until it is used to make better marketing decisions. Thus, the marketing information system must make the information available to the managers and others who make marketing decisions or deal with customers. In some cases, this means providing regular reports and updates; in other cases it means making nonroutine information available for special situations and on-the-spot decisions. Many firms use company intranets and extranets to facilitate this process. Thanks to modern technology, today's marketing managers can gain direct access to the information system at any time and from virtually any location.

5. **Discuss the special issues some marketing researchers face, including public policy and ethics issues.**

Some marketers face special marketing research situations, such as those conducting research in small business, nonprofit, or international situations. Marketing research can be conducted effectively by small businesses and nonprofit organizations with limited budgets. International marketing researchers follow the same steps as domestic researchers but often face more and different problems. All organizations need to respond responsibly to major public policy and ethical issues surrounding marketing research, including issues of intrusions on consumer privacy and misuse of research findings.

Reviewing the Key Terms

Causal research 101
Customer relationship management (CRM) 112
Descriptive research 101
Ethnographic research 104
Experimental research 105

Exploratory research 101
Focus group interviewing 106
Internal databases 98
Marketing information system (MIS) 97

Marketing intelligence 99
Marketing research 100
Observational research 104
Online databases 103
Online marketing research 106

Primary data 102
Sample 108
Secondary data 102
Survey research 105

Discussing the Concepts

1. Figure 4.1 describes four marketing information system activities for developing information. In groups of four, determine how these activities would apply to Reebok developing the information it needs to market a new running shoe.

2. Assume that you are a regional marketing manager for a cellular phone company. List at least three different sources of internal data and discuss how these data would help you create cellular services that provide greater customer value and satisfaction.

3. Marketing research over the Internet has increased significantly in the past decade. Outline the strengths and weaknesses of marketing research conducted online.

4. According to the text, "The most common cause of CRM failures is that companies mistakenly view CRM only as a technology and software solution." What does this statement mean?

5. How does your college use an intranet to help its students access data?

6. Small businesses and nonprofit organizations often lack the resources to conduct extensive market research. Assume that you are the director of fundraising for a small nonprofit organization that focuses on a social issue. List three ways, using limited resources, that you could gather information about your primary donor group.

Applying the Concepts

1. Imagine you are an owner of a small children's retail clothing store that specializes in upscale girls' fashions from sizes 2 to 6. You have found a potential clothing line but you are unsure whether the line will generate the sales needed to be profitable. Which type of research methodology (exploratory, descriptive, or causal) is best suited to solve your research objective? Why?

2. Many consumer rights advocates argue that research data can be manipulated to support any conclusion. Assume you are attending a meeting where a research project for a new product in a new market is being presented. List five questions that you would ask to test the interpretation and objectivity of the findings being presented.

3. Visit zoomerang.com or another free online Web survey site. Using the tools at the site, design a short five-question survey on the dining services for your school. Send the survey to six friends and look at the results. What did you think of the online survey method?

Focus on Technology

Several companies offer technology that assists marketers in observational research. These techniques include cameras to monitor a shopper's movements, Web-tracking software to follow a visitor's click stream, and mechanisms to monitor the movement of a consumer's eyeballs. Visit eyetracking.com to learn more about eye-tracking devices. A visit to the "solutions" area of the Web site provides many examples of consumer marketing solutions, including television commercials, Web site branding, and package design. Eye-tracking measurements can help a television advertiser know whether the brand is noticed and, amazingly, report on whether the viewer's emotional reaction to the ad was pleasing or aversive.

1. What can marketers learn from eye-tracking technology in areas other than television advertising?

2. How can marketers use this technology to improve their marketing?

3. What might be some weaknesses with this technology?

Focus on Ethics

In 2001, Procter & Gamble (P&G) created Tremor, a network of approximately 280,000 young consumers ages 13-19. Tremor uses these teens, identified as being very connected to and influential with others, to spread word of mouth regarding not just its own products but also those of companies as diverse as AOL, Coca-Cola, and Toyota. Tremor does not pay the teens. Nor does it tell them what to say about specific products. But does provide them with extensive free samples and the knowledge that their input will be important to marketing decisions.

1. How might P&G identify, attract, and then qualify teens to be members of Tremor?

2. What do you think of using teens to spread word of mouth about products and brands? Are there any ethics issues?

Video Case

Burke

For more than 75 years, Burke has been helping marketers to understand the marketplace and build stronger relationships with customers. As a full-service, custom marketing research firm, the company helps its clients better understand everything from how consumers make purchase decisions to what drives customer loyalty. In the beginning in 1931, researchers with Burke went door to door to gather information. Today, the company uses a rich array of avenues to reach consumers, including telephone and Web interviewing, direct mail, and online surveys.

Burke helps marketers discover information about customers, competitors, products, and marketing programs. But more than just gathering information, Burke's services help clients use the information. With sophisticated computer analysis, Burke offers the right information, in the right form, at the right time to help them make better marketing decisions.

After viewing the video featuring Burke, answer the following questions about marketing research.

1. What process does Burke use to define the research question?

2. How does Burke's process for marketing research compare to the steps outlined in the chapter?

3. How does Burke help clients build strong relationships with customers?

Company Case

Enterprise Rent-A-Car: Measuring Service Quality

SURVEYING CUSTOMERS

Kevin Kirkman wheeled his shiny blue BMW coupe into his driveway, put the gearshift into park, set the parking brake, and got out to check his mailbox as he did every day when he returned home. As he flipped through the deluge of catalogs and credit card offers, he noticed a letter from Enterprise Rent-A-Car. He wondered why Enterprise would be writing him.

THE WRECK

Then he remembered. Earlier that month, Kevin had been involved in a wreck. As he was driving to work one rainy morning, another car had been unable to stop on the slick pavement and had plowed into his car as he waited at a stoplight. Thankfully, neither he nor the other driver was hurt, but both cars had sustained considerable damage. In fact, he was not able to drive his car.

Kevin had used his cell phone to call the police, and while he was waiting for the officers to come, he had called his auto insurance agent. The agent had assured Kevin that his policy included coverage to pay for a rental car while he was having his car repaired. He told Kevin to have the car towed to a nearby auto repair shop and gave him the telephone number for the Enterprise Rent-A-Car office that served his area. The agent noted that his company recommended using Enterprise for replacement rentals and that Kevin's policy would cover up to $20 per day of the rental fee.

Once Kevin had checked his car in at the body shop and made the necessary arrangements, he telephoned the Enterprise office. Within 10 minutes, an Enterprise employee had driven to the repair shop and picked him up. They drove back to the Enterprise office, where Kevin completed the paperwork and rented a Ford Taurus. He drove the rental car for 12 days before the repair shop completed work on his car.

"Don't know why Enterprise would be writing me," Kevin thought. "The insurance company paid the $20 per day, and I paid the extra because the Taurus cost more than that. Wonder what the problem could be?"

TRACKING SATISFACTION

Kevin tossed the mail on the passenger's seat and drove up the driveway. Once inside his house, he opened the Enterprise letter to find that it was a survey to determine how satisfied he was with his rental. The survey itself was only one page long and consisted of 13 questions (see Exhibit 1).

Exhibit 1

SERVICE QUALITY SURVEY

Please mark the box that best reflects your response to each question.

1. Overall, how satisfied were you with your recent car rental from Enterprise on January 1, 2003?

Completely Satisfied	Somewhat Satisfied	Neither Satisfied Nor Dissatisfied	Somewhat Dissatisfied	Completely Dissatisfied
☐	☐	☐	☐	☐

2. What, if anything, could Enterprise have done better? *(Please be specific)*

_____

3a. Did you experience any problems during the rental process?

Yes ☐
No ☐

3b. If you mentioned any problems to Enterprise, did they resolve them to your satisfaction?

Yes ☐
No ☐
Did not mention ☐

4. If you personally called Enterprise to reserve a vehicle, how would you rate the telephone reservation process?

Excellent	Good	Fair	Poor	N/A
☐	☐	☐	☐	☐

5. Did you go to the Enterprise office. . . .

Both at start and end of rental	Just at start of rental	Just at end of rental	Neither time
☐	☐	☐	☐

6. Did an Enterprise employee give you a ride to help with your transportation needs. . . .

Both at start and end of rental	Just at start of rental	Just at end of rental	Neither time
☐	☐	☐	☐

7. After you arrived at the Enterprise office, how long did it take you to:

	Less than 5 minutes	5–10 minutes	11–15 minutes	16–20 minutes	21–30 minutes	More than 30 minutes	N/A
⊛ pick up your rental car?	☐	☐	☐	☐	☐	☐	☐
⊛ return your rental car?	☐	☐	☐	☐	☐	☐	☐

8. How would you rate the . . .

	Excellent	Good	Fair	Poor	N/A
⊛ timeliness with which you were either picked up at the start of the rental or dropped off afterwards?	☐	☐	☐	☐	☐
⊛ timeliness with which the rental car was either brought to your location and left with you or picked up from your location afterwards?	☐	☐	☐	☐	☐
⊛ Enterprise employee who handled your paperwork . . . at the START of the rental?	☐	☐	☐	☐	☐
at the END of the rental?	☐	☐	☐	☐	☐
⊛ mechanical condition of the car?	☐	☐	☐	☐	☐
⊛ cleanliness of the car interior/exterior?	☐	☐	☐	☐	☐

9. If you asked for a specific type or size of vehicle, was Enterprise able to meet your needs?

Yes	No	N/A
☐	☐	☐

10. For what reason did you rent this car?

Car repairs due to accident	All other car repairs/ maintenance	Car was stolen	Business	Leisure/ vacation	Some other reason
☐	☐	☐	☐	☐	☐

11. The next time you need to pick up a rental car in the city or area in which you live, how likely are you to call Enterprise?

Definitely will call	Probably will call	Might or might not call	Probably will not call	Definitely will not call
☐	☐	☐	☐	☐

12. Approximately how many times in total have you rented from Enterprise (including this rental)?

Once—this was first time	2 times	3–5 times	6–10 times	11 or more times
☐	☐	☐	☐	☐

13. Considering *all rental companies,* approximately how many times *within the past year* have you rented a car in the city or area in which you live (including this rental)?

0 times	1 time	2 times	3–5 times	6–10 times	11 or more times
☐	☐	☐	☐	☐	☐

(case continues)

(case continued)

Enterprise's executives believed that the company had become the largest rent-a-car company in the U.S. (in terms of number of cars, rental locations, and revenue) because of its laserlike focus on customer satisfaction and because of its concentration on serving the home-city replacement market. It aimed to serve customers like Kevin who were involved in wrecks and suddenly found themselves without a car. While the more well known companies like Hertz and Avis battled for business in the cutthroat airport market, Enterprise quietly built its business by cultivating insurance agents and body-shop managers as referral agents so that when one of their clients or customers needed a replacement vehicle, they would recommend Enterprise. Although such replacement rentals accounted for about 80 percent of the company's business, it also served the discretionary market (leisure/vacation rentals), and the business market (renting cars to businesses for their short-term needs). It had also begun to provide on-site and off-site service at some airports.

Throughout its history, Enterprise had followed founder Jack Taylor's advice. Taylor believed that if the company took care of its customers and employees first, profits would follow. So the company was careful to track customer satisfaction.

CONTINUOUS IMPROVEMENT

Meanwhile, back at Enterprise's St. Louis headquarters, the company's top managers were interested in taking the next steps in their customer satisfaction program. Enterprise had used the percentage of customers who were completely satisfied to develop its Enterprise Service Quality index (ESQi). It used the survey results to calculate an overall average ESQi score for the company and a score for each individual branch. The company's branch managers believed in and supported the process.

About one in 20 randomly selected customers received a letter like Kevin's. An independent company mailed the letter and a postage-paid return envelope to the selected customers. Customers who completed the survey used the envelope to return it to the independent company. That company compiled the results and provided them to Enterprise.

However, top management believed that to really "walk the walk" on customer satisfaction, it needed to make the ESQi a key factor in the promotion process. The company wanted to take the ESQi for the branch or branches a manager supervised into consideration when it evaluated that manager for a promotion. Top management believed that such a process would ensure that its managers and all its employees would focus on satisfying Enterprise's customers.

However, the top managers realized they had two problems in taking the next step. First, they wanted a better survey response rate. Although the company got a 25 percent response rate, which was good for this type of survey, it was concerned that it might still be missing important information. Second, it could take up to two months to get results back, and Enterprise believed it needed a process that would get the customer satisfaction information more quickly, at least on a monthly basis, so its branch managers could identify and take action on customer service problems quickly and efficiently.

Enterprise's managers wondered how they could improve the customer-satisfaction-tracking process.

Questions for Discussion

1. Analyze Enterprise's Service Quality Survey. What information is it trying to gather? What are its research objectives?

2. What decisions has Enterprise made with regard to primary data collection—research approach, contact methods, sampling plan, and research instruments?

3. In addition to or instead of the mail survey, what other means could Enterprise use to gather customer satisfaction information?

4. What specific recommendations would you make to Enterprise to improve the response rate and the timeliness of feedback from the process?

Source: Officials at Enterprise Rent-A-Car contributed to and supported development of this case. See also Company Case in Chapter 18 for more details on Enterprise Rent-A-Car.

Consumer Markets and Consumer Buyer Behavior

Previewing the Concepts

In the previous chapter, you studied how marketers obtain, analyze, and use information to understand the marketplace and to assess marketing programs. In this and the next chapter, we'll continue with a closer look at the most important element of the marketplace—customers. The aim of marketing is to affect how customers think about and behave toward the organization and its market offerings. To affect the *whats, whens,* and *hows* of buying behavior, marketers must first understand the *whys.* In this chapter, we look at *final consumer* buying influences and processes. In the next chapter, we'll study the buyer behavior of *business customers.* You'll see that understanding buyer behavior is an essential but very difficult task.

To get a better sense of the importance of understanding consumer behavior, let's look first at Harley-Davidson, maker of the nation's top-selling heavyweight motorcycles. Who rides these big Harley "Hogs"? What moves them to tattoo their bodies with the Harley emblem, abandon home and hearth for the open road, and flock to Harley rallies by the hundreds of thousands? *You* might be surprised, but Harley-Davidson knows *very* well.

Few brands engender such intense loyalty as that found in the hearts of Harley-Davidson owners. Harley buyers are granitelike in their devotion to the brand. "You don't see people tattooing Yamaha on their bodies," observes the publisher of *American Iron,* an industry publication. And according to another industry insider, "For a lot of people, it's not that they want a motorcycle; it's that they want a Harley—the brand is that strong."

Each year, in early March, more than 350,000 Harley bikers rumble through the streets of Daytona Beach, Florida, to attend Harley-Davidson's Bike Week celebration. Bikers from across the nation lounge on their low-slung Harleys, swap biker tales, and sport T-shirts proclaiming "I'd rather push a Harley than drive a Honda."

Riding such intense emotions, Harley-Davidson has rumbled its way to the top of the heavyweight motorcycle market. Harley's "Hogs" capture 23 percent of all U.S. bike sales and almost 50 percent of the heavyweight segment. For several years running, sales have outstripped supply, with customer waiting lists of up to two years for popular models and street prices running well above suggested list prices. During just the past 5 years, Harley sales have increased more than 50 percent, and earnings have jumped more than 75 percent. By 2006, the company had experienced 20 straight years of record sales and income.

Harley-Davidson's marketers spend a great deal of time thinking about customers and their buying behavior. They want to know who their customers are, what they think and how they feel, and why they buy a Harley Fat Boy Softail rather than a Yamaha or a Kawasaki or a big Honda American Classic. What is it that makes Harley buyers so fiercely loyal? These are difficult questions; even Harley owners themselves don't know exactly what motivates their buying. But Harley management puts top priority on understanding customers and what makes them tick.

Who rides a Harley? You might be surprised. It's no longer just the Hell's Angels crowd—the burly, black-leather-jacketed rebels and biker chicks who once made up Harley's core clientele. Motorcycles are attracting a new breed of riders—older, more affluent, and better educated. Harley now appeals more to "rubbies" (rich urban bikers) than to rebels. "While the outlaw bad-boy biker image is what we might typically associate with Harley riders," says an analyst, "they're just as likely to be CEOs and investment bankers." The average Harley customer is a 46-year-old husband with a median household income of $82,000. More than 10 percent of Harley purchases today are made by women.

Harley-Davidson makes good bikes, and to keep up with its shifting market, the company has upgraded its showrooms and sales approaches. But Harley customers are buying a lot more than just a quality bike and a smooth sales pitch. To gain a better understanding of customers' deeper motivations, Harley-Davidson conducted focus groups in which it invited bikers to make cut-and-paste collages of pictures that expressed their feelings about Harley-Davidsons. (Can't you just see a bunch of hard-core bikers doing this?) It then mailed out 16,000 surveys containing a typical battery of psychological, sociological, and demographic questions as well as subjective questions such as "Is Harley more typified by a brown bear or a lion?"

The research revealed seven core customer types: adventure-loving traditionalists, sensitive pragmatists, stylish status seekers, laid-back campers, classy capitalists, cool-headed loners, and cocky misfits. However, all owners appreciated their Harleys for the same basic reasons. "It didn't matter if you were the guy who swept the floors of the factory or if you were the CEO at that factory, the attraction to Harley was very similar," says a Harley executive. "Independence, freedom, and power were the universal Harley appeals."

"It's much more than a machine," says the analyst. "It is part of their own self-expression and lifestyle." Another analyst suggests that owning a Harley makes you "the toughest, baddest guy on the block. Never mind that [you're] a dentist or an accountant. You [feel] wicked astride all that power." Your Harley renews your spirits and announces your independence. As the Harley Web site's home page announces, "Thumbing the starter of a Harley-Davidson does a lot more than fire the engine. It fires the imagination." Adds a Harley dealer: "We sell a dream here." The classic look, the throaty sound, the very idea of a Harley—all contribute to its mystique. Owning this "American legend" makes you a part of something bigger, a member of the Harley family.

Such strong emotions and motivations are captured in a classic Harley-Davidson advertisement. The ad shows a close-up of an arm, the bicep adorned with a Harley-Davidson tattoo. The headline asks, "When was the last time you felt this strongly about anything?" The ad copy outlines the problem and suggests a solution: "Wake up in the morning and life picks up where it left off. . . . What once seemed exciting has now become part of the numbing routine. It all begins to feel the same. Except

Objectives

After studying this chapter, you should be able to

1. define the consumer market and construct a simple model of consumer buyer behavior
2. name the four major factors that influence consumer buyer behavior
3. list and define the major types of buying decision behavior and the stages in the buyer decision process
4. describe the adoption and diffusion process for new products

when you've got a Harley-Davidson. Something strikes a nerve. The heartfelt thunder rises up, refusing to become part of the background. Suddenly things are different. Clearer. More real. As they should have been all along. Riding a Harley changes you from within. The effect is permanent. Maybe it's time you started feeling this strongly. Things are different on a Harley."[1]

Consumer buyer behavior

The buying behavior of final consumers—individuals and households who buy goods and services for personal consumption.

Consumer market

All the individuals and households who buy or acquire goods and services for personal consumption.

The Harley-Davidson example shows that many different factors affect consumer buyer behavior. Buyer behavior is never simple, yet understanding it is the essential task of marketing management. **Consumer buyer behavior** refers to the buying behavior of final consumers—individuals and households who buy goods and services for personal consumption. All of these final consumers combine to make up the **consumer market**. The American consumer market consists of more than 300 million people who consume more than $12 trillion worth of goods and services each year, making it one of the most attractive consumer markets in the world. The world consumer market consists of more than 6.5 *billion* people who annually consume an estimated $61 trillion worth of goods and services.[2]

Consumers around the world vary tremendously in age, income, education level, and tastes. They also buy an incredible variety of goods and services. How these diverse consumers relate with each other and with other elements of the world around them impacts their choices among various products, services, and companies. Here we examine the fascinating array of factors that affect consumer behavior.

Model of Consumer Behavior

Consumers make many buying decisions every day. Most large companies research consumer buying decisions in great detail to answer questions about what consumers buy, where they buy, how and how much they buy, when they buy, and why they buy. Marketers can study actual consumer purchases to find out what they buy, where, and how much. But learning about the *whys* of consumer buying behavior is not so easy—the answers are often locked deep within the consumer's mind.

"For companies with billions of dollars on the line, the buying decision is the most crucial part of their enterprise," states one consumer behavior analyst. "Yet no one really knows how the human brain makes that choice." Often, consumers themselves don't know exactly what influences their purchases. "Buying decisions are made at an unconscious level," says the analyst, "and . . . consumers don't generally give very reliable answers if you simply ask them, 'Why did you buy this?'"[3]

The central question for marketers is: How do consumers respond to various marketing efforts the company might use? The starting point is the stimulus response model of buyer behavior shown in Figure 5.1. This figure shows that marketing and other stimuli enter the consumer's "black box" and produce certain responses. Marketers must figure out what is in the buyer's black box.

Marketing stimuli consist of the Four Ps: product, price, place, and promotion. Other stimuli include major forces and events in the buyer's environment: economic, technological, political, and cultural. All these inputs enter the buyer's black box, where they are turned into a set of observable buyer responses: product choice, brand choice, dealer choice, purchase timing, and purchase amount.

The marketer wants to understand how the stimuli are changed into responses inside the consumer's black box, which has two parts. First, the buyer's characteristics influence how he

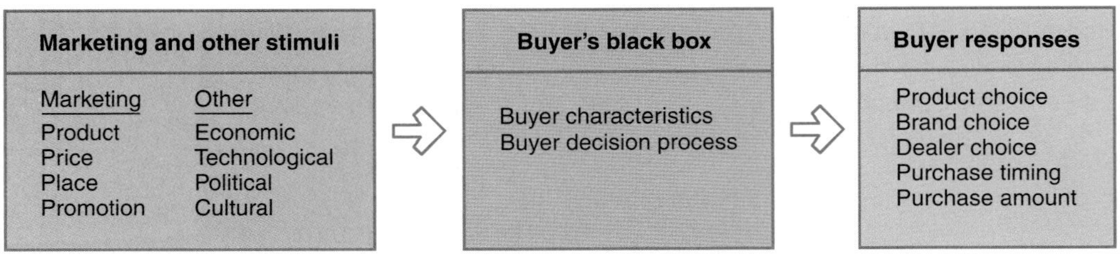

FIGURE 5.1
Model of buyer behavior

Marketing and other stimuli		Buyer's black box	Buyer responses
Marketing	**Other**	Buyer characteristics	Product choice
Product	Economic	Buyer decision process	Brand choice
Price	Technological		Dealer choice
Place	Political		Purchase timing
Promotion	Cultural		Purchase amount

or she perceives and reacts to the stimuli. Second, the buyer's decision process itself affects the buyer's behavior. We look first at buyer characteristics as they affect buyer behavior and then discuss the buyer decision process.

Characteristics Affecting Consumer Behavior

Consumer purchases are influenced strongly by cultural, social, personal, and psychological characteristics, shown in Figure 5.2. For the most part, marketers cannot control such factors, but they must take them into account.

Cultural Factors

Cultural factors exert a broad and deep influence on consumer behavior. The marketer needs to understand the role played by the buyer's *culture, subculture,* and *social class.*

Culture

Culture is the most basic cause of a person's wants and behavior. Human behavior is largely learned. Growing up in a society, a child learns basic values, perceptions, wants, and behaviors from the family and other important institutions. A child in the United States normally learns or is exposed to the following values: achievement and success, activity and involvement, efficiency and practicality, progress, material comfort, individualism, freedom, humanitarianism, youthfulness, and fitness and health. Every group or society has a culture, and cultural influences on buying behavior may vary greatly from country to country. Failure to adjust to these differences can result in ineffective marketing or embarrassing mistakes.

Marketers are always trying to spot *cultural shifts* in order to discover new products that might be wanted. For example, the cultural shift toward greater concern about health and fitness has created a huge industry for health-and-fitness services, exercise equipment and clothing, more-natural foods, and a variety of diets. The shift toward informality has resulted in more demand for casual clothing and simpler home furnishings.

Subculture

Each culture contains smaller **subcultures**, or groups of people with shared value systems based on common life experiences and situations. Subcultures include nationalities, religions, racial groups, and geographic regions. Many subcultures make up important market segments, and marketers often design products and marketing programs tailored to their needs. Examples of four such important subculture groups include Hispanic, African American, Asian American, and mature consumers.

HISPANIC CONSUMERS The U.S. *Hispanic market*—Americans of Cuban, Mexican, Central American, South American, and Puerto Rican descent—consists of more than 41 million consumers. It's the fastest growing U.S. subsegment—one in every two new Americans since 2000 is Hispanic. By 2050, this group will make up about 25 percent of the U.S. population. Hispanic

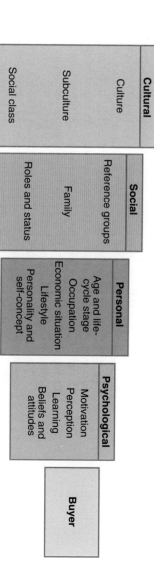

FIGURE 5.2
Factors influencing consumer behavior

Culture
The set of basic values, perceptions, wants, and behaviors learned by a member of society from family and other important institutions.

Subculture
A group of people with shared value systems based on common life experiences and situations.

Cultural	Social	Personal	Psychological	Buyer
Culture	Reference groups	Age and life-cycle stage	Motivation	
Subculture	Family	Occupation	Perception	
Social class	Roles and status	Economic situation	Learning	
		Lifestyle	Beliefs and attitudes	
		Personality and self-concept		

purchasing power, estimated at $700 billion annually, is expected to increase to more than $1 trillion by 2010. One out of every ten U.S. small businesses is Hispanic owned.[4]

Hispanic consumers tend to buy more branded, higher-quality products—generics don't sell well to this group. They tend to make shopping a family affair, and children have a big say in what brands they buy. Perhaps more important, Hispanics are very brand loyal, and they favor companies who show special interest in them.

Most major marketers now produce products tailored to the Hispanic market and promote them using Spanish-language ads and media. For example, Procter & Gamble, one of the nation's leading multicultural marketers, spent almost $160 million last year on Hispanic print and television advertising for major brands such as Pantene, Tide, Crest, and Pampers.[5] It creates special Hispanic versions of some of its products. For instance, its Pantene Extra Liso (extra straight) line of hair-care products is specially formulated with Hispanic women in mind.

But P&G's Hispanic marketing efforts run much deeper. Consider the following example:[6]

Julieta Parilla, a new mother living in a predominantly Hispanic working-class suburb of Los Angeles, is a diehard Pampers fan. She first heard about Pampers from her sister. But strong marketing from Procter & Gamble has turned the 21-year-old single mother into a very loyal customer. Julieta recalls a Pampers television ad she liked, broadcast in both English and Spanish, showing a smiling baby crawling in the diapers. The nurses at the medical center where she had her baby, Fatima, gave her free samples of Pampers as she checked out, along with other P&G brands such as Crest and Tide. At a local health clinic, Julieta picked up a copy of *Avanzando con Tu Familia* (Helping Your Family Move Ahead), a P&G-published, *Martha Stewart Living*–type magazine for recent Hispanic immigrants that reaches a million homes across the country. Besides coupons for P&G products, the magazine provides recipes, exercise tips, and lifestyle advice. Julieta especially liked a story on how to clean her newborn, and she has been impressed by P&G's support for the Hispanic Scholarship Fund.

Over the past five years, such targeted marketing efforts have helped P&G to increase Pampers' share of the Hispanic market by 25 percent. More broadly, 6 of the 12 brands managed by P&G's ethnic-marketing division are now ranked number one among Hispanics in their categories, and five others rank second.

AFRICAN AMERICAN CONSUMERS With annual buying power of $762 million, estimated to reach $981 billion by 2010, the nation's 39.7 million *African American* consumers also attract much marketing attention. The U.S. black population is growing in affluence and sophistication. Although more price conscious than other segments, blacks are also strongly motivated by quality and selection. Brands are important. So is shopping—black consumers seem to enjoy shopping more than other groups, even for something as mundane as groceries. Black consumers are also the most fashion conscious of the ethnic groups.[7]

In recent years, many companies have developed special products and services, appeals, and marketing programs to reach African Americans consumers. For example, Hallmark launched its Afrocentric brand, Mahogany, with only 16 cards in 1987. Today the brand features more than 800 cards designed to celebrate African American culture, heritage, and traditions.[8] St. Joseph Aspirin, focusing on unique African American health issues, runs print ads noting that their aspirin comes in the dosage recommended by the Association of Black Cardiologists for daily heart therapy.

Financial services provider J.P. Morgan Chase makes a special effort to target black consumers with home financing products and services. Rather than the standard approach of touting low interest rates, Chase stresses the benefits of home ownership. It sponsors and participates in hundreds of conferences for minority professional groups, such as the National

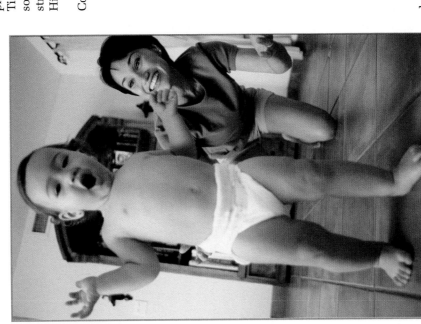

■ Procter & Gamble spends heavily on marketing to Hispanics. As a result, consumers like Julieta Parilla are diehard fans of Pampers and other P&G brands.

Association of Real Estate Brokers, the Urban League, 100 Black Men, and local gatherings of community leaders and politicians.[9]

A wide variety of magazines, television channels, and other media now target African American consumers. Marketers are also reaching out to the African American virtual community. Per capita, black consumers spend twice as much as white consumers for online services. African Americans are increasingly turning to Web sites such as BlackPlanet.com, an African American community site with more than 13 million registered users. BlackPlanet.com's mission is to enable members to "cultivate meaningful personal and professional relationships, stay informed about the world, and gain access to goods and services that allow members to do more in life." Other popular sites include BET.com and BlackVoices.com.[10]

ASIAN AMERICAN CONSUMERS   *Asian Americans* are the most affluent U.S. demographic segment. They now number more than 14.4 million and wield more than $396.5 billion in annual spending power. They are the second-fastest-growing population subsegment after Hispanics. Chinese Americans constitute the largest group, followed by Filipinos, Japanese Americans, Asian Indians, and Korean Americans. The U.S. Asian American population is expected to more than double by 2050, when it will make up more than 9 percent of the U.S. population.[11]

Asian consumers may be the most tech-savvy segment—more than 85 percent of English-speaking Asian Americans go online regularly and are most comfortable with Internet technologies such as online banking and instant messaging. As a group, Asian consumers shop frequently and are the most brand conscious of all the ethnic groups. They can be fiercely brand loyal.[12]

Because of the segment's rapidly growing buying power, many firms are now targeting the Asian American market. For example, consider Wal-Mart. Today, in one Seattle store, where Asian Americans represent over 13 percent of the population, Wal-Mart stocks a large selection of CDs and videos from Asian artists, Asian-favored health and beauty products, and children's learning videos that feature multiple language tracks. The giant retailer recently launched an Asian-language television, radio, and print advertising blitz in markets with high concentrations of Asian Americans, such as Los Angeles, San Francisco, San Diego, and Houston. The ads feature actual Asian American shoppers speaking in their native languages about why they shop at Wal-Mart. In a Chinese ad, a family recounts how its weekly Wal-Mart shopping trip is a family bonding experience.[13]

MATURE CONSUMERS   As the U.S. population ages, *mature consumers* are becoming a very attractive market. Now 68 million strong, the population of U.S. seniors will more than double in the next 25 years. The 65-and-over crowd alone numbers close to 37 million, more than 12 percent of the population. Mature consumers are better off financially than are younger consumer groups. Because mature consumers have more time and money, they are an ideal market for exotic travel, restaurants, high-tech home entertainment products, leisure goods and services, designer furniture and fashions, financial services, and health care services.[14]

Their desire to look as young as they feel also makes more-mature consumers good candidates for cosmetics and personal care products, health foods, fitness products, and other items that combat the effects of aging. The best strategy is to appeal to their active, multidimensional lives. For example, Kellogg aired a TV spot for All-Bran cereal in which individuals ranging in age from 53 to 81 are featured playing ice hockey, water skiing, running hurdles, and playing baseball, all to the tune of "Wild Thing." A Pepsi ad features a young man at a rock concert who turns around to see his father rocking out nearby. And an Aetna commercial portrays a senior who, after retiring from a career as a lawyer, fulfills a lifelong dream of becoming an archeologist.

■ Targeting Asian American consumers: Wal-Mart print ads feature actual Asian American shoppers speaking in their native languages about why they shop at Wal-Mart. In this Chinese ad, a family recounts how its weekly Wal-Mart shopping trip is a family bonding experience.

Social Class

Social class

Relatively permanent and ordered divisions in a society whose members share similar values, interests, and behaviors.

Almost every society has some form of social class structure. **Social classes** are society's relatively permanent and ordered divisions whose members share similar values, interests, and behaviors. Social scientists have identified the seven American social classes shown in Figure 5.3.

Social class is not determined by a single factor, such as income, but is measured as a combination of occupation, income, education, wealth, and other variables. In some social systems, members of different classes are reared for certain roles and cannot change their social positions. In the United States, however, the lines between social classes are not fixed and rigid; people can move to a higher social class or drop into a lower one.

Marketers are interested in social class because people within a given social class tend to exhibit similar buying behavior. Social classes show distinct product and brand preferences in areas such as clothing, home furnishings, leisure activity, and automobiles.

Social Factors

A consumer's behavior also is influenced by social factors, such as the consumer's *small groups*, *family*, and *social roles* and *status*.

Groups

Group

Two or more people who interact to accomplish individual or mutual goals.

A person's behavior is influenced by many small **groups**. Groups that have a direct influence and to which a person belongs are called membership groups. In contrast, reference groups

Upper Class

Upper Uppers (1 percent): The social elite who live on inherited wealth. They give large sums to charity, own more than one home, and send their children to the finest schools.

Lower Uppers (2 percent): Americans who have earned high income or wealth through exceptional ability. They are active in social and civic affairs and buy expensive homes, educations, and cars.

Middle Class

Upper Middles (12 percent): Professionals, independent businesspersons, and corporate managers who possess neither family status nor unusual wealth. They believe in education, are joiners and highly civic minded, and want the "better things in life."

Middle Class (32 percent): Average-pay white- and blue-collar workers who live on "the better side of town." They buy popular products to keep up with trends. Better living means owning a nice home in a nice neighborhood with good schools.

Working Class

Working Class (38 percent): Those who lead a "working-class lifestyle," whatever their income, school background, or job. They depend heavily on relatives for economic and emotional support, for advice on purchases, and for assistance in times of trouble.

Lower Class

Upper Lowers (9 percent): The working poor. Although their living standard is just above poverty, they strive toward a higher class. However, they often lack education and are poorly paid for unskilled work.

Lower Lowers (7 percent): Visibly poor, often poorly educated unskilled laborers. They are often out of work and some depend on public assistance. They tend to live a day-to-day existence.

Wealth   Education   Occupation   Income

FIGURE 5.3

The major American social classes

serve as direct (face-to-face) or indirect points of comparison or reference in forming a person's attitudes or behavior. People often are influenced by reference groups to which they do not belong. For example, an aspirational group is one to which the individual wishes to belong, as when a young girl soccer player hopes to someday emulate Mia Hamm and play on the U.S. women's Olympic soccer team.

Marketers try to identify the reference groups of their target markets. Reference groups expose a person to new behaviors and lifestyles, influence the person's attitudes and self-concept, and create pressures to conform that may affect the person's product and brand choices. The importance of group influence varies across products and brands. It tends to be strongest when the product is visible to others whom the buyer respects.

Manufacturers of products and brands subjected to strong group influence must figure out how to reach **opinion leaders**—people within a reference group who, because of special skills, knowledge, personality, or other characteristics, exert social influence on others. Some experts call this 10 percent of Americans *the influentials* or *leading adopters*. These consumers "drive trends, influence mass opinion and, most importantly, sell a great many products," says one expert. They often use their big circle of acquaintances to "spread their knowledge on what's good and what's bad."[15]

Marketers often try to identify opinion leaders for their products and direct marketing efforts toward them. They use *buzz marketing* by enlisting or even creating opinion leaders to spread the word about their brands. For example, Tremor and Vocalpoint, separate marketing arms of Procter & Gamble, have enlisted armies of buzzers to create word of mouth, not just for P&G products but for those of other client companies as well (see Real Marketing 5.1).

In the past few years, a new type of social interaction has exploded onto the scene—online *social networking*—carried out over Internet media ranging from blogs to social networking sites such as MySpace.com and Facebook.com. This new form of high-tech buzz has big implications for marketers.

Personal connections—forged through words, pictures, video, and audio posted just for the [heck] of it—are the life of the new Web, bringing together the estimated 60 million bloggers, [an unbelievable] 72 million MySpace.com users, and millions more on single-use social networks where people share one category of stuff, like Flickr (photos), Del.icio.us (links), Digg (news stories), Wikipedia (encyclopedia articles), and YouTube (video). . . . It's hard to overstate the coming impact of these new network technologies on business: They hatch trends and build immense waves of interest in specific products. They serve [up] giant, targeted audiences to advertisers. They edge out old media with the loving labor of amateurs. They effortlessly provide hyperdetailed data to marketers. If your customers are satisfied, networks can help build fanatical loyalty; if not, they'll amplify every complaint until you do something about it. [The new social networking technologies] provide an authentic, peer-to-peer channel of communication that is far more credible than any corporate flackery.[16]

Marketers are working to harness the power of these new social networks to promote their products and build closer customer relationships. For example, when Volkswagen set up a MySpace.com site for Helga, the German-accented, dominatrix-type blonde who appears in its controversial Volkswagen GTI ads, tens of thousands of fans signed up as "friends."[17] And companies regularly post ads or custom videos on video-sharing sites such as YouTube.

When Adidas recently reintroduced its adicolor shoe, a customizable white-on-white sneaker with a set of seven color markers, it signed on seven top creative directors to develop innovative videos designed especially for downloading to iPods and other

Opinion leader
Person within a reference group who, because of special skills, knowledge, personality, or other characteristics, exerts social influence on others.

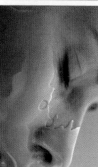

■ Social networking: Adidas harnessed the power of social networks to reintroduce its customizable adicolor shoe. It developed innovative downloadable videos that celebrate color and personal expression—here in pink—and then released them through e-mail and social networking sites like YouTube.

Real Marketing | Tremor and Vocalpoint: What's the Latest Buzz?

5.1 Gina Lavagna is the ideal pitch gal. After receiving information about Sony's latest compact digital music player and six $10-off coupons, she rushed four of her teen chums to a mall near her home to show them the cool new device, which sells for $99 and up. "I've probably told 20 people about it," she says, adding, "At least 10 are extremely interested in getting one." Her parents got her one for Christmas.

Procter & Gamble couldn't ask for a better salesperson than Donna Wetherell. The gregarious Columbus, Ohio, mom works at a customer service call center unaffiliated with P&G, where she knows some 300 coworkers by name. Lately, Wetherell has spent so much time at work talking about P&G products and handing out discount coupons that her colleagues have given her a nickname. "I am called the coupon lady," Wetherell says.

Multiply Gina Lavagna by 250,000 teens, and Donna Wetherell by 600,000 moms, and you'll get a notion of the size and impact of P&G's huge and carefully cultivated stealth marketing force. Gina and Donna aren't just any consumers. They're members of P&G's Tremor and Vocalpoint word-of-mouth marketing arms—natural-born buzzers on a mission to spread the word about P&G and other companies' brands among their peers.

It all started five years ago when P&G created Tremor, a word-of-mouth network to reach teens. Teens are maddeningly difficult to reach through traditional channels—more than other consumer groups, they tend to ignore mass-media messages or even to resent them. Tremor taps the power of peer-to-peer personal endorsements that cut through the advertising clutter. Tremorites deliver the word in school cafeterias, at sleepovers, by cell phone, and by e-mail.

Initially focused only on P&G brands, Tremor's forces were soon being tapped to talk up other companies' brands. More than 80 percent of Tremor's campaigns are now for non-P&G brands, such as Coca-Cola, Toyota, Kraft, and shoe company Vans. Tremor has been so successful that P&G has built a massive new network—Vocalpoint—focusing on moms. The moms market is a much bigger and more affluent target than teens, and a market that's more relevant to most P&G products. Initially, Vocalpoint has focused on moms with school-age kids, women who interact more with other moms.

To fill their enormous ranks, Tremor and Vocalpoint recruit online for what they call "connectors"—people with vast networks of friends and a gift for gab. For example, whereas average teens have only about 30 names on their instant messaging buddy lists, Tremorites average 150 to 200 names. Vocalpoint moms have five to six times the average number of friends and acquaintances. These connectors are carefully screened—only about 10 percent of those

who apply are accepted. In addition to connectedness, the company is looking for natural talkers with large doses of inquisitiveness and persuasiveness.

Except for educating Tremorites and Vocalpointers about products and supplying them samples and coupons, the company doesn't coach the teens and moms. The connectors themselves choose whether or not to pitch the product to friends and what to say. For example, when Gina Lavagna learned from Tremor about Clairol Herbal Essences Fruit Fusions Shampoo and Noxzema face wash, it was her own idea to invite her pals over so they could try it.

Tremorites and Vocalpointers also do the work without pay. What's in it for them? For one thing, they receive a steady flow of coupons and samples. But more than that, says CEO Knox, the company promises two things. First, it "provides you with cool new ideas before your friends have them," with the thrill of being an insider. Second, it gives them a voice. "They're filled with great ideas, and they don't think anybody listens to them," says Knox. "It's an empowering proposition [just to be heard]."

Buzz marketing is one of today's hottest new marketing practices. Still, jumping onto the buzz bandwagon carries some risks. For example, because Tremor and Vocalpoint connectors aren't coached or controlled, word of mouth can quickly backfire. If the teens and moms like what they see, they'll be quick to share the good news. If not, they might be even quicker to share the bad. Says one word-of-mouth expert, it's "like playing with fire: It can be a positive force when harnessed for the good, but fires are very destructive when they are out of control. If word of mouth goes against you, you're sunk."

Moreover, some advocacy groups and others question the ethics, even the legality, of recruiting people to promote products by word of mouth without disclosing that fact. One such group, Commercial Alert, has filed a complaint with the FTC against Tremor and several small buzz marketing agencies. But Tremor insiders ardently defend their own campaigns and buzz marketing in general. "We encourage [connectors] to talk freely, whether positively or negatively. We do not give them a script," says a company spokeswoman. "We think that's a very important part of the model," agrees Knox. "The connectors need to be free to say whatever it is they want to say. It's [really just] natural human behavior. . . . People like talking to people about things they think help them."

Despite the risks and criticisms, Tremor and Vocalpoint are producing striking results. According to one analyst, most companies see a 10 to 30 percent boost in sales after employing the word-of-mouth networks. Consider these examples:

Shamrock Farms of Phoenix launched a new chocolate-malt-flavored milk in Phoenix and Tucson. The launch tactics were

handhelds. The directors were given complete creative control to interpret their assigned color as they saw fit. "The directors that we chose we feel have a good deal of underground street cred," says an Adidas marketing executive. The project was not tied specifically to the product. Rather, the directors were asked to "celebrate color, customization, and personal expression." The diverse set of short films was then released, one film a week, via e-mail and sites such as YouTube. The films drew more than 2.1 million viewers within three weeks, 20 million within the first two months, and the numbers were growing exponentially with each new release.[18]

identical in both cities, with one exception: 2,100 Phoenix Tremorites received product information, coupons, and stickers. Shamrock reports that after 23 weeks, sales of the new milk flavor were 18 percent higher in Phoenix than in Tucson. Coupon redemption in Phoenix was 21 percent, higher than the dairy had ever achieved. To Shamrock's pleasant surprise, overall milk sales in Phoenix rose by 4 percent as well.

In traditional ads introducing new Dawn Direct Foam, P&G stressed its potent grease-cutting power. But in packets mailed to Vocalpoint moms, it showed the detergent and a smiling girl on the outside with these words in big letters: "Mom, can I help?" A pamphlet inside explained that the soap is so fun to use that kids would want to help out with the dishes. To reinforce the point, the packet included a little sponge in the shape of a child's foot, plus a dozen $1.50 coupons. "We have to enable a conversation to take place," CEO Knox says. "Kids not doing enough chores is a conversation taking place among moms." Donna Wetherell, the Vocalpoint connector in Columbus, says she talked about Dawn Direct Foam with about 100 female coworkers at her call center. "There are a lot of women there who have kids," says Wetherell, 51, who has a daughter, 17. "We were all interested." Adds Lavonda Harrington, 28, another Columbus connector: "My daughter loves the foot-shaped sponge." That kind of buzz may explain the explosive sales results in the three test markets. Dawn unit sales in those locations were double those of markets without a Vocalpoint effort.

Thus, business is buzzing at P&G—and the Tremor and Vocalpoint grapevines are growing faster then Jack's beanstalk. Says CEO Knox, "We know that the most powerful form of marketing is [a]

But marketers need to be careful when tapping into online social networking. Ultimately, the users control the content, and online network marketing attempts can easily backfire. For example, when Chevrolet recently launched a Web contest inviting folks to create their own ads for its Chevy Tahoe, it quickly lost control. Says one observer, "the entries that got passed around, blogged about, and eventually covered in the mainstream media were all about the SUV's abysmal gas mileage and melting polar ice caps." One user-generated ad proclaimed, "Like this snowy wilderness? Better get your fill of it now. Then say hello to global warming." Another concluded, "$70 to fill up the tank, which will last less than 400 miles. Chevy Tahoe."[19]

The Tremor Crew

TREMOR

Do you like to Influence your friends?

Companies listen to Tremor Teens

TREMOR MEMBER APPROVED!

Tremor and Vocalpoint, separate marketing arms of Procter & Gamble, have enlisted armies of buzzers to create word-of-mouth for brands. "We know that the most powerful form of marketing is a message from a trusted friend."

Sources: Extracts adapted from Robert Berner, "I Sold It through the Grapevine," *BusinessWeek,* May 29, 2006, pp. 32–34; and Melanie Wells, "Kid Nabbing," *Forbes,* February 2, 2004, p. 84. Quotes and other information from Samar Farah, "Making Waves," *CMO Magazine,* July 2005; Jeff Gelles, "Tremor: Shaky Stuff," *The Seattle Times,* December 4, 2005, p. L6; Bruce Horovitz, "P&G 'Buzz Marketing' Unit Hit With Complaint," *USA Today,* October 19, 2005, p. 1B; Todd Wasserman, "Q+A: P&G Buzz Program Tremor Moving on to Mothers," *Brandweek,* September 26, 2006, p. 15; and Jack Neff, "P&G Provides Product Launchpad, A Buzz Network Of Moms," *Advertising Age,* March 20, 2006, p. 1.

Family

Family members can strongly influence buyer behavior. The family is the most important consumer buying organization in society, and it has been researched extensively. Marketers are interested in the roles and influence of the husband, wife, and children on the purchase of different products and services.

Husband-wife involvement varies widely by product category and by stage in the buying process. Buying roles change with evolving consumer lifestyles. In the United States, the wife traditionally has been the main purchasing agent for the family in the areas of food, household products, and clothing. But with 70 percent of women holding jobs outside the home and the willingness of husbands to do more of the family's purchasing, all this is changing. Men now account for about 40 percent of all food-shopping dollars. And whereas women make up just 40 percent of drivers, they now influence more than 80 percent of car-buying decisions. In all, women now make almost 85 percent of all purchases, spending $6 trillion each year.[20]

Such changes suggest that marketers in industries that have sold their products to only men or only women are now courting the opposite sex. For example, after realizing that women today account for 50 percent of all technology purchases, Dell has stepped up its efforts to woo women buyers.[21]

Managers from Dell's marketing and public relations staff met earlier this year with editors and sales reps at a dozen publications. Their mission wasn't too surprising: Get editors to print more about Dell's computers, televisions, and pocketPCs. It was the choice of magazines that was unusual, including Oprah Winfrey's *O at Home*, *Ladies' Home Journal*, and *CosmoGIRL*—not exactly publications on the company's regular radar screen. In barely six months, though, Dell's laser printer, plasma TV, and notebook computer were featured as must-haves in gift guides in shelter magazines *Real Simple* and *O at Home*. And in a recent issue, *CosmoGIRL* gave Dell's Inspiron 700m, four-pound notebook a "kiss of approval." Why the new emphasis on women buyers? Dell's has realized that women are its fastest-growing customer group and a key to its growth strategy, especially as it branches out to TVs and MP3 players. Its own research shows that women make up half of its buyers and are as likely as men to prefer buying PCs online. So besides the women's magazines, Dell is running ads on women-centric cable-TV channels such as Oxygen and Lifetime Television. Until recently, says Dell's director of customer experience, "you wouldn't have seen any Dell ads on these women's channels."

Children may also have a strong influence on family buying decisions. The nation's 36 million kids age 3 to 11 wield an estimated $18 billion in disposable income. They also influence an additional $115 billion that their families spend on them in areas such as food, clothing, entertainment, and personal care items. For example, one recent study found that kids significantly influence family decisions about where they take vacations and what cars and cell phones they buy. As a result, marketers of cars, full-service restaurants, cell phones, and travel destinations are now placing ads on networks such as Cartoon Network and Toon Disney. Nickelodeon recently signed multimillion-dollar advertising deals with Chevrolet and Kia. Chevrolet runs TV ads on Nickelodeon television and print ads in *Nickelodeon Magazine* for its Uplander sports van.[22]

■ Children may have a strong influence on family buying decisions for everything from cell phones to restaurants to cars. To capture such family buying influences, Chevrolet runs ads like this one for its Uplander sports van in kid-focused Nickelodeon Magazine, featuring a family Big Wish Sweepstakes.

Roles and Status

A person belongs to many groups—family, clubs, and organizations. The person's position in each group can be defined in terms of both role and status. A role consists of the activities people are expected to perform according to the persons around them. Each role carries a status reflecting the general esteem given to it by society.

People usually choose products appropriate to their roles and status. Consider the various roles a working mother plays. In her company, she plays the role of a brand manager; in her family, she plays the role of wife and mother; at her favorite sporting events, she plays the role of avid fan. As a brand manager, she will buy the kind of clothing that reflects her role and status in her company.

Personal Factors

A buyer's decisions also are influenced by personal characteristics such as the buyer's *age and life-cycle stage, occupation, economic situation, lifestyle, and personality and self-concept*.

Age and Life-Cycle Stage

People change the goods and services they buy over their lifetimes. Tastes in food, clothes, furniture, and recreation are often age related. Buying is also shaped by the stage of the family life cycle—the stages through which families might pass as they mature over time. Marketers often define their target markets in terms of life-cycle stage and develop appropriate products and marketing plans for each stage.

Traditional family life-cycle stages include young singles and married couples with children. Today, however, marketers are increasingly catering to a growing number of alternative, nontraditional stages such as unmarried couples, singles marrying later in life, childless couples, same-sex couples, single parents, extended parents (those with young adult children returning home), and others.

RBC Royal Bank has identified five life-stage segments. The *youth* segment includes customers younger than 18. *Getting Started* consists of customers aged 18 to 35 who are going through first experiences, such as graduation, first credit card, first car, first loan, marriage, and first child. *Builders*, customers aged 35 to 50, are in their peak earning years. As they build careers and family, they tend to borrow more than they invest. *Accumulators*, aged 50 to 60, worry about saving for retirement and investing wisely. Finally, *Preservers*, customers over 60, want to maximize their retirement income to maintain a desired lifestyle. RBC markets different services to the different segments. For example, with *Builders*, who face many expenses, it emphasizes loans and debt-load management services.[23]

Occupation

A person's occupation affects the goods and services bought. Bluecollar workers tend to buy more rugged work clothes, whereas executives buy more business suits. Marketers try to identify the occupational groups that have an above-average interest in their products and services. A company can even specialize in making products needed by a given occupational group.

For example, Carhartt makes rugged, durable, no-nonsense work clothes—what it calls "original equipment for the American worker. From coats to jackets, bibs to overalls . . . if the apparel carries the name Carhartt, the performance will be legendary." Its Web site carries real-life testimonials of hard-working Carhartt customers. One electrician, battling the cold in Canada's arctic region, reports wearing Carhartt's lined Arctic bib overalls, Arctic jacket, and other clothing for more than two years without a single

■ Occupation: Carhartt makes rugged, durable, no-nonsense work clothes—what it calls "original equipment for the American worker."

"popped button, ripped pocket seam, or stuck zipper." And an animal trainer in California says of his favorite pair of Carhartt jeans: "Not only did they keep me warm but they stood up to one playful lion and her very sharp claws."[24]

Economic Situation

A person's economic situation will affect product choice. Marketers of income-sensitive goods watch trends in personal income, savings, and interest rates. If economic indicators point to a recession, marketers can take steps to redesign, reposition, and reprice their products closely. Some marketers target consumers who have lots of money and resources, charging prices to match. For example, Rolex positions its luxury watches as "a tribute to elegance, an object of passion, a symbol for all time." Other marketers target consumers with more modest means. Timex makes more affordable watches that "take a licking and keep on ticking."

Lifestyle

Lifestyle

A person's pattern of living as expressed in his or her activities, interests, and opinions.

People coming from the same subculture, social class, and occupation may have quite different lifestyles. **Lifestyle** is a person's pattern of living as expressed in his or her psychographics. It involves measuring consumers' major AIO dimensions—activities (work, hobbies, shopping, sports, social events), interests (food, fashion, family, recreation), and opinions (about themselves, social issues, business, products). Lifestyle captures something more than the person's social class or personality. It profiles a person's whole pattern of acting and interacting in the world. When used carefully, the lifestyle concept can help marketers understand changing consumer values and how they affect buying behavior.

Several research firms have developed lifestyle classifications. The one most widely used is SRI Consulting Business Intelligence's VALS™ typology (see Figure 5.4). VALS classifies people by psychological characteristics and four demographics that correlate with purchase behavior—

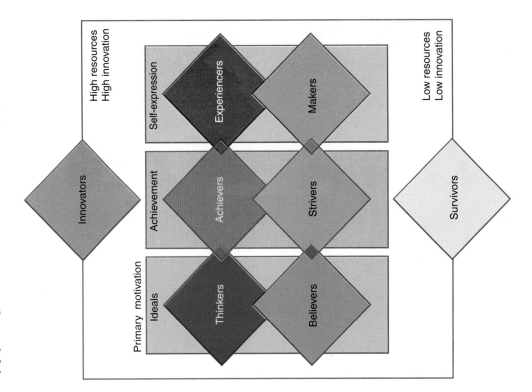

FIGURE 5.4
VALS™ lifestyle classifications

how they spend their time and money. It divides consumers into eight groups based on two major dimensions: primary motivation and resources. *Primary motivations* include ideals, achievement, and self-expression. According to SRI-BI, consumers who are primarily motivated by *ideals* are guided by knowledge and principles. Consumers who are primarily motivated by *achievement* look for products and services that demonstrate success to their peers. Consumers who are primarily motivated by *self-expression* desire social or physical activity, variety, and risk.

Consumers within each orientation are further classified into those with *high resources* and those with *low resources*, depending on whether they have high or low levels of income, education, health, self-confidence, energy, and other factors. Consumers with either very high or very low levels of resources are classified without regard to their primary motivations (Innovators, Survivors). Innovators are people with so many resources that they exhibit all three primary motivations in varying degrees. In contrast, Survivors are people with so few resources that they do not show a strong primary motivation. They must focus on meeting needs rather than fulfilling desires.

Iron City beer, a well-known brand in Pittsburgh, used VALS to update its image and improve sales. Iron City was losing sales—its aging core users were drinking less beer, and younger men weren't buying the brand. VALS research showed that one VALS segment, male Experiencers, drink the most beer, followed by Strivers. Men in these segments perceived Iron City drinkers as blue-collar steelworkers stopping off at the local bar. However, they saw themselves as more modern, hardworking, and fun loving. They strongly rejected the outmoded, heavy-industry image of Pittsburgh. Based on this research, Iron City created ads linking its beer to the new self-image of Pittsburgh. The ads mingled images of the old Pittsburgh with those of the new, dynamic city and scenes of young Experiencers and Strivers having fun and working hard. Within just one month of the start of the campaign, Iron City sales shot up by 26 percent.[25]

Personality and Self-Concept

Personality
The unique psychological characteristics that lead to relatively consistent and lasting responses to one's own environment.

Each person's distinct personality influences his or her buying behavior. **Personality** refers to the unique psychological characteristics that lead to relatively consistent and lasting responses to one's own environment. Personality is usually described in terms of traits such as self-confidence, dominance, sociability, autonomy, defensiveness, adaptability, and aggressiveness. Personality can be useful in analyzing consumer behavior for certain product or brand choices. For example, coffee marketers have discovered that heavy coffee drinkers tend to be high on sociability. Thus, to attract customers, Starbucks and other coffeehouses create environments in which people can relax and socialize over a cup of steaming coffee.

Brand personality
The specific mix of human traits that may be attributed to a particular brand.

The idea is that brands also have personalities, and that consumers are likely to choose brands with personalities that match their own. A **brand personality** is the specific mix of human traits that may be attributed to a particular brand. One researcher identified five brand personality traits:[26]

1. Sincerity (down-to-earth, honest, wholesome, and cheerful)
2. Excitement (daring, spirited, imaginative, and up-to-date)
3. Competence (reliable, intelligent, and successful)
4. Sophistication (upper class and charming)
5. Ruggedness (outdoorsy and tough)

The researcher found that a number of well-known brands tended to be strongly associated with one particular trait: Levi's with "ruggedness," MTV with "excitement," CNN with "competence," and Campbell with "sincerity." Hence, these brands will attract persons who are high on the same personality traits.

Many marketers use a concept related to personality—a person's *self-concept* (also called *self-image*). The basic self-concept premise is that people's possessions contribute to and reflect their identities; that is, "we are what we have." Thus, in order to understand consumer behavior, the marketer must first understand the relationship between consumer self-concept and possessions.

Apple applies this concept in a recent set of ads that characterize two people as computers—one guy plays the part of an Apple Mac and the other plays a PC. "Hello, I'm a Mac," says the guy on the right, who's younger and dressed in jeans. "And I'm a PC," says the one on the left, who's wearing dweeby glasses and a jacket and tie. The two men discuss the relative advantages of Macs versus PCs, with the Mac coming out on top. The ad presents the Mac brand personality as young, laid back, and hip. The PC is portrayed as buttoned down, corporate, and a bit dorky. The message? If you see yourself as young and with it, you need a Mac.[27]

Psychological Factors

A person's buying choices are further influenced by four major psychological factors: *motivation, perception, learning,* and *beliefs* and *attitudes.*

Motivation

Motive (or drive)
A need that is sufficiently pressing to direct the person to seek satisfaction of the need.

A person has many needs at any given time. Some are biological, arising from states of tension such as hunger, thirst, or discomfort. Others are psychological, arising from the need for recognition, esteem, or belonging. A need becomes a motive when it is aroused to a sufficient level of intensity. A **motive** (or drive) is a need that is sufficiently pressing to direct the person to seek satisfaction. Psychologists have developed theories of human motivation. Two of the most popular—the theories of Sigmund Freud and Abraham Maslow—have quite different meanings for consumer analysis and marketing.

Sigmund Freud assumed that people are largely unconscious about the real psychological forces shaping their behavior. He saw the person as growing up and repressing many urges. These urges are never eliminated or under perfect control; they emerge in dreams, in slips of the tongue, in neurotic and obsessive behavior, or ultimately in psychoses.

Freud's theory suggests that a person's buying decisions are affected by subconscious motives that even the buyer may not fully understand. Thus, an aging baby boomer who buys a sporty BMW 330Ci convertible might explain that he simply likes the feel of the wind in his thinning hair. At a deeper level, he may be trying to impress others with his success. At a still deeper level, he may be buying the car to feel young and independent again.

The term *motivation research* refers to qualitative research designed to probe consumers' hidden, subconscious motivations. Consumers often don't know or can't describe just why they act as they do. Thus, motivation researchers use a variety of probing techniques to uncover underlying emotions and attitudes toward brands and buying situations. These sometimes bizarre techniques range from sentence completion, word association, and inkblot or cartoon interpretation tests, to having consumers form daydreams and fantasies about brands or buying situations. One writer offers the following tongue-in-cheek summary of a motivation research session:[28]

Good morning, ladies and gentlemen. We've called you here today for a little consumer research. Now, lie down on the couch, toss your inhibitions out the window, and let's try a little free association. First, think about brands as if they were your *friends.* Imagine you could talk to your TV dinner. What would he say? And what would you say to him? . . . Now, think of your shampoo as an animal. Go on, don't be shy. Would it be a panda or a lion? A snake or a wooly worm? For our final exercise, let's all sit up and pull out our magic markers. Draw a picture of a typical cake-mix user. Would she wear an apron or a negligee? A business suit or a can-can dress?

Such projective techniques seem pretty goofy, and some marketers dismiss such motivation research as mumbo jumbo. But many marketers routinely use such touchy-feely approaches to dig deeply into consumer psyches and develop better marketing strategies.

Many companies employ teams of psychologists, anthropologists, and other social scientists to carry out motivation research. One ad agency routinely conducts one-on-one, therapy-like interviews to delve into the inner workings of consumers. Another company asks consumers to describe their favorite brands as animals or cars (say, Cadillacs versus Chevrolets) in order to assess the prestige associated with various brands. Still others rely on hypnosis, dream therapy, or soft lights and mood music to plumb the murky depths of consumer psyches.

■ Motivation: An aging baby boomer who buys a sporty convertible might explain that he simply likes to feel the wind in his thinning hair. At a deeper level, he may be buying the car to feel young and independent again.

FIGURE 5.5
Maslow's hierarchy of needs

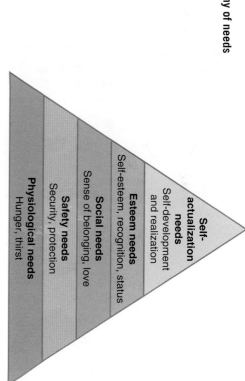

Self-
actualization
needs
Self-development
and realization

Esteem needs
Self-esteem, recognition, status

Social needs
Sense of belonging, love

Safety needs
Security, protection

Physiological needs
Hunger, thirst

Perception

The process by which people select, organize, and interpret information to form a meaningful picture of the world.

Abraham Maslow sought to explain why people are driven by particular needs at particular times. Why does one person spend much time and energy on personal safety and another on gaining the esteem of others? Maslow's answer is that human needs are arranged in a hierarchy, as shown in Figure 5.5, from the most pressing at the bottom to the least pressing at the top.[29] They include *physiological needs, safety needs, social needs, esteem needs,* and *self-actualization needs.*

A person tries to satisfy the most important need first. When that need is satisfied, it will stop being a motivator and the person will then try to satisfy the next most important need. For example, starving people (physiological need) will not take an interest in the latest happenings in the art world (self-actualization needs), nor in how they are seen or esteemed by others (social or esteem needs), nor even in whether they are breathing clean air (safety needs). But as each important need is satisfied, the next most important need will come into play.

Perception

A motivated person is ready to act. How the person acts is influenced by his or her own perception of the situation. All of us learn by the flow of information through our five senses: sight, hearing, smell, touch, and taste. However, each of us receives, organizes, and interprets this sensory information in an individual way. **Perception** is the process by which people select, organize, and interpret information to form a meaningful picture of the world.

People can form different perceptions of the same stimulus because of three perceptual processes: selective attention, selective distortion, and selective retention. People are exposed to a great amount of stimuli every day. For example, people are exposed to an estimated 3,000 to 5,000 ad messages every day.[30] It is impossible for a person to pay attention to all these stimuli. *Selective attention*—the tendency for people to screen out most of the information to which they are exposed—means that marketers must work especially hard to attract the consumer's attention.

Even noticed stimuli do not always come across in the intended way. Each person fits incoming information into an existing mind-set. *Selective distortion* describes the tendency of people to interpret information in a way that will support what they already believe. For example, if you distrust a company, you might perceive even honest ads from the company as questionable. Selective distortion means that marketers must try to understand the mind-sets of consumers and how these will affect interpretations of advertising and sales information.

People also will forget much of what they learn. They tend to retain information that supports their attitudes and beliefs. Because of *selective retention,* consumers are likely to remember good points made about a brand they favor and to forget good points made about competing brands. Because of selective exposure, distortion, and retention, marketers must work hard to get their messages through. This fact explains why marketers use so much drama and repetition in sending messages to their market.

Interestingly, although most marketers worry about whether their offers will be perceived at all, some consumers worry that they will be affected by marketing messages without even knowing it—through *subliminal advertising.* In 1957, a researcher announced that he had

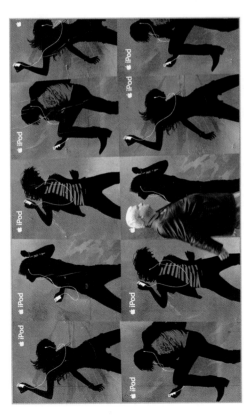

■ Selective perception: It's impossible for people to pay attention to the thousands of ads they're exposed to every day, so they screen most of them out.

flashed the phrases "Eat popcorn" and "Drink Coca-Cola" on a screen in a New Jersey movie theater every five seconds for 1/300th of a second. He reported that although viewers did not consciously recognize these messages, they absorbed them subconsciously and bought 58 percent more popcorn and 18 percent more Coke. Suddenly advertisers and consumer-protection groups became intensely interested in subliminal perception. People voiced fears of being brainwashed, and California and Canada declared the practice illegal. Although the researcher later admitted to making up the data, the issue has not died. Some consumers still fear that they are being manipulated by subliminal messages.

Numerous studies by psychologists and consumer researchers have found little or no link between subliminal messages and consumer behavior. It appears that subliminal advertising simply doesn't have the power attributed to it by its critics. Most advertisers scoff at the notion of an industry conspiracy to manipulate consumers through "invisible" messages. Says one industry insider: "[Some consumers believe we are] wizards who can manipulate them at will. Ha! Snort! Oh my sides! As we know, just between us, most of [us] have difficulty getting a 2 percent increase in sales with the help of $50 million in media and extremely liminal images of sex, money, power, and other [motivators] of human emotion. The very idea of [us] as puppeteers, cruelly pulling the strings of consumer marionettes, is almost too much to bear."[31]

Learning

When people act, they learn. **Learning** describes changes in an individual's behavior arising from experience. Learning theorists say that most human behavior is learned. Learning occurs through the interplay of drives, stimuli, cues, responses, and reinforcement.

A *drive* is a strong internal stimulus that calls for action. A drive becomes a motive when it is directed toward a particular *stimulus object*. For example, a person's drive for self-actualization might motivate him or her to look into buying a digital camera. The consumer's response to the idea of buying a camera is conditioned by the surrounding cues. *Cues* are minor stimuli that determine when, where, and how the person responds. For example, the person might spot several camera brands in a shop window, hear of a special sale price, or discuss cameras with a friend. These are all cues that might influence a consumer's *response* to his or her interest in buying the product.

Suppose the consumer buys a Nikon digital camera. If the experience is rewarding, the consumer will probably use the camera more and more, and his or her response will be *reinforced*. Then, the next time the consumer shops for a camera, or for binoculars or some similar product, the probability is greater that he or she will buy a Nikon product. The practical significance of learning theory for marketers is that they can build up demand for a product by associating it with strong drives, using motivating cues, and providing positive reinforcement.

Beliefs and Attitudes

Through doing and learning, people acquire beliefs and attitudes. These, in turn, influence their buying behavior. A **belief** is a descriptive thought that a person has about something. Beliefs may be based on real knowledge, opinion, or faith and may or may not carry an emotional charge. Marketers are interested in the beliefs that people formulate about specific products and services, because these beliefs make up product and brand images that affect buying behavior. If some of the beliefs are wrong and prevent purchase, the marketer will want to launch a campaign to correct them.

People have attitudes regarding religion, politics, clothes, music, food, and almost everything else. **Attitude** describes a person's relatively consistent evaluations, feelings, and tendencies toward an object or idea. Attitudes put people into a frame of mind of liking or disliking things, of moving toward or away from them. Our digital camera buyer may hold attitudes such as "Buy the best," "The Japanese make the best electronics products in the

Learning
Changes in an individual's behavior arising from experience.

Belief
A descriptive thought that a person has about something.

Attitude
A person's relatively consistent evaluations, feelings, and tendencies toward an object or idea.

world," and "Creativity and self-expression are among the most important things in life." If so, the Nikon camera would fit well into the consumer's existing attitudes.

Attitudes are difficult to change. A person's attitudes fit into a pattern, and to change one attitude may require difficult adjustments in many others. Thus, a company should usually try to fit its products into existing attitudes rather than attempt to change attitudes. Of course, there are exceptions in which the cost of trying to change attitudes may pay off handsomely:

By 1994, milk consumption had been in decline for 20 years. The general perception was that milk was unhealthy, outdated, just for kids, or good only with cookies and cake. To counter these notions, the National Fluid Milk Processors Education Program (MilkPEP) began an ad campaign featuring milk-bemustached celebrities and the tag line Got Milk? The campaign has not only been wildly popular, it has been successful as well—not only did it stop the decline, milk consumption actually increased. The campaign is still running. Although initially the target market was women in their 20s, the campaign has been expanded to other target markets and has gained cult status with teens, much to their parents' delight. Teens collect the print ads featuring celebrities ranging from music stars Kelly Clarkson and Nelly, to actors such as Jessica Alba and Lindsay Lohan, to sports idols such as Jeff Gordon, Tracy McGrady, and Venus and Serena

Crowd-pleaser.

Milk has a lot of fans. And I'm one of them. Its nine essential nutrients help me give strong performances day after day. What can it do for you?

got milk?

Williams. Building on this popularity with teens, the industry set up a Web site (www.whymilk.com) where young folks can make their own mustache, check out the latest Got Milk? ads, or get facts about "everything you ever need to know about milk." The industry also promotes milk to them through grassroots marketing efforts. It recently launched an online promotion searching for America's 50 healthiest student bodies. People who enter their school can win prizes from various sponsors and a grant to support fitness and nutrition programs in the winner's school.[32]

We can now appreciate the many forces acting on consumer behavior. The consumer's choice results from the complex interplay of cultural, social, personal, and psychological factors.

Types of Buying Decision Behavior

Buying behavior differs greatly for a tube of toothpaste, an iPod, financial services, and a new car. More complex decisions usually involve more buying participants and more buyer deliberation. Figure 5.6 shows types of consumer buying behavior based on the degree of buyer involvement and the degree of differences among brands.

Complex Buying Behavior

Consumers undertake **complex buying behavior** when they are highly involved in a purchase and perceive significant differences among brands. Consumers may be highly involved when the product is expensive, risky, purchased infrequently, and highly self-expressive. Typically, the

Complex buying behavior
Consumer buying behavior in situations characterized by high consumer involvement in a purchase and significant perceived differences among brands.

■ Attitudes are difficult to change, but the National Fluid Milk Processor's wildly popular milk moustache campaign succeeded in changing attitudes toward milk.

FIGURE 5.6

Four types of buying behavior

Source: Adapted from Henry Assael, *Consumer Behavior and Marketing Action* (Boston: Kent Publishing Company, 1987), p. 87. Copyright © 1987 by Wadsworth, Inc. Printed by permission of Kent Publishing Company, a division of Wadsworth, Inc.

	High involvement	Low involvement
Significant differences between brands	Complex buying behavior	Variety-seeking buying behavior
Few differences between brands	Dissonance-reducing buying behavior	Habitual buying behavior

consumer has much to learn about the product category. For example, a PC buyer may not know what attributes to consider. Many product features carry no real meaning: a "3.4GHz Pentium processor," "WUXGA active matrix screen," or "4GB dual-channel DDR2 DRAM memory."

This buyer will pass through a learning process, first developing beliefs about the product, then attitudes, and then making a thoughtful purchase choice. Marketers of high-involvement products must understand the information-gathering and evaluation behavior of high-involvement consumers. They need to help buyers learn about product-class attributes and their relative importance. They need to differentiate their brand's features, perhaps by describing the brand's benefits using print media with long copy. They must motivate store salespeople and the buyer's acquaintances to influence the final brand choice.

Dissonance-Reducing Buying Behavior

Dissonance-reducing buying behavior

Consumer buying behavior in situations characterized by high involvement but few perceived differences among brands.

Dissonance-reducing buying behavior occurs when consumers are highly involved with an expensive, infrequent, or risky purchase, but see little difference among brands. For example, consumers buying carpeting may face a high-involvement decision because carpeting is expensive and self-expressive. Yet buyers may consider most carpet brands in a given price range to be the same. In this case, because perceived brand differences are not large, buyers may shop around to learn what is available, but buy relatively quickly. They may respond primarily to a good price or to purchase convenience.

After the purchase, consumers might experience *postpurchase dissonance* (after-sale discomfort) when they notice certain disadvantages of the purchased carpet brand or hear favorable things about brands not purchased. To counter such dissonance, the marketer's after-sale communications should provide evidence and support to help consumers feel good about their brand choices.

Habitual Buying Behavior

Habitual buying behavior

Consumer buying behavior in situations characterized by low consumer involvement and few significant perceived brand differences.

Habitual buying behavior occurs under conditions of low consumer involvement and little significant brand difference. For example, take salt. Consumers have little involvement in this product category—they simply go to the store and reach for a brand. If they keep reaching for the same brand, it is out of habit rather than strong brand loyalty. Consumers appear to have low involvement with most low-cost, frequently purchased products.

In such cases, consumer behavior does not pass through the usual belief-attitude-behavior sequence. Consumers do not search extensively for information about the brands, evaluate brand characteristics, and make weighty decisions about which brands to buy. Instead, they passively receive information as they watch television or read magazines. Ad repetition creates *brand familiarity* rather than *brand conviction*. Consumers do not form strong attitudes toward a brand; they select the brand because it is familiar. Because they are not highly involved with the product, consumers may not evaluate the choice even after purchase. Thus, the buying process involves brand beliefs formed by passive learning, followed by purchase behavior, which may or may not be followed by evaluation.

Because buyers are not highly committed to any brands, marketers of low-involvement products with few brand differences often use price and sales promotions to stimulate product trial. In advertising for a low-involvement product, ad copy should stress only a few key points. Visual symbols and imagery are important because they can be remembered easily and associated with the brand. Ad campaigns should include high repetition of short-duration messages. Television is usually more effective than print media because it is a low-involvement medium suitable for passive learning. Advertising planning should be based on classical conditioning theory, in which buyers learn to identify a certain product by a symbol repeatedly attached to it.

Variety-Seeking Buying Behavior

Consumers undertake **variety-seeking buying behavior** in situations characterized by low consumer involvement but significant perceived brand differences. In such cases, consumers often do a lot of brand switching. For example, when buying cookies, a consumer may hold some beliefs, choose a cookie brand without much evaluation, and then evaluate that brand during consumption. But the next time, the consumer might pick another brand out of boredom or simply to try something different. Brand switching occurs for the sake of variety rather than because of dissatisfaction.

In such product categories, the marketing strategy may differ for the market leader and minor brands. The market leader will try to encourage habitual buying behavior by dominating shelf space, keeping shelves fully stocked, and running frequent reminder advertising. Challenger firms will encourage variety seeking by offering lower prices, special deals, coupons, free samples, and advertising that presents reasons for trying something new.

◼ The Buyer Decision Process

Now that we have looked at the influences that affect buyers, we are ready to look at how consumers make buying decisions. Figure 5.7 shows that the buyer decision process consists of five stages: *need recognition, information search, evaluation of alternatives, purchase decision,* and *postpurchase behavior.* Clearly, the buying process starts long before the actual purchase and continues long after. Marketers need to focus on the entire buying process rather than on just the purchase decision.[33]

The figure suggests that consumers pass through all five stages with every purchase. But in more routine purchases, consumers often skip or reverse some of these stages. A woman buying her regular brand of toothpaste would recognize the need and go right to the purchase decision, skipping information search and evaluation. However, we use the model in Figure 5.7 because it shows all the considerations that arise when a consumer faces a new and complex purchase situation.

Need Recognition

The buying process starts with **need recognition**—the buyer recognizes a problem or need. The need can be triggered by *internal stimuli* when one of the person's normal needs—hunger, thirst, sex—rises to a level high enough to become a drive. A need can also be triggered by *external stimuli.* For example, an advertisement or a discussion with a friend might get you thinking about buying a new car. At this stage, the marketer should research consumers to find out what kinds of needs or problems arise, what brought them about, and how they led the consumer to this particular product.

Information Search

An interested consumer may or may not search for more information. If the consumer's drive is strong and a satisfying product is near at hand, the consumer is likely to buy it then. If not, the consumer may store the need in memory or undertake an **information search** related to the need. For example, once you've decided you need a new car, at the least, you will probably pay more attention to car ads, cars owned by friends, and car conversations. Or you may actively look for reading material, phone friends, and gather information in other ways. The amount of searching you do will depend on the strength of your drive, the amount of information you start with, the ease of obtaining more information, the

---

Variety-seeking buying behavior
Consumer buying behavior in situations characterized by low consumer involvement but significant perceived brand differences.

Need recognition
The first stage of the buyer decision process, in which the consumer recognizes a problem or need.

Information search
The stage of the buyer decision process in which the consumer is aroused to search for more information; the consumer may simply have heightened attention or may go into active information search.

FIGURE 5.7 Buyer decision process

 Need recognition ⇨ Information search ⇨ Evaluation of alternatives ⇨ Purchase decision ⇨ Postpurchase behavior

■ Need recognition can be triggered by advertising. This inventive ad from The LEGO Company invites consumers to think about where the first little block might lead—"imagine. . . ."

value you place on additional information, and the satisfaction you get from searching.

Consumers can obtain information from any of several sources. These include *personal sources* (family, friends, neighbors, acquaintances), *commercial sources* (advertising, salespeople, Web sites, dealers, packaging, displays), *public sources* (mass media, consumer-rating organizations, Internet searches), and *experiential sources* (handling, examining, using the product). The relative influence of these information sources varies with the product and the buyer. Generally, the consumer receives the most information about a product—those controlled by the marketer. The most effective sources, however, tend to be personal. Commercial sources normally *inform* the buyer, but personal sources *legitimize* or *evaluate* products for the buyer. As one

marketer states, "It's rare that an advertising campaign can be as effective as a neighbor leaning over the fence and saying, 'This is a wonderful product.'"[34]

As more information is obtained, the consumer's awareness and knowledge of the available brands and features increase. In your car information search, you may learn about the several brands available. The information might also help you to drop certain brands from consideration. A company must design its marketing mix to make prospects aware of and knowledgeable about its brand. It should carefully identify consumers' sources of information and the importance of each source.

Evaluation of Alternatives

We have seen how the consumer uses information to arrive at a set of final brand choices. How does the consumer choose among the alternative brands? The marketer needs to know about **alternative evaluation**—that is, how the consumer processes information to arrive at brand choices. Unfortunately, consumers do not use a simple and single evaluation process in all buying situations. Instead, several evaluation processes are at work.

The consumer arrives at attitudes toward different brands through some evaluation procedure. How consumers go about evaluating purchase alternatives depends on the individual consumer and the specific buying situation. In some cases, consumers use careful calculations and logical thinking. At other times, the same consumers do little or no evaluating; instead they buy on impulse and rely on intuition. Sometimes consumers make buying decisions on their own; sometimes they turn to friends, consumer guides, or salespeople for buying advice.

Suppose you've narrowed your car choices to three brands. And suppose that you are primarily interested in four attributes—styling, operating economy, warranty, and price. By this time, you've probably formed beliefs about how each brand rates on each attribute. Clearly, if one car rated best on all the attributes, we could predict that you would choose it. However, the brands will no doubt vary in appeal. You might base your buying decision on only one attribute, and your choice would be easy to predict. If you wanted styling above everything else, you would buy the car that you think has the best styling. But most buyers consider several attributes, each with different importance. If we knew the importance that you assigned to each of the four attributes, we could predict your car choice more reliably.

Marketers should study buyers to find out how they actually evaluate brand alternatives. If they know what evaluative processes go on, marketers can take steps to influence the buyer's decision.

Purchase Decision

In the evaluation stage, the consumer ranks brands and forms purchase intentions. Generally, the consumer's **purchase decision** will be to buy the most preferred brand,

Alternative evaluation
The stage of the buyer decision process in which the consumer uses information to evaluate alternative brands in the choice set.

Purchase decision
The buyer's decision about which brand to purchase.

Postpurchase behavior
The stage of the buyer decision process in which the consumers takes further action after purchase, based on their satisfaction or dissatisfaction.

Cognitive dissonance
Buyer discomfort caused by postpurchase conflict.

but two factors can come between the purchase *intention* and the purchase *decision*. The first factor is the *attitudes of others*. If someone important to you thinks that you should buy the lowest-priced car, then the chances of your buying a more expensive car are reduced.

The second factor is *unexpected situational factors*. The consumer may form a purchase intention based on factors such as expected income, expected price, and expected product benefits. However, unexpected events may change the purchase intention. For example, the economy might take a turn for the worse, a close competitor might drop its price, or a friend might report being disappointed in your preferred car. Thus, preferences and even purchase intentions do not always result in actual purchase choice.

Postpurchase Behavior

The marketer's job does not end when the product is bought. After purchasing the product, the consumer will be satisfied or dissatisfied and will engage in **postpurchase behavior** of interest to the marketer. What determines whether the buyer is satisfied or dissatisfied with a purchase? The answer lies in the relationship between the *consumer's expectations* and the product's *perceived performance*. If the product falls short of expectations, the consumer is disappointed; if it meets expectations, the consumer is satisfied; if it exceeds expectations, the consumer is delighted.

The larger the gap between expectations and performance, the greater the consumer's dissatisfaction. This suggests that sellers should promise only what their brands can deliver so that buyers are satisfied. Some sellers might even understate product performance levels to boost later consumer satisfaction. For example, Boeing's salespeople tend to be conservative when they estimate the potential benefits of their aircraft. They almost always underestimate fuel efficiency—they promise a 5 percent savings that turns out to be 8 percent. Customers are delighted with better-than-expected performance; they buy again and tell other potential customers that Boeing lives up to its promises.

Almost all major purchases result in **cognitive dissonance**, or discomfort caused by postpurchase conflict. After the purchase, consumers are satisfied with the benefits of the chosen brand and are glad to avoid the drawbacks of the brands not bought. However, every purchase involves compromise. Consumers feel uneasy about acquiring the drawbacks of the chosen brand and about losing the benefits of the brands not purchased. Thus, consumers feel at least some postpurchase dissonance for every purchase.[35]

Why is it so important to satisfy the customer? Customer satisfaction is a key to building profitable relationships with consumers—to keeping and growing consumers and reaping their customer lifetime value. Satisfied customers buy a product again, talk favorably to others about the product, pay less attention to competing brands and advertising, and buy other products from the company. Many marketers go beyond merely *meeting* the expectations of customers—they aim to *delight* the customer (see Real Marketing 5.2).

A dissatisfied consumer responds differently. Bad word of mouth often travels farther and faster than good word of mouth. It can quickly damage consumer attitudes about a company and its products. But companies cannot simply rely on dissatisfied customers to volunteer their complaints when they are dissatisfied. Most unhappy customers never tell the company about their problem. Therefore, a company should measure customer satisfaction regularly. It should set up systems that *encourage* customers to complain. In this way, the company can learn how well it is doing and how it can improve.

But what should companies do about dissatisfied customers? At a minimum, most companies offer toll-free numbers and Web sites to handle complaints and inquiries. For example, over the past 25 years, the Gerber help line (1-800-4-GERBER) has received millions of calls. Help line staffers, most of them mothers or grandmothers themselves, handle customer concerns and provide baby care advice 24 hours a day, 365 days a year to more than 2,400 callers a day. Customers can also log onto the Gerber Web site (www.gerber.com/contactus) and enter a phone number, and a staffer will call them.

By studying the overall buyer decision, marketers may be able to find ways to help consumers move through it. For example, if consumers are not buying a new product because they do not perceive a need for it, marketing might launch advertising messages that trigger the need and show how the product solves customers' problems. If customers know about the product but are not buying because they hold unfavorable attitudes toward it, the marketer must find ways either to change the product or change consumer perceptions.

Real Marketing   Lexus: Delighting Customers to Keep Them Coming Back

5.2 Close your eyes for a minute and picture a typical car dealership. Not impressed? Talk to a friend who owns a Lexus, and you'll no doubt get a very different picture. The typical Lexus dealership is . . . well, anything but typical. And some Lexus dealers will go to almost any extreme to take care of customers and keep them coming back:

Jordan Case has big plans for the ongoing expansion of his business. He's already put in wireless Internet access. He's adding a café. And he's installing a putting green for customers who want to hone their golf skills while waiting for service. Case isn't the manager of a swank hotel or restaurant. He's the president of Park Place Lexus, an auto dealership with two locations in the Dallas area, and he takes pride that his dealership is, well, the anti-dealership. "Buying a car doesn't rank up there with the top five things you like to do," Case says. "So we try to make the experience different." In addition to the café, putting green, and Internet access, customer perks include free car washes and portable DVD players with movies loaned to waiting service clients.

These ideas sprung from constant customer feedback, including a focus group of more than 20 Lexus and non-Lexus customers who vetoed some ideas (while-you-wait manicures got a thumbs down) and helped gauge expectations in other areas (wait times for receiving newly bought cars should be only two minutes, they said). "They don't cut corners here," says a Park Place salesperson. "The dealer spends an exorbitant amount of

Delighting customers: Lexus and its dealers—such as Park Place Lexus near Dallas—go to almost any extreme to take care of customers. "They don't cut corners here," says a Park Place salesperson. "It's like walking into a Ritz-Carlton."

money on renovations, and there are fresh flowers everywhere. It's like walking into a Ritz-Carlton. Last year, Park Place Lexus's passion for customer service earned it a Malcolm Baldrige National Quality Award, a business-excellence honor bestowed by the U.S. government, making it the first automotive dealership ever in the award's 18-year history to win the Baldrige."

Lexus knows that good marketing doesn't stop with making the sale. Keeping customers happy *after* the sale is the key to building lasting relationships. Dealers across the country have a common goal: to delight customers and keep them coming back. Lexus believes that if you "delight the customer, and continue to delight the

The Buyer Decision Process for New Products

We have looked at the stages buyers go through in trying to satisfy a need. Buyers may pass quickly or slowly through these stages, and some of the stages may even be reversed. Much depends on the nature of the buyer, the product, and the buying situation.

We now look at how buyers approach the purchase of new products. A **new product** is a good, service, or idea that is perceived by some potential customers as new. It may have been around for a while, but our interest is in how consumers learn about products for the first time and make decisions on whether to adopt them. We define the **adoption process** as "the mental process through which an individual passes from first learning about an innovation to final adoption," and *adoption* as the decision by an individual to become a regular user of the product.[36]

Stages in the Adoption Process

Consumers go through five stages in the process of adopting a new product:

New product
A good, service, or idea that is perceived by some potential customers as new.

Adoption process
The mental process through which an individual passes from first hearing about an innovation to final adoption.

customer, you will have a customer for life." And Lexus understands just how valuable a customer can be—it estimates that the average lifetime value of a Lexus customer is $600,000.

Despite the amenities, few Lexus customers spend much time hanging around the dealership. Lexus knows that the best dealership visit is the one that you don't have to make at all. So it builds customer-pleasing cars to start with—high-quality cars that need little servicing. In its "Lexus Covenant," the company vows that it will make "the finest cars ever built." In survey after industry survey, Lexus rates at or near the top in quality. Last year's J.D. Powers Initial Quality Study rated Lexus highest in 6 of 19 model segments. Other than the Toyota brand, which topped four categories, no other brand led in more than one segment. Lexus has had the study's top-rated vehicle in five of the last six years.

Still, when a car does need to be serviced, Lexus goes out of its way to make it easy and painless. Most dealers will even pick up the car and then return it when the maintenance is finished. And the car comes back spotless, thanks to a complimentary cleaning to remove bugs and road grime from the exterior and smudges from the leather interior. You might even be surprised to find that they've touched up a door ding to help restore the car to its fresh-from-the-factory luster. "My wife will never buy another car except a Lexus," says one satisfied Lexus owner. "They come to our house, pick up the car, do an oil change, [spiff it up,] and bring it back. She's sold for life."

And when a customer does bring a car in, Lexus repairs it right the first time, on time. Dealers know that their well-heeled customers have money, "but what they don't have is time." So dealers like Mike Sullivan of California are testing a system that uses three technicians instead of one for 35,000-mile service checkups. The new system will cut a customer's wait in half. "I'm not in the car business," says one dealer. "I'm in the service business."

According to its Web site, from the very start, Lexus set out to "revolutionize the automotive experience with a passionate commitment to the finest products, supported by dealers who create the most satisfying ownership experience the world has ever seen. We vow to value the customer as an important individual. To do things right the first time. And to always exceed expectations." Jordan Case of Park Place Lexus fully embraces this philosophy: "You've got to do it right, on time, and make people feel like they are the only one in the room."

At Lexus, exceeding customer expectations sometimes means fulfilling even seemingly outrageous customer requests. Dave Wilson, owner of several Lexus dealerships in Southern California, tells of a letter he received from an angry Lexus owner who spent $374 to repair her car at his dealership. She'd owned four prior Lexus vehicles without a single problem. She said in her letter that she resented paying to fix her current one. Turns out, she thought they were maintenance free—as in get in and drive . . . and drive and drive. "She didn't think she had to do anything to her Lexus," says Wilson. "She had 60,000 miles on it, and never had the oil changed." Wilson sent back her $374.

By all accounts, Lexus has lived up to its ambitious customer-satisfaction promise. It has created what appear to be the world's most satisfied car owners. Lexus regularly tops not just the J.D. Power quality ratings but also its customer-satisfaction ratings, and not just in the United States, but worldwide. In 2004, in the United Kingdom, Lexus achieved the highest J.D. Power customer-satisfaction score ever in the rating's 12-year history. Customer satisfaction translates into sales and customer loyalty. Last year, for the sixth straight year, Lexus was this nation's number one selling luxury car. And once a Lexus customer, always a Lexus customer—Lexus retains 84 percent of customers who've gone to the dealership for service.

Sources: The Park Place Lexus example is adapted from Julia Chang, "At Your Service," Sales & Marketing Management, June 2006, pp. 42–43. Other information and quotes from Steve Finlay, "At Least She Put Fuel in It," Ward's Dealer Business, August 1, 2003; "Lexus Roars for Loyal Customers," B&T Magazine, November 27, 2003; Jeremy W. Peters, "Lexus Tops Owners Survey for Fifth Year," New York Times, May 19, 2005, p. C10; "Porsche Tops Quality Survey: Toyota, Lexus Top Most Vehicle Segments in Revised J.D. Power Initial Quality Study," June 8, 2006, accessed at www.cnn.com/2006/AUTOS/06/07/jdpower_iqs/index.html; "Lexus Covenant," accessed at www.lexus.com/about/corporate/covenant.html, December 2006.

- Awareness: The consumer becomes aware of the new product, but lacks information about it.
- Interest: The consumer seeks information about the new product.
- Evaluation: The consumer considers whether trying the new product makes sense.
- Trial: The consumer tries the new product on a small scale to improve his or her estimate of its value.
- Adoption: The consumer decides to make full and regular use of the new product.

This model suggests that the new-product marketer should think about how to help consumers move through these stages. A luxury car producer might find that many potential customers know about and are interested in its new model but aren't buying because of uncertainty about the model's benefits and the high price. The producer could launch a "take one home for the weekend" promotion to high-value prospects to move them into the trial process and lead them to purchase.

Individual Differences in Innovativeness

People differ greatly in their readiness to try new products. In each product area, there are "consumption pioneers" and early adopters. Other individuals adopt new products much

low involvement and little significant brand difference. In situations characterized by low involvement but significant perceived brand differences, consumers engage in *variety-seeking buying behavior.*

When making a purchase, the buyer goes through a decision process consisting of *need recognition, information search, evaluation of alternatives, purchase decision,* and *postpurchase behavior.* The marketer's job is to understand the buyer's behavior at each stage and the influences that are operating. During *need recognition,* the consumer recognizes a problem or need that could be satisfied by a product or service in the market. Once the need is recognized, the consumer is aroused to seek more information and moves into the *information search* stage. With information in hand, the consumer proceeds to *alternative evaluation,* during which the information is used to evaluate brands in the choice set. From there, the consumer makes a *purchase decision* and actually buys the product. In the final stage of the buyer decision process, *postpurchase behavior,* the consumer takes action based on satisfaction or dissatisfaction.

4. Describe the adoption and diffusion process for new products.

The product adoption process is comprised of five stages: awareness, interest, evaluation, trial, and adoption. Initially, the consumer

must become aware of the new product. *Awareness* leads to *interest,* and the consumer seeks information about the new product. Once information has been gathered, the consumer enters the *evaluation* stage and considers buying the new product. Next, in the *trial* stage, the consumer tries the product on a small scale to improve his or her estimate of its value. If the consumer is satisfied with the product, he or she enters the *adoption* stage, deciding to use the new product fully and regularly.

With regard to diffusion of new products, consumers respond at different rates, depending on the consumer's characteristics and the product's characteristics. Consumers may be innovators, early adopters, early majority, late majority, or laggards. *Innovators* are willing to try risky new ideas; *early adopters*—often community opinion leaders—accept new ideas early but carefully; the *early majority*—rarely leaders—decide deliberately to try new ideas, doing so before the average person does; the *late majority* try an innovation only after a majority of people have adopted it; whereas *laggards* adopt an innovation only after it has become a tradition itself. Manufacturers try to bring their new products to the attention of potential early adopters, especially those who are opinion leaders.

Reviewing the Key Terms

Adoption process 150	Consumer market 130	Learning 144	Personality 141
Alternative evaluation 148	Culture 131	Lifestyle 140	Postpurchase behavior 149
Attitude 144	Dissonance-reducing buying	Motive (or drive) 142	Purchase decision 148
Belief 144	behavior 146	Need recognition 147	Social class 134
Brand personality 141	Group 134	New product 150	Subculture 131
Cognitive dissonance 149	Habitual buying behavior 146	Opinion leader 135	Variety-seeking buying
Complex buying behavior 145	Information search 147	Perception 143	behavior 147
Consumer buyer behavior 130			

Discussing the Concepts

1. According to the model of consumer behavior, the buyer's black box consists of buyer characteristics and decision processes. Explain why the text calls this a black box.

2. Explain the cultural, social, and personal characteristics that affect people when they choose a restaurant at which to celebrate their birthdays.

3. A bank used SRI's Consulting Business Intelligence Values and Lifestyles (VALS) research to profile customer segments that did not use any automated or electronic services. Based on your knowledge of this lifestyle classification system, speculate what might be the primary and secondary VALS type for this customer segment.

4. The vice president of marketing for a regional doughnut retailer says, "We believe our customers exhibit high-involvement buying behaviors." Do you agree? Why or why not?

5. Form small groups and discuss how a consumer goes through the buyer decision process when choosing a college.

6. According to Figure 5.8, which adopter category is just now buying 'a' digital camera? Which group is now adding TiVo? Which category describes you? Why?

Applying the Concepts

1. Soft drink marketers spend about $400 million on television advertising each year. From a consumer behavior perspective, why is this important?

2. You are the vice president of marketing for a small software company that has developed new and novel spam-blocking software. You are charged with selecting the target market for the product launch. How would you use Roger's *Diffusion of Innovations* framework to help you with this decision? What are some of the likely characteristics of this customer group?

3. The chapter defines "alternative evaluation" as "how the consumer processes information to arrive at brand choices." Suppose that, as discussed in the chapter, you have narrowed your choice of new cars to brand A, B, or C. You have finalized the four most important new-car attributes and their weights and have created the evaluation [matrix]. Which new-car brand will you likely select?

Attributes	Importance Weight	New Car Alternatives		
		Brand A	Brand B	Brand C
Styling	0.5	3	7	4
Operating Economy	0.2	6	5	7
Warranty	0.1	5	5	6
Price	0.2	8	7	8

■ Focus on Technology

Many Internet sites use collaborative filtering technology to assist consumers in decision making. The process begins by *collaborating* the purchasing or product rating behavior of a vast group of consumers. Then, the technology filters this information to offer recommendations to a single user based on individual search, rating, or purchasing behavior. Originated by Amazon.com for book recommendations, the technology is now used by many marketers, including iTunes and Netflix.

1. At which step of the consumer behavior decision process does collaborative filtering most help the consumer?

2. What are the drawbacks of collaborative filtering?

3. How could your college use this technology to help its consumers?

■ Focus on Ethics

Marketing to "tweens," 9–12-year-old consumers, has increased dramatically in recent years. This age group, which once purchased toys, is now more involved in electronics, clothing, and the media. In general, they aspire to be more like their older teen counterparts. Most companies market responsibly to this group, but there is concern that some companies prey on the immature nature of tweens. Abercrombie and Fitch, as well as Victoria's Secret have been criticized as having products, a retail atmosphere, and advertisements that are targeted to tweens as well as teens and young adults. To help parents and tweens understand marketing, PBS has set up an area of its Web site called "Don't Buy It"

(http://pbskids.org/dontbuyit). The site covers topics such as food advertising tricks, secrets of a magazine cover model, and how to see through the sales pitch.

After viewing the video featuring Wild Planet, answer the following questions about consumer buyer behavior.

1. Why is this age group considered so vulnerable as consumers?

2. Visit pbskids.org/dontbuyit and comment on the effectiveness of this site.

3. Can you think of any other products or services that are targeted to this younger group with inappropriate or dangerous products or messages?

Chances are that when you hear the term *socially responsible business*, a handful of companies leap to mind, companies such as Ben & Jerry's and The Body Shop. Although these companies and their founders led the revolution for socially responsible business, a new generation of activist entrepreneurs has now taken up the reins. Today, socially responsible businesses and their founders not only have a passion to do good, they also have the know-how to connect with consumers.

For example, Wild Planet markets high-quality, nonsexist, nonviolent toys that encourage kids to be imaginative and creative and to explore the world around them. But Wild Planet sells more than just toys. It sells positive play experiences. To better understand those experiences, the company conducts a tremendous amount of consumer research to delve into consumer buyer behavior. Wild Planet even created a Toy Opinion

Panel to evaluate current products and develop new product ideas. The panel helps Wild Planet to understand why parents and kids buy the toys they buy.

After viewing the video featuring Wild Planet, answer the following questions about consumer buyer behavior.

1. Which of the four sets of factors affecting consumer behavior do you believe most strongly affect consumers' choices to buy toys from Wild Planet?

2. What demographic segment of consumers is Wild Planet targeting?

3. Visit the Wild Planet Web site at www.wildplanet.com to learn more about the company. How does the Web site help consumers through the buyer decision process?

When most people think of Victoria's Secret, they think of lingerie. Indeed, the Limited Brands division has done a very good job of developing this association by placing images of supermodels donning its signature bras, panties, and "sleepwear" in everything from standard broadcast and print advertising to the controversial prime-time television fashion shows that the company airs each year. Such promotional tactics have paid off for Victoria's Secret, a subsidiary of Limited Brands, which continues to achieve healthy sales and profit growth.

How does a successful company ensure that its hot sales don't cool off? One approach is to sell more to existing customers. Another is to find new customers. Victoria's Secret is doing plenty of both. One key component in its quest to find new customers is the launch and growth of its new brand, Pink.

EXPANDING THE TARGET MARKET

Victoria's Secret launched its line of Pink products in 50 test markets in 2003. Based on very positive initial results, the company expanded the subbrand quickly to a national level. With the Pink introduction, Victoria's Secret hoped to add a new segment to its base: young, hip, and fashionable customers. "Young" in this case means 18 to 30 years of age. More specifically, Pink is geared toward college coeds. According to company spokesman Anthony Hebron, "It's what you see around the dorm. It's the fun, playful stuff she needs, but is still fashionable."

The company classifies the Pink product line as "loungewear," a very broad term that includes sweatpants, T-shirts, pajamas, bras and panties, pillows and bedding, and even dog accessories. In keeping with the "young and fun" image, the product line includes bright colors (Pink is not a misnomer) and often incorporates stripes and polka-dots. The garments feature comfortable cuts and mostly soft cotton fabrics. To keep things fresh for the younger segment, stores introduce new Pink products every three or four weeks.

According to those at Victoria's Secret, in sharp contrast to the sexy nature of the core brand, Pink is positioned as cute and playful. "It's spirited and collegiate. It's not necessarily sexy—it's not sexy at all—but young, hip, and casual. It's fashion forward and accessible," said Mary Beth Wood, a spokeswoman for Victoria's Secret. The Pink line does include underwear that some might consider to be on par with standard Victoria's Secret items. But management is quick to point out that the designs such as heart-covered thongs are more cute than racy. Displays of Pink merchandise often incorporate stuffed animals, and many articles display Pink's trademark mascot, a pink dog.

Pink is currently a store-within-a-store concept. According to Les Wexner, chairman and chief executive of parent company Limited Brands, the company intended this from the beginning. "Two years ago, we did not believe Pink was a stand-alone concept, and I'm still not sure that it is, but it's possible." But with Pink sales expected to reach $700 million for 2006, the company is giving far more serious consideration to opening freestanding Pink lifestyle shops in several markets by early 2007.

To aid in the expansion of Pink, Victoria's Secret has enlisted the help of the PR firm Alison Brod. Although the company plans to stay committed to fashion-advertising vehicles such as Vogue and Lucky, it also plans to expand its promotional campaigns to include nontraditional avenues. Lisette Sand-Freedman, VP of fashion and lifestyle for Alison Brod, indicates that it "will seek different arenas to be in, ways to get the word out," focusing on "more lifestyle angles and bigger campaigns." The company will also leverage the star power of trend-setting young Hollywood personalities such as Lindsay Lohan and Sophia Bush. This will be accomplished through formal product placements and through the placement of Pink products in the personal wardrobes of celebrities.

A KEY DRIVER OF VICTORIA'S SECRET'S FUTURE GROWTH

Limited Brands has been experiencing good times. First-quarter earnings for 2006 were up 19 percent over the same period from the year before. Victoria's Secret has been a huge part of that success. Already the largest component in the Limited Brands portfolio (which includes Bath & Body Works, Express, and Limited stores), Victoria's Secret accounts for more than 1,000 of the parent company's 3,559 stores and more than half of total sales. For 2005, most of Victoria's Secret's product lines posted better-than-anticipated sales and profits.

But Wexner is not content to let the chain rest. "The Victoria brand is really the power of the business," he says. "We can double the Victoria's Secret business in the next five years." This would mean increasing the division's sales from $5 billion to $10 billion. The umbrella strategy for achieving this growth is to continually broaden the customer base. This will include a focus on new and emerging lines, such as IPEX and Angels Secret Embrace (bras), Intimissimi (a line of Italian lingerie for women and men appealing to younger customers), and Sexy Sport (a collection of sports bras, yoga pants, tennis apparel, and dancewear). Pink is a key component of this strategy.

The future of Victoria's Secret will also include a move toward bigger stores. Currently, the typical Victoria's Secret store is approximately 6,000 square feet. Wexner believes that this is far too small. "We're very undersized, and we've proven that to ourselves. We believe we should have at a minimum stores of 10,000 to 15,000 square feet." Larger stores will allow the company to give more space and attention to the store-within-a-store brands, such as Pink.

BROADENING THE CUSTOMER BASE . . . TOO FAR?

Although Victoria's Secret's introduction and expansion of Pink seems well founded, it has raised some eyebrows. As young and cute Pink's line has expanded rapidly, it has become apparent that the brand's appeal goes far beyond that of its intended target market. Some women much older than 30 have shown an interest (41-year-old Courtney Cox Arquette was photographed wearing Pink sweats). But stronger interest is being shown by girls younger than 18.

Girls as young as 11 are visiting Victoria's Secret stores to buy Pink items, with and without their mothers.

Two such 11-year-olds, Lily Feingold and Brittany Garrison, were interviewed while shopping at a Victoria's Secret store with Lily's mother. As they browsed exclusively through the Pink merchandise, the two confessed that Victoria's Secret was one of their favorite stores. Passing up cotton lounge pants because each already had multiple pairs, both girls bought $68 pairs of sweatpants with the "Pink" label emblazoned on the derriere. The girls denied buying the items because they wanted to seem more grown up, instead saying that they simply liked the clothes.

The executives at Victoria's Secret are quick to say that they are not targeting girls younger than 18. Perhaps that is due to the backlash that retailer Abercrombie & Fitch experienced not long ago for targeting teens and preteens with sexually charged promotional materials and merchandise. But regardless of Victoria's Secret's intentions, Pink is fast becoming popular among teens and "tweens," one of the newest generational market segments, loosely defined by a range of about 8 to 14 years of age. Most experts agree that by the time children reach 10, they are rejecting childlike images and aspiring to more mature things associated with being a teenager. Called "age compression," it explains the trend toward preteens leaving their childhoods earlier and giving up traditional toys for more mature interests, such as cell phones, consumer electronics, and fashion products.

Tweens are growing in size and purchase power. The 33 million teens (ages 12 to 19) in the United States spend more than $175 billion annually (over 60 percent have jobs), and the 25 million tweens spend $51 billion annually, a number that continues to increase. But even more telling is the $170 billion per year that is spent by parents and other family members directly for the younger consumers who may not have as much income as their older siblings. Although boys are a part of this group, it is widely recognized that girls account for the majority of dollars spent. With this kind of purchase power behind them, as they find revenue for their older target markets leveling off, marketers everywhere are focusing on the teen and tween segments.

Although executives at Victoria's Secret deny targeting the youth of America, experts disagree. David Morrison, president of marketing research agency TwentySomething, says he is not surprised that Victoria's Secret denies marketing to teens and preteens. "If Victoria's Secret is blatantly catering to seventh and eighth graders, that might be considered exploitative." Morrison also acknowledges that the age group is drawn to the relative maturity and sophistication of the Pink label.

Natalie Weathers, assistant professor of fashion-industry management at Philadelphia University, says that Victoria's Secret is capitalizing on a trend known as coshopping—mothers and tweens shopping together. "They are advising their daughters about their purchases, and their daughters are advising them," she said. This type of activity may have been strange 20 years ago, but according to Weathers, the preteens of today are more savvy and, therefore, more likely to be shopping partners for moms. "They are not little girls, and they aren't teenagers, but they have a lot of access to sophisticated information about what the media says is beautiful, what is pretty, what is hot and stylish and cool. They are very visually literate."

In general, introducing a brand to younger consumers is considered a sound strategy for growth and for creating long-term relationships. Marketers of everything from packaged foods to shampoo use this strategy. In most cases, it's not considered controversial to engender aspirational motives in young consumers through an entry-level product line. But many critics have questioned the aspirations engendered in tweens as they identify with Pink because of what they are aspiring to. Based on years of experience working as a creative director for ad agencies in New York, Timothy Matz calls Pink "beginner-level lingerie." Matz does not question the practice of gateway marketing (getting customers to use the brand at an earlier age). But he admits that a "gateway" to a sexy lingerie shop may make parents nervous. "Being a 45-year-old dad, do I want my 10-year-old going to Victoria's Secret?"

Thus far, Victoria's Secret has avoided the negative reactions of the masses who opposed Abercrombie & Fitch's blatant marketing of thong underwear to preteens. Perhaps that's because it adamantly professes its exclusive focus on young adults. Nonetheless, many question Victoria's Secret's appeal to the preadult crowd, whether intentional or unintentional. Big tobacco companies have been under fire for years for using childlike imagery to draw the interest of youth to an adult product. Is Pink the Joe Camel of early adolescent sexuality? Are Pink's extreme low-rise string bikini panties the gateway drug to pushup teddies and Pleasure State Geisha thongs? These are questions that Victoria's Secret may have to address more directly at some point in the near future.

Questions for Discussion

1. Analyze the buyer decision process of a typical Pink customer.

2. Apply the concept of aspirational groups to Victoria's Secret Pink line. Should marketers have boundaries with regard to this concept?

3. Explain how both positive and negative consumer attitudes toward a brand like Pink develop. How might someone's attitude toward Pink change?

4. What role does Pink appear to be playing in the self-concept of preteens, teens, and young adults?

Sources: Alycia De Mesa, "Marketing and Tweens," BusinessWeek Online, October 12, 2005; Fae Goodman, "Lingerie Is Luscious and Lovely—For Grown-Ups," Chicago Sun Times, February 19, 2006, p. B02; Vivian McInerny, "Pink Casual Loungewear Brand Nicely Colors Teen Girls' World," The Oregonian, May 7, 2006, p. O13; Randy Schmelzer, "Victoria's Secret Has Designs on Putting Everyone in the Pink," PR Week, March 13, 2006, p. 3; Jeffrey Sheben, "Victoria's Secret to Expand," Columbus Dispatch, May 18, 2006, p. 01B; Jane M. Von Bergen, "Victoria's Secret? Kids," Philadelphia Inquirer, December 22, 2005.

6

Business Markets and Business Buyer Behavior

Previewing the Concepts

In the previous chapter, you studied *final consumer* buying behavior and factors that influence it. In this chapter, we'll do the same for *business customers*—those that buy goods and services for use in producing their own products and services or for resale to others.

To start, let's look at UPS. You probably know UPS as your neighborhood small package delivery company. It turns out, however, that a majority of UPS's business comes not from residential consumers like you and me, but from large *business* customers. To succeed in its business-to-business markets, UPS must do more than just pick up and deliver packages. It must work closely and deeply with its business customers to become a strategic logistics partner.

ention UPS, and most people envision one of those familiar brown trucks with a friendly driver, rumbling around their neighborhood dropping off parcels. That makes sense. The company's 88,000 brown-clad drivers deliver more than 3.75 billion packages annually, an average of 14.8 million each day.

For most of us, seeing a brown UPS truck evokes fond memories of past package deliveries. If you close your eyes and listen, you can probably imagine the sound of the UPS truck pulling up in front of your home. Even the company's brown color has come to mean something special to customers. "We've been referred to for years as Big Brown," says a UPS marketing executive. "People love our drivers, they love our brown trucks, they love everything we do." Thus was born UPS's current "What Can Brown Do for You?" advertising theme.

For most residential consumers, the answer to the question "What can Brown do for you?" is pretty simple: "Deliver my package as quickly as possible." But most of UPS's revenues come not from the residential customers who receive the packages, but from the *business* customers who send them. And for these business customers, UPS does more than just get Grandma's holiday package there on time. Whereas residential consumers might look to "Brown" simply for fast, friendly, low-cost package delivery, business customers usually have much more complex needs.

For businesses, package delivery is just part of a much more complex logistics process that involves purchase orders, inventory, order status checks, invoices, payments, returned merchandise, and fleets of delivery vehicles. Beyond the physical package flow, companies must also handle the accompanying information and money flows. They need timely information about packages—what's in them, where they're currently located, to whom they are going, when they will get there, how much has been paid, and how much is owed. UPS knows that for many companies, all these work-a-day logistical concerns can be a nightmare. Moreover, most companies don't see these activities as strategic competencies that provide competitive advantage.

That's where Big Brown comes in. These are exactly the things that UPS does best. Over the years, UPS has grown to become much more than a neighborhood small package delivery service. It is now a $43 billion corporate giant providing a broad range of logistics solutions. UPS handles the logistics, allowing customers to focus on what they do best. It offers everything from ground and air package distribution, freight delivery (air, ocean, rail, and road), and mail services to inventory management, third-party logistics, international trade management, logistics management software and e-commerce solutions, and even financing. If it has to do with logistics, at home or abroad, UPS can probably do it better than anyone else can.

UPS has the resources to handle the logistics needs of just about any size business. It employs 407,000 people, some 92,000 vehicles (package cars, vans, tractors, and motorcycles), 600 aircraft, and about 1,800 warehouse facilities in 200 countries. UPS now moves an astounding 6 percent of the gross domestic product in the United States, links 1.8 million sellers with 6.1 million buyers every day, and processes more than 460 million electronic transactions every week. It serves 90 percent of the world population and 99 percent of businesses in the Fortune 1000. UPS invests $1 billion a year in information technology to support its highly synchronized, by-the-clock logistics services and to provide customers with information at every point in the process.

Beyond moving their packages around the United States, UPS can also help business customers to navigate the complexities of international shipping, with some 700 international flights per day to or from 377 international destinations. For example, although most residential customers don't need next-day air service to or from China, many businesses do seek help shipping to and from the burgeoning Asian manufacturing zones. UPS helps ensure the timely flow of crucial business documents, prototypes, high-value goods (such as semiconductors), and emergency repair parts that wing their way across the Pacific every day.

UPS even offers expedited U.S. Customs services, with fast inspection and clearance processes that help get goods into the country quickly. "When you're trading internationally, you're entire investment could be hanging on a single clause," says one UPS ad. "We don't get you over oceans, mountains, and deserts only to be delayed by Chapter 3, Part 319, Regulation 40-2 of CFR Title 7. . . . Leave the burden of global compliance to UPS."

In addition to shipping and receiving packages, UPS provides a wide range of financial services for its business customers. For example, its UPS Capital division will handle client's accounts receivable—UPS shippers can choose to be reimbursed immediately and have UPS collect payment from the recipient. Other financial services include credit cards for small businesses and programs to fund inventory, equipment leasing, and asset financing. UPS even bought a bank to underpin UPS Capital's operations.

We don't get you over oceans, mountains and deserts only to be delayed by Chapter 3, Part 319, Regulation 40-2 of CFR Title 7.

When you're trading internationally, your entire investment could be hanging on a single clause. Whether it's a rule overlooked out of hundreds of laws and trade agreements or a misinterpretation by one of dozens of third parties, mistakes like these can cause costly delays.

Fortunately, there's a simple solution. Leave the burden of global compliance to UPS. With over 80 years of experience in international trade, we have the resources and network of people all over

the world to head off problems and facilitate the movement of your goods. And since we deal with the thorniest compliance issues every day, we're up on the very latest, most accurate information.

As your single source for customs brokerage and international trade management solutions, we'll help make sure nothing stands in the way of your global transactions. Including that mountain of paper.

1-800-PICK-UPS

Objectives

After studying this chapter, you should be able to

1. define the business market and explain how business markets differ from consumer markets

2. identify the major factors that influence business buyer behavior

3. list and define the steps in the business buying decision process

4. compare the institutional and government markets and explain how institutional and government buyers make their buying decisions

At a deeper level, UPS can provide the advice and technical resources needed to help business customers large and small improve their own logistics operations. UPS Consulting advises companies on redesigning logistics systems to align them better with business strategies. UPS Supply Chain Solutions helps customers to synchronize the flow of goods, funds, and information up and down their supply chains. UPS Logistics Technologies supplies software that improves customers' distribution efficiency, including street-level route optimization, territory planning, mobile delivery execution, real-time wireless dispatch, and GPS tracking.

So, what can Brown do for you? As it turns out, the answer depends on who you are. For its residential consumers, UPS uses those familiar chugging brown trucks to provide simple and efficient package pickup and delivery services. But in its business-to-business markets, it develops deeper and more involved customer relationships. The company's "What Can Brown Do for You?" ads feature a variety of business professionals discussing how UPS's broad range of services makes their jobs easier. But such ad promises have little meaning if not reinforced by actions. Says former UPS CEO Jim Kelly, "A brand can be very hollow and lifeless . . . if the people and the organization . . . are not 100 percent dedicated to living out the brand promise every day."

For UPS, that means that employees around the world must do more than just deliver packages from point A to point B for their business customers. They must roll up their sleeves and work hand in hand with customers to help solve their complex logistics problems. More than just providing shipping services, they must become strategic logistics partners.[1]

In one way or another, most large companies sell to other organizations. Companies such as DuPont, Boeing, IBM, Caterpillar, and countless other firms, sell *most* of their products to other businesses. Even large consumer products companies, which make products used by final consumers, must first sell their products to other businesses. For example, General Mills makes many familiar consumer brands—Big G cereals (Cheerios, Wheaties, Total, Golden Grahams); baking products (Pillsbury, Betty Crocker, Gold Medal flour), snacks (Nature Valley, Chex Mix, Pop Secret); Yoplait Yogurt; Häagen-Dazs ice cream, and others. But to sell these products to consumers, General Mills must first sell them to its wholesaler and retailer customers, who in turn serve the consumer market.

Business buyer behavior refers to the buying behavior of the organizations that buy goods and services for use in the production of other products and services that are sold, rented, or supplied to others. It also includes the behavior of retailing and wholesaling firms that acquire goods to resell or rent them to others at a profit. In the **business buying process**, business buyers determine which products and services their organizations need to purchase and then find, evaluate, and choose among alternative suppliers and brands. *Business-to-business (B-to-B) marketers* must do their best to understand business markets and business buyer behavior. Then, like businesses that sell to final buyers, they must build profitable relationships with business customers by creating superior customer value.

Business buyer behavior
The buying behavior of the organizations that buy goods and services for use in the production of other products and services or for the purpose of reselling or renting them to others at a profit.

Business buying process
The decision process by which business buyers determine which products and services their organizations need to purchase, and then find, evaluate, and choose among alternative suppliers and brands.

Business Markets

The business market is *huge*. In fact, business markets involve far more dollars and items than do consumer markets. For example, think about the large number of business transactions involved in the production and sale of a single set of Goodyear tires. Various suppliers sell Goodyear the rubber, steel, equipment, and other goods that it needs to produce the tires. Goodyear then sells the finished tires to retailers, who in turn sell them to consumers. Thus, many sets of *business* purchases were made for only one set of *consumer* purchases. In addition, Goodyear sells tires as original equipment to manufacturers who install them on new vehicles, and as replacement tires to companies that maintain their own fleets of company cars, trucks, buses, or other vehicles.

In some ways, business markets are similar to consumer markets. Both involve people who assume buying roles and make purchase decisions to satisfy needs. However, business markets differ in many ways from consumer markets. The main differences, shown in Table 6.1, are in *market structure and demand*, the *nature of the buying unit*, and the *types of decisions and the decision process involved*.

Market Structure and Demand

The business marketer normally deals with *far fewer but far larger buyers* than the consumer marketer does. Even in large business markets, a few buyers often account for most of the purchasing. For example, when Goodyear sells replacement tires to final consumers, its potential market includes the owners of the millions of cars currently in use in the United States and around the world. But Goodyear's fate in the business market depends on getting orders from one of only a handful of large automakers. Similarly, Black & Decker sells its power tools and outdoor equipment to tens of millions of consumers worldwide. However, it must sell these products through three huge retail customers—Home Depot, Lowe's, and Wal-Mart—which combined account for more than half its sales.

Business markets are also *more geographically concentrated*. More than half the nation's business buyers are concentrated in eight states: California, New York, Ohio, Illinois, Michigan, Texas, Pennsylvania, and New Jersey. Further, business demand is *derived demand*—it ultimately derives from the demand for consumer goods. Hewlett-Packard and Dell buy Intel microprocessor chips because consumers buy personal computers. If consumer demand for PCs drops, so will the demand for computer chips.

Therefore, B-to-B marketers sometimes promote their products directly to final consumers to increase business demand. For example, Intel advertises heavily to personal computer buyers, selling them on the virtues of Intel microprocessors. The increased demand for Intel chips boosts demand for the PCs containing them, and both Intel and its business partners win.

Similarly, INVISTA promotes DuPont Teflon directly to final consumers as a key branded ingredient in stain-repellent and wrinkle-free fabrics and leathers. You see Teflon Fabric Protector hangtags on clothing lines such as Nautica and Tommy Hilfiger and on home furnishing brands such as Kravet.[2] By making Teflon familiar and attractive to final buyers, INVISTA also makes the products containing it more attractive.

Many business markets have *inelastic demand*; that is, total demand for many business products is not affected much by price changes, especially in the short run. A drop in the price of leather will not cause shoe manufacturers to buy much more leather unless it results in lower shoe prices that, in turn, will increase consumer demand for shoes.

Finally, business markets have more *fluctuating demand*. The demand for many business goods and services tends to change more—and more quickly—than the demand for consumer goods and services does. A small percentage increase in consumer demand can cause large increases in business demand. Sometimes a rise of only 10 percent in consumer demand can cause as much as a 200 percent rise in business demand during the next period.

TABLE 6.1
Characteristics of Business Markets

Marketing Structure and Demand

Business markets contain *fewer but larger buyers.*

Business customers are *more geographically concentrated.*

Business buyer demand is *derived* from final consumer demand.

Demand in many business markets is *more inelastic*—not affected as much in the short run by price changes.

Demand in business markets *fluctuates more*, and more quickly.

Nature of the Buying Unit

Business purchases involve *more buyers.*

Business buying involves a *more professional purchasing effort.*

Types of Decisions and the Decision Process

Business buyers usually face *more complex buying decisions.*

The business buying process is *more formalized.*

In business buying, buyers and sellers work closely together and build long-term *relationships.*

Derived demand

Business demand that ultimately comes from (derives from) the demand for consumer goods.

Nature of the Buying Unit

Compared with consumer purchases, a business purchase usually involves *more decision participants and a more professional purchasing effort.* Often, business buying is done by trained purchasing agents who spend their working lives learning how to buy better. The more complex the purchase, the more likely it is that several people will participate in the decisionmaking process. Buying committees made up of technical experts and top management are common in the buying of major goods.

Beyond this, many companies are now upgrading their purchasing functions to "supply management" or "supplier development" functions. B-to-B marketers now face a new breed of higher-level, better-trained supply managers. These supply managers sometimes seem to know more about the supplier company than it knows about itself. Therefore, business marketers must have well trained marketers and salespeople to deal with these well trained buyers.

Types of Decisions and the Decision Process

Business buyers usually face *more complex* buying decisions than do consumer buyers. Purchases often involve large sums of money, complex technical and economic considerations, and interactions among many people at many levels of the buyer's organization. Because the purchases are more complex, business buyers may take longer to make their decisions. The business buying process also tends to be *more formalized* than the consumer buying process. Large business purchases usually call for detailed product specifications, written purchase orders, careful supplier searches, and formal approval.

Finally, in the business buying process, the buyer and seller are often much *more dependent* on each other. Consumer marketers are often at a distance from their customers. In contrast, B-to-B marketers may roll up their sleeves and work closely with their customers during all stages of the buying process—from helping customers define problems, to finding solutions, to supporting after sale operations. They often customize their offerings to individual customer needs. In the short run, sales go to suppliers who meet buyers' immediate product and service needs. In the long run, however, B-to-B marketers keep a customer's sales by meeting current needs *and* by partnering with customers to help them solve their problems.

In recent years, relationships between customers and suppliers have been changing from downright adversarial to close and chummy. In fact, many customer companies are now practicing **supplier development**, systematically developing networks of supplier-partners to ensure an appropriate and dependable supply of products and materials that they will use in making their own products or resell to others. For example, Caterpillar no longer calls its buyers "purchasing agents"—they are managers of "purchasing and supplier development." Wal-Mart doesn't have a "Purchasing Department," it has a "Supplier Development Department." And giant Swedish furniture retailer IKEA doesn't just buy from its suppliers, it involves them deeply in the process of delivering a stylish and affordable lifestyle to IKEA's customers (see Real Marketing 6.1).

Business Buyer Behavior

At the most basic level, marketers want to know how business buyers will respond to various marketing stimuli. Figure 6.1 shows a model of business buyer behavior. In this model, marketing and other stimuli affect the buying organization and produce certain buyer responses.

■ Derived demand: Intel advertises heavily to personal computer buyers, selling them on the virtues of Intel microprocessors—both Intel and its business partners benefit.

Supplier development
Systematic development of networks of supplier-partners to ensure an appropriate and dependable supply of products and materials for use in making products or reselling them to others.

FIGURE 6.1
A model of business buyer behavior

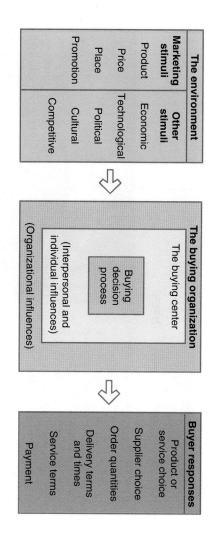

The environment		The buying organization	Buyer responses
Marketing stimuli	**Other stimuli**	The buying center	Product or service choice
Product	Economic		Supplier choice
Price	Technological	Buying decision process	Order quantities
Place	Political	(Interpersonal and individual influences)	Delivery terms and times
Promotion	Cultural	(Organizational influences)	Service terms
	Competitive		Payment

As with consumer buying, the marketing stimuli for business buying consist of the Four Ps: product, price, place, and promotion. Other stimuli include major forces in the environment: economic, technological, political, cultural, and competitive. These stimuli enter the organization and are turned into buyer responses: product or service choice; supplier choice; order quantities; and delivery, service, and payment terms. In order to design good marketing mix strategies, the marketer must understand what happens within the organization to turn stimuli into purchase responses.[3]

Within the organization, buying activity consists of two major parts: the buying center, made up of all the people involved in the buying decision, and the buying decision process. The model shows that the buying center and the buying decision process are influenced by internal organizational, interpersonal, and individual factors as well as by external environmental factors.

The model in Figure 6.1 suggests four questions about business buyer behavior: What buying decisions do business buyers make? Who participates in the buying process? What are the major influences on buyers? How do business buyers make their buying decisions?

Major Types of Buying Situations

There are three major types of buying situations.[4] At one extreme is the *straight rebuy*, which is a fairly routine decision. At the other extreme is the *new task*, which may call for thorough research. In the middle is the *modified rebuy*, which requires some research.

In a **straight rebuy**, the buyer reorders something without any modifications. It is usually handled on a routine basis by the purchasing department. Based on past buying satisfaction, the buyer simply chooses from the various suppliers on its list. "In" suppliers try to maintain product and service quality. They often propose automatic reordering systems so that the purchasing agent will save reordering time. "Out" suppliers try to find new ways to add value or exploit dissatisfaction so that the buyer will consider them.

In a **modified rebuy**, the buyer wants to modify product specifications, prices, terms, or suppliers. The modified rebuy usually involves more decision participants than does the straight rebuy. The "in" suppliers may become nervous and feel pressured to put their best foot forward to protect an account. "Out" suppliers may see the modified rebuy situation as an opportunity to make a better offer and gain new business.

A company buying a product or service for the first time faces a **new-task** situation. In such cases, the greater the cost or risk, the larger the number of decision participants and the greater their efforts to collect information will be. The new-task situation is the marketer's greatest opportunity and challenge. The marketer not only tries to reach as many key buying influences as possible but also provides help and information.

The buyer makes the fewest decisions in the straight rebuy and the most in the new-task decision. In the new-task situation, the buyer must decide on product specifications, suppliers, price limits, payment terms, order quantities, delivery times, and service terms. The order of these decisions varies with each situation, and different decision participants influence each choice.

Many business buyers prefer to buy a packaged solution to a problem from a single seller. Instead of buying and putting all the components together, the buyer may ask sellers to supply the components *and* assemble the package or system. The sale often goes to the firm that provides the most complete system meeting the customer's needs. Thus,

Straight rebuy
A business buying situation in which the buyer routinely reorders something without any modifications.

Modified rebuy
A business buying situation in which the buyer wants to modify product specifications, prices, terms, or suppliers.

New task
A business buying situation in which the buyer purchases a product or service for the first time.

Real Marketing

IKEA: Working with Suppliers to Keep Customers Clamoring for More

6.1 IKEA, the world's largest furniture retailer, is the quintessential global cult brand. Last year, more than 410 million shoppers flocked to the Scandinavian retailer's 236 huge stores in 34 countries, generating more than $18 billion in sales. Most of the shoppers are loyal IKEA customers—many are avid apostles. From Beijing to Moscow to Middletown, Ohio, all are drawn to the IKEA lifestyle, one built around trendy but simple and practical furniture at affordable prices. According to *BusinessWeek*:

Perhaps more than any other company in the world, IKEA has become a curator of people's lifestyles, if not their lives. At a time when consumers face so many choices for everything they buy, IKEA provides a one-stop sanctuary for coolness. IKEA is far more than a furniture merchant. It sells a lifestyle that customers around the world embrace as a signal that they've arrived, that they have good taste and recognize value. "If it wasn't for IKEA," writes British design magazine *Icon*, "most people would have no access to affordable contemporary design."

As the world's Ambassador of Kul (Swedish for fun), IKEA is growing at a healthy clip. Sales have leapt 31 percent in just the past two years. IKEA plans to open 19 new megastores this year, including outlets in Western China and Japan. In the United States, it plans to expand from its current 28 stores to more than 50 stores by 2013. In fact, the biggest obstacle to growth isn't opening new stores and attracting customers. Rather, it's finding enough of the right kinds of goods *suppliers* to help design and produce the billions of dollars of goods that those customers will carry out of its stores. IKEA currently relies on about 1,800 suppliers in more than 50 countries to stock its shelves. If the giant retailer continues at its current rate of growth, it will need to double its supply network by 2010. "We can't increase by

more than 20 stores a year because supply is the bottleneck," says IKEA's country manager for Russia.

Giant Swedish furniture retailer IKEA doesn't just buy from its suppliers, it involves them deeply in the process of delivering a stylish and affordable lifestyle to IKEA's customers worldwide—here in Saudi Arabia.

It turns out that creating beautiful, durable furniture at low prices is no easy proposition. It calls for a resolute focus on design and an obsession for low costs. IKEA knows that it can't go it alone. Instead, it must develop close partnerships with suppliers around the globe who can help it develop simple new designs and keep costs down. Here's how the company describes its approach, and the importance of suppliers:

To manufacture beautiful, durable furniture at low prices is not so easy. . . . We can't do it alone. . . . First we do our part. Our designers work with manufacturers to find smart ways to make furniture using existing production processes. Then our buyers look all over the world for good suppliers with the most suitable raw materials. Next, we buy in bulk—on a global scale—

Systems selling

Systems selling is often a key business marketing strategy for winning and holding accounts. For example, ChemStation provides a complete solution for its customers' industrial cleaning problems:

ChemStation sells industrial cleaning chemicals to a wide range of business customers, ranging from car washes to the U.S. Air Force. Whether a customer is washing down a fleet or a factory, a store or a restaurant, a distillery or an Army base, ChemStation comes up with the right cleaning solution every time. It supplies thousands of products in hundreds of industries. But ChemStation does more than just sell chemicals. First, ChemStation works closely with each individual customer to concoct a soap formula specially designed for that customer. It has brewed special formulas for cleaning hands, feathers, eggs, mufflers, flutes, perfume vats, cosmetic eye makeup containers, yacht-making molds, concrete

Systems selling
Buying a packaged solution to a problem from a single seller, thus avoiding all the separate decisions involved in a complex buying situation.

so that we can get the best deals, and you can get the lowest price. Then you do your part. Using the IKEA catalog and visiting the store, you choose the furniture yourself and pick it up at the self-serve warehouse. Because most items are packed flat, you can get them home easily, and assemble them yourself. This means we don't charge you for things you can easily do on your own. So together we save money . . . for a better everyday life.

At IKEA, design is important. But no matter how good the design, a product won't find its way to the showroom unless it's also affordable. IKEA goes to the ends of the earth to find supply partners who can help it to create just the right product at just the right price. According to the *BusinessWeek* writer, IKEA "once contracted with ski makers—experts in bent wood—to manufacture its Poang armchairs, and it has tapped makers of supermarket carts to turn out durable sofas."

The design process for a new IKEA product can take up to three years. IKEA's designers start with a basic customer value proposition. Then, they work closely with key suppliers to bring that proposition to market. Consider IKEA's Olle chair, developed in the late 1990s. Based on customer feedback, designer Evamaria Ronnegard set out to create a sturdy, durable kitchen chair that would fit into any décor, priced at $52. Once her initial design was completed and approved, IKEA's 45 trading offices searched the world and matched the Olle with a Chinese supplier, based on both design and cost efficiencies.

Together, Ronnegard and the Chinese supplier refined the design to improve the chair's function and reduce its costs. For example, the supplier modified the back leg angle to prevent the chair from tipping easily. This also reduced the thickness of the seat without compromising the chair's strength, reducing both costs and shipping weight. However, when she learned that the supplier planned to use traditional wood joinery methods to attach the chair back to the seat, Ronnegard intervened. That would require that the chair be shipped in a costly L-shape, which by itself would inflate the chair's retail price to $58. Ronnegard convinced the supplier to go with metal bolts instead. The back-and-forth design process worked well. IKEA introduced its still-popular Olle chair at the $52 target price. (Through continued design and manufacturing refinements, IKEA and its supplier have now reduced the price to just $29.)

Throughout the design and manufacturing process, Ronnegard was impressed by the depth of the supplier partnership. "My job really hit home when I got a call from the supplier in China, who had a question about some aspect of the chair," she recalls. "There he was, halfway around the world, and he was calling me about my chair." Now, Ronnegard is often on-site in China or India or Vietnam, working face to face with suppliers as they help to refine her designs.

Another benefit of close collaboration with suppliers is that they can often help IKEA to customize its designs to make them sell better in local markets. In China, for example, at the suggestion of a local supplier, IKEA stocked 250,000 plastic place mats commemorating the year of the rooster. The place mats sold out in only three weeks.

Thus, before IKEA can sell the billions of dollars worth of products its customer covet, it must first find suppliers who can help it design and make all those products. IKEA doesn't just rely on spot suppliers who might be available when needed. Instead, it has systematically developed a robust network of supplier-partners that reliably provide the more than 10,000 items it stocks. And more than just buying from suppliers, IKEA involves them deeply in the process of designing and making stylish but affordable products to keep IKEA's customers coming back. Working together, IKEA and its suppliers have kept fans like Jen Segrest clamoring for more:

At least once a year, Jen Segrest, a 36-year-old freelance Web designer, and her husband travel 10 hours round-trip from their home in Middletown, Ohio, to the IKEA in Schaumburg, Illinois, near Chicago. "Every piece of furniture in my living room is IKEA—except for an end table, which I hate. And next time I go to IKEA I'll replace it," says Segrest. To lure the retailer to Ohio, Segrest has even started a blog called OH! IKEA. The banner on the home page reads "IKEA in Ohio—Because man cannot live on Target alone."

Sources: Extracts, quotes, and other information from Kerry Capell, "How the Swedish Retailer Became a Global Cult Brand," *BusinessWeek*, November 14, 2005, p. 103; Shari Kulha, "Behind the Scenes at IKEA," *The Guardian*, September 29, 2005, p. 8; Greta Guest, "Inside IKEA's Formula for Global Success," *Detroit Free Press*, June 3, 2006; and "Our Vision: A Better Everyday Life," accessed at www.ikea.com, December 2006.

trucks, oceangoing trawlers, and about anything else you can imagine. Next, ChemStation delivers the custom-made mixture to a tank installed at the customer's site. Finally, it maintains the tank by monitoring usage and automatically refilling the tank when supplies run low. Thus, ChemStation sells an entire system for dealing with the customer's special cleaning problems. The company's motto: "Our system is your solution!" Partnering with an individual customer to find a full solution creates a lasting relationship that helps ChemStation to lock out the competition. As noted in an issue of *Insights*, ChemStation's customer newsletter, "Our customers . . . oftentimes think of us as more of a partner than a supplier." [5]

Sellers increasingly have recognized that buyers like this method and have adopted systems selling as a marketing tool. Systems selling is a two-step process. First, the supplier

■ System selling: ChemStation does more than simply supply its customers with cleaning chemicals. "Our customers . . . think of us as more of a partner than a supplier."

plier sells a group of interlocking products. For example, the supplier sells not only glue, but also applicators and dryers. Second, the supplier sells a system of production, inventory control, distribution, and other services to meet the buyer's need for a smooth-running operation.

Systems selling is a key business marketing strategy for winning and holding accounts. The contract often goes to the firm that provides the most complete solution to the customer's needs. For example, the Indonesian government requested bids to build a cement factory near Jakarta. An American firm's proposal included choosing the site, designing the cement factory, hiring the construction crews, assembling the materials and equipment, and turning the finished factory over to the Indonesian government. A Japanese firm's proposal included all of these services, plus hiring and training workers to run the factory, exporting the cement through their trading companies, and using the cement to build some needed roads and new office buildings in Jakarta. Although the Japanese firm's proposal cost more, it won the contract. Clearly, the Japanese viewed the problem not as just building a cement factory (the narrow view of systems selling) but of running it in a way that would contribute to the country's economy. They took the broadest view of the customer's needs. This is true systems selling.[6]

Participants in the Business Buying Process

Who does the buying of the trillions of dollars' worth of goods and services needed by business organizations? The decision-making unit of a buying organization is called its **buying center**: all the individuals and units that play a role in the purchase decision-making process. This group includes the actual users of the product or service, those who make the buying decision, those who influence the buying decision, those who do the actual buying, and those who control the buying information.

The buying center includes all members of the organization who play any of five roles in the purchase decision process.[7]

■ **Users** are members of the organization who will use the product or service. In many cases, users initiate the buying proposal and help define product specifications.

■ **Influencers** often help define specifications and also provide information for evaluating alternatives. Technical personnel are particularly important influencers.

■ **Buyers** have formal authority to select the supplier and arrange terms of purchase. Buyers may help shape product specifications, but their major role is in selecting vendors and negotiating. In more complex purchases, buyers might include high-level officers participating in the negotiations.

■ **Deciders** have formal or informal power to select or approve the final suppliers. In routine buying, the buyers are often the deciders, or at least the approvers.

■ **Gatekeepers** control the flow of information to others. For example, purchasing agents often have authority to prevent salespersons from seeing users or deciders. Other gatekeepers include technical personnel and even personal secretaries.

The buying center is not a fixed and formally identified unit within the buying organization. It is a set of buying roles assumed by different people for different purchases. Within the organization, the size and makeup of the buying center will vary for different products and for different buying situations. For some routine purchases, one person—say a purchasing agent—may assume all the buying center roles and serve as the only person involved in the buying decision. For more complex purchases, the buying center may include 20 or 30 people from different levels and departments in the organization.

Buying center
All the individuals and units that play a role in the purchase decision-making process.

Users
Members of the buying organization who will actually use the purchased product or service.

Influencers
People in an organization's buying center who affect the buying decision; they often help define specifications and also provide information for evaluating alternatives.

Buyers
The people in the organization's buying center who make an actual purchase.

The buying center concept presents a major marketing challenge. The business marketer must learn who participates in the decision, each participant's relative influence, and what evaluation criteria each decision participant uses. For example, the medical products and services group of Cardinal Health sells disposable surgical gowns to hospitals. It identifies the hospital personnel involved in this buying decision as the vice president of purchasing, the operating room administrator, and the surgeons. Each participant plays a different role. The vice president of purchasing analyzes whether the hospital should buy disposable gowns or reusable gowns. If analysis favors disposable gowns, then the operating room administrator compares competing products and prices and makes a choice. This administrator considers the gown's absorbency, antiseptic quality, design, and cost and normally buys the brand that meets requirements at the lowest cost. Finally, surgeons affect the decision later by reporting their satisfaction or dissatisfaction with the brand.

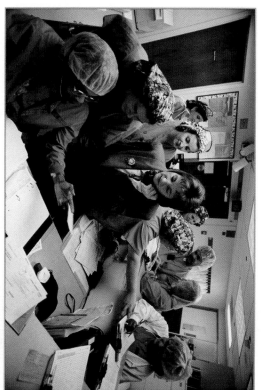

■ Buying Center: Cardinal Health deals with a wide range of buying influences, from purchasing executives and hospital administrators to the surgeons who actually use its products.

Deciders

People in the organization's buying center who have formal or informal power to select or approve the final suppliers.

Gatekeepers

People in the organization's buying center who control the flow of information to others.

The buying center usually includes some obvious participants who are involved formally in the buying decision. For example, the decision to buy a corporate jet will probably involve the company's CEO, chief pilot, a purchasing agent, some legal staff, a member of top management, and others formally charged with the buying decision. It may also involve less obvious, informal participants, some of whom may actually make or strongly affect the buying decision. Sometimes, even the people in the buying center are not aware of all the buying participants. For example, the decision about which corporate jet to buy may actually be made by a corporate board member who has an interest in flying and who knows a lot about airplanes. This board member may work behind the scenes to sway the decision. Many business buying decisions result from the complex interactions of ever-changing buying center participants.

Major Influences on Business Buyers

Business buyers are subject to many influences when they make their buying decisions. Some marketers assume that the major influences are economic. They think buyers will favor the supplier who offers the lowest price or the best product or the most service. They concentrate on offering strong economic benefits to buyers. However, business buyers actually respond to both economic and personal factors. Far from being cold, calculating, and impersonal, business buyers are human and social as well. They react to both reason and emotion.

Today, most B-to-B marketers recognize that emotion plays an important role in business buying decisions. For example, you might expect that an advertisement promoting large trucks to corporate fleet buyers would stress objective technical, performance, and economic factors. However, one ad for Volvo heavy-duty trucks shows two drivers arm-wrestling and claims, "It solves all your fleet problems. Except who gets to drive." It turns out that, in the face of an industry-wide driver shortage, the type of truck a fleet provides can help it to attract qualified drivers. The Volvo ad stresses the raw beauty of the truck and its comfort and roominess, features that make it more appealing to drivers. The ad concludes that Volvo trucks are "built to make fleets more profitable and drivers a lot more possessive."[8]

When suppliers' offers are very similar, business buyers have little basis for strictly rational choice. Because they can meet organizational goals with any supplier, buyers can allow personal factors to play a larger role in their decisions. However, when competing products differ greatly, business buyers are more accountable for their choice and tend to pay more attention to economic factors. Figure 6.2 lists various groups of influences on business buyers—environmental, organizational, interpersonal, and individual.[9]

■ Emotions play an important role in business buying: This Volvo truck ad mentions objective factors, such as efficiency and ease of maintenance. But it stresses more emotional factors such as the raw beauty of the truck and its comfort and roominess, features that make "drivers a lot more possessive."

Environmental Factors

Business buyers are heavily influenced by factors in the current and expected *economic environment*, such as the level of primary demand, the economic outlook, and the cost of money. Another environmental factor is shortages in key materials. Many companies now are more willing to buy and hold larger inventories of scarce materials to ensure adequate supply. Business buyers also are affected by technological, political, and competitive developments in the environment. Finally, culture and customs can strongly influence business buyer reactions to the marketer's behavior and strategies, especially in the international marketing environment (see Real Marketing 6.2). The business buyer must watch these factors, determine how they will affect the buyer, and try to turn these challenges into opportunities.

Organizational Factors

Each buying organization has its own objectives, policies, procedures, structure, and systems, and the business marketer must understand these factors well. Questions such as these arise: How many people are involved in the buying decision? Who are they? What are their evaluative criteria? What are the company's policies and limits on its buyers?

Interpersonal Factors

The buying center usually includes many participants who influence each other, so *interpersonal factors* also influence the business buying process. However, it is often difficult to assess such interpersonal factors and group dynamics. Buying center participants do not

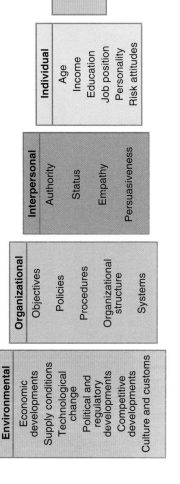

FIGURE 6.2 Major influences on business buyer behavior

wear tags that label them as "key decision maker" or "not influential." Nor do buying center participants with the highest rank always have the most influence. Participants may influence the buying decision because they control rewards and punishments, are well liked, have special expertise, or have a special relationship with other important participants. Interpersonal factors are often very subtle. Whenever possible, business marketers must try to understand these factors and design strategies that take them into account.

Individual Factors

Each participant in the business buying decision process brings in personal motives, perceptions, and preferences. These individual factors are affected by personal characteristics such as age, income, education, professional identification, personality, and attitudes toward risk. Also, buyers have different buying styles. Some may be technical types who make indepth analyses of competitive proposals before choosing a supplier. Other buyers may be intuitive negotiators who are adept at pitting the sellers against one another for the best deal.

The Business Buying Process

Figure 6.3 lists the eight stages of the business buying process.[10] Buyers who face a new-task buying situation usually go through all stages of the buying process. Buyers making modified or straight rebuys may skip some of the stages. We will examine these steps for the typical new-task buying situation.

Problem Recognition

The buying process begins when someone in the company recognizes a problem or need that can be met by acquiring a specific product or service. **Problem recognition** can result from internal or external stimuli. Internally, the company may decide to launch a new product that requires new production equipment and materials. Or a machine may break down and need new parts. Perhaps a purchasing manager is unhappy with a current supplier's product quality, service, or prices. Externally, the buyer may get some new ideas at a trade show, see an ad, or receive a call from a salesperson who offers a better product or a lower price. In fact, in their advertising, business marketers often alert customers to potential problems and then show how their products provide solutions. For example, Kodak Health Imaging ads point out the complexities of hospital imaging and suggest that with Kodak, "complexity becomes clarity."

General Need Description

Having recognized a need, the buyer next prepares a **general need description** that describes the characteristics and quantity of the needed item. For standard items, this process presents few problems. For complex items, however, the buyer may need to work with others—engineers, users, consultants—to define the item. The team may want to rank the importance of reliability, durability, price, and other attributes desired in the item. In this phase, the alert business marketer can help the buyers define their needs and provide information about the value of different product characteristics.

Product Specification

The buying organization next develops the item's technical **product specifications**, often with the help of a value analysis engineering team. **Value analysis** is an approach to cost reduction in which components are studied carefully to determine if they can be

---

Problem recognition
The first stage of the business buying process in which someone in the company recognizes a problem or need that can be met by acquiring a good or a service.

General need description
The stage in the business buying process in which the company describes the general characteristics and quantity of a needed item.

Product specification
The stage of the business buying process in which the buying organization decides on and specifies the best technical product characteristics for a needed item.

Value analysis
An approach to cost reduction in which components are studied carefully to determine if they can be redesigned, standardized, or made by less costly methods of production.

Problem recognition → General need description → Product specification → Supplier search → Proposal solicitation → Supplier selection → Order-routine specification → Performance review

FIGURE 6.3 Stages of the business buying process

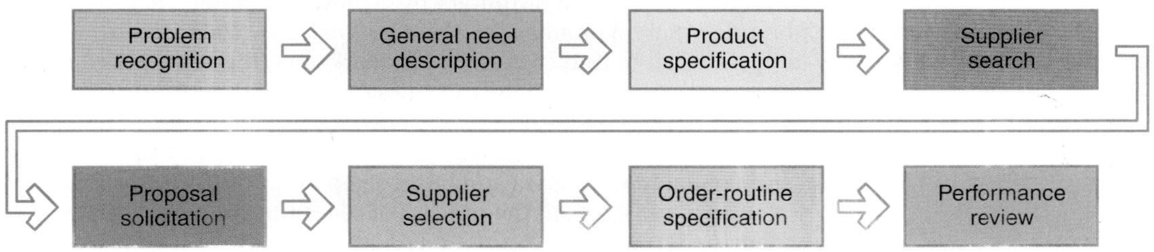

Real Marketing   International Marketing Manners: When in Rome, Do as the Romans Do

6.2   Picture this: Consolidated Amalgamation, Inc., thinks it's time that the rest of the world enjoyed the same fine products it has offered American consumers for two generations. It dispatches Vice President Harry E. Slicksmile to Europe, Africa, and Asia to explore the territory. Mr. Slicksmile stops first in London, where he makes short work of some bankers—he rings them up on the phone. He handles Parisians with similar ease: After securing a table at La Tour d'Argent, he greets his luncheon guest, the director of an industrial engineering firm, with the words, "Just call me Harry, Jacques."

In Germany, Mr. Slicksmile is a powerhouse. Whisking through a lavish, state-of-the-art marketing presentation, complete with flip charts and audiovisuals, he shows 'em that this Georgia boy *knows* how to make a buck. Heading on to Milan, Harry strikes up a conversation with the Japanese businessman sitting next to him on the plane. He flips his card onto the guy's tray and, when the two say good-bye, shakes hands warmly and clasps the man's right arm. Later, for his appointment with the owner of an Italian packaging design firm, our hero wears his comfy corduroy sport coat, khaki pants, and Topsiders. Everybody knows Italians are zany and laid back.

Mr. Slicksmile next swings through Saudi Arabia, where he coolly presents a potential client with a multimillion-dollar proposal in a classy pigskin binder. His final stop is Beijing, China, where he talks business over lunch with a group of Chinese executives. After completing the meal, he drops his chopsticks into his bowl of rice and presents each guest with an elegant Tiffany clock as a reminder of his visit.

A great tour, sure to generate a pile of orders, right? Wrong. Six months later, Consolidated Amalgamation has nothing to show for the trip but a stack of bills. Abroad, they weren't wild about Harry.

This hypothetical case has been exaggerated for emphasis. Americans are seldom such dolts. But experts say success in international business has a lot to do with knowing the territory and its people. By learning English and extending themselves in other ways, the world's business leaders have met Americans more than halfway. In contrast, Americans too often do little except assume that others will march to their music. "We want things to be 'American' when we travel. Fast. Convenient. Easy. So we become 'ugly Americans' by

American companies must help their managers understand international customers and customs. For example, Japanese people revere the business card as an extension of self—they do not hand it out to people, they present it.

redesigned, standardized, or made by less costly methods of production. The team decides on the best product characteristics and specifies them accordingly. Sellers, too, can use value analysis as a tool to help secure a new account. By showing buyers a better way to make an object, outside sellers can turn straight rebuy situations into new-task situations that give them a chance to obtain new business.

Supplier Search

Supplier search
The stage of the business buying process in which the buyer tries to find the best vendors.

The buyer now conducts a **supplier search** to find the best vendors. The buyer can compile a small list of qualified suppliers by reviewing trade directories, doing computer searches, or phoning other companies for recommendations. Today, more and more companies are turning to the Internet to find suppliers. For marketers, this has leveled the playing field—the Internet gives smaller suppliers many of the same advantages as larger competitors.

The newer the buying task, and the more complex and costly the item, the greater the amount of time the buyer will spend searching for suppliers. The supplier's task is to get listed in major directories and build a good reputation in the marketplace. Salespeople should watch for companies in the process of searching for suppliers and make certain that their firm is considered.

Proposal Solicitation

In the **proposal solicitation** stage of the business buying process, the buyer invites qualified suppliers to submit proposals. In response, some suppliers will send only a catalog or a salesperson. However, when the item is complex or expensive, the buyer will usually require detailed written proposals or formal presentations from each potential supplier.

Business marketers must be skilled in researching, writing, and presenting proposals in response to buyer proposal solicitations. Proposals should be marketing documents, not just technical documents. Presentations should inspire confidence and should make the marketer's company stand out from the competition.

Supplier Selection

The members of the buying center now review the proposals and select a supplier or suppliers. During **supplier selection**, the buying center often will draw up a list of the desired supplier attributes and their relative importance. In one survey, purchasing executives listed the following attributes as most important in influencing the relationship between supplier and customer: quality products and services, on-time delivery, ethical corporate behavior, honest communication, and competitive prices. Other important factors include repair and servicing

Proposal solicitation
The stage of the business buying process in which the buyer invites qualified suppliers to submit proposals.

Supplier selection
The stage of the business buying process in which the buyer reviews proposals and selects a supplier or suppliers.

---

demanding that others change," says one American world trade expert. "I think more business would be done if we tried harder."

Poor Harry tried, all right, but in all the wrong ways. The British do not, as a rule, make deals over the phone as much as Americans do. It's not so much a "cultural" difference as a difference in approach. A proper Frenchman neither likes instant familiarity—questions about family, church, or alma mater—nor refers to strangers by their first names. "That poor fellow, Jacques, probably wouldn't show anything, but he'd recoil. He'd *not* be pleased," explains an expert on French business practices. "It's considered poor taste," he continues. "Even after months of business dealings, I'd wait for him or her to make the invitation [to use first names]. . . . You are always right, in Europe, to say 'Mister.' "

Harry's flashy presentation would likely have been a flop with the Germans, who dislike overstatement and showiness. According to one German expert, however, German businessmen have become accustomed to dealing with Americans. Although differences in body language and customs remain, the past 20 years have softened them. "I hugged an American woman at a business meeting last night," he said. "That would be normal in France, but [older] Germans still have difficulty [with the custom]." He says that calling secretaries by their first names would still be considered rude: "They have a right to be called by the surname. You'd certainly ask—and get—permission first." In Germany, people address each other formally and correctly—someone with two doctorates (which is fairly common) must be referred to as "Herr Doktor Doktor."

When Harry Slicksmile grabbed his new Japanese acquaintance by the arm, the executive probably considered him disrespectful and presumptuous. Japan, like many Asian countries, is a "no-contact culture" in which even shaking hands is a strange experience. Harry made matters worse by tossing his business card. Japanese people revere the business card as an extension of self and as an indicator of rank. They do not *hand* it to people, they *present* it—with both hands. In addition, the Japanese are sticklers about rank. Unlike Americans, they don't heap praise on subordinates in a room; they will praise only the highest-ranking official present.

Hapless Harry also goofed when he assumed that Italians are like Hollywood's stereotypes of them. The flair for design and style that has characterized Italian culture for centuries is embodied in the businesspeople of Milan and Rome. They dress beautifully and admire flair, but they blanch at garishness or impropriety in others' attire.

To the Saudi Arabians, the pigskin binder would have been considered vile. An American salesman who really did present such a binder was unceremoniously tossed out and his company was black-listed from working with Saudi businesses. In China, Harry's casually dropping his chopsticks could have been misinterpreted as an act of aggression. Stabbing chopsticks into a bowl of rice and leaving them signifies death to the Chinese. The clocks Harry offered as gifts might have confirmed such dark intentions. To "give a clock" in Chinese sounds the same as "seeing someone off to his end."

Thus, to compete successfully in global markets, or even to deal effectively with international firms in their home markets, companies must help their managers to understand the needs, customs, and cultures of international business buyers. "When doing business in a foreign country and a foreign culture—particularly a non-Western culture—assume nothing," advises an international business specialist. "Take nothing for granted. Turn every stone. Ask every question. Dig into every detail. Because cultures really are different, and those differences can have a major impact." So the old advice is still good advice: When in Rome, do as the Romans do.

Sources: Portions adapted from Susan Harte, "When in Rome, You Should Learn to Do What the Romans Do," *The Atlanta Journal-Constitution*, January 22, 1990, pp. D1, D6. Additional examples can be found in David A. Ricks, *Blunders in International Business Around the World* (Malden, MA: Blackwell Publishing, 2000); Terri Morrison, Wayne A. Conway, and Joseph J. Douress, *Dun & Bradstreet's Guide to Doing Business* (Upper Saddle River, NJ: Prentice Hall, 2000); Jame K. Sebenius, "The Hidden Challenge of Cross-Border Negotiations," *Harvard Business Review*, March 2002, pp. 76–85; Ross Thompson, "Lost in Translation," *Medical Marketing and Media*, March 2005, p. 82; and information accessed at www.executiveplanet.com, December 2006.

capabilities, technical aid and advice, geographic location, performance history, and reputation. The members of the buying center will rate suppliers against these attributes and identify the best suppliers.

Buyers may attempt to negotiate with preferred suppliers for better prices and terms before making the final selections. In the end, they may select a single supplier or a few suppliers. Many buyers prefer multiple sources of supplies to avoid being totally dependent on one supplier and to allow comparisons of prices and performance of several suppliers over time. Today's supplier development managers want to develop a full network of supplier-partners that can help the company bring more value to its customers.

Order-Routine Specification

Order-routine specification
The stage of the business buying process in which the buyer writes the final order with the chosen supplier(s), listing the technical specifications, quantity needed, expected time of delivery, return policies, and warranties.

The buyer now prepares an **order-routine specification**. It includes the final order with the chosen supplier or suppliers and lists items such as technical specifications, quantity needed, expected time of delivery, return policies, and warranties. In the case of maintenance, repair, and operating items, buyers may use blanket contracts rather than periodic purchase orders. A blanket contract creates a longterm relationship in which the supplier promises to resupply the buyer as needed at agreed prices for a set time period.

Many large buyers now practice *vendor-managed inventory*, in which they turn over ordering and inventory responsibilities to their suppliers. Under such systems, buyers share sales and inventory information directly with key suppliers. The suppliers then monitor inventories and replenish stock automatically as needed.

Performance Review

Performance review
The stage of the business buying process in which the buyer assesses the performance of the supplier and decides to continue, modify, or drop the arrangement.

In this stage, the buyer reviews supplier performance. The buyer may contact users and ask them to rate their satisfaction. The **performance review** may lead the buyer to continue, modify, or drop the arrangement. The seller's job is to monitor the same factors used by the buyer to make sure that the seller is giving the expected satisfaction.

The eight stage buying-process model provides a simple view of the business buying as it might occur in a new-task buying situation. The actual process is usually much more complex. In the modified rebuy or straight rebuy situation, some of these stages would be compressed or bypassed. Each organization buys in its own way, and each buying situation has unique requirements.

Different buying center participants may be involved at different stages of the process. Although certain buying-process steps usually do occur, buyers do not always follow them in the same order, and they may add other steps. Often, buyers will repeat certain stages of the process. Finally, a customer relationship might involve many different types of purchases ongoing at a given time, all in different stages of the buying process. The seller must manage the total customer relationship, not just individual purchases.

E-Procurement: Buying on the Internet

During the past few years, advances in information technology have changed the face of the B-to-B marketing process. Online purchasing, often called *eprocurement*, has grown rapidly.

Companies can do e-procurement in any of several ways. They can set up their own *company buying sites*. For example, GE operates a company trading site on which it posts its buying needs and invites bids, negotiates terms, and places orders. Or the company can create *extranet links* with key suppliers. For instance, they can create direct procurement accounts with suppliers such as Dell or Office Depot through which company buyers can purchase equipment, materials, and supplies.

B-to-B marketers can help customers who wish to purchase online by creating well-designed, easy-to-use Web sites. For example, *BtoB* magazine regularly rates Hewlett-Packard's B-to-B Web site among very best.

The HP site consists of some 1,900 site areas and 2.5 million pages. It integrates an enormous amount of product and company information, putting it within only a few mouse clicks of customers' computers. IT buying decision makers can enter the site, click directly into their customer segment—large enterprise business; small or medium business; or government, health, or educational institution—and quickly find product overviews, detailed technical information, and purchasing solutions.

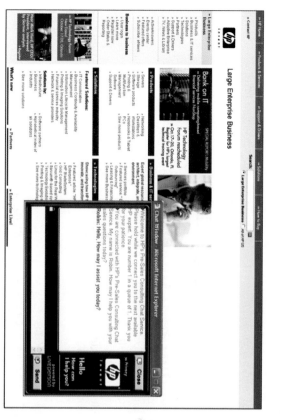

■ To help customers who wish to purchase online, HP's Web site consists of some information, purchasing solutions, e-newsletters, live chats with sales reps, online classes, and real-time customer support.

The site lets customers create customized catalogs for frequently purchased products, set up automatic approval routing for orders, and conduct end-to-end transaction processing. To build deeper, more personalized online relationships with customers, HP.com features flash demos that show how to use the site, e-newsletters, live chats with sales reps, online classes, and real-time customer support. The site has really paid off. Roughly 55 percent the company's total sales now come from the Web site.[11]

E-procurement gives buyers access to new suppliers, lowers purchasing costs, and hastens order processing and delivery. In turn, business marketers can connect with customers online to share marketing information, sell products and services, provide customer support services, and maintain ongoing customer relationships.

So far, most of the products bought online are MRO materials—maintenance, repair, and operations. For instance, Hewlett-Packard spends 95 percent of its $13 billion MRO budget via e-procurement. And last year Delta Air Lines purchased $6.2 billion worth of fuel online. National Semiconductor has automated almost all of the company's 3,500 monthly requisitions to buy materials ranging from the sterile booties worn in its fabrication plants to state-of-the-art software. Even the Baltimore Aquarium uses e-procurement to buy everything from exotic fish to feeding supplies. It recently spent $6 billion online for architectural services and supplies to help construct a new exhibit, "Animal Planet Australia: Wild Extremes."[12]

The actual dollar amount spent on these types of MRO materials pales in comparison to the amount spent for items such as airplane parts, computer systems, and steel tubing. Yet, MRO materials make up 80 percent of all business orders and the transaction costs for order processing are high. Thus, companies have much to gain by streamlining the MRO buying process on the Web.

Business-to-business e-procurement yields many benefits. First, it shaves transaction costs and results in more efficient purchasing for both buyers and suppliers. A Web-powered purchasing program eliminates the paperwork associated with traditional requisition and ordering procedures. One recent study found that e-procurement cuts down requisition-to-order costs by an average of 58 percent.[13]

E-procurement reduces the time between order and delivery. Time savings are particularly dramatic for companies with many overseas suppliers. Adaptec, a leading supplier of computer storage, used an extranet to tie all of its Taiwanese chip suppliers together in a kind of virtual family. Now messages from Adaptec flow in seconds from its headquarters to its Asian partners, and Adaptec has reduced the time between the order and delivery of its chips from as long as 16 weeks to just 55 days—the same turnaround time for companies that build their own chips.

Finally, beyond the cost and time savings, e-procurement frees purchasing people to focus on more-strategic issues. For many purchasing professionals, going online means reducing drudgery and paperwork and spending more time managing inventory and working creatively with suppliers. "That is the key," says the HP executive. "You can now focus people on value-added activities. Procurement professionals can now find different sources and work with suppliers to reduce costs and to develop new products."[14]

The rapidly expanding use of e-purchasing, however, also presents some problems. For example, at the same time that the Web makes it possible for suppliers and customers to share business data and even collaborate on product design, it can also erode decades-old customer-supplier relationships. Many firms are using the Web to search for better suppliers.

E-purchasing can also create potential security disasters. Although e-mail and home banking transactions can be protected through basic encryption, the secure environment that businesses need to carry out confidential interactions is often still lacking. Companies are spending millions for research on defensive strategies to keep hackers at bay. Cisco Systems, for example, specifies the types of routers, firewalls, and security procedures that its partners must use to safeguard extranet connections. In fact, the company goes even further—it sends its own security engineers to examine a partner's defenses and holds the partner liable for any security breach that originates from its computer.

Institutional and Government Markets

So far, our discussion of organizational buying has focused largely on the buying behavior of business buyers. Much of this discussion also applies to the buying practices of institutional and government organizations. However, these two nonbusiness markets have additional characteristics and needs. In this final section, we address the special features of institutional and government markets.

Institutional Markets

Institutional market
Schools, hospitals, nursing homes, prisons, and other institutions that provide goods and services to people in their care.

The **institutional market** consists of schools, hospitals, nursing homes, prisons, and other institutions that provide goods and services to people in their care. Institutions differ from one another in their sponsors and in their objectives. For example, Tenet Healthcare runs 70 for-profit hospitals in 12 states. By contrast, the Shriners Hospitals for Children is a nonprofit organization that provides free specialized health care for children, and the government-run Veteran Affairs Medical Centers located across the country provide special services to veterans.[15] Each institution has different buying needs and resources.

Many institutional markets are characterized by low budgets and captive patrons. For example, hospital patients have little choice but to eat whatever food the hospital supplies. A hospital purchasing agent must decide on the quality of food to buy for patients. Because the food is provided as a part of a total service package, the buying objective is not profit. Nor is strict cost minimization the goal—patients receiving poor-quality food will complain to others and damage the hospital's reputation. Thus, the hospital purchasing agent must search for institutional-food vendors whose quality meets or exceeds a certain minimum standard and whose prices are low.

Many marketers set up separate divisions to meet the special characteristics and needs of institutional buyers. For example, Heinz produces, packages, and prices its ketchup and other condiments, canned soups, frozen desserts, pickles, and other products differently to better serve the requirements of hospitals, colleges, and other institutional markets. Nearly 20 percent of the company's sales come from its U.S. Foodservice division, which includes institutional customers.[16]

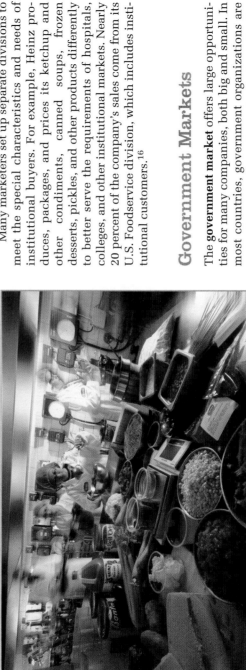

■ Institutional markets: Heinz produces, packages, and prices its products differently to better serve the requirements of hospitals, colleges, and other institutional markets.

Government market
Governmental units—federal, state, and local—that purchase or rent goods and services for carrying out the main functions of government.

Government Markets

The **government market** offers large opportunities for many companies, both big and small. In most countries, government organizations are major buyers of goods and services. In the United States alone, federal, state, and local governments contain more than 82,000 buying units. Government buying and business buying are similar in many ways. But there are also differences that must be understood by companies that wish to sell products and services to governments. To succeed in the government market, sellers must locate key decision makers, identify the factors that affect buyer behavior, and understand the buying decision process.

Government organizations typically require suppliers to submit bids, and normally they award the contract to the lowest bidder. In some cases, the government unit will make allowance for the supplier's superior quality or reputation for completing contracts on time.

Governments will also buy on a negotiated contract basis, primarily in the case of complex projects involving major R&D costs and risks, and in cases where there is little competition.

Government organizations tend to favor domestic suppliers over foreign suppliers. A major complaint of multinationals operating in Europe is that each country shows favoritism toward its nationals in spite of superior offers that are made by foreign firms. The European Economic Commission is gradually removing this bias.

Like consumer and business buyers, government buyers are affected by environmental, organizational, interpersonal, and individual factors. One unique thing about government buying is that it is carefully watched by outside publics, ranging from Congress to a variety of private groups interested in how the government spends taxpayers' money. Because their spending decisions are subject to public review, government organizations require considerable paperwork from suppliers, who often complain about excessive paperwork, bureaucracy, regulations, decision-making delays, and frequent shifts in procurement personnel.

Given all the red tape, why would any firm want to do business with the U.S. government? The reasons are quite simple: The U.S. government is the world's largest buyer of products and services—and its checks don't bounce. For example, last year, the federal government spent a whopping $65 billion on information technology alone. The Transportation Security Agency spent more than $380 million just for electronic baggage screening technology.[17]

Most governments provide would-be suppliers with detailed guides describing how to sell to the government. For example, the U.S. Small Business Administration publishes a guide entitled *U.S. Government Purchasing, Specifications, and Sales Directory*, which lists products and services frequently bought by the federal government and the specific agencies most frequently buying them. The Government Printing Office issues the *Commerce Business Daily*, which lists major current and planned purchases and recent contract awards, both of which can provide leads to subcontracting markets. The U.S. Commerce Department publishes *Business America*, which provides interpretations of government policies and programs and gives concise information on potential worldwide trade opportunities.

In several major cities, the General Services Administration operates *Business Service Centers* with staffs to provide a complete education on the way government agencies buy, the steps that suppliers should follow, and the procurement opportunities available. Various trade magazines and associations provide information on how to reach schools, hospitals, highway departments, and other government agencies. And almost all of these government organizations and associations maintain Internet sites offering up-to-date information and advice.

Still, suppliers must master the system and find ways to cut through the red tape, especially for large government purchases. Consider Envisage Technologies, a small software development company that specializes in Internet-based training applications and human resource management platforms. All of its contracts fall in the government sector; 65 percent are with the federal government. Envisage uses the General Services Administration (GSA) Web site to gain access to smaller procurements, often receiving responses within 14 days. However, it puts the most sweat into seeking large, highly coveted contracts. A comprehensive bid proposal for one of these contracts can easily run from 600 to 700 pages because of federal paperwork requirements. And the company's president estimates that to prepare a single bid proposal the firm has spent as many as 5,000 man-hours over the course of a few years.[18]

Noneconomic criteria also play a growing role in government buying. Government buyers are asked to favor depressed business firms and areas; small business firms; minority-owned firms; and business firms that avoid race, gender, or age discrimination. Sellers need to keep these factors in mind when deciding to seek government business.

Many companies that sell to the government have not been very marketing oriented for a number of reasons. Total government spending is determined by elected officials rather than by any marketing effort to develop this market. Government buying has emphasized price, making suppliers invest their effort in technology to bring costs down. When the product's characteristics are specified carefully, product differentiation is not a marketing factor. Nor do advertising or personal selling matter much in winning bids on an open-bid basis.

Several companies, however, have established separate government marketing departments, including GE, CDW, Kodak, and Goodyear. These companies anticipate government needs and projects, participate in the product specification phase, gather competitive intelligence, prepare bids carefully, and produce stronger communications to describe and enhance their companies' reputations.

Other companies have set up customized marketing programs for government buyers. For example, Dell has specific business units tailored to meet the needs of federal as well as state and local government buyers. Dell offers its customers tailor-made Premier Dell.com Web pages that include special pricing, online purchasing, and service and support for each city, state, and federal government entity.

During the past decade, a great deal of the government's buying has gone online. The Federal Business Opportunities Web site (www.FedBizOpps.gov) acts as a single government point of entry for federal government procurement opportunities over the amount of $25,000. The three federal agencies that act as purchasing agents for the rest of government have also launched Web sites supporting online government purchasing activity. The GSA, which influences more than one-quarter of the federal government's total procurement dollars, has set up a GSA Advantage! Web site (www.gsaadvantage.gov). The Defense Logistics Agency offers a Procurement Gateway (http://progate.daps.dla.mil) for purchases by America's military services. And the Department of Veteran Affairs facilitates e-procurement through its VA Advantage! Web site (https://vaadvantage.gsa.gov).

Such sites allow authorized defense and civilian agencies to buy everything from office supplies, food, and information technology equipment to construction services through online purchasing. The GSA, VA, and DLA not only sell stocked merchandise through their Web sites but also create direct links between buyers and contract suppliers. For example, the branch of the DLA that sells 160,000 types of medical supplies to military forces transmits orders directly to vendors such as Bristol-Myers. Such Internet systems promise to eliminate much of the hassle sometimes found in dealing with government purchasing.[19]

Reviewing the Concepts

Business markets and consumer markets are alike in some key ways. For example, both include people in buying roles who make purchase decisions to satisfy needs. But business markets also differ in many ways from consumer markets. For one thing, the business market is *enormous*, far larger than the consumer market. Within the United States alone, the business market includes organizations that annually purchase trillions of dollars' worth of goods and services.

1. Define the business market and explain how business markets differ from consumer markets.

Business buyer behavior refers to the buying behavior of the organizations that buy goods and services for use in the production of other products and services that are sold, rented, or supplied to others. It also includes the behavior of retailing and wholesaling firms that acquire goods for the purpose of reselling or renting them to others at a profit.

As compared to consumer markets, business markets usually have fewer, larger buyers who are more geographically concentrated. Business demand is *derived*, largely *inelastic*, and more *fluctuating*. More buyers are usually involved in the business buying decision, and business buyers are better trained and more professional than are consumer buyers. In general, business purchasing decisions are more complex, and the buying process is more formal than consumer buying.

2. Identify the major factors that influence business buyer behavior.

Business buyers make decisions that vary with the three types of *buying situations*: straight rebuys, modified rebuys, and new tasks. The decision-making unit of a buying organization—the *buying center*—can consist of many different persons playing many different roles. The business marketer needs to know the following: Who are the major buying center participants? In what decisions do they exercise influence and to what degree? What evaluation criteria does each decision participant use? The business marketer also needs to understand the major environmental, organizational, interpersonal, and individual influences on the buying process.

3. List and define the steps in the business buying decision process.

The *business buying decision process* itself can be quite involved, with eight basic stages: problem recognition, general need description, product specification, supplier search, proposal solicitation, supplier selection, order-routine specification, and performance review. Buyers who face a new-task buying situation usually go through all stages of the buying process. Buyers making modified or straight rebuys may skip some of the stages. Companies must manage the overall customer relationship, which often includes many different buying decisions in various stages of the buying decision process.

Recent advances in information technology have given birth to "e-procurement," by which business buyers are purchasing all kinds of products and services online. The Internet gives business buyers access to new suppliers, lowers purchasing costs, and hastens order processing and delivery. However, e-procurement can also erode customer-supplier relationships and create potential security problems. Still, business marketers are increasingly connecting with customers online to share marketing information, sell products and services, provide customer support services, and maintain ongoing customer relationships.

4. Compare the institutional and government markets and explain how institutional and government buyers make their buying decisions.

The *institutional market* consists of schools, hospitals, prisons, and other institutions that provide goods and services to people in their care. These markets are characterized by low budgets and captive patrons. The *government market*, which is vast, consists of government units—federal, state, and local—that purchase or rent goods and services for carrying out the main functions of government.

Government buyers purchase products and services for defense, education, public welfare, and other public needs. Government buying practices are highly specialized and specified, with open bidding or negotiated contracts characterizing most of the buying. Government buyers operate under the watchful eye of Congress and many private watchdog groups. Hence, they tend to require more forms and signatures and to respond more slowly and deliberately when placing orders.

Reviewing the Key Terms

Discussing the Concepts

1. How do the market structure and demand of the business markets for Intel's microprocessor chips differ from those of final consumer markets?

2. Discuss several ways in which a straight rebuy differs from a new-task situation.

3. In a buying center purchasing process, which buying center participant—a buyer, decider, gatekeeper, influencer, or user—is most likely to make each of the following statements?
   - "This bonding agent better be good, because I have to put this product together."
   - "I specified this bonding agent on another job, and it worked for them."
   - "Without an appointment, no sales rep gets in to see Mr. Johnson."

4. Outline the major influences on business buyers. Why is it important for the business-to-business buyer to understand these major influences?
   - "Okay, it's a deal—we'll buy it."
   - "I'll place the order first thing tomorrow."

5. How does the business buying process differ from the consumer buying process?

6. Suppose that you own a small printing firm and have the opportunity to bid on a federal government contract that could bring a considerable amount of new business to your company. List three advantages and three disadvantages of working in a contract situation with the federal government.

Applying the Concepts

1. Burst-of-Energy is a food product positioned in the extreme sports market as a performance enhancer. A distributor of the product has seen an upward shift in the demand for the product (depicted in the figure at the right). The manufacturer has done nothing to generate this demand, but there have been a couple of reports that two popular celebrities were photographed with the product. Could something like this happen? Based on the figure, how would you characterize the demand for the product? Is it elastic or inelastic? Would you call this an example of fluctuating demand? Support your answers.

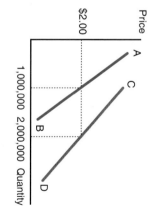

2. Assume that you own a market research consulting firm that specializes in conducting focus groups for food manufacturers. Your customers are marketing managers and market research managers at these large firms. Outline your business consumers' buying process and explain how you can improve your chances of being hired at each step of the process.

3. Form a small group and compare the similarities and differences between a buyer at a Veteran's Administration Hospital and a buyer at a for-profit hospital like Humana. Compare the buyers on the following four factors: environmental, organizational, interpersonal, and individual.
   a. An InnerSell.com member, who sells real estate, talks to a prospect or customer and learns that it has a need for $50,000 worth of photocopiers.

Focus on Technology

Social networking is a hot topic in Internet marketing. Web sites including friendster.com and myspace.com are crowded meeting grounds for Web visitors who are hoping to get connected online. Social networking is also a growing technology for B-to-B interactions. From finding services, locating opportunities, even recruiting board members, these sites offer what business consumers need. InnerSell.com is a company that is using social networking to drive real business for clients by locating prospects. A sample scenario on InnerSell.com works like this:

b. The member enters the need (lead) into InnerSell.com and sees a list of trusted photocopier vendors along with their ratings and their finder's fee.

c. The member views each vendor's ratings and selects two photocopier vendors who pay a 10 percent finder's fee.

d. The selected vendors receive an e-mail advising them that they've been chosen and instructing them to log into InnerSell.com to see the details of the opportunity.

e. When a selected vendor sees the lead, contacts the customer, and wins the business, it pays InnerSell.com its 10 percent finder's fee (in this case, $5,000).

f. InnerSell.com then passes $3,500 of the winning vendor's finder's fee to the member who entered the winning lead.

1. At what stage(s) of the business buying process does InnerSell.com operate?

2. What types of businesses is this best suited to serve?

3. What are some weaknesses with this technology?

Focus on Ethics

You are the senior buyer for a growing medical products company and an avid baseball fan. You have just opened an invitation to attend the World Series this coming fall. The invitation is from a supplier company that has been trying to sell you its new line of products for the past year. The supplier will pay for everything—travel, room, meals—and you'll even get an opportunity to meet some of the players. You have read the newly released employee manual and there is no reference or rule that specifically states that an employee cannot accept a fully paid trip from a vendor, although there are some vague restrictions on lunches and dinners paid for by suppliers.

1. Do you accept or decline the invitation?

2. Just because it is not specifically mentioned in the employee manual, would you be acting ethically if you accepted?

3. Do you think the supplier will expect "special" treatment in the next buying situation?

4. How would other company employees interpret your acceptance of this invitation?

Video Case   Eaton

With nearly 60,000 employees doing business in 125 countries and sales last year of more than $11 billion, Eaton is one of the world's largest suppliers of diversified industrial goods. Eaton's products make cars more peppy, 18 wheelers safer to drive, and airliners more fuel efficient. So why haven't you heard of the company? Because Eaton sells its products not to end consumers but to other businesses.

At Eaton, B-to-B marketing means working closely with customers to develop a better product. So the company partners with its sophisticated, knowledgeable clients to create total solutions that meet their needs. Along the way, Eaton maps the decision-making process to better understand the concerns and interests of decision makers. In the end, Eaton's

success depends on its ability to provide high-quality, dependable customer service and product support. Through service and support, Eaton develops a clear understanding of consumer needs and builds stronger relationships with clients.

After viewing the video featuring Eaton, answer the following questions about business markets and business buyer behavior.

1. What is Eaton's value proposition?

2. To which decision makers does Eaton market its products and services?

3. How does Eaton add value to its products and services?

Company Case   Kodak: Changing the Picture

MEMORIES

"You press the button—we do the rest." With that simple slogan, George Eastman unveiled the first Kodak camera in 1888—yes, 1888, more than 118 years ago. In 1900, Kodak launched its famous Brownie cameras, which it priced at $1.00, opening the photography market to millions. Throughout the twentieth century, Kodak dominated the photography business. By 2000, Kodak was one of the most recognized and trusted brands in the world. Many people referred to the company as "Big Yellow." The company saw

itself as being in the memory business, not in the photography business.

GOING NEGATIVE

Despite its storied past, however, entering the new millennium, Kodak faced many new challenges that would require it to rethink and perhaps redesign its business strategy. The company's stock price, which had reached an historic peak of $90 in 1997, had been plummeting, and the company had begun to lay off workers.

Several factors were causing Kodak's problems. First, although Kodak had been the first company to produce a digital camera in 1976, it had been reluctant to develop the technology. The core of Kodak's business strategy had always been the three-fold foundation of commercial and consumer photography: film, photo-developing chemicals, and light-sensitive paper. Like many other companies, Kodak believed that consumers would be slow to adopt digital technology. But what held the company back even more was that a shift toward digital would to some extent have been a shift away from George Eastman's legacy. Thus, Kodak saw every digital camera consumers purchased as another nail in the coffin of the company's heart and soul.

Second, despite Kodak's dominance in traditional photography, many competitors, especially Fuji, were exposing flaws in Kodak's marketing and stealing market share. Third, competition from an unexpected source—cellular phone manufacturers—surprised Kodak. Nokia introduced the first cellular phone with a built-in camera in November 2001. Although many people thought such phones would only be toys, consumers began snapping them up. By 2003, sales of camera phones doubled the sales of conventional digital cameras. Further, analysts predicted correctly that the number of cell phones with cameras would increase dramatically during the early 2000s.

Finally, consumers who owned digital cameras or cell-phone cameras were increasingly using their PCs and print-ers to download and print their own pictures, if they printed them at all. Analysts discovered that consumers printed only 2 percent of camera-phone pictures in the United States, versus 10 percent in Japan.

THE PROOF IS IN THE PICTURE—WALGREENS

Up through the 1980s, when consumers wanted to develop pictures, they took their film rolls to local drugstores, discount department stores, or photo shops. These stores sent the film to regional labs run by Kodak and others, which produced the prints and returned them to the store for pickup. This process took many days. Then, with the development of the self-contained photo lab, retailers could place a machine directly in their store that would do all the photo processing. These photo labs allowed the retailers to offer faster service—even one-hour service.

As consumers demanded more one-hour photo developing, Kodak agreed to help Walgreens, the nation's largest drugstore chain, set up a national one-hour photo business. Kodak had been the exclusive supplier of photo-developing services to Walgreens for years. In response to the request, Kodak provided minilabs, which it bought from a Swiss manufacturer, that handled the photo developing on-site, collecting fees for leasing the equipment. Kodak even loaned Walgreens $31.6 million, interest free, to help it implement the system.

Problems developed, however, when the minilabs proved to be unreliable. They broke down up to 11 times a month due to paper jams and software glitches. It often took two to three days to get the machines serviced, and when they were, customers' film in the machines was exposed to light when service people opened the machines.

As a result, in 2001, Walgreens quietly began to install Fuji minilabs in some of its California stores. Fuji's machines, in addition to handling traditional film, also allowed consumers to make prints from their digital cameras' memory devices, something Kodak's did not do. Kodak began selling kits to allow its minilabs to handle digital prints, but Walgreens officials believed Kodak's prints were lower quality. By early 2004, Fuji had 1,500 minilabs in Walgreens' almost 4,300 outlets.

Walgreens also approached Kodak about developing a Walgreens Internet site that would allow consumers to upload digital photos over the Web. Kodak would then store images and allow customers to order prints, which would then be mailed to them. Walgreens did not like Kodak's proposal as it minimized the Walgreens role and allowed Kodak to keep the pictures on its site, gaining an advantage in future customer orders. Despite these concerns, Walgreens was about to sign a deal with Kodak when two top officials, who favored Kodak, retired. The company then nixed the deal and started developing its own Web site with Fuji, which was comfortable with a less prominent role. Walgreens launched its Web service in 2003, with Fuji carrying out the photo developing.

A NEW DEVELOPMENT

Given all this, in early 2003, Kodak reevaluated its strategy. It recognized that the time had come to fully embrace the digital age. In September 2003, Kodak announced a historic shift in its strategy. It would now focus on digital imaging for consumers, businesses, and health care providers. The company would reduce its dependence on traditional film, boost investment in nonphotographic markets, and pursue digital markets, such as inkjet printers and high-end digital printing. These moves would put it in direct competition with entrenched competitors, such as HP, Canon, Seiko, Epson, and Xerox. It was a necessary but risky shift—at the time, traditional film and photography accounted for 70 percent of Kodak's revenue and all of its operating profits.

By 2004, Kodak had laid out a complete four-year restructuring plan. The plan was that Kodak's traditional business would progressively contribute less as a percentage of revenues and earnings while the digital business would contribute more. As a part of the shift in strategy, Kodak stopped selling reloadable film cameras in the United States, Canada, and Europe. In 2005, Kodak focused intensely on further executing the strategic plan. CEO Antonio Perez even asserted, "Soon, I'm not going to be answering questions about film because I won't know. It will be too small for me to get involved." Given the criticism that Kodak had taken for its sluggish move to a digital strategy, this was a welcome statement to many.

CEO Perez made some dramatic moves. He divided the company into four distinct units: imaging, commercial and print, medical, and traditional film. To assist in phasing out the film business and to stop the "bleeding year after year,"

(case continues)

chapter 7

Customer-Driven Marketing Strategy

Creating Value for Target Customers

Previewing the Concepts

So far, you've learned what marketing is and about the importance of understanding consumers and the marketplace environment. With that as background, you're now ready to delve deeper into marketing strategy and tactics. This chapter looks further into key customer-driven marketing strategy decisions—how to divide up markets into meaningful customer groups (*segmentation*), choose which customer groups to serve (*targeting*), create market offerings that best serve target customers (*differentiation*), and position the offerings in the minds of consumers (*positioning*). Then, the chapters that follow explore the tactical marketing tools—the Four Ps—by which marketers bring these strategies to life.

As an opening example of segmentation, targeting, differentiation, and positioning at work, let's look at Dunkin' Donuts. Dunkin', a largely Eastern U.S. coffee chain, has ambitious plans to expand into a national powerhouse, on a par with Starbucks. But Dunkin' is no Starbucks. In fact, it doesn't want to be. It targets a very different kind of customer with a very different value proposition. Grab yourself some coffee and read on.

L ast year, Dunkin' Donuts paid dozens of faithful customers in Phoenix, Chicago, and Charlotte, North Carolina, $100 a week to buy coffee at Starbucks instead. At the same time, the no-frills coffee chain paid Starbucks customers to make the opposite switch. When it later debriefed the two groups, Dunkin' says it found them so polarized that company researchers dubbed them "tribes"—each of whom loathed the very things that made the other tribe loyal to their coffee shop. Dunkin' fans viewed Starbucks as pretentious and trendy, whereas Starbucks loyalists saw Dunkin' as plain and unoriginal. "I don't get it," one Dunkin' regular told researchers after visiting Starbucks. "If I want to sit on a couch, I stay at home."

William Rosenberg opened the first Dunkin' Donuts in Quincy, Massachusetts, in 1950. Residents flocked to his store each morning for the coffee and fresh doughnuts. Rosenberg started franchising the Dunkin' Donuts name, and the chain grew rapidly throughout the Midwest and Southeast. By the early 1990s, however, Dunkin' was losing breakfast sales to morning sandwiches at McDonald's and Burger King. Starbucks and other high-end cafes began sprouting up, bringing more competition. Sales slid as the company clung to its strategy of selling sugary doughnuts by the dozen.

In the mid-1990s, however, Dunkin' shifted its focus from doughnuts to coffee in the hope that promoting a more frequently consumed item would drive store traffic. The coffee push worked—coffee now makes up 62 percent of sales. And Dunkin's sales are growing at a double-digit clip, with profits up 35 percent over the past two years. Based on this recent success, Dunkin' now has ambitious plans to expand into a national coffee powerhouse, on a par with Starbucks, the nation's largest coffee chain. Over the next three years, Dunkin' plans to remake its nearly 5,000 U.S. stores and to grow to triple that number in less than 15 years.

But Dunkin' is not Starbucks. In fact, it doesn't want to be. To succeed, it must have its own clear vision of just which customers it wants to serve (what *segments* and *targeting*) and how (what *positioning* or *value proposition*). Dunkin' and Starbucks target very different customers, who want very different things from their favorite coffee shop. Starbucks is strongly positioned as a sort of high-brow "third place"—outside the home and office—featuring couches, eclectic music, wireless Internet access, and art-splashed walls. Dunkin' has a decidedly more low-brow, "everyman" kind of positioning.

With its makeover, Dunkin' plans to move upscale—a bit but not too far—to rebrand itself as a quick but appealing alternative to specialty coffee shops and fast-food chains. A prototype Dunkin' store in Euclid, Ohio, outside Cleveland, features rounded granite-style coffee bars, where workers make espresso drinks face-to-face with customers. Open-air pastry cases brim with yogurt parfaits and fresh fruit, and a carefully orchestrated pop-music soundtrack is piped throughout.

Yet Dunkin' built itself on serving simple fare to working-class customers. Inching upscale without alienating that base will prove tricky. There will be no couches in the new stores. And Dunkin' renamed a new hot sandwich a "stuffed melt" after customers complained that calling it a "panini" was too fancy. "We're walking that [fine] line," says Regina Lewis, the chain's vice president of consumer insights. "The thing about the Dunkin' tribe is, they see through the hype."

Dunkin's research showed that although loyal Dunkin' customers want nicer stores, they were bewildered and turned off by the atmosphere at Starbucks. They groused that crowds of laptop users made it difficult to find a seat. They didn't like Starbucks' "tall," "grande," and "venti" lingo for small, medium, and large coffees. And they couldn't understand why anyone would pay as much as $4 for a cup of coffee. "It was almost as though they were a group of Martians talking about a group of Earthlings," says an executive from Dunkin's ad agency. One customer told researchers that lingering in a Starbucks felt like "celebrating Christmas with people you don't know." The Starbucks customers that Dunkin' paid to switch were equally uneasy in Dunkin' shops. "The Starbucks people couldn't bear that they weren't special anymore," says the ad executive.

Objectives

After studying this chapter, you should be able to

1. define the four major steps in designing a customer-driven market strategy: market segmentation, market targeting, differentiation, and positioning

2. list and discuss the major bases for segmenting consumer and business markets

3. explain how companies identify attractive market segments and choose a market targeting strategy

4. discuss how companies position their products for maximum competitive advantage in the marketplace

Such opposing opinions aren't surprising, given the differences in the two stores' customers. About 45 percent of Dunkin' Donuts customers have an annual household income between $45,000 and $100,000 a year, with 30 percent earning less than that and 25 percent earning more. Dunkin's customers include blue- and white-collar workers across all age, race, and income demographics. By contrast, Starbucks targets a higher-income, more professional group.

But Dunkin' researchers concluded that it wasn't income that set the two tribes apart, as much as an ideal: Dunkin' tribe members want to be part of a crowd, whereas members of the Starbucks tribe want to stand out as individuals. "The Starbucks tribe, they seek out things to make them feel more important," says Dunkin' VP Lewis. Members of the Dunkin' Donuts tribe "don't need to be any more important than they are."

Based on such findings, Dunkin' executives have made dozens of store-redesign decisions, big and small, ranging from where to put the espresso machines to how much of its signature pink and orange color scheme to retain to where to display its fresh baked goods. Out went the square laminate tables, to be replaced by round imitation-granite tabletops and sleek chairs. Dunkin' covered store walls in espresso brown and dialed down the pink and orange tones. Executives considered but held off on installing wireless Internet access because customers "just don't feel it's Dunkin' Donuts." Executives continue to discuss dropping the word "donuts" from its signs to convey that its menu is now broader.

To grab a bigger share of customers, Dunkin' is expanding its menu beyond breakfast with hearty snacks that can substitute for meals, such as smoothies and dough-wrapped pork bites. The new Euclid store is doing three times the sales of other stores in its area, partly because more customers are coming after 11 A.M. for new gourmet cookies and Dunkin' Dawgs, hot dogs wrapped in dough. Focus groups liked hot flatbreads and smoothies, but balked at tiny pinwheels of dough stuffed with various fillings. Customers said "they felt like something at a fancy cocktail hour," says Lewis, and they weren't substantial enough.

Stacey Stevens, a 34-year-old Euclid resident who recently visited the new Dunkin' prototype store, said she noticed it felt different than other Dunkin' locations. "I don't remember there being lots of music," she said, while picking up a dozen doughnuts. "I like it in here." She said it felt "more upbeat" than Starbucks. One Euclid store manager even persuaded Richard Wandersleben to upgrade from a regular coffee to a $2.39 latte during a recent visit. The 73- year-old retired tool-and-die maker, who drinks about three cups of coffee a day, says the Dunkin' Donuts latte suited him fine. "It's a little creamier" than regular coffee, he said.

Dunkin' knows that it'll take some time to refresh its image. And whatever else happens, it plans to stay true to the needs and preferences of the Dunkin' tribe. Dunkin's "not going after the Starbucks coffee snob," says one analyst, it's "going after the average Joe." Dunkin's positioning and value proposition are pretty well summed up in its new ad campaign, which features the slogan "America Runs on Dunkin'." The ads show everyone from office and construction workers to harried families relying on the chain to get them through their day. Says one ad, "It's where everyday people get things done every day."[1]

Companies today recognize that they cannot appeal to all buyers in the marketplace, or at least not to all buyers in the same way. Buyers are too numerous, too widely scattered, and too varied in their needs and buying practices. Moreover, the companies themselves vary widely in their abilities to serve different segments of the market. Instead, like Dunkin' Donuts, a company must identify the parts of the market that it can serve best and most profitably. It must design customer-driven marketing strategies that build the *right* relationships with the *right* customers.

Thus, most companies have moved away from mass marketing and toward *target marketing*—identifying market segments, selecting one or more of them, and developing products and marketing programs tailored to each. Instead of scattering their marketing efforts (the "shotgun" approach), firms are focusing on the buyers who have greater interest in the values they create best (the "rifle" approach).

Figure 7.1 shows the four major steps in designing a customer-driven marketing strategy. In the first two steps, the company selects the customers that it will serve. **Market segmentation** involves dividing a market into smaller groups of buyers with distinct needs, characteristics, or behaviors who might require separate products or marketing mixes. The company

Market segmentation

Dividing a market into smaller groups with distinct needs, characteristics, or behaviors who might require separate products or marketing mixes.

Market targeting
The process of evaluating each market segment's attractiveness and selecting one or more segments to enter.

Differentiation
Actually differentiating the firm's market offering to create superior customer value.

Positioning
Arranging for a product to occupy a clear, distinctive, and desirable place relative to competing products in the minds of target consumers.

Geographic segmentation
Dividing a market into different geographical units such as nations, states, regions, counties, cities, or neighborhoods.

FIGURE 7.1 Steps in market segmentation, targeting, and positioning

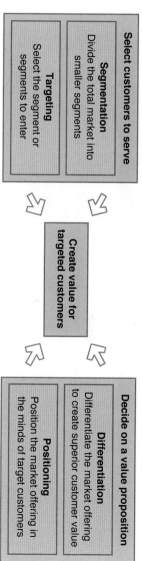

Select customers to serve

Segmentation	Targeting
Divide the total market into smaller segments	Select the segment or segments to enter

Create value for targeted customers

Decide on a value proposition

Differentiation	Positioning
Differentiate the market offering to create superior customer value	Position the market offering in the minds of target customers

identifies different ways to segment the market and develops profiles of the resulting market segments. **Market targeting** (or **targeting**) consists of evaluating each market segment's attractiveness and select one or more market segments to enter.

In the final two steps, the company decides on a value proposition—on how it will create value for target customers. **Differentiation** involves actually differentiating the firm's market offering to create superior customer value. **Positioning** consists of arranging for a market offering to occupy a clear, distinctive, and desirable place relative to competing products in the minds of target consumers. We discuss each of these steps in turn.

■ Market Segmentation

Markets consist of buyers, and buyers differ in one or more ways. They may differ in their wants, resources, locations, buying attitudes, and buying practices. Through market segmentation, companies divide large, heterogeneous markets into smaller segments that can be reached more efficiently and effectively with products and services that match their unique needs. In this section, we discuss four important segmentation topics: segmenting consumer markets, segmenting business markets, segmenting international markets, and requirements for effective segmentation.

Segmenting Consumer Markets

There is no single way to segment a market. A marketer has to try different segmentation variables, alone and in combination, to find the best way to view the market structure. Table 7.1 outlines the major variables that might be used in segmenting consumer markets. Here we look at the major *geographic, demographic, psychographic,* and *behavioral* variables.

Geographic Segmentation

Geographic segmentation calls for dividing the market into different geographical units such as nations, regions, states, counties, cities, or neighborhoods. A company may decide to operate in one or a few geographical areas, or to operate in all areas but pay attention to geographical differences in needs and wants.

Many companies today are localizing their products, advertising, promotion, and sales efforts to fit the needs of individual regions, cities, and even neighborhoods. For example, one consumer products company shipped additional cases of its low-calorie snack foods to stores in neighborhoods near Weight Watchers clinics. Kraft developed Post's Fiesta Fruity Pebbles cereal for areas with high Hispanic populations. Coca-Cola developed four ready-to-drink canned coffees for the Japanese market, each targeted to a specific geographic region. Procter & Gamble introduced Curry Pringles in England and Funky Soy Sauce Pringles in Asia.[2]

Other companies are seeking to cultivate as-yet untapped geographic territory. For example, many large companies are fleeing the fiercely competitive major cities and suburbs to set up shop in small-town America. Consider Applebee's, the nation's largest casual-dining chain:

Applebee's is now making sure that even far-flung suburbs and small towns can have a neighborhood bar and grill. It's extending into what it calls STAR (small-town Applebee's restaurant) markets with fewer that 50,000 people, breaking down the misconception that small-market Americans aren't interested in anything that can't be bought at Wal-Mart (or its restaurant equivalent). How's the strategy working? Just check out the dozen or more parties lined up on a typical Friday night outside an Applebee's in Hays, Kansas, a small town of 21,000 people located in an area known

TABLE 7.1   Major Segmentation Variables for Consumer Markets

Geographic

World region or country	North America, Western Europe, Middle East, Pacific Rim, China, India, Canada, Mexico
Country region	Pacific, Mountain, West North Central, West South Central, East North Central, East South Central, South Atlantic, Middle Atlantic, New England
City or metro size	Under 5,000; 5,000–20,000; 20,000–50,000; 50,000–100,000; 100,000–250,000; 250,000–500,000; 500,000–1,000,000; 1,000,000–4,000,000; over 4,000,000
Density	Urban, suburban, rural
Climate	Northern, southern

Demographic

Age	Under 6, 6–11, 12–19, 20–34, 35–49, 50–64, 65+
Gender	Male, female
Family size	1–2, 3–4, 5+
Family life cycle	Young, single; young, married, no children; young, married with children; older, married, no children; under 18; older, single; other
Income	Under $10,000; $10,000–$20,000; $20,000–$30,000; $30,000–$50,000; $50,000–$100,000; $100,000 and over
Occupation	Professional and technical; managers, officials, and proprietors; clerical; sales; craftspeople; supervisors; operatives; farmers; retired; students; homemakers; unemployed
Education	Grade school or less; some high school; high school graduate; some college; college graduate
Religion	Catholic, Protestant, Jewish, Muslim, Hindu, other
Race	Asian, Hispanic, Black, White
Generation	Baby boomer, Generation X, Generation Y
Nationality	North American, South American, British, French, German, Italian, Japanese

Psychographic

Social class	Lower lowers, upper lowers, working class, middle class, upper middles, lower uppers, upper uppers
Lifestyle	Achievers, strivers, survivors
Personality	Compulsive, gregarious, authoritarian, ambitious

Behavioral

Occasions	Regular occasion; special occasion
Benefits	Quality, service, economy, convenience, speed
User status	Nonuser, ex-user, potential user, first-time user, regular user
User rates	Light user, medium user, heavy user
Loyalty status	None, medium, strong, absolute
Readiness stage	Unaware, aware, informed, interested, desirous, intending to buy
Attitude toward product	Enthusiastic, positive, indifferent, negative, hostile

as "the middle of nowhere" between Denver and Kansas City. Although sales in such smaller communities average 10 percent less than at a suburban Applebee's, that's offset by cheaper real estate and less-complicated zoning laws. And there is no real casual-dining competition in Hays. No Chili's. No Houlihan's. Not even a Bennigan's. "If you want to take someone out on a date," says one young diner, "you're not going to take them to the Golden Corral," an all-you-can-eat family restaurant next door. That's a telling statement, given that the young man is a management trainee at the Golden Corral. So far, Applebee's has opened some 156 small-town restaurants. Considering that there are about 2,200 counties in the United States with populations under 50,000, it has a lot more room to grow.[3]

In contrast, other retailers are developing new store concepts that will give them access to higher-density urban areas. For example, Home Depot has been introducing urban neighborhood stores that look a lot like its traditional stores but at about two-thirds the size. It is placing these stores in high-density markets, such as Manhattan, where full-size stores are impractical. Similarly, Wal-Mart has been opening small, supermarket-style Neighborhood Market grocery stores to complement its supercenters.[4]

Demographic Segmentation

Demographic segmentation divides the market into groups based on variables such as age, gender, family size, family life cycle, income, occupation, education, religion, race, generation, and nationality. Demographic factors are the most popular bases for segmenting customer groups. One reason is that consumer needs, wants, and usage rates often vary closely with demographic variables. Another is that demographic variables are easier to measure than most other types of variables. Even when market segments are first defined using other bases, such as benefits sought or behavior, their demographic characteristics must be known in order to assess the size of the target market and to reach it efficiently.

AGE AND LIFE-CYCLE STAGE Consumer needs and wants change with age. Some companies use **age and life-cycle segmentation**, offering different products or using different marketing approaches for different age and life-cycle groups. For example, for kids, Procter & Gamble sells Crest Spinbrushes featuring favorite children's characters. For adults, it sells more serious models, promising "a dentist-clean feeling twice a day." And Nintendo, long known for its youth-oriented video games, has launched a subbrand, Touch Generations, which targets aging baby boomers. Touch Generations offers video games such as *Brain Training: How Old Is Your Brain?*, designed to "exercise the noggin" and keep the mind young. The aim is to "lure in older nongamers by offering skill-building—or at least less violent, less fantasy-based—titles that might appeal to [older consumers] more than, say, *Grand Theft Auto* or *World of Warcraft*."[5]

Marketers must be careful to guard against stereotypes when using age and life-cycle segmentation. For example, although some 70-year-olds require wheelchairs, others play tennis. Similarly, whereas some 40-year-old couples are sending their children off to college, others are just beginning new families. Thus, age is often a poor predictor of a person's life cycle, health, work or family status, needs, and buying power. Companies marketing to mature consumers usually employ positive images and appeals. For example, ads for Olay ProVital—designed to improve the elasticity and appearance of the "maturing skin" of women over 50—feature attractive older spokeswomen and uplifting messages.

GENDER **Gender segmentation** has long been used in clothing, cosmetics, toiletries, and magazines. For example, Procter & Gamble was among the first with Secret, a brand specially formulated for a woman's chemistry, packaged and advertised to reinforce the female image. More recently, many mostly women's cosmetics makers have begun marketing men's lines. For example, L'Oreal offers Men's Expert skin care products and a VIVE For Men grooming line. Ads proclaim, "Now L'Oreal Paris brings its grooming technology and expertise to men . . . because you're worth it too."

Nike has recently stepped up its efforts to capture the women's sports apparel market. It wasn't until 2000 that Nike made women's shoes using molds made from women's feet, rather than simply using a small man's foot mold. Since then, however, Nike has changed its approach to women. It has overhauled its women's apparel line—called Nikewomen—to create better fitting, more colorful, more fashionable workout clothes for women. Its revamped Nikewomen.com Web site now features the apparel, along with workout trend highlights. And Nike has been opening Nikewomen stores in several major cities.[6]

A growing number of Web sites and media networks also target women, such as iVillage, Oxygen, Lifetime, and WE. For example, WE TV is "the network dedicated to helping women

---

Demographic Segmentation

Demographic segmentation divides the market into groups based on variables such as age, gender, family size, family life cycle, income, occupation, education, religion, race, generation, and nationality.

Demographic segmentation
Dividing a market into groups based on variables such as age, gender, family size, family life cycle, income, occupation, education, religion, race, generation, and nationality.

Age and life-cycle segmentation
Dividing a market into different age and life-cycle groups.

Gender segmentation
Dividing a market into different groups based on gender.

■ Gender segmentation: Nike has recently stepped up its efforts to capture the women's sports apparel market by overhauling its women's apparel lines, revamping the Nikewomen.com Web site, and opening Nikewomen stores in several major cities.

connect to one another and the world around them." Its WE Empowers Women initiative helps women "find your voice and feel good doing it" by supporting causes that are important to women.[7]

Income segmentation
Dividing a market into different income groups.

INCOME Income segmentation has long been used by the marketers of products and services such as automobiles, clothing, cosmetics, financial services, and travel. Many companies target affluent consumers with luxury goods and convenience services. Stores such as Neiman Marcus pitch everything from expensive jewelry and fine fashions to glazed Australian apricots priced at $20 a pound. And credit-card companies offer superpremium credit cards dripping with perks, such as VISA's Signature Card, MasterCard's World card, and American Express's super-elite Centurion card. The much-coveted black Centurian card is issued by invitation only, to customers who spend more than $250,000 a year on other AmEx cards. Then, the select few who do receive the card pay a $2,500 annual fee just for the privilege of carrying it.

However, not all companies that use income segmentation target the affluent. For example, many retailers—such as the Dollar General, Family Dollar, and Dollar Tree store chains—successfully target low- and middle-income groups. The core market for such stores is families with incomes under $30,000. When Family Dollar real-estate experts scout locations for new stores, they look for lower-middle-class neighborhoods where people wear less expensive shoes and drive old cars that drip a lot of oil.

With their low-income strategies, the dollar stores are now the fastest growing retailers in the nation. They have been so successful that giant discounters are taking notice. For example, Target has installed a dollar aisle—the "1 Spot"—in its stores. And supermarkets such as Kroger to A&P are launching "10 for $10" promotions. And some experts predict that, to meet the dollar store threat, Wal-Mart will eventually buy one of these chains or start one of its own.[8]

Psychographic Segmentation

Psychographic segmentation
Dividing a market into different groups based on social class, lifestyle, or personality characteristics.

Psychographic segmentation divides buyers into different groups based on social class, lifestyle, or personality characteristics. People in the same demographic group can have very different psychographic makeups.

In Chapter 5, we discussed how the products people buy reflect their *lifestyles. As a* result, marketers often segment their markets by consumer lifestyles and base their marketing strategies on lifestyle appeals. For example, American Express promises "a card that fits your life." It's "My life. My card." campaign provides glimpses into the lifestyles of famous people with whom consumers might want to identify, from pro surfer Laird Hamilton and television personality Ellen DeGeneres to screen stars Robert DeNiro and Kate Winslet.

Pottery Barn, with its different store formats, sells more than just home furnishings. It sells all that its customers aspire to be. Pottery Barn Kids offers idyllic scenes of the perfect childhood,

■ The American Express "My life. My card." campaign provides glimpses into the lifestyles of famous people with whom consumers might identify, here Ellen DeGeneres.

whereas PB Teens offers trendy fashion-forward self-expression. The flagship Pottery Barn stores serve an upscale yet casual, family- and friend-focused lifestyle—affluent but sensibly so:[9]

Shortly after Hadley MacLean got married, she and her husband, Doug, agreed that their old bed had to go. It was a mattress and box spring on a cheap metal frame, a relic of Doug's Harvard days. But Hadley never anticipated how tough it would be to find a new bed. "We couldn't find anything we liked, even though we were willing to spend the money," says Hadley, a 31-year-old marketing director. It turned out to be much more than just finding a piece of furniture at the right price. It was a matter of emotion: They needed a bed that meshed with their lifestyle—with who they are and where they are going. The couple finally ended up at the Pottery Barn on Boston's upscale Newbury Street, where Doug fell in love with a mahogany sleigh bed that Hadley had spotted in the store's catalog. The couple was so pleased with how great it looked in their Dutch Colonial home that they hurried back to the store for a set of end tables. And then they bought a quilt. And a mirror for the living room. And some stools for the dining room. "We got kind of addicted," Hadley confesses.

Marketers also have used *personality* variables to segment markets. For example, marketing for Honda motor scooters *appears* to target hip and trendy 22-year-olds. But it is *actually* aimed at a much broader personality group. One old ad, for example, showed a delighted child bouncing up and down on his bed while the announcer says, "You've been trying to get there all your life." The ad reminded viewers of the euphoric feelings they got when they broke away from authority and did things their parents told them not to do. Thus, Honda is appealing to the rebellious, independent kid in all of us. In fact, 22 percent of its scooters riders are retirees. Competitor Vespa sells more than a quarter of its scooters to the over-50 set. "The older buyers are buying them for kicks," says one senior. "They never had the opportunity to do this as kids."[10]

Behavioral Segmentation

Behavioral segmentation divides buyers into groups based on their knowledge, attitudes, uses, or responses to a product. Many marketers believe that behavior variables are the best starting point for building market segments.

OCCASIONS Buyers can be grouped according to occasions when they get the idea to buy, actually make their purchase, or use the purchased item. **Occasion segmentation** can help firms build up product usage. For example, eggs are most often consumed at breakfast. But the American Egg Board, with its "incredible, edible egg" theme, promotes eating eggs at all times of the day. Its Web site offers basic egg facts and lots of recipes for egg appetizers, snacks, main dishes, and desserts.

Some holidays, such as Mother's Day and Father's Day, were originally promoted partly to increase the sale of candy, flowers, cards, and other gifts. And many marketers prepare special offers and ads for holiday occasions. For example, Altoids offers a special "Love Tin," the "curiously strong valentine." Peeps creates different shaped sugar and fluffy marshmallow treats for Easter, Valentine's Day, Halloween, and Christmas when it captures most of its sales but advertises that Peeps are "Always in Season" to increase the demand for non-holiday occasions.

BENEFITS SOUGHT A powerful form of segmentation is to group buyers according to the different *benefits* that they seek from the product. **Benefit segmentation** requires finding the major benefits people look for in the product class, the kinds of people who look for each benefit, and the major brands that deliver each benefit.

Champion athletic wear segments its markets according to benefits that different consumers seek from their activewear. For example,

---

Behavioral segmentation
Dividing a market into groups based on consumer knowledge, attitude, use, or response to a product.

Occasion segmentation
Dividing a market into groups according to occasions when buyers get the idea to buy, actually make their purchase, or use the purchased item.

Benefit segmentation
Dividing a market into groups according to the different benefits that consumers seek from the product.

■ Occasion segmentation: Peeps creates different shaped marshmallow treats for special holidays when it captures most of its sales but advertises that Peeps are "Always in Season" to increase the demand for non-holiday occasions.

Peeps
Ready for Summer!

ABOUT PEEPS... | "ALWAYS IN SEASON" | FEATURED RECIPES & CRAFTS | PEEPS' FAN CLUB | PEEPS' TALK

Check Out PEEPS' Summer Travels! Click here!

PEEPS' Fan Club

Easter | Valentine's Day | Halloween | Christmas

"Fit and Polish" consumers seek a balance between function and style—they exercise for results but want to look good doing it. "Serious Sports Competitors" exercise heavily and live in and love their activewear—they seek performance and function. By contrast, "Value-Seeking Moms" have low sports interest and low activewear involvement—they buy for the family and seek durability and value. Thus, each segment seeks a different mix of benefits. Champion must target the benefit segment or segments that it can serve best and most profitably using appeals that match each segment's benefit preferences.

USER STATUS Markets can be segmented into nonusers, ex-users, potential users, first-time users, and regular users of a product. For example, blood banks cannot rely only on regular donors. They must also recruit new first-time donors and remind ex-donors—each will require different marketing appeals.

Included in the potential user group are consumers facing life-stage changes—such as newlyweds and new parents—who can be turned into heavy users. For example, P&G acquires the names of parents-to-be and showers them with product samples and ads for its Pampers and other baby products in order to capture a share of their future purchases. It invites them to visit Pampers.com and join MyPampers.com, giving them access to expert parenting advice, Parent Pages e-mail newsletters, and coupons and special offers.

USAGE RATE Markets can also be segmented into light, medium, and heavy product users. Heavy users are often a small percentage of the market but account for a high percentage of total consumption. For example, fast-feeder Burger King targets what it calls "Super Fans," young (age 18 to 34), Whopper-wolfing males who make up 18 percent of the chain's customers but account for almost half of all customer visits. They eat at Burger King an average of 16 times a month.[11]

Burger King targets these Super Fans openly with ads that exalt monster burgers containing meat, cheese, and more meat and cheese that can turn "innies into outies." It's "Manthem" ad parodies the Helen Reddy song "I Am Woman." In the ad, young Super Fans who are "too hungry to settle for chick food" rebel by burning their briefs, pushing a minivan off a bridge, chowing down on decadent Texas Double Whoppers, and proclaiming "Eat like a man, man!" Although such ads puzzled many a casual fast-food patron, they really pushed the hungry buttons of Burger King's heavy users.

Despite claims by some consumers that the fast-food chains are damaging their health, these heavy users are extremely loyal. "They insist they don't need saving," says one analyst, "protesting that they are far from the clueless fatties anti-fast-food activists make them out to be." Even the heaviest users "would have to be stupid not to know that you can't eat only burgers and fries and not exercise," he says.[12]

LOYALTY STATUS A market can also be segmented by consumer loyalty. Consumers can be loyal to brands (Tide), stores (Nordstrom), and companies (Toyota). Buyers can be divided into groups according to their degree of loyalty. Some consumers are completely loyal—they buy one brand all the time. For example, Apple has a small but almost cultlike following of loyal users.[13]

It's the "Cult of the Mac," and it's popularized by "macolytes." Urbandictionary.com defines a *macolyte* as "One who is fanatically devoted to Apple products, especially the Macintosh computer. Also known as a Mac Zealot." (Sample usage: "He's a macolyte; don't even *think* of mentioning Microsoft within earshot.") How about Anna Zisa, a graphic designer from Milan who doesn't really like tattoos but stenciled an Apple tat on her behind. "It just felt like the most me thing to have," says Zisa. "I like computers. The apple looks good and sexy. All the comments I have heard have been positive, even from Linux and Windows users."

■ Consumer loyalty: "Macolytes"—fanatically loyal Apple users—helped keep Apple afloat during the lean years, and they are now at the forefront of Apple's burgeoning iPod and iTunes empire.

And then there's Taylor Barcroft, who has spent the past 11 years traveling the country in an RV on a mission to be the Mac cult's ultimate "multimedia historical videographer." He goes to every Macworld Expo, huge trade shows centered on the Mac, as well as all kinds of other tech shows—and videotapes anything and everything Apple. He's accumulated more than 3,000 hours of footage. And he's never been paid a dime to do any of this, living off an inheritance. Barcroft owns 17 Macs. Such fanatically loyal users helped keep Apple afloat during the lean years, and they are now at the forefront of Apple's burgeoning iPod-iTunes empire.

Others consumers are somewhat loyal—they are loyal to two or three brands of a given product or favor one brand while sometimes buying others. Still other buyers show no loyalty to any brand. They either want something different each time they buy or they buy whatever's on sale.

A company can learn a lot by analyzing loyalty patterns in its market. It should start by studying its own loyal customers. For example, by studying "macolytes," Apple can better pinpoint its target market and develop marketing appeals. By studying its less loyal buyers, the company can detect which brands are most competitive with its own. By looking at customers who are shifting away from its brand, the company can learn about its marketing weaknesses.

Using Multiple Segmentation Bases

Marketers rarely limit their segmentation analysis to only one or a few variables. Rather, they are increasingly using multiple segmentation bases in an effort to identify smaller, better-defined target groups. Thus, a bank may not only identify a group of wealthy retired adults but also, within that group, distinguish several segments based on their current income, assets, savings and risk preferences, housing, and lifestyles.

One good example of multivariable segmentation is "geodemographic" segmentation. Several business information services—such as Claritas, Experian, Acxiom, and MapInfo—have arisen to help marketing planners link U.S. Census and consumer transaction data with consumer lifestyle patterns to better segment their markets down to zip codes, neighborhoods, and even households.

One of the leading lifestyle segmentation systems is the PRIZM NE (New Evolution) system by Claritas. The PRIZM NE system classifies every American household based on a host of demographic factors—such as age, educational level, income, occupation, family composition, ethnicity, and housing—and behavioral and lifestyle factors—such as purchases, free-time activities, and media preferences. Using PRIZM NE, marketers can use where you live to paint a surprisingly precise picture of who you are and what you might buy:

You're a 23-year-old first-generation college graduate, working as a marketing assistant in a small publishing company. Starting on the bottom rung of the job ladder, you make just enough money to chip in your half of the rent for a no-frills, walk-up apartment you share downtown with an old college friend. You drive a one-year-old Kia Spectra and spend your Friday nights socializing at the local nightclubs. Instead of cooking, you'd much rather order pizza from Papa John's and eat a few slices as you watch a rerun of *The Mind of Mencia* on Comedy

Central picture shows an advertisement:

Choose Wisely.

#18
Kids & Cul-de-Sacs

#21
Gray Power

Choose Claritas.
Solve your marketing challenges with segmentation solutions from Claritas. Our industry-standard segmentation systems, PRIZM® NE, P$YCLE® and ConneXions™ help you know your audience so you can tailor your marketing programs to them. Depth of knowledge gives you leverage for reaching and retaining your most profitable customers and prospects.

And, through our special analytics company, Integras, you can create a segmentation system that is specific to your company—the ultimate in precision marketing!

Choose wisely and call us today!

1-800-234-5973
www.claritas.com

CLARITAS
Adding
Intelligence
to Information

■ Using Claritas' PRIZM NE system, marketers can paint a surprisingly precise picture of who you are and what you might buy. PRIZM NE segments carry such exotic names as "Kids & Cul-de-Sacs," "Gray Power," "Blue Blood Estates," "Shotguns & Pickups," and "Bright Lites L'il City."

Central. You spend most Sunday afternoons doing laundry at the local laundromat, while drinking your usual large cup of coffee from the café down the block and reading a recent issue of *Spin*. You're living out your own, individual version of the good life. You're unique—not some demographic cliché. Right? Wrong. You're a prime example of PRIZM NE's "City Startups" segment. If you consume, you can't hide from Claritas.[14]

PRIZM NE classifies U.S. households into 66 unique segments, organized into 14 different social groups. PRIZM NE segments carry such exotic names as "Kids & Cul-de-Sacs," "Gray Power," "Blue Blood Estates," "Mayberry-ville," "Shotguns & Pickups," "Old Glories," "Multi-Culti Mosaic," "Big City Blues," and "Bright Lites L'il City." "Those image-triggered nicknames save a lot of time and geeky technical research terms explaining what you mean," says one marketer. "It's the names that bring the clusters to life," says another.[15]

Regardless of what you call the categories, such systems can help marketers to segment people and locations into marketable groups of like-minded consumers. Each segment exhibits unique characteristics and buying behavior. For example, "Blue Blood Estates" neighborhoods, part of the Elite Suburbs social group, are suburban areas populated by elite, superich families. People in this segment are more likely to take a golf vacation, watch major league soccer, eat at fast-food restaurants picked by kids, and read *Fortune*. In contrast, the "Shotguns & Pickups" segment, part of the Middle America social group, is populated by rural blue-collar workers and families. People in this segment are more likely to go hunting, buy hard rock music, drive a GMC Sierra 2500, watch the Daytona 500 on TV, and read *Field & Stream*.

Such segmentation provides a powerful tool for marketers of all kinds. It can help companies to identify and better understand key customer segments, target them more efficiently, and tailor market offerings and messages to their specific needs.

Segmenting Business Markets

Consumer and business marketers use many of the same variables to segment their markets. Business buyers can be segmented geographically, demographically (industry, company size), or by benefits sought, user status, usage rate, and loyalty status. Yet, business marketers also use some additional variables, such as customer *operating characteristics, purchasing approaches, situational factors,* and *personal characteristics.* By going after segments instead of the whole market, companies can deliver just the right value proposition to each segment served and capture more value in return.

Almost every company serves at least some business markets. For example, we've discussed American Express as the "My life. My card." company that offers credit cards to end consumers. But American Express also targets businesses in three segments—merchants, corporations, and small businesses. It has developed distinct marketing programs for each segment.

In the merchants segment, American Express focuses on convincing new merchants to accept the card and on managing relationships with those that already do. For larger corporate customers, the company offers a corporate card program, which includes extensive employee expense and travel management services. It also offers this segment a wide range of asset management, retirement planning, and financial education services.

Finally, for small business customers, American Express has created the OPEN: Small Business

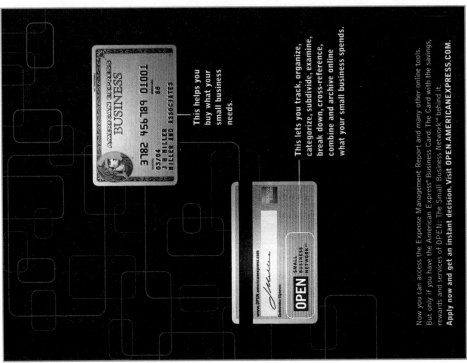

This helps you buy what your small business needs.

This lets you track, organize, categorize, subdivide, examine, break down, cross-reference, combine and archive online what your small business spends.

Now you can access the Expense Management Report and many other online tools. But only if you have the American Express® Business Card. The Card with the savings, rewards and services of OPEN: The Small Business Network™ behind it.
Apply now and get an instant decision. Visit OPEN.AMERICANEXPRESS.COM.

■ Segmenting business markets: For small business customers, American Express has created the OPEN: Small Business Network, "the one place that's all about small business."

Network, "the one place that's all about small business." Small business cardholders can access the network for everything from account and expense management software to expert small business management advice and connecting with other small business owners to share ideas and get recommendations.[16]

Many companies set up separate systems for dealing with larger or multiple-location customers. For example, Steelcase, a major producer of office furniture, first segments customers into 10 industries, including banking, insurance, and electronics. Next, company salespeople work with independent Steelcase dealers to handle smaller, local, or regional Steelcase customers in each segment. But many national, multiple-location customers, such as ExxonMobil or IBM, have special needs that may reach beyond the scope of individual dealers. So Steelcase uses national accounts managers to help its dealer networks handle its national accounts.

Within a given target industry and customer size, the company can segment by purchase approaches and criteria. As in consumer segmentation, many marketers believe that *buying behavior* and *benefits* provide the best basis for segmenting business markets.

Segmenting International Markets

Few companies have either the resources or the will to operate in all, or even most, of the countries that dot the globe. Although some large companies, such as Coca-Cola or Sony, sell products in more than 200 countries, most international firms focus on a smaller set. Operating in many countries presents new challenges. Different countries, even those that are close together, can vary greatly in their economic, cultural, and political makeup. Thus, just as they do within their domestic markets, international firms need to group their world markets into segments with distinct buying needs and behaviors.

Companies can segment international markets using one or a combination of several variables. They can segment by *geographic location*, grouping countries by regions such as Western Europe, the Pacific Rim, the Middle East, or Africa. Geographic segmentation assumes that nations close to one another will have many common traits and behaviors. Although this is often the case, there are many exceptions. For example, although the United States and Canada have much in common, both differ culturally and economically from neighboring Mexico. Even within a region, consumers can differ widely. For example, some U.S. marketers lump all Central and South American countries together. However, the Dominican Republic is no more like Brazil than Italy is like Sweden. Many Central and South Americans don't even speak Spanish, including 140 million Portuguese-speaking Brazilians and the millions in other countries who speak a variety of Indian dialects.

World markets can also be segmented on the basis of *economic factors*. For example, countries might be grouped by population income levels or by their overall level of economic development. A country's economic structure shapes its population's product and service needs and, therefore, the marketing opportunities it offers. Countries can be segmented by *political and legal factors* such as the type and stability of government, receptivity to foreign firms, monetary regulations, and the amount of bureaucracy. Such factors can play a crucial role in a company's choice of which countries to enter and how. *Cultural factors* can also be used, grouping markets according to common languages, religions, values and attitudes, customs, and behavioral patterns.

Segmenting international markets based on geographic, economic, political, cultural, and other factors assumes that segments should consist of clusters of countries. However, many companies use a different approach called **intermarket segmentation**. They form segments of consumers who have similar needs and buying behavior even though they are located in different countries. For example, Mercedes-

Intermarket segmentation
Forming segments of consumers who have similar needs and buying behavior even though they are located in different countries.

■ Intermarket segmentation: Teens show surprising similarity no matter where they live—these teens could be from almost anywhere. Thus, many companies target teens with worldwide marketing campaigns.

Benz targets the world's well-to-do, regardless of their country. And Swedish furniture giant IKEA targets the aspiring global middle class—it sells good-quality furniture that ordinary people worldwide can afford.

MTV targets the world's teenagers. The world's 1.2 billion teens have a lot in common: They study, shop, and sleep. They are exposed to many of the same major issues: love, crime, homelessness, ecology, and working parents. In many ways, they have more in common with each other than with their parents. "Last year I was in 17 different countries," says one expert, "and it's pretty difficult to find anything that is different, other than language," among a teenager in Japan, a teenager in the UK, and a teenager in China." Says another, "Global teens in Buenos Aires, Beijing, and Bangalore swing to the beat of MTV while sipping Coke." MTV bridges the gap between cultures, appealing to what teens around the world have in common. Sony, Adidas, Nike, and many other firms also actively target global teens. For example, Adidas's "Impossible Is Nothing" theme appeals to teens the world over.[17]

Requirements for Effective Segmentation

Clearly, there are many ways to segment a market, but not all segmentations are effective. For example, buyers of table salt could be divided into blond and brunette customers. But hair color obviously does not affect the purchase of salt. Furthermore, if all salt buyers bought the same amount of salt each month, believed that all salt is the same, and wanted to pay the same price, the company would not benefit from segmenting this market.

To be useful, market segments must be

- *Measurable:* The size, purchasing power, and profiles of the segments can be measured. Certain segmentation variables are difficult to measure. For example, there are 32.5 million left-handed people in the United States—almost equaling the entire population of Canada. Yet few products are targeted toward this left-handed segment. The major problem may be that the segment is hard to identify and measure. There are no data on the demographics of lefties, and the U.S. Census Bureau does not keep track of left-handedness in its surveys. Private data companies keep reams of statistics on other demographic segments but not on left-handers.

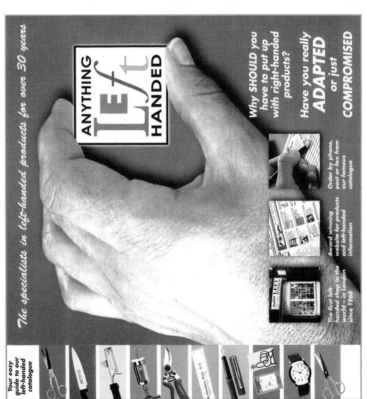

■ The "Leftie" segment can be hard to identify and measure. As a result, few companies tailor their offers to left-handers. However, some nichers such as Anything Left-Handed targets this segment.

- *Accessible:* The market segments can be effectively reached and served. Suppose a fragrance company finds that heavy users of its brand are single men and women who stay out late and socialize a lot. Unless this group lives or shops at certain places and is exposed to certain media, its members will be difficult to reach.

- *Substantial:* The market segments are large or profitable enough to serve. A segment should be the largest possible homogenous group worth pursuing with a tailored marketing program. It would not pay, for example, for an automobile manufacturer to develop cars especially for people whose height is greater than seven feet.

- *Differentiable:* The segments are conceptually distinguishable and respond differently to different marketing mix elements and programs. If married and unmarried women respond similarly to a sale on perfume, they do not constitute separate segments.

- *Actionable:* Effective programs can be designed for attracting and serving the segments. For example, although one small airline identified seven market segments, its staff was too small to develop separate marketing programs for each segment.

Market Targeting

Market segmentation reveals the firm's market segment opportunities. The firm now must evaluate the various segments and decide how many and which segments it can serve best. We now look at how companies evaluate and select target segments.

Evaluating Market Segments

In evaluating different market segments, a firm must look at three factors: segment size and growth, segment structural attractiveness, and company objectives and resources. The company must first collect and analyze data on current segment sales, growth rates, and expected profitability for various segments. It will be interested in segments that have the right size and growth characteristics. But "right size and growth" is a relative matter. The largest, fastest-growing segments are not always the most attractive ones for every company. Smaller companies may lack the skills and resources needed to serve the larger segments. Or they may find these segments too competitive. Such companies may target segments that are smaller and less attractive, in an absolute sense, but that are potentially more profitable for them.

The company also needs to examine major structural factors that affect long-run segment attractiveness.[18] For example, a segment is less attractive if it already contains many strong and aggressive *competitors*. The existence of many actual or potential *substitute products* may limit prices and the profits that can be earned in a segment. The relative *power of buyers* also affects segment attractiveness. Buyers with strong bargaining power relative to sellers will try to force prices down, demand more services, and set competitors against one another—all at the expense of seller profitability. Finally, a segment may be less attractive if it contains *powerful suppliers* who can control prices or reduce the quality or quantity of ordered goods and services.

Even if a segment has the right size and growth and is structurally attractive, the company must consider its own objectives and resources. Some attractive segments can be dismissed quickly because they do not mesh with the company's long-run objectives. Or the company may lack the skills and resources needed to succeed in an attractive segment. The company should enter only segments in which it can offer superior value and gain advantages over competitors.

Selecting Target Market Segments

After evaluating different segments, the company must now decide which and how many segments it will target. A **target market** consists of a set of buyers who share common needs or characteristics that the company decides to serve.

Because buyers have unique needs and wants, a seller could potentially view each buyer as a separate target market. Ideally, then, a seller might design a separate marketing program for each buyer. However, although some companies do attempt to serve buyers individually, most face larger numbers of smaller buyers and do not find individual targeting worthwhile. Instead, they look for broader segments of buyers. More generally, market targeting can be carried out at several different levels. Figure 7.2 shows that companies can target very broadly (undifferentiated marketing), very narrowly (micromarketing), or somewhere in between (differentiated or concentrated marketing).

Undifferentiated Marketing

Using an **undifferentiated marketing** (or **mass-marketing**) strategy, a firm might decide to ignore market segment differences and target the whole market with one offer. This mass-marketing strategy focuses on what is *common* in the needs of consumers rather than on what

---

Target market
A set of buyers sharing common needs or characteristics that the company decides to serve.

Undifferentiated (mass) marketing
A market-coverage strategy in which a firm decides to ignore market segment differences and go after the whole market with one offer.

FIGURE 7.2
Target marketing strategies

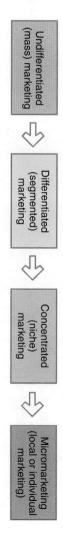

| Undifferentiated (mass) marketing | → | Differentiated (segmented) marketing | → | Concentrated (niche) marketing | → | Micromarketing (local or individual marketing) |

| **Targeting broadly** | | | | | | **Targeting narrowly** |

is *different*. The company designs a product and a marketing program that will appeal to the largest number of buyers.

As noted earlier in the chapter, most modern marketers have strong doubts about this strategy. Difficulties arise in developing a product or brand that will satisfy all consumers. Moreover, mass marketers often have trouble competing with more-focused firms that do a better job of satisfying the needs of specific segments and niches.

Differentiated (segmented) marketing

A market-coverage strategy in which a firm decides to target several market segments and designs separate offers for each.

Differentiated Marketing

Using a **differentiated marketing** (or **segmented marketing**) strategy, a firm decides to target several market segments and designs separate offers for each. General Motors tries to produce a car for every "purse, purpose, and personality." Gap Inc. has created four different retail store formats—Gap, Banana Republic, Old Navy, and it's most recent addition, Forth & Towne—to serve the varied needs of different fashion segments. And Estée Lauder offers hundreds of different products aimed at carefully defined segments:

Estée Lauder is an expert in creating differentiated brands that serve the tastes of different market segments. Five of the top-ten best-selling prestige perfumes in the United States belong to Estée Lauder. So do eight of the top-ten prestige makeup brands. There's the original Estée Lauder brand, with its gold and blue packaging, which appeals to older, 501 baby boomers. Then there's Clinique, the company's most popular brand, perfect for the middle-aged mom with no time to waste and for younger women attracted to its classic free gift offers. For young, fashion-forward consumers, there's M.A.C., which provides makeup for clients like Pamela Anderson and Marilyn Manson. For the young and trendy, there's the Stila line, containing lots of shimmer and uniquely packaged in clever containers. And, for the New Age type, there's upscale Aveda, with its salon, makeup, and lifestyle products, based on the art and science of earthy origins and pure flower and plant essences, celebrating the connection between Mother Nature and human nature.[19]

By offering product and marketing variations to segments, companies hope for higher sales and a stronger position within each market segment. Developing a stronger position within several segments creates more total sales than undifferentiated marketing across all segments. Estée Lauder's combined brands give it a much greater market share than any single brand could. The Estée Lauder and Clinique brands alone reap a combined 40 percent share of the prestige cosmetics market. Similarly, Procter & Gamble markets six different brands of laundry detergent, which compete with each other on supermarket shelves. Yet together, these multiple brands capture four times the market share of nearest rival Unilever (see Real Marketing 7.1).

But differentiated marketing also increases the costs of doing business. A firm usually finds it more expensive to develop and produce, say, 10 units of 10 different products than 100 units of one product. Developing separate marketing plans for the separate segments requires extra marketing research, forecasting, sales analysis, promotion planning, and channel

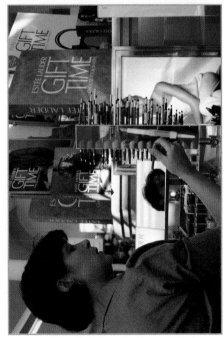

■ Differentiated marketing: Estée Lauder offers hundreds of different products aimed at carefully defined segments, from its original Estée Lauder brand appealing to age 50+ baby boomers to Aveda, with earthy origins that appeal to younger new age types.

management. And trying to reach different market segments with different advertising increases promotion costs. Thus, the company must weigh increased sales against increased costs when deciding on a differentiated marketing strategy.

Concentrated Marketing

Concentrated (niche) marketing
A market-coverage strategy in which a firm goes after a large share of one or a few segments or niches.

A third market-coverage strategy, **concentrated marketing** (or **niche marketing**), is especially appealing when company resources are limited. Instead of going after a small share of a large market, the firm goes after a large share of one or a few smaller segments or niches. For example, Oshkosh Truck is the world's largest producer of airport rescue trucks and front-loading concrete mixers. Tetra sells 80 percent of the world's tropical fish food, and Steiner Optical captures 80 percent of the world's military binoculars market.

Through concentrated marketing, the firm achieves a strong market position because of its greater knowledge of consumer needs in the niches it serves and the special reputation it acquires. It can market more *effectively* by fine-tuning its products, prices, and programs to the needs of carefully defined segments. It can also market more *efficiently*, targeting its products or services, channels, and communications programs toward only consumers that it can serve best and most profitably.

Whereas segments are fairly large and normally attract several competitors, niches are smaller and may attract only one or a few competitors. Niching offers smaller companies an opportunity to compete by focusing their limited resources on serving niches that may be unimportant to or overlooked by larger competitors. Consider Apple Computer. Although it once enjoyed a better than 13 percent market share, Apple is now a PC market nicher, capturing less than 2 percent of the personal computer market worldwide. Rather than competing head-on with other PC makers as they slash prices and focus on volume, Apple invests in research and development, making it the industry trendsetter. For example, when the company introduced the iPod and iTunes, it captured more than 70 percent of the music download market. Such innovation has created a loyal base of consumers who are willing to pay more for Apple's cutting edge products.[20]

Many companies start as nichers to get a foothold against larger, more resourceful competitors, then grow into broader competitors. For example, Southwest Airlines began by serving intrastate, no-frills commuters in Texas but is now one of the nation's largest airlines. In contrast, as markets change, some megamarketers develop niche markets to create sales growth. For example, in recent years, Pepsi has introduced several niche products, such as Sierra Mist, Pepsi Twist, Mountain Dew Code Red, and Mountain Dew LiveWire. Initially, these brands combined accounted for barely 5 percent of Pepsi's overall soft-drink sales. However, Sierra Mist quickly blossomed and now is the number two lemon-lime soft drink behind Sprite, and Code Red and LiveWire have revitalized the Mountain Dew brand. Says Pepsi-Cola North America's chief marketing officer, "The era of the mass brand has been over for a long time."[21]

Today, the low cost of setting up shop on the Internet makes it even more profitable to serve seemingly minuscule niches. Small businesses, in particular, are realizing riches from serving small niches on the Web. Here is a "Webpreneur" who achieved astonishing results:

Sixty-three-year-old British artist Jacquie Lawson taught herself to use a computer only a few years ago. Last year, her online business had sales of over $4 million. What does she sell? Online cards. Lawson occupies a coveted niche in the electronic world: a profitable, subscription-based Web site (www.jacquielawson.com) where she sells her highly stylized e-cards without a bit of advertising. While the giants—Hallmark and American Greetings—offer hundreds of e-cards for every occasion, Lawson only offers about 50 in total, the majority of which she intricately designed herself. Revenue comes solely from members—81 percent from the United States—who pay $8 a year. Last year, membership climbed from 300,000 to 500,000 and the membership renewal rate is close to 70 percent. Last December, Lawson's Web site attracted 22.7 million visitors, more than double that of closest rival AmericanGreetings.com. Lawson's success with a business model that has stumped many media giants speaks to both the Internet's egalitarian nature and her own stubborn belief that doing it her way is the right way.[22]

Concentrated marketing can be highly profitable. At the same time, it involves higher-than-normal risks. Companies that rely on one or a few segments for all of their business will suffer greatly if the segment turns sour. Or larger competitors may decide to enter the same segment with greater resources. For these reasons, many companies prefer to diversify in several market segments.

Real Marketing   P&G: Competing with Itself—and Winning

7.1 Procter & Gamble is one of the world's premier consumer-goods companies. Some 99 percent of all U.S. households use at least one of P&G's more than 300 brands, and the typical household regularly buys and uses from one to two *dozen* P&G brands.

P&G sells six brands of laundry detergent in the United States (Tide, Cheer, Gain, Era, Dreft, and Ivory Snow). It also sells six brands of bath soap (Ivory, Safeguard, Camay, Olay, Zest, and Old Spice); seven brands of shampoo (Pantene, Head & Shoulders, Aussie, Herbal Essences, Infusium 23, Pert Plus, and Physique); four brands of dishwashing detergent (Dawn, Ivory, Joy, and Cascade); three brands each of tissues and paper towels (Charmin, Bounty, and Puffs), skin care products (Olay, Gillette Complete Skincare, and Noxzema), and deodorant (Secret, Sure, and Old Spice); and two brands each of fabric softener (Downy and Bounce), cosmetics (CoverGirl and Max Factor), and disposable diapers (Pampers and Luvs).

Moreover, P&G has many additional brands in each category for different international markets. For example, it sells 16 different laundry product brands in Latin America and 19 in Europe, the Middle East, and Africa. (See P&G's Web site at www.pg.com for a full glimpse of the company's impressive lineup of familiar brands.)

These P&G brands compete with one another on the same super-market shelves. But why would P&G introduce several brands in one category instead of concentrating its resources on a single leading brand? The answer lies in the fact that different people want different *mixes of benefits* from the products they buy. Take laundry deter-

Differentiated marketing: Procter & Gamble markets six different laundry detergents, including Tide—each with multiple forms and formulations—that compete with each other on store shelves. Yet together, these multiple brands capture four times the market share of nearest rival Unilever.

gents as an example. People use laundry detergents to get their clothes clean. But they also want other things from their detergents—such as economy, strength or mildness, bleaching power, fabric softening, fresh smell, and lots of suds or only a few. We all want *some of* every one of these benefits from our detergent, but we may have different *priorities* for each benefit. To some people, cleaning and bleaching power are most important; to others, fabric softening matters most; still others want a mild, fresh scented detergent. Thus,

Micromarketing

Differentiated and concentrated marketers tailor their offers and marketing programs to meet the needs of various market segments and niches. At the same time, however, they do not customize their offers to each individual customer. **Micromarketing** is the practice of tailoring products and marketing programs to suit the tastes of specific individuals and locations. Rather than seeing a customer in every individual, micromarketers see the individual in every customer. Micromarketing includes *local marketing and individual marketing.*

LOCAL MARKETING **Local marketing** involves tailoring brands and promotions to the needs and wants of local customer groups—cities, neighborhoods, and even specific stores. Citibank provides different mixes of banking services in each of its branches, depending on neighborhood demographics. Kroger designates its supermarkets as "upscale," "mainstream," or "value" based on customer purchase behavior and adjusts its merchandise to match store customer profiles. And Wal-Mart customizes its merchandise store by store to meet the needs of local shoppers.

Wal-Mart's real-estate teams deeply research the local customer base when scouting for locations. Designers then create a new store's format accordingly—

Micromarketing
The practice of tailoring products and marketing programs to the needs and wants of specific individuals and local customer groups—includes *local marketing and individual marketing.*

Local marketing
Tailoring brands and promotions to the needs and wants of local customer groups—cities, neighborhoods, and even specific stores.

each segment of laundry detergent buyers seeks a special combination of benefits.

Procter & Gamble has identified at least six important laundry detergent segments, along with numerous subsegments, and has developed a different brand designed to meet the special needs of each. The six brands are positioned for different segments as follows:

- *Tide* provides "fabric cleaning and care at its best." It's the all-purpose family detergent that "gets to the bottom of dirt and stains to help keep your whites white and your colors bright."

- *Cheer* is the "color expert." It helps protect against fading, color transfer, and fabric wear, with or without bleach. *Cheer Free* is "dermatologist tested . . . contains no irritating perfume or dye."

- *Gain*, originally P&G's "enzyme" detergent, was repositioned as the detergent that gives you "great cleaning power and the smell that says clean." It "cleans and freshens like sunshine."

- *Era* "provides powerful stain removal and pretreating for physically active families." It contains advanced enzymes to fight a family's tough stains and help get the whole wash clean. *Era Max* has three types of active enzymes to help fight many stains that active families encounter.

- *Ivory Snow* is "Ninety-nine and forty-four one-hundredths percent pure." It provides "mild cleansing benefits for a gentle, pure, and simple clean."

- *Dreft* is specially formulated "to help clean tough baby and toddler stains." It "rinses out thoroughly, leaving clothes soft next to a baby's delicate skin."

Within each segment, P&G has identified even *narrower* niches. For example, you can buy regular Tide (in powder or liquid form) or any of several formulations:

- *Tide Powder* helps keep everyday laundry clean and new. It comes in regular and special scents: *Tide Mountain Spring* ("the scent of crisp mountain air and fresh wildflowers"); *Tide Clean Breeze* (the fresh scent of laundry line-dried in a clean breeze); *Tide Tropical Clean* (a fresh tropical scent); and *Tide Free* ("has no scent at all—leaves out the dyes or perfumes").

- *Tide Liquid* combines all the great stain-fighting qualities you've come to expect in Tide powder with the pretreating ease of a liquid detergent. Available in original and Mountain Spring, Clean Breeze, Tropical Clean, and Free scents.

- *Tide with Bleach* helps to "clean even the dirtiest laundry without the damaging effects of chlorine bleach." Keeps "your family's whites white and colors bright." Available in Clean Breeze or Mountain Spring scents.

- *Tide Liquid with Bleach Alternative* is the "smart alternative to chlorine bleach." It uses active enzymes in pretreating and washing to break down and remove the toughest stains while whitening whites.

- *Tide with a Touch of Downy* provides "outstanding Tide clean with a touch of Downy softness and freshness." Available in April Fresh, Clean Breeze, and Soft Ocean Mist scents.

- *Tide Coldwater* is specially formulated to help reduce your energy bills by delivering outstanding cleaning, even on the toughest stains, in cold water. Available in both liquid and powder formulas and in two new cool scents—Fresh Scent and Glacier.

- *Tide HE* is specially formulated to unlock the cleaning potential of high-efficiency washers and provides excellent cleaning with the right level of sudsing. Available in Original, Free, and Clean Breeze scents.

By segmenting the market and having several detergent brands, P&G has an attractive offering for consumers in all important preference groups. As a result, P&G is really cleaning up in the $4.9 billion U.S. laundry detergent market. Tide, by itself, captures a whopping 40 percent of the detergent market. All P&G brands combined take an impressive 60 percent market share—more than four times that of nearest rival Unilever and much more than any single brand could obtain by itself.

Sources: See LeeAnn Prescott, "Case Study: Tide Boosts Traffic 9-Fold," *iMedia Connection,* November 30, 2005, accessed at www.imediaconnection.com; Doris de Guzman, "Household Products Struggle," *Chemical Market Reporter,* March 20–26, 2006, pp. 46–47; and information accessed at www.pg.com and www.tide.com, December 2006.

stores near office parks, for example, contain prominent islands featuring ready-made meals for busy workers. Through its Retail Link program, Wal-Mart works with suppliers to tailor store merchandise with similar precision. Retail Link provides both local Wal-Mart managers and suppliers with a two-year history of every item's daily sales in every Wal-Mart store. Using Retail Link, Wal-Mart and its suppliers can determine which merchandise should be stocked when and where. For example, Wal-Mart stocks about 60 types of canned chili but carries only three nationwide. The rest are allocated according to local tastes. Similarly, Wal-Mart uses more than 200 finely tuned planograms (shelf plans) to match product packaging to match local preferences. For example, Wal-Mart found that although ant and roach killer sells well in the southern United States, consumers in the northern states are turned off by the word "roach." After labeling the pesticide as "ant killer" in northern states, the company has seen sales increase dramatically.[23]

Local marketing has some drawbacks. It can drive up manufacturing and marketing costs by reducing economies of scale. It can also create logistics problems as companies try to meet the varied requirements of different regional and local markets. Further, a brand's overall image might be diluted if the product and message vary too much in different localities.

Still, as companies face increasingly fragmented markets, and as new supporting technologies develop, the advantages of local marketing often outweigh the drawbacks. Local marketing helps a company to market more effectively in the face of pronounced regional and local differences in demographics and lifestyles. It also meets the needs of the company's first-line customers—retailers—who prefer more fine-tuned product assortments for their neighborhoods.

Individual marketing

Tailoring products and marketing programs to the needs and preferences of individual customers—also labeled "markets-of-one marketing," "customized marketing," and "one-to-one marketing."

INDIVIDUAL MARKETING In the extreme, micromarketing becomes **individual marketing**—tailoring products and marketing programs to the needs and preferences of individual customers. Individual marketing has also been labeled *one-to-one marketing, mass customization,* and *markets-of-one marketing.*

The widespread use of mass marketing has obscured the fact that for centuries consumers were served as individuals: The tailor custom-made the suit, the cobbler designed shoes for the individual, the cabinetmaker made furniture to order. Today, however, new technologies are permitting many companies to return to customized marketing. More powerful computers, detailed databases, robotic production and flexible manufacturing, and interactive communication media such as e-mail and the Internet—all have combined to foster "mass customization." Mass customization is the process through which firms interact one-to-one with masses of customers to design products and services tailor-made to individual needs.[24]

Dell creates custom-configured computers. Hockey-stick maker Branches Hockey lets customers choose from more than two dozen options—including stick length, blade patterns, and blade curve—and turns out a customized stick in five days. Visitors to Nike's NikeID Web site can personalize their sneakers by choosing from hundreds of colors and putting an embroidered word or phrase on the tongue. And at Target's "Target to a T" Web site, customers can personalize selected clothing items to "create a clothing look that's all you." The "Target to a T Web site proclaims: "You'll experience the perfect fit—for your personality, your lifestyle, your wardrobe, your body—without setting foot in a dressing room."

Companies selling all kinds of products—from computers, candy, clothing, and golf clubs to fire trucks—are customizing their offerings to the needs of individual buyers. Consider this example:

The LEGO Company recently launched LEGO Factory, a Web site (LEGOFactory. com) where LEGO fans can "design their own ultimate LEGO model, show it off, and bring it to life." Using free, downloadable Digital Designer software, customers can create any structure they can imagine. Then, if they decide to actually build their creation, the software, which keeps track of which pieces are required, sends the order to the LEGO warehouse. There, employees put all the pieces into a box, along with instructions, and ship it off. Customers can even design their own boxes. The software also lets proud users share their creations with others in the LEGO community, one of the traditional building blocks of the company's customer loyalty. The LEGO Factory Gallery features winning designs and lets users browse and order the inspired designs of others.[25]

Consumer goods marketers aren't the only ones going one-to-one. Business-to-business marketers are also finding new ways to customize their offerings. For example, John Deere manufactures seeding equipment that can be configured in more than two million versions to individual customer specifications. The seeders

■ Individual marketing: At the LEGO Factory Web site, fans can design their own ultimate LEGO model, show it off, and bring it to life.

are produced one at a time, in any sequence, on a single production line. Mass customization provides a way to stand out against competitors. Consider Oshkosh Truck:

Oshkosh Truck specializes in making heavy-duty fire, airport-rescue, cement, garbage, snow-removal, ambulance, and military vehicles. According to one account, "Whether you need to plow your way through Sahara sands or Buffalo snow, Oshkosh has your vehicle, by gosh." Oshkosh has grown rapidly and profitably over the past decade. What's its secret? Mass customization—the ability to personalize its products and services to the needs of individual customers. For example, when firefighters order a truck from Oshkosh, it's an event. They travel to the plant to watch the vehicle, which may cost as much as $800,000, take shape. The firefighters can choose from 19,000 options. A stripped-down fire truck costs $130,000, but 75 percent of Oshkosh's customers order lots of extras, like hideaway stairs, ladders, special doors, compartments, and firefighting foam systems for those difficult-to-extinguish fires. Some bring along paint chips so they can customize the color of their fleet. Others are content just to admire the vehicles, down to the water tanks and hideaway ladders. "Some chiefs even bring their wives; we encourage it," says the president of Oshkosh's firefighting unit, Pierce Manufacturing. "Buying a fire truck is a very personal thing." Indeed, Pierce customers are in town so often that the Holiday Inn renamed its lounge the Hook and Ladder. Through such customization and personalization, Oshkosh has gained a big edge over its languishing larger rivals.26

Unlike mass production, which eliminates the need for human interaction, one-to-one marketing has made relationships with customers more important than ever. Just as mass production was the marketing principle of the twentieth century, mass customization is becoming a marketing principle for the twenty-first century. The world appears to be coming full circle—from the good old days when customers were treated as individuals, to mass marketing when nobody knew your name, and back again.

The move toward individual marketing mirrors the trend in consumer *self-marketing*. Increasingly, individual customers are taking more responsibility for determining which products and brands to buy. Consider two business buyers with two different purchasing styles. The first sees several salespeople, each trying to persuade him to buy his or her product. The second sees no salesperson but rather logs onto the Internet. She searches for information on available products; interacts electronically with various suppliers, users, and product analysts; and then makes up her own mind about the best offer. The second purchasing agent has taken more responsibility for the buying process, and the marketer has had less influence over her buying decision.

As the trend toward more interactive dialogue and less advertising monologue continues, self-marketing will grow in importance. As more buyers look up consumer reports, join Internet product-discussion forums, and place orders via phone or online, marketers will need to influence the buying process in new ways. They will need to involve customers more in all phases of the product development and buying processes, increasing opportunities for buyers to practice self-marketing.

Choosing a Targeting Strategy

Companies need to consider many factors when choosing a market targeting strategy. Which strategy is best depends on *company resources.* When the firm's resources are limited, concentrated marketing makes the most sense. The best strategy also depends on the degree of *product variability.* Undifferentiated marketing is more suited for uniform products such as grapefruit or steel. Products that can vary in design, such as cameras and automobiles, are more suited to differentiation or concentration. The *product's life-cycle stage* also must be considered. When a firm introduces a new product, it may be practical to launch only one version, and undifferentiated marketing or concentrated marketing may make the most sense. In the mature stage of the product life cycle, however, differentiated marketing begins to make more sense.

Another factor is *market variability.* If most buyers have the same tastes, buy the same amounts, and react the same way to marketing efforts, undifferentiated marketing is appropriate. Finally, *competitors' marketing strategies* are important. When competitors use differentiated or concentrated marketing, undifferentiated marketing can be suicidal. Conversely, when competitors use undifferentiated marketing, a firm can gain an advantage by using differentiated or concentrated marketing.

Socially Responsible Target Marketing

Smart targeting helps companies to be more efficient and effective by focusing on the segments that they can satisfy best and most profitably. Targeting also benefits consumers—companies reach specific groups of consumers with offers carefully tailored to satisfy their needs. However, target marketing sometimes generates controversy and concern. The biggest issues usually involve the targeting of vulnerable or disadvantaged consumers with controversial or potentially harmful products.

For example, over the years, the cereal industry has been heavily criticized for its marketing efforts directed toward children. Children make up almost half of the $8.9 billion U.S. cereal market. Critics worry that premium offers and high-powered advertising appeals presented through the mouths of lovable animated characters will overwhelm children's defenses. The marketers of toys and other children's products have been similarly battered, often with good justification.[27]

Other problems arise when the marketing of adult products spills over into the kid segment—intentionally or unintentionally. For example, the Federal Trade Commission (FTC) and citizen action groups have accused tobacco and beer companies of targeting underage smokers and drinkers. For instance, a recent Adbowl poll found that, in the most recent Super Bowl, Bud Light and Budweiser ads ranked first through fourth in popularity among viewers under age 17.[28] Some critics have even called for a complete ban on advertising to children. To encourage responsible advertising, the Children's Advertising Review Unit, the advertising industry's self-regulatory agency, has published extensive children's advertising guidelines that recognize the special needs of child audiences.

Cigarette, beer, and fast-food marketers have also generated much controversy in recent years by their attempts to target inner-city minority consumers. For example, McDonald's and other chains have drawn criticism for pitching their high-fat, salt-laden fare to low-income, urban residents who are much more likely than are suburbanites to be heavy consumers. Similarly, R.J. Reynolds took heavy flak in the early 1990s when it announced plans to market Uptown, a menthol cigarette targeted toward low-income blacks. It quickly dropped the brand in the face of a loud public outcry and heavy pressure from black leaders.

The meteoric growth of the Internet and other carefully targeted direct media has raised fresh concerns about potential targeting abuses. The Internet allows increasing refinement of audiences and, in turn, more precise targeting. This might help makers of questionable products or deceptive advertisers to more readily victimize the most vulnerable audiences. Unscrupulous marketers can now send tailor-made deceptive messages directly to the computers of millions of unsuspecting consumers. For example, the FBI's Internet Crime Complaint Center Web site alone received more than 231,000 complaints last year, an increase of more than 85 percent over the past two years.[29]

Not all attempts to target children, minorities, or other special segments draw such criticism. In fact, most provide benefits to targeted consumers. For example, Colgate makes a large selection of toothbrushes and toothpaste flavors and packages for children—from Colgate Barbie, Blues Clues, and SpongeBob SquarePants Sparkling Bubble Fruit toothpastes to Colgate LEGO BIONICLE and Bratz character toothbrushes. Such products help make tooth brushing more fun and get children to brush longer and more often.

American Girl appropriately targets minority consumers with African American, Mexican, and American Indian versions of its highly acclaimed dolls and books. And Nacara Cosmetiques markets a multiethnic cosmetics line for "ethnic women who have a thirst for the exotic." The line is specially formulated to complement the darker skin tones of African American women and dark-skinned women of Latin American, Indian, and Caribbean origins.

Thus, in target marketing, the issue is not really *who* is targeted but rather *how* and for *what*. Controversies arise when marketers attempt to profit at the expense of targeted segments—when they unfairly target vulnerable segments or target them with questionable

The multiethnic cosmetic line
La ligne de maquillage multiethnique

Make up your mind!
La beauté du succès

nacara

■ Most target marketing benefits both the marketer and the consumer. Nacara Cosmetiques markets cosmetics for "ethnic women who have a thirst for the exotic."

products or tactics. Socially responsible marketing calls for segmentation and targeting that serve not just the interests of the company but also the interests of those targeted.

■ Differentiation and Positioning

Beyond deciding which segments of the market it will target, the company must decide on a *value proposition*—on how it will create differentiated value for targeted segments and what positions it wants to occupy in those segments. A **product's position** is the way the product is *defined by consumers* on important attributes—the place the product occupies in consumers' minds relative to competing products. "Products are created in the factory, but brands are created in the mind," says a positioning expert.[30]

Tide is positioned as a powerful, all-purpose family detergent; Ivory Snow is positioned as the gentle detergent for fine washables and baby clothes. At Subway restaurants, you "Eat Fresh"; at Olive Garden, "When You're Here, You're Family"; and at Applebee's, you're "Eatin' Good in the Neighborhood." In the automobile market, the Toyota Yaris and Honda Fit are positioned on economy, Mercedes and Cadillac on luxury, and Porsche and BMW on performance. Volvo positions powerfully on safety. And Toyota positions its fuel-efficient, hybrid Prius as a high-tech solution to the energy shortage. "How far will you go to save the planet?" it asks.

Consumers are overloaded with information about products and services. They cannot reevaluate products every time they make a buying decision. To simplify the buying process, consumers organize products, services, and companies into categories and "position" them in their minds. A product's position is the complex set of perceptions, impressions, and feelings that consumers have for the product compared with competing products.

Consumers position products with or without the help of marketers. But marketers do not want to leave their products' positions to chance. They must *plan* positions that will give their products the greatest advantage in selected target markets, and they must design marketing mixes to create these planned positions.

Positioning Maps

In planning their differentiation and positioning strategies, marketers often prepare *perceptual positioning maps*, which show consumer perceptions of their brands versus competing products on important buying dimensions. Figure 7.3 shows a positioning map for the U.S. large luxury sport utility vehicle market.[31] The position of each circle on the map indicates the brand's perceived positioning on two dimensions—price and orientation (luxury versus performance). The size of each circle indicates the brand's relative market share. Thus, customers view the market-leading Cadillac Escalade as a moderately-priced large luxury SUV with a balance of luxury and performance.

The original Hummer H1 is positioned as a very high-performance SUV with a price tag to match. Hummer targets the current H1 Alpha toward a small segment of well-off rugged individualists. According to the H1 Web site, "The H1 was built around one central philosophy: function—the most functional off-road vehicle ever made available to the civilian market. The H1 Alpha not only sets you apart, but truly sets you free."

By contrast, although also oriented toward performance, the Hummer H2 is positioned as a more luxury-oriented and more reasonably priced luxury SUV. The H2 is targeted toward a larger segment of urban and suburban professionals. "In a world where SUVs have begun to look like their owners, complete with love handles and mushy seats, the H2 proves that there is still one out there that can drop and give you 20," says the H2 Web site. The H2 "strikes a perfect balance between interior comfort, on-the-road capability, and off-road capability."

Choosing a Differentiation and Positioning Strategy

Some firms find it easy to choose a differentiation and their positioning strategy. For example, a firm well known for quality in certain segments will go for this position in a new segment if there are enough buyers seeking quality. But in many cases, two or more firms will go after the same position. Then, each will have to find other ways to set itself apart. Each firm must differentiate its offer by building a unique bundle of benefits that appeals to a substantial group within the segment.

Product position

The way the product is defined by consumers on important attributes—the place the product occupies in consumers' minds relative to competing products.

FIGURE 7.3
Positioning map: Large luxury SUVs

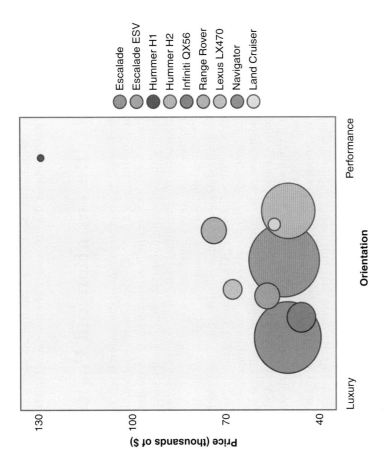

Competitive advantage
An advantage over competitors gained by offering consumers greater value, either through lower prices or by providing more benefits that justify higher prices.

The differentiation and positioning task consists of three steps: identifying a set of possible customer value differences that provide competitive advantages upon which to build a position, choosing the right competitive advantages, and selecting an overall positioning strategy. The company must then effectively communicate and deliver the chosen position to the market.

Identifying Possible Value Differences and Competitive Advantages

To build profitable relationships with target customers, marketers must understand customer needs better than competitors do and deliver more customer value. To the extent that a company can differentiate and position itself as providing superior value, it gains **competitive advantage.**

But solid positions cannot be built on empty promises. If a company positions its product as *offering* the best quality and service, it must actually differentiate the product so that it *delivers* the promised quality and service. Companies must do much more than simply shout out their positions in ad slogans and taglines. They must first *live* the slogan. For example, when Staples' research revealed that it should differentiate itself on the basis of "an easier shopping experience," the office supply retailer held back its "Staples: That was easy" marketing campaign for more than a year. First, it remade its stores to actually deliver the promised positioning (see Real Marketing 7.2).

To find points of differentiation, marketers must think through the customer's entire experience with the company's product or service. An alert company can find ways to differentiate itself at every customer contact point. In what specific ways can a company differentiate itself or its market offer? It can differentiate along the lines of *product, services, channels, people,* or *image.*

Product differentiation takes place along a continuum. At one extreme we find physical products that allow little variation: chicken, steel, aspirin. Yet even here some meaningful differentiation is possible. For example, Perdue claims that its branded chickens are better—fresher and more tender—and gets a 10 percent price premium based on this differentiation. At the other extreme are products that can be highly differentiated, such as automobiles, clothing, and furniture. Such products can be differentiated on features, performance, or style and design. Thus, Volvo provides new and better safety features; Whirlpool designs its dishwasher to run more quietly; Bose positions its speakers on their striking design and sound characteristics. Similarly, companies can differentiate their products on such attributes as consistency, durability, reliability, or repairability.

Real Marketing

Staples: Positioning Made easy

7.2

These days, Staples really is riding the easy button. But only five years ago, things weren't so easy for the office-supply superstore—or for its customers. The ratio of customer complaints to compliments was running an abysmal eight to one at Staples stores. The company's slogan—"Yeah, we've got that"—had become laughable. Customers griped that items were often out of stock and said the sales staff was unhelpful to boot.

After weeks of focus groups and interviews, Shira Goodman, Staples' executive VP for marketing, had a revelation. "Customers wanted an easier shopping experience," she says. That simple revelation has resulted in one of the most successful marketing campaigns in recent history, built around the now-familiar "Staples: That was easy" tagline. But Staples' positioning turnaround took a lot more than simply bombarding customers with a new slogan. Before it could promise customers a simplified shopping experience, Staples had to actually deliver one. First, it had to *live* the slogan.

When it launched in 1986, Staples all but invented the office-supply superstore. Targeting small and medium-size businesses, it aimed to sell everything for the office under one roof. But by the mid-1990s, the marketplace was crowded with retailers such as Office Depot, not to mention Target, Wal-Mart, and a slew of other online and offline sellers. Partly as a result of that competition, Staples' same-store sales fell for the first time in 2001.

Customer research conducted by Goodman and her team revealed that although shoppers expected Staples and its competitors to have everything in stock, they placed little importance on price. Instead, customers overwhelmingly requested a simple, straightforward shopping experience. "They wanted knowledgeable and helpful associates and hassle-free shopping," Goodman says. The "Staples: That was easy" tagline was the simple—yet inspired—outgrowth of that realization.

The slogan, however, was kept under wraps until the company could give its stores a major makeover. Staples removed from its inventory some 800 superfluous items, such as Britney Spears backpacks, that had little use in the corporate world. Office chairs, which had been displayed in the rafters, were moved to the floor so customers could try them out. Staples also added larger signs and retrained sales associates to walk shoppers to the correct aisle. Because customers revealed that the availability of ink was one of their biggest concerns, the company introduced an in-stock guarantee on printer cartridges. Even communications were simplified—a four-paragraph letter sent to prospective customers was cut to two sentences.

Only when all of the customer-experience pieces were in place did Staples begin communicating its new positioning to customers. It took about a year to get the stores up to snuff, Goodman says, but "once we felt that the experience was significantly easier, we changed the tagline."

For starters, the company hired a new ad agency, McCann-Erickson Worldwide, which had also created MasterCard's nine-year-old "Priceless" campaign. A group of McCann copywriters and art directors held a marathon brainstorming session to find ways to illustrate the concept of "easy." As the creative session dragged on, the group's creative director mentioned how nice it would be if she could just push a button to come up with a great ad, so they could go to lunch. The Easy Button was born. "It took an amorphous concept and made it tangible," Goodman says.

Now there's an easy button for your business. It's called Staples.

Wouldn't it be nice if daily tasks around the office got a little easier? When you shop Staples, it will be as easy as – well – pressing a button. Visit us at **staples.com/easy** *to find out what our Easy Button™ can do for you today.*

STAPLES that was easy.

The "Staples: That was easy" marketing campaign has played a major role in repositioning Staples. But marketing promises count for little if not backed by the reality of the customer experience.

The Easy Button soon birthed a string of humorous and popular television commercials, which premiered in January 2005 and also aired during the Super Bowl a month later. In one spot, called "The Wall," an emperor uses the button to erect a giant barrier as marauders approach; another shows an office worker causing printer cartridges to rain down from above. Online, Staples created a download-able Easy Button toolbar, which took shoppers directly from their desktops to Staples.com, and billboards reminded commuters that an Easy Button would be helpful in snarled traffic.

As a result of the advertising onslaught, customers began asking about buying real Easy Buttons, so Staples again took the cue. It began selling $5 three-inch red plastic buttons that when pushed say "That was easy." Staples promised to donate $1 million in button profits to charity each year, and by mid-2006, it had sold its millionth button. By selling the Easy Button as a sort of modern-day stress ball, Staples has turned its customers into advertisers. Homegrown movies starring the button have appeared on video-sharing site

(continues)

(continued)

YouTube, and a blogger at Sexy Red-Headed Nuns hacked the button to create a garage door opener; the post was picked up by Digg.com and other sites. "The Easy Button is bigger than its category," says a McCann executive creative director.

In all, the repositioning campaign has met with striking success. The five-year rebranding odyssey has helped make $16.1 billion Staples the runaway leader in office retail. In addition to the viral success of the buttons, Staples says customer recall of its advertising has doubled to about 70 percent, compared with the industry average of 43. Last year, Staples' profits were up 18 percent—in a year when competitor Office Depot's earnings slid 18 percent and OfficeMax posted a loss of $73.8 million. According to Goodman, Staples now receives twice as many compliments as complaints at its stores.

No doubt about it, the "Staples: That was easy" marketing campaign has played a major role in repositioning Staples. Beyond pulling customers to the company's stores and Web site, the Easy Button seems to have insinuated itself into popular culture. But marketing promises count for little if not backed by the reality of the customer experience. Marketing VP Goodman attributes Staples' recent success more to the easy-does-it push within stores than to the "That was easy" catchphrase and campaign. "What has happened at the store has done more to drive the Staples brand than all the marketing in the world," she says.

Source: Adapted from portions of Michael Myser, "Marketing Made Easy," *Business 2.0,* June 2006, pp. 43–44.

Beyond differentiating its physical product, a firm can also differentiate the services that accompany the product. Some companies gain *services differentiation* through speedy, convenient, or careful delivery. For example, Commerce Bank has positioned itself as "the most convenient bank in America"—it remains open seven days a week, including evenings, and you can get a debit card while you wait. Installation service can also differentiate one company from another, as can repair services. Many an automobile buyer will gladly pay a little more and travel a little farther to buy a car from a dealer that provides top-notch repair services.

Some companies gain service differentiation by providing customer training service or consulting services—data, information systems, and advising services that buyers need. McKesson Corporation, a major drug wholesaler, consults with its 12,000 independent pharmacists to help them set up accounting, inventory, and computerized ordering systems. By helping its customers compete better, McKesson gains greater customer loyalty and sales.

Firms that practice *channel differentiation* gain competitive advantage through the way they design their channel's coverage, expertise, and performance. Amazon.com, Dell, and GEICO set themselves apart with their smooth-functioning direct channels. Caterpillar's success in the construction-equipment industry is based on superior channels. Its dealers worldwide are renowned for their first-rate service.

Companies can gain a strong competitive advantage through *people differentiation*—hiring and training better people than their competitors do. Disney people are known to be friendly and upbeat. And Singapore Airlines enjoys an excellent reputation, largely because of the grace of its flight attendants. People differentiation requires that a company select its customer-contact people carefully and train them well. For example, Disney trains its theme park people thoroughly to ensure that they are competent, courteous, and friendly—from the hotel check-in agents, to the monorail drivers, to the ride attendants, to the people who sweep Main Street USA. Each employee is carefully trained to understand customers and to "make people happy."

Even when competing offers look the same, buyers may perceive a difference based on company or brand *image differentiation*. A company or brand image should convey the product's distinctive benefits and positioning. Developing a strong and distinctive image calls for creativity and hard work. A company cannot develop an image in the public's mind overnight using only a few advertisements. If Ritz-Carlton means quality, this image must be supported by everything the company says and does.

Symbols—such as the McDonald's golden arches, the Prudential rock, the Nike swoosh, or Google's colorful logo—can provide strong company or brand recognition and image differentiation. The company might build a brand around a famous person, as Nike did with its Air Jordan basketball shoes and Tiger Woods golfing products. Some companies even become associated with colors, such as IBM (blue), UPS (brown), or Coco-Cola (red). The chosen symbols, characters, and other image elements must be communicated through advertising that conveys the company's or brand's personality.

■ People differentiation: Singapore Airlines enjoys an excellent reputation, largely because of the grace of its flight attendants.

Choosing the Right Competitive Advantages

Suppose a company is fortunate enough to discover several potential differentiations that provide competitive advantages. It now must choose the ones on which it will build its positioning strategy. It must decide *how many* differences to promote and *which ones.*

HOW MANY DIFFERENCES TO PROMOTE Many marketers think that companies should aggressively promote only one benefit to the target market. Ad man Rosser Reeves, for example, said a company should develop a *unique selling proposition* (USP) for each brand and stick to it. Each brand should pick an attribute and tout itself as "number one" on that attribute. Buyers tend to remember number one better, especially in this overcommunicated society. Thus, Crest toothpaste consistently promotes its anticavity protection and Wal-Mart promotes its always low prices.

Other marketers think that companies should position themselves on more than one differentiator. This may be necessary if two or more firms are claiming to be best on the same attribute. Today, in a time when the mass market is fragmenting into many small segments, companies are trying to broaden their positioning strategies to appeal to more segments. For example, Unilever introduced the first three-in-one bar soap—Lever 2000—offering cleansing, deodorizing, *and* moisturizing benefits. Clearly, many buyers want all three benefits. The challenge was to convince them that one brand can deliver all three. Judging from Lever 2000's outstanding success, Unilever easily met the challenge. However, as companies increase the number of claims for their brands, they risk disbelief and a loss of clear positioning.

WHICH DIFFERENCES TO PROMOTE Not all brand differences are meaningful or worthwhile; not every difference makes a good differentiator. Each difference has the potential to create company costs as well as customer benefits. A difference is worth establishing to the extent that it satisfies the following criteria:

■ *Important:* The difference delivers a highly valued benefit to target buyers.

■ *Distinctive:* Competitors do not offer the difference, or the company can offer it in a more distinctive way.

■ *Superior:* The difference is superior to other ways that customers might obtain the same benefit.

■ *Communicable:* The difference is communicable and visible to buyers.

■ *Preemptive:* Competitors cannot easily copy the difference.

■ *Affordable:* Buyers can afford to pay for the difference.

■ *Profitable:* The company can introduce the difference profitably.

Many companies have introduced differentiations that failed one or more of these tests. When the Westin Stamford Hotel in Singapore once advertised that it is the world's tallest hotel, it was a distinction that was not important to most tourists—in fact, it turned many off. Polaroid's Polarvision, which produced instantly developed home movies, bombed too. Although Polarvision was distinctive and even preemptive, it was inferior to another way of capturing motion, namely, camcorders. Thus, choosing competitive advantages upon which to position a product or service can be difficult, yet such choices may be crucial to success.

Value proposition
The full positioning of a brand—the full mix of benefits upon which it is positioned.

Selecting an Overall Positioning Strategy

The full positioning of a brand is called the brand's **value proposition**—the full mix of benefits upon which the brand is differentiated and positioned. It is the answer to the customer's question "Why should I buy your brand?" Volvo's value proposition hinges on safety but also includes reliability, roominess, and styling, all for a price that is higher than average but seems fair for this mix of benefits.

Figure 7.4 shows possible value propositions upon which a company might position its products. In the figure, the five green cells represent winning value propositions—differentiation and positioning that gives the company competitive advantage. The red cells, however, represent losing value propositions. The center yellow cell represents at best a marginal proposition. In the following sections, we discuss the five winning value propositions upon which companies can position their products: more for more, more for the same, the same for less, less for much less, and more for less.

MORE FOR MORE "More-for-more" positioning involves providing the most upscale product or service and charging a higher price to cover the higher costs. Ritz-Carlton Hotels, Mont Blanc writing instruments, Mercedes automobiles, Viking appliances—each claims superior quality, craftsmanship, durability, performance, or style and charges a price to match. Not only is the market offering high in quality, it also gives prestige to the buyer. It symbolizes status and a loftier lifestyle. Often, the price difference exceeds the actual increment in quality.

Sellers offering "only the best" can be found in every product and service category, from hotels, restaurants, food, and fashion to cars and household appliances. Consumers are sometimes surprised, even delighted, when a new competitor enters a category with an unusually high-priced brand. Starbucks coffee entered as a very expensive brand in a largely commodity category. Dyson came in as a premium vacuum cleaner with a price to match, touting "No clogged bags, no clogged filters, and no loss of suction means only one thing. It's a Dyson."

In general, companies should be on the lookout for opportunities to introduce a "more-for-more" brand in any underdeveloped product or service category. Yet "more-for-more" brands can be vulnerable. They often invite imitators who claim the same quality but at a lower price. Luxury goods that sell well during good times may be at risk during economic downturns when buyers become more cautious in their spending.

MORE FOR THE SAME Companies can attack a competitor's more-for-more positioning by introducing a brand offering comparable quality but at a lower price. For example, Toyota introduced its Lexus line with a "more-for-the-same" value proposition versus Mercedes and BMW. Its first ad headline read: "Perhaps the first time in history that trading a $72,000 car for a $36,000 car could be considered trading up." It communicated the high quality of its new Lexus through rave reviews in car magazines and through a widely distributed videotape showing side-by-side comparisons of Lexus and Mercedes automobiles. It published surveys showing that Lexus dealers were providing customers with better sales and service experiences than were Mercedes dealerships. Many Mercedes owners switched to Lexus, and the Lexus repurchase rate has been 60 percent, twice the industry average.

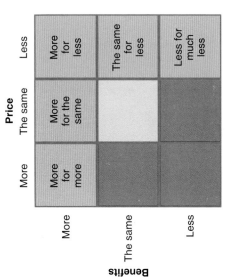

FIGURE 7.4
Possible value propositions

THE SAME FOR LESS Offering "the same for less" can be a powerful value proposition—everyone likes a good deal. For example, Dell offers equivalent quality computers at a lower "price for performance." Discounts stores such as Wal-Mart and "category killers" such as Best Buy, Circuit City, and Sportmart also use this positioning. They don't claim to offer different or better products. Instead, they offer many of the same brands as department stores and specialty stores but at deep discounts based on superior purchasing power and lower-cost operations. Other companies develop imitative but lower-priced brands in an effort to lure customers away from the market leader. For example, AMD makes less-expensive versions of Intel's market-leading microprocessor chips.

LESS FOR MUCH LESS A market almost always exists for products that offer less and therefore cost less. Few people need, want, or can afford "the very best" in everything they buy. In many cases, consumers will gladly settle for less than optimal performance or give up some of the bells and whistles in exchange for a lower price. For example, many travelers seeking lodgings prefer not to pay for what they consider unnecessary extras, such as a pool, attached restaurant, or mints on the pillow. Hotel chains such as Ramada Limited suspend some of these amenities and charge less accordingly.

"Less-for-much-less" positioning involves meeting consumers' lower performance or quality requirements at a much lower price. For example, Family Dollar and Dollar General stores offer more affordable goods at very low prices. Sam's Club and Costco warehouse stores offer less merchandise selection and consistency and much lower levels of service; as a result, they charge rock-bottom prices. Southwest Airlines, the nation's most consistently profitable air carrier, also practices less-for-much-less positioning.

From the start, Southwest has positioned itself firmly as the no-frills, low-price airline. Southwest's passengers have learned to fly without the amenities. For example, the airline provides no meals—just peanuts. It offers no first-class section, only three-across seating in all of its planes. And there's no such thing as a reserved seat on a Southwest flight. Why, then, do so many passengers love Southwest? Perhaps most importantly, Southwest excels at the basics of getting passengers where they want to go on time, and with their luggage. Beyond the basics, however, Southwest offers shockingly low prices. In fact, prices are so low that when Southwest enters a market, it actually increases total air traffic by attracting customers who might otherwise travel by car or bus.

No frills and low prices, however, don't mean drudgery. Southwest's cheerful employees go out of their way to amuse, surprise, or somehow entertain passengers. For example, veteran Southwest fliers know to listen up to announcements over the intercom. On one recent flight, a flight attendant offered the following safety advice: "In the unlikely event of a sudden loss of cabin pressure, oxygen masks will descend from the ceiling. Stop screaming, grab the mask, and pull it over your face. If you have small children traveling with you, secure your mask before assisting with theirs. If you are traveling with two small children, decide now which one you love more." One analyst sums up Southwest's less-for-much-less positioning this way: "It is not luxurious, but it's cheap and it's fun."

MORE FOR LESS Of course, the winning value proposition would be to offer "more for less." Many companies claim to do this. And, in the short run, some companies can actually achieve such lofty positions. For example, when it first opened for business, Home Depot had

■ Less-for-much-less positioning: Southwest has positioned itself firmly as the no-frills, low-price airline. But no frills doesn't mean drudgery—Southwest's cheerful employees go out of their way to amuse, surprise, or somehow entertain passengers.

arguably the best product selection, the best service, *and* the lowest prices compared to local hardware stores and other home improvement chains.

Yet in the long run, companies will find it very difficult to sustain such best-of-both positioning. Offering more usually costs more, making it difficult to deliver on the "for-less" promise. Companies that try to deliver both may lose out to more focused competitors. For example, facing determined competition from Lowe's stores, Home Depot must now decide whether it wants to compete primarily on superior service or on lower prices.

All said, each brand must adopt a positioning strategy designed to serve the needs and wants of its target markets. "More for more" will draw one target market, "less for much less" will draw another, and so on. Thus, in any market, there is usually room for many different companies, each successfully occupying different positions. The important thing is that each company must develop its own winning positioning strategy, one that makes it special to its target consumers.

Developing a Positioning Statement

Positioning statement
A statement that summarizes company or brand positioning—it takes this form: *To (target segment and need) our (brand) is (concept) that (point of difference).*

Company and brand positioning should be summed up in a **positioning statement**. The statement should follow the form: *To (target segment and need) our (brand) is (concept) that (point of difference).*[32] For example: *"To busy, mobile professionals who need to always be in the loop, BlackBerry is a wireless connectivity solution that allows you to stay connected to data, people, and resources while on the go, easily and reliably—more so than competing technologies."* Sometimes a positioning statement is more detailed:

To young, active soft-drink consumers who have little time for sleep, Mountain Dew is the soft drink that gives you more energy than any other brand because it has the highest level of caffeine. With Mountain Dew, you can stay alert and keep going even when you haven't been able to get a good night's sleep.

Note that the positioning first states the product's membership in a category (Mountain Dew is a soft drink) and then shows its point of difference from other members of the category (has more caffeine). Placing a brand in a specific category suggests similarities that it might share with other products in the category. But the case for the brand's superiority is made on its points of difference.

Sometimes marketers put a brand in a surprisingly different category before indicating the points of difference. DiGiorno is a frozen pizza whose crust rises when the pizza is heated. But instead of putting it in the frozen pizza category, the marketers positioned it in the delivered pizza category. Their ad shows party guests asking which pizza delivery service the host used. But, says the host, "It's not delivery, it's DiGiorno!" This helped highlight DiGiorno's fresh quality and superior taste over the normal frozen pizza.

Communicating and Delivering the Chosen Position

Once it has chosen a position, the company must take strong steps to deliver and communicate the desired position to target consumers. All the company's marketing mix efforts must support the positioning strategy.

Positioning the company calls for concrete action, not just talk. If the company decides to build a position on better quality and service, it must first *deliver* that position. Designing the marketing mix—product, price, place, and promotion—involves working out the tactical details of the positioning strategy. Thus, a firm that seizes on a more-for-more position knows that it must produce high-quality products, charge a high price, distribute through high-quality dealers, and advertise in high-quality media. It must hire and train more service people, find retailers who have a good reputation for service, and develop sales and advertising messages that broadcast its superior service. This is the only way to build a consistent and believable more-for-more position.

Companies often find it easier to come up with a good positioning strategy than to implement it. Establishing a position or changing one usually takes a long time. In contrast, positions that have taken years to build can quickly be lost. Once a company has built the desired position, it must take care to maintain the position through consistent performance and communication. It must closely monitor and adapt the position over time to match changes in consumer needs and competitors' strategies. However, the company should avoid abrupt changes that might confuse consumers. Instead, a product's position should evolve gradually as it adapts to the ever-changing marketing environment.

Reviewing the Concepts

In this chapter, you've learned about the major elements of a customer-driven marketing strategy: segmentation, targeting, differentiation, and positioning. Marketers know that they cannot appeal to all buyers in their markets, or at least not to all buyers in the same way. Buyers are too numerous, too widely scattered, and too varied in their needs and buying practices. Therefore, most companies today practice *target marketing*—identifying market segments, selecting one or more of them, and developing products and marketing mixes tailored to each.

1. Define the major steps in designing a customer-driven marketing strategy: market segmentation, targeting, differentiation, and positioning.

Customer-driven marketing strategy begins with selecting which customers to serve and deciding on a value proposition that best serves the targeted customers. It consists of four steps. *Market segmentation* is the act of dividing a market into distinct groups of buyers with different needs, characteristics, or behaviors who might require separate products or marketing mixes. Once the groups have been identified, *market targeting* evaluates each market segment's attractiveness and selects one or more segments to serve. Market targeting consists of *designing strategies to build the *right relationships* with the *right customers*. *Differentiation* involves actually differentiating the market offering to create superior customer value. *Positioning* consists of positioning the market offering in the minds of target customers.

2. List and discuss the major bases for segmenting consumer and business markets.

There is no single way to segment a market. Therefore, the marketer tries different variables to see which give the best segmentation opportunities. For consumer marketing, the major segmentation variables are geographic, demographic, psychographic, and behavioral. In *geographic segmentation*, the market is divided into different geographical units such as nations, regions, states, counties, cities, or neighborhoods. In *demographic segmentation*, the market is divided into groups based on demographic variables, including age, gender, family size, family life cycle, income, occupation, education, religion, race, generation, and nationality. In *psychographic segmentation*, the market is divided into different groups based on social class, lifestyle, or personality characteristics. In *behavioral segmentation*, the market is divided into groups based on consumers' knowledge, attitudes, uses, or responses to a product.

Business marketers use many of the same variables to segment their markets. But business markets also can be segmented by business consumer *demographics* (industry, company size), *operating*

characteristics, *purchasing approaches, situational factors, and personal characteristics*. The effectiveness of segmentation analysis depends on finding segments that are *measurable, accessible, substantial, differentiable,* and *actionable*.

3. Explain how companies identify attractive market segments and choose a market targeting strategy.

To target the best market segments, the company first evaluates each segment's size and growth characteristics, structural attractiveness, and compatibility with company objectives and resources. It then chooses one of four market targeting strategies—ranging from very broad to very narrow targeting. The seller can ignore segment differences and target broadly using *undifferentiated (or mass) marketing.* This involves mass producing, mass distributing, and mass promoting about the same product in about the same way to all consumers. Or the seller can adopt *differentiated marketing*—developing different market offers for several segments. *Concentrated marketing (or niche marketing)* involves focusing on only one or a few market segments. Finally, *micromarketing* is the practice of tailoring products and marketing programs to suit the tastes of specific individuals and locations. Micromarketing includes *local marketing* and *individual marketing.* Which targeting strategy is best depends on company resources, product variability, product life-cycle stage, market variability, and competitive marketing strategies.

4. Discuss how companies differentiate and position their products for maximum competitive advantage in the marketplace.

Once a company has decided which segments to enter, it must decide on its *differentiation and positioning strategy.* The differentiation and positioning task consists of three steps: identifying a set of possible differentiations that create competitive advantage, choosing advantages upon which to build a position, choosing the right competitive advantages, and selecting an overall positioning strategy. The brand's full positioning is called its *value proposition*—the full mix of benefits upon which the brand is positioned. In general, companies can choose from one of five winning value propositions upon which to position their products: more for more, more for the same, the same for less, less for much less, or more for less. Company and brand positioning are summarized in positioning statements that state the target segment and need, positioning concept, and specific points of difference. The company must then effectively communicate and deliver the chosen position to the market.

Reviewing the Key Terms

Discussing the Concepts

1. Explain which segmentation variables would be most important to marketers of the following products: vitamins, credit cards, coffee.

2. How can a company segment international markets for its products? How might Apple segment the international market for its iPod?

3. What is micromarketing? When should a company practice micromarketing?

4. The chapter discusses five requirements for effective segmentation. Suppose you are a product manager in a regional fast-food restaurant company. You are listening to a presentation on a new sand-

wich wrap idea (chicken breast and basil) and it is your turn to ask questions. Write five questions that you would ask the person presenting this product idea. Each question should be directed at one of the five segmentation requirements.

5. In the context of marketing, what does the term "product positioning" mean? Why is it so important?

6. Using the value propositions presented in Figure 7.4, describe the value proposition of Toys "R" Us. Is the Toys "R" Us value proposition clear? Is it appropriate?

Applying the Concepts

1. As discussed in the chapter, PRIZM is one of the leading lifestyle segmentation systems. Go to "http://www.tetrad.com/pcensus/usa/prizmlst.html" and review the 67 PRIZM clusters. Which cluster(s) would each of the following retailers most likely target?
   a. Tiffany's
   b. Macy's
   c. Wal-Mart

2. You are a product manager of a financial services product that is being sold directly to consumers over the Internet. The most important measure to the company is customer acquisition cost—the cost associated with convincing a consumer to buy the service. You have been conducting tests with both a concentrated and undifferentiated segmentation strategy, and the results are presented here.

Concentrated segmentation outcome

- Purchased 10,000 very targeted exposures on Web sites such Yahoo Financial and keywords such as retirement, IRA, and ROTH.
- Paid $80 per thousand exposures
- Obtained 400 clicks to the site, 40 trials, and 20 repeat customers

Undifferentiated segmentation outcome

- Purchased 1,000,000 run-of-site exposures on Web sites
- Paid $1.60 per thousand exposures
- Obtained 2,000 clicks to the site, 100 trials, and 40 repeat customers

3. Form a small group and create an idea for a new reality television show. What competitive advantage does this show have over existing shows? How many and which differences would you promote? Develop a positioning statement for this television show.

Focus on Technology

Marketers of technological products such as cell phones have become very focused on segmentation. They segment on benefits sought, allowing consumers to pick from many popular phone features including Bluetooth technology, camera, games, video screens, speakerphone, and voice dialing. Consumers make choices based on style and price, with most prices ranging from $20 to $800. To move style to the next level and to target the high-end consumer, Nokia offers Vertu, the luxury brand, which comes in platinum and gold. Vertu prices begin at around $5,000, with diamond-studded phones selling at more than $30,000. Visit Vertu

on the Web at http://www.vertu.com and compare this site to Nokia's general site at "www.nokia.com".

1. Explain how the design of each Web site relates to positioning of the products featured.

2. What do you think of the Vertu luxury brand?

3. Nokia uses a different brand name for its luxury brands. Is this a good decision? How else might this product be marketed differently than other Nokia brands? Consider distribution and promotion.

Focus on Ethics

Pharmaceutical companies work very hard to get the word out to patients with specific illnesses when they have a new drug to treat that illness. They segment on benefits sought, allowing consumers to pick from a wide range of diseases have benefited from the advances in pharmaceutical research. But some are concerned by the way some companies market specific medications. Doctors worry about "disease-mongering," corporate-sponsored exaggeration of maladies that drives consumers to request and receive unnecessary medications. Diagnoses of rare diseases are soaring, and even mild cases of maladies are being treated with drugs. Diseases cited include restless legs syndrome, social anxiety disorder, irritable bowel syndrome, and bipolar disorder. The drug makers say they are only trying to educate patients and that labels con-

tain important information on the product. In addition, the pharmaceutical companies stress that the final decision for any medication is made by the doctor.

1. How do pharmaceutical marketers segment the market?

2. How do they position their medications?

3. Are these marketing strategies socially responsible?

See "Hey, You Don't Look So Good," *BusinessWeek*, May 8, 2006, pp. 30–32.

Video Case

Procter & Gamble

Procter & Gamble has one of the world's largest and strongest brand portfolios, including such familiar brands Pampers, Tide, Ariel, Always, Pantene, Bounty, Folgers, Pringles, Charmin, Downy, Iams, Crest, Secret, and Olay. In fact, in the United States, P&G offers seven shampoo brands, six detergent brands, and six soap brands . In each of these categories, P&G's products compete against each other, in addition to products offered by other companies, for share of the customer's wallet.

How can a company with more than 300 brands sold in more than 140 countries maximize profits without cannibalizing its own sales? It all starts with a solid understanding of consumers and how a brand fits into consumers' lives. P&G believes that a brand must stand for something singular in a consumer's life. As a result, each brand is carefully positioned to target a very specific segment of the market. The result? P&G had nearly $57 billion in sales last year.

After viewing the video featuring Procter & Gamble, answer the following questions about segmentation, targeting, and positioning.

1. Visit the Procter & Gamble Web site, choose a specific product category, and review the brands in that category. How does P&G use positioning to differentiate the brands in the product category you selected?

2. What bases of segmentation does P&G use to differentiate the products in the category you selected?

3. How does P&G use its variety of brands to build relationships with the right customers?

Company Case

Saturn: An Image Makeover

Things are about to change at Saturn. The General Motors brand had only three iterations of the same compact car for the entire decade of the 1990s. But Saturn will soon introduce an all-new lineup of vehicles that includes a mid-sized sport sedan, an eight-passenger crossover vehicle, a two-seat roadster, a new compact, and a hybrid SUV. Having anticipated the brand's renaissance for years, Saturn executives, employees, and customers are beside themselves with glee.

But with all this change, industry observers are wondering whether Saturn will be able to maintain the very characteristics that have distinguished the brand since its inception. Given that Saturn established itself based on a very narrow line of compact vehicles, many believe that the move from targeting one segment of customers to targeting multiple segments will be challenging. Will a newly positioned Saturn still meet the needs of one of the most loyal cadres of customers in the automotive world?

A NEW KIND OF CAR COMPANY

In 1980, GM recognized its inferiority to the Japanese big three (Honda, Toyota, and Datsun) with respect to compact vehicles. The Japanese had a lower cost structure, yet built better cars. In an effort to offer a more competitive economy car, GM actually turned to the enemy. It entered into a joint venture with Toyota to build small cars. Soon, a Toyota plant in Northern California was turning out Corollas on one assembly line while making very similar Chevy Novas on a second. Meanwhile, in a long-term effort to make better small cars, GM gave the green light to Group 99, a secretive task force that resulted in formation of the Saturn Corporation in 1985.

From the beginning, Saturn set out to break through the GM bureaucracy and become "A different kind of car. A different kind of company." As the single-most defining characteristic of the new company, Saturn proclaimed that its sole focus would be people: customers, employees, and communities. Saturn put significant resources into customer research and product development. The first Saturn cars were made "from scratch," without any allegiance to the GM parts bin or suppliers. The goal was to produce not only a high-quality vehicle, but one known for safety and innovative features that would "wow" the customer.

Saturn's focus on employees began with an unprecedented contract with United Auto Workers (UAW). The contract was so simple, it fit in a shirt pocket. It established progressive work rules, with special emphasis given to benefits, work teams, and the concept of empowerment At the retail end, Saturn selected dealers based on carefully crafted criteria. It paid service personnel and sales associates a salary rather than commission. This would help create an environment that would reverse the common customer perception of the dealer as a nemesis.

Finally, in addition to customer and employee relations, Saturn focused on social responsibility. Human resources policies gave equal opportunities to women, ethnic minorities, and people with disabilities. Saturn designed environmentally responsible manufacturing processes, even going beyond legal requirements. The company also gave heavy philanthropic support to various causes. All of these actions earned Saturn a number of awards recognizing its environmentally and socially responsible actions.

(case continues)

When the first Saturn vehicles rolled off the assembly line on July 30, 1990, the company offered a sedan, a coupe, and a wagon in two trim levels each, all based on a single compact vehicle platform. In spite of this minimal approach, sales quickly exceeded expectations. By 1992, Saturn had sold 500,000 vehicles. That same year, the company achieved the highest new-car sales per retail outlet, something that had not been done by a domestic car company for 15 years.

Indeed, customers were drawn to all the things that Saturn had hoped they would be. They loved the innovations, such as dent resistant body panels, the high-tech paint job designed to resist oxidization and chipping longer than any in the industry, and safety features such as traction control, antilock brakes, and unparalleled body reinforcements. They were overwhelmed by the fresh sales approach that included no-haggle pricing, a 30-day return policy, and no hassle from the sales associates. The noncommissioned associates spent as much time with each customer as they wished, even going on extended test drives. Absent were typical high-pressure tactics so commonly used by automotive salespeople.

By 1994, Saturn had developed an unusually loyal customer base. The depth of customer relationships became apparent when 38,000 Saturn loyalists made the trek to company headquarters in Tennessee to celebrate the first five years at the company's Spring Hill Homecoming. It was "just like Woodstock without all the patchouli oil," beamed one proud SL2 owner. The homecoming set the mold for many company-sponsored customer gatherings to follow.

As Saturn's customer base grew, it became apparent that the Saturn brand was attracting customers who would not have otherwise purchased a GM vehicle. Interestingly, the typical Saturn buyer did not appear to be all that different from a Chevrolet buyer. With respect to household income, age, gender, and education, typical Saturn buyers appeared to represent the same Chevy-like cross section of middle-class America. But Wisconsin megadealer John Bergstrom said his network of 22 GM dealerships draws different types of customers to the two brands. With trucks accounting for 65 percent of his Chevrolet sales, he described the Chevy owner as "a true-blue, bow-tie America consumer." However, "the Saturn guest is a little different guest. They might buy an Asian car or a Korean car or a Saturn. They are very much into safety and value, and how they're treated is critically important. I don't think we'd get those kinds of people in our Chevy stores if we didn't have the Saturn brand."

During Saturn's first years of operations, the accolades rolled in. The list included "Best Car" picks from numerous magazines and organizations, along with awards for quality, engineering, safety, and ease of maintenance. But the crowning achievement occurred in 1995, as the 1,000,000th Saturn took to the road. That year, Saturn ranked number one out of all automotive nameplates on the J.D. Power and Associates Sales Satisfaction Index Study, achieving the

highest score ever given by the organization. It would be the only company ever to achieve the highest marks in all three categories ranked by the satisfaction index (salesperson performance, delivery activities, and initial product quality). Saturn earned that honor for an astounding four consecutive years, and it was the only nonluxury brand to be at or near the top of J.D. Power's scores for the better part of a decade.

THE HONEYMOON ENDS

Despite the initially strong sales levels, overall Saturn revenues tapered off quickly (sales peaked in 1994 at 286,000, settling in at an average of about 250,000 units per year). This may have been due partly to the fact that Saturn released no new models in the 1990s. Finally, in the 2000 model year, Saturn introduced its long-awaited mid-sized L-series with an optional V6 engine. But unlike the S-series, the L-series was reviewed as a generally bland and forgettable car.

In 2002, Saturn broadened the lineup with the Vue, a compact SUV model. In January of 2003, it replaced the S-series with the Ion, a totally new compact that offered more options than before. But although these new vehicles addressed the issue of a lack of model options, they brought with them a new concern. Saturn's history of high quality and its long-cherished J.D. Power ratings began to slide. In the early part of the new millennium, not only was Saturn's J.D. Power initial-quality rating not near the top, it fell to below the industry average.

Even with the new models, Saturn's sales did not improve. In fact, they declined. This was partly due to an industry-wide downturn in sales wrought by a recession. Still, L-series production ended in 2004, only five years after it began. In 2005, Saturn sales fell to a low of 213,000 units, only about 1 percent of the overall market. It seemed that sales of the L-series and Vue were coming almost entirely from loyal Saturn customers who were trading up to something different, something bigger, and, unfortunately, something not as good.

Looking back, Saturn unquestionably defied the odds. To launch an all-new automotive company in such a fiercely competitive and barrier-entrenched industry is one thing. To achieve the level of sales, the customer base, and the list of awards that Saturn achieved in such a short period of time is truly remarkable. But as GM and Saturn executives faced the reality of declining quality, plummeting sales, and annual losses of up to $1 billion, they knew they had to do something dramatic. In 2006, Saturn general manager Jill Lajdziak said, "Saturn's initial image as a smart innovation small-car company was blurred by bumps in quality and slow model turnover. We didn't grow the portfolio fast enough, and this year we're growing in a huge way."

A NEW KIND OF SATURN

With all that Saturn has done wrong, the fact that dealers still moved 213,000 vehicles in 2005 against competitors with better reputations and better cars testifies to the things it has done right. With its rock-solid dealer network, high purchase process satisfaction ratings, and loyal customer base, Saturn has valuable assets to build upon.

And GM plans to do just that as it addresses product quality and model selection problems. GM is currently investing heavily in a Saturn turnaround. Showering $3 billion on Saturn, it hopes to perform a makeover between 2006 and 2008 that is similar to the one achieved with Cadillac earlier this decade. GM, the world's biggest carmaker, lost $10.6 billion in 2005. It's clearly putting some faith in one of its smallest brands to help turn the tide. GM wants to raise Saturn's sales to 400,000 units by the end of 2007. If all goes as planned, sales could reach 500,000 not long after that. With higher prices and margins, this would represent an even greater growth in revenues and profits.

Key to the Saturn makeover will be an infusion of European styling from GM's German division, Opel. In fact, some of the new cars already hitting showrooms are largely rebadged Opels. In the future, new-product development will be carried out in a joint-venture fashion between the two divisions. For a company that in the past has been known as making the "car for people who hate cars," this is a 180-degree turnaround. Saturn clearly hopes to change its humdrum image to boost profits with higher-priced vehicles.

If the first of four new Saturn models is any indication, Saturn is moving in the right direction. The Sky two-seat roadster hit showroom floors in early 2006 with long waiting lists. Based on the Opel GT, the Sky is a head-turning performance vehicle, dubbed by one observer as the "cub-Vette." For dealer John Bergstrom, this new model presented an unexpected but welcome dilemma. "Sky is just a flat-out home run," said Bergstrom, referring to the waiting lists that he has started at all six of his dealerships. "I've never had that before," he says, noting that those on the waiting lists are people who have never even considered a Saturn before.

In the fall of 2006, Saturn launched 2007 models of the mid-sized Aura sport sedan (based on the Opel Vectra) and the eight-passenger Outlook crossover vehicle (based on GM's Lambda platform being sold by Chevrolet, Buick, and GMC). For 2008, after a year without a compact car, Saturn will replace the Ion with a mildly changed Opel Astra, already a European hit in its fifth generation. The new lineup will also include the Green Line, which will add hybrid technology to multiple models, starting with the 2007 Vue. The Green Line promises to make full-hybrid technology available at a price much lower than any other hybrid offering.

"The biggest advantage to rebranding Opel vehicles as Saturn is it doesn't mean additional costs to GM," said Guido Vildozo, a senior market analyst and industry forecaster at Global Insight Inc. "And since Opel is a kind of sporty European brand, Saturn will adopt this image too, or at least that is what they hope to happen." Some industry analysts suggest that because Saturn is such a new company, it can reposition itself more easily than other brands.

GM makes it clear that with Saturn, it's not trying to make another Chevrolet. Chevrolet will remain the only GM brand positioned as "all things to all people." Along with the other GM brands, Saturn will play a niche role and target a specific segment of the market. In fact, GM says that it's just trying to help Saturn do more of what it has been doing all along—reach the type of import-buying customer it can't reach with any of its other brands. Indeed, top executives at GM acknowledge that many Saturn owners already believe their car is an Asian brand, not a domestic one. "Saturn has always been the one brand in the GM lineup suitable for attracting import-intenders," says a GM executive.

However, some questions remain as to what segment Saturn will actually target. After seeing the new Saturn lineup at the New York auto show, Tom Libby of Power Information Network says he's confused about what the brand is trying to do. He's worried that Saturn will stop focusing on the retail experience and shift to emphasizing styling. "What's the message they're trying to get out?" he asks. "I'm just puzzled by the whole thing." Is Saturn losing focus, or is it simply adding style to its current image of providing a good value and an honest dealer experience? Many analysts believe that because Saturn's current image is only loosely based on the actual car, the company has plenty of room to add style to the formula.

Questions for Discussion

1. Using the full spectrum of segmentation variables, describe how GM has segmented the automobile market.

2. What segment(s) is Saturn now targeting? How is GM now positioning Saturn? How do these strategies differ from those employed with the original Saturn S-series?

3. Describe the role that social responsibility plays in Saturn's targeting strategy.

4. Do you think that GM will accomplish its goals with the "new Saturn"? Why or why not?

5. What segmentation, targeting, and positioning recommendations would you make to GM for future Saturn models?

Sources: Leslie J. Allen, "Saturn's Rebirth Vexes Chevy Dealers," Automotive News, February 20, 2006, p. 1; Sharon Silke Carty, "Saturn Puts Its Models Where Its Mouth Is," USA Today, April 21, 2006, accessed at www.usatoday.com; Barbara Powell, "GM's Saturn Seeks to Shake Up Humdrum Image," Ottawa Citizen, April 12, 2006, p. F7; David Welch, "Saturn's Second Liftoff?" BusinessWeek Online, April 13, 2006, accessed at www.businessweek.com; and "Our Story," accessed at www.saturn.com, May 2006.

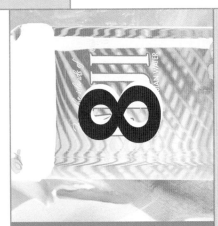

chapter

8

FIJIAN WATER

Product, Services, and Branding Strategy

Previewing the Concepts

Now that you've had a good look at marketing strategy, we'll take a deeper look at the marketing mix—the tactical tools that marketers use to implement their strategies. In this and the next chapter, we'll study how companies develop and manage products and brands. Then, in the chapters that follow, we'll look at pricing, distribution, and marketing communication tools. The product is usually the first and most basic marketing consideration. We'll start with a seemingly simple question: What *is* a product? As it turns out, however, the answer is not so simple.

To start things off, remember that seemingly simple question—what is a product? Well, what is water? That's right, *water*. As it turns out, to a FIJI Water customer, water is more than just a liquid you draw out of the tap to wash down a sandwich or to quench your thirst after a workout. FIJI Water is "the nature of water."

The best things in life are free. *That's what the old song says.* The flowers in spring, the robins that sing, the sunbeams that shine, they're yours, they're mine! *The air that we breathe, the water we drink . . . oops, not so fast. The water we drink? Free? Consider the following account:*

At Jean-Georges, a celebrated Manhattan restaurant known for its artful cuisine and fine wines, a waiter lifts a tall silver decanter and fills three goblets from the bottle cradled within. Its contents must be precious: Chef Jean-Georges Vongerichten even uses this beverage as an ingredient in broths and sorbets. A rare vintage, perhaps? Try again. It's FIJI Natural Artesian Water, the latest bottled water brand to elevate the world's simplest drink to celebrity status. Today, at all of his restaurants, Mr. Vongerichten exclusively pours FIJI, which looks and sounds almost as exotic as the French dishes on his menu.

FIJI water may be one of the best things in life, but it's certainly not free. A quick check of the Jean-Georges menu shows that FIJI sells there for $10 a bottle. $10! Shop around, perhaps at a lesser restaurant, and you might find a bottle at the bargain price of $2.75. And you thought gas was expensive. Why would anyone pay those kinds of prices for water, something they could get for free out of the tap?

Well, it turns out the FIJI water is very, very good water. Drawn from an underground source on Viti Levu, the main island of the South Pacific country of Fiji, it has an ultraclean taste and contains not a hint of impurities or pollutants. But when you drink FIJI Water, you're getting a lot more than just pure, good-tasting water. According to the company, not all waters are created equal. FIJI water is untouched by man—it's "the nature of water."

Rainfall in a Fijian forest is a symphony of sound in a theater of green. Somewhere overhead, raindrops strike palm fronds that move with the wind, clicking and tapping like hundreds of castanets. Around you is a glimpse of Eden: giant leaves large enough to lie on, ferns like trees, bamboo and grasses taller than a man. And the rain, formed in clouds above the blue Pacific, dances down through the forest canopy and seeps into the rich volcanic soil, wending its way to the aquifer far below the forest floor. Water, like wine, gets its taste from the terrain that forms it. FIJI Water comes from a virgin ecosystem deep in the South Pacific, from tropical rain filtered for hundreds of years through volcanic stone. This natural artesian water is known for its signature soft, smooth taste and well-balanced mineral content including a

216

high level of silica, a youth-preserving antioxidant. You can taste the purity in every sip. It's The Nature of Water!

Everything about FIJI Water contributes to this "nature of water" brand experience—from its name, packaging, and label to the places that sell and serve it, to the celebrities that drink and endorse it. The name was a natural—FIJI Natural Artesian Water evokes visions of unspoiled natural beauty and purity. The name also set the bottle and colorful labeling also set the brand apart. The unique square bottle and colorful labeling also set the brand apart. The clear plastic front label presents the FIJI name with a flower resting below. Looking through the front label to the inside of the back label, you see an image of palm leaves. In combination, the front and back labels create a striking 3-D picture that emphasizes FIJI Water's clarity and purity. "The bottle appears to have a magic in it," says a company official.

Skillful marketing has also helped to build the brand's ultrachic image. Initial ads played up FIJI's exotic origins—raindrops falling into Fiji's pristine tropical forests and filtering through layers of volcanic rock. "We're sure you'll agree, it was worth the 450-year wait," said the ads. To boost the brand's status, the company sent samples to movies stars, athletes, and other celebrities, and it pursued product placements in films and TV shows. For example, in the movie *Dodgeball*, Lance Armstrong, the seven-time Tour de France winner, sat at a bar while drinking FIJI water. And Drew Barrymore clutched a bottle of FIJI in "50 First Dates." Such efforts

Objectives

After studying this chapter, you should be able to

1. define *product* and the major classifications of products and services

2. describe the decisions companies make regarding their individual products and services, product lines, and product mixes

3. discuss branding strategy—the decisions companies make in building and managing their brands

4. identify the four characteristics that affect the marketing of a service and the additional marketing considerations that services require

The Nature of Water

have given FIJI top billing as what one observer calls "the bottled water of the stars." Further adding to the brand's allure, Estée Lauder even released new Island Michael Kors FIJI fragrance—each bottle contains a splash of FIJI Water.

At the same time, the company convinced luxury hotels and restaurants of the merits of FIJI Water, urging that superb food and atmosphere needed to be paired with water of the same quality. It trained restaurant wait staff to educate consumers on the brand's taste and purity. The company even convinced chefs at leading restaurants to use FIJI Water as a *cooking ingredient* in their kitchens. "Great chefs spend all their time carefully choosing ingredients and crafting a wine list, then they use a water that doesn't complement the taste of either," notes FIJI's chief executive. Finally, to make FIJI Water's plastic bottles more table worthy, the company came up with its own distinctive silver serving sleeve, custom-made to fit FIJI's square bottle. That silver sleeve tells everyone in a restaurant that the customer who ordered FIJI water appreciates the best and can afford it.

So not all waters are created equal. When you need something to quench your thirst after a good workout, gulping a glass of tap water might do the trick. But for special occasions, you may want something more—something that tastes really good, or that makes you feel special, or that tells others something about who you are. On such occasions, the FIJI brand promises a special experience— much like a fine wine with a gourmet meal. When FIJI sells water, it sells more than just the tangible liquid. It sells purity and great taste, good health, refinement, status, and exclusivity.

But, still, could any water be worth $10 a bottle, or even $2.75? Apparently so! Despite an increasingly crowded bottled-water market, FIJI is scrambling to keep up with surging demand. Last year, while primary competitor Evian's U.S. sales volume decreased 23 percent, FIJI's sales shot up 61 percent. And the company recently added a new bottling line that tripled its capacity. Thus, more and more people are buying into FIJI's "The Nature of Water" brand promise, despite the high price—or maybe because of it.[1]

Clearly, water is more than just water when FIJI sells it. This chapter begins with a deceptively simple question: *What is a product?* After answering this question, we look at ways to classify products in consumer and business markets. Then we discuss the important decisions that marketers make regarding individual products, product lines, and product mixes. Next, we look into the critically important issue of how marketers build and manage brands. Finally, we examine the characteristics and marketing requirements of a special form of product—services.

What Is a Product?

We define a **product** as anything that can be offered to a market for attention, acquisition, use, or consumption that might satisfy a want or need. Products include more than just tangible goods. Broadly defined, products include physical objects, services, events, persons, places, organizations, ideas, or mixes of these entities. Throughout this text, we use the term *product* broadly to include any or all of these entities. Thus, an Apple iPod, a Toyota Camry, and a Caffé Mocha at Starbucks are products. But so are a European vacation, Fidelity online investment services, and advice from your family doctor.

Because of their importance in the world economy, we give special attention to services. **Services** are a form of product that consists of activities, benefits, or satisfactions offered for sale that are essentially intangible and do not result in the ownership of anything. Examples are banking, hotel, airline, retail, tax preparation, and home-repair services. We will look at services more closely later in this chapter.

Products, Services, and Experiences

Product is a key element in the overall *market offering*. Marketing-mix planning begins with formulating an offering that brings value to target customers. This offering becomes the basis upon which the company builds profitable relationships with customers.

Product
Anything that can be offered to a market for attention, acquisition, use, or consumption that might satisfy a want or need.

Service
Any activity or benefit that one party can offer to another that is essentially intangible and does not result in the ownership of anything.

A company's market offering often includes both tangible goods and services. Each component can be a minor or a major part of the total offer. At one extreme, the offer may consist of a *pure tangible good*, such as soap, toothpaste, or salt—no services accompany the product. At the other extreme are *pure services*, for which the offer consists primarily of a service. Examples include a doctor's exam or financial services. Between these two extremes, however, many goods-and-services combinations are possible.

Today, as products and services become more commoditized, many companies are moving to a new level in creating value for their customers. To differentiate their offers, beyond simply making products and delivering services, they are creating and managing customer *experiences* with their products or company.

Experiences have always been important in the entertainment industry—Disney has long manufactured memories through its movies and theme parks. Today, however, all kinds of firms are recasting their traditional goods and services to create experiences. For example, American Girl Inc. does more than just make and sell high-end dolls. It takes additional steps to create special experiences between the dolls and the girls who adore them.[2]

To extend its reach and to put more smiles on the faces of the girls who adore their American Girl dolls, the company has opened American Girl Places in Chicago, New York, and Los Angeles. Inside a Place—which has become as much of a destination spot as it is a store—are a series of wonderfully engaging experiences for girls, mothers, and grandmothers (not to mention the occasional male who's either dragged into the Place or who loves his daughter very much). There's a theater with a live play centered on the doll collection; there's a café for a grown-up dining experience; there's a salon to style a doll's hair; and a doll hospital to fix one up as good as new. Before, during, and after all these experiences, shopping does go on—and the purchases become memorabilia for the experiences visitors have. Moreover, these same visitors buy more from the catalog, frequent the Web site to purchase items more often, and tell their friends about their American Girl Place experience. Much more than a store that sells dolls, says the company, "it's the place where imaginations soar—from boutiques to special events, from the café to the theater and beyond."

■ Marketing experiences: American Girl, Inc., does more than just make and sell high-end dolls. It now takes additional steps to create special experiences between the dolls and the girls who adore them.

Companies that market experiences realize that customers are really buying much more than just products and services. They are buying what those offers will *do* for them.

Levels of Product and Services

Product planners need to think about products and services on three levels (see Figure 8.1). Each level adds more customer value. The most basic level is the *core benefit*, which addresses the question *What is the buyer really buying?* When designing products, marketers must first define the core, problem-solving benefits or services that consumers seek. A woman buying lipstick buys more than lip color. Charles Revson of Revlon saw this early: "In the factory, we make cosmetics; in the store, we sell hope." And people who buy a BlackBerry are buying more than a wireless mobile phone, e-mail and Web-browsing device, or personal organizer. They are buying freedom and on-the-go connectivity to people and resources.

At the second level, product planners must turn the core benefit into an *actual product*. They need to develop product and service features, design, a quality level, a brand name, and packaging. For example, the BlackBerry is an actual product. Its name, parts, styling, features, packaging, and other attributes have all been combined carefully to deliver the core benefit of staying connected.

FIGURE 8.1
Three levels of product

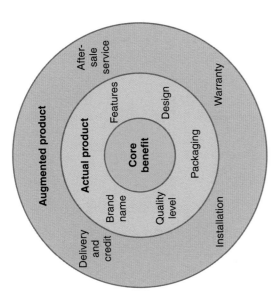

Consumer product
Product bought by final consumer for personal consumption.

Convenience product
Consumer product that the customer usually buys frequently, immediately, and with a minimum of comparison and buying effort.

Finally, product planners must build an *augmented product* around the core benefit and actual product by offering additional consumer services and benefits. BlackBerry must offer more than just a communications device. It must provide consumers with a complete solution to mobile connectivity problems. Thus, when consumers buy a BlackBerry, the company and its dealers also might give buyers a warranty on parts and workmanship, instructions on how to use the device, quick repair services when needed, and a toll-free telephone number and Web site to use if they have problems or questions.

Consumers see products as complex bundles of benefits that satisfy their needs. When developing products, marketers first must identify the *core* consumer needs the product will satisfy. They must then design the *actual* product and find ways to *augment* it in order to create the bundle of benefits that will provide the most satisfying customer experience.

Product and Service Classifications

Products and services fall into two broad classes based on the types of consumers that use them—*consumer products* and *industrial products*. Broadly defined, products also include other marketable entities such as experiences, organizations, persons, places, and ideas.

Consumer Products

Consumer products are products and services bought by final consumers for personal consumption. Marketers usually classify these products and services further based on how consumers go about buying them. Consumer products include *convenience products*, *shopping products*, *specialty products*, and *unsought products*. These products differ in the ways consumers buy them and therefore in how they are marketed (see Table 8.1).

Convenience products are consumer products and services that the customer usually buys frequently, immediately, and with a minimum of comparison and buying effort.

■ Core, actual, and augmented product: People who buy a Blackberry are buying more than a wireless mobile phone, e-mail and Web-browsing device, or personal organizer. They are buying freedom and on-the-go connectivity to people and resources.

TABLE 8.1 Marketing Considerations for Consumer Products

Marketing Considerations	Type of Consumer Product			
	Convenience	Shopping	Specialty	Unsought
Customer buying behavior	Frequent purchase, little planning, little comparison or shopping effort, low customer involvement	Less frequent purchase, much planning and shopping effort, comparison of brands on price, quality, style	Strong brand preference and loyalty, special purchase effort, little comparison of brands, low price sensitivity	Little product awareness, knowledge (or, if aware, little or even negative interest)
Price	Low price	Higher price	High price	Varies
Distribution	Widespread distribution, convenient locations	Selective distribution in fewer outlets	Exclusive distribution in only one or a few outlets per market area	Varies
Promotion	Mass promotion by the producer	Advertising and personal selling by both producer and resellers	More carefully targeted promotion by both producer and resellers	Aggressive advertising and personal selling by producer and resellers
Examples	Toothpaste, magazines, laundry detergent	Major appliances, televisions, furniture, clothing	Luxury goods, such as Rolex watches or fine crystal	Life insurance, Red Cross blood donations

Shopping product

Consumer good that the customer, in the process of selection and purchase, characteristically compares on such bases as suitability, quality, price, and style.

Specialty product

Consumer product with unique characteristics or brand identification for which a significant group of buyers is willing to make a special purchase effort.

Unsought product

Consumer product that the consumer either does not know about or knows about but does not normally think of buying.

Industrial product

Product bought by individuals and organizations for further processing or for use in conducting a business.

Examples include soap, candy, newspapers, and fast food. Convenience products are usually low priced, and marketers place them in many locations to make them readily available when customers need them.

Shopping products are less frequently purchased consumer products and services that customers compare carefully on suitability, quality, price, and style. When buying shopping products and services, consumers spend much time and effort in gathering information and making comparisons. Examples include furniture, clothing, used cars, major appliances, and hotel and airline services. Shopping products marketers usually distribute their products through fewer outlets but provide deeper sales support to help customers in their comparison efforts.

Specialty products are consumer products and services with unique characteristics or brand identification for which a significant group of buyers is willing to make a special purchase effort. Examples include specific brands and types of cars, high-priced photographic equipment, designer clothes, and the services of medical or legal specialists. A Lamborghini automobile, for example, is a specialty product because buyers are usually willing to travel great distances to buy one. Buyers normally do not compare specialty products. They invest only the time needed to reach dealers carrying the wanted products.

Unsought products are consumer products that the consumer either does not know about or knows about but does not normally think of buying. Most major new innovations are unsought until the consumer becomes aware of them through advertising. Classic examples of known but unsought products and services are life insurance, preplanned funeral services, and blood donations to the Red Cross. By their very nature, unsought products require a lot of advertising, personal selling, and other marketing efforts.

Industrial Products

Industrial products are those purchased for further processing or for use in conducting a business. Thus, the distinction between a consumer product and an industrial product is based on the *purpose* for which the product is bought. If a consumer buys a lawn mower for use around home, the lawn mower is a consumer product. If the same consumer buys

Industrial product

Product bought by individuals and organizations for further processing or for use in conducting a business.

the same lawn mower for use in a landscaping business, the lawn mower is an industrial product.

The three groups of industrial products and services include materials and parts, capital items, and supplies and services. *Materials and parts* include raw materials and manufactured materials and parts. Raw materials consist of farm products (wheat, cotton, livestock, fruits, vegetables) and natural products (fish, lumber, crude petroleum, iron ore). Manufactured materials and parts consist of component materials (iron, yarn, cement, wires) and component parts (small motors, tires, castings). Most manufactured materials and parts are sold directly to industrial users. Price and service are the major marketing factors; branding and advertising tend to be less important.

Capital items are industrial products that aid in the buyer's production or operations, including installations and accessory equipment. Installations consist of major purchases such as buildings (factories, offices) and fixed equipment (generators, drill presses, large computer systems, elevators). Accessory equipment includes portable factory equipment and tools (hand tools, lift trucks) and office equipment (computers, fax machines, desks). They have a shorter life than installations and simply aid in the production process.

The final group of industrial products is *supplies and services*. Supplies include operating supplies (lubricants, coal, paper, pencils) and repair and maintenance items (paint, nails, brooms). Supplies are the convenience products of the industrial field because they are usually purchased with a minimum of effort or comparison. Business services include maintenance and repair services (window cleaning, computer repair) and business advisory services (legal, management consulting, advertising). Such services are usually supplied under contract.

Organizations, Persons, Places, and Ideas

In addition to tangible products and services, in recent years marketers have broadened the concept of a product to include other market offerings—organizations, persons, places, and ideas.

Organizations often carry out activities to "sell" the organization itself. *Organization marketing* consists of activities undertaken to create, maintain, or change the attitudes and behavior of target consumers toward an organization. Both profit and not-for-profit organizations practice organization marketing. Business firms sponsor public relations or *corporate image advertising* campaigns to polish their images and market themselves to various publics. For example, BASF ads say "We don't make a lot of the products you buy, we make a lot of the products you buy better." Similarly, not-for-profit organizations, such as churches, colleges, charities, museums, and performing arts groups, market their organizations in order to raise funds and attract members or patrons.

People can also be thought of as products. *Person marketing* consists of activities undertaken to create, maintain, or change attitudes or behavior toward particular people. People ranging from presidents, entertainers, and sports figures to professionals such as doctors, lawyers, and architects use person marketing to build their reputations. And businesses, charities, and other organizations use well-known personalities to help sell their products or causes. For example, more than a dozen different companies—including Nike, Apple, Tag Heuer, Buick, American Express, Wheaties, and Accenture—combine to pay more than $80 million a year to link themselves with golf superstar Tiger Woods.[3]

The skillful use of person marketing can turn a person's name into a powerhouse brand. The brand power of Oprah Winfrey's name has made her a billionaire: Oprah-branded products include her television show, TV and feature movies, *O, The Oprah Magazine*, Oprah's Angel Network, Oprah's Boutiques online shop, and Oprah's Book Club. And businessman Donald Trump has slapped his well-known name on everything from skyscrapers and casinos to bottled water, magazines, and reality TV programs:

Donald Trump has made and lost fortunes as a real-estate developer. But Trump's genius is in brand building, and he is the brand. Thanks to tireless self-promotion, "The Donald" has established the Trump brand as a symbol of quality, luxury, and success. What's the value of the Trump brand? Trump's name now adorns everything from magazines and bottled water (Trump Ice) to fashion (Donald J. Trump Signature Collection) and reality TV shows (*The Apprentice*). Trump does commercials for Verizon, was host of *Saturday Night Live*, and even unveiled a Trump Rewards Visa card, which rewards cardholders with casino discounts. "He's like P.T. Barnum on steroids," says a friend. "What's his greatest asset? It's his name. He's a skillful marketing person, and what he markets is his name."[4]

Place marketing involves activities undertaken to create, maintain, or change attitudes or behavior toward particular places. Cities, states, regions, and even entire nations compete to attract tourists, new residents, conventions, and company offices and factories. Texas advertises "It's Like a Whole Other Country" and New York state shouts, "I Love New York!" The Iceland Tourist Board invites visitors to Iceland by advertising that it has "Discoveries the Entire Year." Icelandair, the only airline that serves the island, partners with the tourist board to sell world travelers on the wonders of Iceland—everything from geothermal spas and glacier tours to midnight golf and clubbing.[5]

Ideas can also be marketed. In one sense, all marketing is the marketing of an idea, whether it is the general idea of brushing your teeth or the specific idea that Crest toothpastes "create smiles every day." Here, however, we narrow our focus to the marketing of *social ideas*. This area has been called **social marketing**, defined by the Social Marketing Institute as the use of commercial marketing concepts and tools in programs designed to influence individuals' behavior to improve their well-being and that of society.[6]

Social marketing programs include public health campaigns to reduce smoking, alcoholism, drug abuse, and overeating. Other social marketing efforts include environmental campaigns to promote wilderness protection, clean air, and conservation. Still others address issues such as family planning, human rights, and racial equality. The Ad Council of America has developed dozens of social advertising campaigns, involving issues ranging from preventive health, education, and personal safety to environmental preservation.

But social marketing involves much more than just advertising—the Social Marketing Institute (SMI) encourages the use of a broad range of marketing tools. "Social marketing goes well beyond the promotional 'P' of the marketing mix to include every other element to achieve its social change objectives," says the SMI's executive director.[7]

SOME OF NEW YORK'S MOST INFLUENTIAL ROLE MODELS WILL NEVER WEAR THE YANKEE UNIFORM.

JOIN NEW YORK'S BRIGHTEST
T E A C H N Y C
WWW.TEACHNYC.NET

NYC DEPARTMENT OF EDUCATION

AdCouncil.org

Appleseed FOUNDATION

■ Social marketing: The Ad Council has created thousands of public service campaigns that have created positive and lasting social change. For example, it joined with the New York City Department of Education and the Appleseed Foundation to create ads like this one that helped recruit promising young teachers to New York City public schools.

Social marketing

The use of commercial marketing concepts and tools in programs designed to influence individuals' behavior to improve their well-being and that of society.

▉ Product and Service Decisions

Marketers make product and service decisions at three levels: individual product decisions, product line decisions, and product mix decisions. We discuss each in turn.

Individual Product and Service Decisions

Figure 8.2 shows the important decisions in the development and marketing of individual products and services. We will focus on decisions about *product attributes*, *branding*, *packaging*, *labeling*, and *product support services*.

Product and Service Attributes

Developing a product or service involves defining the benefits that it will offer. These benefits are communicated and delivered by product attributes such as *quality*, *features*, and *style and design*.

FIGURE 8.2
Individual product decisions

| Product attributes | ⇨ | Branding | ⇨ | Packaging | ⇨ | Labeling | ⇨ | Product support services |

Product quality

The characteristics of a product or service that bear on its ability to satisfy stated or implied customer needs.

PRODUCT QUALITY **Product quality** is one of the marketer's major positioning tools. Quality has a direct impact on product or service performance; thus, it is closely linked to customer value and satisfaction. In the narrowest sense, quality can be defined as "freedom from defects." But most customer-centered companies go beyond this narrow definition. Instead, they define quality in terms of creating customer value and satisfaction. The American Society for Quality defines quality as the characteristics of a product or service that bear on its ability to satisfy stated or implied customer needs. Similarly, Siemens defines quality this way: "Quality is when our customers come back and our products don't."[8]

Total quality management (TQM) is an approach in which all the company's people are involved in constantly improving the quality of products, services, and business processes. For most top companies, customer-driven quality has become a way of doing business. Today, companies are taking a "return on quality" approach, viewing quality as an investment and holding quality efforts accountable for bottom-line results.[9]

Product quality has two dimensions—level and consistency. In developing a product, the marketer must first choose a *quality level* that will support the product's positioning. Here, product quality means *performance quality*—the ability of a product to perform its functions. For example, a Rolls-Royce provides higher performance quality than a Chevrolet: It has a smoother ride, provides more "creature comforts," and lasts longer. Companies rarely try to offer the highest possible performance quality level—few customers want or can afford the high levels of quality offered in products such as a Rolls-Royce automobile, a Viking range, or a Rolex watch. Instead, companies choose a quality level that matches target market needs and the quality levels of competing products.

Beyond quality level, high quality also can mean high levels of quality consistency. Here, product quality means *conformance quality*—freedom from defects and *consistency* in delivering a targeted level of performance. All companies should strive for high levels of conformance quality. In this sense, a Chevrolet can have just as much quality as a Rolls-Royce. Although a Chevy doesn't perform as well as a Rolls-Royce, it can as consistently deliver the quality that customers pay for and expect.

PRODUCT FEATURES A product can be offered with varying features. A stripped-down model, one without any extras, is the starting point. The company can create higher-level models by adding more features. Features are a competitive tool for differentiating the company's product from competitors' products. Being the first producer to introduce a valued new feature is one of the most effective ways to compete.

How can a company identify new features and decide which ones to add to its product? The company should periodically survey buyers who have used the product and ask these questions: How do you like the product? Which specific features of the product do you like most? Which features could we add to improve the product? The answers provide the company with a rich list of feature ideas. The company can then assess each feature's *value* to customers versus its *cost* to the company. Features that customers value highly in relation to costs should be added.

PRODUCT STYLE AND DESIGN Another way to add customer value is through distinctive *product style and design*. Design is a larger concept than style. *Style* simply describes the appearance of a product. Styles can be eye catching or yawn producing. A sensational style may grab attention and produce pleasing aesthetics, but it does not necessarily make the product *perform* better. Unlike style, *design* is more than skin deep—it goes to the very heart of a product. Good design contributes to a product's usefulness as well as to its looks.

Good design begins with a deep understanding of customer needs. More than simply creating product or service attributes, it involves shaping the customer's product-use experience. Consider the design process behind Procter & Gamble's Swiffer CarpetFlick.

P&G's innovative Swiffer home-cleaning gadget was really cleaning up. However, it worked only on hardwood, tile, and linoleum floors, and some 75 percent of U.S. floors are carpeted. P&G needed to find a way to "Swiffer" a carpet. Award-winning design firm IDEO set out to help P&G design a solution. But IDEO didn't start in its labs with R&D-like scientific research. Instead, IDEO designers went into people's homes, snapping photos and asking questions about how folks cleaned their carpets. There was a young mother who complained that the noise of the vacuum scared her child, but she had time to vacuum only when he was asleep. There was an older woman with a busted knee who relied on two vacuums—a heavy one for once-a-

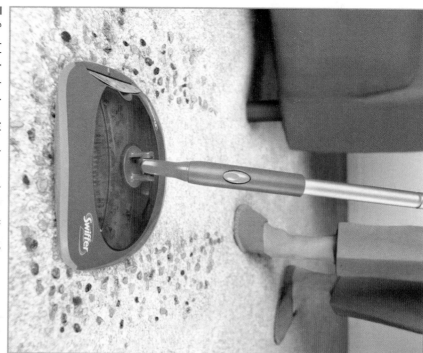

■ Good design begins with a deep understanding of customer needs. P&G's Swiffer CarpetFlick looks good, but it works even better than it looks.

week cleaning when she took painkillers for her knee, and one she could easily lift for spot cleaning. Most consumers found vacuum cleaners bulky, noisy, and hard to use; carpet sweepers were more convenient but not very effective.

With this deep understanding of customer needs, IDEO's design team immersed itself in an intensive, 10-month development effort, attacking countless messy carpet squares—sucking, scraping, stamping, sticking, and trying anything else they could come up with to clean carpet. The result was a revolutionary new carpet sweeping system, the Swiffer CarpetFlick, which flicks dirt, crumbs, and other small bits off the carpet and traps them onto a disposable adhesive cartridge. The CarpetFlick design certainly *looks* good—it is sleek, stylish, and very "Swifferesque." But it *works* even better than it looks. It is quiet, convenient, and effective—just the thing for "quick carpet clean-ups between vacuuming."[10]

Thus, product designers should think less about product attributes and technical specifications and more about how customers will use and benefit from the product. IDEO has used this same customer-experience approach to develop award-winning designs for everything from high-tech consumer electronics products and more user-friendly software to more satisfying and functional hotel rooms, retail stores, and health clinic layouts.[11]

Just as good design can improve customer value, cut costs, and create strong competitive advantage, poor design can result in lost sales and embarrassment.

When you're a bike-lock maker whose slogan is "Tough World, Tough Locks," it doesn't get much tougher than finding out that most of the locks you've been making for the past 30 years can be picked with a Bic pen. That, sadly, is what happened to Ingersoll-Rand subsidiary Kryptonite, after bloggers began posting videos showing just how easy it was to pop open the company's ubiquitous U-shaped locks. Kryptonite reacted quickly, agreeing to exchange old locks for new Bic-proof ones. But the damage was already done. The news spread quickly through cycling chat rooms and blogs, and within weeks the company was sued for alleged product defects. The design mistake damaged Kryptonite's pocketbook as well as its reputation. Exchanging the locks cost the company an estimated $10 million. In the meantime, many dealers have received no shipments of new locks, costing Kryptonite as much as an additional $6 million in sales.[12]

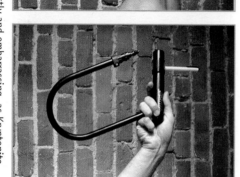

■ Poor product design can be costly and embarrassing, as Kryptonite learned when bloggers revealed that most of the locks it had been making for the past 30 years could be picked with a Bic pen.

Branding

Perhaps the most distinctive skill of professional marketers is their ability to build and manage brands. A **brand** is a name, term, sign, symbol, or design, or a combination of these, that identifies the maker or seller of a product or service. Consumers view a brand

Brand

A name, term, sign, symbol, or design, or a combination of these that identifies the products or services of one seller or group of sellers and differentiates them from those of competitors.

as an important part of a product, and branding can add value to a product. For example, most consumers would perceive a bottle of White Linen perfume as a high-quality, expensive product. But the same perfume in an unmarked bottle would likely be viewed as lower in quality, even if the fragrance was identical.

Branding has become so strong that today hardly anything goes unbranded. Salt is packaged in branded containers, common nuts and bolts are packaged with a distributor's label, and automobile parts—spark plugs, tires, filters—bear brand names that differ from those of the automakers. Even fruits, vegetables, dairy products, and poultry are branded—Sunkist oranges, Dole Classic Iceberg Salads, Horizon Organic milk, and Perdue chickens.

Branding helps buyers in many ways. Brand names help consumers identify products that might benefit them. Brands also say something about product quality and consistency—buyers who always buy the same brand know that they will get the same features, benefits, and quality each time they buy. Branding also gives the seller several advantages. The brand name becomes the basis on which a whole story can be built around a product's special qualities. The seller's brand name and trademark provide legal protection for unique product features that otherwise might be copied by competitors. And branding helps the seller to segment markets. For example, General Mills can offer Cheerios, Wheaties, Chex, Total, Kix, Golden Grahams, Trix, and many other cereal brands, not just one general product for all consumers. We will discuss branding strategy in more detail later in the chapter.

Packaging

Packaging

The activities of designing and producing the container or wrapper for a product.

Packaging involves designing and producing the container or wrapper for a product. Traditionally, the primary function of the package was to hold and protect the product. In recent times, however, numerous factors have made packaging an important marketing tool. Increased competition and clutter on retail store shelves means that packages must now perform many sales tasks—from attracting attention, to describing the product, to making the sale.

Companies are realizing the power of good packaging to create instant consumer recognition of the company or brand. For example, in an average supermarket, which stocks 15,000 to 17,000 items, the typical shopper passes by some 300 items per minute, and more than 60 percent of all purchases are made on impulse. In this highly competitive environment, the package may be the seller's last chance to influence buyers. "Not long ago, the package was merely the product's receptacle, and the brand message was elsewhere—usually on TV," says a packaging expert. But changes in the marketplace environment are now "making the package itself an increasingly important selling medium."[13]

Poorly designed packages can cause headaches for consumers and lost sales for the company. By contrast, innovative packaging can give a company an advantage over competitors and boost sales. Sometimes even seemingly small packaging improvements can make a big difference. For example, Heinz revolutionized the 170-year-old condiments industry by inverting the good old ketchup bottle, letting customers quickly squeeze out even the last bit of ketchup. In the year following the new bottle's debut, Heinz ketchup sales grew at three times the industry rate. It started a packaging trend that quickly spread to other categories. Similarly, Kraft learned that many Chips Ahoy customers were frustrated by those hard-to-use, endopening bags. They often transferred the cookies into jars for easier access and to keep them fresh. Kraft solved both problems by creating a resealable bag that opens from the top. In the following year, the new packaging raked in sales nearly double those of the old packaging. "Companies make a lot of money by making things less annoying," says a packaging expert.[14]

In recent years, product safety has also become a major packaging concern. We have all learned to deal with hard-to-open "childproof" packaging. And after the rash of product tampering scares during the 1980s, most drug producers and food makers now put their products in tamper-resistant packages. In making packaging decisions, the company also must heed growing environmental concerns. Fortunately, many companies have gone "green" by reducing their packaging and using environmentally responsible packaging materials.

■ Innovative packaging can give a company an advantage over competitors and boost sales. When Heinz inverted the good old ketchup bottle, nextyear sales grew at three times the industry rate.

Labeling

Labels range from simple tags attached to products to complex graphics that are part of the package. They perform several functions. At the very least, the label *identifies* the product or brand, such as the name Sunkist stamped on oranges. The label might also *describe* several things about the product—who made it, where it was made, when it was made, its contents, how it is to be used, and how to use it safely. Finally, the label might help to *promote* the product and support its positioning.

For example, in the never-ending search for ways to stand out, the apparel industry seems to be rediscovering the promotional value of the product label.

Some clothing labels send strong messages. A "booklet tag" hanging from a workout garment might reinforce the brand's positioning, describing in detail how the garment is used by certain high-profile athletes or what types of special materials are used in its construction. Other brasher statements include pocket flashers and "lenticular tags," which generate 3-D or animation effects. At the other extreme, tagless heat-transfer labels are replacing sewn-in woven labels, promising ultimate comfort. Even low-key labels are using more brilliant colors or elaborate graphics, beautifying the product and reinforcing the brand message. Rich treatments on labels add pizzazz to luxury items; futuristic tags support emerging technical, man-made fabrications; tags adorned with playful characters evoke a sense of fun for kids' garments. "The product label is a key cog in branding strategy," says a labeling expert. "The look, feel, or even smell of the label—if done creatively—can complement a brand."[15]

Along with the positives, labeling also raises concerns. There has been a long history of legal concerns about packaging and labels. The Federal Trade Commission Act of 1914 held that false, misleading, or deceptive labels or packages constitute unfair competition. Labels can mislead customers, fail to describe important ingredients, or fail to include needed safety warnings. As a result, several federal and state laws regulate labeling. The most prominent is the Fair Packaging and Labeling Act of 1966, which set mandatory labeling requirements, encouraged voluntary industry packaging standards, and allowed federal agencies to set packaging regulations in specific industries.

Labeling has been affected in recent times by *unit pricing* (stating the price per unit of standard measure), *open dating* (stating the expected shelf life of the product), and *nutritional labeling* (stating the nutritional values in the product). The Nutritional Labeling and Educational Act of 1990 requires sellers to provide detailed nutritional information on food products, and recent sweeping actions by the Food and Drug Administration regulate the use of health-related terms such as *low fat, light,* and *high fiber.* Sellers must ensure that their labels contain all the required information.

Product Support Services

Customer service is another element of product strategy. A company's offer usually includes some support services, which can be a minor or a major part of the total offering. Later in the chapter, we will discuss services as products in themselves. Here, we discuss services that augment actual products.

The first step is to survey customers periodically to assess the value of current services and to obtain ideas for new ones. For example, Cadillac holds regular focus group interviews with owners and carefully watches complaints that come into its dealerships. From this careful monitoring, Cadillac has learned that buyers are very upset by repairs that are not done correctly the first time.

Once the company has assessed the value of various support services to customers, it must next assess the costs of providing these services. It can then develop a package of services that will both delight customers and yield profits to the company. Based on its consumer interviews, Cadillac has set up a system directly linking each dealership with a group of 10 engineers who can help walk mechanics through difficult repairs. Such actions helped Cadillac jump, in one year, from 14th to 7th in independent rankings of service. For the past several years, Cadillac has rated at or near the top of its industry on the American Customer Satisfaction Index.[16]

Many companies are now using a sophisticated mix of phone, e-mail, fax, Internet, and interactive voice and data technologies to provide support services that were not possible before. Consider the following examples:

Some online merchants are watching where you surf, then opening a chat window on your screen to ask—just as they would in the store—if you have questions about the goods they see you eyeing. For example, at the Scion Web site, clicking on the Scion Chat button puts you in real-time touch with someone who can answer your questions or help you to design your personalized Scion. Hewlett-Packard sends pop-up chat boxes to visitors who are shopping on HP.com's pages for digital-photography products. If a shopper loiters a few minutes over some gear, up pops a photo of an attractive woman with the words, "Hello, need information? An HP live chat representative is standing by to assist you." Click on "Go" and type a question, and a live sales agent responds immediately. Since launching its pop-up chat feature, HP has seen a 65 percent surge in online questions. SunTrust Banks is taking proactive chat one step further by experimenting with co-browsing. This feature essentially lets chat agents take control of a customer's computer screen, opening Web pages directly on their browser to help them find what they're looking for. In the future, "call cams" will even let customers see an agent on their screen and talk directly through voice-over-Web capabilities.[17]

■ Product support services: Many companies are now using a sophisticated mix of interactive technologies to provide support services that were not possible before. For example, at the Scion Web site, clicking the Scion Chat button puts you in realtime touch with someone who can answer your questions or help you to design your own personalized Scion.

Product line

A group of products that are closely related because they function in a similar manner, are sold to the same customer groups, are marketed through the same types of outlets, or fall within given price ranges.

Product Line Decisions

Beyond decisions about individual products and services, product strategy also calls for building a product line. A **product line** is a group of products that are closely related because they function in a similar manner, are sold to the same customer groups, are marketed through the same types of outlets, or fall within given price ranges. For example, Nike produces several lines of athletic shoes and apparel, and Charles Schwab produces several lines of financial services.

The major product line decision involves *product line length*—the number of items in the product line. The line is too short if the manager can increase profits by adding items; the line is too long if the manager can increase profits by dropping items. Managers need to conduct a periodic *product line analysis* to assess each product item's sales and profits and to understand how each item contributes to the line's performance.

Product line length is influenced by company objectives and resources. For example, one objective might be to allow for upselling. Thus BMW wants to move customers up from its 3-series models to 5- and 7-series models. Another objective might be to allow cross-selling: Hewlett-Packard sells printers as well as cartridges. Still another objective might be to protect against economic swings: Gap runs several clothing-store chains (Gap, Old Navy, Banana Republic, Forth & Towne) covering different price points.

A company can lengthen its product line in two ways: by *line stretching* or by *line filling*. *Product line stretching* occurs when a company lengthens its product line beyond its current range. The company can stretch its line downward, upward, or both ways.

Companies located at the upper end of the market can stretch their lines *downward*. A company may stretch downward to plug a market hole that otherwise would attract a new competitor or to respond to a competitor's attack on the upper end. Or it may add low-end products because it finds faster growth taking place in the low-end segments. DaimlerChrysler stretched its Mercedes line downward for all these reasons. Facing a slow-growth luxury car market and attacks by Japanese automakers on its high-end positioning, it successfully introduced its Mercedes C-Class cars. These models sell in the $30,000 range without harming the firm's ability to sell other Mercedes at much higher prices.

Companies at the lower end of a market can stretch their product lines *upward*. Sometimes, companies stretch upward in order to add prestige to their current products. Or they may be attracted by a faster growth rate or higher margins at the higher end. For example, each of the leading Japanese auto companies introduced an upmarket automobile: Toyota

Product line stretching: Marriott offers a full line of hotel brands, each aimed at a different target market.

launched Lexus; Nissan launched Infinity; and Honda launched Acura. They used entirely new names rather than their own names.

Companies in the middle range of the market may decide to stretch their lines in *both directions*. Marriott did this with its hotel product line. Along with regular Marriott hotels, it added new branded hotel lines to serve both the upper and lower ends of the market. Renaissance Hotels & Resorts aims to attract and please top executives; Marriott, upper and middle managers; Courtyard by Marriott, salespeople and other "road warriors"; and Fairfield Inn by Marriott, vacationers and business travelers on a tight travel budget. Marriott ExecuStay provides temporary housing for those relocating or away on long-term assignments of 30 days or longer. Residence Inn by Marriott provides a relaxed, residential atmosphere—a home away from home for people who travel for a living. TownePlace Suites by Marriott pro-vide a comfortable atmosphere at a moderate price for extended-stay travelers. And SpringHill Suites by Marriott has 25 percent more space than an average hotel room—offering a separate living and work space for business travelers.[18] The major risk with this strategy is that some travelers will trade down after finding that the lower-price hotels in the Marriott chain give them pretty much everything they want. However, Marriott would rather capture its customers who move downward than lose them to competitors.

An alternative to product line stretching is *product line filling*—adding more items within the present range of the line. There are several reasons for product line filling: reach-ing for extra profits, satisfying dealers, using excess capacity, being the leading full-line com-pany, and plugging holes to keep out competitors. However, line filling is overdone if it results in cannibalization and customer confusion. The company should ensure that new items are noticeably different from existing ones.

Product Mix Decisions

An organization with several product lines has a product mix. A **product mix (or product portfo-lio)** consists of all the product lines and items that a particular seller offers for sale. Colgate's prod-uct mix consists of four major product lines: oral care, personal care, home care, and pet nutrition. Each product line consists of several sublines. For example, the home care line consists of dish-washing, fabric conditioning, and household cleaning products. Each line and subline has many individual items. Altogether, Colgate's product mix includes hundreds of items.

A company's product mix has four important dimensions: width, length, depth, and con-sistency. Product mix *width* refers to the number of different product lines the company car-ries. For example, Colgate markets a fairly contained product mix, consisting of personal and home care products that you can "trust to care for yourself, your home, and the ones you love." By comparison, 3M markets more than 60,000 products, a typical Wal-Mart stocks 100,000 to 120,000 items, and GE manufactures as many as 250,000 items, ranging from light-bulbs to jet engines.

Product mix *length* refers to the total number of items the company carries within its product lines. Colgate typically carries many brands within each line. For example, its

Margin notes

Product mix (or product portfolio)
The set of all product lines and items that a particular seller offers for sale.

personal care line includes Softsoap liquid soaps and body washes, Irish Spring bar soaps, Speed Stick and Crystal Clean deodorants, and Skin Bracer and Afta aftershaves.

Product mix *depth* refers to the number of versions offered of each product in the line. Colgate toothpastes come in 11 varieties, ranging from Colgate Total, Colgate Tartar Control, Colgate 2in1, and Colgate Cavity Protection to Colgate Sensitive, Colgate Fresh Confidence, Colgate Max Fresh, Colgate Simply White, Colgate Sparkling White, Colgate Kids Toothpastes, and Colgate Baking Soda & Peroxide. Then, each variety comes in its own special forms and formulations. For example, you can buy Colgate Total in regular, mint fresh stripe, whitening paste and gel, advanced fresh gel, or 2in1 liquid gel versions.[19] (Talk about niche marketing! Remember our Chapter 7 discussion?)

Finally, the *consistency* of the product mix refers to how closely related the various product lines are in end use, production requirements, distribution channels, or some other way. Colgate's product lines are consistent insofar as they are consumer products that go through the same distribution channels. The lines are less consistent insofar as they perform different functions for buyers.

These product mix dimensions provide the handles for defining the company's product strategy. The company can increase its business in four ways. It can add new product lines, widening its product mix. In this way, its new lines build on the company's reputation in its other lines. The company can lengthen its existing product lines to become a more full-line company. Or it can add more versions of each product and thus deepen its product mix. Finally, the company can pursue more product line consistency—or less— depending on whether it wants to have a strong reputation in a single field or in several fields.

Branding Strategy: Building Strong Brands

Some analysts see brands as *the* major enduring asset of a company, outlasting the company's specific products and facilities. John Stewart, co-founder of Quaker Oats, once said, "If this business were split up, I would give you the land and bricks and mortar, and I would keep the brands and trademarks, and I would fare better than you." A former CEO of McDonald's agrees: "If every asset we own, every building, and every piece of equipment were destroyed in a terrible natural disaster, we would be able to borrow all the money to replace it very quickly because of the value of our brand. . . . The brand is more valuable than the totality of all these assets."[20]

Thus, brands are powerful assets that must be carefully developed and managed. In this section, we examine the key strategies for building and managing brands.

Brand Equity

Brands are more than just names and symbols. They are a key element in the company's relationships with consumers. Brands represent consumers' perceptions and feelings about a product and its performance—everything that the product or service *means* to consumers. In the final analysis, brands exist in the minds of consumers.

The real value of a strong brand is its power to capture consumer preference and loyalty. Brands vary in the amount of power and value they have in the marketplace. Some brands— such as Coca-Cola, Tide, Nike, Harley-Davidson, Disney, and others—become larger-than-life icons that maintain their power in the market for years, even generations. These brands win in the marketplace not simply because they deliver unique benefits or reliable service. Rather, they succeed because they forge deep connections with customers.

Consumers sometimes bond *very* closely with specific brands. Consider the feelings of one Michigan couple about Black & Decker's DeWalt power tool brand:[21]

Rick and Rose Whitaker weren't comfortable with the idea of a white-gown-and-tux wedding. They kept coming back to the fact that Rick, a carpenter, had a passion for power tools. Specifically, DeWalt power tools. So at the July nuptials, 50-plus guests gathered in Rick's backyard wearing DeWalt's trademark yellow-and-black T-shirts. The Michigan couple—both are now 44—dressed in shirts emblazoned with an image of DeWalt-sponsored NASCAR driver Matt Kenseth. They made their way to a wooden chapel that they had built with their DeWalt gear. There they exchanged power tools, cutting the cake with a power saw.

A powerful brand has high *brand equity*. **Brand equity** is the positive differential effect that knowing the brand name has on customer response to the product or service. One measure of a brand's equity is the extent to which customers are willing to pay more for the brand. One study found that 72 percent of customers would pay a 20 percent premium for their brand of choice relative to the closest competing brand; 40 percent said they would pay a 50 percent premium. Tide and Heinz lovers are willing to pay a 100 percent premium.[22]

A brand with strong brand equity is a very valuable asset. *Brand valuation* is the process of estimating the total financial value of a brand. Measuring such value is difficult. However, according to one estimate, the brand value of Coca-Cola is $67 billion, Microsoft is $57 billion, and IBM is $56 billion. Other brands rating among the world's most valuable include GE, Intel, Nokia, Toyota, Disney, McDonald's, and Mercedes-Benz.[23]

High brand equity provides a company with many competitive advantages. A powerful brand enjoys a high level of consumer brand awareness and loyalty. Because consumers expect stores to carry the brand, the company has more leverage in bargaining with resellers. Because the brand name carries high credibility, the company can more easily launch line and brand extensions. A powerful brand offers the company some defense against fierce price competition.

Above all, however, a powerful brand forms the basis for building strong and profitable customer relationships. The fundamental asset underlying brand equity is *customer equity*—the value of the customer relationships that the brand creates. A powerful brand is important, but what it really represents is a profitable set of loyal customers. The proper focus of marketing is building customer equity, with brand management serving as a major marketing tool. Says one marketing expert, "Companies need to be thought of as portfolios of products."[24]

Building Strong Brands

Branding poses challenging decisions to the marketer. Figure 8.3 shows that the major brand strategy decisions involve brand positioning, brand name selection, brand sponsorship, and brand development.

Brand Positioning

Marketers need to position their brands clearly in target customers' minds. They can position brands at any of three levels.[25] At the lowest level, they can position the brand on *product attributes*. Thus, The Body Shop marketers can talk about their products' natural, environmentally friendly ingredients, unique scents, and special textures. However, attributes are the least desirable level for brand positioning. Competitors can easily copy attributes. More

■ Consumers sometimes bond very closely with specific brands. Jokes the bride: "He loves DeWalt nearly as much as he loves me."

Brand equity

The positive differential effect that knowing the brand name has on customer response to the product or service.

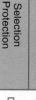

FIGURE 8.3 Major brand strategy decisions

Brand positioning	Brand name selection	Brand sponsorship	Brand development
Attributes Benefits Beliefs and values	Selection Protection	Manufacturer's brand Private brand Licensing Co-branding	Line extensions Brand extensions Multibrands New brands

important, customers are not interested in attributes as such; they are interested in what the attributes will do for them.

A brand can be better positioned by associating its name with a desirable *benefit*. Thus, The Body Shop can go beyond product ingredients and talk about the resulting beauty benefits, such as clearer skin from its Tea Tree Oil Facial Wash and sun-kissed cheeks from its Bronzing Powder. Some successful brands positioned on benefits are Volvo (safety), FedEx (guaranteed on-time delivery), Nike (performance), and Lexus (quality).

The strongest brands go beyond attribute or benefit positioning. They are positioned on strong *beliefs and values*. These brands pack an emotional wallop. Thus, The Body Shop can talk not just about environmentally friendly ingredients and skin-care benefits, but about how purchasing these products empowers its socially conscious customer to "make up your mind, not just your face."26 Successful brands engage customers on a deep, emotional level. Brands such as Starbucks, Victoria's Secret, and Godiva rely less on a product's tangible attributes and more on creating surprise, passion, and excitement surrounding a brand.

When positioning a brand, the marketer should establish a mission for the brand and a vision of what the brand must be and do. A brand is the company's promise to deliver a specific set of features, benefits, services, and experiences consistently to the buyers. The brand promise must be simple and honest. Motel 6, for example, offers clean rooms, low prices, and good service but does not promise expensive furniture or large bathrooms. In contrast, The Ritz-Carlton offers luxurious rooms and a truly memorable experience but does not promise low prices.

The New Godiva Gold Collection

Get lost in a golden moment. Luscious new pieces and your favorite classics all created with your utmost chocolate desires in mind.

793 Madison Avenue
godiva.com

SOME WOMEN
FOLLOW THE TRENDS.
THE
GODIVA
Chocolatier
DEVOUR THEM.

■ Brand positioning: The strongest brands go beyond attribute or benefit positioning. Godiva engages customers on a deeper level, touching universal emotions.

Brand Name Selection

A good name can add greatly to a product's success. However, finding the best brand name is a difficult task. It begins with a careful review of the product and its benefits, the target market, and proposed marketing strategies. After that, naming a brand becomes part science, part art, and a measure of instinct (see Real Marketing 8.1).

Desirable qualities for a brand name include the following: (1) It should suggest something about the product's benefits and qualities. Examples: Beautyrest, Craftsman, Curves, OFF! bug spray. (2) It should be easy to pronounce, recognize, and remember. Short names help. Examples: Tide, Silk, JetBlue. But longer ones are sometimes effective. Example: "I Can't Believe It's Not Butter" margarine. (3) The brand name should be distinctive. Examples: Lexus, Kodak, Oracle. (4) It should be extendable: Amazon.com began as an online bookseller but chose a name that would allow expansion into other categories. (5) The name should translate easily into foreign languages. Before spending $100 million to change its name to Exxon, Standard Oil of New Jersey tested several names in 54 languages in more than 150 foreign markets. It found that the name Enco referred to a stalled engine when pronounced in Japanese. (6) It should be capable of registration and legal protection. A brand name cannot be registered if it infringes on existing brand names.

Once chosen, the brand name must be protected. Many firms try to build a brand name that will eventually become identified with the product category. Brand names such as Kleenex, Levi's, Jell-O, BAND-AID, Scotch Tape, Formica, Ziploc, and Fiberglass have succeeded in this way. However, their very success may threaten the company's rights to the name. Many originally protected brand names—such as cellophane, aspirin, nylon, kerosene, linoleum, yo-yo, trampoline, escalator, thermos, and shredded wheat—are now generic names that any seller can use. To protect their brands, marketers present them carefully using the word "brand" and the registered trademark symbol, as in "BAND-AID® Brand Adhesive Bandages."

Brand Sponsorship

A manufacturer has four sponsorship options. The product may be launched as a *manufacturer's brand* (or national brand), as when Kellogg and Apple sell their output under their own manufacturer's brand names. Or the manufacturer may sell to resellers who give it a *private brand* (also called a *store brand* or *distributor brand*). Although most manufacturers create their own brand names, others market *licensed brands*. Finally, two companies can join forces and *co-brand* a product.

MANUFACTURER'S BRANDS VERSUS PRIVATE BRANDS Manufacturers' brands have long dominated the retail scene. In recent times, however, an increasing number of retailers and wholesalers have created their own **private brands** (or **store brands**). And in many industries, these private brands are giving manufacturers' brands a real run for their money:

Melanie Turner has forgotten her shopping list, but the 42-year-old pension consultant doesn't seem to mind. Entering her local Costco store, Turner knows right where she's going. In the dish detergent section, her hand goes past Procter & Gamble's Cascade to grab two 96-ounce bottles of Kirkland Signature, the in-store brand that Costco has plastered on everything from cashews to cross-trainer sneakers. Trolling for some fresh fish for dinner, she hauls in a 2 1/2-pound package of tilapia—it, too, emblazoned with the bold red, white, and black Kirkland logo. Then it's off to the paper aisle, where she picks up mammoth packs of Kirkland dinner napkins, Kirkland toilet paper, and . . . wait, where are the Kirkland paper towels? Her eyes scan the store's maze of hulking pallets—no sign of them—before coming to rest on a 12-pack of P&G's Bounty. A moment of decision. "I'll wait on this," she says finally.

And there, in microcosm, is why Procter & Gamble, Unilever, Kraft, and just about every consumer-goods company out there. Her shopping cart is headed for the checkout aisle, and there's hardly a national brand in it. . . . A subtle tectonic shift has been reshaping the world of brands. Retailers—once the lowly peddlers of brands that were made and marketed by big, important manufacturers—are now behaving like full-fledged marketers.[27]

Private brand (or store brand)
A brand created and owned by a reseller of a product or service.

■ An increasing number of retailers have created their own store brands. Costco's Kirkland brand adorns everything from baby wipes to barbeques.

It seems that almost every retailer now carries its own store brands. Wal-Mart offers Sam's Choice beverages and food products, Equate pharmacy and health and beauty products, and White Cloud brand toilet tissue, diapers, detergent, and fabric softener. More than half the products at your local Target are private brands, and grocery giant Kroger markets some 8,000 items under a variety of private brands, such as Private Selection, Kroger Brand, F.M.V. (For Maximum Value), Naturally Preferred, and Everyday Living. And private labels make up more than 80 percent of Trader Joe's merchandise. At the other end of the spectrum, upscale retailer Saks Fifth Avenue carries its own clothing line, which features $98 men's ties, $200 halter-tops, and $250 cotton dress shirts.

In all, private brands capture more than 20 percent of all U.S. consumer products sales. Private-label apparel, such as Gap, The Limited, Arizona Jeans (JC Penney), and Liz Lange (Target), captures a 36 percent share of all U.S. apparel sales.[28]

■ Licensing: Nickelodeon has developed a stable full of hugely popular characters—such as Dora the Explorer, the Rugrats clan, and SpongeBob SquarePants—which generate more than $5 billion in annual retail sales.

sales. "When it comes to licensing its brands for consumer products, Nickelodeon has proved that it has the Midas touch," states a brand licensing expert.[30]

Co-branding

Co-branding
The practice of using the established brand names of two different companies on the same product.

CO-BRANDING Although companies have been **co-branding** products for many years, there has been a recent resurgence in co-branded products. Last year alone, 524 new co-branded products were introduced. Co-branding occurs when two established brand names of different companies are used on the same product. For example, Bravo! Foods (which markets Slammers dairy brands) co-branded with MasterFoods (which markets M&Ms, Snickers, Starburst, and many other familiar candy brands) to create Starburst Slammers, 3 Musketeers Slammers, and Milky Way Slammers. GE worked with Culligan to develop its Water by Culligan Profile Performance refrigerator with a built-in Culligan water filtration system. In most co-branding situations, one company licenses another company's well-known brand to use in combination with its own.

Co-branding offers many advantages. Because each brand dominates in a different category, the combined brands create broader consumer appeal and greater brand equity. Co-branding also allows a company to expand its existing brand into a category it might otherwise have difficulty entering alone. For example, consider the co-branding efforts of SunTrust Banks and Wal-Mart, through which SunTrust is setting up in-store branches co-branded as "Wal-Mart Money Center by SunTrust." The arrangement gives SunTrust a presence in Wal-Mart's massive supercenters. In return, it gives Wal-Mart a foothold in financial services and lets it serve its customers better by offering check cashing, money transfers, money orders, and other services.[31]

Co-branding also has limitations. Such relationships usually involve complex legal contracts and licenses. Co-branding partners must carefully coordinate their advertising, sales promotion, and other marketing efforts. Finally, when co-branding, each partner must trust the other will take good care of its brand. For example, consider the marriage between Kmart and the Martha Stewart Everyday housewares brand. When Kmart declared bankruptcy, it cast a shadow on the Martha Stewart brand. In turn, when Martha Stewart was convicted and jailed for illegal financial dealings, it created negative associations for Kmart. Kmart was further embarrassed when Martha Stewart recently struck a major licensing agreement with

Macy's, announcing that it would separate from Kmart when the current contract ends in 2009. Thus, as one manager puts it, "Giving away your brand is a lot like giving away your child—you want to make sure everything is perfect."[32]

Brand Development

A company has four choices when it comes to developing brands (see Figure 8.4). It can introduce *line extensions*, *brand extensions*, *multibrands*, or *new brands*.

FIGURE 8.4
Brand development strategies

	Product category	
Brand name	Existing	New
Existing	Line extension	Brand extension
New	Multibrands	New brands

LINE EXTENSIONS **Line extensions** occur when a company extends existing brand names to new forms, colors, sizes, ingredients, or flavors of an existing product category. Thus, Yoplait introduced several line extensions, including new yogurt flavors, a yogurt smoothie, and a yogurt with added cholesterol reducers. And Morton Salt has expanded its line to include regular iodized salt plus Morton Course Kosher Salt, Morton Sea Salt, Morton Lite Salt (low in sodium), Morton Popcorn Salt, Morton Salt Substitute, and several others. The vast majority of all new-product activity consists of line extensions.

A company might introduce line extensions as a low-cost, low-risk way to introduce new products. Or it might want to meet consumer desires for variety, to use excess capacity, or simply to command more shelf space from resellers. However, line extensions involve some risks. An overextended brand name might lose its specific meaning, or heavily extended brands can cause consumer confusion or frustration.

Want a Coke? Not so easy. Pick from more than 16 varieties. In zero-calorie versions alone, Coke comes in three subbrands—Diet Coke, Diet Coke with Splenda, and Coca-Cola Zero. Throw in the flavored and free versions—Diet Cherry Coke, Diet Coke with Lemon, Diet Coke with Lime, Diet Coke Black Cherry Vanilla, and Caffeine-Free Diet Coke—and you reach a dizzying nine diets from Coke. And that doesn't count "mid-calorie" Coca-Cola C2. Each subbrand has its own hype—Diet Coke tells you to "light it up," and Coke Zero allows you to "enjoy Coke-ness with zero calories." And Coca-Cola C2 has "1/2 the carbs, 1/2 the calories, all the great taste." But it's unlikely that many consumers fully appreciate the differences. Instead, the glut of extensions will likely cause what one expert calls "profusion confusion." Laments one cola consumer, "How many versions of Diet Coke do they need?"[33]

BRAND EXTENSIONS A **brand extension** extends a current brand name to new or modified products in a new category. For example, Kimberly-Clark extended its market-leading Huggies brand from disposable diapers to a full line of toiletries for tots, from shampoos, lotions, and diaper-rash ointments to baby wash, disposable washclothes, and disposable changing pads. Victorinox extended its venerable Swiss Army brand from multitool knives to products ranging from cutlery and ball point pens to watches, luggage, and apparel. And Brinks leveraged its strong reputation in commercial security to launch Brink's Home Security systems.

A brand extension gives a new product instant recognition and faster acceptance. It also saves the high advertising costs usually required to build a new brand name. At the same

Another risk is that sales of an extension may come at the expense of other items in the line. For example, the original Hershey's Kisses have now morphed into a full line of Kisses, including such morsels as Rich Dark Chocolate Hershey's Kisses, Hershey Kisses Filled with Caramel, Hershey Kisses Filled with Dulce de Leche, and a dozen others. Although all are doing well, the original Hershey's Kiss brand now seems like just another flavor. A line extension works best when it takes sales away from competing brands, not when it "cannibalizes" the company's other items.

Line extension
Extending an existing brand name to new forms, colors, sizes, ingredients, or flavors of an existing product category.

Brand extension
Extending an existing brand name to new product categories.

time, a brand extension strategy involves some risk. Brand extensions such as Bic pantyhose, Heinz pet food, LifeSavers gum, and Clorox laundry detergent met early deaths. The extension may confuse the image of the main brand. And if a brand extension fails, it may harm consumer attitudes toward the other products carrying the same brand name.

Further, a brand name may not be appropriate to a particular new product, even if it is well made and satisfying—would you consider buying a Harley-Davidson cake-decorating kit or an Evian water-filled padded bra (both failed)? Companies that are tempted to transfer a brand name must research how well the brand's associations fit the new product.[34]

MULTIBRANDS Companies often introduce additional brands in the same category. Thus, Procter & Gamble markets many different brands in each of its product categories. *Multibranding* offers a way to establish different features and appeal to different buying motives. It also allows a company to lock up more reseller shelf space.

A major drawback of multibranding is that each brand might obtain only a small market share, and none may be very profitable. The company may end up spreading its resources over many brands instead of building a few brands to a highly profitable level.

These companies should reduce the number of brands they sell in a given category and set up tighter screening procedures for new brands.

NEW BRANDS A company might believe that the power of its existing brand name is waning and a new brand name is needed. Or it may create a new brand name when it enters a new product category for which none of the company's current brand names are appropriate. For example, Toyota created the separate Scion brand, targeted toward GenY consumers. Japan's Matsushita uses separate names for its different families of consumer electronics products: Panasonic, Technics, JVC, and Quasar, to name just a few.

As with multibranding, offering too many new brands can result in a company spreading its resources too thin. And in some industries, such as consumer packaged goods, consumers and retailers have become concerned that there are already too many brands, with too few differences between them. Thus, Procter & Gamble, Frito-Lay, and other large consumer product marketers are now pursuing *megabrand* strategies—weeding out weaker brands and focusing their marketing dollars only on brands that can achieve the number-one or number-two market share positions in their categories. "We . . . sort through our smaller brands," says P&G's CEO, and "divest the ones that don't have a strategic role or cannot deliver."[35]

Managing Brands

Companies must manage their brands carefully. First, the brand's positioning must be continuously communicated to consumers. Major brand marketers often spend huge amounts on advertising to create brand awareness and to build preference and loyalty. For example, Verizon spends more than $1.7 billion annually to promote its brand. Coca-Cola spends $317 million on its Coca-Cola and Diet Coke brands.[36]

Such advertising campaigns can help to create name recognition, brand knowledge, and maybe even some brand preference. However, the fact is that brands are not maintained by advertising but by the *brand experience*. Today, customers come to know a brand through a wide range of contacts and touch points. These include advertising, but also personal experience with the brand, word of mouth, company Web pages, and many others. The company must put as much care into managing these touch points as it does into producing its ads. "A brand is a living entity," says former Disney chief executive Michael Eisner, "and it is enriched or undermined cumulatively over time, the product of a thousand small gestures."[37]

The brand's positioning will not take hold fully unless everyone in the company lives the brand. Therefore the company needs to train its people to be customer centered. Even better,

Brand extensions: Brinks leveraged its strong reputation in commercial security to launch Brink's Home Security systems.

the company should carry on internal brand building to help employees understand and be enthusiastic about the brand promise. Many companies go even further by training and encouraging their distributors and dealers to serve their customers well.

All of this suggests that managing a company's brand assets can no longer be left only to brand managers. Brand managers do not have enough power or scope to do all the things necessary to build and enhance their brands. Moreover, brand managers often pursue short-term results, whereas managing brands as assets calls for longer-term strategy. Thus, some companies are now setting up brand asset management teams to manage their major brands. Canada Dry and Colgate-Palmolive have appointed *brand equity managers* to maintain and protect their brands' images, associations, and quality and to prevent short-term actions by overeager brand managers from hurting the brand.

Finally, companies need to periodically audit their brands' strengths and weaknesses.[38] They should ask: Does our brand excel at delivering benefits that consumers truly value? Is the brand properly positioned? Do all of our consumer touch points support the brand's positioning? Do the brand's managers understand what the brand means to consumers? Does the brand receive proper, sustained support? The brand audit may turn up brands that need more support, brands that need to be dropped, or brands that must be rebranded or repositioned because of changing customer preferences or new competitors.

▐ Services Marketing

Services have grown dramatically in recent years. Services now account for close to 79 percent of U.S. gross domestic product. And the service industry is growing. By 2014, it is estimated that nearly four out of five jobs in the United States will be in service industries. Services are growing even faster in the world economy, making up 37 percent of the value of all international trade.[39]

Service industries vary greatly. *Governments* offer services through courts, employment services, hospitals, military services, police and fire departments, postal services, and schools. *Private not-for-profit organizations* offer services through museums, charities, churches, colleges, foundations, and hospitals. A large number of *business organizations* offer services—airlines, banks, hotels, insurance companies, consulting firms, medical and legal practices, entertainment companies, real-estate firms, retailers, and others.

Nature and Characteristics of a Service

A company must consider four special service characteristics when designing marketing programs: *intangibility, inseparability, variability,* and *perishability* (see Figure 8.5).

Service intangibility means that services cannot be seen, tasted, felt, heard, or smelled before they are bought. For example, people undergoing cosmetic surgery cannot see the result before the purchase. Airline passengers have nothing but a ticket and the promise that they and their luggage will arrive safely at the intended destination, hopefully at the same time. To reduce uncertainty, buyers look for "signals" of service quality. They draw conclusions about quality from the place, people, price, equipment, and communications that they can see.

FIGURE 8.5
Four service characteristics

Service intangibility
A major characteristic of services—they cannot be seen, tasted, felt, heard, or smelled before they are bought.

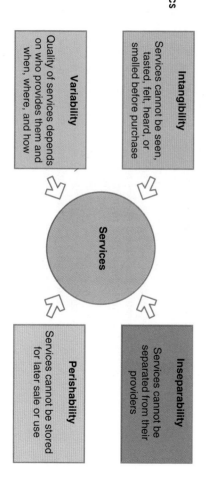

Intangibility
Services cannot be seen, tasted, felt, heard, or smelled before purchase

Variability
Quality of services depends on who provides them and when, where, and how

Services

Inseparability
Services cannot be separated from their providers

Perishability
Services cannot be stored for later sale or use

Therefore, the service provider's task is to make the service tangible in one or more ways and to send the right signals about quality. One analyst calls this *evidence management*, in which the service organization presents its customers with organized, honest evidence of its capabilities. The Mayo Clinic practices good evidence management:[40]

When it comes to hospitals, it's very hard for the average patient to judge the quality of the "product." You can't try it on, you can't return it if you don't like it, and you need an advanced degree to understand it. And so, when we're considering a medical facility, most of us unconsciously turn detective, looking for evidence of competence, caring, and integrity. The Mayo Clinic doesn't leave that evidence to chance. By carefully managing a set of visual and experiential clues, Mayo offers patients and their families concrete evidence of its strengths and values. For example, staff people at the clinic are trained to act in a way that clearly signals its patient-first focus. "My doctor calls me at home to check on how I am doing," marvels one patient. "She wants to work with what is best for my schedule." Mayo's physical facilities also send the right signals. They've been carefully designed to relieve stress, offer a place of refuge, create positive distractions, convey caring and respect, signal competence, accommodate families, and make it easy to find your way around. The result? Exceptionally positive word of mouth and abiding customer loyalty, which have allowed Mayo Clinic to build what is arguably the most powerful brand in health care—with very little advertising.

Physical goods are produced, then stored, later sold, and still later consumed. In contrast, services are first sold, then produced and consumed at the same time. **Service inseparability** means that services cannot be separated from their providers, whether the providers are people or machines. If a service employee provides the service, then the employee becomes a part of the service. Because the customer is also present as the service is produced, *provider-customer interaction* is a special feature of services marketing. Both the provider and the customer affect the service outcome.

Service variability means that the quality of services depends on who provides them as well as when, where, and how they are provided. For example, some hotels—say, Marriott—have reputations for providing better service than others. Still, within a given Marriott hotel, one registration-counter employee may be cheerful and efficient, whereas another standing just a few feet away may be unpleasant and slow. Even the quality of a single Marriott employee's service varies according to his or her energy and frame of mind at the time of each customer encounter.

Service perishability means that services cannot be stored for later sale or use. Some doctors charge patients for missed appointments because the service value existed only at that point and disappeared when the patient did not show up. The perishability of services is not a problem when demand is steady. However, when demand fluctuates, service firms often have difficult problems. For example, because of rush-hour demand, public transportation companies have to own much more equipment than they would if demand were even throughout the day. Thus, service firms often design strategies for producing a better match between demand and supply. Hotels and resorts charge lower prices in the off-season to attract more guests. And restaurants hire part-time employees to serve during peak periods.

Marketing Strategies for Service Firms

Just like manufacturing businesses, good service firms use marketing to position themselves strongly in chosen target markets. Target promises "Expect more, pay less." The Ritz-Carlton Hotels positions itself as offering a memorable experience that "enlivens the senses, instills well-being, and fulfills even the unexpressed wishes and needs of our guests." At the Mayo Clinic, "the needs of the patient come first." These and other service firms establish their positions through traditional marketing mix activities. However, because services differ from tangible products, they often require additional marketing approaches.

The Service-Profit Chain

In a service business, the customer and front-line service employee *interact* to create the service. Effective interaction, in turn, depends on the skills of front-line service employees and on the support processes backing these employees. Thus, successful service companies focus their attention on *both* their customers and their employees. They understand the **service-**

Service inseparability

A major characteristic of services—they are produced and consumed at the same time and cannot be separated from their providers.

Service variability

A major characteristic of services—their quality may vary greatly, depending on who provides them and when, where, and how.

Service perishability

A major characteristic of services—they cannot be stored for later sale or use.

Service-profit chain

The chain that links service firm profits with employee and customer satisfaction.

profit chain, which links service firm profits with employee and customer satisfaction. This chain consists of five links:[41]

- *Internal service quality:* superior employee selection and training, a quality work environment, and strong support for those dealing with customers, which results in . . .
- *Satisfied and productive service employees:* more satisfied, loyal, and hardworking employees, which results in . . .
- *Greater service value:* more effective and efficient customer value creation and service delivery, which results in . . .
- *Satisfied and loyal customers:* satisfied customers who remain loyal, repeat purchase, and refer other customers, which results in . . .
- *Healthy service profits and growth:* superior service firm performance.

Therefore, reaching service profits and growth goals begins with taking care of those who take care of customers (see Real Marketing 8.2). In fact, legendary founder and former CEO of Southwest Airlines, Herb Kelleher, always put employees first, not customers. His reasons? "If they're happy, satisfied, dedicated, and energetic, they'll take good care of customers," he says. "When the customers are happy, they come back, and that makes shareholders happy."[42] Consider Wegmans, a 71-store grocery chain in the Mid-Atlantic States.

Wegmans customers have a zeal for the store that borders on obsession. Says one regular, "Going there isn't just shopping, it's an event." A recent national survey of food retailer customer satisfaction put Wegmans at the top. Last, year, Wegmans received more than 7,000 letters from around the country, about half of them asking Wegmans to come to their town. The secret? Wegmans knows that happy, satisfied employees produce happy, satisfied customers. So Wegmans takes care of its employees. It pays higher salaries, shells out money for employee college scholarships, covers 100 percent of health insurance premiums for employees making less than $55,000 a year, and invests heavily in employee training. In fact, last year Wegmans topped *Fortune* magazine's best-companies-to-work-for list. "The biggest reason Wegmans is a shopping experience like no other is that it is an employer like no other," says a Wegmans watcher.[43]

Thus, service marketing requires more than just traditional external marketing using the Four Ps. Figure 8.6 shows that service marketing also requires *internal marketing* and *interactive marketing.* **Internal marketing** means that the service firm must orient and motivate its front-line service employees and supporting service people to work as a team to provide customer satisfaction. Marketers must get everyone in the organization customer-centered. In fact, internal marketing must precede external marketing.

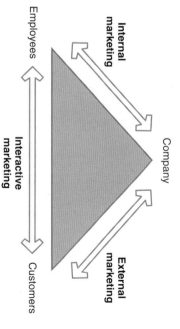

FIGURE 8.6
Three types of service marketing

- The service-profit chain: Happy employees make for happy customers. "The biggest reason Wegmans is a shopping experience like no other is that it is an employer like no other."

Real Marketing   The Ritz-Carlton: Taking Care of Those Who Take Care of Customers

8.2 The Ritz-Carlton, a chain of luxury hotels renowned for outstanding service, caters to the top 5 percent of corporate and leisure travelers. The company's Credo sets lofty customer-service goals: "The Ritz-Carlton Hotel is a place where the genuine care and comfort of our guests is our highest mission. . . . The Ritz-Carlton experience enlivens the senses, instills well-being, and fulfills even the unexpressed wishes and needs of our guests."

The Credo is more than just words on paper—The Ritz-Carlton delivers on its promises. In surveys of departing guests, some 95 percent report that they've had a truly memorable experience. In fact, at The Ritz-Carlton, exceptional service encounters have become almost commonplace. Take the experiences of Nancy and Harvey Heffner of Manhattan, who stayed at the Ritz-Carlton Naples, in Naples, Florida (recently rated the best hotel in the United States and fourth best in the world, by *Travel + Leisure* magazine). As reported in the *New York Times*:

"The hotel is elegant and beautiful," Mrs. Heffner said, "but more important is the beauty expressed by the staff. They can't do enough to please you." When the couple's son became sick last year in Naples, the hotel staff brought him hot tea with honey at all hours of the night, she said. When Mr. Heffner had to fly home on business for a day and his return flight was delayed, a driver for the hotel waited in the lobby most of the night.

Or how about this account: "An administrative assistant at The Ritz-Carlton Philadelphia overheard a guest lamenting that he'd forgotten to pack a pair of formal shoes and would have to wear hiking boots to an important meeting. Early the next morning, she delivered to the awestruck man a new pair of formal shoes in his size and favorite color."

Such personal, high-quality service has also made The Ritz-Carlton a favorite among conventioneers. For six straight years, the luxury hotel came out on top in *Business Travel News*'s Top U.S. Hotel Chain Survey of business travel buyers. "They not only treat us like kings when we hold our top-level meetings in their hotels, but we just never get any complaints," comments one convention planner. Says another, who had recently held a meeting at The Ritz-Carlton at Half Moon Bay, "The . . . first-rate catering and service-oriented convention services

its customer-contact employees and supporting service people to work as a *team* to provide customer satisfaction. Marketers must get everyone in the organization to be customer centered. In fact, internal marketing must *precede* external marketing. For example, The Ritz-Carlton orients its employees carefully, instills in them a sense of pride, and motivates them by recognizing and rewarding outstanding service deeds.

Interactive marketing means that service quality depends heavily on the quality of the buyer-seller interaction during the service encounter. In product marketing, product quality often depends little on how the product is obtained. But in services marketing, service quality depends on both the service deliverer and the quality of the delivery. Service marketers, therefore, have to master interactive marketing skills. Thus, Ritz-Carlton selects only "people who care about people" and instructs them carefully in the fine art of interacting with customers to satisfy their every need.

In today's marketplace, companies must know how to deliver interactions that are not only "high-tech" but also "high-touch." For example, customers can log onto the Charles Schwab Web site and access account information, investment research, real-time quotes, after-hours trading, and the Schwab learning center. They can also participate in live online events and chat online with customer service representatives. Customers seeking more-

The Ritz-Carlton knows that to deliver on its promise of creating truly memorable experiences, it must first take care of those who take care of customers.

Internal marketing
Orienting and motivating customer-contact employees and the supporting service people to work as a team to provide customer satisfaction.

Interactive marketing
Training service employees in the fine art of interacting with customers to satisfy their needs.

staff [and] The Ritz-Carlton's ambiance and beauty—the elegant, Grand Dame-style lodge, nestled on a bluff between two championship golf courses overlooking the Pacific Ocean—makes a day's work there seem anything but."

Since its incorporation in 1983, The Ritz-Carlton has received virtually every major award that the hospitality industry bestows. In addition, it's the only hotel company ever to win the prestigious Malcolm Baldrige National Quality Award and one of only two companies from any industry to win the award twice. The recent *Consumer Reports* Hotels issue ranked The Ritz-Carlton Hotel Company the number-one luxury hotel company in all areas, including value, service, upkeep, and problem resolution. More than 90 percent of The Ritz-Carlton customers return. And despite its hefty room rates, the chain enjoys a 70 percent occupancy rate, almost nine points above the industry average.

Most of the responsibility for keeping guests satisfied falls to The Ritz-Carlton's customer-contact employees. Thus, the hotel chain takes great care in finding just the right personnel. The Ritz-Carlton goes to great lengths to "rigorously—even fanatically—select and train employees, instill pride, and compensate generously," says an industry insider. "We don't hire or recruit, we select," says Ritz-Carlton's director of human resources. "We want only people who care about people," notes the company's vice president of quality. Once selected, employees are given intensive training in the art of coddling customers. New employees attend a two-day orientation, in which top management drums into them the 12 Ritz-Carlton "Service Values." "Service Value number one: "I build strong relationships and create Ritz-Carlton guests for life."

Employees are taught to do everything they can never to lose a guest. "There's no negotiating at The Ritz-Carlton when it comes to solving customer problems," says the quality executive. Staff learn that *anyone* who receives a customer complaint *owns* that complaint until it's resolved (Ritz-Carlton Service Value number six). They are trained to drop whatever they're doing to help a customer—no matter what they're doing or what their department. The Ritz-Carlton employees are empowered to handle problems on the spot, without consulting higher-ups. Each employee can spend up to $2,000 to redress a guest grievance. And each is allowed to break from his or her routine for as long as needed to make a guest happy. Thus, while

competitors are still reading guest comment cards to learn about customer problems, The Ritz-Carlton has already resolved them.

The Ritz-Carlton instills a sense of pride in its employees. "You serve," they are told, "but you are not servants." The company motto states, "We are ladies and gentlemen serving ladies and gentlemen." Employees understand their role in The Ritz-Carlton's success. "We might not be able to afford a hotel like this," says employee Tammy Patton, "but we can make it so people who can afford it will want to keep coming here." As the general manager of The Ritz-Carlton Naples puts it, "When you invite guests to your house, you want everything to be perfect."

The Ritz-Carlton recognizes and rewards employees who perform feats of outstanding service. Under its 5-Star Awards program, outstanding performers are nominated by peers and managers, and winners receive plaques at dinners celebrating their achievements. For on-the-spot recognition, managers award Gold Standard Coupons, redeemable for items in the gift shop and free weekend stays at the hotel. The Ritz-Carlton further motivates its employees with events such as Super Sports Day, an employee talent show, luncheons celebrating employment anniversaries and birthdays, a family picnic, and special themes in employee dining rooms. As a result, The Ritz-Carlton's employees appear to be just as satisfied as its customers. Employee turnover is less than 25 percent a year, compared with 44 percent at other luxury hotels.

The Ritz-Carlton's success is based on a simple philosophy: To take care of customers, you must first take care of those who take care of customers. Satisfied employees deliver high service value, which then creates satisfied customers. Satisfied customers, in turn, create sales and profits for the company.

Sources: Quotes and other information from Duff McDonald, "Roll Out the Blue Carpet," *Business 2.0,* May 2004, pp. 53–54; Marshall Krantz, "Buyers Say Four Seasons Is Most Luxurious," *Meeting News,* May 9, 2005, pp. 1–3; Edwin McDowell, "Ritz-Carlton's Keys to Good Service," *New York Times,* March 31, 1993, p. D1; "The Ritz-Carlton, Half Moon Bay," *Successful Meetings,* November 2001, p. 40; Bruce Serlen, "Ritz-Carlton Retains Hold on Corporate Deluxe Buyers," *Business Travel News,* February 7, 2005, pp. 15–17; Peter Sanders, "Takin' Off the Ritz—A Tad," *Wall Street Journal,* June 23, 2006, p. B1; and The Ritz-Carlton Web site at www.ritzcarlton.com, August 2006.

personal interactions can contact service reps by phone or visit a local Schwab branch office. Thus, Schwab has mastered interactive marketing at all three levels—calls, clicks, *and* visits.

Today, as competition and costs increase, and as productivity and quality decrease, more service marketing sophistication is needed. Service companies face three major marketing tasks: They want to increase their *service differentiation, service quality,* and *service productivity.*

Managing Service Differentiation

In these days of intense price competition, service marketers often complain about the difficulty of differentiating their services from those of competitors. To the extent that customers view the services of different providers as similar, they care less about the provider than the price.

The solution to price competition is to develop a differentiated offer, delivery, and image. The *offer* can include innovative features that set one company's offer apart from competitors' offers. Some hotels offer car-rental, banking, and business-center services in their lobbies and free high-speed Internet connections in their rooms. Airlines differentiate their offers through frequent-flyer award programs and special services. For example, Qantas offers personal entertainment screens at every seat and "Skybeds" for international business class flyers.

Lufthansa provides wireless Internet access and real-time surfing to every seat—it makes "an airplane feel like a cyber café." And British Airways offers spa services at its Arrivals Lounge at Heathrow airport and softer in-flight beds, plumper pillows, and cozier blankets. Says one ad: "Our goal is simple: to deliver the best service you can ask for, without you having to ask."

Service companies can differentiate their service *delivery* by having more able and reliable customer-contact people, by developing a superior physical environment in which the service product is delivered or by designing a superior delivery process. For example, many grocery chains now offer online shopping and home delivery as a better way to shop than having to drive, park, wait in line, and tote groceries home.

Finally, service companies also can work on differentiating their *images* through symbols and branding. The Harris Bank of Chicago adopted the lion as its symbol on its stationery, in its advertising, and even as stuffed animals offered to new depositors. The well-known Harris lion confers an image of strength on the bank. Other well-known service symbols include Merrill Lynch's bull, MGM's lion, McDonald's Golden Arches, and Allstate's "good hands."

Managing Service Quality

A service firm can differentiate itself by delivering consistently higher quality than its competitors do. Like manufacturers before them, most service industries have now joined the customer-driven quality movement. And like product marketers, service providers need to identify what target customers expect concerning service quality.

Unfortunately, service quality is harder to define and judge than product quality. For instance, it is harder to agree on the quality of a haircut than on the quality of a hair dryer. Customer retention is perhaps the best measure of quality—a service firm's ability to hang onto its customers depends on how consistently it delivers value to them.

Top service companies set high service-quality standards. They watch service performance closely, both their own and that of competitors. They do not settle for merely good service; they aim for 100 percent defect-free service. A 98 percent performance standard may sound good, but using this standard, UPS would lose or misdirect 296,000 packages each day and U.S. pharmacists would misfill close to 1.4 million prescriptions each week.[44]

Unlike product manufacturers who can adjust their machinery and inputs until everything is perfect, service quality will always vary, depending on the interactions between employees and customers. As hard as they try, even the best companies will have an occasional late delivery, burned steak, or grumpy employee. However, good *service recovery* can turn angry customers into loyal ones. In fact, good recovery can win more customer purchasing and loyalty than if things had gone well in the first place. Therefore, companies should take steps not only to provide good service every time but also to recover from service mistakes when they do occur.

The first step is to *empower* front-line service employees—to give them the authority, responsibility, and incentives they need to recognize, care about, and tend to customer needs. At Marriott, for example, well-trained employees are given the authority to do whatever it takes, on the spot, to keep guests happy. They are also expected to help management ferret out the cause of guests' problems and to inform managers of ways to improve overall hotel service and guests' comfort.

Managing Service Productivity

With their costs rising rapidly, service firms are under great pressure to increase service productivity. They can do so in several ways. They can train current employees better or hire

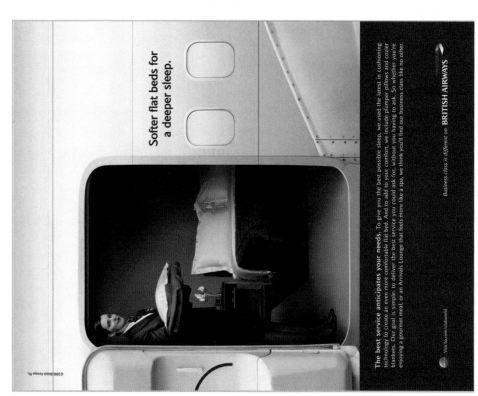

Softer flat beds for a deeper sleep.

The best service anticipates your needs. To give you the best possible sleep, we used the latest in cushioning technology to create an even more comfortable flat bed. And to add to your comfort, we include plumper pillows and cozier blankets. Our goal is simple: to deliver the best service you could ask for, without you having to ask. So whether you're enjoying a gourmet meal, or an Arrivals Lounge that feels more like a spa, we think you'll find our business class like no other.

Business class is different on **BRITISH AIRWAYS**

Visit ba.com/cluFworld

■ Service differentiation: At British Airways, says this ad, "Our goal is simple: to deliver the best service you can ask for, without you having to ask."

new ones who will work harder or more skillfully. Or they can increase the quantity of their service by giving up some quality. The provider can "industrialize the service" by adding equipment and standardizing production, as in McDonald's assembly-line approach to fast-food retailing. Finally, the service provider can harness the power of technology. Although we often think of technology's power to save time and costs in manufacturing companies, it also has great—and often untapped—potential to make service workers more productive.

However, companies must avoid pushing productivity so hard that doing so reduces quality. Attempts to industrialize a service or to cut costs can make a service company more efficient in the short run. But they can also reduce its longer-run ability to innovate, maintain service quality, or respond to consumer needs and desires. Many airlines are learning this lesson the hard way as they attempt to streamline and economize in the face of rising costs.

Over the past year, Northwest Airlines has stopped offering free magazines, pillows, movies, and even minibags of pretzels on its domestic flights. Passengers can still get an in-flight snack of raisins and nuts, but it costs $1. The airline is also charging a $15 fee for a roomier seat on the aisle or in an exit row. Combine that with higher fares and a sharply curtailed schedule, and it's little wonder that flyers rate Northwest dead last among the nation's major airlines. "If at all possible, I don't fly Northwest," says one veteran traveler, "I have found a lack of interest in the customer." A services marketing expert agrees: "The upshot is that some companies, in their passion to drive down costs, have mangled their relationships with customers."[45]

■ Pushing service productivity too far—in its passion to drive down costs, Northwest Airlines "mangled its relationships with customers."

Thus, in attempting to improve service productivity, companies must be mindful of how they create and deliver customer value. In short, they should be careful not to take the "service" out of service.

Reviewing the Concepts

1. Define *product* and the major classifications of products and services.

A product is more than a simple set of tangible features. In fact, many market offerings consist of combinations of both tangible goods and services, ranging from *pure tangible goods* at one extreme to *pure services* at the other. Each product or service offered to customers can be viewed on three levels. The *core product* consists of the core problem-solving benefits that consumers seek when they buy a product. The *actual product* exists around the core and includes the quality level, features, design, brand name, and packaging. The *augmented product* is the actual product plus the various services and benefits offered with it, such as warranty, free delivery, installation, and maintenance.

Products and services fall into two broad classes based on the types of consumers that use them. *Consumer products*—those bought by final consumers—are usually classified according to consumer shopping habits (convenience products, shopping products, specialty prod-

ucts, and unsought products). *Industrial products*—purchased for further processing or for use in conducting a business—include materials and parts, capital items, and supplies and services. Other marketable entities—such as organizations, persons, places, and ideas—can also be thought of as products.

2. Describe the decisions companies make regarding their individual products and services, product lines, and product mixes.

Individual product decisions involve product attributes, branding, packaging, labeling, and product support services. *Product attribute* decisions involve product quality, features, and style and design. *Branding* decisions include selecting a brand name and developing a brand strategy. *Packaging* provides many key benefits, such as protection, economy, convenience, and promotion. Package decisions often include designing *labels*, which identify, describe, and possibly promote the product. Companies also develop *product support services* that enhance customer service and satisfaction and safeguard against competitors.

Most companies produce a product line rather than a single product. A *product line* is a group of products that are related in function, customer-purchase needs, or distribution channels. *Line stretching* involves extending a line downward, upward, or in both directions to occupy a gap that might otherwise by filled by a competitor. In contrast, *line filling* involves adding items within the present range of the line. All product lines and items offered to customers by a particular seller make up the *product mix*. The mix can be described by four dimensions: width, length, depth, and consistency. These dimensions are the tools for developing the company's product strategy.

3. Discuss branding strategy—the decisions companies make in building and managing their brands.

Some analysts see brands as *the* major enduring asset of a company. Brands are more than just names and symbols—they embody everything that the product or service *means* to consumers. *Brand equity* is the positive differential effect that knowing the brand name has on customer response to the product or service. A brand with strong brand equity is a very valuable asset.

In building brands, companies need to make decisions about brand positioning, brand name selection, brand sponsorship, and brand development. The most powerful *brand positioning* builds around strong consumer beliefs and values. *Brand name selection* involves finding the best brand name based on a careful review of product benefits, the target market, and proposed marketing strategies. A manufacturer has four *brand sponsorship* options: it can launch a *manufacturer's brand* (or national brand), sell to resellers who use a *private brand*, market *licensed brands*, or join forces with another company to *co-brand* a product. A company also has four choices when it comes to developing brands. It can introduce *line extensions*, *brand extensions*, *multibrands*, or *new brands*.

Companies must build and manage their brands carefully. The brand's positioning must be continuously communicated to con-sumers. Advertising can help. However, brands are not maintained by advertising but by the *brand experience*. Customers come to know a brand through a wide range of contacts and interactions. The company must put as much care into managing these touch points as it does into producing its ads. Thus, managing a company's brand assets can no longer be left only to brand managers. Some companies are now setting up brand asset management teams to manage their major brands. Finally, companies must periodically audit their brands' strengths and weaknesses. In some cases, brands may need to be repositioned because of changing customer preferences or new competitors.

4. Identify the four characteristics that affect the marketing of a service and the additional marketing considerations that services require.

Services are characterized by four key characteristics: they are *intangible, inseparable, variable,* and *perishable*. Each characteristic poses problems and marketing requirements. Marketers work to find ways to make the service more tangible, to increase the productivity of providers who are inseparable from their products, to standardize the quality in the face of variability, and to improve demand movements and supply capacities in the face of service perishability.

Good service companies focus attention on *both* customers and employees. They understand the *service-profit chain*, which links service firm profits with employee and customer satisfaction. Services marketing strategy calls not only for external marketing but also for *internal marketing* to motivate employees and *interactive marketing* to create service delivery skills among service providers. To succeed, service marketers must create *competitive differentiation*, offer high *service quality*, and find ways to increase *service productivity*.

Reviewing the Key Terms

Brand 226
Brand equity 231
Brand extension 237
Co-branding 236
Consumer product 220
Convenience product 220
Industrial product 221

Interactive marketing 242
Internal marketing 242
Line extension 237
Packaging 226
Private brand (or store brand) 233
Product 218

Product line 228
Product mix (or product portfolio) 229
Product quality 224
Service 218
Service inseparability 240
Service intangibility 239

Service perishability 240
Service-profit chain 240
Service variability 240
Shopping product 221
Social marketing 223
Specialty product 221
Unsought product 221

Discussing the Concepts

1. Is Microsoft's Windows XP Professional operating software a product or a service? Describe the core, actual, and augmented levels of this software offering.

2. Classify the following consumer products as convenience, shopping, specialty, or unsought goods: a laptop computer, a surgeon, automobile tires.

3. What is a brand? Describe the value of branding for both the buyer and seller.

4. Brand positioning can occur on three levels. How is Old Navy's brand positioned on these three levels?

5. What are the four brand sponsorship options a manufacturer faces? How does a manufacturer decide which one makes the most sense for its products?

6. Merrill Lynch is one of the world's leading financial services and advisory companies (see www.ml.com). Do Merrill Lynch's financial advising activities meet the four special characteristics of a service? Explain.

Applying the Concepts

1. Using the six qualities that a good brand name should possess, create a brand name for a personal care product that has the following positioning statement: "Intended for X-Games sports participants and enthusiasts, _____ is a deodorant that combines effective odor protection with an enduring and seductive fragrance that will enhance your romantic fortunes."

2. You are the marketing director for a snowboard manufacturer that holds 45 percent of the men's 18–29-year-old segment. Using the four brand development strategies discussed in the chapter, give examples of products you could add to your brand.

3. Farber Cancer Institute has been a leading hospital providing care for cancer patients and their families. Describe how the service-profit chain is essential for this organization's success.

Focus on Technology

For decades, consumers have dreamed of owning home robots. Industry uses many production-line robots, and many companies are now working on products for the consumer. Some basic products currently available for consumers include navigation systems, home security robots, cleaning tools such as robotic vacuums, and toys that provide some elementary robotic functions. Several companies are working on the next step—humanoid robots that can serve consumers. In designing these products, companies must determine what features are most desirable to consumers and the benefits their products can offer.

Two leading products are Honda's Asimo and Sony's QRIO. The products, both in the development stage, will offer companionship to humans. Honda's Asimo stands four feet tall and can walk smoothly on its two feet in any direction, including slopes and steps. It has voice and visual recognition, which allows it to greet people by name and follow basic commands. In Japan, Asimo is now being used by museums as a guide and

by some high-tech companies to greet visitors. It is not yet available for purchase in the United States. Sony's QRIO has many of the same features. Like Honda, Sony is developing the product to make people's lives easier. In addition, Sony's wants to make life fun and happy and to provide a navigator as the world becomes more complex. See the corporate Web sites for more information on Asimo (http://world.honda.com/ASIMO/) and QRIO (www.sony.net/SonyInfo/QRIO/).

1. Explain the core, actual, and augmented levels of a home robot.

2. When these products are available, how might corporate branding and the brand name of the robot tie into the consumer's purchase decision? Would you keep or change the current names?

3. How must Honda and Sony consider services marketing when they eventually sell this product to end consumers?

Focus on Ethics

The U.S. organic foods market has exploded in the past ten years. Now a $15-billion industry, organic foods have moved past specialty manufacturers and Whole Foods Markets to national manufacturers and retailers. Recently Kellogg introduced organic versions of three major cereal brands, including Raisin Bran, Rice Krispies, and Frosted Mini Wheats. As many other food manufacturers look to the organic market, they are also keeping a keen eye on the U.S. government's strict standards on the use of the word "organic." Regulations state that foods labeled as "organic" must consist of at least 95 percent organically produced ingredients, and those labeled "made with organic ingredients" must contain at least 70 percent organic ingredients. If a product contains less than 70 percent organic ingredients, the term organic cannot

be used anywhere on the front of the package. In addition, operations that process organic food must be certified by one of 60 USDA-accredited certifying agents. A civil penalty of up to $10,000 will be levied for any person who knowingly mislabels a product.

1. Explain the product line reasoning behind Kellogg's adding organic products.

2. Do you think that average consumers know the differences in organic label designations? Do you?

3. General Mills markets organic cereals under the Cascadian Farm brand name. Compare its brand development strategy for organic cereals to Kellogg's strategy.

Video Case

Accenture

Remember Andersen Consulting? One of the world's largest consulting firms, Andersen Consulting enjoyed tremendous name recognition and worked with some of the largest companies worldwide, include 87 of the *Fortune* Global 100. But, today, you're probably more familiar with the company's new name, Accenture. Accenture is a global management consulting, technology services, and outsourcing company. In 2001, a court ruling forced the company to change its name, jeopardizing the firm's brand equity. Rather than viewing the name change as a setback, Accenture's marketing executives used it as an opportunity to reposition the company and reintroduce it to customers.

The name Accenture, a combination of the words accent and future, was suggested by an Andersen employee and was received with considerable excitement by customers. Some skeptics wondered about the effectiveness of a "made-up" name that had no real meaning. However,

others saw it as an opportunity to start fresh and create new positioning with a name that carried no previous baggage. Today, Accenture's annual revenues total more than $15 billion. Perhaps more importantly, the new company enjoys the same or even more brand recognition and brand equity than it did under its old name.

After viewing the video featuring Accenture, answer the following questions about branding strategy.

1. How did Accenture transfer the brand equity from its original name, Andersen Consulting, to the new company name?

2. Evaluate the Accenture brand name using the six criteria detailed in the chapter.

3. How did Accenture use the requirement to rename the company as an opportunity to reposition itself?

The first Olympic basketball team wore them; they dominated the basketball courts—amateur and professional—for more than 40 years; Dr. J made them famous; Kurt Cobain died in them. What are they? Converse All Stars—more particularly the famous Chuck Taylor All Stars, known around the world as Chucks.

Compared to today's marvels of performance engineering, Chucks have always been very basic shoes. The first Chucks were introduced in 1923 as high-top canvas lace-ups with rubber-covered toes in black, white, and red with a blue label on the back that read "Made in the U.S.A." More than 80 years and 750 million pairs later, that formula has changed very little. They may be basic, but they are also downright affordable. A standard pair of Chuck Taylor high-tops still costs only about $38.

Converse invented basketball shoes, and by the mid-1970s, 70 to 80 percent of basketball players still wore Converse. But by the year 2000, the company's market share had dwindled to only about 1 percent of the total athletic shoe market. In 2001, Converse declared Chapter 11 bankruptcy and was purchased by an investment group. In 2003, Nike bought the wavering company for $305 million. What would a behemoth like Nike want with a bankrupt brand? Before dealing with that question, let's look at Converse's history.

THE LEGEND BEGINS

Converse was founded in 1908 in North Reading, Massachusetts by Marquis. In 1917, the company introduced a canvas, high-top called the All Star. By 1923, it was renamed the Chuck Taylor, after a semiprofessional basketball player from Akron, Ohio. After his basketball career ended, Charles "Chuck" Taylor became an aggressive member of the Converse sales force. He drove throughout the Midwest, stopping at playgrounds to sell the high-tops to players. Some consider Taylor to be the original Phil Knight, Nike's CEO, who also started out selling his shoes at track meets from the back of his van. Throughout the '30s, '40s, '50s, and '60s, Chucks were *the* shoes to have.

By the early 1980s, with a secure hold on the basketball shoe market (it thought), Converse branched out, introducing both tennis and running shoes. This strategy appeared to be successful, helping to boost revenue in 1983 by 21 percent to $209 million. By 1986, however, Converse's fortunes had taken a turn for the worse, and it was acquired by consumer products maker and retailer Interco for approximately $132 million. By the late 1980s, Converse had been overtaken by a host of competitors. In 1989, the top four athletic shoe companies were Nike with a 26 percent market share, Reebok with 23 percent, L.A. Gear with 13 percent, and Converse with 5 percent. Strangely, while Nike was grabbing basketball shoe sales at a rapid clip, Converse was still the official shoe of the NBA, which gave it the right to use the NBA logo in its advertising.

By 1993, an ailing Converse had changed its positioning strategy. Instead of focusing on basketball and Chucks, it aimed at capitalizing on an image that was both sexy and streetwise. Converse launched a provocative, edgy ad campaign where nothing was sacred. And without the aid of advertising, the venerable Chuck Taylor All Star was dissoci-

ated from basketball and given new life as a fashion statement. Candy Pratts, fashion director of shoes and accessories at Vogue, used high-top canvas sneakers on models in numerous layouts. The best part, according to Candy, was that this trend didn't come from advertising, but from the kids on the street.

But financially, things only continued to get worse for Converse. In 1992, it was forced to abandon the treasured "Made in the U.S.A." label, sending manufacturing to India in order to cut costs. In 1996, Converse restructured, cutting 594 jobs from a little over 2,000 and reorganizing its product line into four categories: basketball, athletic-leisure, cross-training, and children's. (Notice the absence of tennis and running shoes, although Converse had once been big in those areas.) To boost its basketball shoes, Converse put the famous Chuck Taylor signature patch on a new line of performance wear—the All Star 2000 collection.

Encouraged by the successful relaunch of the All Star 2000, the company chose to launch another new line called Dr. J 2000. A remake of a '70s shoe, it was backed by heavy advertising. Dr. J was chosen because kids told Converse researchers that Dr. J was cool enough to have a shoe. The campaign tagline was "Take the Soul to the Hole," and ads consisted of a cartoon Julius Irving performing his famous moves to a Stevie Wonder soundtrack. Unfortunately, the Dr. J 2000 produced disappointing results.

At the turn of the century, nostalgia was in. Jimi Hendrix was on Rolling Stone and the VW Beetle was a hot-selling car. Consumers were looking for "retro," so companies were redesigning classic products. And no athletic shoe was more classic than Chucks. So Converse introduced an updated black shoe, the EZ Chucks.

In addition to this bump from the nostalgia trend, classic Chucks enjoyed a counterculture following that dated back to the punk rock movement of the '70s and '80s. In the 1990s, street kids had begun wearing Converse because of their affordability. In 2000, Converse capitalized on this segment and introduced a line of shoes for skateboarders. The company became a favorite of the antiestablishment, anticorporate crowd, fueled by the unfortunate fact that it had such a small market presence and did very little advertising. Converse also appealed to the antiflash group, tired of polyester and synthetic, Michael Jordan-endorsed shoes. This segment wanted "antibrands" reflecting its antiglobalization perspective. Punk rocker Joey Ramone wore Chucks in the 70s. Molly Ringwald's record-store clerk wore them in 1986's "Pretty in Pink." And in 1994, Kurt Cobain donned a pair when he committed suicide.

NIKE TO THE RESCUE

Converse was hanging in, but only by the skin of its teeth. In 2001, the company had 180 employees and sales of $185 million. But Converse had global brand recognition and strong brand equity in the market. The question was, "Could the company make the products to back up its reputation?" Enter Nike and the buy-out. Initially, Nike left Converse management alone to implement its own business strategy. It also allowed Converse products to go without the famous Swoosh, unlike other acquired brands such as Bauer hockey equipment (now Nike Bauer Hockey). But Nike did help Converse with advertising dollars. In 2001, Converse had spent a mere $163,500 on promotions. In 2004, Nike poured more than $4 million into advertising for Converse, quadrupling promotional expenses in 2005 to over $17 million.

After nearly a decade-long absence from TV advertising, Converse produced ads with the tagline "The first school." The focus was on basketball, not famous players. The ads featured a basketball being dribbled and shot, but no player. They were "narrated" by Mos Def. "Before Mr. Taylor taught the world to play. Before fiberglass. Before parquet. Before the word 'doctor' was spelled with a J. And ballrooms were ball courts where renaissance played. Before the hype and before the dunk. After the rhythm, but before the funk. Before the money and before the fame. Before new and old school. Before school had a name. There was only the ball and the soul of the game." The ad ended with shots of the Converse logo or the Chuck Taylor All Star.

So, back to the original question. What does a megabrand like Nike do with a fading icon like Converse? Converse's new parent gave that question considerable thought. Some observers believed that Converse should become a second-tier brand. Nike could use Converse to sell millions and millions of shoes in Wal-Mart and Target—a sort of "Sam Walton meets Chuck Taylor" scenario. But Nike filled that void in 2004 when it bought Exeter Brands Group, the maker of the lower-price Starter line of apparel and footwear that now sell in Wal-Mart.

Instead, Nike has taken Converse in two different directions. After many years without the endorsement of a professional athlete, Converse is back on pro basketball courts as a performance shoe. The "Wade," named for Miami Heat superstar Dwyane Wade, hit the shelves of athletic footwear chains in 2005. So far, sales are promising. Converse now offers a special edition of the classic Converse Pro Leather. Originally made famous by Julius "Dr. J" Erving, it features a sockliner map of Dwyane Wade's hometown of Chicago. And, it comes only in blue and gold, a nod to Wade's days at Marquette University where he led his team to the Final Four.

A DIFFERENT KIND OF CHUCKS?

But while Converse is currently retesting the waters of the performance shoe market, it is springboarding off the Chucks' trendy roots and doing a cannonball dive into the fashion shoe market. The current line-up of the longest-selling athletic shoe includes the classic high- and low-top canvas Chucks. But pricey variations include gold-metallic Chucks ($72), knee-high shearling-lined Chucks ($175), tattooed Chucks ($52), and customer-designed Chucks ($65 and up); there's even a "limited edition" snakeskin high-top going for $1,800. In all, Converse currently offers more than 1,000 different types of Chucks in outlets ranging from retail chains such as Foot Locker and Journeys to upscale stores such as Saks, Bloomingdales, and Barneys. This may seem like a big order for the tiny 12-person design team at Converse. But Nike has opened the doors to its creative labs, giving the team access to its designers, engineers, and biomechanics experts.

As if this weren't enough, Converse has enlisted the talent of designer John Varvatos to not only design a line of Chucks, but to put the "C. Taylor" label on a full line of men's and women's clothing that includes blazers, merino wool hoodies, military coats, jeans, and T-shirts. Prices range from $55 to $125 for T-shirts and from $295 for outerwear and jackets.

But this new fashion strategy begs an interesting question. Can the affordable, antiestablishment image of the Chuck Taylor All Star survive what can only be viewed as the antithesis? Some of the Converse old guard are not pleased with Nike's handiwork. One skate-shop manager says the new Chucks don't have the same vibe as the classics. "What's happening is that Converse has now gotten greedy. That's why those are not as cool."

Converse may well lose some of its devoted Chuck Taylor customer base. But given that U.S. sales of Converse footwear hit $400 million in 2005, it may not care. That's still only 1.5 percent of the market, but it's more than double the company's revenue from just four years earlier. And sales are continuing on an upward trend. Converse plans more fashion variations for the Chucks line, asserting that the possibilities are endless. And encouraged by the success of the Wade, Converse is set to launch "All Star Revolution," a shoe with the Chuck Taylor look but performance features and technology. In light of this drastic turnaround at Converse, it appears that Nike may have once again demonstrated its magic touch.

Questions for Discussion

1. What are the core, actual, and augmented product benefits of the Converse Chuck?

2. When Converse outsourced production of its shoes to India, it entered into a licensing arrangement. What are the benefits and risks of that action? Do you think it has helped or hurt the company? The brand?

3. What are the sources of brand equity for both Converse and Chuck Taylor All Stars?

4. Analyze the Nike-era direction of Converse. (a) Assess the benefits and risks of the fashion and performance strategies individually, and of the combined two-tiered approach. (b) What targeting and positioning would you recommend for the Converse brand in the future?

Sources: Stephanie Kang, "Nike Takes Chuck Taylors from Antifashion to Fashionista," Wall Street Journal, June 23, 2006, p. B1; Michelle Jeffers, "Word on the Street," Adweek, May 16, 2005; Hilary Cassidy, "Shoe Companies Use Body and Sole to Track Down Sales," Brandweek, June 21, 2004, p. S.50; Lisa van der Pool and David Gianatasio, "Converse Hearkens Back to Roots in New Campaign," Adweek, August 4, 2003, p. 10; Jennifer Laabs, "Converse Will Restructure and Cut Jobs," Personnel Journal, January 1996, p. 12; Kevin Goldman, "Converse Sneaker Seeks Statement of Fashion Instead of Foul Shots," Wall Street Journal, May 6, 1993, p. B6; Brian Bagot, "Shoeboom!" M&MD, June 1990, p. 89; Donna Goodison, "Converse is Convert to Designer Clothing," Boston Herald, May 16, 2006, p. 36; and "From Court to Street, Converse Kicks It Double Time with Dwyane Wade Signature Product in Two-Pack," PR Newswire, February 13, 2006.

9

New-Product Development and Product Life-Cycle Strategies

Previewing the Concepts

In the previous chapter, you learned how marketers manage individual brands and entire product mixes. In this chapter, we'll look into two additional product topics: developing new products and managing products through their life cycles. New products are the lifeblood of an organization. However, new-product development is risky, and many new products fail. So, the first part of this chapter lays out a process for finding and growing successful new products. Once introduced, marketers want their products to enjoy a long and happy life. In the second part of the chapter, you'll see that every product passes through several life-cycle stages and that each stage poses new challenges requiring different marketing strategies and tactics. Finally, we'll wrap up our product and services discussion by looking at two additional considerations, social responsibility in product decisions and international product and services marketing.

For openers, consider Apple Computer. An early new-product innovator, Apple got off to a fast and impressive start. But only a decade later, as its creative fires cooled, Apple found itself on the brink of extinction. That set the stage for one of the most remarkable turnarounds in corporate history. Read on to see how Apple's cofounder, Steve Jobs, used lots of innovation and creative new products to first start the company and then to remake it again 20 years later.

From the very start, the tale of Apple Computer has been a tale of dazzling creativity and customer-driven innovation. Under the leadership of its cofounder and creative genius, Steve Jobs, Apple's very first personal computers, introduced in the late 1970s, stood apart because of their user-friendly look and feel. The company's Macintosh computer, unveiled in 1984, and its LazerWriter printers, blazed new trails in desktop computing and publishing, making Apple an early industry leader in both innovation and market share.

But then things took an ugly turn for Apple. In 1985, after tumultuous struggles with the new president he'd hired only a year earlier, Steve Jobs left Apple. With Jobs gone, Apple's creative fires cooled. By the late 1980s, the company's fortunes dwindled as a new wave of PC machines, sporting Intel chips and Microsoft software, swept the market. By the mid- to late-1990s, Apple's sales had plunged to $5 billion, 50 percent off previous highs. And its once-commanding share of the personal-computer market had dropped to a tiny 2 percent. Even the most ardent Apple fans—the "macolytes"—wavered, and the company's days seemed numbered.

Yet Apple has engineered a remarkable turnaround. Last year's sales soared to a record $16 billion, more than double sales just two years earlier. Profits rose a stunning 20-fold in that same two-year period. "To say Apple Computer is hot just doesn't do the company justice," said one analyst. "Apple is smoking, searing, blisteringly hot, not to mention hip, with a side order of funky. . . . Gadget geeks around the world have crowned Apple the keeper of all things cool."

What caused this breathtaking turnaround? Apple rediscovered the magic that had made the company so successful in the first place: customer-driven creativity and new-product innovation. The remarkable makeover began with the return of Steve Jobs in 1997. Since leaving Apple, Jobs had started a new computer company, NeXT. He'd then bought out Pixar Animation Studios, turning it into an entertainment-industry powerhouse. Jobs returned to Apple determined to breathe new creative life and customer focus into the company he'd cofounded 20 years earlier.

Jobs' first task was to revitalize Apple's computer business. For starters, in 1998, Apple launched the iMac personal computer, which featured a sleek, egg-shaped monitor and hard drive, all in one unit, in a futuristic translucent turquoise casing. With its one-button Internet access, this machine was designed specifically for cruising the Internet (hence the "i" in "iMac"). The dramatic iMac won raves for design and lured buyers in droves. Within a year, it had sold more than a million units.

Apple next unleashed Mac OS X, a ground-breaking new Apple operating system that one observer called "the equivalent of a cross between a Porsche and an

Abram's tank." OS X served as the launching pad for a new generation of Apple computers and software products. Consider iLife, a bundle of programs that comes with every new iMac. It includes applications such as iMovie (for video editing), iDVD (for recording movies, digital-photo slide shows, and music onto TV-playable DVDs), iPhoto (for managing and touching up digital pictures), GarageBand (for making and mixing your own music), and iWork (for making presentations and newsletters).

The iMac and Mac OS X put Apple back on the map in personal computing. But Jobs knew that Apple, still a nicher claiming less than a 5 percent share of the U.S. market, would never catch up in computers with dominant competitors Dell and HP. Real growth and stardom would require even more creative thinking. And it just doesn't get much more creative than iPod and iTunes, innovations that would utterly change the way people acquire and listen to music.

A music buff himself, Jobs noticed that kids by the millions were using computers and CD writers to download digital songs from then-illegal online services, such as Napster, and then burning their own music CDs. He moved quickly to make CD burners standard equipment on all Macs. Then, to help users download music and manage their music databases, Apple's programmers created state-of-the-art juke-box software called iTunes.

Even before iTunes hit the streets, according to Apple watcher Brent Schendler, Jobs "recognized that although storing and playing music on your computer was

Objectives

After studying this chapter, you should be able to

1. explain how companies find and develop new-product ideas
2. list and define the steps in the new-product development process and the major considerations in managing this process
3. describe the stages of the product life cycle
4. describe how marketing strategies change during the product's life cycle
5. discuss two additional product and services issues: socially responsible product decisions and international product and services marketing

pretty cool, wouldn't it be even cooler if there was a portable, Walkman-type player that could hold all your digital music so that you could listen to it anywhere?" Less than nine months later, Apple introduced the sleek and sexy iPod, a tiny computer with an amazing capacity to store digital music and an easy-to-use interface for managing and playing it. In another 18 months, the Apple iTunes Music Store opened on the Web, enabling consumers to legally download CDs and individual songs.

The results have been astonishing. The iPod now ranks as one of the greatest consumer electronics hits of all time. By January of 2006, Apple had sold more than 50 million iPods, and more than one billion songs had been downloaded from the iTunes Music Store. "We had hoped to sell a million songs in the first six months, but we did that in the first six days," notes an Apple spokesman. And the iPod has now created a whole new market for downloadable videos, everything from music videos to television shows. Since last year's debut of the video iPod, users have downloaded more 35 million videos. Both iPod and the iTunes Music Store are capturing more than 75 percent shares of their respective markets.

Apple's success is attracting a horde of large, resourceful competitors. To stay ahead, the company must keep its eye on the consumer and continue to innovate. So, Apple isn't standing still. It recently introduced a line of new, easy-to-use wireless gadgets that link home and business computers, stereos, and other devices. Its .Mac (pronounced dot-Mac) online subscription service has signed up more than 600,000 members. Apple has also opened more than 150 chic and gleaming Apple Stores. And observers see a host of new products just on or just over the horizon: an iHome (a magical device that powers all your digital home entertainment devices), an iPhone (a combination iPod and cell phone), and an iPod on Wheels (a digital hub that integrates your iPod with your car's entertainment system).

For the second straight year, Apple was named the world's most innovative company in Boston Consulting Group's "Most Innovative Company" survey of 940 senior executives in 68 countries. Apple received an amazing 25 percent of the votes, twice the number of runner-up 3M and three times that of third-place Microsoft.

Thus, almost overnight, it seems, Steve Jobs has transformed Apple from a failing niche computer maker to a major force in consumer electronics, digital music and video, and who knows what else in the future. And he's done it through innovation—by helping those around him to "Think Different" (Apple's motto) in their quest to bring value to customers. *Time* magazine sums it up this way:

[Steve Jobs]'s recipe for success? He's a marketing and creative genius with a rare ability to get inside the imaginations of consumers and understand what will captivate them. He is obsessed with the Apple user's experience. . . . For every product his companies have released, it's clear that someone actually asked, How can we "think different" about this? . . . Whether it's the original Macintosh, the iMac, the iPod, the flat-panel monitor, even the Apple operating system, most of the company's products over the past three decades have had designs that are three steps ahead of the competition. . . . Jobs has a drive and vision that renews itself, again and again. It leaves you waiting for his next move.[1]

As the Apple story suggests, a company must be good at developing and managing new products. Every product seems to go through a life cycle—it is born, goes through several phases, and eventually dies as newer products come along that better serve consumer needs. This product life cycle presents two major challenges: First, because all products eventually decline, a firm must be good at developing new products to replace aging ones (the challenge of *new-product development*). Second, the firm must be good at adapting its marketing strategies in the face of changing tastes, technologies, and competition as products pass through life-cycle stages (the challenge of *product life-cycle strategies*). We first look at the problem of finding and developing new products and then at the problem of managing them successfully over their life cycles.

New-Product Development Strategy

Given the rapid changes in consumer tastes, technology, and competition, companies must develop a steady stream of new products and services. A firm can obtain new products in two ways. One is through *acquisition*—by buying a whole company, a patent, or a license to produce someone else's product. The other is through *new product development* in the company's own research-and-development department. By *new products* we mean original products, product improvements, product modifications, and new brands that the firm develops through its own research-and-development efforts. New products are important—to both customers and the marketers who serve them. "Both consumers and companies love new products," declares a new-product consultant, "consumers because they solve problems and bring variety to their lives, and companies because they are a key source of growth."[2]

Yet, innovation can be very expensive and very risky. For example, Texas Instruments lost $660 million before withdrawing from the home computer business, Webvan burned through a staggering $1.2 billion trying to create a new online grocery business before shutting its cyberdoors for a lack of customers. And despite a huge investment and fevered speculation that it could be even bigger than the Internet, Segway sold only 6,000 of its human transporters in the 18 months following its launch, a tiny fraction of projected sales. Segway has yet to do more than gain small footholds in niche markets, such as urban touring and police departments.[3]

New products face tough odds. Other costly product failures from sophisticated companies include New Coke (Coca-Cola Company), Eagle Snacks (Anheuser-Busch), Zap Mail electronic mail (FedEx), Premier "smokeless" cigarettes (R.J. Reynolds), Arch Deluxe sandwiches (McDonald's), and Breakfast Mates cereal-and-milk combos (Kellogg). Studies indicate that up to 90 percent of all new consumer products fail. For example, of the 30,000 new food, beverage, and beauty products launched each year, and estimated 70 to 90 percent fail within just 12 months.[4]

Why do so many new products fail? There are several reasons. Although an idea may be good, the company may overestimate market size. The actual product may be poorly designed. Or it might be incorrectly positioned, launched at the wrong time, priced too high, or poorly advertised. A high-level executive might push a favorite idea despite poor marketing research findings. Sometimes the costs of product development are higher than expected, and sometimes competitors fight back harder than expected. However, the reasons behind some new-product failures seem pretty obvious. Try the following on for size:[5]

Strolling the aisles at Robert McMath's New Product Works collection is like finding yourself in some nightmare version of a supermarket. There's Gerber food for

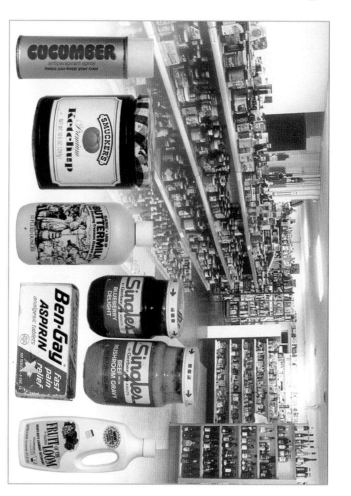

New-product development

The development of original products, product improvements, product modifications, and new brands through the firm's own R&D efforts.

■ Product failures: Visiting the New Product Showcase and Learning Center is like finding yourself in some nightmare version of a supermarket. Each product failure represents squandered dollars and hopes.

adults (pureed sweet-and-sour pork and chicken Madeira), Hot Scoop microwaveable ice cream sundaes, Premier smokeless cigarettes, and Miller Clear Beer. How about Richard Simmons Dijon Vinaigrette Salad Spray? Most of the 82,135 products on display were abject flops. Behind each of them are squandered dollars and hopes.

McMath, the genial curator of this Smithsonian of consumerism, gets lots of laughs when he asks his favorite question, "What were they thinking?" Some companies failed because they attached trusted brand names to something totally out of character. For example, when you hear the name Ben-Gay, you immediately think of the way Ben-Gay cream sears and stimulates your skin. Can you imagine swallowing Ben-Gay aspirin? Other misbegotten attempts to stretch a good name include Cracker Jack cereal, Smucker's premium ketchup, Fruit of the Loom laundry detergent, and Harley-Davidson cake-decorating kits. Looking back, what *were* they thinking? You can tell that some innovative products were doomed as soon as you hear their names: Toaster Eggs. Cucumber antiperspirant spray. Health-Sea sea sausage. Look of Buttermilk shampoo. Dr. Care Aerosol Toothpaste (many parents questioned the wisdom of arming their kids with something like this!). Really, what were they thinking?

▌The New-Product Development Process

So companies face a problem—they must develop new products, but the odds weigh heavily against success. In all, to create successful new products, a company must understand its consumers, markets, and competitors and develop products that deliver superior value to customers. It must carry out strong new-product planning and set up a systematic *new-product development process* for finding and growing new products. Figure 9.1 shows the eight major steps in this process.

Idea Generation

New-product development starts with **idea generation**—the systematic search for new-product ideas. A company typically has to generate many ideas in order to find a few good ones. According to one management consultant, on average, companies "will run through 3,000 ideas before they hit a winner." For instance, one brainstorming session for Prudential Insurance Company came up with 1,500 ideas and only 12 were considered even usable.[6]

Major sources of new-product ideas include internal sources and external sources such as customers, competitors, distributors and suppliers, and others.

Internal Idea Sources

Using *internal sources*, the company can find new ideas through formal research and development. It can pick the brains of its executives, scientists, engineers, manufacturing staff, and salespeople. Some companies have developed successful "intrapreneurial" programs that encourage employees to think up and develop new-product ideas. For example, 3M's well-known "15 percent rule" allows employees to spend 15 percent of their time "bootlegging"—

Idea generation
The systematic search for new-product ideas.

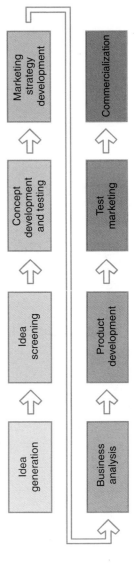

FIGURE 9.1 Major stages in new-product development

working on projects of personal interest, whether or not those projects directly benefit the company.

Samsung has even built a special center to encourage and support new-product innovation internally—its Value Innovation Program (VIP) Center in Suwon, South Korea. The VIP Center is the ultimate round-the-clock idea factory in which company researchers, engineers, and designers co-mingle to come up with new-product ideas and processes. The invitation-only center features workrooms, dorm rooms, training rooms, a kitchen, and a basement filled with games, a gym, and a sauna. Almost every week, the center announces a "world's first" or "world's largest" innovation. Recent ideas sprouting from the VIP Center include a 102-inch plasma HDTV and a process to reduce material costs on a multifunction printer by 30 percent. The center has helped Samsung, once know as the maker of cheap knock-off products, become one of the world's most innovative and profitable consumer electronics companies.[7]

Not all companies have such "innovation incubators." However, any business can obtain new ideas from employees, even small businesses. A recent survey of small companies revealed that three-quarters of them directly encourage employees to make new-product and service suggestions. More than half of these small businesses give bonuses or other recognition to those whose ideas are used.[8]

Everyone in the company can contribute good new-product ideas. "Most companies operate under the assumption that big ideas come from a few big brains: the inspired founder, the eccentric inventor, the visionary boss," says one analyst. But in today's fast-moving and competitive environment, "it's time to invent a less top-down approach to innovation, to make it everybody's business to come up with great ideas."[9]

External Idea Sources

Good new-product ideas also come from *customers*. The company can analyze customer questions and complaints to find new products that better solve consumer problems. Or company engineers or salespeople can meet with and work alongside customers to get suggestions and ideas.

LEGO did just that when it invited 250 LEGO train-set enthusiasts to visit its New York office to assess new designs. "We pooh-poohed them all," says one LEGO fan, an Intel engineer from Portland. But the group gave LEGO lots of new ideas, and the company put them to good use. "We literally produced what they told us to produce," says a LEGO executive. The result was the "Santa Fe Super Chief" set. Thanks to "word-of-mouse" endorsements from the

■ Product ideas from customers: Advice from 250 train-set enthusiasts resulted in the LEGO Santa Fe Super Chief set, a blockbuster new product that sold out in less than two weeks.

250 enthusiasts, LEGO sold out the first 10,000 units in less than two weeks with no additional marketing.[10]

Consumers often create new products and uses on their own, and companies can benefit by putting them on the market. For example, for years customers were spreading the word that Avon Skin-So-Soft bath oil and moisturizer was also a terrific bug repellent. Whereas some consumers were content simply to bathe in water scented with the fragrant oil, others carried it in their backpacks to mosquito-infested campsites or kept a bottle on the decks of their beach houses. Avon turned the idea into a complete line of Skin-So-Soft Bug Guard products, including Bug Guard Mosquito Repellent Moisturizing Towelettes and Bug Guard Plus, a combination moisturizer, insect repellent, and sunscreen.[11]

Finally, some companies even give customers the tools and resources to design their own products. Notes one expert, "Not only is the customer king, now he is market-research head, R&D chief, and product development manager, too."[12] For example, computer games maker Electronic Arts (EA) noticed that its customers were making new content for existing games and posting it online for others to use freely. It began shipping basic game development tools with its games and feeding customer innovations to its designers to use in creating new games. "The fan community has had a tremendous influence on game design," says an EA executive, "and the games are better as a result."[13]

Companies must be careful not to rely too heavily on customer input when developing new products. For some products, especially highly technical ones, customers may not know what they need. "Merely giving people what they want isn't always enough," says one innovation management consultant. "People want to be surprised; they want something that's better than they imagined, something that stretches them in what they like."[14]

Beyond customers, companies can tap several other external sources. For example, *competitors* can be a good source of new-product ideas. Companies watch competitors' ads to get clues about their new products. They buy competing new products, take them apart to see how they work, analyze their sales, and decide whether they should bring out a new product of their own.

Distributors and suppliers can also contribute many good new-product ideas. Distributors are close to the market and can pass along information about consumer problems and new-product possibilities. Suppliers can tell the company about new concepts, techniques, and materials that can be used to develop new products. Other idea sources include trade magazines, shows, and seminars; government agencies; new-product consultants; advertising agencies; marketing research firms; university and commercial laboratories; and inventors.

Some companies seek the help of outside design firms, such as IDEO or Frog Design, for new-product ideas and design. For example, Frog Design helped Tupperware find a new-product solution to a common customer problem—organizing that closet full of randomly stacked plastic storage containers and matching the lids with the bases. From idea generation to final prototypes, Frog Design developed Tupperware's FlatOut series, flexible containers that can be collapsed, stacked, and stored flat with the lid attached. The new product received several design awards.[15]

Idea Screening

The purpose of idea generation is to create a large number of ideas. The purpose of the succeeding stages is to *reduce* that number. The first idea-reducing stage is **idea screening**, which helps spot good ideas and drop poor ones as soon as possible. Product development costs rise greatly in later stages, so the company wants to go ahead only with the product ideas that will turn into profitable products.

Many companies require their executives to write up new-product ideas on a standard form that can be reviewed by a new-product committee. The write-up describes the product, the target market, and the competition. It makes some rough estimates of market size, product price, development time and costs, manufacturing costs, and rate of return. The committee then evaluates the idea against a set of general criteria.

For example, at Kao Corporation, the large Japanese consumer products company, the new-product committee asks questions such as these: Is the product truly useful to consumers and society? Is it good for our particular company? Does it mesh well with the company's objectives and strategies? Do we have the people, skills, and resources to make it succeed? Does it deliver more value to customers than do competing products? Is it easy to advertise and distribute? Many companies have well-designed systems for rating and screening new-product ideas.

Concept Development and Testing

Product concept
A detailed version of the new-product idea stated in meaningful consumer terms.

An attractive idea must be developed into a **product concept**. It is important to distinguish between a product idea, a product concept, and a product image. A *product idea* is an idea for a possible product that the company can see itself offering to the market. A *product concept* is a detailed version of the idea stated in meaningful consumer terms. A *product image* is the way consumers perceive an actual or potential product.

Concept Development

After more than a decade of development, DaimlerChrysler is beginning to commercialize its experimental fuel-cell-powered electric car. This car's nonpolluting fuel-cell system runs directly on hydrogen, which powers the fuel cell with only water as a by-product. It is highly fuel efficient and gives the new car an environmental advantage over even today's superefficient gasoline-electric hybrid cars.

DaimlerChrysler has released 30 "F-Cell" cars in California and 100 more around the world so that they can be tested under varying weather conditions, traffic situations, and driving styles. Based on the tiny Mercedes A-Class, the car accelerates from 0 to 60 in 16 seconds, reaches speeds of 85 miles per hour, and has a 100-mile driving range, giving it a huge edge over battery-powered electric cars that travel only about 80 miles before needing 3 to 12 hours of recharging.[16]

Now DaimlerChrysler's task is to develop this new product into alternative product concepts, find out how attractive each concept is to customers, and choose the best one. It might create the following product concepts for the fuel-cell electric car:

Concept 1 A moderately priced subcompact designed as a second family car to be used around town. The car is ideal for running errands and visiting friends.

Concept 2 A medium-cost sporty compact appealing to young people.

Concept 3 An inexpensive subcompact "green" car appealing to environmentally conscious people who want practical, low-polluting transportation.

Concept 4 A high-end SUV appealing to those who love the space SUVs provide but lament the poor gas mileage.

Concept Testing

Concept testing
Testing new-product concepts with a group of target consumers to find out if the concepts have strong consumer appeal.

Concept testing calls for testing new-product concepts with groups of target consumers. The concepts may be presented to consumers symbolically or physically. Here, in words, is concept 3:

An efficient, peppy, fun-to-drive, fuel-cell-powered electric subcompact car that seats four. This hydrogen-powered high-tech wonder provides practical and reliable transportation with virtually no pollution. It goes up to 85 miles per hour and, unlike battery-powered electric cars, it never needs recharging. It's priced, fully equipped, at $25,000.

For some concept tests, a word or picture description might be sufficient. However, a more concrete and physical presentation of the concept will increase the reliability of the concept test. After being exposed to the concept, consumers then may be asked to react to it by answering questions such as those in Table 9.1.

The answers to such questions will help the company decide which concept has the strongest appeal. For example, the last question asks about the consumer's intention to

TABLE 9.1

Questions for Fuel-Cell-Powered Electric Car Concept Test

1. Do you understand the concept of a fuel-cell-powered electric car?
2. Do you believe the claims about the car's performance?
3. What are the major benefits of the fuel-cell-powered electric car compared with a conventional car?
4. What are its advantages compared with a battery-powered electric car?
5. What improvements in the car's features would you suggest?
6. For what uses would you prefer a fuel-cell-powered electric car to a conventional car?
7. What would be a reasonable price to charge for the car?
8. Who would be involved in your decision to buy such a car? Who would drive it?
9. Would you buy such a car (definitely, probably, probably not, definitely not)?

Marketing strategy development

Designing an initial marketing strategy for a new product based on the product concept.

buy. Suppose 10 percent of consumers say they "definitely" would buy, and another 5 percent say "probably." The company could project these figures to the full population in this target group to estimate sales volume. Even then, the estimate is uncertain because people do not always carry out their stated intentions.

Many firms routinely test new-product concepts with consumers before attempting to turn them into actual new products. For example, AcuPOLL, a global brand-building research company, tests thousands of new product concepts every year. In past polls, M&M Mini's, "teeny-tiny" M&Ms sold in a tube container, received a rare A+ concept rating, meaning that consumers thought it was an outstanding concept that they would try and buy. Other products such as Glad Stand & Zip Bags, Clorox Wipes, the Mead Inteli-Gear learning system, and Elmer's 3D Paint Pens were also big hits.

Other product concepts didn't fare so well. Consumers didn't think much of Excedrin Tension Headache Cooling Pads. Nor did they care for Nubrush Anti-Bacterial Toothbrush Spray disinfectant, from Applied Microdontics, which received an F. Most consumers don't think they have a problem with "infected" toothbrushes. Another concept that fared poorly was Chef Williams 5 Minute Marinade, which comes with a syringe customers use to inject the marinade into meat. Some consumers found the thought of injecting something into meat a bit repulsive, and "it's just so politically incorrect to have this syringe on there," comments an AcuPOLL executive.[17]

Marketing Strategy Development

Suppose DaimlerChrysler finds that concept 3 for the fuel-cell-powered electric car tests best. The next step is **marketing strategy development**, designing an initial marketing strategy for introducing this car to the market.

The *marketing strategy statement* consists of three parts. The first part describes the target market; the planned product positioning; and the sales, market share, and profit goals for the first few years. Thus:

The target market is younger, well-educated, moderate-to-high-income individuals, couples, or small families seeking practical, environmentally

Food,
moisture,
and
lots of
places
to hide.
No wonder
a billion germs
call your sponge
home.

Don't spread germs. Kill them.

CLOROX DISINFECTING WIPES

©2005 The Clorox Company

■ AcuPOLL tests thousands of new-product concepts every year. Its polls correctly predicted that CLOROX® Wipes would be a big hit with consumers.

responsible transportation. The car will be positioned as more fun to drive and less polluting than today's internal combustion engine or hybrid cars. It is also less restricting than battery-powered electric cars, which must be recharged regularly. The company will aim to sell 100,000 cars in the first year, at a loss of not more than $15 million. In the second year, the company will aim for sales of 120,000 cars and a profit of $25 million.

The second part of the marketing strategy statement outlines the product's planned price, distribution, and marketing budget for the first year:

The fuel-cell-powered electric car will be offered in three colors—red, white, and blue—and will have optional air-conditioning and power-drive features. It will sell at a retail price of $25,000—with 15 percent off the list price to dealers. Dealers who sell more than 10 cars per month will get an additional discount of 5 percent on each car sold that month. An advertising budget of $50 million will be split 50-50 between a national media campaign and local advertising. Advertising will emphasize the car's fun spirit and low emissions. During the first year, $100,000 will be spent on marketing research to find out who is buying the car and their satisfaction levels.

The third part of the marketing strategy statement describes the planned long-run sales, profit goals, and marketing mix strategy:

DaimlerChrysler intends to capture a 3 percent long-run share of the total auto market and realize an after-tax return on investment of 15 percent. To achieve this, product quality will start high and be improved over time. Price will be raised in the second and third years if competition permits. The total advertising budget will be raised each year by about 10 percent. Marketing research will be reduced to $60,000 per year after the first year.

Business Analysis

Once management has decided on its product concept and marketing strategy, it can evaluate the business attractiveness of the proposal. **Business analysis** involves a review of the sales, costs, and profit projections for a new product to find out whether they satisfy the company's objectives. If they do, the product can move to the product development stage.

To estimate sales, the company might look at the sales history of similar products and conduct surveys of market opinion. It can then estimate minimum and maximum sales to assess the range of risk. After preparing the sales forecast, management can estimate the expected costs and profits for the product, including marketing, R&D, operations, accounting, and finance costs. The company then uses the sales and costs figures to analyze the new product's financial attractiveness.

Product Development

So far, for many new-product concepts, the product may have existed only as a word description, a drawing, or perhaps a crude mock-up. If the product concept passes the business test, it moves into **product development**. Here, R&D or engineering develops the product concept into a physical product. The product development step, however, now calls for a large jump in investment. It will show whether the product idea can be turned into a workable product.

The R&D department will develop and test one or more physical versions of the product concept. R&D hopes to design a prototype that will satisfy and excite consumers and that can be produced quickly and at budgeted costs. Developing a successful prototype can take days, weeks, months, or even years.

Often, products undergo rigorous tests to make sure that they perform safely and effectively or that consumers will find value in them. Here are some examples of such product tests:[18]

Thunk. Thunk. Thunk. Behind a locked door in the basement of Louis Vuitton's elegant Paris headquarters, a mechanical arm hoists a brown-and-tan handbag a half-meter off the floor—then drops it. The bag, loaded with an 8-pound weight, will be lifted and dropped, over and over again, for four days. This is Vuitton's test laboratory,

Business analysis
A review of the sales, costs, and profit projections for a new product to find out whether these factors satisfy the company's objectives.

Product development
Developing the product concept into a physical product in order to ensure that the product idea can be turned into a workable product.

a high-tech torture chamber for its fabled luxury goods. Another piece of lab equipment bombards handbags with ultraviolet rays to test resistance to fading. Still another tests zippers by tugging them open and shutting them 5,000 times. There's even a mechanized mannequin hand, with a Vuitton charm bracelet around its wrist, being shaken vigorously to make sure none of the charms fall off.

At Gillette, almost everyone gets involved in new-product testing. Every working day at Gillette, 200 volunteers from various departments come to work unshaven, troop to the second floor of the company's gritty South Boston plant, and enter small booths with a sink and mirror. There they take instructions from technicians on the other side of a small window as to which razor, shaving cream, or aftershave to use. The volunteers evaluate razors for sharpness of blade, smoothness of glide, and ease of handling. In a nearby shower room, women perform the same ritual on their legs, underarms, and what the company delicately refers to as the "bikini area." "We bleed so you'll get a good shave at home," says one Gillette employee.

A new product must have the required functional features and also convey the intended psychological characteristics. The fuel-cell electric car, for example, should strike consumers as being well built, comfortable, and safe. Management must learn what makes consumers decide that a car is well built. To some consumers, this means that the car has "solid-sounding" doors. To others, it means that the car is able to withstand heavy impact in crash tests. Consumer tests are conducted in which consumers test-drive the car and rate its attributes.

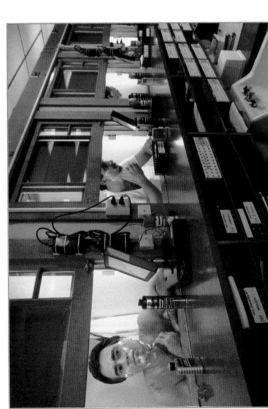

■ Product testing: Gillette uses employee-volunteers to test new shaving products—"We bleed so you'll get a good shave at home," says a Gillette employee.

Test Marketing

If the product passes concept and product tests, the next step is **test marketing**, the stage at which the product and marketing program are introduced into more realistic market settings. Test marketing gives the marketer experience with marketing the product before going to the great expense of full introduction. It lets the company test the product and its entire marketing program—positioning strategy, advertising, distribution, pricing, branding and packaging, and budget levels.

The amount of test marketing needed varies with each new product. Test marketing costs can be high, and it takes time that may allow competitors to gain advantages. When the costs of developing and introducing the product are low, or when management is already confident about the new product, the company may do little or no test marketing. In fact, test marketing by consumer-goods firms has been declining in recent years. Companies often do not test-market simple line extensions or copies of successful competitor products.

However, when introducing a new product requires a big investment, or when management is not sure of the product or marketing program, a company may do a lot of test marketing. For instance, for more than two years, McDonald's has tested the *redbox* concept of automated DVD rental kiosks in its own restaurants and in supermarkets throughout major U.S. markets. Using the kiosks, consumers can rent DVDs for $1 per night using their debit or credit cards. Based on the success of these test markets—in Denver tests alone, the *redbox* kiosks now command more than a 15 percent share of all DVD rentals.[19]

Although test-marketing costs can be high, they are often small when compared with the costs of making a major mistake. Still, test marketing doesn't guarantee success. For example, Procter & Gamble tested its Fit produce rinse heavily for five years and Olay cosmetics for three years. Although market tests suggested the products would be successful, P&G pulled the plug on both shortly after their introductions.[20]

When using test marketing, consumer products companies usually choose one of three approaches—standard test markets, controlled test markets, or simulated test markets.

Standard Test Markets

Using standard test markets, the company finds a small number of representative test cities, conducts a full marketing campaign in these cities, and uses store audits, consumer and distributor surveys, and other measures to gauge product performance. The results are used to forecast national sales and profits, discover potential product problems, and fine-tune the marketing program.

Standard test markets have some drawbacks. They can be very costly and they may take a long time—some last as long as three to five years. Moreover, competitors can monitor test market results or interfere with them by cutting their prices in test cities, increasing their promotion, or even buying up the product being tested. Finally, test markets give competitors a look at the company's new product well before it is introduced nationally. Thus, competitors may have time to develop defensive strategies, and may even beat the company's product to the market. For example, while Clorox was still test marketing its new detergent with bleach in selected markets, P&G launched Tide with Bleach nationally. Tide with Bleach quickly became the segment leader; Clorox later withdrew its detergent.

Despite these disadvantages, standard test markets are still the most widely used approach for major in-market testing. However, many companies today are shifting toward quicker and cheaper controlled and simulated test marketing methods.

Controlled Test Markets

Several research firms keep controlled panels of stores that have agreed to carry new products for a fee. Controlled test marketing systems such as ACNielsen's Scantrack and Information Resources Inc.'s (IRI) BehaviorScan track individual consumer behavior for new products from the television set to the checkout counter.

In each BehaviorScan market, IRI maintains a panel of shoppers who report all of their purchases by showing an identification card at check-out in participating stores and by using a handheld scanner at home to record purchases at nonparticipating stores.[21] Within test stores, IRI controls such factors as shelf placement, price, and in-store promotions for the product being tested. IRI also measures TV viewing in each panel household and sends special commercials to panel member television sets. Direct mail promotions can also be tested.

Detailed scanner information on each consumer's purchases is fed into a central computer, where it is combined with the consumer's demographic and TV viewing information and reported daily. Thus, BehaviorScan can provide store-by-store, week-by-week reports on the sales of tested products. Such panel purchasing data enables in-depth diagnostics not possible with retail point-of-sale data alone, including repeat purchase analysis, buyer demographics, and earlier, more accurate sales forecasts after just 12 to 24 weeks in market. Most importantly, the system allows companies to evaluate their specific marketing efforts.

Controlled test markets, such as Behaviorscan, usually cost less than standard test markets. Also, because retail distribution is "forced" in the first weeks of the test, controlled test markets can be completed much more quickly than standard test markets. As in standard test markets, controlled test markets allow competitors to get a look at the company's new product. And some companies are concerned that the limited number of controlled test markets used by the research services may not be representative of their products' markets or target consumers. However, the research firms are experienced in projecting test market results to broader markets and can usually account for biases in the test markets used.

■ Test marketing: Based on two years of test marketing in six major U.S. cities, McDonald's now plans to roll out Redbox DVD rental kiosks in all of its restaurants and in a slew of supermarkets across the country.

■ Controlled Test Markets: IRI's BehaviorScan system tracks individual consumer behavior for new products from the television set to the checkout counter.

Simulated Test Markets

Companies can also test new products in a simulated shopping environment. The company or research firm shows ads and promotions for a variety of products, including the new product being tested, to a sample of consumers. It gives consumers a small amount of money and invites them to a real or laboratory store where they may keep the money or use it to buy items. The researchers note how many consumers buy the new product and competing brands.

This simulation provides a measure of trial and the commercial's effectiveness against competing commercials. The researchers then ask consumers the reasons for their purchase or nonpurchase. Some weeks later, they interview the consumers by phone to determine product attitudes, usage, satisfaction, and repurchase intentions. Using sophisticated computer models, the researchers then project national sales from results of the simulated test market. Recently, some marketers have begun to use interesting new high-tech approaches to simulated test market research, such as virtual reality and the Internet.

Simulated test markets overcome some of the disadvantages of standard and controlled test markets. They usually cost much less, can be run in eight weeks, and keep the new product out of competitors' view. Yet, because of their small samples and simulated shopping environments, many marketers do not think that simulated test markets are as accurate or reliable as larger, real-world tests.

Still, simulated test markets are used widely, often as "pretest" markets. Because they are fast and inexpensive, they can be run to quickly assess a new product or its marketing program. If the pretest results are strongly positive, the product might be introduced without further testing. If the results are very poor, the product might be dropped or substantially redesigned and retested. If the results are promising but indefinite, the product and marketing program can be tested further in controlled or standard test markets.

Commercialization

Commercialization
Introducing a new product into the market.

Test marketing gives management the information needed to make a final decision about whether to launch the new product. If the company goes ahead with **commercialization**—introducing the new product into the market—it will face high costs. The company may have to build or rent a manufacturing facility. And, in the case of a major new consumer packaged good, it may spend hundreds of millions of dollars for advertising, sales promotion, and other marketing efforts in the first year. For example, when Procter & Gamble introduced its new Fusion six-blade razor, it spent an eye-popping $1 billion on global marketing support, $300 million in the United States alone.[22]

The company launching a new product must first decide on introduction *timing*. If DaimlerChrysler's new fuel-cell electric car will eat into the sales of the company's other cars, its introduction may be delayed. If the car can be improved further, or if the economy is

■ Commercialization: Procter & Gamble introduced its new Gillette Fusion six-blade razor with an eye-popping $1 billion of global marketing support. It spent $300 million in the United States alone, complete with Super Bowl ads and star-studded launch spectaculars.

down, the company may wait until the following year to launch it. However, if competitors are ready to introduce their own fuel-cell models, DaimlerChrysler may push to introduce the car sooner.

Next, the company must decide *where* to launch the new product—in a single location, a region, the national market, or the international market. Few companies have the confidence, capital, and capacity to launch new products into full national or international distribution. They will develop a planned *market rollout* over time. In particular, small companies may enter attractive cities or regions one at a time. Larger companies, however, may quickly introduce new models into several regions or into the full national market. For example, Procter & Gamble launched the Gillette Fusion razor with a full national blitz. The launch began with 2006 Super Bowl ads costing more than $6 million. Within the first week of launch, P&G had blanketed U.S. stores with some 180,000 Fusion displays. After three months, Fusion brand awareness exceeded 60 percent, and the new brand contributed to a 44 percent rise in overall U.S. sales of nondisposable razors.[23]

Companies with international distribution systems may introduce new products through global rollouts. P&G did this with its SpinBrush low-priced, battery-powered toothbrush. In a swift and successful global assault—its fastest global rollout ever—P&G quickly introduced the new product into 35 countries. Such rapid worldwide expansion overwhelmed rival Colgate's Actibrush brand. Within a year of its introduction, SpinBrush was outselling Colgate's Actibrush by a margin of two to one.[24]

Managing New-Product Development

The new-product development process shown in Figure 9.1 highlights the important activities needed to find, develop, and introduce new products. However, new-product development involves more than just going through a set of steps. Companies must take a holistic approach to managing this process. Successful new-product development requires a customer-centered, team-based, and systematic effort.

Customer-Centered New-Product Development

Above all else, new-product development must be customer centered. When looking for and developing new products, companies often rely too heavily on technical research in their R&D labs. But like everything else in marketing, successful new-product development begins with a thorough understanding of what consumers need and value. **Customer-centered new-product development** focuses on finding new ways to solve customer problems and create more customer-satisfying experiences.

One recent study found that the most successful new products are ones that are differentiated, solve major customer problems, and offer a compelling customer value proposition.[25] Thus, for products ranging from bathroom cleaners to jet engines, today's innovative companies are getting out of the research lab and mingling with customers in the search for new customer value. Consider these examples:[26]

People at all levels of Procter & Gamble, from brand managers to the CEO, look for fresh ideas by tagging along with and talking to customers as they shop for and use

Customer-centered new-product development
New-product development that focuses on finding new ways to solve customer problems and create more customer-satisfying experiences.

the company's products. When one P&G team tackled the problem of "reinventing bathroom cleaning," it started by "listening with its eyes." The group spent many hours watching consumers clean their bathrooms. They focused on "extreme users," ranging from a professional house cleaner who scrubbed grout with his fingernail to four single guys whose idea of cleaning the bathroom was pushing a filthy towel around the floor with a big stick. If they could make both users happy, they figured they had a home run. One big idea—a cleaning tool on a removable stick that could both reach shower walls and get into crannies—got the green light quickly. Consumers loved the prototype, patched together with repurposed plastic, foam, and duct tape. Some refused to return it. The idea became P&G's highly successful Mr. Clean Magic Reach bathroom cleaning tool.

GE wants to infuse customer-centered new-product development thinking into all of its diverse divisions. Executives from the GE Money division—which offers credit cards, loans, and other consumer finance solutions—recently took a tour of San Francisco. During the tour, they watched how people use money—where they get it, how they spend it, even how they carry it. Similarly, to unleash creativity in 15 top executives from GE's jet-engine business, the company took them out to talk with airplane pilots and mechanics. "We even went to meet Larry Flynt's private jet team," says a manager who arranged the trip. "It's a way to . . . increase their empathy and strengthen their ability to make innovation decisions."

Thus, customer-centered new-product development begins and ends with solving customer problems. As one expert asks: "What is innovation after all, if not products and services that offer fresh thinking in a way that meets the needs of customers?"[27]

Team-Based New-Product Development

Good new-product development also requires a total-company, cross-functional effort. Some companies organize their new-product development process into the orderly sequence of steps shown in Figure 9.1, starting with idea generation and ending with commercialization. Under this *sequential product development* approach, one company department works individually to complete its stage of the process before passing the new product along to the next department and stage. This orderly, step-by-step process can help bring control to complex and risky projects. But it also can be dangerously slow. In fast-changing, highly competitive markets, such slow-but-sure product development can result in product failures, lost sales and profits, and crumbling market positions.

In order to get their new products to market more quickly, many companies use a **team-based new-product development** approach. Under this approach, company departments work closely together in cross-functional teams, overlapping the steps in the product development process to save time and increase effectiveness. Instead of passing the new product from department to department, the company assembles a team of people from various departments that stays with the new product from start to finish. Such teams usually include people from the marketing, finance, design, manufacturing, and legal departments, and even supplier and customer companies. In the sequential process, a bottleneck at one phase can seriously slow the entire project. In the simultaneous approach, if one functional area hits snags, it works to resolve them while the team moves on.

The team-based approach does have some limitations. For example, it sometimes creates more organizational tension and confusion than the more orderly sequential approach. However, in rapidly changing industries facing increasingly shorter product life cycles, the rewards of fast and flexible product development far exceed the risks. Companies that combine both a customer-centered approach with team-based new-product development gain a big competitive edge by getting the right new products to market faster (see Real Marketing 9.1).

Systematic New-Product Development

Finally, the new-product development process should be holistic and systematic rather than haphazard. Otherwise, few new ideas will surface, and many good ideas will sputter and die. To avoid these problems, a company can install an *innovation management system* to collect, review, evaluate, and manage new-product ideas.

Team-based new-product development

An approach to developing new products in which various company departments work closely together, overlapping the steps in the product development process to save time and increase effectiveness.

Real Marketing

9.1 Electrolux: Cleaning Up with Customer-Centered, Team-Based New-Product Development

You will never meet Catherine, Anna, Maria, or Monica. But the future success of Swedish home appliances maker Electrolux depends on what these four women think. Catherine, for instance, a type A career woman who is a perfectionist at home, loves the idea of simply sliding her laundry basket into a washing machine, instead of having to lift the clothes from the basket and into the washer. That product idea has been moved onto the fast track for consideration.

So, just who are Catherine and the other women? Well, they don't actually exist. They are composites based on in-depth interviews with some 160,000 consumers from around the globe. To divine the needs of these mythical customers, 53 Electrolux employees—in teams that included designers, engineers, and marketers hailing from various divisions—gathered in Stockholm last November for a weeklong brainstorming session. The Catherine team began by ripping photographs out of a pile of magazines and sticking them onto poster boards. Next to a picture of a woman wearing a sharply tailored suit, they scribbled some of Catherine's attributes: driven, busy, and a bit overwhelmed.

With the help of these characters, Electrolux product developers are searching for the insights they'll need to dream up the next batch of hot products. It's a new way of doing things for Electrolux, but then again, a lot is new at the company. When Chief Executive Hans Straberg took the helm in 2002, Electrolux—which sells products under the Electrolux, Eureka, and Frigidaire brands—was the world's number-two home appliances maker behind Whirlpool. The company faced spiraling costs, and its middle-market products were gradually losing out to cheaper goods from Asia and Eastern Europe. Competition in the United States, where Electrolux gets 40 percent of its sales, was ferocious. The company's stock was treading water. Straberg had to do something radical, especially in the area of new-product innovation. So he began breaking down barriers between departments and forcing his designers, engineers, and mar-

keters to work together to come up with new products. He also introduced an intense focus on the customer. He set out to become "the leader in our industry in terms of systematic development of new products based on consumer insight."

At the Stockholm brainstorming session, for example, group leader Kim Scott urges everyone "to think of yourselves as Catherine." The room buzzes with discussion. Ideas are refined, sketches drawn up. The group settles on three concepts: Breeze, a clothes steamer that also removes stains; an Ironing Center, similar to a pants press but for shirts; and Ease, the washing machine that holds a laundry basket inside its drum.

Half the group races off to the machine shop to turn out a prototype for Breeze, while the rest stay upstairs to bang out a marketing plan. Over the next hour, designer Lennart Johansson carves and sandpapers a block of peach-colored polyurethane until a contraption that resembles a cross between an electric screwdriver and a handheld vacuum begins to emerge. The designers in the group want the Breeze to be smaller, but engineer Giuseppe Frucco points out that would leave too little space for a charging station for the 1,500-watt unit.

For company veterans such as Frucco, who works at Electrolux's fabric care research and development center in Porcia, Italy, this dynamic groupthink is a refreshing change: "We never used to create new products together," he says. "The designers would come up with something and then tell us to build it." The new way saves time and money by avoiding the technical glitches that crop up as a new design moves from the drafting table to the factory floor. The ultimate goal is to come up with new products that consumers will gladly pay a premium for: Gadgets with drop-dead good looks and clever features that ordinary people can understand without having to pore through a thick users' manual. "Consumers are prepared to pay for good design and good performance," says CEO Straberg.

Few companies have pulled off the range of hot new offerings that Electrolux has. One clear hit is a cordless stick and hand vacuum,

Customer-centered new-product development: Electrolux's new-product team starts by watching and talking with consumers to understand their problems. Here, they build a bulletin board packed with pictures and post-its detailing consumers struggling with household cleaning chores and possible product solutions. Then the team moves to the lab to create products that solve customer problems. "We were thinking of you when we developed this product," says Electrolux.

(continues)

(continued)

called Pronto in the United States. Available in an array of metallic hues with a rounded, ergonomic design, this is the Cinderella of vacuums. Too attractive to be locked up in the broom closet, it calls out to be displayed in your kitchen. In Europe, it now commands 50 percent of the market for stick vacs, a coup for a product with fewer than two years on the market. The Pronto is cleaning up in the United States, too. Stacy Silk, a buyer at retail chain Best Buy, says it is one of her hottest sellers, even though it retails for around $100, double the price of comparable models. A recent check at Best Buy's online site shows that the Pronto is currently out of stock. "The biggest thing is the aesthetics," Silk says. "That gets people to walk over and look."

Electrolux is crafting such new products even while moving away from many traditional customer research tools. The company relies less heavily on focus groups and now prefers to interview people in their homes where they can be videotaped pushing a vacuum or shoving laundry into the washer. "Consumers think they know what they want, but they often have trouble articulating it," says Electrolux's senior vice-president for global design. "But when we watch them, we can ask, 'Why do you do that?' We can change the product and solve their problems."

This customer-centered, team-based new-product development approach is producing results. Under the new approach, new-product launches have almost doubled in quantity, and the proportion of new-product launches that result in outsized unit sales is now running at 50 percent of all introductions, up from around 25 percent

previously. As a result, Electrolux's sales, profits, and share price are all up sharply.

It all boils down to understanding consumers and giving them what they need and want. According to a recent Electrolux annual report:

"Thinking of you" sums up our product offering. That is how we create value for our customers—and thereby for our shareholders. All product development and marketing starts with understanding consumer needs, expectations, dreams, and motivation. That's why we contact tens of thousands of consumers throughout the world every year. . . . The first steps in product development are to ask questions, observe, discuss, and analyze. So we can actually say, "We were thinking of you when we developed this product."

Thanks to such thinking, Electrolux has now grown to become the world's biggest household appliances company. Catherine and the other women would be pleased.

Source: Portions adapted from Arlene Sains and Stanley Reed, "Electrolux Cleans Up," *BusinessWeek*, February 27, 2006, pp. 42–43; with quotes and extracts adapted from "Products Developed on the Basis of Consumer Insight," *Acceleration . . . Electrolux Annual Report*, April 7, 2006, p. 7; accessed at www.electrolux.com/node60.aspx. Additional information from Caroline Perry, "Electrolux Doubles Spend with New Strategy," *Marketing Week*, February 16, 2006, pp. 7–9.

The company can appoint a respected senior person to be the company's innovation manager. It can set up Web-based idea management software and encourage all company stakeholders—employees, suppliers, distributors, dealers—to become involved in finding and developing new products. It can assign a cross-functional innovation management committee to evaluate proposed new-product ideas and help bring good ideas to market. It can create recognition programs to reward those who contribute the best ideas.[28]

The innovation management system approach yields two favorable outcomes. First, it helps create an innovation-oriented company culture. It shows that top management supports, encourages, and rewards innovation. Second, it will yield a larger number of new-product ideas, among which will be found some especially good ones. The good new ideas will be more systematically developed, producing more new-product successes. No longer will good ideas wither for the lack of a sounding board or a senior product advocate.

Thus, new-product success requires more than simply thinking up a few good ideas, turning them into products, and finding customers for them. It requires a holistic approach for finding new ways to create valued customer experiences, from generating and screening new-product ideas to creating and rolling out want-satisfying products to customers.

More than this, successful new-product development requires a whole-company commitment. At companies known for their new-product prowess—such as Apple, Google, 3M, Procter & Gamble, and GE—the entire culture encourages, supports, and rewards innovation. Consider 3M, which year after year rates among the world's most innovative companies:[29]

You see the headline in every 3M ad: "Innovation Working for You." But at 3M, innovation isn't just an advertising pitch. Throughout its history, 3M has been one of America's most innovative companies. The company markets more than 50,000 products, ranging from sandpaper, adhesives, and hundreds of sticky tapes to contact lenses, heart-lung machines, and futuristic synthetic ligaments. Each year 3M invests $1.1 billion in research and launches more than 200 new products. But these

1 The world wants thinner electronics.

2 We're getting it all on tape.

3M has pioneered a whole new technology: Microflex Circuits – the world's leading mass-produced electronic circuits on tape.

They're thinner, smaller, highly reliable, and allow for more connections than rigid circuit boards. They'll go anywhere a designer can dream up: phones, pagers, laptops and printers. We expand the possibilities because we make the leap *from need to…*

3M Innovation

For more information, call 1-800-3M-HELPS, or Internet: http://www.mmm.com

■ Innovation: At 3M, new products don't just happen. The company's entire culture encourages, supports, and rewards innovation.

new products don't just happen. 3M works hard to create an entrepreneurial culture that fosters innovation. For more than a century, 3M's culture has encouraged employees to take risks and try new ideas. 3M knows that it must try thousands of new-product ideas to hit one big jackpot. Trying out lots of new ideas often means making mistakes, but 3M accepts blunders and dead ends as a normal part of creativity and innovation.

In fact, "blunders" have turned into some of 3M's most successful products. Old-timers at 3M love to tell the story about 3M scientist Spencer Silver. Silver started out to develop a super-strong adhesive; instead he came up with one that didn't stick very well at all. He sent the apparently useless substance on to other 3M researchers to see whether they could find something to do with it. Nothing happened for several years. Then Arthur Fry, another 3M scientist, had a problem—and an idea. As a choir member in a local church, Mr. Fry was having trouble marking places in his hymnal—the little scraps of paper he used kept falling out. He tried dabbing some of Mr. Silver's weak glue on one of the scraps. It stuck nicely and later peeled off without damaging the hymnal. Thus were born 3M's Post-It Notes, a product that is now one of the top selling office supply products in the world.

Product life cycle (PLC)
The course of a product's sales and profits over its lifetime. It involves five distinct stages: product development, introduction, growth, maturity, and decline.

Product Life-Cycle Strategies

After launching the new product, management wants the product to enjoy a long and happy life. Although it does not expect the product to sell forever, the company wants to earn a decent profit to cover all the effort and risk that went into launching it. Management is aware that each product will have a life cycle, although its exact shape and length is not known in advance.

Figure 9.2 shows a typical **product life cycle** (PLC), the course that a product's sales and profits take over its lifetime. The product life cycle has five distinct stages:

1. *Product development* begins when the company finds and develops a new-product idea. During product development, sales are zero and the company's investment costs mount.
2. *Introduction* is a period of slow sales growth as the product is introduced in the market. Profits are nonexistent in this stage because of the heavy expenses of product introduction.
3. *Growth* is a period of rapid market acceptance and increasing profits.
4. *Maturity* is a period of slowdown in sales growth because the product has achieved acceptance by most potential buyers. Profits level off or decline because of increased marketing outlays to defend the product against competition.
5. *Decline* is the period when sales fall off and profits drop.

Not all products follow this product life cycle. Some products are introduced and die quickly; others stay in the mature stage for a long, long time. Some enter the decline stage and

FIGURE 9.2
Sales and profits over the product's life from inception to decline

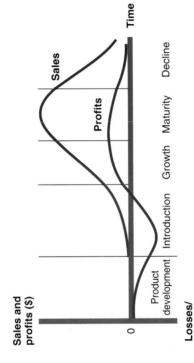

Style
A basic and distinctive mode of expression.

Fashion
A currently accepted or popular style in a given field.

are then cycled back into the growth stage through strong promotion or repositioning. It seems that a well-managed brand could live forever. Such venerable brands as Coca-Cola, Gillette, Budweiser, American Express, Wells-Fargo, and Tabasco, for instance, are still going strong after more than 100 years.

The PLC concept can describe a *product class* (gasoline-powered automobiles), a *product form* (SUVs), or a *brand* (the Ford Escape). The PLC concept applies differently in each case. Product classes have the longest life cycles—the sales of many product classes stay in the mature stage for a long time. Product forms, in contrast, tend to have the standard PLC shape. Product forms such as "dial telephones" and "cassette tapes" passed through a regular history of introduction, rapid growth, maturity, and decline.

A specific brand's life cycle can change quickly because of changing competitive attacks and responses. For example, although laundry soaps (product class) and powdered detergents (product form) have enjoyed fairly long life cycles, the life cycles of specific brands have tended to be much shorter. Today's leading brands of powdered laundry soap are Tide and Cheer; the leading brands 75 years ago were Fels Naptha, Octagon, and Kirkman.[30]

The PLC concept also can be applied to what are known as styles, fashions, and fads. Their special life cycles are shown in Figure 9.3. A **style** is a basic and distinctive mode of expression. For example, styles appear in homes (colonial, ranch, transitional, clothing (formal, casual), and art (realist, surrealist, abstract). Once a style is invented, it may last for generations, passing in and out of vogue. A style has a cycle showing several periods of renewed interest. A **fashion** is a currently accepted or popular style in a given field. For example, the more formal "business attire" look of corporate dress of the 1980s and early 1990s gave way to the "business casual" look of today. Fashions tend to grow slowly, remain popular for a while, and then decline slowly.

Fads are temporary periods of unusually high sales driven by consumer enthusiasm and immediate product or brand popularity.[31] A fad may be part of an otherwise normal lifecycle, as in the case of recent surges in the sales of scooters and yo-yos. Or the fad may comprise a brand's or product's entire lifecycle. "Pet rocks" are a classic example. Upon hearing his friends complain about how expensive it was to care for their dogs, advertising copywriter Gary Dahl joked about his pet rock. He soon wrote a spoof of a dog-training manual for it, titled "The Care and Training of Your Pet Rock."

■ Product life cycle: Some products die quickly; others stay in the mature stage for a long, long time. TABASCO Sauce is "over 130 years old and yet still able to totally whup your butt!"

FIGURE 9.3
Styles, fashions, and fads

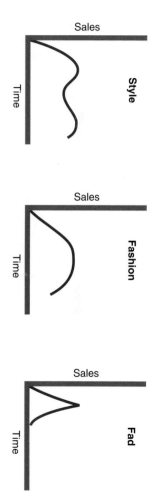

Style	Fashion	Fad
Sales / Time	Sales / Time	Sales / Time

Fad
A temporary period of unusually high sales driven by consumer enthusiasm and immediate product or brand popularity.

Introduction stage
The product life-cycle stage in which the new product is first distributed and made available for purchase.

■ Fads: Pet rocks, introduced one October, had sunk like a stone by the next February.

Soon Dahl was selling some 1.5 million ordinary beach pebbles at $4 a pop. Yet the fad, which broke one October, had sunk like a stone by the next February. Dahl's advice to those who want to succeed with a fad: "Enjoy it while it lasts." Other examples of such fads include the Rubik's Cube, lava lamps, and low-carb diets.³²

The PLC concept can be applied by marketers as a useful framework for describing how products and markets work. And when used carefully, the PLC concept can help in developing good marketing strategies for different stages of the product life cycle. But using the PLC concept for forecasting product performance or for developing marketing strategies presents some practical problems. For example, managers may have trouble identifying which stage of the PLC the product is in or pinpointing when the product moves into the next stage. They may also find it hard to determine the factors that affect the product's movement through the stages.

In practice, it is difficult to forecast the sales level at each PLC stage, the length of each stage, and the shape of the PLC curve. Using the PLC concept to develop marketing strategy also can be difficult because strategy is both a cause and a result of the product's life cycle. The product's current PLC position suggests the best marketing strategies, and the resulting marketing strategies affect product performance in later life-cycle stages.

Moreover, marketers should not blindly push products through the traditional stages of the product life cycle. "As marketers instinctively embrace the old life-cycle paradigm, they needlessly consign their products to following the curve into maturity and decline," notes one marketing professor. Instead, marketers often defy the "rules" of the life cycle and position their products in unexpected ways. By doing this, "companies can rescue products foundering in the maturity phase of their life cycles and return them to the growth phase. And they can catapult new products forward into the growth phase, leapfrogging obstacles that could slow consumers' acceptance."³³

We looked at the product development stage of the product life cycle in the first part of the chapter. We now look at strategies for each of the other life-cycle stages.

Introduction Stage

The **introduction stage** starts when the new product is first launched. Introduction takes time, and sales growth is apt to be slow. Well-known products such as instant coffee and frozen foods lingered for many years before they entered a stage of rapid growth.

In this stage, as compared to other stages, profits are negative or low because of the low sales and high distribution and promotion expenses. Much money is needed to attract distributors and build their inventories. Promotion spending is relatively high to inform consumers of the new product and get them to try it. Because the market is not generally ready for product refinements at this stage, the company and its few competitors produce basic versions of the product. These firms focus their selling on those buyers who are the most ready to buy.

A company, especially the *market pioneer*, must choose a launch strategy that is consistent with the intended product positioning. It should realize that the initial strategy is just the first step in a grander marketing plan for the product's entire life cycle. If the pioneer chooses its launch strategy to make a "killing," it may be sacrificing long-run revenue for the sake of short-run gain. As the pioneer moves through later stages of the life cycle, it must continuously formulate new pricing, promotion, and other marketing strategies. It has the best chance of building and retaining market leadership if it plays its cards correctly from the start.

Growth Stage

Growth stage
The product life-cycle stage in which a product's sales start climbing quickly.

If the new product satisfies the market, it will enter a **growth stage**, in which sales will start climbing quickly. The early adopters will continue to buy, and later buyers will start following their lead, especially if they hear favorable word of mouth. Attracted by the opportunities for profit, new competitors will enter the market. They will introduce new product features, and the market will expand. The increase in competitors leads to an increase in the number of distribution outlets, and sales jump just to build reseller inventories. Prices remain where they are or fall only slightly. Companies keep their promotion spending at the same or a slightly higher level. Educating the market remains a goal, but now the company must also meet the competition.

Profits increase during the growth stage, as promotion costs are spread over a large volume and as unit manufacturing costs fall. The firm uses several strategies to sustain rapid market growth as long as possible. It improves product quality and adds new product features and models. It enters new market segments and new distribution channels. It shifts some advertising from building product awareness to building product conviction and purchase, and it lowers prices at the right time to attract more buyers.

In the growth stage, the firm faces a trade-off between high market share and high current profit. By spending a lot of money on product improvement, promotion, and distribution, the company can capture a dominant position. In doing so, however, it gives up maximum current profit, which it hopes to make up in the next stage.

Maturity Stage

Maturity stage
The product life-cycle stage in which sales growth slows or levels off.

At some point, a product's sales growth will slow down, and the product will enter a **maturity stage**. This maturity stage normally lasts longer than the previous stages, and it poses strong challenges to marketing management. Most products are in the maturity stage of the life cycle, and therefore most of marketing management deals with the mature product.

The slowdown in sales growth results in many producers with many products to sell. In turn, this overcapacity leads to greater competition. Competitors begin marking down prices, increasing their advertising and sales promotions, and upping their R&D budgets to find better versions of the product. These steps lead to a drop in profit. Some of the weaker competitors start dropping out, and the industry eventually contains only well-established competitors.

Although many products in the mature stage appear to remain unchanged for long periods, most successful ones are actually evolving to meet changing consumer needs. Product managers should do more than simply ride along with or defend their mature products—a good offense is the best defense. They should consider modifying the market, product, and marketing mix.

In *modifying the market*, the company tries to increase the consumption of the current product. It may look for new users and new market segments, as when John Deere targeted the retiring baby-boomer market with the Gator, a vehicle traditionally used on a farm. For this new market, Deere has repositioned the Gator, promising that it can "take you from a do-it-yourselfer to a do-it-a-lot-easier."

The manager may also look for ways to increase usage among present customers. Amazon.com does this by sending permission-based e-mails to regular customers letting them know when their favorite authors or performers publish new books or CDs. The WD-40 Company has shown a real knack for expanding the market by finding new uses for its popular substance.

Nip dirt and rust in the bud. For clean, smooth operation and perennial protection from the elements, spray your hand tools with WD-40® before and after each use.

wd40.com

■ The WD-40 Company's knack for finding new uses has made this popular substance one of the truly essential survival items in most American homes.

In 2000, the company launched a search to uncover 2,000 unique uses for WD-40. After receiving 300,000 individual submissions, it narrowed the list to the best 2,000 and posted it on the company's Web site. Some consumers suggest simple and practical uses. One teacher uses WD-40 to clean old chalkboards in her classroom. "Amazingly, the boards started coming to life again," she reports. "Not only were they restored, but years of masking and Scotch tape residue came off as well." Others, however, report some pretty unusual applications. One man uses WD-40 to polish his glass eye; another uses it to remove a prosthetic leg. And did you hear about the nude burglary suspect who had wedged himself in a vent at a cafe in Denver? The fire department extracted him with a large dose of WD-40. Or how about the Mississippi naval officer who used WD-40 to repel an angry bear? Then there's the college student who wrote to say that a friend's nightly amorous activities in the next room were causing everyone in his dorm to lose sleep—he solved the problem by treating the squeaky bedsprings with WD-40.[34]

The company might also try *modifying the product*—changing characteristics such as quality, features, style, or packaging to attract new users and to inspire more usage. It might improve the product's quality and performance—its durability, reliability, speed, taste. It can improve the product's styling and attractiveness. Thus, car manufacturers restyle their cars to attract buyers who want a new look. The makers of consumer food and household products introduce new flavors, colors, ingredients, or packages to revitalize consumer buying.

Or the company might add new features that expand the product's usefulness, safety, or convenience. For example, WD-40 has recently introduced a new Smart Straw can featuring a permanently attached straw that never gets lost. And it brought out a No-Mess Pen, with a handy pen-shaped applicator that lets users "put WD-40 where you want it and nowhere else."

Finally, the company can try *modifying the marketing mix*—improving sales by changing one or more marketing mix elements. It can launch a better advertising campaign or use aggressive sales promotions—trade deals, cents-off, premiums, and contests. In addition to pricing and promotion, the company can also move into larger market channels, using mass merchandisers, if these channels are growing. Finally, the company can offer new or improved services to buyers.

Decline Stage

The sales of most product forms and brands eventually dip. The decline may be slow, as in the case of oatmeal cereal, or rapid, as in the cases of cassette and VHS tapes. Sales may plunge to zero, or they may drop to a low level where they continue for many years. This is the **decline stage.**

Sales decline for many reasons, including technological advances, shifts in consumer tastes, and increased competition. As sales and profits decline, some firms withdraw from the market. Those remaining may prune their product offerings. They may drop smaller market segments and marginal trade channels, or they may cut the promotion budget and reduce their prices further.

Decline stage
The product life-cycle stage in which a product's sales decline.

Real Marketing P&G: Working at Both Ends of the Product Life Cycle

9.2 Not so long ago, Procter & Gamble was a slumbering giant. Mired in mature markets with megabrands such as Tide, Crest, Pampers, and Pantene, growth had slowed and earnings languished. But no longer. Now, thanks to a potent mixture of renewed creativity and marketing muscle, P&G is once again on the move. In the past five years, P&G's stock price and profits have doubled.

The key to this success has been a renewed knack for innovation and a string of successful new products. As you've no doubt noted, P&G innovations have popped up repeatedly as examples in this chapter. "From its Swiffer mop to battery-powered Crest SpinBrush toothbrushes and Whitestrip tooth whiteners," says one observer, "P&G has simply done a better job than rivals of coming up with new products that consumers crave."

But it's not just *new* products—P&G has been working at both ends of the product life cycle. Along with creating innovative new products, P&G has become adept at turning yesterday's faded favorites into today's hot new products. Here are two examples.

Mr. Clean

Mr. Clean's share of the all-purpose household cleaner market had plunged more than 45 percent in just ten years. But rather than abandon the 48-year-old iconic brand, P&G chose to modify and extend it. First, it reformulated the core Mr. Clean all-purpose liquid cleaner, adding antibacterial properties and several new scents. Then came some real creativity. P&G extended the brand to include several revolutionary new products.

The first was Mr. Clean Magic Eraser, a soft, disposable self-cleaning pad that acts like an eraser to lift away tough dirt, including difficult scuff and crayon marks. The Magic Eraser was soon followed by products such as the Mr. Clean AutoDry Carwash system, which gives your car a spot-free clean and shine with no need to hand dry, and the Mr. Clean MagicReach bathroom cleaner,

Cleans tables, chairs, stairs, you name it:
Mr. Clean Magic Eraser. Cleans like magic.

Working at both ends of the product life cycle: Along with creating innovative new products, P&G has become adept at turning yesterday's faded favorites into today's hot new products. For example, its Mr. Clean brand has now muscled its way back into a market-leading position.

Carrying a weak product can be very costly to a firm, and not just in profit terms. There are many hidden costs. A weak product may take up too much of management's time. It often requires frequent price and inventory adjustments. It requires advertising and sales-force attention that might be better used to make "healthy" products more profitable. A product's failing reputation can cause customer concerns about the company and its other products. The biggest cost may well lie in the future. Keeping weak products delays the search for replacements, creates a lopsided product mix, hurts current profits, and weakens the company's foothold on the future.

For these reasons, companies need to pay more attention to their aging products. The firm's first task is to identify those products in the decline stage by regularly reviewing sales, market shares, costs, and profit trends. Then, management must decide whether to maintain, harvest, or drop each of these declining products.

Management may decide to *maintain* its brand without change in the hope that competitors will leave the industry. For example, Procter & Gamble made good profits by remaining in

which helps ease the tough job of cleaning those hard-to-reach bathroom spots.

As for the marketing muscle, P&G backed the new-product launches with millions of dollars in marketing support. It spent $75 million on marketing the first version of the AutoDry Carwash alone. Now, after a decade of playing the 98-pound weakling, Mr. Clean has muscled its way back to a market-leading position as a P&G billion-dollar brand.

Old Spice

When P&G acquired Old Spice in 1990, the brand was largely a has-been. It consisted mainly of a highly fragrant aftershave, marketed to a rapidly graying customer base through ads featuring a whistling sailor with a girl in every port. Old Spice deodorant ranked a dismal tenth in market share. But in a surprisingly short time, P&G has transformed a small stagnating brand into a men's personal care powerhouse. Old Spice is now one of the top-selling brands in the deodorant, antiperspirant, and body spray category, with 10 percent share of the almost $2.4 billion market.

To get there, P&G pulled off one of the hardest tricks in marketing: reviving a familiar brand. To shed the image of "your father's aftershave," and to appeal to younger buyers, P&G refocused on performance, launching Old Spice High Endurance deodorant in 1994. It ditched the sailor ads and targeted guys 18 to 34. The deodorant business grew steadily, but P&G still wasn't drawing in men 25 to 45, who still remembered Old Spice as a relic from Dad's era.

So P&G skipped a generation and aimed Old Spice at first-time deodorant users. It started handing out samples of High Endurance to fifth-grade health classes, covering 90 percent of the nation's schools. In 2000, P&G launched Old Spice Red Zone, a sub-brand that offered even more protection than High Endurance. Sales took off, and by 2001, Old Spice was edging out Right Guard as the top teen brand.

To reach teen boys, who spend less time watching TV, P&G's marketing for Old Spice has gone well beyond the 30-second TV commercial to include lots of grassroots marketing. P&G hands out Old Spice samples at skateboarding events and gets the product into locker rooms by sponsoring a contest for high-school football player of the year. Old Spice has even partnered with P&G brand Always to assemble sex-education packages for fifth-grade classrooms, entitled "Always Changing: About You—Puberty and Stuff." For boys, the package comes complete with reading material, a video, and Old Spice product samples.

P&G now has that Old Spice sailor whistling a whole new tune. The once old and stodgy is young again, and hot. Beyond deodorant, P&G sees Old Spice as a beachhead into other products. It has already launched Old Spice body sprays and body washes and has licensed sales of razors and shaving cream. What was old just over five years ago is new again—and a lot younger.

Sources: Examples adapted from portions of Robert Berner, "Extreme Makeover," *Business Week*, November 1, 2004, pp. 105-106; and Jack Neff, "Mr. Clean Gets $50 Million Push," *Advertising Age*, August 18, 2003, pp. 3, 32; with quotes and other information from Todd Wasserman, "Mr. Clean AutoDry Gets an Overhaul," *Brandweek*, February 28, 2005, p. 17; Marek Fuchs, "Sex Ed, Provided by Old Spice," *New York Times*, May 29, 2005, p. 14WC.1; Jack Neff, "Who's No. 1? Depends on Who's Analyzing the Data," *Advertising Age*, June 12, 2006, p. 8; Constantine von Hoffman, "A Washout or a Clean Sweep," *Brandweek*, June 19, 2006, pp. S52–S54; P&G 2005 Annual Report, accessed at www.PG.com, July 2006; and information accessed at www.homemadesimple.com/mrclean/, December 2006.

the declining liquid soap business as others withdrew. Or management may decide to reposition or reinvigorate the brand in hopes of moving it back into the growth stage of the product life cycle. Procter & Gamble has done this with several brands, including Mr. Clean and Old Spice (see Real Marketing 9.2).

Management may decide to *harvest* the product, which means reducing various costs (plant and equipment, maintenance, R&D, advertising, sales force) and hoping that sales hold up. If successful, harvesting will increase the company's profits in the short run. Or management may decide to *drop* the product from the line. It can sell it to another firm or simply liquidate it at salvage value. In recent years, Procter & Gamble has sold off a number of lesser or declining brands such as Crisco and Jif peanut butter. If the company plans to find a buyer, it will not want to run down the product through harvesting.

Table 9.2 summarizes the key characteristics of each stage of the product life cycle. The table also lists the marketing objectives and strategies for each stage.[35]

TABLE 9.2
Summary of Product Life-Cycle Characteristics, Objectives, and Strategies

Characteristics	Introduction	Growth	Maturity	Decline
Sales	Low sales	Rapidly rising sales	Peak sales	Declining sales
Costs	High cost per customer	Average cost per customer	Low cost per customer	Low cost per customer
Profits	Negative	Rising profits	High profits	Declining profits
Customers	Innovators	Early adopters	Middle majority	Laggards
Competitors	Few	Growing number	Stable number beginning to decline	Declining number
Marketing Objectives				
	Create product awareness and trial	Maximize market share	Maximize profit while defending market share	Reduce expenditure and milk the brand
Strategies				
Product	Offer a basic product	Offer product extensions, service, warranty	Diversify brand and models	Phase out weak items
Price	Use cost-plus	Price to penetrate market	Price to match or beat competitors	Cut price
Distribution	Build selective distribution	Build intensive distribution	Build more intensive distribution	Go selective: phase out unprofitable outlets
Advertising	Build product awareness among early adopters and dealers	Build awareness and interest in the mass market	Stress brand differences and benefits	Reduce to level needed to retain hard-core loyals
Sales Promotion	Use heavy sales promotion to entice trial	Reduce to take advantage of heavy consumer demand	Increase to encourage brand switching	Reduce to minimal level

Source: Philip Kotler, *Marketing Management*, 12th ed. (Upper Saddle River, NJ: Prentice Hall, 2006), p. 332.

Additional Product and Service Considerations

Here, we'll wrap up our discussion of products and services with two additional considerations: social responsibility in product decisions and issues of international product and service marketing.

Product Decisions and Social Responsibility

Product decisions have attracted much public attention. Marketers should carefully consider public policy issues and regulations involving acquiring or dropping products, patent protection, product quality and safety, and product warranties.

Regarding new products, the government may prevent companies from adding products through acquisitions if the effect threatens to lessen competition. Companies dropping products must be aware that they have legal obligations, written or implied, to their suppliers, dealers, and customers who have a stake in the dropped product. Companies must also obey U.S. patent laws when developing new products. A company cannot make its product illegally similar to another company's established product.

Manufacturers must comply with specific laws regarding product quality and safety. The Federal Food, Drug, and Cosmetic Act protects consumers from unsafe and adulterated food, drugs, and cosmetics. Various acts provide for the inspection of sanitary conditions in the meat- and poultry-processing industries. Safety legislation has been passed to regulate fabrics, chemical substances, automobiles, toys, and drugs and poisons. The Consumer Product Safety Act of 1972 established a Consumer Product Safety Commission, which has the authority to ban or seize potentially harmful products and set severe penalties for violation of the law.

If consumers have been injured by a product that has been designed defectively, they can sue manufacturers or dealers. Product liability suits are now occurring in federal courts at the rate of almost 24,000 per year. Although manufacturers are found at fault in only 6 percent of all product liability cases, when they are found guilty, the median jury award is $1.5 million, and individual awards can run into the tens or even hundreds of millions of dollars. For example, a jury recently ordered Ford to pay nearly $369 million to a woman paralyzed in a rollover accident involving a Ford Explorer.[36]

This phenomenon has resulted in huge increases in product liability insurance premiums, causing big problems in some industries. Some companies pass these higher rates along to consumers by raising prices. Others are forced to discontinue high-risk product lines. Some companies are now appointing "product stewards," whose job is to protect consumers from harm and the company from liability by proactively ferreting out potential product problems.

Many manufacturers offer written product warranties to convince customers of their products' quality. To protect consumers, Congress passed the Magnuson-Moss Warranty Act in 1975. The act requires that full warranties meet certain minimum standards, including repair "within a reasonable time and without charge" or a replacement or full refund if the product does not work "after a reasonable number of attempts" at repair. Otherwise, the company must make it clear that it is offering only a limited warranty. The law has led several manufacturers to switch from full to limited warranties and others to drop warranties altogether.

International Product and Services Marketing

International product and service marketers face special challenges. First, they must figure out what products and services to introduce and in which countries. Then, they must decide how much to standardize or adapt their products and services for world markets.

On the one hand, companies would like to standardize their offerings. Standardization helps a company to develop a consistent worldwide image. It also lowers the product design, manufacturing, and marketing costs of offering a large variety of products. On the other hand, markets and consumers around the world differ widely. Companies must usually respond to these differences by adapting their product offerings. For example, Cadbury sells kiwi-filled Cadbury Kiwi Royale in New Zealand. Frito-Lay sells Nori Seaweed Lay's potato chips for Thailand and A la Turca corn chips with poppy seeds and a dried tomato flavor for Turkey.[37]

Packaging also presents new challenges for international marketers. Packaging issues can be subtle. For example, names, labels, and colors may not translate easily from one country to another. A firm using yellow flowers in its logo might fare well in the United States but meet with disaster in Mexico, where a yellow flower symbolizes death or disrespect. Similarly, although Nature's Gift might be an appealing name for gourmet mushrooms in America, it would be deadly in Germany, where *gift* means poison. Packaging may also need to be tailored to meet the physical characteristics of consumers in various parts of the world. For instance, soft drinks are sold in smaller cans in Japan to fit the smaller Japanese hand better. Thus, although product and package standardization can produce benefits, companies must usually adapt their offerings to the unique needs of specific international markets.

Service marketers also face special challenges when going global. Some service industries have a long history of international operations. For example, the commercial banking industry was one of the first to grow internationally. Banks had to provide global services in order to meet the foreign exchange and credit needs of their home country clients wanting to sell overseas. In recent years, many banks have become truly global. Germany's Deutsche Bank, for example, serves more than 13 million customers in 73 countries. For its clients around the world who wish to grow globally, Deutsche Bank can raise money not only in Frankfurt but also in Zurich, London, Paris, and Tokyo.[38]

Professional and business services industries such as accounting, management consulting, and advertising have also globalized. The international growth of these firms followed the globalization of the client companies they serve. For example, as more clients employ worldwide marketing and advertising strategies, advertising agencies have responded by globalizing their own operations. McCann Worldgroup, a large U.S.-based advertising and marketing services agency, operates in more than 130 countries. It serves international clients such as Coca-Cola, General Motors, ExxonMobile, Microsoft, MasterCard, Johnson & Johnson, and Unilever in markets ranging from the United States and Canada to Korea and Kazakhstan. Moreover, McCann Worldgroup is one company in the Interpublic Group of Companies, an immense, worldwide network of advertising and marketing services companies.[39]

Retailers are among the latest service businesses to go global. As their home markets become saturated, American retailers such as Wal-Mart, Office Depot, and Saks Fifth Avenue are expanding into faster-growing markets abroad. For example, since 1995, Wal-Mart has entered 14 countries; its international division's sales grew more than 11 percent last year, skyrocketing to more than $62.7 billion. Foreign retailers are making similar moves. Asian shoppers can now buy American products in French-owned Carrefour stores. Carrefour, the world's second-largest retailer behind Wal-Mart, now operates in more than 11,000 stores in more than 30 countries. It is the leading retailer in Europe, Brazil, and Argentina and the largest foreign retailer in China.[40]

The trend toward growth of global service companies will continue, especially in banking, airlines, telecommunications, and professional services. Today service firms are no longer simply following their manufacturing customers. Instead, they are taking the lead in international expansion.

▌ Reviewing the Concepts

A company's current products face limited life spans and must be replaced by newer products. But new products can fail—the risks of innovation are as great as the rewards. The key to successful innovation lies in a total-company effort, strong planning, and a systematic *new-product development* process.

1. Explain how companies find and develop new-product ideas.

Companies find and develop new-product ideas from a variety of sources. Many new-product ideas stem from *internal sources*. Companies conduct formal research and development, pick the brains of their employees, and brainstorm at executive meetings. Other ideas come from *external sources*. By conducting surveys and analyzing *customer* questions and complaints, companies can generate new-product ideas that will meet specific consumer needs. Companies track *competitors'* offerings and inspect new products, dismantling them, analyzing their performance, and deciding whether to introduce a similar or improved product. *Distributors and suppliers* are close to the market and can pass along information about consumer problems and new-product possibilities.

2. List and define the steps in the new-product development process and the major considerations in managing this process.

The new-product development process consists of eight sequential stages. The process starts with *idea generation*. Next comes *idea screening*, which reduces the number of ideas based on the company's own criteria. Ideas that pass the screening stage continue through *product concept development*, in which a detailed version of the new-product idea is stated in meaningful consumer terms. In the next stage, *concept testing*, new-product concepts are tested with a group of target consumers to determine whether the concepts have strong consumer appeal. Strong concepts proceed to *marketing strategy development*, in which an initial marketing strategy for the new product is developed from the product concept. In the *business-analysis* stage, a review of the sales, costs, and profit projections for a new product is conducted to determine whether the new product is

likely to satisfy the company's objectives. With positive results here, the ideas become more concrete through *product development* and *test marketing* and finally are launched during *commercialization*.

New-product development involves more than just going through a set of steps. Companies must take a systematic, holistic approach to managing this process. Successful new-product development requires a customer-centered, team-based, systematic effort.

3. Describe the stages of the product life cycle.

Each product has a *life cycle* marked by a changing set of problems and opportunities. The sales of the typical product follow an S-shaped curve made up of five stages. The cycle begins with the *product development stage* when the company finds and develops a new-product idea. The *introduction stage* is marked by slow growth and low profits as the product is distributed to the market. If successful, the product enters a *growth stage*, which offers rapid sales growth and increasing profits. Next comes a *maturity stage* when sales growth slows and profits stabilize. Finally, the product enters a *decline stage* in which sales and profits dwindle. The company's task during this stage is to recognize the decline and to decide whether it should maintain, harvest, or drop the product.

4. Describe how marketing strategies change during the product's life cycle.

In the *introduction stage*, the company must choose a launch strategy consistent with its intended product positioning. Much money is needed to attract distributors and build their inventories and to inform consumers of the new product and achieve trial. In the *growth stage*, companies continue to educate potential consumers and distributors. In addition, the company works to stay ahead of the competition and sustain rapid market growth by improving product quality, adding new product features and models, entering new market segments and distribution channels, shifting advertising from building product awareness to building product conviction and purchase, and lowering prices at the right time to attract new buyers.

In the *maturity stage*, companies continue to invest in maturing products and consider modifying the market, the product, and the marketing mix. When *modifying the market*, the company attempts to increase the consumption of the current product. When *modifying the product*, the company changes some of the product's characteristics—such as quality, features, or style—to attract new users or inspire more usage. When *modifying the marketing mix*, the company works to improve sales by changing one or more of the marketing-mix elements. Once the company recognizes that a product has entered the *decline stage*, management must decide whether to *maintain* the brand without change, hoping that competitors will drop out of the market; *harvest* the product, reducing costs and trying to maintain sales; or *drop* the product, selling it to another firm or liquidating it at salvage value.

5. Discuss two additional product issues: socially responsible product decisions and international product and services marketing.

Marketers must consider two additional product issues. The first is *social responsibility*. This includes public policy issues and regulations involving acquiring or dropping products, patent protection, product quality and safety, and product warranties. The second involves the special challenges facing international product and service marketers. International marketers must decide how much to standardize or adapt their offerings for world markets.

Reviewing the Key Terms

Discussing the Concepts

1. Why is concept testing important?

2. Under what conditions would you consider marketing a product? Describe a product or service that meets these no-need-to-test criteria.

3. Compare the sequential product development to the team-based approach. Is one approach better than the other? Explain.

4. Identify and discuss some potential problems with the product life cycle.

5. The chapter states that "In the growth stage of the product life cycle, the firm faces a trade-off between high market share and high current profit." Explain this statement.

6. What are some of the major reasons a product reaches the decline stage of the product life cycle?

Applying the Concepts

1. Form a small group. Generate ideas for a new consumer product that fills an existing need but does not currently exist. Select the one idea that you think is best. What process did your group use for idea generation and screening?

2. Write a marketing strategy statement for a new full-functioning but folding bicycle.

3. You are a product manager in a firm that manufactures and markets a line of branded action figure toys. The branded toy line is five years old. Annual sales and profits for this period are presented in the chart. Prepare a one-sentence strategy for each of the 4 Ps based on the brand's current product life-cycle position.

Focus on Technology

In the United States, there are over 250,000 deaths per year from sudden cardiac arrest. That's 100,000 more deaths than the number caused by traffic accidents, house fires, handguns, breast cancer, and AIDS combined. Defibrillators are medical devices that are commonly used by firefighters and paramedics to treat victims of sudden cardiac arrest with an electrical charge that restarts their hearts. With more than 80 percent of sudden cardiac arrests occurring at home, and only 5 percent of victims receiving the lifesaving electrical charge, Philips is now marketing a portable consumer defibrillator called the HeartStart. The product, which is about the size of a handheld video game, can be operated by any individual and does not need a trained medical provider. Voice activation guides a consumer through each step, and smart technology gives specific instructions based on feedback to the main system. The FDA-approved product, priced at $1,495, is available online from amazon.com and drugstore.com. Visit http://www.heartstart.com for recent information on this new product.

1. Explain how this product might have moved through the stages of new-product development.

2. How might the marketing strategy for HeartStart change as it moves through the product life cycle?

HD DVD forum claims that new issues this time around will give its technology the advantage. For starters, manufacturing costs for Blu-ray will be significantly higher. (The Blu-ray camp counters that the cost difference is minimal and will likely disappear as volumes increase.) HD DVD software will also allow consumers to make copies of their discs to computer hard drives and portable devices. And with its iHD technology, HD DVD discs promise greater interactivity by allowing for enhanced content and navigation, as well as fancy features such as picture-in-picture capability.

However, additional new issues could tilt the scales in favor of Blu-ray. Although Toshiba and HD DVD enjoy a brief first-to-market advantage, Blu-ray will likely experience a huge bump in market share when Sony introduces its long-awaited PlayStation 3 gaming platform in late 2006. The PlayStation 3 not only uses Blu-ray technology for its game discs, it will be able to play all Blu-ray movies as well. This could put millions of Blu-ray players into homes very quickly via the video consoles.

WILL THE POINT BE MOOT?

Drawing comparisons to the Beta/VHS format war assumes that one of the two current competing formats will ultimately win and the other will die out. However, two other possibilities exist. First, both formats could succeed and do well. Most of the issues mentioned previously may become nonissues as the Blu-ray and HD DVD technologies evolve. Either of the two technologies could adopt features of the other. Additionally, at some point, hardware manufacturers may well release dual-format players, capable of playing both Blu-ray and HD DVD discs. Such a development could reduce the relevance of format labels.

Stephen Nickerson, senior vice president at Warner Home Video, believes that both formats could easily succeed. Although most analysts compare the DVD format war to the VCR format war, he suggests another analogy. "The [video] games industry since the early '90s has had two or three incompatible formats and it hasn't slowed the adoption of game platforms."

However, there is another potential outcome. Both formats might fail. Ted Schadler, analyst with Forrester Research, believes that most people are missing an important point. "The irony of this format war is that it comes at the tail end of the century-long era of physical media. While a high-definition video format does bring benefits over today's standard-definition discs, in movies as in music, consumers are moving beyond shiny discs." Schadler's statement refers to the fact that the consumption of all kinds of entertainment products, even television programming, has evolved dramatically since the mid-1990s. Consumers have far more options than they used to, and the dust has yet to settle on which options will dominate for any given type of product.

For home video, more customers are choosing on-demand, nonphysical media, including online video and video-on-demand television. One in six cable subscribers has demonstrated significant interest in watching video-on-demand. As cable providers increase their video libraries and technologies improve, that number will only grow. Internet video is also spreading rapidly, with 46 percent of online consumers now watching movies via the Web. Additionally, with the success of the video iPod, major Hollywood studios aren't just considering which DVD formats to support. They're assessing how they can make money by selling movies directly to consumers in a file format that can be played on portable devices. According to Ted Schadler, the device more consumers age 12 to 21 now say they can't live without isn't their TV, it's their PC. Even Bill Gates has his doubts about the current DVD format war. "Understand that this is the last physical format there will ever be. Everything's going to be streamed directly or on a hard disk."

Although these predictions may very well be true, there is likely still plenty of steam left in the DVD market. Physical discs still hold many advantages over the non-physical media. Even with the significant threat of VHS, Beta survived for eight years. And no format will last forever. Only nine years passed between the introductions of the first home DVD and HD DVD players. So although there's clearly a home video war looming, the big questions concern who will be fighting and on what fronts.

Questions for Discussion

1. Classify the high-definition DVD market using the product life-cycle framework. Based on this analysis, what objectives and strategies should Sony and the other competitors pursue? Are any of the competitors deviating from this formula?

2. As sales of the new DVD players increase, what will happen to the characteristics of the home video market and the strategies employed by Sony and other competitors?

3. Analyze the development of Blu-ray and HD DVD according to the stages of the new-product development process.

4. Who are the current combatants in the battle for the home video market? Who will they be in five years?

Sources: Beth Snyder Bulik, "Marketing War Looms for Dueling DVD Formats," *Advertising Age,* April 10, 2006, p. 20; Gary Gentile, "Beta/VHS-Like Battle Shaping Up for New High-Def DVDs," *Associated Press Worldstream,* January 6, 2006; Ann Steffora Mutschler, "The Convergence War," *Electronic Business,* May 1, 2006, p. 44; Sue Zeidler, "Hold On Tight; Going to the Store to Rent a DVD May Soon Be a Thing of the Past," *Calgary Sun,* p. 40; information on Beta and VHS accessed online at www.totalrewind.org.

Pricing Products
Understanding and Capturing Customer Value

Previewing the Concepts

Next, we look at a second major marketing mix tool—pricing. According to one pricing expert, pricing lets a company "get paid for the value it creates for customers."1 If effective product development, promotion, and distribution sow the seeds of business success, effective pricing is the harvest. Firms successful at creating customer value with the other marketing mix activities must still capture some of this value in the prices they earn. Yet, despite its importance, many firms do not handle pricing well. In this chapter, we'll look at internal and external considerations that affect pricing decisions and examine general pricing approaches. In the next chapter, we dig into pricing strategies.

Pricing decisions can make or break a company. For openers, consider Toys 'R' Us, whose low-cost, everyday-low-price strategy years ago helped it to sweep aside smaller competitors and become the nation's largest toy seller. But what goes around comes around. Once-dominant Toys 'R' Us is now fighting for survival in the toy market against an even more ruthless low-price competitor. (Can you guess which one?!)

Finding the right pricing strategy and implementing it well can be critical to a company's success—even to its survival. Perhaps no company knows this better than giant toy retailer Toys 'R' Us. More than three decades ago, Toys 'R' Us taught smaller independent toy retailers and department-store chains in its industry a hard pricing lesson, driving many of them to extinction. In recent years, however, Toys 'R' Us has gotten a bitter taste of its own pricing medicine in return.

In the late 1970s, Toys 'R' Us emerged as a toy retailing "category killer," offering consumers a vast selection of toys at everyday low prices. The then-prevalent smaller toy stores, and toy sections of larger department stores, soon fell by the wayside because they couldn't match Toys 'R' Us's selection, convenience, and low prices. Throughout the 1980s and early 1990s, Toys 'R' Us grew explosively to become the nation's largest toy retailer, grabbing as much as a 25 percent share of the U.S. toy market.

However, in the 1990s, Toys 'R' Us's heady success seemed to vanish almost overnight with the emergence of—you guessed it—Wal-Mart as a toy retailing force. Wal-Mart offered toy buyers an even more compelling value proposition. Like Toys 'R' Us, it offered good toy selection and convenience. But on prices, it did Toys 'R' Us one better. Wal-Mart offered not just *everyday low prices* on toys, it offered *rock-bottom* prices.

Says one analyst, "With its mammoth stores, diverse array of products, and super efficient supply chain, Wal-Mart can provide consumers good quality, high levels of choice and convenience, and [incredibly low] prices." What's more, he continues, "Because it is a mass retailer with a broad, diverse inventory, Wal-Mart can afford to use toys as a loss-leader, losing money on toy purchases to lure in customers who then purchase higher-margin goods. Focused retailers such as Toys 'R' Us just don't have that luxury." In 1998, Wal-Mart pushed Toys 'R' Us aside to become the country's largest toy seller.

Toys 'R' Us fought back by trying to match Wal-Mart's super low prices, but with disastrous results. Consider this *Business Week* account of the 2003 Christmas season:

He sings, he dances, he shakes it all about. For thousands of toddlers, Hokey Pokey Elmo was one of the great things about Christmas, 2003. But for Toys 'R' Us, Elmo was the fuzzy red embodiment of all that went wrong: He was just too cheap. In October, two months before the heart of the holiday rush, Wal-Mart stores surprised all of its competition by dropping Elmo's price from $25 to $19.50, a full $4.50 below what many retailers had paid for it. Within days,

Toys 'R' Us dropped its price to $19.99. The price war dominoed all the way down the toy aisle. "Our choice was short-term profit vs. long-term market share; we chose to protect market share," says [former] CEO John Eyler, who thinks all stores could have sold out of the popular doll at $29.99.

That's profit Toys 'R' Us couldn't afford to lose. The holiday season [its third disappointing one in a row] resulted in a 5 percent drop in sales at Toys 'R' Us stores open at least a year. Net income for the year fell 27 percent. Wal-Mart, on the other hand, [was] all smiles. . . . CEO Lee Scott called 2003 "an excellent toy season" and toys "a very profitable category with a very strong gross margin." Clearly, Toys 'R' Us has little hope of competing on price with Wal-Mart. "I wouldn't want to play that game," says [an industry expert].

By early 2005, Wal-Mart held a 25 percent share of the toy market; Toys 'R' Us's share had fallen to 15 percent. Later that year, new ownership took Toys 'R' Us private. Despite rumors that the once-dominant toy retailer would exit the toy business altogether and focus on its growing and profitable Babies 'R' Us unit, the new owners vowed to remain a player in the toy industry.

However, Toys 'R' Us is now playing out a dramatically new game plan. For starters, management has closed nearly 100 underperforming stores to cut costs, and it's refocusing its marketing strategy. For example, the chain has stepped back from cut-throat price wars that it simply can't win. Instead, it's dropping slow-selling products and emphasizing top-selling brands and higher-margin exclusive items, such as special Bratz or Barbie dolls sold only at its stores.

And in an effort to differentiate itself from the likes of Wal-Mart and Target, Toys 'R' Us is making a big push to improve store atmospheres, shopper experiences, and customer service. It's cleaning up its stores, uncluttering its aisles, and hiring more helpful employees who can offer customers toy-buying advice. Says CEO Gerald Storch, "When you go to a large, multiproduct discount chain, you'll be lucky to find someone who can point you to the toy department or will even take you there, much less answer specific questions. When a customer comes in our

Objectives

After studying this chapter, you should be able to

1. answer the question "What is price?" and discuss the importance of pricing in today's fast-changing environment
2. discuss the importance of understanding customer value perceptions when setting prices
3. discuss the importance of company and product costs in setting prices
4. identify and define the other important internal and external factors affecting a firm's pricing decisions

store, our people can tell them what's a great toy for a ten-year-old boy for their birthday, because all we do is toys." Storch hopes that brighter, less-cluttered stores and better service will support higher prices and margins.

Still, Toys 'R' Us faces an uphill battle in its efforts to win back the now-price-sensitive toy buyers it helped to create decades ago. Consider this example.

Aurore Boone of Alpharetta, Georgia, was recently at her local Wal-Mart checking out kids' bikes. She shops at Toys 'R' Us to see what's on the shelves, but of the roughly $500 she and her husband Mark spend on toys a year, more than half goes to Wal-Mart, the rest to stores such as Target. It's cheaper, and she can do her other shopping there, too.

It isn't a matter of whether Toys 'R' Us can *sell* toys—with more than $11 billion in sales, the company remains one of the world's largest retailers. It's a matter of whether Toys 'R' Us can sell toys *profitably* (despite big sales, it's still posting losses). And to do that, it must find the right customer value and pricing formulas. As *Business Week* concludes: "It's a harsh new world for Toys 'R' Us, which, as the industry's original 800-pound gorilla, wiped out legions of small toy stores in the '60s and '70s with its cut-price, no-frills, big-box outlets. Now, having taught consumers that toys should be cheap, the chain is finding that they learned the lesson all too well."2

Companies today face a fierce and fast-changing pricing environment. Increasing customer price consciousness has put many companies in a "pricing vise." "Thank the Wal-Mart phenomenon," says one analyst. "These days, we're all cheapskates in search of a spend-less strategy."3 In response, it seems that almost every company is looking for ways to slash prices, and that is hurting their profits.

Yet, cutting prices is often not the best answer. Reducing prices unnecessarily can lead to lost profits and damaging price wars. It can signal to customers that the price is more important than the customer value a brand delivers. Instead, companies should sell value, not price. They should persuade customers that paying a higher price for the company's brand is justified by the greater value they gain. The challenge is to find the price that will let the company make a fair profit by getting paid for the customer value it creates. "Give people something of value," says Ronald Shaich, CEO of Panera Bread Company, "and they'll happily pay for it."4

In this chapter and the next, we focus on the process of setting prices. This chapter defines prices, looks at the factors marketers must consider when setting prices, and examines general pricing approaches. In the next chapter, we look at pricing strategies for new-product pricing, product mix pricing, price adjustments for buyer and situational factors, and price changes.

What Is a Price?

In the narrowest sense, **price** is the amount of money charged for a product or service. More broadly, price is the sum of all the values that customers give up in order to gain the benefits of having or using a product or service. Historically, price has been the major factor affecting buyer choice. In recent decades, non-price factors have gained increasing importance. However, price still remains one of the most important elements determining a firm's market share and profitability.

Price is the only element in the marketing mix that produces revenue; all other elements represent costs. Price is also one of the most flexible marketing mix elements. Unlike prod-

Price
The amount of money charged for a product or service, or the sum of the values that consumers exchange for the benefits of having or using the product or service.

Pricing: The challenge is to harvest the customer value the company creates. Says Panera's CEO, pictured here, "Give people something of value, and they'll happily pay for it."

uct features and channel commitments, prices can be changed quickly. At the same time, pricing is the number-one problem facing many marketing executives, and many companies do not handle pricing well. One frequent problem is that companies are too quick to reduce prices in order to get a sale rather than convincing buyers that their product's greater value is worth a higher price. Other common mistakes include pricing that is too cost oriented rather than customer-value oriented, and pricing that does not take the rest of the marketing mix into account.

Some managers view pricing as a big headache, preferring instead to focus on the other marketing mix elements. However, smart managers treat pricing as a key strategic tool for creating and capturing customer value. Prices have a direct impact on a firm's bottom line. According to one expert, "a 1 percent price improvement generates a 12.5 percent profit improvement for most organizations."[5] More importantly, as a part of a company's overall value proposition, price plays a key role in creating customer value and building customer relationships. "Instead of running away from pricing," says the expert, "savvy marketers are embracing it."

▮ Factors to Consider When Setting Prices

The price the company charges will fall somewhere between one that is too high to produce any demand and one that is too low to produce a profit. Figure 10.1 summarizes the major considerations in setting price. Customer perceptions of the product's value set the ceiling for prices. If customers perceive that the price is greater than the product's value, they will not buy the product. Product costs set the floor for prices. If the company prices the product below its costs, company profits will suffer. In setting its price between these two extremes, the company must consider a number of other internal and external factors, including its overall marketing strategy and mix, the nature of the market and demand, and competitors' strategies and prices.

In the end, the customer will decide whether a product's price is right. Pricing decisions, like other marketing mix decisions, must start with customer value. When customers buy a product, they exchange something of value (the price) in order to get something of value (the benefits of having or using the product). Effective, customer-oriented pricing involves understanding how much value consumers place on the benefits they receive from the product and setting a price that captures this value.

Value-Based Pricing

Good pricing begins with a complete understanding of the value that a product or service creates for customers. **Value-based pricing** uses buyers' perceptions of value, not the seller's cost, as the key to pricing. Value-based pricing means that the marketer cannot design a product and marketing program and then set the price. Price is considered along with the other marketing mix variables *before* the marketing program is set.

Figure 10.2 compares value-based pricing with cost-based pricing. Cost-based pricing is product driven. The company designs what it considers to be a good product, adds up the costs of making the product, and sets a price that covers costs plus a target profit. Marketing must then convince buyers that the product's value at that price justifies its purchase. If the price turns out to be too high, the company must settle for lower markups or lower sales, both resulting in disappointing profits.

Value-based pricing reverses this process. The company sets its target price based on customer perceptions of the product value. The targeted value and price then drive

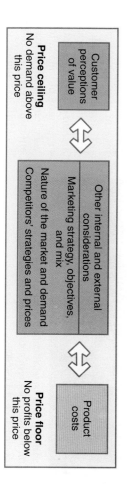

FIGURE 10.1
Considerations in setting price

Value-based pricing
Setting prices based on buyers' perceptions of value rather than on the seller's cost.

Customer
perceptions
of value

Price ceiling
No demand above
this price

Other internal and external
considerations
Marketing strategy, objectives,
and mix
Nature of the market and demand
Competitors' strategies and prices

Product
costs

Price floor
No profits below
this price

FIGURE 10.2
Value-based pricing versus cost-based pricing

Source: Thomas T. Nagle and Reed K. Holden, *The Strategy and Tactics of Pricing*, 3rd ed. (Upper Saddle River, NJ: Prentice Hall, 2002), p. 4. Reproduced by permission of Pearson Education, Inc., Upper Saddle River, New Jersey.

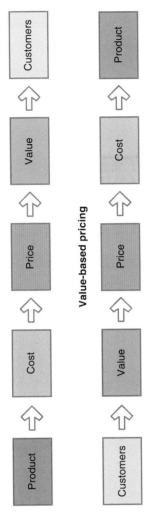

Cost-based pricing

Product ⇨ Cost ⇨ Price ⇨ Value ⇨ Customers

Value-based pricing

Customers ⇨ Value ⇨ Price ⇨ Cost ⇨ Product

decisions about product design and what costs can be incurred. As a result, pricing begins with analyzing consumer needs and value perceptions, and price is set to match consumers' perceived value.

It's important to remember that "good value" is not the same as "low price." For example, prices for a Hermes Birkin Bag start at $6,000—a less expensive handbag might carry as much, but some consumers place great value on the intangibles they receive from a one-of-a-kind handmade bag that has a year-long waiting list. Similarly, some car buyers consider the luxurious Bentley Continental GT automobile a real value, even at an eye-popping price of $150,000:

Stay with me here, because I'm about to [tell you why] a certain automobile costing $150,000 is not actually expensive, but is in fact a tremendous value. Every Bentley GT is built by hand, an Old World bit of automaking requiring 160 hours per vehicle. Craftsmen spend 18 hours simply stitching the perfectly joined leather of the GT's steering wheel, almost as long as it takes to assemble an entire VW Golf. The results are impressive: Dash and doors are mirrored with walnut veneer, floor pedals are carved from aluminum, window and seat toggles are cut from actual metal rather than plastic, and every air vent is perfectly chromed. . . . The sum of all this is a fitted cabin that approximates that of a $300,000 vehicle, matched to an engine the equal of a $200,000 automobile, within a car that has brilliantly incorporated . . . technological sophistication. As I said, the GT is a bargain. [Just ask anyone on the lengthy waiting list.] The waiting time to bring home your very own GT is currently half a year.[6]

A company using value-based pricing must find out what value buyers assign to different competitive offers. However, companies often find it hard to measure the value customers will attach to its product. For example, calculating the cost of ingredients in a meal at a fancy restaurant is relatively easy. But assigning a value to other satisfactions such as taste, environment, relaxation, conversation, and status is very hard. And these values will vary both for different consumers and different situations.

Still, consumers will use these perceived values to evaluate a product's price, so the company must

THE BENTLEY CONTINENTAL GT

PURE ANTICIPATION.

A seamless bloodline of grand touring cars, taken into a breathtaking new future. 550 hp AWD. 6.0 liter 12 cylinder twin turbo. Over 190 mph.* Coming Spring 2004.

BENTLEY

For further information visit a Bentley dealer. Call 1 877 300 8853 or visit www.bentleymotors.com

■ Value-based pricing: "Good value" is not the same as "low price." Some car buyers consider the luxurious Bentley Continental GT automobile a real value, even at an eye-popping price of $150,000.

work to measure them. Sometimes, companies ask consumers how much they would pay for a basic product and for each benefit added to the offer. Or a company might conduct experiments to test the perceived value of different product offers. According to an old Russian proverb, there are two fools in every market—one who asks too much and one who asks too little. If the seller charges less, its products sell very well. But they produce less revenue than if they were priced at the level of perceived value.

We now examine two types of value-based pricing: *good-value pricing* and *value-added pricing.*

Good-Value Pricing

During the past decade, marketers have noted a fundamental shift in consumer attitudes toward price and quality. Many companies have changed their pricing approaches to bring them into line with changing economic conditions and consumer price perceptions. More and more, marketers have adopted **good-value pricing** strategies—offering just the right combination of quality and good service at a fair price.

In many cases, this has involved introducing less-expensive versions of established, brand name products. Fast-food restaurants such as Taco Bell and McDonald's offer "value menus." Armani offers the less-expensive, more casual Armani Exchange fashion line. Procter & Gamble created Charmin Basic—it is "slightly less 'squeezably soft' but it's a lot less pricey than Procter & Gamble's other toilet paper." It's "Soft. Strong. Sensible."[7] In other cases, good-value pricing has involved redesigning existing brands to offer more quality for a given price or the same quality for less.

An important type of good-value pricing at the retail level is *everyday low pricing (EDLP).* EDLP involves charging a constant, everyday low price with few or no temporary price discounts. In contrast, *high-low pricing* involves charging higher prices on an everyday basis but running frequent promotions to lower prices temporarily on selected items. In recent years, high-low pricing has given way to EDLP in retail settings ranging from Saturn car dealerships to furniture store Room & Board.

The king of EDLP is Wal-Mart, which practically defined the concept. Except for a few sale items every month, Wal-Mart promises everyday low prices on everything it sells. In contrast, Kmart's recent attempts to match Wal-Mart's EDLP strategy failed. To offer everyday low prices, a company must first have everyday low costs. However, because Kmart's costs are much higher than Wal-Mart's, it could not make money at the lower prices and quickly abandoned the attempt.[8]

Value-Added Pricing

In many business-to-business marketing situations, the challenge is to build the company's *pricing power*—its power to escape price competition and to justify higher prices and margins without losing market share. To retain pricing power, a firm must retain or build the value of its market offering. This is especially true for suppliers of commodity products, which are characterized by little differentiation and intense price competition. If companies "rely on price to capture and retain business, they reduce whatever they're selling to a commodity," says an analyst. "Once that happens, there is no customer loyalty."[9]

To increase their pricing power, many companies adopt **value-added pricing** strategies. Rather than cutting prices to match competitors, they attach value-added features and services to differentiate their offers and thus support higher prices (see Real Marketing 10.1). "Even in today's economic environment, it's not about price," says a pricing expert. "It's about keeping customers loyal by providing service they can't find anywhere else."[10]

Good-value pricing
Offering just the right combination of quality and good service at a fair price.

Value-added pricing
Attaching value-added features and services to differentiate a company's offers and to support charging higher prices.

Good-value pricing: Procter & Gamble's Charmin Basic is still "squeezably soft" but it's a lot less pricey than P&G's other toilet paper. It's "the quality toilet tissue at the price you'll love."

Charmin

PRODUCTS | OFFERS & EVENTS | FUN FACTS

CHARMIN MEGA ROLL *OUR LARGEST SIZE!*
CHARMIN ULTRA
CHARMIN PLUS *WITH LOTION*
CHARMIN SCENTS
CHARMIN BASIC
CHARMIN FRESH MATES

ROLL OVER THE PACKAGES TO LEARN MORE ABOUT SIZES AND VARIETIES.

Packaging Information

VIEW SIZING CHART

Charmin Basic

Introducing Charmin® Basic—the quality toilet tissue at a price you'll love. Charmin Basic is softness, strength, and value rolled into one! Look for it on shelves now.

Real Marketing Pricing Power: The Value of Value Added

10.1 When a company finds its major competitors offering a similar product at a lower price, the natural tendency is to try to match or beat that price. Although the idea of undercutting competitors' prices and watching customers flock to you is tempting, there are dangers. Successive rounds of price-cutting can lead to price wars that erode the profit margins of all competitors in an industry. Or worse, discounting a product can cheapen it in the minds of customers, greatly reducing the seller's power to maintain profitable prices in the long term.

So, how can a company keep its pricing power when a competitor undercuts its price? Often, the best strategy is not to price below the competitor, but rather to price above and convince customers that the product is worth it. The company should ask, "What is the value of the product to the customer?" and then stand up for what the product is worth. In this way, the company shifts the focus from price to value.

But what if the company is operating in a "commodity" business, in which the products of all competitors seem pretty much alike? In such cases, the company must find ways to "decommoditize" its products—to create superior value for customers. It can do this by developing value-added features and services that differentiate its offer and justify higher prices and margins. Here are some examples of how suppliers are using value-added features and services to give them a competitive edge:

■ *Caterpillar:* Caterpillar charges premium prices for its heavy construction and mining equipment by convincing customers that its products and service justify every additional cent—or, rather, the extra tens of thousands of dollars. Caterpillar typically reaps a 20 to 30 percent price premium over competitors that can amount to an extra $200,000 or more on one of those huge yellow million-dollar dump trucks.

When a large potential customer says, "I can get it for less from a competitor," the Caterpillar dealer doesn't discount the price. Instead, the dealer explains that, even at the higher price,

Cat offers the best value. Caterpillar equipment is designed with modular components that can be removed and repaired quickly, minimizing machine downtime. Caterpillar dealers carry an extensive parts inventory and guarantee delivery within 48 hours anywhere in the world, again minimizing downtime. Cat's products are designed to be rebuilt, providing a "second life" that competitors cannot match. As a result, Caterpillar used-equipment prices are often 20 percent to 30 percent higher. Beyond its high-quality equipment and maintenance, Caterpillar offers a wide range of value-adding services, from financing and insurance to equipment training and investment management advice.

In all, the dealer explains, even at the higher initial price, Caterpillar equipment delivers the lowest total cost per cubic yard of earth moved, ton of coal uncovered, or mile of road graded over the life of the product—guaranteed! Most customers seem to agree with Caterpillar's value proposition—the market-leading company dominates its markets with a more than 37 percent worldwide market share. And the big cat just keeps purring. In the past two years, sales are up 60 percent and profits have rocketed 250 percent. Despite its higher prices, demand is so strong that Caterpillar is having trouble making equipment fast enough to fill orders.

■ *Pioneer Hi-Bred International:* A major producer of commercial seeds and other agricultural products often thought of as commodities, DuPont subsidiary Pioneer Hi-Bred International (PHI) hardly acts like a commodity supplier. Its patented hybrid seeds yield 10 percent more crops than competitors' seeds. PHI's researchers harvest tens of thousands of test plots worldwide each year to perfect product yields and traits.

But beyond producing a superior product, PHI also provides a bundle of value-added services. For example, it equips its sales reps with laptop PCs and software that allow them to provide farmers with customized information and advice. The rep can plug in the type of hybrid that a farmer is using, along with infor-

Company and Product Costs

Whereas customer-value perceptions set the price ceiling, costs set the floor for the price that the company can charge. **Cost-based pricing** involves setting prices based on the costs for producing, distributing, and selling the product plus a fair rate of return for its effort and risk. A company's costs may be an important element in its pricing strategy. Many companies, such as Southwest Airlines, Wal-Mart, and Dell, work to become the "low-cost producers" in their industries. Companies with lower costs can set lower prices that result in greater sales and profits.

Types of Costs

A company's costs take two forms, fixed and variable. **Fixed costs** (also known as **overhead**) are costs that do not vary with production or sales level. For example, a company must pay each month's bills for rent, heat, interest, and executive salaries, whatever the company's output. **Variable costs** vary directly with the level of production. Each PC produced by Hewlett-Packard involves a cost of computer chips, wires, plastic, packaging, and other inputs. These costs tend to be the same for each unit produced. They are called variable because their total varies with the number of units produced. **Total costs** are the sum of the fixed and variable

Cost-based pricing
Setting prices based on the costs for producing, distributing, and selling the product plus a fair rate of return for effort and risk.

Fixed costs (overhead)
Costs that do not vary with production or sales level.

Variable costs
Costs that vary directly with the level of production.

Value added: Caterpillar offer its dealers a wide range of value-added services—from guaranteed parts delivery to investment management advice and equipment training. Such added value supports a higher price.

mation about pricing, acreage, and yield characteristics, and then advise the farmer on how to do a better job of farm management. The reps can also supply farmers with everything from agricultural research reports to assistance in comparison shopping. To add even more value, PHI offers farmers crop insurance, financing, and marketing services.

Backing its claim "We believe in customer success" with superior products and value-added services gives PHI plenty of pricing power. Despite charging a significant price premium—or perhaps because of it—the company's share of the North American corn market has grown from 35 percent during the mid-1980s to its current level of 44 percent.

■ *Microsystems Engineering Company:* "The way we sell on value is by differentiating ourselves," says Mark Beckman, director of

sales for Microsystems, a software company. "My product is twice as much as my nearest competitor's, but we sell as much as—if not more than—our competition." Rather than getting into price wars, Microsystems adds value to its products by adding new components and services. It builds close, value-added relationships with customers. "We foster strong working relationships with our clients," declares the company's Web site, "and have built our industry-leading reputation on going the extra mile for them." As a result, customers "get more for their money," says Beckman. "We get the price because we understand what people want." When customers see the extra value, price becomes secondary. Ultimately, Beckman asserts, "let the customer decide whether the price you're charging is worth all the things they're getting." What if the answer is no? Beckman would suggest that dropping the price is the last thing you want to do. Instead, look to the value of value added.

Sources: William F. Kendy, "The Price Is Too High," *Selling Power*, April 2006, pp. 30-33; Ian Brat, "Caterpillar Posts 38% Profit Rise, Raises Outlook on Strong Demand," *Wall Street Journal*, July 22, 2006, p. A2; Michael Arndt, "Cat Claws Its Way into Services," *BusinessWeek*, December 5, 2005, pp. 56-59; Erin Stout, "Keep Them Coming Back for More," *Sales & MarketingManagement*, February 2002, pp. 51-52; "Global Construction & Farm Machinery: Industry Profile," Datamonitor, June 2006, accessed at www.datamonitor.com; and information accessed online at www.pioneer.com, www.caterpillar.com, and www.microsystems.com/about.php, December 2006.

Costs for any given level of production. Management wants to charge a price that will at least cover the total production costs at a given level of production.

The company must watch its costs carefully. If it costs the company more than it costs competitors to produce and sell its product, the company must charge a higher price or make less profit, putting it at a competitive disadvantage.

Costs at Different Levels of Production

To price wisely, management needs to know how its costs vary with different levels of production. For example, suppose Texas Instruments (TI) has built a plant to produce 1,000 calculators per day. Figure 10.3A shows the typical shortrun average cost (SRAC) curve. It shows that the cost per calculator is high if TI's factory produces only a few per day. But as production moves up to 1,000 calculators per day, average cost falls. This is because fixed costs are spread over more units, with each one bearing a smaller share of the fixed cost. TI can try to produce more than 1,000 calculators per day, but average costs will increase because the plant becomes inefficient. Workers wait for machines, the machines break down more often, and workers get in each other's way.

Total costs

The sum of the fixed and variable costs for any given level of production.

FIGURE 10.3

Cost per unit at different levels of production per period

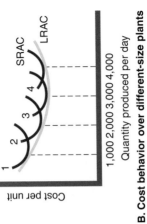

Cost per unit

1,000

Quantity produced per day

A. Cost behavior in a fixed-size plant

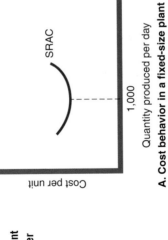

Cost per unit

1 2 3 4

LRAC

SRAC

1,000 2,000 3,000 4,000

Quantity produced per day

B. Cost behavior over different-size plants

If TI believed it could sell 2,000 calculators a day, it should consider building a larger plant. The plant would use more efficient machinery and work arrangements. Also, the unit cost of producing 2,000 calculators per day would be lower than the unit cost of producing 1,000 units per day, as shown in the long-run average cost (LRAC) curve (Figure 10.3B). In fact, a 3,000-capacity plant would even be more efficient, according to Figure 10.3B. But a 4,000-daily production plant would be less efficient because of increasing diseconomies of scale—too many workers to manage, paperwork slowing things down, and so on. Figure 10.3B shows that a 3,000-daily production plant is the best size to build if demand is strong enough to support this level of production.

Costs as a Function of Production Experience

Suppose TI runs a plant that produces 3,000 calculators per day. As TI gains experience in producing calculators, it learns how to do it better. Workers learn shortcuts and become more familiar with their equipment. With practice, the work becomes better organized, and TI finds better equipment and production processes. With higher volume, TI becomes more efficient and gains economies of scale. As a result, average cost tends to fall with accumulated production experience. This is shown in Figure 10.4.[11] Thus, the average cost of producing the first 100,000 calculators is $10 per calculator. When the company has produced the first 200,000 calculators, the average cost has fallen to $9. After its accumulated production experience doubles again to 400,000, the average cost is $7. This drop in the average cost with accumulated production experience is called the **experience curve** (or the **learning curve**).

If a downward-sloping experience curve exists, this is highly significant for the company. Not only will the company's unit production cost fall, but it will fall faster if the company makes and sells more during a given time period. But the market must stand ready to buy the higher output. And to take advantage of the experience curve, TI must get a large market share early in the product's life cycle. This suggests the following pricing strategy: TI should price its calculators low; its sales will then increase, and its costs will decrease through gaining more experience, and then it can lower its prices further.

Some companies have built successful strategies around the experience curve. For example, Bausch & Lomb solidified its position in the soft contact lens market by using computerized lens design and steadily expanding its one Soflens plant. As a result, its market share climbed steadily to 65 percent.

However, a single-minded focus on reducing costs and exploiting the experience curve will not always work. Experience-curve pricing carries some major risks. The aggressive pricing might give the product a cheap image. The strategy also assumes that competitors are weak and not willing to fight it out by meeting the company's price cuts. Finally, while the company is building volume under one technology, a competitor may find a lower-cost technology that lets it start at prices lower than those of the market leader, who still operates on the old experience curve.

Cost-Based Pricing

The simplest pricing method is **cost-plus pricing**—adding a standard markup to the cost of the product. Construction companies, for example, submit job bids by estimating the total project cost and adding a standard markup for profit. Lawyers, accountants, and other professionals typically price by adding a standard markup to their costs. Some sellers tell their cus-

Experience curve (learning curve)
The drop in the average per-unit production cost that comes with accumulated production experience.

Cost-plus pricing
Adding a standard markup to the cost of the product.

FIGURE 10.4

Cost per unit as a function of accumulated production:
The experience curve

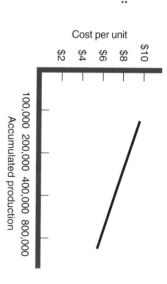

tomers they will charge cost plus a specified markup; for example, aerospace companies price this way to the government.

To illustrate markup pricing, suppose a toaster manufacturer had the following costs and expected sales:

Variable cost	$10
Fixed costs	$300,000
Expected unit sales	50,000

Then the manufacturer's cost per toaster is given by:

$$\text{Unit Cost} = \text{Variable Cost} + \frac{\text{Fixed Costs}}{\text{Unit Sales}} = \$10 + \frac{\$300,000}{50,000} = \$16$$

Now suppose the manufacturer wants to earn a 20 percent markup on sales. The manufacturer's markup price is given by:[12]

$$\text{Markup Price} = \frac{\text{Unit Cost}}{(1 - \text{Desired Return on Sales})} = \frac{\$16}{1 - .2} = \$20$$

The manufacturer would charge dealers $20 per toaster and make a profit of $4 per unit. The dealers, in turn, will mark up the toaster. If dealers want to earn 50 percent on the sales price, they will mark up the toaster to $40 ($20 + 50% of $40). This number is equivalent to a *markup on cost of 100 percent ($20/$20)*.

Does using standard markups to set prices make sense? Generally, no. Any pricing method that ignores demand and competitor prices is not likely to lead to the best price. Such cost-plus pricing wrongly assumes that prices can be set without affecting sales volume. In our toaster example, suppose that consumers saw the $40 retail price as too high relative to competitors' prices, reducing demand to only 30,000 toasters instead of 50,000. Then the producer's unit cost would have been higher because the fixed costs are spread over fewer units, and the realized percentage markup on sales would have been lower. Markup pricing works only if that price actually brings in the expected level of sales.

Still, markup pricing remains popular for many reasons. First, sellers are more certain about costs than about demand. By tying the price to cost, sellers simplify pricing—they do not have to make frequent adjustments as demand changes. Second, when all firms in the industry use this pricing method, prices tend to be similar and price competition is thus minimized. Third, many people feel that cost-plus pricing is fairer to both buyers and sellers. Sellers earn a fair return on their investment but do not take advantage of buyers when buyers' demand becomes great.

Break-Even Analysis and Target Profit Pricing

Another cost-oriented pricing approach is **break-even pricing** (or a variation called **target profit pricing**). The firm tries to determine the price at which it will break even or make the target profit it is seeking. Such pricing is used by General Motors, which prices its automobiles to achieve a 15 to 20 percent profit on its investment. This pricing method is also used by public utilities, which are constrained to make a fair return on their investment.

Target pricing uses the concept of a *break-even chart*, which shows the total cost and total revenue expected at different sales volume levels. Figure 10.5 shows a break-even chart for the toaster manufacturer discussed here. Fixed costs are $300,000 regardless of sales volume. Variable costs are added to fixed costs to form total costs, which rise with volume. The total

(case continued)

Being the low-cost leader has some disadvantages. Because Southwest already has such a lean cost structure, it has much less room for improvement. For example, travel agent commissions have been at zero for some time (Southwest doesn't work through agents). Sixty-five percent of Southwest customers already buy their tickets online, minimizing its expense for call centers. And Southwest is losing another of its traditional cost advantages. For years, though some smartly negotiated fuel-hedging contracts, Southwest has enjoyed fuel prices far below those paid by the rest of the industry. But the most lucrative of those contracts are expiring. At a time when fuel prices are surging for the entire industry, this means that Southwest's fuel expenses are rising faster than those of its competitors. In the first quarter of 2006, Southwest paid 63 percent more for fuel that it did for the year-earlier period.

As these factors have quickly turned the tables on Southwest, some analysts are questioning the company's current strategic direction. "Slowly, Southwest is becoming what its competitors used to be," says industry consultant Steven Casley. Serving congested hub airports, linking with rivals through code sharing, and hunting the big boys on their own turf are all things that Southwest would previously have never considered.

But Gary Kelly, Southwest's new CEO, defends the company's actions. "Hey, I can admit it, our competitors are getting better," says Kelly. "Sure, we have an enormous cost advantage. Sure, we're the most efficient. The problem is, I just don't see how that can be indefinitely sustained without some sacrifice." Kelly has hinted that such sacrifices could include modest fare increases and more conservative labor contracts. In direct contrast to its well-known "first-come" boarding policy, Southwest is even experimenting with an assigned-seating system. And when asked if he was worried about Southwest losing its competitive advantage, Mr. Kelly responded confidently:

We know people shop first for fares, and we've got the fares. [But] ultimately, our industry is a customer-service business, and we have the best people to provide that special customer service . . . that's our core advantage. Since the U.S. Department of Transportation began collecting and publishing operating statistics, we've excelled at on-time performance, baggage handling, fewest complaints, and fewest canceled flights. Besides, we're still the low-cost producer and the low-fare leader in the U.S. We have no intention of conceding that position.

By almost any measure, Southwest is still the healthiest airline in the business. However, that might be like saying it's the least sick patient in the hospital. As the industry as a whole has suffered in the post-September 11th world, Southwest's 2005 earnings of $313 million were half of what the company made in 2000. The airline's stock prices hover at around $15 a share, more than 30 percent below 2001 levels. And as the other patients get better, Southwest may have to find some new medicine.

Questions for Discussion

1. How do Southwest's marketing objectives and its marketing mix strategy affect its pricing decisions?

2. Discuss factors that have affected the nature of costs in the airline industry since the year 2000. How have these factors affected pricing decisions?

3. How do the nature of the airline market and the demand for airline service affect Southwest's decisions?

4. What general pricing approaches have airlines pursued?

5. Do you think that Southwest will be able to continue to maintain a competitive advantage based on price? What will happen if others carriers match the low-price leader?

Sources: Chris Walsh, "A Philadelphia Success Story; Southwest's Quick Growth in City Shows Its Potential in Denver," Rocky Mountain News, December 30, 2005, p. 1B; Susan Warren, "Keeping Ahead of the Pack," Wall Street Journal, December 19, 2005, p. B1; Barney Gimbel, "Southwest's New Flight Plan," Fortune, May 16, 2005, accessed at www.fortune.com; "Let the Battle Begin," Air Transport World, May 2004, p. 9; Micheline Maynard, "Southwest Comes Calling, and a Race Begins," New York Times, May 10, 2004; Melanie Trottman, "Destination: Philadelphia," Wall Street Journal, May 4, 2004, p. B1; Andy Serwer and Kate Bonamici, "Southwest Airlines: The Hottest Thing in the Sky," Fortune, March 8, 2004, p. 86.

RYANAIR.CO

HOME | TRAVEL QUESTIONS | DESTINA

ONLI CHEC IN

○ Return   ○ One Way
Select Your Journey

Origin

Pricing Products
Pricing Strategies

Previewing the Concepts

In the last chapter, you explored the many internal and external factors that affect a firm's pricing decisions and examined three general approaches to setting prices. In this chapter, we'll look at pricing strategies available to marketers—new-product pricing strategies, product mix pricing strategies, price-adjustment strategies, and price reaction strategies.

Most U.S. airlines are facing tough times these days. One of the biggest issues is figuring out how to price their services in the face of fierce competition, high fuel costs, and already-disgruntled passengers. But Ryanair—Europe's original, largest, and most profitable low-fares airline—appears to have found a radical new pricing solution: Fly *free!* But surely this strategy is doomed to failure. How can Ryanair make money on free tickets?

The major airlines are facing very difficult pricing strategy decisions in these tough air-travel times. Pricing strategies vary widely. Some airlines offer no-frills flights and charge rock-bottom prices (Southwest, JetBlue, Frontier). Others offer luxury and charge higher prices to match (Virgin, Singapore Airlines). But most airlines haven't yet figured it out, leaving air-travel passengers generally grumpy when it comes to the topic of airline ticket prices. For example, when Northwest Airlines recently charged full fares but still cut basic perks (such as free magazines, pillows, and pretzels) and tacked on irksome new charges for things competitors provide for free (such as in-flight snacks and aisle seats), it dropped to dead last in the industry's customer satisfaction ratings.

But now, one airline appears to have found a radical new pricing solution, one that customers are sure to love: Make flying *free!* That's right, Michael O'Leary, chief executive of Ireland's Ryanair, Europe's most profitable airline, wants to make air travel free. Not free as in free from regulation, but free as in zero cost. By the end of the decade, he promises, "more than half of our passengers will fly free." The remarkable thing is, few analysts think his prediction is far-fetched: Ryanair already offers free fares to a quarter of its customers.

Even without free flights, Ryanair has become one of Europe's most popular carriers. Last year it flew 35 million passengers to more than 100 European destinations, while its customers paid an average fare of just $53. The airline enjoyed revenues of $1.7 billion, up 20 percent over the previous year, at a time when most competitors were stuck in a holding pattern. Even more impressive, Ryanair reaped an industry-leading 22 percent net profit margin. (By comparison, profitable Southwest Airlines' net margin was 7.2 percent.) "Ryanair has the strongest financials in the European airline industry," says an airlines analyst.

The secret? Ryanair's austere cost structure makes even cost-conscious Southwest look like a reckless spender. In addition, the Irish airline puts a price on virtually everything except tickets, from baggage check-in to seat-back advertising space. As a result, last year Ryanair collected $265 million—15.6 percent of overall revenues—from sources other than ticket sales. "We weren't the first to figure this out," O'Leary says. "But we do it better than everybody else."

The similarities to the Southwest model are hardly coincidental. In 1991, when Ryanair was just another struggling European regional carrier, CEO O'Leary went to

Dallas to meet Southwest executives and look for lessons he could take back to Ireland. The visit prompted a wholesale reconsideration of how the airline did business. Following Southwest's lead, Ryanair embraced a single type of aircraft—the venerable Boeing 737. Likewise, it focused on smaller, secondary airports and began to offer open (unassigned) passenger seating.

But Ryanair has since taken the low-cost pricing model even further. An accountant who spent several years at big-four global accounting firm KPMG, O'Leary is maniacal about keeping costs down. "We want to be known as the Wal-Mart of flying," he says. Like the retail giant, each time Ryanair comes up with a new way to cut costs by a few million dollars—for example, by removing seat-back pockets to reduce weight and cleaning expense—O'Leary passes the savings along to customers in the form of lower fares.

It also means charging passengers for practically every amenity they might consume. There are no free peanuts or beverages on Ryanair flights; 27 million passengers bought in-flight refreshments on the airline last year, generating sales of $61 million, or an average of $2.25 per person. Last March, Ryanair eliminated its free checked-bag allowance and began charging $3.50 per piece—a "revenue-neutral" fee that was offset by cutting ticket prices by an average of $3.50. Ryanair expects the move to save $36 million a year by reducing fuel and handling costs.

The airline is just as aggressive in its efforts to develop new sources of revenue. Today, 98 percent of Ryanair's passengers book their flights online, and the company's Web site sees roughly 15 million unique visitors a month—making it Europe's most popular travel site. The airline uses that traffic as a marketing tool for related services; each time a passenger books a rental car or a hotel room, Ryanair earns a percentage of the sale. Linking customers to such services brought in more than $100 million last year.

O'Leary is also starting to turn his planes into media and entertainment venues. He's offered advertisers the opportunity to repaint the exteriors of Ryanair's planes, effectively turning them into giant billboards. (Hertz, Jaguar, and Vodafone have purchased space on the fuselages of Ryanair's 737s.) For passengers seeking distraction,

Objectives

After studying this chapter, you should be able to

1. describe the major strategies for pricing initiative and new products

2. explain how companies find a set of prices that maximize the profits from the total product mix

3. discuss how companies adjust their prices to take into account different types of customers and situations

4. discuss the key issues related to initiating and responding to price changes

Ryanair intends to offer in-flight gambling in 2007, with the airline earning a tiny cut off of each wager. O'Leary thinks gambling could double Ryanair's profits over the next decade, but he's not stopping there. He also envisions a day when the airline can charge passengers for the ability to use their cell phones at 35,000 feet. And he's expressed interest in partnering with operators of airport parking lots and concession stands to capture a bigger slice of the cash that passengers spend on the ground getting to and from his planes.

Add it all up—relentless cost cutting on the operations side, combined with innovative efforts to extract more revenue from each traveler—and O'Leary's plan to give away half of Ryanair's seats by 2010 starts to look quite sane. Sure, taking to the skies on Ryanair may feel more like riding in a subway car than an airplane, but you can't beat the prices. And financially-strapped U.S. carriers should take note: Flying people from here to there for free could truly be liberating. For Ryanair, not even the sky's the limit.[1]

As the Ryanair example illustrates, pricing decisions are subject to a complex and fascinating array of company, environmental, and competitive forces. To make things even more complex, a company sets not a single price but rather a *pricing structure* that covers different items in its line. This pricing structure changes over time as products move through their life cycles. The company adjusts product prices to reflect changes in costs and demand and to account for variations in buyers and situations. As the competitive environment changes, the company considers when to initiate price changes and when to respond to them.

This chapter examines the major dynamic pricing strategies available to marketers. In turn, we look at *new-product pricing strategies* for products in the introductory stage of the product life cycle, *product mix pricing strategies* for related products in the product mix, *price-adjustment strategies* that account for customer differences and changing situations, and strategies for initiating and responding to *price changes*.[2]

New-Product Pricing Strategies

Pricing strategies usually change as the product passes through its life cycle. The introductory stage is especially challenging. Companies bringing out a new product face the challenge of setting prices for the first time. They can choose between two broad strategies: *market-skimming pricing* and *market-penetration pricing*.

Market-Skimming Pricing

Market-skimming pricing

Setting a high price for a new product to skim maximum revenues layer by layer from the segments willing to pay the high price; the company makes fewer but more profitable sales.

Many companies that invent new products set high initial prices to "skim" revenues layer by layer from the market. Sony frequently uses this strategy, called **market-skimming pricing**. When Sony introduced the world's first high-definition television (HDTV) to the Japanese market in 1990, the high-tech sets cost $43,000. These televisions were purchased only by customers who could afford to pay a high price for the new technology. Sony rapidly reduced the price over the next several years to attract new buyers. By 1993 a 28-inch HDTV cost a Japanese buyer just over $6,000. In 2001, a Japanese consumer could buy a 40-inch HDTV for about $2,000, a price that many more customers could afford. An entry level HDTV set now sells for less than $500 in the United States, and prices continue to fall. In this way, Sony skimmed the maximum amount of revenue from the various segments of the market.[3]

Market skimming makes sense only under certain conditions. First, the product's quality and image must support its higher price, and enough buyers must want the product at that price. Second, the costs of producing a smaller volume cannot be so high that they cancel the advantage of charging more. Finally, competitors should not be able to enter the market easily and undercut the high price.

Market-Penetration Pricing

Rather than setting a high initial price to skim off small but profitable market segments, some companies use **market-penetration pricing**. They set a low initial price in order to *penetrate* the market quickly and deeply—to attract a large number of buyers quickly and win a large market share. The high sales volume results in falling costs, allowing the company to cut its price even further. For example, Wal-Mart and other discount retailers use penetration pricing. And Dell used penetration pricing to enter the personal computer market, selling high-quality computer products through lower-cost direct channels. Its sales soared when IBM, Apple, and other competitors selling through retail stores could not match its prices.

Several conditions must be met for this low-price strategy to work. First, the market must be highly price sensitive so that a low price produces more market growth. Second, production and distribution costs must fall as sales volume increases. Finally, the low price must help keep out the competition, and the penetration pricer must maintain its low-price position—otherwise, the price advantage may be only temporary. For example, Dell faced difficult times when IBM and other competitors established their own direct distribution channels. However, through its dedication to low production and distribution costs, Dell has retained its price advantage and established itself as the industry's number-one PC maker.

Mutually inclusive.

like no other

SONY

BRAVIA.

BRAVIA™ LCD TV. THE WORLD'S FIRST TELEVISION FOR MEN AND WOMEN.

■ Market-skimming pricing: Sony priced it's early HDTVs high, then reduced prices gradually over the years to attract new buyers.

Market-penetration pricing

Setting a low price for a new product in order to attract a large number of buyers and a large market share.

■ ■ **Product Mix Pricing Strategies**

The strategy for setting a product's price is often changed when the product is part of a product mix. In this case, the firm looks for a set of prices that maximizes the profits on the total product mix. Pricing is difficult because the various products have related demand and costs and face different degrees of competition. We now take a closer look at the five product mix pricing situations summarized in Table 11.1: *product line pricing, optional-product pricing, captive-product pricing, by-product pricing,* and *product bundle pricing.*

Product Line Pricing

Companies usually develop product lines rather than single products. For example, Snapper makes many different lawn mowers, ranging from simple walk-behind versions starting at

---

TABLE 11.1
Product Mix Pricing Strategies

Strategy	Description
Product line pricing	Setting price steps between product line items
Optional-product pricing	Pricing optional or accessory products sold with the main product
Captive-product pricing	Pricing products that must be used with the main product
By-product pricing	Pricing low-value by-products to get rid of them
Product bundle pricing	Pricing bundles of products sold together

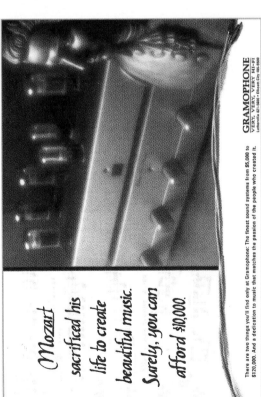

There are two things you'll find only at Gramophone: The finest sound systems from $5,000 to $120,000. And a dedication to music that matches the passion of the people who created it.

GRAMOPHONE
VERY, VERY, VERY HI-FI
Lutherville 821-5600 • Ellicott City 465-5500

■ Product line pricing. Gramophone sells a complete line of high quality sound systems, ranging in price from $5,000 to $120,000.

Product line pricing
Setting the price steps between various products in a product line based on cost differences between the products, customer evaluations of different features, and competitors' prices.

Optional-Product Pricing

Optional-product pricing
The pricing of optional or accessory products along with a main product.

$349.00, to elaborate "Yard Cruisers" and lawn tractors priced at $2,200 or more. Each successive lawn mower in the line offers more features. And Gramophone makes a complete line of high-quality sound systems, ranging in price from $5,000 to $120,000. In **product line pricing**, management must decide on the price steps to set between the various products in a line.

The price steps should take into account cost differences between the products in the line, customer evaluations of their different features, and competitors' prices. In many industries, sellers use well-established *price points* for the products in their line. Thus, men's clothing stores might carry men's suits at three price levels: $185, $325, and $495. The customer will probably associate low-, average-, and high-quality suits with the three price points. Even if the three prices are raised a little, men normally will buy suits at their own preferred price points. The seller's task is to establish perceived quality differences that support the price differences.

Many companies use **optional-product pricing**—offering to sell optional or accessory products along with their main product. For example, a car buyer may choose to order alloy wheels and a CD changer. Refrigerators come with optional ice makers. And an iPod buyer can also choose from a bewildering array of accessories, everything from travel chargers and FM transmitters to external speakers and armband carrying cases.

Pricing these options is a sticky problem. Automobile companies must decide which items to include in the base price and which to offer as options. Until recent years, General Motors' normal pricing strategy was to advertise a stripped-down model at a base price to pull people into showrooms and then to devote most of the showroom space to showing option-loaded cars at higher prices. The economy model was stripped of so many comforts and conveniences that most buyers rejected it. Then, GM and other U.S. car makers followed the examples of the Japanese and German automakers and included in the sticker price many useful items previously sold only as options. Most advertised prices today represent well-equipped cars.

Captive-Product Pricing

Companies that make products that must be used along with a main product are using **captive-product pricing**. Examples of captive products are razor blade cartridges, video games, and printer cartridges. Producers of the main products (razors, video game consoles, and printers) often price them low and set high markups on the supplies. Thus, Gillette sells low-priced razors but makes money on the replacement cartridges. HP makes very low margins on its printers but very high margins on printer cartridges and other supplies. Sony and other video games makers sell game consoles at low prices and obtain the majority of their profits from the video games. Last year alone, total industry sales of consoles were $190 million, compared with total games sales of nearly $6.1 billion.[4]

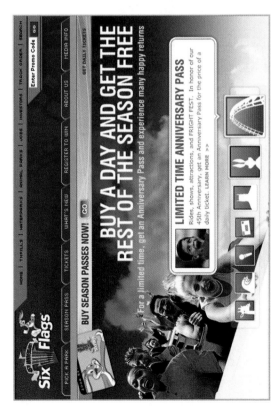

■ Captive-product pricing: At Six Flags, you pay a daily ticket or season pass charge plus additional fees for food and other in-park features.

In the case of services, this strategy is called *two-part pricing*. The price of the service is broken into a *fixed fee* plus a *variable usage rate*. Thus, at Six Flags and other amusement parks, you pay a daily ticket or season pass charge plus additional fees for food and other in-park features. Theaters charge admission and then generate additional revenues from concessions. And cell phone companies charge a flat rate for a basic calling plan, then charge for minutes over what the plan allows. The service firm must decide how much to charge for the basic service and how much for the variable usage. The fixed amount should be low enough to induce usage of the service; profit can be made on the variable fees.

By-Product Pricing

In producing processed meats, petroleum and agricultural products, chemicals, and other products, there are often by-products. If the by-products have no value and if getting rid of them is costly, this will affect the pricing of the main product. Using **by-product pricing**, the manufacturer will seek a market for these by-products and should accept any price that covers more than the cost of storing and delivering them.

By-products can even turn out to be profitable. For example, papermaker MeadWestvaco has turned what was once considered chemical waste into profit-making products.

MeadWestvaco created a separate company, Asphalt Innovations, which creates useful chemicals entirely from the by-products of MeadWestvaco's wood-processing activities. In fact, Asphalt Innovations has grown to become the world's biggest supplier of specialty chemicals for the paving industry. Using the salvaged chemicals, paving companies can pave roads at a lower temperature, create longer-lasting roads, and more easily recycle road materials when roads need to be replaced. What's more, salvaging the by-product chemicals eliminates the costs and environmental hazards once associated with disposing of them.[5]

Sometimes, companies don't realize how valuable their by-products are. For example, most zoos don't realize that one of their by-products—their occupants' manure—can be an excellent source of additional revenue. But the Zoo Doo Compost Company has helped many zoos understand the costs and opportunities involved with these by-products. Zoo Doo licenses its name to zoos and receives royalties on manure sales. So far, novelty sales have been the largest segment, with tiny containers of Zoo Doo (and even "Love, Love Me Doo" valentines) available in 160 zoo stores and 700 additional retail outlets. You can also buy Zoo Doo products online ("the easiest way to buy our crap," says Zoo Doo) or even send a friend (or perhaps a foe) a free Poopy Greeting via e-mail. Other zoos sell their by-products on their own. For example, the Woodland Park Zoo in Seattle sponsors annual Fecal Fests, selling processed manure by the trash can and truck load to lucky lottery winners. In all, the zoo creates 1 million pounds of compost each year, saving $60,000 a year in disposal costs.[6]

Captive-product pricing
Setting a price for products that must be used along with a main product, such as blades for a razor and film for a camera.

By-product pricing
Setting a price for by-products in order to make the main product's price more competitive.

■ By-products can be profitable: Woodland Park Zoo in Seattle sponsors annual Fecal Fests, selling processed manure by the trash can and truck load to lucky lottery winners. "It's not just compost . . . it's a movement."

WWW.ZOO.ORG

WOODLAND PARK ZOO DOO™

Woodland Park Zoo Doo™ is a rich, sweet-smelling compost made from the manure and bedding materials (straw, sawdust, etc.) from the zoo's herbivorous (plant-eating) animals.

it's not just compost . . . it's a movement.

Product Bundle Pricing

Product bundle pricing
Combining several products and offering the bundle at a reduced price.

Using **product bundle pricing**, sellers often combine several of their products and offer the bundle at a reduced price. For example, fast-food restaurants bundle a burger, fries, and a soft drink at a combo price. Resorts sell specially priced vacation packages that include airfare, accommodations, meals, and entertainment. And Comcast and other cable companies bundle cable service, phone service, and high-speed Internet connections at a low combined price. Price bundling can promote the sales of products consumers might not otherwise buy, but the combined price must be low enough to get them to buy the bundle.[7]

Price-Adjustment Strategies

Companies usually adjust their basic prices to account for various customer differences and changing situations. Here we examine the seven price-adjustment strategies summarized in Table 11.2: *discount and allowance pricing, segmented pricing, psychological pricing, promotional pricing, geographical pricing, dynamic pricing,* and *international pricing.*

Discount and Allowance Pricing

Discount
A straight reduction in price on purchases during a stated period of time.

Most companies adjust their basic price to reward customers for certain responses, such as early payment of bills, volume purchases, and off-season buying. These price adjustments—called *discounts* and *allowances*—can take many forms.

The many forms of **discounts** include a *cash discount,* a price reduction to buyers who pay their bills promptly. A typical example is "2/10, net 30," which means that although payment is due within 30 days, the buyer can deduct 2 percent if the bill is paid within 10 days. A *quantity discount* is a price reduction to buyers who buy large volumes. Such discounts provide an incentive to the customer to buy more from one given seller, rather than from many different sources.

Allowance
Promotional money paid by manufacturers to retailers in return for an agreement to feature the manufacturer's products in some way.

A *functional discount* (also called a *trade discount*) is offered by the seller to trade-channel members who perform certain functions, such as selling, storing, and record keeping. A *seasonal discount* is a price reduction to buyers who buy merchandise or services out of season. For example, lawn and garden equipment manufacturers offer seasonal discounts to retailers during the fall and winter months to encourage early ordering in anticipation of the heavy spring and summer selling seasons. Seasonal discounts allow the seller to keep production steady during an entire year.

Allowances are another type of reduction from the list price. For example, *trade-in allowances* are price reductions given for turning in an old item when buying a new one. Trade-in allowances are most common in the automobile industry but are also given for other durable goods. *Promotional allowances* are payments or price reductions to reward dealers for participating in advertising and sales support programs.

Segmented Pricing

Segmented pricing
Selling a product or service at two or more prices, where the difference in prices is not based on differences in costs.

Companies will often adjust their basic prices to allow for differences in customers, products, and locations. In **segmented pricing,** the company sells a product or service at two or more prices, even though the difference in prices is not based on differences in costs.

TABLE 11.2
Price-Adjustment Strategies

Strategy	Description
Discount and allowance pricing	Reducing prices to reward customer responses such as paying early or promoting the product
Segmented pricing	Adjusting prices to allow for differences in customers, products, or locations
Psychological pricing	Adjusting prices for psychological effect
Promotional pricing	Temporarily reducing prices to increase short-run sales
Geographical pricing	Adjusting prices to account for the geographic location of customers
Dynamic pricing	Adjusting prices continually to meet the characteristics and needs of individual customers and situations
International pricing	Adjusting prices for international markets

Product-form pricing: Evian water in a 1-liter bottle might cost you 5 cents an ounce at your local supermarket, whereas the same water might run $2.28 an ounce when sold in 5-ounce aerosol cans as Evian Brumisateur Mineral Water Spray moisturizer.

Segmented pricing takes several forms. Under *customer-segment pricing*, different customers pay different prices for the same product or service. Museums, for example, may charge a lower admission for students and senior citizens. Under *product-form pricing*, different versions of the product are priced differently but not according to differences in their costs. For instance, a 1-liter bottle (about 34 ounces) of Evian mineral water may cost $1.59 at your local supermarket. But a 5-ounce aerosol can of Evian Brumisateur Mineral Water Spray sells for a suggested retail price of $11.39 at beauty boutiques and spas. The water is all from the same source in the French Alps, and the aerosol packaging costs little more than the plastic bottles. Yet you pay about 5 cents an ounce for one form and $2.28 an ounce for the other.

Using *location pricing*, a company charges different prices for different locations, even though the cost of offering each location is the same. For instance, theaters vary their seat prices because of audience preferences for certain locations, and state universities charge higher tuition for out-of-state students. Finally, using *time pricing*, a firm varies its price by the season, the month, the day, and even the hour. Some public utilities vary their prices to commercial users by time of day and weekend versus weekday. Resorts give weekend and seasonal discounts.

Segmented pricing goes by many names. Robert Cross, a long-time consultant to the airlines, calls it *revenue management*. According to Cross, the practice ensures that "companies will sell the right product to the right consumer at the right time for the right price." Airlines, hotels, and restaurants call it *yield management* and practice it religiously. The airlines, for example, routinely set prices hour-by-hour—even minute-by-minute—depending on seat availability, demand, and competitor price changes.

Continental Airlines launches more than 3,200 flights every day. Each flight has between 10 and 20 prices. Continental starts booking flights 330 days in advance, and every flying day is different from every other flying day. As a result, at any given moment, Continental may have nearly 7 million prices in the market. It's a daunting marketing task—all of those prices need to be managed, all of the time. For Continental, setting prices is a complex process of balancing demand and customer satisfaction against company profitability.[8]

The airlines know full well that we are puzzled by the frantic pricing and repricing that they do—puzzled, that is, when we aren't infuriated. "I do not set the prices," says Jim Compton, senior vice president of pricing and revenue management at Continental Airlines. "The market sets prices." That's point one. Point two: "I have a really perishable product. It's gone when the door of the plane closes. An empty seat is lost revenue." The most valuable airline seat is the one that somebody must have an hour before takeoff and is willing to pay almost any price for. An airline seat gets more profitable with time—right up to the moment it goes from being worth $1,000 one-way to being worth $0.

Here's how Compton and his colleagues think about this: You want to sell every seat on the plane, except that you also want to have a handful left at the very end, for your most profitable (not to mention most grateful) customers. The airlines could easily sell out every seat, every flight, every day. They'd price 'em pretty low, book 'em up, and wait for takeoff. But that would mean there'd never be any seats available two or three weeks before a flight took off. How exasperated would customers be to call and find no seats three days out? When you understand that dilemma, all of a sudden, airline prices don't seem so exploitive. Although all of the seats on that New York-Miami flight are going to the same place, they aren't the same product. You pay less when you commit to a ticket four weeks in advance; Continental assumes a risk for holding a seat until the end—and wants to be paid a lot to balance the times when saving that last seat for you means that the seat flies empty.

For segmented pricing to be an effective strategy, certain conditions must exist. The market must be segmentable, and the segments must show different degrees of demand. The costs of segmenting and watching the market cannot exceed the extra revenue obtained from the price difference. Of course, the segmented pricing must also be legal. Most importantly, segmented prices should reflect real differences in customers' perceived value. Otherwise, in the long run, the practice will lead to customer resentment and ill will.

Psychological Pricing

Price says something about the product. For example, many consumers use price to judge quality. A $100 bottle of perfume may contain only $3 worth of scent, but some people are willing to pay the $100 because this price indicates something special.

In using **psychological pricing**, sellers consider the psychology of prices and not simply the economics. For example, consumers usually perceive higher-priced products as having higher quality. When they can judge the quality of a product by examining it or by calling on past experience with it, they use price less to judge quality. But when they cannot judge quality because they lack the information or skill, price becomes an important quality signal:

Some years ago, Heublein produced Smirnoff, then America's leading vodka brand. Smirnoff was attacked by another brand, Wolfschmidt, which claimed to have the same quality as Smirnoff but was priced at one dollar less per bottle. To hold on to market share, Heublein considered either lowering Smirnoff's price by one dollar or holding Smirnoff's price but increasing advertising and promotion expenditures. Either strategy would lead to lower profits and it seemed that Heublein faced a no-win situation. At this point, however, Heublein's marketers thought of a third strategy. They *raised* the price of Smirnoff by one dollar! Heublein then introduced a new brand, Relska, to compete with Wolfschmidt. Moreover, it introduced yet another brand, Popov, priced even *lower* than Wolfschmidt. This clever strategy positioned Smirnoff as the elite brand and Wolfschmidt as an ordinary brand, producing a large increase in Heublein's overall profits. The irony is that Heublein's three brands were pretty much the same in taste and manufacturing costs. Heublein knew that a product's price signals its quality. Using price as a signal, Heublein sold roughly the same product at three different quality positions.

Psychological pricing
A pricing approach that considers the psychology of prices and not simply the economics; the price is used to say something about the product.

Reference prices
Prices that buyers carry in their minds and refer to when they look at a given product.

Another aspect of psychological pricing is **reference prices**—prices that buyers carry in their minds and refer to when looking at a given product. The reference price might be formed by noting current prices, remembering past prices, or assessing the buying situation. Sellers can influence or use these consumers' reference prices when setting price. For example, a company could display its product next to more expensive ones in order to imply that it belongs in the same class. Department stores often sell women's clothing in separate departments differentiated by price: Clothing found in the more expensive department is assumed to be of better quality.

For most purchases, consumers don't have all the skill or information they need to figure out whether they are paying a good price. They don't have the time, ability, or inclination to research different brands or stores, compare prices, and get the best deals. Instead, they may rely on certain cues that signal whether a price is high or low. For example, the fact that a product is sold in a prestigious department store might signal that it's worth a higher price.

Interestingly, such pricing cues are often provided by sellers. A retailer might show a high manufacturer's suggested price next to the marked price, indicating that the product was originally priced much higher. Or the retailer might sell a selection of familiar products for which consumers have accurate price knowledge at very low prices, suggesting that the store's prices on other, less familiar products are low as well. The use of such pricing cues has become a common marketing practice (see Real Marketing 11.1).

■ Psychological pricing: What do the prices marked on this tag suggest about the product and buying solution.

11.1

It's Saturday morning and you stop by your local supermarket to pick up a few items for tonight's backyard barbeque. Cruising the aisles, you're bombarded with price signs, all suggesting that you just can't beat this store's deals. A 10-pound bag of Kingsford Charcoal Briquets goes for only $3.99 with your frequent shopper card ($4.39 without the card). Cans of Van Camps Pork & Beans are 4 for $1.00 (4 for $2.16 without the card). An aisle display hawks big bags of Utz potato chips at an "everyday low price" of just $1.99. And a sign atop a huge mass of Coke 12-packs advertises 2 for $7.

These sure look like good prices, but *are they?* If you're like most shoppers, you don't really know. In a recent *Harvard Business Review* article, two pricing researchers conclude, "for most of the items they buy, consumers don't have an accurate sense of what the price should be." In fact, customers often don't even know what prices they're actually paying. In one recent study, researchers asked supermarket shoppers the price of an item just as they were putting it into their shopping carts. Fewer than half the shoppers gave the right answer.

To know for sure if you're paying the best price, you'd have to compare the marked price to past prices, prices of competing brands, and prices in other stores. For most purchases, consumers just don't bother. Instead, they rely on a most unlikely source. "Remarkably, . . . they rely on the retailer to tell them if they're getting a good price," say the researchers. "In subtle and not-so-subtle ways, retailers send signals [or pricing cues] to customers, telling them whether a given price is relatively high or low." In their article, the researchers outline the following common retailer pricing cues.

■ *Sale Signs.* The most straightforward retail pricing cue is a sale sign. It might take any of several familiar forms: "Sale!" "Reduced!" "New low price!" "Price after rebate!" or "Now 2 for only. . . !" Such signs can be very effective in signaling low prices to consumers and increasing sales for the retailer. The researchers' studies in retail stores and mail-order catalogs reveal that using the word "sale" beside a price (even without actually varying the price) can increase demand by more than 50 percent.

Sales signs can be effective, but overuse or misuse can damage both the seller's credibility and its sales. Unfortunately, some retailers don't always use such signs truthfully. Still, consumers trust sale signs. Why? "Because they are accurate most of the time," say the researchers. "And besides, customers are not that easily fooled." They quickly become suspicious when sale signs are used improperly.

■ *Prices Ending in 9.* Just like a sale sign, a 9 at the end of a price often signals a bargain. You see such prices everywhere. For example, browse the Web sites of discounters such as Target, Best Buy, or PetsMart: It's almost impossible to find even one price that *doesn't* end in 9 (really, try it!). "In fact, this pricing tactic is so common," say the researchers, "you'd think cus-tomers would ignore it. Think again. Response to this pricing cue is remarkable. "Normally, you'd expect that demand for an item would fall as the price goes up. Yet in one study involving women's clothing, raising the price of a dress from $34 to $39 *increased* demand by a third. By comparison, raising the price from $34 to $44 yielded no difference in demand.

Pricing cues such as sales signs and prices ending in 9 can be effective in signaling low prices to consumers and increasing sales for the retailer.

But are prices ending in 9 accurate as pricing cues? "The answer varies," the researchers report. "Some retailers do reserve prices that end in 9 for their discounted items. For instance, J. Crew and Ralph Lauren generally use 00-cent end-ings on regularly priced merchandise and 99-cent endings on discounted items. Comparisons of prices at major department stores reveal that this is common, particularly for apparel. But at some stores, prices that end in 9 are a miscue—they are used on all products regardless of whether the items are discounted."

■ *Signpost Pricing (or Loss-Leader Pricing).* Unlike sale signs or prices that end in 9, signpost pricing is used on frequently pur-chased products about which consumers tend to have accurate price knowledge. For example, you probably know a good price on a 12-pack of Coke when you see one. New parents usually know how much they should expect to pay for disposable diapers.

(continues)

(continued)

Research suggests that customers use the prices of such "sign-post" items to gauge a store's overall prices. If a store has a good price on Coke or Pampers or Tide, they reason, it probably also has good prices on other items.

Retailers have long known the importance of signpost pricing, often called "loss-leader pricing." They offer selected signpost items at or below cost to pull customers into the store, hoping to make money on the shopper's other purchases. For instance, Best Buy often sells recently released DVDs at several dollars below wholesale price. Customers get a really good deal. And although Best Buy loses money on every DVD sold, the low DVD prices increase store traffic and purchases of higher-margin complementary products, such as DVD players.

Pricing-Matching Guarantees. Another widely used retail pricing cue is price matching, whereby stores promise to meet or beat any competitor's price. Best Buy, for example, says "we'll meet or beat any local competitor's price, guaranteed!" If you find a better price within 30 days on something you bought at Best Buy, the retailer will refund the difference plus 10 percent. Tweeter, a New England consumer-electronics retailer, even offers a self-enforced price-matching policy. When Tweeter finds a competitor advertising a lower advertised price, it mails a check for the difference to any customers who paid a higher price at Tweeter in the previous 30 days.

Evidence suggests that customers perceive that stores offering price-matching guarantees have overall lower prices than competing stores, especially in markets where they perceive price comparisons to be relatively easy. But are such perceptions accurate? "The evidence is mixed," say the researchers. Consumers can usually be confident that they'll pay the lowest price on eligible items. However, some manufacturers make it hard to take advantage of price-matching policies by introducing "branded variants"—slightly different versions of products with

different model numbers for different retailers. "When Tweeter introduced its highly effective automatic price-matching policy," the researchers note, "only 6 percent of its transactions were actually eligible for refunds."

Used properly, pricing cues can help consumers. Careful buyers really can take advantage of signals such as sale signs, 9-endings, loss-leaders, and price guarantees to locate good deals. Used improperly, however, these pricing cues can mislead consumers, tarnishing a brand and damaging customer relationships.

The researchers conclude: "Customers need price information, just as they need products. They look to retailers to provide both. Retailers must manage pricing cues in the same way that they manage quality. . . . No retailer . . . interested in [building profitable long-term relationships with customers] would purposely offer a defective product. Similarly, no retailer who [values customers] would deceive them with inaccurate pricing cues. By reliably signaling which prices are low, companies can retain customers' trust—and [build more solid relationships]."

Sources: Quotes and other information from Eric Anderson and Duncan Simester, "Mind Your Pricing Cues," *Harvard Business Review,* September 2003, pp. 96–103. Also see Joydeep Srivastava and Nicholas Lurie, "Price-Matching Guarantees as Signals of Low Store Prices: Survey and Experimental Evidence," *Journal of Retailing,* volume 80, issue 2, 2004, pp. 117–128; Bruce McWilliams and Eitan Gerstner, "Offering Low Price Guarantees to Improve Customer Retention," *Journal of Retailing,* June 2006, pp. 105–113; Manoj Thomas and Vicki Morvitz, "Penny Wise and Pound Foolish: The Double-Digit Effect in Price Cognition," *Journal of Consumer Research,* June 2005, pp. 54–64; and Heyong Min Kim and Luke Kachersky, "Dimensions of Price Salience: A Conceptual Framework for Perceptions of Multi-Dimensional Prices," *Journal of Product and Brand Management,* 2006, vol. 15, no. 2, pp. 139–147.

Even small differences in price can signal product differences. Consider a stereo priced at $300 compared to one priced at $299.99. The actual price difference is only 1 cent, but the psychological difference can be much greater. For example, some consumers will see the $299.99 as a price in the $200 range rather than the $300 range. The $299.99 will more likely be seen as a bargain price, whereas the $300 price suggests more quality. Some psychologists argue that each digit has symbolic and visual qualities that should be considered in pricing. Thus, 8 is round and even and creates a soothing effect, whereas 7 is angular and creates a jarring effect.[9]

Promotional Pricing

Promotional pricing
Temporarily pricing products below the list price, and sometimes even below cost, to increase short-run sales.

With **promotional pricing,** companies will temporarily price their products below list price and sometimes even below cost to create buying excitement and urgency. Promotional pricing takes several forms. Supermarkets and department stores will price a few products as *loss leaders* to attract customers to the store in the hope that they will buy other items at normal markups. For example, supermarkets often sell disposable diapers at less than cost in order to attract family buyers who make larger average purchases per trip. Sellers will also use *special-event pricing* in certain seasons to draw more customers. Thus, linens are promotionally priced every January to attract weary Christmas shoppers back into stores.

Manufacturers sometimes offer *cash rebates* to consumers who buy the product from dealers within a specified time; the manufacturer sends the rebate directly to the customer. Rebates have been popular with automakers and producers of durable goods and small appli-

ances, but they are also used with consumer packaged goods. Some manufacturers offer *low-interest financing, longer warranties,* or *free maintenance* to reduce the consumer's "price." This practice has become another favorite of the auto industry. Or, the seller may simply offer *discounts* from normal prices to increase sales and reduce inventories.

Promotional pricing, however, can have adverse effects. Used too frequently and copied by competitors, price promotions can create "deal-prone" customers who wait until brands go on sale before buying them. Or, constantly reduced prices can erode a brand's value in the eyes of customers. Marketers sometimes use price promotions as a quick fix instead of sweating through the difficult process of developing effective longer-term strategies for building their brands. In fact, one observer notes that price promotions can be downright addicting to both the company and the customer: "Price promotions are the brand equivalent of heroin: easy to get into but hard to get out of. Once the brand and its customers are addicted to the short-term high of a price cut, it is hard to wean them away to real brand building.... But continue and the brand dies by 1,000 cuts."[10]

The frequent use of promotional pricing can also lead to industry price wars. Such price wars usually play into the hands of only one or a few competitors—those with the most efficient operations. For example, until recently, Computer companies, including IBM, Hewlett-Packard, and Gateway, showed strong profits as their new technologies were snapped up by eager consumers. When the market cooled, however, many competitors began to unload PCs at discounted prices. In response, Dell, the industry's undisputed low-cost leader, started a brutal price war that only it could win. The result was nothing short of a rout. IBM has since sold off its PC unit to Lenovo, and Gateway struggles with razor thin profit margins. HP PC profit margins average just 3.9 percent compared to Dell's 6.4 percent. Dell has emerged atop the worldwide PC industry.[11]

The point is that promotional pricing can be an effective means of generating sales for some companies in certain circumstances. But it can be damaging for other companies or if taken as a steady diet.

Geographical Pricing

A company also must decide how to price its products for customers located in different parts of the country or world. Should the company risk losing the business of more-distant customers by charging them higher prices to cover the higher shipping costs? Or should the company charge all customers the same prices regardless of location? We will look at five **geographical pricing** strategies for the following hypothetical situation:

The Peerless Paper Company is located in Atlanta, Georgia, and sells paper products to customers all over the United States. The cost of freight is high and affects the companies from whom customers buy their paper. Peerless wants to establish a geographical pricing policy. It is trying to determine how to price a $100 order to three specific customers: Customer A (Atlanta), Customer B (Bloomington, Indiana), and Customer C (Compton, California).

One option is for Peerless to ask each customer to pay the shipping cost from the Atlanta factory to the customer's location. All three customers would pay the same factory price of $100, with Customer A paying, say, $10 for shipping; Customer B, $15; and Customer C, $25. Called **FOB-origin pricing,** this practice means that the goods are placed *free on board* (hence,

Geographical pricing
Setting prices for customers located in different parts of the country or world.

FOB-origin pricing
A geographical pricing strategy in which goods are placed free on board a carrier; the customer pays the freight from the factory to the destination.

■ Promotional pricing: Companies offer promotional prices to create buying excitement and urgency.

FOB) a carrier. At that point the title and responsibility pass to the customer, who pays the freight from the factory to the destination. Because each customer picks up its own cost, supporters of FOB pricing feel that this is the fairest way to assess freight charges. The disadvantage, however, is that Peerless will be a high-cost firm to distant customers.

Uniform-delivered pricing is the opposite of FOB pricing. Here, the company charges the same price plus freight to all customers, regardless of their location. The freight charge is set at the average freight cost. Suppose this is $15. Uniform-delivered pricing therefore results in a higher charge to the Atlanta customer (who pays $15 freight instead of $10) and a lower charge to the Compton customer (who pays $15 freight instead of $25). Although the Atlanta customer would prefer to buy paper from another local paper company that uses FOB-origin pricing, Peerless has a better chance of winning over the California customer. Other advantages of uniform-delivered pricing are that it is fairly easy to administer and it lets the firm advertise its price nationally.

Zone pricing falls between FOB-origin pricing and uniform-delivered pricing. The company sets up two or more zones. All customers within a given zone pay a single total price; the more distant the zone, the higher the price. For example, Peerless might set up an East Zone and charge $10 freight to all customers in this zone, a Midwest Zone in which it charges $15, and a West Zone in which it charges $25. In this way, the customers within a given price zone receive no price advantage from the company. For example, customers in Atlanta and Boston pay the same total price to Peerless. The complaint, however, is that the Atlanta customer is paying part of the Boston customer's freight cost.

Using **basing-point pricing**, the seller selects a given city as a "basing point" and charges all customers the freight cost from that city to the customer location, regardless of the city from which the goods are actually shipped. For example, Peerless might set Chicago as the basing point and charge all customers $100 plus the freight from Chicago to their locations. This means that an Atlanta customer pays the freight cost from Chicago to Atlanta, even though the goods may be shipped from Atlanta. If all sellers used the same basing-point city, delivered prices would be the same for all customers and price competition would be eliminated. Industries such as sugar, cement, steel, and automobiles used basing-point pricing for years, but this method has become less popular today. Some companies set up multiple basing points to create more flexibility: They quote freight charges from the basing-point city nearest to the customer.

Finally, the seller who is anxious to do business with a certain customer or geographical area might use **freight-absorption pricing**. Using this strategy, the seller absorbs all or part of the actual freight charges in order to get the desired business. The seller might reason that if it can get more business, its average costs will fall and more than compensate for its extra freight cost. Freight-absorption pricing is used for market penetration and to hold on to increasingly competitive markets.

Dynamic Pricing

Throughout most of history, prices were set by negotiation between buyers and sellers. *Fixed price* policies—setting one price for all buyers—is a relatively modern idea that arose with the development of large-scale retailing at the end of the nineteenth century. Today, most prices are set this way. However, some companies are now reversing the fixed pricing trend. They are using **dynamic pricing**—adjusting prices continually to meet the characteristics and needs of individual customers and situations.

For example, think about how the Internet has affected pricing. From the mostly fixed pricing practices of the past century, the Web seems now to be taking us back—into a new age of fluid pricing. "Potentially, [the Internet] could push aside sticker prices and usher in an era of dynamic pricing," says one writer, "in which a wide range of goods would be priced according to what the market will bear—instantly, constantly."[12]

Dynamic pricing offers many advantages for marketers. For example, Internet sellers such as Amazon.com can mine their databases to gauge a specific shopper's desires, measure his or her means, instantaneously tailor products to fit that shopper's behavior, and price products accordingly. Catalog retailers such as L.L. Bean or Spiegel can change prices on the fly according to changes in demand or costs, changing prices for specific items on a day-by-day or even hour-by-hour basis.

Many direct marketers monitor inventories, costs, and demand at any given moment and adjust prices instantly. For example, Dell uses dynamic pricing to achieve real-time balancing of supply and demand for computer components. Author Thomas Friedman describes Dell's dynamic pricing system this way:[13]

Uniform-delivered pricing
A geographical pricing strategy in which the company charges the same price plus freight to all customers, regardless of their location.

Zone pricing
A geographical pricing strategy in which the company sets up two or more zones. All customers within a zone pay the same total price; the more distant the zone, the higher the price.

Basing-point pricing
A geographical pricing strategy in which the seller designates some city as a basing point and charges all customers the freight cost from that city to the customer.

Freight-absorption pricing
A geographical pricing strategy in which the seller absorbs all or part of the freight charges in order to get the desired business.

Dynamic pricing
Adjusting prices continually to meet the characteristics and needs of individual customers and situations.

[Dell's] supply chain symphony—from my order over the phone to production to delivery to my house—is one of the wonders of the flat world. . . . Demand shopping goes on constantly. . . . It works like this: At 10 A.M. Austin time, Dell discovers that so many customers have ordered notebooks with 40-gigabyte hard drives since the morning that its supply chain will run short in two hours. That signal is automatically relayed to Dell's marketing department and to Dell.com and to all the Dell phone operators taking orders. If you happen to call to place your Dell order at 10:30 A.M., the Dell representative will say to you, "Tom, it's your lucky day! For the next hour we are offering 60-gigabyte hard drives with the notebook you want—for only $10 more than the 40-gig drive. And if you act now, Dell will throw in a carrying case along with your purchase, because we so value you as a customer." In an hour or two, using such promotions, Dell can reshape the demand for any part of any notebook or desktop to correspond with the projected supply in its global supply chain. Today memory might be on sale, tomorrow it might be CD-ROMs.

Buyers also benefit from the Web and dynamic pricing. A wealth of *shopping bots*—such as Froogle.com, Yahoo! Shopping, Bizrate.com, NexTag.com, epinions.com, PriceGrabber.com, mySimon.com, and PriceScan.com—offer instant product and price comparisons from thousands of vendors. Epinions.com, for instance, lets shoppers browse by category or search for specific products and brands. It then searches the Web and reports back links to sellers offering the best prices along with customer reviews. In addition to simply finding the best product and the vendor with the best price for that product, customers armed with price information can often negotiate lower prices.

Buyers can also negotiate prices at online auction sites and exchanges. Suddenly the centuries-old art of haggling is back in vogue. Want to sell that antique pickle jar that's been collecting dust for generations? Post it on eBay, the world's biggest online flea market. Want to name your own price for a hotel room or rental car? Visit Priceline.com or another reverse auction site. Want to bid on a ticket to a Coldplay show? Check out Ticketmaster.com, which now offers an online auction service for concert tickets.

Dynamic pricing can also be controversial. Most customers would find it galling to learn that the person in the next seat on that flight from Gainesville to Galveston paid 10 percent less just because he or she happened to call at the right time or buy through the right sales channel. Amazon.com learned this some years ago when it experimented with lowering prices to new customers in order to woo their business. When regular customers learned through Internet chatter that they were paying generally higher prices than first-timers, they protested loudly. An embarrassed Amazon.com halted the experiments.

Dynamic pricing makes sense in many contexts—it adjusts prices according to market forces, and it often works to the benefit of the customer. But marketers need to be careful not to use dynamic pricing to take advantage of certain customer groups, damaging important customer relationships. Especially in the online retail environment, customer loyalty can be fragile. According to one online retail researcher, "A consumer [can] switch in a heartbeat. Price shopping is done as a matter of course, and it wouldn't be all that hard [for a consumer] to identify [himself or herself] as someone else just to see the price on that site. Get caught, and you're dead."14

Comparison shop the new-fashioned way.

YAHOO! shopping
Search. Compare. Save.
shopping.yahoo.com

■ Buyers benefit from the Web and dynamic pricing. Sites like Yahoo! Shopping give instant product and price comparisons from thousands of vendors, arming customers with price information they need to get the lowest prices.

International Pricing

Companies that market their products internationally must decide what prices to charge in the different countries in which they operate. In some cases, a company can set a uniform worldwide price. For example, Boeing sells its jetliners at about the same price everywhere, whether in the United States, Europe, or a third-world country. However, most companies adjust their prices to reflect local market conditions and cost considerations.

The price that a company should charge in a specific country depends on many factors, including economic conditions, competitive situations, laws and regulations, and development of the wholesaling and retailing system. Consumer perceptions and preferences also may vary from country to country, calling for different prices. Or the company may have different marketing objectives in various world markets, which require changes in pricing strategy. For example, Samsung might introduce a new product into mature markets in highly developed countries with the goal of quickly gaining mass-market share—this would call for a penetration-pricing strategy. In contrast, it might enter a less developed market by targeting smaller, less price-sensitive segments; in this case, market-skimming pricing makes sense.

■ Companies that market products internationally must decide what prices to charge in the different countries.

Costs play an important role in setting international prices. Travelers abroad are often surprised to find that goods that are relatively inexpensive at home may carry outrageously higher price tags in other countries. A pair of Levi's selling for $30 in the United States might go for $63 in Tokyo and $88 in Paris. A McDonald's Big Mac selling for a modest $2.90 here might cost $6.00 in Reykjavik, Iceland, and an Oral-B toothbrush selling for $2.49 at home may cost $10 in China. Conversely, a Gucci handbag going for only $140 in Milan, Italy, might fetch $240 in the United States. In some cases, such *price escalation* may result from differences in selling strategies or market conditions. In most instances, however, it is simply a result of the higher costs of selling in another country—the additional costs of product modifications, shipping and insurance, import tariffs and taxes, exchange-rate fluctuations, and physical distribution.

For example, Campbell found that distribution in the United Kingdom cost 30 percent more than in the United States. U.S. retailers typically purchase soup in large quantities—48-can cases of a single soup by the dozens, hundreds, or carloads. In contrast, English grocers purchase soup in small quantities—typically in 24-can cases of *assorted* soups. Each case had to be hand-packed for shipment. To handle these small orders, Campbell had to add a costly extra wholesale level to its European channel. The smaller orders also meant that English retailers ordered two or three times as often as their U.S. counterparts, bumping up billing and order costs. These and other factors caused Campbell to charge much higher prices for its soups in the United Kingdom.[15]

Thus, international pricing presents some special problems and complexities. We discuss international pricing issues in more detail in Chapter 19.

▮ Price Changes

After developing their pricing structures and strategies, companies often face situations in which they must initiate price changes or respond to price changes by competitors.

Initiating Price Changes

In some cases, the company may find it desirable to initiate either a price cut or a price increase. In both cases, it must anticipate possible buyer and competitor reactions.

Initiating Price Cuts

Several situations may lead a firm to consider cutting its price. One such circumstance is excess capacity. Another is falling demand in the face of strong price competition. In such cases, the firm may aggressively cut prices to boost sales and share. But as the airline, fast-food, automobile, and other industries have learned in recent years, cutting prices in an industry loaded with excess capacity may lead to price wars as competitors try to hold on to market share.

A company may also cut prices in a drive to dominate the market through lower costs. Either the company starts with lower costs than its competitors, or it cuts prices in the hope of gaining market share that will further cut costs through larger volume. Bausch & Lomb used an aggressive low-cost, low-price strategy to become an early leader in the competitive soft contact lens market. And Dell used this strategy in the PC market.

Initiating Price Increases

A successful price increase can greatly increase profits. For example, if the company's profit margin is 3 percent of sales, a 1 percent price increase will increase profits by 33 percent if sales volume is unaffected. A major factor in price increases is cost inflation. Rising costs squeeze profit margins and lead companies to pass cost increases along to customers. Another factor leading to price increases is overdemand: When a company cannot supply all that its customers need, it may raise its prices, ration products to customers, or both. Consider the worldwide oil and gas industry.

When raising prices, the company must avoid being perceived as a price gouger. Customers have long memories, and they will eventually turn away from companies or even whole industries that they perceive as charging excessive prices. There are some techniques for avoiding this problem. One is to maintain a sense of fairness surrounding any price increase. Price increases should be supported by company communications telling customers why prices are being raised. Making low-visibility price moves first is also a good technique: Some examples include dropping discounts, increasing minimum order sizes, and curtailing production of low-margin products. The company sales force should help business customers find ways to economize.

Wherever possible, the company should consider ways to meet higher costs or demand without raising prices. For example, it can consider more cost-effective ways to produce or distribute its products. It can shrink the product or substitute less expensive ingredients instead of raising the price. Or it can "unbundle" its marketing—removing features, packaging, or services and separately pricing elements that were formerly part of the offer. IBM, for example, now offers training and consulting as separately priced services.

Buyer Reactions to Price Changes

Customers do not always interpret price changes in a straightforward way. They may view a price cut in several ways. For example, what would you think if Joy perfume, "the costliest fragrance in the world," were to cut its price in half? Or what if Sony suddenly cut its PC prices drastically? You might think that the computers are about to be replaced by newer models or that they have some fault and are not

■ Buyer reactions to price changes: What would you think if the price of Joy was suddenly cut in half?

selling well. You might think that Sony is abandoning the computer business and may not stay in this business long enough to supply future parts. You might believe that quality has been reduced. Or you might think that the price will come down even further and that it will pay to wait and see.

Similarly, a price *increase*, which would normally lower sales, may have some positive meanings for buyers. What would you think if Sony *raised* the price of its latest PC model? On the one hand, you might think that the item is very "hot" and may be unobtainable unless you buy it soon. Or you might think that the computer is an unusually good performer. On the other hand, you might think that Sony is greedy and charging what the traffic will bear.

Competitor Reactions to Price Changes

A firm considering a price change must be concerned about the reactions of its competitors as well as those of its customers. Competitors are most likely to react when the number of firms involved is small, when the product is uniform, and when the buyers are well informed about products and prices.

How can the firm anticipate the likely reactions of its competitors? The problem is complex because, like the customer, the competitor can interpret a company price cut in many ways. It might think the company is trying to grab a larger market share, or that it's doing poorly and trying to boost its sales. Or it might think that the company wants the whole industry to cut prices to increase total demand.

The company must guess each competitor's likely reaction. If all competitors behave alike, this amounts to analyzing only a typical competitor. In contrast, if the competitors do not behave alike—perhaps because of differences in size, market shares, or policies—then separate analyses are necessary. However, if some competitors will match the price change, there is good reason to expect that the rest will also match it.

Responding to Price Changes

Here we reverse the question and ask how a firm should respond to a price change by a competitor. The firm needs to consider several issues: Why did the competitor change the price? Is the price change temporary or permanent? What will happen to the company's market share and profits if it does not respond? Are other competitors going to respond? Besides these issues, the company must also consider its own situation and strategy and possible customer reactions to price changes.

Figure 11.1 shows the ways a company might assess and respond to a competitor's price cut. Suppose the company learns that a competitor has cut its price and decides that this price cut is likely to harm company sales and profits. It might simply decide to hold its current price and profit margin. The company might believe that it will not lose too much market share, or that it would lose too much profit if it reduced its own price. Or it might decide that

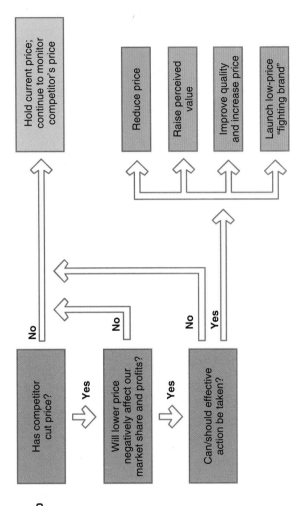

FIGURE 11.1
Assessing and responding to competitor price changes

it should wait and respond when it has more information on the effects of the competitor's price change. However, waiting too long to act might let the competitor get stronger and more confident as its sales increase.

If the company decides that effective action can and should be taken, it might make any of four responses. First, it could *reduce its price* to match the competitor's price. It may decide that the market is price sensitive and that it would lose too much market share to the lower-priced competitor. Cutting the price will reduce the company's profits in the short run. Some companies might also reduce their product quality, services, and marketing communications to retain profit margins, but this will ultimately hurt long-run market share. The company should try to maintain its quality as it cuts prices.

Alternatively, the company might maintain its price but *raise the perceived value* of its offer. It could improve its communications, stressing the relative value of its product over that of the lower-price competitor. The firm may find it cheaper to maintain price and spend money to improve its perceived value than to cut price and operate at a lower margin. Or, the company might *improve quality and increase price*, moving its brand into a higher price-value position. The higher quality creates greater customer value, which justifies the higher price. In turn, the higher price preserves the company's higher margins.

Finally, the company might *launch a low-price "fighting brand"*—adding a lower-price item to the line or creating a separate lower-price brand. This is necessary if the particular market segment being lost is price sensitive and will not respond to arguments of higher quality. Thus, when challenged on price by Southwest Airlines and JetBlue, Delta created low-fare Song airlines and United created Ted. To counter store brands and other low-price entrants, Procter & Gamble turned a number of its brands into fighting brands, including Luvs disposable diapers, Joy dishwashing detergent, Charmin Basic toilet paper, and Camay beauty soap. In turn, P&G competitor Kimberly-Clark positions its value-priced Scott Towels brand as "the Bounty killer." It advertises that "Scott makes good sense." The brand scores well on customer satisfaction measures but sells for a lower price than P&G's Bounty brand. The Scott products Web site offers printable coupons to support the brand's good-value positioning.

■ Fighting brands: Kimberly-Clark offers its value-priced Scott brand as "the Bounty killer." It scores well on customer satisfaction but sells for a lower price than P&G's Bounty. "Scott makes good sense."

■ Public Policy and Pricing

Price competition is a core element of our free-market economy. In setting prices, companies are not usually free to charge whatever prices they wish. Many federal, state, and even local laws govern the rules of fair play in pricing. In addition, companies must consider broader societal pricing concerns (see Real Marketing 11.2). The most important pieces of legislation affecting pricing are the Sherman, Clayton, and Robinson-Patman acts, initially adopted to curb the formation of monopolies and to regulate business practices that might unfairly restrain trade. Because these federal statutes can be applied only to interstate commerce, some states have adopted similar provisions for companies that operate locally.

Figure 11.2 shows the major public policy issues in pricing. These include potentially damaging pricing practices within a given level of the channel (price-fixing and predatory pricing) and across levels of the channel (retail price maintenance, discriminatory pricing, and deceptive pricing).[16]

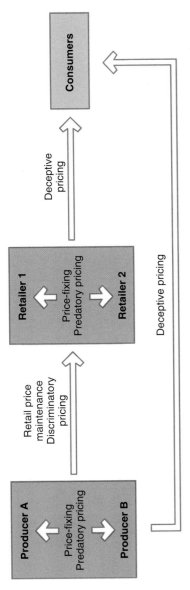

FIGURE 11.2 Public policy issues in pricing

Source: Adapted with permission from Dhruv Grewal and Larry D. Compeau, "Pricing and Public Policy: A Research Agenda and Overview of Special Issue," *Journal of Public Policy and Marketing,* Spring 1999, pp. 3–10, Figure 1.

Pricing Within Channel Levels

Federal legislation on *price-fixing* states that sellers must set prices without talking to competitors. Otherwise, price collusion is suspected. Price-fixing is illegal per se—that is, the government does not accept any excuses for price-fixing. Companies found guilty of such practices can receive heavy fines. Recently, governments at the state and national levels have been aggressively enforcing price-fixing regulations in industries ranging from gasoline, insurance, and concrete to credit cards, CDs, and computer chips. For example, Samsung and two other computer memory-chip makers agreed to pay $160 million to settle a suit alleging a four-year price-fixing conspiracy to artificially constrict the supply of D-Ram (dynamic random access memory) chips to computer makers such as Dell and Apple. This control of the supply helped keep prices artificially high, producing higher profits for the conspiring companies. Since that settlement, U.S. state and federal governments have filed additional price-fixing lawsuits against various computer memory-chip makers.[17]

Sellers are also prohibited from using *predatory pricing*—selling below cost with the intention of punishing a competitor or gaining higher long-run profits by putting competitors out of business. This protects small sellers from larger ones who might sell items below cost temporarily or in a specific locale to drive them out of business. The biggest problem is determining just what constitutes predatory pricing behavior. Selling below cost to sell off excess inventory is not considered predatory; selling below cost to drive out competitors is. Thus, the same action may or may not be predatory depending on intent, and intent can be very difficult to determine or prove.

In recent years, several large and powerful companies have been accused of predatory pricing. For example, Wal-Mart has been sued by dozens of small competitors charging that it lowered prices in their specific areas to drive them out of business. In fact, the State of New York passed a bill requiring companies to price gas at or above 98 percent of cost to "address the more extreme cases of predatory pricing by big-box stores" such as Wal-Mart. Yet, in North Dakota, the same gas pricing proposal was rejected because state representatives did not view the practice as predatory pricing.[18]

Pricing Across Channel Levels

The Robinson-Patman Act seeks to prevent unfair *price discrimination* by ensuring that sellers offer the same price terms to customers at a given level of trade. For example, every retailer is entitled to the same price terms from a given manufacturer, whether the retailer is Sears or your local bicycle shop. However, price discrimination is allowed if the seller can prove that its costs are different when selling to different retailers—for example, that it costs less per unit to sell a large volume of bicycles to Sears than to sell a few bicycles to the local dealer.

The seller can also discriminate in its pricing if the seller manufactures different qualities of the same product for different retailers. The seller must prove that these differences are proportional. Price differentials may also be used to "match competition" in "good faith," provided the price discrimination is temporary, localized, and defensive rather than offensive.

11.2 GlaxoSmithKline: Pricing for More Than Sales and Profits

The U.S. pharmaceutical industry has historically been one of the nation's most profitable industries. Since the mid-1990s, annual industry revenues have grown by an average of 10 percent per year, a trend that few industries can match. As the world's second-largest pharmaceuticals company, GlaxoSmithKline (GSK) has played a large role in the industry's success. It produces a medicine cabinet full of well-known prescription drugs that combat infections, depression, skin conditions, asthma, heart and circulatory disease, and cancer. It also makes dozens of familiar over-the-counter remedies, from Contac, Nicorette, and Sensodyne to Tagamet and Tums.

GlaxoSmithKline is doing very well in a high-performing industry. Its sales last year grew by 7 percent; earnings per share grew 18 percent. Around the world, more than 1,100 prescriptions are written for GSK products every minute. And with more drugs in its research and development pipeline than most of its competitors, it appears that GSK's future will be just as bright.

In most situations, we applaud companies for strong profit performance. However, when it comes to pharmaceuticals firms, critics claim that healthy profits may not be so healthy for consumers. Learning that GlaxoSmithKline is reaping big profits leaves a bad taste in the mouths of many consumers—it's like learning that the oil companies are profiting as gas prices soar. Although most consumers appreciate the steady stream of beneficial drugs produced by the U.S. pharmaceutical companies, they sense that the industry's huge success may be coming at their own expense—literally.

Americans spend more than $200 billion a year on prescription medications, nearly half of worldwide spending, and this spending is expected to exceed $450 billion by 2015. Prescription prices have risen rapidly over the years and healthcare costs continue to jump. An AARP survey of 193 brand-name prescription drugs found that their average wholesale prices increased 3.9 percent over just the first three months of 2006, almost four times the general inflation rate. The prices of many of the most important drugs are skyrocketing. High drug prices have sent many consumers, especially seniors with limited budgets and fixed incomes, to Mexico or Canada in search of cheaper alternatives. Says one senior after a visit to Mexico, "If we couldn't get cheap meds, I wouldn't live."

The critics claim that competitive forces don't operate well in the pharmaceutical market, allowing GSK and other companies to charge excessive prices. Unlike purchases of other consumer products, drug purchases cannot be postponed. And consumers don't usually shop for the best deal on medicines—they simply take what the doctor orders. Because physicians who write the prescriptions don't pay for the medicines they recommend, they have little incentive to be price conscious. Finally, because of patents and FDA approvals, few competing brands exist to force lower prices, and existing brands don't go on sale. The critics claim that these market

factors leave pharmaceutical companies free to practice monopoly pricing resulting in unfair practices and price gouging.

To add insult to injury, the critics say, drug companies pour $7.5 billion a year into direct-to-consumer advertising and another $16 billion into sampling. These marketing efforts dictate higher prices at the same time that they build demand for more expensive remedies. Even when doctors or pharmacists recommend less-expensive generic drugs, consumers may pay substantial markups. Pharmacies may look like good guys when they encourage the use of generics to save consumers money, but they also pocket a handsome profit. One recent study found that drugstores and pharmacies are marking up the price of some generics by more than 1,000 percent.

As a pharmaceuticals industry leader, GlaxoSmithKline has borne its share of the criticism. For example, as the largest producer of AIDS-fighting antiretroviral drugs, GSK has been accused of pricing its drugs out of the reach of the poor people who need them the most. And the company recently settled claims by the U.S. Department of Justice and 40 states alleging that it had inflated the wholesale prices of drugs used by cancer patients and others. Thus, the severest critics say, GSK may be profiting unfairly—or even at the expense of human life.

But there's another side to the drug-pricing issue. Industry proponents point out that, over the years, GSK has developed a steady stream of medicines that transform people's lives. Developing such new drugs is a risky and expensive endeavor, involving legions of scientists, expensive technology, and years of effort with no certainty of success. The pharmaceuticals industry invests nearly $50 billion a year in R&D—GSK alone invested $5.4 billion last year. GSK now has 149 prescription drugs and vaccines under development. On average,

Most consumers appreciate the steady stream of beneficial drugs produced by pharmaceutical companies like GlaxoSmithKline. However, with the prices of many of the most important drugs skyrocketing, others protest that the industry's huge success may be coming at consumers' own expense—literally.

(continues)

(continued)

each new drug takes 15 years to develop at a cost of close to $800 million. Then, 70 percent of new drugs never generate enough revenue to recover the cost of development. Although the prices of prescription drugs seem high, they're needed to fund the development of important future drugs.

A recent GlaxoSmithKline ad notes that it took 15 years to complete all the tests and to find the exact right compound for a new heart medicine, at a cost of more than the price of a space shuttle mission. Profits from the heart drug will help to fund critical research on diseases such as Multiple Sclerosis and Alzheimer's. The ad concludes: "Inventing new medicines isn't easy, but it's worth it. . . . Today's medicines finance tomorrow's miracles."

And so the controversy continues. As drug prices climb, GSK and the industry are facing pressures from the federal government, insurance companies, managed-care providers, and advocacy groups to exercise restraint in setting prices. Rather than waiting for tougher legislation on prices—or simply because it's the right thing to do—GSK has undertaken several initiatives to make drugs available to those who need but can't afford them. For some years now, it has priced its HIV/AIDS and malaria medicines at cost to customers and not-for-profit organizations in developing countries. In the United States and other developed countries, GSK sponsors patient assistance programs and discount cards that provide prescription medi-

cines to low-income, uninsured patients free or at minimal cost. And GSK regularly donates free medicines in response to disaster relief efforts around the globe.

The pharmaceuticals pricing controversy will no doubt continue. For GlaxoSmithKline, it's more than a matter of sales and profits. In setting prices, short-term financial goals must be tempered by broader societal considerations. GSK's heartfelt mission is "to improve the quality of human life by enabling people to do more, feel better, and live longer." Accomplishing this mission won't come cheap. Most consumers understand that one way or another they'll have to pay the price. All they really ask is that they be treated fairly in the process.

Sources: Milt Freudenheim, "Drug Prices Up Sharply This Year," *New York Times*, June 21, 2006, p. C1; "Drug Spending to Soar, but Not as Quickly as Expected," *Formulary*, April 2006, p. 203; Jane Wardell, "GlaxoSmithKline Sees 25 Percent Profit Rise," *Associated Press Online*, April 27, 2006; Joel Millman, "Not Your Generic Smugglers—American Seniors Flock to Border Town for Cheap Prescriptions," *Wall Street Journal*, March 20, 2003, p. D.3; Cole Ollinger, "A Tough Pill to Swallow," *Manufacturing Business Technology*, February 2006, pp. 22–23; "GSK to Settle Pricing Claims," *The News & Observer*, August 11, 2006, p. 2D; and information from www.gsk.com, December 2006.

Laws also prohibit *retail (or resale) price maintenance*—a manufacturer cannot require dealers to charge a specified retail price for its product. Although the seller can propose a manufacturer's *suggested* retail price to dealers, it cannot refuse to sell to a dealer who takes independent pricing action, nor can it punish the dealer by shipping late or denying advertising allowances. For example, the Florida attorney general's office investigated Nike for allegedly fixing the retail price of its shoes and clothing. It was concerned that Nike might be withholding items from retailers who were not selling its most expensive shoes—such as the Air Jordan and Shox lines—at prices the company considered suitable.

Deceptive pricing occurs when a seller states prices or price savings that mislead consumers or are not actually available to consumers. This might involve bogus reference or comparison prices, as when a retailer sets artificially high "regular" prices then announces "sale" prices close to its previous everyday prices. For example, Overstock.com recently came under scrutiny for inaccurately listing manufacturer's suggested retail prices, often quoting them higher than the actual price. Such comparison pricing is widespread.

Comparison pricing claims are legal if they are truthful. However, the FTC's *Guides Against Deceptive Pricing* warns sellers not to advertise a price reduction unless it is a saving from the usual retail price, not to advertise "factory" or "wholesale" prices unless such prices are what they are claimed to be, and not to advertise comparable value prices on imperfect goods.[19]

Other deceptive pricing issues include *scanner fraud* and price confusion. The widespread use of scanner-based computer checkouts has led to increasing complaints of retailers overcharging their customers. Most of these

■ Deceptive pricing concerns: The widespread use of checkout scanners has led to increasing complaints of retailers overcharging their customers.

overcharges result from poor management—from a failure to enter current or sale prices into the system. Other cases, however, involve intentional overcharges. *Price confusion* results when firms employ pricing methods that make it difficult for consumers to understand just what price they are really paying. For example, consumers are sometimes misled regarding the real price of a home mortgage or car leasing agreement. In other cases, important pricing details may be buried in the "fine print."

Many federal and state statutes regulate against deceptive pricing practices. For example, the Automobile Information Disclosure Act requires automakers to attach a statement to new-car windows stating the manufacturer's suggested retail price, the prices of optional equipment, and the dealer's transportation charges. However, reputable sellers go beyond what is required by law. Treating customers fairly and making certain that they fully understand prices and pricing terms is an important part of building strong and lasting customer relationships.

Reviewing the Concepts

1. **Describe the major strategies for pricing imitative and new products.**

   Pricing is a dynamic process. Companies design a *pricing structure* that covers all their products. They change this structure over time and adjust it to account for different customers and situations. Pricing strategies usually change as a product passes through its life cycle. The company can decide on one of several price-quality strategies for introducing an imitative product, including premium pricing, economy pricing, good value, or overcharging. In pricing innovative new products, it can use *market-skimming pricing* by initially setting high prices to "skim" the maximum amount of revenue from various segments of the market. Or it can use *market-penetrating pricing* by setting a low initial price to penetrate the market deeply and win a large market share.

2. **Explain how companies find a set of prices that maximizes the profits from the total product mix.**

   When the product is part of a product mix, the firm searches for a set of prices that will maximize the profits from the total mix. In *product line pricing*, the company decides on price steps for the entire set of products it offers. In addition, the company must set prices for *optional products* (optional or accessory products included with the main product), *captive products* (products that are required for use of the main product), *by-products* (waste or residual products produced when making the main product), and *product bundles* (combinations of products at a reduced price).

3. **Discuss how companies adjust their prices to take into account different types of customers and situations.**

   Companies apply a variety of *price-adjustment strategies* to account for differences in consumer segments and situations. One is *discount and allowance pricing*, whereby the company establishes cash, quantity, functional, or seasonal discounts, or varying types of allowances. A second strategy is *segmented pricing*, where the company sells a product at two or more prices to accommodate different customers, product forms, locations, or times. Sometimes companies consider more than economics in their pricing decisions, using *psychological pricing* to better communicate a product's intended position. In *promotional pricing*, a company offers discounts or temporarily sells a product below list price as a special event, sometimes even selling below cost as a loss leader. Another approach is *geographical pricing*, whereby the company decides how to price to distant customers, choosing from such alternatives as FOB pricing, uniform-delivered pricing, zone pricing, basing-point pricing, and freight-absorption pricing. Finally, *international pricing* means that the company adjusts its price to meet different conditions and expectations in different world markets.

4. **Discuss the key issues related to initiating and responding to price changes.**

   When a firm considers initiating a *price change*, it must consider customers' and competitors' reactions. There are different implications to *initiating price cuts* and *initiating price increases*. Buyer reactions to price changes are influenced by the meaning customers see in the price change. Competitors' reactions flow from a set reaction policy or a fresh analysis of each situation.

   There are also many factors to consider in responding to a competitor's price changes. The company that faces a price change initiated by a competitor must try to understand the competitor's intent as well as the likely duration and impact of the change. If a swift reaction is desirable, the firm should preplan its reactions to different possible price actions by competitors. When facing a competitor's price change, the company might sit tight, reduce its own price, raise perceived quality, improve quality and raise price, or launch a fighting brand.

Reviewing the Key Terms

Allowance 312
Basing-point pricing 318
By-product pricing 311
Captive-product pricing 311
Discount 312

Dynamic pricing 318
FOB-origin pricing 317
Freight-absorption pricing 318
Geographical pricing 317
Market-penetration pricing 309

Market-skimming pricing 308
Optional-product pricing 310
Product bundle pricing 312
Product line pricing 310
Promotional pricing 316

Psychological pricing 314
Reference prices 314
Segmented pricing 312
Uniform-delivered pricing 318
Zone pricing 318

Discussing the Concepts

1. Why would Palm choose market-skimming pricing rather than market-penetration pricing for a new line of smartphones?

2. Why is product bundle pricing effective?

3. Psychological pricing is a pricing-adjustment strategy often used by retailers. Explain this pricing strategy. How it is tied to the concept of reference prices?

4. Discuss the difficulties an international company would encounter if it set a uniform worldwide price for a commodity-type product.

5. Continental Cruise Lines is increasing the price for its Boston-to-Bermuda five-day cruise from $700 per person to $1,000 per per-son. How might consumers interpret this price increase? How might Continental reduce possible negative reactions?

6. Lawful price discrimination by sellers is a common practice. Discuss the conditions under which price discrimination practice becomes unlawful.

Applying the Concepts

1. Visit the Web sites of two wireless phone companies (say, Sprint and Cingular). Compare their pricing strategies for cellular services. What types of product-mix and price-adjustment strategies do you observe?

2. Promotional pricing generates a sense of urgency and excitement. However, recognizing the dangers of this pricing approach, your boss has requested that you design an alternative pricing strategy that will generate the greater long-term sales and customer loyalty. What pricing strategy do you recommend? Will this strategy work as well as promotional pricing in the short term? Explain.

3. You are an owner of a small independent chain of coffee houses competing head-to-head with Starbucks. The retail price your cus-tomers pay for coffee is exactly the same as at Starbucks. The wholesale price you pay for roasted coffee beans has increased by 25 percent. You understand that you cannot absorb this increase and that it must be passed on to your customers. However, you are concerned about the consequences of an open price increase. Discuss three alternative price-increase strategies that address your concerns.

Focus on Technology

Space travel for the average person once seemed probable only in sci-ence fiction stories. But on April 28, 2001, the world saw its first true pay-ing civilian astronaut when Dennis Tito, a California multimillionaire, became the first-ever space tourist. Tito traveled on a Russian Soyuz cap-sule and proved that an everyday citizen could endure this trip. Tito's trip, along with advances in rocket technology, accelerated the opportunities for space tourism. A pioneer in this area, Virgin Group founder Richard Branson has established Virgin Galactic, which will begin offering a fleet of space ships for travel into outer space. Virgin Galactic, which will set up its world headquarters in New Mexico, plans to build a $200-million spaceport on a 27-square-mile area in the southern part of the state.

Virgin Galactic is already collecting refundable deposits of $20,000 for the first year of travel. The deposits will be applied to the full fare of $200,000 for each trip into outer space. Visit www.virgingalactic.com to learn more about space tourism.

1. How should a company go about setting price for a new, high-technology product or service? What new-product pricing strategy is Virgin Galactic using for its space trips?

2. How might the entrance of a competitor affect the pricing?

3. How might Virgin Galactic bundle other products with space travel?

Focus on Ethics

Technology products, especially high-speed Internet delivery services, differ in their prices throughout the world. Such geographical price adjustments are often justified on the basis of increased communication costs in local markets. But in rare instances, prices are lowered in a coun-try based on an initiative by corporate leaders, even if the country's infra-structure would support high prices. For example, in June 2006, Microsoft and South Africa's largest cellular operator, MTM, announced a project to offer cheap Internet connections throughout Africa. According to Microsoft cofounder and CEO Bill Gates, mobile connectivity is a key to growth in this country, and the current structure causes high prices in urban areas and makes connectivity prohibitive in rural areas. The Microsoft-MTM program offers affordable options for consumers who purchase Internet connectivity and a PC running Microsoft's Windows starter edition software.

1. What are the benefits of this program to Microsoft?

2. What do you think of this program? Does it present any ethical issues?

3. What pricing strategies from the chapter are involved in this initiative?

Video Case

GE

When you think of GE, you might think first of products such as appliances and light bulbs. But GE is much, much more. The giant $150 billion company also owns NBC, provides commercial and consumer financial services, develops and markets medical imaging equipment, and provides fundamental technology to build infrastructure in developing countries—all under its tagline "imagination at work."

Despite all of its growth and success, however, several years ago GE found its appliances business in decline. Prices were dropping and GE's brands stood largely undifferentiated from others on the market. In response, GE applied its considerable marketing muscle to revamp, rebrand, and reprice its entire appliances line. Rather than accepting lower prices, GE invested heavily in new-product innovation to add more customer value that would support higher prices and margins. In addition to its core mass-market GE appliance brand, the company added the GE Monogram and GE Profile lines. GE Profile targeted the upper quartile of the market, offering "the marriage of style and innovation" with "the best in contemporary design matched with the latest kitchen technologies."

GE Monogram targeted the ultrahigh end of the market, offering built-in products with "depth and breadth of design choices that allow you to customize your home and make it your own." The result? The average retail price paid for GE appliance products has increased more than 15 percent. At the same time, GE's appliances business has delivered five years of double-digit earnings growth.

After viewing the video featuring GE, answer the following questions about pricing strategies.

1. Which of the product-mix pricing strategies discussed in the book most closely describes GE's approach?

2. How did the new positioning statements for the Monogram and Profile lines affect pricing decisions?

3. Visit the Web site for GE's three appliance brands, GE, GE Profile, and GE Monogram. How do the sites support the positioning and pricing of the three brands?

Company Case

ExxonMobil: Achieving Big Profits During Hard Times

One fine spring day in 2006, Joe Tyler watched the gas pump dials spin as he filled up his 1998 Toyota at the neighborhood Exxon station. What he saw shocked him right down to the core of his wallet. It had just cost him $30.30 to fill up his economy car. How could this be? Sure, the tank was completely empty and took almost 11 gallons. And, yes, gas prices were on the rise. But at $2.77 per gallon, this was the first time that a fill-up had cost him more than $30.

Joe usually didn't even look at his gas receipts. Even though gas prices had risen dramatically over the past few years, it was still relatively cheap by world standards; still cheaper than bottled water. And his Toyota rolled along consistently at 32-34 miles per gallon. Until now, Joe didn't think that his gas expenses were affecting his budget all that much. But crossing the $30 line gave him a wakeup call. Although it was far less than the $100 fill-ups he's heard about for SUV drivers in places like Los Angeles, it didn't seem that long ago that he'd routinely filled his tank for less than $10. In 1998, gas prices were really low. In fact, he remembered once paying only $.88 a gallon to fill this same car. Now, he was starting to feel the frustration expressed by so many other gas buyers. What had happened?

About the same time that Joe was waking up to high gas prices, a man named Lee Raymond probably wasn't too concerned about how much it cost him to fill up his own car—or his jet for that matter. After 13 years, Mr. Raymond had just retired as the chairman and CEO of ExxonMobil. Including all his pension payoffs and stock options, Raymond's retirement package was valued at a mindboggling $400 million. And why not? While at the helm of the giant oil company, Raymond had kept ExxonMobil at or near the top of the Fortune 500 list year after year. Upon his

retirement, ExxonMobil had reclaimed the number-one position from Wal-Mart after four years at number-two with revenue of $340 billion, the most ever posted by any company in the world. The company's 2005 annual profits of $36 billion was also a record and represented a 44 percent increase over the prior year. ExxonMobil's fourth-quarter revenues alone exceeded the annual gross domestic product of some major oil-producing nations, including the United Arab Emirates and Kuwait.

Was it just a coincidence that ExxonMobil and the other major oil companies were posting record numbers at a time when consumers were getting hit so hard? Most consumers didn't think so—and they cried "foul." In an effort to calm irate consumers, politicians and consumer advocates were calling for action. Maria Cantwell (D-WA) was one of four U.S. senators who backed legislation that would give the government more oversight of oil, gas, and electricity markets. "Right now excuses from oil companies on why gas prices are so high are like smoke and mirrors," Senator Cantwell said. "The days of Enron taught us the painful lesson that fierce market manipulation does happen, and I don't want American consumers to have to experience that again."

Several state attorneys general also launched investigations. Even the Bush administration demanded a federal investigation into gasoline pricing. In a speech to the country, President Bush said, "Americans understand by and large that the price of crude oil is going up and that [gas] prices are going up, but what they don't want and will not accept is manipulation of the market, and neither will I."

(case continues)

(case continued)

Just as many of these investigations were beginning, and as the market heated up for the summer of 2006, the FTC reported on its investigation of fuel markets in the wake of the 2005 hurricanes, Katrina and Rita. Although it had found various examples of price gouging, most were explainable, and it found no evidence of widespread market manipulation.

DEMAND AND SUPPLY: IS IT REALLY THAT SIMPLE?

Although many parties disagree on where to place the blame for skyrocketing gas prices, there is a high level of consistency among economists and industry observers. They agree that crude oil and even gasoline are commodities. Like corn and pork bellies, there is little if any differentiation in the products producers are turning out. And even though ExxonMobil has tried hard to convince customers that its gasoline differs from other brands based on a proprietary cocktail of detergents and additives, consumers do not generally perceive a difference. Thus, the market treats all offerings as the same.

Walter Lukken, a member of the U.S. Commodity Futures Trading Commission, has stated publicly what many know to be true about the pricing of commodities. In a testimony before Congress on the nature of gasoline prices, Mr. Lukken said, "the commission thinks the markets accurately reflect tight world energy supplies and a pickup in growth and demand this year." But is it really as simple as demand and supply?

Let's look at demand. In 1995, when oil was cheap, global demand was around 70 million barrels a day (mbd). Ten years later, world consumption had risen to 84 mbd and was expected to rise another 2 mbd in 2006. Many environmentalists point the finger at the driving habits of North Americans and their gas-swilling SUVs—with good reason. The United States continues to be one of the world's leading petroleum consumers, with an appetite that grows every year. And as much as U.S. consumers cry about high gas prices, they've done little to change how much gas they consume.

However, although the United States consumes more gas than any other country, this consumption has grown only moderately. Over the past decade, the rise in global demand for oil has been much more the result of the exploding needs of emerging economies. The biggest contributors are China and India, which together account for 37 percent of the world's population. Both countries have a growing appetite for oil that reflects their rapid economic growth. With manufacturing and production increasing and with more individuals trading in bicycles for cars, China and India have the fastest-growing economies in the world, with annual growth rates of 10 percent and 8 percent, respectively.

Now, let's look at supply. Recent spikes in the global price of crude are occurring at a time when rising demand coincides with constrained supply. Supply constraints exist at various levels of production, including drilling, refining, and distributing. In the past decade, oil companies have had little incentive to invest in exploration and to expand capacity. Oil has been cheap, and environmental regula-

tions created more constraints. Oil-producing countries claim that they are producing at or near capacity. Many analysts support this, noting that global consumption of oil is pressing up against the limits of what the world can produce.

Similar constraints place limits on other stages of the supply chain. For example, U.S. refineries no longer have the capacity to meet the country's demand for petroleum-based fuels. And as regulations dictate more gasoline blends for different regions, refineries feel an even greater pinch and distribution lines experience bottlenecks.

But as much as supply and demand account for fluctuations in gas prices, there is a third factor. At a time when supply is stretched so tightly across a growing level of demand, price volatility may result more from the global petroleum futures trading than from anything else. Modern futures markets function on speculation. When factors point to a rise in prices, traders buy futures contracts in hopes of profiting. When oil seems overvalued, they sell. The net effect of all the buying and selling is a constant tweaking of oil prices, which reflects both the fundamental supply-demand situation as well as the constantly changing risk of a major political crisis or natural disaster.

Some policymakers and consumer advocates have pointed to speculative futures trading as a cause of high gas prices. But according to Walter Lukken, "Blaming the futures markets for high commodity prices is like blaming a thermometer for it being hot outside." Although it is true that the oil futures trading can artificially inflate prices in the short term, economists have found that such activities have more of a stabilizing effect in the long run. Speculators absorb risk, often stepping in when nobody else wants to buy or sell. In fact, as with other commodities, the more traders in a given commodity market, the smaller the gap between the buying and selling price for petroleum. This reduces costs for companies at all stages of the value chain, which should ultimately lower prices for customers. Accordingly, if not for the global oil futures market, price spikes and crashes would probably be even bigger and occur more frequently.

THE ANATOMY OF THE PRICE OF A GALLON OF GAS

Consumers like Joe Tyler wonder not only what makes the price of gas go up, but just how much of the price of each gallon they buy goes into big oil's pockets. They might be surprised to learn the breakdown on the price of a gallon of gas. Roughly 75 percent of the retail price of gas covers sales taxes and the cost of crude. In the United States, the excise tax on gasoline varies from state to state, averaging about 40 cents a gallon in 2005. Between 2004 and 2006, the price of crude more than doubled to more than $70 a barrel. Thus, it should come as no surprise that gasoline prices have risen in tandem.

Refining, distribution, and marketing costs account for most of the rest of the price. This leaves less for oil companies than most consumers might imagine. In 2005, the oil industry as a whole made a net profit of 8.5 percent. Although this was higher than the average for all industries, it was less than half the profit margins for health care, financial services, and pharmaceuticals. Still, the absolute profits for big oil companies are among the highest of all industries. ExxonMobil representatives are quick to point out a simple reason: scale. ExxonMobil had the highest profits in 2005 because it had the highest revenues. And when a company like General Motors (number three on the Fortune 500) actually loses more than $10 billion, ExxonMobil's $36 billion net profit really stands out.

Given the nature of commodity pricing, it should be clear that the cost of producing crude has nothing to do with the price. ExxonMobil can't just add 10 percent onto the price of producing oil. Neither can OPEC. Thus, as market forces drive up the price of crude, ExxonMobil's cost remains relatively stable. Thus, good times for oil companies and good times for consumers occur at opposite ends of the price spectrum.

WHAT TO DO?

If gas prices are determined in the way that so many experts say, it seems odd that so many people point the finger of scandal. Yet, given the impact of gas prices on personal budgets and national economies, it is understandable that people want answers. But even if the investigations were to actually produce evidence of wrongdoing, many experts believe that this would only distract from examining the real factors that govern the price of oil.

Proposed solutions for gas price woes span a very broad spectrum. At one end, some call for extreme government intervention and regulation. On the other end are those who suggest that no action be taken. "I don't think the government should be involved, trying to change the supply-and-demand equation here," said Evan Smith, a fund manager with U.S. Global Investors in San Antonio. "I really don't think anything they might do will [make] much of a difference anyway." In a time of such turmoil, ExxonMobil must consider not only how it might help alleviate the problem, but how actions by others might impact its operations.

Questions for Discussion

1. Which, if any, of the pricing strategies discussed in the chapter are being applied by ExxonMobil and other oil companies? Could they adopt any other strategies?
2. Discuss buyer reactions to changes in the gas prices. How can you explain these reactions?
3. How should ExxonMobil react to gasoline price changes by other large and small oil companies? Can ExxonMobil keep its prices stable (or even lower them) when the market price is increasing? Should it?
4. Consider the public policy issues within and across channel levels of the oil industry. Is ExxonMobil acting illegally or irresponsibly by reaping record profits while consumers are hurting at the pumps?
5. How would you "fix" the problem of rising gas prices? Consider solutions for different groups, including governments, corporations, nonprofit groups, and consumers. What are the advantages and disadvantages of your proposed solutions?

Sources: Harold Brubaker, "Why Prices Are Sky High," *Philadelphia Enquirer*, April 26, 2006; Patricia Hill, "Market Fuel Prices Drop, Relief Ahead as Demand Slows and Supplies Rise," *Washington Times*, April 28, 2006, p. A01; Katherine Reynolds Lewis, "Oil Market Is Running on Fear," *New Orleans Times-Picayune*, May 6, 2006, p. M1; "High Gasoline Prices Not Due to Manipulation, Regulators Say," *Calgary Herald*, April 28, 2006, p. E5; Robert J. Samuelson, "The Oil Factor," *Newsweek*, May 8, 2006, p. 37; John W. Schoen, "OPEC Says It Has Lost Control of Oil Prices," accessed online at www.msnbc.com; May 16, 2006; John W. Schoen, "Why Do Gas Pump Prices Rise Faster than Costs?" accessed online at www.msnbc.com, April 28, 2006; "Exxon Dethrones Wal-Mart atop Fortune 500," *Associated Press*, April 3, 2006, accessed online at www.msnbc.com; and "High Oil Prices Drive Up Exxon Mobil's Profit," *Associated Press*, May 3, 2006, accessed online at www.msnbc.com.

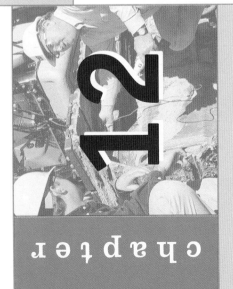

12

Marketing Channels and Supply Chain Management

Previewing the Concepts

We now arrive at the third marketing mix tool—distribution. Firms rarely work alone in creating value for customers and building profitable customer relationships. Instead, most are only a single link in a larger supply chain and marketing channel. As such, an individual firm's success depends not only on how well *it* performs but also on how well its *entire marketing channel* competes with competitors' channels. To be good at customer relationship management, a company must also be good at partner relationship management. The first part of this chapter explores the nature of marketing channels and the marketer's channel design and management decisions. We then examine physical distribution—or logistics—an area that is growing dramatically in importance and sophistication. In the next chapter, we'll look more closely at two major channel intermediaries—retailers and wholesalers.

We'll start with a look at Caterpillar. You might think that Caterpillar's success, and its ability to charge premium prices, rests on the quality of the heavy construction and mining equipment that it produces. But Caterpillar sees things differently. The company's dominance, it claims, results from its unparalleled distribution and customer support system—from the strong and caring partnerships that it has built with independent Caterpillar dealers. Read on and see why.

For more than seven decades, Caterpillar has dominated the world's markets for heavy construction, mining, and logging equipment. Its familiar yellow tractors, crawlers, loaders, bulldozers, and trucks are a common sight at any construction area. Caterpillar sells more than 300 products in nearly 200 countries, with sales approaching $40 billion annually. Over the past two years, sales have grown 60 percent; profits have shot up 250 percent. The big Cat captures some 37 percent of the worldwide construction and farm equipment business, more than double that of number-two Komatsu. The waiting line for some of Caterpillar's biggest equipment is years long.

Many factors contribute to Caterpillar's enduring success—high-quality products, flexible and efficient manufacturing, and a steady stream of innovative new products. Yet these are not the most important reasons for Caterpillar's dominance. Instead, Caterpillar credits its focus on customers and its corps of 200 outstanding independent dealers worldwide, who do a superb job of taking care of every customer need. According to former Caterpillar CEO Donald Fites:

After the product leaves our door, the dealers take over. They are the ones on the front line. They're the ones who live with the product for its lifetime. They're the ones customers see. . . . They're out there making sure that when a machine is delivered, it's in the condition it's supposed to be in. They're out there training a customer's operators. They service a product frequently throughout its life, carefully monitoring a machine's health and scheduling repairs to prevent costly downtime. The customer . . . knows that there is a [$40-billion-plus] company called Caterpillar. But the dealers create the image of a company that doesn't just stand *behind* its products but *with* its products, anywhere in the world. Our dealers are the reason that our motto—Buy the Iron, Get the Company—is not an empty slogan.

"Buy the Iron, Get the Company"—that's a powerful value proposition. It means that when you buy Cat equipment, you become a member of the Caterpillar family. Caterpillar and its dealers work in close harmony to find better ways to bring value to customers. Dealers play a vital role in almost every aspect of Caterpillar's operations, from product design and delivery, to product service and support, to market intelligence and customer feedback.

In the heavy-equipment industry, in which equipment downtime can mean big losses, Caterpillar's exceptional service gives it a huge advantage in winning and keeping customers. Consider Freeport-McMoRan, a Cat customer that operates one of the world's largest copper and gold mines, 24 hours a day, 365 days a year. High in the mountains of Indonesia, the mine is accessible only by aerial cableway or helicopter. Freeport-McMoRan relies on more than 500 pieces of Caterpillar mining and construction equipment—worth several hundred million dollars—including loaders, tractors, and mammoth 240-ton, 2,000-plus-horsepower trucks. Many of these machines cost well over $1 million apiece. When equipment breaks down, Freeport-McMoRan loses money fast. Freeport-McMoRan gladly pays a premium price for machines and service it can count on. It knows that it can count on Caterpillar and its outstanding distribution network for superb support.

The close working relationship between Caterpillar and its dealers comes down to more than just formal contracts and business agreements. The powerful partnership rests on a handful of basic principles and practices:

■ *Dealer profitability:* Caterpillar's rule: "Share the gain as well as the pain." When times are good, Caterpillar shares the bounty with its dealers rather than trying to grab all the riches for itself. When times are bad, Caterpillar protects its dealers. In the mid-1980s, facing a depressed global construction-equipment market and cutthroat competition, Caterpillar sheltered its dealers by absorbing much of the economic damage. It lost almost $1 billion dollars in just three years but didn't

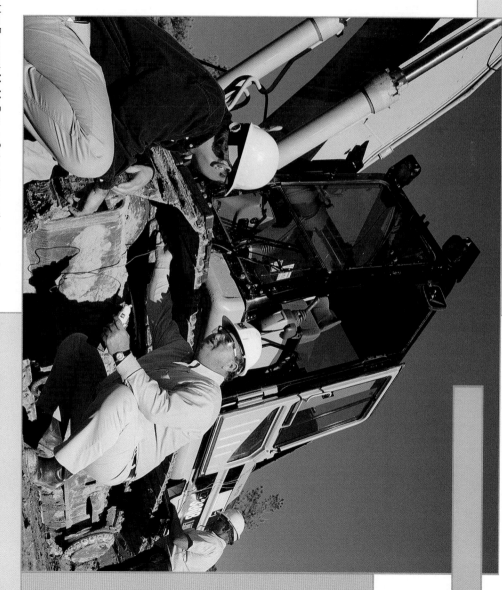

After studying this chapter, you should be able to

1. explain why companies use marketing channels and discuss the functions these channels perform

2. discuss how channel members interact and how they organize to perform the work of the channel

3. identify the major channel alternatives open to a company

4. explain how companies select, motivate, and evaluate channel members

5. discuss the nature and importance of marketing logistics and integrated supply chain management

lose a single dealer. In contrast, competitors' dealers struggled and many failed. As a result, Caterpillar emerged with its distribution system intact and its competitive position stronger than ever.

■ *Extraordinary dealer support:* Nowhere is this support more apparent than in the company's parts delivery system, the fastest and most reliable in the industry. Caterpillar maintains 36 distribution centers and 1,500 service facilities around the world, which stock 320,000 different parts and ship 84,000 items per day, every day of the year. In turn, dealers have made huge investments in inventory, warehouses, fleets of trucks, service bays, diagnostic and service equipment, and information technology. Together, Caterpillar and its dealers guarantee parts delivery within 48 hours anywhere in the world. The company ships 80 percent of parts orders immediately and 99 percent on the same day the order is received. In contrast, it's not unusual for competitors' customers to wait four or five days for a part.

■ *Communications:* Caterpillar communicates with its dealers—fully, frequently, and honestly. According to Fites, "There are no secrets between us and our dealers. We have the financial statements and key operating data of every dealer in the world. . . . In addition, virtually all Caterpillar and dealer employees have real-time access to continually updated databases of service information, sales trends and forecasts, customer satisfaction surveys, and other critical data."

■ *Dealer performance:* Caterpillar does all it can to ensure that its dealerships are run well. It closely monitors each dealership's sales, market position, service capability, financial situation, and other performance measures. It genuinely wants each dealer to succeed, and when it sees a problem, it jumps in to help. As a result, Caterpillar dealerships, many of which are family businesses, tend to be stable and profitable.

■ *Personal relationships:* In addition to more formal business ties, Cat forms close personal ties with its dealers in a kind of family relationship. One Caterpillar executive relates the following example: "When I see Chappy Chapman, a retired executive vice-president . . . , out on the golf course, he always asks about particular dealers or about their children, who may be running the business now. And every time I see those dealers, they inquire, 'How's Chappy?' That's the sort of relationship we have. . . . I consider the majority of dealers personal friends."

Thus, Caterpillar's superb distribution system serves as a major source of competitive advantage. The system is built on a firm base of mutual trust and shared dreams. Caterpillar and its dealers feel a deep pride in what they are accomplishing together. As Fites puts it, "There's a camaraderie among our dealers around the world that really makes it more than just a financial arrangement. They feel that what they're doing is good for the world because they are part of an organization that makes, sells, and tends to the machines that make the world work."[1]

Most firms cannot bring value to customers by themselves. Instead, they must work closely with other firms in a larger value delivery network.

Supply Chains and the Value Delivery Network

Producing a product or service and making it available to buyers requires building relationships not just with customers, but also with key suppliers and resellers in the company's *supply chain*. This supply chain consists of "upstream" and "downstream" partners. Upstream from the company is the set of firms that supply the raw materials, components, parts, information, finances, and expertise needed to create a product or service. Marketers, however, have traditionally focused on the "downstream" side of the supply chain—on the *marketing channels* or *distribution channels* that look forward toward the customer. Downstream marketing channel partners, such as wholesalers and retailers, form a vital connection between the firm and its customers.

Both upstream and downstream partners may also be part of other firms' supply chains. But it is the unique design of each company's supply chain that enables it to deliver superior value to customers. An individual firm's success depends not only on how well *it* performs, but also on how well its entire supply chain and marketing channel competes with competitors' channels.

The term *supply chain* may be too limited—it takes a *make-and-sell* view of the business. It suggests that raw materials, productive inputs, and factory capacity should serve as the starting point for market planning. A better term would be *demand chain* because it suggests a *sense-and-respond* view of the market. Under this view, planning starts with the needs of target customers, to which the company responds by organizing a chain of resources and activities with the goal of creating customer value.

Even a demand chain view of a business may be too limited, because it takes a step-by-step, linear view of purchase-production-consumption activities. With the advent of the Internet and other technologies, however, companies are forming more numerous and complex relationships with other firms. For example, Ford manages numerous supply chains. It also sponsors or transacts on many B2B Web sites and online purchasing exchanges as needs arise. Like Ford, most large companies today are engaged in building and managing a continuously evolving *value delivery network*.

As defined in Chapter 2, a **value delivery network** is made up of the company, suppliers, distributors, and ultimately customers who "partner" with each other to improve the performance of the entire system. For example, Palm, the leading manufacturer of handheld devices, manages a whole community of suppliers and assemblers of semiconductor components, plastic cases, LCD displays, and accessories. Its network also includes offline and online resellers, and 45,000 complementors who have created more than 5,000 applications for the Palm operating systems. All of these diverse partners must work effectively together to bring superior value to Palm's customers.

This chapter focuses on marketing channels—on the downstream side of the value delivery network. However, it is important to remember that this is only part of the full value network. To bring value to customers, companies need upstream supplier partners just as they need downstream channel partners. Increasingly, marketers are participating in and influencing their company's upstream activities as well as its downstream activities. More than marketing channel managers, they are becoming full value-network managers.

The chapter examines four major questions concerning marketing channels: What is the nature of marketing channels and why are they important? What problems do companies face in designing and managing their channels? What role do physical distribution and supply chain management play in attracting and satisfying customers? In Chapter 13, we will look at marketing channel issues from the viewpoint of retailers and wholesalers.

The Nature and Importance of Marketing Channels

Few producers sell their goods directly to the final users. Instead, most use intermediaries to bring their products to market. They try to forge a **marketing channel** (or **distribution channel**)—a set of interdependent organizations that help make a product or service available for use or consumption by the consumer or business user.

Value delivery network
The network made up of the company, suppliers, distributors, and ultimately customers who "partner" with each other to improve the performance of the entire system.

Marketing channel (distribution channel)
A set of interdependent organizations that help make a product or service available for use or consumption by the consumer or business user.

■ Value delivery network: Palm, Inc., manages a whole community of suppliers, assemblers, resellers, and complementors who must work effectively together to make life easier for Palm's customers.

How do channel firms interact and organize to do the work of the channel? They try to forge a marketing channel.

A company's channel decisions directly affect every other marketing decision. Pricing depends on whether the company works with national discount chains, uses high-quality specialty stores, or sells directly to consumers via the Web. The firm's sales force and communications decisions depend on how much persuasion, training, motivation, and support its channel partners need. Whether a company develops or acquires certain new products may depend on how well those products fit the capabilities of its channel members.

Companies often pay too little attention to their distribution channels, sometimes with damaging results. In contrast, many companies have used imaginative distribution systems to *gain* a competitive advantage. FedEx's creative and imposing distribution system made it a leader in express delivery. Dell revolutionized its industry by selling personal computers directly to consumers rather than through retail stores. Amazon.com pioneered the sales of books and a wide range of other goods via the Internet. And Calyx & Corolla led the way in selling fresh flowers and plants direct to consumers by phone and from its Web site, cutting a week or more off the time it takes flowers to reach consumers through conventional retail channels.

Distribution channel decisions often involve long-term commitments to other firms. For example, companies such as Ford, Hewlett-Packard, or McDonald's can easily change their advertising, pricing, or promotion programs. They can scrap old products and introduce new ones as market tastes demand. But when they set up distribution channels through contracts with franchisees, independent dealers, or large retailers, they cannot readily replace these channels with company-owned stores or Web sites if conditions change. Therefore, management must design its channels carefully, with an eye on tomorrow's likely selling environment as well as today's.

How Channel Members Add Value

Why do producers give some of the selling job to channel partners? After all, doing so means giving up some control over how and to whom they sell their products. Producers use intermediaries because they create greater efficiency in making goods available to target markets. Through their contacts, experience, specialization, and scale of operation, intermediaries usually offer the firm more than it can achieve on its own.

■ Innovative marketing channels: Calyx & Corolla sells fresh flowers and plants directly to consumers by phone and from its Web site, cutting a week or more off the time it takes flowers to reach consumers through conventional retail channels.

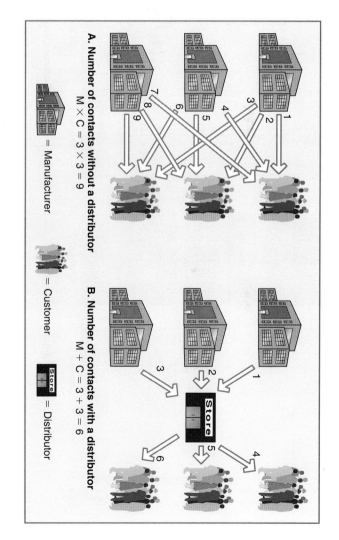

A. Number of contacts without a distributor
M × C = 3 × 3 = 9

B. Number of contacts with a distributor
M + C = 3 + 3 = 6

= Manufacturer   = Customer   = Distributor

Figure 12.1 shows how using intermediaries can provide economies. Figure 12.1A shows three manufacturers, each using direct marketing to reach three customers. This system requires nine different contacts. Figure 12.1B shows the three manufacturers working through one distributor, which contacts the three customers. This system requires only six contacts. In this way, intermediaries reduce the amount of work that must be done by both producers and consumers.

From the economic system's point of view, the role of marketing intermediaries is to transform the assortments of products made by producers into the assortments wanted by consumers. Producers make narrow assortments of products in large quantities, but consumers want broad assortments of products in small quantities. Marketing channel members buy large quantities from many producers and break them down into the smaller quantities and broader assortments wanted by consumers.

For example, Unilever makes millions of bars Lever 2000 hand soap each day, but you want to buy only a few bars at a time. So big food, drug, and discount retailers, such as Kroger, Walgreens, and Wal-Mart, buy Lever 2000 by the truckload and stock it on their store's shelves. In turn, you can buy a single bar of Lever 2000, along with a shopping cart full of small quantities of toothpaste, shampoo, and other related products as you need them. Thus, intermediaries play an important role in matching supply and demand.

In making products and services available to consumers, channel members add value by bridging the major time, place, and possession gaps that separate goods and services from those who would use them. Members of the marketing channel perform many key functions. Some help to complete transactions:

- *Information:* Gathering and distributing marketing research and intelligence information about actors and forces in the marketing environment needed for planning and aiding exchange.
- *Promotion:* Developing and spreading persuasive communications about an offer.
- *Contact:* Finding and communicating with prospective buyers.
- *Matching:* Shaping and fitting the offer to the buyer's needs, including activities such as manufacturing, grading, assembling, and packaging.
- *Negotiation:* Reaching an agreement on price and other terms of the offer so that ownership or possession can be transferred.

Others help to fulfill the completed transactions:

- *Physical distribution:* Transporting and storing goods.
- *Financing:* Acquiring and using funds to cover the costs of the channel work.
- *Risk taking:* Assuming the risks of carrying out the channel work.

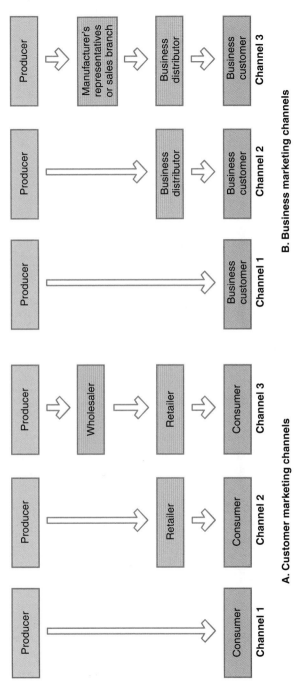

A. Customer marketing channels

B. Business marketing channels

FIGURE 12.2 **Consumer and business marketing channels**

Channel level
A layer of intermediaries that performs some work in bringing the product and its ownership closer to the final buyer.

Direct marketing channel
A marketing channel that has no intermediary levels.

Indirect marketing channel
Channel containing one or more intermediary levels.

The question is not *whether* these functions need to be performed—they must be—but rather *who* will perform them. To the extent that the manufacturer performs these functions, its costs go up and its prices become higher. When some of these functions are shifted to intermediaries, the producer's costs and prices may be lower, but the intermediaries must charge more to cover the costs of their work. In dividing the work of the channel, the various functions should be assigned to the channel members who can add the most value for the cost.

Number of Channel Levels

Companies can design their distribution channels to make products and services available to customers in different ways. Each layer of marketing intermediaries that performs some work in bringing the product and its ownership closer to the final buyer is a **channel level**. Because the producer and the final consumer both perform some work, they are part of every channel.

The *number of intermediary levels* indicates the *length* of a channel. Figure 12.2A shows several consumer distribution channels of different lengths. Channel 1, called a **direct marketing channel**, has no intermediary levels; the company sells directly to consumers. For example, Mary Kay and Amway sell their products door-to-door, through home and office sales parties, and on the Web; GEICO sells direct via the telephone and the Internet. The remaining channels in Figure 12.2A are **indirect marketing channels**, containing one or more intermediaries.

Figure 12.2B shows some common business distribution channels. The business marketer can use its own sales force to sell directly to business customers. Or it can sell to various types of intermediaries, who in turn sell to these customers. Consumer and business marketing channels with even more levels can sometimes be found, but less often. From the producer's point of view, a greater number of levels means less control and greater channel complexity. Moreover, all of the institutions in the channel are connected by several types of *flows*. These include the *physical flow* of products, the *flow of ownership*, the *payment flow*, the *information flow*, and the *promotion flow*. These flows can make even channels with only one or a few levels very complex.

▌ Channel Behavior and Organization

Distribution channels are more than simple collections of firms tied together by various flows. They are complex behavioral systems in which people and companies interact to accomplish individual, company, and channel goals. Some channel systems consist only of informal interactions among loosely organized firms. Others consist of formal interactions guided by strong organizational structures. Moreover, channel systems do not stand still—new types of intermediaries emerge and whole new channel systems evolve. Here we look at channel behavior and at how members organize to do the work of the channel.

Channel Behavior

A marketing channel consists of firms that have partnered for their common good. Each channel member depends on the others. For example, a Ford dealer depends on Ford to design cars that meet consumer needs. In turn, Ford depends on the dealer to attract consumers, persuade them to buy Ford cars, and service cars after the sale. Each Ford dealer also depends on other dealers to provide good sales and service that will uphold the brand's reputation. In fact, the success of individual Ford dealers depends on how well the entire Ford marketing channel competes with the channels of other auto manufacturers.

Each channel member plays a specialized role in the channel. For example, Samsung's role is to produce consumer electronics products that consumers will like and to create demand through national advertising. Best Buy's role is to display these Samsung products in convenient locations, to answer buyers' questions, and to complete sales. The channel will be most effective when each member assumes the tasks it can do best.

Ideally, because the success of individual channel members depends on overall channel success, all channel firms should work together smoothly. They should understand and accept their roles, coordinate their activities, and cooperate to attain overall channel goals. However, individual channel members rarely take such a broad view. Cooperating to achieve overall channel goals sometimes means giving up individual company goals. Although channel members depend on one another, they often act alone in their own short-run best interests. They often disagree on who should do what and for what rewards. Such disagreements over goals, roles, and rewards generate **channel conflict.**

Horizontal conflict occurs among firms at the same level of the channel. For instance, some Ford dealers in Chicago might complain the other dealers in the city steal sales from them by pricing too low or by advertising outside their assigned territories. Or Holiday Inn franchisees might complain about other Holiday Inn operators overcharging guests or giving poor service, hurting the overall Holiday Inn image.

Vertical conflict, conflicts between different levels of the same channel, is even more common. For example, Goodyear created hard feelings and conflict with its premier independent-dealer channel when it began selling through mass-merchant retailers (see Real Marketing 12.1). Similarly, Revlon came into serious conflict with its department store channels when it cozied up to mass merchants:[2]

A few years back, Revlon made a big commitment to mass-market retailers such as Wal-Mart, Target, and CVS, all but snubbing better department stores. That strategy worked well initially. However, the mass merchants are sophisticated and demanding, and they quickly abandon brands that aren't working. That happened recently with Revlon's important new Vital Radiance line of cosmetics targeted toward aging boomers. When Revlon failed to deliver on the promised marketing support for Vital Radiance—it spent only $700,000 during the three-month launch versus P&G's $9 million during the same period for its own CoverGirl Advanced Radiance cosmetics—the mass-merchant channels backed away from the brand. For example, only 647 of CVS's 5,300 stores carried the new line. Meanwhile, the snubbed department stores are now lukewarm toward Revlon's prestige lines. An alienated Federated Department Stores, which operates Macy's and Bloomingdale's, refused to carry Revlon's new Flair prestige fragrance altogether. Says one retailing expert, "The prestige channel doesn't trust Revlon not to run back to the discount channel if sales for Flair don't fly."

Some conflict in the channel takes the form of healthy competition. Such competition can be good for the channel—without it, the channel could become passive and noninnovative. But severe or prolonged conflict, as in the case of Goodyear and Revlon, can disrupt channel effectiveness and cause lasting harm to channel relationships. Companies should manage channel conflict to keep it from getting out of hand.

Channel conflict

Disagreement among marketing channel members on goals and roles—who should do what and for what rewards.

Real Marketing   Goodyear Rolls, but No Longer over Its Dealers

12.1 For more than 60 years, Goodyear sold replacement tires exclusively through its premier network of 5,300 independent Goodyear dealers. Both Goodyear and its dealers profited from this partnership. Goodyear received the undivided attention and loyalty of its single-brand dealers, and the dealers gained the exclusive right to sell the highly respected Goodyear tire line. In mid-1992, however, Goodyear shattered tradition and jolted its dealers by agreeing to sell its tires through Sears auto centers. Similar pacts soon followed with Wal-Mart and Sam's Club, placing dealers in direct competition with the nation's most potent retailers.

To add insult to injury, beyond selling its branded tires through large retailers, Goodyear began selling private-branded tires though Wal-Mart and other discounters. It even opened its own no-frills, quick-serve Just Tires discount stores designed to fend off low-priced competitors. All of these moves created fierce new competition for Goodyear's independent dealers.

Goodyear claimed that the channel changes were essential. Tires had become more of an impulse item, and value-minded tire buyers were increasingly buying from cheaper, multibrand discount outlets and department stores. The market share of these outlets had grown 30 percent in the previous

Channel conflict: Following more than a decade of damaging conflict with its prized independent dealer network, Goodyear has actively set about repairing fractured dealer relations. The result: a remarkable turnaround that has Goodyear now rolling, rolling, rolling.

Vertical Marketing Systems

For the channel as a whole to perform well, each channel member's role must be specified and channel conflict must be managed. The channel will perform better if it includes a firm, agency, or mechanism that provides leadership and has the power to assign roles and manage conflict.

Historically, *conventional distribution channels* have lacked such leadership and power, often resulting in damaging conflict and poor performance. One of the biggest channel developments over the years has been the emergence of *vertical marketing systems* that provide channel leadership. Figure 12.3 contrasts the two types of channel arrangements.

A **conventional distribution channel** consists of one or more independent producers, wholesalers, and retailers. Each is a separate business seeking to maximize its own profits, perhaps even at the expense of the system as a whole. No channel member has much control over the other members, and no formal means exists for assigning roles and resolving channel conflict.

In contrast, a **vertical marketing system (VMS)** consists of producers, wholesalers, and retailers acting as a unified system. One channel member owns the others, has contracts with them, or wields so much power that they must all cooperate. The VMS can be dominated by the producer, wholesaler, or retailer.

We look now at three major types of VMSs: *corporate, contractual,* and *administered.* Each uses a different means for setting up leadership and power in the channel.

Conventional distribution channel
A channel consisting of one or more independent producers, wholesalers, and retailers, each a separate business seeking to maximize its own profits even at the expense of profits for the system as a whole.

Vertical marketing system (VMS)
A distribution channel structure in which producers, wholesalers, and retailers act as a unified system. One channel member owns the others, has contracts with them, or has so much power that they all cooperate.

five years, while that of tire dealers had fallen 4 percent. Marketing research showed that one out of four Wal-Mart customers was a potential Goodyear buyer and that these buyers came from a segment unlikely to be reached by independent Goodyear dealers. By selling exclusively through its dealer network, Goodyear claimed, it simply wasn't putting its tires where many consumers were going to buy them.

The shifts in consumer buying were also causing problems for dealers. Unfortunately, however, as Goodyear expanded into the needed new channels, it took few steps to protect its prized dealer network. Although it offered an ample variety of premium lines, Goodyear provided its dealers with none of the lower-priced lines that many consumers were demanding. Dealers complained not just about competition from megaretailers but also about shoddy treatment and unfair pricing from Goodyear. For example, to sell more tires, Goodyear offered volume discounts to its biggest retailers and wholesalers. "The result was pricing insanity," notes one observer. "Some smaller dealers were paying more for tires than what Sears charged at retail!"

Not surprisingly, Goodyear's aggressive moves into new channels set off a surge of dysfunctional channel conflict, and dealer relations deteriorated rapidly. Some of Goodyear's best dealers defected to competitors. Other angry dealers struck back by taking on competing brands and by aggressively promoting cheaper, private-label tires that offered higher margins to dealers and more appeal to value-conscious consumers. U.S. dealers in California even took Goodyear to court in a class action suit, causing Goodyear to somewhat restrict the tire lines sold through its new channels there. Says one former dealer, "After someone punches you in the face a few times, you say, 'Enough is enough.'"

Such dealer actions weakened the Goodyear name and the premium price that it could command. Goodyear's replacement tire sales—which make up 72 percent of the company's revenues—went

flat, dropping the company into a decade-long profit funk. By 2002, Goodyear was fighting off rumors of bankruptcy.

In 2003, however, Goodyear regained its senses and refocused its strategy. After years of chasing volume by selling low-margin tires to mid-market buyers, the company began focusing on higher-performance, higher-margin tire lines. More importantly, Goodyear actively set about repairing fractured dealer relations. It began supporting dealers with more fair and consistent pricing, on-time order fulfillment, strong marketing support, and hot new products sold exclusively through the dealer network.

The new strategic direction had an immediate and impressive impact. In the two years following the redirection, Goodyear's sales exploded 30 percent, profits went from searing red to healthy black, and the company's stock price quadrupled. Goodyear is now rolling, rolling, rolling. And dealer relations have turned around dramatically. At a recent meeting with dealers in Nashville, Tennessee, Goodyear chief executive Robert Keegan received a "roaring standing ovation" from dealers.

Despite its recent successes, however, the company still faces many bumps in the road ahead. Completely patching Goodyear's dealer relations, damaged over many years, will take time. "We still have a long way to go on this," admits Goodyear's VP for replacement tire sales. "We lost sight of the fact that it's in our interest that our dealers succeed." An industry analyst agrees: "Goodyear...must stay proactive about keeping dealers satisfied. It's an everyday effort involving all of the company's interactions with dealers."

Sources: Quotes and other information from "No Time to Rest for Goodyear," *Tire Business,* February 13, 2006, p. 8; Kevin Kelleher, "Giving Dealers a Raw Deal," *Business 2.0,* December 2004, pp. 82-84; Jonathan Fahey, "Rolling, Rolling, Rolling," *Forbes,* November 28, 2005, pp. 54-56; and Goodyear annual reports and other information accessed at www.goodyear.com, September 2006.

FIGURE 12.3
Comparison of conventional distribution channel with vertical marketing system

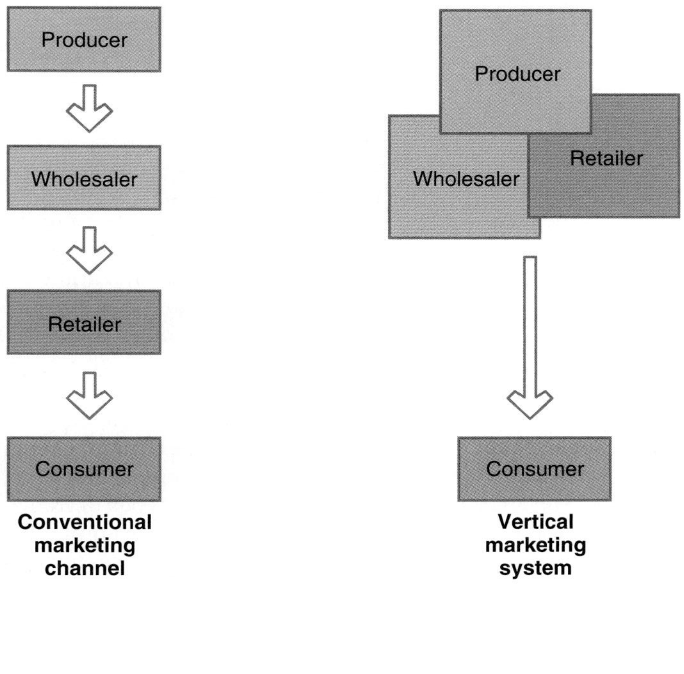

Corporate VMS

Corporate VMS
A vertical marketing system that combines successive stages of production and distribution under single ownership—channel leadership is established through common ownership.

A **corporate VMS** integrates successive stages of production and distribution under single ownership. Coordination and conflict management are attained through regular organizational channels. For example, grocery giant Kroger owns and operates 42 factories that crank out more than 8,000 private label items found on its store shelves. Giant Food Stores operates an ice-cube processing facility, a soft-drink bottling operation, its own dairy, an ice cream plant, and a bakery that supplies Giant stores with everything from bagels to birthday cakes. And little-known Italian eyewear maker Luxottica produces many famous eyewear brands—including Ray-Ban, Vogue, Anne Klein, Ferragamo, and Bvlgari. It then sells these brands through two of the world's largest optical chains, LensCrafters and Sunglass Hut, which it also owns.³

Controlling the entire distribution chain has turned Spanish clothing chain Zara into the world's fastest-growing fashion retailer.

The secret to Zara's success is its control over almost every aspect of the supply chain, from design and production to its own worldwide distribution network. Zara makes 40 percent of its own fabrics and produces more than half of its own clothes, rather than relying on a hodgepodge of slow-moving suppliers. More than 11,000 new items every season take shape in Zara's own design centers, supported by real-time sales data. New designs feed into Zara manufacturing centers, which ship finished products directly to 918 Zara stores in 64 countries, saving time, eliminating the need for warehouses, and keeping inventories low. Effective vertical integration makes Zara faster, more flexible, and more efficient than international competitors such as Gap, Benetton, and H&M. Its finely tuned distribution systems makes Zara seem more like Dell or Wal-Mart than Gucci or Louis Vuitton. Zara can make a new line from start to finish in less than 15 days, so a look seen on MTV can be in Zara stores within a month, versus an industry average of nine months. And Zara's low costs let it offer midmarket chic at downmarket prices. The company's stylish but affordable offerings have attracted a cult following, and Zara store sales grew more than 18 percent last year to $4.4 billion.⁴

■ Corporate VMS: Zara's success stems from its control over almost every aspect of the supply chain, from design and production to its own worldwide distribution network.

Contractual VMS

Contractual VMS
A vertical marketing system in which independent firms at different levels of production and distribution join together through contracts to obtain more economies or sales impact than they could achieve alone.

Franchise organization
A contractual vertical marketing system in which a channel member, called a franchiser, links several stages in the production-distribution process.

A **contractual VMS** consists of independent firms at different levels of production and distribution who join together through contracts to obtain more economies or sales impact than each could achieve alone. Coordination and conflict management are attained through contractual agreements among channel members.

The **franchise organization** is the most common type of contractual relationship—a channel member called a *franchisor* links several stages in the production-distribution process. In the United States alone, more 760,000 franchise outlets account for more than $1.5 trillion in annual sales. Industry analysts estimate that a new franchise outlet opens somewhere in the United States every eight minutes and that about one out of every 12 retail business outlets is a franchised business.⁵ Almost every kind of business has been franchised—from motels and fast-food restaurants to dental centers and dating services, from wedding consultants and maid services to fitness centers and funeral homes.

There are three types of franchises. The first type is the *manufacturer-sponsored retailer franchise system*—for example, Ford and its network of independent franchised dealers. The second type is the *manufacturer-sponsored wholesaler franchise system*—Coca-Cola licenses bottlers (wholesalers) in various markets who buy Coca-Cola syrup concentrate and then bottle and sell the finished product to retailers in local markets. The third type is the *service-*

firm-sponsored retailer franchise system—examples are found in the auto-rental business (Hertz, Avis), the fast-food service business (McDonald's, Burger King), and the motel business (Holiday Inn, Ramada Inn).

The fact that most consumers cannot tell the difference between contractual and corporate VMSs shows how successfully the contractual organizations compete with corporate chains. Chapter 13 presents a fuller discussion of the various contractual VMSs.

Administered VMS

In an **administered VMS**, leadership is assumed not through common ownership or contractual ties but through the size and power of one or a few dominant channel members. Manufacturers of a top brand can obtain strong trade cooperation and support from resellers. For example, GE, Procter & Gamble, and Kraft can command unusual cooperation from resellers regarding displays, shelf space, promotions, and price policies. Large retailers such as Wal-Mart, Home Depot, and Barnes & Noble can exert strong influence on the manufacturers that supply the products they sell.

Horizontal Marketing Systems

Another channel development is the **horizontal marketing system**, in which two or more companies at one level join together to follow a new marketing opportunity. By working together, companies can combine their financial, production, or marketing resources to accomplish more than any one company could alone.

Companies might join forces with competitors or noncompetitors. They might work with each other on a temporary or permanent basis, or they may create a separate company. For example, McDonald's now places "express" versions of its restaurants in Wal-Mart stores.

McDonald's benefits from Wal-Mart's heavy store traffic, while Wal-Mart keeps hungry shoppers from having to go elsewhere to eat. McDonald's also recently joined forces with Sinopec, China's largest gasoline retailer, to place restaurants at its more than 30,000 gas stations. The move greatly speeds McDonald's expansion into China while at the same time pulling hungry motorists into Sinopec gas stations.[6]

Such channel arrangements also work well globally. For example, because of its excellent coverage of international markets, Nestlé jointly sells General Mills' cereal brands in 80 countries outside North America. Similarly, Coca-Cola and Nestlé formed a joint venture, Beverage Partners Worldwide, to market ready-to-drink coffees, teas, and flavored milks in more than 40 countries worldwide. Coke provides worldwide experience in marketing and distributing beverages, and Nestlé contributes two established brand names—Nescafé and Nestea.[7]

Multichannel Distribution Systems

In the past, many companies used a single channel to sell to a single market or market segment. Today, with the proliferation of customer segments and channel possibilities, more and more companies have adopted **multichannel distribution systems**—often called *hybrid marketing channels*. Such multichannel marketing occurs when a single firm sets up two or more marketing channels to reach one or more customer segments. The use of multichannel systems has increased greatly in recent years.

Figure 12.4 shows a multichannel distribution system. In the figure, the producer sells directly to consumer segment 1 using direct-mail catalogs, telemarketing, and the Internet and reaches consumer segment 2 through retailers. It sells indirectly to business segment 1 through distributors and dealers and to business segment 2 through its own sales force.

Administered VMS
A vertical marketing system that coordinates successive stages of production and distribution, not through common ownership or contractual ties, but through the size and power of one of the parties.

Horizontal marketing system
A channel arrangement in which two or more companies at one level join together to follow a new marketing opportunity.

Multichannel distribution system
A distribution system in which a single firm sets up two or more marketing channels to reach one or more customer segments.

■ Horizontal marketing systems: McDonald's recently joined forces with Sinopec, China's largest gasoline retailer, to place restaurants at its more than 30,000 gas stations. Here, the presidents of the two companies shake hands while announcing the partnership.

FIGURE 12.4
Multichannel distribution system

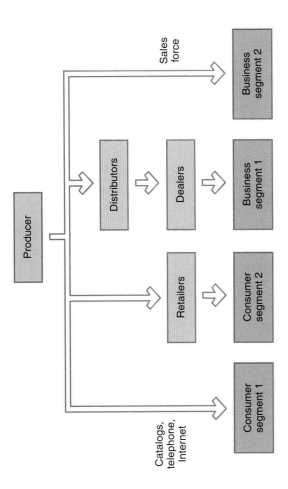

These days, almost every large company and many small ones distribute through multiple channels. Fidelity Investments reaches customers by telephone, over the Internet, and through its branch offices. It invites its customer to "call, click, or visit" Fidelity. Urban Outfitters markets itself through its traditional retail outlets, a direct-response Internet site, its mail-order catalog, and as a retailer on Amazon.com.

Hewlett-Packard uses multiple channels to serve dozens of segments and niches, ranging from large corporate and institutional buyers to small businesses to home office buyers. The HP sales force sells the company's information technology equipment and services to large and mid-size business customers. HP also sells through a network of distributors and value-added resellers, which sell HP computers, systems, and services to a variety of special business segments. Home office buyers can buy HP personal computers and printers from specialty computer stores or any of several large retailers, such as Best Buy or Circuit City. And business, government, and home office buyers can buy directly from HP by phone or online from the company's Web site (www.hp.com).

Multichannel distribution systems offer many advantages to companies facing large and complex markets. With each new channel, the company expands its sales and market coverage and gains opportunities to tailor its products and services to the specific needs of diverse customer segments. But such multichannel systems are harder to control, and they generate conflict as more channels compete for customers and sales. For example, when HP began selling directly to customers through its own Web site, many of its retail dealers cried "unfair competition." Many salespeople felt that they were being undercut by the new "inside channels."

Changing Channel Organization

Changes in technology and the explosive growth of direct and online marketing are having a profound impact on the nature and design of marketing channels. One major trend is toward **disintermediation**—a big term with a clear message and important consequences. Disintermediation occurs when product or service producers cut out intermediaries and go directly to final buyers, or when radically new types of channel intermediaries displace traditional ones.

Thus, in many industries, traditional intermediaries are dropping by the wayside. For example, companies such as Dell and Southwest Airlines sell directly to final buyers, cutting retailers from their marketing channels altogether. In other cases, new forms of resellers are displacing traditional brick-and-mortar retailers. For example, online marketing is growing rapidly, taking business from traditional brick-and-mortar retailers. Consumers can buy electronics from sonystyle.com; clothes and accessories from bluefly.com; and books, videos, toys, jewelry, sports, consumer electronics, home and garden items, and almost anything else from Amazon.com; all without ever stepping into a traditional retail store. And online music download services such as iTunes and Musicmatch are threatening the very existence of traditional music-store retailers (see Real Marketing 12.2).

Disintermediation
The cutting out of marketing channel intermediaries by product or service producers, or the displacement of traditional resellers by radical new types of intermediaries.

12.2 Disintermediation: The Music Industry Dances to a New iTune

Buying music can be a pretty frustrating experience. Perhaps you can identify with the following scenario:

You whistle a happy tune as you stroll into Tower Records to do a little music shopping. But when you pick up *The Essential Bruce Springsteen*, your temperature starts to rise. You should be ecstatic at the discovery of 12 new releases by the Boss, but instead you're furious: You can't buy them unless you shell out $25.99 for the entire three-CD set that includes 30 "career-spanning classics" that you already own from his other hit records. You shove Bruce back into his display case and pick up *The Ragpicker's Dream*, by Mark Knopfler. It has one funny, tender tune that you love, called "Devil Baby"—but what about those other 16 songs? It'll cost you $23.99 to find out. Suddenly, every-thing seems like a crapshoot. Why do they keep insisting that you buy an entire CD when you can just go online and get only the tunes you really want from *iTunes* or *Musicmatch* for 99 cents each? Fed up, you walk away without buying anything.

Experiences like these, coupled with revolutionary changes in the way music is being distributed and purchased, have thrown the music industry into turmoil. Today, online music download services, such as Yahoo's Musicmatch, AOL's MusicNow, Buy.com's BuyMusic, and Apple's iTunes, offer an attractive alternative to buy-ing overpriced standard CDs from the limited assortments of tradi-tional music retailers. Instead, you can go online, choose from hun-dreds of thousands of individual tracks, digitally download one or a dozen in any of several formats, burn them onto a CD or dump them into your iPod, and listen to them wherever and whenever you please.

It seems like everyone is getting into the music download busi-ness these days. Coffee chain Starbucks opened an in-store music service—Hear Music—letting customers burn downloaded tracks onto CDs while sipping their lattes. Mobile phone makers are now unveiling music-purchase service to go with their music-playing phones that can hold thousands of downloaded songs. And fearsome competitors such as Microsoft and Sony have launched their own online music stores.

These new distribution options are great for consumers. But the new channel forms threaten the very existence of traditional music retailers. There's even a fancy word to describe this phenomenon—*disintermediation*. Strictly speaking, disintermediation means the elimination of a layer of intermediaries from a marketing channel—skipping a step between the source of a product or service and its consumers. For example, when Dell began selling personal computers directly to consumers, it eliminated—or disintermediated—retailers from the traditional PC distribution channel.

More broadly, disintermediation includes not only the elimination of channel intermediaries but also the displacement

Disintermediation: Online music download services are threatening to make traditional CD sellers obsolete. For example, once-dominant Tower Records recently closed its doors for good.

of traditional resellers by radically new types of intermediaries. For example, only a few decades ago, most recorded music was sold through independent music retailers or small chains. Many of these smaller retailers were later disintermediated by large specialty music superstores, such as Tower Records, Virgin Records, and Musicland. The superstores, in turn, have faced growing competition from broad-line discount retailers such as Wal-Mart and Best Buy. In fact, Wal-Mart is currently the world's number-one CD seller. Within the past decade, sales of CDs by traditional music retailers has slipped from 50 percent to less than 32 percent, while Wal-Mart and other super-stores have seen their share jump from 28 percent to 54 percent.

Now, the surge of new online music sellers is threatening to make traditional CD sellers obsolete. "Tower Records and the other music-store chains are in a dizzying tailspin," comments one industry expert. Overall retail CD sales have dropped nearly 20 percent since 1999—the year Napster (the original music download site) was launched. Over the past five years, Tower Records has been in and out of bank-ruptcy, closing more than half of its stores to help pay off debts. Number-two Musicland declared bankruptcy, shuttered more than two-thirds of its stores (only 345 remain), and sold out to Trans World Entertainment. Smaller chains such as National Record Mart have disappeared altogether. Things will likely get worse before they get better. One retail consultant predicts that half of today's music stores will be out of business within five years and that, eventually, "CDs, DVDs, and other forms of physical media will become obsolete."

How are the traditional retailers responding to the disintermediation threat? Some are following the "if you can't beat them, join them" prin-ciple by creating their own downloading services. For example, Best Buy partnered with Napster to offer music downloading services, as did Virgin Records. Wal-Mart offers in-store and online downloads at a bargain rate of only 88 cents a song. And Tower Records recently unveiled a down-load service to complement its brick-and-mortar locations.

(continues)

(continued)

Music stores do still have several advantages over their online counterparts. The stores have a larger base of existing customers, and a physical store provides a shopping experience for customers that's difficult to duplicate online. Retailers can morph their stores into comfortable, sociable gathering spots were people hang out, chat with friends, listen to music, go to album signings, and perhaps attend a live performance. Taking advantage of this notion, Musicland recently unveiled a new store-within-a-store concept called Graze, a mesh-enclosed lounge complete with couches, a video wall, a sound system, and pumped-in smells of citrus and chocolate. "Musicland execs are betting that the new ambiance will persuade shoppers to linger, listen—and buy," says an analyst.

But the traditional store retailers also face daunting economics. Store rents are rising while CD prices are falling. And running stores generates considerable inventory and store operating costs. New online entrants face none of those traditional distribution costs. Moreover, whereas store retailers can physically stock only a limited number of in-print titles, the music download sites can provide millions of selections and offer out-of-print songs.

What's more, whereas music stores are stuck selling pre-compiled CDs at high album prices, music download sites let customers buy only the songs they want at low per-song rates. Finally, the old retailing model of selling CDs like they were LP vinyl records doesn't work so well anymore. That was fine in an era when people had one stereo in the living room and maybe one in the kids' room. But now consumers want music in a variety of formats that they can play anywhere, anytime: on boomboxes, car stereos, computers, and digital players such as Apple's iPod, which can store thousands of songs in a nifty credit-card-sized device.

Thus, disintermediation is a big word but the meaning is clear. Disintermediation occurs only when a new channel form succeeds in serving customers better than the old channels. Marketers who continually seek new ways to create value for customers have little to fear. However, those who fall behind in adding value risk being swept aside. Will today's music-store retailers survive? Stay iTuned.

Sources: Opening extract adapted from Paul Keegan, "Is the Music Store Over?" *Business 2.0,* March 2004, pp. 114–118. Other quotes and information from Rob Levine, "Luring MP3ers Back to the Mall," *Business 2.0,* January–February 2006, p. 32; Lorin Cipolla, "Music's on the Menu," *Promo,* May 1, 2004; Mike Hughlett, "More Companies Enter Musical Phone Field," *Knight Ridder Tribune News,* June 16, 2005, p. 1; "How to Get Your Music Mobile," *Music Week,* June 25, 2005, p. S11; Jon Ortiz, "As Big Chains Flail, He's Got the Beat," *Sacramento Bee,* March 9, 2006, p. D1; Dale Kasler, "Tower Gets New Leader," *Sacramento Bee,* July 29, 2006, p. D1; Chris Serres, "Buyer Surfaces for Bankrupt Musicland," *Star Tribune,* February 26, 2006, p. 1D.

Disintermediation presents problems and opportunities for both producers and intermediaries. To avoid being swept aside, traditional intermediaries must find new ways to add value in the supply chain. To remain competitive, product and service producers must develop new channel opportunities, such as Internet and other direct channels. However, developing these new channels often brings them into direct competition with their established channels, resulting in conflict.

To ease this problem, companies often look for ways to make going direct a plus for the entire channel. For example, Black & Decker knows that many customers would prefer to buy its power tools and outdoor power equipment online. But selling directly through its Web site would create conflicts with important and powerful retail partners, such as Home Depot, Lowe's, Target, Wal-Mart, and Amazon.com. So, although Black & Decker's Web site provides detailed information about the company's products, you can't buy a Black & Decker cordless drill, laser level, leaf blower, or anything else there. Instead, the Black & Decker site refers you to resellers' Web sites and stores. Thus, Black & Decker's direct marketing helps both the company and its channel partners.

Channel Design Decisions

We now look at several channel decisions manufacturers face. In designing marketing channels, manufacturers struggle between what is ideal and what is practical. A new firm with limited capital usually starts by selling in a limited market area. Deciding on the best channels might not be a problem: The problem might simply be how to convince one or a few good intermediaries to handle the line.

If successful, the new firm can branch out to new markets through the existing intermediaries. In smaller markets, the firm might sell directly to retailers; in larger markets, it might sell through distributors. In one part of the country, it might grant exclusive franchises; in another, it might sell through all available outlets. Then, it might add a Web store that sells directly to hard-to-reach customers. In this way, channel systems often evolve to meet market opportunities and conditions.

- Avoiding disintermediation problems: Black & Decker's Web site provides detailed information, but you can't buy any of the company's products there. Instead, Black & Decker refers you to resellers' Web sites and stores.

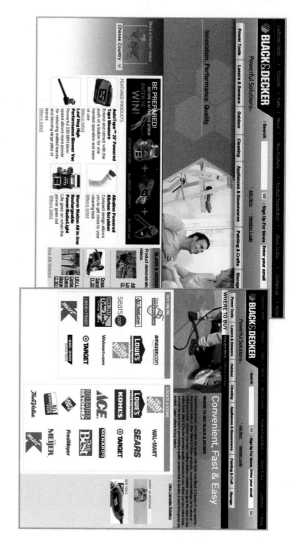

For maximum effectiveness, however, channel analysis and decision making should be more purposeful. Designing a channel system calls for analyzing consumer needs, setting channel objectives, identifying major channel alternatives, and evaluating them.

Analyzing Consumer Needs

As noted previously, marketing channels are part of the overall *customer value delivery network*. Each channel member adds value for the customer. Thus, designing the marketing channel starts with finding out what target consumers want from the channel. Do consumers want to buy from nearby locations or are they willing to travel to more distant centralized locations? Would they rather buy in person, over the phone, through the mail, or online? Do they value breadth of assortment or do they prefer specialization? Do consumers want many add-on services (delivery, credit, repairs, installation), or will they obtain these elsewhere? The faster the delivery, the greater the assortment provided, and the more add-on services supplied, the greater the channel's service level.

Providing the fastest delivery, greatest assortment, and most services may not be possible or practical. The company and its channel members may not have the resources or skills needed to provide all the desired services. Also, providing higher levels of service results in higher costs for the channel and higher prices for consumers. The company must balance consumer needs not only against the feasibility and costs of meeting these needs but also against customer price preferences. The success of discount retailing shows that consumers will often accept lower service levels in exchange for lower prices.

Setting Channel Objectives

Companies should state their marketing channel objectives in terms of targeted levels of customer service. Usually, a company can identify several segments wanting different levels of service. The company should decide which segments to serve and the best channels to use in each case. In each segment, the company wants to minimize the total channel cost of meeting customer service requirements.

The company's channel objectives are also influenced by the nature of the company, its products, its marketing intermediaries, its competitors, and the environment. For example, the company's size and financial situation determine which marketing functions it can handle itself and which it must give to intermediaries. Companies selling perishable products may require more direct marketing to avoid delays and too much handling.

In some cases, a company may want to compete in or near the same outlets that carry competitors' products. In other cases, producers may avoid the channels used by competitors. Mary Kay Cosmetics, for example, sells direct to consumers through its corps of more than one million independent beauty consultants in 34 markets worldwide rather than going head-to-head with other cosmetics makers for scarce positions in retail stores. And GEICO Direct markets auto and homeowner's insurance directly to consumers via the telephone and Web rather than through agents.

Finally, environmental factors such as economic conditions and legal constraints may affect channel objectives and design. For example, in a depressed economy, producers want to distribute their goods in the most economical way, using shorter channels and dropping unneeded services that add to the final price of the goods.

Identifying Major Alternatives

When the company has defined its channel objectives, it should next identify its major channel alternatives in terms of *types* of intermediaries, the *number* of intermediaries, and the *responsibilities* of each channel member.

Types of Intermediaries

A firm should identify the types of channel members available to carry out its channel work. For example, suppose a manufacturer of test equipment has developed an audio device that detects poor mechanical connections in machines with moving parts. Company executives think this product would have a market in all industries in which electric, combustion, or steam engines are made or used. The company's current sales force is small, and the problem is how best to reach these different industries. The following channel alternatives might emerge:

Company sales force: Expand the company's direct sales force. Assign outside salespeople to territories and have them contact all prospects in the area, or develop separate company sales forces for different industries. Or, add an inside telesales operation in which telephone salespeople handle small or midsize companies.

Manufacturer's agency: Hire manufacturer's agents—independent firms whose sales forces handle related products from many companies—in different regions or industries to sell the new test equipment.

Industrial distributors: Find distributors in the different regions or industries who will buy and carry the new line. Give them exclusive distribution, good margins, product training, and promotional support.

Number of Marketing Intermediaries

Companies must also determine the number of channel members to use at each level. Three strategies are available: intensive distribution, exclusive distribution, and selective distribution. Producers of convenience products and common raw materials typically seek **intensive distribution**—a strategy in which they stock their products in as many outlets as possible. These products must be available where and when consumers want them. For example, toothpaste, candy, and other similar items are sold in millions of outlets to provide maximum brand exposure and consumer convenience. Kraft, Coca-Cola, Kimberly-Clark, and other consumer-goods companies distribute their products in this way.

By contrast, some producers purposely limit the number of intermediaries handling their products. The extreme form of this practice is **exclusive distribution**, in which the producer gives only a limited number of dealers the exclusive right to distribute its products in their territories. Exclusive distribution is often found in the distribution of luxury automobiles and prestige women's clothing. For example, Bentley dealers are few and far between—even large cities may have only one dealer. By granting exclusive distribution, Bentley gains

Intensive distribution
Stocking the product in as many outlets as possible.

Exclusive distribution
Giving a limited number of dealers the exclusive right to distribute the company's products in their territories.

Exclusive distribution: Luxury car makers such as Bentley sell exclusively through a limited number of retailers. Such limited distribution enhances the car's image and generates stronger retailer support.

Selective distribution

The use of more than one, but fewer than all, of the intermediaries who are willing to carry the company's products.

stronger distributor selling support and more control over dealer prices, promotion, credit, and services. Exclusive distribution also enhances the car's image and allows for higher markups.

Between intensive and exclusive distribution lies **selective distribution**—the use of more than one, but fewer than all, of the intermediaries who are willing to carry a company's products. Most television, furniture, and home appliance brands are distributed in this manner. For example, KitchenAid, Whirlpool, and GE sell their major appliances through dealer networks and selected large retailers. By using selective distribution, they can develop good working relationships with selected channel members and expect a better-than-average selling effort. Selective distribution gives producers good market coverage with more control and less cost than does intensive distribution.

Responsibilities of Channel Members

The producer and intermediaries need to agree on the terms and responsibilities of each channel member. They should agree on price policies, conditions of sale, territorial rights, and specific services to be performed by each party. The producer should establish a list price and a fair set of discounts for intermediaries. It must define each channel member's territory, and it should be careful about where it places new resellers.

Mutual services and duties need to be spelled out carefully, especially in franchise and exclusive distribution channels. For example, McDonald's provides franchisees with promotional support, a record-keeping system, training at Hamburger University, and general management assistance. In turn, franchisees must meet company standards for physical facilities, cooperate with new promotion programs, provide requested information, and buy specified food products.

Evaluating the Major Alternatives

Suppose a company has identified several channel alternatives and wants to select the one that will best satisfy its long-run objectives. Each alternative should be evaluated against economic, control, and adaptive criteria.

Using *economic criteria*, a company compares the likely sales, costs, and profitability of different channel alternatives. What will be the investment required by each channel alternative, and what returns will result? The company must also consider *control issues*. Using intermediaries usually means giving them some control over the marketing of the product, and some intermediaries take more control than others. Other things being equal, the company prefers to keep as much control as possible. Finally, the company must apply *adaptive criteria*. Channels often involve long-term commitments, yet the company wants to keep the channel flexible so that it can adapt to environmental changes. Thus, to be considered, a channel involving long-term commitments should be greatly superior on economic and control grounds.

Designing International Distribution Channels

International marketers face many additional complexities in designing their channels. Each country has its own unique distribution system that has evolved over time and changes very slowly. These channel systems can vary widely from country to country. Thus, global marketers must usually adapt their channel strategies to the existing structures within each country.

In some markets, the distribution system is complex and hard to penetrate, consisting of many layers and large numbers of intermediaries. At the other extreme, distribution systems in developing countries may be scattered and inefficient, or altogether lacking. For example, China and India are huge markets, each with populations over one billion. However, because of inadequate distribution systems, most companies can profitably access only a small portion of the population located in each country's most affluent cities. "China is a very decentralized market," notes a China trade expert. "[It's] made up of two dozen distinct markets sprawling across 2,000 cities. Each has its own culture. . . . It's like operating in an asteroid belt." China's distribution system is so fragmented that logistics costs amount to 15 percent of the nation's GDP, far higher than in most other countries. After ten years of effort, even Wal-Mart executives admit that they have been unable to assemble an efficient supply chain in China.[8]

Sometimes customs or government regulation can greatly restrict how a company distributes products in global markets. For example, it wasn't an inefficient distribution structure that caused problems for Avon in China—it was restrictive government regulations. Fearing the growth of multilevel marketing schemes, the Chinese government banned door-to-door selling altogether in 1998. Forced to abandon its traditional direct marketing approach and to try selling through retail shops, Avon fell behind its more store-oriented competitors. The Chinese government has only recently given Avon permission to sell door to door, and the company has much catching up to do.[9]

International marketers face a wide range of channel alternatives. Designing efficient and effective channel systems between and within various country markets poses a difficult challenge. We discuss international distribution decisions further in Chapter 19.

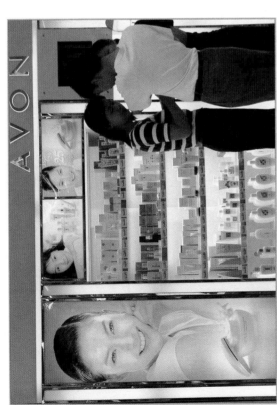

■ International channel complexities: Barred from door-to-door selling in China, Avon fell behind trying to sell through retail stores. Here, Chinese consumers buy Avon products at a supermarket in Shanghai. The Chinese government only recently gave Avon permission to sell door to door.

Channel Management Decisions

Once the company has reviewed its channel alternatives and decided on the best channel design, it must implement and manage the chosen channel. Channel management calls for selecting, managing, and motivating individual channel members and evaluating their performance over time.

Selecting Channel Members

Producers vary in their ability to attract qualified marketing intermediaries. Some producers have no trouble signing up channel members. For example, when Toyota first introduced its Lexus line in the United States, it had no trouble attracting new dealers. In fact, it had to turn down many would-be resellers.

At the other extreme are producers who have to work hard to line up enough qualified intermediaries. When Polaroid started, for example, it could not get photography stores to carry its new cameras, and it had to go to mass-merchandising outlets. Similarly, when the U.S. Time Company first tried to sell its inexpensive Timex watches through regular jewelry stores, most jewelry stores refused to carry them. The company then managed to get its watches into mass-merchandise outlets. This turned out to be a wise decision because of the rapid growth of mass merchandising.

When selecting intermediaries, the company should determine what characteristics distinguish the better ones. It will want to evaluate each channel member's years in business, other lines carried, growth and profit record, cooperativeness, and reputation. If the intermediaries are sales agents, the company will want to evaluate the number and character of other lines carried and the size and quality of the sales force. If the intermediary is a retail store that wants exclusive or selective distribution, the company will want to evaluate the store's customers, location, and future growth potential.

Managing and Motivating Channel Members

Once selected, channel members must be continuously managed and motivated to do their best. The company must sell not only *through* the intermediaries but *to* and *with* them. Most companies see their intermediaries as first-line customers and partners. They practice strong *partner relationship management (PRM)* to forge long-term partnerships with channel members. This creates a marketing system that meets the needs of both the company *and* its marketing partners.

In managing its channels, a company must convince distributors that they can succeed better by working together as a part of a cohesive value delivery system. Thus, Procter & Gamble and Wal-Mart work together to create superior value for final consumers. They jointly plan merchandising goals and strategies, inventory levels, and advertising and promotion plans. Similarly, GE Appliances has created an alternative distribution system called *CustomerNet* to coordinate, support, and motivate its dealers.

GE CustomerNet gives dealers instant online access to GE Appliances' distribution and order-processing system, 24 hours a day, 7 days a week. By logging on to the GE CustomerNet Web site, dealers can obtain product specifications, photos, feature lists, and side-by-side model comparisons for hundreds of GE appliance models.

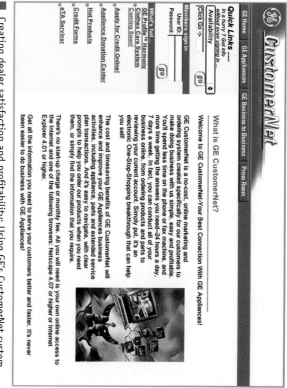

They can check on product availability and prices, place orders, and review order status. They can even create custom brochures, order point-of-purchase materials, or download "advertising slicks"—professionally prepared GE appliance ads ready for insertion in local media. GE promises next-day delivery on most appliance models, so dealers need carry only display models in their stores. This greatly reduces inventory costs, making even small dealers more price competitive. GE CustomerNet also helps dealers to sell GE appliances more easily and effectively. A dealer can put a computer terminal on the showroom floor, where salespeople and customers together can use the system to dig through detailed product descriptions and check availability for GE's entire line of appliances. Perhaps the biggest benefit to GE Appliances, however, is that the system builds strong bonds between the company and its dealers and motivates dealers to put more push behind the company's products.[10]

Creating dealer satisfaction and profitability: Using GE's CustomerNet system, dealers have instant online access to GE Appliances' distribution system, 24 hours a day, 7 days a week to check on product availability and prices, place orders, and review order status. "Simply put, it's an electronic one-stop shopping breakthrough that can help you sell."

Many companies are now installing integrated high-tech partner relationship management systems to coordinate their whole-channel marketing efforts. Just as they use customer relationship management (CRM) software systems to help manage relationships with important customers, companies can now use PRM and supply chain management (SCM) software to help recruit, train, organize, manage, motivate, and evaluate relationships with channel partners.

Evaluating Channel Members

The producer must regularly check channel member performance against standards such as sales quotas, average inventory levels, customer delivery time, treatment of damaged and lost goods, cooperation in company promotion and training programs, and services to the customer. The company should recognize and reward intermediaries who are performing well and adding good value for consumers. Those who are performing poorly should be assisted or, as a last resort, replaced. A company may periodically "requalify" its intermediaries and prune the weaker ones.

Finally, manufacturers need to be sensitive to their dealers. Those who treat their dealers poorly risk not only losing dealer support but also causing some legal problems. The next section describes various rights and duties pertaining to manufacturers and their channel members.

Public Policy and Distribution Decisions

For the most part, companies are legally free to develop whatever channel arrangements suit them. In fact, the laws affecting channels seek to prevent the exclusionary tactics of some companies that might keep another company from using a desired channel. Most channel law deals with the mutual rights and duties of the channel members once they have formed a relationship.

Text within the GE CustomerNet screen image:

GE CustomerNet

GE Home | GE Appliances | GE Business to Business | Press Room

Quick Links ....
In a hurry? Get in
without even signing in .....

Availability
[click Go >] [go]

Members sign in ....
User ID:
Password: [go]

What's hot ......
GE Profile™ Harmony
Clothes Care System
Coming Soon!

Apply for Credit Online!
Appliance Donation Center
Hot Products
Credit Forms
eTA Service!

What is GE CustomerNet?

Welcome to GE CustomerNet-Your Best Connection With GE Appliances!

GE CustomerNet is a no-cost, online marketing and ordering system created specifically for our customers to make doing business with us simple, easy and profitable. You'll spend less time on the phone or fax machine, and more time getting the answers you need–24 hours a day, 7 days a week. In fact, you can conduct all of your business online, from ordering products and parts to reviewing your current account. Simply put, it's an electronic One-Stop-Shopping breakthrough that can help you sell!

The cost and timesaving benefits of GE CustomerNet will enhance and improve your GE Appliances business activities, including appliance, parts and extended service plan transactions. And it's easy to navigate, with clear prompts to help you order our products when you need them, or simply find the information that you require.

There's no start-up charge or monthly fee. All you will need to access to the Internet and one of the following browsers: Netscape 4.07 or higher or Internet Explorer 4.01 or higher.

Get all the information you need to serve your customers better and faster. It's never been easier to do business with GE Appliances!

Many producers and wholesalers like to develop exclusive channels for their products. When the seller allows only certain outlets to carry its products, this strategy is called *exclusive distribution*. When the seller requires that these dealers not handle competitors' products, its strategy is called *exclusive dealing*. Both parties can benefit from exclusive arrangements: The seller obtains more loyal and dependable outlets, and the dealers obtain a steady source of supply and stronger seller support. But exclusive arrangements also exclude other producers from selling to these dealers. This situation brings exclusive dealing contracts under the scope of the Clayton Act of 1914. They are legal as long as they do not substantially lessen competition or tend to create a monopoly and as long as both parties enter into the agreement voluntarily.

Exclusive dealing often includes *exclusive territorial agreements*. The producer may agree not to sell to other dealers in a given area, or the buyer may agree to sell only in its own territory. The first practice is normal under franchise systems as a way to increase dealer enthusiasm and commitment. It is also perfectly legal—a seller has no legal obligation to sell through more outlets than it wishes. The second practice, whereby the producer tries to keep a dealer from selling outside its territory, has become a major legal issue.

Producers of a strong brand sometimes sell it to dealers only if the dealers will take some or all of the rest of the line. This is called full-line forcing. Such *tying agreements* are not necessarily illegal, but they do violate the Clayton Act if they tend to lessen competition substantially. The practice may prevent consumers from freely choosing among competing suppliers of these other brands.

Finally, producers are free to select their dealers, but their right to terminate dealers is somewhat restricted. In general, sellers can drop dealers "for cause." However, they cannot drop dealers if, for example, the dealers refuse to cooperate in a doubtful legal arrangement, such as exclusive dealing or tying agreements.[11]

Marketing Logistics and Supply Chain Management

In today's global marketplace, selling a product is sometimes easier than getting it to customers. Companies must decide on the best way to store, handle, and move their products and services so that they are available to customers in the right assortments, at the right time, and in the right place. Physical distribution and logistics effectiveness has a major impact on both customer satisfaction and company costs. Here we consider the nature and importance of logistics management in the supply chain, goals of the logistics system, major logistics functions, and the need for integrated supply chain management.

Nature and Importance of Marketing Logistics

To some managers, marketing logistics means only trucks and warehouses. But modern logistics is much more than this. **Marketing logistics**—also called **physical distribution**—involves planning, implementing, and controlling the physical flow of goods, services, and related information from points of origin to points of consumption to meet customer requirements at a profit. In short, it involves getting the right product to the right customer in the right place at the right time.

In the past, physical distribution typically started with products at the plant and then tried to find low-cost solutions to get them to customers. However, today's marketers prefer customer-centered logistics thinking, which starts with the marketplace and works backward to the factory, or even to sources of supply. Marketing logistics involves not only *outbound distribution* (moving products from the factory to resellers and ultimately to customers) but also *inbound distribution* (moving products and materials from suppliers to the factory) and *reverse distribution* (moving broken, unwanted, or excess products returned by consumers or resellers). That is, it involves entire **supply chain management**—managing upstream and downstream value-added flows of materials, final goods, and related information among suppliers, the company, resellers, and final consumers, as shown in Figure 12.5.

The logistics manager's task is to coordinate activities of suppliers, purchasing agents, marketers, channel members, and customers. These activities include forecasting, information systems, purchasing, production planning, order processing, inventory, warehousing, and transportation planning.

Marketing logistics (physical distribution)
The tasks involved in planning, implementing, and controlling the physical flow of materials, final goods, and related information from points of origin to points of consumption to meet customer requirements at a profit.

Supply chain management
Managing upstream and downstream value-added flows of materials, final goods, and related information among suppliers, the company, resellers, and final consumers.

FIGURE 12.5
Supply chain management

Suppliers → Company → Resellers → Customers

Inbound logistics → Outbound logistics

Reverse logistics

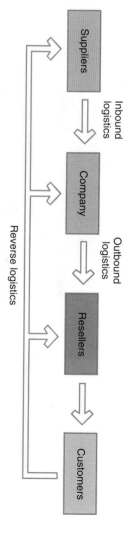

Companies today are placing greater emphasis on logistics for several reasons. First, companies can gain a powerful competitive advantage by using improved logistics to give customers better service or lower prices. Second, improved logistics can yield tremendous cost savings to both the company and its customers. As much as 20 percent of an average product's price is accounted for by shipping and transport alone. This far exceeds the cost of advertising and many other marketing costs. Last year, American companies spent almost $1.2 trillion—about 9.6 percent of gross domestic product—to wrap, bundle, load, unload, sort, reload, and transport goods. By itself, Ford has more than 500 million tons of finished vehicles, production parts, and aftermarket parts in transit at any given time, running up an annual logistics bill of around $4 billion.[12] Shaving off even a small fraction of these costs can mean substantial savings.

Third, the explosion in product variety has created a need for improved logistics management. For example, in 1911 the typical A&P grocery store carried only 270 items. The store manager could keep track of this inventory on about 10 pages of notebook paper stuffed in a shirt pocket. Today, the average A&P carries a bewildering stock of more than 25,000 items. A Wal-Mart Supercenter store carries more than 100,000 products, 30,000 of which are grocery products.[13] Ordering, shipping, stocking, and controlling such a variety of products presents a sizable logistics challenge.

Finally, improvements in information technology have created opportunities for major gains in distribution efficiency. Today's companies are using sophisticated supply chain management software, Web-based logistics systems, point-of-sale scanners, uniform product codes, satellite tracking, and electronic transfer of order and payment data. Such technology lets them quickly and efficiently manage the flow of goods, information, and finances through the supply chain.

■ The importance of logistics: At any given time, Ford has more than 500 million tons of finished vehicles, production parts, and aftermarket parts in transit, running up an annual logistics bill of around $4 billion.

Goals of the Logistics System

Some companies state their logistics objective as providing maximum customer service at the least cost. Unfortunately, no logistics system can *both* maximize customer service *and* minimize distribution costs. Maximum customer service implies rapid delivery, large inventories, flexible assortments, liberal returns policies, and other services—all of which raise distribution costs. In contrast, minimum distribution costs imply slower delivery, smaller inventories, and larger shipping lots—which represent a lower level of overall customer service.

The goal of marketing logistics should be to provide a *targeted* level of customer service at the least cost. A company must first research the importance of various distribution services to customers and then set desired service levels for each segment. The objective is to maximize *profits*, not sales. Therefore, the company must weigh the benefits of providing higher levels of service against the costs. Some companies offer less service than their competitors and charge a lower price. Other companies offer more service and charge higher prices to cover higher costs.

Major Logistics Functions

Given a set of logistics objectives, the company is ready to design a logistics system that will minimize the cost of attaining these objectives. The major logistics functions include *warehousing, inventory management, transportation,* and *logistics information management.*

Warehousing

Production and consumption cycles rarely match. So most companies must store their tangible goods while they wait to be sold. For example, Snapper, Toro, and other lawn mower manufacturers run their factories all year long and store up products for the heavy spring and summer buying seasons. The storage function overcomes differences in needed quantities and timing, ensuring that products are available when customers are ready to buy them.

A company must decide on *how many* and *what types* of warehouses it needs and *where* they will be located. The company might use either *storage warehouses* or *distribution centers.* Storage warehouses store goods for moderate to long periods. They are large and highly automated warehouses designed to receive goods from various plants and suppliers, take orders, fill them efficiently, and deliver goods to customers as quickly as possible.

For example, Wal-Mart operates a network of more than 100 huge U.S. distribution centers and another 57 around the globe. A single center, which might serve the daily needs of 120 Wal-Mart stores, typically contains some 1.2 million square feet of space (about 29 football fields) under a single roof. One huge center near Williamsburg, Virginia, contains more than 3 million square feet. At a typical center, laser scanners route as many as 190,000 cases of goods per day along 11 miles of conveyor belts, and the center's 1,000 workers load or unload some 500 trucks daily. Wal-Mart's Monroe, Georgia, distribution center contains a 127,000-square-foot freezer that can hold 10,000 pallets—room enough for 58 million Popsicles.[14]

Like almost everything else these days, warehousing has seen dramatic changes in technology in recent years. Older, multistoried warehouses with outdated materials-handling methods are steadily being replaced by newer, single-storied *automated warehouses* with advanced, computer-controlled materials-handling systems requiring few employees. Computers and scanners read orders and direct lift trucks, electric hoists, or robots to gather goods, move them to loading docks, and issue invoices.

Inventory Management

Inventory management also affects customer satisfaction. Here, managers must maintain the delicate balance between carrying too little inventory and carrying too much. With too little stock, the firm risks not having products when customers want to buy. To remedy this, the firm may need costly emergency shipments or production. Carrying too much inventory results in higher-than-necessary inventory-carrying costs and stock obsolescence. Thus, in managing inventory, firms must balance the costs of carrying larger inventories against resulting sales and profits.

Many companies have greatly reduced their inventories and related costs through *just-in-time* logistics systems. With such systems, producers and retailers carry only small inventories of parts or merchandise, often only enough for a few days of operations. For example, Dell, a master just-in-time producer, carries just 2 to 3 days of inventory, whereas competitors might carry 40 days or even 60.[15] New stock arrives exactly when needed, rather than being stored in inventory until being used. Just-in-time systems require accurate forecasting along with fast, frequent, and flexible delivery so that new supplies will be available when needed. However, these systems result in substantial savings in inventory-carrying and handling costs.

Marketers are always looking for new ways to make inventory management more efficient. In the not-too-distant future, handling inventory might even become fully automated. For example, in Chapter 3, we discussed RFID or "smart tag" technology, by which

Distribution center
A large, highly automated warehouse designed to receive goods from various plants and suppliers, take orders, fill them efficiently, and deliver goods to customers as quickly as possible.

 Logistics technology: In the not-to-distant future, RFID or "smart tag" technology could make the entire supply chain—which accounts for nearly 75 percent of a product's cost—intelligent and automated.

small transmitter chips are embedded in or placed on products and packaging on everything from flowers and razors to tires. "Smart" products could make the entire supply chain—which accounts for nearly 75 percent of a product's cost—intelligent and automated.

Companies using RFID would know, at any time, exactly where a product is located physically within the supply chain. "Smart shelves" would not only tell them when it's time to reorder, but would also place the order automatically with their suppliers. Such exciting new information technology applications will revolutionize distribution as we know it. Many large and resourceful marketing companies, such as Procter & Gamble, IBM, Wal-Mart, Levi Strauss, and Best Buy, are investing heavily to make the full use of RFID technology a reality.[16]

Transportation

The choice of transportation carriers affects the pricing of products, delivery performance, and condition of the goods when they arrive—all of which will affect customer satisfaction. In shipping goods to its warehouses, dealers, and customers, the company can choose among five main transportation modes: truck, rail, water, pipeline, and air, along with an alternative mode for digital products—the Internet.

Trucks have increased their share of transportation steadily and now account for nearly 35 percent of total cargo ton-miles (more than 60 percent of actual tonnage).[17] Each year in the United States, trucks travel more than 216 billion miles—a distance that has more than dou-

bled over the past 20 years—carrying 11 billion tons of freight worth over $9 trillion. Trucks are highly flexible in their routing and time schedules, and they can usually offer faster service than railroads. They are efficient for short hauls of high-value merchandise. Trucking firms have added many services in recent years. For example, Roadway Express now offers everything from satellite tracking and 24-hour shipment information to logistics planning software and "border ambassadors" who expedite cross-border shipping operations.

Railroads account for 31 percent of total cargo ton-miles moved. They are one of the most cost-effective modes for shipping large amounts of bulk products—coal, sand, minerals, and farm and forest products—over long distances. In recent years, railroads have increased their customer services by designing new equipment to handle special categories of goods, providing flatcars for carrying truck trailers by rail (piggyback), and providing in-transit services such as the diversion of shipped goods to other destinations en route and the processing of goods en route.

Water carriers, which account for about 11 percent of cargo ton-miles, transport large amounts of goods by ships and barges on U.S. coastal and inland waterways. Although the cost of water transportation is very low for shipping bulky, low-value, nonperishable products such as sand, coal, grain, oil, and metallic ores, water transportation is the slowest mode and may be affected by the weather.

Pipelines, which also account for about 16 percent of cargo ton-miles, are a specialized means of shipping petroleum, natural gas, and chemicals from sources to markets. Most pipelines are used by their owners to ship their own products.

Although *air* carriers transport less than 5 percent of the nation's goods, they are an important

- Roadway and other transportation firms have added many services in recent years—everything from satellite tracking to logistics planning software and "border ambassadors" who expedite cross-border shipping operations. The Roadway Customer Care Teams focus on specific customer's needs: "With the entire Roadway team in your corner, you get transportation solutions that are simple, smart, and effective. And that makes everything better for you."

transportation mode. Airfreight rates are much higher than rail or truck rates, but airfreight is ideal when speed is needed or distant markets must be reached. Among the most frequently air-freighted products are perishables (fresh fish, cut flowers) and high-value, low-bulk items (technical instruments, jewelry). Companies find that airfreight also reduces inventory levels, packaging costs, and the number of warehouses needed.

The *Internet* carries digital products from producer to customer via satellite, cable modem, or telephone wire. Software firms, the media, music companies, and education all make use of the Internet to transport digital products. Although these firms primarily use traditional transportation to distribute CDs, newspapers, and more, the Internet holds the potential for lower product distribution costs. Whereas planes, trucks, and trains move freight and packages, digital technology moves information bits.

Shippers also use **intermodal transportation**—combining two or more modes of transportation. *Piggyback* describes the use of rail and trucks; *fishyback*, water and trucks; *trainship*, water and rail; and *airtruck*, air and trucks. Combining modes provides advantages that no single mode can deliver. Each combination offers advantages to the shipper. For example, not only is piggyback cheaper than trucking alone but it also provides flexibility and convenience.

In choosing a transportation mode for a product, shippers must balance many considerations: speed, dependability, availability, cost, and others. Thus, if a shipper needs speed, air and truck are the prime choices. If the goal is low cost, then water or pipeline might be best.

Intermodal transportation
Combining two or more modes of transportation.

Logistics Information Management

Companies manage their supply chains through information. Channel partners often link up to share information and to make better joint logistics decisions. From a logistics perspective, information flows such as customer orders, billing, inventory levels, and even customer data are closely linked to channel performance. The company wants to design a simple, accessible, fast, and accurate process for capturing, processing, and sharing channel information.

Information can be shared and managed in many ways—by mail or telephone, through salespeople, or through traditional or Internet-based *electronic data interchange (EDI)*, the computerized exchange of data between organizations. Wal-Mart, for example, maintains EDI links with almost all of its 91,000 suppliers. And where it once took eight weeks, using EDI, Krispy Kreme can now turn around 1,000 supplier invoices and process the checks in only a single week.[18]

In some cases, suppliers might actually be asked to generate orders and arrange deliveries for their customers. Many large retailers—such as Wal-Mart and Home Depot—work closely with major suppliers such as Procter & Gamble or Black & Decker to set up *vendor-managed inventory* (VMI) systems or *continuous inventory replenishment* systems. Using VMI, the customer shares real-time data on sales and current inventory levels with the supplier. The supplier then takes full responsibility for managing inventories and deliveries. Some retailers even go so far as to shift inventory and delivery costs to the supplier. Such systems require close cooperation between the buyer and seller.

Integrated Logistics Management

Today, more and more companies are adopting the concept of **integrated logistics management**. This concept recognizes that providing better customer service and trimming distribution costs require *teamwork*, both inside the company and among all the marketing channel organizations. Inside, the company's various departments must work closely together to maximize the company's own logistics performance. Outside, the company must integrate its logistics system with those of its suppliers and customers to maximize the performance of the entire distribution system.

Cross-Functional Teamwork Inside the Company

In most companies, responsibility for various logistics activities is assigned to many different departments—marketing, sales, finance, operations, purchasing. Too often, each function tries to optimize its own logistics performance without regard for the activities of the other functions. However, transportation, inventory, warehousing, and order-processing activities interact, often in an inverse way. Lower inventory levels reduce inventory-carrying costs. But they may also reduce customer service and increase costs from stockouts, back orders, special production runs, and costly fast-freight shipments. Because distribution activities involve

Integrated logistics management
The logistics concept that emphasizes teamwork, both inside the company and among all the marketing channel organizations, to maximize the performance of the entire distribution system.

strong trade-offs, decisions by different functions must be coordinated to achieve better over-all logistics performance.

The goal of integrated supply chain management is to harmonize all of the company's logistics decisions. Close working relationships among departments can be achieved in several ways. Some companies have created permanent logistics committees, made up of managers responsible for different physical distribution activities. Companies can also create supply chain manager positions that link the logistics activities of functional areas. For example, Procter & Gamble has created supply chain managers, who manage all of the supply chain activities for each of its product categories. Many companies can employ sophisticated, systemwide supply chain management software, now available from wide range of software enterprises large and small, from SAP to RiverOne and Logility.[19] The important thing is that the company must coordinate its logistics and marketing activities to create high market satisfaction at a reasonable cost.

Building Logistics Partnerships

Companies must do more than improve their own logistics. They must also work with other channel partners to improve whole-channel distribution. The members of a marketing channel are linked closely in creating customer value and building customer relationships. One company's distribution system is another company's supply system. The success of each channel member depends on the performance of the entire supply chain. For example, IKEA can create its stylish but affordable furniture and deliver the "IKEA lifestyle" only if its entire supply chain—consisting of thousands of merchandise designers and suppliers, transport companies, warehouses, and service providers—operates at maximum efficiency and customer-focused effectiveness.

Smart companies coordinate their logistics strategies and forge strong partnerships with suppliers and customers to improve customer service and reduce channel costs. Many companies have created *cross-functional, cross-company teams*. For example, Procter & Gamble has a team of more than 200 people working in Bentonville, Arkansas, home of Wal-Mart.[20] The P&Gers work jointly with their counterparts at Wal-Mart to find ways to squeeze costs out of their distribution system. Working together benefits not only P&G and Wal-Mart but also their shared final consumers.

Other companies partner through *shared projects*. For example, many large retailers are working closely with suppliers on in-store programs. Home Depot allows key suppliers to use its stores as a testing ground for new merchandising programs. The suppliers spend time at Home Depot stores watching how their product sells and how customers relate to it. They then create programs specially tailored to Home Depot and its customers. Clearly, both the supplier and the customer benefit from such partnerships. The point is that all supply chain members must work together in the cause of bringing value to final consumers.

Third-Party Logistics

Most big companies love to make and sell their products. But many loathe the associated logistics "grunt work." They detest the bundling, loading, unloading, sorting, storing, reloading, transporting, customs clearing, and tracking required to supply their factories and to get products out to customers. They hate it so much that a growing number of firms now outsource some or all of their logistics to **third-party logistics (3PL) providers**.

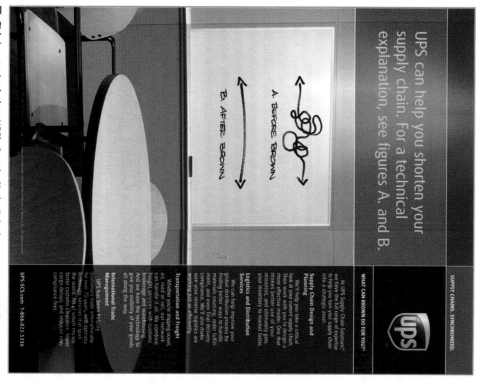

SUPPLY CHAINS, SYNCHRONIZED.

UPS can help you shorten your supply chain. For a technical explanation, see figures A. and B.

A. BEFORE BROWN

B. AFTER BROWN

WHAT CAN BROWN DO FOR YOU?

Supply Chain Design and Planning

Logistics and Distribution Services

International Trade Management

Transportation and Freight

UPS-SCS.com 1-866-822-5336

■ Third party logistics: UPS's Supply Chain Solutions group can help a company shorten its supply chains and turn it into a strategic asset.

(case continued)

Asia. But Zara makes 40 percent of its own fabrics and produces more than half of its own clothes, rather than relying on a hodgepodge of slow-moving suppliers. Even things that are farmed out are done locally in order to maximize time efficiency. Nearly all Zara clothes for its stores worldwide are produced in its remote Northeast corner of Spain.

As it completes designs, Zara cuts fabric in-house. It then sends the designs to one of several hundred local co-operatives for sewing, minimizing the time for raw material distribution. When items return to Zara's facilities, they are ironed by an assembly line of workers who specialize in a specific task (lapels, shoulders, on so on). Clothing items are wrapped in plastic and transported on conveyor belts to a group of giant warehouses.

Zara's warehouses are a vision of modern automation as swift and efficient as any automotive or consumer electronics plant. Human labor is a rare sight in these cavernous buildings. Customized machines patterned after the equipment used by overnight parcel services process up to 80,000 items an hour. The computerized system sorts, packs, labels, and allocates clothing items to every one of Zara's 1,000-plus stores. For stores within a 24-hour drive, Zara delivers goods by truck, whereas it ships merchandise via cargo jet to stores farther away.

DOMESTIC MANUFACTURING PAYS OFF

The same philosophy that has produced such good results for Zara has led parent company Inditex to diversify. Its other chains now include underwear retailer Oysho, teen-oriented Bershka and Stradivarius, children's Kiddy's Class, menswear Massimo Duti, and casual and sportswear chain Pull & Bear. Recently, Inditex opened its first non-clothing chain, Zara Home. Each chain operates under the same style of vertical integration honed at Zara.

Making speed the main goal of its supply chain has really paid off for Inditex. In 2005, sales grew by a whopping 21 percent over the prior year to $8.15 billion (retail revenue growth worldwide averages single-digit increases). That puts Inditex ahead of H&M in the fast-fashion category for the first time. During the same period, profits soared by 26 percent to $973 million. Most of this performance was driven by Zara, now ranked number 73 on Interbrand's list of top 100 most valuable worldwide brands. Although Inditex has grown rapidly, it only wants more. In 2005, it opened 448 new stores (H&M added only 145) and had plans for 490 more. With more than one ribbon-cutting ceremony per day, Inditex could increase its number of stores from the current 2,900 to as many as 5,000 stores in 70 countries by the end of this decade.

European fast-fashion retailers have thus far expanded very cautiously in the United States (Zara has only 19 stores stateside). But the threat has U.S. clothing retailers rethinking the models they have relied on for years. According to one analyst, the industry may soon experience a reversal from outsourcing to China to "Made in the U.S.A":

"U.S. retailers are finally looking at lost sales as lost revenue. They know that in order to capture maximum sales they need to turn their inventory much quicker. The disadvantage of importing from China is that it requires a longer lead time of between three to six months from the time an order is placed to when the inventory is stocked in stores. By then the trends may have changed and you're stuck with all the unsold inventory. If retailers want to refresh their merchandise quicker, they will have to consider sourcing at least some of the merchandise locally."

So being the fastest of the fast-fashion retailers has not only paid off for Zara, its model has reconfigured the fashion landscape everywhere. Zara has blazed a trail for cheaper and cheaper fashion-led mass retailers, has put the squeeze on mid-priced fashion, and has forced luxury brands to scramble to find ways to set themselves apart from Zara's look-a-like designs. Leadership certainly has its perks.

Questions for Discussion

1. As completely as possible, sketch the supply chain for Zara from raw materials to consumer purchase.

2. Discuss the concepts of horizontal and vertical conflict as they relate to Zara.

3. Which type of vertical marketing system does Zara exhibit? List all the benefits that Zara receives by having adopted this system.

4. Does Zara incur disadvantages from its "fast-fashion" distribution system? Are these disadvantages offset by the advantages?

5. How does Zara add value for the customer through major logistics functions?

Sources: "The Future of Fast Fashion," *The Economist,* June 18, 2005; Rachel Tiplady, "Zara: Taking the Lead in Fast Fashion," *BusinessWeek Online,* April 4, 2006; John Tagliabue, "A Rival to Gap that Operates Like Dell," *New York Times,* May 30, 2003, p. W1; Elizabeth Nash, "Dressed for Success," *The Independent,* March 31, 2006, p. 22; Parija Bhatnagar, "Is 'Made in U.S.A.' Back in Vogue?" www.CNNMoney.com, March 1, 2005; Sarah Mower, "The Zara Phenomenon," *The Evening Standard,* January 13, 2006, p. 30; and www.inditex.com, August 2006.

13

Retailing and Wholesaling

Previewing the Concepts

In the previous chapter, you learned the basics of distribution channel design and management. Now, we'll look more deeply into the two major intermediary channel functions, retailing and wholesaling. You already know something about retailing—you're served every day by retailers of all shapes and sizes. However, you probably know much less about the hoard of wholesalers that work behind the scenes. In this chapter, we'll examine the characteristics of different kinds of retailers and wholesalers, the marketing decisions they make, and trends for the future.

To start the tour, we'll look at Whole Foods Market. In today's marketing world, almost every retailer, large or small, worries about competing with Wal-Mart, the world's largest retailer—the world's second-largest *company*. Few retailers *can* compete directly with Wal-Mart and survive. Yet, little Whole Foods is thriving in the shadow of the giant.

These days, Wal-Mart sells just about everything. That means that it competes ruthlessly with almost every other retailer, no matter what the product category. Wal-Mart outsells Toys 'R' Us in the toy market and sells half again as many groceries as the leading groceries-only retailer, Kroger. It gives Blockbuster big headaches in DVD and video sales, and puts a big dent in Best Buy's consumer electronics business. Almost every retailer, large or small, has its hands full devising strategies by which it can compete with Wal-Mart and survive.

So, how *do* you compete with a behemoth like Wal-Mart? The best answer: You don't—at least not directly. Perhaps the worst strategy is trying to out-Wal-Mart Wal-Mart. Instead of competing head-to-head, smart competitors choose their turf carefully.

In fact, this story isn't even about Wal-Mart—we'll cover that colossus later in the chapter. Instead, this is a David-and-Goliath story about Whole Foods Market, a small, upscale grocery chain that's doing very well by carving out its own turf in the giant's shadow. Whole Foods has only 184 stores versus Wal-Mart's more than 6,500 worldwide, and its annual sales total about $4.7 billion, compared to Wal-Mart's $312 billion.

Although it may not seem like a fair fight, Whole Foods is thriving. It succeeds through careful positioning—specifically, by positioning *away* from Wal-Mart. Rather than pursuing mass-market sales volume and razor-thin margins, Whole Foods targets a select group of upscale customers and offers them "organic, natural, and gourmet foods, all swaddled in Earth Day politics." As one analyst puts it, "While other grocers are looking over their shoulder, watching and worrying about Wal-Mart, Whole Foods is going about business as usual. The tofu is still selling; the organic eggs are fresh in the back dairy cooler; and meats are still hormone free."

Whole Foods' value proposition is summed up in its motto: "Whole Foods, Whole People, Whole Planet."

Counters groan with creamy hunks of artisanal cheese. Medjool dates beckon amid rows of exotic fruit. Savory breads rest near fruit-drenched pastries, and prepared dishes like sesame-encrusted tuna rival what's sold in fine restaurants. In keeping with the company's positioning, most of the store's goods carry labels proclaiming "organic," "100% natural," and "contains no additives." Staff people smile, happy to suggest wines that go with a particular cheese, or pause to debate the virtues of peanut butter maltballs. And it's all

Printer Friendly Version

Welcome to Whole Foods Market

Founded in 1980 as one small store in Austin, Texas, Whole Foods Market® is now the world's leading retailer of natural and organic foods, with 180 stores in North America and the United Kingdom. To date Whole Foods Market remains uniquely mission driven: We're highly selective about what we sell, dedicated to stringent Quality Standards, and committed to sustainable agriculture.

We believe in a virtuous circle entwining the food chain, human beings and Mother Earth: each is reliant upon the others through a beautiful and delicate symbiosis.

Whole Foods

We obtain our products locally and from all ov... uniquely dedicated food artisans. We strive to processed, most flavorful and naturally preserv... in its purest state—unadulterated by artificial a... and preservatives—is the best tasting and most...

Whole People

We recruit the best people we can to become them to make their own decisions, creating people who are treated fairly and are highly motiv... people who are passionate about food. Our t... rounded human beings. They play a critical rol... a profitable and beneficial part of its communit...

Whole Planet

We believe companies, like individuals, m... responsibility as tenants of Planet Earth. O... support organic farming—the best method... agriculture and protecting the environment and... basis, we are actively involved in our communit... sponsoring neighborhood events, compensat... community service work, and contributing at... profits to not-for-profit organizations.

done against a backdrop of eye-pleasing earth-toned hues and soft lighting. This is grocery shopping? Well, not as most people know it. Whole Foods Market has cultivated its mystique with shoppers . . . by being anything but a regular supermarket chain. Whole Foods is, well, special.

The Whole Foods Web site reinforces the company's positioning. The site offers up recipes for healthy eating, such as "Sweet Potato Pancakes with Creamy Dill Sauce," "Baked Basmati & Currant Stuffed Trout," and "Beginner's Tips for Tofu, Tempeh, and Other Soy Foods." The site bursts at the seams with information on a wide range of health and wellness issues, from sources such as the WholeHealthMD reference library and the American Botanical Council. You'll find all you ever wanted to know about topics ranging from the potential medical uses of over 100 herbs to alternative therapies such as acupuncture, reflexology, and homeopathy.

Both online and in the flesh, a visit to Whole Foods is more than just a shopping trip, it's an experience. And the experience is anything but what you'd find at Wal-Mart. "We create store environments that are inviting, fun, unique, informal, comfortable, attractive, nurturing, and educational," the company claims. "We want our stores to become community meeting places where our customers come to join their friends and to make new ones."

Objectives

After studying this chapter, you should be able to

1. explain the roles of retailers and wholesalers in the distribution channel
2. describe the major types of retailers and give examples of each
3. describe the major types of wholesalers and give examples of each
4. explain the marketing decisions facing retailers and wholesalers

By design, Whole Foods is not for everyone—the upscale retailer caters to a carefully selected segment of consumers. Whole Foods customers are affluent, liberal, educated people living in university towns such as Austin, Texas, Boulder, Colorado, and Ann Arbor, Michigan. Their median annual household income exceeds the U.S. average by almost $8,000. Whole Foods customers live a health-conscious lifestyle, care about the food they eat, and worry about the environment. They tend to be social do-gooders who abhor soulless corporate greed. Whole Foods doesn't really need to compete with mass merchandisers such as Wal-Mart for these customers. In fact, a Whole Foods customer is more likely to boycott the local Wal-Mart than to shop at it.

Whole Foods customers like the fact that the store's commitment to quality reaches far beyond what's on its shelves. In its "Declaration of Interdependence," the company recognizes that living up to its "Whole Foods, Whole People, Whole Planet" motto means doing more than simply selling food. It means caring about the well-being and quality of life of everyone associated with the business, from customers and employees, to suppliers, to the broader communities in which it operates.

Its concern for customers runs deep. "We go to extraordinary lengths to satisfy and delight our customers," says a company spokesperson. "We want to meet or exceed their expectations on every shopping trip." Whole Foods also cares about its employees—for the past nine years, it's been listed among *Fortune* magazine's "Top 100 Companies to Work for in America." Whole Foods cares about its suppliers. The Declaration of Interdependence states, "We view our trade partners as allies in serving our stakeholders. We treat them with respect, fairness, and integrity, and expect the same in return." To back this up, the company supports sustainable, environmentally friendly agriculture practices, offering organically grown foods almost exclusively.

Whole Foods also cares about its communities. It provides financial support for employees doing voluntary community service. And it invests in the local environment. One store in Berkeley, California, gets most of its electrical power from roof-top solar panels. A special electrical system and energy-conserving features make the most of the sun. Perhaps most telling of Whole Foods' broad community commitment: It donates 5 percent of its after-tax profits to not-for-profit organizations.

Such commitment, along with strong targeting and positioning, have made Whole Foods one of the nation's fastest growing and most profitable food retailers. It's now the world's number-one natural food chain. Its upscale stores ring up an average of $689 in sales per square foot, almost twice that of a traditional grocer. And the chain reaps 35 percent gross margins, half again as large as those of traditional competitors such as Kroger. Whereas other grocers have faced limited sales and profit growth or even declines in the face of the withering Wal-Mart assault, Whole Foods' sales and profits have doubled over the past four years.

So, Whole Foods can't compete directly with the Wal-Marts of the world. It can't match Wal-Mart's massive economies of scale, incredible volume purchasing power, ultraefficient logistics, wide selection, and hard-to-beat prices. But then again, it doesn't even try. Instead, it targets customers that Wal-Mart can't serve, offering them value that Wal-Mart can't deliver. By positioning away from Wal-Mart and other mainstream grocers, Whole Foods has found its own very profitable place in the world. Says Whole Foods chief executive, "Not everyone is concerned with getting mediocre food at the lowest price."[1]

The Whole Foods story sets the stage for examining the fast-changing world of today's resellers. This chapter looks at *retailing* and *wholesaling*. In the first section, we look at the nature and importance of retailing, major types of store and nonstore retailers, the decisions retailers make, and the future of retailing. In the second section, we discuss these same topics as they relate to wholesalers.

Retailing

What is retailing? We all know that Wal-Mart, Home Depot, Macy's, and Target are retailers, but so are Avon representatives, Amazon.com, the local Hampton Inn, and a doctor seeing patients. **Retailing** includes all the activities involved in selling products or services directly to final consumers for their personal, nonbusiness use. Many institutions—manufacturers, wholesalers, and retailers—do retailing. But most retailing is done by **retailers:** businesses whose sales come *primarily* from retailing.

Although most retailing is done in retail stores, in recent years *nonstore retailing* has been growing much faster than has store retailing. Nonstore retailing includes selling to final consumers through direct mail, catalogs, telephone, the Internet, TV home-shopping shows, home and office parties, door-to-door contact, vending machines, and other direct-selling approaches. We discuss such direct-marketing approaches in detail in Chapter 17. In this chapter, we focus on store retailing.

Types of Retailers

Retail stores come in all shapes and sizes, and new retail types keep emerging. The most important types of retail stores are described in Table 13.1 and discussed in the following sections. They can be classified in terms of several characteristics, including the *amount of service* they offer, the breadth and depth of their *product lines,* the *relative prices* they charge, and how they are *organized.*

Amount of Service

Different products require different amounts of service, and customer service preferences vary. Retailers may offer one of three levels of service—self-service, limited service, and full service.

Self-service retailers serve customers who are willing to perform their own "locate-compare-select" process to save money. Self-service is the basis of all discount operations and

---

Retailing
All activities involved in selling goods or services directly to final consumers for their personal, nonbusiness use.

Retailer
A business whose sales come *primarily* from retailing.

TABLE 13.1 Major Store Retailer Types

Specialty Stores: Carry a narrow product line with a deep assortment, such as apparel stores, sporting-goods stores, furniture stores, florists, and bookstores. A clothing store would be a *single-line* store, a men's clothing store would be a *limited-line* store, and a men's custom-shirt store would be a *superspecialty* store. Examples: Gap, The Athlete's Foot, Williams-Sonoma.

Department Stores: Carry several product lines—typically clothing, home furnishings, and household goods—with each line operated as a separate department managed by specialist buyers or merchandisers. Examples: Sears, Macy's, Neiman Marcus.

Supermarkets: A relatively large, low-cost, low-margin, high-volume, self-service operation designed to serve the consumer's total needs for grocery and household products. Examples: Safeway, Kroger, Albertsons, Publix.

Convenience Stores: Relatively small stores located near residential areas, open long hours seven days a week, and carrying a limited line of high-turnover convenience products at slightly higher prices. Examples: 7-Eleven, Stop-N-Go, Circle K.

Discount Stores: Carry standard merchandise sold at lower prices with lower margins and higher volumes. Examples: Wal-Mart, Target, Kohl's.

Off-Price Retailers: Sell merchandise bought at less-than-regular wholesale prices and sold at less than retail, often leftover goods, overruns, and irregulars obtained at reduced prices from manufacturers or other retailers. These include *factory outlets* owned and operated by manufacturers (example: Mikasa); *independent off-price retailers* owned and run by entrepreneurs or by divisions of larger retail corporations (example: TJ Maxx); and *warehouse (or wholesale) clubs* selling a limited selection of brand-name groceries, appliances, clothing, and other goods at deep discounts to consumers who pay membership fees (examples: Costco, Sam's, BJ's Wholesale Club).

Superstores: Very large stores traditionally aimed at meeting consumers' total needs for routinely purchased food and nonfood items. Includes *category killers,* which carry a deep assortment in a particular category and have a knowledgeable staff (examples: Best Buy, PetSmart, Staples); *supercenters,* combined supermarket and discount stores (examples: Wal-Mart Supercenters, SuperTarget, Super Kmart Center, Meijer); and *hypermarkets* with up to 220,000 square feet of space combining supermarket, discount, and warehouse retailing (examples: Carrefour [France], Pyrca [Spain]).

is typically used by sellers of convenience goods (such as supermarkets) and nationally branded, fast-moving shopping goods (such as Wal-Mart).

Limited-service retailers, such as Sears or JC Penney, provide more sales assistance because they carry more shopping goods about which customers need information. Their increased operating costs result in higher prices. In *full-service retailers*, such as specialty stores and first-class department stores, salespeople assist customers in every phase of the shopping process. Full-service stores usually carry more specialty goods for which customers like to be "waited on." They provide more services resulting in much higher operating costs, which are passed along to customers as higher prices.

Product Line

Retailers also can be classified by the length and breadth of their product assortments. Some retailers, such as **specialty stores,** carry narrow product lines with deep assortments within those lines. Today, specialty stores are flourishing. The increasing use of market segmentation, market targeting, and product specialization has resulted in a greater need for stores that focus on specific products and segments.

In contrast, **department stores** carry a wide variety of product lines. In recent years, department stores have been squeezed between more focused and flexible specialty stores on the one hand, and more efficient, lower-priced discounters on the other. In response, many have added promotional pricing to meet the discount threat. Others have stepped up the use of store brands and single-brand "designer shops" to compete with specialty stores. Still others are trying mail-order, telephone, and Web selling. Service remains the key differentiating factor. Retailers such as Nordstrom, Saks, Neiman Marcus, and other high-end department stores are doing well by emphasizing high-quality service.

Supermarkets are the most frequently shopped type of retail store. Today, however, they are facing slow sales growth because of slower population growth and an increase in competition from discount food stores and supercenters on the one hand, and upscale specialty food stores on the other. Supermarkets also have been hit hard by the rapid growth of out-of-home eating. In fact, supermarkets' share of the groceries and consumables market plunged from 73 percent in 1998 to 51 percent in 2005.[2] Thus, many traditional supermarkets are facing hard times.

Many supermarkets are making improvements to attract more customers. In the battle for "share of stomachs," many large supermarkets are moving upscale, providing improved store environments and higher-quality food offerings, such as from-scratch bakeries, gourmet deli counters, and fresh seafood departments. For example, Safeway recently converted 300 of its stores to "lifestyle" formats, featuring subdued lighting, hardwood floors and display cabinets, and home departments. Others are cutting costs, establishing more efficient operations, and lowering prices in order to compete more effectively with food discounters. Finally, a few have added Web-based sales. Today, one-quarter of all grocery stores sell their goods online—including Safeway, Albertsons, D'Agostino, and others—the number is slowly growing. Forrester Research estimates that online grocery buying will grow to $17.4 billion by 2008.[3]

Convenience stores are small stores that carry a limited line of high-turnover convenience goods. After several years of stagnant sales, convenience stores are now experiencing healthy growth. Last year, U.S. convenience stores posted sales of $474 billion, a 20 percent increase over the previous year. More than 69 percent of convenience store revenues come

Specialty store
A retail store that carries a narrow product line with a deep assortment within that line.

Department store
A retail organization that carries a wide variety of product lines—each line is operated as a separate department managed by specialist buyers or merchandisers.

Supermarket
Large, low-cost, low-margin, high-volume, self-service store that carries a wide variety of grocery and household products.

Convenience store
A small store, located near a residential area, that is open long hours seven days a week and carries a limited line of high-turnover convenience goods.

■ Facing increased competition, many supermarkets are providing improved store environments and higher quality food offerings. For example, Safeway recently converted 300 of its stores to "lifestyle" formats, featuring subdued lighting, hardwood floors and display cabinets, and home departments.

from sales of gasoline; a majority of in-store sales are from tobacco products (38 percent) and beer and other beverages (25 percent).[4]

In recent years, convenience store chains have tried to expand beyond their primary market of young, blue-collar men, redesigning their stores to attract female shoppers. They are shedding the image of a "truck stop" where men go to buy beer, cigarettes, and magazines, and instead offer fresh prepared foods and cleaner, safer, more upscale environments. Consider this example:[5]

There's something familiar about the place, with its muted orange-and-green color scheme. The aisles are wider, though, and the displays tonier. Chilling in the fridge is the house Chardonnay, not far from a glass case packed with baguettes and cream cheese croissants that come piping-hot out of the onsite oven. An aisle away is the snazzy cappuccino machine, which offers up bananas foster and pumpkin spice java. There's sushi and, of course, bouquets of fresh-cut flowers. They're right next to the Slurpee machine. Yes, this decidedly upscale little shoppe is a 7-Eleven—or it will be, once the company's team of ace technologists, trendspotters, and product developers wrap up one of the most ambitious makeovers in business history.

The convenience king, most commonly known for lowbrow though popular features such as the Big Gulp and around-the-clock access to Twinkies, is moving up the food chain in search of more affluent customers and fatter margins. After all, the majority of convenience store sales come from gasoline and cigarettes—two increasingly stagnant categories. So 7-Eleven is banking on a new, inventive inventory mix that competes more with Starbucks than with Shell. The transformation seems to be working. After declaring bankruptcy in 1990, the company's fortunes turned around last year. Sales were up 12 percent; profits jumped 66 percent.

■ Convenience store makeover: 7-Eleven is shedding its "truck stop" image and transforming its stores to offer more upscale assortments and environments.

Superstore

A store much larger than a regular supermarket that offers a large assortment of routinely purchased food products, nonfood items, and services.

Category killer

Giant specialty store that carries a very deep assortment of a particular line and is staffed by knowledgeable employees.

food products, nonfood items, and services. Wal-Mart, Target, Meijer, and other discount retailers offer *supercenters,* very large combination food and discount stores. Supercenters are growing in the United States at an annual rate of 25 percent, compared with a supermarket industry growth rate of only 1 percent. Wal-Mart, which opened its first supercenter in 1988, now has almost 2,000 worldwide, capturing more than 70 percent of all supercenter volume.[6]

Recent years have also seen the explosive growth of superstores that are actually giant specialty stores, the so-called **category killers.** They feature stores the size of airplane hangars that carry a very deep assortment of a particular line with a knowledgeable staff. Category killers are prevalent in a wide range of categories, including books, baby gear, toys, electronics, home-improvement products, linens and towels, party goods, sporting goods, even pet supplies. Another superstore variation, a *hypermarket,* is a huge superstore, perhaps as large as six football fields. Although hypermarkets have been very successful in Europe and other world markets, they have met with little success in the United States.

Finally, for some retailers, the product line is actually a service. Service retailers include hotels and motels, banks, airlines, colleges, hospitals, movie theaters, tennis clubs, bowling alleys, restaurants, repair services, hair salons, and dry cleaners. Service retailers in the United States are growing faster than product retailers.

Superstores

Superstores are much larger than regular supermarkets and offer a large assortment of routinely purchased

Relative Prices

Retailers can also be classified according to the prices they charge (see Table 13.1). Most retailers charge regular prices and offer normal-quality goods and customer service. Others

Real Marketing   Wal-Mart: The World's Largest Retailer

13.1   Wal-Mart is the world's largest retailer, and it's play-ing tag-team with ExxonMobil for the title of the world's largest *company*. Wal-Mart is almost unimaginably big. It rang up an incredible $316 billion in sales last year—that's 1.7 times the sales of competitors Costco, Target, Sears/Kmart, JC Penney, and Kohl's *combined*.

Wal-Mart is the number-one seller in several categories of con-sumer products, including groceries, toys, CDs, and pet-care prod-ucts. It sells more clothes than the Gap and Limited combined and almost twice as many groceries as Kroger, the leading grocery-only food retailer. Incredibly, Wal-Mart sells 30 percent of the disposable diapers purchased in the United States each year, 30 percent of the hair-care products, 26 percent of the toothpaste, and 20 percent of the pet food. On average, some 130 million people visit Wal-Mart stores each week.

It's also hard to fathom Wal-Mart's impact on the U.S. economy. It's the nation's largest employer—one out of every 230 men, women, and children in the United States is a Wal-Mart associate. Its sales of $1.52 billion on one day in 2003 exceeded the GDPs of 26 countries. According to one study, Wal-Mart was responsible for some 25 per-cent of the nation's astonishing productivity gains during the 1990s. Another study found that—through its own low prices and through its impact on competitors' prices—Wal-Mart saved the American public $263 billion in 2004 alone—or $2,329 per household.

What are the secrets behind this spectacular success? First and foremost, Wal-Mart is passionately dedicated to its winning value proposition of "Always Low Prices, *Always!*" Its mission is to "lower the world's cost of living." To accomplish this mission, Wal-Mart offers a broad selection of carefully selected goods at unbeatable prices. No other retailer has come nearly so close to mastering the concepts of everyday low prices and one-stop shopping. As one analyst puts it, "The company gospel . . . is relatively simple: Be an agent for customers—find out what they want, and sell it to them for the lowest possible price." Says Wal-Mart's president and chief executive, "We're obsessed with delivering value to customers."

How does Wal-Mart make money with such low prices? The answer is deceptively simple. Wal-Mart is a lean, mean, distribution

machine—it has the lowest cost structure in the industry. Low costs let the giant retailer charge lower prices but still reap higher profits. For example, grocery prices drop an average of 10 to 15 percent in

Leading discounters, such as Wal-Mart, now dominate the retail scene. First and foremost, Wal-Mart is passionately dedicated to its value proposition of "Always Low Prices, Always!"

offer higher-quality goods and service at higher prices. The retailers that feature low prices are discount stores and "off-price" retailers.

A **discount store** sells standard merchandise at lower prices by accepting lower margins and selling higher volume. The early discount stores cut expenses by offering few services and operating in warehouselike facilities in low-rent, heavily traveled dis-tricts. Today's discounters have improved their store environments and increased their services, while at the same time keeping prices low through lean, efficient operations. Leading discounters, such as Wal-Mart, now dominate the retail scene (see Real Marketing 13.1).

As the major discount stores traded up, a new wave of **off-price retailers** moved in to fill the ultralow-price, high-volume gap. Ordinary discounters buy at regular wholesale prices and accept lower margins to keep prices down. In contrast, off-price retailers buy at less-than-regular wholesale prices and charge consumers less than retail. Off-price retailers can be found in all areas, from food, clothing, and electronics to no-frills banking and discount brokerages.

Discount store

A retail operation that sells standard merchandise at lower prices by accepting lower margins and selling at higher volume.

Off-price retailer

Retailer that buys at less-than-regular wholesale prices and sells at less than retail. Examples are factory outlets, independents, and warehouse clubs.

Independent off-price retailer

Off-price retailer that is either owned and run by entrepreneurs or is a division of a larger retail corporation.

Factory outlet

Off-price retailing operation that is owned and operated by a manufacturer and that normally carries the manufacturer's surplus, discontinued, or irregular goods.

The three main types of off-price retailers are *independents, factory outlets,* and *warehouse clubs.* **Independent off-price retailers** either are owned and run by entrepreneurs or are divisions of larger retail corporations. Although many off-price operations are run by smaller independents, most large off-price retailer operations are owned by bigger retail chains. Examples include store retailers such as TJ Maxx and Marshall's, owned by TJX Companies, and Web sellers such as Overstock.com.

Factory outlets—producer-operated stores by firms such as Liz Claiborne, Carters, Levi Strauss, and others—sometimes group together in *factory outlet malls* and *value-retail centers,* where dozens of outlet stores offer prices as low as 50 percent below retail on a wide range of items. Whereas outlet malls consist primarily of manufacturers' outlets, value-retail centers combine manufacturers' outlets with off-price retail stores and department store clearance centers, such as Nordstrom Rack, Neiman Marcus Last Call Clearance Centers, and Off 5th (Saks Fifth Avenue outlets). Factory outlet malls have become one of the hottest growth areas in retailing.

The malls now are moving upscale—and even dropping "factory" from their descriptions—narrowing the gap between factory outlet and more traditional forms of retailers. As the gap

markets Wal-Mart has entered, and Wal-Mart's food prices average 20 percent less than its grocery store rivals. Lower prices attract more shoppers, producing more sales, making the company more efficient, and enabling it to lower prices even more.

Wal-Mart's low costs result in part from superior management and more sophisticated technology. Its Bentonville, Arkansas, headquarters contains a computer communications system that the U.S. Defense Department would envy, giving managers around the country instant access to sales and operating information. And its huge, fully automated distribution centers employ the latest technology to supply stores efficiently.

Wal-Mart also keeps costs down through good old "tough buying." The company is known for the calculated way it wrings low prices from suppliers. "Don't expect a greeter and don't expect friendly," says one supplier's sales executive after a visit to Wal-Mart's buying offices. "Once you are ushered into one of the spartan little buyers' rooms, expect a steely eye across the table and be prepared to cut your price. They are very, very focused people, and they use their buying power more forcefully than anyone else in America."

Some critics argue that Wal-Mart squeezes its suppliers too hard, driving some out of business. Wal-Mart proponents counter, however, that it is simply acting in its customers' interests by forcing suppliers to be more efficient. "Wal-Mart is tough," says an industry consultant. "Wal-Mart has forced manufacturers to get their act together."

Despite its incredible success over the past four decades, some analysts see chinks in the seemingly invincible Wal-Mart's armor. For example, its same-store sales are growing at a slower clip than those of Target and other spryer competitors, causing Wal-Mart's stock to languish. And to many higher-income consumers, Wal-Mart seems downright dowdy compared with the younger, hipper Target. "Many of its upscale customers . . . come into the store for vegetables, cereal, detergent, and the like—but turn up their noses at higher margin items such as apparel and electronics," says an analyst.

So, to reignite growth and to extend its customer base by capturing a larger share-of-wallet from higher-income consumers, Wal-Mart recently began giving itself a modest image facelift. It's sprucing up

its stores and adding new, higher-quality merchandise. For example, many urban Wal-Marts now carry a slew of higher-end consumer electronics products, from Sony plasma televisions to Toshiba laptops to Apple iPods. And it's now dressing up its apparel racks with more stylish fashion lines under brand names such as Metro 7 and George by designer Mark Eisen.

Wal-Mart is also beefing up its spending on more stylish advertising. Gone are the old bouncing smiley-face, "roll back the prices" ads. In their place are ads that look more like, well, Target ads. Maybe that's because Wal-Mart's new chief marketing executive—and the architect of the image makeover—is a 20-year Target marketing veteran.

Even with its slightly more upscale image, however, in no way will Wal-Mart ever give up its core "Always Low Prices—Always" value proposition. After all, it is and always will be a discount store. And despite some growing pains, Wal-Mart appears well on its way to becoming the world's first trillion-dollar corporation. This leads some observers to wonder if an ever-larger Wal-Mart can retain its customer focus and positioning. The company's managers are betting on it. No matter where it operates, Wal-Mart's announced policy is to take care of customers "one store at a time." Says one top executive: "We'll be fine as long as we never lose our responsiveness to the consumer."

Sources: Quotes and other information from Bill Saporito and Jerry Useem, "One Nation Under Wal-Mart," *Fortune,* March 3, 2003, pp. 65–78; Don Longo, "Wal-Mart on Its Way to Becoming the First Trillion Dollar Corporation," *Retail Merchandiser,* March 2005, p. 7; Pallavi Gogoi, "Wal-Mart Gets the Fashion Bug," *BusinessWeek Online,* October 7, 2006, accessed at www.businessweek.com; Luke Boggs, "Why I'm Fighting for Wal-Mart," *DSN Retailing Today* December 19, 2005, p. 11; "The Fortune 500," *Fortune,* April 17, 2006, pp. F1–F3; Theresa Howard, "Ads Try to Expand Customer Base," *USA Today,* February 21, 2006; Stuart Elliott and Michael Barbaro, "Wal-Mart on the Hunt for an Extreme Makeover," May 4, 2006, pp. C1, C13; Robert Berner, "Fashion Emergency at Wal-Mart," *BusinessWeek,* July 31, 2006, p. 67; and www.walmartstores.com January 2007.

narrows, the discounts offered by outlets are getting smaller. However, a growing number of outlet malls now feature brands such as Coach, Polo, Ralph Lauren, Dolce & Gabbana, Giorgio Armani, Gucci, and Versace, causing department stores to protest to the manufacturers of these brands. Given their higher costs, the department stores must charge more than the off-price outlets. Manufacturers counter that they send last year's merchandise and seconds to the factory outlet malls, not the new merchandise that they supply to the department stores. Still, the department stores are concerned about the growing number of shoppers willing to make weekend trips to stock up on branded merchandise at substantial savings.

Warehouse club

Off-price retailer that sells a limited selection of brand name grocery items, appliances, clothing, and a hodgepodge of other goods at deep discounts to members who pay annual membership fees.

Warehouse clubs (or *wholesale clubs* or *membership warehouses*), such as Sam's Club, Costco, and BJ's, operate in huge, drafty, warehouselike facilities and offer few frills. Customers themselves must wrestle furniture, heavy appliances, and other large items to the checkout line. Such clubs make no home deliveries and often accept no credit cards. However, they do offer ultralow prices and surprise deals on selected branded merchandise.

Although they account for only about 8 percent of total U.S. retail sales, warehouse clubs have grown rapidly in recent years. These retailers appeal not just to low-income consumers seeking bargains on bare-bones products; they appeal to all kinds of customers shopping for a wide range of goods, from necessities to extravagances. Consider Costco, the nation's largest warehouse retailer:

What Costco has come to stand for is a retail segment where high-end products meet deep-discount prices. It's the U.S.'s biggest seller of fine wines (including the likes of a Chateau Cheval-Blanc Bordeaux for $229.99 a bottle) and baster of poultry (55,000 rotisserie chickens a day). Last year it sold 45 million hot dogs at $1.50 each and 60,000 carats of diamonds at up to $100,000. It even offered a Pablo Picasso drawing at Costco.com for only $129,999.99! Yuppies seek the latest gadgets there. Even people who don't have to pinch pennies shop at Costco.

There was a time when only the great unwashed shopped at off-price stores. But warehouse clubs attract a breed of urban sophisticates attuned to what one retail consultant calls the "new luxury." These shoppers shun Seiko watches for TAG Heuer; Jack Nicklaus golf clubs for Callaway; Maxwell House coffee (it goes without saying) for Starbucks. They "trade up," eagerly spending more for items that make their hearts pound and for which they don't have to pay full price. Then they "trade down" to private labels for things like paper towels, detergent, and vitamins. Catering to this fast-growing segment, Costco has exploded too. "It's the ultimate concept in trading up and trading down," says the consultant. "It's a brilliant innovation for the new luxury."[7]

■ Off-price retailers: Shoppers at warehouse clubs such as Costco "trade down" to private labels for things like paper towels, detergent, and vitamins. At the same time, they "trade up," getting good prices on items that make their hearts pound. Costco even offered a Pablo Picasso drawing at its Web site—for only $129,999.99.

Chain stores

Two or more outlets that are commonly owned and controlled.

Organizational Approach

Although many retail stores are independently owned, others band together under some form of corporate or contractual organization. The major types of retail organizations—*corporate chains, voluntary chains* and *retailer cooperatives, franchise organizations,* and *merchandising conglomerates*—are described in Table 13.2.

Chain stores are two or more outlets that are commonly owned and controlled. They have many advantages over independents. Their size allows them to buy in large quantities at lower prices and gain promotional economies. They can hire specialists to deal with areas such as pricing, promotion, merchandising, inventory control, and sales forecasting.

The great success of corporate chains caused many independents to band together in one of two forms of contractual associations. One is the *voluntary chain*—a wholesaler-sponsored

TABLE 13.2 Major Types of Retail Organizations

Type	Description	Examples
Corporate chain stores	Two or more outlets that are commonly owned and controlled, employ central buying and merchandising, and sell similar lines of merchandise. Corporate chains appear in all types of retailing, but they are strongest in department stores, food stores, drug stores, shoe stores, and women's clothing stores.	Sears, Safeway (grocery stores), CVS (drug stores), Williams-Sonoma (cookware, dinnerware, and housewares)
Voluntary chains	Wholesaler-sponsored groups of independent retailers engaged in bulk buying and common merchandising.	Independent Grocers Alliance (IGA), Do-It Best hardware, Western Auto, True Value
Retailer cooperatives	Groups of independent retailers who set up a central buying organization and conduct joint promotion efforts.	Associated Grocers (groceries), Ace (hardware)
Franchise organizations	Contractual association between a franchiser (a manufacturer, wholesaler, or service organization) and franchisees (independent businesspeople who buy the right to own and operate one or more units in the franchise system). Franchise organizations are normally based on some unique product, service, or method of doing business, or on a trade name or patent, or on goodwill that the franchiser had developed.	McDonald's, Subway, Pizza Hut, Jiffy Lube, Meineke Mufflers, 7-Eleven
Merchandising conglomerates	Free-form corporations that combine several diversified retailing lines and forms under central ownership, along with some integration of their distribution and management functions.	Limited Brands

Franchise

A contractual association between a manufacturer, wholesaler, or service organization (a franchiser) and independent businesspeople (franchisees) who buy the right to own and operate one or more units in the franchise system.

group of independent retailers that engages in group buying and common merchandising—which we discussed in Chapter 12. Examples include Independent Grocers Alliance (IGA), Western Auto, and Do-It Best hardware. The other type of contractual association is the *retailer cooperative*—a group of independent retailers that bands together to set up a jointly owned, central wholesale operation and conducts joint merchandising and promotion efforts. Examples are Associated Grocers and Ace Hardware. These organizations give independents the buying and promotion economies they need to meet the prices of corporate chains.

Another form of contractual retail organization is a **franchise.** The main difference between franchise organizations and other contractual systems (voluntary chains and retail cooperatives) is that franchise systems are normally based on some unique product or service; on a method of doing business; or on the trade name, goodwill, or patent that the franchiser has developed. Franchising has been prominent in fast foods, health and fitness centers, hair-cutting, auto rentals, motels, travel agencies, real estate, and dozens of other product and service areas.

But franchising covers a lot more than just burger joints and fitness centers. Franchises have sprung up to meet about any need. Franchiser Mad Science Group franchisees put on science programs for schools, scout troops, and birthday parties. Mr. Handyman provides repair services for homeowners, and Merry Maids tidies up their houses.

Once considered upstarts among independent businesses, franchises now command 40 percent of all retail sales in the United States. These days, it's nearly impossible to stroll down a city block or drive on a suburban street without seeing a McDonald's, Subway, Jiffy Lube, or Holiday Inn. One of the best-known and most successful franchisers, McDonald's, now has nearly 32,000 stores in 119 countries. It serves nearly 50 million customers a day and racks up more than $39 billion in annual systemwide sales. Some 58 percent of McDonald's restaurants worldwide are owned and operated by franchisees. Gaining fast is Subway Sandwiches and Salads, one of the fastest-growing franchises, with more than 26,000 shops in 85 countries, including over 20,000 in the United States.[8]

Finally, *merchandising conglomerates* are corporations that combine several different retailing forms under central ownership. An example is Limited Brands, which operates The Limited (fashion-forward women's clothing), Express (trendy private-label women's and men's apparel), Victoria's Secret (glamorous lingerie and beauty products), Bath & Body

■ Franchising: These days, it's nearly impossible to stroll down a city block or drive on a suburban street without seeing a McDonald's, Jiffy Lube, Subway, or Holiday Inn.

Works (natural but luxurious beauty and body-care products), and The White Barn Candle Company (home fragrance and décor items). Such diversified retailing, similar to a multibranding strategy, provides superior management systems and economies that benefit all the separate retail operations.

Retailer Marketing Decisions

Retailers are always searching for new marketing strategies to attract and hold customers. In the past, retailers attracted customers with unique product assortments and more or better services. Today, retail assortments and services are looking more and more alike. Nationalbrand manufacturers, in their drive for volume, have placed their branded goods everywhere. Such brands are found not only in department stores but also in mass-merchandise discount stores, off-price discount stores, and on the Web. Thus, it's now more difficult for any one retailer to offer exclusive merchandise.

Service differentiation among retailers has also eroded. Many department stores have trimmed their services, whereas discounters have increased theirs. Customers have become smarter and more price sensitive. They see no reason to pay more for identical brands, especially when service differences are shrinking. For all these reasons, many retailers today are rethinking their marketing strategies.

As shown in Figure 13.1, retailers face major marketing decisions about their *target market* and *positioning, product assortment and services, price, promotion, and place.*

Target Market and Positioning Decision

Retailers must first define their target markets and then decide how they will position themselves in these markets. Should the store focus on upscale, midscale, or downscale shoppers? Do target shoppers want variety, depth of assortment, convenience, or low prices? Until they define and profile their markets, retailers cannot make consistent decisions about product assortment, services, pricing, advertising, store décor, or any of the other decisions that must support their positions.

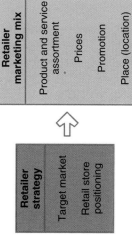

Retailer strategy		Retailer marketing mix
Target market	⇨	Product and service assortment
Retail store positioning		Prices
		Promotion
		Place (location)

FIGURE 13.1
Retailer marketing decisions

Retail positioning: To avoid dog-eat-dog competition with Wal-Mart and cost-focused market leader PetSmart, Petco has transformed itself into an emporium of luxury pet supplies.

Too many retailers fail to define their target markets and positions clearly. They try to have "something for everyone" and end up satisfying no market well. In contrast, successful retailers define their target markets well and position themselves strongly. For example, Wal-Mart positions itself strongly on low prices. In a recent survey testing consumers on their recall of the slogans for American brands, 67 percent of consumers associated Wal-Mart with its "Always low prices. *Always*" promise. Sprite, in second place, scored just 35 percent recognition.[9]

If Wal-Mart owns the low-price position, how can other discounters hope to compete? Again, the answer is good targeting and positioning. For example, rather than facing Wal-Mart head-on, Target—or Tar-*zhay* as many fans call it—thrives by aiming at a seemingly oxymoronic "upscale discount" niche. It has become the nation's number-two discount chain by offering discount prices but rising above the discount fray with upmarket style and design and higher-grade service. Target's "expect more, pay less" positioning sets it apart and helps insulate it from Wal-Mart.

In the same way, pet-supply chain Petco competes effectively with low-priced competitors Wal-Mart and PetSmart by positioning upscale:

With Gen Xers postponing child rearing and baby boomers coping with empty nests, more Americans are treating pets like spoiled kids with fur. "The way people view animals in the household has changed dramatically" in recent years, says a Petco executive, noting that 55 percent of pet canines now sleep in their owners' beds. People are now spending "more on what could be considered frivolous products," adds an industry consultant, "such as things to coddle their pets."

This trend has been a boon for pets everywhere, but Sparky's not the only one wagging his tail. It's also been good for Petco. Ten years ago Petco made most of its money selling food. Today two-thirds of its revenue comes from services like grooming and training, and from specialty goods like $7.50 beef-flavored toothpaste and $30 pheromone-emitting stress reducers. This shift to pricier offerings has helped Petco avoid a catfight with Wal-Mart, a growing pet-supply power. Of Petco's 10,000 offerings, only 40 overlap with Wal-Mart's. And going upscale has given Petco higher operating margins than the more warehouse-focused PetSmart, the industry's top dog. Such smart targeting and positioning have earned Petco more than 12 consecutive years of double-digit income growth.[10]

Product Assortment and Services Decision

Retailers must decide on three major product variables: *product assortment, services mix,* and *store atmosphere.*

The retailer's *product assortment* should differentiate the retailer while matching target shoppers' expectations. One strategy is to offer merchandise that no other competitor carries. For example, Saks gets exclusive rights to carry a well-known designer's labels. It also offers its own private-label lines—the Saks Fifth Avenue Signature, Classic, and Sport collections. At JC Penney, private-label brands account for 40 percent of sales.[11]

Another strategy is to feature blockbuster merchandising events—Bloomingdale's is known for running spectacular shows featuring goods from a certain country, such as India or China. Or the retailer can offer surprise merchandise, as when Costco offers surprise assortments of seconds, overstocks, and closeouts. Finally, the retailer can differentiate itself by offering a highly targeted product assortment—Lane Bryant carries plus-size clothing; Brookstone offers an unusual assortment of gadgets in what amounts to an adult toy store.

The *services mix* can also help set one retailer apart from another. For example, some retailers invite customers to ask questions or consult service representatives in person or via phone or keyboard. Home Depot offers a diverse mix of services to do-it-yourselfers, from "how-to" classes to a proprietary credit card. Nordstrom promises to "take care of the customer, no matter what it takes."

The *store's atmosphere* is another element in the reseller's product arsenal. Every store has a physical layout that makes moving around in it either hard or easy. Each store has a "feel"; one store is cluttered, another cheerful, a third plush, a fourth somber. The retailer must design an atmosphere that suits the target market and moves customers to buy. For example, Apple's retail stores are very seductive places. They're what one analyst calls "a Space-Age vision of a Kubrickian future—full of gleaming white and dull silver hardware."[12] The store design is clean, simple, and just oozing with style—much like an Apple iPod or Mac PC. Shoppers are invited to stay a while, use the equipment, and soak up all of the exciting new technology. One shopper sums up the Apple store atmosphere and experience this way:

It has become something of a second home to me—or, as I jokingly call it, "my temple." I've been known to spend hours at a time there. It seems a trifling thing that I can walk up to any terminal in the place during a . . . shopping break, log in to my e-mail account, and attend to my electronic correspondence. I am also able to freely Web-surf, instant-message, or do a bit of e-shopping (heck, even buy a new Mac or iPod on the online Apple Store). No one rushes or hassles me. It seems like a family room (albeit a gigantic one), with its comfortable theater seating in the back, its library-style shelves lined neatly with Mac software, books and magazines, its rows of flat-panel screens flashing Pixar trailers, its speaker-connected iPods cranking out catchy tunes, its low-to-the-ground kids' table and ball-shaped chairs for iMac gaming, and its Genius Bar, to which visitors could cozy up for guidance or troubleshooting with an Apple supergeek. That's why I sometimes don't want to leave. In fact, I wrote part of this essay on a MacBook laptop while reclining in one of those airport-style chairs. It's a testament to Apple retail savvy that I felt totally at ease while typing away.[13]

Store atmosphere: Apple's retail stores are very seductive places. Here, people wait in line to enter the new Apple store on Fifth Avenue in New York City. "It has become something of a second home to me," says one shopper, "or, as I jokingly call it, 'my temple.'"

It's no wonder that Apple stores "are going gangbusters," says the analyst. "The stores are attracting up to 10,000 visitors per week each, or 18.1 million visitors a year in total." By comparison, Gateway's more pedestrian retail stores pulled in an average of only 250 people a week.

Other retailers practice "experiential retailing." At an REI store, consumers can try out climbing equipment on a huge wall in the store, or they can test Gore-Tex raincoats by going under a simulated rain shower. At Lifestyles Spa in Van Nuys, California, shoppers are invited to wear their bathing suits to the store and slip into water-filled Jacuzzis and hot tubs for a "test drive." Similarly, Maytag has set up "try-before-you-buy" stores in which it displays products in realistic home kitchen and laundry room settings, beckoning customers to try out products before making a choice. They can do a load of laundry, bake a sheet of cookies, or listen to a dishwasher to see whether it's really quiet.[14]

Increasingly, retailers are turning their stores into theaters that transport customers into unusual, exciting shopping environments. For example, outdoor goods retailer Cabela's stores are as much natural history museums as they are retail outlets (see Real Marketing 13.2). And the huge Mall of America near Minneapolis is a veritable playground that attracts as many as 42 million visitors each year. Under a single roof, it shelters more than 520 specialty stores, some 50 restaurants, a wedding chapel that has married over 4,000 couples, a college campus, an enormous LEGO Imagination Center, an ice-skating rink, an aquarium, a two-story miniature golf course, and Underwater Adventures, which features hundreds of marine specimens and a dolphin show. Shoppers who wear themselves out can visit the new nap store, which features walls thick enough to shut out the sounds of screaming kids or the amusement park attractions. It sells shut-eye for 70 cents a minute.[15]

All of this confirms that retail stores are much more than simply assortments of goods. They are environments to be experienced by the people who shop in them. Store atmospheres offer a powerful tool by which retailers can differentiate their stores from those of competitors.

Price Decision

A retailer's price policy must fit its target market and positioning, product and service assortment, and competition. All retailers would like to charge high markups and achieve high volume, but the two seldom go together. Most retailers seek either high markups on lower volume (most specialty stores) or low markups on higher volume (mass merchandisers and discount stores).

Thus, Bijan's boutique with locations in New York City and on Rodeo Drive in Beverly Hills sells "the most expensive menswear in the world." Its million-dollar wardrobes include $50 socks, $375 silk ties, and $19,000 ostrich-skin vests. Its "by appointment only" policy is designed to make its wealthy, high-profile clients comfortable with these prices. Says Mr. Bijan, "If a man is going to spend $400,000 on his visit, don't you think it's only fair that he have my full attention?"[16] Bijan's sells a low volume but makes hefty profits on each sale. At the other extreme, TJ Maxx sells brand-name clothing at discount prices, setting for a lower margin on each sale but selling at a much higher volume.

Retailers must also decide on the extent to which they will use sales and other price promotions. Some retailers use no price promotions at all, competing instead on product and service quality rather than on price. For example, it's difficult to imagine Bijan's holding a two-for-the-price-of-one sale. Other retailers practice "high-low" pricing—charging higher prices on an everyday basis, coupled with frequent sales and other price promotions to increase store traffic, clear out unsold merchandise, create a low-price image, or attract customers who will buy other goods at full prices. Still others—such as Wal-Mart, Costco, Home Depot, and other mass retailers—practice everyday low pricing (EDLP), charging constant, everyday low prices with few sales or discounts. Which strategy is best depends on the retailer's marketing strategy and the pricing approaches of competitors.[17]

Promotion Decision

Retailers use any or all of the promotion tools—advertising, personal selling, sales promotion, public relations, and direct marketing—to reach consumers. They advertise in newspapers, magazines, radio, television, and on the Internet. Advertising may be supported by newspaper inserts and direct mail. Personal selling requires careful training of salespeople in how to greet customers, meet their needs, and handle their complaints. Sales promotions may include in-store demonstrations, displays, contests, and visiting celebrities. Public relations activities, such as press conferences and speeches, store openings, special events, newsletters, magazines, and public service activities, are always available to retailers. Most retailers have also set up Web sites, offering customers information and other features and often selling merchandise directly.

Real Marketing   Cabela's: Creating a Sense of Wonder for People Who Hate to Shop

13.2 At first glance, outdoor-products retailer Cabela's seems to break all the rules of retailing. First, it locates its stores in tiny, off-the-beaten-path locations—places like Sidney, Nebraska, Prairie du Chien, Wisconsin, Dundee, Michigan, Lehi, Utah, and Owatonna, Minnesota. Then, to make matters worse, it targets customers who hate to shop! The typical Cabela's customer is a reclusive male outdoorsman who yearns for the great outdoors, someone who detests jostling crowds and shopping.

So how do you explain Cabela's surging success? Over the past decade, Cabela's has evolved from a popular mail-order catalog business into one of the nation's hottest store retailers. Despite Cabela's often-remote locations, customers are flocking to its 15 superstores (soon to be 30) to buy hunting, fishing, and outdoor gear. A typical Cabela's store draws 4.4 million customers a year—an average of 40,000 customers on a Saturday and 50,000 to 100,000 on a holiday weekend. Half of Cabela's customers drive 100 miles or more to get there, and many travel up to 350 miles. Schools even send busloads of kids.

In fact, Cabela's stores have become tourist destinations. Its store in Michigan is the state's largest tourist attraction, drawing more than 6 million people a year. The Minnesota store trails only the Mall of America in the number of annual visitors. And the Cabela's in Sidney, Nebraska, a town of only 6,000 people located 150 miles from the nearest city (Denver), attracts 1.2 millions visitors a year, making it Nebraska's second-largest tourist attraction behind The Omaha Zoo.

Just what is it that attracts these hordes of otherwise reluctant shoppers to Cabela's remote stores? Part of the answer lies in all the stuff the stores sell. Cabela's huge 230,000-square-foot superstores (one and one-half times larger than a typical Wal-Mart supercenter) house a vast assortment of quality merchandise at reasonable prices. Cabela's competes on price with discounters, but carries a selection that's six to ten times deeper—more than 200,000 kinds of items for hunting, fishing, boating, camping, and archery. "I'd have to go to two or three different stores to find all the brands they have at Cabela's," says Jason Gies, a 26-year-old mechanical engineer who drove 150 miles to purchase a vintage used Remington shotgun.

Cabela's also sells lines of branded clothing and gifts that appeal to customers' wives and children, making it a popular stop for the

Cabela's: "This is more than a place to get fishhooks . . . "

whole family. And to top things off, Cabela's offers first-class service. It staffs its departments with a generous supply of employees, all of whom must pass a 100-question test on the products they sell. For customers who stop by during hunting trips, Cabela's even offers use of outdoor kennels and corrals to house their hunting dogs or horses while they shop. Hunters with rifles are welcomed.

But deep product assortments and good service don't explain the huge crowds that show up at Cabela's. The retailer's real magic lies in the *experiences* it creates for those who visit. "This is more than a place to go get fishhooks," says a Cabela's spokesperson. "The Cabelas"—Nebraska brothers Dick and Jim—"wanted to create a sense of wonder." Mission accomplished! In each of its stores, Cabela's has created what amounts to a natural history theme park for outdoor enthusiasts.

Take the store near Fort Worth, Texas, for example. Cabela's 11th store and the largest so far. Dominating the center of the store is Conservation Mountain, a two-story mountain replica with two waterfalls and cascading streams. The mountain is divided into four ecosystems and five bioregions: a Texas prairie, an Alaskan habitat, an Arctic ice cap, an American woodland, and an Alpine mountaintop. Each bioregion is populated by lifelike, museum-quality taxidermy animals in action poses—everything from prairie dogs, deer,

Place Decision

Retailers often point to three critical factors in retailing success: *location, location, and location!* It's very important that retailers select locations that are accessible to the target market in areas that are consistent with the retailer's positioning. For example, Apple locates its stores in high-end malls and trendy shopping districts—such as the "Miracle Mile" on Chicago's Michigan Avenue or Fifth Avenue in Manhattan—not low-rent strip malls on the edge of town. Small retailers may have to settle for whatever locations they can find or afford. Large retailers, however, usually employ specialists who select locations using advanced methods.

Cabela's spares no expense in developing this sportsman's paradise. A stuffed polar bear can cost up to $10,000. The Fort Worth store presents 800 such animals, right down to a Texas rattlesnake. Cabela's even created a new post—Taxidermy Purchasing Specialist—an executive who seeks out stuffed animals and mounts them in authentic scenes—two grizzly bears locked in battle, a leopard leaping for a monkey—even the droppings are real. "The muscle tone of the animal, the eyes, the posture—everything must be just right," says the executive. The taxidermy collection at Cabela's Fort Worth store is twice as large as the one at the Fort Worth Museum of Science and History.

So, if you scratch a little deeper, you find that far from breaking the rules, Cabela's is doing all the right things. It's creating total experiences that delight the senses as well as the wallets of carefully targeted customers. Put it all together and you've got a powerful magnet for outdoorsmen and their families. Just ask one of the millions of anything-but-reluctant Cabela's customers:

"I'll do just about anything to avoid shopping," says John Brown, a small-business owner in Cheyenne, Wyoming. In 35 years of marriage, his wife says she's persuaded him to go shopping only twice. Yet one day last month he invited her to drive 100 miles with him for a day of shopping at Cabela's. "I'm like a kid in a candy store here," he says, dropping a new tackle box into his cart.

The trick . . . is appealing to the family member who is usually most reluctant to shop: Dad. One recent morning, Lara Miller was trying to round up her husband and three kids, as their morning trip to Cabela's stretched into afternoon. Mrs. Miller—normally the only family member who likes to shop—now was the one most ready to leave. "We haven't had breakfast yet," she moaned. Her husband, Darren Miller, a farmer in Jerome, Idaho, said, "I love this place."

Sources: Extracts, quotes, and other information from Heather Landy, "Plenty in Store," *Knight Ridder Tribune Business News*, May 22, 2005, p. 1; Kevin Helliker, "Hunter Gatherer: Rare Retailer Scores by Targeting Men Who Hate to Shop," *Wall Street Journal*, December 17, 2002, p. A1; Landry, "Many Counting on New Cabela's to Be Quite a Draw," *Knight Ridder Tribune Business News*, May 22, 2005, p. 1; John Seward, "Outdoor Retailers Plan for Expansion," *Wall Street Journal*, June 8, 2005, p. 1; Bud Kennedy, "Bud Kennedy Column," *Fort Worth Star-Telegram*, May 26, 2005, p. 1; "The Art of Service," *Fast Company*, October 2005, pp. 47–58; Dan Benson, "Booming Times: Cabela's Pushes Up Interest, Price for Land in Area," *Milwaukee Journal Sentinel*, March 5, 2006; and www.cabelas.com, December 2006.

". . . we want to create a sense of wonder."

elk, and caribou to brown bears, polar bears, musk oxen, and mountain goats.

Elsewhere in the store, Cabela's has created an African diorama, complete with African animals depicted in their natural habitats—an elephant, a rhinoceros, a Cape buffalo, and lions downing their prey. Other store attractions include a trophy deer museum and three walk-through aquariums, where visitors can view trophy-quality freshwater fish and learn to identify them. Getting hungry? Drop by the Mesquite Grill café for an elk, ostrich, or wild boar sandwich—no Big Macs here! The nearby General Store offers old-fashioned candy and snacks.

Most stores today cluster together to increase their customer pulling power and to give consumers the convenience of one-stop shopping. *Central business districts* were the main form of retail cluster until the 1950s. Every large city and town had a central business district with department stores, specialty stores, banks, and movie theaters. When people began to move to the suburbs, however, these central business districts, with their traffic, parking, and crime problems, began to lose business. Downtown merchants opened branches in suburban shopping centers, and the decline of the central business districts continued. In recent years, many cities have joined with merchants to try to revive downtown shopping areas by building malls and providing underground parking.

Shopping center
A group of retail businesses planned, developed, owned, and managed as a unit.

A **shopping center** is a group of retail businesses planned, developed, owned, and managed as a unit. A *regional shopping center*, or *regional shopping mall*, the largest and most dramatic shopping center, contains from 40 to over 200 stores. It is like a covered mini-downtown and attracts customers from a wide area. A *community shopping center* contains between 15 and 40 retail stores. It normally contains a branch of a department store or variety store, a supermarket, specialty stores, professional offices, and sometimes a bank. Most shopping centers are *neighborhood shopping centers or strip malls* that generally contain between 5 and 15 stores. They are close and convenient for consumers. They usually contain a supermarket, perhaps a discount store, and several service stores—dry cleaner, self-service laundry, drugstore, video-rental outlet, barber or beauty shop, hardware store, or other stores.

A recent addition to the shopping center scene is the so-called *power center.* These huge unenclosed shopping centers consist of a long strip of retail stores, including large, freestanding anchors such as Wal-Mart, Home Depot, Costco, Best Buy, Michaels, OfficeMax, and CompUSA. Each store has its own entrance with parking directly in front for shoppers who wish to visit only one store. Power centers have increased rapidly during the past few years to challenge traditional indoor malls.

Combined, the nation's nearly 48,500 shopping centers now account for about 75 percent of U.S. retail activity (not counting cars and gasoline). The average American makes 2.9 trips to the mall a month, shopping for an average of 80 minutes per trip and spending about $86. However, many experts suggest that America is now "over-malled." During the 1990s, mall shopping space grew at about twice the rate of population growth. As a result, as many as 20 percent of America's shopping malls are either dead or dying. There "is a glut of retail space," says one insider. "There's going to have to be a shakeout."[18]

Thus, despite the recent development of many new "megamalls," such as the spectacular Mall of America, the current trend is toward value-oriented outlet malls and power centers on the one hand, and smaller "lifestyle centers" on the other. These lifestyle centers—smaller malls with upscale stores, convenient locations, and expensive atmospheres—are usually located near affluent residential neighborhoods and cater to the retail needs of consumers in their areas. "Think of lifestyle centers as part Main Street and part Fifth Avenue," comments an industry observer. "The idea is to combine the hominess and community of an old-time village square with the cachet of fashionable urban stores; the smell and feel of a neighborhood park with the brute convenience of a strip center." The future of malls "will be all about creating places to be rather than just places to buy."[19]

■ Shopping centers: The spectacular Mall of America contains more than 520 specialty stores, 50 restaurants, a 7-acre indoor theme park, an Underwater World featuring hundreds of marine specimens and a dolphin show, and a two-story miniature golf course.

The Future of Retailing

Retailers operate in a harsh and fast-changing environment, which offers threats as well as opportunities. For example, the industry suffers from chronic overcapacity, resulting in fierce competition for customer dollars. Consumer demographics, lifestyles, and shopping patterns are changing rapidly, as are retailing technologies. To be successful, then, retailers will need to choose target segments carefully and position themselves strongly. They will need to take the following retailing developments into account as they plan and execute their competitive strategies.

New Retail Forms and Shortening Retail Life Cycles

New retail forms continue to emerge to meet new situations and consumer needs, but the life cycle of new retail forms is getting shorter. Department stores took about 100 years to reach the mature stage of the life cycle; more recent forms, such as warehouse stores, reached maturity in about 10 years. In such an environment, seemingly solid retail positions can crumble quickly. Of the top ten discount retailers in 1962 (the year that Wal-Mart and Kmart began), not one still exists today.

Consider the Price Club, the original warehouse store chain. When Sol Price pioneered his first warehouse store outside San Diego in 1976, he launched a retailing revolution. Selling everything from tires and office supplies to five-pound tubs of peanut butter at super low prices, his store chain was generating $2.6 billion a year in sales within 10 years. But Price refused to expand beyond its California base. And as the industry quickly matured, Price ran headlong into wholesale clubs run by such retail giants as Wal-Mart and Kmart. (In his autobiography, Sam Walton confesses: "I guess I've stolen—I actually prefer the word 'borrowed'—as many ideas from Sol Price as from anybody else in the business.") Only 17 years later, in a stunning reversal of fortune, a faltering Price sold out to competitor Costco. Price's rapid rise and fall shows that even the most successful retailers can't sit back with a winning formula. To remain successful, they must keep adapting.[20]

Many retailing innovations are partially explained by the **wheel-of-retailing concept**.[21] According to this concept, many new types of retailing forms begin as low-margin, low-price, low-status operations. They challenge established retailers that have become "fat" by letting their costs and margins increase. The new retailers' success leads them to upgrade their facilities and offer more services. In turn, their costs increase, forcing them to increase their prices. Eventually, the new retailers become like the conventional retailers they replaced. The cycle begins again when still newer types of retailers evolve with lower costs and prices. The wheel-of-retailing concept seems to explain the initial success and later troubles of department stores, supermarkets, and discount stores and the recent success of off-price retailers.

Growth of Nonstore Retailing

Most of us still make most of our purchases the old-fashioned way: We go to the store, find what we want, wait patiently in line to plunk down our cash or credit card, and bring home the goods. However, consumers now have an array of alternatives, including mail-order, television, phone, and online shopping. Americans are increasingly avoiding the hassles and crowds at malls by doing more of their shopping by phone or computer. Although such retailing advances may threaten some traditional retailers, they offer exciting opportunities for others. Most store retailers have now developed direct-retailing channels. In fact, more online retailing is conducted by "click-and-brick" retailers than by "click-only" retailers. In a recent ranking of the top 50 online retail sites, 35 were multichannel retailers.[22]

Online retailing is the newest form of nonstore retailing. Only a few years ago, prospects for online retailing were soaring. As more and more consumers flocked to the Web, some experts even saw a day when consumers would bypass stodgy "old economy" store retailers and do almost all of their shopping via the Internet. However, the dot-com meltdown of 2000 dashed these overblown expectations. Many once-brash Web sellers crashed and burned and expectations reversed almost overnight. The experts began to predict that e-tailing was destined to be little more than a tag-on to in-store retailing.

However, today's online retailing is alive, well, and growing. With easier-to-use Web sites, improved online service, and the increasing sophistication of search technologies, online business is booming. In fact, online buying is growing at a much brisker pace than retail buying as a whole. Last year's U.S. online retail sales reached $113.6 billion, a 28 percent leap over the previous year, representing 4.7 percent of all retail sales.[23]

All types of retailers now use the Web as an important marketing tool. The online sales of giant brick-and-mortar retailers, such as Sears, Wal-Mart, Staples, and Gap, are increasing rapidly. Several large click-only retailers—Amazon.com, online auction site eBay, online travel companies such as Travelocity and Expedia, and others—are now making it big on the Web. At the other extreme, hordes of niche marketers are using the Web to reach new markets and expand their sales. Today's more sophisticated search engines (Google, Yahoo!) and comparison shopping sites (Shopping.com, Buy.com, Shopzilla, and others) put almost any e-tailer within a mouse click or two's reach of millions of customers.

Still, much of the anticipated growth in online sales will go to multichannel retailers—the click-and-brick marketers who can successfully merge the virtual and physical worlds. Consider office-supply retailer Staples. Based on two years of research, Staples recently redesigned its Web site to extend its "Staples—That was easy" marketing promise to online shoppers. The retailer's online sales are now growing at an even faster clip than its store sales. Sales through Staples.com jumped 27 percent last year, now accounting for almost one-quarter of Staples's revenues. But Staples online operations aren't robbing from store sales. Instead, the in-store and online channels compliment one another. For example, customers can buy conveniently online and then return unwanted or defective merchandise to their local Staples store. And in-store Staples.com kiosks ensure that customers never leave the store without finding what they need. As a result, for example, the average yearly spending of small-business customers jumps more than fourfold when they combine shopping online with shopping in the store.[24]

■ Online retailing: Today's online retailing is alive, well, and growing, especially for click-and-brick retailers like Staples. Its Web site, staples.com, now accounts for almost one-quarter of sales. "That was easy!"

Retail Convergence

Today's retailers are increasingly selling the same products at the same prices to the same consumers in competition with a wider variety of other retailers. For example, you can buy books at outlets ranging from independent local bookstores to warehouse clubs such as Costco, superstores such as Barnes & Noble or Borders, or Web sites such as Amazon.com. When it comes to brand-name appliances, department stores, discount stores, home improvement stores, off-price retailers, electronics superstores, and a slew of Web sites all compete for the same customers. So if you can't find the microwave oven you want at Sears, just step across the street and find one for a better price at Lowe's or Home Depot—or just order one online from Amazon.com.

This merging of consumers, products, prices, and retailers is called *retail convergence*. "Where you go for what you want—that has created the biggest challenge facing retailers," says one retailing expert. "Customers of all income levels are shopping at the same stores, often for the same goods. Old distinctions such as discount store, specialty store, and department store are losing significance: The successful store must match a host of rivals on selection, service, and price."[25]

Such convergence means greater competition for retailers and greater difficulty in differentiating offerings. The competition between chain superstores and smaller, independently owned stores has become particularly heated. Because of their bulk-buying power and high sales volume, chains can buy at lower costs and thrive on smaller margins. The arrival of a superstore can quickly force nearby independents out of business. For example, the decision by electronics superstore Best Buy to sell CDs as loss leaders at rock-bottom prices pushed a number of specialty record-store chains into bankruptcy. And with its everyday low prices, Wal-Mart has been accused of destroying independents in countless small towns around the country who sell the same merchandise.

Yet the news is not all bad for smaller companies. Many small, independent retailers are thriving. They are finding that sheer size and marketing muscle are often no match for the personal touch small stores can provide or the specialty merchandise niches that small stores fill for a devoted customer base.

The Rise of Megaretailers

The rise of huge mass merchandisers and specialty superstores, the formation of vertical marketing systems, and a rash of retail mergers and acquisitions have created a core of superpower megaretailers. Through their superior information systems and buying power, these giant retailers can offer better merchandise selections, good service, and strong price savings to consumers. As a result, they grow even larger by squeezing out their smaller, weaker competitors.

The megaretailers are also shifting the balance of power between retailers and producers. A relative handful of retailers now control access to enormous numbers of consumers, giving them the upper hand in their dealings with manufacturers. For example, in the United States, Wal-Mart's revenues are more than five times those of Procter & Gamble, and Wal-Mart generates almost 20 percent of P&G's revenues. Wal-Mart can, and often does, use this power to wring concessions from P&G and other suppliers.[26]

Growing Importance of Retail Technology

Retail technologies are becoming critically important as competitive tools. Progressive retailers are using advanced information technology and software systems to produce better forecasts, control inventory costs, order electronically from suppliers, send information between stores, and even sell to customers within stores. They are adopting checkout scanning systems, online transaction processing, electronic data interchange, in-store television, and improved merchandise-handling systems.

Perhaps the most startling advances in retailing technology concern the ways in which today's retailers are connecting with customers. Many retailers now routinely use technologies such as touch-screen kiosks, customer-loyalty cards, electronic shelf labels and signs, handheld shopping assistants, smart cards, self-scanning systems, and virtual-reality displays. For example, in its new pilot store—Bloom—southeastern grocery chain Food Lion is using technology to make shopping easier for its customers:

Ever stood in the wine aisle at the grocery store and felt intimidated? You think that bottle of Shiraz looks pretty good but you're not sure what it goes with. It's the sort of problem the creators of Food Lion's new concept store —Bloom—thought about, and one they will use technology to solve. The store relies on technology to enhance the shopping experience and to help customers find products, get information, and check out with greater ease. A computerized kiosk in the wine section lets you scan a bottle and get serving suggestions. The kiosk, and a second one in the meat section, lets you print recipes off the screen. Eight stations with touch screens and scanners around the store let you check an item's price or locate it on the map. To make it easier to keep track of purchases and check out, you can pick up a personal handheld scanner as you walk in the door, then scan and bag items as you shop. Checkout then is just a simple matter of paying as you leave. The personal scanners also give you a running total of the items you've selected as you shop, helping you stay within your budget and avoid surprises at the checkout. And if you drop off a prescription, the pharmacy can send a message to your scanner when your order is ready.[27]

■ Retail technology: In its new pilot store—Bloom—Southeastern grocery chain Food Lion is using technology to make shopping easier for its customers.

Global Expansion of Major Retailers

Retailers with unique formats and strong brand positioning are increasingly moving into other countries. Many are expanding internationally to escape mature and saturated home markets. Over the years, some giant U.S. retailers, such as McDonald's, have become globally prominent as a result of their marketing prowess. Others, such as Wal-Mart, are rapidly establishing a global presence. Wal-Mart, which now operates more than 2,700 stores in 14 countries abroad, sees exciting global potential. Its international division alone last year racked up sales of more than $67 billion, an increase of 11.4 percent over the previous year and 27 percent more than rival Target's *total* sales. Profits from international operations increased more than 26 percent last year.[28]

However, most U.S retailers are still significantly behind Europe and Asia when it comes to global expansion. Ten of the world's top 20 retailers are U.S. companies; only two of these retailers have set up stores outside of North America (Wal-Mart and Costco). Of the 10 non-U.S. retailers in the world's top 20, nine have stores in at least 10 countries. Among foreign retailers that have gone global are France's Carrefour, Germany's Metro and Aldi chains, the Netherlands' Royal Ahold, Britain's Tesco, Japan's Yaohan supermarkets, and Sweden's IKEA home furnishings stores.[29]

French discount retailer Carrefour, the world's second-largest retailer after Wal-Mart, has embarked on an aggressive mission to extend its role as a leading international retailer:

The Carrefour Group has an interest in more than 12,000 stores in 29 countries in Europe, Asia, and the Americas, including 926 hypermarkets. It leads Europe in supermarkets and the world in hypermarkets. Carrefour is outpacing Wal-Mart in several emerging markets, including South America, China, and the Pacific Rim. It's the leading retailer in Brazil and Argentina, where it operates close to 1,000 stores, compared to Wal-Mart's 300 units in those two countries. Carrefour is the largest foreign retailer in China, where it operates more than 300 stores versus Wal-Mart's 60. In short, Carrefour is forging ahead of Wal-Mart in most markets outside North America. The only question: Can the French retailer hold its lead? Although no one retailer can safely claim to be in the same league with Wal-Mart as an overall retail presence, Carrefour stands a better chance than most to hold its own in global retailing.[30]

Retail Stores as "Communities" or "Hangouts"

With the rise in the number of people living alone, working at home, or living in isolated and sprawling suburbs, there has been a resurgence of establishments that, regardless of the product or service they offer, also provide a place for people to get together. These places include coffee shops and cafes, shopping malls, bookstores, children's play spaces, super-stores, and urban greenmarkets. For example, today's bookstores have become part book-store, part library, part living room, and part coffee house. On an early evening at your local Barnes & Noble, you'll likely find back-pack-toting high school students doing homework with friends in the coffee bar. Nearby, retirees sit in cushy chairs thumbing through travel or gardening books while parents read aloud to their children. Barnes & Noble sells more than just books, it sells comfort, relaxation, and community.

And retailers don't create communities only in their brick-and-mortar stores. Many also build virtual communities on the Internet. For example, Nike creates community in its giant, interactive Niketown retail stores, but it also creates online gathering places:

In just over a decade, Nike's global soccer presence has grown dramatically—from roughly $40 million of sales in 1994 to almost $1.5 billion today. So, when Nike discovered that rival Adidas had gotten the exclusive deal to broadcast ads in the United States during the 2006 World Cup, it had to be innovative. In partnership with Google, Nike created Joga.com, a social networking site for soccer fans. Launched quietly in February of 2006, the site became an instant hit—a bustling online soccer community. More than 1 million members from 140 countries signed up by mid-July. On Joga.com, fans can blog, create communities around favorite teams or players, organize pickup games, download videos, and rant about the encroaching commercialism of the game. Some of the most downloaded videos are clips containing Nike products. According to one marketing analyst, "By enrolling consumers in shaping the [content], Nike is . . . nurturing deeper bonds of loyalty and advocacy." Nike's CEO agrees: "When someone joins a Nike community or invites Nike into their community, a strong relationship is created." [31]

■ Nike creates community in its giant, interactive Niketown retail stores, but it also creates community in its online gathering place, Joga.com, a social networking site that allows soccer fans to blog, create communities around favorite teams or players, organize pickup games, download videos, and rant about the encroaching commercialism of the game.

Wholesaling
All activities involved in selling goods and services to those buying for resale or business use.

Wholesaler
A firm engaged *primarily* in wholesaling activities.

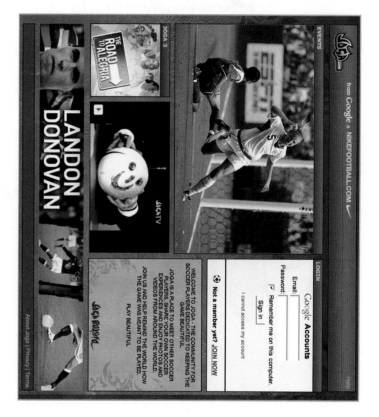

■ Wholesaling

Wholesaling includes all activities involved in selling goods and services to those buying for resale or business use. We call **wholesalers** those firms engaged *primarily* in wholesaling activities.

Wholesalers buy mostly from producers and sell mostly to retailers, industrial consumers, and other wholesalers. As a result, many of the nation's largest and most important wholesalers are largely unknown to final consumers. For example, you may never have heard of Grainger, even though it's very well known and much valued by its more than 1.7 million business and institutional customers across North America.

Grainger may be the biggest market leader you've never heard of. It's a $5.5 billion business that offers more than 800,000 maintenance, repair, and operating (MRO) products to more than 1.7 million customers. Through its branch network, service centers, sales reps, catalog, and Web site, Grainger links customers with the supplies they need to keep their facilities running smoothly—everything from light bulbs, cleaners, and display cases to nuts and bolts, motors, valves, power tools, and test equipment. Grainger's nearly 600 North American branches, 20 distribution centers, more than 16,700 employees, and innovative Web site handle more than 100,000 transactions a day. Its customers include organizations ranging from factories, garages, and grocers to schools and military bases. Most American businesses are located within 20 minutes of a Grainger branch. Customers include notables such as Abbott Laboratories, General Motors, Campbell Soup, American Airlines, DaimlerChrysler, and the U.S. Postal Service.

Grainger operates on a simple value proposition: to make it easier and less costly for customers to find and buy MRO supplies. It starts by acting as a one-stop shop for products to maintain facilities. On a broader level, it builds lasting relationships with customers by helping them find *solutions* to their overall MRO problems. Acting as consultants, Grainger sales reps help buyers with everything from improving their supply chain management to reducing inventories and streamlining warehousing operations. So, how come you've never heard of Grainger? Maybe it's because the company operates in the not-so-glamorous world of MRO supplies, which are important to every business but not so important to consumers. More likely, it's because Grainger is a wholesaler. And like most wholesalers, it operates behind the scenes, selling only to other businesses.[32]

■ Wholesaling: Many of the nation's largest and most important wholesalers—like Grainger—are largely unknown to final consumers. But they are very well known and much valued by the business customers they serve.

Why are wholesalers important to sellers? For example, why would a producer use wholesalers rather than selling directly to retailers or consumers? Simply put, wholesalers add value by performing one or more of the following channel functions:

■ *Selling and promoting:* Wholesalers' sales forces help manufacturers reach many small customers at a low cost. The wholesaler has more contacts and is often more trusted by the buyer than the distant manufacturer.

■ *Buying and assortment building:* Wholesalers can select items and build assortments needed by their customers, thereby saving the consumers much work.

■ *Bulk-breaking:* Wholesalers save their customers money by buying in carload lots and breaking bulk (breaking large lots into small quantities).

■ *Warehousing:* Wholesalers hold inventories, thereby reducing the inventory costs and risks of suppliers and customers.

■ *Transportation:* Wholesalers can provide quicker delivery to buyers because they are closer than the producers.

■ *Financing:* Wholesalers finance their customers by giving credit, and they finance their suppliers by ordering early and paying bills on time.

■ *Risk bearing:* Wholesalers absorb risk by taking title and bearing the cost of theft, damage, spoilage, and obsolescence.

■ *Market information:* Wholesalers give information to suppliers and customers about competitors, new products, and price developments.

■ *Management services and advice:* Wholesalers often help retailers train their salesclerks, improve store layouts and displays, and set up accounting and inventory control systems.

Types of Wholesalers

Wholesalers fall into three major groups (see Table 13.3): *merchant wholesalers, agents and brokers,* and *manufacturers' sales branches and offices.* **Merchant wholesalers** are the largest single group of wholesalers, accounting for roughly 50 percent of all wholesaling. Merchant wholesalers include two broad types: full-service wholesalers and limited-service wholesalers. *Full-service wholesalers* provide a full set of services, whereas the various *limited-service wholesalers* offer fewer services to their suppliers and customers. The several different

Merchant wholesaler
Independently owned business that takes title to the merchandise it handles.

TABLE 13.3 Major Types of Wholesalers

Type	Description
Merchant wholesalers	Independently owned businesses that take title to the merchandise they handle. In different trades they are called *jobbers*, *distributors*, or *mill supply houses*. They include *full-service wholesalers* and *limited-service wholesalers*.
Full-service wholesalers	Provide a full line of services: carrying stock, maintaining a sales force, offering credit, making deliveries, and providing management assistance. There are two types:
Wholesale merchants	Sell primarily to retailers and provide a full range of services. *General merchandise wholesalers* carry several merchandise lines, whereas *general line wholesalers* carry one or two lines in great depth. *Specialty wholesalers* specialize in carrying only part of a line. Examples: health food wholesalers, seafood wholesalers.
Industrial distributors	Sell to manufacturers rather than to retailers. Provide several services, such as carrying stock, offering credit, and providing delivery. May carry a broad range of merchandise, a general line, or a specialty line.
Limited-service wholesalers	Offer fewer services than full-service wholesalers. Limited-service wholesalers are of several types:
Cash-and-carry wholesalers	Carry a limited line of fast-moving goods and sell to small retailers for cash. Normally do not deliver. Example: A small fish store retailer may drive to a cash-and-carry fish wholesaler, buy fish for cash, and bring the merchandise back to the store.
Truck wholesalers (or truck jobbers)	Perform primarily a selling and delivery function. Carry limited line of semiperishable merchandise (such as milk, bread, snack foods), which they sell for cash as they make their rounds to supermarkets, small groceries, hospitals, restaurants, factory cafeterias, and hotels.
Drop shippers	Do not carry inventory or handle the product. On receiving an order, they select a manufacturer, who ships the merchandise directly to the customer. The drop shipper assumes title and risk from the time the order is accepted to its delivery to the customer. They operate in bulk industries, such as coal, lumber, and heavy equipment.
Rack jobbers	Serve grocery and drug retailers, mostly in nonfood items. They send delivery trucks to stores, where the delivery people set up toys, paperbacks, hardware items, health and beauty aids, or other items. They price the goods, keep them fresh, set up point-of-purchase displays, and keep inventory records. Rack jobbers retain title to the goods and bill the retailers only for the goods sold to consumers.
Producers' cooperatives	Are owned by farmer members and assemble farm produce to sell in local markets. The co-op's profits are distributed to members at the end of the year. They often attempt to improve product quality and promote a co-op brand name, such as Sun Maid raisins, Sunkist oranges, or Diamond walnuts.
Mail-order wholesalers	Send catalogs to retail, industrial, and institutional customers featuring jewelry, cosmetics, specialty foods, and other small items. Maintain no outside sales force. Main customers are businesses in small outlying areas. Orders are filled and sent by mail, truck, or other transportation.
Brokers and agents	Do not take title to goods. Main function is to facilitate buying and selling, for which they earn a commission on the selling price. Generally specialize by product line or customer type.
Brokers	Chief function is bringing buyers and sellers together and assisting in negotiation. They are paid by the party who hired them and do not carry inventory, get involved in financing, or assume risk. Examples: food brokers, real estate brokers, insurance brokers, and security brokers.
Agents	Represent either buyers or sellers on a more permanent basis than brokers do. There are several types:
Manufacturers' agents	Represent two or more manufacturers of complementary lines. A formal written agreement with each manufacturer covers pricing, territories, order handling, delivery service and warranties, and commission rates. Often used in such lines as apparel, furniture, and electrical goods. Most manufacturers' agents are small businesses, with only a few skilled salespeople as employees. They are hired by small manufacturers who cannot afford their own field sales forces and by large manufacturers who use agents to open new territories or to cover territories that cannot support full-time salespeople.

(continues)

TABLE 13.3 Major Types of Wholesalers—*continued*

Type	Description
Selling agents	Have contractual authority to sell a manufacturer's entire output. The manufacturer either is not interested in the selling function or feels unqualified. The selling agent serves as a sales department and has significant influence over prices, terms, and conditions of sale. Found in product areas such as textiles, industrial machinery and equipment, coal and coke, chemicals, and metals.
Purchasing agents	Generally have a long-term relationship with buyers and make purchases for them, often receiving, inspecting, warehousing, and shipping the merchandise to the buyers. They provide helpful market information to clients and help them obtain the best goods and prices available.
Commission merchants	Take physical possession of products and negotiate sales. Normally, they are not employed on a long-term basis. Used most often in agricultural marketing by farmers who do not want to sell their own output and do not belong to producers' cooperatives. The commission merchant takes a truckload of commodities to a central market, sells it for the best price, deducts a commission and expenses, and remits the balance to the producers.
Manufacturers' and retailers' branches and offices	Wholesaling operations conducted by sellers or buyers themselves rather than through independent wholesalers. Separate branches and offices can be dedicated to either sales or purchasing.
Sales branches and offices	Set up by manufacturers to improve inventory control, selling, and promotion. *Sales branches* carry inventory and are found in industries such as lumber and automotive equipment and parts. *Sales offices* do not carry inventory and are most prominent in dry-goods and notions industries.
Purchasing officers	Perform a role similar to that of brokers or agents but are part of the buyer's organization. Many retailers set up purchasing offices in major market centers such as New York and Chicago.

types of limited-service wholesalers perform varied specialized functions in the distribution channel.

Brokers and *agents* differ from merchant wholesalers in two ways: They do not take title to goods, and they perform only a few functions. Like merchant wholesalers, they generally specialize by product line or customer type. A **broker** brings buyers and sellers together and assists in negotiation. **Agents** represent buyers or sellers on a more permanent basis. *Manufacturers' agents* (also called manufacturers' representatives) are the most common type of agent wholesaler. The third major type of wholesaling is that done in **manufacturers' sales branches and offices** by sellers or buyers themselves rather than through independent wholesalers.

Wholesaler Marketing Decisions

Wholesalers now face growing competitive pressures, more demanding customers, new technologies, and more direct-buying programs on the part of large industrial, institutional, and retail buyers. As a result, they have taken a fresh look at their marketing strategies. As with retailers, their marketing decisions include choices of target markets, positioning, and the marketing mix—product assortments and services, price, promotion, and place (see Figure 13.2).

Target Market and Positioning Decision

Like retailers, wholesalers must define their target markets and position themselves effectively—they cannot serve everyone. They can choose a target group by size of customer (only large retailers), type of customer (convenience stores only), need for service (customers who need credit), or other factors. Within the target group, they can identify the more profitable customers, design stronger offers, and build better relationships with them. They can propose automatic reordering systems, set up management-training and advising systems, or even sponsor a voluntary chain. They can discourage less profitable customers by requiring larger orders or adding service charges to smaller ones.

Broker
A wholesaler who does not take title to goods and whose function is to bring buyers and sellers together and assist in negotiation.

Agent
A wholesaler who represents buyers or sellers on a relatively permanent basis, performs only a few functions, and does not take title to goods.

Manufacturers' sales branches and offices
Wholesaling by sellers or buyers themselves rather than through independent wholesalers.

FIGURE 13.2
Wholesaler marketing
decisions

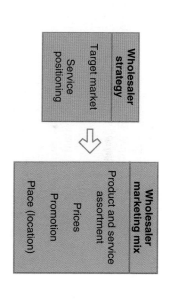

Wholesaler strategy		Wholesaler marketing mix
Target market		Product and service assortment
Service positioning		Prices
		Promotion
		Place (location)

Marketing Mix Decisions

Like retailers, wholesalers must decide on product assortment and services, prices, promotion, and place. The wholesaler's "product" is the assortment of *products and services* that it offers. Wholesalers are under great pressure to carry a full line and to stock enough for immediate delivery. But this practice can damage profits. Wholesalers today are cutting down on the number of lines they carry, choosing to carry only the more profitable ones. Wholesalers are also rethinking which services count most in building strong customer relationships and which should be dropped or charged for. The key is to find the mix of services most valued by their target customers.

Price is also an important wholesaler decision. Wholesalers usually mark up the cost of goods by a standard percentage—say, 20 percent. Expenses may run 17 percent of the gross margin, leaving a profit margin of 3 percent. In grocery wholesaling, the average profit margin is often less than 2 percent. Wholesalers are trying new pricing approaches. They may cut their margin on some lines in order to win important new customers. They may ask suppliers for special price breaks when they can turn them into an increase in the supplier's sales.

Although *promotion* can be critical to wholesaler success, most wholesalers are not promotion minded. Their use of trade advertising, sales promotion, personal selling, and public relations is largely scattered and unplanned. Many are behind the times in personal selling—they still see selling as a single salesperson talking to a single customer instead of as a team effort to sell, build, and service major accounts. Wholesalers also need to adopt some of the nonpersonal promotion techniques used by retailers. They need to develop an overall promotion strategy and to make greater use of supplier promotion materials and programs.

Finally, *place* is important—wholesalers must choose their locations, facilities, and Web locations carefully. Wholesalers typically locate in low-rent, low-tax areas and tend to invest little money in their buildings, equipment, and systems. As a result, their materials-handling and order-processing systems are often outdated. In recent years, however, large and progressive wholesalers are reacting to rising costs by investing in automated warehouses and online ordering systems. Orders are fed from the retailer's system directly into the wholesaler's computer, and the items are picked up by mechanical devices and automatically taken to a shipping platform where they are assembled. Most large wholesalers are using technology to carry out accounting, billing, inventory control, and forecasting. Modern wholesalers are adapting their services to the needs of target customers and finding cost-reducing methods of doing business.

Trends in Wholesaling

Today's wholesalers face considerable challenges. The industry remains vulnerable to one of the most enduring trends of the last decade—fierce resistance to price increases and the winnowing out of suppliers who are not adding value based on cost and quality. Progressive wholesalers constantly watch for better ways to meet the changing needs of their suppliers and target customers. They recognize that, in the long run, their only reason for existence comes from adding value by increasing the efficiency and effectiveness of the entire marketing channel. For example, Grainger succeeds by making life easier and more efficient for the commercial and institutional buyers and sellers it serves:

Beyond making it easier for customers to find the products they need, Grainger also helps them streamline their acquisition processes. For most companies, acquiring MRO supplies is a very costly process. In fact, 40 percent of the cost of MRO supplies stems from the purchase process, including finding a supplier, negotiating the best deal, placing the order, receiving the order, and paying the invoice. Grainger constantly seeks ways to reduce the costs associated with MRO supplies acquisition, both internally and externally. One company found that working with Grainger cut MRO requisition time by more than 60 percent; lead times went from days to hours. Its supply chain dropped from 12,000 suppliers to 560—significantly reducing expenses. Similarly, a large timber and paper-products company has come to appreciate Grainger's selection and stream-lined ordering process. It orders two-thirds of its supplies from Grainger's Web site at an annual acquisition cost of only $300,000. By comparison, for the remainder of its needs, this company deals with more than 1,300 small distributors at an acquisition cost of $2.4 million each year—eight times the cost of dealing with Grainger for half of the vol-ume. The company is now looking for ways to buy all of its MRO supplies from Grainger. As one Grainger branch manager puts it, "If we don't save [customers] time and money every time they come [to us], they won't come back."[33]

McKesson, the nation's leading wholesaler of pharmaceuticals, health and beauty care, home health care, and medical supply and equipment products, provides another example of progressive, value-adding wholesaling. To survive, McKesson has to remain more cost effec-tive than manufacturers' sales branches. Thus, the company has built efficient automated warehouses, established direct computer links with drug manufacturers, and set up extensive online supply-management and accounts-receivable systems for customers. It offers retail pharmacists a wide range of online resources, including supply-management assistance, cata-log searches, real-time order tracking, and an account-management system. It has also created solutions such as automated pharmaceutical-dispensing machines that assist pharmacists by reducing costs and improving accuracy.

Retailers can even use the McKesson system to maintain medical profiles on their cus-tomers. McKesson's medical-surgical supply and equipment customers receive a rich assortment of online solutions and supply-management tools, including an online order-management sys-tem and real-time information on products and pricing, inventory availability, and order status. According to McKesson, it adds value in the channel by providing "supply, information, and health-care-management products and services designed to reduce costs and improve quality across health care."[34]

The distinction between large retailers and large wholesalers continues to blur. Many retailers now operate formats such as wholesale clubs and hypermarkets that perform many wholesale functions. In return, many large wholesalers are setting up their own retailing oper-ations. For example, until recently, SuperValu was classified as a food wholesaler, with a majority of its business derived from supplying grocery products to independent grocery retailers. However, over the past decade, SuperValu has started or acquired several retail food chains of its own—including Albertsons, Jewel-Osco, Save-A-Lot, Cub Foods, and others—to become the nation's third-largest food retailer. Thus, even though it remains the country's largest food wholesaler, because 80 percent of its $44 billion in sales come from retailing, SuperValu is now classified as a retailer.[35]

Wholesalers will continue to increase the services they provide to retailers—retail pricing, cooperative advertising, marketing and management information reports, accounting services, online transactions, and others. Rising costs on the one hand, and the demand for increased services on the other, will put the squeeze on wholesaler profits. Wholesalers who do not find efficient ways to deliver value to their customers will soon drop by the wayside. However, the increased use of computerized, automated, and Web-based systems will help wholesalers to contain the costs of ordering, shipping, and inventory holding, boosting their productivity.

Finally, facing slow growth in their domestic markets and such developments as the North American Free Trade Agreement, many large wholesalers are now going global. For example, in 1991, McKesson bought out its Canadian partner, Provigo. The company now receives about 3 percent of its total revenues from Canada. Its Information Solutions group operates widely throughout North America, the United Kingdom, and other European countries.

Reviewing the Concepts

In this chapter, we looked at the nature and importance of retailing, major types of retailers, the decisions retailers make, and the future of retailing. We then examined these same topics for wholesalers.

1. **Explain the roles of retailers and wholesalers in the distribution channel.**
   Retailing and wholesaling consist of many organizations bringing goods and services from the point of production to the point of use. *Retailing* includes all activities involved in selling goods or services

directly to final consumers for their personal, nonbusiness use. *Wholesaling* includes all the activities involved in selling goods or ser-vices to those who are buying for the purpose of resale or for business use. Wholesalers perform many functions, including selling and pro-moting, buying and assortment building, bulk breaking, warehousing, transporting, financing, risk bearing, supplying market information, and providing management services and advice.

2. Describe the major types of retailers and give examples of each.

Retail stores come in all shapes and sizes, and new retail types keep emerging. Store retailers can be classified by the *amount of service* they provide (self-service, limited service, or full service), *product line sold* (specialty stores, department stores, supermarkets, convenience stores, superstores, and service businesses), and *relative prices* (discount stores and off-price retailers). Today, many retailers are banding together in corporate and contractual *retail organizations* (corporate chains, voluntary chains and retailer cooperatives, franchise organizations, and merchandising conglomerates).

3. Describe the major types of wholesalers and give examples of each.

Wholesalers fall into three groups. First, *merchant wholesalers* take possession of the goods. They include *full-service wholesalers* (wholesale merchants, industrial distributors) and *limited-service wholesalers* (cash-and-carry wholesalers, truck wholesalers, drop shippers, rack jobbers, producers' cooperatives, and mail-order

wholesalers). Second, *brokers and agents* do not take possession of the goods but are paid a commission for aiding buying and selling. Finally, *manufacturers' sales branches and offices* are wholesaling operations conducted by nonwholesalers to bypass the wholesalers.

4. Explain the marketing decisions facing retailers and wholesalers.

Each retailer must make decisions about its target markets and positioning, product assortment and services, price, promotion, and place. Retailers need to choose target markets carefully and position themselves strongly. Today, wholesaling is holding its own in the economy. Progressive wholesalers are adapting their services to the needs of target customers and are seeking cost-reducing methods of doing business. Faced with slow growth in their domestic markets and developments such as the North American Free Trade Agreement, many large wholesalers are also now going global.

Reviewing the Key Terms

Agent 388	Factory outlet 371	Off-price retailer 370
Broker 388	Franchise 373	Retailer 367
Category killer 369	Independent off-price retailer 371	Retailing 367
Chain stores 372	Manufacturers' sales branches and offices 388	Shopping center 380
Convenience store 368	Merchant wholesaler 386	Specialty store 368
Department store 368		Supermarket 368
Discount store 370		Superstore 369

Warehouse club 372	
Wheel-of-retailing concept 381	
Wholesaler 385	
Wholesaling 385	

Discussing the Concepts

1. Why have warehouse clubs grown in popularity over the past several years?

2. Describe the similarities and differences between corporate chain stores and franchise organizations.

3. Explain why it is important for retailers to define their target markets and to decide how they will position themselves in these markets. Give an example of a national specialty retailer that has done this well.

4. What is the wheel-of-retailing concept? Does it apply to online retailing?

5. What is retail convergence? How has it helped or harmed small retailers?

6. What is the primary challenge facing a wholesaler who wishes to remain a viable part of the marketing channel? Explain.

Applying the Concepts

1. Choose three retailers that you buy from often. Classify these retailers in terms of the characteristics presented in the chapter. Next, use Table 13.1 to categorize each retailer.

2. Jordan's Furniture differentiates itself through its store atmosphere. Visit it on the Web at www.jordans.com and take a virtual tour of its

Natick store. Does Jordan's Furniture do a good job of differentiating itself?

3. Suppose that you are a manufacturer's agent for three lines of complementary women's apparel. Discuss what types of marketing mix decisions you will be making.

Focus on Technology

Imagine having a friend who helps you with your grocery shopping by reminding you about how much you have spent, what you usually purchase, and what's on sale this week that you have purchased in the past. Stop & Shop Supermarket Company, the largest food retailer in New England, will soon introduce the Shopping Buddy. According to the company, "Shopping Buddy can help you organize your shopping trip and save money! The Shopping Buddy is a small tablet that you activate with your Stop & Shop card. Once activated, the Shopping Buddy displays your personal savings coupons and shopping history by aisle, based on your location. It's easy to see the things that you normally buy that are on

sale in each aisle. You can also use Buddy to keep a running total of today's purchases, order deli without waiting in line, and scan and bag your items as you shop for quick checkout." Stop & Shop will soon be testing this new technology in 20 of its 360 stores.

1. What advantages does Stop & Shop gain by offering this technology?

2. What do you think of the Shopping Buddy concept? Would you use this technology?

3. Visit Stop & Shop at www.stopandshop.com. What other services does this retailer offer that differentiate its store from competitors' stores?

Focus on Ethics

Purchase a television, computer, or other electronic device and you are bound to be asked whether you would like to purchase a service contract. Most large electronics retailers carefully train their salespeople and cashiers to ask this important question. In fact, some retailers urge their salespeople to exert strong sales pressure to sell these contracts. It's no wonder, because service contracts provide extremely high profits for the retailers, several times the profit margins realized from the equipment you are purchasing. But do you know when to say yes and when to pass on a contract? Most consumers are confused and will buy the contract because the price seems low in comparison to the price of that new

plasma television. Experts, such as those at Consumer Reports, generally recommend that buyers pass on these contracts. With increased product reliability and decreasing prices that make replacement more reasonable, such contracts are rarely worth the price. If most consumers do not need them, should retailers continue to offer and promote them?

1. Is it ethical for retailers to offer and strongly promote service contracts?

2. When should you purchase a service contract?

3. Why do retailers continue to offer these contracts, even under criticism from customer advocacy groups?

Video Case   Wellbeing

In 2003, Dan Wales and Matt Lennox opened their first Wellbeing restaurant. Their goal was to offer consumers a healthy alternative to typical fast-food options. Working with fresh ingredients, bright and open stores, and a well-crafted, healthy menu, the new chain offered something new. "There are few truly healthy fast-food chains," says Wales. "People have been desperate for healthy options." So it came as no surprise that customers responded with enthusiasm to Wellbeing's new choices as they gobbled up sandwiches, salads, soups, juices, smoothies, and fruit salads. In only a few years, the chain has expanded to 18 stores and expects to nearly double that number in the next two years.

After viewing the video featuring Wellbeing, answer the following questions about retailing and wholesaling.

1. Categorize Wellbeing according to the four characteristics of retailers discussed in the chapter.

2. How is Wellbeing positioned in the marketplace? Which consumers does the chain target? Are its product assortment, pricing, promotion, and place decisions consistent with this targeting and positioning?

3. Which trend affecting the future of retailing do you think will most impact Wellbeing in the coming years?

Company Case   Peapod: Thriving in the World of Online Groceries

After years of marketing consumer products for both Procter & Gamble and Kraft Foods, Andrew Parkinson was ready for a change. His brother Thomas, who owned a software company, was also ready for something new. The two decided to partner and enter the online grocery business. Given that the Internet grocery business has produced a high number of casualties, it may seem that venture was a suicide mission. But this case is very different from that of other online grocery companies. Andrew and Thomas Parkinson made their decision to start a company selling groceries online in 1989, years before the Internet and the World Wide Web would become available to the public. Today, not only is their company, Peapod LLC, still in business, it is the leader in online grocery retailing.

FROM IDEA TO REALITY

For decades, the retail grocery industry has been characterized by fierce competition, low margins, and powerful chains. In the late 1980s, most of these chains differentiated themselves based on price. But the Parkinson broth-

ers perceived a niche that was not being satisfied by grocers. In the early 1900s, the most common way to purchase groceries was through a full-service neighborhood grocer. However, not since the industry made the shift to the more-familiar supermarket format has a grocery chain focused on differentiation through full service. The Parkinson brothers not only saw this as an opportunity, they wanted to take the service concept further than it had ever been taken. Their vision included giving customers the ability to place orders from their homes at any hour of the day, have the orders hand assembled and then have them delivered to customers' homes, even to be placed on the kitchen counter if desired.

Aspiring to succeed in the online grocery business in 1989 was indeed a pioneering venture. At that time, the general public had no concept of online communications. Peapod had to supply customers with a modem and software that would allow their home PCs to dial in and communicate with the company system. Given that most customers had never used a modem, they had to be taught how to do that as well. In the first few years of operations, Peapod focused exclusively on the metro Chicago area. Andrew and Thomas took care of all the aspects of running the business, from selling the service to packing orders and delivering them in their own cars.

From the beginning, Andrew and Thomas settled on a concept that would serve as the foundation for their business model: partnering with existing grocery chains. Rather than trying to tackle the challenges of online order fulfillment along with those of starting a freestanding grocery chain, it was clear to them that it would be better to serve as the order and delivery service for existing chains. In Chicago in the early 1990s, they partnered with Jewel Food Stores. As Peapod grew, they partnered with Safeway in San Francisco, Kroger in Columbus, and Stop & Shop in Boston. In 2001, Netherlands-based Royal Ahold, the parent company of Stop & Shop, purchased all existing shares of Peapod, making it a wholly owned subsidiary. This not only provided capital, it created a direct partnership with Stop & Shop and Giant, another Royal Ahold grocery chain on the east coast.

As of 2006, Peapod has delivered more than eight million orders to over 240,000 customers. It currently serves the Chicago area as well as east coast metropolitan markets where Stop & Shop and Giant have a presence. The online grocer assembles orders in one of two 75,000-square-foot warehouses, and in more than a dozen 7,500-square-foot "warerooms" located adjacent to partner stores. Although Peapod is far from providing service on a national level, the company covers 1,500 zip codes containing almost 13,000,000 households. Peapod has grown conservatively, yet it has averaged 25 percent annual revenue increases, a phenomenal feat in an industry characterized by single-digit growth rates.

PROVIDING CUSTOMER VALUE BY OVERCOMING NEGATIVE PERCEPTIONS

Customers most commonly cite convenience as their reason for purchasing groceries online. Many find the benefit of grocery shopping at any hour of the day from the comfort of home or the office very motivating. Yet many potential customers perceive numerous disadvantages that prevent them from ever trying online grocery services. The Parkinson brothers have always focused on providing customer value by addressing the following commonly perceived disadvantages.

Ordering on the Web is too complex and time consuming. Retail experts have widely recognized that the Internet is not well suited to shopping for and purchasing low-dollar, routinely purchased consumables. If it takes customers 30 minutes online to find the type and brand of bread, milk, cheese, and apples they want, they might as well just stop by the store on the way home from work. The basic Peapod system requires an initial account setup that includes establishing a shopping list of commonly purchased items. Given that most people buy many of the same items regularly, this list becomes the basis for

each order. The customer's core list is flexible to additions and deletions. As customers purchase new items, the Peapod system remembers those items and makes them available for future purchases without searching. Being able to quickly find an item through a keyword search can be much easier than trying to locate the same item in the aisles of a grocery store.

Finding new items is enhanced by Express Shop. This feature lets shoppers jot down an entire list and then provides matching products instantly. Any resulting products being compared can be sorted by price, nutritional content (sodium, fat, carbs, etc.), or even best-seller status. In a similar manner, shoppers can also personalize their lists around dietary needs or recipe requirements. To keep searching and browsing simple, Peapod offers a maximum of 8,000 items, as opposed to the 30,000 to 40,000 items available in the typical partner store.

People often do not know what they want until they browse the store. Even as customers go to the store with shopping lists, they often discover things as they walk the aisles. The Peapod Web site approximates in-store shopping by letting the customer browse for products in a traditional grocery store aisle format if they choose. Additionally, a "New Arrivals" icon highlights new products that customers might not think of before shopping. Shoppers can also easily find hundreds of weekly specials by clicking on the "Specials" tab, or by looking for red tags in normal browsing.

The quality of the delivered products might not be as good. The vast majority of food purchased in grocery stores is prepackaged. However, a commonly cited reason consumers give for not getting groceries online is that an unknown, unseen person will select their produce, meats, and bakery items. EMarketing analyst David Berkowitz says, "People who go in and feel fruit have no idea what they're doing, but it's still so important for them."

However, Peapod believes that it can do a better job of selecting foods and of transporting those foods in a way that maximizes quality. It trains order assemblers so that they know what to look for in a piece of produce. "I would pick your fruit the way I pick fruit for myself," said one trained shopper. Many customers don't stop to consider that the interior of a car on a hot summer day can wreak havoc on fresh produce, dairy products, and frozen foods. But Peapod equips its facilities and delivery vans with multiple climate-controlled zones, so the produce stays warm, the produce stays cool, and the ice cream stays rock hard.

Online groceries are too high priced. For the most part, Peapod's grocery prices match those found in partner stores. Peapod adds a modest flat fee that covers the cost of delivery: $6.95 for orders greater than $100 and $9.95 for orders between $50 and $100 (orders have a $50 minimum). Moreover, Peapod offers easily located "in-store" specials,

(case continues)

(case continued)

and drivers accept all manufacturer coupons and credits them to the next order.

Waiting to meet the delivery person is too inconvenient. When considering Peapod's delivery option, many potential customers envision spending hours "waiting for the cable installer." In actuality, customers can choose a two-hour delivery window that is convenient for them. What's more, they can place orders seven days a week, to be delivered as soon as the next day or as far as two weeks ahead. For people living in high-rise apartments, orders can be left with the doorman at any time.

THE COMPETITIVE LANDSCAPE

The first thing that comes to mind when most people think of online groceries is the string of high-profile dot-com failures of the late 1990s. The most notable failure was Webvan in California. Despite its grandiose predictions, the company burned through $830 million in venture capital and declared bankruptcy in 2001, without ever turning a profit. Experts now agree that Webvan grew too fast and took on too many of the aspects of the business without first establishing a foundation.

Whereas examples such as Webvan have left most people with the impression that the Internet grocery business failed completely, other companies have been slowly and quietly expanding. Peapod's growth model allowed the company not only to achieve operational stability prior to the dot-com blitz of online grocers but also to weather the storm and emerge strong and profitable. Since the dot-com bust, Peapod and others have gone quietly about their business. The current list of notable online grocers consists almost entirely of existing grocery chain companies that have ventured into the online sector. The list includes Safeway, Albertson's, Pathmark, Shoprite, Waldbaum's, Roche Bros., and Sam's Club. New York-based Freshdirect.com is the only other online grocer without a brick-and-mortar chain to have achieved a measurable level of success.

Each of these companies has rolled out services on a regional basis. The regions generally correspond to where chains have a brick-and-mortar presence. Companies are also wisely expanding in urban areas that are densely populated with potential customers that fit the profile. That profile is characterized by affluent, Internet-savvy, time-pressed consumers. This includes high-income households that are also two-paycheck or single-parent households. As a secondary market, people with physical disabilities are attracted to grocery delivery service.

Because the existing Internet grocers serve only select regional areas, they are often not in competition with each other. The most notable competitors of Peapod are Safeway in the Washington D.C./Baltimore area, Roche Bros. in Boston and Cape Cod, and Freshdirect.com in Westchester County, New York. These companies have many comparable features. But each company also has some points of differentiation. For example, Roche Bros. does not have a minimum order price, offers 20,000 items, and does not allow tipping (Peapod encourages it).

These points of differentiation don't concern Peapod much at this time. In any given market, Peapod faces at most one other formidable competitor. And although some experts have questioned whether or not a single metro area can support two major online grocers, Peapod believes that there is plenty of business to go around. Addressing the issue of competition, Peapod spokesperson Elana Margolis is more welcoming than concerned. "It validates the service. People are recognizing what we've realized all along, that people want options," she says. "It's a big enough market I think it can hold more than one grocery delivery business."

The industry is indeed growing. Whereas many local chains have experienced varying degrees of success with online sales, the major players are doing well. According to Jupiter Research analyst Patti Freeman Evans, online grocery sales reached $2.4 billion in 2004, just 0.4 percent of the total $570 billion grocery market. However, by 2008, overall online grocery sales are expected to hit $6.5 billion. Although that still represents only about 1 percent of the total market, it amounts to an annual growth rate of 42 percent, as much as 10 times that of the overall industry. Safeway expects that Internet sales could account for up to 5 percent of its total sales within a few years, without significant cannibalization.

If the past is any predictor of success, Peapod has a bright future. However, as overall sales for online grocers continue to grow, Peapod and its competitors will likely find emerging challenges. According to Claes Fornell, a professor of business at the University of Michigan, "more Internet shopping options have given consumers the upper hand in brick-and-mortar retail stores. [Consumers] are more powerful relative to the seller than they ever have been in the past. There is more pressure on the company to try to satisfy the customer." As Peapod continues to face the challenges of growing its business today, it will likely deal with a rising bar in the future.

Questions for Discussion

1. Visit www.Peapod.com and click on the "Groceries for your home" link. Enter a Chicago-area zip code (say 60602), and click on the "Learn More" arrow. Compare the Peapod customer experience to a brick-and-mortar grocery shopping experience. What benefits can a customer receive by using Peapod? What are the disadvantages?

2. Using the various characteristics for classifying types of retailers, develop a profile of Peapod.

3. Who does Peapod target? How does it position itself in this market? Does its marketing mix support this targeting and positioning?

4. Apply the wheel-of-retailing concept to the entire grocery industry, defining Peapod's role.

5. What does the future hold for Peapod, in both the short term and the long term?

Source: Steve Adams, "Fresh Rivalry," The Patriot Ledger, October 29, 2005, p. 37; Dina ElBoghdady, "Safeway Rolls Out Online Shopping," Washington Post, September 19, 2005, p. D01; Jen Haberkorn, "Going the Extra Smile," Washington Times, November 16, 2005; Bruce Mohl, "Like Peapod, Roche Bros. Now Aims to Deliver," Boston Globe, October 23, 2005, p. D1; Jason Straziuso, "After Flashy Failures, Online Groceries Quietly Grow," www.cnn.com, May 19, 2004; and Eileen Gunn, "Picking Up an Online Grocery Order," Wall Street Journal, April 6, 2006, p. D4. Also see "Company Information" at www.peapod.com/.

Communicating Customer Value

Integrated Marketing Communications Strategy

Previewing the Concepts

In this and the next three chapters, we'll examine the last of the marketing mix tools—promotion. Companies must do more than just create customer value. They must also use promotion to clearly and persuasively communicate that value. You'll find that promotion is not a single tool but rather a mix of several tools. Ideally, under the concept of *integrated marketing communications*, the company will carefully coordinate these promotion elements to deliver a clear, consistent, and compelling message about the organization and its products. We'll begin by introducing you to the various promotion mix tools. Next, we'll examine the rapidly changing communications environment and the need for integrated marketing communications. Finally, we'll discuss the steps in developing marketing communications and the promotion budgeting process. In the next three chapters, we'll visit the specific marketing communications tools.

To start this chapter, let's look behind the scenes at an award-winning advertising agency—Crispin Porter + Bogusky (Crispin). As it turns out, Crispin's success reflects all the current trends in the fast-changing world of modern integrated marketing communications. As one advertising insider puts it: "Crispin is right where it's at in today's advertising." Let's take a closer look.

Inside its sparkling steel-and-granite Miami headquarters, ad agency Crispin Porter + Bogusky was unveiling pieces of the campaign for then-new client Virgin Atlantic Airways. At presentations like this, agency executives typically hold up TV commercial storyboards and explain why everyone is going to love this particular dancing cat or flatulent horse. This morning, however, the presenters from Crispin—led by a pregnant woman, a young dude with a flop of unruly blond curls, and a guy with Elvis sideburns—had no TV storyboards. But they certainly had a lot of other stuff, and it came flying from all sides at the three Virgin clients.

There were ads designed to look like those flight safety cards found in airplane seat backs. There were samples of a newspaper comic strip called *The Jet Set*, as well as a mock-up for a lifestyle magazine titled *Jetrosexual*, a term Crispin created to describe Virgin's target audience. Both played off the Virgin campaign's theme, "Go Jet Set, Go!" There was something titled *Night-Night Jet Set, Night-Night* that resembled an illustrated children's book, although it actually contained bedtime ditties for adult business flyers—something that flight attendants would leave on pillows in Virgin's sleeping cabins.

And speaking of those flight attendants? Crispin wouldn't mind hiring a high-fashion designer to spruce up the uniforms. And how about staging "concert flights"? And wouldn't it be cool to hire celebrities to work as "guest flight attendants"? And by the way, could the pilots fly at a higher altitude so Virgin can claim it soars above the competition? And there's one more thing—well, no, actually there were 160 more, because that was how many far-flung ideas Crispin had come up with since starting work on the campaign.

Welcome to advertising as practiced by Crispin Porter + Bogusky, the agency of the moment. Crispin is as hot as South Beach on a Saturday night, and it's at the epicenter of all that's current in today's advertising world. The agency has snapped up every top advertising creative award lately while reeling in prime new accounts, including some big ones.

Early on, working with modest ad budgets, Crispin riveted customers' attention with startling guerrilla tactics, unconventional uses of media, and holistic marketing strategies that tied together everything from product design to packaging to event marketing to stuff that can't even be categorized. "Anything and everything is an ad," preaches Crispin's 40-something creative director, Alex Bogusky. What the agency used sparingly, however, at least until recently, is the traditional TV commercial. This was very close to heresy in a business that grew fat on those million-dollar 30-second spots.

In its celebrated BMW MINI campaign, Crispin created a huge buzz for the quirky, anything-but-ordinary little British-made MINI car with an anything-but-ordinary *Let's Motor* campaign. The campaign employed a rich mix of unconventional media, carefully integrated to create personality for the car and a tremendous buzz of excitement among consumers. The *Let's Motor* campaign was a smashing success, creating an almost cult-like following for the personable little car. And suddenly everyone—from Virgin Atlantic to big old Burger King, Coca-Cola, Miller Lite, and even Volkswagen—wanted a piece of Crispin.

How does Crispin do it? For starters, the agency swings for the fences on each new brand assignment, going beyond cute slogans to try to start a consumer movement behind the brand. "The jet set" was a mobilizing idea for Virgin, as was "motoring" in a MINI. Once a central theme is in place, the ad making begins—and this is where Crispin really turns the process upside down. Most copywriters and art directors instinctively start by sketching ideas for print ads and TV commercials. But Crispin begins with a blank slate. The goal is to figure out the best places to reach the target audience and the most interesting vehicles to carry the message, even if those vehicles have to be invented.

This leads to another Crispin difference: The agency often sticks its nose into things unrelated to advertising. For example, the agency convinced Virgin Atlantic to brand its flights by giving them names, such as "The Fly Chi" for flight number 020, San Francisco to London. Similarly, it got the brewer Molson to spend $1 million retooling its bottling plant to put labels on the backs of bottles for Crispin to use as an ad canvas with funny pickup lines. And it persuaded MINI to rewrite its lease agreement to match the tone of the overall MINI campaign. What does Crispin know about car leases? "Nothing," Bogusky admits, but that doesn't stop him from trying to ensure that every consumer "touch point" conveys the same message as the ad campaign. Crispin turns away clients who don't give it access to every part of the company.

Crispin is now at a turning point—rapidly evolving from a scrappy, nimble little creative shop to an industry giant. As it accepts larger, more conservative new accounts, such as Burger King, Miller Lite, and Volkswagen, many analysts wonder if Crispin will be able to retain the fast, edgy culture that has made it so successful. So far, so good. Rather than having its style crimped by these clients, Crispin seems to be infecting the clients with freewheeling cultures of their own.

Objectives

After studying this chapter, you should be able to

1. discuss the process and advantages of integrated marketing communications in communicating customer value
2. define the five promotion tools and discuss the factors that must be considered in shaping the overall promotion mix
3. outline the steps in developing effective marketing communications
4. explain the methods for setting the promotion budget and factors that affect the design of the promotion mix

For example, Crispin has breathed new purpose, personality, and profitability into an ailing Burger King®. It focused on "Superfans"—young, mostly male, Whopper-wolfing consumers who eat fast food six to eight times per week and account for nearly half of all Burger King visits. It brought the old "Have It Your Way" theme back to life, but with a modern "personalization" twist relevant to the Superfans. In an un-Crispin-like move, the Burger King campaign began with big-budget television ads. But the commercials themselves were uniquely Crispin: "Whopperettes"—commercials in which singing and dancing burger ingredients combined to make a Whopper your way; a "Manthem" ad in which young, brief-burning male Superfans spurned "chick food," chomped into man-size Texas Double Whoppers, and sang an all-male parody of the Helen Reddy song "I am Woman"; "Wake Up with the King" ads in which consumers met nose-to-nose with a freaky but likeable new ceramic-faced version of the Burger King, a character who rapidly became a pop culture icon.

And in typical fashion, Crispin's Burger King campaign reached way beyond television advertising. It created a bawdy but wildly successful "Subservient Chicken" Internet site, in which a man in a dingy apartment wearing a chicken suit and garter belt hangs out in front of his Web cam and does almost anything you ask him to—have it your way, get it? The site has drawn a staggering 460 million hits in two years. Crispin has placed its creative stamp on everything from Burger King packaging, tray liners, and door pulls to a new version of the Burger King employee's manual.

Also typical—Crispin's Burger King campaign is working: Sales grew 11 percent last year, firmly reestablishing Burger King as the nation's number two burger joint, behind McDonald's. And formerly disgruntled franchisees are now enthusiastic. "I think our competitors are scared of the King," says one franchisee. "They should be."

Although unconventional, or perhaps because of it, Crispin Porter + Bogusky just keeps winning awards, including top honors at last year's 2004 International Advertising Festival and a remarkable 2005 Grand Clio for its Subservient Chicken campaign. Last year, both *Advertising Age* and *Creativity* magazine named Crispin their agency of the year. Crispin "has been redefining what consumers even recognize as advertising," says the head of a rival agency. But to Alex Bogusky, it's all pretty simple. Advertising is "anything that makes our clients famous."[1]

Building good customer relationships calls for more that just developing a good product, pricing it attractively, and making it available to target customers. Companies must also *communicate* their value propositions to customers, and what they communicate should not be left to chance. All of their communications must be planned and blended into carefully integrated marketing communications programs. Just as good communication is important in building and maintaining any kind of relationship, it is a crucial element in a company's efforts to build profitable customer relationships.

The Promotion Mix

A company's total **promotion mix**—also called its **marketing communications mix**—consists of the specific blend of advertising, sales promotion, public relations, personal selling, and direct-marketing tools that the company uses to persuasively communicate customer value and build customer relationships. Definitions of the five major promotion tools follow:[2]

Advertising: Any paid form of nonpersonal presentation and promotion of ideas, goods, or services by an identified sponsor.

Sales promotion: Short-term incentives to encourage the purchase or sale of a product or service.

Public relations: Building good relations with the company's various publics by obtaining favorable publicity, building up a good corporate image, and handling or heading off unfavorable rumors, stories, and events.

Promotion mix (marketing communications mix)
The specific blend of advertising, sales promotion, public relations, personal selling, and direct-marketing tools that the company uses to persuasively communicate customer value and build customer relationships.

Advertising
Any paid form of nonpersonal presentation and promotion of ideas, goods, or services by an identified sponsor.

Sales promotion
Short-term incentives to encourage the purchase or sale of a product or service.

Public relations
Building good relations with the company's various publics by obtaining favorable publicity, building up a good "corporate image," and handling or heading off unfavorable rumors, stories, and events.

Personal selling
Personal presentation by the firm's sales force for the purpose of making sales and building customer relationships.

Direct marketing
Direct connections with carefully targeted individual consumers to both obtain an immediate response and cultivate lasting customer relationships.

Personal selling: Personal presentation by the firm's sales force for the purpose of making sales and building customer relationships.

Direct marketing: Direct connections with carefully targeted individual consumers to both obtain an immediate response and cultivate lasting customer relationships—the use of direct mail, the telephone, direct-response television, e-mail, the Internet, and other tools to communicate directly with specific consumers.

Each category involves specific promotional tools used to communicate with consumers. For example, advertising includes broadcast, print, Internet, outdoor, and other forms. Sales promotion includes discounts, coupons, displays, and demonstrations. Personal selling includes sales presentations, trade shows, and incentive programs. Public relations includes press releases, sponsorships, special events, and Web pages. And direct marketing includes catalogs, telephone marketing, kiosks, the Internet, and more.

At the same time, marketing communication goes beyond these specific promotion tools. The product's design, its price, the shape and color of its package, and the stores that sell it—*all* communicate something to buyers. Thus, although the promotion mix is the company's primary communication activity, the entire marketing mix—promotion *and* product, price, and place—must be coordinated for greatest communication impact.

Integrated Marketing Communications

In past decades, marketers have perfected the art of mass marketing—selling highly standardized products to masses of customers. In the process, they have developed effective mass-media communications techniques to support these mass-marketing strategies. Large companies routinely invest millions or even billions of dollars in television, magazine, or other mass-media advertising, reaching tens of millions of customers with a single ad. Today, however, marketing managers face some new marketing communications realities.

The New Marketing Communications Landscape

Two major factors are changing the face of today's marketing communications. First, as mass markets have fragmented, marketers are shifting away from mass marketing. More and more, they are developing focused marketing programs designed to build closer relationships with customers in more narrowly defined micromarkets. Second, vast improvements in information technology are speeding the movement toward segmented marketing. With today's new information technologies, marketers can amass detailed customer information and keep closer track of customer needs.

Improved information technology has also caused striking changes in the ways in which companies and customers communicate with each other. The digital age has spawned a host of new information and communication tools—from cell phones, iPods, and the Internet to satellite and cable television systems and digital video recorders (DVRs). The new technologies give companies exciting new media tools for interacting with targeted consumers. They also give consumers more control over the nature and timing of messages they choose to send and receive.

The Shifting Marketing Communications Model

The shift toward segmented marketing and the explosive developments in information and communications technology have had a dramatic impact on marketing communications. Just as marketing once gave rise to a new generation of mass-media communications, the shift toward targeted marketing and the changing communications environment are giving birth to a new marketing communications model. Although television, magazines, and other mass media remain very important, their dominance is now declining. Advertisers are now adding a broad selection of more specialized and highly targeted media to reach smaller customer segments with more personalized messages. The new media range from specialty magazines, cable television channels, and video on demand (VOD) to product placements in television programs and video games, Internet catalogs, e-mails, and podcasts. In all, companies are doing less *broadcasting* and more *narrowcasting*.

Some advertising industry experts even predict a doom-and-gloom "chaos scenario," in which the old mass-media communications model will collapse entirely. They believe that marketers will increasingly abandon traditional mass media in favor of "the glitzy promise of new digital technologies—from Web sites and e-mail to cell phone content and video on demand. . . . Fragmentation, the bane of network TV and mass marketers everywhere, will become the Holy Grail, the opportunity to reach—and have a conversation with—small clusters of consumers who are consuming not what is force-fed them, but exactly what they want."[3]

Just think about what's happening to television viewing these days. "Adjust your set," says one reporter, "television is changing as quickly as the channels. It's on cell phones. It's on digital music players. It's on almost anything with a screen. Shows can be seen at their regular times or when you want [with or without the commercials]. Some 'TV' programs aren't even on cable or network or satellite; they're being created just for Internet viewing."[4]

Consumers, especially younger ones, appear to be turning away from the major television networks in favor of cable TV or altogether different media. According to a recent study:

Only one in four 12- to 34-year-olds can name all four major broadcast networks: ABC, NBC, CBS, and Fox. Teens may not be able to name the big four, but they know MTV, Cartoon Network, and Comedy Central. The most popular activity? That would be surfing the Internet, which 84 percent said they did during their idle periods. Hanging out with friends came in second at 76 percent, watching movies third at 71 percent, and TV viewing fourth at 69 percent.[5]

As a result, marketers are losing confidence in television advertising. As mass-media costs rise, audiences shrink, ad clutter increases, and more and more viewers use VOD and TiVo-like systems to skip past disruptive television commercials, many skeptics even predict the demise of the old mass-media mainstay—the 30-second television commercial. In a recent survey, 70 percent of major brand advertisers said that they believe DVRs and VOD will reduce or destroy the effectiveness of traditional 30-second commercials.[6]

Thus, many large advertisers are shifting their advertising budgets away from network television in favor of more targeted, cost-effective, interactive, and engaging media. "The ad industry's plotline used to be a lot simpler: Audiences are splintering off in dozens of new directions, watching TV shows on iPods, watching movies on videogame players, and listening to radio on the Internet," observes one analyst. So marketers must "start planning how to reach consumers in new and unexpected ways."[7]

Rather than a "chaos scenario," however, other industry insiders see a more gradual shift to the new marketing communications model. They note that broadcast television and other mass media still capture a lion's share of the promotion budgets of most major marketing firms, a fact that isn't likely to change quickly. Although some may question the future of the 30-second spot, it's still very much in use today. And although ad spending on the major TV networks decreased last year, cable ad spending increased 11 percent. Moreover, television offers many promotional opportunities beyond the 30-second commercial." One advertising expert advises: "Because TV is at the forefront of 30 technological advances [such as DVRs and VOD], its audience will continue to increase. So if you think that TV is an aging dinosaur, or you're a national advertiser who is thinking of moving ad dollars away from TV, maybe you should think again."[8]

Thus, it seems likely that the new marketing communications model will consist of a gradually shifting mix of both traditional mass media and a wide array of exciting new, more targeted, more personalized media. For example, in its Let's Motor campaign, MINI uses a rich mix of media—conventional but clever magazine ads coupled with novel displays, quirky promotions, and attention-grabbing Web pages. "We need to reinvent the way we market to consumers," says A.G. Lafley, chief executive of Procter & Gamble. "Mass marketing still has an important role, [but] we need new models to initially coexist with mass marketing, and eventually to succeed it."[9]

The Need for Integrated Marketing Communications

The shift toward a richer mix of media and communication approaches poses a problem for marketers. Consumers today are bombarded by commercial messages from a broad range of sources. But consumers don't distinguish between message sources the way marketers do. In the consumer's mind, messages from different media and promotional approaches all become part of a single message about the company. Conflicting messages from these different sources can result in confused company images, brand positions, and customer relationships.

■ The shifting marketing communications model: MINI Let's Motor campaign uses a rich mix of media: conventional but clever magazine ads coupled with novel displays—here an actual MINI that looks like a children's ride ("Rides $16,850. Quarters only") and airport displays featuring oversize newspaper vending machines next to billboards proclaiming, "Makes everything else seem a little too big."

LET'S SHOW THE WORLD WHAT MAKES US DIFFERENT. Let's give our handling a name. Let's call it go-kart-like. Let's call it hairpin-ready. Let's call it turndicious. Let's call it "whiptastic." Let's trademark it pronto. Let's stick it on the boot. Let's whip it. Let's whip it good. **LET'S MOTOR.**

All too often, companies fail to integrate their various communications channels. The result is a hodgepodge of communications to consumers. Mass-media advertisements say one thing, while a price promotion sends a different signal, and a product label creates still another message. Company sales literature says something altogether different, and the company's Web site seems out of sync with everything else.

The problem is that these communications often come from different parts of the company. Advertising messages are planned and implemented by the advertising department or an advertising agency. Personal selling communications are developed by sales management. Other company specialists are responsible for public relations, sales promotion events, Internet marketing, and other forms of marketing communications.

However, whereas these companies have separated their communications, customers won't. According to one marketing communications expert:[10]

The truth is, most [consumers] won't compartmentalize their use of the [different media]. They won't say, "Hey, I'm going off to do a bit of Web surfing. Burn my TV, throw out all my radios, cancel all my magazine subscriptions and, by the way, take out my telephone and don't deliver any mail anymore." It's not that kind of world for consumers, and it shouldn't be that kind of world for marketers either.

Today, more companies are adopting the concept of **integrated marketing communications (IMC)**. Under this concept, as illustrated in Figure 14.1, the company carefully integrates its many communications channels to deliver a clear, consistent, and compelling message about the organization and its brands.[11]

IMC calls for recognizing all contact points where the customer may encounter the company and its brands. Each *brand contact* will deliver a message, whether good, bad, or indifferent. The company wants to deliver a consistent and positive message with each contact. IMC leads to a total marketing communication strategy aimed at building strong customer relationships by showing how the company and its products can help customers solve their problems.

IMC ties together all of the company's messages and images. The company's television and print advertisements have the same message, look, and feel as its e-mail and personal selling communications. And its public relations materials project the same image as its Web site. For example, Ford recently created a nicely integrated promotion campaign for its Escape Hybrid model.

It kicked off the Escape Hybrid campaign with a blockbuster Super Bowl ad, in which Kermit the Frog lamented "It's not easy being green" before discovering that it

Integrated marketing communications (IMC)
Carefully integrating and coordinating the company's many communications channels to deliver a clear, consistent, and compelling message about the organization and its products.

FIGURE 14.1
Integrated marketing communications

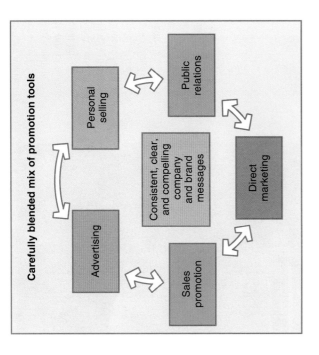

Carefully blended mix of promotion tools

Advertising

Personal selling

Consistent, clear, and compelling company and brand messages

Sales promotion

Direct marketing

Public relations

really is easy being green with the Escape Hybrid. Ford followed up with print ads in major magazines, featuring Kermit and reinforcing the "I guess it is easy being green" theme. The Super Bowl and print ads helped to build consumer awareness and preference for the Escape Hybrid brand. But the ads also pointed viewers to a special Web site (www.fordvehicles.com/suvs/escapehybrid), which extended the Kermit theme with a number of relationship-building and sales-building features. Visitors to the site could view the Super Bowl commercial again and then watch a charming video on the making of the "Easy Being Green" commercial—narrated by Kermit, of course. The site also offered lots of help with very little hype to serious car buyers, letting them learn more about the benefits of the Escape Hybrid, build and price a model, and find a dealer online. Later, at the dealership, Ford salespeople communicated the "Easy Being Green" message in person while customers kicked the tires and tested the Escape Hybrid's ride before deciding to purchase.

In the past, no one person or department was responsible for thinking through the communication roles of the various promotion tools and coordinating the promotion mix. To help implement integrated marketing communications, some companies appoint a marketing communications director who has overall responsibility for the company's communications efforts. This helps to produce better communications consistency and greater sales impact. It places the responsibility in someone's hands—where none existed before—to unify the company's image as it is shaped by thousands of company activities.

A View of the Communication Process

Integrated marketing communications involves identifying the target audience and shaping a well-coordinated promotional program to obtain the desired audience response. Too often, marketing communications focus on immediate awareness, image, or preference goals in the target market. But this approach to communication is too shortsighted. Today, marketers are moving toward viewing communications as *managing the customer relationship over time.*

Because customers differ, communications programs need to be developed for specific segments, niches, and even individuals. And, given the new interactive communications technologies, companies must ask not only, "How can we reach our customers?" but also, "How can we find ways to let our customers reach us?"

Thus, the communications process should start with an audit of all the potential contacts target customers may have with the company and its brands. For example, someone purchasing a new kitchen appliance may talk to others, see television ads, read articles and ads in newspapers and magazines, visit various Web sites, and check out appliances in one or more stores. The marketer needs to assess what influence each of these communications experiences will have at different stages of the buying process. This understanding will help marketers allocate their communication dollars more efficiently and effectively.

To communicate effectively, marketers need to understand how communication works. Communication involves the nine elements shown in Figure 14.2. Two of these elements are the major parties in a communication—the *sender* and the *receiver*. Another two are the major communication tools—the *message* and the *media*. Four more are major communication functions—*encoding*, *decoding*, *response*, and *feedback*. The last element is *noise* in the system. Definitions of these elements follow and are applied to an ad for Hewlett-Packard (HP) LaserJet color copiers.

- *Sender:* The party sending the message to another party—here, HP.
- *Encoding:* The process of putting thought into symbolic form—HP's advertising agency assembles words and illustrations into an advertisement that will convey the intended message.
- *Message:* The set of symbols that the sender transmits—the actual HP copier ad.
- *Media:* The communication channels through which the message moves from sender to receiver—in this case, the specific magazines that HP selects.
- *Decoding:* The process by which the receiver *assigns meaning to the symbols encoded by the sender*—a consumer reads the HP copier ad and interprets the words and illustrations it contains.
- *Receiver:* The *party receiving the message sent by another party*—the home office or business customer who reads the HP copier ad.
- *Response:* The *reactions of the receiver after being exposed to the message*—any of hundreds of possible responses, such as the consumer is more aware of the attributes of HP copiers, visits the HP Web site for more information, actually buys an HP copier, or does nothing.
- *Feedback:* The part of the *receiver's response communicated back to the sender*—HP research shows that consumers are struck by and remember the ad, or consumers write or call HP praising or criticizing the ad or HP's products.
- *Noise:* The *unplanned static or distortion during the communication process*, which results in the receiver's getting a different message than the one the sender sent—the consumer is distracted while reading the magazine and misses the HP ad or its key points.

For a message to be effective, the sender's encoding process must mesh with the receiver's decoding process. The best messages consist of words and other symbols that are familiar to the receiver. The more the sender's field of experience overlaps with that of the receiver, the more effective the message is likely to be. Marketing communicators may not always *share* their consumer's field of experience. For example, an advertising copywriter from one socioeconomic stratum might create ads for consumers from another stratum—say,

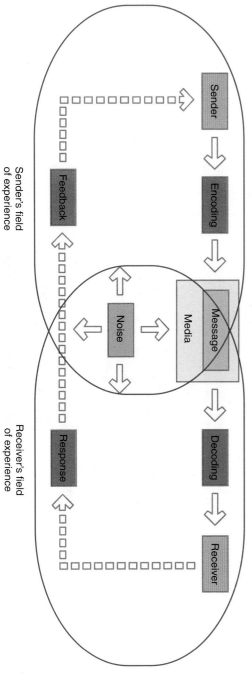

FIGURE 14.2 Elements in the communication process

Sender's field
of experience

Receiver's field
of experience

Sender → Encoding → Message / Media → Decoding → Receiver

Noise

Feedback ← Response

wealthy business owners. However, to communicate effectively, the marketing communicator must *understand* the consumer's field of experience.

This model points out several key factors in good communication. Senders need to know what audiences they wish to reach and what responses they want. They must be good at encoding messages that take into account how the target audience decodes them. They must send messages through media that reach target audiences, and they must develop feedback channels so that they can assess the audience's response to the message.

Steps in Developing Effective Communication

We now examine the steps in developing an effective integrated communications and promotion program. Marketers must do the following: Identify the target audience; determine the communication objectives; design a message; choose the media through which to send the message; select the message source; and collect feedback.

Identifying the Target Audience

A marketing communicator starts with a clear target audience in mind. The audience may be potential buyers or current users, those who make the buying decision or those who influence it. The audience may be individuals, groups, special publics, or the general public. The target audience will heavily affect the communicator's decisions on *what* will be said, *how* it will be said, *when* it will be said, *where* it will be said, and *who* will say it.

Determining the Communication Objectives

Once the target audience has been defined, the marketers must decide what response they seek. Of course, in many cases, they will seek a *purchase* response. But a purchase results from a long consumer decision-making process. The marketing communicator needs to know where the target audience now stands and to what stage it needs to be moved. The target audience may be in any of six **buyer-readiness stages**, the stages consumers normally pass through on their way to making a purchase. These stages include *awareness, knowledge, liking, preference, conviction,* and *purchase* (see Figure 14.3).

The marketing communicator's target market may be totally unaware of the product, know only its name, or know only a few things about it. The communicator must first build *awareness* and *knowledge.* For example, when Daimler-Chrysler first introduced its Chrysler 300 model, it used "teaser ads" to create initial awareness and curiosity. The ads showed the car but not its name. Later ads and the company's Web site created knowledge by informing potential buyers of the car's high quality and its many innovative features. Edy's ran similar teaser ads when it introduced Edy's Slow-Churned ice cream. Print ads show a blank package with the headline "You've been waiting for this." The ads directed consumers to the slowchurned.com Web site, where they could learn more about the new product and receive a chance to win a lifetime supply of Edy's ice cream.

Assuming target consumers *know* about the product, how do they *feel* about it? Once potential buyers knew about the Chrysler 300, Chrysler's marketers wanted to move them through successively stronger stages of feelings toward the car. These stages included *liking* (feeling favorable about the car); *preference* (preferring Chrysler 300 to other car brands); and *conviction* (believing that Chrysler 300 is the best car for them). Chrysler marketers used a combination of the promotion mix tools to create positive feelings and conviction. Advertising built an emotional brand connection and extolled the 300's advantages over competing brands—with this car, it tells them, "inspiration comes standard." Press releases and other public relations activities stressed the car's innovative features and performance. Dealer salespeople told buyers about options, value for the price, and after-sale service.

Buyer-readiness stages
The stages consumers normally pass through on their way to purchase, including awareness, knowledge, liking, preference, conviction, and purchase.

FIGURE 14.3 **Buyer-readiness stages**

Awareness ⇨ Knowledge ⇨ Liking ⇨ Preference ⇨ Conviction ⇨ Purchase

Finally, some members of the target market might be convinced about the product, but not quite get around to making the *purchase*. Potential Chrysler buyers might have decided to wait for more information or for the economy to improve. The communicator must lead these consumers to take the final step. Actions might include offering special promotional prices, rebates, or premiums. Salespeople might call or write to selected customers, inviting them to visit the dealership for a special showing. The Chrysler 300 Web site explains various financing options and invites potential buyers to sign up for a test drive.

Of course, marketing communications alone cannot create positive feelings and purchases for the Chrysler 300. The car itself must provide superior value for the customer. In fact, outstanding marketing communications can actually speed the demise of a poor product. The more quickly potential buyers learn about the poor product, the more quickly they become aware of its faults. Thus, good marketing communication calls for "good deeds followed by good words."

Designing a Message

Having defined the desired audience response, the communicator turns to developing an effective message. Ideally, the message should get *Attention*, hold *Interest*, arouse *Desire*, and obtain *Action* (a framework known as the *AIDA model*). In practice, few messages take the consumer all the way from awareness to purchase, but the AIDA framework suggests the desirable qualities of a good message.

When putting the message together, the marketing communicator must decide what to say (*message content*) and how to say it (*message structure and format*).

YOU'VE BEEN WAITING FOR THIS.™

Get a sneak peek at *SlowChurned.com!*

Enter to **WIN** a "lifetime" supply!

Edy's

■ Moving customers through the buyer-readiness stages: Edy's teaser ads built initial awareness and curiosity for the company's new Slowed-Churned ice cream and directed consumers to a Web site where they could learn more about the new product.

Message Content

The marketer has to figure out an appeal or theme that will produce the desired response. There are three types of appeals: rational, emotional, and moral. *Rational appeals* relate to the audience's self-interest. They show that the product will produce the desired benefits. Examples are messages showing a product's quality, economy, value, or performance. Thus, Tylenol runs a series of ads that inform customers about pain relievers and why Tylenol is the best choice. The ads say, "Stop. Think. Tylenol."

Emotional appeals attempt to stir up either negative or positive emotions that can motivate purchase. Communicators may use positive emotional appeals such as love, pride, joy, and humor. For example, advocates for humorous messages claim that they attract more attention and create more liking and belief in the sponsor. In a RoperASW survey, Americans picked humor as their favorite ad approach, with 85 percent saying they like ads with humorous themes. Other favorite emotional themes in the post-September 11, 2001, era include such reassuring ones as "safety and security" (77 percent), "family closeness" (76 percent), "giving to others" (74 percent), "patriotism" (74 percent), and "optimism" (64 percent).[12]

These days, it seems as though every company is using humor in its advertising, from consumer product firms such as Anheuser-Busch to the scholarly American Heritage Dictionary. Advertising in recent Super Bowls appears to reflect consumers' preferences for humor. For example, 14 of the top 15 most popular ads in *USA Today's* ad meter consumer rankings of 2006 Super Bowl advertisements used humor. Anheuser-Busch used humor to claim six of the top 10 ad spots. Its Bud Light ads featured everything from young men wor-shiping a neighbor's rotating magic fridge stocked with Bud Light to an office manager who motivates employees by hiding bottles of Bud Light throughout the office.[13]

■ Humor in advertising: These days, it seems as though almost every company is using humor in its advertising, even the scholarly American Heritage Dictionary.

Properly used, humor can capture attention, make people feel good, and give a brand personality. Anheuser-Busch has used humor effectively for years, helping consumers relate to its brands. However, advertisers must be careful when using humor. Used poorly, it can detract from comprehension, wear out its welcome fast, overshadow the product, or even irritate consumers. For example, many consumers and ad critics took exception to some of the humor used in the 2004 Super Bowl ads, including Anheuser-Busch ads.

Advertising professionals agreed that the quality of Super Bowl ads [in 2004] had declined, mostly from the use of "toilet bowl" humor that insulted viewers' intelligence. They pointed to Budweiser ads featuring a crotch-biting dog, a male monkey wooing a human female, and a gas-passing horse that spoiled a sleigh-ride date. Many critics and consumers complained that such ads showed that Budweiser was "reaching for the lowest common denominator in commercials aimed at the most frequent beer drinkers—men from 21 to 25 years old—resulting in a race to the bottom to fill commercials with bathroom humor, double entendres, crude sight gags and vulgarisms." As a result of such criticism, Anheuser-Busch [rethought] the tone and content of its ads for future Super Bowls. "We are taking a more cautious approach to our creative," says Anheuser-Busch president August Busch IV. "[Bud Light] is about fun, being with friends, and good times," says a senior Budweiser ad agency executive, "and we can do that within the boundaries of good taste."[14]

Communicators can also use negative emotional appeals, such as fear, guilt, and shame that get people to do things they should (brush their teeth, eat better, buy new tires) or to stop doing things they shouldn't (smoke, drink too much, eat unhealthy foods). For example, an ad for TLC's show *Honey We're Killing the Kids* (a reality show that tries to get families to eat healthier) teaches "Life Lesson #74: Sometimes being their best friend isn't being their best friend." And Etonic ads ask, "What would you do if you couldn't run?" They go on to note that Etonic athletic shoes are designed to avoid injuries—they're "built so you can last."

Moral appeals are directed to the audience's sense of what is "right" and "proper." They are often used to urge people to support social causes such as a cleaner environment, better race relations, equal rights for women, and aid to the disadvantaged. An example of a moral appeal is the Salvation Army headline, "While you're trying to figure out what to get the man who has everything, don't forget the man who has nothing."

Message Structure

Marketers must also decide how to handle three message structure issues. The first is whether to draw a conclusion or leave it to the audience. Research suggests that in many cases, rather than drawing a conclusion, the advertiser is better off asking questions and letting buyers come to their own conclusions. The second message structure issue is whether to present the strongest arguments first or last. Presenting them first gets strong attention but may lead to an anticlimactic ending.

The third message structure issue is whether to present a one-sided argument (mentioning only the product's strengths) or a two-sided argument (touting the product's strengths while also admitting its shortcomings). Usually, a one-sided argument is more effective in sales presentations—except when audiences are highly educated or likely to hear opposing claims, or when the communicator has a negative association to overcome. In this spirit, Heinz ran the message "Heinz Ketchup is slow good" and Listerine ran the message "Listerine tastes bad twice a day." In such cases, two-sided messages can enhance the advertiser's credibility and make buyers more resistant to competitor attacks.

Message Format

The marketing communicator also needs a strong *format* for the message. In a print ad, the communicator has to decide on the headline, copy, illustration, and color. To attract attention, advertisers can use novelty and contrast; eye-catching pictures and headlines; distinctive formats; message size and position; and color, shape, and movement. If the message is to be carried over the radio, the communicator has to choose words, sounds, and voices. The "sound" of an ad promoting banking services should be different from one promoting an iPod.

If the message is to be carried on television or in person, then all these elements plus body language must be planned. Presenters plan every detail—their facial expressions, gestures, dress, posture, and hairstyles. If the message is carried on the product or its package, the communicator has to watch texture, scent, color, size, and shape. For example, age and other demographics affect the way in which consumers perceive and react to color. Here are examples:

How do you sell margarine—stodgy, wholesome margarine—to today's kids? One answer: color. "We knew we wanted to introduce a color product. It's been a big trend with kids since the blue M&M," says a Parkay spokesperson. So Parkay tried out margarine in blue, pink, green, and purple. "When we tested four different colors in focus groups, kids had a blast." Electric blue and shocking pink margarine emerged as clear favorites. In contrast, as we get older, our eyes mature and our vision takes on a yellow cast. Color looks less bright to older people, so they gravitate to white and other bright tones. A recent survey found 10 percent of people 55 years and older want the brightness of a white car, compared with 4 percent of 21- to 34-year-olds and 2 percent of teens. Lexus, which skews toward older buyers, makes sure that 60 percent of its cars are light in color.[15]

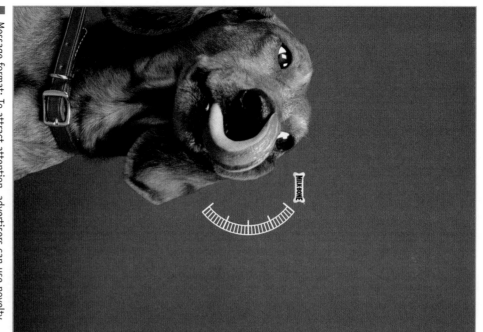

■ Message format: To attract attention, advertisers can use novelty and contrast, eye-catching pictures and headlines, and distinctive formats, as in this Milkbone ad.

Choosing Media

The communicator must now select *channels of communication.* There are two broad types of communication channels—*personal* and *nonpersonal.*

Personal Communication Channels

In **personal communication channels,** two or more people communicate directly with each other. They might communicate face to face, on the phone, through mail or e-mail, or even through an Internet "chat." Personal communication channels are effective because they allow for personal addressing and feedback.

Some personal communication channels are controlled directly by the company. For example, company salespeople contact target buyers. But other personal communications about the product may reach buyers through channels not directly controlled by the company.

Thus, in designing effective marketing communications, marketers must consider color and other seemingly unimportant details carefully.

Personal Communication Channels

Personal communication channels
Channels through which two or more people communicate directly with each other, including face to face, on the phone, through mail or e-mail, or even through an Internet "chat."

Word-of-mouth influence
Personal communication about a product between target buyers and neighbors, friends, family members, and associates.

These channels might include independent experts—consumer advocates, online buying guides, and others—making statements to buyers. Or they might be neighbors, friends, family members, and associates talking to target buyers. This last channel, known as **word-of-mouth influence**, has considerable effect in many product areas.

Personal influence carries great weight for products that are expensive, risky, or highly visible. Consider the power of simple customer reviews on Amazon.com:

It doesn't matter how loud or often you tell consumers your "truth," few today are buying a big-ticket item before they know what existing users have to say about the product. This is a low-trust world. That's why "recommendation by a relative or friend" comes out on top in just about every survey of purchasing influences. A recent study found that more than 90 percent of customers trust "recommendations from consumers," whereas trust in ads runs from a high of about 40 percent to less than 10 percent. It's also a major reason for Amazon's success in growing sales per customer. Who hasn't made an Amazon purchase based on another customer's review or the "Customers who bought this also bought . . ." section? And it explains what a recent Shop.org survey found—that 96 percent of retailers find ratings and reviews to be an effective tactic in lifting online sales.[16]

Companies can take steps to put personal communication channels to work for them. For example, they can create *opinion leaders* for their brands—people whose opinions are sought by others—by supplying influencers with the product on attractive terms or by educating them so that they can inform others. **Buzz marketing** involves cultivating opinion leaders and getting them to spread information about a product or service to others in their communities. Consider BzzAgent, a Boston marketing firm that creates word-of-mouth campaigns for many of the country's best-known companies.

Buzz marketing
Cultivating opinion leaders and getting them to spread information about a product or service to others in their communities.

BzzAgent has assembled a nationwide volunteer army of 130,000 natural-born buzzers, and they will channel their chatter toward products and services they deem authentically worth talking about. "Our goal is to find a way to capture honest word of mouth," says David Balter, BzzAgent's founder, "and to build a network that will turn passionate customers into brand evangelists." Once a client signs on, BzzAgent searches its database for "agents" matching the demographic and psychographic profile of target customers of the product or service. Selected volunteers receive a sample product and a training manual for buzz-creating strategies. These volunteers aren't just mall rats on cell phones. Some 65 percent are over 25, 60 percent are women, and two are Fortune 500 CEOs. They've buzzed products as diverse as Estee Lauder facial masks, Lee Jeans, Rock Bottom Restaurants, and The March of Dimes. In Alabama, Bzzagent ArnoldGinger123 buttonholed her probation officer to chat up a tush-flattering new brand of jeans. In Illinois, BzzAgent GeminiDreams spent a family Christmas party extolling the features of Monster.com's new networking site.

■ Taking advantage of personal communications channels: BzzAgent's army of 130,000 natural-born buzzers creates word-of-mouth chatter for many of the world's best-known brands.

And, in an especially moving final tribute in New Jersey, BzzAgent Karri buzzed her grandpa into the great beyond with a round of Anheuser World Select beer at the old gent's wake. The service's appeal is its authenticity. "What I like is that BzzAgents aren't scripted," says Steve Cook, vice president of worldwide strategic marketing at Coca-Cola. "[The company tells its agents,] 'Here's the information; if you believe in it, say whatever you think.' It's . . . genuine."[17]

Nonpersonal Communication Channels

Nonpersonal communication channels are media that carry messages without personal contact or feedback. They include major media, atmospheres, and events. Major *media* include print media (newspapers, magazines, direct mail), broadcast media (radio, television), display media (billboards, signs, posters), and online media (e-mail, Web sites). *Atmospheres* are designed environments that create or reinforce the buyer's leanings toward buying a product. Thus, lawyers' offices and banks are designed to communicate confidence and other qualities that might be valued by clients. *Events* are staged occurrences that communicate messages to target audiences. For example, public relations departments arrange press conferences, grand openings, shows and exhibits, public tours, and other events.

Nonpersonal communication affects buyers directly. In addition, using mass media often affects buyers indirectly by causing more personal communication. Communications first flow from television, magazines, and other mass media to opinion leaders and then from these opinion leaders to others. Thus, opinion leaders step between the mass media and their audiences and carry messages to people who are less exposed to media. This suggests that mass communicators should aim their messages directly at opinion leaders, letting them carry the message to others.

Interestingly, marketers often use nonpersonal communications channels to replace or stimulate personal communications by embedding consumer endorsements or word-of-mouth testimonials in their ads and other promotions. JetBlue's recent "Sincerely, JetBlue" promotion campaign does this (see Real Marketing 14.1).

Selecting the Message Source

In either personal or nonpersonal communication, the message's impact on the target audience is also affected by how the audience views the communicator. Messages delivered by highly credible sources are more persuasive. Thus, many food companies promote to doctors, dentists, and other health care providers to motivate these professionals to recommend their products to patients. And marketers hire celebrity endorsers—well-known athletes, actors,

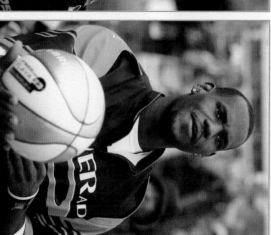

■ Marketers hire celebrities to deliver their messages: NASCAR superstar Jeff Gordon pitches everything from DuPont to Pepsi and Edy's ice cream, basketball pro LeBron James vouches for Coca-Cola's Powerade and Sprite brands, and young golfer Michelle Wie lends her image to Nike.

Nonpersonal communication channels
Media that carry messages without personal contact or feedback, including major media, atmospheres, and events.

Real Marketing   JetBlue: Hearing It from People You Know and Trust

14.1 Trying to choose the right airline? There's no need to ask your friends, relatives, or neighbors about their airline experiences, or about which airline provides the best service. JetBlue has already done that for you. And it's sharing their stories with you and other travelers in a promotional campaign called "Sincerely, JetBlue." The campaign features a series of offbeat commercials in which actual customers share their JetBlue experiences.

The goal of the campaign is to retain JetBlue's upstart, small-airline personality in the face of ambitious expansion plans. JetBlue is now the nation's number two discount airline, behind Southwest, and it's adding planes and routes at a rapid pace. As it grows, it wants to hang onto the underdog, grassroots appeal that's made it successful in the dog-eat-dog airline industry.

Some airlines have built their images through lush, big-budget ad campaigns. Not so for JetBlue. "This brand was created almost entirely on an experience, then on word of mouth about that experience," says the chief creative director at JWT, the New York ad agency that created the "Sincerely, JetBlue" campaign. "When [JetBlue founder and CEO] David Neeleman came to us," recounts another JWT executive, "he said the thing that keeps him up at night is how he can grow the airline and keep the JetBlue experience." The answer: Let the JetBlue faithful themselves give voice to that experience. "Allowing our customers to tell our story [will help the airline] keep a local, small feel as JetBlue becomes more national in scope," says JetBlue's chief marketing executive.

JetBlue has built a huge infrastructure for breeding and collecting customer stories to use in the "Sincerely" ads. It has erected futuristic JetBlue "story booths" in eighteen cities, where passersby can recount and record their experiences flying on JetBlue. According to one observer, the booths are "less like circus tents and more like futuristic spaceships. [They're] made of high-tech honeycomb mesh and have LED screens underneath the shell, pressure-sensitive floors, and voice-activated walls." Inside the booths, a virtual crew member guides customer-storytellers through their experiences. JetBlue also invites customers to submit stories at its

Web site, and it places postcards in seatback pockets, which passengers can use to keep and submit minijournals on their JetBlue journeys.

Once collected, the stories are incorporated into simple but colorful, cleverly animated commercials in which customers themselves share their JetBlue experiences. "You take this little story and you give it to an animator and they turn it into something marvelous," says a JWT creative director. In one ad, customer Melissa confides, "Let me tell you, I wanted to not like you, if only because everyone seems to love you. I got on a flight with a pen and paper, waiting to take down every irritating detail." But, she continues, "two flights later, I was staring at the same blank piece of paper. You've done nothing wrong and everything more than right, if that's possible." After detailing all the right things the airline does, she mock-laments, "JetBlue, I wanted to not like you, but it can't be done—at all. Sincerely, Melissa McCall, Portland, Oregon."

In a similar fashion, in other ads: Brian relates how a JetBlue flight attendant dashed from the plane just before takeoff to retrieve a brand-new iPod he'd left in a rental car. Ann recounts how, when her JetBlue flight was delayed by a snowstorm, the airline eased the long wait by providing pizza and even a live band. "My [three-year-old] son was dancing. I was dancing," she remembers. "It was a great time! It made a horrible experience really nice." And the Steins tell about the time they arrived late at night for a family vacation in Florida with their three very tired small children only to learn that their hotel wouldn't take them in. Jason Stein recalls, "Out of nowhere we heard a voice from behind us, go ahead, take my room." His wife Nancy continues: "A superhero in a JetBlue pilot's uniform, who sacrificed his room graciously, saved our night. And we slept like babies. Thank you, JetBlue. Sincerely, Nancy and Jason Stein, Darien, Connecticut."

The tone and crafting of the ads makes them appealing and believable. It's almost like talking to your next-door neighbor, but with colorful, intriguing animations that help to bring their stories to life. (Check out all of these stories and others at the JetBlue Web site at

and even cartoon characters—to deliver their messages. Golfer Tiger Woods speaks for Nike, Buick, Accenture, and a dozen other brands. Basketball pro LeBron James vouches for Nike and Coca-Cola's Powerade and Sprite brands. NASCAR superstar Jeff Gordon pitches everything from Ray-Ban sunglasses to Pepsi and Edy's ice cream. And young golfer Michelle Wie lends her image to brands such as Nike and Sony.

But companies must be careful when selecting celebrities to represent their brands. Picking the wrong spokesperson can result in embarrassment and a tarnished image. McDonald's, Sprite, and Nutella found this out when superspokesperson Kobe Bryant was charged with sexual assault. H&M, Chanel, and Burberry had to publicly dismiss supermodel Kate Moss after she was reportedly photographed using cocaine. And Pepsi, McDonald's, Roots, and Ford faced embarrassment when gambling scandals threatened to dirty the squeaky-clean image of their spokesperson, hockey great Wayne Gretzky. "Arranged marriages between brands and celebrities are inherently risky," notes an expert. "Today it's standard practice to sign a celeb only after an extensive background check. But accidents still happen."18

JetBlue's recent "Sincerely, JetBlue" campaign uses nonpersonal communications channels to replace or stimulate personal communications by embedding consumer testimonials in ads. In one ad, Brian relates how a JetBlue flight attendant dashed from the plane just before takeoff to retrieve a brand-new iPod he'd left in a rental car.

http://jetblue.com/experience/index.html?intcmp=jwt_1001). "The various illustrations—including animation, paper cutouts, and miniature doll pieces—have a wonderful rhythm and flow," comments an advertising analyst, "and the stories have an on-the-fly populist quality, which fits the brand."

In all, the campaign just seems to work. It's the ultimate word of mouth. Says the JWT executive, "The best way to get people who haven't tried the airline to try it is for them to hear from people they know and trust."

Sources: Quotes and other information from Stuart Elliot, "JetBlue May Be Big, but It Wants Fliers to Think Small," *New York Times*, March 30, 2006, p. C3; and Barbara Lippert, "Voices Carry," *Adweek*, April 17, 2006, p. 32; and www.jetblue.com, December 2006.

Collecting Feedback

After sending the message, the communicator must research its effect on the target audience. This involves asking the target audience members whether they remember the message, how many times they saw it, what points they recall, how they felt about the message, and their past and present attitudes toward the product and company. The communicator would also like to measure behavior resulting from the message—how many people bought a product, talked to others about it, or visited the store.

Feedback on marketing communications may suggest changes in the promotion program or in the product offer itself. For example, JetBlue Airways uses television and newspaper advertising to inform area consumers about the airline, its routes, and its fares. Suppose feedback research shows that 80 percent of all fliers in an area recall seeing the airline's ads and are aware of its flights and prices. Sixty percent of these aware fliers have flown JetBlue, but only 20 percent of those who tried it were satisfied. These results suggest that although promotion is creating *awareness*, the airline isn't giving consumers the *satisfaction* they expect.

Therefore, JetBlue needs to improve its service while staying with the successful communication program. In contrast, suppose the research shows that only 40 percent of area consumers are aware of the airline, only 30 percent of those aware have tried it, but 80 percent of those who have tried it return. In this case, JetBlue needs to strengthen its promotion program to take advantage of its power to create customer satisfaction.

Setting the Total Promotion Budget and Mix

We have looked at the steps in planning and sending communications to a target audience. But how does the company decide on the total *promotion budget* and its division among the major promotional tools to create the *promotion mix*? By what process does it blend the tools to create integrated marketing communications? We now look at these questions.

Setting the Total Promotion Budget

One of the hardest marketing decisions facing a company is how much to spend on promotion. John Wanamaker, the department store magnate, once said, "I know that half of my advertising is wasted, but I don't know which half. I spent $2 million for advertising, and I don't know if that is half enough or twice too much." Thus, it is not surprising that industries and companies vary widely in how much they spend on promotion. Promotion spending may be 10 to 12 percent of sales for consumer packaged goods and less than 1 percent for industrial machinery products. Within a given industry, both low and high spenders can be found.[19]

How does a company decide on its promotion budget? We look at four common methods used to set the total budget for advertising: the *affordable method*, the *percentage-of-sales method*, the *competitive-parity method*, and the *objective-and-task method*.[20]

Affordable Method

Affordable method
Setting the promotion budget at the level management thinks the company can afford.

Some companies use the **affordable method**: They set the promotion budget at the level they think the company can afford. Small businesses often use this method, reasoning that the company cannot spend more on advertising than it has. They start with total revenues, deduct operating expenses and capital outlays, and then devote some portion of the remaining funds to advertising.

Unfortunately, this method of setting budgets completely ignores the effects of promotion on sales. It tends to place promotion last among spending priorities, even in situations in which advertising is critical to the firm's success. It leads to an uncertain annual promotion budget, which makes long-range market planning difficult. Although the affordable method can result in overspending on advertising, it more often results in underspending.

Percentage-of-Sales Method

Percentage-of-sales method
Setting the promotion budget at a certain percentage of current or forecasted sales or as a percentage of the unit sales price.

Other companies use the **percentage-of-sales method**, setting their promotion budget at a certain percentage of current or forecasted sales. Or they budget a percentage of the unit sales price. The percentage-of-sales method has advantages. It is simple to use and helps management think about the relationships between promotion spending, selling price, and profit per unit.

Despite these claimed advantages, however, the percentage-of-sales method has little to justify it. It wrongly views sales as the *cause* of promotion rather than as the *result*. Although studies have found a positive correlation between promotional spending and brand strength, this relationship often turns out to be effect and cause, not cause and effect. Stronger brands with higher sales can afford the biggest ad budgets.

Thus, the percentage-of-sales budget is based on availability of funds rather than on opportunities. It may prevent the increased spending sometimes needed to turn around falling sales. Because the budget varies with year-to-year sales, long-range planning is difficult. Finally, the method does not provide any basis for choosing a *specific* percentage, except what has been done in the past or what competitors are doing.

Competitive-Parity Method

Competitive-parity method
Setting the promotion budget to match competitors' outlays.

Still other companies use the **competitive-parity method**, setting their promotion budgets to match competitors' outlays. They monitor competitors' advertising or get industry promotion spending estimates from publications or trade associations, and then they set their budgets based on the industry average.

Two arguments support this method. First, competitors' budgets represent the collective wisdom of the industry. Second, spending what competitors spend helps prevent promotion wars. Unfortunately, neither argument is valid. There are no grounds for believing that the competition has a better idea of what a company should be spending on promotion than does the company itself. Companies differ greatly, and each has its own special promotion needs. Finally, there is no evidence that budgets based on competitive parity prevent promotion wars.

Objective-and-Task Method

The most logical budget-setting method is the **objective-and-task method**, whereby the company sets its promotion budget based on what it wants to accomplish with promotion. This budgeting method entails (1) defining specific promotion objectives, (2) determining the tasks needed to achieve these objectives, and (3) estimating the costs of performing these tasks. The sum of these costs is the proposed promotion budget.

The advantage of the objective-and-task method is that it forces management to spell out its assumptions about the relationship between dollars spent and promotion results. But it is also the most difficult method to use. Often, it is hard to figure out which specific tasks will achieve stated objectives. For example, suppose Sony wants 95 percent awareness for its latest camcorder model during the six-month introductory period. What specific advertising messages and media schedules should Sony use to attain this objective? How much would these messages and media schedules cost? Sony management must consider such questions, even though they are hard to answer.

Shaping the Overall Promotion Mix

The concept of integrated marketing communications suggests that the company must blend the promotion tools carefully into a coordinated *promotion mix.* But how does the company determine what mix of promotion tools it will use? Companies within the same industry differ greatly in the design of their promotion mixes. For example, Mary Kay spends most of its promotion funds on personal selling and direct marketing, whereas CoverGirl spends heavily on consumer advertising. HP relies on advertising and promotion to retailers, whereas Dell uses more direct marketing. We now look at factors that influence the marketer's choice of promotion tools.

Objective-and-task method
Developing the promotion budget by (1) defining specific objectives; (2) determining the tasks that must be performed to achieve these objectives; and (3) estimating the costs of performing these tasks. The sum of these costs is the proposed promotion budget.

■ Promotion Mix: Companies within the same industry may use different mixes. Mary Kay relies heavily on personal selling and direct marketing; CoverGirl devotes significant resources to advertising.

The Nature of Each Promotion Tool

Each promotion tool has unique characteristics and costs. Marketers must understand these characteristics in shaping the promotion mix.

ADVERTISING Advertising can reach masses of geographically dispersed buyers at a low cost per exposure, and it enables the seller to repeat a message many times. For example, television advertising can reach huge audiences. An estimated 141 million Americans tuned in to at least part of the most recent Super Bowl; about 38 million people watched at least part of the last Academy Awards broadcast; and 33.6 million fans tuned in to watch the debut episode of the fourth season of *American Idol.* For companies that want to reach a mass audience, TV is the place to be.[21]

Beyond its reach, large-scale advertising says something positive about the seller's size, popularity, and success. Because of advertising's public nature, consumers tend to view advertised products as more legitimate. Advertising is also very expressive—it allows the company to dramatize its products through the artful use of visuals, print, sound, and color. On the one hand, advertising can be used to build up a long-term image for a product (such as Coca-Cola ads). On the other hand, advertising can trigger quick sales (as when Kohl's advertises weekend specials).

Advertising also has some shortcomings. Although it reaches many people quickly, advertising is impersonal and cannot be as directly persuasive as can company salespeople. For the most part, advertising can carry on only a one-way communication with the audience, and the audience does not feel that it has to pay attention or respond. In addition, advertising can be very costly. Although some advertising forms, such as newspaper and radio advertising, can be done on smaller budgets, other forms, such as network TV advertising, require very large budgets.

PERSONAL SELLING Personal selling is the most effective tool at certain stages of the buying process, particularly in building up buyers' preferences, convictions, and actions. It involves personal interaction between two or more people, so each person can observe the other's needs and characteristics and make quick adjustments. Personal selling also allows all kinds of customer relationships to spring up, ranging from matter-of-fact selling relationships to personal friendships. An effective salesperson keeps the customer's interests at heart in order to build a long-term relationship by solving customer problems. Finally, with personal selling, the buyer usually feels a greater need to listen and respond, even if the response is a polite "No thank you."

These unique qualities come at a cost, however. A sales force requires a longer-term commitment than does advertising—advertising can be turned on and off, but sales force size is harder to change. Personal selling is also the company's most expensive promotion tool, costing companies $329 on average per sales call. In some industries, the average cost of a sales call reaches $452.[22] U.S. firms spend up to three times as much on personal selling as they do on advertising.

SALES PROMOTION Sales promotion includes a wide assortment of tools—coupons, contests, cents-off deals, premiums, and others—all of which have many unique qualities. They attract consumer attention, offer strong incentives to purchase, and can be used to dramatize product offers and to boost sagging sales.

■ With personal selling, the customer feels a greater need to listen and respond, even if the response is a polite "No thank you."

Sales promotions invite and reward quick response—whereas advertising says, "Buy our product," sales promotion says, "Buy it now." Sales promotion effects are often short-lived, however, and often are not as effective as advertising or personal selling in building long-run brand preference and customer relationships.

PUBLIC RELATIONS Public relations is very believable—news stories, features, sponsorships, and events seem more real and believable to readers than ads do. Public relations can also reach many prospects who avoid salespeople and advertisements—the message gets to the buyers as "news" rather than as a sales-directed communication. And, as with advertising, public relations can dramatize a company or product. Marketers tend to underuse public relations or to use it as an afterthought. Yet a well-thought-out public relations campaign used with other promotion mix elements can be very effective and economical.

DIRECT MARKETING Although there are many forms of direct marketing—direct mail and catalogs, telephone marketing, online marketing, and others—they all share four distinctive characteristics. Direct marketing is *nonpublic*: The message is normally directed to a specific person. Direct marketing is *immediate* and *customized*: Messages can be prepared very quickly and can be tailored to appeal to specific consumers. Finally, direct marketing is *interactive*: It allows a dialogue between the marketing team and the consumer, and messages can be altered depending on the consumer's response. Thus, direct marketing is well suited to highly targeted marketing efforts and to building one-to-one customer relationships.

Promotion Mix Strategies

Marketers can choose from two basic promotion mix strategies—*push* promotion or *pull* promotion. Figure 14.4 contrasts the two strategies. The relative emphasis on the specific promotion tools differs for push and pull strategies. A **push strategy** involves "pushing" the product through marketing channels to final consumers. The producer directs its marketing activities (primarily personal selling and trade promotion) toward channel members to induce them to carry the product and to promote it to final consumers.

Using a **pull strategy**, the producer directs its marketing activities (primarily advertising and consumer promotion) toward final consumers to induce them to buy the product. If the pull strategy is effective, consumers will then demand the product from channel members, who will in turn demand it from producers. Thus, under a pull strategy, consumer demand "pulls" the product through the channels.

Some industrial goods companies use only push strategies; some direct-marketing companies use only pull strategies. However, most large companies use some combination of both. For example, Kraft uses mass-media advertising and consumer promotions to pull its products and a large sales force and trade promotions to push its products through the channels. In recent years, consumer goods companies have been decreasing the pull portions of their mixes in favor of more push. This has caused concern that they may be driving short-run sales at the expense of long-term brand equity (see Real Marketing 14.2).

Push strategy

A promotion strategy that calls for using the sales force and trade promotion to push the product through channels. The producer promotes the product to channel members to induce them to carry the product and to promote it to final consumers.

Pull strategy

A promotion strategy that calls for spending a lot on advertising and consumer promotion to induce final consumers to buy the product. If the pull strategy is effective, consumers will then demand the product from channel members, who will in turn demand it from producers.

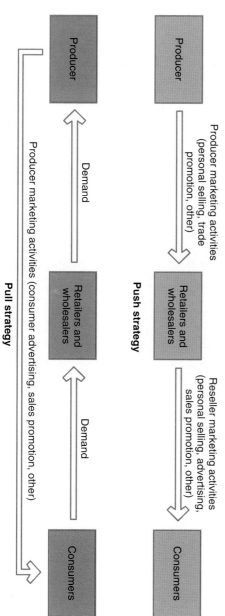

FIGURE 14.4 Push versus pull promotion strategy

Push strategy

Producer → Retailers and wholesalers → Consumers

Producer marketing activities (personal selling, trade promotion, other)

Reseller marketing activities (personal selling, advertising, sales promotion, other)

Pull strategy

Producer → Retailers and wholesalers → Consumers

Demand ← Demand ←

Producer marketing activities (consumer advertising, sales promotion, other)

Real Marketing   Are Consumer Goods Companies Too Pushy?

14.2 Consumer packaged-goods companies such as Procter & Gamble, Kraft Foods, Kellogg, and General Mills grew into giants by using mostly pull promotion strategies. They used massive doses of national advertising to differentiate their products, gain market share, and build brand equity and customer loyalty. But during the past few decades, such companies have gotten more "pushy," deemphasizing national advertising and putting more of their marketing budgets into trade and consumer sales promotions.

General trade promotions (trade allowances, displays, cooperative advertising, and slotting fees aimed at retailers) now account for 58 percent of total marketing spending by consumer product companies. That represents a six-percentage-point increase in trade spending in just the past eight years. Consumer promotions (coupons, discounts, premiums) account for another 16 percent of the typical marketing budget. That leaves less than 26 percent of total marketing spending for mass-media advertising, down from 42 percent twenty years ago.

Why have these companies shifted so heavily toward push strategies? One reason is that mass-media campaigns have become more expensive and less effective in recent years. Network television costs have risen sharply, while audiences have fallen off, making national advertising less cost effective. Companies are also tailoring their marketing programs more narrowly, making national advertising less suitable than localized retailer promotions. And in these days of brand extensions and me-too products, companies sometimes have trouble

finding meaningful product differences to feature in advertising. So they have differentiated their products through price reductions, premium offers, coupons, and other push techniques.

Another factor speeding the shift from pull to push has been the growing strength of retailers. Retail giants such as Wal-Mart, Target, Kroger, and Safeway now have the power to demand and get what they want—and what they want is more push. Whereas national advertising bypasses them on its way to the masses, push promotion benefits them directly. Thus, producers must often use push just to obtain good shelf space and other support from important retailers.

Too pushy? Some categories tend to self-destruct by always being on sale. For example, when automakers get promotion happy, the market just sits back and waits for a deal while the car companies lose money on profit-eating incentives.

Companies consider many factors when designing their promotion mix strategies, including *type of product/market* and the *product life-cycle stage.* For example, the importance of different promotion tools varies between consumer and business markets. Business-to-consumer (B2C) companies usually "pull" more, putting more of their funds into advertising, followed by sales promotion, personal selling, and then public relations. In contrast, business-to-business (B2B) marketers tend to "push" more, putting more of their funds into personal selling, followed by sales promotion, advertising, and public relations. In general, personal selling is used more heavily with expensive and risky goods and in markets with fewer and larger sellers.

The effects of different promotion tools also vary with stages of the product life cycle. In the introduction stage, advertising and public relations are good for producing high awareness, and sales promotion is useful in promoting early trial. Personal selling must be used to get the trade to carry the product. In the growth stage, advertising and public relations continue to be powerful influences, whereas sales promotion can be reduced because fewer incentives are needed. In the mature stage, sales promotion again becomes important relative to advertising. Buyers know the brands, and advertising is needed only to remind them of the product. In the decline stage, advertising is kept at a reminder level, public relations is dropped, and salespeople give the product only a little attention. Sales promotion, however, might continue to be strong.

However, many marketers are concerned that the reckless use of push will lead to fierce price competition and a never-ending spiral of price slashing and deal making. If used improperly, push promotion can mortgage a brand's future for short-term gains. Sales promotion buys short-run reseller support and consumer sales, but advertising builds long-run brand equity and consumer preference. By robbing the media advertising budget to pay for more sales promotion, companies might win the battle for short-run earnings but lose the war for long-run brand equity, consumer loyalty, and market share. In fact, some analysts blame the shift away from advertising dollars for a recent two-decade-long drop in the percentage of consumers who buy only well-known brands.

Of special concern is the overuse of price promotions. The regular use of price as a selling tool can destroy brand equity by encouraging consumers to seek value through price rather than through the benefits of the brand. For example, one recent study showed that decreased TV spending and increased trade promotions for Diet Coke and Coca-Cola Classic over a five-year period eroded equity for both brands, while at the same time increasing consumer price and promotion sensitivity.

In cases where price is a key part of the brand's positioning, featuring price makes sense. But for brands where price does not underlie price value, "price promotions are really desperate acts by brands that have their backs against the wall," says one marketing executive. "Generally speaking, it is better to stick to your guns with price and invest in advertising to drive sales."

Jack Trout, a well-known marketing consultant, cautions that some categories tend to self-destruct by always being on sale. Furniture, automobile tires, airline tickets, and many other categories of goods are rarely sold at anything near list price. And when automakers get rebate happy, the market just sits back and waits for a deal while the car companies lose money on profit-eating incentives. For example, in 2004, General Motors doled out billions of dollars in sales incentives—discounted prices, rebates, and low-cost financing—to move cars out of its showrooms. "While pinching pennies on its $3.5 billion media-buying budget," says an industry expert, "it's giving away $17 billion in incentives—undermining its brand-building efforts." Such promotion tactics have done little to win profits or customer loyalty over the years. Last year, GM lost a staggering $10.5 billion, and its domestic market share has dwindled to less than 25 percent, down from 44.5 percent in 1980.

Trout offers several "Commandments of Discounting," such as "Thou shalt not offer discounts because everyone else does," "Thou shalt be creative with your discounting," "Thou shalt put time limits on the deal," and "Thou shalt stop discounting as soon as you can."

Thus, many consumer companies are now rethinking their promotion strategies and reversing the trend by shifting their promotion budgets back toward advertising. They realize that it's not a question of sales promotion versus advertising, or of push versus pull. Success lies in finding the best mix of the two: consistent advertising to build long-run brand value and consumer preference, and sales promotion to create short-run trade support and consumer excitement. The company needs to blend both push and pull elements into an integrated marketing communications program that meets immediate consumer and retailer needs as well as long-run strategic needs.

Sources: Promotion spending statistics from *2005 Trade Promotion Spending & Merchandising Industry Study* (Cannondale Associates, Wilton, CT, May 2006), p. 13. Other information from Jack Trout, "Prices: Simple Guidelines to Get Them Right," *Journal of Business Strategy*, November-December 1998, pp. 13–16; Alan Mitchell, "When Push Comes to Shove, It's All About Pull," *Marketing Week*, January 9, 2003, pp. 26–27; E. Craig Stacey, "Abandon TV at Your Own Risk," *Advertising Age*, June 7, 2004, p. 32; Jean Halliday, "GM Bleeds as Incentives Undermine Brand Value," *Advertising Age*, March 21, 2005, pp. 1, 37; and "General Motors Corporation," *Hoover's Company Records*, May 15, 2006, p. 10640.

Integrating the Promotion Mix

Having set the promotion budget and mix, the company must now take steps to see that all of the promotion mix elements are smoothly integrated. Here is a checklist for integrating the firm's marketing communications.[23]

- *Analyze trends—internal and external—that can affect the company's ability to do business.* Look for areas where communications can help the most. Determine the strengths and weaknesses of each communications function. Develop a combination of promotional tactics based on these strengths and weaknesses.

- *Audit the pockets of communications spending throughout the organization.* Itemize the communications budgets and tasks and consolidate these into a single budgeting process. Reassess all communications expenditures by product, promotional tool, stage of the life cycle, and observed effect.

- *Identify all customer touch points for the company and its brands.* Work to ensure that communications at each touch point are consistent with the overall communications strategy and that communications efforts are occurring when, where, and how *customers* want them.

- *Team up in communications planning.* Engage all communications functions in joint planning. Include customers, suppliers, and other stakeholders at every stage of communications planning.
- *Create compatible themes, tones, and quality across all communications media.* Make sure each element carries the company's unique primary messages and selling points. This consistency achieves greater impact and prevents the unnecessary duplication of work across functions.
- *Create performance measures that are shared by all communications elements.* Develop systems to evaluate the combined impact of all communications activities.
- *Appoint a director responsible for the company's persuasive communications efforts.* This move encourages efficiency by centralizing planning and creating shared performance measures.

Socially Responsible Marketing Communication

In shaping its promotion mix, a company must be aware of the large body of legal and ethical issues surrounding marketing communications. Most marketers work hard to communicate openly and honestly with consumers and resellers. Still, abuses may occur, and public policy makers have developed a substantial body of laws and regulations to govern advertising, sales promotion, personal selling, and direct-marketing activities. In this section, we discuss issues regarding advertising, sales promotion, and personal selling. We discuss issues regarding direct marketing in Chapter 17.

Advertising and Sales Promotion

By law, companies must avoid false or deceptive advertising. Advertisers must not make false claims, such as suggesting that a product cures something when it does not. They must avoid ads that have the capacity to deceive, even though no one actually may be deceived. An automobile cannot be advertised as getting 32 miles per gallon unless it does so under typical conditions, and a diet bread cannot be advertised as having fewer calories simply because its slices are thinner.

Sellers must avoid bait-and-switch advertising that attracts buyers under false pretenses. For example, a large retailer advertised a sewing machine at $179. However, when consumers tried to buy the advertised machine, the seller downplayed its features, placed faulty machines on showroom floors, understated the machine's performance, and took other actions in an attempt to switch buyers to a more expensive machine. Such actions are both unethical and illegal.

A company's trade promotion activities also are closely regulated. For example, under the Robinson-Patman Act, sellers cannot favor certain customers through their use of trade promotions. They must make promotional allowances and services available to all resellers on proportionately equal terms.

Beyond simply avoiding legal pitfalls, such as deceptive or bait-and-switch advertising, companies can use advertising and other forms of promotion to encourage and promote socially responsible programs and actions. For example, Caterpillar is one of several companies and environmental groups forming the Tropical Forest Foundation, which is working to save the great Amazon rain forest. Caterpillar promotes the cause through advertising and pages on its Web site. Similarly, Mont Blanc supports the National Arts Education Initiative in its efforts to raise awareness about the need for arts education in schools. Its ads state: "Time is precious. Use it wisely. To invest in our future, we must nurture our children's fantasies and inspire their creativity." And for more than a decade, Avon has sponsored the Avon Breast Cancer Crusade, dedicated to funding access to care and finding a cure for breast cancer. Through advertising and a variety of promotions—such as the Avon Walk for Breast Cancer, charity cruises, and the sale of pink ribbon products—Avon's crusade has raised more than the $400 million for this worthwhile cause.[24]

Personal Selling

A company's salespeople must follow the rules of "fair competition." Most states have enacted deceptive sales acts that spell out what is not allowed. For example, salespeople may not lie to consumers or mislead them about the advantages of buying a product. To avoid bait-and-switch practices, salespeople's statements must match advertising claims.

Different rules apply to consumers who are called on at home versus those who go to a store in search of a product. Because people called on at home may be taken by surprise and may be especially vulnerable to high-pressure selling techniques, the Federal Trade Commission (FTC) has adopted a *three-day cooling-off rule* to give special protection to customers who are not seeking products. Under this rule, customers who agree in their own homes to buy something costing more than $25 have 72 hours in which to cancel a contract or return merchandise and get their money back, no questions asked.

Much personal selling involves business-to-business trade. In selling to businesses, salespeople may not offer bribes to purchasing agents or to others who can influence a sale. They may not obtain or use technical or trade secrets of competitors through bribery or industrial espionage. Finally, salespeople must not disparage competitors or competing products by suggesting things that are not true.[25]

Reviewing the Concepts

In this chapter, you've learned how companies use integrated marketing communications (IMC) to communicate customer value. Modern marketing calls for more than just creating customer value by developing a good product, pricing it attractively, and making it available to target customers. Companies also must clearly and persuasively *communicate* that value to current and prospective customers. To do this, they must blend five promotion mix tools, guided by a well-designed and implemented integrated marketing communications strategy.

1. **Discuss the process and advantages of integrated marketing communications in communicating customer value.**

   Recent shifts toward targeted or one-to-one marketing, coupled with advances in information and communication technology, have had a dramatic impact on marketing communications. As marketing communicators adopt richer but more fragmented media and promotion mixes to reach their diverse markets, they risk creating a communications hodgepodge for consumers. To prevent this, more companies are adopting the concept of *integrated marketing communications* (*IMC*). Guided by an overall IMC strategy, the company works out the roles that the various promotional tools will play and the extent to which each will be used. It carefully coordinates the promotional activities and the timing of when major campaigns take place. Finally, to help implement its integrated marketing strategy, the company appoints a marketing communications director who has overall responsibility for the company's communications efforts.

2. **Define the five promotion tools and discuss factors that must be considered in shaping the overall promotion mix.**

   A company's total *promotion mix*—also called its *marketing communications mix*—consists of the specific blend of *advertising*, *personal selling*, *sales promotion*, *public relations*, and *direct-marketing* tools that the company uses to persuasively communicate customer value and build customer relationships. Advertising includes any paid form of nonpersonal presentation and promotion of ideas, goods, or services by an identified sponsor. In contrast, public relations focuses on building good relations with the company's various publics by obtaining favorable unpaid publicity. Personal selling is any form of personal

   presentation by the firm's sales force for the purpose of making sales and building customer relationships. Firms use sales promotion to provide short-term incentives to encourage the purchase or sale of a product or service. Finally, firms seeking immediate response from targeted individual customers use nonpersonal direct-marketing tools to communicate with customers.

3. **Outline the steps in developing effective marketing communications.**

   In preparing marketing communications, the communicator's first task is to *identify the target audience* and its characteristics. Next, the communicator must determine the *communication objectives* and define the response sought, whether it be *awareness*, *knowledge*, *liking*, *preference*, *conviction*, or *purchase*. Then a *message* should be constructed with an effective content and structure. *Media* must be selected, both for personal and nonpersonal communication. The communicator must find highly credible sources to deliver messages. Finally, the communicator must collect *feedback* by watching how much of the market becomes aware, tries the product, and is satisfied in the process.

4. **Explain the methods for setting the promotion budget and factors that affect the design of the promotion mix.**

   The company must decide how much to spend for promotion. The most popular approaches are to spend what the company can afford, to use a percentage of sales, to base promotion on competitors' spending, or to base it on an analysis and costing of the communication objectives and tasks.

   The company divides the *promotion mix* among the major tools to create the *promotion mix*. Companies can pursue a *push* or a *pull* promotional strategy, or a combination of the two. The best specific blend of promotion tools depends on the type of product/market, the buyer's readiness stage, and the product life-cycle stage.

   People at all levels of the organization must be aware of the many legal and ethical issues surrounding marketing communications. Companies must communicate openly, honestly, and agreeably with their customers and resellers.

Reviewing the Key Terms

Discussing the Concepts

1. Many companies are adopting the Integrated Marketing Communication concept. Discuss two major problems that this marketing communications philosophy is designed to remedy.

2. Outline the nine elements of the communications process. Why do marketers need to understand these elements?

3. Why does the marketing communicator need to know the target market's readiness stage? Give an example of an ad targeting each stage.

4. Why might the Northwestern Mutual Life Insurance Company choose a rational appeal for its life insurance products targeted to 28- to 38-year-old males? Why might it choose a humor appeal?

5. Explain how a brand manager for Colgate toothpaste might use each of the common methods for setting total advertising budgets.

6. Name at least five types of sales that are exempt from the FTC's three-day cooling-off rule.

Applying the Concepts

1. Find and describe examples of advertisements or promotions that are examples of narrowcasting, nontraditional advertising, and innovative media technologies.

2. In your judgment who would be the best and the worst celebrity endorsers for each of these products/services: MADD, Dell, Lamborghini.

3. Assume that Energizer is introducing a new line of batteries that provide a longer life than its existing Titanium models. The brand manager for the new line believes most of the promotion budget should be spent on consumer and trade promotions, but the assistant brand manager thinks that the promotion mix should emphasize television advertising. Partner with another student. Play the roles of the brand manager and assistant brand manager and debate their opposing views on advertising versus promotion.

Focus on Technology

As network television viewership declines and fragments, many large advertisers are looking for alternative media. In fact, the 18- to 34-year-old male target market has reduced its hours watching television in favor of video gaming. According to Nielson Entertainment, consumers in this segment watch 9.8 hours of television a week versus 12.5 hours a week playing video games. Until recently, video game advertising posed many challenges for advertisers, including long lead times, technological issues, and the inability to change the advertising message packaged in the game.

Today, with more video games played on the Internet, in-game advertising has exploded. Companies such as Double Fusion (www.doublefusion.com) now offer dynamic, real-time advertising for online gamers. They state that this ultimate "lean-forward" environment offers unique opportunities for marketers. Advertisers can now rotate their advertising during the gaming experience, and they can use online metrics to track the advertising impressions they generate. Software giant Microsoft recently purchased Massive Inc., a pioneer of in-game advertising and is expected to take a lead in this field. The question remains as to how receptive gamers will be to such advertising. Massive hopes to enhance game realism by integrating brands into game items such as soda cans, pizza boxes, billboards, and televisions.

1. How can marketers use in-game advertising to practice IMC?

2. What might Double Fusion mean by a "lean-forward" environment? How might such an environment appeal to marketers when considering buyer-readiness stages?

3. What social responsibility concerns might in-game advertising raise?

Focus on Ethics

Interference Inc. (www.interferenceinc.com) offers guerrilla marketing approaches that enable brands to communicate with target consumers through guerrilla intercept, street teams, stunt and publicity events, and other high-impact creative executions. The company's case studies include many promotions for the Discovery Channel, including a promotion for Discovery's Nefertiti special. The Nefertiti promotion, which included 27 actors in three major cities dressed in historically accurate twelfth-century BC Egyptian costume, was credited with helping the show exceed its national ratings goal. But a recent promotion by Sony Ericsson caught the attention of marketing critics. In the promotion, Sony Ericsson used actor couples pretending to be tourists visiting popular locations to promote a new cell phone. The couples asked passersby to take their pictures with the new cell phone's camera. Sony Ericsson also used actors posing as patrons to visit popular bars and strike up conversations that introduced the new phone to unsuspecting other patrons.

1. Why do you think guerrilla marketing is so effective?

2. What do you think of the Nefertiti guerrilla marketing tactics?

3. Do you consider the Sony Ericsson campaign to be ethical? Explain your opinion.

When you think of Motorola, what comes to mind? A sleek RAZR phone? Or maybe it's the impossibly thin SLVR, a cell phone, camera, and MP3 player all in one. Not so long ago, the Motorola brand wasn't quite so cutting edge. Competitors, such as Nextel, offered products that were more advanced and better designed. So Motorola redesigned it's products and hired Ogilvy & Mather, a global communications firm, to redefine and reposition the Motorola brand. Centered on a core, universal idea—"intelligence everywhere"—the "Moto" campaign hopes to enliven Motorola's image. Rather than convincing consumers by making direct appeals to sign contracts and buy phones, the campaign relies on a simple tagline—Moto—that Motorola hopes consumers will associate with edgy innovation.

More than just ads, the campaign reaches out to consumers through a variety of media. Ogilvy calls it "360-degree brand stewardship." In addition to print, radio, and television ads, the agency crafted interactive e-mails and helped design Motorola's Web site to convey the same lifestyle and value messages that consumers found in print and television ads. The result? Motorola, once seen as stodgy and out of date, is now a hip company with high-tech, sexy phones and annual U.S. sales of more than $31.3 billion.

After watching the video featuring Motorola, answer the following questions about integrated marketing communications.

1. How did Ogilvy & Mather apply the concepts of integrated marketing communications to build Motorola's communications strategy? What was the goal of the campaign that resulted?

2. What were Motorola's communication objectives?

3. How did Motorola's budget for the Moto campaign influence its development and success?

PASS THE MUSTARD

In early 2004, as Burger King's CEO Brad Blum reviewed the company's 2003 performance, he decided once again that he must do something to spice up BK's bland performance. Industry leader McDonald's had just reported a 9 percent sales jump in 2003 to a total of $22.1 billion, while number-two BK's U.S. sales had *slipped* about 5 percent to $7.9 billion. Further, number-three Wendy's sales had spiked 11 percent to $7.4 billion, putting it in position to overtake BK.

Blum surprised the fast-food industry by abruptly firing the firm's advertising agency, Young & Rubicam (Y&R), and awarding its global creative account to a small, Miami-based, upstart firm Crispin Porter + Bogusky (Crispin). The switch marked the fifth time in four years that BK had moved its account! Ad agency Y&R had gotten the $350 million BK account only ten months earlier. To help revive BK's sales, it had developed a campaign with the theme "The Fire's Ready," which focused on BK's flame-broiled versus frying cooking method. However, observers found the message to be flat and uninspiring, and the sales decline sealed Y&R's fate.

With the move to Crispin, there was no shortage of speculation that the fickle Burger King would soon move again. Many saw BK as a bad client, impossible to work for. Others noted that the "win" of this account would ruin Crispin's culture.

CHALLENGING CONVENTIONAL WISDOM

In announcing the Crispin selection, Blum indicated he had challenged the firm to develop "groundbreaking, next-level, results-oriented, and innovative advertising that strongly connects with our core customers." BK automatically became the small firm's largest customer, but Crispin was not without an impressive track record.

Chuck Porter joined Crispin Advertising in 1988. A middle-aged windsurfer, he wanted to be near the water. Alex Bogusky joined the firm later as a 24-year-old art director who raced motorbikes. The Porter-Bogusky combination clicked, and Crispin Porter + Bogusky racked up local awards for its ad campaigns. A Sunglass Hut billboard featured a huge pair of sunglasses with the headline "What to Wear to a Nude Beach." Because its clients often had little money for advertising, Crispin found inexpensive ways to gain attention. For a local homeless shelter, it placed ads on shopping carts, trash dumpsters, and park benches.

In 1997, with Bogusky serving as creative director, Crispin finally got national attention with its unconventional "Truth" campaign aimed at convincing Florida teens to stop smoking. The campaign was so successful, the American Legacy Foundation picked it up and turned it

(case continues)

into a national promotion, leading to a big-budget ad at the Super Bowl—the "Shards O'Glass Freeze Pop." Crispin followed with award-winning, low-budget campaigns for BMW's MINI Cooper, IKEA furniture, and Virgin Atlantic Airways, forging Crispin's reputation as an out-of-the-box, results-oriented agency. Along the way, Crispin developed some loose "rules." Among them were:

- Zero in on the product.
- Kick the TV commercial habit.
- Find the sweet spot (the overlap between product characteristics and customer needs).
- Surprise = buzz = exposure.
- Don't be timid.
- Think of advertising as a product rather than a service.

BACK TO THE FUTURE

Within a month of getting BK's account, rather than recommending some outrageous new idea, Crispin recommended going back to the firm's "Have It Your Way" tagline, developed by BK's second advertising agency, BBDO, in 1974. Crispin argued that it could take that old phrase and make it relevant to today's customers.

Although Crispin's pitch may have initially seemed "same-old," it was anything but. Uncharacteristically, Crispin kicked off the new campaign with TV commercials. In a series of off-beat ads that were a takeoff on a British comedy series, *The Office*, office workers competed and compared their "made my way" BK burgers, reinforcing the message that each customer could have a custom-made burger—no matter how unusual it might be. Crispin planned an entire package of promotions around the new-old theme, including everything from in-store signage to messages on cups.

Although *The Office* ads were unusual and catchy, they were also mainstream media. The TV campaign created an environment for the real Crispin approach to emerge. To promote BK's TenderCrisp chicken, Crispin launched a Web site, www.subservientchicken.com. When people visited the site, they saw what appeared to be a Web camera focused on a somewhat seedy living room. In the room was a man dressed like a chicken (except for one subtle accessory, a lady's garter belt). The site invited the visitor to "Get chicken just the way you like it. Type in your command here." The visitor could type in a command, such as "stand on your head" or "do jumping jacks" and the chicken would respond. If someone typed in a risqué request, the chicken would wave a wing at the camera, as if to say "no-no."

Below the chicken video area were five other icons. "Subservient TV" featured three video clips with various people "having their way" with the chicken. "Photos" presented five "glamour" shots of the chicken. The "Chicken Mask" icon produced a printable chicken mask that one could print, cut out, and wear. The mask's instructions were to "cut along dotted line, put on chicken face, be subservient." A fourth icon, "Tell a Friend," pulled up an Outlook Express e-mail document that invited you to send an e-mail to a friend with the text: "Finally, somebody in a chicken costume who will do whatever you want. Check it out. www.subservientchicken.com." The last icon was marked "BK TenderCrisp" and was linked to the Burger King home page. This was the only indication of BK's sponsorship on the site, reflecting Crispin's desire to avoid seeming too commercial and "uncool." Unless a visitor clicked on that last icon, he or she would have no indication that the site had anything to do with Burger King.

When Crispin launched the site, it told only 20 people—all of whom were friends of people who worked at the agency. Within the first ten *days*, 20 million people visited the site, with the average visitor spending more than seven minutes. Many visitors apparently selected the "tell a friend" icon, sending e-mails flying like feathers.

SUBSERVIENT CHICKEN—CHAPTER 2

In 2005, as a follow-up to the Subservient Chicken promotion, Crispin created a campaign to launch a new BK product, Chicken Fries. The promotion was based on a heavy metal band called Coq Roq with lead singer, Fowl Mouth. Crispin set up a Web site, www.coqroq.com, in world-class rock band fashion. It showcased the band's songs, including "Bob Your Head," "One-Armed Bandit," and "Nice Box." There was even a video for the "hit song" "Cross the Road," directed by music video biggie Paul Hunter. Fans could purchase T-shirts, CDs, cell-phone ring tones, and other fowl merchandise. There was even talk of a tour and a DVD! Was this a real band or just a promotion? Crispin's Coq Roq campaign was so well done, it was difficult to tell. Soon after the Web site launch, Hunter-directed music-video-style ads began airing on MTV and VH-1.

Crispin targeted this campaign squarely at what it perceived to be the main BK target market—young men. Although the campaign was well received by this target segment, many others groups were not so entertained. The campaign ruffled the feathers of real metal band Slipknot. It filed suit, claiming violation of publicity and trademark rights. Other critics saw the campaign for what it was—a crude attempt to generate buzz among teenagers through childish genital humor. In fact, with relations already rocky between Burger King and its franchisees, the campaign only threw more fuel on the fire. The franchisees hated it, as they did the eerie 2004 campaign that featured a bobblehead-looking ceramic King with a gargantuan head. But none of this bothered Burger King's sales. The fast feeder sold more than 100 million orders of Chicken Fries in the first four weeks of the new product launch.

A VIRAL TURNAROUND

Crispin clearly demonstrated with both the Subservient Chicken and the Coq Roq campaigns that it was a master at viral marketing—using unusual methods to get attention and to generate buzz and word of mouth. Despite the success of these campaigns in producing lots of Web site hits, many analysts wondered if they would lead to increased sales and turn around BK's sliding market share. There was also speculation as to whether or not Crispin could continue to produce ideas that would keep BK strong in the fast-food fights.

But at Burger King's 2006 annual franchisee convention, the feeling in the air was "long live the king." CEO Blum debuted a new Crispin ad entitled "Manthem." A parody of the Helen Reddy song "I Am Woman," the spot was yet another example of BK's strategy to unapologetically embrace the young, male, fast-food "super fan." "Manthem's" lyrics spurned "chick food" and gleefully exalted the meat, cheese, and more meat and cheese combos that can turn "innies into outies," all the while showing guys burning their briefs and pushing a minivan off a bridge.

After openly revolting at the convention the year before, BK's restaurant operators rose to their feet in a thunderous ovation, demanding an encore. They now embraced the kind of uncomfortably edgy advertising that they had rejected not so long before. Why this sudden change of heart?

Perhaps it was because Burger King was on the verge of a public offering. Or maybe it was because sales and profits go a long way in healing wounds. "I feel much better this year than I have in the last three, four, or five years," said Mahendra Nath, owner-operator of 90 stores in the upper Midwest and Florida. "I've been up 7.8 percent in 2004, 4.8 percent for 2005, and up 2.8 percent for this quarter so far. Now I think we are believers, and hopefully the trend is going to keep going." Alex Salgueiro, another franchisee who was seeing results similar to Nath's, said, "I think our competitors are scared of the King . . . they should be. They say, 'What's with the King?' and my answer is, 'It's better than clowns.'"

With BK's fortunes apparently changing, franchisees are much less likely to question the irreverent Crispin promotional tactics, whether they like them or not.

And why would they? With the young male demographic providing nearly half of all Burger King visits, Mr. Salguiero said it best: "All opinions boil down to traffic and sales. Once that happens, everybody has to shut up with their opinion. We have a very old franchisee base at this point, and some of us don't understand our customers. We have a lot of gray hair."

Questions for Discussion

1. What are Burger King's communication objectives for its target audience?

2. With its focus on the "super fan," does BK risk alienating other customers? What are the implications of this?

3. Why is viral or buzz marketing effective? Analyze the design of the subservient chicken Web site's message, including content, structure, and format. What can you conclude from this analysis?

4. Do the TV and viral elements of BK's campaigns work well together? What additional elements and media might Crispin add to the integrated marketing communications campaign?

5. What other recommendations would you make to BK and Crispin to help them improve the integration of BK's promotion mix?

Sources: Kate MacArthur, "BK Rebels Fall in Love with King," Advertising Age, May 1, 2006, p. 1; Elaine Walker, "Burger King Works to Mend Rift," Miami Herald, March 27, 2006; Michael Paoletta and Susan Butler, "For BK and Slipknot, a Game of Chicken," Billboard, September 3, 2005; Bob Garfield, "Garfield's Ad Review," Advertising Age, August 1, 2005, p. 29; Bob Garfield, "Garfield's Ad Review," Advertising Age, April 26, 2004, p. 103; Catharine P. Taylor, "Playing Chicken," Adweek, April 19, 2004, p. 19; Brian Steinberg and Suzanne Vranica, "Burger King Seeks Some Web Heat," Wall Street Journal, April 15, 2004, p. B3; Warren Berger, "Dare-Devils: The Ad World's Most Buzzed-About Agency Is Miami's Crispin Porter & Bogusky," Business 2.0, April 2004, p. 110; Kate MacArthur, "Burger King's Big Idea: Have It Your Way, Again," Advertising Age, February 16, 2004, p. 1.

Previewing the Concepts

Now that we've looked at overall integrated marketing communications planning, let's dig more deeply into the specific marketing communications tools. In this chapter, we'll explore advertising and public relations. Advertising involves communicating the company's or brand's value proposition by using paid media to inform, persuade, and remind consumers. Public relations involves building good relations with various company publics—from consumers and the general public to the media, investor, donor, and government publics. As with all of the promotion mix tools, advertising and public relations must be blended into the overall integrated marketing communications program. In the next two chapters, we'll discuss the remaining promotion mix tools: personal selling, sales promotion, and direct marketing.

Let's start by examining some outstanding advertising. Until about ten years ago, GEICO was a little-known nicher in the auto insurance industry. But now, thanks in large part to an industry-changing advertising campaign featuring a likable spokes-lizard and an enduring tagline, GEICO has grown to become a major industry player. Here's the story.

ounded in 1936, GEICO initially targeted a select customer group of government employees and noncommissioned military officers with exceptional driving records. Unlike its much larger competitors, GEICO has no agents. Instead, the auto insurer markets directly to customers. For nearly 60 years, little GEICO relied almost entirely on direct-mail advertising and the telephone to market its services to its select clientele.

In 1994, however, when the company decided to expand its customer base, it knew that it must also expand its marketing. So it hired The Martin Agency, an advertising firm located in Richmond, Virginia. GEICO's advertising adventure began modestly. In 1995, the company spent a paltry $10 million to launch its first national TV, radio, and print ads to support its direct-mail marketing. Then, in 1996, billionaire investor Warren Buffet bought the company and told the marketing group to "speed things up." Did it ever! Over the next 10 years, GEICO's ad spending jumped 30-fold, to more than $300 million.

By now, you probably know a lot about GEICO and its smooth-talking gecko. But at the start, The Martin Agency faced a tough task—introducing a little-known company with a funny name to a national audience. Like all good advertising, the GEICO campaign began with a simple but enduring theme, one that highlights the convenience and savings advantages of GEICO's direct-to-customers system. Every single one of the more than 130 commercials produced in the campaign so far drives home the now-familiar tagline: "15 minutes could save you 15 percent or more on car insurance."

But what really set GEICO's advertising apart was the inspired way the company chose to bring its value proposition to life. At the time, competitors were using serious and sentimental pitches—"You're in good hands with Allstate" or "Like a good neighbor, State Farm is there." To help make its advertising stand out, GEICO decided to deliver its punch line with humor. The creative approach worked and sales began to climb.

As the brand grew, it became apparent that customers had difficulty pronouncing the GEICO name (which once stood for Government Employees Insurance Company). Too often, GEICO became "gecko." Enter the charismatic green lizard. In 1999, GEICO ran a 15-second spot in which the now-famous, British-accented gecko calls a press conference and pleads: "I am a gecko, not to be confused with a GEICO, which could save you hundreds on car insurance. So stop calling me." The ad was supposed to be a "throwaway." "It was an odd spot that didn't fit," says Ted Ward, GEICO vice president of marketing, "but we thought it was funny." Consumers agreed. They quickly flooded the company with calls and letters begging to see more of the gecko. The rest, as they say, is history.

Not only has the gecko helped people to pronounce and remember GEICO's name, it's become a pop culture icon. The unlikely lizard has become so well known that it was voted one of America's top two favorite icons by attendees of last year's Advertising Week in New York, one of the ad industry's largest and most important gatherings.

Although the gecko ads remain a fixture, over the past seven years, to keep its advertising fresh and entertaining, GEICO has added several new minicampaigns. Each new campaign emphasizes a different dimension of the brand's positioning. For example, "Good News" spots address the difficulties of getting drivers to switch insurance companies. The humorous spots appear to be about other products or TV programming, say a soap opera or a home improvement program, until one of the characters unexpectedly announces, "I have good news. I just saved a bunch of money on my car insurance by switching to GEICO."

Another minicampaign, called "Caveman," is designed to bring younger buyers to the GEICO Web site by showing them how easy it is to purchase insurance online. In the first spot, a caveman is livid when a pitchman making a GEICO ad announces, "It's so easy to use GEICO.com, a caveman could do it." In the second spot, two cavemen see the ad and are outraged. In the final spot, the spokesman takes the cavemen to dinner to apologize for insulting them. "Seriously, we apologize. We had no idea you guys were still around," he says. "Next time, maybe do a little research," responds one of the cavemen.

In yet another subcampaign, designed to appeal to young drivers, GEICO launched an Internet site, www.goldengecko.com, at which it invites people to post their own 15-second ads. The only restrictions: The ads must use the gecko and they must be funny. So far, the site has produced some remarkably clever ads.

Although different, all of these minicampaigns have a distinctly GEICO flavor. And each closes strongly with the crucial "15 minutes could save you 15 percent" tagline. Also, as we've come to expect, "the ads are fun," says a branding expert. "What makes GEICO so good is that the ads entertain, deliver a message, and satisfy a need."

Just how good is GEICO's advertising? In each of the past five years, GEICO has experienced double-digit market share gains. Rising from relative obscurity only a dozen years ago, the upstart direct marketer now serves more than seven million customers, making it the fourth largest insurance company, behind State Farm, Allstate, and Progressive, all of which do most of their business through agents.

Not only has the gecko helped GEICO grow, it's changed the face of the auto insurance industry. Many analysts credit GEICO with changing the way insurance companies market their products in this traditionally boring category. "GEICO is spicing it up, and other companies are having to respond," says a communications consultant. "GEICO is exponentially ahead of its competitors in this category." Says another industry observer, "When your advertising has become part of the [pop culture], you have hit a home run."[1]

Objectives

After studying this chapter, you should be able to

1. define the roles of advertising in the promotion mix
2. describe the major decisions involved in developing an advertising program
3. define the role of public relations in the promotion mix
4. explain how companies use public relations to communicate with and influence important publics

As we discussed in the previous chapter, companies must do more that simply create customer value. They must also clearly and persuasively communicate that value to target consumers. In this chapter, we'll take a closer look at two marketing communications tools, *advertising* and *public relations*.

Advertising

Advertising can be traced back to the very beginnings of recorded history. Archaeologists working in the countries around the Mediterranean Sea have dug up signs announcing various events and offers. The Romans painted walls to announce gladiator fights, and the Phoenicians painted pictures promoting their wares on large rocks along parade routes. During the Golden Age in Greece, town criers announced the sale of cattle, crafted items, and even cosmetics. An early "singing commercial" went as follows: "For eyes that are shining, for cheeks like the dawn / For beauty that lasts after girlhood is gone / For prices in reason, the woman who knows / Will buy her cosmetics from Aesclyptos."

Modern advertising, however, is a far cry from these early efforts. U.S. advertisers now run up an estimated annual advertising bill of more than $271 billion; worldwide ad spending exceeds an estimated $604 billion. Procter & Gamble, the world's largest advertiser, last year spent almost $4.6 billion on U.S. advertising and more than $7.9 billion worldwide.[2]

Although advertising is used mostly by business firms, a wide range of not-for-profit organizations, professionals, and social agencies also use advertising to promote their causes to various target publics. In fact, the 27th largest advertising spender is a not-for-profit organization—the U.S. government. Advertising is a good way to inform and persuade, whether the purpose is to sell Coca-Cola worldwide or to get consumers in a developing nation to use birth control.

Marketing management must make four important decisions when developing an advertising program (see Figure 15.1): *setting advertising objectives, setting the advertising budget, developing advertising strategy* (*message decisions* and *media decisions*), and *evaluating advertising campaigns*.

Setting Advertising Objectives

The first step is to set *advertising objectives*. These objectives should be based on past decisions about the target market, positioning, and the marketing mix, which define the job that advertising must do in the total marketing program. The overall advertising objective is to help build customer relationships by communicating customer value. Here, we discuss specific advertising objectives.

An **advertising objective** is a specific communication *task* to be accomplished with a specific *target* audience during a specific period of *time*. Advertising objectives can be classified by primary purpose—whether the aim is to *inform, persuade,* or *remind.* Table 15.1 lists examples of each of these specific objectives.

Advertising
Any paid form of nonpersonal presentation and promotion of ideas, goods, or services by an identified sponsor.

Advertising objective
A specific communication *task* to be accomplished with a specific *target* audience during a specific period of *time.*

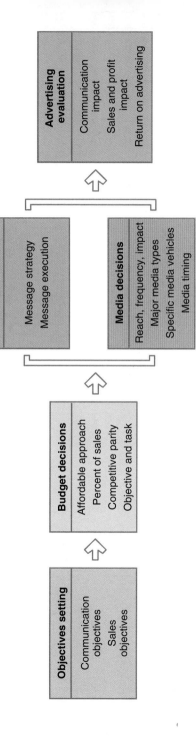

FIGURE 15.1 Major advertising decisions

Objectives setting
Communication objectives
Sales objectives

Budget decisions
Affordable approach
Percent of sales
Competitive parity
Objective and task

Message decisions
Message strategy
Message execution

Media decisions
Reach, frequency, impact
Major media types
Specific media vehicles
Media timing

Advertising evaluation
Communication impact
Sales and profit impact
Return on advertising

TABLE 15.1
Possible Advertising Objectives

Informative Advertising

Communicating customer value	Informing the market of a price change
Telling the market about a new product	Describing available services
Explaining how the product works	Correcting false impressions
Suggesting new uses for a product	Building a brand and company image

Persuasive Advertising

Building brand preference	Persuading customers to purchase now
Encouraging switching to your brand	Persuading customers to receive a sales call
Changing customer's perception of product attributes	Convincing customers to tell others about the brand

Reminder Advertising

Maintaining customer relationships	Reminding consumers where to buy the product
Reminding consumers that the product may be needed in the near future	Keeping the brand in customer's minds during off-seasons

Campbell's Condensed Chicken & Stars

Progresso Chicken Noodle

Now that the kids are gone, life just keeps getting better.

It's time to go Progresso.

This is a time for discovery. So maybe it's time you discovered a soup with a more adult taste. One that tastes better than the condensed you served your kids. Progresso Chicken Noodle. With tender chunks of all white meat chicken, bigger veggies, and wide curly noodles. This is your time. Enjoy a better soup, . . better than the condensed you served your kids. Progresso Chicken Noodle soup and Campbell's Condensed Chicken & Stars. Campbell's is a registered trademark of the Campbell Soup Company. Visit us at www.progressosoup.com

Based on a national taste test comparing Progresso

■ Comparative advertising: Progresso makes side-by-side comparisons of its soup versus Campbell's, inviting consumers to "Enjoy a better soup . . . with a more adult taste."

Informative advertising is used heavily when introducing a new product category. In this case, the objective is to build primary demand. Thus, early producers of DVD players first had to inform consumers of the image quality and convenience benefits of the new product. *Persuasive advertising* becomes more important as competition increases. Here, the company's objective is to build selective demand. For example, once DVD players became established, Sony began trying to persuade consumers that *its* brand offered the best quality for their money.

Some persuasive advertising has become *comparative advertising*, in which a company directly or indirectly compares its brand with one or more other brands. Comparative advertising has been used for products ranging from soft drinks, beer, and pain relievers to computers, batteries, car rentals, and credit cards. For example, in its classic comparative campaign, Avis positioned itself against market-leading Hertz by claiming, "We try harder."

More recently, Suave ran ads featuring a woman with beautiful hair questioning, "Suave or Matrix? Can You Tell?" The ad then explains that you can't tell because Suave hair products perform just as well as Matrix products, "even though Matrix costs five times as much." Similarly, Procter & Gamble ran an ad comparing its Tide with Bleach to Oxy10. In the ad, consumers spread iodine, tomato sauce, mud, and grass on a white T-shirt that was then cut in half and treated with the two detergents. All the while, "Anything You Can Do I Can Do Better" played in the background. Of course, Tide did a better job of removing the stains. Advertisers should use comparative advertising with caution. All too often, such ads invite competitor responses, resulting in an advertising war that neither competitor can win.

Reminder advertising is important for mature products—it helps to maintain customer relationships

Informative advertising is used heavily when introducing a new product category. In this case, the objective is to build primary demand. Thus, early producers of DVD players first had to inform consumers of the image quality and convenience benefits of the new product. Persuasive advertising becomes more important as competition increases. Here, the company's objective is to build selective demand. For example, once DVD players became established, Sony began trying to persuade consumers that its brand offered the best quality for their money.

and keep consumers thinking about the product. Expensive Coca-Cola television ads primarily build and maintain the Coca-Cola brand relationship rather than informing or persuading customers to buy in the short run.

Advertising's goal is to move consumers through the buyer-readiness stages discussed in the previous chapter. Some advertising is designed to move people to immediate action. For example, a direct-response television ad by Sharper Image for its Bionic Breeze air purifier urges consumers to pick up the phone and order right away, and a Sears newspaper ad for a weekend sale encourages store visits. However, many of the other ads focus on building or strengthening long-term customer relationships. For example, a Nike television ad in which well-known athletes "just do it" never directly asks for a sale. Instead, the goal is to somehow change the way the customers think or feel about the brand.

Setting the Advertising Budget

Advertising budget
The dollars and other resources allocated to a product or company advertising program.

After determining its advertising objectives, the company next sets its **advertising budget** for each product. Four commonly used methods for setting promotion budgets are discussed in Chapter 14. Here we discuss some specific factors that should be considered when setting the advertising budget.

A brand's advertising budget often depends on its *stage in the product life cycle*. For example, new products typically need large advertising budgets to build awareness and to gain consumer trial. In contrast, mature brands usually require lower budgets as a ratio to sales. *Market share* also impacts the amount of advertising needed: Because building the market or taking market share from competitors requires larger advertising spending than does simply maintaining current share, low-share brands usually need more advertising spending as a percentage of sales. Also, brands in a market with many competitors and high advertising clutter must be advertised more heavily to be noticed above the noise in the market. Undifferentiated brands—those that closely resemble other brands in their product class (soft drinks, laundry detergents)—may require heavy advertising to set them apart. When the product differs greatly from competitors, advertising can be used to point out the differences to consumers.

No matter what method is used, setting the advertising budget is no easy task. How does a company know if it is spending the right amount? Some critics charge that large consumer packaged-goods firms tend to spend too much on advertising and business-to-business marketers generally underspend on advertising. They claim that, on the one hand, the large consumer companies use lots of image advertising without really knowing its effects. They overspend as a form of "insurance" against not spending enough. On the other hand, business advertisers tend to rely too heavily on their sales forces to bring in orders. They underestimate the power of company and product image in preselling to industrial customers. Thus, they do not spend enough on advertising to build customer awareness and knowledge.

Companies such as Coca-Cola and Kraft have built sophisticated statistical models to determine the relationship between promotional spending and brand sales and to help determine the "optimal investment" across various media. Still, because so many factors, some controllable and others not, affect advertising effectiveness, measuring the results of advertising spending remains an inexact science. In most cases, managers must rely on large doses of judgment along with more quantitative analysis when setting advertising budgets.[3]

Developing Advertising Strategy

Advertising strategy
The strategy by which the company accomplishes its advertising objectives. It consists of two major elements: creating advertising messages and selecting advertising media.

Advertising strategy consists of two major elements: creating advertising *messages* and selecting advertising *media*. In the past, companies often viewed media planning as secondary to the message-creation process. The creative department first created good advertisements, and then the media department selected and purchased the best media for carrying these advertisements to desired target audiences. This often caused friction between creatives and media planners.

Today, however, media fragmentation, soaring media costs, and more-focused target marketing strategies have promoted the importance of the media-planning function. More and more, advertisers are orchestrating a closer harmony between their messages and the media that deliver them.

■ Media-creative partnerships: In its now classic campaign, Absolut vodka developed a wonderful assortment of creative ads that were tightly targeted to the audiences of the media in which they appeared.

A long-simmering Madison Avenue debate is boiling anew: Should the people who create clever commercials work more closely with the people who decide where those same commercials appear? It used to be that creative executives who crafted commercials were the top dogs of Madison Avenue. Media buyers and planners played a much less glamorous role, figuring out which TV network or magazine an advertiser should use and then buying the time or space needed. Many large agency holding companies have widened the creative-media gap by splitting off their media planning and buying functions into separate divisions. More recently, however, what was a humdrum media job has become vastly more important. The fragmentation of audiences among a growing array of new-media technologies is forcing marketers to put less emphasis on traditional outlets, such as television, and more on narrowly targeted media. As a result, the decision about which medium to use for an ad campaign—iPod, Web site, video on demand, broadcast or cable television, or e-mail—is now sometimes more critical than the creative elements of the campaign.

Now, marketers are asking ad agencies for strategies that integrate creative ideas with media placement. An example is satellite-TV operator DirecTV, which targets some of its marketing so narrowly that it aims at individual zip codes. The geographic area helps determine the types of ads used. People in a city dependent on cars are more likely to see a DirecTV billboard than are target customers in a mass-transit hotspot such as New York. In such cases, the creative content of the commercials is sometimes determined only after deciding on the types of media. DirecTV recently moved its advertising and media accounts, previously handled separately, to a single agency. "It's just easier and more coordinated and better executed" when creative and media planning are "all under one roof," says DirecTV's chief marketing officer. An executive of a large ad agency agrees: "The stupidest thing that ever happened in our industry is when media planners left the building."[4]

Some companies have long recognized the importance of tight media-creative partnerships. For example, for more than 25 years, Absolut created a wonderful assortment of creative ads that were tightly targeted to the audiences of the media in which they appeared. In New York-area magazines, "Absolut Manhattan" ads featured a satellite photo of Manhattan, with Central Park assuming the distinctive outline of an Absolut bottle. In London, ads showed the famous entry to the Prime Minister's residence at No. 10 Downing Street with the door in the shape of an Absolut bottle. An "Absolut Bravo" ad in playbills had roses adorning a clear bottle, and an "Absolute Primary" ad run during the political season featured the well-known bottle spattered with mud. And in "Absolut Love," run in February to celebrate Valentine's Day, two Absolut bottles embrace, silhouetted by a shining heart in the background. This pioneering campaign helped make Absolut the nation's number-one imported vodka and the number-three liquor brand overall.[5]

Creating the Advertising Message

No matter how big the budget, advertising can succeed only if advertisements gain attention and communicate well. Good advertising messages are especially important in today's costly and cluttered advertising environment. In 1950, the average U.S. household received just three network television channels and a handful of major national magazines. Today, there are seven networks and 263 subscription channels, and consumers have more than 22,000 magazines from which to choose.[6] Add the countless radio stations and a continuous barrage of catalogs, direct mail, Internet e-mail and online ads, and out-of-home media, and consumers are being bombarded with ads at home, at work, and at all points in between. One expert estimates that the average person is exposed to some 3,000 ad messages a day. Another puts the number at an eye-popping 5,000 ads a day.[7]

BREAKING THROUGH THE CLUTTER If all this advertising clutter bothers some consumers, it also causes big problems for advertisers. Take the situation facing network television advertisers. They pay an average of $338,000 to make a single thirty-second commercial. Then, each time they show it, they regularly pay $300,000 or more for thirty seconds of advertising time during a popular prime-time program. They pay even more if it's an especially popular program such as *American Idol* (as much as $705,000), *Desperate Housewives* ($560,000), *CSI* ($478,000), or a megaevent such as the *American Idol* season finale ($1.3 million) or the Super Bowl ($2.5 million per 30 seconds!).[8]

Then, their ads are sandwiched in with a clutter of other commercials, announcements, and network promotions, totaling more than 15 minutes of nonprogram material per prime-time hour, more than 21 minutes per daytime hour. Such clutter in television and other ad media has created an increasingly hostile advertising environment. According to one recent study, 65 percent of Americans say they are "constantly bombarded with too much" advertising and about two-thirds say that their view of advertising is "much more negative than just a few years ago."[9]

Until recently, television viewers were pretty much a captive audience for advertisers. But today's digital wizardry has given consumers a rich new set of information and entertainment choices. With the growth in cable and satellite TV, the Internet, video on demand (VOD), and DVD rentals, today's viewers have many more options. Digital technology has also armed consumers with an arsenal of weapons for choosing what they watch or don't watch. Increasingly, consumers are choosing *not* to watch ads. They "zap" commercials by fast-forwarding through recorded programs. With the remote control, they mute the

■ Advertising clutter: If advertising clutter bothers some consumers, it also causes big problems for advertisers. They might pay $1 million or more for 30 seconds of advertising time around a popular prime-time TV program like the final episode of American Idol, then have their ads sandwiched in with a glut of other commercials, announcements, and network promotions.

sound during a commercial or "zip" around the channels to see what else is on. A recent study found that 40 percent of all television viewers now switch channels when the commercial break starts.[10]

Adding to the problem is the rapid growth of TiVo-style DVR (digital video recorder) systems. Almost 20 percent of American homes now have DVR technology, and it is expected that 39 percent of households will have it by 2010. And TiVo reports that when its customers watch recorded programs, they skip 70 percent of the commercials. One ad agency executive calls DVR systems "electronic weed whackers." "In time, the number of people using them to obliterate commercials will totally erode faith in the 30-second commercial," he declares. Similarly, the number of VOD viewers is expected to quadruple during the next five years. These viewers will be able to watch programming on their own time terms, with or without commercials.[11]

Thus, advertisers can no longer force-feed the same old cookie-cutter ad messages to captive consumers through traditional media. Just to gain and hold attention, today's advertising messages must be better planned, more imaginative, more entertaining, and more rewarding to consumers. "Interruption or disruption as the fundamental premise of marketing" no longer works, says one advertising executive. "You have to create content that is interesting, useful, or entertaining enough to invite [consumers]." According to another, advertisers must now "draw people in. Tell a story. Encourage them to engage in it, and reward them when they do. If you do it right, they'll want to see your ads again and again."[12]

In fact, many marketers are now subscribing to a new merging of advertising and entertainment, dubbed **"Madison & Vine."** You've probably heard of Madison Avenue. It's the New York City street that houses the headquarters of many of the nation's largest advertising agencies. You may also have heard of Hollywood & Vine, the intersection of Hollywood Avenue and Vine Street in Hollywood, California, long the symbolic heart of the U.S. entertainment industry. Now, Madison Avenue and Hollywood & Vine are coming together to form a new intersection—*Madison & Vine*—that represents the merging of advertising and entertainment in an effort to break through the clutter and create new avenues for reaching consumers with more engaging messages (see Real Marketing 15.1).

MESSAGE STRATEGY The first step in creating effective advertising messages is to plan a *message strategy*—to decide what general message will be communicated to consumers. The purpose of advertising is to get consumers to think about or react to the product or company in a certain way. People will react only if they believe that they will benefit from doing so. Thus, developing an effective message strategy begins with identifying customer *benefits* that can be used as advertising appeals. Ideally, advertising message strategy will follow directly from the company's broader positioning and customer value strategies.

Message strategy statements tend to be plain, straightforward outlines of benefits and positioning points that the advertiser wants to stress. The advertiser must next develop a compelling **creative concept**—or *"big idea"*—that will bring the message strategy to life in a distinctive and memorable way. At this stage, simple message ideas become great ad campaigns. Usually, a copywriter and art director will team up to generate many creative concepts, hoping that one of these concepts will turn out to be the big idea. The creative concept may emerge as a visualization, a phrase, or a combination of the two.

The creative concept will guide the choice of specific appeals to be used in an advertising campaign. *Advertising appeals* should have three characteristics: First, they should be *meaningful*, pointing out benefits that make the product more desirable or interesting to consumers. Second, appeals must be *believable*—consumers must believe that the product or service will deliver the promised benefits.

However, the most meaningful and believable benefits may not be the best ones to feature. Appeals should also be *distinctive*—they should tell how the product is better than the competing brands. For example, the most meaningful benefit of owning a wristwatch is that it keeps accurate time, yet few watch ads feature this benefit. Instead, based on the distinctive benefits they offer, watch advertisers might select any of a number of advertising themes. For years, Timex has been the affordable watch that "Takes a lickin' and keeps on tickin'." In contrast, Fossil has featured style and fashion, whereas Rolex stresses luxury and status.

Madison & Vine
A term that has come to represent the merging of advertising and entertainment in an effort to break through the clutter and create new avenues for reaching consumers with more engaging messages.

Creative concept
The compelling "big idea" that will bring the advertising message strategy to life in a distinctive and memorable way.

Real Marketing

Madison & Vine: The New Intersection of Advertising and Entertainment

15.1 Welcome to the ever-busier intersection of Madison & Vine, where the advertising industry meets the entertainment industry. In today's cluttered advertising environment, Madison Avenue knows that it must find new ways to engage ad-weary consumers with more compelling messages. The answer? Entertainment! And who knows more about entertainment than the folks at Hollywood & Vine? The term "Madison & Vine" has come to represent the merging of advertising and entertainment. It takes one of two primary forms: *advertainment* or *branded entertainment.*

The aim of *advertainment* is to make ads themselves so entertaining, or so useful, that people *want* to watch them. It's advertising by invitation rather than by intrusion. There's no chance that you'd watch ads on purpose, you say? Think again. For example, the Super Bowl has become an annual advertainment showcase. Tens of millions of people tune in to the Super Bowl each year, as much to watch the entertaining ads as to see the game.

And rather than bemoaning TiVo and other DVR systems, many advertisers are now using them as a new medium for showing useful or entertaining ads that consumers actually volunteer to watch. For example, TiVo recently launched Product Watch, a service offering special on-demand ads to subscribers from companies such as Kraft Foods, Ford, Lending Tree, and Pioneer Electronics. Longer than traditional 30-second spots, these ads allow consumers to research products before buying them or simply to learn something new. Kraft, for instance, offered 20 different cooking videos creating meals using its products. And Pioneer sponsored a four-minute video ad on the ins and outs of buying a plasma-screen high-definition television.

Interestingly, a recent study found that DVR users aren't necessarily skipping all the ads. According to the study, 55 percent of DVR users take their finger off the fast-forward button to watch a commercial that is entertaining or relevant, sometimes even watching it more than once. "If advertising is really entertaining, you don't zap it," notes an industry observer. "You might even go out of your way to see it."

Beyond making their regular ads more entertaining, advertisers are also creating new advertising forms that look less like ads and more like short films or shows. For example, as part of a $100 million campaign to introduce its Sunsilk line of hair care products in the United States, Unilever is producing a series of two-minute short programs that resemble sitcom episodes more than ads.

The series, titled "Sunsilk Presents Max and Katie," will run on the TBS cable network. The miniepisodes present a humorous look at the hectic life of a 20-something woman—not coincidentally, the Sunsilk target audience. In all, Unilever will produce 85 miniepisodes of "Max and Katie," with 65 intended for TBS and the rest to be available online, on cell phones, through e-mail, and at displays in stores. The woman at whom Sunsilk will be aimed "has grown up being marketed to her

whole life," says a Unilever marketing manager. "She's open to advertising, if it's entertaining to her."

Similarly, Procter & Gamble produced a series of 90-second advertising sitcoms called "At the Poocherellas," shown on Nick at Night, featuring a family of dogs and promoting its Febreze brand. Each miniepisode includes the expected commercial break, which lasts

---

Welcome to Madison & Vine. As this book cover suggests, in today's cluttered advertising environment, Madison Avenue must find new ways to engage ad-weary consumers with more compelling messages. The answer? Entertainment!

MESSAGE EXECUTION The advertiser now must turn the big idea into an actual ad execution that will capture the target market's attention and interest. The creative team must find the best approach, style, tone, words, and format for executing the message. Any message can be presented in different **execution styles**, such as the following:

- *Slice of life:* This style shows one or more "typical" people using the product in a normal setting. For example, two mothers at a picnic discuss the nutritional benefits of Jif peanut butter.

Execution style
The approach, style, tone, words, and format used for executing an advertising message.

just long enough to say, "Febreze, it's fresh." "We don't really think of this as advertising," says a media executive. "We create an environment where a brand's character and equity live in a show."

Branded entertainment (or brand integrations) involves making the brand an inseparable part of some other form of entertainment. The most common form of branded entertainment is product placements—imbedding brands as props within other programming. In all, advertisers paid an estimated $1.2 billion on product placements last year, up 30 percent from the previous year. The nature of the placement can vary widely. It might be a brief glimpse of a Starbucks coffee cup sitting on a table on HBO's *Entourage* or the judges on *American Idol* drinking out of Coca-Cola cups. Or it might involve scripting products into the theme of the program. For example, the boss of *The Office* frequents Chili's restaurant and orders his "awesome blossom, extra awesome"—in one episode, he even broke into the restaurant's catchy "baby back ribs" jingle while entertaining a client there.

Costs of product placements range widely. "A car manufacturer might be willing to pay $100,000 to $150,000 to show the mirror turns upside down," says one expert. "Going in and completely crafting a whole segment from scratch where the brand is a key player could be a million bucks." For example, blue-chip companies such as Procter & Gamble, General Motors, Staples, Unilever, and Burger King paid $1 to $4 million per episode to integrate their brands into the reality show, *The Apprentice.*

Perhaps no company has gotten more mileage out of such brand integrations than GM's Pontiac division. It all started with an extraordinary giveaway on a popular talk show:

When *The Oprah Winfrey Show* opened its 19th season with a "Wildest Dreams" theme, Oprah electrified the studio audience by giving every one of the 276 people in attendance a new, fully loaded Pontiac G6 sedan worth $28,400. The Oprah giveaway set a new benchmark in the field of branded entertainment. It cost Pontiac about $8 million but generated an estimated $20 million in unpaid media coverage and favorable PR.

Pontiac followed quickly with another stunningly successful placement, this time on *The Apprentice.* Generally viewed as the most successful *Apprentice* brand integration ever, Pontiac used the show to announce a national early-order program for its then-new Solstice two-seat roadster. In a show that included photo shoots of the sleek new car and discussions of Solstice benefits, *Apprentice* teams pulled all-nighters to create Solstice promotion brochures. The result: Pontiac's Web site traffic skyrocketed 1,400 percent the night the episode aired, and some 41,000 people registered online for a chance to place an early order. Expecting to sell 1,000 cars within 10 days, Pontiac blew by that goal in just 41 minutes after the cars went on sale the next day. In all, Pontiac chalked up

Or a Silk soymilk "Rise and Shine" ad shows a young professional starting the day with a healthier breakfast and high hopes.

■ *Lifestyle:* This style shows how a product fits in with a particular lifestyle. For example, an ad for Liquidlogic Kayaks shows kayakers challenging some serious white water and states, "2/3 of the earth is covered in playground—live wet."

7,116 orders during the promotion, more Solstices than it planned to build for the entire year.

Originally created with TV in mind, branded entertainment has spread quickly into other sectors of the entertainment industry. It's widely used in movies—think about Ray Ban sunglasses in *Men in Black*, or the Land Rover LR3 in *Mission: Impossible III*. And when DreamWorks built the terminal for its movie *The Terminal*, along with United Airlines, more than 35 companies chipped in millions to build real stores—Brookstone, Discovery Store, Borders Books, Paul Mitchell—as well as a working food court with a Starbucks, Baskin-Robbins, Burger King, and Baja Fresh. If you look carefully, you'll also see subtle and not-so-subtle product placements in online video games, magazines, Internet sites, and just about anything else—from comic books to Broadway musicals. For example, the script for *Sweet Charity* was revised to fit Jose Cuervo's Gran Centenario tequila into a scene.

So, Madison & Vine is *the* new meeting place for the advertising and entertainment industries. When done right, advertisement and branded entertainment can pay big dividends. However, experts caution that Madison & Vine can also be a dangerous crossing. They worry that making ads too entertaining might detract from the seller's brand message—consumers will remember the clever ad but forget the brand or advertiser. And they note that the intersection is getting pretty congested. With all these new ad formats and product placements, Madison & Vine threatens to create even more of the very clutter that it's designed to break through.

They also worry about potential customer resentment and backlash. Some TV shows outright bristle with product placements. A heavily branded show like *American Idol* contains, on average, more than 36 product placement shots per hour. During the fall season last year, the 10 prime-time TV shows with the most placements included 9,019 "brand shout-outs," up from 5,821 the year before. At what point will consumers decide that the intersection of Madison & Vine is just too congested and take yet a different route?

Sources: Quotes and information from Michael Applebaum, "Early Bird Apprentice Draws Solstice Buyers," *Brandweek*, March 13, 2006, pp. R4–R5; Gail Schiller, "Win, Draw for Burnett Branding," *The Hollywood Reporter*, June 1, 2005, accessed at www.hollywoodreporter.com; "Study Spots Ad-Skipping Trends," August 19, 2005, accessed at www.hollywoodreporter.com; Jim Edwards, "There's Less Than Meets the Eye in TV Placement Economy," *Brandweek*, December 19–26, 2005, p. 15; Lynn Smith, "Television: When the Plot Pushes Product," *Los Angeles Times*, February 12, 2006, p. E5; Stuart Elliot, "Pay Attention to the Story, but Please Also Notice the Goods," *New York Times*, March 13, 2006, p. C8; Stuart Elliot, "A Sponsor and Its Show, Intertwined," *New York Times*, April 17, 2006, p. C8; and Brian Steinberg, "TiVo Latest Viewing Option: Commercials," *Wall Street Journal*, May 8, 2006, p. B3.

- *Fantasy:* This style creates a fantasy around the product or its use. For instance, many ads are built around dream themes. One commercial for the Adidas1 shoes features a guy dreaming he can out-run everything wearing his Adidas. It closes with the statement "Impossible is nothing."

- *Mood or image:* This style builds a mood or image around the product or service, such as beauty, love, or serenity. Few claims are made about the product except through suggestion. For example, ads for Singapore Airlines feature soft lighting and refined flight attendants pampering relaxed and happy customers.

- *Musical:* This style shows people or cartoon characters singing about the product. For example, one of the most famous ads in history was a Coca-Cola ad built around the song "I'd Like to Teach the World to Sing." Similarly, Oscar Mayer has long run ads showing children singing its now-classic "I wish I were an Oscar Mayer wiener . . ." jingle. And is there anyone who doesn't know the Chili's advertising song, "I love my baby-back, baby-back, baby-back, . . . baby-back ribs"?

- *Personality symbol:* This style creates a character that represents the product. The character might be *animated* (Mr. Clean, Tony the Tiger, the GEICO gecko) or *real* (the Marlboro man, Ol' Lonely the Maytag repairman, or the AFLAC duck).

- *Technical expertise:* This style shows the company's expertise in making the product. Thus, Maxwell House shows one of its buyers carefully selecting coffee beans, and Jim Koch of the Boston Beer Company tells about his many years of experience in brewing Samuel Adams beer.

- *Scientific evidence:* This style presents survey or scientific evidence that the brand is better or better liked than one or more other brands. For years, Crest toothpaste has used scientific evidence to convince buyers that Crest is better than other brands at fighting cavities.

- *Testimonial evidence or endorsement:* This style features a highly believable or likable source endorsing the product. It could be ordinary people saying how much they like a given product—as in the JetBlue ads discussed in the previous chapter. Or it might be a celebrity presenting the product. For example, Gatorade ran an ad showing how Gatorade helped triathlete Chris Legh win an Ironman triathlon victory following a near-fatal collapse a few years earlier due to dehydration.

The advertiser also must choose a *tone* for the ad. Procter & Gamble always uses a positive tone: Its ads say something very positive about its products. P&G usually avoids humor that might take attention away from the message. In contrast, many advertisers now use edgy humor to break through the commercial clutter.

The advertiser must use memorable and attention-getting *words* in the ad. For example, rather than claiming simply that "a BMW is a well-engineered automobile," BMW uses more creative and higher-impact phrasing: "The ultimate driving machine." Instead of stating that "K9 Advantix is a topical serum that keeps ticks, fleas, and mosquitoes off your dog," Bayer states it more colorfully—with K9 Advantix, "There ain't no bugs on me!" The World Wildlife Fund doesn't say, "We need your money to help save nature." Instead, it says, "We share the sky. We share the future. Together, we can be a force of nature."

Finally, *format* elements make a difference in an ad's impact as well as in its cost. A small change in ad design can make a big difference in its effect. In a print ad, the *illustration* is the first thing the reader notices—it must be strong enough to draw attention. Next, the *headline*

Lifestyle execution style: This LiquidLogic Kayaks ad shows kayakers challenging some serious white water and states, "2/3 of the earth is covered in playground—live wet."

must effectively entice the right people to read the copy. Finally, the *copy*—the main block of text in the ad—must be simple but strong and convincing. Moreover, these three elements must effectively work *together* to persuasively present customer value.

Selecting Advertising Media

The major steps in **advertising media** selection are (1) deciding on *reach, frequency,* and *impact*; (2) choosing among major *media types*; (3) selecting specific *media vehicles*; and (4) deciding on *media timing*.

DECIDING ON REACH, FREQUENCY, AND IMPACT To select media, the advertiser must decide on the reach and frequency needed to achieve advertising objectives. *Reach* is a measure of the *percentage* of people in the target market who are exposed to the ad campaign during a given period of time. For example, the advertiser might try to reach 70 percent of the target market during the first three months of the campaign. *Frequency* is a measure of how many *times* the average person in the target market is exposed to the message. For example, the advertiser might want an average exposure frequency of three.

But advertisers want to do more than just reach a given number of consumers a specific number of times. The advertiser also must decide on the desired *media impact*—the *qualitative value* of a message exposure through a given medium. For example, the same message in one magazine (say, *Newsweek*) may be more believable than in another (say, the *National Enquirer*). For products that need to be demonstrated, messages on television may have more impact than messages on radio because television uses sight *and* sound. Products for which consumers provide input on design or features might be better promoted at a Web site than in a direct mailing.

More generally, the advertiser wants to choose media that will *engage* consumers rather than simply reach them. For example, for television advertising, "how relevant a program is for its audience and where the ads are inserted are likely to be much more important than whether the program was a Nielsen winner" numbers-wise, says one expert. "This is about 'lean to' TV rather than 'lean back.'" Although Nielsen is beginning to measure levels of television *media engagement*, such measures are hard to come by for most media. "All the measurements we have now are media metrics: ratings, readership, listenership, click-through rates," says an executive of the Advertising Research Foundation, but engagement "happens inside the consumer, not inside the medium. What we need is a way to determine how the targeted prospect connected with, got engaged with, the brand idea. With engagement, you're on your way to a relationship. . . ."[13]

CHOOSING AMONG MAJOR MEDIA TYPES The media planner must know the reach, frequency, and impact of each of the major media types. As summarized in Table 15.2, the major media types are television, newspapers, direct mail, magazines, radio, outdoor, and the Internet. Each medium has advantages and limitations. Media planners consider many factors when making their media choices. They want to choose media that will effectively and efficiently present the advertising message to target customers. Thus, they must consider each medium's impact, message effectiveness, and cost.

The mix of media must be reexamined regularly. For a long time, television and magazines dominated in the media mixes of national advertisers, with other media often neglected. However, as discussed in the previous chapter, the media mix appears to be shifting. As mass-media costs rise, audiences shrink, and exciting new digital media emerge, many advertisers are finding new ways to reach consumers. They are supplementing the traditional mass media with more specialized and highly targeted media that cost less, target more effectively, and engage consumers more fully.

For example, cable television and satellite television systems are booming. Such systems allow narrow programming formats such as all sports, all news, nutrition, arts, home improvement and gardening, cooking, travel, history, finance, and others that target select groups. Time Warner, Comcast, and other cable operators are even testing systems that will let them target specific types of ads to specific neighborhoods or to specific types of customers. For example, ads for a Spanish-language newspaper would run only in Hispanic neighborhoods, or only pet owners would see ads from pet food companies.[14]

Advertisers can take advantage of such "narrowcasting" to "rifle in" on special market segments rather than use the "shotgun" approach offered by network broadcasting. Cable and

Advertising media
The vehicles through which advertising messages are delivered to their intended audiences.

TABLE 15.2
Profiles of Major Media Types

Medium	Advantages	Limitations
Television	Good mass-marketing coverage; low cost per exposure; combines sight, sound, and motion; appealing to the senses	High absolute costs; high clutter; fleeting exposure; less audience selectivity
Newspapers	Flexibility; timeliness; good local market coverage; broad acceptability; high believability	Short life; poor reproduction quality; small pass-along audience
Direct mail	High audience selectivity; flexibility; no ad competition within the same medium; allows personalization	Relatively high cost per exposure, "junk mail" image
Magazines	High geographic and demographic selectivity; credibility and prestige; high-quality reproduction; long life and good pass-along readership	Long ad purchase lead time; high cost; no guarantee of position
Radio	Good local acceptance; high geographic and demographic selectivity; low cost	Audio only, fleeting exposure; low attention ("the half-heard" medium); fragmented audiences
Outdoor	Flexibility; high repeat exposure; low cost; low message competition; good positional selectivity	Little audience selectivity; creative limitations
Internet	High selectivity; low cost; immediacy; interactive capabilities	Demographically skewed audience; relatively low impact; audience controls exposure

satellite television media seem to make good sense. But, increasingly, ads are popping up in far less likely places. In their efforts to find less costly and more highly targeted ways to reach consumers, advertisers have discovered a dazzling collection of "alternative media" (see Real Marketing 15.2).

Another important trend affecting media selection is the rapid growth in the number of "media multitaskers," people who absorb more than one medium at a time:

It looks like people who aren't satisfied with "just watching TV" are in good company. According to a recent survey, three-fourths of U.S. TV viewers read the newspaper while they watch TV, and two-thirds of them go online during their TV time. According to the study, 70 percent of media users say they at one time or another try to absorb two or more forms of media at once. What's more, if today's kids are any indication, media multitasking is on the rise. Americans aged 8 to 18 are managing to cram an average 8.5 hours of media consumption into 6.5 hours. It's not uncommon to find a teenage boy chasing down photos of Keira Knightly on Google, IMing several friends at once, listening to a mix of music on iTunes, and talking on the cell phone to a friend all the while, in the midst of the multimedia chaos, trying to complete an essay he's got open in a Word file a few layers down on his desktop.[15]

Media planners need to take such media interactions into account when selecting the types of media they will use.

SELECTING SPECIFIC MEDIA VEHICLES   The media planner now must choose the best *media vehicles*—specific media within each general media type. For example, television vehicles include *Scrubs* and *ABC World News Tonight. Magazine* vehicles include *Newsweek, People,* and *ESPN The Magazine.*

Media planners must compute the cost per thousand persons reached by a vehicle. For example, if a full-page, four-color advertisement in the U.S. national edition of *Newsweek* costs $220,500 and *Newsweek's* readership is 3.1 million people, the cost of reaching each group of 1,000 persons is about $71. The same advertisement in *Business Week* may cost only $99,500 but reach only 971,000 persons—at a cost per thousand of about $102. The media planner ranks each

15.2 Alternative Media: Ads Popping Up in Unlikely Places

As consumers, we're used to ads on television, in magazines and newspapers, at Web sites, on the radio, and along the roadways. But these days, no matter where you go or what you do, you will probably run into some new form of advertising.

Tiny billboards attached to shopping carts, ads on shopping bags, and even advertising decals on supermarket floors urge you to buy Jell-O Pudding Pops or Pampers. Signs atop parking meters hawk everything from Jeeps to Minolta cameras to Recipe dog food. A city bus rolls by, fully wrapped for Trix cereal, or a school bus displays ads for a local toy store or realtor. You escape to the ballpark, only to find billboard-size video screens running Budweiser ads while a blimp with an electronic message board circles lazily overhead. How about a quiet trip to the country? Sorry—you find an enterprising farmer using his milk cows as four-legged billboards mounted with ads for Ben & Jerry's ice cream.

You pay to see a movie at your local theater, only to learn that the movie is full of not-so-subtle promotional plugs for Pepsi, Domino's Pizza, MasterCard, Mercedes, Ray Ban sunglasses, or any of a dozen other products. You head home for a little TV to find your favorite sitcom full of "virtual placements" of Coca-Cola, Sony, or Miller Lite products digitally inserted into the program. You pop in the latest video game and find your action character jumping into a Jeep on the way to the skateboarding park.

At the local rail station, it's the Commuter Channel; at the airport, you're treated to the CNN Airport Network. Shortly after your plane lifts off the runway, you look out the window and spot a 500-foot-diameter crop circle carved into a farmer's field depicting Monster.com's mascot and corporate logo. As you wait to pick up your luggage, ads for Sony, or Miller Lite products digitally inserted into the program. You pop in the latest video game and find your action character roll by on the baggage carousel conveyor belt.

These days, you're likely to find ads—well, anywhere. Boats cruise along public beaches flashing advertising messages for Sundown Sunscreen as sunbathers spread their towels over ads for Snapple pressed into the sand. Taxi cabs sport electronic messaging signs tied to GPS location sensors that can pitch local stores and restaurants wherever they roam. Ad space is being sold on DVD cases, parking-lot tickets, golf scorecards, delivery trucks, pizza boxes, gas pumps, ATMs, municipal garbage cans, police cars, and church bulletins. One agency even leases space on the foreheads of college students for temporary advertising tattoos. And the group meeting at the office water cooler has a new member—a "cooleristing" ad sitting on top of the water cooler jug trying to start up a conversation about the latest episode of *American Idol*.

The following account takes a humorous look ahead at what might be in store for the future:

Tomorrow your alarm clock will buzz at 6 a.m., as usual. Then the digital readout will morph into an ad for Burger King's breakfast special. Hungry for an Enormous Omelet Sandwich, you settle for a bagel that you plop into the toaster. The coils burn a Toastmaster brand onto the sides. Biting into your

Marketers have discovered a dazzling array of "alternative media."

embossed bread, you pour a cup of coffee as the familiar green-and-white Starbucks logo forms on the side. Sipping the brew, you slide on your Nikes to go grab the newspaper. The pressure sensitive shoes leave a temporary trail of swooshes behind them wherever you step. Walking outside, you pick up the *Times* and gaze at your lawn, where the fertilizer you put down last month time-releases ads for Scotts Turf Builder, Toro lawn mowers, Weber grills. . . .

Even some of the current alternative media seem a bit far-fetched, and they sometimes irritate consumers who resent it all as "ad nauseam." But for many marketers, these media can save money and provide a way to hit selected consumers where they live, shop, work, and play. "We like to call it the captive pause," says an executive of an alternative-media firm, where consumers "really have nothing else to do but either look at the person in front of them or look at some engaging content as well as 15-second commercials"—the average person waits in line about 30 minutes a day. Many spend even more time on mass transit. So, companies such as Target, Snapple, Calvin Klein, and American Express are testing new technologies to reach captive consumers. Riders on Manhattan's subway system now see a series of light boxes speed by that create a moving commercial in the subway car's windows.

Of course, this may leave you wondering if there are any commercial-free havens remaining for ad-weary consumers. Public elevators, perhaps, or stalls in a public restroom? Forget it! Each has already been invaded by innovative marketers.

Sources: See Cara Beardi, "From Elevators to Gas Stations, Ads Multiplying," *Advertising Age*, November 13, 2000, pp. 40–42; Charles Pappas, "Ad Nauseam," *Advertising Age*, July 10, 2000, pp. 16–18; Sam Jaffe, "Easy Riders," *American Demographics*, March 2004, pp. 20–23; David H. Freedman, "The Future of Advertising Is Here," *Inc.*, August 2005, pp. 70–78; Emily Bazar, "Advertisers Catch the School Bus," *USA Today*, December 26, 2005, p. 3A; David Kiley, "Rated M for Mad Ave," *BusinessWeek*, February 26, 2006, pp. 76–77; and "Global Trends Watch—Innovative Advertising," *Brand Strategy*, April 10, 2006, p. 14.

magazine by cost per thousand and favors those magazines with the lower cost per thousand for reaching target consumers.[16]

The media planner must also consider the costs of producing ads for different media. Whereas newspaper ads may cost very little to produce, flashy television ads can be very costly. For example, the set of extravagant Burger King Whopperettes commercials discussed in the chapter-opening story of Chapter 14 cost millions of dollars to produce. And a few years ago, a two-minute Chanel No. 5 commercial featuring Nicole Kidman and filmed by the director of *Moulin Rouge*, Baz Luhrmann, cost an almost unimaginable $14 million to create.[17]

In selecting specific media vehicles, the media planner must balance media costs against several media effectiveness factors. First, the planner should evaluate the media vehicle's *audience quality*. For a Huggies disposable diapers advertisement, for example, *Parenting* magazine would have a high exposure value; *Gentlemen's Quarterly* would have a low exposure value. Second, the media planner should consider *audience engagement*. Readers of *Vogue*, for example, typically pay more attention to ads than do *Newsweek* readers. Third, the planner should assess the vehicle's *editorial quality*—*Time* and the *Wall Street Journal* are more believable and prestigious than the *National Enquirer*.

DECIDING ON MEDIA TIMING The advertiser must also decide how to schedule the advertising over the course of a year. Suppose sales of a product peak in December and drop in March. The firm can vary its advertising to follow the seasonal pattern, to oppose the seasonal pattern, or to be the same all year. Most firms do some seasonal advertising. For example, The Picture People, the national chain of portraits studios, advertises more heavily before major holidays such as Christmas, Easter, and Valentines Day. Some marketers do *only* seasonal advertising: For instance, Hallmark advertises its greeting cards only before major holidays.

Finally, the advertiser must choose the pattern of the ads. *Continuity* means scheduling ads evenly within a given period. *Pulsing* means scheduling ads unevenly over a given time period. Thus, 52 ads could either be scheduled at one per week during the year or pulsed in several bursts. The idea behind pulsing is to advertise heavily for a short period to build awareness that carries over to the next advertising period. Those who favor pulsing feel that it can be used to achieve the same impact as a steady schedule but at a much lower cost. However, some media planners believe that although pulsing achieves maximal awareness, it sacrifices depth of advertising communications.

Media Timing: The Picture People, the national chain of family portrait studios, advertises more heavily before special holidays.

Evaluating Advertising Effectiveness and Return on Advertising Investment

Advertising accountability and **return on advertising investment** have become hot issues for most companies. Increasingly, top management is asking: "How do we know that we're spending the right amount on advertising?" and "What return are we getting on our advertising investment?" According to a recent survey by the Association of National Advertisers (ANA), measuring advertising's efficiency and effectiveness is the number-one issue in the minds of today's advertisers. In the survey, 61.5 percent of respondents said that it is important that they define, measure, and take action in the area of advertising accountability.[18]

Return on advertising investment

The net return on advertising investment divided by the costs of the advertising investment.

Advertisers should regularly evaluate two types of advertising results: the communication effects and the sales and profit effects. Measuring the *communication effects* of an ad or ad campaign tells whether the ads and media are communicating the ad message well. Individual ads can be tested before or after they are run. Before an ad is placed, the advertiser can show it to consumers, ask how they like it, and measure message recall or attitude changes resulting from it. After an ad is run, the advertiser can measure how the ad affected consumer recall or product awareness, knowledge, and preference. Pre- and post-evaluations of communication effects can be made for entire advertising campaigns as well.

Advertisers have gotten pretty good at measuring the communication effects of their ads and ad campaigns. However, *sales and profits* effects of advertising are often much harder to measure. For example, what sales and profits are produced by an ad campaign that increases brand awareness by 20 percent and brand preference by 10 percent? Sales and profits are affected by many factors besides advertising—such as product features, price, and availability.

One way to measure the sales and profit effects of advertising is to compare past sales and profits with past advertising expenditures. Another way is through experiments. For example, to test the effects of different advertising spending levels, Coca-Cola could vary the amount it spends on advertising in different market areas and measure the differences in the resulting sales and profit levels. More complex experiments could be designed to include other variables, such as differences in the ads or media used.

However, because so many factors, some controllable and others not, affect advertising effectiveness, measuring the results of advertising spending remains an inexact science. For example, despite the growing importance of advertising accountability, only 19 percent of ANA study respondents were satisfied with their ability to measure return on advertising investments. When asked if they would be able to "forecast the impact on sales" of a 10 percent cut in advertising spending, 63 percent said no.

"Marketers are tracking all kinds of data and they still can't answer basic questions" about advertising accountability, says a marketing analyst, "because they don't have real models and metrics by which to make sense of it."[19] Thus, although the situation is improving as marketers seek more answers, managers often must rely on large doses of judgment along with quantitative analysis when assessing advertising performance.

Other Advertising Considerations

In developing advertising strategies and programs, the company must address two additional questions. First, how will the company organize its advertising function—who will perform which advertising tasks? Second, how will the company adapt its advertising strategies and programs to the complexities of international markets?

Organizing for Advertising

Different companies organize in different ways to handle advertising. In small companies, advertising might be handled by someone in the sales department. Large companies set up advertising departments whose job it is to set the advertising budget, work with the ad agency, and handle other advertising not done by the agency. Most large companies use outside advertising agencies because they offer several advantages.

How does an **advertising agency** work? Advertising agencies were started in the mid-to-late 1800s by salespeople and brokers who worked for the media and received a commission for selling advertising space to companies. As time passed, the salespeople began to help customers prepare their ads. Eventually, they formed agencies and grew closer to the advertisers than to the media.

Today's agencies employ specialists who can often perform advertising tasks better than the company's own staff can. Agencies also bring an outside point of view to solving the company's problems, along with lots of experience from working with different clients and situations. So, today, even companies with strong advertising departments of their own use advertising agencies.

Some ad agencies are huge—the largest U.S. agency, McCann Erickson Worldwide, has worldwide annual gross revenue of more than $1.4 billion. In recent years, many agencies have grown by gobbling up other agencies, thus creating huge agency holding companies. The largest of these agency "megagroups," Omnicom Group, includes several large advertising, public relations, and promotion agencies with combined worldwide revenues of almost $10.5 billion.[20] Most large advertising agencies have the staff and resources to handle all phases of an advertising campaign for their clients, from creating a marketing plan to developing ad campaigns and preparing, placing, and evaluating ads.

Advertising agency
A marketing services firm that assists companies in planning, preparing, implementing, and evaluating all or portions of their advertising programs.

International Advertising Decisions

International advertisers face many complexities not encountered by domestic advertisers. The most basic issue concerns the degree to which global advertising should be adapted to the unique characteristics of various country markets. Some large advertisers have attempted to support their global brands with highly standardized worldwide advertising, with campaigns that work as well in Bangkok as they do in Baltimore. For example, Jeep has created a worldwide brand image of ruggedness and reliability; Coca-Cola's Sprite brand uses standardized appeals to target the world's youth. Ads for Gillette's Venus razors are almost identical worldwide, with only minor adjustments to suit the local culture.

Standardization produces many benefits—lower advertising costs, greater global advertising coordination, and a more consistent worldwide image. But it also has drawbacks. Most importantly, it ignores the fact that country markets differ greatly in their cultures, demographics, and economic conditions. Thus, most international advertisers "think globally but act locally." They develop global advertising *strategies* that make their worldwide advertising efforts more efficient and consistent. Then they adapt their advertising *programs* to make them more responsive to consumer needs and expectations within local markets. For example, Coca-Cola has a pool of different commercials that can be used in or adapted to several different international markets. Some can be used with only minor changes—such as language—in several different countries. Local and regional managers decide which commercials work best for which markets.

Global advertisers face several special problems. For instance, advertising media costs and availability differ vastly from country to country. Countries also differ in the extent to which they regulate advertising practices. Many countries have extensive systems of laws restricting how much a company can spend on advertising, the media used, the nature of advertising claims, and other aspects of the advertising program. Such restrictions often require advertisers to adapt their campaigns from country to country.

For example, alcoholic products cannot be advertised in India or in Muslim countries. In many countries, Sweden and Norway, for example, food ads are banned from kids' TV. To play it safe, McDonald's advertises itself as a family restaurant in Sweden. Comparative ads, while acceptable and even common in the United States and Canada, are less commonly used in the United Kingdom, unacceptable in Japan, and illegal in India and Brazil. China bans sending e-mail for advertising purposes to people without their permission, and all advertising e-mail that is sent must be titled "advertisement."

China also has restrictive censorship rules for TV and radio advertising; for example, the words *the best* are banned, as are ads that "violate social customs" or present women in "improper ways." McDonald's once avoided government sanctions there by publicly apologizing for an ad that crossed cultural norms by showing a customer begging for a discount. Similarly, Coca-Cola's Indian subsidiary was forced to end a promotion that offered prizes,

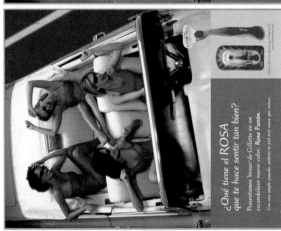

■ Standardized worldwide advertising: Gillette's ads for its Gillette for Women Venus razors are almost identical worldwide, with only minor adjustments to suit the local culture.

such as a trip to Hollywood, because it violated India's established trade practices by encouraging customers to buy in order to "gamble."[21]

Thus, although advertisers may develop global strategies to guide their overall advertising efforts, specific advertising programs must usually be adapted to meet local cultures and customs, media characteristics, and advertising regulations.

Public Relations

Another major mass-promotion tool is **public relations (PR)**—building good relationships with the company's various publics by obtaining favorable publicity, building a good corporate image, and handling or heading off unfavorable rumors, stories, and events. Public relations departments may perform any or all of the following functions:[22]

- *Press relations or press agency:* Creating and placing newsworthy information in the news media to attract attention to a person, product, or service
- *Product publicity:* Publicizing specific products
- *Public affairs:* Building and maintaining national or local community relations
- *Lobbying:* Building and maintaining relations with legislators and government officials to influence legislation and regulation
- *Investor relations:* Maintaining relationships with shareholders and others in the financial community
- *Development:* Public relations with donors or members of nonprofit organizations to gain financial or volunteer support

Public relations is used to promote products, people, places, ideas, activities, organizations, and even nations. Companies use public relations to build good relationships with consumers, investors, the media, and their communities. Trade associations have used public relations to rebuild interest in declining commodities such as eggs, apples, milk, and potatoes. The state of New York turned its image around when its "I ♥ New York!" publicity and advertising campaign took root, bringing in millions more tourists. Johnson & Johnson's masterly use of public relations played a major role in saving Tylenol from extinction after its product-tampering scare. Nations have used public relations to attract more tourists, foreign investment, and international support.

Public relations (PR)
Building good relations with the company's various publics by obtaining favorable publicity, building a good corporate image, and handling or heading off unfavorable rumors, stories, and events.

The Role and Impact of Public Relations

Public relations can have a strong impact on public awareness at a much lower cost than advertising can. The company does not pay for the space or time in the media. Rather, it pays for a staff to develop and circulate information and to manage events. If the company develops an interesting story or event, it could be picked up by several different media, having the same effect as advertising that would cost millions of dollars. And it would have more credibility than advertising.

Public relations results can sometimes be spectacular. Here's how publisher Scholastic, Inc., used public relations to turn a simple new book introduction into a major international event, all on a very small budget:

Secret codes. A fiercely guarded text. Huddled masses lined up in funny hats at the witching hour. Welcome to one of the biggest literary events in history. As the clock creeps past midnight, kids worldwide rush to buy the next installment of Harry Potter. It's the fastest-shrinking book pile in history. *Harry Potter and the Half-Blood Prince*, the sixth book in the series, sold an astonishing 8.9 million copies in just the first 24 hours in the United States and Britain alone—some 370,000 per hour. How do you whip up a consumer frenzy with a miserly $1.8 million promotion budget and only a few well-placed ads? The spellbinding plots, written by Scottish welfare-mom-turned-millionaire J. K. Rowling, captivate kids everywhere. But the hidden hand of public relations plays a large role, too. Publisher Scholastic works behind the scenes with retailers to prepare contests, theme parties, and giveaways leading up to each new release. It communicates through amateur fan sites such as The Leaky Cauldron and MuggleNet.com to keep fans informed about print runs and store events. It works with the mainstream media to create a sense of celebration and excitement. NBC's *Today Show* ran an entire week of "Countdown to Harry" events leading up to the publication of the *Half-Blood Prince*. Scholastic's Web site reaches out to obsessed fans with essay contests and video clips. Scholastic heightens the tension by keeping each new book's title and book jacket under wraps almost until the last minute, even forcing booksellers to sign secrecy agreements. With all this PR hype, by the time the book hits the shelves, conditions are hot for Harry. And the hype made a lasting impact— the book went on to become the nation's best selling book of the year.[23]

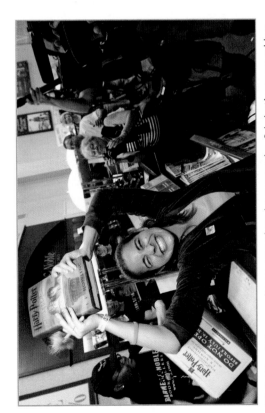

■ Public relations results can sometimes, be spectacular. Scholastic sponsored low-cost sleepovers, games, and costume contests to whip up consumer frenzy for the last installment of its Harry Potter series.

tives may be ignored. Marketing managers and public relations practitioners do not always speak the same language. Many public relations practitioners see their job as simply communicating. In contrast, marketing managers tend to be much more interested in how advertising and public relations affect brand building, sales and profits, and customer relationships.

This situation is changing, however. Although public relations still captures only a small portion of the overall marketing budgets of most firms, PR is playing an increasingly important brand-building role. Public relations can be a powerful brand-building tool. Two well-known marketing consultants even go so far as to conclude that advertising doesn't build brands, PR does. In their book *The Fall of Advertising & the Rise of PR*, the consultants proclaim that the dominance of advertising is over and that public relations is quietly becoming the most powerful marketing communications tool.

The birth of a brand is usually accomplished with [public relations], not advertising. Our general rule is [PR] first, advertising second. [Public relations] is the nail, advertising the hammer. [PR] creates the credentials that provide the credibility for advertising. . . . Anita Roddick built the Body Shop into a major brand with no advertising at all. Instead, she traveled the world on a relentless quest for publicity. . . . Until recently Starbucks Coffee didn't spend a hill of beans on advertising, either. In 10 years, the company spent less than $10 million on advertising, a trivial amount for a brand that delivers annual sales of [in the billions]. Wal-Mart Stores became the world's largest retailer . . . with very little advertising. . . . On the Internet, Amazon.com became a powerhouse brand with virtually no advertising.[24]

Although the book created much controversy, and most advertisers wouldn't agree about the "fall of advertising" part of the title, the point is a good one. Advertising and public relations should work hand in hand to build and maintain brands.

Major Public Relations Tools

Public relations uses several tools. One of the major tools is *news*. PR professionals find or create favorable news about the company and its products or people. Sometimes news stories occur naturally, and sometimes the PR person can suggest events or activities that would create news. *Speeches* can also create product and company publicity. Increasingly, company executives must field questions from the media or give talks at trade associations or sales meetings, and these events can either build or hurt the company's image. Another common PR tool is *special events*, ranging from news conferences, press tours, grand openings, and fireworks displays to laser shows, hot air balloon releases, multimedia presentations, star-studded spectaculars, or educational programs designed to reach and interest target publics.

Public relations people also prepare *written materials* to reach and influence their target markets. These materials include annual reports, brochures, articles, and company newsletters

Despite its potential strengths, public relations is sometimes described as a marketing stepchild because of its often limited and scattered use. The public relations department is usually located at corporate headquarters. Its staff is so busy dealing with various publics—stockholders, employees, legislators, the press—that public relations programs to support product marketing objec-

and magazines. *Audiovisual materials*, such as films, slide-and-sound programs, DVDs, and online videos are being used increasingly as communication tools. *Corporate identity materials* can also help create a corporate identity that the public immediately recognizes. Logos, stationery, brochures, signs, business forms, business cards, buildings, uniforms, and company cars and trucks—all become marketing tools when they are attractive, distinctive, and memorable. Finally, companies can improve public goodwill by contributing money and time to *public service activities*.

As we discussed in Chapter 5, many marketers are now also designing *buzz marketing* campaigns to generate excitement and favorable word-of-mouth for their brands. Buzz marketing takes advantage of *social networking* processes by getting consumers themselves to spread information about a product or service to others in their communities. For example, UPN used buzz marketing to reach often tuned-out and cynical teen girls:

High schools are always abuzz with talk of one kind or another: sports, music, clothes, and whatever else teens consider indispensable at any given time. But last year, one piece of chatter weaving its way through select high schools across America was very specific. It was about the TV series *America's Next Top Model*, then entering its fourth season. While teens did the talking, UPN, the network that airs the series, was listening very closely. It had to. UPN was essentially sponsoring the whole conversation.

The plan worked like this. With the help of Alloy.com, a shopping and lifestyle site aimed at teen girls, UPN created a list of 500 "insiders" who could generate buzz about Top Model, which needed a ratings boost. Alloy monitored chat within the site and compiled a list of 7,000 girls who, in the course of their banter, had expressed interest in the show. It cut that list to the 500 girls who seemed the best-connected—those who had frequently shown up on instant-messaging buddy lists. Alloy then provided these gossipy, in-crowd teens with party kits and encouraged them to invite an average of four friends over to their homes for gatherings themed around—you guessed it—*America's Next Top Model*. The girls knew that UPN's cash was behind the kits, and "it wasn't a tough sell," says an Alloy marketing executive. Tough sell or not, it seems to have worked. "The ratings have been very good," says the executive, "especially among that age group." Whereas most reality shows don't stick around that long, *America's Next Top Model* is now in its sixth season.[25]

Another recent public relations development is *mobile tour marketing*—traveling promotional tours that bring the brand to consumers. Mobile tour marketing has emerged as an effective way to build one-to-one relationships with targeted consumers. These days, it seems that almost every company is putting its show on the road. For example, Home Depot recently brought do-it-yourself home project workshops and demonstrations to 26 NASCAR racetracks. Microsoft teams with local partners to field Across America Mobile Solutions Centers, 27-foot techie dream vans that visit information technology workers in offices around the country to demonstrate Microsoft's latest software products. And Charmin's "Potty Palooza" serves as a rolling showcase for—you guessed it—toilet paper (see Real Marketing 15.3).[26]

A company's Web site can be a good public relations vehicle. Consumers and members of other publics can visit the site for information and entertainment. Such sites can be extremely popular. For example, Butterball's site (www.butterball.com), which features cooking and carving tips, once received 550,000 visitors in one day during Thanksgiving week. The Web site supplements the Butterball Turkey Talk-Line (1-800-BUTTERBALL)—called by some the "granddaddy of all help lines"—staffed by 50 home economists and nutritionists who respond to more than 100,000 questions each November and December.[27]

Web sites can also be ideal for handling crisis situations. For example, when several bottles of Odwalla apple juice sold on the West Coast were found to contain E. coli bacteria. Odwalla initiated a massive product recall. Within only three hours, it set up a Web site laden with information about the crisis and Odwalla's response. Company staffers also combed the Internet looking for newsgroups discussing Odwalla and posted links to the site. In all, in this age where "it's easier to disseminate information through e-mail marketing, blogs, and online chat," notes an analyst, "public relations is becoming a valuable part of doing business in a digital world."[28]

As with the other promotion tools, in considering when and how to use product public relations, management should set PR objectives, choose the PR messages and vehicles, implement the PR plan, and evaluate the results. The firm's public relations should be blended smoothly with other promotion activities within the company's overall integrated marketing communications effort.

Real Marketing   Marketing on a Roll: Charmin's Potty Palooza

15.3   The real highlight of the annual Covered Bridge Festival in Mansfield, Indiana, isn't a bridge at all. It's Potty Palooza. "People walk from half a mile away," says John Baker, a festival organizer. No wonder: Charmin's 27-room traveling bathroom facility, painted sky blue with white clouds and latched to the bed of an 18-wheeler, inspires awe wherever it goes. "It's like a ride at the state fair," Baker marvels. "They wait in line 10 to 15 minutes sometimes!"

Depending on your point of view, Potty Palooza represents either the epitome or the pits of experiential, mobile marketing—a marketing approach that touches consumers in places no advertising campaign would go. It's a showroom on wheels, a rolling free trial for . . . toilet paper.

"The media is fracturing, costs are rising," says Charmin's brand manager at Procter & Gamble. "It's difficult to reach consumers these days." Unless, that is, you've got a big semi and a trailer fitted with flushing porcelain toilets, hardwood floors, and air conditioning—plus aromatherapy, skylights, changing stations, a "Little Squirts" stall for kids, and an LCD video screen in every room.

Since its debut in 2002, the Potty Palooza truck has been on the road 11 months a year, visiting 25 to 30 events annually—from the Super Bowl to the Arizona Balloon Festival. All told, Charmin's 5 million annual guests go through some 10,000 cushioned rolls. (A supply truck joins in the Potty Palooza caravan.)

As guests wait, they take part in the full branding experience. The Charmin Bear teaches the Charmin dance while smiling brand reps guide visitors to and from stalls and spruce up rooms after every use. At the Covered Bridge Festival, that can mean cleaning up after 5,000 guests a day. Says the director of the Palooza road team: "We can't budge when that thing is full. We have to empty the black water 5 to 10 times a day."

Yuck. Is it worth it? P&G claims the truck is part of one of the biggest consumer sampling programs anywhere. And, you must admit, it's one of the most unique. By creating a comfortable, if not heavenly, public restroom experience at events where the experience is usually the opposite, Charmin has turned a commodity into a trusted brand with a dedicated following. After Potty Palooza made its first appearance at the Covered Bridge Festival, 30,000 people signed a petition to keep it coming back. By engaging families at the point of use, the tour has help lift sales of Charmin by 14 percent.

Source: Adapted from Lucas Conley, "On a Roll," *Fast Company,* February 2005, p. 28. Additional information from "How Does Charmin Engage Consumers at the Point of Use and Take Commodity Out of the Bath Tissue Equation?" Gigunda Group, Inc., accessed at www.gigundagroup.com, May 15, 2006.

Mobile marketing: Charmin's Potty Palooza serves as a rolling showcase for—you guessed it—toilet paper.

Reviewing the Concepts

Companies must do more than make good products—they must inform consumers about product benefits and carefully position products in consumers' minds. To do this, they must master *advertising* and *public relations*.

1. Define the role of advertising in the promotion mix.

Advertising—the use of paid media by a seller to inform, persuade, and remind buyers about its products or organization—is an important promotion tool for communicating the value that marketers create for their customers. American marketers spend more than $264 billion each year on advertising, and worldwide ad spending exceeds $600 billion. Advertising takes many forms and has many uses. Although advertising is used mostly by business firms, a wide range of not-for-profit organizations, professionals, and social agencies also use advertising to promote their causes to various target publics. *Public relations*—gaining favorable publicity and creating a favorable company image—is the least used of the major promotion tools, although it has great potential for building consumer awareness and preference.

2. Describe the major decisions involved in developing an advertising program.

Advertising decision making involves decisions about the advertising objectives, the budget, the message, the media, and, finally, the evaluation of results. Advertisers should set clear target, task, and timing *objectives*, whether the aim is to inform, persuade, or remind buyers. Advertising's goal is to move consumers through the buyer-readiness stages discussed in the previous chapter. Some advertising is designed to move people to immediate action. However, many of the ads you see today focus on building or strengthening long-term customer relationships. The advertising *budget* can be based on sales, on competitors' spending, or on the objectives and tasks of the advertising program. The size and allocation of the budget depends on many factors.

Advertising strategy consists of two major elements: creating advertising *messages* and selecting advertising *media*. The *message decision* calls for planning a message strategy and executing it effectively. Good advertising messages are especially important in today's costly and cluttered advertising environment. Just to gain and hold attention, today's advertising messages must be better planned, more imaginative, more entertaining, and more rewarding to consumers. In fact, many marketers are now subscribing to a new merging of advertising and entertainment, dubbed "Madison & Vine." The *media decision* involves defining reach, frequency, and impact goals; choosing major media types; selecting media vehicles; and deciding on media timing. Message and media decisions must be closely coordinated for maximum campaign effectiveness.

Finally, *evaluation* calls for evaluating the communication and sales effects of advertising before, during, and after the advertising is placed. Advertising accountability has become a hot issue for most companies. Increasingly, top management is asking: "What return are we getting on our advertising investment?" and "How do we know that we're spending the right amount?" Other important advertising issues involve *organizing* for advertising and dealing with the complexities of international advertising.

3. Define the role of public relations in the promotion mix.

Public relations—gaining favorable publicity and creating a favorable company image—is the least used of the major promotion tools, although it has great potential for building consumer awareness and preference. Public relations is used to promote products, people, places, ideas, activities, organizations, and even nations. Companies use public relations to build good relationships with consumers, investors, the media, and their communities. Public relations can have a strong impact on public awareness at a much lower cost than advertising can, and public relations results can sometimes be spectacular. Although public relations still captures only a small portion of the overall marketing budgets of most firms, PR is playing an increasingly important brand-building role.

4. Explain how companies use public relations to communicate with their publics.

Companies use public relations to communicate with their publics by setting PR objectives, choosing PR messages and vehicles, implementing the PR plan, and evaluating PR results. To accomplish these goals, public relations professionals use several tools, such as *news*, *speeches*, and *special events*. They also prepare *written*, *audiovisual*, and *corporate identity materials* and contribute money and time to *public service activities*. *Buzz marketing* is a form of public relations that gets consumers themselves to spread word-of-mouth information about the company and its brands. The Internet has also become a major public relations tool.

Reviewing the Key Terms

Discussing the Concepts

1. What factors make management's task of setting advertising budgets difficult?

2. Why is it important that the advertising media and creative departments work closely together?

3. How do an advertisement's appeals differ from its execution style?

4. Evaluate why Maybelline New York might decide to remove all its advertising from MTV and instead place more advertising in *Seventeen* magazine.

5. Discuss three potential problems facing a pharmaceutical manufacturer who decides to advertise in Europe. Are these problems different from those the manufacturer would encounter when advertising in Asia?

6. Why is public relations sometimes referred to as a *marketing stepchild*? What can be done to correct this problem?

Applying the Concepts

1. Form a small group and choose three advertising media for a campaign to introduce a new line of men's personal care products under a LeBron James label.

2. Locate a magazine advertisement for a household cleaning product. Describe how the appeals in this ad display the three characteristics of a good advertising appeal.

3. How might Campbell Soup Company go about evaluating the effectiveness of an advertising campaign for a new "heat-and-drink" soup product?

Focus on Technology

ALLERCA creates truly unique products—the world's first scientifically proven hypoallergenic cats (see them at www.allerca.com). Genetically engineered, the medium-sized ALLERCA GD cat weighs 10–15 pounds and is fully mature at age 3. According to ALLERCA, the cats have long life expectancies and possess sweet and affectionate dispositions. For a price of about $3,000, you receive a 12-week-old kitten, complete with all shots and vaccinations, an embedded microchip identifier implant, and a one-year guarantee. Customers purchase kittens over the Internet and must pay approximately $1,000 for processing and transportation. The high shipping cost occurs because commercial air shipping is stressful to the animal; therefore, the kitten travels in a specialized private jet courier. According to ALLERCA, the current waiting time for the ALLERCA GD kitten is approximately two years. Potential buyers may reduce their wait times to just a few months by paying $2,000 for one of the few kittens in the Premium Placement Program.

1. This product is sold over the Internet. How can ALLERCA use Internet advertising technologies to reach its target market? (Visit the Internet Advertising Bureau at www.iab.net to learn about recent technologies.)

2. What might be the main objectives of advertising and pubic relations for ALLERCA, and what factors will affect ALLERCA's decision about its advertising and PR budgets?

3. In addition to Internet marketing, what other advertising media and PR tools would you choose for promoting ALLERCA and its unique products?

Focus on Ethics

Splenda (sucralose) was introduced to the consumer market in 1999. It is now a common sweetener found in more than 3,500 food products. Splenda's advertising slogan is "made from sugar, so it tastes like sugar." Manufactured and marketed by packaged-goods giant Johnson & Johnson, Splenda now captures a substantial percentage of the artificial sweetener market and is beginning to cut into sugar's market share. But Splenda's campaign has attracted much attention from competitors, social advocacy groups, and nutritional experts. According to these groups, Splenda has clearly violated "truth in advertising" codes with its "made from sugar" slogan. Although currently produced from a sugar molecule, they claim, Splenda is an artificial sweetener that can be produced without sugar. In addition, the chemical name assigned to Splenda—sucralose—is misleading because it closely resembles the chemical name of sugar—sucrose.

The strongest opponent to the Splenda "made from sugar" campaign is The Sugar Association, which has launched a large and expensive campaign of its own to educate the public and to expose Splenda's unethical behavior. The association's Web site (http://www.truthaboutsplenda. com) urges consumers to take action by contacting friends, sending letters to the FTC and the FDA, and sending letters of complaint directly to Johnson & Johnson. Another area of the Web site, labeled Fact vs. Fiction, highlights serious consumer misunderstandings that might result from Splenda's advertising. It describes in detail how Splenda is not natural sugar and notes that there exist no conclusive tests regarding the long-term safety of consuming Splenda.

1. What is the objective of Splenda's "made from sugar, so it tastes like sugar" message and campaign? Is this slogan an effective appeal?

2. What is the objective of The Sugar Association's communications campaign? Is that campaign effective?

3. Check the "truth in advertising" guidelines at the FTC Web site (www.ftc.gov/bcp/conline/pubs/buspubs/ad-faqs.htm). Has Splenda followed these rules?

Video Case   DDB Worldwide

DDB Worldwide, a global communications firm, has crafted imaginative commercials and staged successful marketing events for megamarketers such as Ameriquest, Volkswagen, Budweiser, Pepsi, and Nike. Recently, DDB staged a live round of Monopoly on the streets of London to promote Milton Bradley's updated version of the classic game. Online players "bought" properties throughout the city and selected one of eighteen London cabs to use as a playing piece. The cabs, tracked by GPS, tallied rent payments and receipts for each player as they moved about the streets. More than one million people played and the campaign garnered $3 million in free publicity. As a result, *Monopoly: Here and Now* was one of the best-selling games of the year.

With creativity and results like these, it's easy to understand why DDB is one of the world's most decorated agencies. DDB brought the same creativity to the challenge of reinventing another classic, JC Penney. Relying on extensive consumer research, DDB crafted an ad campaign that built the JC Penney brand, connected with the retailer's core consumers, and brought customers back in droves.

After viewing the video featuring DDB Worldwide, answer the following questions about advertising and public relations.

1. What were DDB's advertising objectives for the JC Penney campaign?

2. How did DDB's consumer research affect the message strategy for the campaign? How did the major advertising appeal have the three

3. characteristics discussed in the text? How did identifying JC Penney's core consumers affect DDB's message execution style? Could JC Penney employ the "Madison & Vine" concept discussed in the chapter? How?

Company Case

Pepsi: Promoting Nothing

WATER WARS

Everyone's familiar with the cola wars—the epic battles between Pepsi Cola and Coca-Cola in the soft-drink market. The war has featured numerous taste tests and mostly friendly, but sometimes not-so-friendly, television ads featuring Pepsi and Coke delivery-truck drivers, each trying to out-do the other. But one of the major problems that Pepsi and Coke face is to not just out-do each other, but to maintain growth, especially when the soda market goes flat. For this reason, both PepsiCo and Coca-Cola each have hundreds if not thousands of brands in soft-drink and snack-food categories. Each is also constantly looking for new ideas to increase sales.

One of those ideas is water. In the early 1990s, the bottled-water market was just a drop in the huge U.S. beverage market bucket. The Evian and Perrier brands dominated the tiny niche and helped establish bottled spring water's clean, healthy image. Pepsi took an early interest in the water market. It tried several different ways to attack this market, with both spring water and sparkling water, but each failed. Then it hit on the idea of taking advantage of a built-in resource—its existing bottlers.

Pepsi's bottlers already had their own water treatment facilities to purify municipal tap water used in making soft drinks. Municipal tap water was already pure and had to pass constant monitoring and rigorous quarterly EPA-prescribed tests. Still, cola bottlers filtered it again before using it in the production process.

Pepsi decided that it would *really* filter the tap water. It experimented with a reverse osmosis process, pushing already-filtered tap water at high pressure through fiber-glass membranes to remove even the tiniest particles. Then, carbon filters removed chlorine and any other particles that might give the water any taste or smell. However, all this filtering removed even good particles that killed bacteria, so Pepsi had to add ozone to the water to keep bacteria from growing. The result? Aquafina—a water with no taste or odor—that Pepsi believed could compete with the spring waters already on the market. Further, Pepsi could license its bottlers to use the Aquafina name and sell them the filtration equipment. Because the process used tap water that was relatively inexpensive, Pepsi's Aquafina would also compete well on price with the spring waters.

The marketing strategy was relatively simple. Whereas Evian and the other early entrants targeted women and high-end consumers, Pepsi wanted consumers to see Aquafina as a "unisex, mainstream" water with an everyday price. When the company launched the product in 1994, it was content just to build distribution using its established system and spent very little money on promotion. Pepsi believed that soft-drink advertising should be for soft drinks, not water.

COME ON IN—THE WATER'S FINE

By 1999, what had been a minor trickle in the beverage market had turned into a geyser—bottled water had become the fastest-growing beverage category, and Pepsi had a big head start. Coca-Cola decided it was time to take the plunge. Like Pepsi, Coca-Cola realized its bottlers were already set up to handle a filtered-water process. Unlike Pepsi, however, rather than taking everything out of the tap water, it wanted to put something in.

Coca-Cola's researchers analyzed tap waters and bottled waters and concocted a combination of minerals they believed would give filtered tap water a fresh, clean taste. The formula included magnesium sulfate, potassium chloride, and salt. Coca-Cola guarded the new water formula just as it had the original Coke recipe. Thus, it could sell the formula to its bottlers, as it does Coke concentrate, and let them make the water. Like Pepsi, Coca-Cola was content initially just to get its water, which it called Dasani, into distribution.

HOW TO PROMOTE WATER

By 2001, however, the bottled-water category had over 800 competitors and had grown to $3.53 billion in U.S. sales. Bottled water's market share of the beverage industry had grown from 7.4 percent in 1997 to 11 percent in 2002. At that time, analysts were predicting that bottled water would become the second-largest beverage category by 2004 (surpassing beer, coffee, and even milk!). There were also predictions that bottled water would account for 15 percent of all U.S. beverage sales by 2007. And while bottled-water sales were erupting, the market share of carbonated soft drinks had lost its fizz, remaining steady at around 28 percent.

(case continues)

(case continued)

Given the rapid market growth rate and all the competition, Pepsi and Coca-Cola decided they had better promote their products, just as they did their soft drinks. In 2001, Pepsi launched a $14 million campaign showing how water was a part of real people's lives. Coca-Cola countered with a $20 million campaign that targeted women and used the tagline: "Treat yourself well. Everyday."

Not to be outdone, Pepsi responded by more than doubling its promotion budget to $40 million in 2002. Included in the advertising was a spot featuring *Friends* star Lisa Kudrow. Lisa described how refreshing and mouthwatering Aquafina was—emphasizing that it made no promises it couldn't keep. She described Aquafina as "Pure nothing." The ads featured the tagline: "We promise nothing."

By 2003, the U.S. wholesale bottled-water market had surged to $8.3 billion, up 6.7 percent from 2002. During that same period, wholesale sales of carbonated beverages inched up only 1.5 percent to $45.7 billion. During 2003, Pepsi spent $24 million on Aquafina's advertising, while Coke spent $19 million on Dasani's. Although these two brands were number one and number two, respectively, with 17.7 and 13 percent market shares, all private-label brands combined took third place with a 10.4 percent market share.

One Aquafina 2003 ad featured black-and-white images of an artist, skier, and guitar player drinking the water and carried the tagline "Aquafina. Purity Guaranteed." In mid-2004, Pepsi altered its purity campaign with a new tagline, "Drink more water." One ad showed people partying at an English pub and a German beer garden. Instead of drinking beer, however, they were chugging Aquafina. Coke also had an ad showing young people sipping Dasani at a nightclub.

HAVE ANOTHER ROUND

By 2006, the beverage market trends had intensified. Soda sales were fizzling and bottled-water sales were gushing. In 2005, U.S. carbonated-soda volume declined for the first time ever by .2 percent, and the drop was expected to triple in 2006. The carbonated-soda category still reigned as the king of all beverages, boasting the top-selling brands and a two-to-one margin over bottled water. But analysts predicted that if trends continued, bottled water could overtake sodas as early as 2013.

According to a beverage industry analyst, "The fastest-growing products are the ones people view as healthier or better for you." Indeed, in addition to bottled water, the categories of energy drinks, sports drinks, juices, and teas were also experiencing rapid growth.

With market conditions so favorable, and Aquafina now the ninth-best-selling beverage brand in the United States (Dasani was number-ten, but Coke still ruled at number one), Pepsi knew that it could not rest on its laurels. But how does a company expand on water? Well, with more water of course. Brands and varieties of bottled water were popping up at a mind-boggling rate. Spring water, mineral water, purified water, sparkling water, flavored water, vitamin-enhanced water, lightly carbonated water—the bottled-water market was fragmenting fast.

In 2003, Pepsi and Coca-Cola both introduced vitamin-enhanced waters with Aquafina Essentials and Dasani NutriWater. Both were quickly discontinued, but Pepsi was not about to give up. It knew that it had to stay ahead of the market. So in 2005, Pepsi created two brand extensions, both Aquafina Sparkling and Aquafina FlavorSplash. Both brands stayed true to the healthy traits that were propelling water sales (no calories, carbs, or sugar). But Pepsi designed each to satisfy different needs within the market. Aquafina Sparkling was carbonated, unsweetened, and came in unflavored and lightly flavored varieties. By contrast, FlavorSplash was noncarbonated, sweetened with Splenda, and had heavier doses of flavor, with Raspberry, Citrus Blend, and Wild Berry varieties.

With Coke hot on its tail with the carbonated Dasani Sensations as well as various flavored Dasanis, Pepsi continued to promote its brands heavily. It fielded a variety of promotional tactics. Aquafina hit the Internet, with ads showing up on the MySpace main page and on commercial and personal destination pages. Pepsi also invested in event sponsorship. Aquafina became a major sponsor of the Olympus Fashion Week in New York and the Mercedes-Benz Fashion Week in Los Angeles. It even ran a sweepstakes-style promotion offering an all-expense-paid trip to these fashion events. Pepsi also had Aquafina doing double duty at indie film festivals, with significant sponsorship presence at both Sundance and South By Southwest.

But Pepsi was not about to give up on television. Two years after the successful launch of its "Drink More Water" campaign, Pepsi continued the water-induced jollity of the original ads. In a remake of a scene from the cult classic *Animal House*, a spot entitled "The Toga" had a John Belushi look-alike convulsing to the song "Shout," performed by the real Otis Day and the Knights. But the big difference between the original movie and this frat-house orgy of excess was that the partiers slammed shots of Aquafina.

ARE THE COLA WARS OVER?

For decades, Pepsi fought to sell more cola than Coke. It now appears that Pepsi may have willingly conceded the number one cola honor to Coke. Although it hasn't given up on keeping the Pepsi brand at a strong number two, it has been quietly taking another route to kicking Coke's can. In fact, in December of 2005, PepsiCo surpassed Coca-Cola in market capitalization for the first time in the 108-year rivalry. In the five previous years, PepsiCo's stock had risen by more than a third while Coke's had dropped by the same amount.

What drove this changing of the guard? Without question, one of the most significant factors is Pepsi's lead in growth categories, such as bottled water. "They were the first to recognize that the consumer was moving to noncarbonated products, and they innovated aggressively," observed the analyst. That noncarbonated beverages are growing so rapidly bodes very well for Pepsi. Some 35 to 40 percent of its beverage sales are in noncarbonated categories, as opposed to only 15 percent for Coca-Cola.

But while Coca-Cola seems to be putting plenty of effort into bottled water, it also may be overly confident in the number one brand. When asked about the trend of sales for carbonated and noncarbonated beverages, a Coca-Cola spokesman insisted that the beverage giant is bucking the trend. "We believe we continue to grow carbonated soft drinks," he said, noting that Coke's soda volume was up 1 percent in the fourth quarter of 2005. But whereas a small increase in a huge, flat market might be one thing, a large increase in expanding markets is quite another. Losing the cola wars may be the best thing that ever happened to Pepsi.

Questions for Discussion

1. What markets should Pepsi target for Aquafina?

2. What recommendations would you make for advertising objectives, message strategy, and message execution for Aquafina?

3. What advertising media recommendations would you make for Aquafina, and how would you evaluate the effectiveness of those media and your advertising?

4. What sales promotion and public relations recommendations would you make for Aquafina?

5. What recommendations would you make for promoting Aquafina Sparkling and FlavorSplash?

6. To what extent is Aquafina's sales growth attributable to advertising and promotion versus the growing dynamics of the market?

Sources: Kate MacArthur, "Bleak Future Predicted for Fizz Biz," Advertising Age, June 26, 2006; Karen Herzog, "DRINK! New Beverages Join the Coke-Pepsi Wars," Milwaukee Journal Sentinel, June 7, 2006, p. 1; Lewis Lazare, "Aqua-Boogie Spots Hit All the Right Notes," Chicago Sun Times, May 10, 2006, p. 71; Katrina Brooker, "How Pepsi Outgunned Coke," Fortune, February 1, 2006, accessed online at www.fortune.com; "Aquafina Brings Flavor and Fizz to the Water Aisle," PR Newswire, January 24, 2005; "Beverage Industry Fact Sheet," accessed at www.bevexpo.com/bevindfactsheet.asp; "No Slowdown in Sight for Bottled Water," Beverage Industry, September 2003, p. 22; Betsy McKay, "In a Water Fight, Coke and Pepsi Try Opposite Tacks," Wall Street Journal, April 18, 2002, p. A1; Betsy McKay, "Coke and Pepsi Escalate Their Water Fight," Wall Street Journal, May 18, 2001, p. B8.

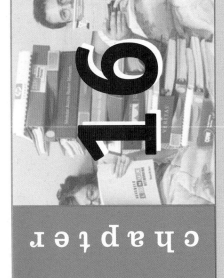

Personal Selling and Sales Promotion

Previewing the Concepts

In the previous two chapters, you learned about communicating customer value through integrated marketing communications (IMC) and about two elements of the promotion mix—advertising and public relations. In this chapter, we'll look at two more IMC elements—personal selling and sales promotion. Personal selling is the interpersonal arm of marketing communications, in which the sales force interacts with customers and prospects to build relationships and make sales. Sales promotion consists of short-term incentives to encourage the purchase or sale of a product or service. As you read on, remember that although this chapter examines personal selling and sales promotion as separate tools, they must be carefully integrated with other elements of the promotion mix.

When someone says "salesperson," what image comes to mind? Perhaps you think about a stereotypical glad-hander who's out to lighten your wallet by selling you something you don't really need. Think again. Today, for most companies, personal selling plays an important role in building profitable customer relationships. Consider CDW Corporation, whose customer-focused sales strategy has helped it grow rapidly while competitors have faltered.

CDW Corporation, a leading provider of multibrand technology products and services, is thriving. In only 22 years since founder Michael Krasny started the business at his kitchen table, CDW has grown to become a high-tech heavyweight in a highly volatile and competitive industry. Even as much of the tech world has slumped, in just the past three years CDW has increased its sales 35 percent, to $6.3 billion annually, while profits have grown 55 percent. Sales last year grew by about 10 percent, almost three times the industry average.

How has CDW managed to grow so profitably? The company owes its success to good old fashioned high-touch personal selling that builds lasting one-to-one customer relationships. The strategy is fueled by a genuine passion for solving customer problems. Under CDW's "Circle of Service" philosophy, "everything revolves around the customer."

CDW sells a complex assortment of more than 100,000 technology products and services—computers, software, accessories, and networking products—including top name brands such as Adobe APC, Apple, Cisco, HP, Lenovo, IBM, Microsoft, Sony, Symantec, Toshiba, and ViewSonic. Many of CDW's competitors chase after a relative handful of very large customers. However, although CDW serves customers of all sizes, one of the company's core customer segments is small and midsize businesses (SMBs). These smaller customers often need lots of advice and support. "Many of our clients don't have IT departments," says one CDW executive, "so they look to us for expertise."

That's where CDW's sales force comes in. The major responsibility for building and managing customer relationships falls to CDW's sales force of over 2,100 account managers. Each customer is assigned an account manager, who helps the customer select the right products and technologies and keep them running smoothly.

Account managers do more than just sell technology products and services. They work closely with customers to find solutions to their technology problems. "This is a big deal to us," says Jim Grass, CDW's senior director of sales. "We want to go beyond fulfilling the order and become the trusted adviser for them. We [want to] talk . . . about what a customer is trying to accomplish and really add value to the sale, as opposed to just sending out a box."

To become trusted advisors and effective customer-relationship builders, CDW account managers really have to know their stuff. And CDW boasts some of the most knowledgeable salespeople in the industry. Before they make a single sales call, new account managers complete a six-week orientation and then a six-month training program. CDW University's College of Sales offers intensive schooling in the science behind the company's products and in the art of consultative selling. But that's just the beginning—the training never ends. Tenured account managers receive ongoing training to enhance their relationship-selling skills. Each year, CDW's sales force completes a whopping 339,000 hours of sales-specific training. John Edwardson, chairman and CEO of CDW and former head of United Airlines, likes to point out that CDW reps get more training than some pilots.

To further support salespeople's customer problem-solving efforts, CDW has also created nine technology teams consisting of more than 120 factory-trained specialists and A+ certified technicians on staff. Account managers can draw on these teams to design customer-specific solutions in technology areas such as mobility/wireless, networking, security, and storage.

Customers who want to access CDW's products and expertise without going through their account manager can do so easily at any of several CDW Web sites. Better yet, CDW will create a free personalized CDW@work extranet site that reflects a given customer's pricing, order status, account history, and special considerations. The extranet site serves as a 24-hour extension of the customer's account manager. This resulted in CDW Web sales of more than $1.7 billion last year. But even here, the ever-present account managers are likely to add personal guidance. Account managers receive immediate notification of their customers' online activities. So if a blurry-eyed SMB manager makes a mistake on an emergency order placed in the middle of the night, chances are good that the account manager will find and correct the error first thing in the morning.

Beyond being knowledgeable and ever present, CDW's account managers are energetic and passionately customer focused. Much of the energy has passed down from CDW founder and former CEO Michael Krasny. Selling has always been a top priority for Krasny, not surprising given that he began the company by selling used personal computers out of his home through classified ads. During his 17-year reign as head of CDW, Krasny created a hardworking and dedicated sales force. One favorite Krasny tale involves a windstorm that ripped off a chunk of the CDW building's roof. Within minutes, Krasny himself was up on the roof, nailing a

Objectives

After studying this chapter, you should be able to

1. discuss the role of a company's salespeople in creating value for customers and building customer relationships

2. identify and explain the six major sales force management steps

3. discuss the personal selling process, distinguishing between transaction-oriented marketing and relationship marketing

4. explain how sales promotion campaigns are developed and implemented

tarp over the hole. When startled employees inside looked up, Krasny shouted down to them to get back to selling.

However, Krasny's most important legacy is the "Circle of Service" culture that he created—a culture that focuses on taking care of customers, and on the CDW employees who serve them (he calls them "coworkers"). "Whenever he made a decision, he'd always ask two questions," says Edwardson: "'What will the reaction of the coworkers be?' and 'What will the response of the customers be?'"

When someone says "salesperson," you may still think of the stereotypical "traveling salesman"—the fast-talking, ever-smiling peddler who travels his territory foisting his wares on reluctant customers. Such stereotypes, however, are out of date. Today, like CDW's account managers, most professional salespeople are well-educated, well-trained men and women who work to build valued customer relationships. They succeed not by taking customers in, but by helping them out—by assessing customer needs and solving customer problems.

CDW's sales force instills loyalty in what are traditionally very price-conscious SMB customers. The company wants to create customer satisfaction at every touch point. Says a former CDW marketing executive, "We're competitively priced, but what's most important is the service and the customers' relationships with their account managers. It's how we actually touch people that creates our most long-lasting [success]."[1]

In this chapter, we examine two more promotion mix tools—*Personal selling* and *sales promotion*. Personal selling consists of interpersonal interactions with customers and prospects to make sales and maintain customer relationships. Sales promotion involves using short-term incentives to encourage customer purchasing, reseller support, and sales force efforts.

Personal Selling

Robert Louis Stevenson once noted that "everyone lives by selling something." Companies all around the world use sales forces to sell products and services to business customers and final consumers. But sales forces are also found in many other kinds of organizations. For example, colleges use recruiters to attract new students and churches use membership committees to attract new members. Museums and fine arts organizations use fund-raisers to contact donors and raise money. Even governments use sales forces. The U.S. Postal Service, for instance, uses a sales force to sell Express Mail and other services to corporate customers. In the first part of this chapter, we examine personal selling's role in the organization, sales force management decisions, and the personal selling process.

The Nature of Personal Selling

Personal selling

Personal presentation by the firm's sales force for the purpose of making sales and building customer relationships.

Personal selling is one of the oldest professions in the world. The people who do the selling go by many names: salespeople, sales representatives, district managers, account executives, sales consultants, sales engineers, agents, and account development reps to name just a few.

People hold many stereotypes of salespeople—including some unfavorable ones. "Salesman," may bring to mind the image of Arthur Miller's pitiable Willy Loman in *Death of a Salesman* or Meredith Willson's cigar-smoking, backslapping, joke-telling Harold Hill in *The Music Man*. These examples depict salespeople as loners, traveling their territories, trying to foist their wares on unsuspecting or unwilling buyers.

However, modern salespeople are a far cry from these unfortunate stereotypes. Today, most salespeople are well-educated, well-trained professionals who work to build and maintain long-term customer relationships. They listen to their customers, assess customer needs, and organize the company's efforts to solve customer problems. Consider Boeing, the aerospace giant competing in the rough-and-tumble worldwide commercial aircraft market. It takes more than fast talk and a warm smile to sell expensive airplanes:

Selling high-tech aircraft at $100 million or more per order is complex and challenging. A single big sale can easily run into billions of dollars. Boeing salespeople

Salesperson
An individual representing a company to customers by performing one or more of the following activities: prospecting, communicating, selling, servicing, information gathering, and relationship building.

■ Professional selling: It takes more than fast talk and a warm smile to sell high-tech aircraft at $100 million or more per order. Success depends on building solid, long-term relationships with customers.

head up an extensive team of company specialists—sales and service technicians, financial analysts, planners, engineers—all dedicated to finding ways to satisfy airline customer needs. The selling process is nerve-rackingly slow—it can take two or three years from the first sales presentation to the day the sale is announced. After getting the order, salespeople then must stay in almost constant touch to keep track of the account's equipment needs and to make certain the customer stays satisfied. Success depends on building solid, long-term relationships with customers, based on performance and trust. "When you buy an airplane, it is like getting married," says the head of Boeing's commercial airplane division. "It is a long-term relationship."[2]

The term **salesperson** covers a wide range of positions. At one extreme, a salesperson might be largely an *order taker*, such as the department store salesperson standing behind the counter. At the other extreme are *order getters*, whose positions demand *creative selling* and *relationship building* for products and services ranging from appliances, industrial equipment, and airplanes to insurance and information technology services. Here, we focus on the more creative types of selling and on the process of building and managing an effective sales force.

The Role of the Sales Force

Personal selling is the interpersonal arm of the promotion mix. Advertising consists largely of one-way, nonpersonal communication with target consumer groups. In contrast, personal selling involves two-way, personal communication between salespeople and individual customers—whether face to face, by telephone, through video or Web conferences, or by other means. Personal selling can be more effective than advertising in more complex selling situations. Salespeople can probe customers to learn more about their problems and then adjust the marketing offer and presentation to fit the special needs of each customer.

The role of personal selling varies from company to company. Some firms have no salespeople at all—for example, companies that sell only online or through catalogs, or companies that sell through manufacturer's reps, sales agents, or brokers. In most firms, however, the sales force plays a major role. In companies that sell business products and services, such as IBM or DuPont, the company's salespeople work directly with customers. In consumer product companies such as Procter & Gamble and Nike, the sales force plays an important behind-the-scenes role. It works with wholesalers and retailers to gain their support and to help them be more effective in selling the company's products.

The sales force serves as a critical link between a company and its customers. In many cases, salespeople serve both masters—the seller and the buyer. First, they *represent the company to customers*. They find and develop new customers and communicate information about the company's products and services. They sell products by approaching customers, presenting their products, answering objections, negotiating prices and terms, and closing sales. In addition, salespeople provide customer service and carry out market research and intelligence work.

At the same time, salespeople *represent customers to the company*, acting inside the firm as "champions" of customers' interests and managing the buyer-seller relationship. Salespeople relay customer concerns about company products and actions back inside to those who can handle them. They learn about customer needs and work with other marketing and nonmarketing people in the company to develop greater customer value. The old view was that salespeople should worry about sales and the company should worry about profit. However, the current view holds that salespeople should be concerned with more than just producing *sales*—they should work with others in the company to produce *customer value* and *company profit*.

Managing the Sales Force

Sales force management

The analysis, planning, implementation, and control of sales force activities. It includes designing sales force strategy and structure and recruiting, selecting, training, supervising, compensating, and evaluating the firm's salespeople.

We define **sales force management** as the analysis, planning, implementation, and control of sales force activities. It includes designing sales force strategy and structure and recruiting, selecting, training, compensating, supervising, and evaluating the firm's salespeople. These major sales force management decisions are shown in Figure 16.1 and are discussed in the following sections.

Designing Sales Force Strategy and Structure

Marketing managers face several sales force strategy and design questions. How should salespeople and their tasks be structured? How big should the sales force be? Should salespeople sell alone or work in teams with other people in the company? Should they sell in the field or by telephone or on the Web?

Sales Force Structure

A company can divide sales responsibilities along any of several lines. The decision is simple if the company sells only one product line to one industry with customers in many locations. In that case the company would use a *territorial sales force structure*. However, if the company sells many products to many types of customers, it might need either a *product sales force structure*, a *customer sales force structure*, or a combination of the two.

Territorial sales force structure

A sales force organization that assigns each salesperson to an exclusive geographic territory in which that salesperson sells the company's full line.

TERRITORIAL SALES FORCE STRUCTURE In the **territorial sales force structure**, each salesperson is assigned to an exclusive geographic area and sells the company's full line of products or services to all customers in that territory. This organization clearly defines each salesperson's job and fixes accountability. It also increases the salesperson's desire to build local customer relationships that, in turn, improve selling effectiveness. Finally, because each salesperson travels within a limited geographic area, travel expenses are relatively small.

A territorial sales organization is often supported by many levels of sales management positions. For example, Campbell Soup uses a territorial structure in which each salesperson is responsible for selling all Campbell Soup products. Starting at the bottom of the organization, *sales merchandisers* report to *sales representatives*, who report to *retail supervisors*, who report to *directors of retail sales operations*, who report to 1 of *22 regional sales managers*. Regional sales managers, in turn, report to 1 of 4 *general sales managers* (West, Central, South, and East), who report to a *vice president and general sales manager*.

Product sales force structure

A sales force organization under which salespeople specialize in selling only a portion of the company's products or lines.

PRODUCT SALES FORCE STRUCTURE Salespeople must know their products—especially when the products are numerous and complex. This need, together with the growth of product management, has led many companies to adopt a **product sales force structure**, in which the sales force sells along product lines. For example, Kodak uses different sales forces for its consumer products than for its industrial products. The consumer products sales force deals with simple products that are distributed intensively, whereas the industrial products sales force deals with complex products that require technical understanding.

The product structure can lead to problems, however, if a single large customer buys many different company products. For example, Cardinal Health, the large health care products and services company, has several product divisions, each with a separate sales force. Using a product sales force structure might mean that several Cardinal salespeople end up calling on the same hospital on the same day. This means that they travel over the same routes and wait to see the same customer's purchasing agents. These extra costs must be compared with the benefits of better product knowledge and attention to individual products.

Customer sales force structure

A sales force organization under which salespeople specialize in selling only to certain customers or industries.

CUSTOMER SALES FORCE STRUCTURE More and more companies are now using a **customer sales force structure**, in which they organize the sales force along customer or industry lines. Separate sales forces may be set up for different industries, for serving current customers ver-

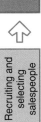

FIGURE 16.1 Major steps in sales force management

Designing sales force strategy and structure ⇨ Recruiting and selecting salespeople ⇨ Training salespeople ⇨ Compensating salespeople ⇨ Supervising salespeople ⇨ Evaluating salespeople

sus finding new ones, and for major accounts versus regular accounts. Many companies even have special sales forces set up to handle the needs of individual large customers. For example, Black & Decker has a Home Depot sales organization and a Lowe's sales organization.

Organizing the sales force around customers can help a company build closer relationships with important customers. Consider Lear Corporation, one of the largest and most successful automotive suppliers in the world.

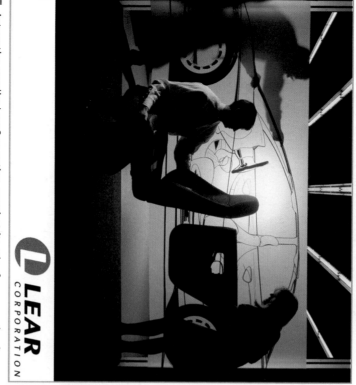

Each year, Lear Corporation produces more than $17 billion worth of automotive interiors—seat systems, instrument panels, door panels, floor and acoustic systems, overhead systems, and electrical distribution systems. Its customers include all of the world's leading automotive companies, from Ford, DaimlerChrysler, General Motors, Toyota, and Volvo to BMW, Ferrari, Rolls-Royce, and more than a dozen others. Perhaps more than any other part of the organization, it's Lear's outstanding 145-person sales force that brings to life the company's credo, "Consumer driven. Customer focused." Lear salespeople work hard at relationship building and doing what's best for the customer. "Our salespeople don't really close deals," notes a senior marketing executive. "They consult and work with customers to learn exactly what's needed and when."

Lear organizes its sales force around major customers. More than that, the company itself is broken up into separate divisions dedicated to specific customers. For example, there's a Ford division, a General Motors, and a Fiat division. This organization lets Lear's sales teams to get very close to their customers. In fact, Lear often locates its sales offices in customers' facilities. For instance, the team that handles GM's light truck division works at GM's truck operation campus. "We can't just be there to give quotes and ask for orders," says the marketing executive. "We need to be involved with customers every step of the way—from vehicle concept through launch."[3]

■ Automotive supplier Lear Corporation organizes its sales force around major customers. In fact, it often locates its sales offices in customers' facilities. "We need to be involved with customers every step of the way—from vehicle concept through launch."

COMPLEX SALES FORCE STRUCTURES

When a company sells a wide variety of products to many types of customers over a broad geographic area, it often combines several types of sales force structures. Salespeople can be specialized by customer and territory, by product and territory, by product and customer, or by territory, product, and customer. No single structure is best for all companies and situations. Each company should select a sales force structure that best serves the needs of its customers and fits its overall marketing strategy.

A good sales structure can mean the difference between success and failure. Companies should periodically review their sales force organizations to be certain that they serve the needs of the company and its customers. Over time, sales force structures can grow complex, inefficient, and unresponsive to customers' needs. This happened recently to technology giant Hewlett-Packard. To correct the problem, the company's new CEO took dramatic steps to restructure HP's corporate sales force (see Real Marketing 16.1).

Sales Force Size

Once the company has set its structure, it is ready to consider *sales force size*. Sales forces may range in size from only a few salespeople to tens of thousands. Some sales forces are huge—for example, American Express employs 23,500 U.S. salespeople, PepsiCo 36,000, and The Hartford Financial Services Group 100,000.[4] Salespeople constitute one of the company's most productive—and most expensive—assets. Therefore, increasing their number will increase both sales and costs.

Real Marketing   Hewlett-Packard Overhauls Its Vast Corporate Sales Force

16.1 Imagine this scenario: You need a new digital camera. You're not sure which one to buy or even what features you need. So you visit your nearest electronics superstore to talk with a salesperson. You walk through the camera section but can't find anyone to help you. When you finally find a salesperson, he yawns and tells you that he's responsible for selling all the products in the store, so he doesn't really know all that much about cameras—maybe you should talk to someone else. You finally find a camera-savvy salesperson. However, after answering a few questions, she disappears to handle some other task, handing you off to someone new. And the new salesperson seems to contradict what the first salesperson said, even quoting different prices on a couple of models you like.

As incredible as it seems, at least until recently, this is the kind of situation that many large business buyers faced when they attempted to buy from technology giant Hewlett-Packard. Before Mark Hurd took over as HP's new CEO in the spring of 2005, the company's revenues and profits had flattened and its stock price had plummeted. To find out why, Hurd first talked directly with 400 corporate customers. Mostly what he heard was gripes about HP's corporate sales force.

Customers complained that they had to deal with too many salespeople, and that HP's confusing management layers made it hard to figure out whom to call. They had trouble tracking down HP sales representatives. And once found, the reps often came across as apathetic, leaving the customer to take the initiative. HP reps were responsible for a broad range of complex products, so they sometimes lacked the needed depth of knowledge on any subset of them. Customers grumbled that they received varying price quotes from different sales reps, and that it often took weeks for reps to respond to seemingly simple requests. In all, HP's corporate customers were frustrated, not a happy circumstance for a company that gets more than 70 percent of its revenues from businesses.

But customers weren't the only ones frustrated by HP's unwieldy and unresponsive sales force structure. HP was organized into three main product divisions: the Personal Systems Group (PSG), the Technology Solutions Group (TSG), and the Image and Printing Group (IPG). However, these divisions had little control over the sales process. Instead, HP's corporate sales force was housed in a fourth

division, the Customer Sales Group (CSG). All salespeople reported directly to the CSG and were responsible for selling products from all three product divisions. To make matters worse, the CSG was bloated and underperforming. According to one reporter, "of the 17,000 people working in HP's corporate sales, only around 10,000 directly sold to customers. The rest were support staff or in management."

HP division executives were frustrated by the CSG structure. They complained that they had little or no direct control over the salespeople who sold their products. And multiple layers of management slowed sales force decision making and customer responsiveness. Finally, salespeople themselves were frustrated by the structure. They weren't being given the time and support they needed to serve their customers well. Burdened with administrative tasks and bureaucratic red tape, they were spending less than a third of their

HP overhauled its vast sales force, reducing salesperson frustration and helping salespeople to create better value for customers.

Many companies use some form of *workload approach* to set sales force size. Using this approach, a company first groups accounts into different classes according to size, account status, or other factors related to the amount of effort required to maintain them. It then determines the number of salespeople needed to call on each class of accounts the desired number of times.

The company might think as follows: Suppose we have 1,000 Type-A accounts and 2,000 Type-B accounts. Type-A accounts require 36 calls a year and Type-B accounts require 12 calls a year. In this case, the sales force's *workload*—the number of calls it must make per year—is 60,000 calls [(1,000 × 36) + (2,000 × 12) = 36,000 + 24,000 = 60,000]. Suppose our average salesperson can make 1,000 calls a year. Thus, we need 60 salespeople (60,000 ÷ 1,000).[5]

Other Sales Force Strategy and Structure Issues

Sales management must also decide who will be involved in the selling effort and how various sales and sales support people will work together.

time with customers. And they had to work through multiple layers of bureaucracy to get price quotes and sample products for customers. "The customer focus was lacking," says an HP sales vice president. "Trying to navigate inside HP was difficult. It was unacceptable."

As CEO Mark Hurd peeled back the layers, it became apparent that HP's organizational problems went deeper than the sales force. The entire company had become so centralized, with so many layers of management, that it was unresponsive and out of touch with customers. Thus began what one observer called "one of Hurd's biggest management challenges: overhauling HP's vast corporate sales force."

For starters, Hurd eliminated the CSG division, instead assigning salespeople directly to the three product divisions. He also did away with three layers of management and cut hundreds of unproductive sales workers. This move gave divisional marketing and sales executives direct control over a leaner, more efficient sales process, resulting in speedier sales decisions and quicker market response.

Hurd also took steps to reduce salesperson and customer frustrations. Eliminating the CSG meant that each salesperson was responsible for selling a smaller number of products and was able to develop expertise in a specific product area. Hurd urged sales managers to cut back on salesperson administrative requirements and to improve sales support so that salespeople could spend more quality time with customers. As a result, salespeople now spend more than 40 percent of their time with customers, up from just 30 percent last year. And HP salespeople are noticing big changes in the sales support they receive:

Salesman Richard Ditucci began noticing some of the changes late last year. At the time, Ditucci was trying to sell computer servers to Staples. As part of the process, Staples had asked him to provide a sample server for the company to evaluate. In the past, such requests typically took two to three weeks to fulfill because of HP's bureaucracy. This time, Ditucci got the server he needed within three days. The quick turnaround helped him win the contract, valued at several million dollars.

To ensure that important customers are carefully tended to, HP assigned each salesperson three or fewer accounts. The top 2,000 accounts were assigned just one salesperson each—"so they'll always know whom to contact." Customers are noticing differences in the attention that they get from HP salespeople:

James Farris, a senior technology executive at Staples, says HP has freed up his salesman to drop by Staples at least twice a month instead of about once a month as before. The extra face time enabled the HP salesman to create more valuable interactions, such as arranging a workshop recently for Staples to explain HP's technology to the retailer's executives. As a result, Farris says he is planning to send more business HP's way. Similarly, Keith Morrow, chief information officer of convenience-store chain 7-Eleven, says his HP sales representative is now "here all the time," and has been more knowledgeable in pitching products tailored to his business. As a result, last October, 7-Eleven began deploying in its U.S. stores 10,000 HP pen pads—a mobile device that helps 7-Eleven workers on the sales floor.

So, HP's sales force restructuring appears to be paying off. Only one year after Mr. Hurd's arrival, HP is now a much leaner and more efficient sales organization. HP's earnings have improved over three consecutive quarters, stock prices are up by over 60 percent, and market share is improving against Dell and other competitors. More importantly, salespeople are happier and more productive, resulting in happier customers. CEO Hurd knows that there's still much more work to be done. But step by step, through restructuring, HP is fixing its sales force to create better value for its business customers. Now, if your local electronics superstore would only do the same for you. . . .

Sources: Quotes and adapted examples from Pui-Wing Tam, "System Reboot: Hurd's Big Challenge at HP: Overhauling Corporate Sales," *Wall Street Journal*, April 3, 2006, p. A1. Other information from Steven Burke and Craig Zarley, "Tables Have Turned; HP Gaining Ground on Dell," *Computer Reseller News*, May 22, 2006, p. 15; Jeffrey Burt, "HP Gets a New Tune," *eWeek*, February 27, 2006, p. 11; "HP Restructures, Putting More Assignments in Play," *Adweek*, March 27, 2006, accessed at www.adweek.com; Craig Zarley and Robert Faletra, "Team Building," *Computer Reseller News*, April 24, 2006, p. 10, and Christopher Hosford, "Rebooting Hewlett-Packard," *Sales & Marketing Management*, July–August 2006, pp. 32–35.

OUTSIDE AND INSIDE SALES FORCES The company may have an **outside sales force** (or *field sales force*), an **inside sales force**, or both. Outside salespeople travel to call on customers in the field. Inside salespeople conduct business from their offices via telephone, the Internet, or visits from buyers.

Some inside salespeople provide support for the outside sales force, freeing them to spend more time selling to major accounts and finding new prospects. For example, *technical sales support people* provide technical information and answers to customers' questions. *Sales assistants* provide administrative backup for outside salespeople. They call ahead and confirm appointments, follow up on deliveries, and answer customers' questions when outside salespeople cannot be reached.

Other inside salespeople do more than just provide support. *Telemarketers and Web sellers* use the phone and Internet to find new leads and qualify prospects or to sell and service accounts directly. Telemarketing and Web selling can be very effective, less costly ways to sell to smaller, harder-to-reach customers. Depending on the complexity of the product and customer, for example, a telemarketer can make from 20 to 33 decision-maker contacts a day,

Outside sales force (or **field sales force**)
Outside salespeople who travel to call on customers in the field.

Inside sales force
Inside salespeople who conduct business from their offices via telephone, the Internet, or visits from prospective buyers.

compared to the average of four that an outside salesperson can make. And whereas an average business-to-business field sales call costs $329 or more, a routine industrial telemarketing call costs only about $5 and a complex call about $20.[6]

For some smaller companies, telephone and Web selling may be the primary sales approaches. However, larger companies also use these tactics, either to sell directly to small and midsize customers or to help out with larger ones. For example, Avaya, a $5 billion global telecommunications firm, recently formed a telemarketing sales force to service its smaller, more routine, less complex accounts. Not only did the telesales force do a better job of selling to these smaller accounts, it freed Avaya's outside salespeople to focus their attentions on the company's highest-value customers and prospects. As a result, the company has experienced 40 percent higher sales in areas where the telesales model is being used.[7]

For many types of products and selling situations, phone or Web selling can be as effective as a personal sales call. Notes a DuPont telemarketer: "I'm more effective on the phone. [When you're in the field], if some guy's not in his office, you lose an hour. On the phone, you lose 15 seconds. . . . Through my phone calls, I'm in the field as much as the rep is." There are other advantages. "Customers can't throw things at you," quips the rep, "and you don't have to outrun dogs."[8]

What's more, although they may seem impersonal, the phone and Internet can be surprisingly personal when it comes to building customer relationships. Remember CDW from our chapter-opening story?

If you're one of CDW Account Manager Ron Kelly's regular customers, you probably know that he's 35 and has a wife named Michelle, a 9-year-old son named Andrew, and a German shepherd named Bones. You know that he majored in journalism and poly sci at SIU (that's Southern Illinois University) and was supposed to attend Northwestern's law school but instead came to work at CDW. You know that he bleeds red and black for the Chicago Blackhawks. You also know that he knows as much, if not more, about you. Kelly, an affable account manager, is a master at relationship-based selling, CDW's specialty. Customers love it. "He's my sales rep, but he's also my friend," says Todd Greenwald, director of operations for Heartland Computers, which sells barcode scanners. "Most of the time we don't even talk about price. I trust Ron."

■ Inside sales force: Although they may seem impersonal, the phone and Internet can be surprisingly personal when it comes to building customer relationships. "He's my business partner," says a CDW customer about her account manager, who manages account relationships almost entirely by phone.

What's particularly impressive is that, for the most part, the interaction occurs over the phone and Internet. Despite the lack of face time, CDW account managers forge close ties. One customer invited his CDW contact to his wedding. Kelly and Greenwald share Blackhawks season tickets. It's not uncommon to find customers and reps whose partnership has outlasted job changes, budget cuts, and marriages. Of course, the relationships aren't based solely on being likable. They're grounded in helping customers succeed. Account managers think like the customer and try to anticipate problems. For instance, before storms rocked Florida one summer, some account managers called or e-mailed clients there with battery and backup-storage solutions. "Instead of just sending a purchase order, we want to ask, 'Why are you buying [that product]?' says a CDW executive. 'That's how you identify customers' needs.'" In this way, to their customers, CDW account managers are much more than just peddlers. When asked if she thinks of her CDW rep as a salesperson anymore, one customer replied, "Never. He's my business partner." And it all happens over the phone or the Web—both supposedly "arms-length" media.[9]

TEAM SELLING   As products become more complex, and as customers grow larger and more demanding, a single salesperson simply can't handle all of a large customer's needs. Instead, most companies now use **team selling** to service large, complex accounts. Sales teams can unearth problems, solutions, and sales opportunities that no individual salesperson could. Such teams might include experts from any area or level of the selling firm—sales, marketing, technical and support services, R&D, engineering, operations, finance, and others. In team selling situations, the salesperson shifts from "soloist" to "orchestrator."

Team selling
Using teams of people from sales, marketing, engineering, finance, technical support, and even upper management to service large, complex accounts.

In many cases, the move to team selling mirrors similar changes in customers' buying organizations. "Today, we're calling on teams of buying people, and that requires more fire-power on our side," says one sales vice president. "One salesperson just can't do it all—can't be an expert in everything we're bringing to the customer. We have strategic account teams, led by customer business managers, who basically are our quarterbacks."[10]

Some companies, such as IBM, Xerox, and Procter & Gamble, have used teams for a long time. P&G sales reps are organized into "customer business development (CBD) teams." Each CBD team is assigned to a major P&G customer, such as Wal-Mart, Safeway, or CVS Pharmacy. Teams consist of a customer business development manager, several account executives (each responsible for a specific category of P&G products), and specialists in marketing strategy, operations, information systems, logistics, and finance. This organization places the focus on serving the complete needs of each important customer. It lets P&G "grow business by work-ing as a 'strategic partner' with our accounts, not just as a supplier. Our goal: to grow their business, which also results in growing ours."[11]

Team selling does have some pitfalls. For example, selling teams can confuse or over-whelm customers who are used to working with only one salesperson. Salespeople who are used to having customers all to themselves may have trouble learning to work with and trust others on a team. Finally, difficulties in evaluating individual contributions to the team sell-ing effort can create some sticky compensation issues.

Recruiting and Selecting Salespeople

At the heart of any successful sales force operation is the recruitment and selection of good salespeople. The performance difference between an average salesperson and a top salesper-son can be substantial. In a typical sales force, the top 30 percent of the salespeople might bring in 60 percent of the sales. Thus, careful salesperson selection can greatly increase over-all sales force performance. Beyond the differences in sales performance, poor selection results in costly turnover. When a salesperson quits, the costs of finding and training a new salesperson—plus the costs of lost sales—can be very high. Also, a sales force with many new people is less productive, and turnover disrupts important customer relationships.

What sets great salespeople apart from all the rest? In an effort to profile top sales per-formers, Gallup Management Consulting Group, a division of the well-known Gallup polling organization, has interviewed hundreds of thousands of salespeople. Its research sug-gests that the best salespeople possess four key talents: intrinsic motivation, disciplined work style, the ability to close a sale, and perhaps most important, the ability to build relation-ships with customers.[12]

Super salespeople are motivated from within. "Different things drive different people—pride, happiness, money, you name it," says one expert. "But all great salespeople have one thing in common: an unrelenting drive to excel." Some salespeople are driven by money, a hunger for recognition, or the satisfaction of competing and winning. Others are driven by the desire to provide service and to build relationships. The best salespeople possess some of each of these motivations.

Whatever their motivations, salespeople must also have a disciplined work style. If salespeople aren't organized and focused, and if they don't work hard, they can't meet the ever-increasing demands customers make these days. Great sales-people are tenacious about laying out detailed, organized plans, then following through in a timely, disciplined way. Says one sales trainer, "Some people say it's all technique or luck. But luck happens to the best salespeople when they

■ Great salespeople: The best salespeople, such as Jennifer Hansen of 3M, possess intrinsic motivation, disciplined work style, the ability to close a sale, and perhaps most important, the ability to build relationships with customers.

get up early, work late, stay up till two in the morning working on a proposal, or keep making calls when everyone is leaving at the end of the day."

Other skills mean little if a salesperson can't close the sale. So what makes for a great closer? For one thing, it takes unyielding persistence. "Great closers are like great athletes," says one sales trainer. "They're not afraid to fail, and they don't give up until they close." Great closers also have a high level of self-confidence and believe that they are doing the right thing.

Perhaps most important in today's relationship-marketing environment, top salespeople are customer problem solvers and relationship builders. They instinctively understand their customers' needs. Talk to sales executives and they'll describe top performers in these terms: Empathetic. Patient. Caring. Responsive. Good listeners. Honest. Top performers can put themselves on the buyer's side of the desk and see the world through their customers' eyes. They don't want just to be liked, they want to add value for their customers.

When recruiting, companies should analyze the sales job itself and the characteristics of its most successful salespeople to identify the traits needed by a successful salesperson in their industry. Then, it must recruit the right salespeople. The human resources department looks for applicants by getting names from current salespeople, using employment agencies, placing classified ads, searching the Web, and working through college placement services. Another source is to attract top salespeople from other companies. Proven salespeople need less training and can be immediately productive.

Recruiting will attract many applicants from whom the company must select the best. The selection procedure can vary from a single informal interview to lengthy testing and interviewing. Many companies give formal tests to sales applicants. Tests typically measure sales aptitude, analytical and organizational skills, personality traits, and other characteristics. But test scores provide only one piece of information in a set that includes personal characteristics, references, past employment history, and interviewer reactions.

Training Salespeople

New salespeople may spend anywhere from a few weeks or months to a year or more in training. Then, most companies provide continuing sales training via seminars, sales meetings, and the Web throughout the salesperson's career. In all, U.S. companies spend more than $7 billion annually on training salespeople. Although training can be expensive, it can also yield dramatic returns. For example, one recent study showed that sales training conducted by a major telecommunications firm paid for itself in 16 days and resulted in a six-month return on investment of 812 percent. Similarly, Nabisco analyzed the return on its two-day Professional Selling Program, which teaches sales reps how to plan for and make professional presentations. Although it cost about $1,000 to put each sales rep through the program, the training resulted in additional sales of more than $122,000 per rep and yielded almost $21,000 of additional profit per rep.[13]

Training programs have several goals. First, salespeople need to know about customers and how to build relationships with them. So the training program must teach them about different types of customers and their needs, buying motives, and buying habits. And it must teach them how to sell effectively and train them in the basics of the selling process. Salespeople also need to know and identify with the company, its products, and its competitors. So an effective training program teaches them about the company's objectives, organization, and chief products and markets and about the strategies of major competitors.

Today, many companies are adding Web-based training to their sales training programs to cut training costs and make training more efficient. One recent study estimates that companies spend 40 cents of every sales training dollar on travel and lodging. Such costs can be greatly reduced through Web-based training. As a result, last year, companies did 33 percent of their corporate training online, up from 24 percent two years earlier.[14]

Online training may range from simple text-based product information to Internet-based sales exercises that build sales skills to sophisticated simulations that re-create the dynamics of real-life sales calls. International Rectifier, a global manufacturer of power management semiconductors, has learned that using the Internet to train salespeople offers many advantages.

To stay competitive in its complex, fast-changing industry, International Rectifier must continually retrain its sales and support people. For example, IR introduces an average of three or more major new products each month. For each new product, the company must coordinate and train hundreds of sales reps, internal sales staffers, field engineers, key executives, and independent inside sales reps across a variety of time zones in 17 locations around the world.

■ Training salespeople: International Rectifier created the online IR University to help keep its hundreds of global sales reps, internal sales staffers, and others trained on the constant stream of new products it introduces.

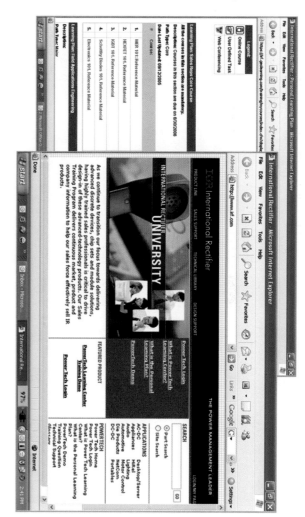

The answer: International Rectifier's online IR University, which provides timely training in advance of new product launches, along with ongoing training on other company and industry developments. The e-learning center provides enhanced presentations, complete with creative animation and streamlined text, to share knowledge accurately but in a way that excites and captures attention. The center also allows for "real-time" visual and audible communications with the presenter via live chat and conference calls. Beyond learning about new products, salespeople can refresh their memories and sharpen their knowledge on almost any topic before meeting with customers. And evaluation diagnostics help sales managers to identify the skill and knowledge levels of each individual salesperson for ongoing support and training.

The sales force is thrilled about being able to "attend" training sessions at times convenient for them, without leaving their home offices. And online training results in significant cost savings. Approximately 500 IR sales and support people have completed more than 5,500 online courses during the past nine months. The cost? Just an estimated $12 per trainee per course. Compared to the costs associated with onsite training, the online learning system has saved the company approximately $250,000 during the past year. In all, online training has reduced IR's training costs by 75 percent.[15]

Compensating Salespeople

To attract good salespeople, a company must have an appealing compensation plan. Compensation is made up of several elements—a fixed amount, a variable amount, expenses, and fringe benefits. The fixed amount, usually a salary, gives the salesperson some stable income. The variable amount, which might be commissions or bonuses based on sales performance, rewards the salesperson for greater effort and success.

Management must decide what *mix* of these compensation elements makes the most sense for each sales job. Different combinations of fixed and variable compensation give rise to four basic types of compensation plans—straight salary, straight commission, salary plus bonus, and salary plus commission. A study of sales force compensation plans showed that 70 percent of all companies surveyed use a combination of base salary and incentives. The average plan consisted of about 60 percent salary and 40 percent incentive pay.[16]

The sales force compensation plan can both motivate salespeople and direct their activities. Compensation should direct the sales force toward activities that are consistent with overall marketing objectives. Table 16.1 illustrates how a company's compensation plan should reflect its overall marketing strategy. For example, if the strategy is to grow rapidly and gain market share, the compensation plan might include a larger commission component, coupled with a new-account bonus to encourage high sales performance and new-account development. In contrast, if the goal is to maximize current account profitability, the compensation plan might contain a larger base-salary component with additional incentives for current account sales or customer satisfaction.

TABLE 16.1   The Relationship between Overall Marketing Strategy and Sales Force Compensation

	Strategic Goal		
	To Gain Market Share Rapidly	*To Solidify Market Leadership*	*To Maximize Profitability*
Ideal salesperson	• An independent self-starter	• A competitive problem solver	• A team player • A relationship manager • Account penetration
Sales focus	• Deal making • Sustained high effort	• Consultative selling	
Compensation role	• To capture accounts • To reward high performance	• To reward new and existing account sales	• To manage the product mix • To encourage team selling • To reward account management

Source: Adapted from Sam T. Johnson, "Sales Compensation: In Search of a Better Solution," *Compensation & Benefits Review*, November–December 1993, p. 52. Copyright © 1998 American Management Association, NY, www.amanet.org. All rights reserved, used with permission.

In fact, more and more companies are moving away from high commission plans that may drive salespeople to make short-term grabs for business. They worry that a salesperson who is pushing too hard to close a deal may ruin the customer relationship. Instead, companies are designing compensation plans that reward salespeople for building customer relationships and growing the long-run value of each customer.

◼ Supervising and Motivating Salespeople

New salespeople need more than a territory, compensation, and training—they need supervision and motivation. The goal of *supervision* is to help salespeople "work smart" by doing the right things in the right ways. The goal of *motivation* is to encourage salespeople to "work hard" and energetically toward sales force goals. If salespeople work smart and work hard, they will realize their full potential, to their own and the company's benefit.

Companies vary in how closely they supervise their salespeople. Many help their salespeople to identify target customers and set call norms. Some may also specify how much time the sales force should spend prospecting for new accounts and set other time management priorities. One tool is the weekly, monthly, or annual *call plan* that shows which customers and prospects to call on and which activities to carry out. Another tool is *time-and-duty analysis*. In addition to time spent selling, the salesperson spends time traveling, waiting, taking breaks, and doing administrative chores.

Figure 16.2 shows how salespeople spend their time. On average, active selling time accounts for only 10 percent of total working time! If selling time could be raised from 10 percent to 30 percent, this would triple the time spent selling.[17] Companies always are looking for ways to save time—simplifying record keeping, finding better sales call and routing plans, supplying

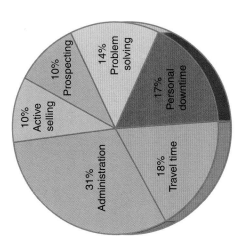

FIGURE 16.2

How salespeople spend their time

Source: Proudfoot Consulting. Data used with permission.

Pie chart segments: 31% Administration, 10% Active selling, 10% Prospecting, 14% Problem solving, 17% Personal downtime, 18% Travel time

more and better customer information, and using phones, e-mail, or video conferencing instead of traveling. Consider the changes GE made to increase its sales force's face-to-face selling time.[18]

When Jeff Immelt became GE's new chairman, he was dismayed to find that members of the sales team were spending far more time on deskbound administrative chores than in face-to-face meetings with customers and prospects. "He said we needed to turn that around," recalls Venki Rao, an IT leader in global sales and marketing at GE Power Systems, a division focused on energy systems and products. "[We need] to spend four days a week in front of the customer and one day for all the admin stuff." GE Power's salespeople spent much of their time at their desks because they had to go to many sources for the information needed to sell multimillion-dollar turbines, turbine parts, and services for the information needed to sell worldwide. To fix the problem, GE created a new sales portal, a kind of "one-stop shop" for just about everything they need. The sales portal connects the vast array of existing GE databases, providing everything from sales tracking and customer data to parts pricing and information on planned outages. GE also added external data, such as news feeds. "Before, you were randomly searching for things," says Bill Snook, a GE sales manager. Now, he says, "I have the sales portal as my home page, and I use it as the gateway to all the applications that I have." The sales portal has freed Snook and 2,500 other users around the globe from once time-consuming administrative tasks, greatly increasing their face time with customers.

Many firms have adopted *sales force automation systems*—computerized, digitized sales force operations that let salespeople work more effectively anytime, anywhere. Companies now routinely equip their salespeople with new-age technologies such as laptops, smart phones, wireless Web connections, Webcams for videoconferencing, and customer-contact and relationship management software. Armed with these technologies, salespeople can more effectively and efficiently profile customers and prospects, analyze and forecast sales, schedule sales calls, make presentations, prepare sales and expense reports, and manage account relationships. The result is better time management, improved customer service, lower sales costs, and higher sales performance.[19]

Perhaps the fastest-growing technology tool is the Internet. The Internet offers explosive potential for conducting sales operations and for interacting with and serving customers. More and more companies are now using the Internet to support their personal selling efforts—not just for selling, but for everything from training salespeople to conducting sales meetings and servicing accounts (see Real Marketing 16.2).

Beyond directing salespeople, sales managers must also motivate them. Some salespeople will do their best without any special urging from management. To them, selling may be the most fascinating job in the world. But selling can also be frustrating. Salespeople often work alone and they must sometimes travel away from home. They may face aggressive competing salespeople and difficult customers. Therefore, salespeople often need special encouragement to do their best.

Management can boost sales force morale and performance through its organizational climate, sales quotas, and positive incentives. *Organizational climate* describes the feeling that salespeople have about their opportunities, value, and rewards for a good performance. Some companies treat salespeople as if they are not very important, and performance suffers accordingly. Other companies treat their salespeople as valued contributors and allow virtually unlimited opportunity for income and promotion. Not surprisingly, these companies enjoy higher sales force performance and less turnover.

■ Sales force automation: Many sales forces have gone high tech, equipping salespeople with everything from smart phones, wireless Web connections, and videoconferencing to customer-contact and relationship management software that helps them to be more effective and efficient.

Real Marketing   Point, Click, and Sell: Welcome to the Web-Based Sales Force

16.2

There are few rules at Fisher Scientific International's sales training sessions. The chemical company's salespeople are allowed to show up for new workshops in their pajamas. And no one flinches if they stroll in at midnight for their first class, take a dozen breaks to call clients, or invite the family cat to sleep in their laps while they take an exam. Sound unorthodox? It would be if Fisher's salespeople were trained in a regular classroom. But for the past few years, the company has been using the Internet to teach the majority of its salespeople in the privacy of their homes, cars, hotel rooms, or wherever else they bring their laptops.

To get updates on Fisher's pricing or refresh themselves on one of the company's highly technical products, all salespeople have to do is log on to the Web site and select from the lengthy index. Any time of the day or night, they can get information on a new product, take an exam, or post messages for product experts—all without ever entering a corporate classroom. Welcome to the world of the Web-based sales force.

Sales organizations around the world are now saving money and time by using a host of Web approaches to train reps, hold sales meetings, and even conduct live sales presentations. Fisher Scientific's reps can dial up the Web site at their leisure, and whereas newer reps might spend hours online going through each session in order, more seasoned sellers might just log on for a quick refresher on a specific product before a sales call. "It allows them to manage their time better, because they're only getting training when they need it, in the doses they need it in," says John Pavlik, director of the company's training department. If salespeople are spending less time on training, Pavlik says, they're able to spend more time on what they do best: selling.

Training is only one of the ways sales organizations are using the Internet. Many companies are using the Web to make sales presentations and service accounts. For example, computer and communications equipment maker NEC Corporation has adopted Web-based selling as an essential marketing tool.

Online selling support: Sales organizations around the world are now using a host of new Web approaches to train reps, hold sales meetings, and even conduct live sales presentations.

After launching a new server line, NEC began looking for ways to cut down on difficult and costly sales force travel. According to Dick Csaplar, marketing manager for the new server line, NEC's old sales approach—traveling to customer sites to pitch NEC products—had become unworkable. Instead, NEC adopted a new Web-based sales approach. Although the initial goal was to cut costs and keep people off airplanes, Web selling has now grown into an intrinsic part of NEC's sales efforts. Web selling certainly does reduce travel time and costs. Whereas the average daily cost of salesperson travel is $663, an hour-long Web conference costs just $60. But more importantly, Web selling lets sales reps meet with more prospective customers than ever before, creating a more efficient and effective sales organization. Csaplar estimates that he's doing 10 customer Web conferences a week, during which he and his sales team show prospects product features and benefits. Customers love it because they get a clear understanding of NEC's technology without

Evaluating Salespeople and Sales-Force Performance

We have thus far described how management communicates what salespeople should be doing and how it motivates them to do it. This process requires good feedback. And good feedback means getting regular information about salespeople to evaluate their performance.

Sales quota
A standard that states the amount a salesperson should sell and how sales should be divided among the company's products.

Many companies motivate their salespeople by setting **sales quotas**—standards stating the amount they should sell and how sales should be divided among the company's products. Compensation is often related to how well salespeople meet their quotas. Companies also use various *positive incentives* to increase sales force effort. *Sales meetings* provide social occasions, breaks from routine, chances to meet and talk with "company brass," and opportunities to air feelings and to identify with a larger group. Companies also sponsor *sales contests* to spur the sales force to make a selling effort above what would normally be expected. Other incentives include honors, merchandise and cash awards, trips, and profit-sharing plans. In all, American companies spend some $100 billion a year on incentive programs to motivate and reward sales-force performance.[20]

having to host the NEC team on-site. And Csaplar was pleased to find that Web-based selling is an effective way to interact with customers and to build customer relationships.

"By the time we're done with the Web-cast, the customer understands the technology, the pricing, and the competition, and we understand the customer's business and needs," he says. Without Web-casts, "we'd be lost on how to communicate with the customer without spending a lot of money," says Csaplar. "I don't see us ever going back to the heavy travel thing."

The Web can be a good channel tool for selling to hard-to-reach customers. For example, the big U.S. pharmaceutical companies currently employ some 87,000 sales reps (often called "detailers") to reach roughly 600,000 practicing physicians. However, these reps are finding it harder than ever to get through to the busy doctors. "Doctors need immense amounts of medical information, but their patient loads limit their ability to see pharmaceutical reps or attend outside conferences," says an industry researcher. The answer: Increasingly, it's the Web. The pharmaceutical companies now regularly use product Web sites, e-mail marketing, and video conferencing to help reps deliver useful information to physicians on their home or office PCs. One study found that last year more than 200,000 physicians participated in "e-detailing"—the process of receiving drug marketing information via the Web—a 400 percent jump in only three years. Using direct-to-doctor Web conferences, companies can make live, interactive medical presentations to any physician with a PC and Web access, saving both the customer's and the rep's time.

The Internet can also be a handy way to hold sales strategy meetings. Consider Cisco Systems, which provides networking solutions for the Internet. Sales meetings used to take an enormous bite out of Cisco's travel budget. Now the company saves about $1 million per month by conducting many of those sessions on the Web. Whenever Cisco introduces a new product, it holds a Web meeting to update salespeople, in groups of one hundred or more, on the product's marketing and sales strategy.

Usually led by the product manager or a vice president of sales, the meetings typically begin with a 10-minute slide presentation that spells out the planned strategy. Then, salespeople spend the next 50 or so minutes asking questions via teleconference. The meeting's leader can direct attendees' browsers to competitors'

Web sites or ask them to vote on certain issues by using the software's instant polling feature. "Our salespeople are actually meeting more online then they ever were face to face," says Mike Mitchell, Cisco's distance learning manager, adding that some salespeople who used to meet with other reps and managers only a few times a quarter are meeting online nearly every day. "That's very empowering for the sales force, because they're able to make suggestions at every step of the way about where we're going with our sales and marketing strategies."

Thus, Web-based technologies can produce big organizational benefits for sales forces. They help conserve salespeople's valuable time, save travel dollars, and give salespeople a new vehicle for selling and servicing accounts. But the technologies also have some drawbacks. For starters, they're not cheap. And such systems can intimidate low-tech salespeople or clients. "As simple as it is, if your salespeople or clients aren't comfortable using the Web, you're wasting your money," says one marketing communications manager. Also, Web tools are susceptible to server crashes and other network difficulties, not a happy event when you're in the midst of an important sales meeting or presentation.

For these reasons, some high-tech experts recommend that sales executives use Web technologies for training, sales meetings, and preliminary client sales presentations, but resort to old-fashioned, face-to-face meetings when the time draws near to close the deal. "When push comes to shove, if you've got an account worth closing, you're still going to get on that plane and see the client in person," says sales consultant Sloane. "Your client is going to want to look you in the eye before buying anything from you, and that's still one thing you just can't do online."

Sources: Portions adapted from Tom Kontzer, "Web Conferencing Embraced," *Information Week*, May 26, 2003, pp. 68–70; Melinda Ligos, "Point, Click, and Sell," *Sales & Marketing Management*, May 1999, pp. 51–55; and Rich Thomaselli, "Pharma Replacing Reps," *Advertising Age*, January 2005, p. 50. Also see Daniel Tynan, "Next Best Thing to Being There," *Sales & Marketing Management*, April 2004, p. 22; Judith Lamont, "Collaboration: Web Conferencing Spans the Distance," *KM World*, June 2005, pp. 16–18; and Rebecca Azronauer, "Looking Good," *Sales & Marketing Management*, April 2006, pp. 41–44.

Management gets information about its salespeople in several ways. The most important source is *sales reports*, including weekly or monthly work plans and longer-term territory marketing plans. Salespeople also write up their completed activities on *call reports* and turn in *expense reports* for which they are partly or wholly repaid. The company can also monitor the sales and profit performance of the salesperson's territory. Additional information comes from personal observation, customer surveys, and talks with other salespeople.

Using various sales force reports and other information, sales management evaluates members of the sales force. It evaluates salespeople on their ability to "plan their work and work their plan." Formal evaluation forces management to develop and communicate clear standards for judging performance. It also provides salespeople with constructive feedback and motivates them to perform well.

On a broader level, management should evaluate the performance of the sales force as a whole. Is the sales force accomplishing its customer relationship, sales, and profit objectives? Is it working well with other areas of the marketing and company organization? Are sales-force costs in line with outcomes? As with other marketing activities, the company wants to measure its *return on sales investment*.[21]

The Personal Selling Process

We now turn from designing and managing a sales force to the actual personal selling process. The **selling process** consists of several steps that the salesperson must master. These steps focus on the goal of getting new customers and obtaining orders from them. However, most salespeople spend much of their time maintaining existing accounts and building long-term customer *relationships*. We discuss the relationship aspect of the personal selling process in a later section.

Steps in the Selling Process

As shown in Figure 16.3, the selling process consists of seven steps: prospecting and qualifying, preapproach, approach, presentation and demonstration, handling objections, closing, and follow-up.

Prospecting and Qualifying

The first step in the selling process is **prospecting**—identifying qualified potential customers. Approaching the right potential customers is crucial to selling success. As one expert puts it: "If the sales force starts chasing anyone who is breathing and seems to have a budget, you risk accumulating a roster of expensive-to-serve, hard-to-satisfy customers who never respond to whatever value proposition you have." He continues, "The solution to this isn't rocket science. [You must] train salespeople to actively scout the right prospects." Another expert concludes: "Increasing your prospecting effectiveness is the fastest single way to boost your sales."[22]

The salesperson must often approach many prospects to get just a few sales. Although the company supplies some leads, salespeople need skill in finding their own. The best source is referrals. Salespeople can ask current customers for referrals and cultivate other referral sources, such as suppliers, dealers, noncompeting salespeople, and bankers. They can also search for prospects in directories or on the Web and track down leads using the telephone and direct mail. Or they can drop in unannounced on various offices (a practice known as "cold calling").

Salespeople also need to know how to *qualify* leads—that is, how to identify the good ones and screen out the poor ones. Prospects can be qualified by looking at their financial ability, volume of business, special needs, location, and possibilities for growth.

Preapproach

Before calling on a prospect, the salesperson should learn as much as possible about the organization (what it needs, who is involved in the buying) and its buyers (their characteristics and buying styles). This step is known as the **preapproach**. The salesperson can consult standard industry and online sources, acquaintances, and others to learn about the company. The salesperson should set *call objectives*, which may be to qualify the prospect, to gather information, or to make an immediate sale. Another task is to decide on the best approach, which might be a personal visit, a phone call, or a letter. The best timing should be considered carefully because many prospects are busiest at certain times. Finally, the salesperson should give thought to an overall sales strategy for the account.

Approach

During the **approach** step, the salesperson should know how to meet and greet the buyer and get the relationship off to a good start. This step involves the salesperson's appearance,

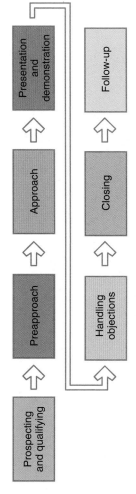

FIGURE 16.3
Major steps in effective selling

Presentation

The step in the selling process in which the salesperson tells the "product story" to the buyer, highlighting customer benefits.

opening lines, and the follow-up remarks. The opening lines should be positive to build goodwill from the beginning of the relationship. This opening might be followed by some key questions to learn more about the customer's needs or by showing a display or sample to attract the buyer's attention and curiosity. As in all stages of the selling process, listening to the customer is crucial.

Presentation and Demonstration

During the **presentation** step of the selling process, the salesperson tells the product "story" to the buyer, presenting customer benefits and showing how the product solves the customer's problems. The problem-solver salesperson fits better with today's marketing concept than does a hard-sell salesperson or the glad-handing extrovert. Buyers today want solutions, not smiles; results, not razzle-dazzle. They want salespeople who listen to their concerns, understand their needs, and respond with the right products and services.

This *need-satisfaction approach* calls for good listening and problem-solving skills. A recent study revealed that 74 percent of 200 purchasers surveyed at companies nationwide said they would be much more likely to buy from a salesperson if the seller would simply listen to them. "To me, sales is listening to customers, finding out what they want, finding out what their concerns are, and then trying to fill them," notes one experienced salesperson. "It's no longer enough to have a good relationship with a client," says another. "You have to understand their problems. You have to feel their pain."[23]

The qualities that buyers *dislike most* in salespeople include being pushy, late, deceitful, and unprepared or disorganized. The qualities they *value most* include good listening, empathy, honesty, dependability, thoroughness, and follow-through. Great salespeople know how to sell, but more importantly they know how to listen and to build strong customer relationships. Says one professional, "Salespeople must have the right answers, certainly, but they also have to learn how to ask those questions and listen."[24]

Today, advanced presentation technologies allow for full multimedia presentations to only one or a few people. CDs and DVDs, online presentation technologies, and handheld and laptop computers with presentation software have replaced the flip chart. Here's an example:[25]

Tina Cox, a technical trainer for Analytical Graphics, a company that produces integrated land, sea, and air analysis software, uses InterWrite software and it's integrated wireless tablet-and-pen capabilities to teach new and potential customers how to use the company's products. Just like TV football commentator John Madden, she writes on her prepared screens during the presentation. She draws on freeze-frame images, just as Madden often does when he directs viewers to the significant elements of the previous football play with his trademark squiggly lines. Cox uses her tablet and pen to show her clients the key elements of the slides. If customers ever lose a thread of her sales presentation, they can easily check the information she circled and almost immediately get back on track. Cox believes the technology greatly enhances her presentations, both Web-based and in person, and customers agree.

Gateway recommends Microsoft® Windows® XP Tablet PC Edition.

■ Today's advanced presentation technologies allow for full multimedia presentations to only one or a few people. Online presentation technologies and hand-held and laptop computers with presentation software, such as Gateway's Convertible Notebook, have replaced the old flip chart.

Handling Objections

Handling objections
The step in the selling process in which the salesperson seeks out, clarifies, and overcomes customer objections to buying.

Customers almost always have objections during the presentation or when asked to place an order. The problem can be either logical or psychological, and objections are often unspoken. In **handling objections**, the salesperson should use a positive approach, seek out hidden objections, ask the buyer to clarify any objections, take objections as opportunities to provide more information, and turn the objections into reasons for buying. Every salesperson needs training in the skills of handling objections.

Closing

Closing
The step in the selling process in which the salesperson asks the customer for an order.

After handling the prospect's objections, the salesperson now tries to close the sale. Some salespeople do not get around to **closing** or do not handle it well. They may lack confidence, feel guilty about asking for the order, or fail to recognize the right moment to close the sale. Salespeople should know how to recognize closing signals from the buyer, including physical actions, comments, and questions. For example, the customer might sit forward and nod approvingly or ask about prices and credit terms.

Salespeople can use one of several closing techniques. They can ask for the order, review points of agreement, offer to help write up the order, ask whether the buyer wants this model or that one, or note that the buyer will lose out if the order is not placed now. The salesperson may offer the buyer special reasons to close, such as a lower price or an extra quantity at no charge.

Follow-Up

Follow-up
The last step in the selling process in which the salesperson follows up after the sale to ensure customer satisfaction and repeat business.

The last step in the selling process—**follow-up**—is necessary if the salesperson wants to ensure customer satisfaction and repeat business. Right after closing, the salesperson should complete any details on delivery time, purchase terms, and other matters. The salesperson then should schedule a follow-up call when the initial order is received, to make sure there is proper installation, instruction, and servicing. This visit would reveal any problems, assure the buyer of the salesperson's interest, and reduce any buyer concerns that might have arisen since the sale.

Personal Selling and Customer Relationship Management

The steps in the selling process as just described are *transaction oriented*—their aim is to help salespeople close a specific sale with a customer. But in most cases, the company is not simply seeking a sale: It has targeted a major customer that it would like to win and keep. The company would like to show that it has the capabilities to serve the customer over the long haul in a mutually profitable *relationship*. The sales force usually plays an important role in building and managing profitable customer relationships.

Today's large customers favor suppliers who can sell and deliver a coordinated set of products and services to many locations, and who can work closely with customer teams to improve products and processes. For these customers, the first sale is only the beginning of the relationship. Unfortunately, some companies ignore these relationship realities. They sell their products through separate sales forces, each working independently to close sales. Their technical people may not be willing to lend time to educate a customer. Their engineering, design, and manufacturing people may have the attitude that "it's our job to make good products" and the salesperson's job to sell them to customers." Their salespeople focus on pushing products toward customers rather than listening to customers and providing solutions.

Other companies, however, recognize that winning and keeping accounts requires more than making good products and directing the sales force to close lots of sales. It requires listening to customers, understanding their needs, and carefully coordinating the whole company's efforts to create customer value and to build lasting relationships.

▌Sales Promotion

Sales promotion
Short-term incentives to encourage the purchase or sale of a product or service.

Personal selling and advertising often work closely with another promotion tool, sales promotion. **Sales promotion** consists of short-term incentives to encourage purchase or sales of a product or service. Whereas advertising offers reasons to buy a product or service, sales promotion offers reasons to buy *now*.

Examples of sales promotions are found everywhere. A freestanding insert in the Sunday newspaper contains a coupon offering $1 off Folgers coffee. An e-mail from EddieBauer.com offers free shipping on your next purchase over $100. The end-of-the-aisle display in the local supermarket tempts impulse buyers with a wall of Coke cases. An executive buys a new Sony laptop and gets a free carrying case, or a family buys a new Explorer and receives a factory rebate of $1,000. A hardware store chain receives a 10 percent discount on selected Black & Decker portable power tools if it agrees to advertise them in local newspapers. Sales promotion includes a wide variety of promotion tools designed to stimulate earlier or stronger market response.

Rapid Growth of Sales Promotion

Sales promotion tools are used by most organizations, including manufacturers, distributors, retailers, and not-for-profit institutions. They are targeted toward final buyers (*consumer promotions*), retailers and wholesalers (*trade promotions*), business customers (*business promotions*), and members of the sales force (*sales force promotions*). Today, in the average consumer packaged-goods company, sales promotion accounts for 74 percent of all marketing expenditures. [26]

Several factors have contributed to the rapid growth of sales promotion, particularly in consumer markets. First, inside the company, product managers face greater pressures to increase their current sales, and promotion is viewed as an effective short-run sales tool. Second, externally, the company faces more competition and competing brands are less differentiated. Increasingly, competitors are using sales promotion to help differentiate their offers. Third, advertising efficiency has declined because of rising costs, media clutter, and legal restraints. Finally, consumers have become more deal oriented, and ever-larger retailers are demanding more deals from manufacturers.

The growing use of sales promotion has resulted in *promotion clutter*, similar to advertising clutter. Consumers are increasingly tuning out promotions, weakening their ability to trigger immediate purchase. Manufacturers are now searching for ways to rise above the clutter, such as offering larger coupon values or creating more dramatic point-of-purchase displays.

In developing a sales promotion program, a company must first set sales promotion objectives and then select the best tools for accomplishing these objectives.

Sales Promotion Objectives

Sales promotion objectives vary widely. Sellers may use *consumer promotions* to urge short-term customer buying or to enhance long-term customer relationships. Objectives for *trade promotions* include getting retailers to carry new items and more inventory, buy ahead, or advertise the company's products and give them more shelf space. For the *sales force*, objectives include getting more sales force support for current or new products or getting salespeople to sign up new accounts.

Sales promotions are usually used together with advertising, personal selling, or other promotion mix tools. Consumer promotions must usually be advertised and can add excitement and pulling power to ads. Trade and sales force promotions support the firm's personal selling process.

In general, rather than creating only short-term sales or temporary brand switching, sales promotions should help to reinforce the product's position and build long-term customer relationships. If properly designed, every sales promotion tool has the potential to build both short-term excitement and long-term consumer relationships. Increasingly, marketers are avoiding "quick fix," price-only promotions in favor of promotions designed to build brand equity.

Examples include all of the "frequency marketing programs" and loyalty clubs that have mushroomed in recent years. Most hotels, supermarkets, and airlines now offer frequent-guest/buyer/flyer programs offering rewards to regular customers. For example, Cendant, which owns hotel chains such as Ramada, Days Inn, Travelodge, Howard Johnson, and Super 8, offers a loyalty program called TripRewards, a program that targets its core market of not-so-frequent leisure travelers.

In designing its TripRewards loyalty program, Cendant knew that Ramada, Days Inn, Travelodge, and the rest of its lodging family could not out-Marriott Marriott Rewards or duplicate the elite tiers of Starwood Preferred Guest. Cendant caters to more budget-minded leisure travelers who venture out on a half dozen trips or fewer annually. Unlike frequent business travelers, these folks don't travel enough to take advantage of most travel loyalty programs. So Cendant put together a network of TripRewards retailers that lets members earn points with everyday purchases. TripRewards members can earn points for purchases at retailers ranging from J.C. Penney and Best Buy to FTD Florists and CheapTickets.com.

Cendant's "It's fun to get more" ad campaign plays up the fun of getting a bonus from everyday shopping transactions. TripRewards' low redemption threshold (as low as 65,000 points for a week-long resort stay versus Marriott Rewards' 140,000) means that Cendant can win the patronage of consumers who would otherwise be decades away from earning anything in a competing program. The TripRewards program drew 2.8 million members in its first eight months, 60 percent of them first-time Cendant hotel customers. It's attracting younger and more affluent consumers with higher average room rates and longer stays—and it keeps them coming back. "They're going to be repeat business," says the manager of one Cendant hotel. "The points add up pretty quick, [and] once we get [guests] through the . . . door, they're not going back to Hilton."[27]

Major Sales Promotion Tools

Many tools can be used to accomplish sales promotion objectives. Descriptions of the main consumer, trade, and business promotion tools follow.

Consumer Promotion Tools

The main **consumer promotion tools** include samples, coupons, cash refunds, price packs, premiums, advertising specialties, patronage rewards, point-of-purchase displays and demonstrations, and contests, sweepstakes, and games.

Samples are offers of a trial amount of a product. Sampling is the most effective—but most expensive—way to introduce a new product or to create new excitement for an existing one. Some samples are free; for others, the company charges a small amount to offset its cost. The sample might be delivered door-to-door, sent by mail, handed out in a store, attached to another product, or featured in an ad. Sometimes, samples are combined into sample packs, which can then be used to promote other products and services. Sampling can be a powerful promotional tool. Consider this example:

Fisherman's Friend throat lozenges used sampling as the centerpiece of a very successful brand-building program. It began by passing out 250,000 samples of its lozenges at more than 25 fairs, sporting events, and other happenings where it was a sponsor. Each sample contained an invitation to visit the Fisherman's Friend Web site, where customers could enter a contest to win a MINI Cooper by submitting a slogan to be used in the future "Tell a Friend" (about Fisherman's Friend) ad campaign. The sampling promotion was a complete success. U.S. sales of Fisherman's Friend lozenges grew 115 percent for the year, 25 percent better than expectations. Some 5,000 people submitted a slogan for the company's new ad campaign. The winner and proud owner of a new MINI Cooper—Shirley Tucker of Pittsburgh—suggested the slogan, "Lose a Cough. Gain a Friend," which is now featured in ads and on the Web site. The successful sampling campaign continues via the company's Web site, which invites consumers to sign themselves and a friend up to receive free samples of Fisherman's Friend in the mail.[28]

Coupons are certificates that give buyers a saving when they purchase specified products. Most consumers love coupons. U.S. companies distributed 323 billion coupons last year with an average face value of $1.16. Consumers redeemed more than 3 billion of them for a total savings of about $3.47 billion.[29] Coupons can promote early trial of a new brand or stimulate sales of a mature brand. However, as a result of coupon clutter, redemption rates have been declining in recent years. Thus, most major consumer goods companies are issuing fewer coupons and targeting them more carefully.

Marketers are also cultivating new outlets for distributing coupons, such as supermarket shelf dispensers, electronic point-of-sale coupon printers, e-mail and online media, or even text-messaging systems. For example, text-message couponing is popular in Europe, India,

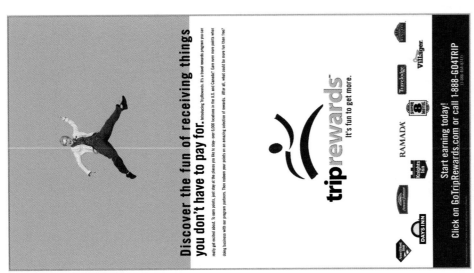

Discover the fun of receiving things you don't have to pay for.

Introducing TripRewards. It's a travel rewards program you can really get excited about. To earn points, just stay at the places you like to stay: over 6,000 locations in the U.S. and Canada*. Earn even more points when doing business with our program partners. Then redeem your points on an amazing selection of rewards. After all, what could be more fun than free?

triprewards
It's fun to get more.

RAMADA
Knights Inn
Wingate Inn
Travelodge
8
villager
Howard Johnson
DAYS INN
AmeriHost

Start earning today!
Click on GoTripRewards.com or call 1-888-604TRIP
(1-888-604-8747)

■ Customer-relationship building promotions: Cendant's TripRewards program makes frequent customers out of not-so-frequent leisure travelers. "It's fun to get more."

Consumer promotion tools
Sales promotion tools used to urge short-term customer buying or to enhance long-term customer relationships.

New forms of coupons: Text message couponing is gaining popularity. At the University of South Florida, local businesses can blast out text message coupons directly to interested students' cell phones via the university's MoBull Plus system.

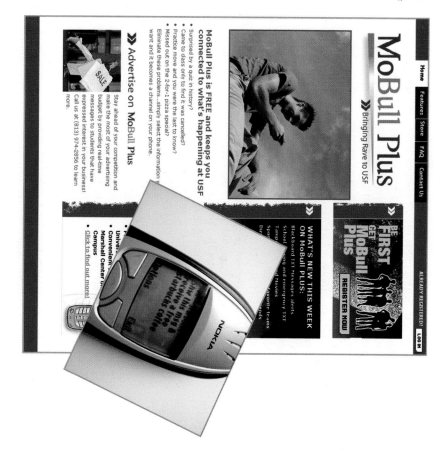

and Japan, and it's slowly gaining popularity in the United States. American Express recently launched Mobile Offers, which sends willing cardholders "coupons" from local merchants via text messages to cell phones. And at the University of South Florida, local businesses can send out text message coupons directly to interested students' cell phones via the university's MoBull Messenger system. For instance, if a local pizza place is having a slow night, it can log in and blast out a two-for-one pizza coupon to students who have opted-in.[30]

Cash refunds (or *rebates*) are like coupons except that the price reduction occurs after the purchase rather than at the retail outlet. The consumer sends a "proof of purchase" to the manufacturer, who then refunds part of the purchase price by mail. For example, Toro ran a clever preseason promotion on some of its snowblower models, offering a rebate if the snowfall in the buyer's market area turned out to be below average. Competitors were not able to match this offer on such short notice, and the promotion was very successful.

Price packs (also called *cents-off deals*) offer consumers savings off the regular price of a product. The producer marks the reduced prices directly on the label or package. Price packs can be single packages sold at a reduced price (such as two for the price of one) or two related products banded together (such as a toothbrush and toothpaste). Price packs are very effective—even more so than coupons—in stimulating short-term sales.

Premiums are goods offered either free or at low cost as an incentive to buy a product, ranging from toys included with kids' products to phone cards and DVDs. A premium may come inside the package (in-pack), outside the package (on-pack), or through the mail. Kellogg often incorporates premiums with its cereals and related products. For instance, it recently offered a free *Cars* racer, based on characters from the Disney/Pixar movie, inside specially marked boxes of Apple Jacks. And buyers of Kellogg Frosted Flakes Cereal & Milk Bars could buy an *Ice Age II: The Meltdown* pop-up tent by mailing in two UPC symbols along with a check for $9.99.

Advertising specialties, also called *promotional products*, are useful articles imprinted with an advertiser's name, logo, or message that are given as gifts to consumers. Typical items include T-shirts and other apparel, pens, coffee mugs, calendars, key rings, mouse pads, matches, tote bags, coolers, golf balls, and caps. U.S. marketers spent more than $18 billion on advertising specialties last year. Such items can be very effective. The "best of them stick around for months, subtly burning a brand name into a user's brain," notes a promotional products expert. In a recent study, 71 percent of all consumers surveyed had received at least one promotional product in the past 12 months. Seventy-six percent of those were able to recall the advertiser's name on the promotional product they received, compared to only 53.5 percent who could recall the name of an advertiser in a print publication they had read in the past week.[31]

Patronage rewards are cash or other awards offered for the regular use of a certain company's products or services. For example, airlines offer frequent flier plans, awarding points for miles traveled that can be turned in for free airline trips. And supermarkets issue frequent shopper cards that dole out a wealth of discounts at the checkout. Office Depot offers frequent-purchase awards—using its Worklife Rewards card, customers who spend at least $200 at Office Depot in three months earn gift cards worth up to $50 that can be used toward future purchases.

Point-of-purchase (POP) promotions include displays and demonstrations that take place at the point of sale. Think of your last visit to the local Safeway, Costco, CVS, or Bed Bath & Beyond. Chances are good that you were tripping over aisle displays, promotional signs, "shelf talkers," or demonstrators offering free tastes of featured food products. Unfortunately, many retailers do not like to handle the hundreds of displays, signs, and posters they receive from manufacturers each year. Manufacturers have responded by offering better POP materials, offering to set them up, and tying them in with television, print, or online messages.

Contests, sweepstakes, and games give consumers the chance to win something, such as cash, trips, or goods, by luck or through extra effort. A *contest* calls for consumers to submit an entry—a jingle, guess, suggestion—to be judged by a panel that will select the best entries. A *sweepstakes* calls for consumers to submit their names for a drawing. A *game* presents consumers with something—bingo numbers, missing letters—every time they buy, which may or may not help them win a prize. A sales contest urges dealers or the sales force to increase their efforts, with prizes going to the top performers.

Trade Promotion Tools

Trade promotion tools
Sales promotion tools used to persuade resellers to carry a brand, give it shelf space, promote it in advertising, and push it to consumers.

Manufacturers direct more sales promotion dollars toward retailers and wholesalers (78 percent) than to final consumers (22 percent).[32] **Trade promotion tools** can persuade resellers to carry a brand, give it shelf space, promote it in advertising, and push it to consumers. Shelf space is so scarce these days that manufacturers often have to offer price-offs, allowances, buy-back guarantees, or free goods to retailers and wholesalers to get products on the shelf and, once there, to keep them on it.

Manufacturers use several trade promotion tools. Many of the tools used for consumer promotions—contests, premiums, displays—can also be used as trade promotions. Or the manufacturer may offer a straight *discount* off the list price on each case purchased during a stated period of time (also called a *price-off, off-invoice,* or *off-list*). Manufacturers also may offer an *allowance* (usually so much off per case) in return for the retailer's agreement to feature the manufacturer's products in some way. An advertising allowance compensates retailers for advertising the product. A display allowance compensates them for using special displays.

Manufacturers may offer *free goods,* which are extra cases of merchandise, to resellers who buy a certain quantity or who feature a certain flavor or size. They may offer *push money*—cash or gifts to dealers or their sales forces to "push" the manufacturer's goods. Manufacturers may give retailers free *specialty advertising items* that carry the company's name, such as pens, pencils, calendars, paperweights, matchbooks, memo pads, and yardsticks.

Business Promotion Tools

Business promotion tools
Sales promotion tools used to generate business leads, stimulate purchases, reward customers, and motivate salespeople.

Companies spend billions of dollars each year on promotion to industrial customers. **Business promotion tools** are used to generate business leads, stimulate purchases, reward customers, and motivate salespeople. Business promotion includes many of the same tools used for consumer or trade promotions. Here, we focus on two additional major business promotion tools—conventions and trade shows, and sales contests.

Many companies and trade associations organize *conventions and trade shows* to promote their products. Firms selling to the industry show their products at the trade show. Vendors receive many benefits, such as opportunities to find new sales leads, contact customers, introduce new products, meet new customers, sell more to present customers, and educate customers with publications and audiovisual materials. Trade shows also help companies reach many prospects not reached through their sales forces.

Some trade shows are huge. For example, at this year's International Consumer Electronics Show, 2,500 exhibitors attracted more than 150,000 professional visitors. Even more impressive, at the BAUMA mining and construction equipment trade show in Munich, Germany, some

■ Some trade shows are huge. At this year's International Consumer Electronics Show, 2,500 exhibitors attracted more than 150,000 professional visitors.

2,800 exhibitors from 47 countries presented their latest product innovations to more than 416,000 attendees from 171 countries. 33

A *sales contest* is a contest for salespeople or dealers to motivate them to increase their sales performance over a given period. Sales contests motivate and recognize good company performers, who may receive trips, cash prizes, or other gifts. Some companies award points for performance, which the receiver can turn in for any of a variety of prizes. Sales contests work best when they are tied to measurable and achievable sales objectives (such as finding new accounts, reviving old accounts, or increasing account profitability).

Developing the Sales Promotion Program

Beyond selecting the types of promotions to use, marketers must make several other decisions in designing the full sales promotion program. First, they must decide on the *size of the incentive*. A certain minimum incentive is necessary if the promotion is to succeed; a larger incentive will produce more sales response. The marketer also must set *conditions for participation*. Incentives might be offered to everyone or only to select groups.

Marketers must decide how to *promote and distribute the promotion program* itself. A $2-off coupon could be given out in a package, at the store, via the Internet, or in an advertisement. Each distribution method involves a different level of reach and cost. Increasingly, marketers are blending several media formats into a total campaign concept. The *length of the promotion* is also important. If the sales promotion period is too short, many prospects (who may not be buying during that time) will miss it. If the promotion runs too long, the deal will lose some of its "act now" force.

Evaluation is also very important. Many companies fail to evaluate their sales promotion programs, and others evaluate them only superficially. Yet marketers should work to measure the returns on their sales promotion investments, just as they should seek to assess the returns on other marketing activities. The most common evaluation method is to compare sales before, during, and after a promotion. Marketers should ask: Did the promotion attract new customers or more purchasing from current customers? Can we hold onto these new customers and purchases? Will the long-run customer relationship and sales gains from the promotion justify its costs?

Clearly, sales promotion plays an important role in the total promotion mix. To use it well, the marketer must define the sales promotion objectives, select the best tools, design the sales promotion program, implement the program, and evaluate the results. Moreover, sales promotion must be coordinated carefully with other promotion mix elements within the overall integrated marketing communications program.

Reviewing the Concepts

This chapter is the third of four chapters covering the final marketing mix element—promotion. The two previous chapters dealt with overall integrated marketing communications and with advertising and public relations. This one investigates personal selling and sales promotion. Personal selling is the interpersonal arm of the communications mix. Sales promotion consists of short-term incentives to encourage the purchase or sale of a product or service.

1. Discuss the role of a company's salespeople in creating value for customers and building customer relationships.

Most companies use salespeople, and many companies assign them an important role in the marketing mix. For companies selling business products, the firm's salespeople work directly with customers. Often, the sales force is the customer's only direct contact with the company and therefore may be viewed by customers as representing the company itself. In contrast, for consumer product companies that sell through intermediaries, consumers usually do not meet salespeople or even know about them. The sales force works behind the scenes, dealing with wholesalers and retailers to obtain their support and helping them become more effective in selling the firm's products.

As an element of the promotion mix, the sales force is very effective in achieving certain marketing objectives and carrying out such activities as prospecting, communicating, selling and servicing, and information gathering. But with companies becoming more market oriented, a customer-focused sales force also works to produce both *customer satisfaction* and *company profit*. The sales force plays a key role in developing and managing profitable *customer relationships*.

2. Identify and explain the six major sales force management steps.

High sales force costs necessitate an effective sales management process consisting of six steps: designing sales force strategy and structure, recruiting and selecting, training, compensating, supervising, and evaluating salespeople and sales force performance.

In designing a sales force, sales management must address strategy issues such as what type of sales force structure will work best (territorial, product, customer, or complex structure); how large the sales force should be; who will be involved in the selling effort; and how its various sales and sales support people will work together (inside or outside sales forces and team selling).

To hold down the high costs of hiring the wrong people, salespeople must be recruited and selected carefully. In recruiting salespeople, a company may look to job duties and the characteristics of its most successful salespeople to suggest the traits it wants in its salespeople. It must then look for applicants through recommendations of current salespeople, employment agencies, classified ads, and the Internet and by contacting college students. In the selection process, the procedure can vary from a single informal interview to lengthy testing and interviewing. After the selection process is complete, training programs familiarize new salespeople not only with the art of selling but also with the company's history, its products and policies, and the characteristics of its market and competitors. The sales force compensation system helps to reward, motivate, and direct salespeople. In compensating salespeople, companies try to have an appealing plan, usually close to the going rate for the type of sales job and needed skills. In addition to compensation, all salespeople need supervision, and many need continuous encouragement

because they must make many decisions and face many frustrations. Periodically, the company must evaluate their performance to help them do a better job. In evaluating salespeople, the company relies on getting regular information gathered through sales reports, personal observations, customers' letters and complaints, customer surveys, and conversations with other salespeople.

3. Discuss the personal selling process, distinguishing between transaction-oriented marketing and relationship marketing.

The art of selling involves a seven-step *selling process: prospecting and qualifying, preapproach, approach, presentation and demonstration, handling objections, closing,* and *follow-up.* These steps help marketers close a specific sale and as such are *transaction oriented.* However, a seller's dealings with customers should be guided by the larger concept of *relationship marketing.* The company's sales force should help to orchestrate a whole-company effort to develop profitable long-term relationships with key customers based on superior customer value and satisfaction.

4. Explain how sales promotion campaigns are developed and implemented.

Sales promotion campaigns call for setting sales promotions objectives (in general, sales promotions should be *consumer relationship building*); selecting tools; and developing and implementing the sales promotion program by using *consumer promotion tools* (coupons, cash refund offers, price packs, premiums, advertising specialties, patronage rewards, point-of-purchase promotions, and contests, sweepstakes, and games), *trade promotion tools* (discounts, allowances, free goods, and push money), and *business promotion tools* (conventions, trade shows, and sales contests) as well as deciding on such things as the size of the incentive, the conditions for participation, how to promote and distribute the promotion package, and the length of the promotion. After this process is completed, the company evaluates its sales promotion results.

Reviewing the Key Terms

Approach 466
Business promotion tools 472
Closing 468
Consumer promotion tools 470
Customer sales force structure 454

Follow-up 468
Handling objections 468
Inside sales force 457
Outside sales force (or field sales force) 457
Personal selling 452
Preapproach 466

Presentation 467
Product sales force structure 454
Prospecting 466
Sales force management 454
Sales promotion 468
Sales quota 464

Salesperson 453
Selling process 466
Team selling 458
Territorial sales force structure 454
Trade promotion tools 472

Discussing the Concepts

1. According to the chapter, salespeople serve "two masters." What does this mean? Is it a good or bad thing?

2. The chapter states that the ability to build relationships with customers is the most important of a salesperson's key talents. Do you agree? Explain.

3. DuPont sells thousands of industrial and consumer products throughout the world. It serves industries as diverse as aerospace, agriculture, and health care. Describe how DuPont can best structure its sales force.

4. A start-up manufacturer of low-carbohydrate muffins wants to sell its product in supermarkets all along the East Coast. It has identified

400 large supermarket chains and 100 smaller chains. The large supermarket chains will require 30 calls per year and the smaller stores 10 calls per year. An average salesperson can make 1,000 calls per year. Using the workload approach for setting sales force size, how many salespeople will this manufacturer need?

5. What are the main differences between sales promotion and advertising?

6. Explain why there has been rapid growth in the use of sales promotions.

Applying the Concepts

1. Who in your class would make a good salesperson? Why?

2. Work in pairs to describe the stages in the selling process for a small Minneapolis company that sells cleaning services to owners of small businesses, such as hair salons, dentists' offices, and clothing stores. Role-play the actual selling process, from approach to close, with one team member acting as the salesperson. The other mem-

ber of the team should act as a customer and raise at least three objections.

3. Suppose you are the marketing coordinator responsible for recommending the sales promotion plan for the market launch of a new brand of Red Bull energy drink sold in supermarkets. What promotional tools would you consider for this task? Explain.

Focus on Technology

High-level salespeople need sophisticated tools to perform more effectively, especially when on the road. They need to gather customer contact information, check updated product inventories, and keep track of order information. Strong customer relationship management systems, such as those offered by SAP (www.sap.com), provide many features that empower the sales force. Visit SAP online to find information on the features of mySAP CRM, which benefit salespeople as follows:

- Sales planning and forecasting
- Territory management
- Account and contact management
- Lead and opportunity management
- Quotation and order management
- Contract management
- Incentive and commission management
- Time and travel management
- Sales analytics

1. Explain which SAP functions apply to sales force management and which tie in more to the salesperson's daily role with the customers.

2. Explain how these SAP functions fit into the personal selling process for an office furniture sales representative selling a new line of office chairs to an existing large customer.

3. Why would a company choose not to use SAP products?

Focus on Ethics

You are the senior sales manager for Johnson Manufacturing. Your company has developed a machine that makes electronic components faster and with a lower defect rate than your major competitor's machines. You call on Haywood Electronics, an important customer, to discuss its purchase of the new machine. Haywood's buyers have been very enthusiastic, but when you arrive, they want to discuss the results of some recent tests they've conducted. They show you output that shows that your competitor's new machine produces components at 1.2 times the rate of your machine with a .01 lower defect rate. Based on this research, they ask for

a reduction on the price of your machine from $800,000 to $500,000. When you return to your company and talk to the vice president of manufacturing, she states that the test results are impossible and that the tests must have been faulty or the results intentionally falsified.

1. What actions would you take?

2. Why is it important that you be careful with your reaction to this situation?

3. Could such a situation really happen? Discuss.

Video Case

Nudie

All across the globe, consumers are seeking all-natural, wholesome foods. Even Wal-Mart, a low-price leader, carries organic and all-natural foods. Nudie, a quirky little company in Australia, makes its own contribution to the fast-growing natural foods market—all-natural fruit juices, fruit crushes, and smoothies that provide a day's fruit in every bottle. Amidst a sea of all-natural products, how did Nudie reach customers and encourage them to try its new products? Through a carefully designed program of personal selling and sales promotion.

Nudie uses well-crafted point-of-purchase displays and a devoted, motivated sales force to work with resellers to reach consumers. As a result, Nudie is the fastest-growing juice maker in Australia, attracting an ever-increasing number of highly devoted customers who love Nudie's

products. Says one Nudie customer, "Don't be a prudie . . . get thee a Nudie." Says another, "Love and happiness are overrated. But Nudies make living worthwhile!"

After viewing the video featuring Nudie, answer the following questions about personal selling and sales promotion.

1. How does Nudie's process for selecting sales representatives compare to the process described in the text?

2. What sales promotion tools does Nudie employ to reach consumers and encourage sales?

3. Select a sales promotion tool not listed in your previous response. How could Nudie use that tool to further promote its products?

Company Case

Personal Selling at the Lear Corporation

When someone says "salesperson," what image comes to mind? Perhaps it's the stereotypical "traveling salesman"—the fast-talking, ever-smiling peddler who travels his territory foisting his wares on reluctant customers. Such stereotypes, however, are sadly out of date. Today, most professional salespeople are well-educated, well-trained men and women who work to build long-term, value-producing relationships with their customers. They succeed not by taking customers in, but by helping them out—by assessing customer needs and solving customer problems.

One company that has been able to employ such a customer-centric sales philosophy is the Lear Corporation. From its humble beginnings in 1917 as a manufacturer of tubular assemblies for the automotive and aircraft industries, Lear has grown into one of the largest and most successful automotive suppliers in the world. In 2005, Lear achieved revenues of $17.1 billion, 127th among the Fortune 500.

For decades, Lear dominated the automotive parts industry as a maker of seat systems. But through 18 major acquisitions since it went public in 1994, Lear has broadened its product line to include all five major vehicle interior systems—instrument panels and cockpits, door and trim, overhead and flooring, and acoustic systems. Lear is also one of the leading global suppliers of automotive electronics and electrical distribution systems.

Lear's customers include most of the world's leading automotive companies, from high-volume producers such as Ford, DaimlerChrysler, General Motors, Fiat, and Toyota, to boutique brands such as Ferrari and Rolls-Royce. Currently, Lear products are found in new products produced by more than 300 nameplates around the world. With 115,000 employees, Lear designs, engineers, and manufactures products in more than 280 facilities in 34 countries.

Along with all this growth, Lear has experienced periods of superb financial performance. The company achieved record-breaking sales and earnings growth throughout the 1990s. During that decade, its "average content per car" in North America increased more than fourfold. Not surprisingly, Lear's revenues more than doubled in the latter half of the '90s. Currently, the company owns roughly 30 percent of the North American interior components market.

Lear has achieved this tremendous growth by focusing on the customer. In a description of its business philosophy, Lear states:

"The success of Lear is a result of our dedication to provide the best possible service to the world's automakers—which includes understanding their customers, the automotive consumer—by delivering increased value through the latest vehicle interior technologies and the continuous improvement of our processes and product quality. All of this is reflected in Lear's exclusive People-Vehicle-Interface Methodology. By utilizing the PVI Method, Lear employs an innovation development discipline that turns market opportunities into the products that consumers want and customers need in their vehicles."

ACHIEVING CUSTOMER ORIENTATION

Lear's customer orientation is evident in all aspects of operations, from design through manufacturing. But perhaps more than any other part of the organization, it's Lear's outstanding sales force that makes the company's credo, "Consumer driven. Customer focused," ring true. Lear's sales force was recently rated by *Sales & Marketing Management* magazine as one of "America's Best Sales Forces." What makes this an outstanding sales force? Lear knows that good selling these days takes much more than just a sales rep covering a territory and convincing customers to buy the product. It takes teamwork, relationship building, and doing what's best for the customer. Lear's sales force excels at these tasks.

Lear's sales depend completely on the success of its customers. If the automakers don't sell cars, Lear doesn't sell interiors. So the Lear sales force strives to create not just sales, but customer success. In fact, Lear salespeople aren't "sales reps," they're "account managers" who function more as consultants than as order getters. "Our salespeople don't really close deals," notes a senior marketing executive. "They consult and work with customers to learn exactly what's needed and when."

Lear's growth and expansion of its product line have been driven by the quest to better meet customers' needs. As Lear has diversified its product line from seats to all parts of a vehicle's interior, it has become a kind of "one-stop shopping" source. As the provision of complete interior solutions benefits customers, it also benefits Lear. "It used to be that we'd build a partnership and then get only a limited amount of revenue from it," the executive says. "Now we can get as much as possible out of our customer relationships."

Lear's heavy customer focus has lead to a structure that is broken up into separate divisions dedicated to specific customers. For example, there's a Ford division and a General Motors division, and each operates as its own profit center. Within each division, high-level "platform teams"—made up of salespeople, engineers, and program managers—work closely with their customer counterparts. These platform teams are closely supported by divisional manufacturing, finance, quality, and advanced technology groups.

The platform team structure has allowed Lear to be very responsive to customer needs. In 1999, leaders at GM wanted to expand their commercial van business. One idea was to create a new model by fitting an existing van shell with deluxe leather seating; flip-down, flat-panel screens, and other high-tech gadgets. "It would have taken two, maybe three years to make a van like this in the GM system," says Larry Szydlowski, GM's program manager for the Express LT. In that time, the demand for such a van might have come and gone. Or, a competitor might have been first to market with a product fitting that concept.

But based on efficiencies derived from its platform teams, Lear confidently predicted that it could go from contract to product in just one year. The claim was so outrageous that GM hesitated. So, Lear took a risk and invested in a physical prototype on its own. GM was so impressed, that it awarded the lucrative contract to Lear. One year later, as promised, the Express LT was in production.

Lear has achieved another sales team efficiency by limiting its customer base to fewer major customers rather than many small-contract customers. This has allowed sales teams to get very close to their customers. "Our teams don't call on purchasers; they're linked to customer operations at all levels," the marketer notes. "We try to put a system in place that creates continuous contact with customers." In fact, Lear often locates its sales offices in customers' plants. For example, the team that handles GM's light truck division works at GM's truck operation campus. "We can't just be there to give quotes and ask for orders," says the marketing executive. "We need to be involved with customers every step of the way—from vehicle concept through launch."

THE TIDE SHIFTS FOR LEAR

Whereas the 1990s were golden years for Lear, numerous factors combined to create a dismal situation as the new millennium unfolded. Despite the fact that Lear captured 2005 revenues of more than $17 billion, it posted a net loss of $1.3 billion. Almost half of that loss came in the fourth quarter alone. Ironically, many of the factors responsible for Lear's earlier success may now be responsible for its current downturn.

For starters, gas prices went up. Although this was nothing that Lear could have stopped, as gas prices have risen, industry-wide vehicle sales have slowed. The biggest casualties have been SUVs and light trucks, models that litter the product lines for the Big Three automakers. Additionally, the downturn in SUV and truck sales has come at an inopportune time. The large American car companies were already losing market share to foreign competitors in other categories as well. Whereas Lear's strategy of limiting its customer base has allowed it to achieve close customer relations, tough times for these large customers are wreaking havoc on Lear's sales.

Lear's product diversification strategy, which has been a key to building customer relationships, is also contributing to current losses. In 2005, the company spent a record $586 million on capital investments, in part to become a total supplier for its largest customers. At the same time, however, these large customers have abandoned their strategy of sourcing all vehicle interior components to one supplier.

As of 2006, things are looking better for Lear, at least in its seating and electronics segments. However, despite overall first-quarter profits of $17.9 million, Lear's interior systems business continues to hemorrhage money, showing a $59.5 million loss. Given that this division has been its poorest performer for some time, Lear is considering the option of selling the business and restructuring it on its own.

Lear also has been struggling to absorb double-digit increases in plastic resin prices and increases in other raw materials. Feeling the pinch from its plastic suppliers, Lear has attempted to work with customers in order to pass on some of those costs. As a result, DaimlerChrysler AG's Chrysler Group sued the company, claiming that Lear threatened to stop shipping parts if Chrysler didn't comply.

Maintaining profitable relationships with large customers takes much more than a nice smile and a firm handshake. And certainly there's no place for the "smoke and mirrors" or "flimflam" sometimes mistakenly associated with personal selling. Success in such a selling environment requires careful teamwork among well-trained, dedicated sales professionals who are bent on profitably taking care of their customers. But even as Lear has focused on these principles, it has found that maintaining solid customer relationships can at times be very difficult.

Questions for Discussion

1. Classify Lear's sales force structure. What role has this structure played in the company's successes and failures?

2. What role does team selling play in Lear's sales force strategy? Should Lear make any changes to this strategy?

3. What implications would selling its interior systems division have on Lear's sales force and its ability to serve its customers? What do you recommend that Lear do?

4. Make other recommendations for how Lear can reverse the difficulties that it now faces. How would you implement each recommendation?

Sources: Jesse Eisinger, "Lear Case Shows Sometimes Investors Can Detect Crises Before Management," *Wall Street Journal,* March 15, 2006, p. C1; Terry Kosdrosky, "Lear Posts $596 Million Loss But Expects Improved 2006," *Wall Street Journal,* January 26, 2006, p. A7; Terry Kosdrosky, "Lear's Profit Climbs 15%," *Wall Street Journal,* April 26, 2006, accessed online at www.wsj.com; Judy Bocklage and Paul Welitzkin, "Lear Profit Soared in First Period, But Borg-Warner Swung to Loss," *Wall Street Journal,* April 23, 2002, p. D5; Andy Cohen, "Top of the Charts: Lear Corporation," *Sales & Marketing Management,* July 1998, p. 40; Fara Warner, "Lear Won't Take a Back Seat," *Fast Company,* June 2001, pp. 178–185; "America's 25 Best Sales Forces," *Sales & Marketing Management,* accessed online at www.salesandmarketing.com, July 2002; "Lear Corporation," *Sales & Marketing Management,* July 1999, p. 62; and "About Lear," accessed online at www.lear.com, June 2006.

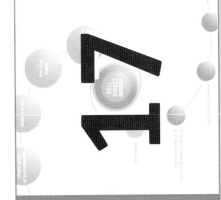
Direct and Online Marketing

Building Direct Customer Relationships

Previewing the Concepts

In the previous three chapters, you learned about communicating customer value through integrated marketing communication (IMC) and about four specific elements of the marketing communications mix—advertising, publicity, personal selling, and sales promotion. In this chapter, we'll look at the final IMC element, direct marketing, and at its fastest-growing form, online marketing. Actually, direct marketing can be viewed as more than just a communications tool. In many ways it constitutes an overall marketing approach—a blend of communication and distribution channels all rolled into one. As you read on, remember that although this chapter examines direct marketing as a separate tool, it must be carefully integrated with other elements of the promotion mix.

To set the stage, let's first look at Dell, the world's largest direct marketer of computer systems and the number-one PC maker worldwide. Ask anyone at Dell and they'll tell you that the company owes its incredible success to what it calls the Dell Direct Model, a model that starts with direct customer relationships and ends with the Dell customer experience. Says one analyst, "There's no better way to make, sell, and deliver PCs than the way Dell does it, and nobody executes [the direct] model better than Dell."

When 19-year-old Michael Dell began selling personal computers out of his college dorm room in 1984, competitors and industry insiders scoffed at the concept of direct computer marketing. Yet young Michael proved the skeptics wrong—way wrong. In little more than two decades, he has turned his dorm-room mail-order business into the burgeoning, $56 billion Dell computer empire.

Dell is now the world's largest direct marketer of computer systems and the number-one PC maker worldwide. In the United States, Dell is number-one in desktop PC sales, number-one in laptops, number-one in servers, and number-two (and gaining) in printers. In fact, Dell flat out dominates the U.S. PC market, with a 33.5 percent market share, compared with number-two HP's 19.4 percent and number-three Gateway's 6.1 percent. Dell has produced a ten-year average annual return to investors of 39 percent, best among all Fortune 100 companies. Investors have enjoyed explosive share gains of more than 28,000 percent since Dell went public fewer than 20 years ago.

What's the secret to Dell's stunning success? Anyone at Dell can tell you without hesitation: It's the company's radically different business model—the *direct model.* "We have a tremendously clear business model," says Michael Dell, the company's 41-year-old founder and chairman. "There's no confusion about what the value proposition is, what the company offers, and why it's great for customers." An industry analyst agrees: "There's no better way to make, sell, and deliver PCs than the way Dell does it, and nobody executes [the direct] model better than Dell."

Dell's direct-marketing approach delivers greater customer value through an unbeatable combination of product customization, low prices, fast delivery, and award-winning customer service. A customer can talk by phone with a Dell representative at 1-800-Buy-Dell or log onto www.dell.com on Monday morning; order a fully customized, state-of-the-art PC to suit his or her special needs; and have the machine delivered to his or her doorstep or desktop by Wednesday—all at a price that's well below competitors' prices for a comparably performing PC. Dell backs its products with high-quality service and support. As a result, Dell consistently ranks among the industry leaders in product reliability and service, and its customers are routinely among the industry's most satisfied.

Dell customers get exactly the machines they need. Michael Dell's initial idea was to serve individual buyers by letting them customize machines with the special features they wanted at low prices. However, this one-to-one approach also appeals strongly to corporate buyers, because Dell can so easily preconfigure each computer

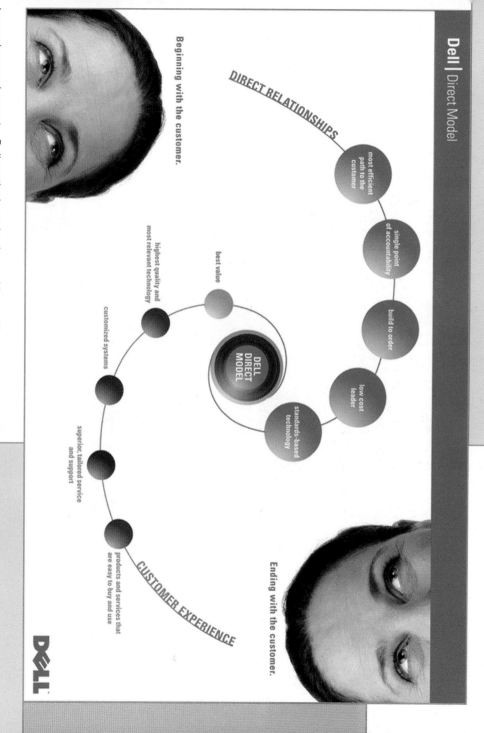

DIRECT RELATIONSHIPS

Beginning with the customer.

Ending with the customer.

- most efficient path to the customer
- single point of accountability
- build to order
- low cost leader
- standards-based technology
- best value
- highest quality and most relevant technology
- customized systems
- superior, tailored service and support
- products and services that are easy to buy and use

DELL DIRECT MODEL

CUSTOMER EXPERIENCE

DELL

Objectives

After studying this chapter, you should be able to

1. define direct marketing and discuss its benefits to customers and companies
2. identify and discuss the major forms of direct marketing
3. explain how companies have responded to the Internet and other powerful new technologies with online marketing strategies
4. discuss how companies go about conducting online marketing to profitably deliver more value to customers
5. overview the public policy and ethical issues presented by direct marketing

---

to precise requirements, Dell routinely preloads machines with a company's own software and even undertakes tedious tasks such as pasting inventory tags onto each machine so that computers can be delivered directly to a given employee's desk. As a result, more than 85 percent of Dell's sales come from business, government, and educational buyers.

The direct model results in more efficient selling and lower costs, which translate into lower prices for customers. "Nobody, but nobody, makes [and markets] computer hardware more efficiently than Dell," says another analyst. "No unnecessary costs: This is an all-but-sacred mandate of the famous Dell direct business model." Because Dell builds machines to order, it carries barely any inventory—less than three days' worth by some accounts. Dealing one-to-one with customers helps the company react immediately to shifts in demand, so Dell doesn't get stuck with PCs no one wants. Finally, by selling directly, Dell has no dealers to pay. As a result, on average, Dell's costs are 12 percent lower than those of its leading PC competitor.

Dell knows that time is money, and the company is obsessed with "speed." According to one account, Dell squeezes "time out of every step in the process—from the moment an order is taken to collecting the cash. [By selling direct, manufacturing to order, and] tapping credit cards and electronic payment, Dell converts the average sale to cash in less than 24 hours." By contrast, competitors selling through dealers might take 35 days or longer.

Such blazing speed results in more satisfied customers and still lower costs. For example, customers are often delighted to find their new computers arriving within as few as 36 hours of placing an order. And because Dell doesn't order parts until an order is booked, it can take advantage of ever-falling component costs. On average, its parts are 60 days newer than those in competing machines, and, hence, 60 days farther down the price curve. This gives Dell a 6 percent profit advantage from parts costs alone.

As you might imagine, competitors are no longer scoffing at Michael Dell's vision of the future. In fact, competing and noncompeting companies alike are studying the Dell direct model closely. "Somehow Dell has been able to take flexibility and speed and build it into their DNA. It's almost like drinking water," says the CEO of another Fortune 500 company, who visited recently to absorb some of the Dell magic to apply to his own company. "I'm trying to drink as much water here as I can."

Still, as Dell grows larger and as the once-torrid growth in the sales of PCs slows, the Dell direct model is facing challenges. After years of rocketing revenue and profit numbers, Dell's recent growth has slowed. Although Dell still dominates in selling PCs, servers, and peripherals to business markets, it appears to be stumbling in its attempts to sell an expanding assortment of high-tech consumer electronics products to final buyers. Some analysts suggest that Dell's vaunted direct model may not work as well for selling LCD TVs, handhelds, MP3 players, digital cameras, and other personal digital devices—products that consumers want to see and experience first-hand before buying. In fact, Dell plans to add retail stores to help bolster the consumer side of its business.

Slowing growth has led some analysts to ask, "Is the much-feared Dell Way running out of gas?" No way, says Dell. There's no question, the company admits, that Dell isn't the high-flying growth company it once was—you can't expect a $56-billion-a-year giant to grow like a full-throttle start-up. But Dell continues to dominate its PC markets, and other companies would kill for Dell's "disappointing" growth numbers—sales last year grew 13.6 percent, and profits were up 17.4 percent. "We still have an outrageous track record," says Dell CEO Kevin Rollins. "Our [direct] model still works very well," Michael Dell agrees. "We wouldn't trade ours for anyone else's!" he says. "In the past ten years our sales are up about 15 times, earnings and the stock price are up about 20 times. Not too shabby!"

It's hard to argue with success, and Michael Dell has been very successful. By following his hunches, at the tender age of 41 he has built one of the world's hottest companies. In the process, he's become one of the world's richest men, amassing a personal fortune of more than $17 billion.[1]

Many of the marketing and promotion tools that we've examined in previous chapters were developed in the context of *mass marketing*: targeting broad markets with standardized messages and offers distributed through intermediaries. Today, however, with the trend toward more narrowly targeted marketing, many companies are adopting *direct marketing*, either as a primary marketing approach or as a supplement to other approaches. In this section, we explore the exploding world of direct marketing.

Direct marketing consists of direct connections with carefully targeted individual consumers to both obtain an immediate response and cultivate lasting customer relationships. Direct marketers communicate directly with customers, often on a one-to-one, interactive basis. Using detailed databases, they tailor their marketing offers and communications to the needs of narrowly defined segments or even individual buyers.

Beyond brand and relationship building, direct marketers usually seek a direct, immediate, and measurable consumer response. For example, as we learned in the chapter-opening story, Dell interacts directly with customers, by telephone or through its Web site, to design built-to-order systems that meet customers' individual needs. Buyers order directly from Dell, and Dell quickly and efficiently delivers the new computers to their homes or offices.

Direct marketing
Direct connections with carefully targeted individual consumers to both obtain an immediate response and cultivate lasting customer relationships.

The New Direct-Marketing Model

Early direct marketers—catalog companies, direct mailers, and telemarketers—gathered customer names and sold goods mainly by mail and telephone. Today, however, fired by rapid advances in database technologies and new marketing media—especially the Internet—direct marketing has undergone a dramatic transformation. According to the head of the Direct Marketing Association, "In recent years, the dramatic growth of the Internet and the increasing sophistication of database technologies have [created] an extraordinary expansion of direct marketing and a seismic shift in what it is, how it's used, and who uses it."[2]

In previous chapters, we've discussed direct marketing as direct distribution—as marketing channels that contain no intermediaries. We also include direct marketing as one element of the promotion mix—as an approach for communicating directly with consumers. In actuality, direct marketing is both these things.

Most companies still use direct marketing as a supplementary channel or medium for marketing their goods and messages. Thus, Lexus markets mostly through mass-media advertising and its high-quality dealer network but also supplements these channels with direct marketing. Its direct marketing includes promotional CDs and other materials mailed directly to prospective buyers and a Web page (www.lexus.com) that provides consumers with information about various models, competitive comparisons, financing, and dealer locations. Similarly, most department stores sell the majority of their merchandise off their store shelves but also sell through direct mail and online catalogs.

However, for many companies today, direct marketing is more than just a supplementary channel or medium. For these companies, direct marketing—especially in its most recent transformation, online marketing—constitutes a complete model for doing business. More than just another marketing channel or advertising medium, this new *direct model* is rapidly changing the way companies think about building relationships with customers.

Rather than using direct marketing and the Internet only as supplemental approaches, firms employing the direct model use it as the *only* approach. Companies such as Dell, Amazon.com, eBay, and GEICO have built their entire approach to the marketplace around direct marketing.

Growth and Benefits of Direct Marketing

Direct marketing has become the fastest-growing form of marketing. According to the Direct Marketing Association, U.S. companies spent $161 billion on direct marketing last year, accounting for whopping 48 percent of total U.S. advertising expenditures. These expenditures generated an estimated $1.85 trillion in direct marketing sales, or about 7 percent of total sales in the U.S. economy. And direct marketing-driven sales are growing rapidly. The DMA estimates that direct marketing sales will grow 6.4 percent annually through 2009, compared with a projected 4.8 percent annual growth for total U.S. sales.[3]

■ The new direct marketing model: Companies such as GEICO have built their entire approach to the marketplace around direct marketing: just visit geico.com or call 1-800-947-auto.

Direct marketing continues to become more Web oriented, and Internet marketing is claiming a fast-growing share of direct marketing spending and sales. The Internet now accounts for only about 16 percent of direct marketing-driven sales. However, the DMA predicts that over the next five years Internet marketing expenditures will grow at a blistering 18 percent a year, three times faster than expenditures in other direct marketing media. Internet-driven sales will grow by 12.6 percent.

Whether employed as a complete business model or as a supplement to a broader integrated marketing mix, direct marketing brings many benefits to both buyers and sellers.

Benefits to Buyers

For buyers, direct marketing is convenient, easy, and private. Direct marketers never close their doors, and customers don't have to battle traffic, find parking spaces, and trek through stores to find products. From the comfort of their homes or offices, they can browse catalogs or company Web sites at any time of the day or night. Business buyers can learn about products and services without tying up time with salespeople.

Direct marketing gives buyers ready access to a wealth of products. For example, unrestrained by physical boundaries, direct marketers can offer an almost unlimited selection to consumers almost anywhere in the world. For example, by making computers to order and selling directly, Dell can offer buyers thousands of self-designed PC configurations, many times the number offered by competitors who sell preconfigured PCs through retail stores. And just compare the huge selections offered by many Web merchants to the more meager assortments of their brick-and-mortar counterparts. For instance, log onto Bulbs.com, "the Web's no. 1 light bulb superstore," and you'll have instant access to every imaginable kind of light bulb or lamp—incandescent bulbs, fluorescent bulbs, projection bulbs, surgical bulbs, automotive bulbs—you name it. No physical store could offer handy access to such a vast selection.

Direct marketing channels also give buyers access to a wealth of comparative information about companies, products, and competitors. Good catalogs or Web sites often provide more information in more useful forms than even the most helpful retail salesperson can. For example, the Amazon.com site offers more information than most of us can digest, ranging from top-10 product lists, extensive product descriptions, and expert and user product reviews to recommendations based on customers' previous purchases. And Sears catalogs offer a treasure trove of information about the store's merchandise and services. In fact, you probably wouldn't think it strange to see a Sears salesperson referring to a catalog in the store while trying to advise a customer on a specific product or offer.

Finally, direct marketing is interactive and immediate—buyers can interact with sellers by phone or on the seller's Web site to create exactly the configuration of information, products, or services they desire, and then order them on the spot. Moreover, direct marketing gives consumers a greater measure of control. Consumers decide which catalogs they will browse and which Web sites they will visit.

Benefits to Sellers

For sellers, direct marketing is a powerful tool for building customer relationships. Using database marketing, today's marketers can target small groups or individual consumers and promote their offers through personalized communications. Because of the one-to-one nature of direct marketing, companies can interact with customers by phone or online, learn more about their needs, and tailor products and services to specific customer tastes. In turn, customers can ask questions and volunteer feedback.

Direct marketing also offers sellers a low-cost, efficient, speedy alternative for reaching their markets. Direct marketing has grown rapidly in business-to-business marketing, partly in response to the ever-increasing costs of marketing through the sales force. When personal sales calls cost an average of more than $400 per contact, they should be made only when necessary and to high-potential customers and prospects. Lower-cost-per-contact media—such as telemarketing, direct mail, and company Web sites—often prove more cost effective. Similarly, online direct marketing results in lower costs, improved efficiencies, and speedier handling of channel and logistics functions, such as order processing, inventory handling, and delivery. Direct marketers such as Amazon.com or Dell also avoid the expense of maintaining a store and the related costs of rent, insurance, and utilities, passing the savings along to customers.

Direct marketing can also offer greater flexibility. It allows marketers to make ongoing adjustments to its prices and programs, or to make immediate and timely announcements and offers. For example, Southwest Airlines' DING! application takes advantage of the flexibility and immediacy of the Web to share low-fare offers directly with customers:[4]

When Jim Jacobs hears a "ding" coming from his desktop computer, he thinks about discount air fares like the $122 ticket he recently bought for a flight from Tampa to Baltimore on Southwest Airlines. Several times a day, Southwest sends Jacobs and hundreds of thousands of other computer users discounts through an application called DING! "If I move quickly," says Jacobs, a corporate telecommunications salesman who lives in Tampa. "I can usually save a lot of money." The fare to Baltimore underbid the airline's own Web site by $36, he says. DING! lets Southwest bypass the reservations system and pass bargain fares directly to interested customers. Eventually, DING! may even allow Southwest to customize fare offers based on each customer's unique characteristics and travel preferences. For now, DING! gets a Southwest icon on the customer's desktop and lets the airline build relationships with customers by helping them to save money. Following its DING! launch in early 2005, Southwest experienced its two biggest online sales days ever. In the first 13 months, two million customers downloaded DING! and the program produced more than $80 million worth of fares.

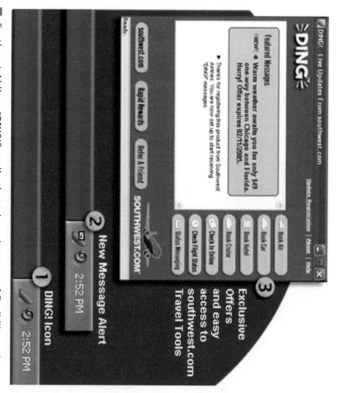

■ Southwest Airlines "DING!" application takes advantage of flexibility and immediacy of the Web to share low-fare offers directly with customers.

Finally, direct marketing gives sellers access to buyers that they could not reach through other channels. Smaller firms can mail catalogs to customers outside their local markets and post 1-800 telephone numbers to handle orders and inquiries. Internet marketing is a truly global medium that allows buyers and sellers to click from one country to another in seconds. A Web surfer from Paris or Istanbul can access an online L.L. Bean catalog as easily as someone living in Freeport, Maine, the direct retailer's hometown. Even small marketers find that they have ready access to global markets.

▮ Customer Databases and Direct Marketing

Effective direct marketing begins with a good customer database. A **customer database** is an organized collection of comprehensive data about individual customers or prospects, including geographic, demographic, psychographic, and behavioral data. A good customer database might contain a customer's demographics (age, income, family members, birthdays), psychographics (activities, interests, and opinions), and buying behavior (buying preferences and the recency, frequency, and monetary value—RFM—of past purchases). In business-to-business marketing, the customer profile might contain the products and services the customer has bought; past volumes and prices; key contacts (and their ages, birthdays, hobbies, and favorite foods); competing suppliers; status of current contracts; estimated customer spending for the next few years; and assessments of competitive strengths and weaknesses in selling and servicing the account.

Many companies confuse a customer database with a customer mailing list. A customer mailing list is simply a set of names, addresses, and telephone numbers. A customer database contains much more information. In consumer marketing, the customer database might contain a customer's demographics (age, income, family members, birthdays), psychographics (activities, interests, and opinions), and buying behavior (buying preferences and the recency, frequency, and monetary value—RFM—of past purchases). In business-to-business marketing, the customer profile might contain the products and services the customer has bought; ing, the customer profile might contain the products and services the customer has bought;

Customer database
An organized collection of comprehensive data about individual customers or prospects, including geographic, demographic, psychographic, and behavioral data.

Some of these databases are huge. For example, casino operator Harrah's Entertainment has built a customer database containing 30 terabytes worth of customer information, roughly three times the number of printed characters in the Library of Congress. Internet portal Yahoo! records every click made by every visitor, adding some 400 billion bytes of data per day to its database—the equivalent of 800,000 books. And Wal-Mart captures data on every item, for every customer, for every store, every day. Its database contains more than 570 terabytes of data—that's 570 trillion bytes, far greater than the storage horsepower of 100,000 personal computers.[6]

Companies use their databases in many ways. They use databases to locate good potential customers and to generate sales leads. They can mine their databases to learn about customers in detail, and then fine-tune their market offerings and communications to the special preferences and behaviors of target segments or individuals. In all, a company's database can be an important tool for building stronger long-term customer relationships. For example, financial services provider USAA uses its database to find ways to serve the long-term needs of customers, regardless of immediate sales impact, creating an incredibly loyal customer base:

USAA provides financial services to U.S. military personnel and their families, largely through direct marketing via the telephone and Internet. It maintains a customer database built from customer purchasing histories and from information collected directly from customers. To keep the database fresh, the organization regularly surveys its more than 5.6 million customers worldwide to learn such things as whether they have children (and if so, how old they are), if they have moved recently, and when they plan to retire. USAA uses the database to tailor direct marketing offers to the specific needs of individual customers. For example, for customers looking toward retirement, it sends information on estate planning. If the family has college-age children, USAA sends those children information on how to manage their credit cards. If the family has younger children, it sends booklets on things such as financing a child's education. One delighted reporter, a USAA customer, recounts how USAA even helped him teach his 16-year-old-daughter to drive. Just before her birthday, but before she received her driver's license, USAA mailed a "package of materials, backed by research, to help me teach my daughter how to drive, help her practice, and help us find ways to agree on what constitutes safe driving later on, when she gets her license." What's more, marvels the reporter, "USAA didn't try to sell me a thing. My take-away: that USAA is investing in me for the long term, that it defines profitability not just by what it sells today." Through such skillful use of its database, USAA serves each customer uniquely, resulting in high levels of customer loyalty and sales growth. The average customer household owns almost five USAA products, and the $12 billion company retains 97 percent of its customers.[7]

Like many other marketing tools, database marketing requires a special investment. Companies must invest in computer hardware, database software, analytical programs, communication links, and skilled personnel. The database system must be user-friendly and available to various marketing groups, including those in product and brand management, new-product development, advertising and promotion, direct mail, telemarketing, Web marketing, field sales, order fulfillment, and customer service. However, a well-managed database should lead to sales and customer-relationship gains that will more than cover its costs.

Forms of Direct Marketing

The major forms of direct marketing—as shown in Figure 17.1—include personal selling, direct-mail marketing, catalog marketing, telephone marketing, direct-response television marketing, kiosk marketing, new digital direct marketing technologies, and online marketing. We examined personal selling in depth in Chapter 16. Here, we examine the other direct-marketing forms.

Direct-Mail Marketing

Direct-mail marketing involves sending an offer, announcement, reminder, or other item to a person at a particular address. Using highly selective mailing lists, direct marketers send out

Direct-mail marketing
Direct marketing by sending an offer, announcement, reminder, or other item to a person at a particular address.

FIGURE 17.1

Forms of direct marketing

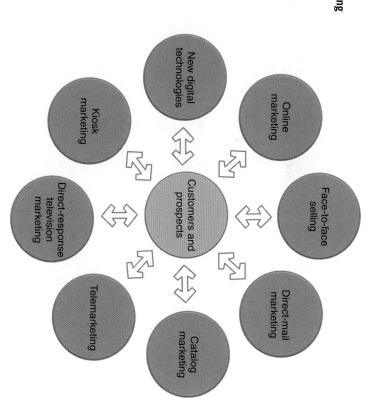

Catalog marketing

Direct marketing through print, video, or electronic catalogs that are mailed to select customers, made available in stores, or presented online.

---

millions of mail pieces each year—letters, catalogues, ads, brochures, samples, CDs and DVDs, and other "salespeople with wings." Direct mail is by far the largest direct marketing medium. The DMA reports that direct mail (including both catalog and non-catalog mail) drives fully one-third of all U.S. direct marketing sales.[8]

Direct mail is well suited to direct, one-to-one communication. It permits high target-market selectivity, can be personalized, is flexible, and allows easy measurement of results. Although direct mail costs more than mass media such as television or magazines per thousand people reached, the people it reaches are much better prospects. Direct mail has proved successful in promoting all kinds of products, from books, music, DVDs, and magazine subscriptions to insurance, gift items, clothing, gourmet foods, and industrial products. Charities also use direct mail heavily to raise billions of dollars each year.

The direct-mail industry constantly seeks new methods and approaches. For example, CDs and DVDs are now among the fastest-growing direct-mail media. One study showed that including a CD or DVD in a marketing offer generates responses between 50 to 600 percent greater than traditional direct mail.[9] New forms of delivery have also become popular, such as *fax mail, voice mail,* and *e-mail.* Fax mail and voice mail are subject to the same do-not-call restrictions as telemarketing, so their use has been limited in recent years. However, e-mail is booming as a direct marketing tool. Today's e-mail messages have moved far beyond the drab text-only messages of old. The new breed of e-mail ad uses animation, interactive links, streaming video, and personalized audio messages to reach out and grab attention.

E-mail and other new forms deliver direct mail at incredible speeds compared to the post office's "snail mail" pace. Yet, much like mail delivered through traditional channels, they may be resented as "junk mail" or SPAM if sent to people who have no interest in them. For this reason, smart marketers are targeting their direct mail carefully so as not waste their money and recipients' time. They are designing permission-based programs, sending e-mail ads only to those who want to receive them. We will discuss e-mail marketing in more detail later in the chapter.

Catalog Marketing

Advances in technology, along with the move toward personalized, one-to-one marketing have resulted in exciting changes in **catalog marketing.** *Catalog Age* magazine used to define a *catalog* as "a printed, bound piece of at least eight pages, selling multiple products, and offering a direct ordering mechanism." Today, only a few years later, this definition is sadly out of date.

With the stampede to the Internet, more and more catalogs are going digital. A variety of Web-only catalogers have emerged, and most print catalogers have added Web-based catalogs to their marketing mixes. For example, click on the Shop by Catalog link at www.llbean.com and you can flip through the latest L.L. Bean catalog page by page online. One study found that consumers now make 36 percent of their catalog purchases online.

However, although the Internet has provided a new avenue for catalog sales, all you have to do is to check your mailbox to know that printed catalogs remain the primary medium. Research shows that print catalogs generate many of those online orders. Customers who receive print catalogs are more likely to buy online, and they spend 16 percent more than customers who did not receive catalogs.[10]

Catalog marketing has grown explosively during the past 25 years. Annual catalog sales amounted to about $133 billion last year and are expected to grow to top $158 billion by 2009.[11] Some large general-merchandise retailers—such as J.C. Penney and Spiegel—sell a full line of merchandise through catalogs. In recent years, these giants have been challenged by thousands of specialty catalogs that serve highly specialized market niches. According to one study, some 10,000 companies now produce 14,000 unique catalog titles in the United States.[12]

Consumers can buy just about anything from a catalog. Sharper Image catalogs hawk everything from $300 robot vacuum cleaners to $4,500 see-through kayaks. Each year Lillian Vernon sends out 22 editions of its 6 catalogs with total circulation of 101 million copies to its 20-million-person database, selling more than 6,000 different items, ranging from shoes to decorative lawn birds and monogrammed oven mitts.[13] Specialty department stores, such as Neiman Marcus, Bloomingdale's, and Saks Fifth Avenue, use catalogs to cultivate upper-middle-class markets for high-priced, often exotic, merchandise.

Catalogs can be an effective sales and relationship builder. A recent study conducted by Frank About Women, a marketing-to-women communications company, found that a majority of women who receive catalogs are actively engaged with them.

Eighty-nine percent of the participants revealed that they do more than just browse through the catalogs they receive in the mail. They circle or "tab" the items that they want, fold over the corners of pages, and tear pages out. Some 69 percent save their catalogs to look through again. More than just a buying tool, many women view catalogs as a source of entertainment and inspiration. Women claim to love perusing catalogs almost like reading a woman's magazine, looking for ideas for everything

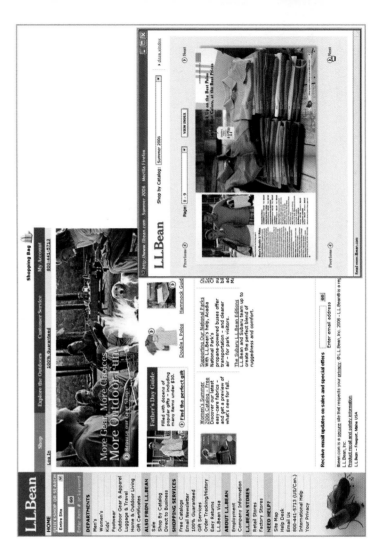

■ More and more catalogs are going digital. For example, click on the Shop by Catalog link at www.llbean.com and you can flip through the latest L.L. Bean catalog page by page online.

from decorating, to fashion, to that extra special gift. More than one-third of women surveyed greet their catalogs with enthusiasm, stating they are the first things they look at when they get their mail. Seventy-five percent of women find catalog brows-ing really enjoyable, fun, and relaxing, with 74 percent agreeing that they get excited when a new catalog arrives.[14]

Web-based catalogs present a number of benefits versus printed catalogs. They save on production, printing, and mailing costs. Whereas print-catalog space is limited, online cata-logs can offer an almost unlimited amount of merchandise. Web catalogs also allow real-time merchandising: Products and features can be added or removed as needed, and prices can be adjusted instantly to match demand. Finally, online catalogs can be spiced up with interac-tive entertainment and promotional features, such as games, contests, and daily specials.

Along with the benefits, however, Web-based catalogs also present challenges. Whereas a print catalog is intrusive and creates its own attention, Web catalogs are passive and must be marketed. Attracting new customers is much more difficult for a Web catalog than for a print catalog. Thus, even catalogers who are sold on the Web are not likely to abandon their print catalogs.

Telephone Marketing

Telephone marketing involves using the telephone to sell directly to consumers and busi-ness customers. Telephone marketing now accounts for 22 percent of all direct marketing-driven sales. We're all familiar with telephone marketing directed toward consumers, but business-to-business marketers also use telephone marketing extensively, accounting for more than 55 percent of all telephone marketing sales.

Marketers use *outbound* telephone marketing to sell directly to consumers and busi-nesses. *Inbound* toll-free 800 numbers are used to receive orders from television and print ads, direct mail, or catalogs. The use of 800 numbers has taken off in recent years as more and more companies have begun using them, and as current users have added new features such as toll-free fax numbers. To accommodate this rapid growth, new toll-free area codes, such as 888, 877, and 866, have been added.

Properly designed and targeted telemarket-ing provides many benefits, including purchas-ing convenience and increased product and ser-vice information. However, the explosion in unsolicited outbound telephone marketing over the years annoyed many consumers, who objected to the almost daily "junk phone calls" that pull them away from the dinner table or fill the answering machine.

In 2003, U.S. lawmakers responded with a National Do-Not-Call Registry, managed by the Federal Trade Commission. The legislation bans most telemarketing calls to registered phone numbers (although people can still receive calls from nonprofit groups, politicians, and companies with which they have recently done business). Delighted consumers have responded enthusiastically. To date, they have registered more than 110 million phone num-bers at www.donotcall.com or by calling 888-382-1222. Businesses that break do-not-call laws can be fined up to $11,000 per violation. As a result, reports an FTC spokesperson, the program "has been exceptionally successful."[15]

Do-not-call legislation has hurt the tele-marketing industry, but not all that much. Two major forms of telemarketing—inbound con-sumer telemarketing and outbound business-to-business telemarketing—remain strong and growing. Telemarketing also remains a major

Careful...you might sprain a taste bud.

Don't wait another day! Call now to place an order or request a catalog. Also, go on line at **www.carolinacookie.com** to place an order, request a catalog or view our entire selection of products.

1-800-447-5797

CAROLINA JUST BAKED COOKIE COMPANY

■ Marketers use inbound toll-free 800 numbers to receive orders from television and print ads, direct mail, or catalogs. Here, the Carolina Cookie Company urges, "Don't wait another day. Call now to place an order or request a catalog."

Telephone marketing
Using the telephone to sell directly to customers.

Telephone Marketing

Telephone marketing involves using the telephone to sell directly to consumers and business customers.

fundraising tool for nonprofits groups. However, many telemarketers are shifting to alternative methods for capturing new customers and sales, from direct mail, direct-response TV, and live-chat Web technology to sweepstakes that prompt customers to call in.

For example, ServiceMaster's TruGreen lawn-care service used to generate about 90 percent of its sales through telemarketing. It now uses more direct mail, as well have having employees go door-to-door in neighborhoods where it already has customers. The new approach appears to be working even better than the old cold-calling one. The company's sales were up last year, and less than 50 percent of sales came from telemarketing. "We were nervous, but were thrilled with what we've accomplished," says ServiceMaster's chief executive.[16]

In fact, do-not-call appears to be helping most direct marketers more than it's hurting them. Many of these marketers are shifting their call-center activity from making cold calls on often resentful customers to managing existing customer relationships. They are developing "opt-in" calling systems, in which they provide useful information and offers to customers who have invited the company to contact them by phone or e-mail. These "sales tactics have [produced] results as good—or even better—than telemarketing," declares one analyst. "The opt-in model is proving [more] valuable for marketers [than] the old invasive one."[17]

Direct-Response Television Marketing

Direct-response television marketing takes one of two major forms. The first is *direct-response television advertising* (DRTV). Direct marketers air television spots, often 60 or 120 seconds long, which persuasively describe a product and give customers a toll-free number or a Web site for ordering. Television viewers also often encounter full 30-minute or longer advertising programs, or *infomercials*, for a single product.

Some successful direct-response ads run for years and become classics. For example, Dial Media's ads for Ginsu knives ran for seven years and sold almost three million sets of knives, worth more than $40 million in sales; its Armourcote cookware ads generated more than twice that much. Bowflex has grossed more than $1.3 billion in infomercial sales. And over the past 40 years, infomercial czar Ron Popeil's company, Ronco, has sold billions of dollars worth of TV-marketed gadgets, including the original Veg-O-Matic, the Pocket Fisherman, Mr. Microphone, "Hair in a Can," the Giant Food Dehydrator and Beef Jerky Machine, and the Showtime Rotisserie & BBQ.[18]

For years, infomercials have been associated with somewhat questionable pitches for juicers and other kitchen gadgets, get-rich-quick schemes, and nifty ways to stay in shape without working very hard at it. In recent years, however, a number of large companies—from Procter & Gamble, Dell, Sears, Disney, Bose, and Revlon to IBM, GM, Land Rover, Anheuser-Busch, and even AARP and the U.S. Navy—have begun using infomercials to sell their wares, refer customers to retailers, send out product information, recruit members, or attract buyers to their Web sites (see Real Marketing 17.1). For example, P&G has used DRTV to market more than a dozen brands, including Dryel, Mr. Clean, CoverGirl, Iams pet food, and Old Spice. An estimated 20 percent of all new infomercials now come to you courtesy of Fortune 1000 companies.[19]

Direct-response TV commercials are usually cheaper to make and the media purchase is less costly. Moreover, unlike most media campaigns, direct-response ads always include a 1-800 number or Web address, making it easier for marketers to track the impact of their pitches. For these reasons, DRTV is growing more quickly than traditional broadcast and cable advertising. Some DRTV experts even predict that in five or ten years, as marketers seek greater returns on their advertising investments, all television advertising will be some form of direct-response advertising. "In a business environment where marketers are obsessed with return on investment," notes one such expert, "direct response is tailor-made—[marketers can] track phone calls and Web-site hits generated by the ads. [They can] use DRTV to build brand awareness while simultaneously generating leads and sales."[20]

Home shopping channels, another form of direct-response television marketing, are television programs or entire channels dedicated to selling goods and services. Some home shopping channels, such as the Quality Value Channel (QVC), Home Shopping Network (HSN), and ShopNBC, broadcast 24 hours a day. Program hosts chat with viewers by phone and offer products ranging from jewelry, lamps, collectible dolls, and clothing to power tools and consumer electronics. Viewers call a toll-free number or go online to order goods. With widespread distribution on cable and satellite television, the top three shopping networks combined now reach 248 million homes worldwide.

Direct-response television marketing
Direct marketing via television, including direct-response television advertising (or infomercials) and home shopping channels.

Real Marketing

17.1 Infomercials: But Wait, There's More!

It's late at night and you can't get to sleep. So you grab the TV remote, surf channels, and chance upon a fast-talking announcer, breathlessly pitching some new must-have kitchen gadget. A grinning blonde coannouncer fawns over the gadget's every feature, and the studio audience roars its approval. After putting the gadget through its paces, the announcer asks, "How much would you expect to pay? Three hundred dollars? Two hundred? Well, think again! This amazing gadget can be yours for just four easy payments of $19.95, plus shipping and handling!" "Oooooh!" the audience screams. "But wait! There's more," declares the announcer. "If you act now, you will also receive an additional gadget, absolutely free. That's two for the price of one." With operators standing by, you don't have a minute to lose.

Sound familiar? We've all seen countless infomercials like this, hawking everything from kitchen gadgets, cleaning compounds, and fitness solutions to psychic advice and get-rich-quick schemes. Traditionally, such pitches have had a kind of fly-by-night feel about them. And in the cold light of day, such a purchase may not seem like such a good deal after all. Such is the reputation of direct-response TV advertising. Yet, behind the hype is a powerful approach to marketing that is becoming more mainstream every day.

Ron Popeil pioneered direct-response product sales. Whether you realize it or not, you've probably been exposed to dozens of Popeil's inventions over the years, and his direct-marketing model has become the standard for the infomercial industry. His company, Ronco, has brought us such classics as the Veg-o-Matic, the Electric Food Dehydrator, the Showtime Rotisserie Oven, the GLH Formula Hair System, the Automatic 5-Minute Pasta and Sausage Maker, the Popeil Pocket Fisherman, the Inside the Egg Shell Electric Egg Scrambler, and the Dial-O-Matic Food Slicer.

The use of infomercials has grown explosively in recent years. Why? Because they can produce spectacular results. Although only one in 60 infomercials turns a profit, "successful pitches can generate annual sales of as much as $50 million," notes one analyst. "And breakout hits become gold mines: Ron Popeil has sold $1 billion worth of Ronco rotisserie ovens, and the Tae-Bo Workout infomercial . . . netted $300 million in its first year. Other benefits include viewer recall that can be three times higher than for traditional 30-second spots and phenomenal brand awareness: Ninety-two percent of consumers have heard of the Nautilus Bowflex home fitness system—about the same number of folks that recognize the Nike brand." Says the head of an infomercial advertising agency, "It's the power of the half-hour."

Moreover, the retail store revenue from a successful infomercial can be many times the actual infomercial sales. For example, more than 85 percent of George Foreman's Mean Lean Grilling Machine sales came from retail locations. Mass retailers have embraced such direct-response staples as Foreman's grill, OxiClean, and Orange Glo. Some, such as drug-chain heavyweight Walgreens, devote entire front-of-store sections to such goods. Whereas it used to take years to get retail distribution for "As seen on TV" products, many now make it to store shelves within a month of going on television.

Such infomercial success hasn't gone unnoticed among the big hitters in corporate America. Direct-response television marketing is rapidly becoming a mainstay weapon in the marketing arsenals of even the most reputable companies. Marketing heavyweights such as Dell, Procter & Gamble, Disney, Time-Life, General Motors, Apple,

Ronco and Ron Popeil, with his Veg-o-Matics, food dehydrators, and electric egg scramblers, paved the way for a host of mainstream marketers who now use direct-response ads.

Motorola, and Sears now use direct-response TV to peddle specific products and promotions and to draw new customers into their other direct-to-consumer channels. For example, Procter & Gamble used a series of infomercials to help propel the Swiffer WetJet past rival Clorox's ReadyMop when other marketing efforts alone failed to do the trick. And P&G launched its Swiffer Dusters product with a campaign that included direct-response ads and a tie-in to the DVD release of the Jennifer Lopez film *Maid in Manhattan*. Consumers contacting the 1-800 number got coupons for both the new Swiffer Duster and the DVD.

Today's infomercials have evolved with the times—most now include highly professional pitches and Web sites to go along with the ever-present toll-free phone number. They also employ a new breed of spokesperson. Once a refuge for Hollywood has-beens such as Suzanne Somers, who squeezed away on her thigh master to bleary-eyed insomniacs, infomercials now are now enlisting A-list celebrities. One of the nation's largest infomercial companies, Guthy-Renker, pays top dollar for a stable of stars to pitch its Proactiv acne treatment. It paid Sean (P. Diddy) Combs $3 million for a four-hour shoot. In four months, the Combs Proactiv infomercial ran an average of more than 10 times on each of 1,400 local TV stations. Other Proactiv ads have featured Jessica Simpson (paid $2.5 million), Vanessa Williams ($2.5 million), Alicia Keys ($3 million), and Britney Spears ($1 million). In all, the ads produced some $650 million in Proactiv sales last year.

Interest in direct-response marketing has now expanded beyond the usual fitness, personal-care, and home-care fare. For instance, submarine-

(continues)

(continued)

sandwich giant Quiznos has turned to late-night infomercials to sell franchises. Trailing only Subway and Starbucks in the number of franchises opened annually, Quiznos created a successful 30-minute spot in which current franchise owners discussed the benefits of owning a Quiznos restaurant and encouraged interested people to attend informational meetings at local hotels. Ice cream chain Carvel also uses infomercials to reach potential franchisees. The results are measurable: "We can push a button to see what commercial ran, how many responses it got, how much revenue it generated if it was selling something, and what the net [return on investment] was," says an executive of the direct-response firm that created the campaign. The results are also impressive: "We got easily four times the normal response than with standard media," says a Carvel marketer.

So, direct-response TV ads are no longer just the province of Ron Popeil and his Veg-o-Matics, food dehydrators, and electric egg scramblers. Although Popeil and his imitators paved the way, their success now has mainstream marketers tuning in to direct-response

ads. In fact, last year marketers spent $21.5 billion on direct-response television advertising, reaping more than $150 billion in revenues in return. What does the future hold for the direct-response TV industry? Wait, there's more!

Sources: Thomas Mucha, "Stronger Sales in Just 28 Minutes," *Business 2.0,* June 2005, pp. 56–60; Jack Neff, "Direct Response Getting Respect," *Advertising Age,* January 20, 2003, p. 4; Kristi Arellano, "Quiznos' Success Not without Problems," *Knight Ridder Tribune Business News,* June 19, 2005, p. 1; Peter Latterman, "So Long Suzanne Somers," *Forbes,* July 4, 2005, p. 60; Victor Grillo, Jr., "Calling All Brands," *Mediaweek,* July 11, 2005, p. 14; Gregg Cebrzynski, "Carvel Joins 'Slicers and Dicers' with Direct-Response Ads," *Nation's Restaurant News,* February 13, 2006, p. 14; Jack Neff, "What Procter & Gamble Learned from Veg-O-Matic," *Advertising Age,* April 10, 2006, pp. 1, 65; and Direct Marketing Association, "The DMA 2006 Statistical Fact Book," June 2006, pp. 249–250.

Despite their lowbrow images, home shopping channels have evolved into highly sophisticated, very successful marketing operations. Consider QVC:

Wired magazine once described QVC as a place appealing to "trailer-park housewives frantically phoning for another ceramic clown." But look past QVC's reputation and you'll find it is one of the world's most successful and innovative retailers. Last year, the company rang up $5.7 billion in sales and $760 million in operating profit, making it nearly as big and roughly twice as profitable as Amazon.com. Although QVC sells no advertising, it's the third-largest U.S. broadcaster in terms of revenue (behind NBC and ABC), and its sales and profits are larger than those of all other TV-based retailers combined. Remarkably, thanks to shrewd coordination with TV programming that drives buyers online, the company's Web site, QVC.com, is now the nation's sixth-largest general merchandise Internet retailer. Moreover, QVC isn't just a place where little-known marketers hawk trinkets and trash at bare-bones prices. Prominent manufacturers such as Estee Lauder, Nextel, and Tourneau now sell through QVC. The network's $80 million single-day sales record happened on Dec. 2, 2001, when Dell sold $65 million worth of PCs in 24 hours. (One month later, Michael Dell went on QVC, doing $48,000 in sales every minute he chatted on air.) Even high-fashion designers such as John Bartlett and Marc Bauer now sell lines on QVC.

QVC has honed the art and science of TV retailing. Its producers react in real time, adjusting offers, camera angles, lighting, and dialogue to maximize sales and profits. QVC has become the gold standard of "retailtainment"—the blending of retailing and entertainment. QVC folks call it the "backyard fence" sell—the feeling that the merchants are neighbors visiting from next door. But according to

■ QVC is more than just a place where little-known sellers hawk trinkets and trash at bare-bones prices. Behind the cameras, it's a sophisticated marketer with sales and profits larger than all other TV-based retailers combined.

QVC's president for U.S. commerce, "we aren't really in the business of selling." Instead, QVC uses products to build relationships with customers.[21]

Kiosk Marketing

As consumers become more and more comfortable with computer and digital technologies, many companies are placing information and ordering machines—called *kiosks* (in contrast to vending machines, which dispense actual products)—in stores, airports, and other locations. Kiosks are popping up everywhere these days, from self-service hotel and airline check-in devices to in-store ordering kiosks that let you order merchandise not carried in the store.

In-store Kodak, Fuji, and HP kiosks let customers transfer pictures from memory sticks, mobile phones, and other digital storage devices, edit them, and make high-quality color prints. Kiosks in Hilton hotel lobbies let guests view their reservations, get room keys, view prearrival messages, check in and out, and even change seat assignments and print boarding passes for flights on any of 18 airlines. Outdoor equipment retailer REI has at least four Web-enabled kiosks in each of its 63 stores that provide customers with product information and let them place orders online. Kiosks in Target stores link to articles from *Consumer Reports* magazine, and Mazda dealers let customers use kiosks to research car and truck values through Kelly Blue Book.[22]

Business marketers also use kiosks. For example, Dow Plastics places kiosks at trade shows to collect sales leads and to provide information on its 700 products. The kiosk system reads customer data from encoded registration badges and produces technical data sheets that can be printed at the kiosk or faxed or mailed to the customer. The system has resulted in a 400 percent increase in qualified sales leads.[23]

New Digital Direct Marketing Technologies

Today, thanks to a wealth of new digital technologies, direct marketers can reach and interact with consumers just about anywhere, at anytime, about almost anything. Here, we look into several exciting new digital direct marketing technologies: mobile phone marketing, podcasts and vodcasts, and interactive TV (ITV).

Mobile Phone Marketing

With almost 200 million Americans now subscribing to wireless services, many marketers view mobile phones as the next big direct marketing medium. According to one expert, "the cell phone, which makes on-the-go conversing so convenient, is morphing into a content device, a kind of digital Swiss Army knife with the capability of filling its owner's every spare minute with games, music, live and on-demand TV, Web browsing, and, oh yes, advertising."[24] A recent survey found that 89 percent of major brands will be marketed via mobile phones by 2008. More than half of those brands will likely spend up to 25 percent of their marketing budgets on mobile phone marketing.[25]

Marketers of all kinds are now integrating mobile phones into their direct marketing. Cell phone promotions include everything from ring-tone give-aways, mobile games, and ad-supported content to text-in contests and sweepstakes. For example, McDonald's recently put a promotion code on 20 million Big Mac packages in a joint sweepstakes contest with the House of Blues, urging participants to enter to win prizes and to text in from concerts. Some 40 percent of contest entries came via text messaging, resulting in a 3 percent sales gain for McDonald's. More importantly, 24 percent of those entering via cell phones opted in to receive future promotions and messages.[26]

Perhaps nowhere is mobile phone marketing more advanced that in Japan. Here's a glimpse of what the future might hold for cell phone marketing in the United States and other countries.

In Japan, life revolves around cell phones, and marketers know it. Take Nami, a 37-year-old graphic designer in Tokyo who regularly uses her phone to send and receive e-mails on the go. Her 11-year-old daughter enjoys downloading wallpaper and animated trailers featuring Disney characters, and Nami's boyfriend relies on his phone's global positioning system to navigate Tokyo's labyrinthine of streets. The family can also use cell phones to buy a can of Coke from high-tech vending machines, receive e-coupons from neighborhood stores, and even have their fortunes told. Digital coupons are taking off, as are GPS-based promotions used by retailers to target people near their stores. Mobile-ad spending in Japan is expected to hit $680 million by 2009, up from just $158 million last year.

Japanese direct marketers are experimenting with new ways to use the mobile devices for brand building. Nestlé, for example, is trying out a new technology called Quick Response (QR) codes, which can be scanned like digital bar codes. QR codes on print and outdoor ads can be read by cell phone cameras, which redirect the user's phone to a designated mobile URL site. Nestlé used QR codes in a campaign to launch a canned drink called Nescafé Shake. It promoted Shake with two 15-minute short films that humorously communicated a sense of fun around the act of "shaking" with a story about a slacker kid who winds up with a dog's wagging tail on his behind. A QR code on promotional materials led cell phone users to a mobile site where they could download the film as well as its original music as songs or ring tones. In the first three weeks after Nestlé's "Nonta's Tail" film debuted, 120,000 people visited the mobile site and another 550,000 watched the film on the Internet.[27]

Mobile phone marketing: To launch its Nescafé Shake canned drink in Japan, Nestlé used Quick Response codes, which can be scanned like UPC codes by a cell phone, to direct consumers to marketing pitches for the new product.

Podcasts and Vodcasts

Podcasting and vodcasting are the latest on-the-go, on-demand technologies. The name *podcast* derives from Apple's now-everywhere iPod. With podcasting, consumers can download audio files (podcasts) or video files (vodcasts) via the Internet to an iPod or other handheld device and then listen to or view them whenever and wherever they wish. They can search for podcast topics through sites such as iTunes or through podcast networks such as PodTrac, Podbridge, or PodShow. These days, you can download podcasts or vodcasts on an exploding array of topics, everything from your favorite National Public Radio show, a recent sit-com episode, or current sports features to the latest music video or Go-Daddy commercial.

One recent study predicts that the U.S. podcast audience will reach 50 million by 2010, up from 5 million in 2005. More than 20 percent of today's podcast listeners make more than $100,000 a year.[28] As a result, this new medium is drawing much attention from marketers. Many are now integrating podcasts and vodcasts into their direct marketing programs in the form of ad-supported podcasts, downloadable ads and informational features, and other promotions.

For example, Volvo sponsors podcasts on Autoblog and Absolut vodka buys ads on PodShow programs. Kraft Foods offers up hundreds of recipes using the iPod's text function and Nestlé Purina publishes podcasts on animal training and behavioral issues. The Walt Disney World Resort offers weekly podcasts on a mix of topics, including behind-the-scenes tours, interviews, upcoming events, and news about new attractions.[29]

Honda recently offered a vodcast as part of a new ad campaign for its Honda Civic. The vodcast consists of a two-minute, "This is what a Honda feels like," ad, in which human voices replicate the sounds that passengers hear in a Honda Civic. The vodcast also includes behind-the-scenes footage of the making of the ad. According to a Honda marketing executive, this dynamic new medium "is enabling people to experience what a Honda feels like from one of their most personal and closest touch points—their iPod."[30]

Interactive TV (ITV)

Interactive TV (ITV) lets viewers interact with television programming and advertising using their remote controls. In the past, ITV has been slow to catch on. However, satellite broadcasting systems such as DirecTV and Echostar are now offering ITV capabilities, and the technology appears poised to take off as a direct marketing medium.

Interactive TV gives marketers an opportunity to reach targeted audiences in an interactive, more involving way. For example, BMW recently ran interactive ads on Echostar that allowed viewers to request catalogs and several screens worth of other information using their remotes. The number of requests exceeded BMW's expectations tenfold. Similarly, Sony uses ITV to interact with TiVo users:[31]

Sony is running ads for its Bravia flat-panel TVs that let viewers, if they have TiVo, choose among different endings, whether they're watching live TV or a recorded program. Five seconds into the commercial, two on-screen choices appear—one aimed at men and one at women. A menu of "male" endings revolves around picture quality and size, and the "female" options focus on the TV's aesthetics. Sony hopes that the interactive and entertaining ad will keep viewers involved. It's even hoping that by offering 12 possible endings for its ad, viewers will be curious enough to watch them all. "If you provide endings for its ad, viewers will be curious enough to absolutely stay engaged," says an executive from the ad agency that created the Bravia campaign.

More broadly, TiVo plans to roll out what may sound like the ultimate in gall: ads on demand. It's not so crazy. Consumers about to spend big money on cars, travel, new kitchens, and the like have shown plenty of interest in watching video about the stuff they plan to buy. TiVo wants to offer that content more conveniently and on viewers' terms. TiVo's budding broadband link to the Net, which, among other things, connects a viewer's TiVo screen with their Yahoo! homepage, is seen as just the beginning of full-blown convergence between interactive TV and the Internet.

Mobile phone marketing, podcasts, and vodcasts, and interactive TV offer exciting direct marketing opportunities. But marketers must be careful to use these new direct marketing approaches wisely. As with other direct marketing forms, marketers who use them risk backlash from consumers who may resent such marketing as an invasion of their privacy. Marketers must target their direct marketing offers carefully, bringing real value to customers rather than making unwanted intrusions into their lives.

Online Marketing

Online marketing
Company efforts to market products and services and build customer relationships over the Internet.

As noted earlier, **online marketing** is the fastest-growing form of direct marketing. Recent technological advances have created a digital age. Widespread use of the Internet and other powerful new technologies are having a dramatic impact on both buyers and the marketers who serve them. In this section, we examine how marketing strategy and practice are changing to take advantage of today's Internet technologies.

Marketing and the Internet

Internet
A vast public web of computer networks that connects users of all types all around the world to each other and to an amazingly large "information repository."

Much of the world's business today is carried out over digital networks that connect people and companies. The **Internet**, a vast public web of computer networks, connects users of all types all around the world to each other and to an amazingly large information repository. Internet usage continues to grow steadily. Last year, Internet household penetration in the United States reached 64 percent, with more than 205 million people now using the Internet at home or at work. The average U.S. Internet user spends some 31 hours a month surfing the Web at home, plus another 78 hours a month at work. Worldwide, some 470 million people now have Internet access.[32]

The Internet has given marketers a whole new way to create value for customers and build customer relationships. The Web has fundamentally changed customers' notions of convenience, speed, price, product information, and service. The amazing success of early click-only companies—the so-called dot-coms such as Amazon.com, eBay, Expedia, and hundreds of others—caused existing brick-and-mortar manufacturers and retailers to reexamine how they served their markets. Now, almost all of these traditional companies have set up their own online sales and communications channels, becoming click-and-mortar competitors. It's hard to find a company today that doesn't have a substantial Web presence.

FIGURE 17.2
Online domains

	Targeted to consumers	Targeted to businesses
Initiated by business	B2C (business to consumer)	B2B (business to business)
Initiated by consumer	C2C (consumer to consumer)	C2B (consumer to business)

Online Marketing Domains

The four major online marketing domains are shown in Figure 17.2. They include B2C (business to consumer), B2B (business to business), C2C (consumer to consumer), and C2B (consumer to business).

Business to Consumer (B2C)

Business-to-consumer (B2C) online marketing
Selling goods and services online to final consumers.

The popular press has paid the most attention to **business-to-consumer (B2C) online marketing**—selling goods and services online to final consumers. Today's consumers can buy almost anything online—from clothing, kitchen gadgets, and airline tickets to computers and cars. Online consumer buying continues to grow at a healthy rate. Some 65 percent of American online users now use the Internet to shop. Last year, U.S. consumers spent an estimated $95 billion online, and consumer Internet spending is expected to reach $144 billion by 2010.[33]

Perhaps more importantly, the Internet now influences 27 percent of total retail sales—sales transacted online plus those carried out offline but encouraged by online research. By 2010, the Internet will influence a staggering 50 percent of total retail sales.[34] Thus, smart marketers are employing integrated multichannel strategies that use the Web to drive sales to other marketing channels.

As more and more people find their way onto the Web, the population of online consumers is becoming more mainstream and diverse. The Web now offers marketers a palette of different kinds of consumers seeking different kinds of online experiences. However, Internet consumers still differ from traditional offline consumers in their approaches to buying and in their responses to marketing. In the Internet exchange process, customer initiate and control the contact. Traditional marketing targets a somewhat passive audience. In contrast, online marketing targets people who actively select which Web sites they will visit and what marketing information they will receive about which products and under what conditions. Thus, the new world of online marketing requires new marketing approaches.

People now go online to order a wide range of goods—clothing from Gap or L.L. Bean, books or electronics from Amazon.com, furniture from Ethan Allen, major appliances from Sears, flowers from Calyx & Corolla, or even home mortgages from Quicken Loans.[35]

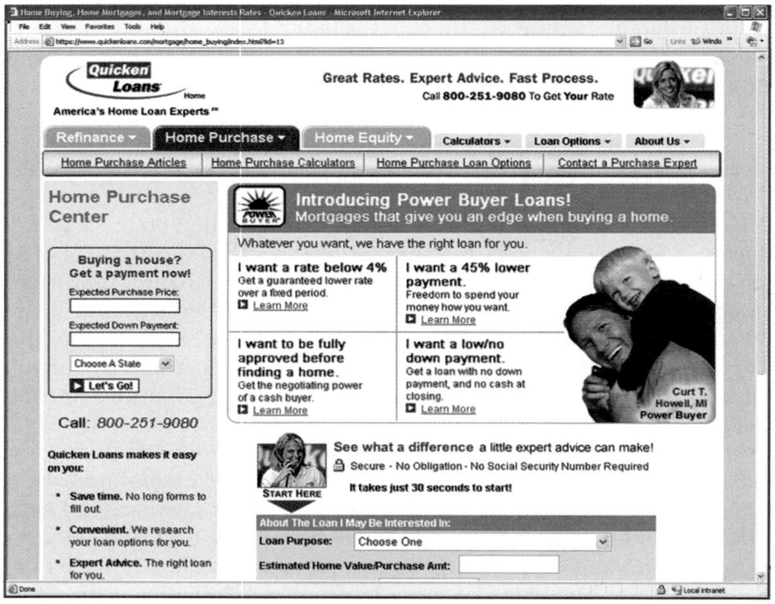

At Quicken Loans (www.quickenloans.com), prospective borrowers receive a high-tech, high-touch, one-stop mortgage shopping experience. At the site, customers can research a wide variety of home-financing and refinancing options, apply for a mortgage, and receive quick loan approval—all without leaving the comfort and security of their homes. The site provides useful interactive tools that help borrowers decide how much house they can afford, whether to rent or buy, whether to refinance a current mortgage, the economics of fixing up their current homes rather than moving, and much more. Customers can receive advice by phone or by chatting online with one of 2,700

■ B2C Web sites: People now go online to order a wide range of goods and services, even home mortgages.

mortgage experts and sign up for later e-mail rate updates. Quicken Loans closed more than $12 billion in mortgage loans last year.

Business-to-business (B2B) online marketing
Using B2B Web sites, e-mail, online product catalogs, online trading networks, and other online resources to reach new business customers, serve current customers more effectively, and obtain buying efficiencies and better prices.

Consumer-to-consumer (C2C) online marketing
Online exchanges of goods and information between final consumers.

Business to Business (B2B)

Although the popular press has given the most attention to B2C Web sites, **business-to-business (B2B) online marketing** is also flourishing. B2B marketers use B2B Web sites, e-mail, online product catalogs, online trading networks, and other online resources to reach new business customers, serve current customers more effectively, and obtain buying efficiencies and better prices.

Most major B2B marketers now offer product information, customer purchasing, and customer support services online. For example, corporate buyers can visit Sun Microsystems' Web site (www.sun.com), select detailed descriptions of Sun's products and solutions, request sales and service information, and interact with staff members. Some major companies conduct almost all of their business on the Web. Networking equipment and software maker Cisco Systems takes more than 80 percent of its orders over the Internet.

Beyond simply selling their products and services online, companies can use the Internet to build stronger relationships with important business customers. For example, Dell has set up customized Web sites for more than 113,000 business and institutional customers worldwide. These individualized Premier Dell.com sites help business customers to more efficiently manage all phases of their Dell computer buying and ownership. Each customer's Premier Dell.com Web site can include a customized online computer store, purchasing and asset management reports and tools, system-specific technical information, links to useful information throughout Dell's extensive Web site, and more. The site makes all the information a customer needs in order to do business with Dell available in one place, 24 hours a day, 7 days a week.[36]

Consumer to Consumer (C2C)

Much **consumer-to-consumer (C2C) online marketing** and communication occurs on the Web between interested parties over a wide range of products and subjects. In some cases, the Internet provides an excellent means by which consumers can buy or exchange goods or information directly with one another. For example, eBay, Amazon.com Auctions, Overstock.com, and other auction sites offer popular marketspaces for displaying and selling almost anything, from art and antiques, coins and stamps, and jewelry to computers and consumer electronics.

EBay's C2C online trading community of more than 181 million registered users worldwide (greater than the combined populations of France, Spain, and Britain!) transacted some $40 billion in trades last year. On any given day, the company's Web site lists more than 16 million items up for auction in more than 45,000 categories. Such C2C sites give people access to much larger audiences than the local flea market or newspaper classifieds (which, by the way, are now also going online). Interestingly, based on its huge success in the C2C market, eBay has now attracted a large number of B2C sellers, ranging from small businesses peddling their regular wares to large businesses liquidating excess inventory at auction.[37]

In other cases, C2C involves interchanges of information through Internet forums that appeal to specific special-interest groups. Such activities may be organized for commercial or noncommercial purposes. An example is Web logs, or *blogs*, online journals where people post their thoughts, usually on a narrowly defined topic. Blogs can be about anything, from politics or baseball to haiku, car repair, or the latest television series. Today's blogosphere consists of more than 10 million blogs, with 40,000 new ones popping up every day. About 16 percent of all American adults now read blogs, and 1 in every 17 Americans has created a blog of his or her own.[38]

Many marketers are now tapping into blogs as a medium for reaching carefully targeted consumers. One way is to advertise on an existing blog or to influence content there. For example, before GE announced a major energy-efficient technology initiative last year, GE executives met with major environmental bloggers to build support. Microsoft reaches out to bloggers to promote its Xbox game systems and other new products. And in an effort to improve its often-battered image, Wal-Mart now works directly with bloggers, feeding them nuggets of positive news, suggesting topics for posting, and even inviting them to visit company headquarters. "Bloggers who agreed to receive the e-mail messages said they were eager to hear Wal-Mart's side of the story, which they . . . felt had been drowned out by critics," say an analyst. The bloggers also "were tantalized by the promise of exclusive news that might attract more visitors to their Web sites."[39]

Other companies set up their own blogs. For example, Coca-Cola set up a blog to add an online community element to its sponsorship of the 2006 Winter Olympics. It enlisted a half-dozen college students from around the world to blog about their trips to the games. Coke paid to fly and accommodate students from China, Germany, Italy, Canada, and Australia, each of whom agreed to post conversations about the positive side of the games. Similarly, before the games began, VisaUSA launched a site where it urged Olympic hopefuls to blog about the games. The blog site allowed for posting photos and comments, podcasting, and video blogging.[40]

As a marketing tool, blogs offer some advantages. They can offer a fresh, original, personal, and cheap way to reach today's fragmented audiences. However, the blogosphere is cluttered and difficult to control. "Blogs may help companies bond with consumers in exciting new ways, but they won't help them control the relationship," says a blog expert. Such Web journals remain largely a C2C medium. "That isn't to suggest companies can't influence the relationship or leverage blogs to engage in a meaningful relationship," says the expert, "but the consumer will remain in control."[41]

In all, C2C means that online buyers don't just consume product information—increasingly, they create it. They join Internet interest groups to share information, with the result that "word of Web" is joining "word of mouth" as an important buying influence.

Consumer to Business (C2B)

The final online marketing domain is **consumer-to-business (C2B) online marketing**. Thanks to the Internet, today's consumers are finding it easier to communicate with companies. Most companies now invite prospects and customers to send in suggestions and questions via company Web sites. Beyond this, rather than waiting for an invitation, consumers can search out sellers on the Web, learn about their offers, initiate purchases, and give feedback. Using the Web, consumers can even drive transactions with businesses, rather than the other way around. For example, using Priceline.com, would-be buyers can bid for airline tickets, hotel rooms, rental cars, cruises, and vacation packages, leaving the sellers to decide whether to accept their offers.

Consumers can also use Web sites such as PlanetFeedback.com to ask questions, offer suggestions, lodge complaints, or deliver compliments to companies. The site provides letter templates for consumers to use based on their moods and reasons for contacting the company. The site then forwards the letters to the customer service manager at each company and helps to obtain a response. "About 80 percent of the companies respond to complaints, some within an hour," says a PlanetFeedback.com spokesperson.[42]

Types of Online Marketers

Companies of all types are now marketing online. In this section, we first discuss the different types of online marketers shown in Figure 17.3. Then, we examine how companies go about conducting online marketing.

Click-Only versus Click-and-Mortar Marketers

The Internet gave birth to a new species of marketers—the *click-only* dot-coms—which operate only online without any brick-and-mortar market presence. In addition, most traditional *brick-and-mortar* companies have now added online marketing operations, transforming themselves into *click-and-mortar* competitors.

Consumer-to-business (C2B) online marketing
Online exchanges in which consumers search out sellers, learn about their offers, and initiate purchases, sometimes even driving transaction terms.

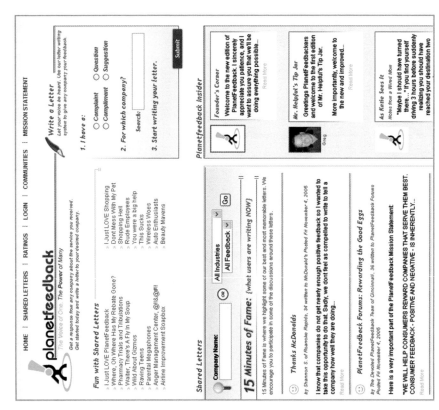

■ C2B e-commerce: Consumers can use Web sites such as PlanetFeedback.com to ask questions, offer suggestions, lodge complaints, or deliver compliments to companies.

Focus on Technology

Indeed, in this Internet age, buying tickets for live events has changed dramatically since Roger's concert-going days. Originators such as Ticketmaster now sell tickets online for everything from Broadway shows to sporting events. Increasingly, however, event tickets are resold through Web sites such as eBay, Craigslist, and newcomer StubHub, the fastest-growing company in the business. According to one survey conducted at a U2 concert, 29 percent of the fans said that they had purchased their tickets from an Internet resale Web site, a statistic that reflects ticket buying industry-wide.

Prices are all over the map, and tickets for sold-out shows of hot events routinely sell for double or triple their face value. In some cases, the markup is astronomical. Prices for a seat at Super Bowl XL in Detroit started at $2,000. Tickets to see Coldplay in San Jose in the spring of 2006 were going for as much as $3,000 each. And a pair of Stones tickets at New York's Madison Square Garden, close enough to see a geriatric Mick Jagger perspire, went for more than $14,000. Extreme cases? Yes, but not uncommon.

When most people think of buying a ticket from a reseller, they probably envision a seedy scalper standing in the shadows near an event venue. But scalping is moving mainstream. Because the Internet and other technologies have allowed professional ticket agents to purchase event tickets in larger numbers, anyone with a computer and broadband connection can instantly become a scalper. And regular folks, even fans, are routinely doing so. "Because we allowed people to buy four [tickets], if they only need two, they put the other two up for sale," said Dave Holmes, manager for Coldplay. This dynamic, occurring for events across the board, has dramatically increased the number of ticket resellers.

STUBHUB ENTERS THE GAME

With the ticket resale market booming, StubHub started operations in 2000 under the name Liquid Seats. It all started with an idea by two first-year students at the Stanford Graduate School of Business. Eric Baker and Jeff Fluhr had been observing the hysteria on the ticket resale market. In their opinion, the market was highly fragmented and rampant with fraud and distorted pricing. Two buyers sitting side-by-side at the same event might find they'd paid wildly different prices for essentially the same product. Even with heavy hitter eBay as the biggest ticket reseller at the time, Baker and Fluhr saw an opportunity to create a system that would bring buyers and sellers together in a more efficient manner.

They entered their proposal in a new-business plan competition. Fluhr was utterly convinced the concept would work, so much so that he withdrew the proposal from the competition and dropped out of school in order to launch the business. At a time when dot-coms were dropping like flies, this might have seemed like a very poor decision. But Fluhr is now CEO of StubHub, the leader and fastest-growing company in a $10-billion-a-year industry.

Home to 200 employees, StubHub utilizes 20,000 square feet of prime office space in San Francisco's pricey financial district, seven satellite offices, and two call centers. Even more telling is the company's financial performance. From

2004 to 2005, StubHub tripled its volume to $200 million worth of tickets sold, generating about $50 million in commissions. Most of that was profit. According to comScore Networks, a firm that tracks Web traffic, StubHub.com is the ticket-resale category.

THE DEVIL IS IN THE DETAILS

Sharing his own experience, a *New York Times* writer provides the following description of how StubHub works:

To test the system I started with the New York Yankees. A series with the Seattle Mariners was coming up, just before the Yankees left town for a long road trip. Good tickets would be scarce. I went to StubHub. Lots of tickets there, many priced stratospherically. I settled on two Main Box seats in Section 313, Row G. They were in the right-field corner, just one section above field level. The price was $35 each, or face price for a season ticket holder. This was a tremendous value for a sold-out game. I registered with StubHub, creating a user name and password, ordered the tickets, then sealed the deal by providing my credit card number. An e-mail message arrived soon after, confirming the order and informing me that StubHub was contacting the seller to arrange for shipment. My card would not be charged until the seller had confirmed to StubHub the time and method of delivery. A second e-mail message arrived a day later giving the delivery details. The tickets arrived on the Thursday before the game, and the seller was paid by StubHub on confirmation of delivery. On Saturday, under a clear, sunny sky, the Yankees were sending a steady stream of screaming line drives into the right-field corner.

From the beginning, Baker and Fluhr set out to provide better options for both buyers and sellers by making StubHub different. Like eBay, StubHub has no ticket inventory of its own, reducing its risk. It simply provides the venue that gives buyers and sellers the opportunity to come together. But it's the differences, perhaps, that have allowed StubHub to achieve such success in such a short period of time.

One of the first differences noticed by buyers and sellers is StubHub's ticket-listing procedure. Sellers can list tickets by auction or at a fixed price, a price that declines as the event gets closer. Whereas eBay charges fees just to list tickets, StubHub lists them for free. Thus, initially, the seller has no risk whatsoever. eBay gets its revenue not only from listing fees, but from additional sliding-scale fees based on sale price. StubHub's system is simpler, and it splits the fee burden between buyer and seller. StubHub charges sellers a 15-percent commission and buyers a 10-percent fee.

StubHub's Web site structure also creates a marketplace that comes closer to pure competition than any other reseller's Web site. It achieves this by minimizing the degree of differentiation between sellers on its site. On eBay, sellers customize their postings through a variety of details. Not only do text, graphics, and conditions of sale differ from seller to seller, so

When marketers and engineers design new products, they rely heavily on input from consumers. At Massachusetts Institute of Technology, researchers are working on a multidisciplinary project known as the Virtual Customer Initiative. The purpose of the initiative is to improve the accuracy and usability of customer input by creating easy-to-use and effective Web-based tools. To see demonstrations of this technology, visit http://conjoint.mit.edu/newdemo/ and click on the "Go" button in the box with a car, labeled "Web-Based Conjoint Analysis." Go through the entire demonstration for the crossover vehicle. The demonstrations show an application of a statistical technique called conjoint analysis. In simple terms, the objective of conjoint analysis is to determine how a consumer

makes trade-offs between different product features—to determine whether a consumer would trade, for instance, less passenger space for more cargo space.

1. What are the advantages and disadvantages of running this type of analysis as a Web-based system as opposed to having subjects come to a research lab and run through the study with a researcher?

2. In addition to cars and cameras, what are some other products that would benefit from this type of Web-based analysis?

3. Why isn't this technology, and conjoint analysis in general, not more widely used?

Focus on Ethics

Technoethics, a recent field of study that examines ethical issues in technology, has recently been applied to many areas in Internet marketing. Blogs are an example of a growing Internet marketing technology that presents many ethical issues. For instance, is it ethical for a company to ask consumers to blog favorably about a product? Is it ethical for companies to pay these consumers to blog? Should a company fire an employee who blogs negative comments about the company? Other technologies, created by leading Internet marketers to improve customer satisfaction on the Internet are also raising issues. Amazon.com, one of the most reputable Internet marketers, has been criticized for its Wish List, which lets

immensely popular online social network, MySpace, is currently suffering with a problem by which some users' sites have been rerouted to adult-content sites. LucasArts updated its Star Wars Galaxies programs and accidentally made it unplayable to players with disabilities, because it could no longer be played with one hand.

1. Is it ethical for an advertiser to pay a consumer to blog favorably about a product? To fire an employee presenting negative issues on his or her blog?

2. What can companies do to reduce the negative public relations effects of such technoethical issues? [69]

Promise to American Consumers." The Privacy Promise requires that all DMA members adhere to a carefully developed set of consumer privacy rules. Members must agree to notify customers when any personal information is rented, sold, or exchanged with others. They must also honor consumer requests to "opt out" of receiving further solicitations or having their contact information transferred to other marketers. Finally, they must abide by the DMA's Preference Service by removing the names of consumers who wish not to receive mail, telephone, or e-mail offers. [69]

Direct marketers know that, left untended, such problems will lead to increasingly negative consumer attitudes, lower response rates, and calls for more restrictive state and federal legislation. "Privacy and customer permission have become the cornerstones of customer trust, [and] trust has become the cornerstone to a continuing relationship," says one expert. Companies must "become the custodians of customer trust and protect the privacy of their customers." [70]

Most direct marketers want the same things that consumers want: honest and well-designed marketing offers targeted only toward consumers who will appreciate and respond to them. Direct marketing is just too expensive to waste on consumers who don't want it.

Reviewing the Concepts

Let's revisit this chapter's key concepts. This chapter is the last of four chapters covering the final marketing mix element—promotion. The previous chapters dealt with advertising, publicity, sales promotion, and personal selling. This one investigates direct and online marketing.

1. Define direct marketing and discuss its benefits to customers and companies.

Direct marketing consists of direct connections with carefully targeted individual consumers to both obtain an immediate response and cultivate lasting customer relationships. Using detailed databases, direct marketers tailor their offers and communications to the needs of narrowly defined segments or even individual buyers.

For buyers, direct marketing is convenient, easy to use, and private. It gives buyers ready access to a wealth of products and information, at home and around the globe. Direct marketing is also immediate and interactive, allowing buyers to create exactly the configuration of information, products, or services they desire, then order them on the spot. For sellers, direct marketing is a powerful tool for building customer relationships. Using database marketing, today's marketers can target small groups or individual consumers, tailor offers to individual needs, and promote these offers through personalized communications. It also offers them a low-cost, efficient alternative for reaching their markets. As a result of these advantages to both buyers and sellers, direct marketing has become the fastest-growing form of marketing.

2. Identify and discuss the major forms of direct marketing.

The main forms of direct marketing include personal selling, direct-mail marketing, catalog marketing, telephone marketing, direct-response television marketing, kiosk marketing, and online marketing. We discussed personal selling in the previous chapter.

Direct-mail marketing, the largest form of direct marketing, consists of the company sending an offer, announcement, reminder, or other item to a person at a specific address. Recently, new forms of "mail delivery" have become popular, such as e-mail marketing. Some marketers rely on catalog marketing—selling through catalogs mailed to a select list of customers, made available in stores, or accessed on the Web. Telephone marketing consists of using the telephone to sell directly to consumers. Direct-response television marketing has two forms: direct-response advertising (or infomercials) and home shopping channels. Kiosks are information and ordering machines that direct marketers place in stores, airports, and other locations. In recent years, a number of new digital direct marketing

technologies have emerged, including mobile phone marketing, podcasts and vodcasts, and interactive TV. Online marketing involves online channels that digitally link sellers with consumers.

3. Explain how companies have responded to the Internet and other powerful new technologies with online marketing.

Online marketing is the fastest-growing form of direct marketing. The Internet enables consumers and companies to access and share huge amounts of information with just a few mouse clicks. In turn, the Internet has given marketers a whole new way to create value for customers and build customer relationships. It's hard to find a company today that doesn't have a substantial Web marketing presence.

Online consumer buying continues to grow at a healthy rate. Some 65 percent of American online users now use the Internet to shop. Perhaps more importantly, by 2010, the Internet will influence a staggering 50 percent of total retail sales. Thus, smart marketers are employing integrated multichannel strategies that use the Web to drive sales to other marketing channels.

4. Discuss how companies go about conducting online marketing to profitably deliver more value to customers.

Companies of all types are now engaged in online marketing. The Internet gave birth to the click-only dot-coms, which operate only online. In addition, many traditional brick-and-mortar companies have now added online marketing operations, transforming themselves into click-and-mortar competitors. Many click-and-mortar companies are now having more online success than their click-only competitors.

Companies can conduct online marketing in any of the four ways: creating a Web site, placing ads and promotions online, setting up or participating in Web communities, or using online e-mail. The first step typically is to set up a Web site. Beyond simply setting up a site, however, companies must make their sites engaging, easy to use, and useful in order to attract visitors, hold them, and bring them back again.

Online marketers can use various forms of online advertising to build their Internet brands or to attract visitors to their Web sites. Beyond online advertising, other forms of online promotion include online display advertising, search-related advertising, content sponsorships, alliances and affiliate programs, and viral marketing, the Internet version of word-of-mouth marketing. Online marketers can also participate in Web communities, which take advantage of the C2C properties of the Web. Finally, e-mail marketing has become a fast-growing tool for both B2C and B2B marketers. Whatever direct marketing tools they use, marketers must work hard to integrate them into a cohesive marketing effort.

About 10,000 people a week go to The Rack, a bar in Boston. . . . One by one, they hand over their driver's licenses to a doorman, who swipes them through a sleek black machine. If a license is valid and its holder is over 21, a red light blinks and the patron is waved through. But most of the customers are not aware that it also pulls up the name, address, birth date, and other personal details from a data strip on the back of the license. Even height, eye color, and sometimes Social Security number are registered. "You swipe the license, and all of a sudden someone's whole life as we know it pops up in front of you," said Paul Barclay, the bar's owner. "It's almost voyeuristic." Mr. Barclay soon found that he could build a database of personal information, providing an intimate perspective on his clientele that can be useful in marketing. Now, for any given night or hour, he can break down his clientele by sex, age, zip code, or other characteristics. If he wanted to, he could find out how many blond women named Karen over 5 feet 2 inches came in over a weekend, or how many of his customers have the middle initial M. More practically, he can build mailing lists based on all that data—and keep track of who comes back.[65]

■ Privacy: The explosion of information technology has put sometimes frightening capabilities into the hands of almost any business. One bar owner discovered the power of information technology after he acquired a simple, inexpensive device to check IDs.

A Need for Action

All of this calls for strong actions by marketers to curb privacy abuses before legislators step in to do it for them. For example, in response to online privacy and security concerns, the federal government has considered numerous legislative actions to regulate how Web operators obtain and use consumer information. State governments are also stepping in. In 2003, California enacted the California Online Privacy Protection Act (OPPA), under which any online business that collects personally identifiable information from California residents must take steps such as posting its privacy policy and notifying consumers about what data will be gathered and how it will be used.[66]

Of special concern are the privacy rights of children. In 1998, the Federal Trade Commission surveyed 212 Web sites directed toward children. It found that 89 percent of the sites collected personal information from children. However, 46 percent of them did not include any disclosure of their collection and use of such information. As a result, Congress passed the Children's Online Privacy Protection Act (COPPA), which requires Web site operators targeting children to post privacy policies on their sites. They must also notify parents about the information they're gathering and obtain parental consent before collecting personal information from children under the age of 13. Under this act, Interstate Bakeries was recently required to rework its Planet Twinkie Web site after the Children's Advertising Review Unit found that the site allowed children under 13 to submit their full name and phone number without parental consent.[67]

Many companies have responded to consumer privacy and security concerns with actions of their own. Still others are taking an industrywide approach. For example, TRUSTe, a nonprofit self-regulatory organization, works with many large corporate sponsors, including Microsoft, AT&T, and Intuit, to audit companies' privacy and security measures and help consumers navigate the Web safely. According to the company's Web site, "TRUSTe believes that an environment of mutual trust and openness will help make and keep the Internet a free, comfortable, and richly diverse community for everyone." To reassure consumers, the company lends it "trustmark" stamp of approval to Web sites that meet its privacy and security standards.[68]

The direct-marketing industry as a whole is also addressing public policy issues. For example, in an effort to build consumer confidence in shopping direct, the Direct Marketing Association (DMA)—the largest association for businesses practicing direct, database, and interactive marketing, with more than 4,800 member companies—launched a "Privacy

2003, Congress passed the CAN-SPAM Act (the Controlling the Assault of Non-Solicited Pornography and Marketing Act), which attempts to clean up the e-mail industry by banning deceptive subject lines, requiring a real return address, and giving consumers a way to "opt out." Such actions have helped somewhat. The number of spam messages received last year dropped by 17 percent over the previous year. However, most of us still get a barrage of e-mail come-ons each day.

Most legitimate e-mail marketers welcome such controls. Left unchecked, they reason, spam will make legitimate e-mail marketing less effective, or even impossible. But the industry worries that solutions such as spam filters and the CAN-SPAM Act often filter out the good e-mails with the bad, dampening the rich potential of e-mail for companies that want to use it as a valid marketing tool. In fact, according to one study, as much as 20 percent of legitimate bulk commercial e-mail—which includes online statements and receipts as well as mail that users sign up to receive—gets caught in spam filters.

So, what's a marketer to do? Permission-based e-mail is the best solution. Companies can send e-mails only to customers who "opt in"—those who grant permission in advance. They can let consumers specify what types of messages they'd like to receive. Financial services firms such as Charles Schwab use configurable e-mail systems that let customers choose what they want to get. Others, such as Yahoo! or Amazon.com, include long lists of opt-in boxes for different categories of marketing material. Amazon.com targets opt-in customers with a limited number of helpful "we thought you'd like to know" messages based on their expressed preferences and previous purchases. Few customers object and many actually welcome such promotional messages.

Permission-based marketing ensures that e-mails are sent only to customers who want them. Still, marketers must be careful not to abuse the privilege. There's a fine line between legitimate e-mail mar-

keting and spam. Companies that cross the line will quickly learn that "opting out" is only a click away for disgruntled consumers.

Sources: Quotes and other information from Jennifer Drumluk and Joe Tyler, "Cracking the E-Mail Marketing Code," *Association Management,* March 2005, pp. 52–56; Matt Haig and Mylene Mangalindan, "Spam Queen: For Bulk E-Mailer, Pestering Millions Offers Path to Profit," *Wall Street Journal,* November 13, 2002, p. A1; Jennifer Wolcott, "You Call It Spam, They Call It a Living," *Christian Science Monitor,* March 22, 2004, p. 12; "AOL Top-10 List Reveals Spammers Are Getting More Sophisticated," *Wireless News,* December 29, 2005, p. 1; Enid Burns, "The Deadly Duo: Spam and Viruses," March 2006, accessed at www.clickz.com; and Jessica E. Vascellaro, "Spam Filters Wild; Spate of Incidents at Verizon, AOL Point to Growing Problem of Blocking Legitimate E-Mail," *Wall Street Journal,* May 3, 2006, p. D1.

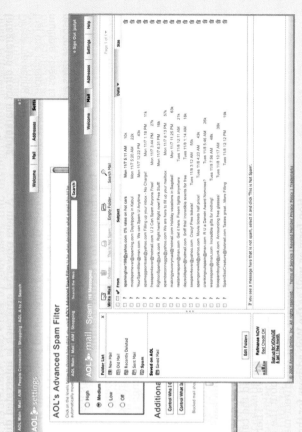

In response to the spam epidemic, Internet service providers such as AOL have created sophisticated spam filters.

ally." However, for most companies, online marketing will remain just one important approach to the marketplace that works alongside other approaches in a fully integrated marketing mix.

Despite the many challenges, companies large and small are quickly integrating online marketing into their marketing strategies and mixes. As it continues to grow, online marketing will prove to be a powerful direct marketing tool for building customer relationships, improving sales, communicating company and product information, and delivering products and services more efficiently and effectively.

Integrated Direct Marketing

Too often, a company's different direct-marketing efforts are not well integrated with one another or with other elements of its marketing and promotion mixes. For example, a firm's media advertising may be handled by the advertising department working with a traditional

Real Marketing

17.2

E-Mail Marketing: The Hot Marketing Medium? Or Pestering Millions for Profit?

E-mail is one hot marketing medium. In mind-boggling numbers, e-mail ads are popping onto our computer screens and filling up our e-mail boxes. And they're no longer just the quiet, plain-text messages of old. The new breed of in-your-face e-mail ad is designed to command your attention—loaded with glitzy features such as animation, interactive links, color photos, streaming video, and personalized audio messages.

But there's a dark side to the exploding use of e-mail marketing. The biggest problem? Spam—the deluge of unsolicited, unwanted commercial messages that now clutter up our e-mail boxes and our lives. Various studies show that spam now accounts for an inbox-clogging 60 to 83 percent of e-mails sent daily throughout the world, up from only 7 percent in 2002. One recent study found that the average consumer received 3,253 spam messages last year.

Despite these dismal statistics, when used properly, e-mail can be the ultimate direct marketing medium. Blue-chip marketers such as Amazon.com, Dell, L.L.Bean, Office Depot, and others use it regularly, and with great success. E-mail lets these marketers send highly targeted, tightly personalized, relationship-building messages to consumers who actually *want* to receive them, at a cost of only a few cents per contact. E-mail ads really can command attention and get customers to act. According to one estimate, well-designed e-mail campaigns sent to internal customer lists typically achieve 10 to 20 percent click-through rates. That's pretty good when compared with the 1 to 2 percent average response rates for traditional direct mail and the less than 1 percent response to traditional banner ads.

However, although carefully designed e-mails may be effective, and may even be welcomed by selected consumers, critics argue that most commercial e-mail messages amount to little more than annoying "junk mail" to the rest of us. Too many bulk e-mailers blast out lowest-common-denominator mailings to anyone with an e-mail address. There is no customization—no relationship building. Everyone gets the same hyperventilated messages. Moreover, too often, the spam comes from shady sources and pitches objectionable products—everything from Viagra and body-enhancement products to pornography and questionable investments. And the messages are often sent from less-than-reputable marketers.

At least in part, it's e-mail economics that are to blame for our overflowing inboxes. Sending e-mail is so easy and so inexpensive that almost anyone can afford to do it, even at paltry response rates. "In the field of direct marketing, it doesn't get much cheaper than spam," says one analyst. "One needs only a credit card (to buy lists of e-mail addresses), a computer, and an Internet connection. Otherwise, it costs nothing to send bulk e-mail, even masses of it."

For example, Touch Media Group once pumped out eight million e-mails a day. That makes the company sound like a big-city direct marketing behemoth. But in reality, it began as a home-based business run by a 44-year-old mother, Laura Betterly, in Dunedin, Florida, dubbed the Spam Queen by the *Wall Street Journal*. Betterly regularly dispatched messages to half a million or more strangers with a single click on the "send" icon. She found that she could make a profit on even very low responses. For example, if only 65 of the half million recipients responded, Betterly's company made $40. In all, Betterly cleared more than $200,000 a year in income from her small business.

The problem, of course, is that it was far easier for Betterly to hit the "send" button on an e-mail to a million and a half strangers than it was for the beleaguered recipients to hit the delete key on all those messages. One analyst calculated that the *recipient* cost of Betterly's e-mails far exceeded the $40 in revenue that it produced for her.

Assume that the average time getting rid of the junk was two seconds, and that the average recipient values his or her time at the mean wage paid in the United States, which is around $14 per hour, or $0.0039 per second. This implies a total cost, incurred by uninterested recipients, of 500,000 times two seconds times $0.0039 per second, which gives $3,900. And such dollar calculations don't begin to account for the sheer frustration of having to deal with all those many junk messages.

The impact of spam on consumers and businesses is alarming. One recent study places the average time spent at work each day deleting spam at 2.8 minutes. This loss in productivity equals $21.6 billion per year based on average U.S. wages.

In response to such costs and frustrations, Internet service providers and Web-browser producers have created sophisticated spam filters. For example, AOL now blocks some 1.5 billion spam messages a day, more than half a trillion a year, from reaching the e-mail boxes of AOL subscribers. It's blocking eight out of every ten attempted e-mails as spam. The government is also stepping in. In

---

walk a fine line between adding value for consumers and being intrusive (see Real Marketing 17.2).

To avoid irritating consumers by sending unwanted marketing e-mail, companies should ask customers for permission to e-mail marketing pitches. They should also tell recipients how to "opt in" or "opt out" of e-mail promotions at any time. This approach, known as *permission-based marketing*, has become a standard model for e-mail marketing.

The Promise and Challenges of Online Marketing

Online marketing continues to offer both great promise and many challenges for the future. Its most ardent apostles still envision a time when the Internet and online marketing will replace magazines, newspapers, and even stores as sources for information and buying. Most marketers, however, hold a more realistic view. To be sure, online marketing will become a successful business model for some companies, Internet firms such as Amazon.com, eBay, and Google, and direct-marketing companies such as Dell. Michael Dell's goal is one day "to have *all* customers conduct *all* transactions on the Internet, glob-

FIGURE 17.3
Types of online marketers

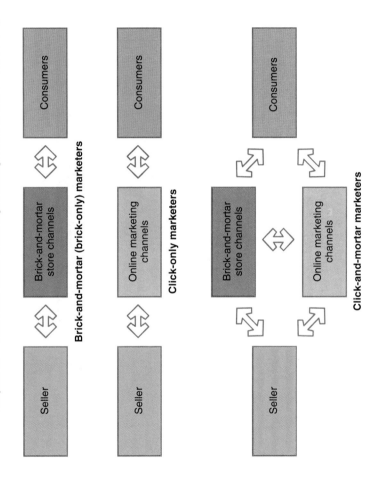

Brick-and-mortar (brick-only) marketers

Click-only marketers

Click-and-mortar marketers

Click-only companies

The so-called dot-coms, which operate only online without any brick-and-mortar market presence.

Click-and-mortar companies

Traditional brick-and-mortar companies that have added online marketing to their operations.

Click-Only Companies

Click-only companies come in many shapes and sizes. They include *e-tailers*, dot-coms that sell products and services directly to final buyers via the Internet. Examples include Amazon.com, Expedia, and Wine.com. The click-only group also includes *search engines and portals*, such as Yahoo!, Google, and MSN, which began as search engines and later added services such as news, weather, stock reports, entertainment, and storefronts, hoping to become the first port of entry to the Internet. *Shopping or price comparison sites*, such as Froogle.com, Yahoo! Shopping, and Bizrate.com, give instant product and price comparisons from thousands of vendors.

Internets service providers (ISPs) such as AOL and Earthlink are click-only companies that provide Internet and e-mail connections for a fee. *Transaction sites*, such as eBay, take commissions for transactions conducted on their sites. Finally, various *content sites*, such as *New York Times* on the Web (www.nytimes.com), ESPN.com, and Encyclopaedia Britannica Online, provide financial, news, research, and other information.

The hype surrounding such click-only Web businesses reached astronomical levels during the "dot-com gold rush" of the late 1990s, when avid investors drove dot-com stock prices to dizzying heights. However, the investing frenzy collapsed in the year 2000, and many high-flying, overvalued dot-coms came crashing back to Earth. Even some of the strongest and most attractive e-tailers—eToys.com, Pets.com, Furniture.com, Garden.com—filed for bankruptcy. Now on firmer footing, many click-only dot-coms are surviving and even prospering in today's marketspace.

Click-and-Mortar Companies

As the Internet grew, established brick-and-mortar companies realized that, to compete effectively with online competitors, they had to go online themselves. Thus, many one-time brick-and-mortar companies are now prospering as **click-and-mortar companies.** For example, Office Depot's more than 1,000 office-supply superstores rack up annual sales of $13.5 billion in more than 23 countries. But you might be surprised to learn that Office Depot's fastest recent growth has come not from its traditional "brick-and-mortar" channels, but from the Internet.

Office Depot's online sales have soared in recent years, now accounting for 27 percent of total sales. Selling on the Web lets Office Depot build deeper, more personalized relationships with customers large and small. "Contract customers"—the 80,000 or so larger businesses that have negotiated relationships with Office Depot—enjoy customized online ordering that includes company-specific product lists and pricing. For

do the sellers' "trustworthiness" ratings. But with StubHub, all sellers are equal. Each posts tickets using the same template. When buyers browse, every posting looks the same. In fact, the seller's identity isn't even included. StubHub even holds the shipping method constant, via FedEx.

This makes the purchase process much more transparent for buyers. They can browse tickets by event, venue, and section. Comparison shopping is very easy, as shoppers can simultaneously view different pairs of tickets in the same section, even in the same row. Although prices still vary, this system makes tickets more of a commodity and allows market forces to narrow the gap considerably from one seller to another. In fact, although tickets often sell for high prices, this also has the effect of pushing ticket prices down below face value.

Perhaps the biggest and most important difference between StubHub and competitors is the company's 100 percent guarantee. Initially, it might seem more risky buying from a seller whose identity is unknown. But StubHub puts the burden of responsibility on the seller, remaining involved after the purchase where competing sites bow out. Buyers aren't charged until they confirm receipt of the tickets. "If you open the package and it contains two squares of toilet paper instead of the tickets," Baker explains, "then we debit the seller's credit card for the amount of the purchase." StubHub will also revoke site privileges for fraudulent or unreliable sellers. In contrast, the eBay system is largely self-policing and does not monitor the shipment or verification of the purchased items.

WHAT THE FUTURE HOLDS

When StubHub was formed, it targeted primary professional ticket brokers and ordinary consumers. In examining individuals as sellers, Baker and Fluhr capitalized on the underexploited assets of sport team season ticket holders. "If you have season tickets to the Yankees, that's 81 games," Mr. Baker said. "Unless you're unemployed or especially passionate, there's no way you're going to attend every game." StubHub entered the equation, not only giving ticket holders a way to recoup some of their investment, but allowing them to have complete control over the process rather than selling to a ticket agent.

It quickly became apparent to StubHub's founders that the benefits of season ticket holders selling off unused tickets extended to the sports franchises as well. Being able to sell unwanted tickets encourages season ticket holders to buy again. It also puts customers in seats that would otherwise go empty—customers who buy hot dogs, souvenirs, and programs. Thus, StubHub began entering into signed agreements with professional sports teams. The teams give official reselling rights to StubHub in exchange for a fee. Originally, this was a percentage of resale profits. But because of the multiple benefits for teams, StubHub now keeps all commissions and instead pays a straight fee to each team for promoting its Web site and providing contact information on season tickets.

This change in contract details has only increased the number of partnerships between StubHub and sports teams.

The company now has signed agreements with numerous NFL, NBA, MLB, and NHL teams to be their official secondary marketplace for season ticket holders. It has also struck deals with USC and the University of Alabama, with more collegiate teams in the pipeline. The deal with USC led directly to a new company record for a single event, the 2006 Rose Bowl between Texas and USC. Although StubHub would not disclose how many tickets it sold, the company acknowledged that it was triple the amount sold for all other 2006 college bowl games combined.

Revenues from sporting events account for more than half of all StubHub sales. So it's not surprising that the company continues to pursue new partnerships with sports teams and even media organizations, such as Sporting News and CBS Sportsline. However, it has arranged similar contractual agreements with big-name performers such as Coldplay, Britney Spears, Jewel, Christina Aguilera, Alanis Morissette, and country music's newest star, Bobby Pinson. Arrangements allow StubHub to offer exclusive event packages with a portion of the proceeds supporting charities designated by the performer.

The reselling of event tickets is here to stay. Although there is more than one channel to buy or sell, StubHub's future looks bright. The company's model of entering into partnerships with event-producing organizations is establishing them as "the official" ticket reseller. Thus, it is more than likely that StubHub's lead over the competition will only increase.

Questions for Discussion

1. Conduct a brief analysis of the marketing environment and the forces shaping the development of StubHub.

2. Discuss StubHub's business model. What general benefits does it afford to buyers and sellers? Which benefits are most important in terms of creating value for buyers and sellers?

3. Discuss StubHub as a new intermediary. What effects has this new type of intermediary had on the ticket industry?

4. Apply the text's e-marketing domains framework to StubHub's business model. What effects has this new type of intermediary had on the ticket industry?

5. What recommendations can you make for improving StubHub's future growth and success?

6. What are the legal or ethical issues, if any, for ticket-reselling Web sites?

Sources: William Grimes, "That Invisible Hand Guides the Game of Ticket Hunting," *New York Times*, June 18, 2004, p. E1; Henry Fountain, "The Price of Admission in a Material World," *New York Times*, April 16, 2006, p. D5; Steve Stecklow, "Can't Get No . . . Tickets?" *Wall Street Journal*, January 7, 2006, p. P1; Steve Stecklow, "StubHub's Ticket to Ride," *Wall Street Journal*, January 17, 2006, p. B1; Bob Tedeschi, "New Era of Ticket Resales: Online and Aboveboard," *New York Times*, August 29, 2005, p. C4; and information from "About Us," accessed online at www.stubhub.com, June, 2006.

18

Creating Competitive Advantage

Previewing the Concepts

In previous chapters, you explored the basics of marketing. You've learned that the aim of marketing is to create value *for* customers in order to capture value *from* consumers in return. In the final three chapters, we'll extend this concept to three special areas—creating competitive advantage, global marketing, and marketing ethics and social responsibility.

In this chapter, we pull all of the marketing basics together. Understanding customers is an important first step in developing profitable customer relationships, but it's not enough. To gain competitive advantage, companies must use this understanding to design market offers that deliver more value than the offers of *competitors* seeking to win the same customers. In this chapter, we look first at competitor analysis, the process companies use to identify and analyze competitors. Then, we examine competitive marketing strategies by which companies position themselves against competitors to gain the greatest possible competitive advantage.

First let's examine Washington Mutual, a very successful financial services company with an unusual formula for building profitable relationships with its middle-American customers. As you read about Washington Mutual, ask yourself: Just what *is* it about this company's marketing strategy that has made it the nation's sixth largest banking company and one of the leading mortgage lenders? Pursuing this strategy, can "WaMu" become the Wal-Mart of the banking industry?

W hen you walk into a Washington Mutual branch for the first time, you'll probably do a double take. This just isn't your usual bank. There are no teller windows or desks, no velvet ropes, and no marble counters. Instead, you'll find a warm and inviting retail environment, complete with a concierge area where WaMulians (that's what employees call themselves) meet and greet customers. According to Washington Mutual, the idea is to create a place where bank customers want to go rather than have to go. "We make our financial centers inviting, not institutional," says the bank. In many respects, a Washington Mutual branch is more like a retail store than a bank.

This is the bank of the future, Washington Mutual style (WaMu, to the faithful). Sales associates are dressed in Gap-like gear: blue shirts, khaki pants, and navy sweaters. But there's not a rack of cargo pants in sight, and denim shirts are in short supply. If you want a mutual fund, however, a young woman is eager to help. If it's a checking account you need, step right up to the concierge station, and a friendly young man will direct you to the right nook. If your kids get fussy while you're chatting about overdraft protection, send them over to the kids corner, called WaMu Kids, where they can amuse themselves with games, books, and other activities.

The bank's look and feel are intended to put the 'retail' back in retail banking. Known internally as Occasio (Latin for "favorable opportunity"), the format grew out of 18 months of intense market research that investigated every customer touch point in a branch. One of the primary innovations of the bank's design is teller towers, pedestals where sales associates stand in front of screens fielding transactions. They handle no money. Customers who need cash (or "wamoola") are given a slip, which they take over to a cash-dispensing machine. This is central to the bank's true goal: cross-selling products by helping customers to find additional products and services they might value. Because they aren't tethered to a cash drawer, tellers who discover that a customer's kid just got into college can march that person over to an education-loan officer. Or they can steer newlyweds to the mortgage desk.

This format might seem unusual for a bank, but it's working for Washington Mutual. The company's 2,600 facilities around the country pull in more than $21 billion in yearly revenues. Last year, revenues grew almost 34 percent; profits were up 19 percent. In little more than ten years, WaMu has grown from an obscure

Northwest thrift into the nation's seventh-largest financial institution, its largest thrift bank, and its number-three mortgage lender.

Washington Mutual's success has resulted from its relentless dedication to a simple competitive marketing strategy: operational excellence. Some companies, such as Ritz-Carlton hotels, create value through customer intimacy—by coddling customers and reaping high prices and margins. Others, such as Microsoft or Intel, create value through product leadership—by offering a continuous stream of leading-edge products. In contrast, Washington Mutual creates value through a Wal-Mart-like strategy of offering convenience and competitive prices.

WaMu's high-tech, innovative retail stores provide customer convenience but cost much less to staff and operate than a typical bank branch. "Their inexpensive branch design allows WaMu to make use of existing retail space and keep personnel low," notes a banking analyst. Leveraging this low cost, WaMu can offer more affordable banking services, which in turn lets it profitably serve the mass market of moderate-income consumers that other banks now overlook. In fact, WaMu wants to be the Wal-Mart of the banking industry:

WaMu's strategy is simple: Deliver great value and convenient service for the everyday Joe. "The blue-collar, lower white-collar end of the market is either underserved or overcharged," says one analyst who has followed WaMu for nearly two decades. The Home Depots, Targets, and Wal-Marts have built empires by focusing on those customers. Now WaMu's CEO, Kerry Killinger, aims to join their ranks. Killinger wants nothing less than to reinvent how people think about banking. "In every retailing industry there are category killers who figure out how to have a very low cost structure and pass those advantages on

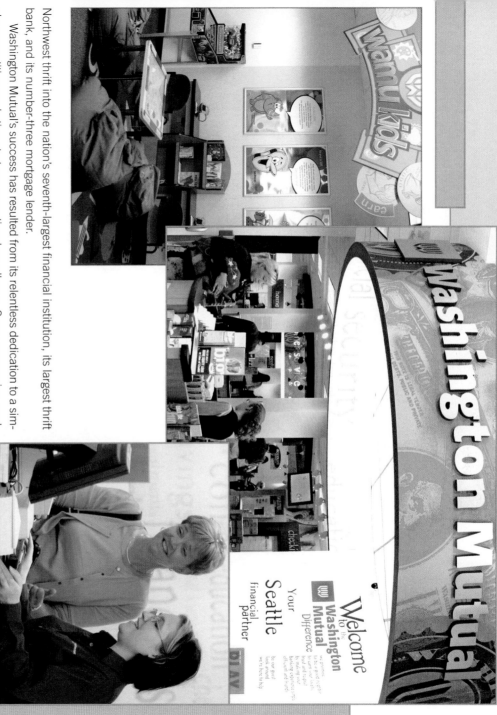

Objectives

After studying this chapter, you should be able to

1. discuss the need to understand competitors as well as customers through competitor analysis
2. explain the fundamentals of competitive marketing strategies based on creating value for customers
3. illustrate the need for balancing customer and competitor orientations in becoming a truly market-centered organization

to customers, day in and day out, with better pricing," he says. "I think we have a shot at doing that in this segment." His goal is to have his company mentioned in the same breath as Wal-Mart and Southwest Airlines. "[We want to] be put into a different category, as a high-growth retailer of consumer financial services," he says, without a trace of doubt. "We'll even start losing the banking label."

WaMu's strategy focuses on building full customer relationships. It begins with offering what the company considers to be its core relationship products: home mortgages and free checking with no minimum balance requirement to avoid a monthly fee. Pretty soon, customers are happily hooked on WaMu's entire range of banking services. According to one account:

"Checking accounts and mortgages are two of the most important products for Main Street America. WaMu can offer a package of products at a better value than you could get by offering those products independently. When you team the convenience and the price value, it's a very powerful combination for the consumer."

WaMu's cross-selling, relationship-building formula is a powerful one. Five years after starting with free checking as their initial relationship, Washington Mutual's households on average maintain more than $23,000 in deposit, investment, and home and consumer loan balances.

WaMu's focus on customer relationships is a primary reason for the bank's success. But the company knows that to build strong customer relationships, it must also take good care of the employees who maintain those relationships. So WaMu has also created an exuberant corporate culture that motivates and supports the WaMulians. "I've never seen an organization that lives its culture the way this organization does," says Steve Rotella, WaMu's president and chief operating officer. Employee surveys show that "they view it as a special place and a place they want to work." All of those warm feelings translate into customer service, satisfaction, and value.

Will Washington Mutual's competitive marketing strategy of bringing value and convenience to middle-Americans make it the Wal-Mart of the banking industry? WaMu is certainly well on its way. "You can have a lucky streak for a few quarters, but you can't accomplish what they've done with just a lucky streak," says an analyst. "They have good people; they have scale; they are very focused on their customers. For WaMu, the best is still to come."[1]

Today's companies face their toughest competition ever. In previous chapters, we argued that to succeed in today's fiercely competitive marketplace, companies will have to move from a product-and-selling philosophy to a customer-and-marketing philosophy. John Chambers, CEO of Cisco Systems put it well: "Make your customer the center of your culture."

This chapter spells out in more detail how companies can go about outperforming competitors in order to win, keep, and grow customers. To win in today's marketplace, companies must become adept not just in *managing products*, but in *managing customer relationships* in the face of determined competition. Understanding customers is crucial, but it's not enough. Building profitable customer relationships and gaining **competitive advantage** requires delivering *more* value and satisfaction to target consumers than *competitors* do.

In this chapter, we examine *competitive marketing strategies*—how companies analyze their competitors and develop successful, value-based strategies for building and maintaining profitable customer relationships. The first step is **competitor analysis**, the process of identifying, assessing, and selecting key competitors. The second step is developing **competitive marketing strategies** that strongly position the company against competitors and give it the greatest possible competitive advantage.

Competitor Analysis

To plan effective marketing strategies, the company needs to find out all it can about its competitors. It must constantly compare its marketing strategies, products, prices, channels, and promotion with those of close competitors. In this way the company can find areas of poten-

---

Competitive advantage
An advantage over competitors gained by offering consumers greater value than competitors offer.

Competitor analysis
The process of identifying key competitors; assessing their objectives, strategies, strengths and weaknesses, and reaction patterns; and selecting which competitors to attack or avoid.

Competitive marketing strategies
Strategies that strongly position the company against competitors and that give the company the strongest possible strategic advantage.

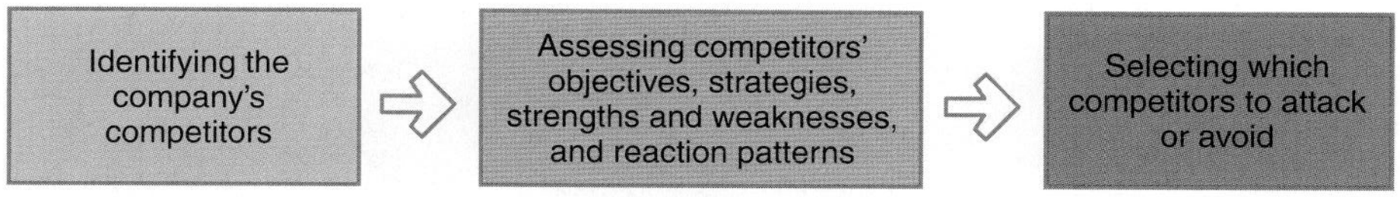

tial competitive advantage and disadvantage. As shown in Figure 18.1, competitor analysis involves first identifying and assessing competitors and then selecting which competitors to attack or avoid.

Identifying Competitors

Normally, identifying competitors would seem a simple task. At the narrowest level, a company can define its competitors as other companies offering similar products and services to the same customers at similar prices. Thus, Pepsi might view Coca-Cola as a major competitor, but not Budweiser or Ocean Spray. Bookseller Barnes & Noble might see Borders as a major competitor, but not Wal-Mart or Costco. Ritz-Carlton might see Four Seasons hotels as a major competitor, but not Holiday Inn Hotels, the Hampton Inn, or any of the thousands of bed-and-breakfasts that dot the nation.

But companies actually face a much wider range of competitors. The company might define competitors as all firms making the same product or class of products. Thus, Ritz-Carlton would see itself as competing against all other hotels. Even more broadly, competitors might include all companies making products that supply the same service. Here Ritz-Carlton would see itself competing not only against other hotels but also against anyone who supplies rooms for weary travelers. Finally, and still more broadly, competitors might include all companies that compete for the same consumer dollars. Here Ritz-Carlton would see itself competing with travel and leisure services, from cruises and summer homes to vacations abroad.

Companies must avoid "competitor myopia." A company is more likely to be "buried" by its latent competitors than its current ones. For example, it wasn't direct competitors that put an end to Western Union's telegram businesses after 161 years; it was cell phones and the Internet. And for decades, Kodak held a comfortable lead in the photographic film business. It saw only Fuji as its major competitor in this market. However, in recent years, Kodak's major new competition has not come from Fuji and other film producers, but from Sony, Canon, and other digital camera makers, and from a host of digital image developers and online image-sharing services.

Because of its myopic focus on film, Kodak was late to enter the digital imaging market. It paid a heavy price. With digital cameras now outselling film cameras, and with film sales plummeting 20 percent every year, Kodak has faced major sales and profit setbacks, massive layoffs, and a 74 percent drop in its stock over the past five years. Kodak is now changing its focus to digital imaging, but the transformation will be difficult. The company has to "figure out not just how to digital imaging, but how to convince consumers to buy its [digital] cameras and home printers but also how to become known as the most convenient and affordable way to process those images," says an industry analyst. "That means home and store printing as well as sending images over the Internet and cell phones."[2]

Companies can identify their competitors from the *industry* point of view. They might see themselves as being in the oil industry, the pharmaceutical industry, or the beverage industry. A company must understand the competitive patterns in its industry if it hopes to be an effective "player" in that industry. Companies can also identify competitors from a *market* point of view. Here they define competitors as companies that are trying to satisfy the same customer need or build relationships with the same customer group.

From an industry point of view, Pepsi might see its competition as Coca-Cola, Dr Pepper, 7UP, and other soft drink makers. From a market point of view, however, the customer really wants "thirst quenching." This need can be satisfied by bottled water, fruit juice, iced tea, or many other fluids. Similarly, Hallmark's Binney & Smith, maker of Crayola crayons, might define its competitors as other makers of crayons and children's drawing supplies. But from a market point of view, it would include all firms making recreational products for children.

In general, the market concept of competition opens the company's eyes to a broader set of actual and potential competitors. One approach is to profile the company's direct and indirect competitors by mapping the steps buyers take in obtaining and using the product. Figure 18.2

FIGURE 18.1
Steps in analyzing competitors

Identifying the company's competitors ⇨ Assessing competitors' objectives, strategies, strengths and weaknesses, and reaction patterns ⇨ Selecting which competitors to attack or avoid

FIGURE 18.2

Competitor map

Source: Based on
Jeffrey F. Rayport and
Bernard J. Jaworski,
e-Commerce (New York:
McGraw-Hill, 2001), p. 53.

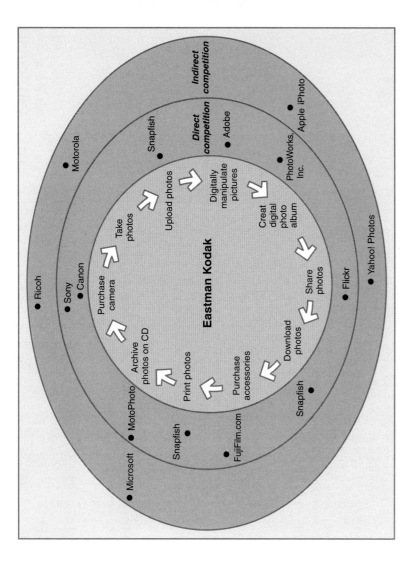

illustrates a *competitor map* of Eastman Kodak in the digital imaging business.[3] In the center is a list of consumer activities: buying a camera, taking photos, creating digital photo albums, printing photos, and others. The first outer ring lists Kodak's main competitors with respect to each consumer activity: Canon and Sony for buying a camera, HP's Snapfish for sharing and printing photos, and so on. The second outer ring lists indirect competitors—Apple, Motorola, Microsoft, and others—who may become direct competitors. This type of analysis highlights both the competitive opportunities and the challenges a company faces.

Assessing Competitors

Having identified the main competitors, marketing management now asks: What are competitors' objectives—what does each seek in the marketplace? What is each competitor's strategy? What are various competitor's strengths and weaknesses, and how will each react to actions the company might take?

Determining Competitors' Objectives

Each competitor has a mix of objectives. The company wants to know the relative importance that a competitor places on current profitability, market share growth, cash flow, technological leadership, service leadership, and other goals. Knowing a competitor's mix of objectives reveals whether the competitor is satisfied with its current situation and how it might react to different competitive actions. For example, a company that pursues low-cost leadership will react much more strongly to a competitor's cost-reducing manufacturing breakthrough than to the same competitor's advertising increase.

A company also must monitor its competitors' objectives for various segments. If the company finds that a competitor has discovered a new segment, this might be an opportunity. If it finds that competitors plan new moves into segments now served by the company, it will be forewarned and, hopefully, forearmed.

Identifying Competitors' Strategies

The more that one firm's strategy resembles another firm's strategy, the more the two firms compete. In most industries, the competitors can be sorted into groups that pursue different strategies. A **strategic group** is a group of firms in an industry following the same or a similar

Strategic group

A group of firms in an
industry following the same or
a similar strategy.

strategy in a given target market. For example, in the major appliance industry, GE and Whirlpool belong to the same strategic group. Each produces a full line of medium-price appliances supported by good service. In contrast, Sub-Zero and Viking belong to a different strategic group. They produce a narrower line of higher-quality appliances, offer a higher level of service, and charge a premium price.

Some important insights emerge from identifying strategic groups. For example, if a company enters one of the groups, the members of that group become its key competitors. Thus, if the company enters the first group, against GE and Whirlpool it can succeed only if it develops strategic advantages over these competitors.

Although competition is most intense within a strategic group, there is also rivalry among groups. First, some of the strategic groups may appeal to overlapping customer segments. For example, no matter what their strategy, all major appliance manufacturers will go after the apartment and homebuilders segment. Second, the customers may not see much difference in the offers of different groups—they may see little difference in quality between Whirlpool and KitchenAid. Finally, members of one strategic group might expand into new strategy segments. Thus, GE Monogram line of appliances competes in the premium quality, premium-price line with Viking and Sub-Zero.

The company needs to look at all of the dimensions that identify strategic groups within the industry. It must understand how each competitor delivers value to its customers. It needs to know each competitor's product quality, features, and mix; customer services; pricing policy; distribution coverage; sales force strategy; and advertising and sales promotion programs. And it must study the details of each competitor's R&D, manufacturing, purchasing, financial, and other strategies.

IMAGINE YOUR LIFE IN A VIKING KITCHEN.

VIKING
1-888-845-4641
vikingrange.com

■ Strategic groups: Viking belongs to the appliance industry strategic group offering a narrow line of higher-quality appliances supported by good service.

Assessing Competitors' Strengths and Weaknesses

Marketers need to assess each competitor's strengths and weaknesses carefully in order to answer the critical question: What *can* our competitors do? As a first step, companies can gather data on each competitor's goals, strategies, and performance over the past few years. Admittedly, some of this information will be hard to obtain. For example, business-to-business marketers find it hard to estimate competitors' market shares because they do not have the same syndicated data services that are available to consumer packaged-goods companies.

Companies normally learn about their competitors' strengths and weaknesses through secondary data, personal experience, and word of mouth. They can also conduct primary marketing research with customers, suppliers, and dealers. Or they can **benchmark** themselves against other firms, comparing the company's products and processes to those of competitors or leading firms in other industries to find ways to improve quality and performance. Benchmarking has become a powerful tool for increasing a company's competitiveness.

Estimating Competitors' Reactions

Next, the company wants to know: What *will* our competitors do? A competitor's objectives, strategies, and strengths and weaknesses go a long way toward explaining its likely actions. They also suggest its likely reactions to company moves such as price cuts, promotion

Benchmarking
The process of comparing the company's products and processes to those of competitors or leading firms in other industries to find ways to improve quality and performance.

increases, or new-product introductions. In addition, each competitor has a certain philosophy of doing business, a certain internal culture and guiding beliefs. Marketing managers need a deep understanding of a given competitor's mentality if they want to anticipate how the competitor will act or react.

Each competitor reacts differently. Some do not react quickly or strongly to a competitor's move. They may feel their customers are loyal; they may be slow in noticing the move; they may lack the funds to react. Some competitors react only to certain types of moves and not to others. Other competitors react swiftly and strongly to any action. Thus, Procter & Gamble does not let a new detergent come easily into the market. Many firms avoid direct competition with P&G and look for easier prey, knowing that P&G will react fiercely if challenged.

In some industries, competitors live in relative harmony; in others, they fight constantly. Knowing how major competitors react gives the company clues on how best to attack competitors or how best to defend the company's current positions.

Selecting Competitors to Attack and Avoid

A company has already largely selected its major competitors through prior decisions on customer targets, distribution channels, and marketing-mix strategy. Management now must decide which competitors to compete against most vigorously.

Strong or Weak Competitors

The company can focus on one of several classes of competitors. Most companies prefer to compete against *weak competitors*. This requires fewer resources and less time. But in the process, the firm may gain little. You could argue that the firm also should compete with *strong competitors* in order to sharpen its abilities. Moreover, even strong competitors have some weaknesses, and succeeding against them often provides greater returns.

A useful tool for assessing competitor strengths and weaknesses is **customer value analysis.** The aim of customer value analysis is to determine the benefits that target customers value and how customers rate the relative value of various competitors' offers. In conducting a customer value analysis, the company first identifies the major attributes that customers value and the importance customers place on these attributes. Next, it assesses the company's and competitors' performance on the valued attributes.

The key to gaining competitive advantage is to take each customer segment and examine how the company's offer compares to that of its major competitor. If the company's offer delivers greater value by exceeding the competitor's offer on all important attributes, the company can charge a higher price and earn higher profits, or it can charge the same price and gain more market share. But if the company is seen as performing at a lower level than its major competitor on some important attributes, it must invest in strengthening those attributes or finding other important attributes where it can build a lead on the competitor.

Close or Distant Competitors

Most companies will compete with *close competitors*—those that resemble them most—rather than *distant competitors*. Thus, Nike competes more against Adidas than against Timberland. And Target competes with Wal-Mart rather than against Neiman Marcus or Nordstrom.

At the same time, the company may want to avoid trying to "destroy," a close competitor. For example, in the late 1970s, Bausch & Lomb moved aggressively against other soft lens manufacturers with great success. However, this forced weak competitors to sell out to larger firms such as Johnson & Johnson. As a result, Bausch & Lomb now faces much larger competitors—and it

Customer value analysis
Analysis conducted to determine what benefits target customers value and how they rate the relative value of various competitors' offers.

■ After driving smaller competitors from the market, Bausch & Lomb faces larger, more resourceful ones, such as Johnson & Johnson's Vistakon division. With Vistakon's Acuvue lenses lending the way, J&J is now the top U.S. contact lens maker.

has suffered the consequences. Johnson & Johnson acquired Vistakon, a small nicher with only $20 million in annual sales. Backed by Johnson & Johnson's deep pockets, however, the small but nimble Vistakon developed and introduced its innovative Acuvue disposable lenses. With Vistakon leading the way, Johnson & Johnson is now the top U.S. contact lens maker with a 33 percent market share, and Bausch & Lomb lags in fourth place with a 13 percent share.[4] In this case, success in hurting a close rival brought in tougher competitors.

■ Good and bad competitors: Digital music download services such as Yahoo! Music Unlimited, Napster, and Rhapsody see Apple as a bad competitor. Music downloaded from their sites can't be played on the Apple's wildly popular iPod, and music from Apples' iTunes Music Store will play only on an iPod.

"Good" or "Bad" Competitors

A company really needs and benefits from competitors. The existence of competitors results in several strategic benefits. Competitors may help increase total demand. They may share the costs of market and product development and help to legitimize new technologies. They may serve less-attractive segments or lead to more product differentiation. Finally, they lower the antitrust risk and improve bargaining power versus labor or regulators. For example, by aggressively pricing its computer chips, $38 billion Intel could make things difficult for smaller rivals such as $6 billion AMD. However, even though AMD may be chipping away at its microprocessor market share, Intel may want to be careful about trying to knock AMD completely out. "If for no other reason than to keep the feds at bay," notes one analyst, "Intel needs AMD . . . and other rivals to stick around." Says another: "If AMD collapsed, the FTC would surely react."[5]

However, a company may not view all of its competitors as beneficial. An industry often contains "good competitors" and "bad competitors."[6] Good competitors play by the rules of the industry. Bad competitors, in contrast, break the rules. They try to buy share rather than earn it, take large risks, and play by their own rules. For example, Yahoo! Music Unlimited sees Napster, Rhapsody, AOL Music, Sony Connect, and most other digital music download services as good competitors. They share a common platform, so that music bought from any of these competitors can be played on almost any playback device. However, it sees Apple's iTunes Music Store as a bad competitor, one that plays by its own rules at the expense of the industry as a whole.

With the iPod, Apple created a closed system with mass appeal. iPods now account for an estimated 73 percent of the 30 million MP3 players currently in use in the United States. In 2003, when the iPod was the only game in town, Apple cut a deal with the Big Five record companies that locked up its device. The music companies wanted to sell songs on iTunes, but they were afraid of Internet piracy. So Apple promised to wrap their songs in its FairPlay software—the only copy-protection software that is iPod-compatible. Other digital music services such as Yahoo! Music Unlimited and Napster have since reached similar deals with the big record labels. But Apple refused to license FairPlay to them. So those companies turned to Microsoft for copy protection. That satisfied fearful music companies, but it means none of the songs sold by those services can be played on the wildly popular iPod. And music downloaded from iTunes will play only on an iPod, making it difficult for other MP3 players that support the Microsoft format to get a toehold. The situation has been a disaster for Apple's competitors. iTunes holds a commanding lead over its rivals, selling more than 75 percent of all digital music. It recently sold its billionth song.[7]

The implication is that "good" companies would like to shape an industry that consists of only well-behaved competitors. A company might be smart to support good competitors, aiming its attacks at bad competitors. Thus, Yahoo! Music Unlimited, Napster, and other digital music competitors will no doubt support one another in trying to break Apple's stranglehold on the market.

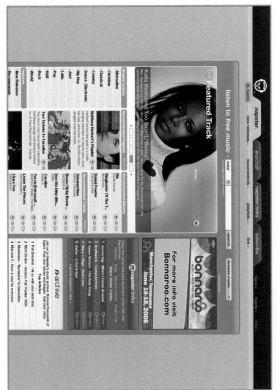

Designing a Competitive Intelligence System

We have described the main types of information that companies need about their competitors. This information must be collected, interpreted, distributed, and used. The cost in money and time of gathering competitive intelligence is high, and the company must design its competitive intelligence system in a cost-effective way.

The competitive intelligence system first identifies the vital types of competitive information and the best sources of this information. Then, the system continuously collects information from the field (sales force, channels, suppliers, market research firms, trade associations, Web sites) and from published data (government publications, speeches, articles). Next, the system checks the information for validity and reliability, interprets it, and organizes it in an appropriate way. Finally, it sends key information to relevant decision makers and responds to inquiries from managers about competitors.

With this system, company managers will receive timely information about competitors in the form of phone calls, e-mails, bulletins, newsletters, and reports. In addition, managers can connect with the system when they need an interpretation of a competitor's sudden move, or when they want to know a competitor's weaknesses and strengths, or when they need to know how a competitor will respond to a planned company move.

Smaller companies that cannot afford to set up formal competitive intelligence offices can assign specific executives to watch specific competitors. Thus, a manager who used to work for a competitor might follow that competitor closely; he or she would be the "in-house expert" on that competitor. Any manager needing to know the thinking of a given competitor could contact the assigned in-house expert.

▐ Competitive Strategies

Having identified and evaluated its major competitors, the company now must design broad competitive marketing strategies by which it can gain competitive advantage through superior customer value. But what broad marketing strategies might the company use? Which ones are best for a particular company, or for the company's different divisions and products?

Approaches to Marketing Strategy

No one strategy is best for all companies. Each company must determine what makes the most sense given its position in the industry and its objectives, opportunities, and resources. Even within a company, different strategies may be required for different businesses or products. Johnson & Johnson uses one marketing strategy for its leading brands in stable consumer markets—such as BAND-AIDs, Tylenol, or Johnson's baby products—and a different marketing strategy for its high-tech health care businesses and products—such as Monocryl surgical sutures or NeuFlex finger joint implants.

Companies also differ in how they approach the strategy-planning process. Many large firms develop formal competitive marketing strategies and implement them religiously. However, other companies develop strategies in a less formal and orderly fashion. Some companies, such as Harley-Davidson, Virgin Atlantic Airways, and BMW's MINI unit succeed by breaking many of the "rules" of marketing strategy. Such companies don't operate large marketing departments, conduct expensive marketing research, spell out elaborate competitive strategies, and spend huge sums on advertising. Instead, they sketch out strategies on the fly, stretch their limited resources, live close to their customers, and create more satisfying solutions to customer needs. They form buyer's clubs, use buzz marketing, and focus on winning customer loyalty. It seems that not all marketing must follow in the footsteps of marketing giants such as IBM and Procter & Gamble.

In fact, approaches to marketing strategy and practice often pass through three stages: entrepreneurial marketing, formulated marketing, and intrepreneurial marketing.[8]

- *Entrepreneurial marketing:* Most companies are started by individuals who live by their wits. They visualize an opportunity, construct flexible strategies on the backs of envelopes, and knock on every door to gain attention. Gary Hirshberg, who started the Stonyfield Farms yogurt company, will tell you that it's not about dumping millions of dollars into marketing and advertising. For Stonyfield, it's about company blogs, snappy packaging, and handing out yogurt from Segway transporters in Boston. And it's about telling the company story to the media. Hirshberg, known for wearing khakis and a vest, started mak-

Entrepreneurial marketing: Stonyfield Farm's idea of marketing strategy—"companies can do better with less advertising, less marketing research, more guerilla marketing, and more acting from the gut."

ing yogurt in Wilton, New Hampshire, with seven cows and a dream. His marketing strategy: building a strong connection with customers using guerilla marketing. His idea is that "companies can do better with less advertising, less marketing research, more guerilla marketing, and more acting from the gut." Using this strategy, Hirshberg has built Stonyfield Farm into a $250 million company.[9]

- *Formulated marketing:* As small companies achieve success, they inevitably move toward more-formulated marketing. They develop formal marketing strategies and adhere to them closely. With 85 percent of the company owned by Groupe Danone (which also owns Dannon yogurt), Stonyfield Farm has developed over the years a formal marketing department that carries out market research and plans strategy. Although Stonyfield may remain less formal in its strategy than the Procter & Gambles of the marketing world, it employs many of the tools used in these more-developed marketing companies.

- *Intrepreneurial marketing:* Many large and mature companies get stuck in formulated marketing. They pore over the latest Nielsen numbers, scan market research reports, and try to fine-tune their competitive strategies and programs. These companies sometimes lose the marketing creativity and passion that they had at the start. They now need to reestablish within their companies the entrepreneurial spirit and actions that made them successful in the first place. They need to encourage more initiative and "intrepreneurship" at the local level. They need to refresh their marketing strategies and try new approaches. Their brand and product managers need to get out of the office, start living with their customers, and visualize new and creative ways to add value to their customers' lives.

The bottom line is that there are many approaches to developing effective competitive marketing strategy. There will be a constant tension between the formulated side of marketing and the creative side. It is easier to learn the formulated side of marketing, which has occupied most of our attention in this book. But we have also seen how marketing creativity and passion in the strategies of many of the company's we've studied—whether small or large, new or mature—have helped to build and maintain success in the marketplace. With this in mind, we now look at broad competitive marketing strategies companies can use.

Basic Competitive Strategies

Almost three decades ago, Michael Porter suggested four basic competitive positioning strategies that companies can follow—three winning strategies and one losing one.[10] The three winning strategies include:

- *Overall cost leadership:* Here the company works hard to achieve the lowest production and distribution costs. Low costs let it price lower than its competitors and win a large market share. Texas Instruments, Dell, and Wal-Mart are leading practitioners of this strategy.

- *Differentiation:* Here the company concentrates on creating a highly differentiated product line and marketing program so that it comes across as the class leader in the industry. Most customers would prefer to own this brand if its price is not too high. IBM and Caterpillar follow this strategy in information technology and services and heavy construction equipment, respectively.

■ Focus: Small but profitable Hohner owns a stunning 85 percent of the harmonica market.

■ *Focus:* Here the company focuses its effort on serving a few market segments well rather than going after the whole market. For example, Ritz-Carlton focuses on the top 5 percent of corporate and leisure travelers. Glassmaker AFG Industries focuses on users of tempered and colored glass. It makes 70 percent of the glass for microwave oven doors and 75 percent of the glass for shower doors and patio tabletops. Similarly, Hohner owns a stunning 85 percent of the harmonica market.[11]

Companies that pursue a clear strategy—one of the above—will likely perform well. The firm that carries out that strategy best will make the most profits. But firms that do not pursue a clear strategy—*middle-of-the-roaders*—do the worst. Sears and Holiday Inn encountered difficult times because they did not stand out as the lowest in cost, highest in perceived value, or best in serving some market segment. Middle-of-the-roaders try to be good on all strategic counts, but end up being not very good at anything.

More recently, two marketing consultants, Michael Treacy and Fred Wiersema, offered new classifications of competitive marketing strategies.[12] They suggested that companies gain leadership positions by delivering superior value to their customers. Companies can pursue any of three strategies—called *value disciplines*—for delivering superior customer value. These are:

■ *Operational excellence:* The company provides superior value by leading its industry in price and convenience. It works to reduce costs and to create a lean and efficient value-delivery system. It serves customers who want reliable, good-quality products or services, but who want them cheaply and easily. Examples include Wal-Mart, Washington Mutual, Southwest Airlines, and Dell.

■ *Customer intimacy:* The company provides superior value by precisely segmenting its markets and tailoring its products or services to match exactly the needs of targeted customers. It specializes in satisfying unique customer needs through a close relationship with and intimate knowledge of the customer. It builds detailed customer databases for segmenting and targeting, and it empowers its marketing people to respond quickly to customer needs. Customer-intimate companies serve customers who are willing to pay a premium to get precisely what they want. They will do almost anything to build long-term customer loyalty and to capture customer lifetime value. Examples include Nordstrom, Ritz-Carlton, Lexus, American Express, and British Airways (see Real Marketing 18.1).

■ *Product leadership:* The company provides superior value by offering a continuous stream of leading-edge products or services. It aims to make its own and competing products obsolete. Product leaders are open to new ideas, relentlessly pursue new solutions, and work to get new products to market quickly. They serve customers who want state-of-the-art products and services, regardless of the costs in terms of price or inconvenience. Examples include Nokia and Microsoft.

Some companies successfully pursue more than one value discipline at the same time. For example, FedEx excels at both operational excellence and customer intimacy. However, such companies are rare—few firms can be the best at more than one of these disciplines. By trying to be *good at all* of the value disciplines, a company usually ends up being *best at none.*

Treacy and Wiersema found that leading companies focus on and excel at a single value discipline, while meeting industry standards on the other two. Such companies design their entire value delivery network to single-mindedly support the chosen discipline. For example,

18.1

Some companies go to extremes to coddle big spenders. From department stores like Nordstrom, to carmakers like Lexus and BMW, to hotels like Ritz-Carlton and Four Seasons, such companies give their well-heeled customers exactly what they need—and even more.

For example, concierge services are no longer the sole province of five-star hotels and fancy credit cards. They are starting to show up at airlines, retailers, and even electronic-goods makers. Sony Electronics, for instance, offers a service for its wealthiest customers, called Cierge, that provides a free personal shopper and early access to new gadgets, as well as "white-glove" help with the installation. (Translation: They will send someone over to set up the new gear.)

And then there's British Airways' "At Your Service" program—available to a hand-picked few of the airline's gold-level elite customers. There's almost nothing that the service won't do for members—tracking down hard-to-get Wimbledon tickets, for example, or running errands around town, sitting in a member's home to wait for the plumber or cable guy, or even planning your wedding, right down to the cake.

But when it comes to stalking the well-to-do, perhaps nowhere is the competition greater than in the credit-card industry. To rise above the credit-card clutter and to attract high-end card holders, the major credit-card companies have created a new top tier of superpremium cards—Visa's Signature card, MasterCard's World card, American Express's super-elite Centurion card. Affluent customers are extremely profitable. While premium cards represent only 1.5 percent of the consumer credit cards issued by Visa, MasterCard, and American Express, they account for 20 percent of the spending. And well-to-do cardholders tend to default a lot less, too.

The World MasterCard program targets what it calls the "mass affluent" and reaches 15 million wealthy households. Visa's Signature card zeros in on "new affluent" households, those with incomes exceeding $125,000. Its seven million cardholders account for 3 percent of Visa's consumer credit cards but 18 percent of Visa sales. Both cards feature a pack of special privileges. For its Signature card, Visa advertises, "The good life isn't only in your reach—it's in your wallet." In addition to the basics, such as no preset spending limit and 24-hour concierge services, Visa promises "upgrades, perks, and discounts" at major airlines, restaurants, and hotels, and special treatment at partners like the Ritz-Carlton, men's fashion designer Ermenegildo Zegna, watchmaker Audemars Piguet.

But when it comes to premium cards, the American Express Centurion card is the "elite of the elite" for luxury card carriers. This mysterious, much-coveted black credit card is issued by invitation only, to customers who *spend* more than $150,000 a year on other AmEx cards and meet other not-so-clear requirements. Then, the select few who do receive the card pay a $2,500 annual fee just for the privilege of carrying it.

But the Centurion card comes dripping with perks and prestige. The elusive plastic, with its elegant matte finish, is coveted by big spenders. "A black card is plastic bling-bling," says an industry observer, "a way for celebrities, athletes, and major business people to express their status."

A real T-shirt-and-jeans kind of guy, Peter H. Shankman certainly doesn't look like a high roller, but American Express knows better. After he was snubbed by salesmen at a Giorgio

---

Targeting affluent customers: Visa's Signature card zeros in on the "new affluent." It offers no preset spending limit, 24-hour concierge services, and loads of "upgrades, perks, and discounts . . . it's not just everywhere you want to be. It's everything you ever wanted."

Armani boutique on Fifth Avenue in New York recently, the 31-year-old publicist saw "an unbelievable attitude reversal" at the cash register when he whipped out his black AmEx Centurion Card. In June, a RadioShack cashier refused the card, thinking it was a fake. "Trust me," I said. 'Run the card,' " recalls the chief executive of Geek Factory, a public-relations and marketing firm. "I could buy a Learjet with this thing."

An exaggeration, perhaps. But AmEx's little black card is decidedly the "it" card for big spenders. Some would-be customers go to absurd lengths to get what they see as a must-have status symbol. Hopefuls have written poems to plead their cases. Others say they'll pay the fee but swear not to use the card—they want it just for show. "Every week I get phone calls or letters, often from prominent people, asking me for the card," says AmEx's head of consumer cards, Alfred F. Kelly Jr. Who, he won't say. In fact, AmEx deliberately builds an air of mystery around the sleek card, keeping hush-hush such details as the number of cards in circulation. Analysts say AmEx earns back many times what it spends on perks for black-card customers in both marketing buzz and fees.

(continues)

(continued)

Basic services on the Centurion card include a personal travel counselor and concierge, available 24/7. Beyond that, almost anything goes. Feel like shopping at Bergdorf Goodman or Saks Fifth Avenue at midnight? No problem. Traveling abroad in first class? Take a pal—the extra ticket is free. The royal treatment often requires elaborate planning. One AmEx concierge arranged a bachelor party for 25, which involved a four-day trip that included 11 penthouse suites, travel by private jet, and a meet-and-greet with an owner of the Sacramento Kings basketball team. The tab was more than $300,000.

How did Shankman earn his card? All the travel and entertainment charges he racks up hosting his clients prompted AmEx to send it to him. It arrived in December, along with a 43-page manual. Recently, Shankman sought reservations for Spice Market, an often-overbooked restaurant in Manhattan, to impress a friend. He called his concierge. "Half an hour later it was done," says Shankman. Membership does have its privileges.

When American Express seeks new Centurion cardholders, it does so discreetly. Last year, when it wanted to expand the elite list in Europe without attracting the ineligible, it mailed invitations to the top 1 percent of its platinum card holders. The mailing contained a card embedded in a glass paperweight with an invitation to meet personally with American Express's European president.

So, how many people actually have a Centurion card? "About the same number of people who can afford a Mercedes Maybach," says Desiree Fish, a spokeswoman for American Express, referring to a luxury car that can list for more than $300,000. The best guess is that only about 5,000 people worldwide have a Centurion card in their back pocket.

Sources: American Express example adapted from Mara Der Hovanesian, "This Black Card Gives You Carte Blanche," *Business Week*, August 9, 2004, p. 54. Quotes and other information from David Carr, "No Name, but Plenty of Bling-Bling for Show," *New York Times*, September 13, 2004, p. C11; Eleena de Lisser, "How to Get an Airline to Wait for Your Plumber—In Battle for Biggest Spenders, British Airways, Sony Rolls Out Hotel-Style 'Concierge' Service," *Wall Street Journal*, July 2, 2002, p. D1; James Tenser, "Cards Play Their Luxury Hand Right," *Advertising Age*, September 13, 2004, pp. S13–S14; Frederick H. Lowe, "Cards for the Rich: They're Different, Indeed," *Credit Card Management*, February 2005, pp. 18–22; Eric Dash, "New Spots for the Credit Card Companies Show Fierce Competition for the High-End Consumer," *New York Times*, May 11, 2005, p. C8; "The 10 Best DM Campaigns," *Campaign*, December 16, 2005, p. 38; and www.visa.com and www.mastercard.com, December 2006.

Wal-Mart knows that customer intimacy and product leadership are important. Compared with other discounters, it offers very good customer service and an excellent product assortment. Still, it purposely offers less customer service and less product depth than do Nordstrom or Williams-Sonoma, which pursue customer intimacy. Instead, Wal-Mart focuses obsessively on operational excellence—on reducing costs and streamlining its order-to-delivery process in order to make it convenient for customers to buy just the right products at the lowest prices.

By the same token, Ritz-Carlton Hotels wants to be efficient and to employ the latest technologies. But what really sets the luxury hotel chain apart is its customer intimacy. Ritz-Carlton creates custom-designed experiences to coddle its customers:

Check into any Ritz-Carlton hotel around the world, and you'll be amazed at how well the hotel's employees anticipate your slightest need. Without ever asking, they seem to know that you want a nonsmoking room with a king-size bed, a nonallergenic pillow, and breakfast with decaffeinated coffee in your room. How does Ritz-Carlton work this magic? At the heart of the system is a huge customer database, which contains information gathered through the observations of hotel employees. Each day, hotel staffers—from those at the front desk to those in maintenance and housekeeping—discreetly record the unique habits, likes, and dislikes of each guest on small "guest preference pads." These observations are then transferred to a corporatewide "guest preference database." Every morning, a "guest historian" at each hotel reviews the files of all new arrivals who have previously stayed at a Ritz-Carlton and prepares a list of suggested extra touches that might delight each guest. Guests have responded strongly to such personalized service. Since inaugurating the guest-history system, Ritz-Carlton has boosted guest retention by 23 percent. An amazing 95 percent of departing guests report that their stay has been a truly memorable experience.

Classifying competitive strategies as value disciplines is appealing. It defines marketing strategy in terms of the single-minded pursuit of delivering superior value to customers. Each value discipline defines a specific way to build lasting customer relationships.

FIGURE 18.3
Hypothetical market structure

Market leader	Market challengers	Market followers	Market nichers
40%	30%	20%	10%

Market leader
The firm in an industry with the largest market share.

Market challenger
A runner-up firm that is fighting hard to increase its market share in an industry.

Market follower
A runner-up firm that wants to hold its share in an industry without rocking the boat.

Market nicher
A firm that serves small segments that the other firms in an industry overlook or ignore.

Competitive Positions

Firms competing in a given target market, at any point in time, differ in their objectives and resources. Some firms are large, others small. Some have many resources, others are strapped for funds. Some are mature and established, others new and fresh. Some strive for rapid market share growth, others for long-term profits. And the firms occupy different competitive positions in the target market.

We now examine competitive strategies based on the roles firms play in the target market—leader, challenger, follower, or nicher. Suppose that an industry contains the firms shown in Figure 18.3. Forty percent of the market is in the hands of the **market leader**, the firm with the largest market share. Another 30 percent is in the hands of **market challengers**, runner-up firms that are fighting hard to increase their market share. Another 20 percent is in the hands of **market followers**, other runner-up firms that want to hold their share without rocking the boat. The remaining 10 percent is in the hands of **market nichers**, firms that serve small segments not being pursued by other firms.

Table 18.1 shows specific marketing strategies that are available to market leaders, challengers, followers, and nichers.[13] Remember, however, that these classifications often do not apply to a whole company, but only to its position in a specific industry. Large companies such as GE, Microsoft, Procter & Gamble, or Disney might be leaders in some markets and nichers in others. For example, Procter & Gamble leads in many segments, such as laundry detergents and shampoo. But it challenges Unilever in the hand soaps and Kimberly-Clark in facial tissues. Such companies often use different strategies for different business units or products, depending on the competitive situations of each.

Market Leader Strategies

Most industries contain an acknowledged market leader. The leader has the largest market share and usually leads the other firms in price changes, new-product introductions, distribution coverage, and promotion spending. The leader may or may not be admired or respected, but other firms concede its dominance. Competitors focus on the leader as a company to challenge, imitate, or avoid. Some of the best-known market leaders are Wal-Mart (retailing), Microsoft (computer software), IBM (information technology services and equipment), Caterpillar (earth-moving equipment), Anheuser-Busch (beer), McDonald's (fast food), Nike (athletic footwear), and Google (Internet search services).

A leader's life is not easy. It must maintain a constant watch. Other firms keep challenging its strengths or trying to take advantage of its weaknesses. The market leader can easily miss a turn in the market and plunge into second or third place. A product innovation may come along and hurt the leader (as when Apple developed the iPod and took the market lead from Sony's Walkman portable audio devices). The leader might grow arrogant or complacent and misjudge the competition (as when Sears lost its lead to Wal-Mart). Or the leader might look old-fashioned against new and peppier rivals (as when Levi's lost serious ground to more current or stylish brands such as Gap, Tommy Hilfiger, DKNY, or Guess).

To remain number one, leading firms can take any of three actions. First, they can find ways to expand total demand. Second, they can protect their current market share through

TABLE 18.1 Strategies for Market Leaders, Challengers, Followers, and Nichers

Market Leader Strategies	Market Challenger Strategies	Market Follower Strategies	Market Nicher Strategies
Expand total market	Full frontal attack	Follow closely	By customer, market, quality-price, service
Protect market share	Indirect attack	Follow at a distance	Multiple niching
Expand market share			

good defensive and offensive actions. Third, they can try to expand their market share further, even if market size remains constant.

Expanding the Total Demand

The leading firm normally gains the most when the total market expands. If Americans purchase more hybrid automobiles, Toyota stands to gain the most because it sells the nation's largest share of hybrids. If Toyota can convince more Americans that hybrid cars are both more economical and more environmentally friendly, it will benefit more than its competitors.

Market leaders can expand the market by developing new users, new uses, and more usage of its products. They usually can find *new users* in many places. For example, Revlon might find new perfume users in its current markets by convincing women who do not use perfume to try it. It might find users in new demographic segments, such as by producing fragrances for men. Or it might expand into new geographic segments, perhaps by selling its fragrances in other countries.

Marketers can expand markets by discovering and promoting *new uses* for the product. For example, Arm & Hammer baking soda, whose sales had flattened after 125 years, discovered that consumers were using baking soda as a refrigerator deodorizer. It launched a heavy advertising and publicity campaign focusing on this use and persuaded consumers in half of America's homes to place an open box of baking soda in their refrigerators and to replace it every few months. Today, its Web site (www.armandhammer.com) features new uses— "Solutions for my home, my family, my body"—ranging from removing residue left behind by hair-styling products and sweetening garbage disposals, laundry hampers, refrigerators, and trash cans to creating a home spa in your bathroom.

■ Creating more usage:
Campbell urges people to eat its soups and other products more often by running ads containing new recipes. It even offers online video clips of guest chefs cooking any of 27 recipes on Campbell's Kitchen TV.

Finally, market leaders can encourage *more usage* by convincing people to use the product more often or to use more per occasion. For example, Campbell urges people to eat soup and other Campbell products more often by running ads containing new recipes. It also offers a toll-free hot line (1-888-MM-MM-GOOD), staffed by live "recipe representatives" who offer recipes to last-minute cooks at a loss for meal ideas. And the Campbell's Kitchen section of the company's Web site (www.campbellsoup.com) lets visitors search for or exchange recipes, set up their own personal recipe box, sign up for a daily or weekly Meal Mail program, and even watch online video clips of guest chefs cooking any of 27 recipes on Campbell's Kitchen TV.

Protecting Market Share

While trying to expand total market size, the leading firm also must protect its current business against competitors' attacks. Dell must also constantly guard against Hewlett-Packard; Caterpillar against Komatsu; Wal-Mart against Target; and McDonald's against Burger King.

What can the market leader do to protect its position? First, it must prevent or fix weaknesses that provide opportunities for competitors. It must always fulfill its value promise. Its prices must remain consistent with the value that customers see in the brand. It must work tirelessly to keep strong relationships with valued customers. The leader should "plug holes" so that competitors do not jump in.

But the best defense is a good offense, and the best response is *continuous innovation*. The leader refuses to be content with the way things are and leads the industry in new products, customer services, distribution effectiveness, and cost cutting. It keeps increasing its competitive effectiveness and value to customers. And when attacked by challengers, the market leader reacts decisively. For example, consider Frito-Lay's reaction to a challenge by a large competitor:

In the early 1990s, Anheuser-Busch attacked Frito-Lay's leadership in salty snacks. The big brewer had noticed that Frito-Lay, a division of PepsiCo, had been distracted by its expansion into cookies and crackers. So Anheuser-Busch began to slip its new Eagle brand salty snacks onto the shelves of its traditional beer outlets—supermarkets and liquor stores—where Frito-Lay was comparatively weak. Frito-Lay reacted ruthlessly. First, to get itself into fighting shape, the salty-snacks leader cut the number of offerings in its product line by half—no more cookies, no more crackers—and invested in product quality, which had slipped below Eagle's. Then, Frito-Lay concentrated its energy, not to mention its 10,000 route drivers, on America's salty-snack aisles. Frito-Lay's strong brands and huge size gave it a clear economic advantage over Anheuser-Busch in the salty-snack business. Armed with a superior offering—better chips, better service, and lower prices—Frito-Lay began to put pressure on one of Eagle's strongholds: potato chips in supermarkets. It sent its salespeople streaming into supermarkets; some even stayed at the largest supermarkets full time, continually restocking the Frito-Lay products. When the dust had settled in 1996, Anheuser-Busch had shuttered its Eagle snack business. In the end, Frito-Lay even bought four of Eagle's plants—at very attractive prices.[14]

Expanding Market Share

Market leaders also can grow by increasing their market shares further. In many markets, small market share increases mean very large sales increases. For example, in the U.S. digital camera market, a 1 percent increase in market share is worth $68 million; in carbonated soft drinks, $660 million![15]

Studies have shown that, on average, profitability rises with increasing market share. Because of these findings, many companies have sought expanded market shares to improve profitability. GE, for example, declared that it wants to be at least number one or two in each of its markets or else get out. GE shed its computer, air-conditioning, small appliances, and television businesses because it could not achieve top-dog position in these industries.

However, some studies have found that many industries contain one or a few highly profitable large firms, several profitable and more focused firms, and a large number of medium-sized firms with poorer profit performance. It appears that profitability increases as a business gains share relative to competitors in its *served market*. For example, Lexus holds only a small share of the total car market, but it earns high profits because it is the leading brand in the luxury-performance car segment. And it has achieved this high share in its served market because it does other things right, such as producing high-quality products, creating good service experiences, and building close customer relationships.

Companies must not think, however, that gaining increased market share will automatically improve profitability. Much depends on their strategy for gaining increased share. There are many high-share companies with low profitability and many low-share companies with high profitability. The cost of buying higher market share may far exceed the returns. Higher shares tend to produce higher profits only when unit costs fall with increased market share, or when the company offers a superior-quality product and charges a premium price that more than covers the cost of offering higher quality.

Market Challenger Strategies

Firms that are second, third, or lower in an industry are sometimes quite large, such as Colgate, Ford, Lowes, Avis, and Hewlett-Packard. These runner-up firms can adopt one of two competitive strategies: They can challenge the leader and other competitors in an aggressive bid for more market share (market challengers). Or they can play along with competitors and not rock the boat (market followers).

A market challenger must first define which competitors to challenge and its strategic objective. The challenger can attack the market leader, a high-risk but potentially high-gain strategy. Its goal might be to take over market leadership. Or the challenger's objective may simply be to wrest more market share. Although it might seem that the market leader has the most going for it, challengers often have what some strategists call a "second-mover advantage." The challenger observes what has made the leader successful and improves upon it. Consider Lowe's, the number-two home-improvement retailer:[16]

Home Depot invented the home-improvement superstore, and it's still putting up good numbers. However, after observing Home Depot's success, No. 2 Lowe's, with its brighter stores, wider aisles, and arguably more helpful salespeople, has positioned itself as the friendly alternative to Big Bad Orange. For Lowe's the advantage has been substantial—and profitable. Although Lowe's still earns barely half of Home Depot's revenues, its sales grew at a 62 percent greater rate last year. And over the past ten years, Lowe's has earned average annual returns of 23.5 percent, versus Home Depot's 14.9 percent. Lowe's isn't the only No. 2 outperforming its industry leaders. Target has been thumping Wal-Mart, PepsiCo is outfizzing Coca-Cola, and Advanced Micro Devices is chipping away at Intel. In fact, *Fortune* magazine analyzed the stock returns of major U.S. companies in ten industries and found that the industry leaders by revenue returned a mere 2 percent over the past year, versus 21 percent for their second bananas. The gap in earnings growth—8 percent versus 24 percent—was almost as great.

Alternatively, the challenger can avoid the leader and instead challenge firms its own size, or smaller local and regional firms. These smaller firms may be underfinanced and not serving their customers well. Several of the major beer companies grew to their present size not by challenging large competitors, but by gobbling up small local or regional competitors. If the company goes after a small local company, its objective may be to put that company out

■ Second mover advantage: After observing Home Depot's success, No. 2 Lowe's, with its brighter stores, wider aisles, and arguably more helpful salespeople, has positioned itself as the friendly alternative to Big Bad Orange.

of business. The important point remains: The challenger must choose its opponents carefully and have a clearly defined and attainable objective.

How can the market challenger best attack the chosen competitor and achieve its strategic objectives? It may launch a full *frontal attack*, matching the competitor's product, advertising, price, and distribution efforts. It attacks the competitor's strengths rather than its weaknesses. The outcome depends on who has the greater strength and endurance. If the market challenger has fewer resources than the competitor, a frontal attack makes little sense. For example, the runner-up razor manufacturer in Brazil attacked Gillette, the market leader. The attacker was asked if it offered the consumer a better razor. "No," was the reply. "A lower price?" "No." "A clever advertising campaign?" "No." "Better allowances to the trade?" "No." "Then how do you expect to take share away from Gillette?" "Sheer determination" was the reply. Needless to say, the offensive failed. Even great size and strength may not be enough to challenge a firmly entrenched, resourceful competitor successfully.

Rather than challenging head-on, the challenger can make an *indirect attack* on the competitor's weaknesses or on gaps in the competitor's market coverage. For example, Netflix found a foothold against giant Blockbuster in the DVD rental market by renting to the consumers through the mail and offering no late fees. Southwest Airlines challenged American and other large carriers by serving the overlooked short-haul, no-frills commuter segment at smaller, out-of-the-way airports. Such indirect challenges make good sense when the company has fewer resources than the competitor.

Market Follower Strategies

Not all runner-up companies want to challenge the market leader. Challenges are never taken lightly by the leader. If the challenger's lure is lower prices, improved service, or additional product features, the leader can quickly match these to defuse the attack. The leader probably has more staying power in an all-out battle for customers. For example, a few years ago, when Kmart launched its renewed low-price "blue-light special" campaign, directly challenging Wal-Mart's everyday low prices, it started a price war that it couldn't win. Wal-Mart had little trouble fending off Kmart's challenge, leaving Kmart worse off for the attempt. Thus, many firms prefer to follow rather than challenge the leader.

Similarly, after years of challenging Procter & Gamble unsuccessfully in the U.S. laundry detergent market, Unilever recently decided to throw in the towel and become a follower instead. P&G captures 55 and 75 percent shares of the liquid and powder detergent markets, respectively, versus Unilever's 17 and 7 percent shares. P&G has outmuscled competitors on every front. For example, it batters competitors with a relentless stream of new and improved products. Recently, P&G spent more than $50 million introducing one new product alone, Tide with Downy. In response to the onslaught, Unilever has cut prices and promotion on its detergents to focus on profit rather than market share.[17]

A follower can gain many advantages. The market leader often bears the huge expenses of developing new products and markets, expanding distribution, and educating the market. By contrast, as with challengers, the market follower can learn from the leader's experience. It can copy or improve on the leader's products and programs, usually with much less investment. Although the follower will probably not overtake the leader, it often can be as profitable.

Following is not the same as being passive or a carbon copy of the leader. A market follower must know how to hold current customers and win a fair share of new ones. It must find the right balance between following closely enough to win customers from the market leader but following at enough of a distance to avoid retaliation. Each follower tries to bring distinctive advantages to its target market—location, services, financing. The follower is often a major target of attack by challengers. Therefore, the market follower must keep its manufacturing costs and prices low or its product quality and services high. It must also enter new markets as they open up.

Market Nicher Strategies

Almost every industry includes firms that specialize in serving market niches. Instead of pursuing the whole market, or even large segments, these firms target subsegments. Nichers are often smaller firms with limited resources. But smaller divisions of larger firms also may pursue niching strategies. Firms with low shares of the total market can be highly successful and profitable through smart niching. For example, Veterinary Pet Insurance is tiny compared with the insurance industry giants, but it captures a profitable 82 percent share of all health insurance policies for our furry—or feathery—friends (see Real Marketing 18.2).

Real Marketing

Niching: Health Insurance for Our Furry—or Feathery—Friends

18.2 Health insurance for pets? MetLife, Prudential, Northwestern Mutual, and most other large insurance companies haven't paid much attention to it. But that leaves plenty of room for more-focused nichers, for whom pet health insurance has become a lucrative business. The largest of the small competitors is Veterinary Pet Insurance (VPI). VPI's mission is to "make the miracles of veterinary medicine affordable to all pet owners."

VPI was founded in 1980 by veterinarian Jack Stephens. He never intended to leave his practice, but his life took a dramatic turn when he visited a local grocery store and was identified by a client's daughter as "the man who killed Buffy." Stephens had euthanized the family dog two weeks earlier. He immediately began researching the possibility of creating medical pet insurance. "There is nothing more frustrating for a veterinarian than knowing that you can heal a sick patient, but the owner lacks the financial resources and instructs you to put the pet down," says Stephens. "I wanted to change that."

Pet insurance is a still-small but fast-growing segment of the insurance business. Insiders think the industry offers huge potential. Currently, there are some 74 million dogs and 91 million cats in the United States—more than 60 percent of all U.S. households own one or the other or both. Another 4.6 million U.S. households own one or more of about 300 species of birds; two million more own pet rabbits. A recent survey showed that 94 percent of pet owners attribute human personality traits to their pets. According to a VPI spokesperson, more than two-thirds have included their pets in holiday celebrations and one-third characterize their pet as a child. Americans now spend a whopping $28.5 billion a year on their pets, including $9.4 billion on pet health care.

Unlike in Britain and Sweden, where almost half of all pet owners carry pet health insurance, relatively few pet owners in the United States now carry such coverage. However, a recent study of pet owners found that nearly 75 percent are willing to go into debt to pay for veterinary care for their furry—or feathery—companions. And for many pet medical procedures, they'd have to! If not diagnosed quickly, even a mundane ear infection in a dog can result in $1,000 worth of medical treatment. Ten days of dialysis treatment can reach $12,000 and cancer treatment as much as $40,000. All of this adds up to a lot of potential growth for pet health insurers.

VPI's plans cover more than 6,400 pet medical problems and conditions. The insurance helps pay for office calls, prescriptions, treatments, lab fees, x-rays, surgery, and hospitalization. Like its handful of competitors, VPI issues health insurance policies for dogs and cats. Unlike its competitors, VPI recently expanded its coverage to a menagerie of exotic pets as well. Among other critters, the Avian and Exotic Pet Plan covers birds, rabbits, ferrets, rats, guinea pigs, snakes (except extra large ones) and other reptiles, iguanas, turtles, hedgehogs, and potbellied pigs. "There's such a vast array of pets", says a VPI executive, "and people love them. We have to respect that."

How's VPI doing in its niche? It's growing like a newborn puppy. VPI is by far the largest of the handful of companies that offer pet insurance, providing more than 60 percent of all U.S. pet insurance policies. Since its inception, VPI has issued more than 1 million policies, and it now serves more than 369,000 policyholders. Sales have grown rapidly, exceeding $110 million in policy premiums last year. That might not amount to much for the likes of MetLife, Prudential, or

FAMILY *Redefined.*

Northwestern Mutual, which rack up tens of billions of dollars in yearly revenues. But it's profitable business for nichers like VPI. And there's room to grow. Less than 5 percent of pet owners currently buy pet insurance.

"Pet health insurance is no longer deemed so outlandish in a world where acupuncture for cats, hospice of dogs, and Prozac for ferrets are part of a veterinarian's routine," says one analyst. Such insurance is a real godsend for VPI's policyholders. Just ask Joe and Paula Sena, whose cocker spaniel, Elvis, is receiving radiation treatments for cancer. "He is not like our kids—he is our kid," says Ms. Sena. "He is a kid in a dog's body." VPI is making Elvis's treatments possible by picking up a lion's share of the costs. "Cost often becomes the deciding factor in the level of care owners can provide," says VPI founder Stephens. VPI will always "strive to make the miracles of modern medicine affordable."

Nichers: Market nicher VPI is growing faster than a new-born puppy. Its mission is to "make the miracles of veterinary medicine affordable to all pet owners."

Sources: Kevin Graman, "Some Pay Premium for Healthy Pets," *Knight Ridder Business News,* April 17, 2006, p. 1; Yilu Zhao, "Break a Leg, Fluffy, If You Have Insurance," *New York Times,* June 30, 2002, p. 9.11; Liz Pulliam Weston, "Should You Buy Pet Insurance?" *MSN Money,* accessed at www.moneycentral.msn.com, May 1, 2004; Damon Darlin, "Vet Bills and the Priceless Pet: What's a Practical Owner to Do?" *New York Times,* May 13, 2006, p. C1; and information accessed at www.petinsurance.com, December 2006.

Why is niching profitable? The main reason is that the market nicher ends up knowing the target customer group so well that it meets their needs better than other firms that casually sell to that niche. As a result, the nicher can charge a substantial markup over costs because of the added value. Whereas the mass marketer achieves high volume, the nicher achieves high margins.

Nichers try to find one or more market niches that are safe and profitable. An ideal market niche is big enough to be profitable and has growth potential. It is one that the firm can serve effectively. Perhaps most importantly, the niche is of little interest to major competitors. And the firm can build the skills and customer goodwill to defend itself against a major competitor as the niche grows and becomes more attractive. Here's an example of a profitable nicher:

Logitech has become a $1.5 billion global success story by focusing on human interface devices—computer mice, game controllers, keyboards, PC video cameras, and others. It makes every variation of computer mouse imaginable. Over the years, Logitech has flooded the world with more than 500 million computer mice of all varieties, mice for left- and right-handed people, wireless mice, travel mice, mini mice, mice shaped like real mice for children, and 3-D mice that let the user appear to move behind screen objects. Breeding mice has been so successful that Logitech dominates the world mouse market, with giant Microsoft as its runner-up. Niching has been very good for Logitech. Its sales and profits have more than doubled in just the past six years.[18]

The key idea in niching is specialization. A market nicher can specialize along any of several markets, customer, product, or marketing mix lines. For example, it can specialize in serving one type of *end user*, as when a law firm specializes in the criminal, civil, or business law markets. The nicher can specialize in serving a given *customer-size group*. Many nichers specialize in serving small and mid-size customers who are neglected by the majors.

Some nichers focus on one or a few *specific customers*, selling their entire output to a single company, such as Wal-Mart or General Motors. Still other nichers specialize by *geographic market*, selling only in a certain locality, region, or area of the world. *Quality-price nichers* operate at the low or high end of the market. For example, Hewlett-Packard specializes in the high-quality, high-price end of the hand-calculator market. Finally, *service nichers* offer services not available from other firms. For example, LendingTree provides online lending and realty services, connecting home buyers and sellers with national networks of mortgage lenders and realtors who compete for the customers' business. "When lenders compete," it proclaims, "you win."

Niching carries some major risks. For example, the market niche may dry up, or it might grow to the point that it attracts larger competitors. That is why many companies practice *multiple niching*. By developing two or more niches, a company increases its chances for survival. Even some large firms prefer a multiple niche strategy to serving the total market. For example, Alberto Culver is a $3.5 billion company that has used a multiple niching strategy to grow profitably without incurring the wrath of a market leader. The company, known mainly for its Alberto VO5 hair products, has focused its marketing muscle on acquiring a stable of smaller niche brands. It niches in hair, skin, and personal care products (Alberto VO5, St. Ives, Motions, Just for Me, Pro-Line, TRESemme, and Consort men's hair products), beauty supplies retailing (Sally Beauty Supply stores), seasonings and sweeteners (Molly McButter, Mrs. Dash, SugarTwin, Baker's Joy), and home products (static-cling fighter Static Guard). Most of its brands are number one in their niches. Alberto Culver's CEO explains the company's philosophy this

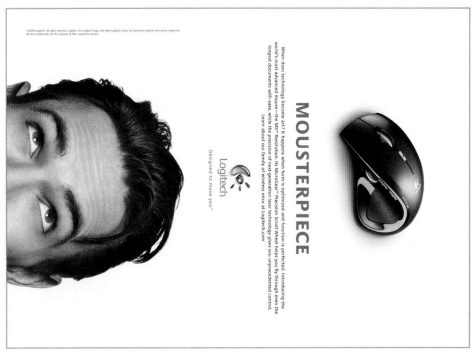

Designed to move you™

Logitech

MOUSTERPIECE

When does technology become art? It happens when form is optimized and function is perfected. Introducing the world's most advanced mouse—the MX™ Revolution. Its MicroGear™ Precision Scroll Wheel helps you fly through even the longest documents with ease, while the precision of next-generation laser technology gives you unprecedented control.

Learn about our family of wireless mice at Logitech.com

■ Profitable niching: Breeding mice has been so successful for Logitech that it dominates the world mouse market, with giant Microsoft as its runner-up.

way: "We know who we are and, perhaps more importantly, we know who we are not. We know that if we try to out-Procter Procter, we will fall flat on our face."[19]

▌ Balancing Customer and Competitor Orientations

Whether a company is a market leader, challenger, follower, or nicher, it must watch its competitors closely and find the competitive marketing strategy that positions it most effectively. And it must continually adapt its strategies to the fast-changing competitive environment. This question now arises: Can the company spend *too* much time and energy tracking competitors, damaging its customer orientation? The answer is yes! A company can become so competitor centered that it loses its even more important focus on maintaining profitable customer relationships.

A **competitor-centered company** is one that spends most of its time tracking competitors' moves and market shares and trying to find strategies to counter them. This approach has some pluses and minuses. On the positive side, the company develops a fighter orientation, watches for weaknesses in its own position, and searches out competitors' weaknesses. On the negative side, the company becomes too reactive. Rather than carrying out its own customer relationship strategy, it bases its own moves on competitors' moves. As a result, it may end up simply matching or extending industry practices rather than seeking innovative new ways to create more value for customers.

A **customer-centered company**, by contrast, focuses more on customer developments in designing its strategies. Clearly, the customer-centered company is in a better position to identify new opportunities and set long-run strategies that make sense. By watching customer needs evolve, it can decide what customer groups and what emerging needs are the most important to serve. Then it can concentrate its resources on delivering superior value to target customers. In practice, today's companies must be **market-centered companies**, watching both their customers and their competitors. But they must not let competitor watching blind them to customer focusing.

Figure 18.4 shows that companies have moved through four orientations over the years. In the first stage, they were product oriented, paying little attention to either customers or competitors. In the second stage, they became customer oriented and started to pay attention to customers. In the third stage, when they started to pay attention to competitors, they became competitor oriented. Today, companies need to be market oriented, paying balanced attention to both customers and competitors. Rather than simply watching competitors and trying to beat them on current ways of doing business, they need to watch customers and find innovative ways to build profitable customer relationships by delivering more value than competitors do. As noted previously, marketing begins with a good understanding of consumers and the marketplace.

Competitor-centered company
A company whose moves are mainly based on competitors' actions and reactions.

Customer-centered company
A company that focuses on customer developments in designing its marketing strategies and on delivering superior value to its target customers.

Market-centered company
A company that pays balanced attention to both customers and competitors in designing its marketing strategies.

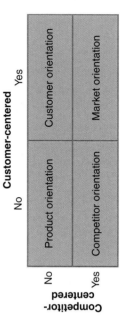

	Customer-centered	
	No	**Yes**
No	Product orientation	Customer orientation
Yes	Competitor orientation	Market orientation

(Competitor-centered — rows labeled No/Yes)

FIGURE 18.4
Evolving company orientations

Reviewing the Concepts

Today's companies face their toughest competition ever. Understanding customers is an important first step in developing strong customer relationships, but it's not enough. To gain competitive advantage, companies must use this understanding to design market offers that deliver more value than the offers of *competitors* seeking to win over the same customers. This chapter examines how firms analyze their competitors and design effective competitive marketing strategies.

1. Discuss the need to understand competitors as well as customers through competitor analysis.

In order to prepare an effective marketing strategy, a company must consider its competitors as well as its customers. Building profitable customer relationships requires satisfying target consumer needs *better than competitors do*. A company must continuously analyze competitors and develop *competitive marketing strategies* that position it effectively against competitors and give it the strongest possible *competitive advantage*.

Competitor analysis first involves identifying the company's major competitors, using both an industry-based and a market-based analysis. The company then gathers information on competitors' objectives, strategies, strengths and weaknesses, and reaction patterns. With this information in hand, it can select competitors to attack or avoid. Competitive intelligence must be collected, interpreted, and distributed continuously. Company marketing managers should be able to obtain full and reliable information about any competitor affecting their decisions.

2. Explain the fundamentals of competitive marketing strategies based on creating value for customers.

Which *competitive marketing strategy* makes the most sense depends on the company's industry and on whether it is a market leader, challenger, follower, or nicher. A *market leader* must mount strategies to expand the total market, protect market share, and expand market share. A *market challenger* is a firm that tries aggressively to expand its market share by attacking the leader, other runner-up companies, or smaller firms in the industry. The challenger can select from a variety of direct or indirect attack strategies.

A *market follower* is a runner-up firm that chooses not to rock the boat, usually from fear that it stands to lose more than it might gain. But the follower is not without a strategy and seeks to use its particular skills to gain market growth. Some followers enjoy a higher rate of return than the leaders in their industry. A *market nicher* is a smaller firm that is unlikely to attract the attention of larger firms. Market nichers often become specialists in some end use, customer size, specific customer, geographic area, or service.

3. Illustrate the need for balancing customer and competitor orientations in becoming a truly market-centered organization.

A competitive orientation is important in today's markets, but companies should not overdo their focus on competitors. Companies are more likely to be hurt by emerging consumer needs and new competitors than by existing competitors. *Market-centered companies* that balance consumer and competitor considerations are practicing a true market orientation.

Reviewing the Key Terms

Discussing the Concepts

1. Discount retailer Target is attempting to identify its competitors but wants to avoid competitor myopia. Name some of its potential competitors from both an industry and market point of view.

2. Why is it important to understand competitor's objectives?

3. What is the difference between entrepreneurial, formulated, and intrepreneurial marketing? What are the advantages and disadvantages of each?

4. Apply Treacy and Wiersema's value disciplines to online search engines. Identify a company that competes according to each discipline.

5. What are the advantages and disadvantages of a market-nicher competitive strategy?

6. Why is it important for a company to maintain a balance between customer and competitor orientations?

Applying the Concepts

1. Form a small group and conduct a customer-value analysis for five local restaurants. Who are the strong and weak competitors? For the strong competitors, what are their vulnerabilities?

2. Dell is the leader in the notebook market, with HP threatening its market share. What are some potential market-leader strategies for Dell?

3. Tiffany & Co. is a high-profile firm in the luxury retail jewelry market. Visit www.tiffany.com/about/Timeline.aspx and review the Tiffany historical timeline for important events. What is Tiffany & Co.'s dominant marketing strategy? Explain.

Focus on Technology

In 1923, Arthur Charles Nielsen introduced consumer marketers to many innovative research methods and techniques. Today, ACNielsen provides market intelligence for most of the world's leading manufacturers and retailers. Its sister company, Nielsen Media Research, is the global leader in television audience measurement and provides the well-known television "Nielsen Ratings." Visit ACNielsen at www.acnielsen.com to find its retail measurement services. The retail measurement service provides consolidated register scanner data from most retail channels, including supermarkets, drugstores, mass merchandisers, and warehouse clubs. In addition to the register data, Nielsen also uses in-store observation to gather data on in-store promotions. Clients can download reports on a daily basis that track sales volume, selling price, observed promotion, and other data points. The information is provided on a company's own

brands as well as competitive brands and is easily examined by brand, category, store, or market.

1. How can a marketer use this to analyze its competitors?

2. How might a market leader such as Procter & Gamble react to increased sales of a store's private brand?

3. What might be a disadvantage of using Nielsen data?

Focus on Ethics

Competitive intelligence offers strong advantages in the area of product development. Knowing the competitor's progress on products, processes, and technology is highly beneficial in competitive markets. A trade secret, information that creates value for a company because it remains a secret, often creates strong competitor curiosity. Companies sometimes go to great lengths to uncover such secrets. They develop creative techniques to access information, sometimes pushing legal and ethical boundaries. One widely used technique is observation. Observational methods include aerial photography of manufacturing plants, dumpster diving to analyze discarded products and materials, and plant tours.

One documented case involves a visit in the 1970s by Steve Jobs and other Apple executives to a Xerox research center. During the tour, Apple executives asked many probing questions about a new technology they observed. After leaving with some proprietary information, Apple subsequently hired some of the Xerox employees to further develop the technology at Apple. Apple's behavior would not be considered illegal.

According to The Uniform Trade Secrets Act (UTSA) of 1985, which attempts to offer some protection for trade secrets, legal protection does not hold if a company did not take reasonable attempts to protect its secrets.

1. Give some examples of the information that might be gleaned from aerial photography of a competitor's plant.

2. Google the Uniform Trade Secrets Act and scan its contents. What else do you observe about this legislation?

3. The Apple incident may not have been illegal, but was it unethical?

See: William Fitzpatrick, "Uncovering Trade Secrets: The Legal and Ethical Conundrum of Creative Competitive Intelligence," *S.A.M. Advanced Management Journal*, Summer 2003, p. 4; and Jim Dalrymple, "Apple Loses Rumor-Site Appeal," *MacWorld*, August 2006, Vol. 23, Issue 8, p. 18.

Video Case   Nike

Nike's mission statement is "to bring inspiration and innovation to every athlete in the world." That's a substantial goal—one goal made even more sizable when you consider that Nike believes that "if you have a body, you're an athlete." Despite the lofty nature of the mission, Nike has made considerable strides in its effort to fulfill it. The Nike swoosh is so ubiquitous in today's market that it may be difficult to believe the symbol appeared just 35 years ago. Since that time, Nike has become the largest sports and fitness company in the world, and 97 percent of Americans recognize the swoosh.

The Nike brand succeeds by staying true to its core values and delivering consistently high-quality, cutting-edge products that appeal to the athlete in all of us, building strong relationships with customers based on real value. By making innovation the centerpiece of its product development and marketing strategy, the Nike brand has become the market

leader, reaching millions of consumers around the globe and raking in annual revenues totaling $15 billion.

After viewing the video featuring Nike, answer the following questions about creating competitive advantage.

1. In the broadest sense, who are Nike's generic competitors? Who are Nike's direct competitors? What competitive strategy does Nike employ?

2. What market leader strategies does Nike rely on to maintain its market position? Identify a competitor pursuing a niche in Nike's market. How do the actions of that competitor benefit Nike? How do they challenge Nike's market share and positioning?

3. How does Nike use partnerships with professional athletes and teams to strengthen its relationships with consumers?

Company Case   Bose: Competing by Being Truly Different

In April of 2006, Forrester Research announced the results of its semiannual survey ranking consumer electronics and personal computer companies on consumer trust. Based on a poll of more than 4,700 customers as to their opinions of 22 of the best-known consumer technology brands, the company drew this conclusion: "Americans' trust in consumer technology companies is eroding."

Why is consumer trust important? Forrester vice president Ted Schadler answered that question this way: "Trust is a powerful way to measure a brand's value and its ability to command a premium price or drive consumers into a higher-profit direct channel. A decline in trust causes brand erosion and price-driven purchase decisions, which in turn correlates with low market growth."

But despite the decline in trust for most technology companies, Forrester made another surprising finding. Consumer trust in the Bose Corporation was riding high. In fact, Bose far outscored all other companies in Forrester's survey. Not bad, considering that it was the first time the company had been included in the survey. Forrester pointed out that these results were no fluke, noting that Bose has 10 million regular users but more than 17 million consumers who aspire to use the brand (compared to 7 million for next-highest Apple).

These high levels of consumer trust result from philosophies that have guided Bose for more than 40 years. Most companies today focus heavily on building revenue, profits, and stock price. They try to outdo the competition by differentiating product lines with features and attributes that other companies do not have. Although Bose pays attention to such factors, its true differentiation derives from the company's unique corporate philosophy.

THE BOSE PHILOSOPHY

You can't understand Bose the company without taking a look at Bose the man. Amar Bose, the company's founder and still its CEO, has been in charge from the start. In the 1950s, Bose was working on his third degree at the Massachusetts Institute of Technology. He had a keen interest in research and studied various areas of electrical engineering. He also had a strong interest in music. When he purchased his first hi-fi system—a model that he believed had the best specifications—he was very disappointed in the system's ability to reproduce realistic sound. So he set out to find his own solution. Thus began a stream of research that would ultimately lead to the founding of the Bose Corporation in 1964.

From those early days, Amar Bose worked around certain core principles that have guided the philosophy of the company. In conducting his first research on speakers and sound, he did something that has since been repeated time and time again at Bose. He ignored existing technologies and started entirely from scratch. Bose president Bob Maresca provides insights on the company today that date back to Amar Bose's original philosophy: "We are not in it strictly to make money," he says. "Dr. Bose is extremely eclectic in his research interests. The business is almost a secondary consideration."

For this reason, Amar Bose plows all of the privately held company's profits back into research. This practice reflects his avid love of research and his belief that it will produce the highest-quality products. But he also does this because he can. Bose has been quoted many times saying, "if I worked for another company, I would have been fired a long time ago," pointing to the fact that publicly held companies have long lists of constraints that don't apply to his privately held company. For this reason, Bose has always vowed that he will never take the company public. "Going public for me would have been the equivalent of losing the company. My real interest is research—that's the excitement—and I wouldn't have been able to do long-term projects with Wall Street breathing down my neck."

This commitment to research and development has led to the high level of trust that Bose customers have for the company. It also explains their almost cultlike loyalty. Customers know that the company cares more about their best interests—about making the best product—than about maximizing profits. But for a company not driven by the bottom line, Bose does just fine. Although performance figures are tightly held, analysts estimate that between 2004 and 2006, the company's revenues increased more than 38 percent, from $1.3 billion to over $1.8 billion. According to market information firm NPD Group, Bose leads the market in home speakers with a 12.6 percent share. Not only were home speakers the company's original product line, but they remain one of its largest and most profitable endeavors.

GROUNDBREAKING PRODUCTS

The company that started so humbly now has a breadth of product lines beyond its core home audio line. Additional lines target a variety of applications that have captured Amar Bose's creative attention over the years, including military, automotive, homebuilding/remodeling, aviation, test equipment, and professional and commercial sound systems. The following are just a few the products that illustrate the innovative breakthroughs produced by the company.

Speakers Bose's first product, introduced 1965, was a speaker. Expecting to sell $1 million worth of speakers that first year, Bose made 60 but sold only 40. The original Bose speaker evolved into the 901 Direct/Reflecting speaker system launched in 1968. The speaker was so technologically advanced that the company still sells it today.

The system was designed around the concept that live sound reaches the human ear via direct as well as reflected channels (off walls, ceilings, and other objects). The configuration of the speakers was completely unorthodox. They were shaped like an eighth of a sphere and mounted facing into a room's corner. The speakers had no woofers or tweeters and were very small compared to the high-end speakers of the day. The design came much closer to the essence and emotional impact of live music than anything else on the market and won immediate industry acclaim.

However, Bose had a hard time convincing customers of the merits of these innovative speakers. At a time when woofers, tweeters, and size were everything, the 901 series initially flopped. In 1968, a retail salesman explained to Amar Bose why the speakers weren't selling:

"Look, I love your speaker but I cannot sell it because it makes me lose all my credibility as a salesman. I can't explain to anyone why the 901 doesn't have any woofers or tweeters. A man came in and saw the small size, and he started looking in the drawers for the speaker cabinets. I walked over to him, and he said, 'Where are you hiding the woofer?' I said to him, 'There is no woofer.' So he said, 'You're a liar,' and he walked out."

(case continues)

(case continued)

Bose eventually worked through the challenges of communicating the virtues of the 901 series to customers through innovative display and demonstration tactics. The product became so successful that Amar Bose now credits the 901 series for building the company.

The list of major speaker innovations at Bose is a long one. In 1975, the company introduced concertlike sound in the bookshelf-size 301 Direct/Reflecting speaker system. Fourteen years of research lead to the 1984 development of acoustic waveguide speaker technology, a technology found today in the award-winning Wave radio, Wave music system, and Acoustic Wave music system. In 1986, the company again changed conventional thinking about the relationship between speaker size and sound. The Acoustimass system enabled palm-size speakers to produce audio quality equivalent to that of high-end systems many times their size. The technological basis of the Acoustimass system is still in use in Bose products today.

Headphones Bob Maresca recalls that, "Bose invested tens of millions of dollars over 19 years developing headset technology before making a profit. Now, headsets are a major part of the business." Initially, Bose focused on noise reduction technologies to make headphones for pilots that would block out the high level of noise interference from planes. Bose headphones combined both passive and active noise reduction methods. Passive methods involve physically blocking out noise with sound-deadening insulation. Active methods are much more complex, involving circuitry that samples ambient noise and then cancels it out by creating sound waves opposite to the "noise" waves. Bose quickly discovered that airline passengers could benefit as much as pilots from its headphone technology. Today, Bose sells its QuietComfort and Triport headphone lines for use in a variety of consumer applications.

Automotive Suspensions Another major innovation at Bose has yet to be introduced. The company has been conducting research since 1980 on a product outside of its known areas of expertise: automotive suspensions. Amar Bose's interest in suspensions dates back to the 1950s when he bought both a Citroen DS-19 C and a Pontiac Bonneville, each riding on unconventional air suspension systems. Since that time, he's been obsessed with the engineering challenge of achieving good cornering capabilities without sacrificing a smooth ride. The Bose Corporation is now on the verge of introducing a suspension that it believes will accomplish this feat better than any system to date.

The basics of the system include an electromagnetic motor installed at each wheel. Based on inputs from road-sensing monitors, the motor can retract and extend almost instantaneously. If there is a bump in the road, the suspension reacts by "jumping" over it. If there is a pothole, the suspension allows the wheel to extend downward, but then retracts it quickly enough that the pothole is not felt. In addition to these comfort-producing capabilities, the wheel

motors are strong enough to prevent the car from rolling and pitching during an aggressive maneuver.

The suspension system has been designed so that it can be bolted right onto the chassis of current production cars, thus minimizing both time and expense for manufacturers. Initially, the cost of the system will put it in the class of luxury automobiles. Currently, Bose is demonstrating the system only to a handful of companies, with the intention of partnering with one manufacturer before rolling it out to others. Eventually, Bose anticipates that wider adoption and higher volume will bring the price down to the point where the suspension could be found in all but the least expensive cars.

At an age when most people have long ago retired, 76-year-old Amar Bose works every day, either at the company's headquarters in Framingham, Massachusetts, or at his home in nearby Wayland. "He's got more energy than an 18-year-old," says Maresca. "Every one of the naysayers only strengthens his resolve." This work ethic illustrates the passion of the man who has shaped one of today's most innovative and yet most trusted companies. His philosophies have produced Bose's long list of groundbreaking innovations. Even now, as the company prepares to enter the world of automotive suspensions, it continues to achieve success by following another one of Dr. Bose's basic philosophies: "The potential size of the market? We really have no idea. We just know that we have a technology that's so different and so much better that many people will want it."

Questions for Discussion

1. Based on the business philosophies of Amar Bose, how do you think the Bose Corporation goes about analyzing its competition?

2. Which of the text's three approaches to marketing strategy best describes Bose's approach?

3. Using the Michael Porter and Treacy and Wiersema frameworks presented in the text, which basic competitive marketing strategies does Bose pursue?

4. What is Bose's competitive position in its industry? Do its marketing strategies match this position?

5. In your opinion, is Bose a customer-centric company?

6. What do you think will happen when Amar Bose leaves the company?

Sources: Brian Dumaine, "Amar Bose," *Fortune Small Business,* September 1, 2004, accessed online at www.money.cnn.com/magazines/fsb/; Olga Kharif, "Selling Sound: Bose Knows," *Business Week Online,* May 15, 2006, accessed online at www.businessweek.com; Mark Jewell, "Bose Tries to Shake Up Auto Industry," *Associated Press,* November 27, 2005; "Bose Introduces New QuietComfort 3 Acoustic Noise-Cancelling Headphones," *Business Wire,* June 8, 2006; "Forrester Research Reveals the Most Trusted Consumer Technology Brands," press release accessed online at www.forrester.com; also see, "About Bose," accessed online at www.bose.com, June, 2006.

19

The Global Marketplace

Previewing the Concepts

You've now learned the fundamentals of how companies develop competitive marketing strategies to create customer value and to build lasting customer relationships. In this chapter, we extend these fundamentals to global marketing. We've visited global topics in each previous chapter—it's difficult to find an area of marketing that doesn't contain at least some international issues. Here, however, we'll focus on special considerations that companies face when they market their brands globally. Advances in communication, transportation, and other technologies have made the world a much smaller place. Today, almost every firm, large or small, faces international marketing issues. In this chapter, we will examine six major decisions marketers make in going global.

Before moving into the chapter, let's look first at one of today's hottest global brands—the National Basketball Association. Yes, the NBA! Just like most other large businesses, the once quintessentially American NBA is now seeking growth opportunities beyond its own national boarders. And when it comes to global marketing, the NBA is jamming down one slam dunk after another. Read on and see how.

What could be more American than basketball? The sport was invented in the United States, and each year tens of millions of excited fans crowd their local gyms or huddle around their television sets to cheer on their favorite rec league, high school, college, or pro teams. But basketball is rapidly becoming a worldwide craze. Although soccer remains the number-one sport in most of the world, basketball—that's right, basketball—is a solid number two.

Lots of companies are going global these days, but few organizations are doing it better than the National Basketball Association (NBA). During the past two decades, under the leadership of Commissioner David Stern, the NBA has become a truly global marketing enterprise. Nowhere was this more apparent than in last year's NBA finals, which were televised to more than 205 countries in 39 languages, from Armenian, Belorussian, Lithuanian, and Norwegian to Arabic, Cantonese, and Macedonian. In fact, as much as 20 percent of the NBA's $900 million in annual TV revenues now comes from international markers. More than half the hits on NBA.com, which now features nine country sites in seven languages, originate outside the United States. And 25 percent of all NBA-licensed basketballs, jerseys, backboards, and other merchandise is sold internationally.

The NBA has become a powerful worldwide brand. A *Fortune* article summarizes:

Deployed by global sponsors such as Coca-Cola, Reebok, and McDonald's, well-paid [NBA superstars] hawk soda, sneakers, burgers, and basketball to legions of mostly young fans [worldwide]. That they are recognized from Santiago to Seoul says a lot about the soaring worldwide appeal of hoops—and about the marketing juggernaut known as the NBA. After watching their favorite stars swoop in and slam-dunk on their local TV stations, fans of the league now cheer the *mate* in Latin America, the *trofsla* in Iceland, and the *smash* in France.

Like many other businesses, the NBA's primary motive for going global is growth. The league now sells out most of its games, and domestic licensing revenues have flattened in recent years. "Globalization is a huge opportunity for us," says Commissioner Stern, who recently called basketball a "universal language about to bloom on a global basis." Stern sees huge worldwide potential for the NBA. "If you watch over the years what percentage of profit Coca-Cola makes from overseas, or how Wal-Mart and others are expanding in Europe and China, you'll understand," he says.

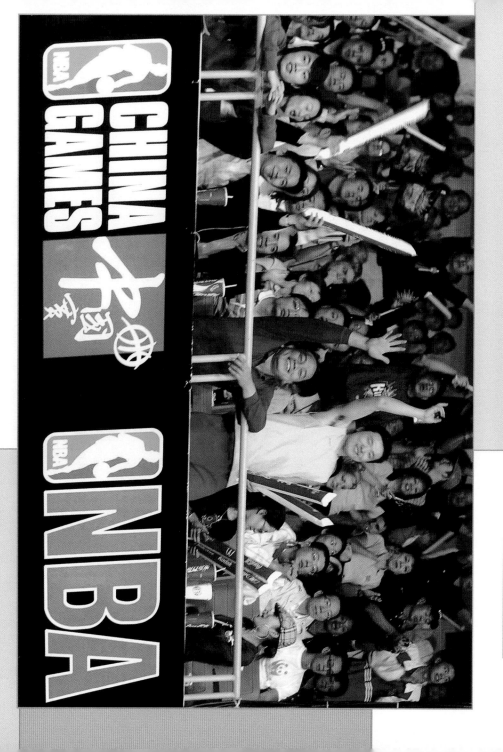

Most experts expect slam dunk after slam dunk for the NBA as it extends its international reach. Adding to the league's global appeal is the growing presence of foreign-born players. Some 82 players (more than 20 percent of all NBA pros) hail from outside the United States, and almost every NBA team boasts at least one non-U.S. star. To name just a few, the list includes Yao Ming from China, Dirk Nowitzki from Germany, Tony Kukoc from Croatia, Pau Gasol from Spain, Manu Ginobili from Argentina, and Peja Stojakovic from Serbia. Such players attract large followings in their home countries. German tennis star Boris Becker credits Dirk Nowitzki for the increase in NBA ratings in his homeland. "Thanks to Dirk, basketball has become very, very popular" in Germany.

And many American basketball superstars have developed their own hoards of fanatical fans abroad. For example, according to one report, "Two years ago in Beijing, police were forced to cancel Michael Jordan's first public appearance in the city on his Asian tour after fans trampled flower beds, blocked sidewalks, damaged a car, and ripped down several billboards while angling so they could get a good view of the retired NBA legend. When police pulled the plug on the event at Dongdan Sports Center before Jordan even arrived, the fans became angry, many shouting Jordan's name in unison. Some had [waited] outside the stadium for hours, waving Jordan posters."

Objectives

After studying this chapter, you should be able to

1. discuss how the international trade system and the economic, political-legal, and cultural environments affect a company's international marketing decisions

2. describe three key approaches to entering international markets

3. explain how companies adapt their marketing mixes for international markets

4. identify the three major forms of international marketing organization

Stern is not content to just sit back and let international things happen. He's investing heavily to build the NBA's popularity and business abroad. The NBA now has nine offices in major world cities, including Paris, Tokyo, and Hong Kong. Its international staff numbers more than 100 people, nearly double the number who ran the entire league just two decades ago. The NBA even has an Hispanic marketing office in Miami, where eight people focus on Latin America and the Hispanic media in other parts of the world.

For Heidi Ueberroth, head of the NBA's international business operations, the U.S. summer off-season is the start of the international marketing season. During the 2006 summer off-season, the league sponsored 132 international events, with 198 players representing all 30 NBA teams appear-ing in 87 cities on five continents. It also started what might be its most ambitious global expansion effort eve—called NBA Europe Live. This program took off-season training for four teams—the Suns, Clippers, Sixers, and Spurs—to European cities. Each team was chosen because it has major foreign-born players with international appeal.

NBA Europe Live does much more than simply showcase team training. Each team competes in exhibition games against host teams from Euroleague basketball. According to Stern, "At the culmina-tion of the exhibition games, there will be a four-team tournament featuring the champion of the Euroleague and the runner-up of Euroleague basketball going against two NBA teams." Given that the bulk of the NBA's international fan base is in Europe, NBA Europe Live makes good business sense. Some even see NBA Europe Live as a significant step toward landing an NBA team overseas. "I think somewhere down the road, a European Division or European Conference is certainly a possibility," says an analyst.

If things look good for the NBA in Europe, the league is positively drooling over its prospects in China, with its more than 1.3 billion people and 300 million basketball fans. According to Ueberroth, basketball in China "is the number one sport for youth 30 and under." It helps that in recent years China's three biggest stars, Yao Ming, Wang ZhiZhi, and Mengke Bateer, left the Chinese Basketball Association to take a shot at NBA careers. The NBA is reaping the benefits. NBA.com's Mandarin lan-guage Web site accounts for 20 percent of all the league's Internet traffic, and 20,000 Chinese retail outlets now sell NBA merchandise. "We have seven games a week on 24 different [Chinese] stations," Ueberroth states, underscoring the NBA's current heavy focus on China. The league even deploys its Jam Van, complete with hoops and interactive NBA video games, to tour China's provinces.

Despite the dazzling prospects, many challenges remain. "Winning the loyalty of [more than a bil-lion Chinese won't be a *kou qui*—a slam dunk," suggests one international sports analyst, "but Stern is, well, bullish. . . . Can Ping-Pong survive an NBA invasion? Stay tuned [and see how the ball bounces].[1]

In the past, U.S. companies paid little attention to international trade. If they could pick up some extra sales through exporting, that was fine. But the big market was at home, and it teemed with opportunities. The home market was also much safer. Managers did not need to learn other languages, deal with strange and changing currencies, face political and legal uncertainties, or adapt their products to different customer needs and expectations. Today, however, the situation is much different. Organizations of all kinds, from Coca-Cola, IBM, and Yahoo! to MTV and even the NBA, are going global.

Global Marketing Today

The world is shrinking rapidly with the advent of faster communication, transportation, and financial flows. Products developed in one country—Gucci purses, Sony electronics, McDonald's hamburgers, Japanese sushi, German BMWs—are finding enthusiastic accep-tance in other countries. We would not be surprised to hear about a German businessman wearing an Italian suit meeting an English friend at a Japanese restaurant who later returns home to drink Russian vodka and watch *American Idol* on TV.

■ McDonald's and many other American companies have made the world their market.

Global firm

A firm that, by operating in more than one country, gains R&D, production, marketing, and financial advantages in its costs and reputation that are not available to purely domestic competitors.

International trade is booming. Since 1969, the number of multinational corporations in the world has grown from 7,000 to more than 70,000. Some of these multinationals are true giants. In fact, of the largest 100 "economies" in the world, only 53 are countries. The remaining 47 are multinational corporations. Exxon Mobil, the world's largest company, has annual revenues greater than the gross domestic product of all but the world's 21 largest-GDP countries.[2]

Since 2003, total world trade has been growing at 6 to 10 percent annually, while global gross domestic product has grown at only 2.5 to 4 percent annually. World trade of products and services was valued at over 12.4 trillion dollars in 2005, which accounted for about 28 percent of gross domestic product worldwide. This trade growth is most visible in developing countries, such as China, which saw their share in world exports rise sharply to 24 percent in 2005.[3]

Many U.S. companies have long been successful at international marketing: Coca-Cola, GE, IBM, Colgate, Caterpillar, Ford, Boeing, McDonald's, and dozens of other American firms have made the world their market. And in the United States, names such as Sony, Toyota, BP, IKEA, Nestlé, Nokia, and Prudential have become household words. Other products and services that appear to be American are in fact produced or owned by foreign companies: Bantam books, Baskin-Robbins ice cream, GE and RCA televisions, Carnation milk, Pillsbury food products, Universal Studios, and Motel 6, to name just a few. Michelin, the oh-so-French tire manufacturer, now does 36 percent of its business in North America; Johnson & Johnson, the maker of quintessentially all-American products such as Band-Aids and Johnson's Baby Shampoo, does 44 percent of its business abroad.[4]

But while global trade is growing, global competition is intensifying. Foreign firms are expanding aggressively into new international markets, and home markets are no longer as rich in opportunity. Few industries are now safe from foreign competition. If companies delay taking steps toward internationalizing,

they risk being shut out of growing markets in Western and Eastern Europe, China and the Pacific Rim, Russia, and elsewhere. Firms that stay at home to play it safe not only might lose their chances to enter other markets but also risk losing their home markets. Domestic companies that never thought about foreign competitors suddenly find these competitors in their own backyards.

Ironically, although the need for companies to go abroad is greater today than in the past, so are the risks. Companies that go global may face highly unstable governments and currencies, restrictive government policies and regulations, and high trade barriers. Corruption is also an increasing problem—officials in several countries often award business not to the best bidder but to the highest briber.

A **global firm** is one that, by operating in more than one country, gains marketing, production, R&D, and financial advantages that are not available to purely domestic competitors. The global company sees the world as one market. It minimizes the importance of national boundaries and develops "transnational" brands. It raises capital, obtains materials and components, and manufactures and markets its goods wherever it can do the best job. For example, Otis Elevator gets its elevators' door systems from France, small geared parts from Spain, electronics from Germany, and special motor drives from Japan. It uses the United States only for systems integration. "Borders are so 20th century," says one global marketing expert. "Transnationals take 'stateless' to the next level."[5]

This does not mean that small and medium-size firms must operate in a dozen countries to succeed. These firms can practice global niching. But the world is becoming smaller, and every company operating in a global industry—whether large or small—must assess and establish its place in world markets.

The rapid move toward globalization means that all companies will have to answer some basic questions: What market position should we try to establish in our country, in our economic region, and globally? Who will our global competitors be, and what are their strategies

Looking at the global marketing environment

Deciding whether to go global

Deciding which markets to enter

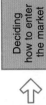
Deciding how to enter the market

Deciding on the global marketing program

Deciding on the global marketing organization

FIGURE 19.1 Major international marketing decisions

and resources? Where should we produce or source our products? What strategic alliances should we form with other firms around the world?

As shown in Figure 19.1, a company faces six major decisions in international marketing. We will discuss each decision in detail in this chapter.

Looking at the Global Marketing Environment

Before deciding whether to operate internationally, a company must understand the international marketing environment. That environment has changed a great deal in the past two decades, creating both new opportunities and new problems.

The International Trade System

U.S. companies looking abroad must start by understanding the international *trade system.* When selling to another country, a firm may face restrictions on trade between nations. Foreign governments may charge *tariffs,* taxes on certain imported products designed to raise revenue or to protect domestic firms. Or they may set *quotas,* limits on the amount of foreign imports that they will accept in certain product categories. The purpose of a quota is to conserve on foreign exchange and to protect local industry and employment. American firms may also face *exchange controls,* which limit the amount of foreign exchange and the exchange rate against other currencies.

The company also may face *nontariff trade barriers,* such as biases against U.S. company bids or restrictive product standards that go against American product features:

For years, Japan has successfully devised nontariff trade barriers to shut foreign products out of its domestic markets. One of the cleverest ways the Japanese have found to keep foreign manufacturers out is to plead "uniqueness." Japanese skin is different, the government argues, so foreign cosmetics companies must test their products in Japan before selling there. The Japanese say their stomachs are small and have room for only the *mikan,* the local tangerine, so imports of U.S. oranges are limited. Now the Japanese have come up with what may be the flakiest argument yet: Their snow is different, so ski equipment should be too.[6]

At the same time, certain forces *help* trade between nations. Examples include the General Agreement on Tariffs and Trade (GATT) and various regional free trade agreements.

The World Trade Organization and GATT

The General Agreement on Tariffs and Trade (GATT) is a 59-year-old treaty designed to promote world trade by reducing tariffs and other international trade barriers. Since the treaty's inception in 1947, member nations (currently numbering 149) have met in eight rounds of GATT negotiations to reassess trade barriers and set new rules for international trade. The first seven rounds of negotiations reduced the average worldwide tariffs on manufactured goods from 45 percent to just 5 percent.[7]

The most recently completed GATT negotiations, dubbed the Uruguay Round, dragged on for seven long years before concluding in 1993. The benefits of the Uruguay Round will be felt for many years as the accord promotes long-term global trade growth. It reduced the world's remaining merchandise tariffs by 30 percent. The agreement also extended GATT to cover trade in agriculture and a wide range of services, and it toughened international protection of copyrights, patents, trademarks, and other intellectual property. Although the financial impact of such an agreement is difficult to measure, research suggests that cutting agriculture, manufacturing, and services trade barriers by one-third would boost the world economy by $613 billion, the equivalent of adding another Australia to the world economy.[8]

Beyond reducing trade barriers and setting global standards for trade, the Uruguay Round set up the World Trade Organization (WTO) to enforce GATT rules. In general, the WTO acts as an umbrella organization, overseeing GATT, mediating global disputes, and imposing trade sanctions. The previous GATT organization never possessed such authorities. A new round of GATT negotiations, the Doha Round, began in Doha, Qatar, in late 2001 and was set to conclude in 2005, but the discussions continue.[9]

Regional Free Trade Zones

Certain countries have formed *free trade zones* or **economic communities**. These are groups of nations organized to work toward common goals in the regulation of international trade. One such community is the *European Union (EU)*. Formed in 1957, the European Union set out to create a single European market by reducing barriers to the free flow of products, services, finances, and labor among member countries and developing policies on trade with nonmember nations. Today, the European Union represents one of the world's single largest markets. By 2007 it will have 27 member countries containing close to half a billion consumers and accounting for more than 20 percent of the world's exports.[10]

European unification offers tremendous trade opportunities for U.S. and other non-European firms. However, it also poses threats. As a result of increased unification, European

companies have grown bigger and more competitive. Perhaps an even greater concern, however, is that lower barriers *inside* Europe will create only thicker walls *outside* Europe. Some observers envision a "Fortress Europe" that heaps favors on firms from EU countries but hinders outsiders by imposing obstacles.

Progress toward European unification has been slow—many doubt that complete unification will ever be achieved. In recent years, 12 member nations have taken a significant step toward unification by adopting the euro as a common currency. Many other countries are expected to follow within the next few years. Widespread adoption of the euro will decrease much of the currency risk associated with doing business in Europe, making member countries with previously weak currencies more attractive markets.[11]

However, even with the adoption of the euro, it is unlikely that the EU will ever go against 2,000 years of tradition and become the "United States of Europe." A community with two dozen different languages and cultures will always have difficulty coming together and acting as a single entity. For example, efforts to forge a single European constitution appear to have failed following French and Dutch "no" votes in mid-2005. And economic disputes between member nations have stalled long-term budget negotiations. Still, although only partly successful so far, unification has made Europe a global force with which to reckon,

with a combined annual GDP of more than $12.1 trillion.[12]

In 1994, the *North American Free Trade Agreement (NAFTA)* established a free trade zone among the United States, Mexico, and Canada. The agreement created a single market of 435 million people who produce and consume over $14.4 trillion worth of goods and services annually. As it is implemented over a 15-year period, NAFTA will eliminate all trade barriers and investment restrictions among the three countries. Thus far, the agreement has allowed

■ The WTO and GATT: The General Agreement on Tariffs and Trade (GATT) promotes world trade by reducing tariffs in other international trade barriers. The WTO oversees GATT, imposes trade sanctions, and mediates global disputes.

Economic community
A group of nations organized to work toward common goals in the regulation of international trade.

WORLD TRADE ORGANIZATION

trade between the countries to flourish. In the dozen years following its establishment, trade among the NAFTA nations has risen 173 percent. U.S. merchandise exports to NAFTA partners grew 133 percent, compared with exports to the rest of the world at 77 percent. Canada and Mexico are now the nation's first and second largest trading partners.[13]

Following the apparent success of NAFTA, in 2005 the Central American Free Trade Agreement (CAFTA) established a free trade zone between the United States and Costa Rica, the Dominican Republic, El Salvador, Guatemala, Honduras, and Nicaragua. And talks have been underway since 1994 to investigate establishing a Free Trade Area of the Americas (FTAA). This mammoth free trade zone would include 34 countries stretching from the Bering Strait to Cape Horn, with a population of 800 million and a combined gross domestic product of about $17 trillion.[14]

Other free trade areas have formed in Latin America and South America. For example, MERCOSUR links ten Latin America and South America countries, and the Andean Community (CAN, for its Spanish initials) links five more. In late 2004, MERCOSUR and CAN agreed to unite, creating the South American Community of Nations (CSN), which will be modeled after the European Union. Complete integration between the two trade blocs is expected by 2007 and all tariffs between the nations are to be eliminated by 2019. With a

■ Economic communities: The European Union represents one of the world's single largest markets. It's current member countries contain more than half a billion consumers and account for 20 percent of the world's exports.

population of more than 370 million, a combined economy of more than $2.8 trillion a year, and exports worth $181 billion, the CSN will make up the largest trading bloc after NAFTA and the European Union.[15]

Although the recent trend toward free trade zones has caused great excitement and new market opportunities, some see it as a mixed blessing. For example, in the United States, unions fear that NAFTA will lead to an exodus of manufacturing jobs to Mexico, where wage rates are much lower. Environmentalists worry that companies that are unwilling to play by the strict rules of the U.S. Environmental Protection Agency will relocate in Mexico, where pollution regulation has been lax.[16]

Each nation has unique features that must be understood. A nation's readiness for different products and services and its attractiveness as a market to foreign firms depend on its economic, political-legal, and cultural environments.

Economic Environment

The international marketer must study each country's economy. Two economic factors reflect the country's attractiveness as a market: the country's industrial structure and its income distribution.

The country's *industrial structure* shapes its product and service needs, income levels, and employment levels. The four types of industrial structures are as follows:

- *Subsistence economies:* In a subsistence economy, the vast majority of people engage in simple agriculture. They consume most of their output and barter the rest for simple goods and services. They offer few market opportunities.

- *Raw material exporting economies:* These economies are rich in one or more natural resources but poor in other ways. Much of their revenue comes from exporting these resources. Examples are Chile (tin and copper), Democratic Republic of Congo (copper, cobalt, and coffee), and Saudi Arabia (oil). These countries are good markets for large equipment, tools and supplies, and trucks. If there are many foreign residents and a wealthy upper class, they are also a market for luxury goods.

■ *Industrializing economies:* In an industrializing economy, manufacturing accounts for 10 to 20 percent of the country's economy. Examples include Egypt, India, and Brazil. As manufacturing increases, the country needs more imports of raw textile materials, steel, and heavy machinery, and fewer imports of finished textiles, paper products, and automobiles. Industrialization typically creates a new rich class and a small but growing middle class, both demanding new types of imported goods.

■ *Industrial economies:* Industrial economies are major exporters of manufactured goods, services, and investment funds. They trade goods among themselves and also export them to other types of economies for raw materials and semifinished goods. The varied manufacturing activities of these industrial nations and their large middle class make them rich markets for all sorts of goods.

The second economic factor is the country's *income distribution.* Industrialized nations may have low-, medium-, and high-income households. In contrast, countries with subsistence economies may consist mostly of households with very low family incomes. Still other countries may have households with only either very low or very high incomes. However, even poor or developing economies may be attractive markets for all kinds of goods, including luxuries. For example, many luxury brand marketers are rushing to take advantage of China's rapidly developing consumer markets:[17]

More than half of China's 1.3 billion consumers can barely afford rice, let alone luxuries. According to The World Bank, more than 400 million Chinese live on less than $2 a day. Yet posh brands—from Gucci and Cartier to BMW and Bentley—are descending on China in force. How can purveyors of $2,000 handbags, $20,000 watches, and $1 million limousines thrive in a developing economy? Easy, says a Cartier executive. "Remember, even medium-sized cities in China . . . have populations larger than Switzerland's. So it doesn't matter if the percentage of people in those cities who can afford our products is very small." Thus, even though China has only 0.2 millionaires per 1,000 residents (compared with 8.4 per 1,000 in the United States), it trails only the U.S., Germany, and the United Kingdom in the total number of millionaires.

Dazzled by the pace at which China's booming economy is minting millionaires and swelling the ranks of the middle class, luxury brands are rushing to stake out shop space, tout their wares, and lay the foundations of a market they hope will eventually include as many as 100 million conspicuous consumers. "The Chinese are a natural audience for luxury goods," notes one analyst. After decades of socialism and poverty, China's elite are suddenly "keen to show off their newfound wealth."

Europe's fashion houses are happy to assist. Giorgio Armani recently hosted a star-studded fashion show to celebrate the opening of his 12,000-square-foot flagship store on Shanghai's waterfront; Armani promises 30 stores in China before the 2008 Beijing Olympics. Gucci recently opened stores in Hangzhou and Chengdu, bringing its China total to six. And it's not just clothes. Cartier, with nine stores in China and seven on the drawing board, has seen its

■ Economic environment: Many luxury brand marketers are rushing to take advantage of China's rapidly developing consumer markets.

China sales double for the past several years. Carmakers, too, are racing in. BMW recently cut the ribbon on a new Chinese factory that has the capacity to produce 50,000 BMWs a year. Audi's sleek A6 has emerged as the car of choice for the Communist Party's senior ranks, despite its $230,000 price tag. Bentley, which sold

70 cars in China in 2003—including 19 limousines priced at more than $1 million each—boasts three dealerships in China, as does Rolls-Royce.

Thus, country and regional economic environments will affect an international marketer's decisions about which global markets to enter and how.

Political-Legal Environment

Nations differ greatly in their political-legal environments. In considering whether to do business in a given country, a company should consider factors such as the country's attitudes toward international buying, government bureaucracy, political stability, and monetary regulations.

Some nations are very receptive to foreign firms; others are less accommodating. For example, India has tended to bother foreign businesses with import quotas, currency restrictions, and other limitations that make operating there a challenge. In contrast, neighboring Asian countries such as Singapore and Thailand court foreign investors and shower them with incentives and favorable operating conditions. Political stability is another issue. For example, India's government is notoriously unstable—the country has elected 10 new governments in the past 20 years—increasing the risk of doing business there. Although most international marketers still find India's huge market attractive, the unstable political situation will affect how they handle business and financial matters.[18]

Companies must also consider a country's monetary regulations. Sellers want to take their profits in a currency of value to them. Ideally, the buyer can pay in the seller's currency or in other world currencies. Short of this, sellers might accept a blocked currency—one whose removal from the country is restricted by the buyer's government—if they can buy other goods in that country that they need themselves or can sell elsewhere for a needed currency. Besides currency limits, a changing exchange rate also creates high risks for the seller.

Most international trade involves cash transactions. Yet many nations have too little hard currency to pay for their purchases from other countries. They may want to pay with other items instead of cash, which has led to a growing practice called **countertrade**. Countertrade takes several forms: *Barter* involves the direct exchange of goods or services, as when Azerbaijan imported wheat from Romania in exchange for crude oil, and Vietnam exchanged rice for Philippine fertilizer and coconuts. Another form is *compensation* (or *buyback*), whereby the seller sells a plant, equipment, or technology to another country and agrees to take payment in the resulting products. Thus, Japan's Fukusuke Corporation sold knitting machines and raw textile materials to Shanghai clothing manufacturer Chinatex in exchange for finished textiles produced on the machines. The most common form of countertrade is *counterpurchase*, in which the seller receives full payment in cash but agrees to spend some of the money in the other country. For example, Boeing sells aircraft to India and agrees to buy Indian coffee, rice, castor oil, and other goods and sell them elsewhere.[19]

Countertrade deals can be very complex. For example, a few years back, DaimlerChrysler agreed to sell 30 trucks to Romania in exchange for 150 Romanian jeeps, which it then sold to Ecuador for bananas, which were in turn sold to a German supermarket chain for German currency. Through this roundabout process, DaimlerChrysler finally obtained payment in German money.

Countertrade
International trade involving the direct or indirect exchange of goods for other goods instead of cash.

Cultural Environment

Each country has its own folkways, norms, and taboos. When designing global marketing strategies, companies must understand how culture affects consumer reactions in each of its world markets. In turn, they must also understand how their strategies affect local cultures.

The Impact of Culture on Marketing Strategy

The seller must examine the ways consumers in different countries think about and use certain products before planning a marketing program. There are often surprises. For example, the average French man uses almost twice as many cosmetics and grooming aids as his wife. The Germans and the French eat more packaged, branded spaghetti than do Italians. Italian children like to eat chocolate bars between slices of bread as a snack. Women in Tanzania will not give their children eggs for fear of making them bald or impotent.

Companies that ignore cultural norms and differences can make some very expensive and embarrassing mistakes. Here are examples:

Nike inadvertently offended Chinese officials when it ran an advertisement featuring LeBron James crushing a number of culturally revered Chinese figures in a kung-fu-themed ad campaign. The Chinese government found that the ad violated regulations to uphold national dignity and respect of the culture and yanked the multi-million-dollar campaign. With egg on its face, Nike released a formal apology. Nike faced a similar situation in Arab countries when Muslims objected to a stylized "Air" logo on its shoes, which resembled "Allah" in Arabic script. Nike apologized for that mistake as well and pulled the shoes from distribution.[20]

■ Overlooking cultural differences can result in embarrassing mistakes. China imposed a nationwide ban on this "blasphemous" kung-fu-themed ad campaign featuring LeBron James crushing a number of culturally revere Chinese figures.

Business norms and behavior also vary from country to country. For example, American executives like to get right down to business and engage in fast and tough face-to-face bargaining. However, Japanese and other Asian businesspeople often find this behavior offensive. They prefer to start with polite conversation, and they rarely say no in face-to-face conversations. As another example, South Americans like to sit or stand very close to each other when they talk business—in fact, almost nose-to-nose. The American business executive tends to keep backing away as the South American moves closer. Both may end up being offended. American business executives need to be briefed on these kinds of factors before conducting business in another country.[21]

By the same token, companies that understand cultural nuances can use them to their advantage when positioning products internationally. Consider the following example:

A television ad running these days in India shows a mother lapsing into a day-dream: Her young daughter is in a beauty contest dressed as Snow White, dancing on a stage. Her flowing gown is an immaculate white. The garments of other contestants, who dance in the background, are a tad gray. Snow White, no surprise, wins the blue ribbon. The mother awakes to the laughter of her adoring family—and glances proudly at her Whirlpool White Magic washing machine. The TV spot is the product of 14 months of research by Whirlpool into the psyche of the Indian consumer. Among other things, [Whirlpool] learned that Indian homemakers prize hygiene and purity, which they associate with white. The trouble is, white garments often get discolored after frequent machine washing in local water. Besides appealing to this love of purity in its ads, Whirlpool custom-designed machines that are especially good with white fabrics. Whirlpool now is the leading brand in India's fast-growing market for fully automatic washing machines.[22]

Thus, understanding cultural traditions, preferences, and behaviors can help companies not only to avoid embarrassing mistakes but also to take advantage of cross-cultural opportunities.

The Impact of Marketing Strategy on Cultures

Whereas marketers worry about the impact of culture on their global marketing strategies, others may worry about the impact of marketing strategies on global cultures. For example, social critics contend that large American multinationals such as McDonald's, Coca-Cola, Starbucks, Nike, Microsoft, Disney, and MTV aren't just "globalizing" their brands, they are "Americanizing" the world's cultures.

Down in the mall, between the fast-food joint and the bagel shop, a group of young people huddles in a flurry of baggy combat pants, skateboards, and slang. They

(case continued)

margin—better than the 3.5 percent overall Wal-Mart margin.

Puerto Rico Puerto Rico is another big success for Wal-Mart. It established its own stores and bought the Supermercados Amigo—Puerto-Rico's second-largest grocery retailer.

Brazil and Argentina Wal-Mart entered Brazil and Argentina in the mid-1990s with disappointing results. The economic situation in both countries was miserable—inflation spiraling out of control, devaluation of currencies, and defaults on loans, plus a political maelstrom in which Argentina's presidency seemed to be a revolving door. To this day, Wal-Mart has opened only 11 stores in Argentina.

But despite the economic situation and considerable competitive woes, Wal-Mart has fared much better in Brazil. Carrefour entered Brazil in 1975 and was well entrenched as the number one retailer. Upon Wal-Mart's entry, Carrefour started a price war and located hypermarkets next to Wal-Mart stores. In retaliation, Wal-Mart opened smaller-format stores called "Todo Dia," which sell mostly groceries and a little general merchandise. These smaller stores give Wal-Mart a presence in crowded Brazilian neighborhoods and enable it to sell to lower-income consumers who buy daily.

In early 2004, Wal-Mart bolstered its market share from sixth to third by buying the 118-unit Bompreco supermarket chain. In late 2005, it bought an additional 140 hypermarkets, supermarkets, and wholesale outlets from Portuguese conglomerate Sonae. Increased market share will generate lower costs and lower prices, making Wal-Mart more competitive with Carrefour and with Companhania Brasiliera de Distribuicao (CBD), the largest grocery retailer in Brazil. Wal-Mart's acquisitions have raised its presence in Brazil to more than 290 stores, including 17 super-centers, 12 Sam's Clubs, and 2 Neighborhood Markets.

Europe

Germany In 1998, Wal-Mart bought the 21-unit Wertkauf chain in Germany, and a year later it purchased the 74-unit Interspar hypermarkets. As the third-largest retail market in the world (behind the United States and Japan), Germany initially looked very attractive. But from the start, it has been a nightmare. First, there were real estate issues: strict zoning laws, scarcity of land, and high real estate prices. Then there were well-entrenched unions, which were unlikely to allow their members to gather in the morning to respond to Wal-Mart's "Give me a W . . . Give me an A . . . ," rallying cheer.

In addition, competition in Germany was much greater—five of the world's top-25 global retailers are German, with two of them in the top ten. Finally, German consumers are among the most demanding in the world. They are extremely quality conscious and are less price conscious. On top of all that, Wal-Mart

had purchased two chains with declining sales, poor locations, and dirty stores.

Wal-Mart executives admit in hindsight that they moved too fast in Germany and failed to take advantage of the managerial expertise in their acquisitions. Although Wal-Mart has not given up on Germany, it has had to close stores there because of poor performance.

United Kingdom Although Wal-Mart struggled in Germany, it scored a homerun when it purchased the UK's ASDA chain. These UK outlets are the biggest contributor to the profits of Wal-Mart's International Division. Why? ASDA had for years modeled itself on the Wal-Mart format—right down to the rah-rah philosophy and low prices. It was not a struggling chain; instead it is a top-notch retailer that "knows food retailing" and shares that knowledge throughout Wal-Mart's other global operations. With Wal-Mart's backing, ASDA cut prices (undercutting rivals), added general merchandise, and took advantage of Wal-Mart's inventory prowess. ASDA has been so successful that its sales per square foot go as high as $2,000, four times higher than a Sam's Club. For the Christmas season in 2003, nine of the ten top-selling Wal-Mart stores worldwide were in the UK. This does not mean a lack of competition; two other UK retailers, Tesco and Sainsbury's, are also in the top-25 global retailers. Wal-Mart's store count in the UK is now at over 280 and growing.

Asia

Hong Kong, Thailand, and Indonesia Wal-Mart's first stop in Southeast Asia was Hong Kong, where it entered a joint venture with Ek Chor Distribution System Co. Ltd. to establish Value Clubs. Because Ek Chor is actually owned by C. P. Pokphand of Bangkog, Wal-Mart was able to locate in Thailand and then Indonesia.

Peoples Republic of China Wal-Mart began operations in China in 1995. Since then, growth has been slow. Today, there are still only 51 stores in China. But Wal-Mart is not taking its eye off this market. And why would it? As the largest market in the world, with more than 1.3 billion people and 170 cities with populations above 1 million, the potential in China is huge. Currently, Wal-Mart is building 20 new stores.

Given its size, China would appear to be one of the only other countries in the world that could sustain a scale similar to that of the U.S. Wal-Mart operation. Chinese consumers couldn't be happier, having embraced the large retailer. But Chinese operations will take awhile to develop. Like Germany, there is a shortage of land and stores tend to be smaller. One of the first Wal-Marts was in a subway station, located to cater to busy commuters. Competition is also a factor. Carrefour and a handful of Chinese supermarket chains are expanding much more rapidly.

But these problems are magnified by a bigger problem: the government. In an effort to limit competition, the government designated territories within which each retailer must locate, and Wal-Mart was confined mostly to southern China. For some time, this meant no stores in Shanghai, the fastest-growing, most-western, highest-income market in China. However, the government is starting to relax these restrictions, and Wal-Mart will open its first supercenters in Shanghai and Beijing by 2007.

To prepare for this growth, Wal-Mart China, Ltd. and CITIC Ltd. (China International Trust and Investment Company) founded the Wal-Mart South China Department Store Co., Ltd. in October 2003. And Gazeley, a Wal-Mart-owned industrial developer, is currently investing $95 million in speculative ventures with Chinese partners.

Japan Wal-Mart entered Japan in 2002 by buying a 38 percent stake in Seiyu Ltd., Japan's fifth-largest supermarket chain. Although Seiyu had 400 stores with good locations, the stores were shabby and the company had declining sales. Anxious not to repeat the German mistake in a land of demanding consumers, Wal-Mart is moving slowly to remodel Seiyu's stores. Unfortunately, this gives Japanese retailers such as Aeon time to get a jump on Wal-Mart.

There are many of the same problems in Japan as in China and Germany, such as pricey real estate and few locations. Until recently, laws restricted store size and opening hours in an effort to protect smaller Japanese retailers, who make up 58 percent of the Japanese retailing system. In addition, there are complicated and sometimes convoluted distribution systems in which retailers go through layers of middlemen with long-standing relationships instead of buying directly from suppliers. As a result, goods may pass through three or more hands before reaching a retailer.

And then there are the Japanese consumers, not only considered to be among the world's quirkiest but also among the most demanding. They want fresher foods, the most orderly and clean stores, short checkout lines, and an abundance of clerks. And they don't understand the EDLP strategy. Trained by Japanese retailers in the past to hunt through newspapers for discounts, consumers still expect discounts and they want to find these in newspaper ads, which must be in color. Shoppers also don't understand jargon such as "rollback," so Wal-Mart must translate terms that it considers standard in the rest of the world. Worse, Japanese consumers think very low prices indicate poor quality. Thus, a strategy of ever-lower prices could hurt sales.

Despite Wal-Mart's elaborate planning, results in Japan have been disappointing. Seiyu has lost money and blames the sluggish economy and unusual weather—not to mention the competition. Wal-Mart has yet to articulate a clear strategy with the struggling chain.

WHAT'S NEXT?

For some time, Wal-Mart's next big move appeared to be Russia. Based on various factors such as market saturation,

political risk, economic growth, and consumer demographics, Russia is currently considered the second most attractive global retail destination. Wal-Mart's developer arm, Gazeley, has been involved in speculative ventures in and around Moscow. But in recent times, Wal-Mart has not shown any concrete signs of opening stores in this large country.

But although Russia may be the second most attractive global retail destination, India is number one, and Wal-Mart is taking serious notice. India has nearly 1.1 billion people and is growing fast. In one year, India's population will grow by over 400,000 people, far outpacing China's growth. India's $350 billion retail market is expected to grow by 13 percent annually. Moreover, India boasts a fast-expanding middle class, one of the fastest-growing economies in the world, and a retail sector that is dominated by small, family-run stores.

Wal-Mart already has 80 employees in India to oversee purchasing of the $600 million worth of goods that it buys each year. But Wal-Mart has also opened an office in India for market research. John Menzer, CEO of Wal-Mart International, has called India a "huge organic growth opportunity." Although no decisions have been made just yet as to how Wal-Mart will enter India or Russia, these two markets alone provide incredible potential for growth. It is also certain that Wal-Mart has plenty of moves up its sleeve for the global market in the future. Stay tuned!

Questions for Discussion

1. In what countries has Wal-Mart done well? Can you identify any common consumer, market, retailer, or entry strategy traits across these countries that might account for Wal-Mart's success?

2. In what countries has Wal-Mart done poorly? Can you identify any common consumer, market, retailer, or entry strategy traits across these countries that might account for Wal-Mart's lack of success?

3. In your opinion, will Wal-Mart be successful in Japan? In Germany? Why or why not?

4. In your opinion, should Wal-Mart enter India? If so, how should it go about this?

5. Beyond India, what countries do you think Wal-Mart should consider entering? What factors are important in making this decision? Be prepared to defend the countries that you chose.

Sources: "India Remains the Most Attractive Destination for Global Retailers," *AFX.COM,* April 30, 2006; Alan Clendenning, "Wal-Mart Buys Brazil Stores for Expansion," *Associated Press,* December 14, 2005; Jon Neale, "Gazeley Targets Russia and China," *Estates Gazette,* December 10, 2005, p. 31; Clay Chandler, "The Great Wal-Mart of China," *Fortune,* July 25, 2005, accessed online at www.fortune.com: Wal-Mart 2005 Annual Report; Laura Heller, "Latin Market Never Looked So Bueno," *DSN Retailing Today,* June 10, 2002, p. 125; Laura Heller, "Southern Hemisphere Woes Persist," *DSN Retailing Today,* June 10, 2002, p. 126; "Germany: Wal-Mart Closings," *New York Times,* July 11, 2002; and www.walmartstores.com, November 2006.

20

Marketing Ethics and Social Responsibility

Previewing the Concepts

In this final chapter, we'll focus on marketing as a social institution. First, we'll look at some common criticisms of marketing as it impacts individual consumers, other businesses, and society as a whole. Then, we'll examine consumerism, environmentalism, and other citizen and public actions to keep marketing in check. Finally, we'll see how companies themselves can benefit from proactively pursuing socially responsible and ethical practices that bring value not just to individual customers, but to society as a whole. You'll see that social responsibility and ethical actions are more than just the right thing to do; they're also good for business.

First, let's visit the concept of social responsibility in business. Perhaps no one gets more fired up about corporate social responsibility than Jeffery Swartz, CEO of footwear-and-apparel maker Timberland. He's on a passionate mission to use the resources of his company to combat the world's social ills. But he knows that to do this, his company must also be profitable. Swartz believes firmly that companies actually can do both—that they can do well by doing good. Here's the story.

Timberland CEO Jeffrey Swartz recently strode purposefully into a New York office packed with McDonald's executives. Dressed in a blazer, jeans, and Timberland boots, he was there to convince the fast-food giant that it should choose his $1.5 billion shoe-and-clothing company to provide its new uniforms. The executives waited expectantly for him to unzip a bag and reveal the sleek new prototype.

"We didn't bring any designs," Swartz said flatly. Eyebrows arched. Instead, he launched into an impassioned speech that had virtually nothing to do with clothes or shoes. What Timberland really had to offer McDonald's, Swartz said, was the benefit to the company—and the world at large—of helping it build a unified, motivated, purposeful workforce. "Other people can do uniforms," Swartz said, his Yankee accent asserting itself. "This is about partnership. We can create a partnership together that will be about value and values."

As unorthodox as it sounds, Swartz wasn't pitching Timberland's creativity or craftsmanship. Rather, he was pitching its culture, and the ways that culture could rub off on McDonald's. Growing more and more animated, Swartz talked about how Timberland's employees get 40 hours paid leave every year to pursue volunteer projects. He discussed Serv-a-palooza, Timberland's daylong burst of do-goodism that this year would host 170 service projects in 27 countries, covering 45,000 volunteer hours of work. And he talked about City Year, the nonprofit that Timberland has supported for more than a decade, which brings young people into public service for a year. As for McDonald's, it was part of practically every community in the country, Swartz explained, but was it helping every community?

The room was silent. Swartz couldn't tell whether they thought he was a touchy-feely freak or whether what he said had struck a deep chord (McDonald's wouldn't make a final decision for many months). Yet Swartz was elated all the same. "I told my team to find me ten more places where I can have this conversation," he said. "No one believes in this more than we do, and that is our competitive advantage."

The "this" that gets Swartz, a third-generation CEO whose grandfather founded the company in 1952, so fired up is expressed in Timberland's slogan: "Boots, Brand, Belief." What Swartz is really trying to do—no kidding—is to use the resources, energy, and profits of a publicly traded footwear-and-apparel company to combat social ills, help the environment, and improve conditions for laborers around the globe. And rather than using his company as a charity, he's using the hard financial metrics of profit, return on investment, and, oh yes, shareholder return, to try to prove that companies actually can do well by doing good.

So far, Swartz has done a more-than-respectable job of proving the point. Over the past five years, the company, which sells outdoor-themed clothes, shoes, and accessories, has seen sales grow at a compound annual rate of 9.7 percent and earnings per share grow at 20 percent. Its stock price has risen 64 percent over the same period. The company is also viewed as a trailblazer by companies many times larger when it comes to corporate social responsibility. But Swartz's big ambitions also draw doubters who question whether Timberland's drive for sustainability is itself sustainable in a profit-driven world—whether the amoral world of capitalism and the spiritual world of service can be merged.

Those who think Timberland must choose between profits and passion have not spent much time with Swartz, an earnest, funny, hyperkinetic 45-year-old who can barely sit still, so anxious is he to discuss the beautiful—and profitable—nexus between, in his words, "commerce and justice." Although Swartz knows the business inside and out, it's hard to get him to talk about it. Asked if he cares about shoes, he looks shocked. "Am I proud of the boots and shoes we make? Desperately." But making good gear, he says, doesn't matter enough. "I can't care enough about shoes or clothes to do what I do unless there is a different kind of purpose to it."

Swartz's quest has created a cohesive culture at Timberland. In the most recent employee survey, 75 percent of employees said they would choose Timberland again if they were looking for work, and 79 percent said Timberland's reputation had

569

Objectives

After studying this chapter, you should be able to

1. identify the major social criticisms of marketing
2. define *consumerism* and *environmentalism* and explain how they affect marketing strategies
3. describe the principles of socially responsible marketing
4. explain the role of ethics in marketing

WE STARTED OUT AS BOOTMAKERS, but we're about much more. Like you, we care about the strength of our neighborhoods, the well-being of our environment, and the quality of life in our communities. We believe in making a difference and invite you to join us.

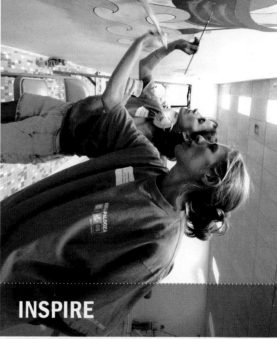

INFORM

INSPIRE

ENGAGE

played a big role in their decision to come to the company. "I love my job," says Michael Moody, a staff attorney. "The core values are humanity, humility, integrity, and excellence, and I see those values used as a touchstone in all conversations."

Betsy Blaisdell, manager for environmental stewardship, laughs when she thinks how horrified she originally was at the thought of working for a big, bad corporation. With Swartz's support, however, she has helped push through such initiatives as a $3,000 cash incentive for employees to purchase hybrid cars (six have taken advantage so far) and the company's $3.5 million solar array at its Ontario, California, distribution center. Although it will provide 60 percent of the center's energy, it may take as many as 20 years to show a return, and that's just fine with Swartz.

For Timberland, service is not something you do once a year. Although volunteer projects are always under way, many of them have been organized under the rubric of Serv-a-palooza, held in late September. Last year's projects included a massive effort to clean up and reclaim public spaces around Lawrence, Massachusetts, and a plan to improve a center for handicapped kids in Ho Chi Minh City, Vietnam. Timberland supports these efforts for their own sake, but the potential corporate benefits do not go unnoticed. As his pitch to McDonald's shows, Swartz also sees service as a powerful differentiator for Timberland with its current and potential customers.

Although Timberland's message seems to be getting through to its business customers, it's not at all clear that consumers have any clue what the brand stands for beyond cool stuff. Nor is it clear that they care. "The vast majority of footwear is purchased by teenagers," says an industry analyst, "and some don't believe in advertising at all, so it's tough to reach them." But Swartz insists that it's simply a matter of time until consumers refuse to patronize companies that don't tell them what they're doing for the community. "I believe that there's a storm coming against the complacent who say good enough is good enough," he says.

Probably Swartz's biggest challenge is getting Wall Street to buy into the doing-good side of the story. Sure, the brand's a success, says the analyst. "But investors would rather see Timberland doing things like increasing dividends or share buybacks. Nobody's investing in Timberland just because Jeff's a nice guy. They expect results."

Although compelling, the lofty notion of serving a doubled bottom line of values and profits will present significant challenges for Timberland. Can one man and his band of devotees really change the role of the corporation? To Swartz, it's only a matter of time. After all, he's trying to save the world. The funny thing is that he's trying to do it by running a large, profitable, publicly traded shoe company. Some call him the messiah for a new age of social awareness. Others think he could be headed for a fall. But all agree he's challenging the system.[1]

Responsible marketers discover what consumers want and respond with market offerings that create value for buyers in order to capture value in return. The *marketing concept* is a philosophy of customer value and mutual gain. Its practice leads the economy by an invisible hand to satisfy the many and changing needs of millions of consumers.

Not all marketers follow the marketing concept, however. In fact, some companies use questionable marketing practices, and some marketing actions that seem innocent in themselves strongly affect the larger society. Consider the sale of cigarettes. On the face of it, companies should be free to sell cigarettes and smokers should be free to buy them. But this private transaction involves larger questions of public policy. For example, the smokers are harming their health and may be shortening their own lives. Smoking places a financial burden on the smoker's family and on society at large. Other people around smokers may suffer discomfort and harm from secondhand smoke. Finally, marketing cigarettes to adults might also influence young people to begin smoking. Thus, the marketing of tobacco products has sparked substantial debate and negotiation in recent years.

This chapter examines the social effects of private marketing practices. We examine several questions: What are the most frequent social criticisms of marketing? What steps have private citizens taken to curb marketing ills? What steps have legislators and government agencies taken to curb marketing ills? What steps have enlightened companies taken to carry out socially responsible and ethical marketing that creates value for both individual customers and society as a whole?

Social Criticisms of Marketing

Marketing receives much criticism. Some of this criticism is justified; much is not. Social critics claim that certain marketing practices hurt individual consumers, society as a whole, and other business firms.

Marketing's Impact on Individual Consumers

Consumers have many concerns about how well the American marketing system serves their interests. Surveys usually show that consumers hold mixed or even slightly unfavorable attitudes toward marketing practices. Consumer advocates, government agencies, and other critics have accused marketing of harming consumers through high prices, deceptive practices, high-pressure selling, shoddy or unsafe products, planned obsolescence, and poor service to disadvantaged consumers.

High Prices

Many critics charge that the American marketing system causes prices to be higher than they would be under more "sensible" systems. They point to three factors—*high costs of distribution, high advertising and promotion costs, and excessive markups.*

HIGH COSTS OF DISTRIBUTION A long-standing charge is that greedy intermediaries mark up prices beyond the value of their services. Critics charge that there are too many intermediaries, that intermediaries are inefficient, or that they provide unnecessary or duplicate services. As a result, distribution costs too much, and consumers pay for these excessive costs in the form of higher prices.

How do resellers answer these charges? They argue that intermediaries do work that would otherwise have to be done by manufacturers or consumers. Markups reflect services that consumers themselves want—more convenience, larger stores and assortments, more service, longer store hours, return privileges, and others. In fact, they argue, retail competition is so intense that margins are actually quite low. For example, after taxes, supermarket chains are typically left with barely 1 percent profit on their sales. If some resellers try to charge too much relative to the value they add, other resellers will step in with lower prices. Low-price stores such as Wal-Mart, Costco, and other discounters pressure their competitors to operate efficiently and keep their prices down.

HIGH ADVERTISING AND PROMOTION COSTS Modern marketing is also accused of pushing up prices to finance heavy advertising and sales promotion. For example, a few dozen tablets of a heavily promoted brand of pain reliever sell for the same price as 100 tablets of less-promoted brands. Differentiated products—cosmetics, detergents, toiletries—include promotion and packaging costs that can amount to 40 percent or more of the manufacturer's price to the retailer. Critics charge that much of the packaging and promotion adds only psychological value to the product rather than functional value.

Marketers respond that advertising does add to product costs. But it also adds value by informing potential buyers of the availability and merits of a brand. Brand name products may cost more, but branding gives buyers assurances of consistent quality. Moreover, consumers can usually buy functional versions of products at lower prices. However, they *want* and are willing to pay more for products that also provide psychological benefits—that make them feel wealthy, attractive, or special. Also, heavy advertising and promotion may be necessary for a firm to match competitors' efforts—the business would lose "share of mind" if it did not match competitive spending. At the same time, companies are cost conscious about promotion and try to spend their money wisely.

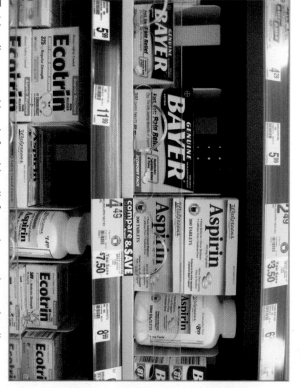

■ A heavily promoted brand of aspirin sells for much more than a virtually identical non-branded or store-branded product. Critics charge that promotion adds only psychological value to the product rather than functional value.

EXCESSIVE MARKUPS Critics also charge that some companies mark up goods excessively. They point to the drug industry, where a pill costing five cents to make may cost the consumer $2 to buy. They point to the pricing tactics of funeral homes that prey on the confused emotions of bereaved relatives and to the high charges for auto repair and other services.

Marketers respond that most businesses try to deal fairly with consumers because they want to build customer relationships and repeat business. Most consumer abuses are unintentional. When shady marketers do take advantage of consumers, they should be reported to Better Business Bureaus and to state and federal agencies. Marketers also respond that consumers often don't understand the reasons for high markups. For example, pharmaceutical markups must cover the costs of purchasing, promoting, and distributing existing medicines plus the high research and development costs of formulating and testing new medicines. As pharmaceuticals company GlaxoSmithKline states in its ads, "Today's medicines finance tomorrow's miracles."

Deceptive Practices

Marketers are sometimes accused of deceptive practices that lead consumers to believe they will get more value than they actually do. Deceptive practices fall into three groups: pricing, promotion, and packaging. *Deceptive pricing* includes practices such as falsely advertising "factory" or "wholesale" prices or a large price reduction from a phony high retail list price. *Deceptive promotion* includes practices such as misrepresenting the product's features or performance or luring the customers to the store for a bargain that is out of stock. *Deceptive packaging* includes exaggerating package contents through subtle design, using misleading labeling, or describing size in misleading terms.

To be sure, questionable marketing practices do occur. Consider the advertising of airline ticket prices:[2]

When is $49 not $49? When it's the advertised price for an airline ticket. In newspaper ads and radio commercials, we are lured with the promise of $49 round--trip tickets to Bermuda. But by the time you add in all the extras, that bargain ticket will cost nearly $200. What ever happened to truth in advertising? Technically, the advertising is legal. But the average airline consumer needs a magnifying glass to get an idea of the actual ticket cost. For the Bermuda ticket, radio commercials warn that the discount price comes with conditions and fees, but you must read the fine print across the bottom of a newspaper ad to discover the true cost. "Prepaid government taxes and fees of up to $86.00, September 11 Security Fees of up to $10.00, and Passenger Facility Charges up to $18.00 per person . . . are not included in listed prices," we're told. "Listed prices include fuel-related and all other increases as of 7/1, but may increase additionally due to unanticipated expenses beyond our control." Add them up, and that ticket costs $163, not counting whatever fuel surcharge may have been imposed over the past nine months. Not quite the $49 in the big print at the top of the ad.

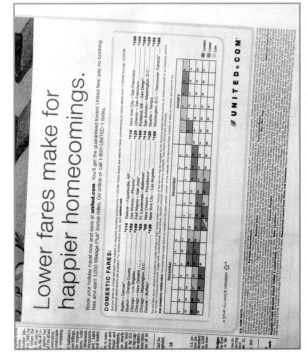

Deceptive practices have led to legislation and other consumer protection actions. For example, in 1938 Congress reacted to such blatant deceptions as Fleischmann's Yeast's claim to straighten crooked teeth by enacting the Wheeler-Lea Act giving the Federal Trade Commission (FTC) power to regulate "unfair or deceptive acts or practices." The FTC has published several guidelines listing deceptive practices. Despite new regulations, some critics argue that deceptive claims are still the norm.

■ Deceptive practices: Technically legal, ads like this one lure readers with promises of low, low prices. But watch out for the small print at the bottom—you will need a magnifying glass to figure out the actual ticket cost.

The toughest problem is defining what is "deceptive." For instance, an advertiser's claim that its powerful laundry detergent "makes your washing machine ten feet tall," showing a surprised homemaker watching her appliance burst through her laundry room ceiling, isn't intended to be taken literally. Instead, the advertiser might claim, it is "puffery"—innocent exaggeration for effect. One noted marketing thinker, Theodore Levitt, once claimed that advertising puffery and alluring imagery are bound to occur—and that they may even be desirable: "There is hardly a company that would not go down in ruin if it refused to provide fluff, because nobody will buy pure functionality. . . . Worse, it denies . . . people's honest needs and values. Without distortion, embellishment, and elaboration, life would be drab, dull, anguished, and at its existential worst."[3]

However, others claim that puffery and alluring imagery can harm consumers in subtle ways, and that consumers must be protected through education:

The real danger to the public . . . comes not from outright lies—in most cases facts can ultimately be proven and mistakes corrected. But . . . advertising uses [the power of images and] emotional appeals to shift the viewer's focus away from facts. Viewers who do not take the trouble to distinguish between provable claims and pleasant but meaningless word play end up buying "the sizzle, not the steak" and often paying high prices. The best defense against misleading ads . . . is not tighter controls on [advertisers], but more education and more critical judgment among . . . consumers. Just as we train children to be wary of strangers offering candy, to count change at a store, and to kick the tires before buying a used car, we must make the effort to step back and judge the value of . . . advertisements, and then master the skills required to separate spin from substance.[4]

Marketers argue that most companies avoid deceptive practices because such practices harm their business in the long run. Profitable customer relationships are built upon a foundation of value and trust. If consumers do not get what they expect, they will switch to more reliable products. In addition, consumers usually protect themselves from deception. Most consumers recognize a marketer's selling intent and are careful when they buy, sometimes to the point of not believing completely true product claims.

High-Pressure Selling

Salespeople are sometimes accused of high-pressure selling that persuades people to buy goods they had no thought of buying. It is often said that insurance, real estate, and used cars are *sold*, not *bought*. Salespeople are trained to deliver smooth, canned talks to entice purchase. They sell hard because sales contests promise big prizes to those who sell the most.

But in most cases, marketers have little to gain from high-pressure selling. Such tactics may work in one-time selling situations for short-term gain. However, most selling involves building long-term relationships with valued customers. High-pressure or deceptive selling can do serious damage to such relationships. For example, imagine a Procter & Gamble account manager trying to pressure a Wal-Mart buyer, or an IBM salesperson trying to browbeat a GE information technology manager. It simply wouldn't work.

Shoddy, Harmful, or Unsafe Products

Another criticism concerns poor product quality or function. One complaint is that, too often, products are not made well and services are not performed well. A second complaint is that many products deliver little benefit, or that they might even be harmful. For example, many critics have pointed out the dangers of today's fat-laden fast food. In fact, McDonald's recently faced a class-action lawsuit charging that its fare has contributed to the nationwide obesity epidemic:

[Four years ago,] the parody newspaper *The Onion* ran a joke article under the headline "Hershey's Ordered to Pay Obese Americans $135 Billion." The hypothesized class-action lawsuit said that Hershey "knowingly and willfully" marketed to children "rich, fatty candy bars containing chocolate and other ingredients of negligible nutritional value," while "spiking" them with "peanuts, crisped rice, and caramel to increase consumer appeal." Some joke. [In 2002] New York City attorney Sam Hirsch filed a strikingly similar suit—against McDonald's—on behalf of a class of obese and overweight children. He alleged that the fast-food chain "negligently, recklessly, carelessly and/or intentionally" markets to children food products that are "high in fat, salt, sugar, and cholesterol" while failing to warn of those ingredients' links to "obesity, diabetes, coronary heart disease, high blood pressure, strokes, elevated cholesterol intake, related cancers," and other conditions. Industry defenders decried the suit as frivolous. It is ridiculous, they claimed, to blame the fast-food industry for consumers' "own nutritional ignorance, lack of willpower, genetic predispositions, failure to exercise, or whatever else may play a role in [their] obesity." A federal judge agreed and dismissed the suit, explaining that "it is not the place of the law to protect them from their own excess." And to prevent similar lawsuits, in 2005 the United States House of Representatives passed The Personal Responsibility in Food Consumption Act, dubbed the "Cheeseburger Bill," which bans obesity-related lawsuits in state and federal courts.[5]

Who's to blame for the nation's obesity problem? And what should responsible food companies do about it? As with most social responsibility issues, there are no easy answers. McDonald's has worked to improve its fare and make its menu and its customers healthier. However, other fast feeders seem to be going the other way. Hardee's, for example, introduced a 1,410-calorie Monster Thickburger, and Burger King launched its Enormous Omelet breakfast sandwich, packing an unapologetic 47 grams of fat. Are these companies being socially irresponsible? Or are they simply serving customers choices they want?[6] (See Real Marketing 20.1.)

A third complaint concerns product safety. Product safety has been a problem for several reasons, including company indifference, increased product complexity, and poor quality control. For years, Consumers Union—the nonprofit testing and information organization that publishes the *Consumer Reports* magazine and Web site—has reported various hazards in tested products: electrical dangers in appliances, carbon monoxide poisoning from room heaters, injury risks from lawn mowers, and faulty automobile design, among many others. The organization's testing and other activities have helped consumers make better buying decisions and encouraged businesses to eliminate product flaws.

However, most manufacturers *want* to produce quality goods. The way a company deals with product quality and safety problems can damage or help its reputation. Companies selling poor-quality or unsafe products risk damaging conflicts with consumer groups and regulators. Moreover, unsafe products can result in product liability suits and large awards for damages. The average compensatory jury award for product liability cases from 1993 through 2002 was $700,000, but individual or class action awards frequently run into the tens of millions of dollars. And proposed legislation could even criminalize product liability, imposing criminal penalties for managers who know about product defects but fail to disclose them to the public.[7]

More fundamentally, consumers who are unhappy with a firm's products may avoid future purchases and talk other consumers into doing the same. Thus, quality missteps can have severe consequences. Today's marketers know that customer-driven quality results in customer value and satisfaction, which in turn creates profitable customer relationships.

Planned Obsolescence

Critics also have charged that some producers follow a program of planned obsolescence, causing their products to become obsolete before they actually should need replacement. For example, consider printer companies and their toner cartridges:

Refilled printer cartridges offer the same or improved performance for about half the price of a new one. A number of businesses, from local shops to Office Depot and other big-box stores,

■ Planned obsolescence: Printer companies continually introduce new cartridge models and tweak designs: "You've got planned obsolescence," says the owner of Laser Logic, a small cartridge refilling company. "It's kind of like a Mission Impossible. At the end of this tape, the toner cartridge will self-destruct."

20.1 The National Obesity Debate: Who's to Blame?

As you've no doubt heard, the United States is facing an obesity epidemic. Everyone seems to agree on the problem—as a nation, we're packing on the pounds. But still unresolved is another weighty issue: Who's to blame? Is it the fault of self-indulgent consumers who just can't say no to sticky buns, fat burgers, and other tempting treats? Or is it the fault of greedy food marketers who are cashing in on vulnerable consumers, turning us into a nation of overeaters?

The problem is a big one. Studies show that some 66 percent of American adults and 17 percent of children and teens are over-weight or obese. According to a Rand Corporation study, the number of people in the United States who are 100 pounds or more overweight quadrupled between 1986 and 2000, from one adult in 200 to one in 50. This weight increase comes despite repeated medical studies showing that excess weight brings increased risks for heart disease, diabetes, and other maladies, even cancer.

So, here's that weighty question again. If we know that we're overweight and that it's bad for us, why do we keep putting on the pounds? Who's to blame? The answer, of course, depends on whom you ask. However, these days, lots of people are blaming food marketers. In the national obesity debate, food marketers have become a favorite target of almost everyone, from politicians, public policy makers, and the press to overweight consumers themselves. And some food marketers are looking pretty much guilty as charged.

Take Hardee's, for example. At a time when other fast-food chains such as McDonald's, Wendy's, and Subway were getting "leaner," Hardee's introduced the decadent Thickburger, featuring a third of a pound of Angus beef. It followed up with the *Monster Thickburger*, two-thirds of a pound of Angus beef, four strips of bacon, and three slices of American cheese, all nestled in a buttered sesame-seed bun slathered with mayonnaise! The Monster Thickburger weighs in at a whopping 1,410 calories and 107 grams of fat, far greater than the government's recommended fat intake for an entire day.

Surely, you say, Hardee's made a colossal blunder here. Not so! At least, not from a profit viewpoint. Sales at Hardee's 1,990 outlets have climbed 20 percent since it introduced the Thickburger line, resulting in fatter profits. It seems that some consumers, especially in Hardee's target market of young men aged 18 to 34, just love fat burgers. A reporter asked a 27-year-old construction worker who was downing a Monster Thickburger if he'd thought about its effect on his health. "I've never even thought about it," he replied, "and to be honest, I don't really care. It just tastes good." Hardee's certainly isn't hiding the nutritional facts. Here's how it describes Thickburgers on its Web site:

There's only one thing that can slay the hunger of a young guy on the move: the Thinkburger line at Hardee's. With nine crav-able varieties, including the classic Original Thickburger and the monument to decadence, the Monster Thickburger, quick-service goes premium with 100% Angus beef and all the fix-

ings. . . . If you want to indulge in a big, delicious, juicy burger, look no further than Hardee's.

Hardee's even offers a Nutrition Calculator on it's Web site showing the calories, fat, and other content of all its menu items.

So, should Hardee's hang its head in shame? Is it being socially irresponsible by aggressively promoting overindulgence to ill-informed or unwary consumers? Or is it simply practicing good marketing, creating more value for its customers by offering a big juicy burger that clearly pings their taste buds and letting them make their own choices? Critics claim the former; industry defenders claim the latter.

Hardee's clearly targets adult men with its products and marketing. However, the question of blame gets even murkier when it comes to child obesity. The debate rages over the marketing of everything from fast food and soft drinks in our nation's school cafeterias to cereal, cookies, and other "not-so-good-for-you" products targeted toward kids and teens, who are seen as especially vulnerable to seductive or misleading marketing pitches. Once again, many public and private advocacy groups point the finger at food marketers. They worry that a five-year-old watching cute characters and fun ads for Trix sugared cereal or Oreo cookies during a Saturday morning cartoon show probably understands little about good nutrition. These critics have called on food marketers to voluntarily adopt more responsible children's marketing practices.

The food industry itself seems split on the issue. Kraft Foods appears to agree. It announced that it would no longer advertise products such as Oreos, Chips Ahoy!, and most of its Oscar Mayer Lunchables meals on programs targeted to children aged 6 to 11—Cereal maker General Mills, however, took just the opposite track. Rather than giving in to pressures from politicians and the press by

The obesity debate: Is Hardee's being socially irresponsible or simply practicing good marketing by giving customers a big juicy burger that clearly pings their taste buds? Judging by the nutrition calculator at its Web site, the company certainly isn't hiding the nutritional facts.

(continues)

(continued)

cutting back on marketing to kids, General Mills fielded its largest-ever kids advertising effort. It proudly launched a "Choose Breakfast" TV campaign, which plays up the health benefits of eating breakfast cereal—including its Trix, Cocoa Puffs, Lucky Charms, and other sugary cereals. To strengthen the wellness message, it's tacking tension trailers on to the ends of commercials promoting the importance of eating a good breakfast. The ten-second spots urge kids to visit a special Web site where they can sign a pledge to "choose a healthy breakfast and to be active each and every day."

With the "Choose Breakfast" campaign, General Mills hopes to present itself as part of the kids' health solution, not the problem. "We have a different point of view than Kraft," says General Mills' chief marketing officer. "We think that kids should be eating cereal, including presweetened cereal." Critics decry the campaign: "The makers of these cereals have done a fabulous marketing job of making people think that these are healthy foods when [in fact] they are cookies," says one. However, The Children's Advertising Review Unit (CARU) of the Council of Better Business Bureaus sides with General Mills. "I think it's responsible advertising," says the CARU's director. "They're encouraging a behavior that is healthful" as opposed to not eating breakfast.

So, back to that big question: Who's to blame for our nation's obesity epidemic? Is it the marketers who promote unhealthy but irresistible fare to vulnerable consumers? Or is it the fault of consumers themselves for failing to take personal responsibility for their own health and well-being? It's a weighty decision for many food marketers. And, as is the case with most social responsibility issues, finding the answer to that question is even harder than trying to take off some of those extra pounds.

Sources: Stephanie Thompson, "Kraft Gets into the Groove," *Advertising Age*, January 23, 2006, p. 25; Steven Gray, "At Fast-Food Chains, Era of the Giant Burger (Plus Bacon) Is Here," *The Wall Street Journal,* January 27, 2005, p. B1; "Obesity Research Ignites Calls for Food Ad Curbs," *Marketing Week*, May 5, 2005, p. 8; John Schmeltzer, "Second Cereal Maker Announces Changes to Child Marketing Campaign," *Knight Ridder Tribune Business News*, June 23, 2005, p. 1; Janet Adamy, "General Mills Touts Sugary Cereal as Healthy Kids Breakfast," *The Wall Street Journal*, June 22, 2005, p. B1; Stephanie Thompson, "General Mills Slaps Down Kraft," *Advertising Age*, June 27, 2005, pp. 1, 53; Sonia Reyes, "Battle Lines Drawn Over Kid Marketing Food Fight," *Brandweek*, December 12, 2005, p. 5; and National Center for Health and Statistics, "Obesity Still a Major Problem," April 14, 2006, accessed at www.cdc.gov.

now offer toner cartridge refill services to businesses. You can refill most cartridges eight to ten times—if you can find the right parts. However, printer companies would prefer to sell their cartridges for $50 or more, rather than allow someone to refill an exhausted one for half the price. So they make it hard for refill operations by continually introducing new models and tweaking inkjet cartridges and laser toner containers. Refill parts manufacturers struggle to keep up, jockeying with the printer companies that are working to thwart refill-enabling rollers, ribbons and other pieces. "You've got planned obsolescence," says the owner of Laser Logic, a small cartridge refilling company, as he disassembles a cartridge to inspect its drum unit, wiper blade, clips, springs and other mechanisms for signs of wear. "It's kind of like a 'Mission Impossible': At the end of this tape, the toner cartridge will self-destruct."[8]

Critics charge that some producers continually change consumer concepts of acceptable styles to encourage more and earlier buying. An obvious example is constantly changing clothing fashions. Other producers are accused of holding back attractive functional features, then introducing them later to make older models obsolete. Critics claim that this occurs in the consumer electronics and computer industries. For example, Intel and Microsoft have been accused over the years of holding back their next-generation computer chips and software until demand is exhausted for the current generation. Still other producers are accused of using materials and components that will break, wear, rust, or rot sooner than they should. One writer put it this way: "The marvels of modern technology include the development of a soda can, which, when discarded, will last forever—and a . . . car, which, when properly cared for, will rust out in two or three years."[9]

Marketers respond that consumers *like* style changes; they get tired of the old goods and want a new look in fashion or a new design in cars. No one has to buy the new look, and if too few people like it, it will simply fail. For most technical products, customers *want* the latest innovations, even if older models still work. Companies that withhold new features run the risk that competitors will introduce the new feature first and steal the market. For example, consider personal computers. Some consumers grumble that the consumer electronics industry's constant push to produce "faster, smaller, cheaper" models means that they must continually buy new machines just to keep up. Others, however, can hardly wait for the latest model to arrive.

Thus, most companies do not design their products to break down earlier, because they do not want to lose customers to other brands. Instead, they seek constant improvement to ensure that products will consistently meet or exceed customer expectations. Much of so-called planned obsolescence is the working of the competitive and technological forces in a free society—forces that lead to ever-improving goods and services.

Poor Service to Disadvantaged Consumers

Finally, the American marketing system has been accused of serving disadvantaged consumers poorly. For example, critics claim that the urban poor often have to shop in smaller stores that carry inferior goods and charge higher prices. The presence of large national chain stores in low-income neighborhoods would help to keep prices down. However, the critics accuse major chain retailers of "redlining," drawing a red line around disadvantaged neighborhoods and avoiding placing stores there.[10]

Similar redlining charges have been leveled at the insurance, consumer lending, banking, and health care industries. Home and auto insurers have been accused of assigning higher premiums to people with poor credit ratings. The insurers claim that individuals with bad credit tend to make more insurance claims, and that this justifies charging them higher premiums. However, critics and consumer advocates have accused the insurers of a new form of redlining. Says one writer, "This is a new excuse for denying coverage to the poor, elderly, and minorities."[11]

More recently, consumer advocates have charged that income tax preparers such as H&R Block and Jackson Hewitt are taking advantage of the working poor by offering them "rapid refunds" after preparing their taxes. Customers receive these rapid refunds when their taxes are prepared, rather than waiting two weeks to a month for the IRS to send the refund. The big prob-lem is that the refunds are not free. In fact, they're "refund anticipation loans" (RALs) with fees starting around $130, which represents an APR (annual percentage rate) of 245 percent of the average working poor person's refund. In one year alone, more than 10.6 million low-income families requested rapid refunds, and tax preparers made more than $1.4 billion in profits on them. Consumer advocates are pressuring state legislatures to pass laws requiring loan materials to be written in a language that the average consumer can understand. And the state of California recently filed a lawsuit against H&R Block for deceptive practices associated with RALs.[12]

Clearly, better marketing systems must be built to service disadvantaged consumers. In fact, many marketers profitably target such consumers with legitimate goods and services that create real value. In cases where marketers do not step in to fill the void, the government likely will. For example, the FTC has taken action against sellers who advertise false values, wrongfully deny services, or charge disadvan-taged customers too much.

■ Public policymakers have charged that income tax preparers such as H&R Block and Jackson Hewitt are taking advantage of vulnerable consumers by offering them "rapid refunds" after preparing their taxes. The big problem is that the refunds are not free.

Marketing's Impact on Society as a Whole

The American marketing system has been accused of adding to several "evils" in American society at large. Advertising has been a special target—so much so that the American Association of Advertising Agencies launched a campaign to defend advertising against what it felt to be common but untrue criticisms.

False Wants and Too Much Materialism

Critics have charged that the marketing system urges too much interest in material possessions. People are judged by what they *own* rather than by who they *are*. This drive for wealth and possessions hit new highs in the 1980s and 1990s, when phrases such as "greed is good" and "shop till you drop" seemed to characterize the times.

In the current decade, many social scientists have noted a reaction against the opulence and waste of the previous decades and a return to more basic values and social commitment. However, our infatuation with material things continues.

If you made a graph of American life since the end of World War II, every line concerning money and the things that money can buy would soar upward, a statistical monument to materialism. Inflation-adjusted income per American has almost tripled. The size of the typical new house has more than doubled. A two-car garage was once a goal; now we're nearly a three-car nation. Designer everything, personal electronics, and other items that didn't even exist a half-century ago are now affordable. Although our time spent shopping has dropped in recent years to just three hours a week, American households currently spend on average $1.22 for every $1 earned. Some consumers will let nothing stand between them and their acquisitions. Recently, in a Florida Wal-Mart, post-Thanksgiving shoppers rushing to buy DVD players (on sale for $29) knocked down a woman, trampled her, and left her unconscious.[13]

The critics do not view this interest in material things as a natural state of mind but rather as a matter of false wants created by marketing. Businesses hire Madison Avenue to stimulate people's desires for goods, and Madison Avenue uses the mass media to create materialistic models of the good life. People work harder to earn the necessary money. Their purchases increase the output of American industry, and industry in turn uses Madison Avenue to stimulate more desire for the industrial output.

Thus, marketing is seen as creating false wants that benefit industry more than they benefit consumers. Some critics even take their concerns to the streets.

For almost a decade Bill Talen, also known as Reverend Billy, has taken to the streets, exhorting people to resist temptation—the temptation to shop. With the zeal of a street-corner preacher and the schmaltz of a street-corner Santa, Reverend Billy will tell anyone willing to listen that people are walking willingly into the hellfires of consumption. He believes that shoppers have almost no resistance to the media messages that encourage them, around the clock, to want things and buy them. He sees a population lost in consumption, the meaning of individual existence vanished in a fog of wanting, buying, and owning too many things. To further his message, Billy started the Church of Stop Shopping. Sporting a televangelist's pompadour, a priest's collar, and a white megaphone, Reverend Billy is often accompanied by his gospel choir when he strides into stores he considers objectionable or shows up at protests like the annual post-Thanksgiving Buy Nothing Day event on Fifth Avenue in Manhattan. When the choir, which is made up of volunteers, erupts in song, it is hard to ignore: "Stop shopping! Stop shopping! We will never shop again!"[14]

■ Materialism: With the zeal of a street-corner preacher and the schmaltz of a street-corner Santa, Reverend Billy—founder of the Church of Stop Shopping—will tell anyone who will listen that people are walking willingly into the hellfires of consumption.

These criticisms overstate the power of business to create needs, however. People have strong defenses against advertising and other marketing tools. Marketers are most effective when they appeal to existing wants rather than when they attempt to create new ones. Furthermore, people seek information when making important purchases and often do not rely on single sources. Even minor purchases that may be affected by advertising messages lead to repeat purchases only if the product delivers the promised customer value. Finally, the high failure rate of new products shows that companies are not able to control demand.

■ Balancing private and public goods: In response to lane-clogging traffic congestion like that above, London now levies a congestion charge. The charge has reduced congestion by 30 percent and raised money to shore up the city's public transportation system.

On a deeper level, our wants and values are influenced not only by marketers but also by family, peer groups, religion, cultural background, and education. If Americans are highly materialistic, these values arose out of basic socialization processes that go much deeper than business and mass media could produce alone.

Too Few Social Goods

Business has been accused of overselling private goods at the expense of public goods. As private goods increase, they require more public services that are usually not forthcoming. For example, an increase in automobile ownership (private good) requires more highways, traffic control, parking spaces, and police services (public goods). The overselling of private goods results in "social costs." For cars, the social costs include traffic congestion, air pollution, gasoline shortages, and deaths and injuries from car accidents.

A way must be found to restore a balance between private and public goods. One option is to make producers bear the full social costs of their operations. The government could require automobile manufacturers to build cars with even more safety features, more efficient engines, and better pollution-control systems. Automakers would then raise their prices to cover extra costs. If buyers found the price of some cars too high, however, the producers of these cars would disappear. Demand would then move to those producers that could support the sum of the private and social costs.

A second option is to make consumers pay the social costs. For example, many cities around the world are starting to charge "congestion tolls" in an effort to reduce traffic congestion. To unclog its streets, the city of London now levies a congestion charge of $16.50 per day per car to drive in an eight-square-mile area downtown. The charge has not only reduced traffic congestion by 30 percent, it raises money to shore up London's public transportation system. Similarly, San Diego has turned some of its HOV (high-occupancy vehicle) lanes into HOT (high-occupancy toll) lanes for drivers carrying too few passengers. Regular drivers can use the HOV lanes, but they must pay tolls ranging from $0.50 off-peak to $4.00 during rush hour. If the costs of driving rise high enough, consumers will travel at nonpeak times or find alternative transportation modes.[15]

Cultural Pollution

Critics charge the marketing system with creating *cultural pollution*. Our senses are being constantly assaulted by marketing and advertising. Commercials interrupt serious programs; pages of ads obscure magazines; billboards mar beautiful scenery; spam fills our e-mail boxes. These interruptions continually pollute people's minds with messages of materialism, sex, power, or status. A recent study found that 65 percent of Americans feel constantly bombarded with too many marketing messages, and some critics call for sweeping changes.[16]

Marketers answer the charges of "commercial noise" with these arguments: First, they hope that their ads reach primarily the target audience. But because of mass-communication channels, some ads are bound to reach people who have no interest in the product and are therefore bored or annoyed. People who buy magazines addressed to their interests—such as *Vogue* or *Fortune*—rarely complain about the ads because the magazines advertise products of interest.

Second, ads make much of television and radio free to users and keep down the costs of magazines and newspapers. Many people think commercials are a small price to pay for these benefits. Finally, today's consumers have alternatives. For example, they can zip and zap TV commercials or avoid them altogether on many cable or satellite channels. Thus, to hold consumer attention, advertisers are making their ads more entertaining and informative.

Too Much Political Power

Another criticism is that business wields too much political power. "Oil," "tobacco," "auto," and "pharmaceuticals" senators support an industry's interests against the public interest. Advertisers are accused of holding too much power over the mass media, limiting media freedom to report independently and objectively. The critics ask: How can magazines afford to tell the truth about the low nutritional value of packaged foods when these magazines are being subsidized by such advertisers as General Foods, Kellogg's, Kraft, and General Mills? How can the major TV networks criticize the practices of the large auto companies when such companies invest billions of dollars a year in broadcast advertising?

American industries do promote and protect their own interests. They have a right to representation in Congress and the mass media, although their influence can become too great. Fortunately, many powerful business interests once thought to be untouchable have been tamed in the public interest. For example, Standard Oil was broken up in 1911, and the meatpacking industry was disciplined in the early 1900s after exposures by Upton Sinclair. Ralph Nader caused legislation that forced the automobile industry to build safer cars, and the Surgeon General's Report resulted in cigarette companies putting health warnings on their packages.

More recently, giants such as AT&T, R.J. Reynolds, Intel, and Microsoft have felt the impact of regulators seeking to balance the interests of big business against those of the public. Moreover, because the media receive advertising revenues from many different advertisers, it is easier to resist the influence of one or a few of them. Too much business power tends to result in counterforces that check and offset these powerful interests.

Marketing's Impact on Other Businesses

Critics also charge that a company's marketing practices can harm other companies and reduce competition. Three problems are involved: acquisitions of competitors, marketing practices that create barriers to entry, and unfair competitive marketing practices.

Critics claim that firms are harmed and competition reduced when companies expand by acquiring competitors rather than by developing their own new products. The large number of acquisitions and rapid pace of industry consolidation over the past several decades have caused concern that vigorous young competitors will be absorbed and that competition will be reduced. In virtually every major industry—retailing, entertainment, financial services, utilities, transportation, automobiles, telecommunications, health care—the number of major competitors is shrinking.

Acquisition is a complex subject. Acquisitions can sometimes be good for society. The acquiring company may gain economies of scale that lead to lower costs and lower prices. A well-managed company may take over a poorly managed company and improve its efficiency. An industry that was not very competitive might become more competitive after the acquisition. But acquisitions can also be harmful and, therefore, are closely regulated by the government.

Critics have also charged that marketing practices bar new companies from entering an industry. Large marketing companies can use patents and heavy promotion spending, and they can tie up suppliers or dealers to keep out or drive out competitors. Those concerned with antitrust regulation recognize that some barriers are the natural result of the economic advantages of doing business on a large scale. Other barriers could be challenged by existing and new laws. For example, some critics have proposed a progressive tax on advertising spending to reduce the role of selling costs as a major barrier to entry.

Finally, some firms have in fact used unfair competitive marketing practices with the intention of hurting or destroying other firms. They may set their prices below costs, threaten to cut off business with suppliers, or discourage the buying of a competitor's products. Various laws work to prevent such predatory competition. It is difficult, however, to prove that the intent or action was really predatory.

In recent years, Wal-Mart, American Airlines, Intel, and Microsoft have all been accused of various predatory practices. For example, Wal-Mart has been accused of using predatory pricing in selected market areas to drive smaller, mom-and-pop retailers out of business. Wal-Mart has become a lightning rod for protests by citizens in dozens of towns who worry that the megaretailer's unfair practices will choke out local businesses. However, whereas critics charge that Wal-Mart's actions are predatory, others question whether this is unfair competition or the healthy competition of a more efficient company against less efficient ones.[17]

■ Predatory business practices: Wal-Mart has become a lightning rod for protests by citizens who worry that the mega-retailer's unfair practices will choke out local businesses. Wal-Mart defenders claim that it's more a matter of healthy competition of a more efficient company against less efficient ones.

Citizen and Public Actions to Regulate Marketing

Because some people view business as the cause of many economic and social ills, grassroots movements have arisen from time to time to keep business in line. The two major movements have been *consumerism* and *environmentalism*.

Consumerism

American business firms have been the target of organized consumer movements on three occasions. The first consumer movement took place in the early 1900s. It was fueled by rising prices, Upton Sinclair's writings on conditions in the meat industry, and scandals in the drug industry. The second consumer movement, in the mid-1930s, was sparked by an upturn in consumer prices during the Great Depression and another drug scandal.

The third movement began in the 1960s. Consumers had become better educated, products had become more complex and potentially hazardous, and people were unhappy with American institutions. Ralph Nader appeared on the scene to force many issues, and other well-known writers accused big business of wasteful and unethical practices. President John F. Kennedy declared that consumers had the right to safety and to be informed, to choose, and to be heard. Congress investigated certain industries and proposed consumer-protection legislation. Since then, many consumer groups have been organized and several consumer laws have been passed. The consumer movement has spread internationally and has become very strong in Europe.

But what is the consumer movement? **Consumerism** is an organized movement of citizens and government agencies to improve the rights and power of buyers in relation to sellers. Traditional *sellers' rights* include:

■ The right to introduce any product in any size and style, provided it is not hazardous to personal health or safety; or, if it is, to include proper warnings and controls.

■ The right to charge any price for the product, provided no discrimination exists among similar kinds of buyers.

■ The right to spend any amount to promote the product, provided it is not defined as unfair competition.

■ The right to use any product message, provided it is not misleading or dishonest in content or execution.

■ The right to use any buying incentive programs, provided they are not unfair or misleading.

Consumerism
An organized movement of citizens and government agencies to improve the rights and power of buyers in relation to sellers.

Traditional *buyers' rights* include:

- The right not to buy a product that is offered for sale.
- The right to expect the product to be safe.
- The right to expect the product to perform as claimed.

Comparing these rights, many believe that the balance of power lies on the seller's side. True, the buyer can refuse to buy. But critics feel that the buyer has too little information, education, and protection to make wise decisions when facing sophisticated sellers. Consumer advocates call for the following additional consumer rights:

- The right to be well informed about important aspects of the product.
- The right to be protected against questionable products and marketing practices.
- The right to influence products and marketing practices in ways that will improve the "quality of life."

Each proposed right has led to more specific proposals by consumerists. The right to be informed includes the right to know the true interest on a loan (truth in lending), the true cost per unit of a brand (unit pricing), the ingredients in a product (ingredient labeling), the nutritional value of foods (nutritional labeling), product freshness (open dating), and the true benefits of a product (truth in advertising). Proposals related to consumer protection include strengthening consumer rights in cases of business fraud, requiring greater product safety, ensuring information privacy, and giving more power to government agencies. Proposals relating to quality of life include controlling the ingredients that go into certain products and packaging, reducing the level of advertising "noise," and putting consumer representatives on company boards to protect consumer interests.

Consumers have not only the *right* but also the *responsibility* to protect themselves instead of leaving this function to someone else. Consumers who believe they got a bad deal have several remedies available, including contacting the company or the media; contacting federal, state, or local agencies; and going to small-claims courts.

Environmentalism

Whereas consumerists consider whether the marketing system is efficiently serving consumer wants, environmentalists are concerned with marketing's effects on the environment and with the costs of serving consumer needs and wants. **Environmentalism** is an organized movement of concerned citizens, businesses, and government agencies to protect and improve people's living environment.

Environmentalists are not against marketing and consumption; they simply want people and organizations to operate with more care for the environment. The marketing system's

Environmentalism
An organized movement of concerned citizens and government agencies to protect and improve people's living environment.

■ Consumerism: Consumer desire for more information led to packing labels with useful facts, from ingredients and nutrition facts to recycling and country of origin information. Jones Soda even puts customer-submitted photos on its labels.

FIGURE 20.1
The environmental sustainability grid

	Internal	External
Tomorrow	**New environmental technology** Is the environmental performance of our products limited by our existing technology base? Is there potential to realize major improvements through new technology?	**Sustainability vision** Does our corporate vision direct us toward the solution of social and environmental problems? Does our vision guide the development of new technologies, markets, products, and processes?
Today	**Pollution prevention** Where are the most significant waste and emission streams from our current operations? Can we lower costs and risks by eliminating waste at the source or by using it as useful input?	**Product stewardship** What are the implications for product design and development if we assume responsibility for a product's entire life cycle? Can we add value or lower costs while simultaneously reducing the impact of our products?

Environmental sustainability

A management approach that involves developing strategies that both sustain the environment and produce profits for the company.

goal, they assert, should not be to maximize consumption, consumer choice, or consumer satisfaction, but rather to maximize life quality. And "life quality" means not only the quantity and quality of consumer goods and services, but also the quality of the environment. Environmentalists want environmental costs included in both producer and consumer decision making.

The first wave of modern environmentalism in the United States was driven by environmental groups and concerned consumers in the 1960s and 1970s. They were concerned with damage to the ecosystem caused by strip-mining, forest depletion, acid rain, loss of the atmosphere's ozone layer, toxic wastes, and litter. They also were concerned with the loss of recreational areas and with the increase in health problems caused by bad air, polluted water, and chemically treated food.

The second wave of modern environmentalism was driven by government, which passed laws and regulations during the 1970s and 1980s governing industrial practices impacting the environment. This wave hit some industries hard. Steel companies and utilities had to invest billions of dollars in pollution control equipment and costlier fuels. The auto industry had to introduce expensive emission controls in cars. The packaging industry had to find ways to reduce litter. These industries and others have often resented and resisted environmental regulations, especially when they have been imposed too rapidly to allow companies to make proper adjustments. Many of these companies claim they have had to absorb large costs that have made them less competitive.

The first two environmentalism waves have now merged into a third and stronger wave in which companies are accepting more responsibility for doing no harm to the environment. They are shifting from protest to prevention, and from regulation to responsibility. More and more companies are adopting policies of **environmental sustainability**. Simply put, environmental sustainability is about generating profits while helping to save the planet. Sustainability is a crucial but difficult societal goal.

Some companies have responded to consumer environmental concerns by doing only what is required to avert new regulations or to keep environmentalists quiet. Enlightened companies, however, are taking action not because someone is forcing them to, or to reap short-run profits, but because it is the right thing to do—for both the company and for the planet's environmental future.

Figure 20.1 shows a grid that companies can use to gauge their progress toward environmental sustainability. At the most basic level, a company can practice *pollution prevention*. This involves more than pollution control—cleaning up waste after it has been created. Pollution prevention means eliminating or minimizing waste before it is created. Companies emphasizing prevention have responded with "green marketing" programs—developing ecologically safer products, recyclable and biodegradable packaging, better pollution controls, and more energy-efficient operations.

For example, Sony has reduced the amount of heavy metals—such as lead, mercury, and cadmium—in its electronic products. Nike produces PVC-free shoes, recycles old sneakers, and educates young people about conservation, reuse, and recycling. And UPS is now turning its fleet of 70,000 boxy brown UPS delivery trucks "green," finding cleaner replacements for the old, smoke-belching diesels. It operates some 1,790 ultralow- and 1,430 low-emission vehicles throughout North America. And it's working with DaimlerChrysler and the U.S. Environmental Protection Agency to test fuel cells that run on hydrogen and other alternative fuels.[18]

At the next level, companies can practice *product stewardship*—minimizing not just pollution from production but all environmental impacts throughout the full product life cycle, and all the while reducing costs. Many companies are adopting *design for environment (DFE)* practices, which involve thinking ahead to design products that are easier to recover, reuse, or recycle. DFE not only helps to sustain the environment, it can be highly profitable for the company.

An example is Xerox Corporation's Equipment Remanufacture and Parts Reuse Program, which converts end-of-life office equipment into new products and parts. Equipment returned to Xerox can be remanufactured reusing 70 to 90 percent by weight of old machine components, while still meeting performance standards for equipment made with all new parts. The program creates benefits for both the environment and for the company. It prevents more than 120 million pounds of waste from entering landfills each year. And it reduces the amount of raw material and energy needed to produce new parts. Energy savings from parts reuse total an estimated 320,000 megawatt hours annually—enough energy to light more than 250,000 U.S. homes for the year.[19]

At the third level, companies look to the future and plan for *new environmental technologies*. Many organizations that have made good sustainability headway are still limited by existing technologies. To develop fully sustainable strategies, they will need to develop new technologies. Wal-Mart is doing this. It recently opened two experimental superstores designed to test dozens of environmentally friendly and energy-efficient technologies:[20]

A 143-foot-tall wind turbine stands outside a Wal-Mart Supercenter in Aurora, Colorado. Incongruous as it might seem, it is clearly a sign that something about this particular store is different. On the outside, the store's facade features row upon row of windows to allow in as much natural light as possible. The landscaping uses native, drought-tolerant plants well adapted to the hot, dry Colorado summers, cutting down on watering, mowing, and the amount of fertilizer and other chemicals needed. Inside the store, an efficient high-output linear fluorescent lighting system saves enough electricity annually from this store alone to supply the needs of 52 single-family homes. The store's heating system burns recovered cooking oil from the deli's fryers. The oil is collected, mixed with waste engine oil from the store's Tire and Lube Express, and burned in the waste-oil boiler. All organic waste, including produce, meats, and paper, is placed in an organic waste compactor, which is then hauled off to a company that turns it into mulch for the garden.

These and dozens more technological touches make the supercenter a laboratory for efficient and Earth-friendly retail operations. In the long run, Wal-Mart's environmental goals are to use 100 percent renewable energy, to create zero waste, and to sell products that sustain its resources and environment. Moreover, Wal-Mart is eagerly spreading the word by encouraging visitors—even from competing companies. "We had Target in here not too long ago, and other retail chains and independents have also taken a tour of the store," notes the store manager. "This is not something we're keeping to ourselves. We want everyone to know about it."

■ Wal-Mart has opened two experimental superstores designed to test dozens of environmentally friendly and energy-efficient technologies. The facade of this store features rows and rows of windows to let in as much natural light as possible, and it's "urban forest" landscaping uses native, well-adapted plants, cutting down on watering, mowing, and the amount of fertilizer and other chemicals needed.

Finally, companies can develop a *sustainability vision*, which serves as a guide to the future. It shows how the company's products and services, processes, and policies must evolve and what new technologies must be developed to get there. This vision of sustainability provides a framework for pollution control, product stewardship, and environmental technology.

Most companies today focus on the lower-left quadrant of the grid in Figure 20.1, investing most heavily in pollution prevention. Some forward-looking companies practice product stewardship and are developing new environmental technologies. Few companies have well-defined sustainability visions. However, emphasizing only one or a few quadrants in the environmental sustainability grid can be shortsighted. Investing only in the bottom half of the grid puts a company in a good position today but leaves it vulnerable in the future. In contrast, a heavy emphasis on the top half suggests that a company has good environmental vision but lacks the skills needed to implement it. Thus, companies should work at developing all four dimensions of environmental sustainability.

Alcoa, the world's leading producer of aluminum is doing just that. For two years running, it has been one of three companies singled out by *Global 100* for superior sustainability excellence:

Alcoa has distinguished itself as a leader through its sophisticated approach to identifying and managing the material sustainability risks that it faces as a company. From pollution prevention via greenhouse gas emissions reduction programs to engaging stakeholders over new environmental technology, such as controversial hydropower projects, Alcoa has the sustainability strategies in place needed to meld its profitability objectives with society's larger environmental protection goals. . . . Importantly, Alcoa's approach to sustainability is firmly rooted in the idea that sustainability programs can indeed add financial value. Perhaps the best evidence is the company's efforts to promote the use of aluminum in transportation, where aluminum—with its excellent strength-to-weight ratio—is making inroads as a material of choice that allows automakers to build low-weight, fuel-efficient vehicles that produce fewer tailpipe emissions. This kind of forward-thinking strategy of supplying the market with the products that will help solve pressing global environmental problems shows a company that sees the future, has plotted a course, and is aligning its business accordingly. Says CEO Alain Belda, "Our values require us to think and act not only on the present challenges, but also with the legacy in mind that we leave for those who will come after us . . . as well as the commitments made by those that came before us."[21]

Public Actions to Regulate Marketing

Citizen concerns about marketing practices will usually lead to public attention and legislative proposals. New bills will be debated—many will be defeated, others will be modified, and a few will become workable laws.

Evironmentalism creates some special challenges for global marketers. As international trade barriers come down and global markets expand, environmental issues are having an ever-greater impact on international trade. Countries in North America, Western Europe, and other developed regions are developing strict environmental standards. In the United States, for example, more than two dozen major pieces of environmental legislation have been enacted since 1970, and recent events suggest that more regulation is on the way. A side accord to the North American Free Trade Agreement (NAFTA) set up a commission for resolving environmental matters. The European Union recently passed "end-of-life" regulations affecting automobiles and consumer electronics products. And the EU's Eco-Management and Audit Scheme provides guidelines for environmental self-regulation.[22]

However, environmental policies still vary widely from country to country. Countries such as Denmark, Germany, Japan, and the United States have fully developed environmental policies and high public expectations. But major countries such as China, India, Brazil, and Russia are in only the early stages of developing such policies. Moreover, environmental factors that motivate consumers in one country may have no impact on consumers in another. For example, PVC soft drink bottles cannot be used in Switzerland or Germany. However, they are preferred in France, which has an extensive recycling process for them. Thus, international companies have found it difficult to develop standard environmental practices that work around the world. Instead, they are creating general policies and then translating these policies into tailored programs that meet local regulations and expectations.

FIGURE 20.2

Major marketing decision areas that may be called into question under the law

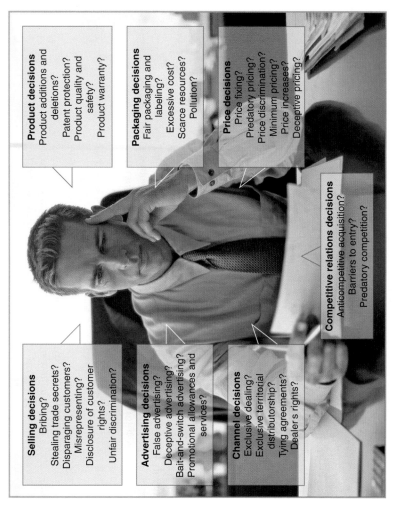

Product decisions
Product additions and
    deletions?
Patent protection?
Product quality and
    safety?
Product warranty?

Packaging decisions
Fair packaging and
    labeling?
Excessive cost?
Scarce resources?
Pollution?

Price decisions
Price fixing?
Predatory pricing?
Price discrimination?
Minimum pricing?
Price increases?
Deceptive pricing?

Selling decisions
Bribing?
Stealing trade secrets?
Disparaging customers?
Misrepresenting?
Disclosure of customer
    rights?
Unfair discrimination?

Advertising decisions
False advertising?
Deceptive advertising?
Bait-and-switch advertising?
Promotional allowances and
    services?

Channel decisions
Exclusive dealing?
Exclusive territorial
    distributorship?
Tying agreements?
Dealer's rights?

Competitive relations decisions
Anticompetitive acquisition?
Barriers to entry?
Predatory competition?

Many of the laws that affect marketing are listed in Chapter 3. The task is to translate these laws into the language that marketing executives understand as they make decisions about competitive relations, products, price, promotion, and channels of distribution. Figure 20.2 illustrates the major legal issues facing marketing management.

Business Actions toward Socially Responsible Marketing

At first, many companies opposed consumerism and environmentalism. They thought the criticisms were either unfair or unimportant. But by now, most companies have grown to embrace the new consumer rights, at least in principle. They might oppose certain pieces of legislation as inappropriate ways to solve specific consumer problems, but they recognize the consumer's right to information and protection. Many of these companies have responded positively to consumerism and environmentalism as a way to create greater customer value and to strengthen customer relationships.

Enlightened Marketing

The philosophy of **enlightened marketing** holds that a company's marketing should support the best long-run performance of the marketing system. Enlightened marketing consists of five principles: *consumer-oriented marketing, customer-value marketing, innovative marketing, sense-of-mission marketing,* and *societal marketing.*

Consumer-Oriented Marketing

Consumer-oriented marketing means that the company should view and organize its market-ing activities from the consumer's point of view. It should work hard to sense, serve, and sat-isfy the needs of a defined group of customers. All of the good marketing companies that

Enlightened marketing
A marketing philosophy holding that a company's marketing should support the best long-run performance of the marketing system.

Consumer-oriented marketing
The philosophy of enlightened marketing that holds that the company should view and organize its marketing activities from the consumer's point of view.

we've discussed in this text have had this in common: an all-consuming passion for delivering superior value to carefully chosen customers. Only by seeing the world through its customers' eyes can the company build lasting and profitable customer relationships.

Customer-Value Marketing

Customer-value marketing
A principle of enlightened marketing that holds that a company should put most of its resources into customer value-building marketing investments.

According to the principle of **customer-value marketing**, the company should put most of its resources into customer value-building marketing investments. Many things marketers do—one-shot sales promotions, cosmetic packaging changes, direct-response advertising—may raise sales in the short run but add less *value* than would actual improvements in the product's quality, features, or convenience. Enlightened marketing calls for building long-run consumer loyalty and relationships by continually improving the value consumers receive from the firm's market offering. By creating value *for* consumers, the company can capture value *from* consumers in return.

Innovative Marketing

Innovative marketing
A principle of enlightened marketing that requires that a company seek real product and marketing improvements.

The principle of **innovative marketing** requires that the company continuously seek real product and marketing improvements. The company that overlooks new and better ways to do things will eventually lose customers to another company that has found a better way. An excellent example of an innovative marketer is Samsung Electronics:

A dozen years ago, Samsung was a copycat consumer electronics brand you bought off a shipping pallet at Costco if you couldn't afford a Sony. But today, the brand holds a high-end, cutting-edge aura. In 1996, Samsung Electronics made an inspired decision. It turned its back on cheap knock-offs and set out to overtake rival Sony. The company hired a crop of fresh, young designers, who unleashed a torrent of new products—not humdrum, me-too products, but sleek, bold, and beautiful products targeted to high-end users. Samsung called them "lifestyle works of art"—from brightly colored cell phones and elegantly thin DVD players to flat-panel TV monitors that hung on walls like paintings. Every new product had to pass the "Wow!" test: If it didn't get a "Wow!" reaction during market testing, it went straight back to the design studio.

Samsung also changed its distribution to match its new caché. It initially abandoned low-end distributors such as Wal-Mart and Kmart, instead building strong relationships with specialty retailers such as Best Buy and Circuit City. Interbrand calculates that Samsung is the world's fastest growing brand over the past five years. It's the world leader in CDMA cell phones and battling for the number two spot in total handsets sold. It's also number-one worldwide in color TVs, flash memory, and LCD panels. "Samsung's performance continues to astound brand watchers," says one analyst. The company has become a model for others that "want to shift from being a cheap supplier to a global brand." Says a Samsung designer, "We're not el cheapo anymore."[23]

Sense-of-Mission Marketing

Sense-of-mission marketing
A principle of enlightened marketing that holds that a company should define its mission in broad social terms rather than narrow product terms.

Sense-of-mission marketing means that the company should define its mission in broad *social* terms rather than narrow *product* terms. When a company defines a social mission, employees feel better about their work and have a clearer sense of direction. Brands linked with broader missions can serve the best long-run interests of both the brand and consumers. For example, Dove wants to do more than just sell its beauty-care products. It's on a mission to discover "real beauty" and to help women be happy just the way they are (see Real Marketing 20.2).

Some companies define their overall corporate missions in broad societal terms. For example, defined in narrow product terms, the mission of Unilever's Ben & Jerry's unit might be "to sell ice cream." However, Ben & Jerry's states its mission more broadly, as one of "linked prosperity," including product, economic, and social missions. From its beginnings, Ben & Jerry's championed a host of social and environmental causes, and it donated a whopping 7.5 percent of pretax profits to support worthy causes. By the mid-1990s, Ben & Jerry's had become the nation's number two superpremium ice cream brand.

However, having a "double bottom line" of values and profits is no easy proposition. Throughout the 1990s, as competitors not shackled by "principles before profits" missions

Real Marketing   Dove on a Mission: "Normal Is the New Beautiful"

20.2 How do you define beauty? Flip open the latest copy of a fashion magazine and check out the ads for cosmetics and beauty-care products. Look at the models in those ads—the classic beauties with incredibly lean, sexy figures and flawless features. Does anyone *you* know look like the women in those ads? Probably not. They're one-of-a-kind supermodels, chosen to portray ideal beauty. The ads are meant to be aspirational. But real women, who compare themselves to these idealized images day in and day out, too often come away feeling diminished by thoughts that they could never really look like that.

Unilever's Dove brand is on a mission to change all of this. Its Dove Campaign for Real Beauty hopes to do much more than just sell Dove beauty creams and lotions. It aims to change the traditional definition of beauty—to "offer in its place a broader, healthier, more democratic view of beauty." It tells women to be happy just the way they are. "In Dove ads," says one advertising expert, "normal is the new beautiful."

It all started with a Unilever study that examined the impact on women of a society that narrowly defines beauty by the images seen in entertainment, in advertising, and on fashion runways. The startling result: Only 2 percent of 3,300 women and girls surveyed in 10 countries around the world considered themselves beautiful. Unilever's research revealed that among women ages 15 to 64 worldwide, 90 percent want to change at least one aspect of their physical appearance; 67 percent withdraw from life-engaging activities because they are uncomfortable with their looks. Unilever's conclusion: It's time to redefine beauty. "We believe that beauty comes in different shapes, sizes, and ages," says Dove marketing director Philippe Harousseau. "Our mission is to make more women feel beautiful every day by broadening the definition of beauty."

Unilever launched the Dove Campaign for Real Beauty globally in 2004, with ads that featured candid and confident images of real

Unilever's Dove brand is on a mission. The Dove Campaign for Real Beauty aims to change the traditional definition of beauty.

women of all types (not actresses or models) and headlines that prompted consumers to ponder their perceptions of beauty. Among others, it featured full-bodied women ("Oversized or Outstanding?"), older women ("Gray or Gorgeous?" "Wrinkled or Wonderful?"), and a heavily freckled woman ("Flawed or Flawless?"). In 2005, the campaign's popularity skyrocketed as Dove introduced six new "real beauties" of various ethnicities and proportions, in sizes ranging from 6 to 14. These women appeared in magazines and on billboards wearing nothing but their underwear and big smiles, with headlines proclaiming, "Let's face it, firming the thighs of a size 2 supermodel is no challenge," or "New Dove Firming: As Tested on Real Curves."

In 2006, Unilever took the Dove campaign to a new level, with a groundbreaking spot in the mother of all ad showcases, the Super Bowl. This ad didn't feature curvy, confident women. Instead, it presented young girls battling self-esteem issues—not models but real

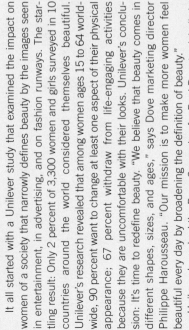

invaded its markets, Ben & Jerry's growth and profits flattened. In 2000, after several years of less than stellar financial returns, Ben & Jerry's was acquired by giant food producer Unilever. Looking back, the company appears to have focused too much on social issues at the expense of sound business management. Cohen once commented, "There came a time when I had to admit 'I'm a businessman.' And I had a hard time mouthing those words."[24]

Such experiences taught the socially responsible business movement some hard lessons. The result is a new generation of activist entrepreneurs—not social activists with big hearts who hate capitalism, but well-trained business managers and company builders with a passion for a cause. For example, consider Honest Tea:

Honest Tea has a social mission. "We strive to live up to our name in the way we conduct our business," states the company's "Philoso-tea." "We do this in every way we

girls picked from schools, sports leagues, and Girl Scout troops. In the ad, one dark-haired girl "wishes she were a blond." Another "thinks she's ugly." A pretty young redhead "hates her freckles." The ad also promoted the Dove Self-Esteem Fund, which supports, among other causes, the Girl Scouts' Uniquely Me program. It urged viewers to "get involved" at the campaignforrealbeauty.com Web site. "We want to raise awareness of self-esteem being a real issue [for a young girl]," says Harousseau. "Every single one of us can get engaged and can change the way we interact with her to increase self-esteem."

As the campaign has taken off, so have sales of Dove products. And calls to Unilever's consumer call center have surged, as has traffic to the campaignforrealbeauty.com Web site. Women, girls, and even men praise Dove for addressing a too-long-ignored social issue. Debora Boyda, managing partner at Ogilvy & Mather, the ad agency that created the campaign, received a phone call from an emotional father. His teenage daughter had just recovered from a four-year battle with anorexia. The father thanked her and stressed how important he thought the ad was. "That to me was the high point of what the ad achieved," says Boyda.

In addition to the positive reactions, however, the Dove Campaign for Real Beauty has also received criticism. Critics point out that the "real women" in the Dove ads are still headturners, with smooth skin, straight teeth, and not an ounce of cellulite. Although these unretouched beauties are more realistic than supermodels, they still represent a lofty standard of beauty. Fans of the campaign counter that, compared with typical ad-industry portrayals, the Dove women represent an image of beauty that is healthy, constructive, and much closer to reality. For example, after seeing a Dove billboard in Chicago, one young woman gushed, "Most girls don't have that (supermodel) type of body and they know they won't get to that. But seeing this [Dove ad] they say, 'I can do that.'"

Others critics claim that the campaign is hypocritical, celebrating less-than-perfect bodies while at the same time selling products designed to restore them, such as firming lotions. "Any change in the culture of advertising that allows for a broader definition of beauty and encourages women to be more accepting and comfortable with their natural appearance is a step in the right direction," says noted psychologist and author Mary Pipher. "But embedded within this is a contradiction. They are still saying you have to use this product to be beautiful." Still, she concedes, "It's better than what we've had in the past."

Yvonne, a woman featured in one of the Dove ads, takes issue with the criticism. "That's like saying, why be into fashion? Women are women. We love to be the best we can be. It's not contradictory; it's just taking care of yourself." Ad executive Boyda also defends Unilever's intentions: "We are telling [women] we want them to take care of themselves, take care of their beauty," she says. "That's very different from sending them the message to look like something they're not."

Still others criticize Unilever for capitalizing on women's low self-esteem just to make a buck. But the company responds that it has created a lot more than just a series of ads. It's promoting a philosophy, one supported by a substantial advertising budget, the Dove Self-Esteem Fund, and a Web site full of resources designed to build the self-esteem of women and young girls.

To be sure, Unilever does have financial objectives for its Dove brand—most consumers understand and except that fact. And if women are not buying the message of Dove about the nature of real beauty, then they aren't buying its products either. But the people behind the Dove brand and the Campaign for Real Beauty have noble motives beyond sales and profits. According to Fernando Acosta, Dove vice president of brand development, the bold and compelling mission of the Dove brand to redefine beauty and reassure women rank well above issues of dollars and cents. "You should see the faces of the people working on this brand now," he says. "There is a real love for the brand."

Sources: Theresa Howard, "Dove Ad Gets Serious for Super Bowl," USA Today, January 23, 2006, accessed at www.usatoday.com; Don Babwin, "Dove Ads with 'Real' Women Get Attention," Associated Press Financial Wire, July 29, 2005; Theresa Howard, "Ad Campaigns Tell Women to Celebrate How They Are," USA Today, August 7, 2005, accessed at www.usatoday.com; Pallavi Gogoi, "From Reality TV to Reality Ads," BusinessWeek Online, August 17, 2005, accessed at www.businessweek.com; "Positioning: Getting Comfy in Their Skin," Brandweek, December 19, 2005, p. 16; Patricia Odell, "Real Girls," Promo, March 1, 2006, p. 24; "Beyond Stereotypes: Rebuilding the Foundation of Beauty Beliefs," February 2006, accessed at www.campaignforrealbeauty.com; Jeani Read, "Women Modeling for Dove Love Challenging Skinny Stereotypes," The Calgary Herald, May 15, 2006, p. C3; and information found at www.campaignforrealbeauty.com, December 2006.

can—whether we are working with growers and suppliers, answering our customers' questions, or trying to leave a lighter environmental footprint." It all starts with a socially responsible product, an "Honest Tea"—tasty, barely sweetened, and made from all-natural ingredients, many purchased from poorer communities seeking to become more self-sufficient. But unlike old revolutionaries like Ben and Jerry, Honest Tea's founders are businesspeople—and proud of it—who appreciate solid business training. Cofounder Seth Goldman won a business-plan competition as a student at the Yale School of Management and later started the company with one of his professors.

Honest Tea's managers know that good deeds alone don't work. They are just as dedicated to building a viable, profitable business as to shaping a mission. For Honest Tea, social responsibility is not about marketing and hype. It goes about its good deeds quietly. A few years ago, Honest Tea became the first (and only) company to sell a Fair Trade bottled tea—every time the company purchases the tea for its

■ Societal marketing: Today's new activist entrepreneurs are not social activists with big hearts who hate capitalism, but well-trained business managers and company builders with a passion for a cause. TeaEO Seth Goldman takes a break with workers in a fair trade tea garden in India.

Peach Oo-la-long tea, a donation is made to the workers who pick the tea leaves. The workers invest the money in their community for a variety of uses, including a computer lab for children in the village and a fund for families. Royalties from sales of Honest Tea's First Nation Peppermint tea go to I'tchik Herbal Tea, a small woman-owned company on the Crow Reservation in Montana, as well as a Native American organization called Pretty Shield Foundation, which includes foster care among its activities. However, "when we first brought out our peppermint tea, our label didn't mention that we were sharing the revenues with the Crow Nation," says Goldman. "We didn't want people to think that was a gimmick."[25]

Thus, today's new activist entrepreneurs are not social activists with big hearts, but well-trained business managers and company builders with a passion for a cause.

Societal Marketing

Societal marketing

A principle of enlightened marketing that holds that a company should make marketing decisions by considering consumers' wants, the company's requirements, consumers' long-run interests, and society's long-run interests.

Deficient products

Products that have neither immediate appeal nor long-run benefits.

Pleasing products

Products that give high immediate satisfaction but may hurt consumers in the long run.

Salutary products

Products that have low appeal but may benefit consumers in the long run.

Following the principle of **societal marketing**, an enlightened company makes marketing decisions by considering consumers' wants and interests, the company's requirements, and society's long-run interests. The company is aware that neglecting consumer and societal long-run interests is a disservice to consumers and society. Alert companies view societal problems as opportunities.

A societally oriented marketer wants to design products that are not only pleasing but also beneficial. The difference is shown in Figure 20.3. Products can be classified according to their degree of immediate consumer satisfaction and long-run consumer benefit. **Deficient products**, such as bad-tasting and ineffective medicine, have neither immediate appeal nor long-run benefits. **Pleasing products** give high immediate satisfaction but may hurt consumers in the long run. Examples include cigarettes and junk food. **Salutary products** have low appeal but may benefit consumers in the long run; for instance, seat belts and air bags. **Desirable products** give both high immediate satisfaction and high long-run benefits, such as a tasty *and* nutritious breakfast food.

Examples of desirable products abound. Philips Lighting's Earth Light compact fluorescent lightbulb provides good lighting at the same time that it gives long life and energy savings. Toyota's hybrid Prius gives both a quiet ride and fuel efficiency. Maytag's front-loading Neptune washer provides superior cleaning along with water savings and energy efficiency. And Haworth's Zody office chair is not only attractive and functional but also environmentally responsible:

Let's talk about your butt—specifically, what it's sitting on. Chances are, your chair is an unholy medley of polyvinyl chloride and hazardous chemicals that drift into your lungs each time you shift your weight. It was likely produced in a fossil-fuel-swilling factory that in turn spews toxic pollution and effluents. And it's ultimately destined for a landfill or incinerator, where it will emit carcinogenic dioxins and endocrine-

FIGURE 20.3
Societal classification of products

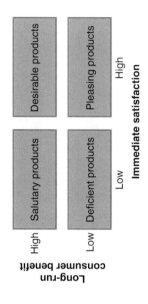

	Immediate satisfaction	
	High	Low
Long-run consumer benefit High	Desirable products	Salutary products
Long-run consumer benefit Low	Pleasing products	Deficient products

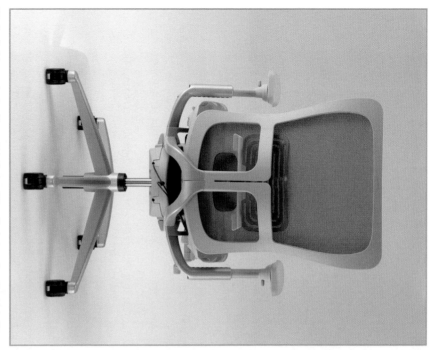

■ Desirable products: Haworth's Zody office chair is not only attractive and functional but also environmentally responsible.

disrupting phthalates, the kind of hormone-mimicking nasties that give male fish female gen-italia and small children cancer (or is it the other way around?). Now, envision what you might be sitting on in 2016. Actually, never mind: Office-furniture outfit Haworth already built it. It's called the Zody, and it's made without PVC, CFCs, chrome, or any other toxic fixin's. Ninety-eight percent of it can be recycled; some 50 per-cent of it already has been. The energy used in the manufacturing process is completely offset by wind-power credits, and when the chair is ready to retire, the company will take it off your hands and reuse its components.[26]

Companies should try to turn all of their products into desirable products. The challenge posed by pleasing products is that they sell very well but may end up hurt-ing the consumer. The product opportunity, therefore, is to add long-run benefits without reducing the product's pleasing qualities. The challenge posed by salutary prod-ucts is to add some pleasing qualities so that they will become more desirable in consumers' minds.

Marketing Ethics

Conscientious marketers face many moral dilemmas. The best thing to do is often unclear. Because not all managers have fine moral sensitivity, companies need to develop *corporate marketing ethics policies*—broad guidelines that everyone in the organization must fol-low. These policies should cover distributor relations, advertising standards, customer service, pricing, prod-uct development, and general ethical standards.

The finest guidelines cannot resolve all the difficult ethical situations the marketer faces. Table 20.1 lists some difficult ethical situations marketers could face during their careers. If marketers choose immediate sales-producing actions in all these cases, their mar-keting behavior might well be described as immoral or even amoral. If they refuse to go along with *any* of the actions, they might be ineffective as marketing managers and unhappy because of the constant moral tension. Managers need a set of principles that will help them figure out the moral importance of each situation and decide how far they can go in good conscience.

But *what* principle should guide companies and marketing managers on issues of ethics and social responsibility? One philosophy is that such issues are decided by the free market and legal system. Under this principle, companies and their managers are not responsible for making moral judgments. Companies can in good conscience do whatever the market and legal systems allow.

A second philosophy puts responsibility not on the system but in the hands of individual companies and managers. This more enlightened philosophy suggests that a company should have a "social conscience." Companies and managers should apply high standards of ethics and morality when making corporate decisions, regardless of "what the system allows." History provides an endless list of examples of company actions that were legal but highly irresponsible.

Each company and marketing manager must work out a philosophy of socially responsi-ble and ethical behavior. Under the societal marketing concept, each manager must look beyond what is legal and allowed and develop standards based on personal integrity, corpo-rate conscience, and long-run consumer welfare. A clear and responsible philosophy will help the company deal with knotty issues such as the one faced recently by 3M:

In late 1997, a powerful new research technique for scanning blood kept turning up the same odd result: Tiny amounts of a chemical 3M had made for nearly 40 years were showing up in blood drawn from people living all across the country. If

Desirable products
Products that give both high immediate satisfaction and high long-run benefits.

TABLE 20.1
Some Morally Difficult Situations in Marketing

1. You work for a cigarette company. Public policy debates over the past many years leave no doubt in your mind that cigarette smoking and cancer are closely linked. Although your company currently runs an "if you don't smoke, don't start" promotion campaign, you believe that other company promotions might encourage young (although legal age) nonsmokers to pick up the habit. What would you do?

2. Your R&D department has changed one of your products slightly. It is not really "new and improved," but you know that putting this statement on the package and in advertising will increase sales. What would you do?

3. You have been asked to add a stripped-down model to your line that could be advertised to pull customers into the store. The product won't be very good, but salespeople will be able to switch buyers up to higher-priced units. You are asked to give the green light for the stripped-down version. What would you do?

4. You are thinking of hiring a product manager who has just left a competitor's company. She would be more than happy to tell you all the competitor's plans for the coming year. What would you do?

5. One of your top dealers in an important territory recently has had family troubles, and his sales have slipped. It looks like it will take him a while to straighten out his family trouble. Meanwhile you are losing sales. Legally, on performance grounds, you can terminate the dealer's franchise and replace him. What would you do?

6. You have a chance to win a big account that will mean a lot to you and your company. The purchasing agent hints that a "gift" would influence the decision. Your assistant recommends sending a fine color television set to the buyer's home. What would you do?

7. You have heard that a competitor has a new product feature that will make a big difference in sales. The competitor will demonstrate the feature in a private dealer meeting at the annual trade show. You can easily send a snooper to this meeting to learn about the new feature. What would you do?

8. You have to choose between three ad campaigns outlined by your agency. The first (a) is a soft-sell, honest, straight-information campaign. The second (b) uses sex-loaded emotional appeals and exaggerates the product's benefits. The third (c) involves a noisy, somewhat irritating commercial that is sure to gain audience attention. Pretests show that the campaigns are effective in the following order: c, b, and a. What would you do?

9. You are interviewing a capable female applicant for a job as salesperson. She is better qualified than the men that you just interviewed. Nevertheless, you know that some of your important customers prefer dealing with men, and you will lose some sales if you hire her. What would you do?

the results held up, it meant that virtually all Americans may be carrying some minuscule amount of the chemical, called perfluorooctane sulfonate (PFOS), in their systems. Even though at the time they had yet to come up with definitive answer as to what harm the chemical might cause, the company reached a drastic decision. In mid-2000, although under no mandate to act, 3M decided to phase out products containing PFOS and related chemicals, including its popular Scotchgard fabric protector. This was no easy decision. Because there was as yet no replacement chemical, it meant a potential loss of $500 million in annual sales. 3M's voluntary actions drew praise from regulators. "3M deserves great credit for identifying the problem and coming forward," says an Environmental Protection Agency administrator. "It took guts," comments another government scientist. "The fact is that most companies . . . go into anger, denial, and the rest of that stuff. [We're used to seeing] decades-long arguments about whether a chemical is really toxic." For 3M, however, it wasn't all that difficult a decision—it was simply the right thing to do.[27]

As with environmentalism, the issue of ethics provides special challenges for international marketers. Business standards and practices vary a great deal from one country to the next. For example, whereas bribes and kickbacks are illegal for U.S. firms, they are standard business practice in many South American countries. One recent study found that companies from some nations were much more likely to use bribes when seeking contracts in emerging-market nations. The most flagrant bribe-paying firms were from Russia and China, with Taiwan and South Korea close behind. Other countries where corruption is common include Turkmenistan, Bangladesh, and Chad. The least corrupt were companies from Iceland, Finland, New Zealand, and Denmark.[28]

The question arises as to whether a company must lower its ethical standards to compete effectively in countries with lower standards. The answer: No. Companies should make a commitment to a common set of shared standards worldwide. For example, John Hancock Mutual Life Insurance Company operates successfully in Southeast Asia, an area that by Western standards has widespread questionable business and government practices. Despite warnings from locals that Hancock would have to bend its rules to succeed, the company set out strict guidelines. "We told our people that we had the same ethical standards, same procedures, and same policies in these countries that we have in the United States, and we do," says Hancock Chairman Stephen Brown. "We just felt that things like payoffs were wrong—and if we had to do business that way, we'd rather not do business." Hancock employees feel good about the consistent levels of ethics. "There may be countries where you have to do that kind of thing," says Brown. "We haven't found that country yet, and if we do, we won't do business there."[29]

Many industrial and professional associations have suggested codes of ethics, and many companies are now adopting their own codes. For example, the American Marketing Association, an international association of marketing managers and scholars, developed the code of ethics shown in Table 20.2. Companies are also developing programs to teach managers about important ethics issues and help them find the proper responses. They hold ethics workshops and seminars and set up ethics committees. Furthermore, most major U.S. companies have appointed high-level ethics officers to champion ethics issues and to help resolve ethics problems and concerns facing employees.

PricewaterhouseCoopers (PwC) is a good example. In 2002, PwC established a global ethics office and comprehensive ethics program, headed by a high-level global ethics officer. The ethics program begins with a code of conduct, called "The Way We Do Business." PwC employees learn about the code of conduct and about how to handle thorny ethics issues in comprehensive ethics training programs, which start when the employee joins the company and continue through the employee's career. The program also includes an ethics help line and regular communications at all levels. "It is obviously not enough to distribute a document," says PwC's CEO, Samuel DiPiazza. "Ethics is in everything we say and do."[30]

Still, written codes and ethics programs do not ensure ethical behavior. Ethics and social responsibility require a total corporate commitment. They must be a component of the overall corporate culture. According to PwC's DiPiazza, "I see ethics as a mission-critical issue...deeply imbedded in who we are and what we do. It's just as important as our product development cycle or our distribution system... . It's about creating a culture based on integrity and respect, not a culture based on dealing with the crisis of the day... . We ask ourselves every day, 'Are we doing the right things?'"[31]

Code of Conduct

The way we do business*

■ Ethics programs: PricewaterhouseCoopers established a comprehensive ethics program, which begins with a code of conduct, called "The Way We Do Business." Says PwC's CEO, "Ethics is in everything we say and do."

TABLE 20.2   **American Marketing Association Code of Ethics**

ETHICAL NORMS AND VALUES FOR MARKETERS

PREAMBLE

The American Marketing Association commits itself to promoting the highest standard of professional ethical norms and values for its members. Norms are established standards of conduct that are expected and maintained by society and/or professional organizations. Values represent the collective conception of what people find desirable, important and morally proper. Values serve as the criteria for evaluating the actions of others. Marketing practitioners must recognize that they not only serve their enterprises but also act as stewards of society in creating, facilitating and executing the efficient and effective transactions that are part of the greater economy. In this role, marketers should embrace the highest ethical norms of practicing professionals and the ethical values implied by their responsibility toward stakeholders (e.g., customers, employees, investors, channel members, regulators and the host community).

GENERAL NORMS

1. Marketers must do no harm. This means doing work for which they are appropriately trained or experienced so that they can actively add value to their organizations and customers. It also means adhering to all applicable laws and regulations and embodying high ethical standards in the choices they make.

2. Marketers must foster trust in the marketing system. This means that products are appropriate for their intended and promoted uses. It requires that marketing communications about goods and services are not intentionally deceptive or misleading. It suggests building relationships that provide for the equitable adjustment and/or redress of customer grievances. It implies striving for good faith and fair dealing so as to contribute toward the efficacy of the exchange process.

Marketers must embrace, communicate and practice the fundamental ethical values that will improve consumer confidence in the integrity of the marketing exchange system. These basic values are intentionally aspirational and include honesty, responsibility, fairness, respect, openness and citizenship.

ETHICAL VALUES

Honesty—to be truthful and forthright in our dealings with customers and stakeholders.

- We will tell the truth in all situations and at all times.
- We will offer products of value that do what we claim in our communications.
- We will stand behind our products if they fail to deliver their claimed benefits.
- We will honor our explicit and implicit commitments and promises.

Responsibility—to accept the consequences of our marketing decisions and strategies.

- We will make strenuous efforts to serve the needs of our customers.
- We will avoid using coercion with all stakeholders.
- We will acknowledge the social obligations to stakeholders that come with increased marketing and economic power.
- We will recognize our special commitments to economically vulnerable segments of the market such as children, the elderly and others who may be substantially disadvantaged.

Fairness—to try to balance justly the needs of the buyer with the interests of the seller.

- We will represent our products in a clear way in selling, advertising and other forms of communication; this includes the avoidance of false, misleading and deceptive promotion.
- We will reject manipulations and sales tactics that harm customer trust.
- We will not engage in price fixing, predatory pricing, price gouging or "bait-and-switch" tactics.
- We will not knowingly participate in material conflicts of interest.

Respect—to acknowledge the basic human dignity of all stakeholders.

- We will value individual differences even as we avoid stereotyping customers or depicting demographic groups (e.g., gender, race, sexual orientation) in a negative or dehumanizing way in our promotions.
- We will listen to the needs of our customers and make all reasonable efforts to monitor and improve their satisfaction on an ongoing basis.
- We will make a special effort to understand suppliers, intermediaries and distributors from other cultures.
- We will appropriately acknowledge the contributions of others, such as consultants, employees and coworkers, to our marketing endeavors.

Openness—to create transparency in our marketing operations.

- We will strive to communicate clearly with all our constituencies.
- We will accept constructive criticism from our customers and other stakeholders.
- We will explain significant product or service risks, component substitutions or other foreseeable eventualities that could affect customers or their perception of the purchase decision.
- We will fully disclose list prices and terms of financing as well as available price deals and adjustments.

TABLE 20.2 American Marketing Association Code of Ethics—continued

Citizenship—to fulfill the economic, legal, philanthropic and societal responsibilities that serve stakeholders in a strategic manner.

- We will strive to protect the natural environment in the execution of marketing campaigns.
- We will give back to the community through volunteerism and charitable donations.
- We will work to contribute to the overall betterment of marketing and its reputation.
- We will encourage supply chain members to ensure that trade is fair for all participants, including producers in developing countries.

Implementation

Finally, we recognize that every industry sector and marketing subdiscipline (e.g., marketing research, e-commerce, direct selling, direct marketing, advertising) has its own specific ethical issues that require policies and commentary. An array of such codes can be accessed through links on the AMA Web site. We encourage all such groups to develop and/or refine their industry and discipline-specific codes of ethics to supplement these general norms and values.

Source: Reprinted with permission of the American Marketing Association.

Reviewing the Concepts

Well—here you are at the end of your introductory marketing travels! In this chapter, we've closed with many important concepts involving marketing's sweeping impact on individual consumers, other businesses, and society as a whole. You learned that responsible marketers discover what consumers want and respond with the right market offerings, priced to give good value to buyers and profit to the producer. A marketing system should deliver customer value and improve the quality of consumers' lives. In working to meet consumer needs, marketers may take some actions that are not to everyone's liking or benefit. Marketing managers should be aware of the main criticisms of marketing.

1. Identify the major social criticisms of marketing.

Marketing's *impact on individual consumer welfare* has been criticized for its high prices, deceptive practices, high-pressure selling, shoddy or unsafe products, planned obsolescence, and poor service to disadvantaged consumers. Marketing's *impact on society* has been criticized for creating false wants and too much materialism, too few social goods, cultural pollution, and too much political power. Critics have also criticized marketing's *impact on other businesses* for harming competitors and reducing competition through acquisitions, practices that create barriers to entry, and unfair competitive marketing practices. Some of these concerns are justified; some are not.

2. Define *consumerism* and *environmentalism* and explain how they affect marketing strategies.

Concerns about the marketing system have led to *citizen action movements*. *Consumerism* is an organized social movement intended to strengthen the rights and power of consumers relative to sellers. Alert marketers view it as an opportunity to serve consumers better by providing more consumer information, education, and protection. *Environmentalism* is an organized social movement seeking to minimize the harm done to the environment and quality of life by marketing practices. The first wave of modern environmentalism was driven by environmental groups and concerned consumers, whereas the second wave was driven by government, which passed laws and reg-

ulations governing industrial practices impacting the environment. The first two environmentalism waves are now merging into a third and stronger wave in which companies are accepting responsibility for doing no environmental harm. Companies now are adopting policies of *environmental sustainability*—developing strategies that both sustain the environment and produce profits for the company.

3. Describe the principles of socially responsible marketing.

Many companies originally opposed these social movements and laws, but most of them now recognize a need for positive consumer information, education, and protection. Some companies have followed a policy of *enlightened marketing*, which holds that a company's marketing should support the best long-run performance of the marketing system. Enlightened marketing consists of five principles: *consumer-oriented marketing, customer-value marketing, innovative marketing, sense-of-mission marketing, and societal marketing.*

4. Explain the role of ethics in marketing.

Increasingly, companies are responding to the need to provide company policies and guidelines to help their managers deal with questions of *marketing ethics*. Of course even the best guidelines cannot resolve all the difficult ethical decisions that individuals and firms must make. But there are some principles that marketers can choose among. One principle states that such issues should be decided by the free market and legal system. A second, and more enlightened principle, puts responsibility not on the system but in the hands of individual companies and managers. Each firm and marketing manager must work out a philosophy of socially responsible and ethical behavior. Under the societal marketing concept, managers must look beyond what is legal and allowable and develop standards based on personal integrity, corporate conscience, and long-term consumer welfare.

Because business standards and practices vary from country to country, the issue of ethics poses special challenges for international marketers. The growing consensus among today's marketers is that it is important to make a commitment to a common set of shared standards worldwide.

Reviewing the Key Terms

Discussing the Concepts

1. In what ways do consumers believe that marketers make products more expensive to the end consumer?

2. What deceptive marketing practices have you witnessed personally? Are they price, promotion, product, or packaging based? Make a list and then briefly describe one incident in detail.

3. Review claims made by critics that marketing creates false wants and too much materialism, too few social goods, cultural pollution, and too much political power. Do you agree or disagree with these claims?

4. Can an organization be focused on both consumerism and environmentalism at the same time? Explain.

5. In what ways do companies benefit from practicing the philosophy of enlightened marketing?

6. Select three moral dilemmas from Table 20.1. Propose an ethical response for each dilemma.

Applying the Concepts

1. Visit adage.com and click on the "why it matters" section on the left-hand column. Choose two reports at this site and discuss how they relate to the ethical and social responsibility topics in this chapter.

2. Recent public concerns over children and the Internet resulted in the Children's Online Privacy Protection Act (COPPA). Among other things, this act requires Web sites that are visited by children under the age of 13 to post a privacy policy detailing any personally identifiable information collected from those children. Do some research and answer the question: What consumer need does COPPA meet?

3. Visit adbuster.org. What is the purpose of this Web site? Do you think it is effective with its message?

Focus on Technology

Cause-related marketing and corporate philanthropy, companies donating a portion of their profits to charity, have been popular for some time. But how do you harness the power of Internet technology to create a business model based on donations? Meet Goodsearch.com, a recent entry into the crowded search engine market. A new competitor in a market that is dominated by Goolge and Yahoo!, Goodsearch differentiates itself on its ability to raise money for thousands of charities. Founded by a brother and sister who lost their mother to cancer, Goodsearch lets people use the power of Yahoo! search engine technology to search the Internet while having money donated to charity. Here's how it works. Choose an existing charity on Goodsearch or add your own charity, including churches, school groups, or local shelters. Each time you search, 50 percent of the advertising revenues are donated to the charity. Each search earns about $.01, so continued searching could reach the following totals in one year.

Charity or School Size	Number of Supporters	Average Searches per Day	Estimated Revenue/Year
Small	100	2	$730
Medium	1,000	2	$7,300
Large	10,000	2	$73,000

1. Were you aware of Goodsearch? If not, why have so few people heard of it?

2. Would you use this Web site? Discuss.

3. What search engine do you use? Why are you loyal to this search engine?

Focus on Ethics

You might be familiar with MADD (Mothers Against Drunk Driving) and other organizations that unite mothers to address serious situations facing kids and teens. Consider Dads and Daughters, known as DAD, a national a nonprofit advocacy group that encourages fathers to be involved in issues facing girls today. DAD's main goal is to use the strength of father-daughter relationships to help transform the pervasive cultural messages that devalue girls and women. Through workshops, publications, e-mails, and books, DAD helps organize fathers and daughters to understand the issues facing young women. It involves fathers and daughters in monthly media action campaigns to change current company advertising or marketing.

A recent campaign targeted Hasbro and its marketing of The Pussycat Dolls—a collection of action figures based on the singing group. The Pussycat Dolls, a popular singing group managed by recording label Interscope, performs music with "mature" lyrics and movements. DAD characterized the Pussycat Doll collection as a set of "stripper" dolls marketed to six-year-old girls. According to DAD's Web site, after a letter-writing initiative from Dads and Daughters, Hasbro pulled the product, saying, "Interscope's current creative direction and images for the record-ing group are focused on a much older target than we had anticipated at the time of our original discussions, thereby making a doll line inappropri-ate for Hasbro."

1. Why does DAD target fathers rather than mothers?

2. To what extent are women portrayed inappropriately in movies and television? Discuss.

3. Can you think of products whose advertising might cast a negative image of women?

Video Case

NFL

Think of the NFL and you might conjure up images of burly football play-ers and adrenaline-filled stadiums. But the league offers fans much more than Sunday afternoons full of football. Players and teams alike consider football and community involvement to be the twin pillars of the NFL. Through more than 20 separate community programs, the NFL focuses considerable manpower on its efforts to give back to the community and encourage others to do the same. In addition, for more than 30 years the NFL has partnered with United Way. NFL teams and players support local United Way chapters by making personal appearances, participating in joint programs, and offering campaign contributions. The NFL and United Way have also created public service television ads featuring NFL stars volunteering in their communities—reading to children, playing shuffle-board with senior citizens, and working at local charities. In total, more than 1,000 such ads have aired during NFL games, making it the longest-running public service ad campaign in history.

It's clear that the partnership benefits United Way. With help from the NFL, United Way fundraising has skyrocketed from $800 million in 1974 to nearly $4 billion today. But the NFL benefits too. Working in the com-munity makes players more accessible and helps to build stronger rela-tionships with fans by connecting with them in their own backyards.

After viewing the video featuring the NFL, answer the following ques-tions about marketing and social responsibility.

1. Why does the NFL partner with United Way? How, if at all, does that partnership impact your opinion of the league? How does it impact your interest in volunteering?

2. Make a list of social criticisms of the NFL. Then visit JoinTheTeam.com and read more about the NFL's outreach pro-grams. Do these efforts alleviate any concerns you have about the league's negative impact on society?

3. By the text's definition, does the NFL practice "enlightened marketing"?

Company Case

Vitango: Fighting Malnutrition

Imagine teaching an elementary school class in which stu-dents are constantly inattentive and falling asleep—not because they are bored but because they are malnourished. In many countries, this is not an unusual problem. Two bil-lion people around the globe suffer from anemia—an iron deficiency. Iron deficiency leads to reduced resistance to disease, lowers learning ability in children, and contributes to the death of one out of five pregnant mothers. Two hun-dred million children do not get enough Vitamin A. As a result 250,000 of them go blind each year and 2.2 million children under five die each year from diarrhea. Many mal-nourished children suffer from zinc deficiency, which leads to growth failure and infections. Close to two billion people do not get enough iodine, and iodine deficiency is the lead-ing cause of preventable mental retardation in the world. If they only used the ordinary iodized table salt found in homes and restaurants all across the United States, this wouldn't happen.

THE PROBLEM

Although estimates vary widely, it is clear that a substantial portion of the world's population suffers from malnutrition of some kind. Malnutrition exists everywhere, but one esti-

mate places as many as 95 percent of the world's malnour-ished people in developing countries, where poverty levels are the highest. Malnutrition is clearly a direct effect of poverty, and it also perpetuates poverty. Malnourished chil-dren are more likely to drop out of school, are less likely to benefit from schooling even if they remain enrolled, and end up having lower incomes as adults. According to Jean-Louis Sarbib, Senior Vice President for Human Development at the World Bank, malnutrition costs developing countries up to 3 percent of their yearly GDP. "Put this in the context that the economies of many developing countries are growing at the rate of 2 to 3 percent annually, and improving nutrition could potentially double these rates," says Sarbib.

THE SOLUTION

What can U.S. businesses do about this deplorable situa-tion? Quite a bit. Companies such as Coca-Cola and Procter & Gamble have invested millions of dollars in research of micronutrients. They are learning how to fortify everyday food and beverages with additional minerals and vitamins to wipe out deficiencies and keep school children around the world alert and mentally prepared for school.

(case continues)

Fortifying foods is not new or unusual in the United States. Iodine has been added to ordinary table salt for decades; milk contains Vitamin D and calcium; and cornflakes list all the micronutrients found in them on the box. A quick check of your pantry reveals that many drinks and other foods have vitamins and minerals added to them. What are new are the efforts of companies to identify deficiencies in specific countries and to develop new technologies for adding micronutrients to foodstuffs in order to eliminate or reduce them. A good example is a Coca-Cola beverage product called Vitango in Botswana.

Coca-Cola spent years developing a powdered beverage that, when mixed with water, looks and tastes like a sweeter version of Hi-C. The beverage is fortified with 12 vitamins and with minerals that are chronically lacking in the diets of people in developing countries. Coca-Cola tested this product in Botswana in Project Mission. Every day for eight weeks, nurses visited schools where they mixed the beverage and passed out paper cups of the "new Hi-C." At the end of the test period, levels of iron and zinc in the children's blood tests had grown. Some parents noted that their children had become more attentive at school. After the Botswana tests, Coca-Cola also ran tests in Peru to determine how well the nutrients are absorbed into the bloodstream.

Coca-Cola, however, is not yet ready to launch Vitango. One issue is the powdered product form. Given the impurities of much of the water in Africa, Coca-Cola wants to package it in a ready-to-drink formula, not in the powdered version now available. That will require reformulation that could actually drive down the price.

Procter & Gamble has also developed micronutrient-enriched drinks for distribution in developing countries. In the 1990s, P&G developed its own proprietary iron, Vitamin A, and iodine fortification technology, which it called GrowthPlus. GrowthPlus was the basic ingredient in a product called Nutridelight that P&G launched in the Philippines. Unfortunately, it didn't sell well—primarily because it was priced at 50 percent above the market price of other powdered drinks.

More recently, P&G has launched another product in Venezuela, Nutristar. Containing eight vitamins and five minerals. Sold at most food stores, it comes in flavors such as mango and passion fruit and promises to produce "taller, stronger, and smarter kids." To date, Nutristar is doing quite well. One reason is that it's available at McDonald's, where it is chosen by consumers with about half of all happy meals sold. P&G is also offering free samples in schools.

PRICING ISSUES

The major problem with both Coca-Cola's and P&G's nutritional products is price. These products were expensive to develop because of long lead times, the need to enlist the help of nutritional experts around the world, and the need to develop products that appeal to the local population's tastes. If offered at "reasonable" prices, they would be out of the reach of the world's desperately poor, the group that needs them most. Consider P&G's Nutristar. The poor people in other countries are *not* eating at McDonald's. In

countries such as Botswana, they are barely existing on cornmeal and rice. They simply cannot afford to buy fortified sweetened drinks or, for that matter, any sweetened drinks.

How can P&G and Coca-Cola market such products without pricing them too high for the intended market? Learning its lesson in the Philippines, P&G priced Nutristar about 25 percent higher than other powdered drinks and 30 percent below carbonated soft drinks. Even so, that's still too high for the poverty stricken. Coca-Cola originally planned to sell Vitango for about 20 cents for an 8-ounce liquid serving but realizes that this price is too high. That's part of the reason for continuing developmental work on the product.

One solution to the pricing problem is to work with governments, but many of them are too poor to be able to afford the products. Many also lack the resources to educate their people on the merits of fortified foods. Additionally, some policy makers fail to recognize the connection between malnutrition and the severe problems that it causes.

GAINING GROUND

Enter GAIN—the Global Alliance for Improved Nutrition—an international consortium set up by the Bill and Melinda Gates Charitable Foundation. GAIN offers assistance to companies in order to profitably market fortified foods in developing countries. One $70 million GAIN program gives money to local governments in order to increase the demand for fortified foods, through means including large-scale public relations campaigns or a government "seal of approval." GAIN also actively lobbies for favorable tariffs and tax rates and for speedier regulatory review of new products in targeted countries. Of course, Coca-Cola and P&G can work with governments on their own, but their actions may be distrusted. After all, these are "for profit" organizations whose motives may be suspect. GAIN has the advantage that it's a not-for-profit organization.

Another GAIN project provides $20 million to fortify salt, flour, and staple foods in developing countries by working directly with a network of more than a dozen manufacturers and retailers. The idea is to motivate food producing and distributing companies to make fortified foods available. After the initial funding period, the companies would then continue fortifying these foods without the need for additional aid money.

In all, once fully implemented, GAIN projects will reach almost 700 million people with fortified food. "We are aiming for a realistic target of eliminating vitamin and mineral deficiencies in the next ten years," said Marc Van Ameringen, executive director of GAIN. "Adding vitamins and minerals to the foods that people eat every day is a proven solution to a genuine health and development problem, and it only costs around 25 cents per person per year."

GAIN seems like a wonderful resource for helping malnourished peoples, but it does have critics. The critics point out that selling or giving away fortified foods does not solve the underlying problem of poverty. Nor does it teach people good nutritional habits. Moreover, in addition to vitamins and minerals, many of the "fortified" foods also contain overly large amounts of fat, sugar, and salt. So, for example, whereas the foods might help reduce iron deficiency, they could also lead to obesity. Some observers claim that it would be better to teach people how to grow fruits and vegetables. The problem is that people will die from malnutrition before poverty is eliminated or trees bear fruit.

Other issues must also be addressed. A fortified beverage such as Vitango will help in dealing with malnutrition but can't eliminate it. People will still need to eat a variety of other foods, which makes education very important. Remember that these products contain no juice. They are intended as supplements, not as substitutes for a proper diet. Lack of understanding about how to use products has landed other companies, such as Nestlé with its infant formula, in trouble when the products were used inappropriately.

Given all these problems, why would Coca-Cola and P&G develop these products in the first place? One answer is future sales and profits. Products such as Nutristar and Vitango could create a basis from which to launch other Coca-Cola or P&G products, such as snack foods or juice drinks. As sales of carbonated beverages around the world have slowed, these fortified drinks pose a growth opportunity for the companies.

Another answer is "goodwill," and not just goodwill for the companies involved. September 11, 2001, taught us in the United States that our country is the focus of both the world's envy and its hatred. Efforts to help share our wealth of technology and research in ways that improve the lot of other peoples may be a major deterrent to future attacks and the growth of terrorism. By helping other nations of the world, U.S. corporations can help create environments where freedom can flourish. One writer insists that when U.S. corporations help people as consumers to buy the goods and services that our companies sell, they also enhance our government's ability to sell our country.

Questions for Discussion

1. Which of the textbook's criticisms of marketing's impact on consumers, if any, are evident in the cases of Vitango and Nutristar?
2. Which of the criticisms of marketing's impact on society are evident in the Vitango and Nutristar case?
3. Could Vitango and Nutristar be considered enlightened marketing efforts? Why or why not?
4. Are the development and marketing of such products as fortified foods and beverages ethical and socially responsible?
5. How should Coca-Cola proceed with the marketing of Vitango?

Sources: Sanjay Suri, "Development: Nutrient-Packed Food Headed for 200 Million," Inter Press Service, April 9, 2006; "World Bank: Malnutrition Causes Heavy Economic Losses," M2 Presswire, March 3, 2006; Jill Bruss, "Reaching the World," Beverage Industry, December 2001, p. 28+; Rance Crain, "U.S. Marketers Must Develop Products to Help Third World," Advertising Age, December 3, 2001, p. 20; Betsy McKay, "Drinks for Developing Countries," Wall Street Journal, November 27, 2001, p. B1, B6; George Carpenter, "P&G and Sustainable Development—Finding Opportunity in Responsibility," April 1, 2003, accessed at www.eu.pg.com/news/speeches/2003040linsideoutcarpenter.html; "Hunger, Malnutrition Kill Six Million Children Annually," Agence France Presse, November 22, 2005; and Betsy McKay, "Effort to Combat Malnutrition Cites Economic Impact," Wall Street Journal, March 3, 2006, p. A6.

MARKETING PLAN

■ The Marketing Plan: An Introduction

As a marketer, you'll need a good marketing plan to provide direction and focus for your brand, product, or company. With a detailed plan, any business will be better prepared to launch a new product or build sales for existing products. Nonprofit organizations also use marketing plans to guide their fundraising and outreach efforts. Even government agencies put together marketing plans for initiatives such as building public awareness of proper nutrition and stimulating area tourism.

The Purpose and Content of a Marketing Plan

Unlike a business plan, which offers a broad overview of the entire organization's mission, objectives, strategy, and resource allocation, a marketing plan has a more limited scope. It serves to document how the organization's strategic objectives will be achieved through specific marketing strategies and tactics, with the customer as the starting point. It is also linked to the plans of other departments within the organization. Suppose a marketing plan calls for selling 200,000 units annually. The production department must gear up to make that many units, the finance department must have funding available to cover the expenses, the human resources department must be ready to hire and train staff, and so on. Without the appropriate level of organizational support and resources, no marketing plan can succeed.

Although the exact length and layout will vary from company to company, a marketing plan usually contains the sections described in Chapter 2. Smaller businesses may create shorter or less formal marketing plans, whereas corporations frequently require highly structured marketing plans. To guide implementation effectively, every part of the plan must be described in considerable detail. Sometimes a company will post its marketing plan on an internal Web site, which allows managers and employees in different locations to consult specific sections and collaborate on additions or changes.

The Role of Research

Marketing plans are not created in a vacuum. To develop successful strategies and action programs, marketers need up-to-date information about the environment, the competition, and the market segments to be served. Often, analysis of internal data is the starting point for assessing the current marketing situation, supplemented by marketing intelligence and research investigating the overall market, the competition, key issues, and threats and opportunities issues. As the plan is put into effect, marketers use a variety of research techniques to measure progress toward objectives and identify areas for improvement if results fall short of projections. Finally, marketing research helps marketers learn more about their customers' requirements, expectations, perceptions, and satisfaction levels. This deeper understanding provides a foundation for building competitive advantage through well-informed segmenting, targeting, and positioning decisions. Thus, the marketing plan should outline what marketing research will be conducted and how the findings will be applied.

The Role of Relationships

The marketing plan shows how the company will establish and maintain profitable customer relationships. In the process, however, it also shapes a number of internal and external relationships. First, it affects how marketing personnel work with each other and with other departments to deliver value and satisfy customers. Second, it affects how the company works with suppliers, distributors, and strategic alliance partners to achieve the objectives listed in the plan. Third, it influences the company's dealings with other stakeholders, including government regulators, the media, and the community at large. All of these relationships are important to the organization's success, so they should be considered when a marketing plan is being developed.

From Marketing Plan to Marketing Action

Companies generally create yearly marketing plans, although some plans cover a longer period. Marketers start planning well in advance of the implementation date to allow time for marketing research, thorough analysis, management review, and coordination between departments. Then, after each action program begins, marketers monitor ongoing results, compare them with projections, analyze any differences, and take corrective steps as needed. Some marketers also prepare contingency plans for implementation if certain conditions emerge. Because of inevitable and sometimes unpredictable environmental changes, marketers must be ready to update and adapt marketing plans at any time.

For effective implementation and control, the marketing plan should define how progress toward objectives will be measured. Managers typically use budgets, schedules, and performance standards for monitoring and evaluating results. With budgets, they can compare planned expenditures with actual expenditures for a given week, month, or other period. Schedules allow management to see when tasks were supposed to be completed—and when they were actually completed. Performance standards track the outcomes of marketing programs to see whether the company is moving forward toward its objectives. Some examples of performance standards are: market share, sales volume, product profitability, and customer satisfaction.

■ Sample Marketing Plan for Sonic

This section takes you inside the sample marketing plan for Sonic, a hypothetical start-up company. The company's first product is the Sonic 1000, a multimedia personal digital assistant (PDA), also known as a handheld computer. Sonic will be competing with Palm, Hewlett-Packard, and other well-established PDA rivals in a crowded, fast-changing marketplace where enhanced cell phones and many other electronics devices have PDA functionality. The annotations explain more about what each section of the plan should contain and why.

Executive Summary

Sonic is preparing to launch a new multimedia PDA product, the Sonic 1000, in a maturing market. Despite the dominance of PDA leader Palm, we can compete because our product offers a unique combination of features at a value-added price. We are targeting specific segments in the consumer and business markets, taking advantage of opportunities indicated by higher demand for easy-to-use PDAs with expanded communications, entertainment, and storage functionality.

The primary marketing objective is to achieve first-year U.S. market share of 3 percent with unit sales of 240,000. The primary financial objectives are to achieve first-year sales revenues of $60 million, keep first-year losses to less than $10 million, and break even early in the second year.

Current Marketing Situation

Sonic, founded 18 months ago by two entrepreneurs with experience in the PC market, is about to enter the now-mature PDA market. Multifunction cell phones, e-mail devices, and wireless communication devices are increasingly popular today; forecasts suggest that annual

Executive summary

This section summarizes the main goals, recommendations, and points as an overview for senior managers who must read and approve the marketing plan. Generally, a table of contents follows this section for management convenience.

Current marketing situation

In this section, marketing managers discuss the overall market, identify the market segments they will target, and provide information about the company's current situation.

sales of such devices will grow at more than 50 percent for the next three years. Competition is therefore more intense even as PDA demand flattens, industry consolidation continues, and pricing pressures squeeze profitability. Yet the worldwide PDA market remains substantial, with annual sales of 10 to 15 million units. To gain market share in this dynamic environment, Sonic must carefully target specific segments with features that deliver benefits valued by each customer group.

Market Description

Sonic's market consists of consumers and business users who prefer to use a single device for communication, information storage and exchange, and entertainment on the go. Specific segments being targeted during the first year include professionals, corporations, students, entrepreneurs, and medical users. Table A1.1 shows how the Sonic 1000 addresses the needs of targeted consumer and business segments.

PDA purchasers can choose between models based on several different operating systems, including systems from Palm, Microsoft, and Symbian, plus Linux variations. Sonic licenses a Linux-based system because it is somewhat less vulnerable to attack by hackers and viruses. With hard drives becoming commonplace in the PDA market, Sonic is equipping its first product with an ultrafast one- gigabyte hard drive for information and entertainment storage. Technology costs are decreasing even as capabilities are increasing, which makes value-priced models more appealing to consumers and to customers with older PDAs who want to trade up to newer, high-end multifunction units.

Product Review

Our first product, the Sonic PDA 1000, offers the following standard features with a Linux OS:

- Voice recognition for hands-free operation
- Built-in cell phone functionality and push-to-talk instant calling
- Digital music/video recording, downloading, and playback
- Wireless Web and e-mail, text messaging, instant messaging

Market description

By describing the targeted segments in detail, marketers provide context for the marketing strategies and detailed action programs discussed later in the plan.

Benefits and product features

Exhibit 1 clarifies the benefits that product features will deliver to satisfy the needs of customers in each targeted segment.

Product review

The product review should summarize the main features for all of the company's products. The information may be organized by product line, by type of customer, by market, or (as here) by order of product introduction.

TABLE A1.1   Needs and Corresponding Features/Benefits of Sonic PDA

Targeted Segment	Customer Need	Corresponding Feature/Benefit
Professionals (consumer market)	• Stay in touch conveniently and securely while on the go	• Built-in cell phone and push-to-talk to communicate anywhere at any time; wireless e-mail/Web access from anywhere; Linux-based operating system less vulnerable to hackers
	• Perform many functions hands-free without carrying multiple gadgets	• Voice-activated applications are convenient; GPS function, camera add value
Students (consumer market)	• Perform many functions hands-free without carrying multiple gadgets	• Compatible with numerous applications and peripherals for convenient, cost-effective note taking and functionality
	• Express style and individuality	• Wardrobe of PDA cases in different colors, patterns, and materials
Corporate users (business market)	• Security and adaptability for proprietary tasks	• Customizable to fit corporate tasks and networks; Linux-based operating system less vulnerable to hackers
	• Obtain driving directions to business meetings	• Built-in GPS allows voice-activated access to directions and maps
Entrepreneurs (business market)	• Organize and access contacts, schedule details, business and financial files	• No-hands, wireless access to calendar, address book, information files for checking appointments and data, connecting with contacts
	• Get in touch fast	• Push-to-talk instant calling speeds up communications
Medical users (business market)	• Update, access, and exchange medical records	• No-hands, wireless recording and exchange of information to reduce paperwork and increase productivity
	• Photograph medical situations to maintain a visual record	• Built-in camera allows fast and easy photography, stores images for later retrieval

- Organization functions, including calendar, address book, synchronization
- Global positioning system for directions and maps
- Connectors for multiple peripherals and applications
- One-gigabyte hard drive with expansion potential
- Interchangeable case wardrobe of different colors and patterns

First-year sales revenues are projected to be $60 million, based on sales of 240,000 Sonic 1000 units at a wholesale price of $250 each. During the second year, we plan to introduce the Sonic 2000, also with Linux OS, as a higher-end product offering the following standard features:

- Global phone and messaging compatibility
- Translation capabilities to send English text as Spanish text (other languages to be offered as add-on options)
- Integrated six-megapixel camera

Competitive Review

Competitive review
The purpose of a competitive review is to identify key competitors, describe their market positions, and briefly discuss their strategies.

The emergence of new multifunction phones, marketed by cell phone manufacturers and carriers, has pressured industry participants to continually add features and cut prices. Competition from specialized devices for text and e-mail messaging, such as BlackBerry devices, is a major factor as well. Key competitors include:

- *Palm.* The trendy Treo PDA-phone combos account for more than half of Palm's $1.6 billion in annual revenues. As the best-known maker of PDAs, Palm has achieved excellent distribution in multiple channels and has alliances with a number of cell phone service carriers in the United States and Europe. Its latest models are available with either the Palm or the Windows operating system.

- *Hewlett-Packard.* HP is targeting business markets with its iPAQ Pocket PC devices, many with wireless capabilities to accommodate corporate users. For extra security, one model allows access by fingerprint match as well as by password. HP enjoys excellent distribution, and its products are priced from below $300 to more than $600.

- *Samsung.* Many of this manufacturer's products combine cell phone capabilities with multifunction PDA features. Its i730, a smartphone based on the Windows operating system, provides wireless Web access and MP3 streaming and downloads, plays videos, and offers PDA functions such as address book, calendar, and speed dial.

- *RIM.* Research in Motion makes the lightweight BlackBerry wireless phone/PDA products that are popular among corporate users. Although legal entanglements have slightly slowed market-share momentum, RIM's continuous innovation and solid customer service support clearly strengthen its competitive standing.

- *Siemens.* This company's latest PDA-phone combinations have several distinctive features. For example, some models dial any phone number that the user writes on the screen with a stylus. Also, on some models, the keyboard slides out of the way when not in use. Siemens is a particularly formidable competitor in European markets.

Despite this strong competition, Sonic can carve out a definite image and gain recognition among the targeted segments. Our voice-recognition system for hands-off operation is a critical point of differentiation for competitive advantage. Also, offering GPS as a standard feature gives our product a competitive edge compared with PDAs in the same general price range. Moreover, our product runs the Linux OS, which is an appealing alternative for customers concerned about security. Table A1.2 shows a selection of competitive PDA products and prices.

Distribution Review

Distribution review
In this section, marketers list the most important channels, provide an overview of each channel arrangement, and mention any new developments or trends.

Sonic-branded products will be distributed through a network of retailers in the top 50 U.S. markets. Among the most important channel partners being contacted are:

- *Office supply superstores.* Office Max and Staples will both carry Sonic products in stores, in catalogs, and online.

TABLE A1.2
Selected PDA Products and Pricing

Competitor	Model	Features	Price
Palm	Treo 700	PDA functions, camera and phone, streaming audio/video, music downloads, Bluetooth connection, high-resolution screen, model P runs Palm OS, model W runs Windows	$349.99
Hewlett-Packard	iPAQ hw6500	PDA functions, backlit keyboard, Bluetooth connection, GPS included, built-in camera, memory slot, wireless radio and messaging capabilities, Windows OS	$549
Samsung	i730 PDA phone	PDA functions, built-in cell phone, Wi-Fi Web access, Bluetooth connection, slide-out keyboard, voice dialing, music streaming and downloads, video playback, Windows OS	$299.99
RIM	BlackBerry 8700c	PDA functions, wireless e-mail and phone functions, multimedia messaging, Bluetooth connection, ergonomic keyboard, light-sensing screen, lightweight (4.7 ounces)	$299.99
Siemens	SX66	PDA functions, Wi-Fi and phone functions, handwriting-recognition dialing, slide-out keyboard, Bluetooth connection, Windows OS, relatively heavy (7.4 ounces)	$499.99

- *Computer stores.* CompUSA will carry Sonic products.
- *Electronics specialty stores.* Circuit City and Best Buy will carry Sonic PDAs.
- *Online retailers.* Amazon.com will carry Sonic PDAs and, for a promotional fee, will give Sonic prominent placement on its home page during the introduction.

Although distribution will initially be restricted to the United States, we plan to expand into Canada and beyond, according to demand. We will emphasize trade sales promotion in the first year.

Strengths, Weaknesses, Opportunities, and Threat Analysis

Sonic has several powerful strengths on which to build, but our major weakness is lack of brand awareness and image. The major opportunity is demand for multimedia PDAs that deliver a number of valued benefits, eliminating the need for customers to carry more than one device. We also face the threat of ever-higher competition from consumer electronics manufacturers, as well as downward pricing pressure. Table A1.3 summarizes Sonic's main strengths, weaknesses, opportunities, and threats.

TABLE A1.3
Sonic's Strengths, Weaknesses, Opportunities, and Threats

Strengths
- Innovative combination of functions operated hands-free in one portable device
- Value pricing
- Security due to Linux-based operating system

Weaknesses
- Lack of brand awareness and image
- Heavier than most competing models

Opportunities
- Increased demand for multimedia models with diverse functions and benefits
- Lower technology costs

Threats
- Intense competition
- Downward pricing pressure
- Compressed product life

Strengths

Strengths are internal capabilities that can help the company reach its objectives.

Sonic can build on three important strengths:

1. *Innovative product.* The Sonic 1000 combines a variety of features that would otherwise require customers to carry multiple devices; these include cell phone and wireless e-mail functionality, GPS capability, and digital video/music storage and playback—all with hands-free operation.

2. *Security.* Our PDA uses a Linux-based operating system that is less vulnerable to hackers and other security threats that can result in stolen or corrupted data.

3. *Pricing.* Our product is priced lower than competing multifunction models—none of which offer the same bundle of features—which gives us an edge with price-conscious customers.

Weaknesses

Weaknesses are internal elements that may interfere with the company's ability to achieve its objectives.

By waiting to enter the PDA market until considerable consolidation of competitors has occurred, Sonic has learned from the successes and mistakes of others. Nonetheless, we have two main weaknesses:

1. *Lack of brand awareness.* Sonic has not yet established a brand or image in the marketplace, whereas Palm and others have strong brand recognition. We will address this area with promotion.

2. *Heavier weight.* The Sonic 1000 is slightly heavier than most competing models because it incorporates multiple features and a sizable hard drive. To counteract this weakness, we will emphasize our unique combination of features and our value-added pricing, two compelling competitive strengths.

Opportunities

Opportunities are external elements that the company may be able to exploit to its advantage.

Sonic can take advantage of two major market opportunities:

1. *Increasing demand for multimedia models with multiple functions.* The market for multimedia, multifunction devices is growing much faster than the market for single-use devices. Customers are now accustomed to seeing users with PDAs in work and educational settings, which is boosting primary demand. Also, customers who bought entry-level models are replacing older models with more-advanced models.

2. *Lower technology costs.* Better technology is now available at a lower cost than ever before. Thus, Sonic can incorporate technically advanced features at a value-added price that allows for reasonable profits.

Threats

Threats are current or emerging external elements that may possibly challenge the company's performance.

We face three main threats at the introduction of the Sonic 1000:

1. *Increased competition.* More companies are entering the U.S. PDA market with models that offer some but not all of the features and benefits provided by Sonic's PDA. Therefore, Sonic's marketing communications must stress our clear differentiation and value-added pricing.

2. *Downward pressure on pricing.* Increased competition and market-share strategies are pushing PDA prices down. Still, our objective of seeking a 10 percent profit on second-year sales of the original model is realistic, given the lower margins in the PDA market.

3. *Compressed product life cycle.* PDAs have reached the maturity stage of their life cycle more quickly than earlier technology products. We have contingency plans to keep sales growing by adding new features, targeting additional segments, and adjusting prices.

Objectives and Issues

Objectives and issues

The company's objectives should be defined in specific terms so management can measure progress and, if needed, take corrective action to stay on track. This section describes any major issues that might affect the company's marketing strategy and implementation.

We have set aggressive but achievable objectives for the first and second years of market entry.

First-year Objectives

During the Sonic 1000's initial year on the market, we are aiming for a 3 percent share of the U.S. PDA market through unit sales volume of 240,000.

Second-year Objectives

Our second-year objectives are to achieve a 6 percent share based on sales of two models and to achieve break-even early in this period.

Issues

In relation to the product launch, our major issue is the ability to establish a well-regarded brand name linked to a meaningful positioning. We must invest heavily in marketing to create a memorable and distinctive brand image projecting innovation, quality, and value. We also must measure awareness and response so we can adjust our marketing efforts as necessary.

Marketing Strategy

Sonic's marketing strategy is based on a positioning of product differentiation. Our primary consumer target is middle- to upper-income professionals who need one portable device to coordinate their busy schedules, communicate with family and colleagues, get driving directions, and be entertained on the go. Our secondary consumer target is high school, college, and graduate students who want a multimedia device. This segment can be described demographically by age (16–30) and education status.

Our primary business target is mid- to large-sized corporations that want to help their managers and employees stay in touch and input or access critical data when out of the office. This segment consists of companies with more than $25 million in annual sales and more than 100 employees. A secondary business target is entrepreneurs and small-business owners. We are also targeting medical users who want to reduce paperwork and update or access patients' medical records.

Positioning

Using product differentiation, we are positioning the Sonic PDA as the most versatile, convenient, value-added model for personal and professional use. The marketing strategy will focus on the hand-free operation of multiple communication, entertainment, and information capabilities differentiating the Sonic 1000.

Product Strategy

The Sonic 1000, including all the features described in the earlier Product Review section, will be sold with a one-year warranty. We will introduce a more compact, powerful high-end model (the Sonic 2000) during the following year. Building the Sonic brand is an integral part of our product strategy. The brand and logo (Sonic's distinctive yellow thunderbolt) will be displayed on the product and its packaging and reinforced by its prominence in the introductory marketing campaign.

Pricing Strategy

The Sonic 1000 will be introduced at $250 wholesale/$350 estimated retail price per unit. We expect to lower the price of this first model when we expand the product line by launching the Sonic 2000, to be priced at $350 wholesale per unit. These prices reflect a strategy of (1) attracting desirable channel partners and (2) taking share from Palm and other established competitors.

Distribution Strategy

Our channel strategy is to use selective distribution, marketing Sonic PDAs through well-known stores and online retailers. During the first year, we will add channel partners until we have coverage in all major U.S. markets and the product is included in the major electronics catalogs and Web sites. We will also investigate distribution through cell-phone outlets maintained by major carriers such as Cingular Wireless. In support of our channel partners, Sonic will provide demonstration products, detailed specification handouts, and full-color photos and displays featuring the product. We will also arrange special trade terms for retailers that place volume orders.

Positioning

A positioning built on meaningful differences, supported by appropriate strategy and implementation, can help the company build competitive advantage.

Marketing tools

These sections summarize the broad logic that will guide decisions made about the marketing tools to be used in the period covered by the plan.

Marketing Communications Strategy

By integrating all messages in all media, we will reinforce the brand name and the main points of product differentiation. Research about media consumption patterns will help our advertising agency choose appropriate media and timing to reach prospects before and during product introduction. Thereafter, advertising will appear on a pulsing basis to maintain brand awareness and communicate various differentiation messages. The agency will also coordinate public relations efforts to build the Sonic brand and support the differentiation message. To attract customer attention and encourage purchasing, we will offer as a limited-time premium a leather carry-case. To attract, retain, and motivate channel partners for a push strategy, we will use trade sales promotions and personal selling. Until the Sonic brand has been established, our communications will encourage purchases through channel partners rather than from our Web site.

Marketing research
Management should explain in this section how marketing research will be used to support development, implementation, and evaluation of strategies and action programs.

Marketing Research

Using research, we are identifying the specific features and benefits that our target market segments value. Feedback from market tests, surveys, and focus groups will help us develop the Sonic 2000. We are also measuring and analyzing customers' attitudes toward competing brands and products. Brand awareness research will help us determine the effectiveness and efficiency of our messages and media. Finally, we will use customer satisfaction studies to gauge market reaction.

Marketing organization
The marketing department may be organized by function, as in this sample, by geography, by product, or by customer (or some combination).

Marketing Organization

Sonic's chief marketing officer, Jane Melody, holds overall responsibility for all of the company's marketing activities. Figure A1.1 shows the structure of the eight-person marketing organization. Sonic has hired Worldwide Marketing to handle national sales campaigns, trade and consumer sales promotions, and public relations efforts.

Action programs
Action programs should be coordinated with the resources and activities of other departments, including production, finance, purchasing, etc.

Action Programs

The Sonic 1000 will be introduced in February. Following are summaries of the action programs we will use during the first six months of next year to achieve our stated objectives.

January We will initiate a $200,000 trade sales promotion campaign to educate dealers and generate excitement for the product launch in February. We will exhibit at the major consumer electronics trade shows, Webcast the product launch, and provide samples to selected product reviewers, opinion leaders, and celebrities as part of our public relations strategy. Our training staff will work with sales personnel at major retail chains to explain the Sonic 1000's features, benefits, and competitive advantages.

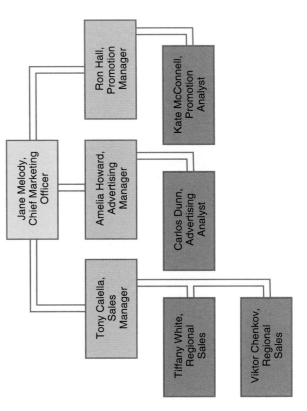

FIGURE A1.1
Sonic's marketing organization

February We will start an integrated print/radio/Internet campaign targeting professionals and consumers. The campaign will show how many functions the Sonic PDA can perform and emphasize the convenience of a single, powerful handheld device. This multimedia campaign will be supported by point-of-sale signage as well as online-only specials.

March As the multimedia advertising campaign continues, we will add consumer sales promotion tactics such as giving away leather carry-cases as a premium. We will also distribute new point-of-purchase displays to support our retailers.

April We will hold a trade sales contest offering prizes for the salesperson and retail organization that sells the most Sonic PDAs during the four-week period.

May We plan to roll out a new national advertising campaign this month. The radio ads will feature celebrity voices telling their Sonic PDAs to perform functions such as initiating a phone call, sending an e-mail, playing a song or video, and so on. The print ads will show these celebrities holding their Sonic PDAs.

June Our radio campaign will add a new voice-over tag line promoting the Sonic 1000 as a graduation gift. We will also exhibit at the semiannual electronics trade show and provide channel partners with new competitive comparison handouts as a sales aid. In addition, we will tally and analyze the results of customer satisfaction surveys for use in future promotions and to provide feedback for product and marketing activities.

Budgets

Total first-year sales revenue for the Sonic 1000 is projected at $60 million, with an average wholesale price of $250 per unit and variable cost per unit of $150 for unit sales volume of 240,000. We anticipate a first-year loss of up to $10 million on the Sonic 1000 model. Break-even calculations indicate that the Sonic 1000 will become profitable after the sales volume exceeds 267,500, early in the product's second year. Our break-even analysis of Sonic's first PDA product assumes per-unit wholesale revenue of $250 per unit, variable cost of $150 per unit, and estimated first-year fixed costs of $26,750,000. Based on these assumptions, the break-even calculation is:

$$\frac{26{,}750{,}000}{\$250 - \$150} = 267{,}500 \text{ units}$$

Controls

We are planning tight control measures to closely monitor quality and customer service satisfaction. This will enable us to react quickly in correcting any problems that may occur. Other early warning signals that will be monitored for signs of deviation from the plan include monthly sales (by segment and channel) and monthly expenses. Given the PDA market's volatility, we are developing contingency plans to address fast-moving environmental changes such as new technology and new competition.

Marketing Plan Tools

Prentice Hall offers two valuable resources to assist you in developing a marketing plan:

- *The Marketing Plan Handbook* by Marian Burk Wood explains the process of creating a marketing plan, complete with detailed checklists and dozens of real-world examples.
- *Marketing Plan Pro* is an award-winning software package that includes sample plans, step-by-step guides, an introductory video, help wizards, and customizable charts for documenting a marketing plan.

Sources: Background information and market data adapted from "Palm 'Hiccup' Highlights EU Enviro Regulations," *RCR Wireless News*, July 10, 2006, p. 6; Arik Hesseldahl, "The Swarm of Killer PDAs," *BusinessWeek*, May 15, 2006, p. 100; Pui-Wing Tam, "The Hand-Helds Strike Back," *Wall Street Journal*, May 18, 2005, pp. D1, D6; Michael V. Copeland, Om Malik, and Rafe Needleman, "The Next Big Thing," *Business 2.0*, July 2003, pp. 62–69; "2005 PDA Shipments Set Record," *Business Communications Review*, April 2006, p. 6; "Smartphone Market Grows Fast Despite Challenges," *Appliance*, March 2006, p. 16; and Sean Ginevan, "A New PDA Is Born," *Network Computing*, July 6, 2006, p. 19.

Budgets

Budgets serve two main purposes: to project profitability and to help managers plan for expenditures, scheduling, and operations related to each action program

Controls

Controls help management assess results after the plan is implemented, identify any problems or performance variations, and initiate corrective action.

MARKETING BY THE NUMBERS

Marketing decisions are coming under increasing scrutiny, and marketing managers must be accountable for the financial implications of their actions. This appendix provides a basic introduction to marketing financial analysis. Such analysis guides marketers in making sound marketing decisions and in assessing the outcomes of those decisions.

The appendix is built around a hypothetical manufacturer of high-definition consumer electronics products—HDX-treme. This company is launching a new product, and we will discuss and analyze the various decisions HDX-treme's marketing managers must make before and after launch.

HDX-treme manufactures high-definition televisions for the consumer market. The company has concentrated on televisions but is now entering the accessories market. Specifically, the company is introducing a high-definition optical disc player (DVD) using the Blu-ray format.

The appendix is organized into three sections. The first section deals with the pricing considerations and break-even and margin analysis assessments that guide the introduction of HDX-treme's new-product launch. The second section begins with a discussion of estimating market potential and company sales. It then introduces the marketing budget, as illustrated through a pro forma profit-and-loss statement followed by the actual profit-and-loss statement. Next, the section discusses marketing performance measures, with a focus on helping marketing managers to better defend their decisions from a financial perspective. In the final section, we analyze the financial implications of various marketing tactics, such as increasing advertising expenditures, adding sales representatives to increase distribution, lowering price, or extending the product line.

At the end of each section, quantitative exercises provide you with an opportunity to apply the concepts you learned in that section to contexts beyond HDX-treme.

■ Pricing, Break-Even, and Margin Analysis

Pricing Considerations

Determining price is one of the most important marketing-mix decisions, and marketers have considerable leeway when setting prices. The limiting factors are demand and costs. Demand factors, such as buyer-perceived value, set the price ceiling. The company's costs set the price floor. In between these two factors, marketers must consider competitors' prices and other factors such as reseller requirements, government regulations, and company objectives.

Current competing high-definition DVD products in this relatively new product category were introduced in 2006 and sell at retail prices between $500 and $1,200. HDX-treme plans to introduce its new product at a lower price in order to expand the market and to gain market share rapidly. We first consider HDX-treme's pricing decision from a cost perspective. Then, we consider consumer value, the competitive environment, and reseller requirements.

Determining Costs

Recall from Chapter 10 that there are different types of costs. **Fixed costs** do not vary with production or sales level and include costs such as rent, interest, depreciation, and clerical and management salaries. Regardless of the level of output, the company must pay these costs. Whereas total fixed costs remain constant as output increases, the fixed cost per unit (or average fixed cost) will decrease as output increases because the total fixed costs are spread across

Fixed costs
Costs that do not vary with production or sales level.

Variable costs
Costs that vary directly with the level of production.

Total costs
The sum of the fixed and variable costs for any given level of production.

Cost-plus pricing (or markup pricing)
Adding a standard markup to the cost of the product.

Relevant costs
Costs that will occur in the future and that will vary across the alternatives being considered.

Break-even price
The price at which total revenue equals total cost and profit is zero.

Return on investment (ROI) pricing (or target-return pricing)
A cost-based pricing method that determines price based on a specified rate of return on investment.

more units of output. **Variable costs** vary directly with the level of production and include costs related to the direct production of the product (such as costs of goods sold—COGS) and many of the marketing costs associated with selling it. Although these costs tend to be uniform for each unit produced, they are called variable because their total varies with the number of units produced. **Total costs** are the sum of the fixed and variable costs for any given level of production.

HDX-treme has invested $10 million in refurbishing an existing facility to manufacture the new DVD product. Once production begins, the company estimates that it will incur fixed costs of $20 million per year. The variable cost to produce each DVD player is estimated to be $250 and is expected to remain at that level for the output capacity of the facility.

Setting Price Based on Costs

HDX-treme starts with the cost-based approach to pricing discussed in Chapter 10. Recall that the simplest method, **cost-plus pricing (or markup pricing)**, simply adds a standard markup to the cost of the product. To use this method, however, HDX-treme must specify an expected unit sales so that total unit costs can be determined. Unit variable costs will remain constant regardless of the output, but *average unit fixed costs* will decrease as output increases.

To illustrate this method, suppose HDX-treme has fixed costs of $20 million, variable costs of $250 per unit, and expects unit sales of 1 million units. Thus, the cost per DVD player is given by:

$$\text{Unit cost} = \text{variable cost} + \frac{\text{fixed costs}}{\text{unit sales}} = \$250 + \frac{\$20,000,000}{1,000,000} = \$270$$

Note that what we do *not* include the initial investment of $10 million in the total fixed cost figure. It is not considered a fixed cost because it is not a *relevant* cost. **Relevant costs** are those that will occur in the future and that will vary across the alternatives being considered. HDX-treme's investment to refurbish the manufacturing facility was a one-time cost that will not reoccur in the future. Such past costs are *sunk costs* and should not be considered in future analyses.

Also notice that if HDX-treme sells its DVD player for $270, the price is equal to the total cost per unit. This is the **break even price**—the price at which unit revenue (price) equals unit cost and profit is zero.

Suppose HDX-treme does not want to merely break even but rather wants to earn a 25% markup on sales. HDX-treme's markup price is:[1]

$$\text{Markup price} = \frac{\text{unit cost}}{(1 - \text{desired return on sales})} = \frac{\$270}{1 - .25} = \$360$$

This is the price that HDX-treme would sell the DVD player to resellers such as wholesalers or retailers to earn a 25% profit on sales.

Another approach HDX-treme could use is called **return on investment (ROI) pricing** (or target-return pricing). In this case, the company *would* consider the initial $10 million investment, but only to determine the dollar profit goal. Suppose the company wants a 30% return on its investment. The price necessary to satisfy this requirement can be determined by:[2]

$$\text{ROI price} = \text{unit cost} + \frac{\text{ROI} \times \text{investment}}{\text{unit sales}} = \$270 + \frac{0.3 \times \$10,000,000}{1,000,000} = \$273$$

That is, if HDX-treme sells its DVD players for $273 each, it will realize a 30% return on its initial investment of $10 million.

In these pricing calculations, unit cost is a function of the expected sales, which were estimated to be 1 million units. But what if actual sales were lower? Then the unit cost would be higher because the fixed costs would be spread over fewer units, and the realized percentage markup on sales or ROI would be lower. Alternatively, if sales are higher than the estimated 1 million units, unit cost would be lower than $270, so a lower price would produce the desired markup on sales or ROI. It's important to note that these cost-based pricing methods are *internally* focused and do not consider demand, competitors' prices, or reseller requirements. Because HDX-treme will be selling these DVD players to consumers through wholesalers and retailers offering competing brands, the company must consider markup pricing from this perspective.

Setting Price Based on External Factors

Whereas costs determine the price floor, HDX-treme also must consider external factors when setting price. HDX-treme does not have the final say concerning the final price to consumers—retailers do. So it must start with its suggested retail price and work back. In doing so, HDX-treme must consider the markups required by resellers that sell the product to consumers.

In general, a dollar **markup** is the difference between a company's selling price for a product and its cost to manufacture or purchase it. For a retailer, then, the markup is the difference between the price it charges consumers and the cost the retailer must pay for the product. Thus, for any level of reseller:

$$\text{Dollar markup} = \text{selling price} - \text{cost}$$

Markups are usually expressed as a percentage, and there are two different ways to compute markups—on *cost* or on *selling price*:

$$\text{Markup percentage on cost} = \frac{\text{dollar markup}}{\text{cost}}$$

$$\text{Markup percentage on selling price} = \frac{\text{dollar markup}}{\text{selling price}}$$

To apply reseller margin analysis, HDX-treme must first set the suggested retail price and then work back to the price at which it must sell the DVD player to a wholesaler. Suppose retailers expect a 30% margin and wholesalers want a 20% margin based on their respective selling prices. And suppose that HDX-treme sets a manufacturer's suggested retail price (MSRP) of $599.99 for its high-definition DVD player.

Recall that HDX-treme wants to expand the market by pricing low and generating market share quickly. HDX-treme selected the $599.99 MSRP because it is much lower than most competitors' prices, which can be as high as $1,200. And the company's research shows that using buyers' perceptions of value and not the seller's cost to determine the MSRP, HDX-treme is using **value-based pricing**. For simplicity, we will use an MSRP of $600 in further analyses.

To determine the price HDX-treme will charge wholesalers, we must first subtract the retailer's margin from the retail price to determine the retailer's cost ($600 − ($600 × 0.30) = $420). The retailer's cost is the wholesaler's price, so HDX-treme next subtracts the wholesaler's margin ($420 − ($420 × 0.20) = $336). Thus, the **markup chain** representing the sequence of markups used by firms at each level in a channel for HDX-treme's new product is:

Suggested retail price: $600
minus retail margin (30%): − $180
Retailer's cost/wholesaler's price: $420
minus wholesaler's margin (20%): − $ 84
Wholesaler's cost/HDX-treme's price: $336

By deducting the markups for each level in the markup chain, HDX-treme arrives at a price for the DVD player to wholesalers of $336.

Break-Even and Margin Analysis

The previous analyses derived a value-based price of $336 for HDX-treme's DVD player. Although this price is higher than the break-even price of $270 and covers costs, that price assumed a demand of 1 million units. But how many units and what level of dollar sales must HDX-treme achieve to break even at the $336 price? And what level of sales must be achieved to realize various profit goals? These questions can be answered through break-even and margin analysis.

Determining Break-Even Unit Volume and Dollar Sales

Based on an understanding of costs, consumer value, the competitive environment, and reseller requirements, HDX-treme has decided to set its price to wholesalers at $336. At that price, what sales level will be needed for HDX-treme to break even or make a profit? **Break-even analysis** determines the unit volume and dollar sales needed to be profitable given a particular price and cost structure.

Markup
The difference between a company's selling price for a product and its cost to manufacture or purchase it.

Value-based pricing
Offering just the right combination of quality and good service at a fair price.

Markup chain
The sequence of markups used by firms at each level in a channel.

Break-even analysis
Analysis to determine the unit volume and dollar sales needed to be profitable given a particular price and cost structure.

cost structure. At the break-even point, total revenue equals total costs and profit is zero. Above this point, the company will make a profit; below it, the company will lose money. HDX-treme can calculate break-even volume using the following formula:[3]

$$\text{Break-even volume} = \frac{\text{fixed costs}}{\text{price} - \text{unit variable cost}}$$

Unit contribution

The amount that each unit contributes to covering fixed costs—the difference between price and variable costs.

The denominator (price − unit variable cost) is called **unit contribution** (sometimes called contribution margin). It represents the amount that each unit contributes to covering fixed costs. Break-even volume represents the level of output at which all (variable and fixed) costs are covered. In HDX-treme's case, break-even unit volume is:

$$\text{Break-even volume} = \frac{\text{fixed cost}}{\text{price} - \text{variable cost}} = \frac{\$20,000,000}{\$336 - \$250} = 232,558.1 \text{ units}$$

Thus, at the given cost and pricing structure, HDX-treme will break even at 232,559 units.

To determine the break-even dollar sales, simply multiply unit break-even volume by the selling price:

$$\text{BE sales} = \text{BE}_{vol} \times \text{price} = 232,559 \text{ units} \times \$336 = \$78,139,824$$

Another way to calculate dollar break-even sales is to use the percentage contribution margin (hereafter referred to as **contribution margin**), which is the unit contribution divided by the selling price:

Contribution margin

The unit contribution divided by the selling price.

$$\text{Contribution margin} = \frac{\text{price} - \text{variable cost}}{\text{price}} = \frac{\$336 - \$250}{\$336} = 0.256 \text{ or } 25.6\%$$

Then,

$$\text{Break-even sales} = \frac{\text{fixed costs}}{\text{contribution margin}} = \frac{\$20,000,000}{0.256} = \$78,125,000$$

Note that the difference between the two break-even sales calculations is due to rounding.

Such break-even analysis helps HDX-treme by showing the unit volume needed to cover costs. If production capacity cannot attain this level of output, then the company should not launch this product. However, the unit break-even volume is well within HDX-treme's capacity. Of course, the bigger question concerns whether HDX-treme can sell this volume at the $336 price. We'll address that issue a little later.

Understanding contribution margin is useful in other types of analyses as well, particularly if unit prices and unit variable costs are unknown or if a company (say, a retailer) sells many products at different prices and knows the percentage of total sales variable costs represent. Whereas unit contribution is the difference between unit price and unit variable costs, total contribution is the difference between total sales and total variable costs. The overall contribution margin can be calculated by:

$$\text{Contribution margin} = \frac{\text{total sales} - \text{total variable costs}}{\text{total sales}}$$

Regardless of the actual level of sales, if the company knows what percentage of sales is represented by variable costs, it can calculate contribution margin. For example, HDX-treme's unit variable cost is $250, or 74% of the selling price ($250 ÷ $336 = 0.74). That means for every $1 of sales revenue for HDX-treme, $0.74 represents variable costs, and the difference ($0.26) represents contribution to fixed costs. But even if the company doesn't know its unit price and unit variable cost, it can calculate the contribution margin from total sales and total variable costs or from knowledge of the total cost structure. It can set total sales equal to 100% regardless of the actual absolute amount and determine the contribution margin:

$$\text{Contribution margin} = \frac{100\% - 74\%}{100\%} = \frac{1 - 0.74}{1} = 1 - 0.74 = 0.26 \text{ or } 26\%$$

Note that this matches the percentage calculated from the unit price and unit variable cost information. This alternative calculation will be very useful later when analyzing various marketing decisions.

Determining "Breakeven" for Profit Goals

Although it is useful to know the break-even point, most companies are more interested in making a profit. Assume HDX-treme would like to realize a $5 million profit in the first year. How many DVD players must it sell at the $336 price to cover fixed costs and produce this profit? To determine this, HDX-treme can simply add the profit figure to fixed costs and again divide by the unit contribution to determine unit sales:[4]

$$\text{Unit volume} = \frac{\text{fixed cost} + \text{profit goal}}{\text{price} - \text{variable cost}} = \frac{\$20,000,000 + \$5,000,000}{\$336 - \$250} = 290,697.7 \text{ units}$$

Thus, to earn a $5 million profit, HDX-treme must sell 290,698 units. Multiply by price to determine dollar sales needed to achieve a $5 million profit:

$$\text{Dollar sales} = 290,698 \text{ units} \times \$336 = \$97,674,528$$

Or use the contribution margin:

$$\text{Sales} = \frac{\text{fixed cost} + \text{profit goal}}{\text{contribution margin}} = \frac{\$20,000,000 + \$5,000,000}{0.256} = \$97,656,250$$

Again, note that the difference between the two break-even sales calculations is due to rounding.

As we saw previously, a profit goal can also be stated as a return on investment goal. For example, recall that HDX-treme wants a 30% return on its $10 million investment. Thus, its absolute profit goal is $3 million ($10,000,000 × 0.30). This profit goal is treated the same way as in the previous example:[5]

$$\text{Unit volume} = \frac{\text{fixed cost} + \text{profit goal}}{\text{price} - \text{variable cost}} = \frac{\$20,000,000 + \$3,000,000}{\$336 - \$250} = 267,442 \text{ units}$$

Or

$$\text{Dollar sales} = 267,442 \text{ units} \times \$336 = \$89,860,512$$

Or

$$\text{Dollar sales} = \frac{\text{fixed cost} + \text{profit goal}}{\text{contribution margin}} = \frac{\$20,000,000 + \$3,000,000}{0.256} = \$89,843,750$$

Finally, HDX-treme can express its profit goal as a percentage of sales, which we also saw in previous pricing analyses. Assume HDX-treme desires a 25% return on sales. To determine the unit and sales volume necessary to achieve this goal, the calculation is a little different from the previous two examples. In this case, we incorporate the profit goal into the unit contribution as an additional variable cost. Look at it this way: If 25% of each sale must go toward profits, that leaves only 75% of the selling price to cover fixed costs. Thus, the equation becomes:[6]

$$\text{Unit volume} = \frac{\text{fixed cost}}{\text{price} - \text{variable cost} - (0.25 \times \text{price})} \quad \text{or} \quad \frac{\text{fixed cost}}{(0.75 \times \text{price}) - \text{variable cost}}$$

So,

$$\text{Unit volume} = \frac{\$20,000,000}{(0.75 \times \$336) - \$250} = 10,000,000 \text{ units}$$

$$\text{Dollar sales necessary} = 10,000,000 \text{ units} \times \$336 = \$3,360,000,000$$

Thus, HDX-treme would need more than $3 billion in sales to realize a 25% return on sales given its current price and cost structure! Could it possibly achieve this level of sales? The major point is this: Although break-even analysis can be useful in determining the level of sales needed to cover costs or to achieve a stated profit goal, it does not tell the company whether it is *possible* to achieve that level of sales at the specified price. To address this issue, HDX-treme needs to estimate demand for this product.

Before moving on, however, let's stop here and practice applying the concepts covered so far. Now that you have seen pricing and break-even concepts in action as they related to HDX-treme's new DVD player, here are several exercises for you to apply what you have learned in other contexts.

Marketing by the Numbers Exercise Set One

Now that you've studied pricing, break-even, and margin analysis as they relate to HDX-treme's new-product launch, use the following exercises to apply these concepts in other contexts.

1.1 Sanborn, a manufacturer of electric roof vents, realizes a cost of $55 for every unit it produces. Its total fixed costs equal $2 million. If the company manufactures 500,000 units, compute the following:

   a. unit cost

   b. markup price if the company desires a 10% return on sales

   c. ROI price if the company desires a 25% return on an investment of $1 million

1.2 An interior decorator purchases items to sell in her store. She purchases a lamp for $125 and sells it for $225. Determine the following:

   a. dollar markup

   b. markup percentage on cost

   c. markup percentage on selling price

1.3 A consumer purchases a toaster from a retailer for $60. The retailer's markup is 20%, and the wholesaler's markup is 15%, both based on selling price. For what price does the manufacturer sell the product to the wholesaler?

1.4 A vacuum manufacturer has a unit cost of $50 and wishes to achieve a margin of 30% based on selling price. If the manufacturer sells directly to a retailer who then adds a set margin of 40% based on selling price, determine the retail price charged to consumers.

1.5 Advanced Electronics manufactures DVDs and sells them directly to retailers who typically sell them for $20. Retailers take a 40% margin based on the retail selling price. Advanced's cost information is as follows:

DVD package and disc	$2.50/DVD
Royalties	$2.25/DVD
Advertising and promotion	$500,000
Overhead	$200,000

   Calculate the following:

   a. contribution per unit and contribution margin

   b. break-even volume in DVD units and dollars

   c. volume in DVD units and dollar sales necessary if Advanced's profit goal is 20% profit on sales

   d. net profit if 5 million DVDs are sold

▌Demand Estimates, the Marketing Budget, and Marketing Performance Measures

Market Potential and Sales Estimates

HDX-treme has now calculated the sales needed to break even and to attain various profit goals on its DVD player. However, the company needs more information regarding demand in order to assess the feasibility of attaining the needed sales levels. This information is also needed for production and other decisions. For example, production schedules need to be developed and marketing tactics need to be planned.

The **total market demand** for a product or service is the total volume that would be bought by a defined consumer group in a defined geographic area in a defined time period in a defined marketing environment under a defined level and mix of industry marketing effort. Total market demand is not a fixed number but a function of the stated conditions. For example, next year's total market demand for high-definition DVD players will depend on how much Samsung, Sony, Pioneer, Toshiba, and other producers spend on marketing their brands. It also depends on many environmental factors, such as government regulations, economic conditions, and the level of consumer confidence in a given market. The upper limit of market demand is called **market potential**.

One general but practical method that HDX-treme might use for estimating total market demand uses three variables: (1) the number of prospective buyers, (2) the quantity purchased

Total market demand

The total volume that would be bought by a defined consumer group in a defined geographic area in a defined time period in a defined marketing environment under a defined level and mix of industry marketing effort.

Market potential

The upper limit of market demand.

by an average buyer per year, and (3) the price of an average unit. Using these numbers, HDX-treme can estimate total market demand as follows:

$$Q = n \times q \times p$$

where

Q = total market demand

n = number of buyers in the market

q = quantity purchased by an average buyer per year

p = price of an average unit

A variation of this approach is the **chain ratio method**. This method involves multiplying a base number by a chain of adjusting percentages. For example, HDX-treme's high-definition DVD player is designed to play high-definition DVD movies on high-definition televisions. Thus, consumers who do not own a high-definition television will not likely purchase this player. Additionally, not all HDTV households will be willing and able to purchase the new high-definition DVD player. HDX-treme can estimate U.S. demand using a chain of calculations like the following:

Total number of U.S. households

$\times$ The percentage of U.S. households owning a high-definition television

$\times$ The percentage of these households willing and able to buy a high-definition DVD player

AC Nielsen, the television ratings company, estimates that there are more than 110 million TV households in the United States.[7] The Consumer Electronics Association estimates that 38% of TV households will own HDTVs by the end of 2006.[8] However, HDX-treme's research indicates that only 44.5% of HDTV households possess the discretionary income needed and are willing to buy a high-definition DVD player. Then, the total number of households willing and able to purchase this product is:

110 million households $\times$ 0.38 $\times$ 0.445 = 18.6 million households

Because HDTVs are relatively new and expensive products, most households have only one of these televisions, and it's usually the household's primary television.[9] Thus, consumers who buy a high-definition DVD player will likely buy only one per household. Assuming the average retail price across all brands is $750 for this product, the estimate of total market demand is as follows:

18.6 million households $\times$ 1 DVD player per household $\times$ $750 = $14 billion

This simple chain of calculations gives HDX-treme only a rough estimate of potential demand. However, more detailed chains involving additional segments and other qualifying factors would yield more accurate and refined estimates. Still, these are only *estimates of market potential*. They rely heavily on assumptions regarding adjusting percentages, average quantity, and average price. Thus, HDX-treme must make certain that its assumptions are reasonable and defendable. As can be seen, the overall market potential in dollar sales can vary widely given the average price used. For this reason, HDX-treme will use unit sales potential to determine its sales estimate for next year. Market potential in terms of units is 18.6 million DVD players (18.6 million households $\times$ 1 DVD player per household).

Assuming that HDX-treme wants to attain 2% market share (comparable to its share of the HDTV market) in the first year after launching this product, then it can forecast unit sales at 18.6 million units $\times$ 0.02 = 372,000 units. At a selling price of $336 per unit, this translates into sales of $124.99 million (372,000 units $\times$ $336 per unit). For simplicity, further analyses will use forecasted sales of $125 million.

This unit volume estimate is well within HDX-treme's production capacity and exceeds not only the break-even estimate (232,559 units) calculated earlier, but also the volume necessary to realize a $5 million profit (290,698 units) or a 30% return on investment (267,442 units). However, this forecast falls well short of the volume necessary to realize a 25% return on sales (10 million units!) and may require that HDX-treme revise expectations.

To assess expected profits, we must now look at the budgeted expenses for launching this product. To do this, we will construct a pro forma profit-and-loss statement.

Chain ratio method

Estimating market demand by multiplying a base number by a chain of adjusting percentages.

The Profit-and-Loss Statement and Marketing Budget

All marketing managers must account for the profit impact of their marketing strategies. A major tool for projecting such profit impact is a **pro forma** (or projected) **profit-and-loss statement** (also called an **income statement** or **operating statement**). A pro forma statement shows projected revenues less budgeted expenses and estimates the projected net profit for an organization, product, or brand during a specific planning period, typically a year. It includes direct product production costs, marketing expenses budgeted to attain a given sales forecast, and overhead expenses assigned to the organization or product. A profit-and-loss statement typically consists of several major components (see Table A2.1):

- ▪ *Net sales*—gross sales revenue minus returns and allowances (for example, trade, cash, quantity, and promotion allowances). HDX-treme's net sales for 2006 are estimated to be $125 million, as determined in the previous analysis.

- ▪ *Cost of goods sold* (sometimes called *cost of sales*)—the actual cost of the merchandise sold by a manufacturer or reseller. It includes the cost of inventory, purchases, and other costs associated with making the goods. HDX-treme's cost of goods sold is estimated to be 50% of net sales, or $62.5 million.

- ▪ *Gross margin (or gross profit)*—the difference between net sales and cost of goods sold. HDX-treme's gross margin is estimated to be $62.5 million.

- ▪ *Operating expenses*—the expenses incurred while doing business. These include all other expenses beyond the cost of goods sold that are necessary to conduct business. Operating expenses can be presented in total or broken down in detail. Here, HDX-treme's estimated operating expenses include *marketing expenses* and *general and administrative expenses*.

  Marketing expenses include sales expenses, promotion expenses, and distribution expenses. The new product will be sold though HDX-treme's sales force, so the company budgets $5 million for sales salaries. However, because sales representatives earn a 10% commission on sales, HDX-treme must also add a variable component to sales expenses of $12.5 million (10% of $125 million net sales), for a total budgeted sales expense of $17.5 million. HDX-treme sets its advertising and promotion to launch this product at $10 million. However, the company also budgets 4% of sales, or $5 million, for cooperative advertising allowances to retailers who promote HDX-treme's new product in their advertising. Thus, the total budgeted advertising and promotion expenses are $15 million ($10 million for advertising plus $5 million in co-op allowances). Finally, HDX-treme budgets 10% of net sales, or $12.5 million, for freight and delivery charges. In all, total marketing expenses are estimated to be $17.5 million + $15 million + $12.5 million = $45 million.

  General and administrative expenses are estimated at $5 million, broken down into $2 million for managerial salaries and expenses for the marketing function and $3 million of indirect overhead allocated to this product by the corporate accountants (such as depreciation, interest, maintenance, and insurance). Total expenses for the year, then, are estimated to be $50 million ($45 million marketing expenses + $5 million in general and administrative expenses).

Pro forma (or projected) **profit-and-loss statement** (or **income statement** or **operating statement**)
A statement that shows projected revenues less budgeted expenses and estimates the projected net profit for an organization, product, or brand during a specific planning period, typically a year.

TABLE A2.1
Pro Forma Profit-and-Loss Statement for the 12-Month Period Ended December 31, 2006

			% of sales
Net Sales		$125,000,000	100%
Cost of Goods Sold		62,500,000	50%
Gross Margin		$ 62,500,000	50%
Marketing Expenses			
Sales expenses	$17,500,000		
Promotion expenses	15,000,000		
Freight	12,500,000	45,000,000	36%
General and Administrative Expenses			
Managerial salaries and expenses	$2,000,000		
Indirect overhead	3,000,000	5,000,000	4%
Net Profit Before Income Tax		$12,500,000	10%

■ *Net profit before taxes*—profit earned after all costs are deducted. HDX-treme's estimated net profit before taxes is $12.5 million.

In all, as Table A2.1 shows, HDX-treme expects to earn a profit on its new DVD player of $12.5 million in 2006. Also note that the percentage of sales that each component of the profit-and-loss statement represents is given in the right-hand column. These percentages are determined by dividing the cost figure by net sales (that is, marketing expenses represent 36% of net sales determined by $45 million ÷ $125 million). As can be seen, HDX-treme projects a net profit return on sales of 10% in the first year after launching this product.

Marketing Performance Measures

Now let's fast-forward a year. HDX-treme's high-definition DVD player has been on the market for one year and management wants to assess its sales and profit performance. One way to assess this performance is to compute performance ratios derived from HDX-treme's **profit-and-loss statement**.

Whereas the pro forma profit-and-loss statement shows *projected* financial performance, the statement given in Table A2.2 shows HDX-treme's *actual* financial performance based on actual sales, cost of goods sold, and expenses during the past year. By comparing the profit-and-loss statement from one period to the next, HDX-treme can gauge performance against goals, spot favorable or unfavorable trends, and take appropriate corrective action.

The profit-and-loss statement shows that HDX-treme lost $1 million rather than making the $12.5 million profit projected in the pro forma statement. Why? One obvious reason is that net sales fell $25 million short of estimated sales. Lower sales translated into lower variable costs associated with marketing the product. However, both fixed costs and the cost of goods sold as a percentage of sales exceeded expectations. Hence, the product's contribution margin was 21% rather than the estimated 26%. That is, variable costs represented 79% of sales (55% for cost of goods sold, 10% for sales commissions, 10% for freight, and 4% for co-op allowances). Recall that contribution margin can be calculated by subtracting that fraction from one $(1 - 0.79 = 0.21)$. Total fixed costs were $22 million, $2 million more than estimated. Thus, the sales that HDX-treme needed to break even given this cost structure can be calculated as:

$$\text{Break-even sales} = \frac{\text{fixed costs}}{\text{contribution margin}} = \frac{\$22,000,000}{0.21} = \$104,761,905$$

If HDX-treme had achieved another $5 million in sales, it would have earned a profit.

Although HDX-treme's sales fell short of the forecasted sales, so did overall industry sales for this product. Overall industry sales were only $2.5 billion. That means that HDX-treme's **market share** was 4% ($100 million ÷ $2.5 billion = 0.04 = 4%), which was higher than forecasted. Thus, HDX-treme attained a higher-than-expected market share but the overall market sales were not as high as estimated.

Profit-and-loss statement (or income statement or operating statement)
A statement that shows actual revenues less expenses and net profit for an organization, product, or brand during a specific planning period, typically a year.

Market share
Company sales divided by market sales.

TABLE A2.2
Profit-and-Loss Statement for the 12-Month Period Ended December 31, 2006

			% *of sales*
Net Sales		$100,000,000	100%
Cost of Goods Sold		55,000,000	55%
Gross Margin		$ 45,000,000	45%
Marketing Expenses			
Sales expenses	$15,000,000		
Promotion expenses	14,000,000		
Freight	10,000,000	39,000,000	39%
General and Administrative Expenses			
Managerial salaries and expenses	$2,000,000		
Indirect overhead	5,000,000	7,000,000	7%
Net Profit Before Income Tax		($1,000,000,	(-1%)

Analytic Ratios

Operating ratios
The ratios of selected operating statement items to net sales.

The profit-and-loss statement provides the figures needed to compute some crucial **operating ratios**—the ratios of selected operating statement items to net sales. These ratios let marketers compare the firm's performance in one year to that in previous years (or with industry standards and competitors' performance in that year). The most commonly used operating ratios are the *gross margin percentage*, the *net profit percentage*, and the *operating expense percentage*. The *inventory turnover rate* and *return on investment (ROI)* are often used to measure managerial effectiveness and efficiency.

Gross margin percentage
The percentage of net sales remaining after cost of goods sold—calculated by dividing gross margin by net sales.

The **gross margin percentage** indicates the percentage of net sales remaining after cost of goods sold that can contribute to operating expenses and net profit before taxes. The higher this ratio, the more a firm has left to cover expenses and generate profit. HDX-treme's gross margin ratio was 45%:

$$\text{Gross margin percentage} = \frac{\text{gross margin}}{\text{net sales}} = \frac{\$45,000,000}{\$100,000,000} = 0.45 = 45\%$$

Note that this percentage is lower than estimated, and this ratio is seen easily in the percentage of sales column in Table A2.2. Stating items in the profit-and-loss statement as a percent of sales allows managers to quickly spot abnormal changes in costs over time. If there was previous history for this product and this ratio was declining, management should examine it more closely to determine why it has decreased (that is, because of a decrease in sales volume or price, an increase in costs, or a combination of these). In HDX-treme's case, net sales were $25 million lower than estimated, and cost of goods sold was higher than estimated (55% rather than the estimated 50%).

Net profit percentage
The percentage of each sales dollar going to profit—calculated by dividing net profits by net sales.

The **net profit percentage** shows the percentage of each sales dollar going to profit. It is calculated by dividing net profits by net sales:

$$\text{Net profit percentage} = \frac{\text{net profit}}{\text{net sales}} = \frac{-\$1,000,000}{\$100,000,000} = -0.01 = -1.0\%$$

This ratio is easily seen in the percent of sales column. HDX-treme's DVD player generated negative profits in the first year, not a good situation given that before the product launch net profits before taxes were estimated at more than $12 million. Later in this appendix, we will discuss further analyses the marketing manager should conduct to defend the product.

Operating expense percentage
The portion of net sales going to operating expenses—calculated by dividing total expenses by net sales.

The **operating expense percentage** indicates the portion of net sales going to operating expenses. Operating expenses include marketing and other expenses not directly related to marketing the product, such as indirect overhead assigned to this product. It is calculated by:

$$\text{Operating expense percentage} = \frac{\text{total expenses}}{\text{net sales}} = \frac{\$46,000,000}{\$100,000,000} = 0.46 = 46\%$$

This ratio can also be quickly determined from the percent of sales column in the profit-and-loss statement by adding the percentages for marketing expenses and general and administrative expenses (39% + 7%). Thus, 46 cents of every sales dollar went for operations. Although HDX-treme wants this ratio to be as low as possible, and 46% is not an alarming amount, it is of concern if it is increasing over time or if a loss is realized.

Inventory turnover rate (or stockturn rate for resellers)
The number of times an inventory turns over or is sold during a specified time period (often one year)—calculated based on costs, selling price, or units.

Another useful ratio is the **inventory turnover rate** (also called *stockturn rate* for resellers). The inventory turnover rate is the number of times an inventory turns over or is sold during a specified time period (often one year). This rate tells how quickly a business is moving inventory through the organization. Higher rates indicate that lower investments in inventory are made, thus freeing up funds for other investments. It may be computed on a cost, selling price, or unit basis. The formula based on cost is:

$$\text{Inventory turnover rate} = \frac{\text{cost of goods sold}}{\text{average inventory at cost}}$$

Assuming HDX-treme's beginning and ending inventories were $30 million and $20 million, respectively, the inventory turnover rate is:

$$\text{Inventory turnover rate} = \frac{\$55,000,000}{(\$30,000,000 + \$20,000,000)/2} = \frac{\$55,000,000}{\$25,000,000} = 2.2$$

That is, HDX-treme's inventory turned over 2.2 times in 2006. Normally, the higher the turnover rate, the higher the management efficiency and company profitability. However, this rate should be compared to industry averages, competitors' rates, and past performance to determine if HDX-treme is doing well. A competitor with similar sales but a higher inventory turnover rate will have fewer resources tied up in inventory, allowing it to invest in other areas of the business.

Companies frequently use **return on investment (ROI)** to measure managerial effectiveness and efficiency. For HDX-treme, ROI is the ratio of net profits to total investment required to manufacture the new product. This investment includes capital investments in land, buildings, and equipment (here, the initial $10 million to refurbish the manufacturing facility) plus inventory costs (HDX-treme's average inventory totaled $25 million), for a total of $35 million. Thus, HDX-treme's ROI for the DVD player is:

$$\text{Return on investment} = \frac{\text{net profit before taxes}}{\text{investment}} = \frac{-\$1,000,000}{\$35,000,000} = -.0286 = -2.86\%$$

ROI is often used to compare alternatives, and a positive ROI is desired. The alternative with the highest ROI is preferred to other alternatives. HDX-treme needs to be concerned with the ROI realized. One obvious way HDX-treme can increase net profit by reducing expenses. Another way is to reduce its investment, perhaps by investing less in inventory and turning it over more frequently.

Marketing Profitability Metrics

Given the above financial results, you may be thinking that HDX-treme should drop this new product. But what arguments can marketers make for keeping or dropping this product? The obvious arguments for dropping the product are that first-year sales were well below expected levels and the product lost money, resulting in a negative return on investment.

So what would happen if HDX-treme did drop this product? Surprisingly, if the company drops the product, the profits for the total organization will decrease by $4 million! How can that be? Marketing managers need to look closely at the numbers in the profit-and-loss statement to determine the *net marketing contribution* for this product. In HDX-treme's case, the net marketing contribution for the DVD player is $4 million, and if the company drops this product, that contribution will disappear as well. Let's look more closely at this concept to illustrate how marketing managers can better assess and defend their marketing strategies and programs.

NET MARKETING CONTRIBUTION **Net marketing contribution (NMC)**, along with other marketing metrics derived from it, measures *marketing* profitability. It includes only components of profitability that are controlled by marketing. Whereas the previous calculation of net profit before taxes from the profit-and-loss statement includes operating expenses not under marketing's control, NMC does not. Referring back to HDX-treme's profit-and-loss statement given in Table A2.2, we can calculate net marketing contribution for the DVD player as:

NMC = net sales − cost of goods sold − marketing expenses
= $100 million − $55 million − $41 million = $4 million

The marketing expenses include sales expenses ($15 million), promotion expenses ($14 million), freight expenses ($10 million), and the managerial salaries and expenses of the marketing function ($2 million), which total $41 million.

Thus, the DVD player actually contributed $4 million to HDX-treme's profits. It was the $5 million of indirect overhead allocated to this product that caused the negative profit. Further, the amount allocated was $2 million more than estimated in the pro forma profit-and-loss statement. Indeed, if only the estimated amount had been allocated, the product would have earned a *profit* of $1 million rather than losing $1 million. If HDX-treme drops the DVD player product, the $5 million in fixed overhead expenses will not disappear—it will simply have to be allocated elsewhere. However, the $4 million in net marketing contribution *will* disappear.

MARKETING RETURN ON SALES AND INVESTMENT To get an even deeper understanding of the profit impact of marketing strategy, we'll now examine two measures of marketing efficiency—*marketing return on sales* (marketing ROS) and *marketing return on investment* (marketing ROI).[10]

Marketing return on sales (or marketing ROS) shows the percent of net sales attributable to the net marketing contribution. For our DVD player, ROS is:

$$\text{Marketing ROS} = \frac{\text{net marketing contribution}}{\text{net sales}} = \frac{\$4,000,000}{\$100,000,000} = 0.04 = 4\%$$

Return on investment (ROI)
A measure of managerial effectiveness and efficiency—net profit before taxes divided by total investment.

Net marketing contribution (NMC)
A measure of marketing profitability that includes only components of profitability controlled by marketing.

Marketing return on sales (or marketing ROS)
The percent of net sales attributable to the net marketing contribution—calculated by dividing net marketing contribution by net sales.

Thus, out of every $100 of sales, the product returns $4 to HDX-treme's bottom line. A high marketing ROS is desirable. But to assess whether this is a good level of performance, HDX-treme must compare this figure to previous marketing ROS levels for the product, the ROSs of other products in the company's portfolio, and the ROSs of competing products.

Marketing return on investment (or marketing ROI) measures the marketing productivity of a marketing investment. In HDX-treme's case, the marketing investment is represented by $41 million of the total expenses. Thus, Marketing ROI is:

$$\text{Marketing ROI} = \frac{\text{net marketing contribution}}{\text{net sales}} = \frac{\$4,000,000}{\$41,000,000} = 0.0976 = 9.76\%$$

As with marketing ROS, a high value is desirable, but this figure should be compared with previous levels for the given product and with the marketing ROIs of competitors' products. Note from this equation that marketing ROI could be greater than 100%. This can be achieved by attaining a higher net marketing contribution and/or a lower total marketing expense.

In this section, we estimated market potential and sales, developed profit-and-loss statements, and examined financial measures of performance. In the next section, we discuss methods for analyzing the impact of various marketing tactics. However, before moving on to those analyses, here's another set of quantitative exercises to help you apply what you've learned to other situations.

Marketing by the Numbers Exercise Set Two

2.1 Determine the market potential for a product that has 50 million prospective buyers who purchase an average of 3 per year and price averages $25. How many units must a company sell if it desires a 10% share of this market?

2.2 Develop a profit-and-loss statement for the Westgate division of North Industries. This division manufactures light fixtures sold to consumers through home improvement and hardware stores. Cost of goods sold represents 40% of net sales. Marketing expenses include selling expenses, promotion expenses, and freight. Selling expenses include sales salaries totaling $3 million per year and sales commissions (5% of sales). The company spent $3 million on advertising last year, and freight costs were 10% of sales. Other costs include $2 million for managerial salaries and expenses for the marketing function and another $3 million for indirect overhead allocated to the division.
   a. Develop the profit-and-loss statement if net sales were $20 million last year.
   b. Develop the profit-and-loss statement if net sales were $40 million last year.
   c. Calculate Westgate's break-even sales.

2.3 Using the profit-and-loss statement you developed in question 2.2b, and assuming that Westgate's beginning inventory was $11 million, ending inventory was $7 million, and total investment was $20 million including inventory, determine the following:
   a. gross margin percentage
   b. net profit percentage
   c. operating expense percentage
   d. inventory turnover rate
   e. return on investment (ROI)
   f. net marketing contribution
   g. marketing return on sales (marketing ROS)
   h. marketing return on investment (marketing ROI)
   i. Is the Westgate division doing well? Explain your answer.

Financial Analysis of Marketing Tactics

Although the first-year profit performance for HDX-treme's DVD player was less than desired, management feels that this attractive market has excellent growth opportunities. Although the sales of HDX-treme's DVD player were lower than initially projected, they were not unreasonable given the size of the current market. Thus, HDX-treme wants to explore new marketing tactics to help grow the market for this product and increase sales for the company.

For example, the company could increase advertising to promote more awareness of the new DVD player and its category. It could add salespeople to secure greater product distribution. HDX-treme could decrease prices so that more consumers could afford its player.

Marketing return on investment (or marketing ROI)

A measure of the marketing productivity of a marketing investment—calculated by dividing net marketing contribution by marketing expenses.

Finally, to expand the market, HDX-treme could introduce a lower-priced model in addition to the higher-priced original offering. Before pursuing any of these tactics, HDX-treme must analyze the financial implications of each.

Increase Advertising Expenditures

Although most consumers understand DVD players, they may not be aware of high-definition DVD players. Thus, HDX-treme is considering boosting its advertising to make more people aware of the benefits of high-definition DVD players in general and of its own brand in particular.

What if HDX-treme's marketers recommend increasing national advertising by 50% to $15 million (assume no change in the variable cooperative component of promotional expenditures)? This represents an increase in fixed costs of $5 million. What increase in sales will be needed to break even on this $5 million increase in fixed costs?

A quick way to answer this question is to divide the increase in fixed cost by the contribution margin, which we found in a previous analysis to be 21%:

$$\text{Increase in sales} = \frac{\text{increase in fixed cost}}{\text{contribution margin}} = \frac{\$5,000,000}{0.21} = \$23,809,524$$

Thus, a 50% increase in advertising expenditures must produce a sales increase of almost $24 million to just break even. That $24 million sales increase translates into an almost 1 percentage point increase in market share (1% of the $2.5 billion overall market equals $25 million). That is, to break even on the increased advertising expenditure, HDX-treme would have to increase its market share from 4% to 4.95% ($123,809,524 ÷ $2.5 billion = 0.0495 or 4.95% market share). All of this assumes that the total market will not grow, which might or might not be a reasonable assumption.

Increase Distribution Coverage

HDX-treme also wants to consider hiring more salespeople in order to call on new retailer accounts and increase distribution through more outlets. Even though HDX-treme sells directly to wholesalers, its sales representatives call on retail accounts to perform other functions in addition to selling, such as training retail salespeople. Currently, HDX-treme employs 60 sales reps who earn an average of $50,000 in salary plus 10% commission on sales. The DVD player is currently sold to consumers through 1,875 retail outlets. Suppose HDX-treme wants to increase that number of outlets to 2,500, an increase of 625 retail outlets. How many additional salespeople will HDX-treme need, and what sales will be necessary to break even on the increased cost?

One method for determining what size sales force HDX-treme will need is the **workload method**. The workload method uses the following formula to determine the salesforce size:

$$NS = \frac{NC \times FC \times LC}{TA}$$

where

NS = number of salespeople

NC = number of customers

FC = average frequency of customer calls per customer

LC = average length of customer call

TA = time an average salesperson has available for selling per year

HDX-treme's sales reps typically call on accounts an average of 20 times per year for about 2 hours per call. Although each sales rep works 2,000 hours per year (50 weeks per year × 40 hours per week), they spent about 15 hours per week on nonselling activities such as administrative duties and travel. Thus, the average annual available selling time per sales rep per year is 1,250 hours (50 weeks × 25 hours per week). We can now calculate how many sales reps HDX-treme will need to cover the anticipated 2,500 retail outlets:

$$NS = \frac{2,500 \times 20 \times 2}{1,250} = 80 \text{ salespeople}$$

Therefore, HDX-treme will need to hire 20 more salespeople. The cost to hire these reps will be $1 million (20 salespeople × $50,000 salary per sales person).

Workload method

An approach to determining sales force size based on the workload required and the time available for selling.

What increase in sales will be required to break even on this increase in fixed costs? The 10% commission is already accounted for in the contribution margin, so the contribution margin remains unchanged at 21%. Thus, the increase in sales needed to cover this increase in fixed costs can be calculated by:

$$\text{Increase in sales} = \frac{\text{increase in fixed cost}}{\text{contribution margin}} = \frac{\$1,000,000}{0.21} = \$4,761,905$$

That is, HDX-treme's sales must increase almost $5 million to break even on this tactic. So, how many new retail outlets will the company need to secure to achieve this sales increase? The average revenue generated per current outlet is $53,333 ($100 million in sales divided by 1,875 outlets). To achieve the nearly $5 million sales increase needed to break even, HDX-treme would need about 90 new outlets ($4,761,905 ÷ $53,333 = 89.3 outlets), or about 4.5 outlets per new rep. Given that current reps cover about 31 outlets apiece (1,875 outlets ÷ 60 reps), this seems very reasonable.

Decrease Price

HDX-treme is also considering lowering its price to increase sales revenue through increased volume. The company's research has shown that demand for most types of consumer electronics products is elastic—that is, the percentage increase in the quantity demanded is greater than the percentage decrease in price. It has also been found that when the price of HDTVs goes down, the quantity of DVD players demanded increases because they are complementary products.

What increase in sales would be necessary to break even on a 10% decrease in price? That is, what increase in sales will be needed to maintain the total contribution that HDX-treme realized at the higher price? The current total contribution can be determined by multiplying the contribution margin by total sales:[11]

Current total contribution = contribution margin × sales = .21 × $100 million = $21 million

Price changes result in changes in unit contribution and contribution margin. Recall that the contribution margin of 21% was based on variable costs representing 79% of sales. Therefore, unit variable costs can be determined by multiplying the original price by this percentage: $336 × 0.79 = $265.44 per unit. If price is decreased by 10%, the new price is $302.40. However, variable costs do not change just because price decreased, so the contribution and contribution margin decrease as follows:

	Old	New (reduced 10%)
Price	$336	$302.40
− Unit variable cost	$265.44	$265.44
= Unit contribution	$70.56	$36.96
Contribution margin	$70.56/$336 = 0.21 or 21%	$36.96/$302.40 = 0.12 or 12%

So a 10% reduction in price results in a decrease in the contribution margin from 21% to 12%.[12] To determine the sales level needed to break even on this price reduction, we calculate the level of sales that must be attained at the new contribution margin to achieve the original total contribution of $21 million:

New contribution margin × new sales level = original total contribution

So,

$$\text{New sales level} = \frac{\text{original contribution}}{\text{new contribution margin}} = \frac{\$21,000,000}{0.12} = \$175,000,000$$

Thus, sales must increase by $75 million ($175 million − $100 million) just to break even on a 10% price reduction. This means that HDX-treme must increase market share to 7% ($175 million ÷ $2.5 billion) to achieve the current level of profits (assuming no increase in the total market sales). The marketing manager must assess whether or not this is a reasonable goal.

Extend the Product Line

As a final option, HDX-treme is considering extending its DVD player product line by offering a lower-priced model. Of course, the new, lower-priced product would steal some sales from

Cannibalization

The situation in which one product sold by a company takes a portion of its sales from other company products.

the higher-priced model. This is called **cannibalization**—the situation in which one product sold by a company takes a portion of its sales from other company products. If the new product has a lower contribution than the original product, the company's total contribution will decrease on the cannibalized sales. However, if the new product can generate enough new volume, it is worth considering.

To assess cannibalization, HDX-treme must look at the incremental contribution gained by having both products available. Recall in the previous analysis we determined that unit variable costs were $265.44 and unit contribution was just over $70. Assuming costs remain the same next year, HDX-treme can expect to realize a contribution per unit of approximately $70 for every unit of the original DVD player sold.

Assume that the first model high-definition DVD player offered by HDX-treme is called HD1 and the new, lower-priced model is called HD2. HD2 will retail for $400, and resellers will take the same markup percentages on price as they do with the higher-priced model. Therefore, HD2's price to wholesalers will be $224 as follows:

Retail price:	$400
minus retail margin (30%):	− $120
Retailer's cost/wholesaler's price:	$280
minus wholesaler's margin (20%):	− $ 56
Wholesaler's cost/HDX-treme's price	$224

If HD2's variable costs are estimated to be $174, then its contribution per unit will equal $50 ($224 − $174 = $50). That means for every unit that HD2 cannibalizes from HD1, HDX-treme will *lose* $20 in contribution toward fixed costs and profit (that is, contribution$_{HD2}$ − contribution$_{HD1}$ = $50 − $70 = −$20). You might conclude that HDX-treme should not pursue this tactic because it appears as though the company will be worse off if it introduces the lower-priced model. However, if HD2 captures enough *additional* sales, HDX-treme will be better off even though some HD1 sales are cannibalized. The company must examine what will happen to *total* contribution, which requires estimates of unit volume for both products.

Originally, HDX-treme estimated that next year's sales of HD1 would be 600,000 units. However, with the introduction of HD2, it now estimates that 200,000 of those sales will be cannibalized by the new model. If HDX-treme sells only 200,000 units of the new HD2 model (all cannibalized from HD1), the company would lose $4 million in total contribution (200,000 units × −$20 per cannibalized unit = −$4 million)—not a good outcome. However, HDX-treme estimates that HD2 will generate the 200,000 of cannibalized sales plus an *additional* 500,000 unit sales. Thus, the contribution on these additional HD2 units will be $25 million (i.e., 500,000 units × $50 per unit = $25 million). The net effect is that HDX-treme will gain $21 million in total contribution by introducing HD2.

The following table compares HDX-treme's total contribution with and without the introduction of HD2:

	HD1 only	HD1 and HD2
HD1 contribution	600,000 units × $70	400,000 units × $70
	= $42,000,000	= $28,000,000
HD2 contribution	0	700,000 units × $50
		= $35,000,000
Total contribution	$42,000,000	$63,000,000

The difference in the total contribution is a net gain of $21 million ($63 million − $42 million). Based on this analysis, HDX-treme should introduce the HD2 model because it results in a positive incremental contribution. However, if fixed costs will increase by more than $21 million as a result of adding this model, then the net effect will be negative and HDX-treme should not pursue this tactic.

Now that you have seen these marketing tactic analysis concepts in action as they related to HDX-treme's new DVD player, here are several exercises for you to apply what you have learned in this section in other contexts.

Marketing by the Numbers Exercise Set Three

3.1 Kingsford, Inc. sells small plumbing components to consumers through retail outlets. Total industry sales for Kingsford's relevant market last year were $80 million, with

Kingsford's sales representing 10% of that total. Contribution margin is 25%. Kingsford's sales force calls on retail outlets and each sales rep earns $45,000 per year plus 1% commission on all sales. Retailers receive a 40% margin on selling price and generate average revenue of $10,000 per outlet for Kingsford.

a. The marketing manager has suggested increasing consumer advertising by $300,000. By how much would dollar sales need to increase to break even on this expenditure? What increase in overall market share does this represent?

b. Another suggestion is to hire three more sales representatives to gain new consumer retail accounts. How many new retail outlets would be necessary to break even on the increased cost of adding three sales reps?

c. A final suggestion is to make a 20% across-the-board price reduction. By how much would dollar sales need to increase to maintain Kingsford's current contribution? (See endnote 12 to calculate the new contribution margin.)

d. Which suggestion do you think Kingsford should implement? Explain your recommendation.

3.2 PepsiCo sells its soft drinks in approximately 400,000 retail establishments, such as supermarkets, discount stores, and convenience stores. Sales representatives call on each retail account weekly, which means each account is called on by a sales rep 52 times per year. The average length of a sales call is 75 minutes (or 1.25 hours). An average salesperson works 2,000 hours per year (50 weeks per year × 40 hours per week), but each spends 10 hours a week on nonselling activities, such as administrative tasks and travel. How many sales people does PepsiCo need?

3.3 Hair Zone manufactures a brand of hair-styling gel. It is considering adding a modified version of the product—a foam that provides stronger hold. Hair Zone's variable costs and prices to wholesalers are:

	Current hair gel	New foam product
Unit selling price	2.00	2.25
Unit variable costs	.85	1.25

Hair Zone expects to sell 1 million units of the new styling foam in the first year after introduction, but it expects that 60% of those sales will come from buyers who normally purchase Hair Zone's styling gel. Hair Zone estimates that it would sell 1.5 million units of the gel if it did not introduce the foam. If the fixed cost of launching the new foam will be $100,000 during the first year, should Hair Zone add the new product to its line? Why or why not?

Appendix 3

CAREERS IN MARKETING

Now that you have completed this course in marketing, you have a good idea of what the field entails. You may have decided you want to pursue a marketing career because it offers constant challenge, stimulating problems, the opportunity to work with people, and excellent advancement opportunities. But you still may not know which part of marketing best suits you—marketing is a very broad field offering a wide variety of career options.

This appendix helps you discover what types of marketing jobs best match your special skills and interests, shows you how to conduct the kind of job search that will get you the position you want in the company of your choice, describes marketing career paths open to you, and suggests other information resources.

◼ Marketing Careers Today

The marketing field is booming, with nearly a third of all Americans now employed in marketing-related positions. Marketing salaries may vary by company, position, and region, and salary figures change constantly. In general, entry-level marketing salaries usually are only slightly below those for engineering and chemistry but equal or exceed starting salaries in economics, finance, accounting, general business, and the liberal arts. Moreover, if you succeed in an entry-level marketing position, it's likely that you will be promoted quickly to higher levels of responsibility and salary. In addition, because of the consumer and product knowledge you will gain in these jobs, marketing positions provide excellent training for the highest levels in an organization.

Overall Marketing Facts and Trends

In conducting your job search, consider the following facts and trends that are changing the world of marketing.

Focus on customers: More and more, companies are realizing that they win in the marketplace only by creating superior value for customers. To capture value from customers, they must first find new and better ways to solve customer problems and improve customer brand experiences. This increasing focus on the customer puts marketers at the forefront in many of today's companies. As the primary customer-facing function, marketing's mission is to get all company departments to "think customer."

Technology: Technology is changing the way marketers work. For example, price coding allows instantaneous retail inventorying. Software for marketing training, forecasting, and other functions is changing the ways we market. And the Internet is creating new jobs and new recruiting rules. Consider the explosive growth in new media marketing. Whereas advertising firms have traditionally recruited "generalists" in account management, "generalist" has now taken on a whole new meaning—advertising account executives must now have both broad and specialized knowledge.

Diversity: The number of women and minorities in marketing continues to rise. Traditionally, women were mainly in retailing. However, women and minorities have now moved fully into all industries. They also are rising rapidly into marketing management. For example, women now outnumber men by nearly two to one as advertising account executives. As marketing becomes more global, the need for diversity in marketing positions will continue to increase, opening new opportunities.

Global: Companies such as Coca-Cola, McDonald's, IBM, MTV, Wal-Mart, and Procter & Gamble have become multinational, with manufacturing and marketing operations in hundreds of countries. Indeed, such companies often make more profit from sales outside the United States than from within. And it's not just the big companies that are involved in international marketing. Organizations of all sizes have moved into the global arena. Many new marketing opportunities and careers will be directly linked to the expanding global marketplace. The globalization of business also means that you will need more cultural, language, and people skills in the marketing world of the twenty-first century.

Not-for-profit organizations: Increasingly, colleges, arts organizations, libraries, hospitals, and other not-for-profit organizations are recognizing the need for effectively marketing their "products" and services to various publics. This awareness has led to new marketing positions—with these organizations hiring their own marketing directors and marketing vice presidents or using outside marketing specialists.

Looking for a Job in Today's Marketing World

To choose and find the right job, you will need to apply the marketing skills you've learned in this course, especially marketing analysis and planning. Follow these eight steps for marketing yourself: (1) Conduct a self-assessment and seek career counseling; (2) examine job descriptions; (3) explore the job market and assess opportunities; (4) develop search strategies; (5) prepare a résumé; (6) write a cover letter and assemble supporting documents; (7) interview for jobs; and (8) follow up.

Conduct a Self-Assessment and Seek Career Counseling

If you're having difficulty deciding what kind of marketing position is the best fit for you, start out by doing some self-testing or get some career counseling. Self-assessments require that you honestly and thoroughly evaluate your interests, strengths, and weaknesses. What do you do well (your best and favorite skills) and not so well? What are your favorite interests? What are your career goals? What makes you stand out from other job seekers?

The answers to such questions may suggest which marketing careers you should seek or avoid. For help in making an effective self-assessment, look at the following books in your local bookstore: Susan Johnston, *The Career Adventure: Your Guide to Personal Assessment, Career Exploration, and Decision Making*, 4th edition (Prentice Hall, 2006) and Richard Bolles, *What Color Is Your Parachute 2007?* (Ten Speed Press, 2006). Many Web sites also offer self-assessment tools, such as the Keirsey Temperament Theory and the Temperament Sorter, a free but broad assessment available at AdvisorTeam.com. For a more specific evaluation, CareerLeader.com offers a complete online business career self-assessment program designed by the Directors of MBA Career Development at Harvard Business School. You can use this for a fee.

For help in finding a career counselor to guide you in making a career assessment, Richard Bolles' *What Color Is Your Parachute 2007?* contains a useful state-by-state sampling. CareerLeader.com also offers personal career counseling. (Some counselors can help you in your actual job search, too.) You can also consult the career counseling, testing, and placement services at your college or university.

Examine Job Descriptions

After you have identified your skills, interests, and desires, you need to see which marketing positions are the best match for them. Two U.S. Labor Department publications (available in your local library or online)—the *Occupation Outlook Handbook* (www.bls.gov/oco) and the *Dictionary of Occupational Titles* (www.occupationalinfo.org)— describe the duties involved in various occupations, the specific training and education needed, the availability of jobs in each field, possibilities for advancement, and probable earnings.

Your initial career shopping list should be broad and flexible. Look for different ways to achieve your objectives. For example, if you want a career in marketing management, consider the public as well as the private sector, and local and regional as well as national and

Explore the Job Market and Assess Opportunities

At this stage, you need to look at the market and see what positions are actually available. You do not have to do this alone. Any of the following may assist you.

Career Development Centers

Your college's career development center is an excellent place to start. Besides checking with your career development center on specific job openings, check the current edition of the National Association of Colleges and Employers *Job Outlook* (www.jobweb.com). It contains a national forecast of hiring intentions of employers as they relate to new college graduates. More and more, college career development centers are also going online. For example, the Web site of the undergraduate career services of Indiana University's Kelley School of Business has a list of career links (http://ucso.indiana.edu/cgi-bin/students/careerResources/) that can help to focus your job search.

In addition, find out everything you can about the companies that interest you by consulting business magazines, Web sites, annual reports, business reference books, faculty, career counselors, and others. Try to analyze the industry's and the company's future growth and profit potential, advancement opportunities, salary levels, entry positions, travel time, and other factors of significance to you.

Job Fairs

Career development centers often work with corporate recruiters to organize on-campus job fairs. You might also use the Internet to check on upcoming career fairs in your region. For example, visit JobWeb's College Career Fairs page at http://www.jobweb.com/employ/fairs/public_fairs.asp.

Networking and the Yellow Pages

Networking, or asking for job leads from friends, family, people in your community, and career centers, is one of the best ways to find a marketing job. A recent study estimated that 60.7 percent of jobs are found through networking. The idea is to spread your net wide, contacting anybody and everybody.

The phone book's yellow pages are another effective way to job search. Check out employers in your field of interest in whatever region you want to work, then call and ask if they are hiring for the position of your choice.

Cooperative Education and Internships

According to the National Association of Colleges and Employers 2004 Experimental Education Survey, employers on average give full-time employment offers to about 58 percent of students who have had internships with their companies. They give offers to more than 67 percent of the students that participate in co-ops with their organizations. Many company Internet sites have separate internship areas. For example, check out WetFeet (www.wetfeet.internshipprograms.com), MonsterTRAK.com (www.monstertrak.monster.com), CampusCareerCenter.com (www.campuscareercenter.com/students/intern.asp), InternJobs.com, and InternAbroad.com. If you know of a company for which you wish to work, go to that company's corporate Web site, enter the human resources area, and check for internships. If none are listed, try e-mailing the human resources department, asking if internships are offered.

The Internet

A constantly increasing number of sites on the Internet deal with job hunting. You can also use the Internet to make contacts with people who can help you gain information on companies and research companies that interest you. The Riley Guide offers a great introduction to what jobs are available (www.rileyguide.com). Other helpful sites are Employment Opportunities for People with Disabilities (www.dol.gov/odep/joblinks/joblinks.htm) and

---

international firms. Be open initially to exploring many options, then focus on specific industries and jobs, listing your basic goals as a way to guide your choices. Your list might include "a job in a start-up company, near a big city on the West Coast, doing new-product planning with a computer software firm."

HireDiversity (www.hirediversity.com), which contains information on opportunities for African Americans, Hispanic Americans, Asian Americans, and Native Americans.

Most companies have their own Web sites on which they post job listings. This may be helpful if you have a specific and fairly limited number of companies that you are keeping your eye on for job opportunities. But if this is not the case, remember that to find out what interesting marketing jobs the companies themselves are posting, you may need to visit hundreds of corporate sites.

Develop Search Strategies

Once you've decided which companies you are interested in, you need to contact them. One of the best ways is through on-campus interviews. But not every company you are interested in will visit your school. In such instances, you can write, e-mail, or phone the company directly or ask marketing professors or school alumni for contacts.

Prepare a Résumé

A résumé is a concise yet comprehensive written summary of your qualifications, including your academic, personal, and professional achievements, that showcases why you are the best candidate for the job. An employer will spend an average of only 15 to 20 seconds reviewing your résumé; therefore, you want to be sure that you prepare a good one.

In preparing your résumé, remember that all information on it must be accurate and complete. Résumés typically begin with the applicant's full name, telephone and fax numbers, and mail and e-mail addresses. A simple and direct statement of career objectives generally appears next, followed by work history and academic data (including awards and internships), and then by personal activities and experiences applicable to the job sought.

The résumé sometimes ends with a list of references the employer may contact (at other times, references may be listed separately). If your work or internship experience is limited, nonexistent, or irrelevant, then it is a good idea to emphasize your academic and nonacademic achievements, showing skills related to those required for excellent job performance.

There are three types of résumés. Reverse *chronological* résumés, which emphasize career growth, are organized in reverse chronological order, starting with your most recent job. They focus on job titles within organizations, describing the responsibilities required for each job. *Functional* résumés focus less on job titles and work history and more on assets and achievements. This format works best if your job history is scanty or discontinuous. *Mixed*, or *combination*, résumés take from each of the other two formats. First, the skills used for a specific job are listed, then the job title is stated. This format works best for applicants whose past jobs are in other fields or seemingly unrelated to the position.

Your local bookstore or library has many books that can assist you in developing your résumé. Popular guides are Brenda Greene, *Get the Interview Every Time : Fortune 500 Hiring Professionals' Tips for Writing Winning Resumes and Cover Letters* (Dearborn Trade, 2004) and Arthur Rosenberg and David Hizer, *The Résumé Handbook* (Adams Media Corporation, 2003). Computer software programs, such as *RésuméMaker Career Edition*, provide hundreds of sample résumés and ready-to-use phrases while guiding you through the résumé preparation process. America's Career InfoNet (www.acinet.org/acinet/resume/resume_intro.asp) offers a step-by-step résumé tutorial, and Monster.com (www.resume.monster.com) offers résumé advice and writing services. Finally, you can even create your own personalized online résumé at sites such as optimalresume.com.

Electronic Résumés

Use of the Internet as a tool in the job search process is increasing, so it's a good idea to have your résumé ready for the online environment. You can forward an electronic résumé to networking contacts or recruiting professionals through e-mail. You can also post it in online databases with the hope that employers and recruiters will find it.

Successful electronic résumés require a different strategy than paper résumés. For instance, when companies search résumé banks, they search key words and industry buzz words that describe a skill or core work required for each job, so nouns are much more important than verbs. Two good resources for preparing electronic résumés are Susan Ireland's Electronic Resume Guide (http://susanireland.com/eresumeguide/) and The Riley Guide (www.rileyguide.com/eresume.html).

After you have written your electronic résumé, you need to post it. The following sites may be good locations to start: Monster.com (www.monster.com) and Yahoo! hotjobs (www.hotjobs.yahoo.com). However, use caution when posting your résumé on various sites. In this era of identity theft, you need to select sites with care so as to protect your privacy. Limit access to your personal contact information and don't use sites that offer to "blast" your résumé into cyberspace.

Résumé Tips

- Communicate your worth to potential employers in a concrete manner, citing examples whenever possible.
- Be concise and direct.
- Use active verbs to show you are a doer.
- Do not skimp on quality or use gimmicks. Spare no expense in presenting a professional résumé.
- Have someone critique your work. A single typo can eliminate you from being considered.
- Customize your résumé for specific employers. Emphasize your strengths as they pertain to your targeted job.
- Keep your résumé compact, usually one page.
- Format the text to be attractive, professional, and readable. Times New Roman is often the font of choice. Avoid too much "design" or gimmicky flourishes.

Write Cover Letter, Follow Up, and Assemble Supporting Documents

Cover Letter

You should include a cover letter informing the employer that a résumé is enclosed. But a cover letter does more than this. It also serves to summarize in one or two paragraphs the contents of the résumé and explains why you think you are the right person for the position. The goal is to persuade the employer to look at the more detailed résumé. A typical cover letter is organized as follows: (1) the name and position of the person you are contacting; (2) a statement identifying the position you are applying for, how you heard of the vacancy, and the reasons for your interest; (3) a summary of your qualifications for the job; (4) a description of what follow-ups you intend to make, such as phoning in two weeks to see if the résumé has been received; (5) an expression of gratitude for the opportunity of being a candidate for the job. America's Career InfoNet (www.acinet.org/acinet/resume/resume_intro.asp) offers a step-by-step tutorial on how to create a cover letter, and Susan Ireland's Web site contains more than 50 cover letter samples (http://susanireland.com/coverletterindex.htm).

Follow-Up

Once you send your cover letter and résumé to perspective employers via the method they prefer—e-mail, their Web site, fax, or regular mail—it's often a good idea to follow up. In today's market, job seekers can't afford to wait for interviews to find them. A quality résumé and an attractive cover letter are crucial, but a proper follow-up may be the key to landing an interview. However, before you engage your potential employer, be sure to research the company. Knowing about the company and understanding its place in the industry will help you shine. When you place a call, send an e-mail, or mail a letter to a company contact, be sure to restate your interest in the position, check on the status of your résumé, and ask the employer about any questions they may have.

Letters of Recommendation

Letters of recommendation are written references by professors, former and current employers, and others that testify to your character, skills, and abilities. Some companies may request letters of recommendation, to be submitted either with the résumé or at the interview. Even if letters of recommendation aren't requested, it's a good idea to bring them with you to the interview. A good reference letter tells why you would be an excellent candidate for the position. In choosing someone to write a letter of recommendation, be confident that the person will give you a good reference. In addition, do not assume the person knows everything about you or the position you are seeking. Rather, provide the person with your résumé and other relevant data. As a courtesy, allow the reference writer at least a month to complete the letter and enclose a stamped, addressed envelope with your materials.

In the packet containing your résumé, cover letter, and letters of recommendation, you may also want to attach other relevant documents that support your candidacy, such as academic transcripts, graphics, portfolios, and samples of writing.

Interview for Jobs

As the old saying goes, "The résumé gets you the interview; the interview gets you the job." The job interview offers you an opportunity to gather more information about the organization, while at the same time allowing the organization to gather more information about you. You'll want to present your best self. The interview process consists of three parts: before the interview, the interview itself, and after the interview. If you pass through these stages successfully, you will be called back for the follow-up interview.

Before the Interview

In preparing for your interview, do the following:

1. Understand that interviewers have diverse styles, including the "chitchat," let's-get-to-know-each-other style; the interrogation style of question after question; and the tough-probing "why, why, why" style, among others. So be ready for anything.

2. With a friend, practice being interviewed and then ask for a critique. Or, videotape yourself in a practice interview so that you can critique your own performance. Your college placement service may also offer "mock" interviews to help you.

3. Prepare at least five good questions whose answers are not easily found in the company literature, such as "What is the future direction of the firm?" "How does the firm differentiate itself from competitors?" "Do you have a new-media division?"

4. Anticipate possible interview questions, such as "Why do you want to work for this company?" or "Why should we hire you?" Prepare solid answers before the interview. Have a clear idea of why you are interested in joining the company and the industry to which it belongs. (See Susan Ireland's site for additional interview questions: http://susanireland.com/interviewwork.html)

5. Avoid back-to-back interviews—they can be exhausting and it is unpredictable how long they will last.

6. Prepare relevant documents that support your candidacy, such as academic transcripts, letters of recommendation, graphics, portfolios, and samples of writing. Bring multiple copies to the interview.

7. Dress conservatively and professionally. Be neat and clean.

8. Arrive 10 minutes early to collect your thoughts and review the major points you intend to cover. Check your name on the interview schedule, noting the name of the interviewer and the room number. Be courteous and polite to office staff.

9. Approach the interview enthusiastically. Let your personality shine through.

During the Interview

During the interview, do the following:

1. Shake hands firmly in greeting the interviewer. Introduce yourself, using the same form of address the interviewer uses. Focus on creating a good initial impression.

2. Keep your poise. Relax. Smile when appropriate, and be upbeat throughout.

3. Maintain eye contact, good posture, and speak distinctly. Don't clasp your hands or fiddle with jewelry, hair, or clothing. Sit comfortably in your chair. Do not smoke, even if it's permitted.

4. Along with the copies of relevant documents that support your candidacy, carry extra copies of your résumé with you.

5. Have your story down pat. Present your selling points. Answer questions directly. Avoid either one-word or too-wordy answers.

6. Let the interviewer take the initiative but don't be passive. Find an opportunity to direct the conversation to things about yourself that you want the interviewer to hear.

7. To end on a high note, make your most important point or ask your most pertinent question during the last part of the interview.

8. Don't hesitate to "close." You might say, "I'm very interested in the position, and I have enjoyed this interview."

9. Obtain the interviewer's business card or address and phone number so that you can follow up later.

A tip for acing the interview: Before you open your mouth, find out *what it's like* to be a brand manager, sales representative, market researcher, advertising account executive, or other position for which you're interviewing. See if you can find a "mentor"—someone in a position similar to the one you're seeking, perhaps with another company. Talk with this mentor about the ins and outs of the job and industry.

After the Interview

After the interview, do the following:

1. After leaving the interview, record the key points that arose. Be sure to note who is to follow up and when a decision can be expected.

2. Analyze the interview objectively, including the questions asked, the answers to them, your overall interview presentation, and the interviewer's responses to specific points.

3. Immediately send a thank-you letter or e-mail, mentioning any additional items and your willingness to supply further information.

4. If you do not hear within the specified time, write, e-mail, or call the interviewer to determine your status.

Follow Up

If your first interview takes place off-site, such as at your college or at a job fair, and if you are successful with that initial interview, you will be invited to visit the organization. The in-company interview will probably run from several hours to an entire day. The organization will examine your interest, maturity, enthusiasm, assertiveness, logic, and company and functional knowledge. You should ask questions about issues of importance to you. Find out about the working environment, job role, responsibilities, opportunity for advancement, current industrial issues, and the company's personality. The company wants to discover if you are the right person for the job, whereas you want to find out if it is the right job for you. The key is to determine if the right *fit* exists between you and the company.

■ Marketing Jobs

This section describes some of the key marketing positions.

Advertising

Advertising is one of today's hottest fields in marketing. In fact, *Money* magazine lists a position in advertising as among the 50 best jobs in America.

Job Descriptions

Key advertising positions include copywriter, art director, production manager, account executive, and media planner/buyer.

- *Copywriters* write advertising copy and help find the concepts behind the written words and visual images of advertisements.

- *Art directors*, the other part of the creative team, help translate the copywriters' ideas into dramatic visuals called "layouts." Agency artists develop print layouts, package designs, television layouts (called "storyboards"), corporate logotypes, trademarks, and symbols.

- *Production managers* are responsible for physically creating ads, in-house or by contracting through outside production houses.

- *Account development executives* research and understand clients' markets and customers and help develop marketing and advertising strategies to impact them.

- *Account executives* serve as liaisons between clients and agencies. They coordinate the planning, creation, production, and implementation of an advertising campaign for the account.

- *Account planners* serve as the voice of the consumer in the agency. They research consumers to understand their needs and motivations as a basis for developing effective ad campaigns.

- *Media planners (or buyers)* determine the best mix of television, radio, newspaper, magazine, and other media for the advertising campaign.

Skills Needed, Career Paths, and Typical Salaries

Work in advertising requires strong people skills in order to interact closely with an often-difficult and demanding client base. In addition, advertising attracts people with high skills in planning, problem solving, creativity, communication, initiative, leadership, and presentation. Advertising involves working under high levels of stress and pressure created by unrelenting deadlines. Advertisers frequently have to work long hours to meet deadlines for a presentation. But work achievements are very apparent, with the results of creative strategies observed by thousands or even millions of people.

Because they are so sought after, positions in advertising sometimes require an MBA. But there are many jobs open for business, graphics arts, and liberal arts undergraduates. Advertising positions often serve as gateways to higher-level management. Moreover, with large advertising agencies opening offices all over the world, there is the possibility of eventually working on global campaigns.

Starting advertising salaries are relatively low compared to some other marketing jobs because of strong competition for entry-level advertising jobs. You may even want to consider working for free to break in. Compensation will increase quickly as you move into account executive or other management positions. For more facts and figures, see the Web pages of *Advertising Age*, a key ad industry publication (www.adage.com, click on the Job Bank button), and the American Association of Advertising Agencies (www.aaaa.org).

Brand and Product Management

Brand and product managers plan, direct, and control business and marketing efforts for their products. They are involved with research and development, packaging, manufacturing, sales and distribution, advertising, promotion, market research, and business analysis and forecasting.

Job Descriptions

A company's brand management team consists of people in several positions.

- *Brand managers* guide the development of marketing strategies for a specific brand.

- *Assistant brand managers* are responsible for certain strategic components of the brand.

- *Product managers* oversee several brands within a product line or product group.

- *Product category managers* direct multiple product lines in the product category.

- *Market analysts* research the market and provide important strategic information to the project managers.

- *Project directors* are responsible for collecting market information on a marketing or product project.

- *Research directors* oversee the planning, gathering, and analyzing of all organizational research.

Skills Needed, Career Paths, and Typical Salaries

Brand and product management requires high problem-solving, analytical, presentation, communication, and leadership skills, as well as the ability to work well in a team. Product management requires long hours and involves the high pressure of running large projects. In consumer goods companies, the newcomer—who usually needs an MBA—joins a brand team as an assistant and learns the ropes by doing numerical analyses and watching senior brand people. This person eventually heads the team and later moves on to manage a larger brand, then several brands.

Many industrial goods companies also have product managers. Product management is one of the best training grounds for future corporate officers. Product management also offers good opportunities to move into international marketing. Product managers command relatively high salaries. Because this job category encourages or requires a master's degree, starting pay tends to be higher than in other marketing categories such as advertising or retailing.

Sales and Sales Management

Sales and sales management opportunities exist in a wide range of profit and not-for-profit organizations and in product and service organizations, including financial, insurance, consulting, and government organizations.

Job Descriptions

Key jobs include consumer sales, industrial sales, national account manager, service support, sales trainers, sales management, and tellesellers.

- *Consumer sales* involves selling consumer products and services through retailers.
- *Industrial sales* involves selling products and services to other businesses.
- *National account managers (NAM)* oversee a few very large accounts.
- *Service support* personnel support salespeople during and after the sale of a product.
- *Sales trainers* train new hires and provide refresher training for all sales personnel.
- *Sales management* includes a sequence of positions ranging from district manager to vice president of sales.
- The *teleseller* (not to be confused with the home consumer telemarketer) offers service and support to field salespeople.

Salespeople enjoy active professional lives, working outside the office and interacting with others. They manage their own time and activities. And successful salespeople can be very well paid. Competition for top jobs can be intense. Every sales job is different, but some positions involve extensive travel, long workdays, and working under pressure. You can also expect to be transferred more than once between company headquarters and regional offices. However, most companies are now working to bring good work-life balance to their salespeople and sales managers.

Skills Needed, Career Paths, and Typical Salaries

Selling is a people profession in which you will work with people every day, all day long. Besides people skills, sales professionals need sales and communication skills. Most sales positions also require high problem-solving, analytical, presentation, and leadership ability as well as creativity and initiative. Teamwork skills are increasingly important.

Career paths lead from salesperson to district, regional, and higher levels of sales management and, in many cases, to the top management of the firm. Today, most entry-level sales management positions require a college degree. Increasingly, people seeking selling jobs are acquiring sales experience in an internship capacity or from a part-time job before graduating. Sales positions are great springboards to leadership positions, with more CEOs starting in sales than in any other entry-level position. Possibly this explains why competition for top sales jobs is intense.

Starting base salaries in sales may be moderate, but compensation is often supplemented by significant commission, bonus, or other incentive plans. In addition, many sales jobs include a company car or car allowance. Successful salespeople are among most companies' highest paid employees.

Other Marketing Jobs

Retailing

Retailing provides an early opportunity to assume marketing responsibilities. Key jobs include store manager, regional manager, buyer, department manager, and salesperson. *Store managers* direct the management and operation of an individual store. *Regional managers* manage groups of stores across several states and report performance to headquarters. *Buyers* select and buy the merchandise that the store carries. The *department manager* acts as store manager of a department, such as clothing, but on the department level. The *salesperson* sells merchandise to retail customers. Retailing can involve relocation, but generally there is little travel, unless you are a buyer. Retailing requires high people and sales skills because retailers are constantly in contact with customers. Enthusiasm, willingness, and communication skills are very helpful for retailers, too.

Retailers work long hours, but their daily activities are often more structured than some types of marketing positions. Starting salaries in retailing tend to be low, but pay increases as you move into management or some retailing specialty job.

Marketing Research

Marketing researchers interact with managers to define problems and identify the information needed to resolve them. They design research projects, prepare questionnaires and samples, analyze data, prepare reports, and present their findings and recommendations to management. They must understand statistics, consumer behavior, psychology, and sociology. A master's degree helps. Career opportunities exist with manufacturers, retailers, some wholesalers, trade and industry associations, marketing research firms, advertising agencies, and governmental and private nonprofit agencies.

New-Product Planning

People interested in new-product planning can find opportunities in many types of organizations. They usually need a good background in marketing, marketing research, and sales forecasting; they need organizational skills to motivate and coordinate others; and they may need a technical background. Usually, these people work first in other marketing positions before joining the new-product department.

Marketing Logistics (Physical Distribution)

Marketing logistics, or physical distribution, is a large and dynamic field, with many career opportunities. Major transportation carriers, manufacturers, wholesalers, and retailers all employ logistics specialists. Increasingly, marketing teams include logistics specialists, and marketing managers' career paths include marketing logistics assignments. Coursework in quantitative methods, finance, accounting, and marketing will provide you with the necessary skills for entering the field.

Public Relations

Most organizations have a public relations staff to anticipate problems with various publics, handle complaints, deal with media, and build the corporate image. People interested in public relations should be able to speak and write clearly and persuasively, and they should have a background in journalism, communications, or the liberal arts. The challenges in this job are highly varied and very people oriented.

Not-for-Profit Services

The key jobs in nonprofits include marketing director, director of development, event coordinator, publication specialist, and intern/volunteers. The *marketing director* is in charge of all marketing activities for the organization. The *director of development* organizes, manages, and directs the fund-raising campaigns that keep a nonprofit in existence. An *event coordinator* directs all aspects of fund-raising events, from initial planning through implementation. The *publication specialist* oversees publications designed to promote awareness of the organization.

Although typically an unpaid position, the *intern/volunteer* performs various marketing functions, and this work can be an important step to gaining a full-time position. The nonprofit sector is typically not for someone who is money driven. Rather, most nonprofits look for people with a strong sense of community spirit and the desire to help others. So starting pay is usually lower than in other marketing fields. However, the bigger the nonprofit, the better your chance of rapidly increasing your income when moving into upper management.

Other Resources

Professional marketing associations and organizations are another source of information about careers. Marketers belong to many such societies. You may want to contact some of the following in your job search:

American Advertising Federation, 1101 Vermont Avenue NW, Suite 500, Washington, D.C. 20005-6306. (202) 898-0089 (www.aaf.org)

American Marketing Association, 311 South Wacker Drive, Suite 5800, Chicago, IL 60606. (800) AMA-1150 (www.ama.org)

Market Research Association, 2189 Silas Deane Highway, Suite 5, Rocky Hill, CT 06067. (860) 257-4008 (www.mra-net.org)

National Association of Sales Professionals, 11000 North 130th Place, Scottsdale, AZ 85259. (480) 951-4311 (www.nasp.com)

National Management Association, 2210 Arbor Boulevard, Dayton, OH 45439. (937) 294-0421 (www.nma1.org)

National Retail Federation, 325 Seventh Street NW, Suite 1100, Washington, D.C. 20004. (800) NRF-HOW2 (www.nrf.com)

Product Development and Management Association, 15000 Commerce Parkway, Suite C, Mount Laurel, NJ 08054. (800) 232-5241 (www.pdma.org)

Public Relations Society of America, 33 Maiden Lane, Eleventh Floor, New York, NY 10038. (212) 460-1400 (www.prsa.org)

Sales and Marketing Executives International, PO Box 1390, Sumas, WA 98295-1390. (312) 893-0751 (www.smei.org)

The Association of Women in Communications, 780 Ritchie Highway, Suite 28-S, Severna Park, MD 21146. (410) 544-7442 (www.womcom.org)

Women Executives in Public Relations, FDR Station, PO Box 7657, New York, NY 10150-7657. (212) 859-7375 (www.wepr.org)

CHAPTER 1

1. Quotes and other information from Paul Farriss, "NASCAR Rides the Fast Track," *Marketing*, April 11, 2005, pp. 11–12; Mark Woods, "Readers Try to Explain Why Racin' Rocks," *Florida Times Union*, February 16, 2003, p. C1; Peter Spiegel, "Heir Gordon," *Forbes*, December 14, 1998, pp. 42–46; Tony Kontzer, "Backseat Drivers—NASCAR Puts You in the Race," *InformationWeek*, March 25, 2002, p. 83; Paul Owens, "Office Depot to Sponsor NASCAR," *Knight Ridder Tribune Business News*, January 28, 2005, p. 1; Nick Daschel, "Drivers Know Daytona Is the One," *The Columbian*, February 15, 2006, p. B1; Howard Schultz, "Lap Chance," *Knight Ridder Tribune Business News*, March 12, 2006, p. 1; Jenny Kincaid, "NASCAR Beefs Up Its Brand Loyalty," *Knight Ridder Tribune Business News*, April 1, 2006, p. 1; Robert McGarvery, "UPS Roars into Action," *Sales & Marketing Management*, May 2005, pp. 58–65; Natalie Finn, "Logistics Fuels Need for Speed," *TelevisionWeek*, May 1, 2006, pp. 35–38; Sora Song, "Days of Thunder," *Time*, May 8, 2006, p. 25; and www.NASCAR.com, December 2006.

2. As quoted in Carolyn P. Neal, "From the Editor," *Marketing Management*, January/February 2006, p. 3.

3. The American Marketing Association offers the following definition: "Marketing is an organizational function and a set of processes for creating, communicating, and delivering value to customers and for managing customer relationships in ways that benefit the organization and its stakeholders." Accessed at www.marketingpower.com/mg-dictionary-view1862.php?, December 2006.

4. Lucas Conley, "Customer-Centered Leader: Winner Maxine Clark," *Fast Company*, October 2005, p. 54; and Dan Scheraga, "IT Is Build-A-Bear's Secret Weapon," *Chain Store Age*, March 2006, p. 76.

5. See Theodore Levitt's classic article, "Marketing Myopia," *Harvard Business Review*, July-August 1960, pp. 45–56. For more recent discussions, see Yves Doz, Jose Santos, and Peter J. Williamson, "Marketing Myopia Re-Visited: Why Every Company Needs to Learn from the World," *Ivey Business Journal*, January–February 2004, p. 1; Lon Zimmerman, "Product Positioning Maps Secure Future," *Marketing News*, October 15, 2005, p. 47.

6. A. G. Lafley, "Getting Along with the New Boss—the Consumer," *Advertising Age*, March 28, 2005, pp. 24, 91.

7. From "The Computer Is Personal Again," an HP ad appearing in *Business 2.0*, June 2006, p. 33. Also see www.hp.com/personal.

8. For an interesting discussion of demarketing, see Ian Gordon, "Relationships Demarketing: Managing Wasteful or Worthless Customer Relationships," *Ivey Business Journal*, March/April 2006, pp. 1–4.

9. See David Lewis, "Southwest Staff Go Nuts (for Customers!)," *Sales & Marketing Institute*, accessed at www.salesmarketing.org.nz/article623.html, May 2005. For more on market orientation and firm performance, see Ahmet H. Kirca, Satish Jayachandran, and William O. Bearden, "Market Orientation: A Meta-Analytic Review and Assessment of Its Antecedents and Impact on Performance," *Journal of Marketing*, April 2005, pp. 24–41; and Paul D. Ellis, "Market Orientation and Performance: A Meta-Analysis and Cross-Cultural Comparisons," *Journal of Management Studies*, July 2006, pp. 1089–1107.

10. See "America's Most Fattening Burger," *Time*, January 3, 2005, p. 186; "For the Health-Unconscious, Era of Mammoth Burger Is Here," *Wall Street Journal*, January 27, 2005, p. B.1; Jim Slater, "New Hardee's Sandwich Piles Meat on More Meat," *Associated Press Wire*, April 19, 2006; and Bruce Horowitz, "Wendy's Will Be 1st Fast Foodie with Healthier Oil," *USA Today*, June 8, 2006, p. 1B.

11. See Alex Taylor III, "Can J&J Keep the Magic Going?" *Fortune*, May 27, 2002, pp. 117–121; Larry Edwards, et al., "75 Years of Ideas," *Advertising Age*, February 14, 2005, p. 14; Liz Torlee, "A Swift Kick in the Credo," *Marketing* magazine, March 21, 2005, p. 25; and www.jnj.com/our_company/our_credo/index.htm, January 2006.

12. Paul A. Eisenstein, "Strategi Vision Puts Toyota, Honda on Top," October 10, 2005, accessed at www.thecarconnection; and Silvio Schindler, "Hybrids and Customers," *Automotive Design & Production*, June 2006, pp. 20–22.

13. Example adapted from Denny Hatch and Ernie Schell, "Delight Your Customers," *Target Marketing*, April 2002, pp. 32–39; with additional information from "Lexus Earns Best-Selling Brand Title for Sixth Consecutive Year," January 4, 2006, accessed at www.lexus.com/about/press_releases/index.html.

14. Information accessed at www.incirlce.com, July 2006.

15. Information about the Harley Owners Group accessed at www.hog.com, September 2006. For more on loyalty programs, see Joseph C. Nunes and Xavier Dreze, "Your Loyalty Program Is Betraying You," *Harvard Business Review*, April 2006, pp. 124–131.

16. See http://supply.mckesson.com/portal/index.jsp?page ID5aboutsmo.

17. Adapted from information found in Elizabeth Esfahani, "How to Get Tough with Bad Customers," *Business 2.0*, October 2004, p. 52. Also see Amey Stone, "Bare Bones, Plump Profits," *BusinessWeek*, March 14, 2005, p. 88; and Steve Bergsman, "The Orange Mortgage," *Mortgage Banking*, June 2006, pp. 48–53.

18. See Phillip E. Pfeifer, "The Optimal Ratio of Acquisition and Retention Costs," *Journal of Targeting*, February 2005, pp. 179–188; and Bruce Clapp, "Common Misconceptions

about Retention Programs," *Bank Marketing*, May 2006, p. 50.

19. Philip Kotler and Kevin Lane Keller, *Marketing Management*, 12th ed. (Upper Saddle River, NJ: Prentice Hall, 2006), p. 27.

20. See John Higgins, "The Math Behind the CW," *Broadcasting & Cable*, January 30, 2006, p. 8; and Jessica Seid, "'Gilmore Girls' Meet 'Smackdown,'" January 24, 2006, accessed at http://money.cnn.com/2006/01/24/news/companies/cbs_warner/.

21. Thor Valdmanis, "Alliances Gain Favor over Risky Mergers," *USA Today*, February 4, 1999, p. 3B. Also see Matthew Schifrin, "Partner or Perish," *Forbes*, May 21, 2001, pp. 26–28; and Kim T. Gordan, "Strong Partnerships Build Marketing Muscle," *CRN*, February 10, 2003, p. 14A.

22. For more discussion of customer delight and loyalty, see Barry Berman, "How to Delight Your Customers," *California Management Review*, Fall 2005, pp. 129–151; Clara Agustin and Jagdip Singh, "Curvilinear Effects of Consumer Loyalty Determinants in Relational Exchanges," *Journal of Marketing Research*, February 2005, pp. 96–108; Ben McConnell and Jackie Huba, "Learning to Leverage the Lunatic Fringe," *Point*, July–August, 2006, pp. 14–15; and Fred Reichheld, *The Ultimate Question: Driving Good Profits and True Growth* (Boston: Harvard Business School Publishing, 2006).

23. "Stew Leonard's," *Hoover's Company Records*, May 1, 2006, p. 104226; and www.stew-leonards.com/html/about.cfm, October 2006.

24. For interesting discussions on assessing and using customer lifetime value, see Charlotte H. Mason, "Tuscan Lifestyles: Assessing Customer Lifetime Value," *Journal of Interactive Marketing*, Autumn 2003, pp. 54–60; Erin Kinikin, "How Valuable Are Your Customers?" September 2001, accessed at www.advisor.com/articles.nsf/aid/KINIE01; Rajkumar Venkatesan and V. Kumar, "A Customer Lifetime Value Framework for Customer Selection and Resource Allocation Strategy," *Journal of Marketing*, October 2004, pp. 106–125; Rajkumar Venkatesan, V. Kumar, and Timothy Bohling, "Selecting Valuable Customers Using a Customer Lifetime Value Framework," Marketing Science Institute, Report No. 05–121, 2005; and Lynette Ryals, "Making Customer Relationships Management Work: The Measurement and Profitable Management of Customer Relationships," *Journal of Marketing*, October 2005, pp. 252–261.

25. Don Peppers and Martha Rogers, "Customer Loyalty: A Matter of Trust," *Sales & Marketing Management*, June 2006, p. 22.

26. Don Peppers and Martha Rogers, "Customers Don't Grow on Trees," *Fast Company*, July 2005, pp. 26.

27. See Roland T. Rust, Valerie A. Zeithaml, and Katherine A. Lemon, *Driving Customer Equity* (New York: Free Press, 2000); Robert C. Blattberg, Gary Getz, Jacquelyn S. Thomas, *Customer Equity* (Boston, MA: Harvard Business School Press, 2001); Rust, Lemon, and Zeithaml, "Return on Marketing: Using Customer Equity to Focus Marketing Strategy," *Journal of Marketing*, January 2004, pp. 109–127; James D. Lenskold, "Customer-Centered Marketing ROI," *Marketing Management*, January/February 2004,

pp. 26–32; Rust,. Zeithaml, and Lemon, "Customer-Centered Brand Management," *Harvard Business Review*, September 2004, p. 110; Don Peppers and Martha Rogers, "Hail to the Customer," *Sales & Marketing Management*, October 2005, pp. 49–51; and Allison Enright, "Serve Them Right," *Marketing News*, May 1, 2006, pp. 21–22.

28. This example is adapted from information in Rust, Lemon, and Zeithaml, "Where Should the Next Marketing Dollar Go?" *Marketing Management*, September–October 2001, pp. 24–28. Also see David Welch and David Kiley, "Can Caddy's Driver Make GM Cool?" *BusinessWeek*, September 20, 2004, pp. 105–106; John K. Teahen, Jr., "Cadillac Kid: 'Gotta Compete,'" *Chicago Tribune*, May 7, 2005, p. 1; and Jamie LaReau, "Cadillac Wants to Boost Sales, Customer Service," *Automotive News*, February 20, 2006, p. 46.

29. Ravi Dhar and Rashi Glazer, "Hedging Customers," *Harvard Business Review*, May 2003, pp. 86–92. Also see Ian Gordon, "Relationship Marketing: Managing Wasteful or Worthless Customer Relationships," *Ivey Business Journal*, March/April 2006, pp. 1–4.

30. Werner Reinartz and V. Kumar, "The Mismanagement of Customer Loyalty," *Harvard Business Review*, July 2002, pp. 86–94. For more on customer equity management, see Sunil Gupta, Donald R. Lehman, and Jennifer Ames Stuart, "Valuing Customers," *Journal of Marketing Research*, February 2004, pp. 7–18; Michael D. Johnson and Fred Selnes, "Customer Portfolio Management: Toward a Dynamic Theory of Exchange Relationships," *Journal of Marketing*, April 2004, pp. 1–17; Sunil Gupta and Donald R. Lehman, *Managing Customers as Investments* (Philadelphia: Wharton School Publishing, 2005); and Roland T. Rust, Katherine N. Lemon, and Das Narayandas, *Customer Equity Management* (Upper Saddle River, NJ: Prentice Hall, 2005).

31. "Population Explosion!" *ClickZ Stats*, April 12, 2006, accessed at www.clickz.com/stats/sectors/geographics/article.php/151151.

32. "JupiterResearch Forecasts Online Retail Spending Will Reach $144 Billion in 2010, a CAGR of 12% from 2005," February 6, 2006, accessed at www.jupitermedia.com/corporate/releases/06.02.06-newjupresearch.html.

33. Anver Versi, "MTV Rolls Out African Channel," *African Business*, January 2005, pp. 58–59; and Johnnie L. Roberts, "World Tour," *Newsweek*, June 6, 2005, pp. 34–35.

34. Quotes and information found at www.patagonia.com/enviro/main_enviro_action.shtml, July 2006.

35. Jessi Hempel, "Selling a Cause? Better Make It Pop," *BusinessWeek*, February 13, 2006, p. 75.

36. Information and quotes from "White Alligator, ZooFest Make Magical Day at SF Zoo," accessed at www.coastnews.com/f001.htm, June 27, 2006; and www.sfzoo.org/kids/about.htm, December 2006.

37. For other examples, and for a good review of nonprofit marketing, see Philip Kotler and Alan R. Andreasen, *Strategic Marketing for Nonprofit Organizations*, 6th ed. (Upper Saddle River, NJ: Prentice Hall, 2003); Philip Kotler and Karen Fox, *Strategic Marketing for Educational Institutions* (Upper Saddle River, NJ: Prentice Hall, 1995); Norman Shawchuck, Philip Kotler, Bruce Wren, and Gustave Rath, *Marketing for Congregations: Choosing to Serve

CHAPTER 2

1. Quotes and other information from Stanley Holmes, "The New Nike," *BusinessWeek*, September 20, 2004, pp. 78–86; "Nike, Inc.," *Hoover's Company Records*, May 15, 2006, p. 14254; Daniel Roth, "Can Nike Still Do It Without Phil Knight?" *Fortune*, April 4, 2005, pp. 59–68; Helen Jung, "Phil Knight's Charity Is Billion Dollar Secret," *The Oregonian*, December 25, 2005, accessed at www.oregonlive. com; Stanley Holmes, "Adidas' World Cup Shutout," *BusinessWeek*. April 3, 2006, pp. 104–106; and www.nikebiz. com. November 2006.

2. For a more detailed discussion of corporate- and business-level strategic planning as they apply to marketing, see Philip Kotler and Kevin Lane Keller, *Marketing Management*, 12th ed. (Upper Saddle River, NJ.: Prentice Hall, 2006), Chapter 2.

3. For more on mission statements, see "Crafting Mission Statements," *Association Management*, January 2004, p. 23; Frank Buytendijk, "Five Keys to Building a High-Performance Organization," *Business Performance Management Magazine*, February 2006, pp. 24–29; and Joseph Peyrefitte and Forest R. David, "A Content Analysis of Mission Statements of United States Firms in Four Industries," *International Journal of Management*, June 2006, pp. 296–301.

4. Nike and eBay mission statements from www.nike.com/nikebiz/nikebiz.jhtml?page=4 and http://pages.ebay.com/aboutebay/thecompany/companyoverview.html, respectively, November 2006.

5. Thomas Walsh, "Mission Statement or Mission: Impossible?" *Central New York Business Journal*, May 26, 2006, pp. 23, 27.

6. Monsanto Company Pledge Report, accessed at http://monsanto.com/monsanto/layout/our_pledge/default. asp. December 2006.

7. The following discussion is based in part on information found at www.bcg.com/this_is_BCG/mission/growth_share_matrix.html, December 2006. For more on strategic planning, see Anthony Lavia, "Strategic Planning in Times of Turmoil," *Business Communications Review*, March 2004, pp. 56–60; Rita Gunther McGrath and Ian C. MacMillan, "Market Busting," *Harvard Business Review*, March 2005, pp. 80–89; and Lloyd C. Harris and Emmanuel Ogbonna, "Initiating Strategic Planning," *Journal of Business Research*, January 2006, pp. 100–111.

8. H. Igor Ansoff, "Strategies for Diversification," *Harvard Business Review*, September-October 1957, pp. 113–124. Quotes and information in the Starbucks examples and in

the growth discussion that follows are from Monica Soto Ouchi, "Starbucks Ratchets Up Growth Forecast," *Knight Ridder Tribune News*, October 15, 2004, p. 1; Patricia Sellers, "Starbucks: The Next Generation," *Fortune*, April 4, 2005, p. 30; Leon Lazaroff, "Starbucks Brews Up Successful Formula for Growth," *Chicago Tribune*, December 18, 2005; Kim Wright Wiley, "Taste of Success," *Selling Power*, April 2006, pp. 51–54; Bruce Horovitz, "Starbucks Nation," *USA Today*, May 19, 2006, accessed at www.usatoday.com/money/industries/food/2006-05-18-starbucks-usat_x.htm; and the company fact sheet, annual report, and other information accessed at www.starbucks. com, July 2006.

9. T. L. Stanley, "Starbucks and Vine Changes the Rules," *Advertising Age*, April 3, 2006, pp. 3–4.

10. Nirmalya Kumar, "Kill a Brand, Keep a Customer," *Harvard Business Review*, December 2003, pp. 87–95. For a more in-depth approach to brand portfolio management, see Kim B. Clark, et al., *Harvard Business School on Managing the Value Chain* (Boston: Harvard Business School Press, 2000); "Buyer Value and the Value Chain," *Business Owner*, September-October 2003, p. 1; and "The Value Chain," accessed at www.quickmba.com/strategy/value-chain, December 2006.

11. Michael E. Porter, *Competitive Advantage: Creating and Sustaining Superior Performance* (New York: Free Press, 1985); and Michel E. Porter, "What Is Strategy?" *Harvard Business Review*, November-December 1996, pp. 61–78. Also see Sam Hill, Richard Ettenson, and Dane Tyson, "Achieving the Ideal Brand Portfolio," *MIT Sloan Management Review*, Winter 2005, pp. 85–90.

12. Kotler, *Kotler on Marketing* (New York: The Free Press, 1999), pp. 20–22; and Marianne Seiler, "Transformation Trek," *Marketing Management*, January–February 2006, pp. 32–39, here p. 37.

13. McDonald's 2006 Fact Sheet, accessed at www.mcdonalds. com/corp/invest/pub/2006_fact_sheet.html, May 2006; "McDonald's Fetes 50th Birthday, Opens Anniversary Restaurant," *Knight Ridder Tribune Business News*, April 15, 2005, p. 1; and "McDonald's Corporation," *Hoover's Company Records*, June 15, 2006, p. 10974.

14. Quotes and other information from Jeffery K. Liker and Thomas Y. Choi, "Building Deep Supplier Relationships," *Harvard Business Review*, December 2004, pp. 104–113; Lindsey Chappell, "Toyota Aims to Satisfy Its Suppliers," *Automotive News*, February 21, 2005, p. 10; and www.toyotasupplier.com, December 2006.

15. Jack Trout, "Branding Can't Exist without Positioning," *Advertising Age*, March 14, 2005, p. 28.

16. "100 Leading National Advertisers," special issue of *Advertising Age*, June 26, 2006, p. 6; and Ford Motor Company 2005 Annual Report, accessed at www.ford.com, March 9, 2006.

17. The four Ps classification was first suggested by E. Jerome McCarthy, *Basic Marketing: A Managerial Approach* (Homewood, IL: Irwin, 1960). For the 4Cs, other proposed classifications, and more discussion, see Robert Lauterborn, "New Marketing Litany: 4P's Passé; C-Words Take Over," *Advertising Age*, October 1, 1990, p. 26; Don E. Schultz, "New Definition of Marketing Reinforces Idea of

People More Effectively (Nashville, TN: Abingdon Press, 1993); Philip Kotler, John Bowen, and James Makens, *Marketing for Hospitality and Tourism*, 3rd ed. (Upper Saddle River, NJ: Prentice Hall, 2003); and "The Nonprofit Marketing Landscape," special section, *Journal of Business Research*, June 2005, pp. 797–862.

38. "National Advertisers Ranked 1 to 50," *Advertising Age*, June 26, 2006, p. 8. For more on social marketing, see Philip Kotler, Ned Roberto, and Nancy R. Lee, *Social Marketing: Improving the Quality of Life*, 2nd ed. (Thousand Oaks, CA: Sage Publications, 2002).

Integration," *Marketing News*, January 15, 2005, p. 8; and Phillip Kotler, "Alphabet Soup," *Marketing Management*, March–April 2006, p. 51.

18. Michael C. Mankins, "Turning Great Strategy into Great Performance," *Harvard Business Review*, July–August 2005, pp. 65–72.

19. Brian Dumaine, "Why Great Companies Last," *Fortune*, January 16, 1995, p. 129. Also see James C. Collins and Jerry I. Porras, *Built to Last: Successful Habits of Visionary Companies* (New York: HarperBusiness, 1995); Jeffrey S. Klein, "Corporate Cultures: Why Values Matter," *Folio*, December 2004, p. 23; Norm Brodsky, "Defining—and Enforcing—Your Company's Culture Might Be Your Most Important Job," *Inc.*, April 2006, pp. 61–62; and Graham Yemm, "Does Your Culture Support or Sabotage Your Strategy?" *Management Services*, Spring 2006, pp. 34–37.

20. For more on brand and product management, see Kevin Lane Keller, *Strategic Brand Management*, 2nd ed. (Upper Saddle River, N.J.: Prentice Hall, 2003).

21. For details, see Kotler and Keller, *Marketing Management*, pp. 719–725. Also see Neil A. Morgan, Bruce H. Clark, and Rich Gooner, "Marketing Productivity, Marketing Audits, and Systems for Marketing Performance Assessment: Integrating Multiple Perspectives," *Journal of Marketing*, May 2002, pp. 363–375.

22. Adapted from Diane Brady, "Making Marketing Measure Up," *BusinessWeek*, December 13, 2004, pp. 112–113; with information from "Kotler Readies World for One-on-One," *Point*, June 2005, p. 3.

23. Mark McMaster, "ROI: More Vital than Ever," *Sales & Marketing Management*, January 2002, pp. 51–52. Also see Paul Hyde, Ed Landry, and Andrew Tipping, "Are CMOs Irrelevant?" Association of National Advertisers/Booz, Allen, Hamilton white paper, p. 4, accessed at www.ana.net/mrc/ANABoozwhitepaper, June 2005; Rob Duboff, "Resisting Gravity," *Marketing Management*, May–June 2006, pp. 37–39; and Gordon A. Wyner, "Beyond ROI," *Marketing Management*, May–June 2006, pp. 8–9.

24. Matthew Creamer, "Shops Push Affinity, Referrals Over Sales," *Advertising Age*, June 20, 2005, p. S4.

25. For more discussion, see Michael Karuss, "Marketing Dashboards Drive Better Decisions," *Marketing News*, October 1, 2005, p. 7; Richard Karpinski, "Making the Most of a Marketing Dashboard," *BtoB*, March 13, 2006, p. 18; and Bruce H. Clark, Andrew V. Abela, and Tim Ambler, "Behind the Wheel," *Marketing Management*, May–June 2006, pp. 19–23.

26. For a full discussion of this model and details on customer-centered measures of return on marketing investment, see Roland T. Rust, Katherine N. Lemon, and Valarie A. Zeithaml, "Return on Marketing: Using Customer Equity to Focus Marketing Strategy," *Journal of Marketing*, January 2004, pp. 109–127; Roland T. Rust, Katherine N. Lemon, and Das Narayandas, *Customer Equity Management* (Upper Saddle River, NJ: Prentice Hall, 2005); and Allison Enright, "Serve Them Right," *Marketing News*, May 1, 2006, pp. 21–22.

27. Deborah L. Vence, "Return on Investment," *Marketing News*, October 15, 2005, pp. 13–14.

CHAPTER 3

1. John O'Connor, "Golden Arches Still Standing After 50 Years," *Knight Ridder Tribune Business News*, April 19, 2005, p. 1; Sherri Day, "After Years at Top, McDonald's Strives To Regain Ground," *New York Times*, March 3, 2003, p. A.1; Amy Garber, "Bistro Gourmet at McDonald's," *Nation's Restaurant News*, January 31, 2005, pp. 34–35; Michael V. Copeland, "Ronald Gets Back in Shape," *Business 2.0*, January/February 2005, pp. 46–47; Kate MacArthur, "McD's to Shops: Make 'Lovin' It' More than Tag," *Advertising Age*, March 13, 2006, p. 8; Pallavi Gogoi, "Mickey D's McMakeover," *BusinessWeek*, May 15, 2006, pp. 42–43; and financial information and other facts accessed at www.mcdonalds.com/corp/invest.html and http://mcdonalds.com/corp/about/factsheets.html, July 2006.

2. Mya Frazier, "Look Who's Putting the Squeeze on Brands," *Advertising Age*, March 27, 2006, pp. 1, 46.

3. See Sarah Lorge, "The Coke Advantage," *Sales & Marketing Management*, December 1998, p. 17; Chad Terhune, "Coke Wins a 10-Year Contract From Subway, Ousting PepsiCo," *Wall Street Journal*, November 28, 2003, p. B.3; and "The Best in Foodservice Just Get Better," *Beverage Industry*, September 2004, pp. 15–16.

4. World POPClock, U.S. Census Bureau, accessed online at www.census.gov, July 2006. This Web site provides continuously updated projections of the U.S. and world populations.

5. Adapted from Frederik Balfour, "Educating the 'Little Emperors' There's a Big Market for Products That Help China's Coddled Kids Get Ahead," *BusinessWeek*, November 10, 2003, p. 22. Also see Clay Chandler, "Little Emperors," *Fortune*, October 4, 2004, pp. 138–150; and "Hothousing Little Tykes," *Beijing Review*, May 5, 2005, accessed at www.bjreview.com.cn/En-2005/05-18-e/china-5.htm.

6. See "China's Golden Oldies," *The Economist*, February 26, 2005, p. 74. See also "China Economy: How Do You Prepare for the Retirement of 1.3bn People?" *EIU ViewsWire*, March 27, 2006.

7. U.S. Census Bureau projections and POPClock Projection, U.S. Census Bureau, accessed at www.census.gov, May 2006.

8. Louise Lee, "Love Those Boomers," *BusinessWeek*, October 24, 2005, pp. 94–102; Tom Ramstack, and "The New Gray: Boomers Spark Retirement Revolution," *Washington Times*, December 29, 2005, p. A1.

9. Dee Depass, "Designed with a Wink, Nod at Boomers," *Minneapolis-St. Paul Star Tribune*, March 17, 2006, accessed at http://seattlepi.nwsource.com/business/263325_boomerbuyers17.html?source=rss.

10. Depass, "Designed with a Wink, Nod at Boomers," p. 1.

11. Linda S. Morris, "Home Is Where Your RV Is," *Knight Ridder Tribune Business News*, February 20, 2005, p. 1. Also see Alina Tugend, "RV's Find a New Fan Base: The Baby Boomers," *New York Times*, January 16, 2005; Thane Peterson, "McMansions on Wheels," *BusinessWeek*, October 17, 2005, pp. 107–107; and Dahleen Glanton, "Wealthy Baby Boomers Increasingly Drawn to Luxury RV Lifestyle," *Chicago Tribune*, April 16, 2006.

12. Stuart Elliott, "Flower Power in Ad Land," *New York Times*, April 11, 2006, p. G2.

13. Scott Schroder and Warren Zeller, "Get to Know Gen X and Its Segments," *Multichannel News*, March 21, 2005, p. 55.

14. Quotes from "Mixed Success: One Who Targeted Gen X and Succeeded—Sort Of," *Journal of Financial Planning*, February 2004, p. 15; and Paul Greenberg, "Move Over, Baby Boomers; Gen Xers Want Far More Collaboration with Companies, Both As Consumers and Employees," *CIO*, March 1, 2006, p. 1.

15. See "Overlooked and Under X-Ploited," *American Demographics*, May 2004, p. 48; Howard Schneider, "Grunge Marketing," *Mortgage Banking*, November 2004, p. 106; and Scott Schroder and Warren Zeller, "Get to Know Gen X and Its Segments," *Multichannel News*, March 21, 2005, p. 55.

16. Mike Brandt, "Young Customers: Who, What, and Y," *ABA Bank Marketing*, March 25, 2005, pp. 37–42; and information from www.wamu.com, August 2006.

17. See "TRU Projects Teens Will Spend $159 Billion in 2005," press release, Teenage Research Unlimited, December 15, 2005, accessed at www.teenresearch.com; and Elizabeth Lazarowitz, "Tutor Teens on Spending," *Daily News (New York)*, February 23, 2006.

18. Quote from Tobi Elkin, "Gen Y Quizzed about On-Demand," *Advertising Age*, February 14, 2003, p. 37. Teen statistics and other information from "Teens Forge Forward with Internet and Other New Technologies," Pew Internet & American Life Project, July 25, 2005, accessed at www.pewinternet.org; and Jessi Hempel, "The MySpace Generation," *BusinessWeek*, December 12, 2005, pp. 86–96.

19. Gregg Bennett and Tony Lachowitz, "Marketing to Lifestyles: Action Sports and Generation Y," *Sports Marketing Quarterly*, 2004, pp. 239–243; and "New Xbox 360 to be Featured in College Campus Tour," *PR Newswire*, March 21, 2006.

20. Julie Bosman, "Hey, Kid, You Want to Buy A Scion?" *New York Times*, June 14, 2006, p. C2.

21. Jason Fields, "America's Families and Living Arrangements: 2003," U.S. Census Bureau, November 2004, accessed at www.census.gov/population/www/socdemo/hh-fam.html.

22. Eduardo Porter, "Stretched to Limit, Women Stall March to Work," *New York Times*, March 2, 2006, accessed at www.nytimes.com.

23. See U.S. Census Bureau, "America's Families and Living Arrangements: 2003," U.S. Census Bureau, November 2004, accessed at www.census.gov/Press-Release/www/releases/archives/families_households/003118.html; Paul Nyhan, "Stay-Home Dads Connect with New Full-Time Job; Pay Stinks, But Benefits Are Great," *Seattle Post-Intelligencer*, April 25, 2006, p. A1.

24. Mary Beth Schweigert, "These Dinners Are a Dream Come True for Harried Cooks," *Knight Ridder Tribune*, February 23, 2005, p. 1; Eileen Gunn, "Cranky Consumer: A New Way to Get a Home-Cooked Meal," *Wall Street Journal*, February 2, 2006, p. D4; and www.dreamdinners.com, accessed May 2006.

25. U.S. Census Bureau, "Geographical Mobility," March 2004, accessed online at www.census.gov/prod/2004pubs/p20-549.pdf; and Jim Taylor, "Manifest Destiny," *American Demographics*, September 2004, pp. 29–34; and Bradley Johnson, "Population Migrates South and West," *American Demographics*, April 4, 2005, p. 41.

26. See U.S. Census Bureau, www.census.gov/population/www/estimates/aboutmetro.html, June 2005; "Redefining Where We Live: New Concepts and Definitions of Statistical Areas," *Industrial Relations*, January 2004, pp. 293–294; "Sales Ablaze in 'Micropolitan' Areas," *Casual Living*, February 2005, pp. 70–74; and Gordon F. Mulligan and Alexander C. Vias, "Growth and Change in Micropolitan Areas," *Annals of Regional Science*, June 2006, p. 203.

27. David L. Margulius, "Telecommuting Gets More Elusive," February 6, 2006, p. 18.

28. Mike Bergman, "College Degree Nearly Doubles Annual Earnings, Census Bureau Reports," U.S. Census Bureau, March 28, 2005, accessed at www.census.gov/Press-Release/www/releases/archives/education/004214.html.

29. See U.S. Bureau of Labor Statistics, "Labor Force, Employment, and Earnings," p. 416, accessed at http://landview.census.gov/prod/2001pubs/statab/sec13.pdf, June 2004; and U.S. Department of Labor, *Occupational Outlook Handbook, 2006-07 Edition*, June 29, 2006, accessed at www.bls.gov/emp/home.htm.

30. See Farai Chideya, "American-Born Hispanic Population Rising," *National Public Radio*, May 16, 2006; "U.S. Diversity Increasing, Census Data Show," May 10, 2006, accessed at www.usinfo.state.gov; and U.S. Census Bureau reports accessed online at www.census.gov, June 2006.

31. Adapted from William F. Gloede, "The Art of Cultural Correctness," *American Demographics*, November 2004, pp. 27–33. See also Meg Green, "Perfect Prospects," *Best Review*, August 2005, pp. 22–26.

32. Information accessed at www.rivendellmarketing.com/ngng/ngng_profiles_set.html, June 2005; Deborah L. Vence, "Younger GLBT Market Spells Opportunities," *Marketing News*, April 1, 2006, pp. 17, 19; Stuart Elliott, "Hey, Gay Spender, Marketers Spending Time with You," *New York Times*, June 26, 2006, p. C8; and www.planetoutinc.com/sales/market.html, July 2006.

33. See John Fetto, Todd Wasserman, "IBM Targets Gay Business Owners," *Adweek*, October 6, 2003, p. 8; and information from www-03.ibm.com/employment/us/diverse/awards.shtml#glbt, July 2006. The Las Vega example is adapted from information found in Chris Jones, "Come Out, Come Out," *Las Vegas Review Journal*, March 5, 2006, p. 1E.

34. Joan Voight, "Accessibility of Disability," *Adweek*, March 27, 2006, p. 20. Also see Stephen Ohlemacher, "Most Disabled Americans Have Jobs," *Associated Press Online*, May 12, 2006.

35. Quotes from Voight, "Accessibility of Disability," *Adweek*, p. 20. Avis example is adapted from "Avis to Sponsor Achilles Track Club Athletes," *PR Newswire*, March 16, 2006.

36. Bradley Johnson, "Recession's Long Gone, but America's Average Income Isn't Budging," *Advertising Age*, April 17, 2006, p. 22.

37. "How Levi Strauss Rekindled the Allure of Brand America," *World Trade*, March 2005, p. 28; Levi Strauss Press Releases, accessed at www.levistrauss.com, May 27, 2006; and Levi's Web site at www.levis.com, July, 2006.

38. Adapted from Lorraine Woellert, "HP Wants Your Old PC Back," *BusinessWeek*, April 10, 2006, pp. 82–83. For more discussion, see the "Environmentalism" section in Chapter 20.

39. Jack Neff, "P&G Products to Wear Wire," *Advertising Age*, December 15, 2004, pp. 1, 32; "Gartner Says Worldwide RFID Spending to Surpass $3 Billion in 2010," *BusinessWire*, December 13, 2005; Renee Boucher, "Wal-Mart Forges Ahead with RFID," *eWeek*, March 6, 2006; Michael Garry, "Wal-Mart Expands RFID Program to Atlanta," *Supermarket News*, June 12, 2006, p. 24; and information accessed online at www.autoidlabs.org, August 2006.

40. See "2006 R&D Funding Improves Amid Increasing Restraints," *R&D*, January 1, 2006.

41. Sarah Pinsky, "KaBoom! and The Home Depot Announce Partnership with Swing-N-Slide," KaBoom! press release, March 9, 2006, accessed at www.kaboom.org; and information accessed at www.causemarketingforum.com/page.asp?ID=442, August 2006.

42. Wendy Meillo, "The Greed for Goodwill," *Adweek*, March 13, 2006, p. 14; and "The Growth of Cause Marketing," accessed at www.causemarketingforum.com/page.asp?ID=188, August 2006.

43. For more on Yankelovich Monitor, see www.yankelovich.com/products/monitor.aspx.

44. Adapted from descriptions found at www.yankelovich.com/products/lists.aspx, August 2006.

45. Adapted from Ronald Grover, "Trading the Bleachers for the Couch," *BusinessWeek*, August 22, 2005, p. 32.

46. "Decked Out," *Inside*, Spring 2006, pp. 76–77.

47. Laura Feldmann, "After 9/11 Highs, America's Back to Good Ol' Patriotism," *Christian Science Monitor*, July 5, 2006, p. 1.

48. L. A. Chung, "New Greetings of Hybrid Fans: Aloha, LOHAS," *Mercury News*, April 29, 2005, accessed at www.mercurynews.com/mld/mercurynews/news/columnists/la_chung/11520890.htm; and Becky Ebenkamp, "Livin' la Vida Lohas," *Brandweek*, May 1, 2006, p. 22.

49. See Doug Desjardins, "Latest Natural-Food Trend Going to the Dogs," *DSN Retailing Today*, March 14, 2005, p. 26; Steven Gray, "Organic Food Goes Mass Market," *Wall Street Journal*, May 4, 2006; and Libby Quib, "Appetite for Organic Outstripping Supply," *Durham Herald Sun*, July 7, 2006, pp. 1, 4.

50. Quotes from Myra Stark, "Celestial Season," *Brandweek*, November 16, 1998, pp. 25–26; and Becky Ebankamp, "The Young and Righteous," *Brandweek*, April 5, 2004, p. 18.

51. See Philip Kotler, *Kotler on Marketing* (New York: Free Press, 1999), p. 3; and Kotler, *Marketing Insights from A to Z* (Hoboken, NJ: John Wiley & Sons, 2003), pp. 23–24.

52. Adapted from Jayne O'Donnell, "Online Rumor Mill Dogs Companies," *USA Today*, October 29, 2005, p. 3B.

1. Quotes and extracts from Ellen Byron, "Case by Case: How Coach Won a Rich Purse by Inventing New Uses for Bags," *Wall Street Journal*, November 17, 2004, p. A1. Other information from Pallavi Gogoi, "I Am Woman, Hear Me Shop," *BusinessWeek Online*, February 14, 2005; Gogoi, "How a Woman Spends Her Money," *BusinessWeek Online*, February 14, 2005; Lauren Foster, "How Coach Pulled into Luxury's Fast Lane," *Financial Times*, June 30, 2004, p. 12; Coach 2005 Annual Report, accessed at www.coach.com; Kate Betts, "It's All in the Bag," *Time*, March 20, 2006, p. 101; Vicki M. Young, "Coach: Jewelry Launch in the Works," *WWD*, April 26, 2006, p. 11; and "Coach, Inc.," *Hoover's Company Records*, June 15, 2006, p. 101101.

2. Mike Freeman, "Data Company Helps Wal-Mart, Casinos, Airlines Analyze Customers," *San Diego Union Tribune*, February 24, 2006.

3. See Christina Le Beau, "Mountains to Mine," *American Demographics*, August 2000, pp. 40–44; Leslie Langnau, "Drowning in Data," *Material Handling Management*, December 2003, p. 22; Daniel Lyons, "Too Much Information," *Forbes*, December 13, 2004, pp. 110–115; and Charles Babcock, "Data, Data, Everywhere," *InformationWeek*, January 9, 2006, pp. 49–53.

4. See Philip Kotler, *Marketing Insights from A to Z* (Hoboken, NJ: John Wiley & Sons, 2003), pp. 80–82.

5. Jennifer Brown, "Pizza Hut Delivers Hot Results Using Data Warehousing," *Computing Canada*, October 17, 2003, p. 24; and "Pizza Hut, Inc.," *Hoover's Company Records*, May 15, 2006, p. 89521.

6. Tracey Tyler, "WestJet Accuses Rival of Trap in Spy Case," *Toronto Star*, February 14, 2006, p. D1.

7. Andy Serwer, "P&G's Covert Operation," *Fortune*, September 17, 2001, pp. 42–44. Also see Andrew Crane, "In the Company of Spies: When Competitive Intelligence Gathering Becomes Industrial Espionage," *Business Horizons*, May–June 2005, pp. 233+; and Kate MacKenzie, "Employees May Be Opening the Door to Criminals," *Financial*, May 31, 2006, p. 4.

8. Fred Vogelstein and Peter Lewis, "Search and Destroy," *Fortune*, May 2, 2005.

9. James Curtis, "Behind Enemy Lines," *Marketing*, May 21, 2001, pp. 28–29. Also see Brian Caufield, "Know Your Enemy," *Business 2.0*, June 2004, p. 89; Michael Fielding, "Damage Control: Firms Must Plan for Counterintelligence," *Marketing News*, September 15, 2004, pp. 19–20; and Bill DeGenaro, "A Case for Business Counterintelligence," *Competitive Intelligence Magazine*, September–October 2005, pp. 5+.

10. For more on research firms that supply marketing information, see Jack Honomichl, "Honomichl 50," special section, *Marketing News*, June 15, 2006, pp. H1–H67. Other information from www.infores.com; www.smrb.com; www.nielsen.com; and http://www.yankelovich.com/products/monitor.aspx, September 2006.

11. Adapted from an example in David Kiley, "Shoot the Focus Group," *BusinessWeek*, November 14, 2005, pp. 120–121.

12. Adapted from an example in Spencer E. Ante, "The Science of Desire," *BusinessWeek*, June 5, 2006, pp. 99–106.

13. Spencer E. Ante, "The Science of Desire," *BusinessWeek*, June 5, 2006, p. 100.

14. David Kiley, "Shoot the Focus Group," *BusinessWeek*, p. 120.

15. *Ibid.*, p. 120.

16. "Online Research: The Time Has Come," Greenfield Online white paper, accessed at www.greenfieldcentral.com/rcwhitepapers.htm, June 2006.

17. Adapted from an example in David Kiley, "Shoot the Focus Group," *BusinessWeek*, November 14, 2005, pp. 120–121.

18. For more on Internet privacy, see James R. Hagerty and Dennis K. Berman, "Caught in the Net: New Battleground over Web Privacy," *Wall Street Journal*, August 27, 2004, p. A1; Alan R. Peslak, "Internet Privacy Policies," *Information Resources Management Journal*, January–March 2005, pp. 29+; and Larry Dobrow, "Privacy Issues Loom for Marketers," *Advertising Age*, March 13, 2006, p. S6.

19. See Gary H. Anthes, "Smile, You're on Candid Computer," *Computerworld*, December 3, 2001, p. 50; Claire Tristram, "Behind BlueEyes," *Technology Review*, May 2001, p. 32; and "Creating Computers That Know How You Feel," accessed at www.almaden.ibm.com/cs/BlueEyes/index.html, September 2006.

20. See David Harding, David Chieftez, Scott DeAngelo, and Elizabeth Ziegler, "CRM's Silver Lining," *Marketing Management*, March–April 2004, pp. 27–32; Ellen Neuborne, "A Second Act of CRM," *Inc.*, March 2005, p. 40; William Boulding et al., "A Customer Relationship Management Roadmap: What Is Known, Potential Pitfalls, and Where to Go," *Journal of Marketing*, October 2005, pp. 155–166; Cindy Wexler, "The Fight Over CRM," *Chief Executive*, January–February 2006, pp. 24–28; and William Band, "The ABCs of CRM Success," *Optimize*, January 2006, accessed at www.optimizemag.com/article/showArticle.jhtml?articleId=175700405.

21. Michael Krauss, "At Many Firms, Technology Obscures CRM," *Marketing News*, March 18, 2002, p. 5. Also see Darrell K. Rigby and Dianne Ledingham, "CRM Done Right," *Harvard Business Review*, November 2004, p. 129; Barton Goldenberg, "Let's Keep to the High Road," *CRM Magazine*, March 2005, p. 22; and Sean Collins, Firish Nair, and Jeffrey Schumacher, "Reaching the Next Level of Performance," *Customer Relationship Management*, May 2006, p. 48.

22. See Robert McLuhan, "How to Reap the Benefits of CRM," *Marketing*, May 24, 2001, p. 35; Stewart Deck, "Data Mining," *Computerworld*, March 29, 1999, p. 76; Jason Compton, "CRM Gets Real," *Customer Relationship Management*, May 2004, pp. 11–12; Ellen Neuborne, "A Second Act of CRM," *Inc.*, March 2005, p. 40; and "Value Added with mySAP CRM," accessed at www.sap.com/solutions/business-suite/crm/pdf/Misc_CRM_Study.pdf, June 2006.

23. See Darell K. Rigby and Vijay Vishwanath, "Localization: The Revolution in Consumer Markets," *Harvard Business Review*, April 2006, pp. 82–92.

24. Adapted from information in Ann Zimmerman, "Small Business: Do the Research," *Wall Street Journal*, May 9, 2005, p. R3; with information from www.bibbentuckers.com, accessed September 2006.

25. For some good advice on conducting market research in a small business, see "Marketing Research...Basics 101," accessed at www.sba.gov/starting_business/marketing/research.html, August 2006; and "Researching Your Market," U.S. Small Business Administration, accessed at www.sba.gov/library/pubs/mt-8.doc, September 2006.

26. Jack Honomichl, "Acquisitions Up, Growth Rate Varies," *Marketing News*, August 15, 2005, pp. H3–H4; Jack Honomichl, "Honomichl 50," special section, *Marketing News*, June 15, 2006, pp. H1–H67; and the ACNielsen International Research Web site, accessed at www.acnielsen.com/company/where.php, September 2006.

27. Phone, PC, and other country media stats are from www.nationmaster.com, July 2006.

28. Subhash C. Jain, *International Marketing Management*, 3rd ed. (Boston: PWS-Kent, 1990), p. 338. Also see Debra L. Vence, "Leave It to the Experts," *Marketing News*, April 28, 2003, p. 37; Gary Kaplan, "Global Research Needs Local Coordination," *Marketing News*, May 15, 2005, p. 43; and C. Samuel Craig and Susan P. Douglas, "International Research Frame Needs Reworking," *Marketing News*, February 15, 2006, pp. 33–34.

29. Adapted from Richard Behar, "Never Heard of Acxiom? Chances Are It's Heard of You," *Fortune*, February 23, 2004, pp. 140–148; with information from www.acxiom.com, September 2006.

30. See "Too Much Information?" *Marketing Management*, January–February 2004, p. 4.

31. Margaret Webb Pressler, "Too Personal to Tell?" *Washington Post*, April 18, 2004, p. F05; and E-Mail Privacy Statistics, accessed at www.relemail.com/statistics.htm, September 2006.

32. "ICC/ESOMAR International Code of Marketing and Social Research Practice," accessed at www.iccwbo.org/home/menu_advert_marketing.asp, July 2006. Also see "Respondent Bill of Rights," accessed at www.cmor.org/rc/tools.cfm?topic=4, July 2006.

33. Jaikumar Vijayan, "Disclosure Laws Driving Data Privacy Efforts, Says IBM Exec," *Computerworld*, May 8, 2006, p. 26.

34. Information accessed at www.americanexpress.com/sif/cda/page/0,1641,14271,00.asp, September 2006.

35. Cynthia Crossen, "Studies Galore Support Products and Positions, but Are They Reliable?" *Wall Street Journal*, November 14, 1991, pp. A1, A9. Also see Allan J. Kimmel, "Deception in Marketing Research and Practice: An Introduction," *Psychology and Marketing*, July 2001, pp. 657–661; and Alvin C. Burns and Ronald F. Bush, *Marketing Research* (Upper Saddle River, NJ: Prentice Hall, 2005), pp. 63–75.

36. Information accessed at www.casro.org/codeofstandards.cfm#intro, September 2006.

CHAPTER 5

1. Quotes and other information from Greg Schneider, "Rebels with Disposable Income: Aging Baby Boomers

Line Up to Buy High-End Versions of Youthful Indulgences," *Washington Post*, April 27, 2003, p. F1; Ian P. Murphy, "Aided by Research, Harley Goes Whole Hog," *Marketing News*, December 2, 1996, pp. 16, 17; Ted Bolton, "Tattooed Call Letters: The Ultimate Test of Brand Loyalty," accessed online at www.boltonresearch.com, April 2003; Jay Palmer, "Vroom at the Top," *Barron's*, March 29, 2004, pp. 17–18; Chris Woodyard, "Motorcycle Sales Rev Up to Top 1 Million," *USA Today*, January 20, 2005; Marc Gerstein, "The Road Ahead for Harley," *Reuters*, April 13, 2006; and the Harley-Davidson Web site at www.Harley-Davidson.com, December 2006.

2. GDP figures from *The World Fact Book*, July 11, 2006, accessed at www.cia.gov/cia/publications/factbook/geos/us.html. Population figures from the World POPClock, U.S. Census Bureau, www.census.gov, September 2006. This Web site provides continuously updated projections of the U.S. and world populations.

3. Jim Edwards, "Why Buy?" *Brandweek*, October 5, 2005, pp. 21–24.

4. Statistics from Deborah L. Vence, "Avoid Shortcuts: Hispanic Audience Requires Distinct, Inventive Marketing," *Marketing News*, February 15, 2006, pp. 23–24; "Hispanics in Business," *Fortune*, April 3, 2006, pp. 132–133; Stanley Perman, "How to Tap the Hispanic Market," *BusinessWeek Online*, July 12, 2006, accessed at www.businessweek.com; and U.S. Census Bureau reports accessed online at www.census.gov, September 2006.

5. Joel Russell, "Big Spenders: Top 50 Advertisers in Hispanic TV and Print Media 2005," *Hispanic Business*, December 2005, accessed at www.hispanicbusiness.com.

6. Example adapted from Sean Gregory, "Diapers for Fatima," *Time*, January 18, 2005, accessed at www.time.com; with information from http://pg.com/company/who_we_are/diversity/multi/hispanic.jhtml, August 2006.

7. Louise Witt, "Color Code Red," *American Demographics*, February 2004, pp. 23–25; Vence, "Companies Target Lifestyle Segments," p. 13; Sonia Alleyne, "Diversity Leader," *Black Enterprise*, March 2005, p. 54; "Increasingly Affluent African American Market Set to Reach $981 Billion by 2010," *PR Newswire*, February 22, 2006; and U.S. Census Bureau reports accessed online at www.census.gov, August 2006.

8. "Facts about Mahogany," accessed at http://pressroom.hallmark.com/mahogany_cards_facts.html, July 2006.

9. See Mike Beirne, "Has This GROUP Been Left BEHIND?" *Brandweek*, March 14, 2005, pp. 33–36.

10. Information accessed at www.communityconnect.com/advertise.html, August 2006; and a list of the most popular African American Web sites at www.blackwebportal.com/web/web_bwptop30.cfm, August 2006.

11. See Vence, "Companies Target Lifestyle Segments," p. 13; U.S. Census Bureau reports accessed at www.census.gov, July 2006; and Randi Schmelzer, "The Asian Answer," *PR Week*, March 13, 2006.

12. Jeffrey M. Humphreys, "The Multicultural Economy 2004," *Georgia Business and Economic Conditions*, The Selig Center for Economic Growth, third quarter 2004; Christopher Reynolds, "Far East Moves West," *American Demographics*, October 2004, p. 56; Mike Troy, "Wal-Mart Unveils Asian Ad Campaign," *DSN Retailing Today*, April 11, 2005, pp. 5–6; Randi Schmelzer, "The Asian Answer," *PR Week*, March 13, 2006; and U.S. Internet Industry Association, *Proposed Legislation and Its Impact on Consumer's Use of Broadband and IP Services*, accessed www.usiia.org, April 11, 2006.

13. Rong-Gong Lin II, "Wal-Mart Pursues Asian Americans," *Los Angeles Times*, April 2, 2005, p. C1; and Randi Schmelzer, "The Asian Answer," *PR Week*, March 13, 2006, p. 1.

14. Information accessed at www.census.gov, September 2006.

15. See Edward Keller and Jonathan Berry, *The Influentials* (New York, NY: The Free Press, 2003); John Battelle, "The Net of Influence," *Business 2.0*, March 2004, p. 70; Alicia Clegg, "Following the Leaders," *Marketing Week*, September 30, 2004, pp. 47–49; Ronald E. Goldsmith, "The Influentials," *Journal of Product & Brand Management*, 2005, pp. 371–372; Matthew Creamer, "Study: Go Traditional to Influence Influencers," *Advertising Age*, March 7, 2005, p. 8; and Dave Balter and Ed Keller, "In Search of True Marketplace Influencers," *Advertising Age*, December 5, 2005, p. 22.

16. Anya Kamenetz, "The Network Unbound," *Fast Company*, June 2006, pp. 69–73.

17. Saul Hansell, "For MySpace, Making Friends Was Easy. Big Profit Is Tougher," *New York Times*, April 23, 2006, p. 3.1.

18. Quote and information from "Colored Vision Adidas Unleashes Seven-Film Mobile Media," *Boards*, May 2006, p. 15.

19. Quote from Anya Kamenetz, "The Network Unbound," *Fast Company*, pp. 73. Also see Julie Bosman, "Chevy Tries a Write-Your-Own-Ad Approach," *New York Times*, April 4, 2006, p. C1.

20. See Sharon Goldman Edry, "No Longer Just Fun and Games," *American Demographics*, May 2001, pp. 36–38; Pallavi Gogoi, "I Am Woman, Hear Me Shop," *Business Week Online*, February 14, 2005, accessed at www.bwonline.com; Amy Gillentine, "Marketing Groups Ignore Women at Their Own Peril," *Colorado Springs Business Journal*, January 20, 2006; and "Finance and Economics: A Guide to Womenomics," *Economist*, April 15, 2006, p. 80.

21. Adapted from Pallavi Gogoi, "Meet Jane Geek," *BusinessWeek*, November 28, 2005, pp. 94–95.

22. Kevin Downey, "What Children Teach Their Parents," *Broadcasting & Cable*, March 13, 2006, p. 26.

23. Alice Dragoon, "How to Do Customer Segmentation Right," *CIO*, October 1, 2005, p. 1.

24. Quotes and examples from www.carhartt.com, September 2006.

25. See Rebecca Piirto, "Measuring Minds in the 1990s," *American Demographics*, December 1990, pp. 35–39; and Rebecca Piirto, "VALS the Second Time," *American Demographics*, July 1991, p. 6. VALS information and examples accessed at www.sric-bi.com/VALS/types.shtml and www.sric-bi.com/VALS/projects.shtml, December 2006.

26. Jennifer Aaker, "Dimensions of Measuring Brand Personality," *Journal of Marketing Research*, May 1999, pp. 45–57; and Audrey Azoulay and Jean-Noel Kapferer, "Do Brand Personality Scales Really Measure Brand Personality?" *Journal of Marketing*, May 1999, pp. 347–356. Also see Aaker, "The Malleable Self: The Role of Self Expression in Persuasion," *Journal of Marketing Research*, August 1997, pp. 347–356.

27. Seth Stevenson, "Ad Report Card: Mac Attack," June 19, 2006, accessed at www.slate.com/id/2143810.

28. Annetta Miller and Dody Tsiantar, "Psyching Out Consumers," *Newsweek*, February 27, 1989, pp. 46–47. Also see Leon G. Schiffman and Leslie L. Kanuk, *Consumer Behavior*, 9th ed. (Upper Saddle River, NJ: 2007), chapter 4.

29. See Abraham. H. Maslow, "A Theory of Human Motivation," *Psychological Review*, 50 (1943), pp. 370–396. Also see Maslow, *Motivation and Personality*, 3rd ed. (New York: HarperCollins Publishers, 1987); and Barbara Marx Hubbard, "Seeking Our Future Potentials," *The Futurist*, May 1998, pp. 29–32.

30. Charles Pappas, "Ad Nauseam," *Advertising Age*, July 10, 2000, pp. 16–18. See also Mark Ritson, "Marketers Need to Find a Way to Control the Contagion of Clutter," *Marketing*, March 6, 2003, p. 16; and David H. Freedman, "The Future of Advertising Is Here," *Inc.*, August 2005, pp. 70–78.

31. Bob Garfield, "'Subliminal' Seduction and Other Urban Myths," *Advertising Age*, September 18, 2000, pp. 4, 105. Also see "We Have Ways of Making You Think," *Marketing Week*, September 25, 2003, p. 14; Si Cantwell, "Common Sense; Scrutiny Helps Catch Catchy Ads," *Wilmington Star-News*, April 1, 2004, p. 1B; and Allison Motluk, "Subliminal Advertising May Work After All," April 28, 2006, accessed at www.newscientist.com.

32. Rebecca Flass, "Got Milk?' Takes a Serious Look Inside the Body," *Adweek*, January 27, 2003, p. 5; Katie Koppenhoefer, "MilkPEP Ads Make Big Impact with Hispanics," press release, International Dairy Foods Association, March 3, 2003, accessed at www.idfa.org/news/gotmilk/2003/milkpepads.cfm; Jeff Manning and Kevin Lane Keller, "Got Advertising That Works?" *Marketing Management*, January–February 2004, pp. 16–20; and information from www.whymilk.com, November 2006.

33. For a deeper discussion of the buyer decision process, see Philip Kotler and Kevin Lane Keller, *Marketing Management*, 12th ed. (Upper Saddle River, NJ: 2006), pp. 191–203.

34. Douglas Pruden and Terry G. Vavra, "Controlling the Grapevine," *Marketing Management*, July–August 2004, pp. 25–30. See also John Goodman, "Treat Your Customers as Prime Media Reps," *Brandweek*, September 12, 2005, pp. 16–17.

35. See Leon Festinger, A Theory of Cognitive Dissonance (Stanford, CA: Stanford University Press, 1957); Schiffman and Kanuk, Consumer Behavior, pp. 219–220; Patti Williams and Jennifer L. Aaker, "Can Mixed Emotions Peacefully Coexist?" PUBLICATION?, March 2002, pp. 636–649; Adam Ferrier, "Young Are Not Marketing Savvy; They're Suckers," *B&T Weekly*, October 22, 2004,

p. 13; and "Cognitive Dissonance and the Stability of Service Quality Perceptions," *The Journal of Services Marketing*, 2004; 2004, p. 433+.

36. The following discussion draws from the work of Everett M. Rogers. See his *Diffusion of Innovations*, 5th ed. (New York: Free Press, 2003). Also see Eric Waarts, Yvonne M. van Everdingen, and Jos van Hillegersberg, "The Dynamics of Factors Affecting the Adoption of Innovations," *The Journal of Product Innovation Management*, November 2002, pp. 412–423; Chaun-Fong Shih and Alladi Venkatesh, "Beyond Adoption: Development and Application of a Use-Diffusion Model," *Journal of Marketing*, January 2004, pp. 59–72; and Richard R. Nelson, Alexander Peterhansl, and Bhaven Sampat, "Why and How Innovations Get Adopted: A Tale of Four Models," *Industrial and Corporate Change*, October 2004, pp. 679–699.

CHAPTER 6

1. Quotes and other information from Dale Buss, "Up with Brown," *Brandweek*, Jan 27, 2003 p. 16; "Business as Usual for Ads on Sunday News Shows," *BtoB*, April 14, 2003, p. 30; "UPS Service Helps Companies Go Global," *Transportation & Distribution*, May 2003, p. 19; "The New Mission of Synchronizing Global Supply Chains," *Inventory Management Report*, May 2003, p. 9; Robert McGarvey, "UPS Builds Millions in Sales," *Selling Power*, June 2004, pp. 56–61; Larry Greenemeier, "On the Line at UPS," *Information Week*, January 23, 2006; and information gathered at www.UPS.com, September 2006.

2. See Kate Macarthur, "Teflon Togs Get $40 Million Ad Push," *Advertising Age*, April 8, 2002, p. 3; "Neat Pants for Sloppy People," *Consumer Reports: Publisher's Edition Including Supplemental Guides*, May 2003, p. 10; "Sales Makes the Wearables World Go 'Round," *Wearables Business*, April 24, 2004, p. 22; and Rosamaria Mancini, *HFN*, May 16, 2005, p. 17; and www.teflon.invista.com, accessed September 2006.

3. For more discussion of business markets and business buyer behavior, see Das Narayandas, "Building Loyalty in Business Markets," *Harvard Business Review*, September 2005, pp. 131–139; and James C. Anderson, James A. Narus, and Wouter van Rossum, "Customer Value Propositions in Business Markets," *Harvard Business Review*, March 2006, pp. 91–99.

4. Patrick J. Robinson, Charles W. Faris, and Yoram Wind, *Industrial Buying Behavior and Creative Marketing* (Boston: Allyn & Bacon, 1967). Also see James C. Anderson and James A. Narus, *Business Market Management*, 2nd ed. (Upper Saddle River, NJ: 2004), chapter 3; and Philip Kotler and Kevin Lane Keller, *Marketing Management*, 12th ed. (Upper Saddle River, NJ: Prentice Hall, 2006), chapter 7.

5. See "BJ's Knows . . . Our System Is Their Solution," *Insights*, March 2002, p. 1; "Soap, Detergent Maker to Open Its First Franchise in Port of Stockton, California," *Knight Ridder Tribune Business News*, September 9, 2003, p. 1; and information accessed online at www.chemstation.com, August 2006.

6. See Philip Kotler, *Marketing Management*, 12th ed. (Upper Saddle River, NJ: Prentice Hall, 2006), pp. 213–214.

7. See Frederick E. Webster Jr. and Yoram Wind, *Organizational Buying Behavior* (Upper Saddle River, NJ: Prentice Hall, 1972), pp. 78–80. Also see James C. Anderson and James A. Narus, *Business Market Management: Understanding, Creating and Delivering Value* (Upper Saddle River, NJ: Prentice Hall, 2004), chapter 3.

8. For more discussion, see Stefan Wuyts and Inge Geyskens, "The Formation of Buyer-Seller Relationships: Detailed Contract Drafting and Close Partner Selection," *Harvard Business Review*, October 2005, pp. 103–117; and Robert McGarvey, "The Buyer's Emotional Side," *Selling Power*, April 2006, pp. 35–36.

9. See Frederick E. Webster, Jr., and Yoram Wind, *Organizational Buying Behavior*, pp. 33–37.

10. Robinson, Faris, and Wind, *Industrial Buying Behavior*, p. 14.

11. For this and other examples, see Kate Maddox, "#1 Hewlett-Packard Co.: www.hp.com," *BtoB*, August 11, 2003, p. 1; "Great Web Sites: www.hp.com," *BtoB Online*, September 13, 2004; and "10 Great Web Sites," *BtoB Online*, September 12, 2005; all accessed at www.btobonline.com.

12. Karen Prema, "National Aquarium Reels in Savings with Online Buying," accessed at www.purchasing.com, March 2, 2006; Karen Prema, "SRM + E-Auctions: Tools in the Toolbox," *Purchasing*, April 6, 2006, pp. 46–47; and Susan Avery, "At HP, Indirect Procurement Takes More of a Leadership Role," accessed at www.purchasing.com, May 25, 2006.

13. Demir Barlas, "E-Procurement: Steady Value," *Line56.com*, January 4, 2005, accessed at www.line56.com.

14. Michael A. Verespej, "E-Procurement Explosion," *Industry Week*, March 2002, pp. 25–28.

15. Information from www.shrinershq.org/Hospitals/_Hospitals_for_Children/; and www.tenethealth.com, September 2006.

16. H.J. Heinz Company Annual Report 2006, p. 20; accessed at http://heinz.com/2006annualreport/2006HeinzAR.pdf.

17. "President Bush's Proposed FY2006 Budget Represents Growth in IT Spending for Federal Government," FedSources press release, February 8, 2005, accessed at http://fedsources.com/about/fsinews/020805_fy06 budget.asp; and "Federal IT Spending to Hit $77B by FY '10, Group Says," *Aerospace Daily and Defense Report*, November 28, 2005, p. 1.

18. Ari Vidali, president of Envisage Technologies, personal communication, July 6, 2006.

19. See Messmer, "The Feds Get into Online Buying," *Network World*, March 5, 2001, p. 67; Patrick E. Clarke, "DLA Shifting from Managing Supplies to Managing Suppliers," May 30, 2002, accessed at www.dla.mil; and information accessed at http://progate.daps.dla. mil/home/; "GSA Organization Overview," accessed as www.gsa.gov, September 2006; and VA Office of Acquisition & Material Management, accessed at www1.va.gov/oamm/, September 2006.

CHAPTER 7

1. Adapted from portions of Janet Adamy, "Battle Brewing; Dunkin' Donuts Tries to Go Upscale, But Not Too Far," *Wall Street Journal*, April 8, 2006, p. A1; with quotes and other information from Julie Bosman, "This Joe's for You," *New York Times*, June 8, 2006, p. C1.

2. For these and other examples, see Darell K. Rigby and Vijay Vishwanath, "Localization: The Revolution in Consumer Markets," *Harvard Business Review*, April 2006, pp. 82–92.

3. Based on information found in Steven Gray, "How Applebee's Is Making It Big in Small Towns," *Wall Street Journal*, August 2, 2004, B1; Applebee's 2005 Annual Report, p. 14, accessed at www.applebees.com; and "Applebee's International, Inc.," *Hoover's Company Records*, Austin, June 1, 2006, p. 13585.

4. See "Customer Experience and 'Small-Marts,'" January 28, 2005, accessed at http://learned.typepad.com/learned_on_women/2005/01/customer_experi.html; Marianne Rohrlich, "Manhattanites Will Soon Find Depots Close to Home," *New York Times*, April 15, 2004, p. F10; Doug Desjardins, "Smaller Format Rolls Dice with Multiple Openings in Vegas," *DSN Retailing Today*, February 28, 2005, p. 46; and Kris Hudson, "Wal-Mart Shelves Dallas Competitors," *Wall Street Journal*, February 15, 2006, p. B3D.

5. Reena Jana, "Nintendo's New Brand Game," June 22, 2006, accessed at www.businessweek.com/innovate/content/jun2006/id20060622_124931.htm?chan=search.

6. See Fara Warner, "Nike Changes Strategy on Women's Apparel," *New York Times*, May 16, 2005, accessed at www.nytimes.com; and Thomas J. Ryan, "Just Do It for Women," *SGB*, March 2006, pp. 25–26.

7. Information accessed at www.we.tv. August 2006.

8. Robert Berner, "Out-Discounting the Discounter," *BusinessWeek*, May 10, 2004, pp. 78–79; "The Almighty Dollar Store," *Wall Street Journal: The Classroom Edition*, March 2005, accessed at www.wsjclassroomedition.com/archive/05mar/econ_dollarstore.htm; Debbie Howell, "Dollar," *DSN Retailing Today*, November 21, 2005, pp. 11–12; and Bernadette Casey, "Retailers Better Learn the Real Value of a Dollar," *DSN Retailing Today*, March 13, 2006, p. 6.

9. Portions adapted from Linda Tischler, "How Pottery Barn Wins with Style," *Fast Company*, June 2003, pp. 106–113; with information from www.potterybarn.com; www.potterybarnkids.com, and www.pbteen.com, September 2006.

10. See Maureen Wallenfang, "Appleton, Wis.-Area Dealers See Increase in Moped Sales," *Knight Ridder Tribune Business News*, August 15, 2004, p. 1; Louise Lee, "Love Those Boomers," *BusinessWeek*, October 24, 2005, pp. 94–100; and Honda's Web site at www.powersports.honda.com/scooters/, September 2006.

11. Kate MacArthur, "BK Rebels Fall in Love with King," *Advertising Age*, May 1, 2006, pp. 1, 86.

12. See Jennifer Ordonez, "Fast-Food Lovers, Unite!" *Newsweek*, May 24, 2004, p. 56.

13. Portions adapted from Alan T. Saracevic, "Author Plumbs Bottomless Depth of Mac Worship," December 12, 2004, accessed at www.sfgate.com. Definition from www.

urbandictionary.com/define.php?term=Macolyte&r=d, September 2006.

14. Based on PRIZM NE cluster information accessed at www.claritas.com, September 2006.

15. John Fetto, "American Neighborhoods' First Page," *American Demographics*, July–August 2003, p. 34. See also the "Prizm NE Lifestyle Segmentation System" brochure, accessed at www.claritas.com, September 2006.

16. Information from http://home.americanexpress.com/home/mt_personal.shtml, August 2006.

17. See Arundhati Parmar, "Global Youth United," *Marketing News*, October 28, 2002, pp. 1, 49; "Impossible Is Nothing' Adidas Launches New Global Brand Advertising Campaign," accessed at www.adidas.com, February 5, 2004; "Teen Spirit," *Global Cosmetic Industry*, March 2004, p. 23; Johnnie L. Roberts, "World Tour," *Newsweek*, June 6, 2005, pp. 34–36; and the MTV Worldwide Web site, www.mtv.com/mtvinternational.

18. See Michael Porter, *Competitive Advantage* (New York: Free Press, 1985), pp. 4–8, 234–236. For more recent discussions, see Stanley Slater and Eric Olson, "A Fresh Look at Industry and Market Analysis," *Business Horizons*, January–February 2002, p. 15–22; Kenneth Sawka and Bill Fiora, "The Four Analytical Techniques Every Analyst Must Know: 2. Porter's Five Forces Analysis," *Competitive Intelligence Magazine*, May–June 2003, p. 57; and Philip Kotler and Kevin Lane Keller, *Marketing Management*, 12th ed. (Upper Saddle River, NJ: Prentice Hall, 2006), pp. 342–343.

19. Nina Munk, "Why Women Find Lauder Mesmerizing," *Fortune*, May 25, 1998, pp. 97–106; Christine Bittar, "New Faces, Same Name," *Brandweek*, March 11, 2002, pp. 28–34; Robin Givhan, "Estee Lauder, Sending a Message in a Bottle," *Washington Post*, April 26, 2004, p. C.01; and information accessed at www.elcompanies.com, www.stila.com, and www.macmakeup.com, September 2006.

20. Arik Hesseldahl, "Apple Set to Take Bigger Bite of the Market," *BusinessWeek Online*, June 16, 2006; and Mark Veverka, "Beyond the iPod: Mac Attack," *Barron's*, July 17, 2006, pp. 20–23.

21. See Gerry Khermouch, "Call It the Pepsi Blue Generation," *BusinessWeek*, February 3, 2003, p. 96; Kathleen Sampey, "Sweet on Sierra Mist," *Adweek*, February 2, 2004, p. 20; Nat Ives, "Mountain Dew Double-Dose for Times Square Passers-By," *New York Times*, April 8, 2004, p. C9; and Phyllis Furman, "Mist-Takes Made Again: New Ads for Sierra Mist," *Knight Ridder Tribune Business News*, April 10, 2006, p. 1.

22. Gwendolyn Bounds, "How an Artist Fell into a Profitable Online Card Business," *Wall Street Journal*, December 21, 2004, p. B1; and David Smith, "UK's Cottage Industry Beats US Internet Giants," *The Observer*, February 12, 2006, accessed at http://oberserver.guardian.co.uk.

23. Adapted from examples in Darell K. Rigby and Vijay Vishwanath, "Localization: The Revolution in Consumer Markets," *Harvard Business Review*, April 2006, pp. 82–92. Also see Jon Springer, "Kroger Looks to New Formats, Positioning," *Supermarket News*, June 26, 2006, p. 1.

24. For a good discussion of mass customization and relationship building, see Don Peppers and Martha Rogers, *Managing Customer Relationships: A Strategic Framework* (Hoboken, NJ: John Wiley & Sons, 2004), chapter 10.

25. Example adapted from Michael Prospero, "Lego's New Building Blocks," *Fast Company*, October 2005, p. 35; with information from http://factory.lego.com/, September 2006.

26. Adapted from information found in Mark Tatge, "Red Bodies, Black Ink," *Forbes*, September 18, 2000, p. 114; "Oshkosh Truck Corporation," *Hoover's Company Records*, July 15, 2006, p. 14345; and information accessed at www.oshkoshtruckcorporation.com, September 2006.

27. See Susan Linn, *Consuming Kids: The Hostile Takeover of Childhood* (New York: The New Press, 2004); Suzy Bashford, "Time to Take More Responsibility?" *Marketing*, May 11, 2005, pp. 32–36; Sonia Reyes, "Kraft Foods Cited for Misleading Kids," August 4, 2005, accessed at www.brandweek.com; and William MacLeod, "Does Advertising Make Us Fat? No!" *Brandweek*, February 20, 2006, p. 19.

28. Andrew Adam Newman, "Youngsters Enjoy Beer Ads, Arousing Industry's Critics," *New York Times*, February 13, 2006, p. C15.

29. See "FBI Internet Crime Complaint Center Releases Stats," *States News Service*, April 6, 2006.

30. Jack Trout, "Branding Can't Exist without Positioning," *Advertising Age*, March 14, 2005, p. 28.

31. Adapted from a positioning map prepared by students Brian May, Josh Payne, Meredith Schakel, and Bryana Sterns, University of North Carolina, April 2003. SUV sales data furnished by WardsAuto.com, June 2006. Price data from www.edmunds.com, June 2006.

32. See Bobby J. Calder and Steven J. Reagan, "Brand Design," in Dawn Iacobucci, ed. *Kellogg on Marketing* (New York: John Wiley & Sons, 2001) p. 61. The Mountain Dew example is from Alice M. Tybout and Brian Sternthal, "Brand Positioning," in Iacobucci, ed., *Kellogg on Marketing*, p. 54.

CHAPTER 8

1. Extracts adapted from Betsy McKay and Cynthia Cho, "Water Works: How FIJI Brand Got Hip to Sip," *Wall Street Journal*, August 16, 2004, p. B1; and information found at www.fijiwater.com, July 2006. Also see Kate Macarthur, "Drink Your Fruits, Veggies: Water's the New Fitness Fad," *Advertising Age*, January 3, 2005, p. 4; and "Designer Michael Kors Partners with FIJI Water in New Fragrance Venture," press release, March 6, 2006, accessed at www.fijiwater.com/michael_kors.html.

2. Adapted from example in B. Joeseph Pine II and James H. Gilmore, "Trade in Ads for Experiences," *Advertising Age*, September 27, 2004, p. 36; with information from www.americangirlplace.com, July 2006. See also Mya Frazier, "$20 Doll Salon?" *American Girl Takes on Hollywood*," *Advertising Age*, March 13, 2006, p. S5; and Josefina Loza, "Moms, Daughters, and Dolls," *Omaha World-Herald*, May 30, 2006, p. 1E.

3. See "The Celebrity 100," *Forbes*, accessed at www.forbes.com, July 2006; and Reed Tucker, "Tiger Woods," *Fortune*, October 17, 2005, p. 142.

4. See Daniel Roth, "The Trophy Life," *Fortune*, April 19, 2004, pp. 70–84; Ryan Underwood, "Bring on the Clown," *Fast Company*, January 2005, p. 28; "New Trump Products on the Market," *Knight Ridder Tribune Business News*, February 26, 2005, p. 1; and "He's Hired: Trump Gets into Jewelry Business," *National-Jeweler.com*, June 1, 2006.

5. For more on marketing places, see Philip Kotler, Donald Haider, and Irving J. Rein, *Marketing Places* (New York: Free Press, 2002). Examples information found in Steve Dougherty, "In a Cold Country, the Nights Are Hot," *New York Times*, December 19, 2004, sect. 5, p. 1; and at www.TravelTex.com, www.iloveny.state.ny.us, and www.visiticeland.com, October 2006.

6. Accessed online at www.social-marketing.org/aboutus.html, October 2006.

7. See Alan R. Andreasen, Rob Gould, and Karen Gutierrez, "Social Marketing Has a New Champion," *Marketing News*, February 7, 2000, p. 38. Also see Philip Kotler, Ned Roberto, and Nancy Lee, *Social Marketing: Improving the Quality of Life*, 2nd ed. (Thousand Oaks, CA: Sage Publications, 2002); and www.social-marketing.org, October 2006.

8. Quotes and definitions from Philip Kotler, *Kotler on Marketing* (New York: Free Press, 1999), p. 17; and www.asq.org, October 2006.

9. See Roland T. Rust, Christine Moorman, and Peter R. Dickson, "Getting Return on Quality: Revenue Expansion, Cost Reduction, or Both?" *Journal of Marketing*, October 2002, pp. 7–24; and Roland T. Rust, Katherine N. Lemon, and Valarie A. Zeithaml, "Return on Marketing: Using Customer Equity to Focus Marketing Strategy," *Journal of Marketing*, January 2004, p. 109.

10. Adapted from information in Sarah Lacy, "How P&G Conquered Carpet," *BusinessWeek Online*, September 23, 2005, accessed at www.businessweek.com/innovate/content/sep2005/id20050923_571639.

11. For these and other examples, see Lee Gomes, "To Design Away Tears, SAP Aims to Make Simpler Software," *Wall Street Journal*, June 21, 2006, p. B1; Lisa Chamberlain, "Going Off the Beaten Path for New Design Ideas," *New York Times*, March 12, 2006; and IDEO's Web site at ideo.com/portfolio/, October 2006.

12. Based on Adam Horowitz et al., "101 Dumbest Moments in Business," *Business 2.0*, January–February 2005, p. 104; and Jason Norman, "Kryptonite's PR Maven Donna Tocci Can Not Be Broken," *Bicycle Retailer and Industry News*, June 1, 2005, p. 39.

13. Kate Fitzgerald, "Packaging Is the Capper," *Advertising Age*, May 5, 2003, p. 22. Also see Rebecca Bedrossian, "Packaging," *Communication Arts*, May/June 2006, pp. 92–101.

14. For these and other examples, see Susanna Hamner, "Packaging that Pays," *Business 2.0*, July 2006, pp. 68–69.

15. Based on Thomas J. Ryan, "Labels Grow Up," *Apparel*, February 2005, pp. 26–29.

16. Bro Uttal, "Companies That Serve You Best," *Fortune*, December 7, 1987, p. 116; Jamie LaReau, "Cadillac Wants to Boost Sales, Customer Service," *Automotive News*, February 20, 2006, p. 46; and American Customer Satisfaction Index ratings accessed at www.theacsi.org/second_quarter.htm#alv, August 2006.

17. Example adapted from Michelle Higgins, "Pop-Up Sales Clerks: Web Sites Try the Hard Sell," *Wall Street Journal*, April 15, 2004, p. D.1. Also see Dawn Chmielewski, "Software That Makes Tech Support Smarter," *Knight Ridder Tribune Business News*, December 25, 2005, p. 1.

18. Information accessed online at www.marriott.com, October 2006.

19. Information about Colgate's product lines accessed at www.colgate.com/app/Colgate/US/Corp/Products.cvsp, August 2006.

20. See "McAtlas Shrugged," *Foreign Policy*, May–June 2001, pp. 26–37; and Philip Kotler and Kevin Lane Keller, *Marketing Management*, 12th ed. (Upper Saddle River, NJ: Prentice Hall, 2006), pp. 290–291.

21. Al Ehrbar, "Breakaway Brands," *Fortune*, October 31, 2005, pp. 153–170. Also see "DeWalt Named Breakaway Brand," *Snips*, January 2006, p. 66.

22. David C. Bello and Morris. B. Holbrook, "Does an Absence of Brand Equity Generalize across Product Classes?" *Journal of Business Research*, October 1995, p. 125; and Scott Davis, *Brand Asset Management: Driving Profitable Growth through Your Brands* (San Francisco: Jossey-Bass, 2000). Also see Kevin Lane Keller, *Building, Measuring, and Managing Brand Equity*, 2nd ed. (Upper Saddle River, NJ: Prentice Hall, 2003), chapter 2; and Kusum Ailawadi, Donald R. Lehman, and Scott A. Neslin, "Revenue Premium as an Outcome Measure of Brand Equity," *Journal of Marketing*, October 2003, pp. 1–17.

23. "The 100 Top Brands," *BusinessWeek*, August 7, 2006, pp. 60–66. For another ranking, see Normandy Madden, "Hold the Phone," *Advertising Age*, April 10, 2006, pp. 4, 64.

24. Larry Selden and Yoko S. Selden, "Profitable Customer: Key to Great Brands," *Point*, July–August 2006, pp. 7–9. Also see Roland Rust, Katherine Lemon, and Valarie Zeithaml, "Return on Marketing: Using Customer Equity to Focus Marketing Strategy," *Journal of Marketing*, January 2004, p. 109; and Connie S. Olasz, "Marketing's Role in a Relationship Age," *Baylor Business Review*, Spring 2006, pp. 2–7.

25. See Scott Davis, *Brand Asset Management*, 2nd ed. (San Francisco: Jossey-Bass, 2002). For more on brand positioning, see Philip Kotler and Kevin Lane Keller, *Marketing Management*, 12th ed. (Upper Saddle River, NJ: Prentice Hall, 2006), chapter 10.

26. See Jacquelyn A. Ottman, Edwin R. Strattford, and Cathy L. Hartman, "Avoiding Green Marketing Myopia," *Environment*, June 2006, pp. 22–37.

27. Example adapted from Matthew Boyle, "Brand Killers," *Fortune*, August 11, 2003, pp. 89–100. See also "Battle of the Brands," *Consumer Reports*, August 2005, pp. 12–15; and Sonia Reyes, "Saving Private Labels," *Brandweek*, May 8, 2006, pp. 30–34.

28. See Sue Stock, "Grocer's Expand Private-Label Marketing Share," *Knight Ridder Tribune Business News*, May 26, 2005, p. 1; and Michael Fielding, "No Longer Plain, Simple," *Marketing News*, May 15, 2006, pp. 11–13.

29. See Margaret Webb Pressler, "Shelf Game; When Stores Force Makers to Pay Them Fees, You Lose," *The Washington Post*, January 18, 2004, p. F.05; and "Legislator Pushing for Disclosure on Slotting Fees," *Gourmet News*, April 2005, p. 3.

30. Jay Sherman, "Nick Puts Muscle Behind EverGirl," *TelevisionWeek*, January 5, 2004, p. 3; and "Nickelodeon Unveils Three New Toy Lines Based on Hit Properties," *PR Newswire*, February 10, 2006.

31. Wendy Zellner, "Your New Banker?" *BusinessWeek*, February 7, 2005, pp. 28–31; and Kathleen Day, "Piggy Banker?" *Washington Post*, February 12, 2006, p. F1.

32. Gabrielle Solomon, "Co-branding Alliances: Arranged Marriages Made by Marketers," *Fortune*, October 12, 1998, p. 188; and "Martha Stewart Upgrading from Kmart to Macys," *FinancialWire*, April 26, 2006, p. 1.

33. Based on information from Kate McArthur, "Cannibalization a Risk as Diet Coke Brand Tally Grows to Seven," *Advertising Age*, March 28, 2005, pp. 3, 123; "Coca-Cola Zero Pops into Stores Today," *Atlanta Business Chronicle*, June 13, 2005, accessed at http://atlanta.bizjournals.com/atlanta/stories/2005/06/13/daily7.html; and www2.coca-cola.com, July 2006.

34. For more on the use of line and brand extensions and consumer attitudes toward them, see Franziska Volckner and Henrik Sattler, "Drivers of Brand Extension Success," *Journal of Marketing*, April 2006, pp. 18–34; and Chris Pullig, Carolyn J. Simmons, and Richard G. Netemeyer, "Brand Dilution: When Do New Brands Hurt Existing Brands?" *Journal of Marketing*, April 2006, pp. 52–66.

35. Constantine von Hoffman, "P&G's House Cleaning May Sweep Away Classics," *Brandweek*, May 15, 2006, p. 5.

36. "100 Leading National Advertisers," supplement to *Advertising Age*, June 26, 2006, pp. 29 and 96.

37. Stephen Cole, "Value of the Brand," *CA Magazine*, May 2005, pp. 39–40.

38. See Kevin Lane Keller, "The Brand Report Card," *Harvard Business Review*, January 2000, pp. 147–157; Keller, *Strategic Brand Management*, pp. 766–767; and David A. Aaker, "Even Brands Need Spring Cleaning," *Brandweek*, March 8, 2004, pp. 36–40.

39. See CIA, *The World Factbook*, accessed at www.cia.gov/cia/publications/factbook/geos/us.html#Econ, August 2006; *International Trade Statistics 2005*, World Trade Organization, p. 23, accessed at www.wto.org; and information from the Bureau of Labor Statistics, www.bls.gov, accessed August 2006.

40. Adapted from information in Leonard Berry and Neeli Bendapudi, "Clueing in Customers," *Harvard Business Review*, February 2003, pp. 100–106; with information accessed at www.mayoclinic.org, October 2006.

41. See James L. Heskett, W. Earl Sasser Jr., and Leonard A. Schlesinger, *The Service Profit Chain: How Leading Companies Link Profit and Growth to Loyalty, Satisfaction, and Value* (New York: Free Press, 1997); Heskett, Sasser, and Schlesinger, *The Value Profit Chain: Treat Employees Like Customers and Customers Like Employees* (New York: Free Press, 2003); and "Recovering from Service Failure," *Strategic Direction*, June 2006, pp. 37–40.

42. William C. Johnson and Larry G. Chiagouris, "So Happy Together," *Marketing Management*, March–April 2006, pp. 47–50.

43. Based on Matthew Boyle, "The Wegmans Way," *Fortune*, January 24, 2005, pp. 62–68; with information from Mark Hamstra, "Wegmans, H-E-B Lead in Customer Satisfaction Study," *Supermarket News*, April 17, 2006, p. 22.

44. See "UPS Fact Sheet," accessed at http://pressroom.ups.com/mediakits/factsheet/0,2305,866,00.html, August 2006; and "Prescription Drug Trends," Kaiser Family Foundation, June 2006, accessed at www.kff.org/rxdrugs/upload/3057-05.pdf.

45. Brian Hindo, "Satisfaction Not Guaranteed," *BusinessWeek*, June 19, 2006, pp. 32–36.

CHAPTER 9

1. Quotes and other information in this Apple story from Terry Semel, "Steve Jobs: Perpetual Innovation Machine," *Time*, April 18, 2005, p. 78; Steve Maich, "Nowhere to Go But Down," *Maclean's*, May 9, 2005, p. 32; Brent Schlender, "How Big Can Apple Get," *Fortune*, February 21, 2005, pp. 67–76; Jim Dalrymple, "Apple's Uphill Climb," *Macworld*, June 2005, p. 16; Paul Sloan and Paul Kaihla, "What's Next for Apple," *Business 2.0*, April 2005; Peter Burrows and Andrew Park, "Apple's Bold Swim Downstream," *BusinessWeek*, January 24, 2005, p. 32; Bruce Nussbaum, "Get Creative!" *BusinessWeek*, August 1, 2005, pp. 61–70; "The World's Most Innovative Companies," *BusinessWeek*, April 24, 2006, p. 62; "Apple Posts Record Earnings," *Apple Matters*, July 20, 2006, p. 62; and Apple annual reports and other information accessed at www.apple.com, October 2006.

2. Robert S. Shulman, "Material Whirl," *Marketing Management*, March–April 2006, pp. 25–27.

3. Rick Romell, "Moving in the Right Direction: Segways Catch on in Niche Markets," *Milwaukee Journal Sentinel*, June 10, 2006, p. 1D.

4. For these and other facts and examples, see Jena McGregor, "How Failure Breeds Success," *BusinessWeek*, July 10, 2006, p. 42; and John T. Gourville, "Eager Sellers & Stony Buyers," *Harvard Business Review*, June 2006, pp. 98–106.

5. Information and examples from Gary Slack, "Innovations and Idiocities," *Beverage World*, November 15, 1998, p. 122; Robert M. McMath and Thom Forbes, *What Were They Thinking? Money-Saving, Time-Saving, Face-Saving Marketing Lessons You Can Learn from Products That Flopped* (New York: Times Business, 1999), various pages; Beatriz Cholo, "Living with Your 'Ex': A Brand New World," *Brandweek*, December 5, 2005, p. 4; and www.newproductworks.com/npw_difference/product_collection.html, September 2006.

6. Joel Berg, "Product Development: Look for Children's Insight," *Central Penn Business*, October 15, 2004, p. 3.

7. Based on material from Peter Lewis, "A Perpetual Crisis Machine," *Fortune*, September 19, 2005, pp. 58–67.

8. Richard Breeden, "By the Numbers—New or Improved," *Wall Street Journal*, July 11, 2006, p. B9.

9. William C. Taylor, "Here's an Idea: Let Everyone Have Ideas," *New York Times*, March 26, 2006, p. 3.3.

10. Based on quotes and information from Robert D. Hof, "The Power of Us," *BusinessWeek*, June 20, 2005, pp. 74–82. See also Robert Weisman, "Firms Turn R&D on Its Head, Looking Outside for Ideas," *Boston Globe*, May 14, 2006, p. E1.

11. Information accessed online at www.avon.com, October 2006.

12. "Business: The Rise of the Creative Consumer; the Future of Innovation," *Economist*, March 12, 2005, p. 75.

13. *Ibid.*, p. 75.

14. Robert Gray, "Not Invented Here," *Marketing*, May 6, 2004, pp. 34–37.

15. Example from www.Frogdesign.com, accessed July 2006.

16. See "DaimlerChrysler Presents California with Three F-Cell Fuel Cell Vehicles," *Fuel Cell Today*, June 1, 2005, accessed at www.fuelcelltoday.com; Steven Ashley, "On the Road to Fuel-Cell Cars," *Scientific American*, March 1, 2005, p. 62; and Kathy Jackson, "Calif. Leads the Way in Fleet Fuel Cell Tests," *Automotive News*, June 5, 2006, p. 35.

17. Becky Ebenkamp, "It's Like Cheers and Jeers, Only for Brands," *Brandweek*, March 19, 2001; Ebenkamp, "The Focus Group Has Spoken," *Brandweek*, April 23, 2001, p. 24; and information furnished by Mark Sneider, General Manager, AcuPoll, October 2004.

18. Examples adapted from those found in Carol Matlack, "The Vuitton Machine," *BusinessWeek*, March 22, 2004, pp. 98–102; and Brendan Koerner, "For Every Sport, A Supper Sock," *New York Times*, March 27, 2005, p. 3.2.

19. Joshua Freed, "Redbox Aims to Up Presence of DVD Kiosks," *Associated Press Online*, April 25, 2006.

20. Jack Neff, "Is Testing the Answer?" *Advertising Age*, July 9, 2001, p. 13; and Dale Buss, "P&G's Rise," *Potentials*, January 2003, pp. 26–30. For more on test marketing, see Philip Kotler and Kevin Lane Keller, *Marketing Management*, 12th ed. (Upper Saddle River, NJ: Prentice Hall, 2006), pp. 653–655.

21. Information on BehaviorScan accessed at www.infores. com/public/us/analytics/productportfolio/bscannew prodtest.htm, November 2006.

22. See Jack Neff, "Six-Blade Blitz," *Advertising Age*, September 9, 2005, pp. 3, 53; and William C. Symonds, "Gillette's New Edge," *BusinessWeek*, February 6, 2006, p. 44.

23. See William C. Symonds, "Gillette's New Edge," *BusinessWeek*, February 6, 2006, p. 44; and "Sales Are Razor Sharp," *Drug Store News*, April 10, 2006, p. 25.

24. See Jack Neff, "New SpinBrush Line Backed by $30 Million," *Advertising Age*, September 9, 2002, p. 36; and Jenn Abelson, "Firms Likely to Shed Some Products," *Knight Ridder Tribune Business News*, June 22, 2005, p.1.

25. Robert G. Cooper, "Formula for Success," *Marketing Management*, March–April 2006, pp. 19–23.

26. Examples adapted from information in Jennifer Reingold, "The Interpreter," *Fast Company*, June 2005, pp. 59–61; and Jonah Bloom, "Beth Has an Idea," *Point*, September 2005, pp. 9–14. Also see Paul Bennett, "Listening Lessons: Make Consumers Part of the Design Process by Tuning In," *Point*, March 2006, pp. 9–10; and Larry Selden and Ian C. MacMillan, "Manage Customer-Centric Innovation—Systematically," *Harvard Business Review*, April 2006, pp. 108–116.

27. Lawrence A. Crosby and Sheree L. Johnson, "Customer-Centric Innovation," *Marketing Management*, March–April 2006, pp. 12–13.

28. See Philip Kotler, *Kotler on Marketing* (New York, NY: The Free Press, 1999), pp. 43–44; Judy Lamont, "Idea Management: Everyone's an Innovator," *KM World*, November/December 2004, pp. 14–16; and J. Roland Ortt, "Innovation Management: Different Approaches to Cope with the Same Trends," *Management*, 2006, pp. 296–318.

29. See Tim Studt, "3M—Where Innovation Rules," *R&D*, April 2003, pp. 20–24; Tim Stevens, "3M Reinvents Its Innovation Process," *Research Technology Management*, March/April 2004, p. 3; Daniel Del Re, "Pushing Past Post-Its," *Business 2.0*, November 2005, pp. 54–56; and "Innovation at 3M," accessed at www.3m.com/about3m/innovation/index.jhtml, October 2006. Also see Blair Sheppard and Michael Canning, "Innovation Culture," *Leadership Excellence*, January 2006, p. 18.

30. Laurie Freeman, "Study: Leading Brands Aren't Always Enduring," *Advertising Age*, February 28, 2000, p. 26. Also see, Veronica MacDonald, "Soaps and Detergents: Going the World Over to Clean," *Chemical Week*, January 6, 2005, pp. 21–24.

31. This definition is based on one found in Bryan Lilly and Tammy R. Nelson, "Fads: Segmenting the Fad-Buyer Market," *Journal of Consumer Marketing*, vol. 20, no. 3, 2003, pp. 252–265.

32. See "Scooter Fad Fades, as Warehouses Fill and Profits Fall," *Wall Street Journal*, June 14, 2001, p. B4; Katya Kazakina, "Toy Story: Yo-Yos Make a Big Splash," *Wall Street Journal*, April 11, 2003, p. W–10; Robert Johnson, "A Fad's Father Seeks a Sequel," *New York Times*, May 30, 2004, p. 3.2; and Tom McGhee, "Spotting Trends, Eschewing Fads," *Denver Post*, May 29, 2006.

33. Youngme Moon, "Break Free from the Product Life Cycle," *Harvard Business Review*, May 2005, pp. 87–94.

34. These and other uses found in "Always Another Use," www.wd40.com/Brands/wd40.cfm, October 2006.

35. For a more comprehensive discussion of marketing strategies over the course of the product life cycle, see Philip Kotler and Kevin Lane Keller, *Marketing Management*, 12th ed. (Upper Saddle River, NJ: Prentice Hall, 2006), pp. 321–335.

36. See "Ford Motor Co.: Jury Orders Auto Maker to Pay $369 in Explorer Case," *Wall Street Journal*, June 4, 2004, p. 1; Lanny R. Berke, "Design for Safety," *Machine Design*, February 17, 2005, pp. 48–49; "Year-by-Year Analysis Reveals an Overall Compensatory Award of $1,500,000 for Products Liability Cases," *Personal Injury Verdict Reviews*, July 3, 2006; and Emily Umbright, "Report Finds Product Lia-

...bility Cases on the Decline," *St. Louis Daily Record*, July 10, 2006.

37. For these and other examples, see Darell K. Rigby and Vijay Vishwanath, "Localization: The Revolution in Consumer Markets," *Harvard Business Review*, April 2006, pp. 82–92.

38. Information accessed online at www.deutsche-bank.com, October 2006.

39. Information accessed online at www.interpublic.com and www.mccann.com, October 2006.

40. See "Wal-Mart International Operations," accessed at www.walmartstores.com, July 2006; "2005 Global Powers of Retailing," *Stores*, January 2005, accessed at www.stores.org; and information accessed at www.carrefour.com/english/groupecarrefour/profil.jsp, October 2006.

CHAPTER 10

1. Thomas T. Nagle and John E. Hogan, *The Strategy and Tactics of Pricing*, 4th ed. (Upper Saddle River, NJ: Prentice Hall, 2006), p. 1.

2. Extracts and quotes from Nanette Byrnes, "Toys 'R' Us: Beaten at Its Own Game," *BusinessWeek*, March 29, 2004, pp. 89–90; and Jeffrey Gold, "Toys 'R' Us," *Raleigh News & Observer*, July 5, 2006, p. 8C. Also see Joan Verdon, "Toys 'R' Us Closes Deal to Go Private," *Knight Ridder Tribune Business News*, July 22, 2005, p. 1; and Doug Desjardins, "Babies 'R' Us Ready for Growth Spurt," *DSNRetailing Today*, May 8, 2006, p. 6.

3. George Mannes, "The Urge to Unbundle," *Fast Company*, February 27, 2005, pp. 23–24.

4. Linda Tischler, "The Price is Right," *Fast Company*, November 2003, pp.83–91. See also Wendy Melillo, "The Gold Standard," *Brandweek*, June 5, 2006, pp. 18–20.

5. Paul S. Hunt, "Seizing the Fourth P," *Marketing Management*, May–June 2005, pp. 40–44.

6. John Tayman, "The Six-Figure Steal," *Business 2.0*, June 2005, pp. 148–150.

7. See Claudia H. Deutsch, "Name Brands Embrace Some Less-Well-Off Kinfolk," *New York Times*, June 24, 2005, p. C7; and information from www.charmin.com/en_us/pages/prod_basic.shtml, August 2006.

8. See Tracy Turner, "Lowering the Bar," *The Columbus Dispatch*, October 26, 2005, p. 1C; and Ruth N. Bolton, Detra Y. Montoya, and Venkatesh Shankar, "Beyond EDLP and HiLo: A New Customized Approach to Retail Pricing," *European Retail Digest*, Spring 2006, pp. 7–10.

9. William F. Kendy, "The Price Is Too High," *Selling Power*, April 2006, pp. 30–33.

10. Erin Stout, "Keep Them Coming Back for More," *Sales & Marketing Management*, February 2002, pp. 51–52. Also see Gerald E. Smith and Thomas T. Nagle, "A Question of Value," *Marketing Management*, July–August 2005, pp. 39–44; and William F. Kendy, "Value as a Sales Tool," *Selling Power*, July–August 2006, pp. 39–41.

11. Here accumulated production is drawn on a semilog scale so that equal distances represent the same percentage increase in output.

12. The arithmetic of markups and margins is discussed in Appendix 2, "Marketing by the Numbers."

13. See Robert Berner, "Why P&G's Smile Is So Bright," *BusinessWeek*, August 12, 2002, pp. 58–60; Jack Neff, "Power Brushes a Hit at Every Level," *Advertising Age*, May 26, 2003, p. 10; Matt Phillips, "Sales of Toothbrushes Decline as Consumers Look to Electric Models," *Knight Ridder Tribune Business News*, November 12, 2004, p. 1; Robert Brenner and William C. Symonds, "Welcome to Procter & Gadget," *Business Week*, February 7, 2005, p. 76; and information accessed at www.spinbrush.com, August 2005.

14. Joshua Rosenbaum, "Guitar Maker Looks for a New Key," *Wall Street Journal*, February 11, 1998, p. B1; and information accessed online at www.gibson.com, October 2006.

15. See Nagle and Hogan, *The Strategy and Tactics of Pricing*, chapter 7.

16. Information and quotes accessed at www.greenmountain.com, December 2004.

17. See Robert J. Dolan, "Pricing: A Value-Based Approach," *Harvard Business School Publishing*, 9-500-071, November 3, 2003.

CHAPTER 11

1. Adapted from Matthew Maier, "A Radical Fix for Airlines: Make Flying Free," *Business 2.0*, April 2006, pp. 32–34. Also see Greg Lindsey, "Airworld Wars," *Advertising Age*, October 24, 2005, pp. 12, 16; "Singapore Airlines Still Flying High," transcript from *Weekend Edition Saturday*, NPR, May 27, 2006; Scott McCartney, "Competition Heats Up over Luxury Flights," *Wall Street Journal*, April 4, 2006, p. D1; and Brian Hindo, "Satisfaction Not Guaranteed," *BusinessWeek*, June 19, 2006, pp. 32–36.

2. For comprehensive discussions of pricing strategies, see Thomas T. Nagle and John E. Hogan, *The Strategy and Tactics of Pricing*, 4th ed. (Upper Saddle River, NJ: Prentice Hall, 2006).

3. See Philip Kotler and Kevin Lane Keller, *Marketing Management*, 12th ed. (Upper Saddle River, NJ: Prentice Hall, 2006), p. 438; and Robert Evatt, "Video Fans Tuning in to HDTV Experience: Prices of High-Definition Television Sets Continue to Fall," *Tulsa World*, July 16, 2006, p. 1.

4. "Shortage of New Xboxes Puts Drag on U.S. Game Industry," *Toronto Star*, January 15, 2006, p. A21.

5. Michael Buettner, "Charleston, S.C.-Based Asphalt Innovations Turns Waste into Helpful Product," *Knight Ridder Tribune Business News*, October 18, 2004, p. 1; and www.meadwestvaco.com, accessed October 2006.

6. Susan Krafft, "Love, Love Me Doo," *American Demographics*, June 1994, pp. 15–16; "That Zoo Doo that You Do So Well," accessed at www.csis.org/states/expzoodoo.html, March 2004; "Time Again for Zoo's Annual Spring Fecal Fest!" Woodland Park Zoo Press Release, February 27, 2004, accessed at www.zoo.org; and "Woodland Park Zoo Doo," accessed at http://zoo.org/zoo_info/special/zoodoo.htm, November 2006.

7. See Nagle and Holden, *The Strategy and Tactics of Pricing*, pp. 244–247; Stefan Stremersch and Gerard J. Tellis,

"Strategic Bundling of Products and Prices: A New Synthesis for Marketing," *Journal of Marketing Research*, January 2002, pp. 55–72; Chris Janiszewski and Marcus Cunha, Jr., "The Influence of Price Discount Framing on the Evaluation of a Product Bundle," *Journal of Marketing Research*, March 2004, pp. 534–546; and "Save a Bundle, Comcast Says," *Tacoma News Tribune*, July 25, 2006.

8. Example adapted from Charles Fishman, "Which Price Is Right?" *Fast Company*, March 2003, pp. 92–96. Additional data from "Continental Airlines Reports July 2006 Operational Performance," Continental Financial and Traffic Releases, accessed at www.continental.com/company/investor/news.asp.

9. For more discussion, see Manoj Thomas and Vicki Morvitz, "Penny Wise and Pound Foolish: The Double-Digit Effect in Price Cognition," *Journal of Consumer Research*, June 2005, pp. 54–64; and Heyong Min Kim and Luke Kachersky, "Dimensions of Price Salience: A Conceptual Framework for Perceptions of Multi-Dimensional Prices," *Journal of Product and Brand Management*, 2006, vol. 15, no. 2, pp. 139–147.

10. Tim Ambler, "Kicking Price Promotion Habit Is Like Getting Off Heroin—Hard," *Marketing*, May 27, 1999, p. 24. Also see Robert Gray, "Driving Sales at Any Price?" *Marketing*, April 11, 2002, p. 24; and Lauren Kellere Johnson, "Dueling Pricing Strategies," *MIT Sloan Management Review*, Spring 2003, pp. 10–11; and Peter R. Darke and Cindy M. Y. Chung, "Effects of Pricing and Promotion on Consumer Perceptions: It Depends of How You Frame It," *Journal of Retailing*, 2005, pp. 35–47.

11. See "Dell, the Conqueror," *BusinessWeek*, September 24, 2001, pp. 92–102; Andy Serwer, "Dell Does Domination," *Fortune*, January 21, 2002, pp. 70–75; and Pui-Wing Tam, "H-P Gains Applause as It Cedes PC Market Share to Dell," *Wall Street Journal*, January 18, 2005, p. C1; Andrea Orr, "Doors Closing on Creaky Gateway," *Daily Deal*, February 10, 2006; Richard Waters, "HP Sees Unexpected Jump in Profits for PCs Computer Technology," *Financial Times*, February 16, 2006, p. 25; and "The Merits of A Diverse Portfolio," *Business Today*, July 2, 2006, p. 10.

12. Robert D. Hof, "Going, Going, Gone," *BusinessWeek*, April 12, 1999, pp. 30–32. Also see Philip Kotler and Kevin Lane Keller, *Marketing Management*, 12th ed. (Upper Saddle River, NJ: Prentice Hall, 2006), pp. 432–433.

13. Thomas L. Friedman, *The World Is Flat: A Brief History of the Twenty-First Century* (New York: Farrar, Straus and Giroux, 2005), pp. 417–418.

14. See Melissa Campanelli, "Getting Personal," *Entrepreneur*, October 2005, pp 44–46.

15. Philip R. Cateora, *International Marketing*, 7th ed. (Homewood, IL: Irwin, 1990), p. 540. Also see Barbara Stottinger, "Strategic Export Pricing: A Long and Winding Road," *Journal of International Marketing*, 2001, pp. 40–63; and Warren J. Keegan and Mark C. Green, *Global Marketing*, 4th ed. (Upper Saddle River, NJ: Prentice Hall, 2005), chapter 11.

16. For discussions of these issues, see Dhruv Grewel and Larry D. Compeau, "Pricing and Public Policy: A Research Agenda and Overview of Special Issue," *Journal of Public Policy and Marketing*, Spring 1999, pp. 3–10; and Michael

V. Marn, Eric V. Roegner, and Craig C. Zawada, *The Price Advantage* (Hoboken, NJ: John Wiley & Sons, 2004), Appendix 2.

17. "Three Chipmakers Settle Antitrust Lawsuit," *Financial Wire*, May 11, 2006, p. 1; and Kevin Allison, "Chipmakers Face Suit over Price-Fixing," *Financial Times*, July 14, 2006, p. 23.

18. "Predatory-Pricing Law Passed by New York Governor," *National Petroleum News*, December 2003, p. 7; and Brenden Timpe, "House Rejects Bill to Protect Gas Stations from Wal-Mart-Style Competition," *Knight Ridder Tribune Business News*, March 26, 2005, p. 1.

19. "FTC Guides Against Deceptive Pricing," accessed at www.ftc.gov/bcp/guides/decptprc.htm, December 2006.

CHAPTER 12

1. Quotes and other information from Donald V. Fites, "Make Your Dealers Your Partners," *Harvard Business Review*, March-April 1996, pp. 84–95; Sandra Ward, "The Cat Comes Back," *Barron's*, February 25, 2002, pp. 21–24; Michael Arndt, "Cat Claws Its Way into Services," *BusinessWeek*, December 5, 2005, pp. 56–59; "Global Construction & Farm Machinery: Industry Profile," *Datamonitor*, June 2006, accessed at www.datamonitor.com; Iian Brat, "Caterpillar Posts 38% Profit Rise, Raises Outlook on Strong Demand," *Wall Street Journal*, July 22, 2006, p. A2; "Caterpillar, Inc.," *BusinessWeek*, April 3, 2006, p. 100; and information accessed at www.caterpillar.com, October 2006.

2. Based on information from Stephanie Thompson and Kack Neff, "Retailer Revolt Causes $40M Loss at Revlon," *Advertising Age*, July 17, 2006, pp. 3, 28.

3. Matthew Boyle, "Brand Killers," *Fortune*, August 11, 2003, pp. 89–100; and information accessed at www.giantfood.com and www.luxottica.com/english/profilo_aziendale/index_keyfacts.html, October 2006.

4. Miguel Helft, "Fashion Fast Forward," *Business 2.0*, May 2002, p. 60; John Tagliabue, "A Rival to Gap That Operates Like Dell," *New York Times*, May 30, 2003, p. W-1; Kasra Ferdows, Michael A. Lewis, and Jose A. D. Machuca, "Rapid-Fire Fulfillment," *Harvard Business Review*, November 2004, pp. 104–110; Brian Dunn, "Inside the Zara Business Model," *DNR*, March 20, 2006, p. 11; Rachael Tiplady, "ZARA: Taking the Lead in Fast-Fashion," *BusinessWeek Online*, April 4, 2006, accessed at www.businessweek.com/globalbiz/content/apr2006/gb20060404_167078.htm; and annual reports and other information from www.inditex.com; October 2006.

5. See Ilan Alon, "The Use of Franchising by U.S.-Based Retailers," *Journal of Small Business Management*, April 2001, pp. 111–122; John Reynolds, "Economics 101: How Franchising Makes Music for the U.S. Economy," *Franchising World*, May 2004, pp. 37–40; Stacy Perman, "Extending the Front Lines of Franchising," *BusinessWeek Online*, April 12, 2005, accessed at www.bwonline.com; and "Answers to the 21 Most Commonly Asked Questions About Franchising," accessed online at the International Franchise Association Web Site, www.franchise.org/content.asp?contentid=379, October 2006.

6. Andrew Yeh, "McDonald's Seeks Heavy Traffic Fast-Food Expansion," *Financial Times*, June 21, 2006, p. 12.

7. Information accessed at www.mind-advertising.com/ch/nestea_ch.htm and www.nestle.com/Our_Brands/Breakfast_Cereals/Overview/Breakfast+Cereals.htm, September 2006. Also see Andrew McMains, "Anomaly to Introduce Gold Peak Tea," July 25, 2006, accessed at www.adweek.com.

8. Quotes and information from Normandy Madden, "Two Chinas," *Advertising Age*, August 16, 2004, pp. 1, 22; Dana James, "Dark Clouds Should Part for International Marketers," *Marketing News*, January 7, 2002, pp. 9, 13; Russell Flannery, "Red Tape," *Forbes*, March 3, 2003, pp. 97–100; and Russell Flannery, "China: The Slow Boat," *Forbes*, April 12, 2004, p. 76.

9. Nanette Byrnes, "Avon Calls, China Opens the Door," *BusinessWeek Online*, February 28, 2006, p. 19.

10. Mitch Betts, "GE Appliance Park Still an IT Innovator," *Computerworld*, January 29, 2001, pp. 20–21; and "What Is GE CustomerNet?" accessed online at www.geappliances.com/ buildwithge/index_cnet.htm, October 2006.

11. For a full discussion of laws affecting marketing channels, see Anne Coughlin, Erin Anderson, Louis W. Stern, and Adel El-Ansary, *Marketing Channels*, 7th ed. (Upper Saddle River, NJ: Prentice Hall, 2006), chapter 10.

12. Martin Piszczalksi, "Logistics: A Difference Between Winning and Losing," *Automotive Manufacturing & Production*, May 2001, pp. 16–18; Neil Shister, "Redesigned Supply Chain Positions Ford for Global Competition," *World Trade*, May 2005, pp. 20–26; and "Logistics Costs on the Rise," *Modern Materials Handling*, July 2006, p. 11.

13. Shlomo Maital, "The Last Frontier of Cost Reduction," *Across the Board*, February 1994, pp. 51–52; "Wal-Mart to Expand Supercenters to California," *Business Journal*, May 15, 2002, accessed online at http://sanjose.bizjournals.com; and information accessed online at www.walmartstores.com, October 2006.

14. Gail Braccidiferro, "One Town's Rejection Is Another's 'Let's Do Business,'" *New York Times*, June 15, 2003, p. 2; Christopher Dinsmore, "Wal-Mart to Add 1 Million Square Feet to Virginia Import Distribution Center," *Knight Ridder Tribune Business News*, May 29, 2004, p. 1; *Hoover's Company Capsules*, August 2006, p. 11600; Dan Scheraga, "Wal-Mart's Muscle," *Chain Store Age*, June 2005, pp. 64–65; and Dan Scheraga, "Wal-Smart," *Chain Store Age*, January 2006 supplement, pp. 16A–21A.

15. "Adding a Day to Dell," *Traffic World*, February 21, 2005, p1; William Hoffman, "Dell Ramps Up RFID," *Traffic World*, April 18, 2005, p. 1; and William Hofman, "Dell Beats the Clock," *Traffic World*, October 24, 2005, p. 1.

16. See Ann Bednarz, "IBM Has Some Tall RFID Plans," *Network World*, May 2, 2005, pp. 17–18; "RFID: From Potential to Reality," *Frozen Food Age*, April 2005, p. 40; Jack Neff, "P&G Products to Wear Wire," *Advertising Age*, December 15, 2004, pp. 1, 32; Tom Van Riper, "Retailers Eye RFID Technology to Make Shopping Easier," *Knight Ridder Tribune Business News*, May 23, 2005, p. 1; John S. McClenahen, "Wal-Mart's Big Gamble," *Industry Week*, April 2005, pp. 42–46; and Mark Roberti, "Using RFID at Item Level," *Chain Store Age*, July 2006, pp. 56–57.

17. Transportation percentages and other figures in this section are from Bureau of Transportation Statistics, "Freight in America," January 2006, accessed at www.bts.gov/publications; and Bureau of Transportation Statistics, "Pocket Guide to Transportation 2006," January 2006, accessed at www.bts.gov/publications/pocket_guide_to_transportation/2006/.

18. Ann Bednarz, "Internet EDI: Blending Old and New," *Network World*, February 23, 2004, pp. 29–31; Laurie Sullivan, "Hey, Wal-Mart, A New Case of Pampers Is on the 100," *Supply & Demand Chain Executive*, July 2006; accessed at www.sdcexec.com/article.asp?article_id=8812.

19. See "Supply Chain Management Systems," *Logistics Today*, 2006, pp.34–42; and Sarah Murray and Andrew K. Reese, "The 2006 Supply & Demand Chain Executive 100," *Supply & Demand Chain Executive*, January 23, 2006, p. 28; and Connie Robbins Gentry, "No More Holes at Krispy Kreme," *Chain Store Age*, July 2006, pp. 64–65.

20. Michael Barbaro, "Upscale Tastes Invade Wal-Mart's Hometown," *Washington Post*, June 27, 2005, p. A1; and Michelle Bradford, "Vendor Families Propel Region's Shift to Affluence," *Arkansas Democrat-Gazette*, February 5, 2006.

21. John Paul Quinn, "3PLs Hit Their Stride," *Logistics Management/Supply Chain Management Review*, July 2006, pp. 3T–8T.

CHAPTER 13

1. Based on quotes and information from Diane Brady, "Eating Too Fast at Whole Foods," *BusinessWeek*, October 24, 2005, pp. 82–84; Samantha Thompson Smith, "Grocer's Success Seems Entirely Natural," *The News & Observer*, May 21, 2004, p. D1; Marianne Wilson, "Retail as Theater, Naturally," *Chain Store Age*, May 25, 2005, p. 182; Julie Schlosser, "After a Dip, Whole Foods Looks Tasty," *Fortune*, April 3, 2006, p. 115; and www.wholefoods.com, October 2006.

2. "Supermarkets' Shrinking Share in Food Retailing Marketing Sparks Opportunities for Alternative Food Retail Channels," *M2PressWIRE*, March 31, 2006.

3. See Robert Manor, "Online Grocers Seek Method that Clicks," *Chicago Tribune*, August 22, 2006, accessed at www.chicagotribune.com; Christopher Conkey, "Green Thumb: Internet Grocers Can Help You Avoid Supermarket, but Is It Worth the Price?" *Wall Street Journal*, July 22, 2006, p. B1; and Justin Hibbard, "Put Your Money Where Your Mouth Is," *BusinessWeek*, September 18, 2006, pp. 61–62.

4. "Convenience Store Industry Sales Hit New Highs in 2005," April 5, 2006, accessed online at www.nacsonline.com/.

5. Adapted from Elizabeth Esfahani, "7-Eleven Gets Sophisticated," *Business 2.0*, January–February 2005, pp. 93–100. Also see Tatiana Serafin, "Smokes and Sandwiches," *Forbes*, February 13, 2006, p. 120.

6. Patricia Callahan and Ann Zimmerman, "Price War in Aisle 3—Wal-Mart Tops Grocery List with Supercenter

References

Format," *Wall Street Journal*, May 27, 2003, p. B-1; Mike Troy, "What Setback? Supercenters Proliferate," *DSN Retailing Today*, May 17, 2004, p. 1; Elliot Zwiebach, "Wal-Mart's Next Weapon," *Supermarket News*, March 7, 2005, p. 14; Lucia Moses, "Supermarkets' Share Seen Fading," *Supermarket News*, February 6, 2006, p. 8; and Wal-Mart 2006 Annual Report, accessed at www.walmartstores.com.

7. Adapted from John Helyar, "The Only Company Wal-Mart Fears," *Fortune*, November 24, 2003, pp. 158–166. Also see Susan Reda, "Filling My Cart at Costco," *Stores*, February 2005, p. 8; David Moin, "The Simple Life: Warehouse Clubs Go Beyond the Basics," *WWD*, July 10, 2006, p. 20B; and Costco Wholesale Corporation, *Hoover's Company Records*, Austin, August 2006, p. 17060.

8. See "Quick Franchise, Franchising, Facts and Statistics," accessed at www.azfranchises.com/franchisefacts.htm, September 2006; and information accessed at www.subway.com and www.mcdonalds.com/corp.html, November 2006.

9. "Who Said That?" *Marketing Management*, January–February 2005, p. 4.

10. Portions adapted from Bridget Finn, "For Petco, Success Is a Bitch," *Business 2.0*, November 2003, p. 54. Also see Petco Animal Supplies, Inc., *Hoover's Company Records*, Austin, August 2006, p. 17256.

11. Laurie Sullivan, "Brand This: Department Stores Capitalize on Their Names," *InformationWeek*, April 18, 2005, pp. 61–67; and David Moin, "Private Label Redux: SFA Plans to Roll Out Three Women's Lines," *WWD*, June 6, 2006, pp. 1, 14.

12. Leander Kahney, "The Genius of Apple's Stores," *WiredNews*, May 2, 2006, accessed at www.wired.com/news/columns/0,70787-0.html.

13. Adapted from "At Home in the Apple Store: A Welcoming Temple to a Devout Member of the Cult," *Saint Paul Pioneer Press*, June 19, 2006.

14. See Lorrie Grant, "Maytag Stores Let Shoppers Try Before They Buy," *USA Today*, June 7, 2004, p. 7B; and Alison Neumer Lara, "Chance to Do Laundry Puts Brand Loyalty to the Test," *Knight Ridder Tribune Business News*, November 16, 2005, p. 1.

15. Information drawn from "The History of Mall of America," accessed online at www.mallofamerica.com, October 2006.

16. Andrea Bermudez, "Bijan Dresses the Wealthy for Success," *Apparel News.Net*, December 1–7, 2000, accessed online at www.apparelnews.net/Archieve/120100/News/newsfeat.htm; Mimi Avins, "FASHION; More is More; Over-the-Top Isn't High Enough for Bijan, Whose Boutique Embraces Excess," *Los Angeles Times*, January 5, 2003, p. E.1; and information accessed at www.bijan.com/boutique, August 2006.

17. For a good discussion of retail pricing and promotion strategies, see Kathleen Seiders and Glenn B. Voss, "From Price to Purchase," *Marketing Management*, November–December 2005, pp. 38–43.

18. Paul Lukas, "Our Malls, Ourselves," *Fortune*, October 18, 2004, pp. 243–256; Ryan Chittum, "Mall-Building Industry Takes Stock," *Wall Street Journal*, May 17, 2006,

p. B7; and information accessed on the International Council of Shopping Centers Web site, www.icsc.org, October 2006.

19. Dean Starkman, "The Mall, Without the Haul—'Lifestyle Centers' Slip Quietly into Upscale Areas, Mixing Cachet and 'Curb Appeal," *Wall Street Journal*, July 25, 2001, p. B1; "To Mall or Not to Mall?" *Buildings*, June 2004, p. 99; Arlyn Tobian Gajilan, "Wolves in Shops' Clothing," *Fortune Small Business*, February 2005, pp. 17–18; Jenny Kincaid, "An Inside Look at Outdoor Malls," *Roanoke Times*, April 9, 2006; and information accessed on the International Council of Shopping Centers Web site, www.icsc.org, October 2006.

20. See Amy Barrett, "A Retailing Pacesetter Pulls Up Lame," *BusinessWeek*, July 12, 1993, pp. 122–123; and John Helyar, "The Only Company Wal-Mart Fears," *Fortune*, November 24, 2003, pp. 158–166; Heather Todd, "Club Stores Pack 'Em In," *Beverage World*, April 15, 2005, pp. 44–45.

21. See Malcolm P. McNair and Eleanor G. May, "The Next Revolution of the Retailing Wheel," *Harvard Business Review*, September–October 1978, pp. 81–91; Stephen Brown, "The Wheel of Retailing: Past and Future," *Journal of Retailing*, Summer 1990, pp. 143–147; Stephen Brown, "Variations on a Marketing Enigma: The Wheel of Retailing Theory," *Journal of Marketing Management*, 7, no. 2, 1991, pp. 131–155; Jennifer Negley, "Retrenching, Reinventing and Remaining Relevant," *Discount Store News*, April 5, 1999, p. 11; and Don E. Schultz, "Another Turn of the Wheel," *Marketing Management*, March–April 2002, pp. 8–9; and Carol Krol, "Staples Preps Easier E-Commerce Site," *BtoB*, March 14, 2005, pp. 3–4.

22. See "Best of the Web—The Top 50 Retailing Sites," *Internet Retailer*, December 2004, accessed at www.internetretailer.com; Sungwook Min and Mary Wolfinbarger, "Market Share, Profit Margin, and Marketing Efficiency of Early Movers, Bricks and Clicks, and Specialists in E-Commerce," *Journal of Business Research*, August 2005, pp. 1030+; and "Peapod and Scholastic Deliver Highest Consistency Rate," *Internet Retailer*, May 10, 2006, accessed at www.internetretailer.com.

23. "Online Sales to Surpass $200 Billion This Year," May 23, 2006, accessed at www.shop.org/press/06/052306.asp.

24. Joseph Pereira, "Staples Posts Strong Earnings on High-Margin Internet Sales," *Wall Street Journal*, March 5, 2004, p. A13; "The BusinessWeek 50: Staples, Inc.," *BusinessWeek*, April 3, 2006, p. 97; and information accessed online at www.staples.com, October 2006.

25. Alice Z. Cuneo, "What's in Store?" *Advertising Age*, February 25, 2002, pp. 1, 30–31. Also see Robert Berner, "Dark Days in White Goods for Sears," *Business Week*, March 10, 2003, pp. 78–79.

26. See "The Fortune 500," *Fortune*, April 17, 2006, p. F1.

27. Adapted form information found in Christina Rexrode, "Concept Store in Bloom," *Herald-Sun*, June 6, 2004, pp. F1, F3; "Food Lion Opens First Bloom Concept Store," press release, May 25, 2004, accessed at www.foodlion.com/news.asp?parm=323; Richard Shulman, "Applied Science," *Progressive Grocer*, April 1, 2005, pp. 22–24; "Food Lion 'Blooms' Outside of North Carolina," *Gourmet Retailer*, June 2006, pp. 12–13; and www.shopbloom.com, December 2006.

28. "Wal-Mart International Operations," September 2006, accessed online at www.walmartstores.com.

29. See "2006 Global Powers of Retailing," *Stores*, January 2006, accessed at www.nxtbook.com/nxtbooks/nrfe/stores0106-globalretail/index.php.

30. See Dexter Roberts, Wendy Zellner, and Carol Matlack, "Let the Retail Wars Begin," *BusinessWeek*, January 17, 2005, pp. 44–45; "Carrefour: At the Intersection of Global," *DSN Retailing Today*, September 18, 2000, p. 16; "Top 250 Global Retailers," *Stores*, January 2006, accessed at www.nxtbook.com/nxtbooks/nrfe/stores0106-globalretail/index.php.; and information from www.carrefour.com, accessed October 2006.

31. Adapted from information in "Nike Will Outfit U.S. Men's National Soccer Team in Germany This Summer," *Business Wire*, May 2, 2006; and Stanley Holmes, "Nike: It's Not a Shoe It's a Community," *BusinessWeek*, July 24, 2006, p. 50.

32. See the Grainger 2006 Fact Book and other information accessed at www.grainger.com, October 2006.

33. See Dale Buss, "The New Deal," *Sales & Marketing Management*, June 2002, pp. 25–30; and Colleen Gourley, "Redefining Distribution," *Warehousing Management*, October 2000, pp. 28–30; Steve Konicki and Eileen Colkin, "Attitude Adjustment," *InformationWeek*, March 25, 2002, pp. 20–22; and Stewart Scharf, "Grainger: Tooled Up for Growth," *BusinessWeek Online*, April 25, 2006, p. 8.

34. "McKesson: Raising Expectations," *Modern Materials Handling*, February 2004, p. 53; and information from "About Us" and "Supply Management Online," accessed online at www.mckesson.com, October 2006.

35. Facts accessed at www.supervalu.com, October 2006.

CHAPTER 14

1. Portions adapted from Warren Berger, "Dare-Devils," *Business 2.0*, April 2004, p. 110; with quotes and other information from David Kiley, "The Craziest Ad Guys in America," *BusinessWeek*, May 22, 2006, pp. 73–80; Matthew Creamer, "Agency of the Year," *Advertising Age*, January 10, 2005, pp. S1-S2; Mae Anderson, "Crispin, Burger King Win Grand Clio," May 24, 2005, accessed at www.adweek.com; "Blood, Sweat, and the Agency of the Year," *Creativity*, December 2005; and Kate MacArthur, "BK Rebels Fall in Love with King," *Advertising Age*, May 1, 2006, pp. 1–2.

2. The first four of these definitions are adapted from Peter D. Bennett, *The AMA Dictionary of Marketing Terms*, 2nd ed. (New York: McGraw-Hill, 1995). Other definitions can be found at www.marketingpower.com/live/mg-dictionary.php?, August 2006.

3. Bob Garfield, "The Chaos Scenario," *Advertising Age*, April 4, 2005, pp. 1, 57+; and "Readers Respond to 'Chaos Scenario'," *Advertising Age*, April 18, 2005, pp. 1+.

4. Chase Squires and Dave Gussow, "The Ways in which We Watch TV Are Changing Right Before Our Eyes," *St. Petersburg Times*, April 27, 2006.

5. Abbey Klaassen, "Study: Only One in Four Teens Can Name Broadcast Networks," *Advertising Age*, May 15, 2006.

6. Abbey Klaassen, "Marketers Lose Confidence in TV Advertising," *Advertising Age*, March 22, 2006, accessed at adage.com/mediaworks/article?article_id=107965.

7. Brian Steinberg and Suzanne Vranica, "As 30-Second Spot Fades, What Will Advertisers Do Next?" *Wall Street Journal*, January 3, 2006, p. A15.

8. Mike Shaw, "Direct Your Advertising Dollars Away from TV at Your Own Risk," *Advertising Age*, February 27, 2006, p. 29. Also see John Consoli, "2005 Spending Rose 4.2 Percent, Says Nielsen Monitor-Plus," *MediaWeek*, March 15, 2006, accessed at www.mediaweek.com; and Claire Atkinson, "Measured Network TV Ad Spending Fell Last Year," *Advertising Age*, March 6, 2006, accessed at www.adage.com.

9. Jack Neff, "P&G Chief: We Need New Model Now," *Advertising Age*, November 15, 2004, pp. 1, 53.

10. Don E. Schultz, "New Media, Old Problem: Keep Marcom Integrated," *Marketing News*, March 29, 1999, p. 11. Also see Don E. Schultz, Stanley I. Tannenbaum, and Robert F. Lauterborn, *Integrated Marketing Communications* (Chicago, IL: NTC, 1992); Claire Atkinson, "Integration Still a Pipe Dream for Many," *Advertising Age*, March 10, 2003, pp. 1, 47; and Randall Rothenberg, "Despite All the Talk, Ad and Media Shops Still Aren't Truly Integrated," *Advertising Age*, March 27, 2006, p. 24.

11. See Don E. Schultz and Philip J. Kitchen, *Communication Globally: An Integrated Marketing Approach* (New York: McGraw-Hill, 2000); and Don E. Schultz and Heidi Schultz, *IMC: The Next Generation* (New York: McGraw-Hill, 2004).

12. Carolyn Setlow, "Humorous, Feel-Good Advertising Hits Home with Consumers," *Dsn Retailing Today*, April 22, 2002, p. 14. Also see Fred K. Beard, "One Hundred Years of Humor in American Advertising," *Journal of Macromarketing*, June 1, 2005, pp. 54+.

13. See "Magic Fridge of Bud Lite Ices a Win," *USA Today*, February 6, 2006, p. 5B.

14. Quotes and other information found in Hillary Chura, "A Creative Low Point," *Advertising Age*, February 9, 2004, p. 49; Stuart Elliott, "Can Beer Ads Extol Great Taste in Good Taste?" *New York Times*, April 2004, p. C2; and Heather Landi, "Madison Avenue's Greatest Hits," *Beverage World*, December 15, 2005, pp. 28–29.

15. For these and other examples, see Pamela Paul, "Color by Numbers," *American Demographics*, February 2002, pp. 31–35; and Arundhati Parmar, "Marketers Ask: Hues on First?" *Marketing News*, February 15, 2004, pp. 8–10.

16. Jonah Bloom, "The Truth Is: Consumers Trust Fellow Buyers Before Marketers," *Advertising Age*, February 13, 2006, p. 25.

17. Example adapted from Linda Tischler, "What's the Buzz?" *Fast Company*, May 2004, p. 76; with information from Matthew Creamer, "BzzAgent Seeks to Turn Word of Mouth into a Saleable Medium," *Advertising Age*, February 2006, p. 12.

18. Eugenia Levenson, "When Celebrity Endorsements Attack," *Fortune*, October 17, 2005, p. 42; and Charlie Gillis, "Thee Shill of Victory," *Maclean's*, February 27, 2006, p. 40.

19. For more on advertising spending by company and industry, see the Advertising Age, "Ad to Sales Ratios 2005 Edition," March 1, 2006, accessed at http://adage.com/datacenter/article.php?article_id=106936.

20. For more on setting promotion budgets, see W. Ronald Lane, Karen Whitehill King, and J. Thomas Russell, Kleppner's Advertising Procedure, 16th ed. (Upper Saddle River, NJ: Prentice Hall, 2005), Chap. 6.

21. See David Barron, "TV Ratings Beat Last Year's," Knight Ridder Tribune Business News, February 7, 2006, p. 1; Nick Madigan and Rob Hiaasen, "Oscar Host Is One Tough Gig," Knight Ridder Tribune Business News, March 7, 2006, p. 1; and Lisa de Moraes, "'American Idol' Belts Out a Huge Opening Number: 33.6 Million," Washington Post, January 20, 2006, p. C1.

22. Roy Chitwood, "Making the Most Out of Each Outside Sales Call," February 4, 2005, accessed at http://seattle.bizjournals.com/seattle/stories/2005/02/07/smallb3.html; and "The Cost of the Average Sales Call Today is More Than $400," Business Wire, February 28, 2006.

23. Based on Matthew P. Gonring, "Putting Integrated Marketing Communications to Work Today," Public Relations Quarterly, Fall 1994, pp. 45-48. Also see Philip Kotler, Marketing Management, 12th ed. (Upper Saddle River, NJ: Prentice Hall, 2006), pp. 558-561.

24. Information accessed at www.tropicalforestfoundation.org/about.html and www.avoncompany.com/women/avoncrusade/, August 2006.

25. For more on the legal aspects of promotion, see Lane, King, and Russell, Kleppner's Advertising Procedure, chapter 25; and William L. Cron and Thomas E. DeCarlo, Dalrymple's Sales Management, 9th ed. (New York: Wiley, 2006), chapter 10.

CHAPTER 15

1. Quotes and other information from "A Legend in Its Time," Best's Review, January 2006, p. 53; Jim Lovel, "Loving the Lizard," Adweek, October 24, 2005, pp. 32-33; and Mya Frazier, "Ad Spending Booms in War of Car Insurers," Advertising Age, March 13, 2006, p. 4.

2. For information on U.S. and international advertising spending, see Lisa Sanders, "Global Ad Spend to Rise to 6 Percent in 2006," Advertising Age, December 5, 2005, p. 1; and "100 Leading National Advertisers," special issue of Advertising Age, June 26, 2006.

3. For more on advertising budgets, see W. Ronald Lane, Karen Whitehill King, and J. Thomas Russell, Kleppner's Advertising Procedure, 16th ed. (Upper Saddle River, NJ: Prentice Hall, 2005), chapter 6.

4. Adapted from Brian Steinberg and Suzanne Vranica, "Agencies Rethink Wall Between Creative, Media; Fragmentation of Audience Undercuts the Rationale for Separate Buying Units," Wall Street Journal, March 1, 2006, p. B3.

5. See the Q&A section at www.absolut.com, August 2006; and "Record Year for Absolut Vodka," press release, January 31, 2006, accessed at www.absolut.com.

6. "Commercial Conundrum," Marketing Management, April 2006, p. 6; and "Number of Magazines by Category,"

7. Charles Pappas, "Ad Nauseam," Advertising Age, July 10, 2000, pp. 16-18; Mark Ritson, "Marketers Need to Find a Way to Control the Contagion of Clutter," Marketing, March 6, 2003, p. 16; and David H. Freedman, "The Future of Advertising Is here," Inc., August 2005, pp. 70-78.

8. See Steve McClellan, "American Idol No. 1 with a $705k Bullet," Mediaweek, September 12, 2005, pp.4-5; Abbey Klaassen and Claire Atkinson, "Super Bowl Spots Lose Their Luster," Advertising Age, February 13, 2006, p. 1; Roberta Bernstein, "Actors' Digital Destiny," Adweek, April 10, 2006, pp. 22-23; and Claire Atkinson, "'Idol' Finale Hits $1.3M High Note," Advertising Age, April 17, 2006, pp. 1, 14.

9. Paul Holmes, "Programs that Demonstrate the Value of Public Relations," Advertising Age, January 24, 2005, pp. C12-C16; Gary Levin, "Ad Glut Turns Off Viewers," USA Today, October 11, 2005, accessed at www.usatoday.com; and John Consoli, "Broadcast, Cable Ad Clutter Continues to Rise," MediaWeek, May 4, 2006, accessed at www.mediaweek.com.

10. John Consoli, "Broadcast, Cable Ad Clutter Continues to Rise," MediaWeek, May 4, 2006, accessed at www.mediaweek.com.

11. Ronald Grover, "The Sound of Many Hands Zapping," BusinessWeek, May 22, 2006, p. 38; David Kiley, "Learning to Love the Dreader TiVo," BusinessWeek, April 17, 2006, p. 88; and Randall Stross, "Someone Has to Pay. But Who? And How?" New York Times, May 7, 2006, p. 3.3.

12. See Theresa Howard, "'Viral' Advertising Spreads through Marketing Plans," USA Today, June 6, 2005, accessed at www.usatoday.com/money/advertising/2005-06-22-viral-usat_x.htm; and Steve McKee, Advertising: Less Is Much More," BusinessWeek Online, May 10, 2006, accessed at www.businessweek.com.

13. Stuart Elliot, "New Rules of Engagement," New York Times, March 21, 2006, p. C7; and Abbey Klaassen, "New Wins Early Battle in Viewer-Engagement War," Advertising Age, March 20, 2006, p. 10.

14. See David Kiley, "Cable's Big Bet on Hyper-Targeting," BusinessWeek, July 4, 2005, pp. 58-59; and David H. Freedman, "The Future of Advertising Is Here," Inc., August 2005, pp. 70-78.

15. Adapted from information found in "Multi-Taskers," Journal of Marketing Management, May-June 2004, p. 6; "Kids Today: Media Multitaskers," March 9, 2005, accessed at www.cbsnews.com/stories/2005/03/09/tech/main678999.shtml; and Claudia Wallis, "The Multitasking Generation," Time, March 27, 2006, accessed at www.time.com.

16. Newsweek and BusinessWeek cost and circulation data accessed online at http://mediakit.businessweek.com and www.newsweekmediakit.com, August 2006.

17. See Marty Bernstein, "Why TV Commercials Are So Costly," Automotive News, May 10, 2004, p. 30H; and Simon Yeaman, "Up Late," The Advertiser, November 10, 2004, p. D5.

18. Stuart Elliot, "How Effective Is This Ad, in Real Numbers? Beats Me.," *New York Times*, July 20, 2005, p. C8.

19. Elliot, "How Effective Is This Ad, in Real Numbers? Beats Me.," p. C8. Also see, Dan Lippe, "Media Scorecard: How ROI Adds Up," *Advertising Age*, June 20, 2005, p. S6; and Pat LaPointe, "For Better ROI, Think Sailing, Not Driving," *Brandweek*, January 30, 2006, pp. 17–18.

20. Information on advertising agency revenues from "Advertising Age's Special Agency Report," *Advertising Age*, May 1, 2006.

21. See Alexandra Jardine and Laurel Wentz, "It's a Fat World After All," *Advertising Age*, March 7, 2005, p. 3; George E. Belch and Michael A. Belch, *Advertising and Promotion*, (New York: McGraw-Hill/Irwin, 2004), pp. 666–668; Jonathan Cheng, "China Demands Concrete Proof of Ads," *Wall Street Journal*, July 8, 2005, p. B1; Cris Prystay, "India's Brewers Cleverly Dodge Alcohol-Ad Ban," *Wall Street Journal*, June 15, 2005, p. B1; and Dean Visser, "China Puts New Restrictions on Cell Phone, E-Mail Advertising," *Marketing News*, March 15, 2006, p. 23.

22. Adapted from Scott Cutlip, Allen Center, and Glen Broom, *Effective Public Relations*, 9th ed. (Upper Saddle River, NJ: Prentice Hall, 2006), chapter 1.

23. Adapted from information found in Diane Brady, "Wizard of Marketing," *BusinessWeek*, July 24, 2000, pp. 84–87; Mira Serrill-Robins, "Harry Potter and the Cyberpirates," *BusinessWeek*, August 1, 2005, p. 9; Keith O'Brien, "Publisher Puts Fans First for New Harry Potter Release," *PRWeek*, July 18, 2005, p. 3; and "Harry Potter Tops U.S. Best-Seller List for 2005," *China Daily*, January 11, 2006, p. 14.

24. Al Ries and Laura Ries, "First Do Some Publicity," *Advertising Age*, February 8, 1999, p. 42. Also see Al Ries and Laura Ries, *The Fall of Advertising and the Rise of PR* (New York: HarperBusiness, 2002). For points and counterpoints and discussions of the role of public relations, see O. Burtch Drake, "'Fall' of Advertising? I Differ," *Advertising Age*, January 13, 2003, p. 23; Robert E. Brown, "Book Review: The Fall of Advertising & the Rise of PR," *Public Relations Review*, March 2003, pp. 91–93; Mark Cheshire, "Roundtable Discussion—Making & Moving the Message," *The Daily Record*, January 30, 2004, p. 1; and David Robinson, "Public Relations Comes of Age," *Business Horizons*, May–June 2006, pp. 247+.

25. Adapted from Todd Wasserman, "Word Games," *Brandweek*, April 24, 2006, pp. 24–28.

26. See Corey Washington, "Software Stops for Corona Demonstration," *Business Press*, February 27, 2006, p. 5; Lucas Conley, "On a Roll," *Fast Company*, February 2005, p. 28; and information from www.microsoft.com/mscorp/acrossamerica/, August 2006.

27. See "Butterball Turkey Talk-Line Fact Sheet," accessed at www.butterball.com/en/files/PDF/Fact_Sheet_2005.PDF, September 2006.

28. Paul Holmes, "Senior Marketers Are Sharply Divided About the Role of PR in the Overall Mix," *Advertising Age*, January 24, 2005, pp. C1–C2.

CHAPTER 16

1. Quotes and other information from Jeff O'Heir, "Michael Krasny—IT Sales Innovator," *Computer Reseller News*, November 18, 2002; Ed Lawler, "Integrated Campaign Winner: CDW Computer Centers," *BtoB*, December 9, 2002, p. 20; "CDW Chooses Richardson to Strengthen Customer Focus," *Business Wire*, July 23, 2003, p. 5397; Scott Campbell, "CDW Snags Companywide Cisco Premier Status," *CRN*, April 12, 2004, p. 12; Chuck Salter, "The Soft Sell," *Fast Company*, January 2005, pp. 72–73; "CDW Corporation," *Hoover's Company Records*, May 15, 2006, p. 16199; Mike Hughlett, "Results Boost CDW's Shares," *Knight Ridder Tribune Business News*, April 26, 2006, p. 1; and www.cdw.com, September 2006.

2. Quote from Laurence Zuckerman, "Selling Airplanes with a Smile," *New York Times*, February 17, 2002, p. 3.2. Also see Joann Muller, "7 Digital 7," *Forbes*, June 21, 2004, p. 117; and Perry Flint, "What Will They Do for an Encore?" *Air Transport World*, March 2006, pp. 22–25.

3. See "Lear Corp. Honored by GM as Supplier of the Year," *St. Charles County Business Record*, May 10, 2006, p. 1; Andy Cohen, "Top of the Charts: Lear Corporation," *Sales & Marketing Management*, July 1998, p. 40; and "Lear Corporation," *Hoover's Company Records*, May 15, 2006, p. 17213.

4. "Selling Power 500," accessed at www.sellingpower.com/sp500/index.asp, October 2006.

5. For more on this and other methods for determining sales force size, see William L. Cron and Thomas E. DeCarlo, *Sales Management*, 9th ed. (New York: John Wiley & Sons, 2006), pp. 84–85.

6. Roy Chitwood, "Making the Most Out of Each Outside Sales Call," February 4, 2005, accessed at http://seattle.bizjournals.com/seattle/stories/2005/02/07/smallb3.html; and "The Cost of the Average Sales Call Today is More Than $400," *Business Wire*, February 28, 2006.

7. Carol Krol, "Telemarketing Team Rings Up Sales for Avaya," *BtoB*, October 10, 2005, p. 34.

8. See Martin Everett, "It's Jerry Hale on the Line," *Sales & Marketing Management*, December 1993, pp. 75–79. Also see Terry Arnold, "Telemarketing Strategy," *Target Marketing*, January 2002, pp. 47–48.

9. Adapted from Chuck Salter, "The Soft Sell," *Fast Company*, January 2005, pp. 72–73. See also "Minding Our Business," *Multichannel Merchant*, March 2006, p. 1.

10. William F. Kendy, "No More Lone Rangers," *Selling Power*, April 2004, pp. 70–74. Also see Michelle Nichols, "Pull Together – Or Fall Apart," *BusinessWeek Online*, December 2, 2005, accessed at www.businessweek.com.

11. "Customer Business Development," accessed at www.pg.com/jobs/jobs_us/work_we_offer/advisor_overview.jhtml?sl=jobs_advisor_business_development, September 2006.

12. Quotes and other information in this section on super salespeople are from Geoffrey Brewer, "Mind Reading: What Drives Top Salespeople to Greatness?" *Sales &*

Marketing Management, May 1994, pp. 82–88; Andy Cohen, "The Traits of Great Sales Forces," *Sales & Marketing Management*, October 2000, pp. 67–72; Julia Chang, "Born to Sell?" *Sales & Marketing Management*, July 2003, pp. 34–38; Henry Canaday, "Recruiting the Right Stuff," *Selling Power*, April 2004, pp. 94–96. Also see Tom Andel, "How to Cultivate Sales Talent," *Official Board Markets*, April 23, 2005, pp. 14–16; and Kevin McDonald, "Therapist, Social Worker or Consultant?" *CRN*, December 2005–January 2006, p. 24.

13. Robert Klein, "Nabisco Sales Soar after Sales Training," *Marketing News*, January 6, 1997, p. 23; and Geoffrey James, "The Return of Sales Training," *Selling Power*, May 2004, pp. 86–91. See also, Anita Sirianni, "How to Build a Sales Training Program That Actually Improves Performance," *Proofs*, January 2005, pp. 66–68.

14. David Chelan, "Revving Up E-Learning to Drive Sales," *EContent*, March 2006, pp. 28–32; and E-Learning Evolves Into Mature Training Tool," *T+D*, April 2006, p. 20.

15. From David Chelan, "Revving Up E-Learning to Drive Sales," *EContent*, March 2006, pp. 28–32; and "International Rectifier Drives Sales with Global E-Leaning Initiative," GeoLearning case study, accessed at www.geolearning.com/main/customers/ir.cfm, June 2006.

16. See *Dartnell's 30th Sales Force Compensation Survey*, Dartnell Corporation, August 1999; and Galea "2006 Compensation Survey," *Sales & Marketing Management*, May 2006, pp. 30–35.

17. See Henry Canaday, "How to Increase the Times Reps Spend Selling," *Selling Power*, March 2005, p. 112; George Reinfeld, "8 Tips to Help Control the Hand of Time," *Printing News*, January 9, 2006, p. 10; and David J. Cichelli, "Plugging Sales 'Time Leaks,'" *Sales & Marketing Management*, April 2006, p. 23.

18. See Gary H Anthes, "Portal Powers GE Sales," Computerworld, June 2, 2003, pp. 31–32. Also see Betsy Cummings, "Increasing Face Time," *Sales & Marketing Management*, January 2004, p. 12; and David J. Cichelli, "Plugging Sales 'Time Leaks,'" *Sales & Marketing Management*, April 2006, p. 23.

19. For extensive discussions of sales force automation, see the May 2005 issue of *Industrial Marketing Management*, which is devoted to the subject.

20. Irwin Speizer, "Incentives Catch on Overseas, But Value of Awards Can Too Easily Get Lost in Translation," *Workforce Management*, November 21, 2005.

21. For more on return on sales investment, see Tim Lukes and Jennifer Stanley, "Bringing Science to Sales," *Marketing Management*, September-October 2004, pp. 36–41.

22. Quotes from Bob Donath, "Delivering Value Starts with Proper Prospecting," *Marketing News*, November 10, 1997, p. 5; and Bill Brooks, "Power-Packed Prospecting Pointers," *Agency Sales*, March 2004, p. 37. See also the audio slide presentation by Mike Trigg and others, "Best Practices for Sales Prospecting," Salesforce.com User & Development Conference 2005, accessed at www.spoke.com/bestpractices, April 2006.

23. Quotes and other information from Dana Ray, "Are You Listening?" *Selling Power*, October 2004, pp. 24–27; Erin

Stout, "Throwing the Right Pitch," *Sales & Marketing Management*, April 2001, pp. 61–63; Betsy Cummings, "Listening for Deals," *Sales & Marketing Management*, August 2005, p. 8; and William Kendy, "Learning to Listen," *Selling Power*, July–August 2006, p. 25. Also see Geoffrey James, "Solution Selling," *Selling Power*, May 2006, pp. 45–48.

24. Betsy Cummings, "Listening for Deals," *Sales & Marketing Management*, August 2005, p. 8.

25. Adapted from Rebecca Aronauer, "Looking Good," *Sales and Marketing Management*, April 2006, pp. 41–45.

26. *2005 Trade Promotion Spending & Merchandising Industry Study* (Cannondale Associates, Wilton, CT, May 2006). p. 13.

27. Adapted from Mike Beirne, "Scoring Points, Having Fun," *Brandweek*, October 18, 2004, pp. 18–19. Also see Jessica Mintz, "Travel Watch," *Wall Street Journal*, March 15, 2005, p. D5.

28. "Casting the Net Wider," *Candy Industry*, February 2005, p. 24; Damian J. Troise, "Fisherman's Friend Coughs Up MINI Cooper for Slogan Contest Winner," *Knight Ridder Tribune Business News*, February 25, 2005, p. 1; and www.fishermansfriendusa.com, accessed August 2006.

29. See Betsy Spethmann, "Clipping Slows," *Promo Magazine*, April 1, 2006; and Direct Marketing Association, "The DMA 2006 Statistical Fact Book," June 2006, p. 90.

30. See Leo Jakobson, "Coupons on the Go," *Incentive*, February 2005, p. 16; and Aman Batheja, "Show Your Text Message, Get a Discount," *Knight Ridder Tribune Business News*, April 22, 2006, p. 1.

31. See "Promotional Products—Impact, Exposure, and Influence" at Promotional Products Association International Web site, www.ppai.org, accessed May 2006; and Stacey Burling, "Your Logo Sells Here," *Philadelphia Enquirer*, May 31, 2006, accessed at www.philly.com/mld/philly/business/14702529.htm.

32. *2005 Trade Promotion Spending & Merchandising Industry Study* (Cannondale Associates, Wilton, CT, May 2006), p. 13.

33. See "Nearly Half a Million Attend Bauma Trade Show," *Pit & Quarry*, May 2004, p. 16; and "Record Breaking 2006 International CES Reflects Strength of Computer Technology Industry," press release at Consumer Electronics Association Web site, www.cesweb.org, January 8, 2006.

CHAPTER 17

1. Quotes and other information from Louise Lee, "It's Dell vs. The Dell Way," *BusinessWeek*, March 6, 2006, pp. 61–62; Andy Serwer, "Dell's Midlife Crisis," *Fortune*, November 28, 2005, pp. 147–152; Kathryn Jones, "The Dell Way," *Business 2.0*, February 2003, pp. 60–66; Serwer, "Dell Does Domination," *Fortune*, January 21, 2002, pp. 71–75; Serwer, "The Education of Michael Dell," *Fortune*, March 7, 2005, pp. 73–78; "Dell Inc.," *Hoover's Company Records*, Austin, May 1, 2006, p. 132692; "Top PC Venders by Market Share," supplement to *Advertising Age*, April 17, 2006, p. 50; Luisa Kroll and Allison Fass, "The World's Billionaires," *Forbes*, March 9, 2006, accessed at www.forbes.com/billionaires; and www.dell.com/us/en/

gen/corporate/access_company_direct_model.htm, December 2006.

2. "Growth Trends Continue for Direct Marketing," press release, Direct Marketing Association, September 2006, accessed at www.the-dma.org.

3. For these and other direct marketing statistics in this section, see Direct Marketing Association, "The DMA 2006 Statistical Fact Book," June 2006, pp. 249–250; Direct Marketing Association, "U.S. Direct Marketing Today: Economic Impact 2005," October, 2005, various pages; and a wealth of other information accessed at www.the-dma.org, September 2006.

4. Portions adapted from Christopher Elliott, "Your Very Own Personal Air Fare," New York Times, August 9, 2005, p. C5. Also see "Southwest Airlines Makes DING! Available to MAC Users," Telecomworldwire, March 21, 2006, p. 1; and "What Is DING!?" accessed at www.southwest.com/ding/, September 2006.

5. Alicia Orr Suman, "Ideas You Can Take to the Bank! 10 Big Things All Direct Marketers Should Be Doing Now," Target Marketing, February 2003, pp. 31–33; and Mary Ann Kleinfelter, "Know Your Customer," Target Marketing, January 2005, pp. 28–31.

6. Daniel Lyons, "Too Much Information," Forbes, December 13, 2004, p. 110; and Mike Freeman, "Data Company Helps Wal-Mart, Casinos, Airlines Analyze Data," Knight Ridder Business Tribune News, February 24, 2006, p. 1.

7. Quotes from Scott Horstein, "Use Care with the Database," Sales & Marketing Management, May 2006, p. 22. Also see Geoffrey Brewer, "The Customer Stops Here," Sales & Marketing Management, March 1998, pp. 31–36; "The Art of Service," Fast Company, October 2005, pp. 47–59; Hoover's Company Records, May 1, 2006, p. 40508; and information from www.usaa.com, September 2006.

8. Direct Marketing Association, "The DMA 2006 Statistical Fact Book," June 2006, p. 250.

9. David Ranii, "Compact Discs, DVDs Get More Use as Promotional Tool," Knight Ridder Tribune Business News, May 5, 2004, p. 1.

10. Jim Emerson, "Print and the Internet Go Hand-in-Hand," Printing News, June 20, 2005, p. 2; and "Abacus Report: Web Sales Soon to Overtake Catalog Sales," August 3, 2005, accessed at http://multichannelmerchant.com/news/Abacus-trend-report-080305/.

11. Direct Marketing Association, "The DMA 2006 Statistical Fact Book," June 2006, p. 250.

12. "Catalog Study Now Available," Business Forms, Labels, and Systems, June 20, 2001, p. 24; Richard S. Hodgson, "It's Still the Catalog Age," Catalog Age, June 2001, p. 156; and Sherry Chiger, "It's Raining Catalogs," Catalog Age, June 2004, p. 12.

13. See "About Lillian Vernon," accessed at www.lillianvernon.com, August 2006; and "Lillian Vernon Corporation," Hoover's Company Records, Austin, May 11, 2006, p. 12111.

14. Janie Curtis, "Catalogs as Portals: Why You Should Keep on Mailing," Multichannel Merchant, November 30, 2005, accessed at http://multichannelmerchant.com/news/catalogs_portal_1130/index.html.

15. Andrea Coombes, "MarketWatch: Hello . . . It's the Do-Not-Call List," Wall Street Journal, January 1, 2006, p. 4.

16. Ira Teinowitz, "Do Not Call' Does Not Hurt Direct Marketing," Advertising Age, April 11, 2005, pp. 3, 95.

17. Teinowitz, "Do Not Call' Does Not Hurt Direct Marketing," p. 3.

18. Ron Donoho, "One-Man Show," Sales & Marketing Management, June 2001, pp. 36–42; and information accessed at www.ronco.com, March 2004; and Brian Steinberg, "Read This Now!; But Wait! There's More! The Infomercial King Explains," Wall Street Journal, March 9, 2005, p. 1.

19. Jack Neff, "What Procter & Gamble Learned from Veg-O-Matic," Advertising Age, April 10, 2006, pp. 1, 65.

20. Steve McLellan, "For a Whole New DRTV Experience, Call Now," Adweek, September 5, 2005, p. 10; and Jack Neff, "What Procter & Gamble Learned from Veg-O-Matic," p. 1.

21. Adapted from portions of Elizabeth Esfahani, "A Sales Channel They Can't Resist," Business 2.0, September 2005, pp. 91–96.

22. Diane Anderson, "HP Developing Retail Kiosks to Reach iMoms," Brandweek, March 6, 2006, p. 12; Chris Jones, "Kiosks Put Shopper in Touch," Knight Ridder Tribune Business News, April 11, 2006, p. 1; and David Eisen, "Hilton Debuts Air Checkin Kiosk," Business Travel News, May 1, 2006, p. 8.

23. "Interactive: Ad Age Names Finalists," Advertising Age, February 27, 1995, pp. 12–14.

24. Alice Z. Cuneo, "Scramble for Content Drives Mobile," Advertising Age, October 24, 2005, p. S6.

25. "Mobile Marketing," Marketing News, April 1, 2006, p. 4.

26. For these and other examples, see Alice Z. Cuneo, "Marketers Get Serious about the Third Screen," Advertising Age, July 11, 2005, p. 6; and Theresa Howard, "Burger King to Send Extended Ad to Customers of Sprint Phone Video," USA Today.com, January 20, 2006, accessed at www.usatoday.com/moneyadvertising/2006-01-20-burger-king-usat_x.htm.

27. Adapted from information found in Normandy Madden, "Cellphones Spawn New 'Fast' Promotions in Japan," Advertising Age, November 7, 2005, p. 14.

28. See Abbey Klaassen and Leslie Taylor, "Few Compete to Settle Podcasting's Wild West," Advertising Age, April 24, 2006, p. 13; and "E-Marketer Sees Big Future for Podcast Ads," BtoB, March 13, 2006, p. 6; Jim Pollock, "Suddenly, It's the Podcast Era," Des Moines Business Record, April 17, 2006, p. 1.

29. For these and other examples, see Karyn Strauss and Derek Gale, Hotels, March 2006, p. 22; and "Disneyland Offers Behind-the-Scenes Podcast," Wireless News, Febraury 19, 2006, p. 1.

30. Susie Haywood, "Honda Scores First with Civic 'Vodcast'," Revolution, February 2006, p. 11.

31. Adapted from David Liley, "Learning to Love the Dreaded TiVo," BusinessWeek, April 17, 2006, p. 88. Also see Daisy Whitney, "Marketers Quick to Say 'Yes' to Opt-In TV Fare," Advertising Age, October 24, 2005, p. S4; and "Nickelodeon Runs SeaWorld iTV Ads," New Media Age, April 27, 2006, p. 3.

32. For these and other statistics on Internet usage, see "United States: Average Web Usage," Nielsen/NetRatings, April 2006, accessed at www.nielsen-netratings.com; Antony Bruno, "Web Adoption Slows, Broadband Grows," *Billboard*, April 15, 2006, p. 16; and Enid Burns, "Global Internet Adoption Slows While Involvement Deepens," *ClickZ Stats*, April 3, 2006, accessed at www.clickz.com.

33. "JupiterResearch Forecasts Online Retail Spending Will Reach $144 Billion in 2010, a CAGR of 12% from 2005," February 6, 2006, accessed at www.jupitermedia.com/corporate/releases/06.02.06-newjupresearch.html. For other estimates, see "Online Retail Sales Grew in 2005," January 5, 2006, accessed at www.clickz.com; and "Consumer Internet Usage," *Interactive Marketing & Media*, a supplement to *Advertising Age*, April 17, 2006, p. 28.

34. "JupiterResearch Forecasts Online Retail Spending Will Reach $144 Billion in 2010, a CAGR of 12% from 2005," February 6, 2006, accessed at www.jupitermedia.com/corporate/releases/06.02.06-new jupresearch.html.

35. Information for this example accessed at http://quicken loans.quicken.com, September 2006.

36. Information for this example accessed at www.dell.com/html/us/segments/pub/premier/tutorial/users_guide.html, September 2006.

37. See Kim Wright Wiley, "Meg Whitman: The $40 Billion eBay Sales Story," *Selling Power*, November–December, 2005, pp. 63–70; "eBay Inc.," *Hoover's Company Records*, May 1, 2006, p. 56307; and facts from eBay annual reports and other information accessed at www.ebay.com, September 2006.

38. Stephen Baker and Heather Green, "Blogs Will Change Your Business," *BusinessWeek*, May 2, 2005, pp. 57–67; and Alan Scott, "Guard Your Rep: Ignore Blogs at the Peril of Brand Image," *Marketing News*, February 15, 2006, pp. 21–22.

39. Michael Barbaro, "Wal-Mart Enlists Bloggers in Its Public Relations Campaign," *New York Times*, March 7, 2006, p. C1.

40. Gavin O'Malley, "Coca-Cola Sends Bloggers to Olympics," *MediaPost Publications*, February 10, 2006, accessed at http://publications.mediapost.com.

41. Pete Blackshaw, "Irrational Exuberance? I Hope We're Not Guilty," *Barcode Blog*, August 26, 2005, accessed at www.barcodefactory.com/wordpress/?p=72.

42. Michelle Slatalla, "Toll-Free Apology Soothes Savage Beast," *New York Times*, February 12, 2004, p. G4; and information from www.planetfeedback.com/consumer, August 2006.

43. "Mass Merchants/Department Stores: Winning by Leveraging More of What the Web Can Do," *Internet Retailer*, December 2004, accessed at www.internetretailer.com; and information from www.officedepot.com, September 2006.

44. See "Best of the Web—The Top 50 Retailing Sites," *Internet Retailer*, December 2004, accessed at www.internetretailer.com; and "Peapod and Scholastic Deliver Highest Consistency Rate," *Internet Retailer*, May 10, 2006, accessed at www.internetretailer.com.

45. Adapted from Jena McGregor, "High-Tech Achiever: MINI USA," *Fast Company*, October 2004, p. 86, with information from www.miniusa.com, September 2006.

46. Jeffrey F. Rayport and Bernard J. Jaworski, *e-Commerce* (New York: McGraw-Hill, 2001), p. 116. Also see Goutam Chakraborty, "What Do Customers Consider Important in B2B Web sites?" *Journal of Advertising*, March 2003, p. 50; and "Looks Are Everything," *Marketing Management*, March/April 2006, p. 7.

47. See Wendy Davis, "Jupiter Research: Internet Ad Spend to Reach $18.9 Billion by 2010," August 9, 2005, accessed at publications.mediapost.com; and "Internet Advertising Revenues Grow 30% to a Record $12.5 Billion in '05," Internet Advertising Bureau, April 20, 2006, accessed at www.iab.net.

48. Ellis Booker, "Vivid 'Experiences' as the New Frontier," *BtoB*, March 14, 2005, p. 14; and Karen J Bannan, "Rich Media Rule Book," *BtoB*, March 13, 2006, pp. 27–30.

49. See Mike Shields, "Google Faces New Rivals," August 22, 2005, accessed at www.mediaweek.com; and "Internet Advertising Revenues Grow 30% to a Record $12.5 Billion in '05," Internet Advertising Bureau, April 20, 2006, accessed at www.iab.net.

50. Adapted from Jon Fine, "Rise of the Lowly Search Ad," *BusinessWeek*, April 24, 2006, p. 24.

51. Kris Oser, "Video in Demand," *Advertising Age*, April 4, 2005, pp. S1–S5.

52. Adapted from information found in Bob Garfield, "War & Peace and Subservient Chicken," April 26, 2004, accessed at www.adage.com; Gregg Cebrzynski, "Burger King Says It's OK to Have Your Way with the Chicken," *Nation's Restaurant News*, May 10, 2004, p. 16; and Ryan Underwood, "Ruling the Roost," *Fast Company*, April 2005, pp. 70–78.

53. Jack Neff, "Taking Package Goods to the Net," *Advertising Age*, July 11, 2005, pp. S1–S3.

54. Information from the iVillage Top-Line Metrics section of www.ivillage.com, October 2006; and www.MyFamily.com, September 2006.

55. Direct Marketing Association, "The DMA 2006 Statistical Fact Book," June 2006, p. 250; and "Jupiter: Email Marketing to Grow, Spam to Drop," February 6, 2006, accessed at www.jupitercommunications.com.

56. Heidi Anderson, "Nintendo Case Study: Rules Are Made to Be Broken," E-Mail Marketing Case Studies, March 6, 2003, accessed online at www.clickz.com.

57. Enid Burns, "The Deadly Duo: Spam and Viruses, March 2006," *ClickZ Stats*, April 28, 2006, accessed at www.clickz.com.

58. Adapted from information found in Carol Krol, "E-Mail Marketing Gains Ground with Integration," *BtoB*, April 3, 2006, p. 1.

59. "Sweepstakes Group Settles with States," *New York Times*, June 27, 2001, p. A14; and "PCH Reaches $34 Million Sweepstakes Settlement with 26 States," *Direct Marketing*, September 2001, p. 6.

60. See National White Collar Crime Center "IC3 2005 Internet Crime Report," 2005, accessed at www.ic3.gov/

61. See Don Oldenburg, "Hook, Line and Sinker: Personalized Phishing Scams Use Customers' Names to Attract Attention," *Washington Post*, April 2, 2006, p. F05; and "How Not to Get Caught by a Phishing Scam," accessed at www.ftc.gov/bcp/online/pubs/alerts/phishingalrt.htm, June 2006.

62. Rob McCann, "Concerns over Online Threats This Holiday Season," *ClickZ Stats*, November 24, 2004, accessed at www.clickz.com. Also see Ann E. Schlosser, Tiffany Barnett White, and Susan M. Lloyd, "Converting Web Site Visitors into Buyers: How Web Site Investment Increases Consumer Trusting Beliefs and Online Purchase Intentions," *Journal of Marketing*, April 2006, pp. 133–148.

63. See "Seventy Percent of US Consumers Worry About Online Privacy, But Few Take Protective Action, Reports Jupiter Media Metrix," Jupiter Media Metrix press release, June 3, 2002, accessed online at www.jup.com; Rob McCann, "Concerns Over Online Threats This Holiday Season," *ClickZ Stats*, November 24, 2004, accessed at www.clickz.com; and Desiree J. Hanford, "Fraud Fears Slow Online Shopping," *Wall Street Journal*, April 13, 2005, p. 1.

64. "14-Year-Old Bids over $3M for Items in eBay Auctions," *USA Today*, April 30, 1999, p. 10B.

65. Jennifer Lee, "Welcome to the Database Lounge," *New York Times*, March 21, 2002, p. G1.

66. See Jaikumar Vijayan, "First Online Data Privacy Law Looms in California," *Computerworld*, June 28, 2004, p. 12; and "Does Your Privacy Policy Comply with the California Online Privacy Protection Act?" Banking and Financial Services Policy Report, January 2005, p. 7.

67. See Jennifer DiSabatino, "FTC OKs Self-Regulation to Protect Children's Privacy," *Computerworld*, February 12, 2001, p. 32; Ann Mack, "Marketers Challenged On Youth Safeguards," *Adweek*, June 14, 2004, p. 12; and Hiawatha Bray, "Google Faces Order to Give Up Records," *Knight Ridder Tribune Business News*, March 15, 2006, p. 1.

68. Information on TRUSTe accessed at www.truste.com, September 2006.

69. Information on the DMA Privacy Promise obtained at www.dmaconsumers.org/privacy.html, September 2006.

70. Debbie A. Connon, "The Ethics of Database Marketing," *Information Management Journal*, May–June 2002, pp. 42–44.

CHAPTER 18

1. Extracts adapted from Linda Tischler, "Bank of (Middle) America," *Fast Company*, March 2003, pp. 104–110. Quotes and other information from Mellissa Allison, "Customers Like WaMu, They Really Do," *Knight Ridder Tribune Business News*, March 1, 2006, p. 1; Michael Sisk, "WaMu Goes after the Middle Man," *USBanker*, November 2003, p. 60; Jacob Ward, "Should a Bank Be a Store?" *USBanker*, April 2004, pp. 36–40; "Washington Mutual, Inc." *Hoover's Company Records*, May 15, 2006, p. 15119; Mary McGarity, "WaMu's Back," *Mortgage Banking*, October 2005, pp. 104–113; and "The WaMu Difference," accessed at www.wamu.com/about, September 2006.

2. Leon Lazaroff, "Kodak Big Picture Focusing on Image Change," *Knight Ridder Tribune Business News*, January 26, 2006. Also see Brad Stone, "What's Kodak's Strategy?" *Newsweek*, January 16, 2006, p. 25.

3. Adapted from Jeffrey F. Rayport and Bernard J. Jaworski, *e-Commerce* (New York: McGraw-Hill, 2001), p. 53.

4. Johanna Bennett, "Turn Around, Bright Eyes," *Barron's*, May 16, 2005, p. 48.

5. Edward F. Moltzen, "Intel, AMD Go At It Again," *CRN*, March 29, 2004, p. 80; Jon Birger, "Second-Mover Advantage," *Fortune*, March 20, 2006, pp. 20–21; and "Advanced Micro Devices," *Hoover's Company Records*, May 15, 2006, p. 10037.

6. See Michael Porter, *Competitive Advantage: Creating and Sustaining Superior Performance* (New York: Free Press, 1998), chap. 6.

7. Adapted from Devin Leonard, "The Player," *Fortune*, March 20, 2006, p. 54.

8. See Philip Kotler and Kevin Lane Keller, *Marketing Management*, 12th ed. (Upper Saddle River, NJ: Prentice Hall, 2006), pp. 13–14; Sam Hill and Glenn Rifkin, *Radical Marketing* (New York: HarperBusiness, 1999); Gerry Khermouch, "Keeping the Froth on Sam Adams," *BusinessWeek*, September 1, 2003, p. 54; and information accessed at www.bostonbeer.com, September 2006.

9. The Stonyfield Story is adapted from Margaret Menge, "Guerilla Marketing Works for NH's Stonyfield Farms," *New Hampshire Union Leader*, November 7, 2005; with information from www.stonyfield.com, September 2006.

10. Michael E. Porter, *Competitive Strategy: Techniques for Analyzing Industries and Competitors* (New York: Free Press, 1980), chap. 2; and Porter, "What Is Strategy?" *Harvard Business Review*, November–December 1996, pp. 61–78. Also see Richard Allen and others, "A Comparison of Competitive Strategies in Japan and the United States," *S.A.M. Advanced Management Journal*, Winter 2006, pp. 24–36.

11. Philip Kotler and Kevin Lane Keller, *Marketing Management*, 12th ed. (Upper Saddle River, NJ: Prentice Hall, 2006), p. 243.

12. See Michael Treacy and Fred Wiersema, "Customer Intimacy and Other Value Disciplines," *Harvard Business Review*, January-February 1993, pp. 84–93; Michael Treacy and Mike Wiersema, *The Discipline of Market Leaders: Choose Your Customers, Narrow Your Focus, Dominate Your Market* (Perseus Press, 1997); Fred Wiersema, *Customer Intimacy: Pick Your Partners, Shape Your Culture, Win Together* (Knowledge Exchange, 1998); and Wiersema, *Double-Digit Growth: How Great Companies Achieve It—No Matter What* (Portfolio, 2003).

13. For more discussion, see Philip Kotler and Kevin Lane Keller, *Marketing Management*, 12th ed., chap. 11.

14. Adapted from an example found in George Stalk, Jr., and Rob Lachenaur, "Hardball: Five Killer Strategies for Trouncing the Competition," *Harvard Business Review*,

April 2004, pp. 62–71. For a discussion of additional defensive-marketing strategies, see John H. Roberts, "Defensive Marketing: How a Strong Incumbent Can Protect Its Position," *Harvard Business Review*, November 2005, pp. 150–157.

15. See "U.S. Digital Camera Market to Reach 6.8 Billion in 2006," www.blogs.zdnet.com, March 6, 2006; and Steve Matthews and Mary Jane Credeur, "Soft-Drink Sales Lag for First Time in Decades," *Chicago Sun Times*, December 13, 2005, p. 57.

16. Adapted from Jon Birger, "Second-Mover Advantage," *Fortune*, March 20, 2006, pp. 20–21; with information from "Fortune 500: Largest U.S. Corporations," *Fortune*, April 17, 2006, p. F1.

17. Jack Neff, "Unilever Cedes Laundry War," *Advertising Age*, May 27, 2002, pp. 1, 47; Veronica MacDonald, "Soaps and Detergents: Going the World Over to Clean," *Chemical Week*, January 26, 2005, pp. 21–23; Jack Neff, "Unilever 3.0: CEO Not Afraid to Copy from P&G," *Advertising Age*, October 23, 2005, p. 8; and Kerri Walsh, "Brand Extensions Clean Up," *Chemical Week*, February 1, 2006, pp. 24+.

18. "Logitech Aims at Convergence for New Growth," *Wall Street Journal*, June 16, 2004, p. 1; Logitech Annual Report, www.logitech.com, April 1, 2006; and "Logitech International S.A.," *Hoover's Company Records*, June 1, 2006, p. 42459.

19. Jim Kirk, "Company Finds Itself, Finds Success: Alberto-Culver Adopts Strategy of Knowing Its Strengths and Promoting Small Brands, Rather Than Tackling Giants," *Chicago Tribune*, January 22, 1998, Business Section, p. 1; "Alberto-Culver Company," *Hoover's Company Records*, June 1, 2006, p. 10048; and www.alberto.com, September 2006.

CHAPTER 19

1. Quotes and other information from John Dorschner, "World Catches NBA Fever," *Miami Herald*, June 15, 2006, accessed online at www.miamiherald.com; Jerry Crowe, "Outside Influence; NBA Finals Being Broadcast in 39 Languages Translates into Big-Time International Drawing Power," *Los Angeles Times*, June 15, 2004; Marc Gunther, "They All Want to Be Like Mike," *Fortune*, July 21, 1997, pp. 51–53; Jon Robinson, "EA Sports Sponsors the NBA's Euroleague Invasion," accessed online at www.sports.ign.com, June 14, 2005; Janny Hu, "Europe Beckons, League Follows," *San Francisco Chronicle*, December 25, 2005, p. C5; and Carol Matlack, "Le Basket Struggles to Score," *BusinessWeek*, May 22, 2006, p. 45.

2. Data from "Fortune 500," *Fortune*, April 17, 2006, p. F-1; United Nations Conference on Trade and Development, World Investment Report 2005, New York and Geneva: United Nations, 2005; the World Bank, "Total GDP 2004," World Development Indicators Database, www.worldbank.org, accessed April 2, 2006; and "List of Countries by GDP," *Wikipedia*, accessed at http://en.wikipedia.org/wiki/List_of_countries_by_GDP_%28nominal%29, September 2006.

3. *Global Economic Prospects, 2006*, World Bank, June 3, 2005, accessed at www.worldbank.org; CIA, *The World Factbook*, accessed at www.cia.gov, June 2006; and WTO, "World Trade Picks Up in Mid-2005: But 2006 Picture Is Uncertain," WTO press release, April 11, 2006, accessed at www.wto.org/english/news_e/pres06_e/pr437_e.htm.

4. Information from www.michelin.com/corporate and www.jnj.com, July 2006.

5. Steve Hamm, "Borders Are So 20th Century," *Business Week*, September 22, 2003, pp. 68–73.

6. "The Unique Japanese," *Fortune*, November 24, 1986, p. 8. Also see James D. Southwick, "Addressing Market Access Barriers in Japan Through the WTO," *Law and Policy in International Business*, Spring 2000, pp. 923–976; U.S. Commercial Service, *Country Commercial Guide Japan, FY 2005*, chap. 5, accessed at www.buyusa.gov, June 18, 2005; and "Japan-U.S. Beef Row Tip of Iceberg: U.S. Lawmaker," *Jiji Press English News Service*, February 16, 2006, p.1.

7. "What Is the WTO?" accessed at www.wto.org/english/thewto_e/whatis_e/whatis_e.htm, September 2006.

8. See *WTO Annual Report 2005*, accessed at www.wto.org, September 2006; and World Trade Organization, "10 Benefits of the WTO Trading System," accessed at www.wto.org/english/thewto_e/whatis_e/whatis_e.htm, September 2006.

9. "Finance and Economics: In the Rough; World Trade Talks," *Economist*, November 5, 2005, p. 102; and Peter Coy, "Why Free-Trade Talks Are in Free Fall," *BusinessWeek*, May 22, 2006, p. 44.

10. "The European Union at a Glance," accessed online at http://europa.eu.int, September 2006.

11. "Overviews of European Union Activities: Economic and Monetary Affairs," accessed at http://europa.eu.int/pol/emu/overview_en.htm, September 2006.

12. See "European Union's Heated Budget Negotiations Collapse," *New York Times*, June 18, 2005, p. A3; "Europe: Desperately Seeking a Policy; France and the European Union," *Economist*, January 21, 2006; CIA, *The World Factbook*, accessed at www.cia.gov, June 2006; and Vito Breda, "A European Constitution in a Multinational Europe or a Multinatioal Constitution for Europe?" *European Law Journal*, May 2006, pp. 330+.

13. Statistics and other information from "List of Countries by GDP," *Wikipedia*, accessed at http://en.wikipedia.org/wiki/List_of_countries_by_GDP_%28nominal%29, July 2006; "Area and Population of Countries," infoplease, accessed at www.infoplease.com/ipa/A0004379.html, July 2006; and "Trade Facts: NAFTA—A Strong Record of Success," Office of the United States Trade Representative, March 2006, accessed at www.ustr.gov/assets/Document_Library/Fact_Sheets/2006/asset_upload_file242_9156.pdf.

14. See Angela Greiling Keane, "Counting on CAFTA," *Traffic World*, August 8, 2005, p. 1; Gilberto Meza, "Is the FTAA Floundering," *Business Mexico*, February 2005, pp. 46–48; Peter Robson, "Integrating the Americas: FTAA and Beyond," *Journal of Common Market Studies*, June 2005, p. 430; Diana Kinch, "Latin America: Mercosul Boosted," *Metal Bulletin Monthly*, February 2006, p. 1; "Foreign Trade Statistics," accessed at www.census.gov, June 2006; and Kevin Z. Jiang, "Americas: Trading Up?" *Harvard International Review*, Spring 2006, pp. 10–12.

15. Richard Lapper, "South American Unity Still a Distant Dream," *Financial Times*, December 9, 2004, accessed at www.news.ft.com; Alan Clendenning, "Venezuela's Entry May Shake Up Mercosur," *AP Financial Wire*, November 30, 2005, p. 1; and Mary Turck, "South American Community of Nations," *Resource Center of the Americas.org*, accessed at www.americas.org, September 2006.

16. See Shanti Gamper-Rabindran, "NAFTA and the Environment: What Can the Data Tell Us?" *Economic Development and Cultural Change*, April 2006, pp. 605–634.

17. Adapted from information found in Clay Chandler, "China Deluxe," *Fortune*, July 26, 2004, pp. 148–156. Also see "Selling to China's Rich and Not So Rich," *Strategic Directions*, June 2005, pp. 5–8; Lisa Movius, "Luxury's China Puzzle," *WWD*, June 15, 2005, p. 1; and Normandy Madden, "After Slow Start, Porsche Cranks Its Chinese Marketing Plan into Top Gear," *Advertising Age*, May 8, 2006, p. 28.

18. See Om Malik, "The New Land of Opportunity," *Business 2.0*, July 2004, pp. 72–79; and "India Economy: South Asia's Worst Business Environment," *EIU ViewsWire*, January 2006.

19. Ricky Griffin and Michael Pustay, *International Business*, 4th ed. (Upper Saddle River, NJ: Prentice Hall, 2005), pp. 522–523.

20. Rebecca Piirto Heath, "Think Globally," *Marketing Tools*, October 1996, pp. 49–54; "The Power of Writing," *National Geographic*, August 1999, pp. 128–129; and Jamie Bryan, "The Mintz Dynasty," *Fast Company*, April 2006, pp. 56–61.

21. For other examples and discussion, see www.executiveplanet.com, December 2006; *Dun & Bradstreet's Guide to Doing Business Around the World* (Upper Saddle River, NJ: Prentice Hall, 2000); Ellen Neuborne, "Bridging the Culture Gap," *Sales & Marketing Management*, July 2003, p. 22; Richard Pooley, "When Cultures Collide," *Management Services*, Spring 2005, pp. 28–31; and Helen Deresky, *International Management*, 5th ed. (Upper Saddle River, NJ: Prentice Hall, 2006).

22. Pete Engardio, Manjeet Kripalani, and Alysha Webb, "Smart Globalization," *BusinessWeek*, August 27, 2001, pp. 132–136.

23. Adapted from Mark Rice-Oxley, "In 2,000 Years, Will the World Remember Disney or Plato?" *Christian Science Monitor*, January 15, 2004, p. 16.

24. Thomas L. Friedman, *The Lexus and the Olive Tree: Understanding Globalization* (New York: Anchor Books, 2000).

25. Robert Berner and David Kiley, "Global Brands," *BusinessWeek*, August 1, 2005, pp. 86–94.

26. Portions adapted from information found in Mark Rice-Oxley, "In 2,000 Years, Will the World Remember Disney or Plato?" *Christian Science Monitor*, January 15, 2004, p. 16.

27. Paulo Prada and Bruce Orwall, "A Certain 'Je Ne Sais Quoi' at Disney's New Park—Movie-Themed Site Near Paris Is Multilingual, Serves Wine—and Better Sausage see 'Euro Disney S. C. A.," *Wall Street Journal*, March 12, 2002, p. B1. Also see "Euro Disney S. C. A.," *Hoover's Company Records*, June 15, 2006, p. 90721.

28. See Jack Neff, "Submerged," *Advertising Age*, March 4, 2002, p. 14; Ann Chen and Vijay Vishwanath, "Expanding in China," *Harvard Business Review*, March 2005, pp. 19–21; and information accessed at www.colgate.com, September 2006.

29. For a good discussion of joint venturing, see James Bamford, David Ernst, and David G. Fubini, "Launching a World-Class Joint Venture," *Harvard Business Review*, February 2004, pp. 91–100.

30. Vanessa O'Connell and Mei Fong, "Saks to Follow Luxury Brands into China," *Wall Street Journal*, April 18, 2006, p. B1.

31. See Cynthia Kemper, "KFC Tradition Sold Japan on Chicken," *Denver Post*, June 7, 1998, p. J4; Milford Prewitt, "Chains Look for Links Overseas," *Nation's Restaurant News*, February 18, 2002, pp. 1, 6; and Yum Brands, Inc. restaurant count, accessed at www.yum.com, September 2006.

32. Quotes from Pankaj Ghemawat, "Regional Strategies for Global Leadership," *Harvard Business Review*, December 2005, pp. 97–108; Douglas B. Holt, John A. Quelch, and Earl L. Taylor, "How Global Brands Compete," *Harvard Business Review*, September 2004, pp. 68–75; and Simon Sherwood, "Building an Advertising Factory," accessed at www.inter-national-ist.com/commentary/commentary% 2020+21%202-18.1.pdf, June 16, 2006.

33. Warren J. Keegan, *Global Marketing Management*, 7th ed. (Upper Saddle River, NJ: Prentice Hall, 2002), pp. 346–351. Also see Phillip Kotler and Kevin Lane Keller, *Marketing Management*, 12th ed. (Upper Saddle River, NJ: 2006), pp. 677–684.

34. Adapted from Normandy Madden, "P&G Launches Cover Girl in China," *Advertising Age*, October 31, 2005, p. 22.

35. See Douglas McGray, "Translating Sony into English," *Fast Company*, January 2003, p. 38; and James Coates, "Chicago Tribune Binary Beat Column," *Chicago Tribune*, January 9, 2005, p. 1.

36. For further information on color and culture see Mubeen M. Aslam, "Are You Selling the Right Colour? A Cross-Cultural Review of Colour as a Marketing Cue," *Journal of Marketing Communications*, March 2006, pp. 15–20.

37. See "Naming Products Is No Game," *BusinessWeek Online*, April 9, 2004, accessed at www.businessweek.com; and Ross Thomson, "Lost in Translation," *Medical Marketing and Media*, March 2005, p. 82.

38. Kate MacArthur, "Coca-Cola Light Employs Local Edge," *Advertising Age*, August 21, 2000, pp. 18–19; and "Case Studies: Coke Light Hottest Guy," Advantage Marketing, msn India, accessed at http://advantage. msn.co.in, March 15, 2004.

39. See Alicia Clegg, "One Ad One World?" *Marketing Week*, June 20, 2002, pp. 51–52; and George E. Belch and Michael A. Belch, *Advertising and Promotion: An Integrated Marketing Communications Perspective*, 7th ed. (New York, NY: McGraw Hill, 2007), Chapter 20.

40. Michael Schroeder, "The Economy: Shrimp Imports to U.S. May Face Antidumping Levy," *Wall Street Journal*, February 18, 2004, p. A2; Woranuj Maneerungsee, "Shrimpers Suspect Rivals of Foul Play," *Knight Ridder*

Tribune Business News, April 28, 2005, p. 1; and David Bierderman, "Tough Journey," *Journal of Commerce,* March 13, 2006, p. 1.

41. Sarah Ellison, "Revealing Price Disparities, the Euro Aids Bargain-Hunters," *Wall Street Journal,* January 30, 2002, p. A15.

42. See Patrick Powers, "Distribution in China: The End of the Beginning," *China Business Review,* July–August, 2001, pp. 8–12; Drake Weisert, "Coca-Cola in China: Quenching the Thirst of a Billion," *China Business Review,* July–August 2001, pp. 52–55; Gabriel Kahn, "Coke Works Harder at Being the Real Thing in Hinterland," *Wall Street Journal,* November 26, 2002, p. B1; Leslie Chang, Chad Terhune, and Betsy McKay, "A Global Journal Report; Rural Thing—Coke's Big Gamble in Asia," *Wall Street Journal,* August 11, 2004, p. A1; and Ann Chen and Vijay Vishwanath, "Expanding in China," *Harvard Business Review,* March 1, 2005.

CHAPTER 20

1. Adapted from Jennifer Reingold, "Walking the Walk," *Fast Company,* November 2005, pp. 81–85. Also see Thomas J. Ryan, "Timberland Introduces 'Nutrition Labels,'" *SGB,* March 2006, p. 14; and Anita Pati, "Timberland Chief Call on Business to Do More," *Third Sector,* May 3, 2006, p. 17.

2. Adapted from Kevin DeMarrais, "You Can't Believe Airlines' Ticket Ads," *Knight Ridder Tribune Business News,* April 2, 2006, p. 1.

3. Theodore Levitt, "The Morality (?) of Advertising," *Harvard Business Review,* July–August 1970, pp. 84–92. For counterpoints, see Heckman, "Don't Shoot the Messenger," pp. 1, 9.

4. Lane Jennings, "Hype, Spin, Puffery, and Lies: Should We Be Scared?" *The Futurist,* January–February 2004, p. 16. For recent examples of deceptive advertising, see "Mobile Providers Sued by New York City," *Telecomworldwire,* July 22, 2005, p. 1; Chad Bray, "Federated to Pay Civil Penalty," *Wall Street Journal,* March 15, 2006, p. B3; and "Pfizer Sues P&G Over Crest Ads," *Wall Street Journal,* March 6, 2006, p. 1.

5. Roger Parloff, "Is Fat the Next Tobacco?" *Fortune,* February 3, 2003, pp. 51–54; "Big Food" Get the Obesity Message," *New York Times,* July 10, 2003, p. A22; Carl Hulse, "Vote in House Offers Shield in Obesity Suits," *New York Times,* March 11, 2004, p. A1; Amy Garber, "Twice-Tossed McD Obesity Suit Back on Docket," *Nation's Restaurant News,* February 7, 2005, p. 11; Marguerite Higgins, "Obesity-Lawsuit Bill Passes in House," *Washington Times,* October 20, 2005, p. C8; and Lisa Bertagnoli, "Capitol Concerns," *Restaurants and Institutions,* January 1, 2006, pp. 47–48.

6. "McDonald's to Cut 'Super Size' Option," *Advertising Age,* March 8, 2004, p. 13; Dave Carpenter, "Hold the Fries, Take a Walk," *News & Observer,* April 16, 2004, p. D1; Michael V. Copeland, "Ronald Gets Back in Shape," *Business 2.0,* January/February 2005, pp. 46–47; David P. Callet and Cheryl A. Falvey, "Is Restaurant Food the New Tobacco?" *Restaurant Hospitality,* May 2005, pp. 94–96; and Kate McArthur, "BK Offers Fat to the Land," *Advertising Age,* April 4, 2005, pp. 1, 60.

7. Gary Bagin, "Products Liability Verdict—Study Releases," press release, Jury Verdict Research, January 15, 2004, accessed at www.juryverdictresearch.com; and Kara Sissell, "Senate Bill Would Allow Criminal Charges in Product Liability Suits," *Chemical Week,* March 22, 2006, p. 43.

8. Adapted from information found in Mark Fagan, "Commodity Driven Market," *Lawrence Journal-World,* May 4, 2005, p. 1. Also see Clint Swett, "High Prices on Printer Cartridges Feeds Marketing for Alternative Industry," *Knight Ridder Tribune Business News,* February 15, 2006, p. 1.

9. Cliff Edwards, "Where Have All the Edsels Gone?" *Greensboro News Record,* May 24, 1999, p. B6. Also see Joel Dryfuss, "Planned Obsolescence Is Alive and Well," *Fortune,* February 15, 1999, p. 192; Tim Cooper, "Inadequate Life? Evidence of Consumer Attitudes to Product Obsolescence," *Journal of Consumer Policy,* December 2004, pp. 421–448; David Hunter, "Planned Obsolescence Well Entrenched in Society," *Knoxville News-Sentinel,* August 15, 2005, p. B5; and Atsuo Utaka, "Planned Obsolescence and Social Welfare," *The Journal of Business,* January 2006, pp. 137–147.

10. For more discussion, see Denver D'Rozario and Jerome D. Williams, "Retail Redlining: Definition, Theory, Typology, and Measurement," *Journal of Macromarketing,* December 2005, pp. 175+.

11. See Brian Grow and Pallavi Gogoi, "A New Way to Squeeze the Weak?" *BusinessWeek,* January 28, 2002, p. 92; Marc Lifsher, "Allstate Settles Over Use of Credit Scores," *Los Angeles Times,* March 2, 2004, p. C.1; Judith Burns, "Study Finds Links in Credit Scores, Insurance Claims," *Wall Street Journal,* February 28, 2005, p. D3; and Erik Eckholm, "Black and Hispanic Home Buyers Pay Higher Interest on Mortgages, Study Finds," *New York Times,* June 1, 2006, p. A22.

12. "Increasing Incomes and Reducing the Rapid Refund Rip-Off," A report from the ACORN Financial Justice Center, September 2004, pp. 3–4; Tracy Turner, "H&R Block Makes Changes in Rapid-Refund Program," *Knight Ridder Tribune Business News,* January 29, 2005, p. 1; Candice Heckman, "Poor Often Fall Victim to Fee on Tax Refund Loans," *Seattle Post-Intelligencer,* February 21, 2005, p. B1; and "California Sues H&R Block," *Knight-Ridder Tribune Business News,* February 16, 2006.

13. Information from "Shop 'til They Drop?" *Christian Science Monitor,* December 1, 2003, p. 8; Gregg Easterbrook, "The Real Truth About MONEY," *Time,* January 17, 2005, pp. 32–35; Bradley Johnson, "Day in the Life: How Consumers Divvy Up All the Time They Have," *Advertising Age,* May 2, 2005; Rich Miller, "Too Much Money," *BusinessWeek,* July 11, 2005, pp. 59–66; and "Bankers Encourage 'Consumer Generation' to Save," *Texas Banking,* March 2006, pp. 25–26.

14. Portions adapted from Constance L. Hays, "Preaching to Save Shoppers from 'Evil' of Consumerism," *New York Times,* January 1, 2003, p. C1. Also see Jo Littler, "Beyond the Boycott," *Cultural Studies,* March 2005, pp. 227–252; and www.revbilly.com, accessed September 2006.

15. See Michael Cabanatuan, "Toll Lanes Could Help Drivers Buy Time," *San Francisco Chronicle,* December 28, 2004, accessed at www.sfgate.com; and "London Mayor Increases

Traffic Toll, Angers Drivers, Retailers," July 3, 2005, accessed at www.bloomberg.com; and Dan Sturges, Gregg Moscoe, and Cliff Henke, "Innovations at Work: Transit and the Changing Urban Landscapes," *Mass Transit*, July/August 2006, pp. 34–38.

16. "Marketing Under Fire," *Marketing Management*, July/August 2004, p. 5. Also see "Media: The Public Wants a Permanent Break from Ad Bombardment," *Marketing Week*, December 1, 2005, p. 27.

17. For more discussion, see Jeremiah Mcwilliams, "Big-Box Retailer Takes Issue with Small Documentary," *Knight Ridder Tribune Business News*, November 15, 2005, p. 1; Nicole Kauffman, "Movie Paints a Dark Picture of Wal-Mart's Impact on Communities," *Knight Ridder Tribune Business News*, January 19, 2006, p. 1; and John Reid Blackwell, "Documentarian Defends Wal-Mart," *Knight Ridder Tribune Business News*, May 12, 2006, p. 1.

18. See "Sustainability Key to UPS Environmental Initiatives," UPS press release, accessed at www.pressroom.ups.com, July 2006.

19. Information from "Xerox Equipment Remanufacture and Parts Reuse," accessed at www.xerox.com, September 2006.

20. Adapted from information found in Joeseph Tarnowski, "Green Monster," *Progressive Grocer*, April 1, 2006, pp. 20–26.

21. Adapted from "The Top 3 in 2005," *Global 100*, accessed at www.global100.org, July 2005. See also, "Alcoa Named One of the Most Sustainable Corporations in the World for Second Straight Year," January 27, 2006, accessed at www.alcoa.com. For further information on Alcoa's sustainability program see Alcoa's Sustainability Report found at www.alcoa.com.

22. See "EMAS: What's New?" accessed at http://europa.eu.int/comm/environment/emas, August 2005; "Special Report: Free Trade on Trial—Ten Years of NAFTA," *The Economist*, January 3, 2004, p. 13; Daniel J. Tschopp, "Corporate Social Responsibility: A Comparison between the United States and Europe," *Corporate Social-Responsibility and Environmental Management*, March 2005, pp. 55–59; and www.epa.gov, accessed September 2006.

23. Information and quotes from Andy Milligan, "Samsung Points the Way for Asian Firms in Global Brand Race," *Media*, August 8, 2003, p. 8; Gerry Khermouch, "The Best Global Brands," *BusinessWeek*, August 5, 2002, p. 92; Leslie P. Norton, "Value Brand," *Barron's*, September 22, 2003, p. 19; "Cult Brands," *BusinessWeek Online*, August 2, 2004, accessed at www.businessweek.com; Bill Breen, "The Seoul of Design," *Fast Company*, December 2005, pp. 91–98; and Samsung Annual Reports and other information accessed at www.samsung.com, September 2006.

24. Information from Mike Hoffman, "Ben Cohen: Ben & Jerry's Homemade, Established in 1978," *Inc.*, April 30, 2001, p. 68; and the Ben & Jerry's Web site at www.benjerrys.com, September 2006.

25. Quotes and other information from Thea Singer, "Can Business Still Save the World?" *Inc.*, April 30, 2001, pp. 58–71; and www.honesttea.com, September, 2006. Also see Elizabeth Fuhrman, "Honest Tea Inc.: Social and Environmental Sinceri-Tea," *Beverage Industry*, April 2005, p. 44.

26. Adapted from Chip Giller and David Roberts, "Resources: The Revolution Begins," *Fast Company*, March 2006, pp. 73–78. Also see Joseph Ogando, "Green Engineering," *Design News*, January 9, 2006, p. 65; and information accessed online at www.haworth.com, August 2006.

27. Joseph Webber, "3M's Big Cleanup," *BusinessWeek*, June 5, 2000, pp. 96–98. Also see Kara Sissell, "3M Defends Timing of Scotchgard Phaseout," *Chemical Week*, April 11, 2001, p. 33; Peck Hwee Sim, "Ausimont Targets Former Scotchgard Markets," *Chemical Week*, August 7, 2002, p. 32; Jennifer Lee, "E.P.A. Orders Companies to Examine Effect of Chemicals," *New York Times*, April 15, 2003, p. F2; and Kara Sissell, "Swedish Officials Propose Global Ban on PFOS," *Chemical Week*, June 22, 2005, p. 35.

28. See "Transparency International Bribe Payers Index" and "Transparency International Corruption Perception Index," accessed at www.transparency.org, August 2006; "Minxin Pei, "The Dark Side of China's Rise," *Foreign Policy*, March/April 2006, pp. 32–40; and "Everybody's Doing It," *Middle East*, April 2006, pp. 20–21.

29. John F. McGee and P. Tanganath Nayak, "Leaders' Perspectives on Business Ethics," *Prizm*, Arthur D. Little, Inc., Cambridge, MA, first quarter 1994, pp. 71–72. Also see Adrian Henriques, "Good Decision—Bad Business?" *International Journal of Management & Decision Making*, 2005, p. 273; and Marylyn Carrigan, Svetla Marinova, and Isabelle Szmigin, "Ethics and International Marketing: Research Background and Challenges," *International Marketing Review*, 2005, pp. 481–494.

30. See Samuel A. DiPiazza, "Ethics in Action," *Executive Excellence*, January 2002, pp. 15–16; Samuel A. DiPiazza, Jr., "It's All Down to Personal Values," accessed online at www.pwcglobal.com, August 2003; and "Code of Conduct: The Way We Do Business," accessed at www.pwcglobal.com/gv/eng/ins-sol/spec-int/ethics/index.html, September 2006. PricewaterhouseCoopers (www.pwc.com) provides industry-focused assurance, tax, and advisory services to build public trust and enhance value for its clients and their stakeholders. More than 130,000 people in 148 countries across its network share their thinking, experience, and solutions to develop fresh perspectives and practical advice. 'PricewaterhouseCoopers' refers to the network of member firms of PricewaterhouseCoopers International limited, each of which is a separate and independent legal entity.

31. DiPiazza, "Ethics in Action," p. 15.

APPENDIX B

1. This is derived by rearranging the following equation and solving for price: Percentage markup = (price − cost) ÷ price.

2. The equation is derived from the basic profit = total revenue − total cost equation. Profit is set to equal the return on investment times the investment (ROI × I), total revenue equals price times quantity (P × Q), and total costs equals quantity times unit cost (Q × UC). Solving for P gives P = ((ROI × I) ÷ Q) + UC.

more effectively, and obtain buying efficiencies and better prices.

Business-to-consumer (B2C) online marketing Selling goods and services online to final consumers.

Buyer-readiness stages The stages consumers normally pass through on their way to purchase, including awareness, knowledge, liking, preference, conviction, and purchase.

Buyers The people in the organization's buying center who make an actual purchase.

Buying center All the individuals and units that play a role in the purchase decision-making process.

Buzz marketing Cultivating opinion leaders and getting them to spread information about a product or service to others in their communities.

By-product pricing Setting a price for by-products in order to make the main product's price more competitive.

Captive-product pricing Setting a price for products that must be used along with a main product, such as blades for a razor and film for a camera.

Catalog marketing Direct marketing through print, video, or electronic catalogs that are mailed to select customers, made available in stores, or presented online.

Category killer Giant specialty store that carries a very deep assortment of a particular line and is staffed by knowledgeable employees.

Causal research Marketing research to test hypotheses about cause-and-effect relationships.

Chain stores Two or more outlets that are commonly owned and controlled.

Channel conflict Disagreement among marketing channel members on goals and roles—who should do what and for what rewards.

Channel level A layer of intermediaries that performs some work in bringing the product and its ownership closer to the final buyer.

Click-and-mortar companies Traditional brick-and-mortar companies that have added online marketing to their operations.

Click-only companies The so-called dot-coms, which operate only online without any brick-and-mortar market presence.

Closing The step in the selling process in which the salesperson asks the customer for an order.

Co-branding The practice of using the established brand names of two different companies on the same product.

Cognitive dissonance Buyer discomfort caused by postpurchase conflict.

Commercialization Introducing a new product into the market.

Communication adaptation A global communication strategy of fully adapting advertising messages to local markets.

Competitive advantage An advantage over competitors gained by offering consumers greater value, either through lower prices or by providing more benefits that justify higher prices.

Competitive marketing strategies Strategies that strongly position the company against competitors and that give the company the strongest possible strategic advantage.

Competitive-parity method Setting the promotion budget to match competitors' outlays.

Competitor analysis The process of identifying key competitors; assessing their objectives, strategies, strengths and weaknesses, and reaction patterns; and selecting which competitors to attack or avoid.

Competitor-centered company A company whose moves are mainly based on competitors' actions and reactions.

Complex buying behavior Consumer buying behavior in situations characterized by high consumer involvement in a purchase and significant perceived differences among brands.

Concentrated (niche) marketing A market-coverage strategy in which a firm goes after a large share of one or a few segments or niches.

Concept testing Testing new-product concepts with a group of target consumers to find out if the concepts have strong consumer appeal.

Consumer buyer behavior The buying behavior of final consumers—individuals and households who buy goods and services for personal consumption.

Consumer market All the individuals and households who buy or acquire goods and services for personal consumption.

Consumer-oriented marketing The philosophy of enlightened marketing that holds that the company should view and organize its marketing activities from the consumer's point of view.

Consumer product Product bought by final consumer for personal consumption.

Consumer promotion tools Sales promotion tools used to urge short-term customer buying or to enhance long-term customer relationships.

Consumerism An organized movement of citizens and government agencies to improve the rights and power of buyers in relation to sellers.

Consumer-to-business (C2B) online marketing Online exchanges in which consumers search out sellers, learn about their offers, and initiate purchases, sometimes even driving transaction terms.

Consumer-to-consumer (C2C) online marketing Online exchanges of goods and information between final consumers.

Contract manufacturing A joint venture in which a company contracts with manufacturers in a foreign market to produce the product or provide its service.

Contractual VMS A vertical marketing system in which independent firms at different levels of production and distribution join together through contracts to obtain more economies or sales impact than they could achieve alone.

Convenience product Consumer product that the customer usually buys frequently, immediately, and with a minimum of comparison and buying effort.

Convenience store A small store, located near a residential area, that is open long hours seven days a week and carries a limited line of high-turnover convenience goods.

Conventional distribution channel A channel consisting of one or more independent producers, wholesalers, and retailers, each a separate business seeking to maximize its own profits even at the expense of profits for the system as a whole.

Corporate VMS A vertical marketing system that combines successive stages of production and distribution under single ownership—channel leadership is established through common ownership.

Corporate Web site A Web site designed to build customer goodwill and to supplement other sales channels, rather than to sell the company's products directly.

Cost-based pricing Setting prices based on the costs for producing, distributing, and selling the product plus a fair rate of return for effort and risk.

Cost-plus pricing Adding a standard markup to the cost of the product.

Countertrade International trade involving the direct or indirect exchange of goods for other goods instead of cash.

Creative concept The compelling "big idea" that will bring the advertising message strategy to life in a distinctive and memorable way.

Cultural environment Institutions and other forces that affect society's basic values, perceptions, preferences, and behaviors.

Culture The set of basic values, perceptions, wants, and behaviors learned by a member of society from family and other important institutions.

Customer-centered company A company that focuses on customer developments in designing its marketing strategies and on delivering superior value to its target customers.

Customer-centered new-product development New-product development that focuses on finding new ways to solve customer problems and create more customer-satisfying experiences.

Customer database An organized collection of comprehensive data about individual customers or prospects, including geographic, demographic, psychographic, and behavioral data.

Customer equity The total combined customer lifetime values of all of the company's customers.

Customer lifetime value The value of the entire stream of purchases that a customer would make over a lifetime of patronage.

Customer perceived value The customer's evaluation of the difference between all the benefits and all the costs of a market offering relative to those of competing offers.

Customer relationship management The overall process of building and maintaining profitable customer relationships by delivering superior customer value and satisfaction.

Customer relationship management (CRM) Managing detailed information about individual customers and carefully managing customer "touch points" in order to maximize customer loyalty.

Customer satisfaction The extent to which a product's perceived performance matches a buyer's expectations.

Customer sales force structure A sales force organization under which salespeople specialize in selling only to certain customers or industries.

Customer value analysis Analysis conducted to determine what benefits target customers value and how they rate the relative value of various competitors' offers.

Customer-value marketing A principle of enlightened marketing that holds that a company should put most of its resources into customer value-building marketing investments.

Decline stage The product life-cycle stage in which a product's sales decline.

Deciders People in the organization's buying center who have formal or informal power to select or approve the final suppliers.

Deficient products Products that have neither immediate appeal nor long-run benefits.

Demand curve A curve that shows the number of units the market will buy in a given time period, at different prices that might be charged.

Demands Human wants that are backed by buying power.

Demographic segmentation Dividing a market into groups based on variables such as age, gender, family size, family life cycle, income, occupation, education, religion, race, generation, and nationality.

Demography The study of human populations in terms of size, density, location, age, gender, race, occupation, and other statistics.

Department store A retail organization that carries a wide variety of product lines—each line is operated as a separate department managed by specialist buyers or merchandisers.

Derived demand Business demand that ultimately comes from (derives from) the demand for consumer goods.

Descriptive research Marketing research to better describe marketing problems, situations, or markets, such as the market potential for a product or the demographics and attitudes of consumers.

Desirable products Products that give both high immediate satisfaction and high long-run benefits.

Differentiation Actually differentiating the firm's market offering to create superior customer value.

Differentiated (segmented) marketing A market-coverage strategy in which a firm decides to target several market segments and designs separate offers for each.

Direct investment Entering a foreign market by developing foreign-based assembly or manufacturing facilities.

Direct marketing Direct connections with carefully targeted individual consumers to both obtain an immediate response and cultivate lasting customer relationships.

Direct marketing channel A marketing channel that has no intermediary levels.

Direct-mail marketing Direct marketing by sending an offer, announcement, reminder, or other item to a person at a particular address.

Direct-response television marketing Direct marketing via television, including direct-response television advertising (or infomercials) and home shopping channels.

Discount A straight reduction in price on purchases during a stated period of time.

Discount store A retail operation that sells standard merchandise at lower prices by accepting lower margins and selling at higher volume.

Disintermediation The cutting out of marketing channel intermediaries by product or service producers, or the displacement of traditional resellers by radical new types of intermediaries.

Dissonance-reducing buying behavior Consumer buying behavior in situations characterized by high involvement but few perceived differences among brands.

Distribution center A large, highly automated warehouse designed to receive goods from various plants and suppliers, take orders, fill them efficiently, and deliver goods to customers as quickly as possible.

Diversification A strategy for company growth through starting up or acquiring businesses outside the company's current products and markets.

Downsizing Reducing the business portfolio by eliminating products of business units that are not profitable or that no longer fit the company's overall strategy.

Dynamic pricing Adjusting prices continually to meet the characteristics and needs of individual customers and situations.

Economic community A group of nations organized to work toward common goals in the regulation of international trade.

Economic environment Factors that affect consumer buying power and spending patterns.

Engel's laws Differences noted over a century ago by Ernst Engel in how people shift their spending across food, housing, transportation, health care, and other goods and services categories as family income rises.

Enlightened marketing A marketing philosophy holding that a company's marketing should support the best long-run performance of the marketing system; its five principles include consumer-oriented marketing, customer-value marketing, innovative marketing, sense-of-mission marketing, and societal marketing.

Environmental sustainability A management approach that involves developing strategies that both sustain the environment and produce profits for the company.

Environmentalism An organized movement of concerned citizens and government agencies to protect and improve people's living environment.

Ethnographic research A form of observational research that involves sending trained observers to watch and interact with consumers in their "natural habitat."

Exchange The act of obtaining a desired object from someone by offering something in return.

Exclusive distribution Giving a limited number of dealers the exclusive right to distribute the company's products in their territories.

Execution style The approach, style, tone, words, and format used for executing an advertising message.

Experience curve (learning curve) The drop in the average per-unit production cost that comes with accumulated production experience.

Experimental research Gathering of primary data by selecting matched groups of subjects, giving them different treatments, controlling related factors, and checking for differences in group responses.

Exploratory research Marketing research to gather preliminary information that will help define problems and suggest hypotheses.

Exporting Entering a foreign market by selling goods produced in the company's home country, often with little modification.

Factory outlet Off-price retailing operation that is owned and operated by a manufacturer and that normally carries the manufacturer's surplus, discontinued, or irregular goods.

Fad A temporary period of unusually high sales driven by consumer enthusiasm and immediate product or brand popularity.

Fashion A currently accepted or popular style in a given field.

Fixed costs (overhead) Costs that do not vary with production or sales level.

FOB-origin pricing A geographical pricing strategy in which goods are placed free on board a carrier; the customer pays the freight from the factory to the destination.

Focus group interviewing Personal interviewing that involves inviting six to ten people to gather for a few hours with a trained interviewer to talk about a product, service, or organization. The interviewer "focuses" the group discussion on important issues.

Follow-up The last step in the selling process in which the salesperson follows up after the sale to ensure customer satisfaction and repeat business.

Franchise A contractual association between a manufacturer, wholesaler, or service organization (a franchiser) and independent businesspeople (franchisees) who buy the right to own and operate one or more units in the franchise system.

Franchise organization A contractual vertical marketing system in which a channel member, called a franchiser, links several stages in the production-distribution process.

Freight-absorption pricing A geographical pricing strategy in which the seller absorbs all or part of the freight charges in order to get the desired business.

Gatekeepers People in the organization's buying center who control the flow of information to others.

Gender segmentation Dividing a market into different groups based on gender.

General need description The stage in the business buying process in which the company describes the general characteristics and quantity of a needed item.

Generation X The 45 million people born between 1965 and 1976 in the "birth dearth" following the baby boom.

Generation Y The 72 million children of the baby boomers, born between 1977 and 1994.

Geographic segmentation Dividing a market into different geographical units such as nations, states, regions, counties, cities, or neighborhoods.

Geographical pricing Setting prices for customers located in different parts of the country or world.

Global firm A firm that, by operating in more than one country, gains R&D, production, marketing, and financial advantages in its costs and reputation that are not available to purely domestic competitors.

Good-value pricing Offering just the right combination of quality and good service at a fair price.

Government market Governmental units—federal, state, and local—that purchase or rent goods and services for carrying out the main functions of government.

Group Two or more people who interact to accomplish individual or mutual goals.

Growth-share matrix A portfolio-planning method that evaluates a company's strategic business units in terms of their market growth rate and relative market share. SBUs are classified as stars, cash cows, question marks, or dogs.

Growth stage The product life-cycle stage in which a product's sales start climbing quickly.

Habitual buying behavior Consumer buying behavior in situations characterized by low consumer involvement and few significant perceived brand differences.

Handling objections The step in the selling process in which the salesperson seeks out, clarifies, and overcomes customer objections to buying.

Horizontal marketing system A channel arrangement in which two or more companies at one level join together to follow a new marketing opportunity.

Idea generation The systematic search for new-product ideas.

Idea screening Screening new-product ideas in order to spot good ideas and drop poor ones as soon as possible.

Income segmentation Dividing a market into different income groups.

Independent off-price retailer Off-price retailer that is either owned and run by entrepreneurs or is a division of a larger retail corporation.

Indirect marketing channel Channel containing one or more intermediary levels.

Individual marketing Tailoring products and marketing programs to the needs and preferences of individual customers—also labeled "markets-of-one marketing," "customized marketing," and "one-to-one marketing."

Industrial product Product bought by individuals and organizations for further processing or for use in conducting a business.

Influencers People in an organization's buying center who affect the buying decision; they often help define specifications and also provide information for evaluating alternatives.

Information search The stage of the buyer decision process in which the consumer is aroused to search for more information; the consumer may simply have heightened attention or may go into active information search.

Innovative marketing A principle of enlightened marketing that requires that a company seek real product and marketing improvements.

Inside sales force Inside salespeople who conduct business from their offices via telephone, the Internet, or visits from prospective buyers.

Institutional market Schools, hospitals, nursing homes, prisons, and other institutions that provide goods and services to people in their care.

Integrated direct marketing Direct-marketing campaigns that use multiple vehicles and multiple stages to improve response rates and profits.

Integrated logistics management The logistics concept that emphasizes teamwork, both inside the company and among all the marketing channel organizations, to maximize the performance of the entire distribution system.

Integrated marketing communications (IMC) Carefully integrating and coordinating the company's many communications channels to deliver a clear, consistent, and compelling message about the organization and its products.

Intensive distribution Stocking the product in as many outlets as possible.

Interactive marketing Training service employees in the fine art of interacting with customers to satisfy their needs.

Intermarket segmentation Forming segments of consumers who have similar needs and buying behavior even though they are located in different countries.

Intermodal transportation Combining two or more modes of transportation.

Internal databases Electronic collections of consumer and market information obtained from data sources within the company network.

Internal marketing Orienting and motivating customer-contact employees and the supporting service people to work as a team to provide customer satisfaction.

Internet A vast public web of computer networks that connects users of all types all around the world to each other and to an amazingly large "information repository."

Introduction stage The product life-cycle stage in which the new product is first distributed and made available for purchase.

Joint ownership A joint venture in which a company joins investors in a foreign market to create a local business in which the company shares joint ownership and control.

Joint venturing Entering foreign markets by joining with foreign companies to produce or market a product or service.

Learning Changes in an individual's behavior arising from experience.

Licensing A method of entering a foreign market in which the company enters into an agreement with a licensee in the foreign market, offering the right to use a manufacturing process, trademark, patent, trade secret, or other item of value for a fee or royalty.

Lifestyle A person's pattern of living as expressed in his or her activities, interests, and opinions.

Line extension Extending an existing brand name to new forms, colors, sizes, ingredients, or flavors of an existing product category.

Local marketing Tailoring brands and promotions to the needs and wants of local customer groups—cities, neighborhoods, and even specific stores.

Macroenvironment The larger societal forces that affect the microenvironment—demographic, economic, natural, technological, political, and cultural forces.

Madison & Vine A term that has come to represent the merging of advertising and entertainment in an effort to break through the clutter and create new avenues for reaching consumers with more engaging messages.

Management contracting A joint venture in which the domestic firm supplies the management know-how to a foreign company that supplies the capital; the domestic firm exports management services rather than products.

Manufacturers' sales branches and offices Wholesaling by sellers or buyers themselves rather than through independent wholesalers.

Market The set of all actual and potential buyers of a product or service.

Market-centered company A company that pays balanced attention to both customers and competitors in designing its marketing strategies.

Market challenger A runner-up firm that is fighting hard to increase its market share in an industry.

Market development A strategy for company growth by identifying and developing new market segments for current company products.

Market follower A runner-up firm that wants to hold its share in an industry without rocking the boat.

Market leader The firm in an industry with the largest market share.

Market nicher A firm that serves small segments that the other firms in an industry overlook or ignore.

Market offering Some combination of products, services, information, or experiences offered to a market to satisfy a need or want.

Market penetration A strategy for company growth by increasing sales of current products to current market segments without changing the product.

Market-penetration pricing Setting a low price for a new product in order to attract a large number of buyers and a large market share.

Market segment A group of consumers who respond in a similar way to a given set of marketing efforts.

Market segmentation Dividing a market into distinct groups of buyers who have distinct needs, characteristics, or behavior and who might require separate products or marketing programs.

Market-skimming pricing Setting a high price for a new product to skim maximum revenues layer by layer from the segments willing to pay the high price; the company makes fewer but more profitable sales.

Market targeting The process of evaluating each market segment's attractiveness and selecting one or more segments to enter.

Marketing The process by which companies create value for customers and build strong customer relationships in order to capture value from customers in return.

Marketing audit A comprehensive, systematic, independent, and periodic examination of a company's environment, objectives, strategies, and activities to determine problem areas and opportunities and to recommend a plan of action to improve the company's marketing performance.

Marketing channel (distribution channel) A set of interdependent organizations that help make a product or service available for use or consumption by the consumer or business user.

Marketing concept The marketing management philosophy that achieving organizational goals depends on knowing the needs and wants of target markets and delivering the desired satisfactions better than competitors do.

Marketing control The process of measuring and evaluating the results of marketing strategies and plans and taking corrective action to ensure that objectives are achieved.

Marketing environment The actors and forces outside marketing that affect marketing management's ability to build and maintain successful relationships with target customers.

Marketing implementation The process that turns marketing strategies and plans into marketing actions in order to accomplish strategic marketing objectives.

Marketing information system (MIS) People, equipment, and procedures to gather, sort, analyze, evaluate, and distribute needed, timely, and accurate information to marketing decision makers.

Marketing intelligence The systematic collection and analysis of publicly available information about competitors and developments in the marketing environment.

Marketing intermediaries Firms that help the company to promote, sell, and distribute its goods to final buyers; they include resellers, physical distribution firms, marketing service agencies, and financial intermediaries.

Marketing logistics (physical distribution) The tasks involved in planning, implementing, and controlling the physical flow of materials, final goods, and related information from points of origin to points of consumption to meet customer requirements at a profit.

Marketing management The art and science of choosing target markets and building profitable relationships with them.

Marketing mix The set of controllable tactical marketing tools—product, price, place, and promotion—that the firm blends to produce the response it wants in the target market.

Marketing myopia The mistake of paying more attention to the specific products a company offers than to the benefits and experiences produced by these products.

Marketing research The systematic design, collection, analysis, and reporting of data relevant to a specific marketing situation facing an organization.

Marketing strategy development Designing an initial marketing strategy for a new product based on the product concept.

Marketing strategy The marketing logic by which the business unit hopes to achieve its marketing objectives.

Marketing Web site A Web site that engages consumers in interactions that will move them closer to a direct purchase or other marketing outcome.

Maturity stage The product life-cycle stage in which sales growth slows or levels off.

Merchant wholesaler Independently owned business that takes title to the merchandise it handles.

Microenvironment The actors close to the company that affect its ability to serve its customers—the company, suppliers, marketing intermediaries, customer markets, competitors, and publics.

Micromarketing The practice of tailoring products and marketing programs to the needs and wants of specific individuals and local customer groups—includes *local marketing* and *individual marketing*.

Mission statement A statement of the organization's purpose—what it wants to accomplish in the larger environment.

Modified rebuy A business buying situation in which the buyer wants to modify product specifications, prices, terms, or suppliers.

Motive (or drive) A need that is sufficiently pressing to direct the person to seek satisfaction of the need.

Multichannel distribution system A distribution system in which a single firm sets up two or more marketing channels to reach one or more customer segments.

Natural environment Natural resources that are needed as inputs by marketers or that are affected by marketing activities.

Need recognition The first stage of the buyer decision process, in which the consumer recognizes a problem or need.

Needs States of felt deprivation.

New product A good, service, or idea that is perceived by some potential customers as new.

New task A business buying situation in which the buyer purchases a product or service for the first time.

New-product development The development of original products, product improvements, product modifications, and new brands through the firm's own R&D efforts.

Nonpersonal communication channels Media that carry messages without personal contact or feedback, including major media, atmospheres, and events.

Objective-and-task method Developing the promotion budget by (1) defining specific objectives; (2) determining the tasks that must be performed to achieve these objectives; and (3) estimating the costs of performing these tasks. The sum of these costs is the proposed promotion budget.

Observational research The gathering of primary data by observing relevant people, actions, and situations.

Occasion segmentation Dividing a market into groups according to occasions when buyers get the idea to buy, actually make their purchase, or use the purchased item.

Off-price retailer Retailer that buys at less-than-regular wholesale prices and sells at less than retail. Examples are factory outlets, independents, and warehouse clubs.

Online advertising Advertising that appears while consumers are surfing the Web, including display ads (banners, interstitials, pop-ups), search-related ads, online classifieds, and other forms.

Online databases Computerized collections of information available from online commercial sources or via the Internet.

Online marketing Company efforts to market products and services and build customer relationships over the Internet.

Online marketing research Collecting primary data through Internet surveys and online focus groups.

Opinion leader Person within a reference group who, because of special skills, knowledge, personality, or other characteristics, exerts social influence on others.

Optional-product pricing The pricing of optional or accessory products along with a main product.

Order-routine specification The stage of the business buying process in which the buyer writes the final order with the chosen supplier(s), listing the technical specifications, quantity needed, expected time of delivery, return policies, and warranties.

Outside sales force (or field sales force) Outside salespeople who travel to call on customers in the field.

Packaging The activities of designing and producing the container or wrapper for a product.

Partner relationship management Working closely with partners in other company departments and outside the company to jointly bring greater value to customers.

Percentage-of-sales method Setting the promotion budget at a certain percentage of current or forecasted sales or as a percentage of the unit sales price.

Perception The process by which people select, organize, and interpret information to form a meaningful picture of the world.

Performance review The stage of the business buying process in which the buyer assesses the performance of the supplier and decides to continue, modify, or drop the arrangement.

Personal communication channels Channels through which two or more people communicate directly with each other, including face to face, on the phone, through mail or e-mail, or even through an Internet "chat."

Personal selling Personal presentation by the firm's sales force for the purpose of making sales and building customer relationships.

Personality The unique psychological characteristics that lead to relatively consistent and lasting responses to one's own environment.

Pleasing products Products that give high immediate satisfaction but may hurt consumers in the long run.

Political environment Laws, government agencies, and pressure groups that influence and limit various organizations and individuals in a given society.

Portfolio analysis The process by which management evaluates the products and businesses making up the company.

Positioning Arranging for a product to occupy a clear, distinctive, and desirable place relative to competing products in the minds of target consumers.

Positioning statement A statement that summarizes company or brand positioning—it takes this form: *To (target segment and need) our (brand) is (concept) that (point of difference).*

Postpurchase behavior The stage of the buyer decision process in which consumers take further action after purchase, based on their satisfaction or dissatisfaction.

Preapproach The step in the selling process in which the salesperson learns as much as possible about a prospective customer before making a sales call.

Presentation The step in the selling process in which the salesperson tells the "product story" to the buyer, highlighting customer benefits.

Price The amount of money charged for a product or service, or the sum of the values that consumers exchange for the benefits of having or using the product or service.

Price elasticity A measure of the sensitivity of demand to changes in price.

Primary data Information collected for the specific purpose at hand.

Private brand (or store brand) A brand created and owned by a reseller of a product or service.

Problem recognition The first stage of the business buying process in which someone in the company recognizes a problem or need that can be met by acquiring a good or a service.

Product Anything that can be offered to a market for attention, acquisition, use, or consumption that might satisfy a want or need.

Product adaptation Adapting a product to meet local conditions or wants in foreign markets.

Product bundle pricing Combining several products and offering the bundle at a reduced price.

Product concept A detailed version of the new-product idea stated in meaningful consumer terms.

Product concept The idea that consumers will favor products that offer the most quality, performance, and features and that the organization should therefore devote its energy to making continuous product improvements.

Product development A strategy for company growth by offering modified or new products to current market segments; Developing the product concept into a physical product in order to ensure that the product idea can be turned into a workable product.

Product invention Creating new products or services for foreign markets.

Product life cycle (PLC) The course of a product's sales and profits over its lifetime. It involves five distinct stages: product development, introduction, growth, maturity, and decline.

Product line A group of products that are closely related because they function in a similar manner, are sold to the same customer groups, are marketed through the same types of outlets, or fall within given price ranges.

Product/market expansion grid A portfolio-planning tool for identifying company growth opportunities through market penetration, market development, product development, or diversification.

Product mix (or product portfolio) The set of all product lines and items that a particular seller offers for sale.

Product position The way the product is defined by consumers on important attributes—the place the product occupies in consumers' minds relative to competing products.

Product quality The characteristics of a product or service that bear on its ability to satisfy stated or implied customer needs.

Product sales force structure A sales force organization under which salespeople specialize in selling only a portion of the company's products or lines.

Product specification The stage of the business buying process in which the buying organization decides on and specifies the best technical product characteristics for a needed item.

Production concept The idea that consumers will favor products that are available and highly affordable and that the organization should therefore focus on improving production and distribution efficiency.

Promotion mix (marketing communications mix) The specific blend of advertising, sales promotion, public relations, personal selling, and direct-marketing tools that the company uses to persuasively communicate customer value and build customer relationships.

Promotional pricing Temporarily pricing products below the list price, and sometimes even below cost, to increase short-run sales.

Proposal solicitation The stage of the business buying process in which the buyer invites qualified suppliers to submit proposals.

Prospecting The step in the selling process in which the salesperson identifies qualified potential customers.

Psychographic segmentation Dividing a market into different groups based on social class, lifestyle, or personality characteristics.

Psychological pricing A pricing approach that considers the psychology of prices and not simply the economics; the price is used to say something about the product.

Public Any group that has an actual or potential interest in or impact on an organization's ability to achieve its objectives.

Public relations Building good relations with the company's various publics by obtaining favorable publicity, building a good corporate image, and handling or heading off unfavorable rumors, stories, and events.

Pull strategy A promotion strategy that calls for spending a lot on advertising and consumer promotion to induce final consumers to buy the product. If the pull strategy is effective, consumers will then demand the product from channel members, who will in turn demand it from producers.

Purchase decision The buyer's decision about which brand to purchase.

Push strategy A promotion strategy that calls for using the sales force and trade promotion to push the product through channels. The producer promotes the product to channel members to induce them to carry the product and to promote it to final consumers.

Reference prices Prices that buyers carry in their minds and refer to when they look at a given product.

Retailer A business whose sales come primarily from retailing.

Retailing All activities involved in selling goods or services directly to final consumers for their personal, nonbusiness use.

Return on advertising investment The net return on advertising investment divided by the costs of the advertising investment.

Return on marketing investment (or marketing ROI) The net return from a marketing investment divided by the costs of the marketing investment.

Sales force management The analysis, planning, implementation, and control of sales force activities. It includes designing sales force strategy and structure and recruiting, selecting, training, supervising, compensating, and evaluating the firm's salespeople.

Salesperson An individual representing a company to customers by performing one or more of the following activities: prospecting, communicating, selling, servicing, information gathering, and relationship building.

Sales promotion Short-term incentives to encourage the purchase or sale of a product or service.

Sales quota A standard that states the amount a salesperson should sell and how sales should be divided among the company's products.

Salutary products Products that have low appeal but may benefit consumers in the long run.

Sample A segment of the population selected for marketing research to represent the population as a whole.

Secondary data Information that already exists somewhere, having been collected for another purpose.

Segmented pricing Selling a product or service at two or more prices, where the difference in prices is not based on differences in costs.

Selective distribution The use of more than one, but fewer than all, of the intermediaries who are willing to carry the company's products.

Selling concept The idea that consumers will not buy enough of the firm's products unless it undertakes a large-scale selling and promotion effort.

Selling process The steps that the salesperson follows when selling, which include prospecting and qualifying, preapproach, approach, presentation and demonstration, handling objections, closing, and follow-up.

Sense-of-mission marketing A principle of enlightened marketing that holds that a company should define its mission in broad social terms rather than narrow product terms.

Service Any activity or benefit that one party can offer to another that is essentially intangible and does not result in the ownership of anything.

Service inseparability A major characteristic of services—they are produced and consumed at the same time and cannot be separated from their providers.

Service intangibility A major characteristic of services—they cannot be seen, tasted, felt, heard, or smelled before they are bought.

Service perishability A major characteristic of services—they cannot be stored for later sale or use.

Service-profit chain The chain that links service firm profits with employee and customer satisfaction.

Service variability A major characteristic of services—their quality may vary greatly, depending on who provides them and when, where, and how.

Share of customer The portion of the customer's purchasing that a company gets in its product categories.

Shopping center A group of retail businesses planned, developed, owned, and managed as a unit.

Shopping product Consumer good that the customer, in the process of selection and purchase, characteristically compares on such bases as suitability, quality, price, and style.

Social class Relatively permanent and ordered divisions in a society whose members share similar values, interests, and behaviors.

Social marketing The use of commercial marketing concepts and tools in programs designed to influence individuals' behavior to improve their well-being and that of society.

Societal marketing A principle of enlightened marketing that holds that a company should make marketing decisions by considering consumers' wants, the company's requirements, consumers' long-run interests, and society's long-run interests.

Societal marketing concept A principle of enlightened marketing that holds that a company should make good marketing decisions by considering consumers' wants, the company's requirements, consumers' long-run interests, and society's long-run interests.

Spam Unsolicited, unwanted commercial e-mail messages.

Specialty product Consumer product with unique characteristics or brand identification for which a significant group of buyers is willing to make a special purchase effort.

Specialty store A retail store that carries a narrow product line with a deep assortment within that line.

Standardized marketing mix An international marketing strategy for using basically the same product, advertising, distribution channels, and other elements of the marketing mix in all the company's international markets.

Straight product extension Marketing a product in a foreign market without any change.

Straight rebuy A business buying situation in which the buyer routinely reorders something without any modifications.

Strategic group A group of firms in an industry following the same or a similar strategy.

Strategic planning The process of developing and maintaining a strategic fit between the organization's goals and capabilities and its changing marketing opportunities.

Style A basic and distinctive mode of expression.

Subculture A group of people with shared value systems based on common life experiences and situations.

Supermarket Large, low-cost, low-margin, high-volume, self-service store that carries a wide variety of grocery and household products.

Superstore A store much larger than a regular supermarket that offers a large assortment of routinely purchased food products, nonfood items, and services.

Supplier development Systematic development of networks of supplier-partners to ensure an appropriate and dependable supply of products and materials for use in making products or reselling them to others.

Supplier search The stage of the business buying process in which the buyer tries to find the best vendors.

Supplier selection The stage of the business buying process in which the buyer reviews proposals and selects a supplier or suppliers.

Supply chain management Managing upstream and downstream value-added flows of materials, final goods, and related information among suppliers, the company, resellers, and final consumers.

Survey research Gathering of primary data by asking people questions about their knowledge, attitudes, preferences, and buying behavior.

SWOT analysis An overall evaluation of the company's strengths (S), weaknesses (W), opportunities (O), and threats (T).

Systems selling Buying a packaged solution to a problem from a single seller, thus avoiding all the separate decisions involved in a complex buying situation.

Target costing Pricing that starts with an ideal selling price, then targets costs that will ensure that the price is met.

Target market A set of buyers sharing common needs or characteristics that the company decides to serve.

Team-based new-product development An approach to developing new products in which various company departments work closely together, overlapping the steps in the product development process to save time and increase effectiveness.

Team selling Using teams of people from sales, marketing, engineering, finance, technical support, and even upper management to service large, complex accounts.

Technological environment Forces that create new technologies, creating new product and market opportunities.

Telephone marketing Using the telephone to sell directly to customers.

Territorial sales force structure A sales force organization that assigns each salesperson to an exclusive geographic territory in which that salesperson sells the company's full line.

Test marketing The stage of new-product development in which the product and marketing program are tested in more realistic market settings.

Third-party logistics (3PL) provider An independent logistics provider that performs any or all of the functions required to get their client's product to market.

Trade promotion tools Sales promotion tools used to persuade resellers to carry a brand, give it shelf space, promote it in advertising, and push it to consumers.

Undifferentiated (mass) marketing A market-coverage strategy in which a firm decides to ignore market segment differences and go after the whole market with one offer.

Uniform-delivered pricing A geographical pricing strategy in which the company charges the same price plus freight to all customers, regardless of their location.

Unsought product Consumer product that the consumer either does not know about or knows about but does not normally think of buying.

Users Members of the buying organization who will actually use the purchased product or service.

Value-added pricing Attaching value-added features and services to differentiate a company's offers and to support charging higher prices.

Value analysis An approach to cost reduction in which components are studied carefully to determine if they can be redesigned, standardized, or made by less costly methods of production.

Value-based pricing Setting prices based on buyers' perceptions of value rather than on the seller's cost.

Value chain The series of departments that carry out value-creating activities to design, produce, market, deliver, and support a firm's products.

Value delivery network The network made up of the company, suppliers, distributors, and ultimately customers who "partner" with each other to improve the performance of the entire system.

Value proposition The full positioning of a brand—the full mix of benefits upon which it is positioned.

Variable costs Costs that vary directly with the level of production.

Variety-seeking buying behavior Consumer buying behavior in situations characterized by low consumer involvement but significant perceived brand differences.

Vertical marketing system (VMS) A distribution channel structure in which producers, wholesalers, and retailers act as a unified system. One channel member owns the others, has contracts with them, or has so much power that they all cooperate.

Viral marketing The Internet version of word-of-mouth marketing—Web sites, e-mail messages, or other marketing events that are so infectious that customers will want to pass them along to friends.

Wants The form human needs take as shaped by culture and individual personality.

Warehouse club Off-price retailer that sells a limited selection of brand name grocery items, appliances, clothing, and a hodgepodge of other goods at deep discounts to members who pay annual membership fees.

Web communities Web sites upon which members can congregate online and exchange views on issues of common interest.

Wheel-of-retailing concept A concept of retailing that states that new types of retailers usually begin as low-margin, low-price, low-status operations but later evolve into higher-priced, higher-service operations, eventually becoming like the conventional retailers they replaced.

Whole-channel view Designing international channels that take into account all the necessary links in distributing the seller's products to final buyers, including the seller's headquarters organization, channels among nations, and channels within nations.

Wholesaler A firm engaged primarily in wholesaling activities.

Wholesaling All activities involved in selling goods and services to those buying for resale or business use.

Word-of-mouth influence Personal communication about a product between target buyers and neighbors, friends, family members, and associates.

Zone pricing A geographical pricing strategy in which the company sets up two or more zones. All customers within a zone pay the same total price; the more distant the zone, the higher the price.

Credits

317 AP Wide World Photos. 317 AP Wide World Photos. 317 AP Wide World Photos. 317 AP Wide World Photos. 319 Courtesy of Yahoo! Inc. 320 Prentice Hall School Division. 321 Courtesy of Joy Perfume. 323 Courtesy of Kimberly Clark. 325 Getty Images. 326 Photo Researchers, Inc.

CHAPTER 12 333 Caterpillar, Inc. 335 Palm, Inc. 336 Courtesy of Calyx & Corolla. 340 Joe Heiner. 342 INDITEK. 343 Getty Images. 345 Redux Pictures. 347 © Black & Decker® Corp. 348 Mike Berray. 350 Corbis/Bettmann. 351 © 2004 General Electric Company. All rights reserved. 353 Fine Image Photography. 354 Redux Pictures. 355 Courtesy of Roadway Express. 357 Courtesy of United Parcel Services.

CHAPTER 13 365 AP Wide World Photos. 368 AP Wide World Photos. 368 OrangeTwice. 369 Corbis/Bettmann. 370 Getty Images. 372 Baerbel Schmidt Photography. 374 Getty Images/Time Life Pictures. 374 AP Wide World Photos. 375 Brad Hines Photography Inc. 375 Dwight Eschliman. 376 Getty Images. 378 Cabela's Incorporated. 379 CORBIS-NY. 380 The Stock Connection. 380 Getty Images. 382 Courtesy of Staples. 383 Food Lion. 385 Courtesy of Google. 386 W. W. Grainger, Inc.

CHAPTER 14 397 The BURGER KING® trademark and King character are used with permission from Burger King Brands, Inc. 401 © 2005 BMW of North America, LLC. All rights reserved. 405 Courtesy of Edy's. 406 © Houghton Mifflin Company and Mullen. All rights reserved. 407 Courtesy of Milkbone. 408 Corbis Royalty Free. 409 Corbis/Bettmann. 409 Corbis/Bettmann. 409 Getty Images. 411 Courtesy of JetBlue. 413 Courtesy of Mary Kay, Inc. All rights reserved. 413 Courtesy of Procter & Gamble Company. All rights reserved. 414 Corbis/Photography veer Inc. 416 Getty Images.

CHAPTER 15 425 © Geico. 427 © General Mills. All rights reserved. 429 Permission by V&S Vin & Sprit AB; ABSOLUT COUNTRY OF SWEDEN VODKA & LOGO, ABSOLUT, ABSOLUT BOTTLE DESIGN AND ABSOLUT CALLIGRAPHY ARE TRADEMARKS OWNED BY V&S VIN AND SPRIT AB. 2004 V&S VIN & SPRIT AB. 430 Getty Images. 432 Cover image of Madison & Vine, by Scott Donaton. © 2004 The McGraw-Hill Companies. Used with permission. 434 Courtesy of Liquid-Logic. 437 Courtesy of Mr. Clean. 438 © 2004 The Picture People Inc. All rights reserved. 440 Used with permission of Gillette. All rights reserved. 442 Getty Images. 444 Courtesy of The Procter & Gamble Company. All rights reserved.

CHAPTER 16 451 © 2004 CDW Corporation. All rights reserved. 453 Boeing Commercial Airplane Group. 455 Courtesy of Lear Corporation. 456 Redux Pictures. 458 Courtesy of CDW Corporation. 459 Linda Ford Photography. 461 Courtesy of International Rectifier. 463 Getty Images, Inc.—Photodisc. 464 Corbis/Bettmann. 467 © 2006 Gateway, Inc., used with permission. 470 Courtesy of Wyndham Worldwide. 471 Courtesy of Mobull Plus. 471 Go2mobile Solutions, Ltd. 473 Consumer Electronics Association (CEA).

CHAPTER 17 479 © 2001 Dell Inc. All rights reserved. 481 © 2005 GEICO. All rights reserved. 483 Courtesy of Southwest Airlines. 486 Courtesy of L.L.Bean Inc. 487 Used with permission of the Carolina Cookie Company. All rights reserved. 489 Chris Corsmeier Photography. 490 Courtesy of QVC. 492 Getty Images. 494 Courtesy of Quicken Loans. 496 Courtesy of Peter Blackshaw. All rights reserved. 498 Courtesy of Office Depot. 499 Courtesy of mini.com. 500 Reprinted with permission of Callard & Bowser—Suchard, Inc. 501 Courtesy of Honda. 502 TM & © 2005 Burger King Brands, Inc. (USA only). TM & © 2005 Burger King Corporation (outside USA). All rights reserved. 503 Procter & Gamble. 505 Copyright 2006 AOL LLC. Used with permission. 508 Getty Images.

CHAPTER 18 515 AP Wide World Photos. 515 AP Wide World Photos. 515 AP Wide World Photos. 519 Courtesy of Viking Range Corp. 520 Johnson & Johnson. 521 Napster logo and marks reprinted with the permission of Napster, LLC. 523 Courtesy of Stonyfield Farm. 524 Courtesy of Hohner, Inc. 525 Courtesy of Visa U.S.A. 528 Courtesy of Campbell's Kitchen. 530 Lowes. 532 Courtesy of VPI Pet Insurance. 533 Courtesy of Logitech.

CHAPTER 19 541 AP Wide World Photos. 543 Still Media. 545 Corbis Royalty Free. 546 Alamy Images. 547 Document China. 549 Getty Images, Inc.—Agence France Presse. 550 Getty Images. 552 Getty Images. 554 Getty Images. 555 Corbis/Getty Images. 556 Getty Images Inc. Liaison. 557 LG Electronics, Inc. 557 LG Electronics, Inc. 557 LG Electronics, Inc. 559 (Both) © Prestige & Collections. 560 © Inter IKEA Systems B. V. 1999–2005. All rights reserved. 561 Audiovisual Library of the European Commission. 562 Emily Flowers.

CHAPTER 20 569 Reprinted with the permission of The Timberland Company © 2006 The Timberland Company. 571 Pearson Education/PH College. 572 Jim Whitmer Photography. 574 LJ-World Photos. 575 Aurora/Getty Images. 577 Corbis/Bettmann. 578 CORBIS- NY. 579 The Image Works. 581 Office of Mayor Jun Choi. 582 Jones Soda Company. 584 Wal-Mart Corporate Communications. 586 Corbis Royalty Free. 588 New York Times Agency. 590 Courtesy of Honest Tea. 591 Haworth, Inc. 593 Reprinted with permission of PricewaterhouseCoopers LLP.

Name, Organization, Brand, Company

Note: Italicized page numbers indicate illustrations.

Subject

Note: Italicized page numbers indicate illustrations.